COMPUTATIONAL SCIENCE AND ENGINEERING

GILBERT STRANG
Massachusetts Institute of Technology

WELLESLEY-CAMBRIDGE PRESS
Box 812060 Wellesley MA 02482

Computational Science and Engineering
Copyright ©2007 by Gilbert Strang
ISBN-10 0-9614088-1-2
ISBN-13 978-0-9614088-1-7

9 8 7 6 5 4 3 2 1

Other texts from Wellesley-Cambridge Press

Introduction to Linear Algebra, Gilbert Strang
ISBN-10 0-9614088-9-8   ISBN-13 978-0-9614088-9-3.

Wavelets and Filter Banks, Gilbert Strang and Truong Nguyen
ISBN-10 0-9614088-7-1   ISBN-13 978-0-9614088-7-9.

Linear Algebra, Geodesy, and GPS, Gilbert Strang and Kai Borre
ISBN-10 0-9614088-6-3   ISBN-13 978-0-9614088-6-2.

Introduction to Applied Mathematics, Gilbert Strang
ISBN-10 0-9614088-0-4   ISBN-13 978-0-9614088-0-0.

An Analysis of the Finite Element Method, Gilbert Strang and George Fix
ISBN-10 0-9614088-8-X   ISBN-13 978-0-9614088-8-6.

Calculus, Gilbert Strang
ISBN-10 0-9614088-2-0   ISBN-13 978-0-9614088-2-4.

Wellesley-Cambridge Press   **gs@math.mit.edu**
Box 812060   **math.mit.edu/~gs**
Wellesley MA 02482 USA   phone (781) 431-8488
www.wellesleycambridge.com   fax (617) 253-4358

LaTeX text preparation by Valutone Solutions, **www.valutone.com**.

LaTeX assembly and book design by Brett Coonley, Massachusetts Institute of Technology.

MATLAB® is a registered trademark of The Mathworks, Inc.

Course materials including syllabus and MATLAB codes and exams are available on the computational science and engineering web site: **math.mit.edu/cse**.
Problem solutions will also be on this **cse** site, with further examples.

Videotaped lectures of the CSE courses 18.085 and 18.086 (which now use this book) are available on the course web sites: **math.mit.edu/18085** and **math.mit.edu/18086**.

Computational Science and Engineering is also included in OpenCourseWare **ocw.mit.edu**.

TABLE OF CONTENTS

TEACHING AND LEARNING FROM THE BOOK

I hope that **mathematics and also engineering departments** will approve of this textbook. It developed from teaching the MIT course 18.085 for thirty years. I thank thousands of engineering and science students for learning this subject with me. I certainly do not teach every single topic! Here is my outline:

1. **Applied linear algebra** (its importance is now recognized)
2. **Applied differential equations** (with boundary values and initial values)
3. **Fourier series** including the Discrete Fourier Transform and convolution.

You will have support from the book and the cse website (and the author). Please select the sections appropriate for the course and the class. What I hope is that this book will serve as a basic text for *all* mathematicians and engineers and scientists, to explain the core ideas of applied mathematics and scientific computing. The subject is beautiful, it is coherent, and *it has moved a long way.*

The course text in earlier years was my book *Introduction to Applied Mathematics* (Wellesley-Cambridge Press). That text contains very substantial material that is not in this book, and vice versa. What naturally happened, from lectures and exams and homeworks and projects over all those years, was a *clearer focus* on how applied and engineering mathematics could be presented. This new book is the result.

This whole book aims to bring ideas and algorithms together. I am convinced that they must be taught and learned in the same course. The algorithm clarifies the idea. The old method, separation of responsibilities, no longer works:

Not perfect — Mathematics courses teach analytical techniques
Engineering courses work on real problems

Even within computational science there is a separation we don't need:

Not efficient — Mathematics courses analyze numerical algorithms
Engineering and computer science implement the software

I believe it is time to teach and learn the reality of computational science and engineering. I hope this book helps to move that beautiful subject forward. Thank you for reading it.

Gilbert Strang is in the Department of Mathematics at MIT. His textbooks have transformed the teaching of linear algebra into a more useful course for many students. His lectures are on the OpenCourseWare website at ocw.mit.edu, where 18.06 is the most frequently visited of 1700 courses. The next course 18.085 evolved in a natural way to become Computational Science and Engineering, and led to this textbook.

Awards have come for research and teaching and mathematical exposition:

Von Neumann Medal in Computational Mechanics
Teaching Prizes from the MIT School of Science
Henrici Prize for Applied Analysis
Haimo Prize for Distinguished Teaching, Mathematical Association of America
Su Buchin Prize, International Congress of Industrial and Applied Mathematics

Gilbert Strang served as President of SIAM (1999–2000) and as chair of the U.S. National Committee on Mathematics.

Earlier books presented the finite element method and the theory of wavelets and the mathematics of GPS. On those topics George Fix and Truong Nguyen and Kai Borre were valuable coauthors. The textbooks *Introduction to Linear Algebra* and *Linear Algebra and Its Applications* are widely adopted by mathematics and engineering departments. With one exception (*LAA*), all books are published by Wellesley-Cambridge Press. They are available also through SIAM.

The present book developed step by step—text first, then problems, MATLAB codes, and video lectures. The response from students has been wonderful. This development will continue on the website math.mit.edu/cse (also /18085 and /18086). Problem solutions will be on that cse site, with further examples.

The crucial need for today's students and readers is to move forward from the older "formula-based" emphasis toward a **solution-based course**. Solving problems is the heart of modern engineering mathematics and scientific computing.

THE COVER OF THE BOOK

Lois Sellers and Gail Corbett created the cover from the "circles" of Section 2.2. The solution to aim for is a true circle, but Euler's method takes discrete steps. When those steps spiral out, they produce the beautiful background on the cover (not the best circle). The spirals and circles and meshes, plus microarrays and the Gibbs phenomenon, are serious parts of Computational Science and Engineering.

It was the inspiration of the cover artists to highlight the three letters **C S E**. Those letters have come to identify an exciting direction for applied mathematics. I hope the book and the cover from birchdesignassociates.com and the evolving website math.mit.edu/cse will give you ideas to work with, and pleasure too.

ACKNOWLEDGEMENTS

I have had wonderful help with this book. For a long time we were a team of two: Brett Coonley prepared hundreds of LaTeX pages. The book would not exist without his steady support. Then new help came from four directions:

1. Per-Olof Persson and Nick Trefethen and Benjamin Seibold and Aslan Kasimov brought the computational part of the book to life. The text explains scientific computing, and their codes do it.

2. The typesetting was completed by www.valutone.com (highly recommended!).

3. Jim Collins and Tim Gardner and Mike Driscoll gave advice on mathematical biology (including the gene microarray on the back cover). From biomechanics to heart rhythms to gene expression, we want and need computational biology.

It became clear that *clustering* is a crucial algorithm in bioinformatics, and far beyond. Des Higham and Inderjit Dhillon and Jon Kleinberg generously helped me to develop the newest section $*2.9$ on Graph Cuts and Gene Clustering.

4. A host of applied mathematicians and engineers told me what to write.

The words came from teaching thousands of students over 40 happy years. The structure of a textbook emerges safely but slowly, it can't be rushed. For ideas of all kinds, I owe thanks to so many (plus Oxford and the Singapore-MIT Alliance):

Stephen Boyd, Bill Briggs, Yeunwoo Cho, Daniel Cremers, Tim Davis, Sohan Dharmaraja, Alan Edelman, Lotti Ekert, Bob Fourer, Michael Friedlander, Mike Giles (especially), Gene Golub, Nick Gould, Mike Heath, David Hibbitt, Nick Higham, Steven Johnson, David Keyes, Brian Kulis, Ruitian Lang, Jorg Liesen, Ross Lippert, Konstantin Lurie, Bill Morton, Jean-Christophe Nave, Jaime Peraire, Raj Rao, John Reid, Naoki Saito, Mike Saunders, Jos Stam, Vasily Strela, Jared Tanner, Kim Chuan Toh, Alar Toomre, Andy Wathen (especially), André Weideman, Chris Wiggins, Karen Willcox, and (on a memorable day at Hong Kong airport) Ding-Xuan Zhou.

May I dedicate this book to my family and friends. They make life beautiful.

Gilbert Strang

INTRODUCTION

When you study a subject as large as applied mathematics, or teach it, or write about it, you first need to organize it. There has to be a pattern and a structure. Then the reader (and the author!) can fit the pieces together. Let me try to separate this subject into manageable pieces, and propose a structure for this book and this course.

A first step is to see two parts—modeling and solving. Those are reflected in the contents of this book. **Applied mathematics** identifies the key quantities in the problem, and connects them by differential equations or matrix equations. Those equations are the starting point for **scientific computing**. In an extreme form, modeling begins with a problem and computing begins with a matrix.

A few more words about those two parts. "Applied mathematics" traditionally includes a study of special functions. These have enormous power and importance (sometimes a complete analysis has to wait for a more advanced course). Also traditionally, "scientific computing" includes a numerical analysis of the algorithm—to test its accuracy and stability. **Our focus stays on the basic problems that everybody meets**:

A. Constructing the equations of equilibrium and of motion (*balance equations*)

B. Solving steady state and time-dependent matrix and differential equations.

Most scientists and engineers, by the nature of our minds and our jobs, will concentrate more heavily on one side or the other. We model the problem, or we use algorithms like the FFT and software like MATLAB to solve it. It is terrific to do both. Doing the whole job from start to finish has become possible, because of fast hardware and professionally written software. So we teach both parts.

The complete effort now defines **Computational Science and Engineering**. New departments are springing up with that name. This is really a text for the basic course in that great (and quickly growing) subject of CSE.

Four Simplifications

We all learn by example. One goal in writing this book and teaching this course is to provide specific examples from many areas of engineering and science. The first section of the first chapter starts with four very particular matrices. Those matrices appear over and over in computational science. The underlying model has been made ***linear***, and ***discrete***, and ***one-dimensional***, with ***constant coefficients***.

I see those as the great simplifications which make it possible to understand applied mathematics. Let me focus on these four steps:

1. **Nonlinear becomes linear**
2. **Continuous becomes discrete**
3. **Multidimensional becomes one-dimensional**
4. **Variable coefficients become constants.**

I don't know if "becomes" is the right word. We can't change the reality of nature. But we do begin to understand the real problem by solving a simpler problem. This is illustrated by Einstein and Newton, the two greatest physicists of all time. Einstein's equations of relativity are not linear (and we are still trying to solve them). Newton *linearized* the geometry of space (and this book works with $F = ma$). His linear equation came 250 years before Einstein connected a nonlinearly to m.

Those four great simplifications are fundamental to the organization of this book. Chapter 1 includes all four, by working with the special matrices K, T, B, and C. Here are K and C:

$$\textbf{Stiffness Matrix} \quad K = \begin{bmatrix} 2 & -1 & & \\ -1 & 2 & -1 & \\ & -1 & 2 & -1 \\ & & -1 & 2 \end{bmatrix} \qquad \textbf{Circulant Matrix} \quad C = \begin{bmatrix} 2 & -1 & & -1 \\ -1 & 2 & -1 & \\ & -1 & 2 & -1 \\ -1 & & -1 & 2 \end{bmatrix}$$

This $-1, 2, -1$ pattern shows **constant coefficients in a one-dimensional problem**. Being matrices, K and C are already linear and discrete. The difference is in the *boundary conditions*, which are always crucial. K is "chopped off" at both ends, while C is cyclic or circular or "periodic." (An interval wraps around into a circle, because of -1 in the corners.) The **Fourier transform** is perfect for C.

Chapter 1 will find K^{-1}, and the triangular factors in $K = LU$, and the eigenvalues of K and C. Then Chapter 2 can solve equilibrium problems $Ku = f$ (steady state equations) and initial-value problems $Mu'' + Ku = f$ (time-dependent equations).

If you get to know this remarkable matrix K, and apply good software when it becomes large (and later multidimensional), you have made a terrific start. K is a *positive definite second difference matrix*, with beautiful properties.

1. Nonlinear becomes linear Chapter 2 models a series of important scientific and engineering and economic problems. In each model, the "physical law" is taken to be linear:

(a) *Hooke's Law in mechanics*: Displacement is proportional to force

(b) *Ohm's Law in networks*: Current is proportional to voltage difference

(c) *Scaling law in economics*: Output is proportional to input

(d) *Linear regression in statistics*: A straight line or a hyperplane can fit the data.

None of those laws is actually true. They are all approximations (no apology for that, false laws can be extremely useful). The truth is that a spring behaves *almost linearly* until the applied force is very large. Then the spring stretches easily. A resistor is also close to linear—but the highly nonlinear transistor has revolutionized electronics. Economies of scale destroy the linearity of input-output laws (and a price-sales law). We work with linear models as long as we can—but eventually we can't.

That was not a complete list of applications—this book gives more. Biology and medicine are rich in the nonlinearities that make our bodies work. So are engineering and chemistry and materials science, and also financial mathematics. Linearization is the fundamental idea of calculus—*a curve is known by its tangent lines.* Newton's method solves a nonlinear equation by a series of linear equations. No wonder that I find linear algebra everywhere.

Let me note that "physical nonlinearity" is easier than "geometric nonlinearity." In the bending of a beam, we replace the true but awful curvature formula $u''/(1+(u')^2)^{3/2}$ by a simple u''. That succeeds when u' is small—typical for many problems. In other cases we can't linearize. If Boeing had assumed ideal flow and ignored the Navier-Stokes equations, the 777 would never fly.

2. Continuous becomes discrete Chapter 3 introduces differential equations. The leading example is *Laplace's equation* $\partial^2 u/\partial x^2 + \partial^2 u/\partial y^2 = 0$, when the magic of complex variables produces a complete family of particular solutions. The solutions come in pairs from $(x+iy)^n$ and $r^n e^{in\theta}$. We call the pairs u and s:

$\boldsymbol{u(x,y)}$	$\boldsymbol{s(x,y)}$	$\boldsymbol{u(r,\theta)}$	$\boldsymbol{s(r,\theta)}$
x	y	$r\cos\theta$	$r\sin\theta$
x^2-y^2	$2xy$	$r^2\cos 2\theta$	$r^2\sin 2\theta$
$\cdots$	$\cdots$	$\cdots$	$\cdots$

Laplace's equation shows (in action) the gradient and divergence and curl. *But real applications solve a discrete form of the differential equation.* That innocent sentence contains two essential tasks: to discretize the continuous equation into $Ku = f$, and to solve for u. Those steps are at the center of scientific computing, and this book concentrates on two methods for each of them:

Continuous to discrete (Chapter 3)	**1. The finite element method** **2. Finite difference methods**
Solving discrete $\boldsymbol{Ku = f}$ (Chapter 7)	**1. Direct elimination** **2. Iterations with preconditioning**

The matrix K can be very large (and very sparse). A good solution algorithm is usually a better investment than a supercomputer. Multigrid is quite remarkable.

Chapter 6 turns to initial-value problems, first for wave and heat equations (convection + diffusion). Waves allow shocks, diffusion makes the solution smooth. These are at the center of scientific computing. The diffusion equation has become famous in finance as the *Black-Scholes equation* for the value of a stock option. Whenever time gets involved, the problem of stability will appear. *When the equations become discrete, are they still stable?* We will find a stability limit on the time step Δt.

3. Multidimensional becomes one-dimensional For linear problems, a key idea (simple when it works) reduces multidimensional problems to one dimension at a time. That idea is *separation of variables.* The unknown $u(x,t)$ becomes a sum of special products $A(x)\,B(t)$. An n-dimensional equation for u is replaced by one-dimensional equations for A and B. This is also part of scientific computing, and the *spectral method* in Chapter 5 has exponential accuracy (when the sum converges quickly). By comparison, finite differences and finite elements solve truly non-separable equations with irregular geometries. Typical errors are of order $(\Delta x)^2 + (\Delta t)^2$.

Among nonlinear equations, $\partial u/\partial t + u\,\partial u/\partial x = 0$ can be solved exactly. This is an important model of a nonlinear possibility: Shocks can develop at a finite time T. A nonlinear wave can break, as surfers know well. In studying fluid flow the equations depend on x, y, z and t, with multiple unknowns. We come to the most demanding problems of computational science. There is a $1,000,000 Clay Prize for a proof that solutions exist—and a big improvement in algorithms would be worth far more.

4. Variable coefficients become constant coefficients It would be impossible to overestimate the importance of this fourth simplification. In a word, Fourier takes over. The key functions become sines and cosines and exponentials e^{ikx} and $e^{i\omega t}$. The *Fourier transform* moves linear problems from the physical domain (x and t) to the frequency domain (k and ω). In that domain there is a separate equation for each frequency, when coefficients are constant. This is the ultimate in separation of variables, transforming a differential equation into ordinary algebra.

You might think that combining all four simplifications would be exceptional and rare. Amazingly, this is not the case. Far from it! Chapter 4 establishes the Fourier transform and its inverse, going from $f(x)$ to its Fourier coefficients and back. The FFT makes both steps fantastically quick and practical (for finite vectors). We devote two full sections to *convolution* and *filtering* and *deconvolution.* Enhancing and denoising and compressing and reconstructing images and data have become extremely important applications of mathematics (they give us high definition).

The **Fast Fourier Transform** takes advantage of every special feature of the complex number $w = e^{2\pi i/N}$. One key is $w^N = 1$ (because $e^{2\pi i} = 1$). The other key is the connection between N and $M = N/2$, the full size and the half size transforms. When you square $e^{2\pi i/N}$ you get $e^{2\pi i/M}$. The FFT continues to $N/4$ and $N/8$ and beyond. It has changed computational science and engineering.

CHAPTER 1

APPLIED LINEAR ALGEBRA

1.1 FOUR SPECIAL MATRICES

An m by n matrix has m rows and n columns and mn entries. We operate on those rows and columns to solve linear systems $Ax = b$ and eigenvalue problems $Ax = \lambda x$. From inputs A and b (and from software like MATLAB) we get outputs x and λ. A fast stable algorithm is extremely important, and this book includes fast algorithms.

One purpose of matrices is to store information, but another viewpoint is more important for applied mathematics. Often we see the matrix as an "operator." ***A acts on vectors x to produce Ax.*** The components of x have a meaning—displacements or pressures or voltages or prices or concentrations. The operator A also has a meaning—in this chapter A takes differences. Then Ax represents pressure differences or voltage drops or price differentials.

Before we turn the problem over to the machine—and also after, when we interpret A\b or eig(A)—it is the meaning we want, as well as the numbers.

This book begins with **four special families of matrices**—simple and useful, absolutely basic. We look first at the properties of these particular matrices K_n, C_n, T_n, and B_n. (Some properties are obvious, others are hidden.) It is terrific to practice linear algebra by working with genuinely important matrices. Here are K_2, K_3, K_4 in the first family, with -1 and 2 and -1 down the diagonals:

$$K_2 = \begin{bmatrix} 2 & -1 \\ -1 & 2 \end{bmatrix} \quad K_3 = \begin{bmatrix} 2 & -1 & 0 \\ -1 & 2 & -1 \\ 0 & -1 & 2 \end{bmatrix} \quad K_4 = \begin{bmatrix} \mathbf{2} & \mathbf{-1} & 0 & 0 \\ \mathbf{-1} & \mathbf{2} & \mathbf{-1} & 0 \\ 0 & \mathbf{-1} & \mathbf{2} & \mathbf{-1} \\ 0 & 0 & \mathbf{-1} & \mathbf{2} \end{bmatrix}$$

What is significant about K_2 and K_3 and K_4, and eventually the n by n matrix K_n? I will give six answers in the same order that my class gave them—starting with four properties of the K's that you can see immediately.

1. These matrices are **symmetric**. The entry in row i, column j also appears in row j, column i. Thus $K_{ij} = K_{ji}$, on opposite sides of the main diagonal. Symmetry can be expressed by transposing the whole matrix at once: $\boldsymbol{K} = \boldsymbol{K}^{\mathrm{T}}$.

2. The matrices K_n are **sparse**. Most of their entries are zero when n gets large. K_{1000} has a million entries, but only $1000 + 999 + 999$ are nonzero.

3. The nonzeros lie in a "band" around the main diagonal, so each K_n is *banded.* The band has only three diagonals, so these matrices are **tridiagonal**.

Because K is a tridiagonal matrix, $Ku = f$ can be quickly solved. If the unknown vector u has a thousand components, we can find them in a few thousand steps (which take a small fraction of a second). For a full matrix of order $n = 1000$, solving $Ku = f$ would take hundreds of millions of steps. Of course we have to ask if the linear equations have a solution in the first place. That question is coming soon.

4. The matrices have **constant diagonals**. Right away that property wakes up Fourier. It signifies that something is not changing when we move in space or time. The problem is shift-invariant or time-invariant. Coefficients are constant. The tridiagonal matrix is entirely determined by the three numbers $-1, 2, -1$. These are actually "second difference matrices" but my class never says that.

The whole world of Fourier transforms is linked to constant-diagonal matrices. In signal processing, the matrix $D = K/4$ is a "highpass filter." Du picks out the rapidly varying (high frequency) part of a vector u. It gives a *convolution* with $\frac{1}{4}(-1, 2, -1)$. We use these words to call attention to the Fourier part (Chapter 4) of this book.

Mathematicians call K a ***Toeplitz matrix***, and MATLAB uses that name:

The command $K = \text{toeplitz}([\,2\ \ -1\ \ \text{zeros}(1,2)\,])$ **constructs** K_4 **from row 1.**

Actually, Fourier will be happier if we make two small changes in K_n. Insert -1 in the southwest and northeast corners. This completes two diagonals (which circle around). All four diagonals of C_4 wrap around in this "*periodic matrix*" or "*cyclic convolution*" or **circulant matrix**:

$$\textbf{Circulant matrix}\qquad C_4 = \begin{bmatrix} 2 & -1 & 0 & -1 \\ -1 & 2 & -1 & 0 \\ 0 & -1 & 2 & -1 \\ -1 & 0 & -1 & 2 \end{bmatrix} = \text{toeplitz}([\,2\ \ -1\ \ 0\ \ -1\,])\,.$$

This matrix is *singular.* It is *not invertible.* Its determinant is zero. Rather than computing that determinant, it is much better to identify a nonzero vector u that solves $C_4 u = 0$. (**If C_4 had an inverse, the only solution to $C_4 u = 0$ would be the zero vector**. We could multiply by C_4^{-1} to find $u = 0$.) For this matrix, the column vector u of all ones (printed as $u = (1, 1, 1, 1)$ with commas) solves $C_4 u = 0$.

The columns of C add to the zero column. This vector $u = \text{ones}(4,1)$ is in the *nullspace* of C_4. The nullspace contains all solutions to $Cu = 0$.

Whenever the entries along every row of a matrix add to zero, the matrix is certainly singular. The same all-ones vector u is responsible. Matrix multiplication Cu adds the column vectors and produces zero. The constant vector $u = (1,1,1,1)$ or $u = (c,c,c,c)$ in the nullspace is like the constant C when we integrate a function. In calculus, this "arbitrary constant" is not knowable from the derivative. In linear algebra, the constant in $u = (c,c,c,c)$ is not knowable from $Cu = 0$.

5. All the matrices $K = K_n$ are **invertible**. They are not singular, like C_n. There is a square matrix K^{-1} such that $K^{-1}K = I =$ *identity matrix.* And if a square matrix has an inverse on the left, then also $KK^{-1} = I$. This "*inverse matrix*" is also symmetric when K is symmetric. *But* K^{-1} *is not sparse.*

Invertibility is not easy to decide from a quick look at a matrix. Theoretically, one test is to compute the determinant. There is an inverse except when $\det K = 0$, because the formula for K^{-1} includes a division by $\det K$. But computing the determinant is almost never done in practice! It is a poor way to find $u = K^{-1}f$.

What we actually do is to go ahead with the elimination steps that solve $Ku = f$. Those steps simplify the matrix, to make it triangular. The nonzero pivots on the main diagonal of the triangular matrix show that the original K is invertible. (Important: We don't want or need K^{-1} to find $u = K^{-1}f$. The inverse would be a full matrix, with all positive entries. All we compute is the solution vector u.)

6. The symmetric matrices K_n are **positive definite**. Those words might be new. One goal of Chapter 1 is to explain what this crucial property means (K_4 has it, C_4 doesn't). Allow me to start by contrasting positive definiteness with invertibility, using the words "pivots" and "eigenvalues" that will soon be familiar. *Please notice the Appendix that summarizes linear algebra.*

   (***Pivots***) An invertible matrix has n *nonzero* pivots.
   A *positive definite* symmetric matrix has n ***positive* pivots**.

   (***Eigenvalues***) An invertible matrix has n *nonzero* eigenvalues.
   A *positive definite* symmetric matrix has n ***positive* eigenvalues**.

   Positive pivots and eigenvalues are tests for positive definiteness, and C_4 fails those tests because it is singular. Actually C_4 has three positive pivots and eigenvalues, so it almost passes. But its fourth eigenvalue is zero (the matrix is singular). Since no eigenvalue is negative ($\lambda \geq 0$), C_4 is **positive *semi*definite**.

The pivots appear on the main diagonal in Section 1.3, when solving $Ku = f$ by elimination. The eigenvalues arise in $Kx = \lambda x$. There is also a determinant test for positive definiteness (not just $\det K > 0$). The proper definition of a symmetric positive definite matrix (it is connected to positive energy) will come in Section 1.6.

Changing K_n to T_n

After K_n and C_n, there are two more families of matrices that you need to know. They are symmetric and tridiagonal like the family K_n. But the $(1, 1)$ entry in T_n is changed from 2 to 1:

$$\mathbf{T_n(1,1) = 1} \qquad T_2 = \begin{bmatrix} \mathbf{1} & -1 \\ -1 & 2 \end{bmatrix} \quad \text{and} \quad T_3 = \begin{bmatrix} \mathbf{1} & -1 & 0 \\ -1 & 2 & -1 \\ 0 & -1 & 2 \end{bmatrix}. \qquad (1)$$

That top row (T stands for top) represents a new boundary condition, whose meaning we will soon understand. Right now we use T_3 as a perfect example of elimination. Row operations produce zeros below the diagonal, and the pivots are circled as they are found. **Two elimination steps reduce T to the upper triangular U.**

Step 1. Add row 1 to row 2, which leaves zeros below the first pivot.

Step 2. Add the new row 2 to row 3, which produces U.

$$T = \begin{bmatrix} \textcircled{1} & -1 & 0 \\ -1 & 2 & -1 \\ 0 & -1 & 2 \end{bmatrix} \xrightarrow{\text{Step 1}} \begin{bmatrix} \textcircled{1} & -1 & 0 \\ 0 & \textcircled{1} & -1 \\ 0 & -1 & 2 \end{bmatrix} \xrightarrow{\text{Step 2}} \begin{bmatrix} \textcircled{1} & -1 & 0 \\ 0 & \textcircled{1} & -1 \\ 0 & 0 & \textcircled{1} \end{bmatrix} = U.$$

All three pivots of T equal 1. We can apply the test for invertibility (three nonzero pivots). T_3 also passes the test for positive definiteness (three *positive* pivots). In fact every T_n in this family is positive definite, with all its pivots equal to 1.

That matrix U has an inverse (which is automatically upper triangular). The exceptional fact for this particular U^{-1} is that *all upper triangular entries are* 1's:

$$U^{-1} = \begin{bmatrix} 1 & -1 & 0 \\ 0 & 1 & -1 \\ 0 & 0 & 1 \end{bmatrix}^{-1} = \begin{bmatrix} 1 & 1 & 1 \\ 0 & 1 & 1 \\ 0 & 0 & 1 \end{bmatrix} = \mathsf{triu(ones(3))}. \qquad (2)$$

This says that the inverse of a 3 by 3 "difference matrix" is a 3 by 3 "**sum matrix.**" This neat inverse of U will lead us to the inverse of T in Problem 2. **The product $U^{-1}U$ is the identity matrix I.** U takes differences, and U^{-1} takes sums. Taking differences and then sums will recover the original vector (u_1, u_2, u_3):

$$\textbf{Differences from } \boldsymbol{U} \qquad \begin{bmatrix} 1 & -1 & 0 \\ 0 & 1 & -1 \\ 0 & 0 & 1 \end{bmatrix} \begin{bmatrix} u_1 \\ u_2 \\ u_3 \end{bmatrix} = \begin{bmatrix} u_1 - u_2 \\ u_2 - u_3 \\ u_3 - 0 \end{bmatrix}$$

$$\textbf{Sums from } \boldsymbol{U^{-1}} \qquad \begin{bmatrix} 1 & 1 & 1 \\ 0 & 1 & 1 \\ 0 & 0 & 1 \end{bmatrix} \begin{bmatrix} u_1 - u_2 \\ u_2 - u_3 \\ u_3 - 0 \end{bmatrix} = \begin{bmatrix} u_1 \\ u_2 \\ u_3 \end{bmatrix}.$$

Changing T_n to B_n

The fourth family B_n has the last entry also changed from 2 to 1. The new boundary condition is being applied at both ends (B stands for both). These matrices B_n are symmetric and tridiagonal, but you will quickly see that they are *not invertible.* The B_n are positive semidefinite but *not positive definite*:

$$\mathbf{B_n(n,n) = 1} \qquad B_2 = \begin{bmatrix} \mathbf{1} & -1 \\ -1 & \mathbf{1} \end{bmatrix} \quad \text{and} \quad B_3 = \begin{bmatrix} \mathbf{1} & -1 & 0 \\ -1 & 2 & -1 \\ 0 & -1 & \mathbf{1} \end{bmatrix}. \tag{3}$$

Again, elimination brings out the properties of the matrix. The first $n-1$ pivots will all equal 1, because those rows are not changed from T_n. But the change from 2 to 1 in the last entry of B produces a change from 1 to 0 in the last entry of U:

$$B = \begin{bmatrix} \textcircled{1} & -1 & 0 \\ -1 & 2 & -1 \\ 0 & -1 & \mathbf{1} \end{bmatrix} \longrightarrow \begin{bmatrix} \textcircled{1} & -1 & 0 \\ 0 & \textcircled{1} & -1 \\ 0 & -1 & \mathbf{1} \end{bmatrix} \longrightarrow \begin{bmatrix} \textcircled{1} & -1 & 0 \\ 0 & \textcircled{1} & -1 \\ 0 & 0 & \mathbf{0} \end{bmatrix} = U. \tag{4}$$

There are only two pivots. (A pivot must be nonzero.) The last matrix U is certainly not invertible. Its determinant is zero, because its third row is all zeros. The constant vector $(1,1,1)$ is in the **nullspace** of U, and therefore it is in the nullspace of B:

$$\begin{bmatrix} 1 & -1 & 0 \\ 0 & 1 & -1 \\ 0 & 0 & 0 \end{bmatrix} \begin{bmatrix} 1 \\ 1 \\ 1 \end{bmatrix} = \begin{bmatrix} 0 \\ 0 \\ 0 \end{bmatrix} \quad \text{and also} \quad \begin{bmatrix} 1 & -1 & 0 \\ -1 & 2 & -1 \\ 0 & -1 & 1 \end{bmatrix} \begin{bmatrix} 1 \\ 1 \\ 1 \end{bmatrix} = \begin{bmatrix} 0 \\ 0 \\ 0 \end{bmatrix}.$$

The whole point of elimination was to simplify a linear system like $Bu = 0$, *without changing the solutions.* In this case we could have recognized non-invertibility in the matrix B, because each row adds to zero. Then the sum of its three columns is the zero column. This is what we see when B multiplies the vector $(1,1,1)$.

Let me summarize this section in four lines (all these matrices are symmetric):

> K_n and T_n are invertible and (more than that) positive definite.
>
> C_n and B_n are singular and (more than that) positive semidefinite.
>
> The nullspaces of C_n and B_n contain all the constant vectors $u = (c, c, \ldots, c)$.
>
> The nullspaces of K_n and T_n contain only the zero vector $u = (0, 0, \ldots, 0)$.

Matrices in MATLAB

It is natural to choose MATLAB for linear algebra, but the reader may select another system. (Octave is very close, and free. Mathematica and Maple are good for symbolic calculation, LAPACK provides excellent codes at no cost in netlib, and there are many other linear algebra packages.) We will construct matrices and operate on them in the convenient language that MATLAB provides.

Our first step is to construct the matrices K_n. For $n = 3$, we can enter the 3 by 3 matrix a row at a time, inside brackets. Rows are separated by a semicolon ;

$$K = [\ 2\ \ -1\ \ 0\ ;\ -1\ \ 2\ \ -1\ ;\ 0\ \ -1\ \ 2\ ]$$

For large matrices this is too slow. We can build K_8 from "eye" and "ones":

eye(8) = 8 by 8 identity matrix   ones(7, 1) = column vector of seven 1's

The diagonal part is 2∗eye(8). The symbol ∗ means multiplication! The −1's above the diagonal of K_8 have the vector −ones(7, 1) along diagonal 1 of the matrix E:

Superdiagonal of −1's $E = -\text{diag}(\text{ones}(7,1), 1)$

The −1's *below* the diagonal of K_8 lie on the diagonal numbered −1. For those we could change the last argument in E from 1 to −1. Or we can simply transpose E, using the all-important symbol E' for E^{T}. Then K comes from its three diagonals:

Tridiagonal matrix K_8 $K = 2 * \text{eye}(8) + E + E'$

Note: The zeroth diagonal (main diagonal) is the default with no second argument, so eye(8)= diag(ones(8,1)). And then diag(eye(8)) = ones(8, 1).

The constant diagonals make K *a Toeplitz matrix.* The toeplitz command produces K, when each diagonal is determined by a single number 2 or −1 or 0. Use the zeros vector for the 6 zeros in the first row of K_8:

Symmetric Toeplitz   row1 = [2 −1 zeros(1, 6)] ; K = toeplitz(row1)

For an unsymmetric constant-diagonal matrix, use toeplitz(col1, row1). Taking col1 = [1 − 1 0 0] and row1 = [1 0 0] gives a 4 by 3 backward difference matrix. It has two nonzero diagonals, 1's and −1's.

To construct the matrices T and B and C from K, just change entries as in the last three lines of this M-file that we have named KTBC.m. Its input is the size n, its output is four matrices of that size. The semicolons suppress display of K, T, B, C:

```
function [K,T,B,C] = KTBC(n)
% Create the four special matrices assuming n>1
K = toeplitz ([2 −1 zeros(1,n−2)]);
T = K; T(1,1) = 1;
B = K; B(1,1) = 1; B(n,n) = 1;
C = K; C(1,n) = −1; C(n,1) = −1;
```

If we happened to want their determinants (we shouldn't!), then with $n = 8$

$$\begin{bmatrix} \det(K) & \det(T) & \det(B) & \det(C) \end{bmatrix} \text{ produces the output } \quad \begin{bmatrix} 9 & 1 & 0 & 0 \end{bmatrix}$$

One more point. MATLAB could not store K_n as a dense matrix for $n = 10{,}000$. **The 10^8 entries need about 800 megabytes unless we recognize K as sparse.** The code sparseKTBC.m on the course website avoids storing (and operating on) all the zeros. It has K, T, B, or C and n as its first two arguments. The third argument is 1 for sparse, 0 for dense (default 0 for narg $= 2$, no third argument).

The input to Sparse MATLAB includes the locations of all nonzero entries. The command $A =$ sparse(i, j, s, m, n) creates an m by n sparse matrix from the vectors i, j, s that list all positions i, j of nonzero entries s. Elimination by lu(A) may produce additional nonzeros (called fill-in) which the software will correctly identify. In the normal "full" option, zeros are processed like all other numbers.

It is best to create the list of triplets i, j, s and then call sparse. Insertions $A(i, j) = s$ or $A(i, j) = A(i, j) + s$ are more expensive. We return to this point in Section 3.6.

The sparse KTBC code on the website uses spdiags to enter the three diagonals. Here is the toeplitz way to form K_8, all made sparse by its sparse vector start:

```
vsp = sparse([2 -1 zeros(1, 6)]) % please look at each output
Ksp= toeplitz(vsp) % sparse format gives the nonzero positions and entries
bsp = Ksp(:, 2)    % colon keeps all rows of column 2, so bsp = column 2 of Ksp
usp = Ksp\bsp      % zeros in Ksp and bsp are not processed, solution: usp(2) = 1
uuu= full(usp)     % return from sparse format to the full uuu = [0 1 0 0 0 0 0 0]
```

The next sections will use all four matrices in these basic tasks of linear algebra:

(**1.2**) The finite difference matrices K, T, B, C include boundary conditions

(**1.3**) Elimination produces pivots in D and triangular factors in LDL^{T}

(**1.4**) Point loads produce inverse matrices K^{-1} and T^{-1}

(**1.5**) The eigenvalues and eigenvectors of K, T, B, C involve sines and cosines.

You will see K\f in **1.2**, lu(K) in **1.3**, inv(K) in **1.4**, eig(K) in **1.5**, and chol(K) in **1.6**.

I very much hope that you will come to know and like these special matrices.

WORKED EXAMPLES

1.1 A $Bu = f$ and $Cu = f$ might be solvable even though B and C are singular!

Show that every vector $f = Bu$ has $f_1 + f_2 + \cdots + f_n = 0$. Physical meaning: **the external forces balance**. Linear algebra meaning: $Bu = f$ is solvable when f is perpendicular to the all-ones column vector $e = (1, 1, 1, 1, \ldots) = \text{ones}(n, 1)$.

Solution Bu is a vector of "differences" of u's. Those differences always add to zero:

$$f = Bu = \begin{bmatrix} 1 & -1 & & \\ -1 & 2 & -1 & \\ & -1 & 2 & -1 \\ & & -1 & 1 \end{bmatrix} \begin{bmatrix} u_1 \\ u_2 \\ u_3 \\ u_4 \end{bmatrix} = \begin{bmatrix} u_1 - u_2 \\ -u_1 + 2u_2 - u_3 \\ -u_2 + 2u_3 - u_4 \\ -u_3 + u_4 \end{bmatrix}$$

All terms cancel in $(u_1 - u_2) + (-u_1 + 2u_2 - u_3) + (-u_2 + 2u_3 - u_4) + (-u_3 + u_4) = 0$. The dot product with $e = (1, 1, 1, 1)$ is that sum $f^{\mathrm{T}}e = f_1 + f_2 + f_3 + f_4 = 0$.

Dot product $\quad f \cdot e = f^{\mathrm{T}}e = f_1e_1 + f_2e_2 + f_3e_3 + f_4e_4 \quad$ (f $'*$e in MATLAB).

A second explanation for $f^{\mathrm{T}}e = 0$ starts from the fact that $Be = 0$. The all-ones vector e is in the nullspace of B. Transposing $f = Bu$ gives $f^{\mathrm{T}} = u^{\mathrm{T}}B^{\mathrm{T}}$, since **the transpose of a product has the individual transposes in reverse order**. This matrix B is symmetric so $B^{\mathrm{T}} = B$. Then

$$f^{\mathrm{T}}e = u^{\mathrm{T}}B^{\mathrm{T}}e \quad \text{is equal to} \quad u^{\mathrm{T}}Be = u^{\mathrm{T}}0 = 0.$$

Conclusion $Bu = f$ is only solvable when f is perpendicular to the all-ones vector e. (*The same is true for* $Cu = f$. Again the differences cancel out.) **The external forces balance** when the f's add to zero. The command B\f will produce Inf because B is square and singular, but the "pseudoinverse" u = pinv(B) $*$ f will succeed. (Or add a zero row to B and f before the command B\f, to make the system rectangular.)

1.1 B The "fixed-free" matrix H changes the *last entry of* K from 2 to 1. Connect H to the "free-fixed" T (*first entry* $= 1$) by using the reverse identity matrix J:

$$H = \begin{bmatrix} 2 & -1 & 0 \\ -1 & 2 & -1 \\ 0 & -1 & \mathbf{1} \end{bmatrix} \quad \begin{array}{l} \text{comes from} \\ JTJ \text{ via the} \\ \textit{reverse identity } J \end{array} \quad J = \begin{bmatrix} 0 & 0 & 1 \\ 0 & 1 & 0 \\ 1 & 0 & 0 \end{bmatrix}.$$

Chapter 2 shows how T comes from a *tower* structure (free at the top). H comes from a *hanging* structure (free at the bottom). Two MATLAB constructions are

$H =$ toeplitz([2 -1 0]); $H(3,3) = 1$ **or** $J =$ fliplr(eye(3)); $H = J * T * J$

Solution JT reverses the rows of T. Then JTJ reverses the columns to give H:

$$T = \begin{bmatrix} 1 & -1 & 0 \\ -1 & 2 & -1 \\ 0 & -1 & 2 \end{bmatrix} \qquad \underset{\text{(rows)}}{JT =} \begin{bmatrix} 0 & -1 & 2 \\ -1 & 2 & -1 \\ 1 & -1 & 0 \end{bmatrix} \qquad \underset{(\textit{columns too})}{(JT)J = H\,.}$$

We could reverse columns first by TJ. Then $J(TJ)$ would be the same matrix H as $(JT)J$. **The parentheses never matter in** $(AB)C = A(BC)$!

Any permutation matrix like J has the rows of the identity matrix I in some order. There are six 3 by 3 permutation matrices because there are six orders for the numbers $1, 2, 3$. *The inverse of every permutation matrix is its transpose.* This particular J is symmetric, so it has $J = J^{\mathrm{T}} = J^{-1}$ as you can easily check:

$$H = JTJ \quad \text{so} \quad H^{-1} = J^{-1}T^{-1}J^{-1} \quad \text{which is} \quad H^{-1} = JT^{-1}J. \tag{5}$$

With back = 3:−1:1, reordering to JTJ is H = T(back, back) in MATLAB.

Problem Set 1.1

Problems 1–4 are about T^{-1} and Problems 5–8 are about K^{-1}.

1 The inverses of T_3 and T_4 (with $T_{11} = 1$ in the top corner) are

$$T_3^{-1} = \begin{bmatrix} 3 & 2 & 1 \\ 2 & 2 & 1 \\ 1 & 1 & 1 \end{bmatrix} \quad \text{and} \quad T_4^{-1} = \begin{bmatrix} 4 & 3 & 2 & 1 \\ 3 & 3 & 2 & 1 \\ 2 & 2 & 2 & 1 \\ 1 & 1 & 1 & 1 \end{bmatrix}.$$

Guess T_5^{-1} and multiply by T_5. Find a simple formula for the entries of T_n^{-1} below the diagonal ($i \geq j$), and then above the diagonal ($i \leq j$).

2 Compute T_3^{-1} in three steps, using U and U^{-1} in equation (2):

1. Check that $T_3 = U^{\mathrm{T}}U$, where U has 1's on the main diagonal and −1's along the diagonal above. Its transpose U^{T} is lower triangular.
2. Check that $UU^{-1} = I$ when U^{-1} has 1's on and above the main diagonal.
3. Invert $U^{\mathrm{T}}U$ to find $T_3^{-1} = (U^{-1})(U^{-1})^{\mathrm{T}}$. *Inverses come in reverse order*!

3 The difference matrix $U = U_5$ in MATLAB is eye(5)−diag(ones(4,1),1). Construct the sum matrix S from triu(ones(5)). (This keeps the upper triangular part of the 5 by 5 all-ones matrix.) Multiply $U * S$ to verify that $S = U^{-1}$.

4 For every n, $S_n = U_n{}^{-1}$ is upper triangular with ones on and above the diagonal. For $n = 4$ check that SS^{T} produces the matrix T_4^{-1} predicted in Problem 1. Why is SS^{T} certain to be a symmetric matrix?

5 The inverses of K_3 and K_4 (please also invert K_2) have fractions $\frac{1}{\det} = \frac{1}{4}, \frac{1}{5}$:

$$K_3^{-1} = \frac{1}{4}\begin{bmatrix} 3 & 2 & 1 \\ 2 & 4 & 2 \\ 1 & 2 & 3 \end{bmatrix} \quad \text{and} \quad K_4^{-1} = \frac{1}{5}\begin{bmatrix} 4 & 3 & 2 & 1 \\ 3 & 6 & 4 & 2 \\ 2 & 4 & 6 & 3 \\ 1 & 2 & 3 & 4 \end{bmatrix}.$$

First *guess* the determinant of $K = K_5$. Then compute $\texttt{det}(K)$ and $\texttt{inv}(K)$ and $\texttt{det}(K) * \texttt{inv}(K)$—any software is allowed.

6 (Challenge problem) Find a *formula* for the i, j entry of K_4^{-1} *below the diagonal* $(i \geq j)$. Those entries grow linearly along every row and up every column. (Section 1.4 will come back to these important inverses.) Problem 7 below is developed in the Worked Example of Section 1.4.

7 **A column u times a row v^{T} is a rank-one matrix uv^{T}.** All columns are multiples of u, and all rows are multiples of v^{T}. $T_4^{-1} - K_4^{-1}$ has rank 1:

$$T_4^{-1} - K_4^{-1} = \frac{1}{5}\begin{bmatrix} 16 & 12 & 8 & 4 \\ 12 & 9 & 6 & 3 \\ 8 & 6 & 4 & 2 \\ 4 & 3 & 2 & 1 \end{bmatrix} = \frac{1}{5}\begin{bmatrix} 4 \\ 3 \\ 2 \\ 1 \end{bmatrix}\begin{bmatrix} 4 & 3 & 2 & 1 \end{bmatrix}$$

Write $K_3 - T_3$ in this special form uv^{T}. Predict a similar formula for $T_3^{-1} - K_3^{-1}$.

8 (a) Based on Problem 7, predict the i, j entry of $T_5^{-1} - K_5^{-1}$ below the diagonal.

(b) Subtract this from your answer to Problem 1 (the formula for T_5^{-1} when $i \geq j$). This gives the not-so-simple formula for K_5^{-1}.

9 Following Example **1.1 A** with C instead of B, show that $e = (1, 1, 1, 1)$ is perpendicular to each column of C_4. Solve $Cu = f = (1, -1, 1, -1)$ with the singular matrix C by $\texttt{u} = \texttt{pinv(C)} * \texttt{f}$. Try $\texttt{u} = \texttt{C\e}$ and $\texttt{C\f}$, before and after adding a fifth equation $0 = 0$.

10 The "hanging matrix" H in Worked Example **1.1 B** changes the last entry of K_3 to $H_{33} = 1$. Find the inverse matrix from $H^{-1} = JT^{-1}J$. Find the inverse also from $H = UU^{\mathrm{T}}$ (check upper times lower triangular!) and $H^{-1} = (U^{-1})^{\mathrm{T}}U^{-1}$.

11 Suppose U is any upper triangular matrix and J is the reverse identity matrix in **1.1 B**. Then JU is a "southeast matrix". What geographies are UJ and JUJ? By experiment, a southeast matrix times a northwest matrix is ____.

12 Carry out elimination on the 4 by 4 circulant matrix C_4 to reach an upper triangular U (or try $[L, U] = \texttt{lu}(C)$ in MATLAB). Two points to notice: The last entry of U is ____ because C is singular. The last column of U has new nonzeros. Explain why this "fill-in" happens.

13 By hand, can you factor the circulant C_4 (with three nonzero diagonals, allowing wraparound) into circulants L times U (with two nonzero diagonals, allowing wraparound so not truly triangular)?

14 Gradually reduce the diagonal $2, 2, 2$ in the matrix K_3 until you reach a singular matrix M. This happens when the diagonal entries reach ____. Check the determinant as you go, and find a nonzero vector that solves $Mu = 0$.

Questions 15–21 bring out important facts about matrix multiplication.

15 How many individual multiplications to create Ax and A^2 and AB?

$$A_{n\,\times\,n}\,x_{n\,\times\,1} \qquad A_{n\,\times\,n}\,A_{n\,\times\,n} \qquad A_{m\,\times\,n}\,B_{n\,\times\,p} = (AB)_{m \times p}$$

16 You can multiply Ax by rows (the usual way) or **by columns** (more important). Do this multiplication both ways:

By rows $\quad \begin{bmatrix} 2 & 3 \\ 4 & 5 \end{bmatrix} \begin{bmatrix} 1 \\ 2 \end{bmatrix} = \begin{bmatrix} \text{inner product using row 1} \\ \text{inner product using row 2} \end{bmatrix}$

By columns $\quad \begin{bmatrix} 2 & 3 \\ 4 & 5 \end{bmatrix} \begin{bmatrix} 1 \\ 2 \end{bmatrix} = 1 \begin{bmatrix} 2 \\ 4 \end{bmatrix} + 2 \begin{bmatrix} 3 \\ 5 \end{bmatrix} = \begin{bmatrix} \textbf{combination} \\ \textbf{of columns} \end{bmatrix}$

17 The product Ax is a **linear combination of the columns of** A. The equations $Ax = b$ have a solution vector x exactly when b is a ____ of the columns.

Give an example in which b is *not in the column space* of A. There is no solution to $Ax = b$, because b is not a combination of the columns of A.

18 Compute $C = AB$ by multiplying the matrix A times each column of B:

$$\begin{bmatrix} 2 & 3 \\ 4 & 5 \end{bmatrix} \begin{bmatrix} 1 & 2 \\ 2 & 4 \end{bmatrix} = \begin{bmatrix} 8 & * \\ 14 & * \end{bmatrix}.$$

Thus, `A * B(:,j) = C(:,j)`.

19 You can also compute AB by multiplying each row of A times B:

$$\begin{bmatrix} 2 & 3 \\ 4 & 5 \end{bmatrix} \begin{bmatrix} 1 & 2 \\ 2 & 4 \end{bmatrix} = \begin{bmatrix} 2 * \text{row } 1 + 3 * \text{row } 2 \\ 4 * \text{row } 1 + 5 * \text{row } 2 \end{bmatrix} = \begin{bmatrix} 8 & 16 \\ * & * \end{bmatrix}.$$

A solution to $Bx = 0$ is also a solution to $(AB)x = 0$. Why? From

$$Bx = \begin{bmatrix} 1 & 2 \\ 2 & 4 \end{bmatrix} \begin{bmatrix} -2 \\ 1 \end{bmatrix} = \begin{bmatrix} 0 \\ 0 \end{bmatrix} \quad \text{how do we know} \quad ABx = \begin{bmatrix} 8 & 16 \\ * & * \end{bmatrix} \begin{bmatrix} -2 \\ 1 \end{bmatrix} = \begin{bmatrix} 0 \\ 0 \end{bmatrix}?$$

20 The four ways to find AB give numbers, columns, rows, and **matrices**:

1 **(*rows of* A) times (*columns of* B)**	C(i,j) = A(i,:) * B(:,j)
2 **A times (*columns of* B)**	C(:,j) = A * B(:,j)
3 **(*rows* of A) times B**	C(i,:) = A(i,:) * B
4 **(columns of A) times (rows of B)**	for k = 1:n, C = C + A(:,k) * B(k,:); end

Finish these 8 multiplications for **columns times rows**. How many for n by n?

$$\begin{bmatrix} 2 & 3 \\ 4 & 5 \end{bmatrix}\begin{bmatrix} 1 & 2 \\ 2 & 4 \end{bmatrix} = \begin{bmatrix} 2 \\ 4 \end{bmatrix}\begin{bmatrix} 1 & 2 \end{bmatrix} + \begin{bmatrix} 3 \\ 5 \end{bmatrix}\begin{bmatrix} 2 & 4 \end{bmatrix} = \begin{bmatrix} 2 & 4 \\ 4 & 8 \end{bmatrix} + \begin{bmatrix} * & * \\ * & * \end{bmatrix} = \begin{bmatrix} 8 & * \\ * & * \end{bmatrix}.$$

21 Which *one* of these equations is true for all n by n matrices A and B?

$$AB = BA \qquad (AB)A = A(BA) \qquad (AB)B = B(BA) \qquad (AB)^2 = A^2B^2.$$

22 Use $n = 1000$; $e =$ ones$(n, 1)$; $K =$ spdiags$([-e, 2 * e, -e], -1{:}1, n, n)$; to enter K_{1000} as a sparse matrix. Solve the sparse equation $Ku = e$ by u = K\e. Plot the solution by plot(u).

23 Create 4-component vectors u, v, w and enter $A =$ spdiags$([u, v, w], -1{:}1, 4, 4)$. Which components of u and w are left out from the -1 and 1 diagonals of A?

24 Build the sparse identity matrix $I =$ sparse$(i, j, s, 100, 100)$ by creating vectors i, j, s of positions i, j with nonzero entries s. (You could use a for loop.) In this case speye(100) is quicker. Notice that sparse(eye(10000)) would be a disaster, since there isn't room to store eye(10000) before making it sparse.

25 The only solution to $Ku = 0$ or $Tu = 0$ is $u = 0$, so K and T are invertible. For proof, suppose u_i is the largest component of u. If $-u_{i-1} + 2u_i - u_{i+1}$ is zero, this forces $u_{i-1} = u_i = u_{i+1}$. Then the next equations force every $u_j = u_i$. At the end, when the boundary is reached, $-u_{n-1} + 2u_n$ only gives zero if $u = 0$.

Why does this "diagonally dominant" argument fail for B and C?

26 For which vectors v is toeplitz(v) a circulant matrix (cyclic diagonals)?

1.2 DIFFERENCES, DERIVATIVES, BOUNDARY CONDITIONS

This important section connects difference equations to differential equations. A typical row in our matrices has the entries $-1, 2, -1$. We want to see how those numbers are producing a **second difference** (or more exactly, *minus* a second difference). The second difference gives a natural approximation to the **second derivative**. The matrices K_n and C_n and T_n and B_n are all involved in approximating the equation

$$-\frac{d^2u}{dx^2} = f(x) \quad \text{with boundary conditions at } x = 0 \text{ and } x = 1\,. \qquad (1)$$

Notice that the variable is x and not t. This is a boundary-value problem and not an initial-value problem. There are boundary conditions at $x = 0$ and $x = 1$, not initial conditions at $t = 0$. Those conditions are reflected in the *first and last rows* of the matrix. They decide whether we have K_n or C_n or T_n or B_n.

We will go from first differences to second differences. All four matrices have the special form $A^{\mathrm{T}}A$ (matrix times transpose). Those matrices A^{T} and A produce first differences, and $A^{\mathrm{T}}A$ produces second differences. So this section has two parts:

I. Differences replace derivatives (and we estimate the error).

II. We solve $-\dfrac{d^2u}{dx^2} = 1$ and then $-\dfrac{\Delta^2 u}{(\Delta x)^2} = 1$ using the matrices K and T.

Part I: Finite Differences

How can we approximate du/dx, the slope of a function $u(x)$? The function might be known, like $u(x) = x^2$. The function might be unknown, inside a differential equation. We are allowed to use values $u(x)$ and $u(x+h)$ and $u(x-h)$, but the stepsize $h = \Delta x$ is fixed. We have to work with $\Delta u/\Delta x$ without taking the limit as $\Delta x \to 0$. So we have "*finite differences*" where calculus has derivatives.

Three different possibilities for Δu are basic and useful. We can choose a forward difference or a backward difference or a centered difference. Calculus textbooks typically take $\Delta u = u(x + \Delta x) - u(x)$, going forward to $x + \Delta x$. **I will use $u(x) = x^2$ to test the accuracy of all three differences.** The derivative of x^2 is $2x$, and that forward difference Δ_+ is usually not the best! Here are Δ_+, Δ_-, and Δ_0:

Forward difference	$\dfrac{\mathbf{u(x+h)-u(x)}}{\mathbf{h}}$	The test gives	$\dfrac{(x+h)^2 - x^2}{h} = \mathbf{2x+h}$
Backward difference	$\dfrac{\mathbf{u(x)-u(x-h)}}{\mathbf{h}}$	The test gives	$\dfrac{x^2 - (x-h)^2}{h} = \mathbf{2x-h}$
Centered difference	$\dfrac{\mathbf{u(x+h)-u(x-h)}}{\mathbf{2h}}$	The test gives	$\dfrac{(x+h)^2 - (x-h)^2}{2h} = \mathbf{2x}$

For $u = x^2$, *the centered difference is the winner.* It gives the exact derivative $2x$, while forward and backward miss by h. Notice the division by $2h$ (not h).

Centered is generally more accurate than one-sided, when $h = \Delta x$ is small. The reason is in the Taylor series approximation of $u(x+h)$ and $u(x-h)$. These first few terms are always the key to understanding the accuracy of finite differences:

$$\textbf{Forward} \qquad u(x+h) = u(x) + hu'(x) + \tfrac{1}{2}h^2u''(x) + \tfrac{1}{6}h^3u'''(x) + \cdots \tag{2}$$

$$\textbf{Backward} \qquad u(x-h) = u(x) - hu'(x) + \tfrac{1}{2}h^2u''(x) - \tfrac{1}{6}h^3u'''(x) + \cdots \tag{3}$$

Subtract $u(x)$ from each side and divide by h. The forward difference is *first order accurate* because the leading error $\frac{1}{2}hu''(x)$ involves the first power of h:

$$\textbf{One-sided is first order} \qquad \frac{u(x+h)-u(x)}{h} = u'(x) + \frac{1}{2}\boldsymbol{hu''(x)} + \cdots \tag{4}$$

The backward difference is also first order accurate, and its leading error is $-\frac{1}{2}hu''(x)$. For $u(x) = x^2$, when $u''(x) = 2$ and $u''' = 0$, the error $\frac{1}{2}hu''$ is exactly h.

For the centered difference, subtract (3) from (2). Then $u(x)$ cancels and also $\frac{1}{2}h^2u''(x)$ cancels (*this gives extra accuracy*). Dividing by $2h$ leaves an h^2 error:

$$\textbf{Centered is second order} \qquad \frac{u(x+h)-u(x-h)}{2h} = u'(x) + \frac{1}{6}\boldsymbol{h^2u'''(x)} + \cdots \tag{5}$$

The centered error is $O(h^2)$ where the one-sided errors were $O(h)$, a significant change. If $h = \frac{1}{10}$ we are comparing a 1% error to a 10% error.

The matrix for centered differences is *antisymmetric* (like the first derivative):

Centered difference matrix $\boldsymbol{\Delta_0}^{\mathrm{T}} = \boldsymbol{-\Delta_0}$

$$\begin{bmatrix} \ddots & & & & \\ & -1 & 0 & 1 & \\ & & -1 & 0 & 1 \\ & & & & \ddots \end{bmatrix} \begin{bmatrix} u_{i-1} \\ u_i \\ u_{i+1} \\ u_{i+2} \end{bmatrix} = \begin{bmatrix} \vdots \\ u_{i+1} - u_{i-1} \\ u_{i+2} - u_i \\ \vdots \end{bmatrix}$$

Transposing Δ_0 reverses -1 and 1. The transpose of the forward difference matrix Δ_+ would be $-$ (backward difference) $= -\Delta_-$. **Centered difference quotients $\Delta_0 u/2h$ are the average of forward and backward** (Figure 1.1 shows $u(x) = x^3$).

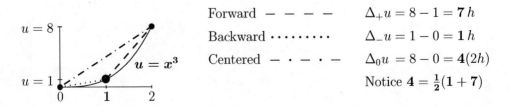

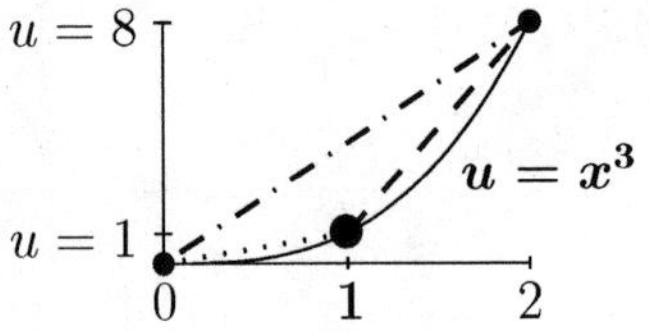

Forward	— — — —	$\Delta_+ u = 8 - 1 = \mathbf{7}\,h$
Backward	·········	$\Delta_- u = 1 - 0 = \mathbf{1}\,h$
Centered	— · — · —	$\Delta_0 u = 8 - 0 = \mathbf{4}(2h)$
		Notice $\mathbf{4} = \frac{1}{2}(\mathbf{1}+\mathbf{7})$

Figure 1.1: Δ_+/h and Δ_-/h and $\Delta_0/2h$ approximate $u' = 3x^2 = 3$ by $7, 1, 4$ at $x = 1$. The *second difference* $\Delta^2 u = 8 - 2(1) + 0$ is exactly $u'' = 6x = 6$ with step $h = 1$.

Second Differences from First Differences

We can propose a basic problem in scientific computing. Find a **finite difference approximation** to this linear second order differential equation:

$$-\frac{d^2u}{dx^2} = f(x) \quad \text{with the boundary conditions } u(0) = 0 \text{ and } u(1) = 0\,. \qquad (6)$$

The derivative of the derivative is the second derivative. In symbols $d/dx(du/dx)$ is d^2u/dx^2. It is natural that the first difference of the first difference should be the second difference. Watch how a second difference $\Delta_-\Delta_+u$ is centered around point i:

Difference of difference $$\frac{1}{h}\left[\left(\frac{u_{i+1}-u_i}{h}\right) - \left(\frac{u_i - u_{i-1}}{h}\right)\right] \quad \text{is} \quad \frac{u_{i+1}-2u_i+u_{i-1}}{h^2}\,. \qquad (7)$$

Those numbers 1, −2, 1 appear on the middle rows of our matrices K and T and B and C (with signs reversed). The denominator is $h^2 = (\Delta x)^2$ under this second difference. Notice the right positions for the superscripts 2, before u and after x:

Second difference $$\frac{d^2u}{dx^2} \approx \frac{\Delta^2 u}{\Delta x^2} = \frac{\boldsymbol{u(x+\Delta x) - 2u(x) + u(x-\Delta x)}}{\boldsymbol{(\Delta x)^2}}\,. \qquad (8)$$

What is the accuracy of this approximation? For $u(x+h)$ we use equation (2), and for $u(x-h)$ we use (3). The terms with h and h^3 cancel out:

$$\Delta^2 u(x) = u(x+h) - 2u(x) + u(x-h) = h^2u''(x) + ch^4u''''(x) + \cdots \qquad (9)$$

Dividing by h^2, $\Delta^2u/(\Delta x)^2$ has ***second order accuracy*** (error ch^2u''''). We get that extra order because Δ^2 is centered. The important tests are on $u(x) = x^2$ and $u(x) = x^3$. *The second difference divided by* $(\Delta x)^2$ *gives the correct second derivative*:

Perfection for $u = x^2$ $$\frac{(x+h)^2 - 2x^2 + (x-h)^2}{h^2} = 2\,. \qquad (10)$$

An equation d^2u/dx^2 = constant and its difference approximation $\Delta^2u/(\Delta x)^2$ = constant will have the *same solutions.* Unless the boundary conditions get in the way...

The Important Multiplications

You will like what comes now. The second difference matrix (with those diagonals $1, -2, 1$) will multiply the most important vectors I can think of. To avoid any problems at boundaries, I am only looking now at the **internal rows**—which are the same for K, T, B, C. These multiplications are a beautiful key to the whole chapter.

$$\boldsymbol{\Delta^2(\text{Squares}) = 2\cdot(\text{Ones}) \qquad \Delta^2(\text{Ramp}) = \text{Delta} \qquad \Delta^2(\text{Sines}) = \lambda\cdot(\text{Sines})} \qquad (11)$$

Here are column vectors whose second differences are special:

Constant	$(1,1,\ldots,1)$	ones(n,1)
Linear	$(1,2,\ldots,n)$	(1:n)′ (in MATLAB notation)
Squares	$(1^2,2^2,\ldots,n^2)$	(1:n)′.^2
Delta at k	$(0,0,\mathbf{1},0,\ldots,0)$	[zeros(k-1,1) ; 1 ; zeros(n-k,1)]
Step at k	$(0,0,\mathbf{1},1,\ldots,1)$	[zeros(k-1,1) ; ones(n-k+1,1)]
Ramp at k	$(0,0,\mathbf{0},1,\ldots,n-k)$	[zeros(k-1,1) ; 0:(n-k)′]
Sines	$(\sin t,\ldots,\sin nt)$	sin((1:n)′*t)
Cosines	$(\cos t,\ldots,\cos nt)$	cos((1:n)′*t)
Exponentials	$(e^{it},\ldots,e^{int})$	exp((1:n)′*i*t)

Now come the multiplications in each group. The second difference of each vector is *analogous* (and sometimes equal!) *to a second derivative.*

I. For constant and linear vectors, the second differences are **zero**:

$$\boldsymbol{\Delta^2}\textbf{(constant)} \qquad \begin{bmatrix} \ddots & & & & \\ & 1 & -2 & 1 & \\ & & 1 & -2 & 1 \\ & & & & \ddots \end{bmatrix} \begin{bmatrix} 1 \\ 1 \\ 1 \\ 1 \end{bmatrix} = \begin{bmatrix} \vdots \\ \mathbf{0} \\ \mathbf{0} \\ \vdots \end{bmatrix}$$

$$\boldsymbol{\Delta^2}\textbf{(linear)} \qquad \begin{bmatrix} \ddots & & & & \\ & 1 & -2 & 1 & \\ & & 1 & -2 & 1 \\ & & & & \ddots \end{bmatrix} \begin{bmatrix} 1 \\ 2 \\ 3 \\ 4 \end{bmatrix} = \begin{bmatrix} \vdots \\ \mathbf{0} \\ \mathbf{0} \\ \vdots \end{bmatrix} \tag{12}$$

For squares, the second differences are constant (the second derivative of x^2 is 2). This is truly important: Matrix multiplication confirms equation (8).

$$\boldsymbol{\Delta^2}\textbf{(squares)} \qquad \begin{bmatrix} \ddots & & & & \\ & 1 & -2 & 1 & \\ & & 1 & -2 & 1 \\ & & & & \ddots \end{bmatrix} \begin{bmatrix} 1 \\ 4 \\ 9 \\ 16 \end{bmatrix} = \begin{bmatrix} \vdots \\ \mathbf{2} \\ \mathbf{2} \\ \vdots \end{bmatrix} \tag{13}$$

Then $Ku =$ **ones** for $\boldsymbol{u} = -\textbf{(squares)}/\mathbf{2}$. Below come boundary conditions.

II. ***Second differences of the ramp vector produce the delta vector***:

$$\boldsymbol{\Delta^2}\textbf{(ramp)} \qquad \begin{bmatrix} \ddots & & & & \\ & 1 & -2 & 1 & \\ & & 1 & -2 & 1 \\ & & & & \ddots \end{bmatrix} \begin{bmatrix} 0 \\ 0 \\ 1 \\ 2 \end{bmatrix} = \begin{bmatrix} 0 \\ \mathbf{1} \\ 0 \\ 0 \end{bmatrix} = \textbf{delta}. \tag{14}$$

Section 1.4 will solve $Ku = \delta$ with boundary conditions included. You will see how each position of the "**1**" in **delta** produces a column u in K^{-1} or T^{-1}.

For functions: *The second derivative of a ramp* $\max(x,0)$ *is a delta function.*

III. Second differences of the **sine** and **cosine** and **exponential** produce $2\cos t - 2$ times those vectors. (Second derivatives of $\sin xt$ and $\cos xt$ and e^{ixt} produce $-t^2$ times the functions.) In Section 1.5, **sines or cosines or exponentials will be eigenvectors of K, T, B, C with the right boundary conditions.**

$$\mathbf{\Delta^2(sines)} \quad \begin{bmatrix} \ddots & & & \\ 1 & -2 & 1 & \\ & 1 & -2 & 1 \\ & & & \ddots \end{bmatrix} \begin{bmatrix} \sin t \\ \sin 2t \\ \sin 3t \\ \sin 4t \end{bmatrix} = (2\cos t - 2) \begin{bmatrix} \sin t \\ \sin 2t \\ \sin 3t \\ \sin 4t \end{bmatrix} \tag{15}$$

$$\mathbf{\Delta^2(cosines)} \quad \begin{bmatrix} \ddots & & & \\ 1 & -2 & 1 & \\ & 1 & -2 & 1 \\ & & & \ddots \end{bmatrix} \begin{bmatrix} \cos t \\ \cos 2t \\ \cos 3t \\ \cos 4t \end{bmatrix} = (2\cos t - 2) \begin{bmatrix} \cos t \\ \cos 2t \\ \cos 3t \\ \cos 4t \end{bmatrix} \tag{16}$$

$$\mathbf{\Delta^2(exponentials)} \quad \begin{bmatrix} \ddots & & & \\ 1 & -2 & 1 & \\ & 1 & -2 & 1 \\ & & & \ddots \end{bmatrix} \begin{bmatrix} e^{it} \\ e^{2it} \\ e^{3it} \\ e^{4it} \end{bmatrix} = (2\cos t - 2) \begin{bmatrix} e^{it} \\ e^{2it} \\ e^{3it} \\ e^{4it} \end{bmatrix} \tag{17}$$

The eigenvalue $2\cos t - 2$ is easiest to see for the **exponential** in (17). It is exactly $e^{it} - 2 + e^{-it}$, which factors out in the matrix multiplication. Then (16) and (15), **cosine** and **sine**, are the real and imaginary parts of (17). Soon t will be θ.

Part II: Finite Difference Equations

We have an approximation $\Delta^2 u/(\Delta x)^2$ to the second derivative d^2u/dx^2. So we can quickly create a discrete form of $-d^2u/dx^2 = f(x)$. ***Divide the interval*** $[0,1]$ ***into equal pieces of length*** $h = \Delta x$. If that meshlength is $h = \frac{1}{n+1}$, then $n+1$ short subintervals will meet at $x = h,\ x = 2h, \ldots,\ x = nh$. The extreme endpoints are $x = 0$ and $x = (n+1)h = 1$. The goal is to compute approximations $u_1, \ldots, u_n$ to the true values $u(h), \ldots, u(nh)$ at those n meshpoints inside the $[0,1]$ interval.

Unknowns $u = \begin{bmatrix} u_1 \\ u_2 \\ \vdots \\ u_n \end{bmatrix}$

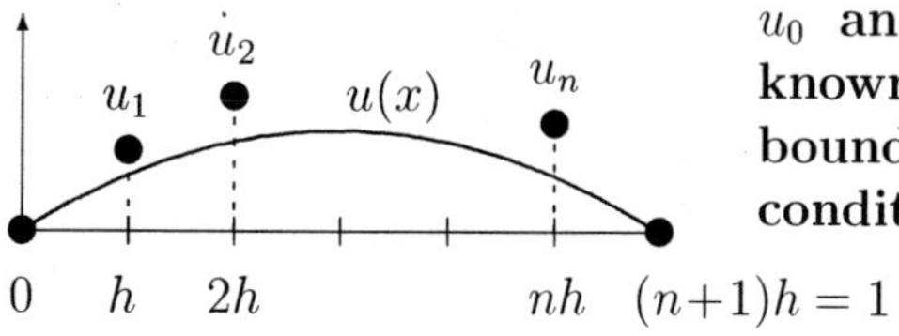

u_0 **and** u_{n+1} **known from boundary conditions**

Figure 1.2: The discrete unknowns $u_1, \ldots, u_n$ approximate the true $u(h), \ldots, u(nh)$.

Certainly $-d^2/dx^2$ is replaced by our $-1, 2, -1$ matrix, divided by h^2 and with the minus sign built in. What to do on the right side? The source term $f(x)$ might be a smooth distributed load or a concentrated point load. If $f(x)$ is smooth as in $\sin 2\pi x$, the first possibility is to use its values f_i at the meshpoints $x = i\Delta x$.

Finite difference equation $$\frac{-u_{i+1}+2u_i-u_{i-1}}{(\Delta x)^2}=f_i \tag{18}$$

The first equation ($i=1$) involves u_0. The last equation ($i=n$) involves u_{n+1}. The boundary conditions given at $x=0$ and $x=1$ will determine what to do. **We now solve the key examples with fixed ends** $u(0)=u_0=0$ **and** $u(1)=u_{n+1}=0$.

Example 1 Solve the differential and difference equations with constant force $f(x)\equiv 1$:

$$-\frac{d^2u}{dx^2}=1 \quad \text{with} \quad u(0)=0 \ \textbf{(fixed end)} \quad \text{and} \quad u(1)=0 \tag{19}$$

$$\frac{-u_{i+1}+2u_i-u_{i-1}}{h^2}=1 \quad \text{with} \quad u_0=0 \quad \text{and} \quad u_{n+1}=0 \tag{20}$$

Solution For every linear equation, the complete solution has two parts. One "particular solution" is added to any solution with *zero on the right side* (no force):

Complete solution $$u_{\textbf{complete}}=u_{\textbf{particular}}+u_{\textbf{nullspace}}\,. \tag{21}$$

This is where linearity is so valuable. Every solution to $Lu=0$ can be added to one particular solution of $Lu=f$. Then by linearity $L(u_{\text{part}}+u_{\text{null}})=f+0$.

Particular solution $-\dfrac{d^2u}{dx^2}=1$ is solved by $u_{\text{part}}(x)=-\frac{1}{2}x^2$

Nullspace solution $-\dfrac{d^2u}{dx^2}=0$ is solved by $u_{\text{null}}(x)=Cx+D$.

The complete solution is $u(x)=-\frac{1}{2}x^2+Cx+D$. The boundary conditions will tell us the constants C and D in the nullspace part. Substitute $x=0$ and $x=1$:

Boundary condition at $x=0$ $u(0)=0$ gives $D=0$ **Solution**

Boundary condition at $x=1$ $u(1)=0$ gives $C=\frac{1}{2}$ $\boldsymbol{u=\frac{1}{2}x-\frac{1}{2}x^2}$

In Figure 1.3, the finite difference solution agrees with this $u(x)$ at the meshpoints. This is special: (19) and (20) have the **same solution** (*a parabola*). A second difference of $u_i=i^2h^2$ gives exactly the correct second derivative of $u=x^2$. The second difference of a linear $u_i=ih$ matches the second derivative (*zero*) of $u=x$:

$$\frac{(i+1)h-2ih+(i-1)h}{h^2}=0 \quad \text{matches} \quad \frac{d^2}{dx^2}(x)=0. \tag{22}$$

The combination of quadratic i^2h^2 and linear ih (particular and nullspace solutions) is exactly right. It solves the equation and satisfies the boundary conditions. We can

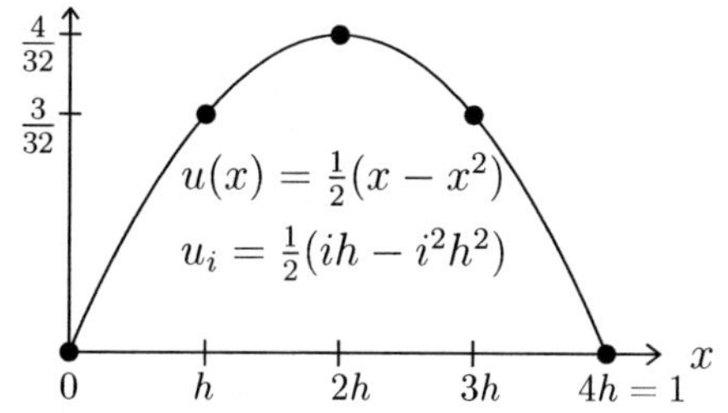

Solution to $-\dfrac{d^2u}{dx^2} = 1$

Solution to $-\dfrac{\Delta^2 u}{\Delta x^2} = \text{ones}$

Figure 1.3: Finite differences give an exact match of $u(x)$ and u_i for the special case $-u'' = 1$ with $u_0 = u_{n+1} = 0$. The discrete values lie right on the parabola.

set $x = ih$ in the true solution $u(x) = \frac{1}{2}(x - x^2)$ to find the correct u_i.

Finite difference solution $\quad u_i = \dfrac{1}{2}(ih - i^2h^2)$ has $u_{n+1} = \dfrac{1}{2}(1 - 1^2) = 0.$

It is unusual to have this perfect agreement between u_i and the exact $u(ih)$. It is also unusual that no matrices were displayed. When $4h = 1$ and $f = 1$, the matrix is $K_3/h^2 = 16K_3$. Then $ih = \frac{1}{4}, \frac{2}{4}, \frac{3}{4}$ leads to $u_i = \frac{3}{32}, \frac{4}{32}, \frac{3}{32}$:

$$\boldsymbol{Ku = f} \qquad 16\begin{bmatrix} 2 & -1 & 0 \\ -1 & 2 & -1 \\ 0 & -1 & 2 \end{bmatrix}\begin{bmatrix} 3/32 \\ 4/32 \\ 3/32 \end{bmatrix} = \begin{bmatrix} 1 \\ 1 \\ 1 \end{bmatrix}. \qquad (23)$$

The -1's in columns 0 and 4 were safely chopped off because $u_0 = u_4 = 0$.

A Different Boundary Condition

Chapter 2 will give a host of physical examples leading to these differential and difference equations. Right now we stay focused on the boundary condition at $x = 0$, changing from zero height to ***zero slope***:

$$-\frac{d^2u}{dx^2} = f(x) \quad \text{with} \quad \frac{du}{dx}(0) = 0 \ (\textbf{free end}) \quad \text{and} \quad u(1) = 0. \qquad (24)$$

With this new boundary condition, the difference equation no longer wants $u_0 = 0$. Instead we could set the *first difference* to zero: $u_1 - u_0 = 0$ means zero slope in the first small interval. With $u_0 = u_1$, the second difference $-u_0 + 2u_1 - u_2$ in row 1 reduces to $u_1 - u_2$. **The new boundary condition changes K_n to T_n.**

Example 2 Solve the differential and difference equations starting from zero slope:

$$\textbf{Free-fixed} \qquad -\frac{d^2u}{dx^2} = 1 \quad \text{with} \quad \frac{du}{dx}(0) = 0 \quad \text{and} \quad u(1) = 0 \qquad (25)$$

$$\frac{-u_{i+1} + 2u_i - u_{i-1}}{h^2} = 1 \quad \text{with} \quad \frac{u_1 - u_0}{h} = 0 \quad \text{and} \quad u_{n+1} = 0 \qquad (26)$$

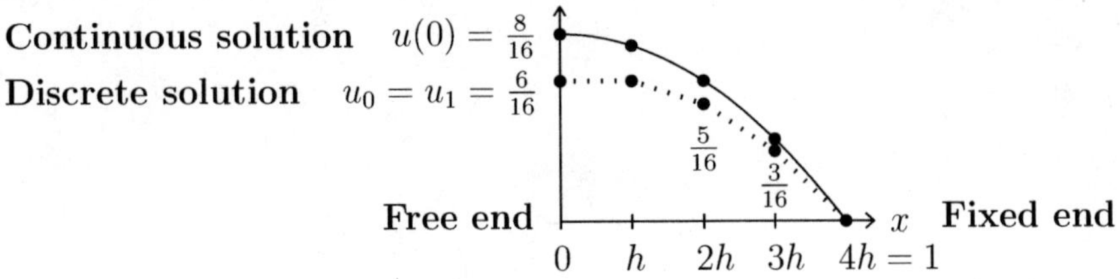

Figure 1.4: u_i is below the true $u(x) = \frac{1}{2}(1 - x^2)$ by an error $\frac{1}{2}h(1 - x)$.

Solution $u(x) = -\frac{1}{2}x^2 + Cx + D$ is still the complete solution to $-u'' = 1$. But the new boundary condition changes the constants to $C = 0$ and $D = \frac{1}{2}$:

$$\frac{du}{dx} = 0 \text{ at } x = 0 \text{ gives } C = 0. \text{ Then } u = 0 \text{ at } x = 1 \text{ gives } D = \frac{1}{2}.$$

The free-fixed solution is $u(x) = \frac{1}{2}(1 - x^2)$.

Figure 1.4 shows this parabola. Example 1 was a symmetric parabola, but now the discrete boundary condition $u_1 = u_0$ is *not exactly satisfied* by $u(x)$. So the finite difference u_i's show small errors. We expect an $O(h)$ correction because of the forward difference $(u_1 - u_0)/h$. For $n = 3$ and $h = \frac{1}{4}$,

$$\frac{1}{h^2}\begin{bmatrix} 1 & -1 & \\ -1 & 2 & -1 \\ & -1 & 2 \end{bmatrix}\begin{bmatrix} u_1 \\ u_2 \\ u_3 \end{bmatrix} = \begin{bmatrix} 1 \\ 1 \\ 1 \end{bmatrix} \quad \text{gives} \quad \begin{bmatrix} u_1 \\ u_2 \\ u_3 \end{bmatrix} = h^2\begin{bmatrix} 6 \\ 5 \\ 3 \end{bmatrix}. \tag{27}$$

Figure 1.4 shows that solution (not very accurate, with three meshpoints). The discrete points will lie much nearer the parabola for large n. The error is $h(1 - x)/2$. For completeness we can go ahead to solve $T_n u = h^2$ ones$(n, 1)$ for every n:

$$T_n = (\textbf{backward})(-\textbf{forward}) = \begin{bmatrix} 1 & 0 & & \\ -1 & 1 & 0 & \\ & \ddots & \ddots & 0 \\ & & -1 & 1 \end{bmatrix}\begin{bmatrix} 1 & -1 & & \\ 0 & 1 & -1 & \\ & \ddots & \ddots & -1 \\ & & 0 & 1 \end{bmatrix} \tag{28}$$

The inverses of those first difference matrices are *sum matrices* (triangles of 1's). The inverse of T_n is an upper triangle times a lower triangle:

$$\boldsymbol{T}_n^{-1}\text{ones} = \begin{bmatrix} 1 & 1 & \ddots & 1 \\ & 1 & 1 & \ddots \\ & & 1 & 1 \\ & & & 1 \end{bmatrix}\begin{bmatrix} 1 & & & \\ 1 & 1 & & \\ \ddots & 1 & 1 & \\ 1 & \ddots & 1 & 1 \end{bmatrix}\begin{bmatrix} 1 \\ 1 \\ \vdots \\ 1 \end{bmatrix} \tag{29}$$

$$\boldsymbol{u} = h^2\boldsymbol{T}_n^{-1}\text{ones} = h^2\begin{bmatrix} 1 + 2 + \cdots + n \\ 2 + \cdots + n \\ \cdots + n \\ n \end{bmatrix} \tag{30}$$

For $n = 3$ we recover $1 + 2 + 3 = 6$ and $2 + 3 = 5$, which appeared in (27). There is a formula for those sums in (30) and it gives the approximation u_i:

Discrete solution $$u_i = \tfrac{1}{2}h^2(n+i)(n+1-i) \qquad (31)$$

This answer has $u_{n+1} = 0$ when $i = n+1$. And $u_0 = u_1$ so the boundary conditions are satisfied. That starting value $u_0 = \frac{1}{2}nh$ is below the correct value $u(0) = \frac{1}{2} = \frac{1}{2}(n+1)h$ only by $\frac{1}{2}h$. This $\frac{1}{2}h$ is the first-order error caused by replacing the zero slope at $x = 0$ by the one-sided condition $u_1 = u_0$.

The worked example removes that $O(h)$ error by centering the boundary condition.

MATLAB Experiment

The function $u(x) = \cos(\pi x/2)$ satisfies free-fixed boundary conditions $u'(0) = 0$ and $u(1) = 0$. It solves the equation $-u'' = f = (\pi/2)^2\cos(\pi x/2)$. How close to u are the solutions U and V of the finite difference equations $T_nU = f$ and $T_{n+1}V = g$?

```
h = 1/(n+1); u = cos(pi*(1:n)'*h/2); c = (pi/2)^2; f = c*u; % Usual matrix T
U = h*h*T\f;              % Solution u_1,...,u_n with one-sided condition u_0 = u_1
e = 1 - U(1)              % First-order error at x = 0
g = [c/2;f]; T = ...;     % Create T_{n+1} as in equation (34) below. Note g(1) = f(0)/2
V = h*h*T\g;              % Solution u_0,...,u_n with centered condition u_{-1} = u_1
E = 1 - V(1)              % Second-order error from centering at x = 0
```

Take $n = 3, 7, 15$ and test T\f with appropriate T and f. Somehow the right mesh has $(n + \frac{1}{2})h = 1$, so the boundary point with $u' = 0$ is halfway between meshpoints. You should find e proportional to h and E proportional to h^2. A big difference.

■ WORKED EXAMPLES ■

1.2 A Is there a way to avoid this $O(h)$ error from the one-sided boundary condition $u_1 = u_0$? Constructing a more accurate difference equation is a perfect example of numerical analysis. This crucial decision comes between the modeling step (by a differential equation) and the computing step (solving the discrete equation).

Solution The natural idea is a **centered difference** $(u_1 - u_{-1})/2h = 0$. This copies the true $u'(0) = 0$ with second order accuracy. It introduces a new unknown u_{-1}, so extend the difference equation to $x = 0$. Eliminating u_{-1} leaves size(T)$= n+1$:

$$-u_{-1} + 2u_0 - u_1 = h^2 f(0) \quad \text{and} \quad u_{-1} = u_1 \quad \text{give} \quad \boldsymbol{u_0 - u_1 = \tfrac{1}{2}h^2 f(0)}\,. \qquad (32)$$

Centering the boundary condition multiplies $f(0)$ by $\frac{1}{2}$. Try $n = 3$ and $h = \frac{1}{4}$:

$$\frac{1}{h^2}\begin{bmatrix} 1 & -1 & & \\ -1 & 2 & -1 & \\ & -1 & 2 & -1 \\ & & -1 & 2 \end{bmatrix}\begin{bmatrix} u_0 \\ u_1 \\ u_2 \\ u_3 \end{bmatrix} = \begin{bmatrix} .5 \\ 1 \\ 1 \\ 1 \end{bmatrix} \quad \text{gives} \quad \begin{bmatrix} u_0 \\ u_1 \\ u_2 \\ u_3 \end{bmatrix} = \frac{1}{16}\begin{bmatrix} 8.0 \\ 7.5 \\ 6.0 \\ 3.5 \end{bmatrix}. \qquad (33)$$

Those numbers u_i are exactly equal to the true $u(x) = \frac{1}{2}(1 - x^2)$ at the nodes. We are back to perfect agreement with the parabola in Figure 1.4. For a varying load $f(x)$ and a non-parabolic solution to $-u'' = f(x)$, the centered discrete equation will have second-order errors $O(h^2)$.

Problem 21 shows a very direct approach to $u_0 - u_1 = \frac{1}{2}h^2 f(0)$.

1.2 B When we multiply matrices, the backward Δ_- times the forward Δ_+ gives 1 and -2 and 1 on the interior rows:

$$\Delta_-\Delta_+ = \begin{bmatrix} 1 & 0 & 0 \\ -1 & 1 & 0 \\ 0 & -1 & 1 \end{bmatrix}\begin{bmatrix} -1 & 1 & 0 \\ 0 & -1 & 1 \\ 0 & 0 & -1 \end{bmatrix} = \begin{bmatrix} -1 & 1 & 0 \\ \mathbf{1} & \mathbf{-2} & \mathbf{1} \\ 0 & 1 & -2 \end{bmatrix}. \qquad (34)$$

We didn't get K_3, for two reasons. First, the signs are still reversed. And the first corner entry is -1 instead of -2. The boundary rows give us T_3, because $\Delta_-(\Delta_+ u)$ sets to zero the first value $\Delta_+ u = (u_1 - u_0)/h$ (not the value of u itself!).

$$-T_3 = \begin{bmatrix} -1 & 1 & 0 \\ 1 & -2 & 1 \\ 0 & 1 & -2 \end{bmatrix} \begin{matrix} \leftarrow \Delta^2 u & \text{boundary row with } u_0 = u_1 \\ \leftarrow \Delta^2 u & \text{typical row } u_2 - 2u_1 + u_0 \\ \leftarrow \Delta^2 u & \text{boundary row with } u_4 = 0 \end{matrix} \qquad (35)$$

The boundary condition at the top is *zero slope.* The second difference $u_2 - 2u_1 + u_0$ becomes $u_2 - u_1$ when $u_0 = u_1$. We will come back to this, because in my experience 99% of the difficulties with differential equations occur at the boundary.

$\boldsymbol{u(0) = 0,\ u(1) = 0}$	K has $u_0 = u_{n+1} = 0$
$\boldsymbol{u'(0) = 0,\ u'(1) = 0}$	B has $u_0 = u_1,\ u_n = u_{n+1}$
$\boldsymbol{u'(0) = 0,\ u(1) = 0}$	T has $u_0 = u_1,\ u_{n+1} = 0$
$\boldsymbol{u(0) = u(1),\ u'(0) = u'(1)}$	C has $u_0 = u_n,\ u_{n+1} = 0$

An infinite tridiagonal matrix, with no boundary, maintains $1, -2, 1$ down its infinitely long diagonals. *Chopping off the infinite matrix would be the same as pretending that u_0 and u_{n+1} are both zero.* That leaves K_n, which has 2's in the corners.

Problem Set 1.2

1 What are the second derivative $u''(x)$ and the second difference $\Delta^2 U_n$? Use $\boldsymbol{\delta(x)}$.

$$u(x) = \begin{cases} Ax & \text{if } x \le 0 \\ Bx & \text{if } x \ge 0 \end{cases} \qquad U_n = \begin{cases} An & \text{if } n \le 0 \\ Bn & \text{if } n \ge 0 \end{cases} = \begin{bmatrix} -2A \\ -A \\ 0 \\ B \\ 2B \end{bmatrix}$$

$u(x)$ and U are piecewise linear with a corner at 0.

2 Solve the differential equation $-u''(x) = \delta(x)$ with $u(-2) = 0$ and $u(3) = 0$. The pieces $u = A(x+2)$ and $u = B(x-3)$ meet at $x = 0$. Show that the vector $U = (u(-1), u(0), u(1), u(2))$ solves the corresponding matrix problem $KU = F = (0,1,0,0)$.

Problems 3–12 are about the "local accuracy" of finite differences.

3 The h^2 term in the error for a centered difference $(u(x+h) - u(x-h))/2h$ is $\frac{1}{6}h^2 u'''(x)$. Test by computing that difference for $u(x) = x^3$ and x^4.

4 Verify that the inverse of the backward difference matrix Δ_- in (28) is the sum matrix in (29). But the centered difference matrix $\Delta_0 = (\Delta_+ + \Delta_-)/2$ might not be invertible! Solve $\Delta_0 u = 0$ for $n = 3$ and $n = 5$.

5 In the Taylor series (2), find the number a in the next term $ah^4 u''''(x)$ by testing $u(x) = x^4$ at $x = 0$.

6 For $u(x) = x^4$, compute the second derivative and second difference $\Delta^2 u/(\Delta x)^2$. From the answers, predict c in the leading error in equation (9).

7 Four samples of u can give fourth-order accuracy for du/dx at the center:

$$\frac{-u_2 + 8u_1 - 8u_{-1} + u_{-2}}{12h} = \frac{du}{dx} + bh^4 \frac{d^5 u}{dx^5} + \cdots$$

1. Check that this is correct for $u = 1$ and $u = x^2$ and $u = x^4$.
2. Expand u_2, u_1, u_{-1}, u_{-2} as in equation (2). Combine the four Taylor series to discover the coefficient b in the h^4 leading error term.

8 *Question* Why didn't I square the centered difference for a good Δ^2?

Answer A centered difference of a centered difference stretches too far:

$$\frac{\Delta_0}{2h}\frac{\Delta_0}{2h} u_n = \frac{u_{n+2} - 2u_n + u_{n-2}}{(2h)^2}$$

The second difference matrix now has $\mathbf{1, 0, -2, 0, 1}$ on a typical row. The accuracy is no better and we have trouble with u_{n+2} at the boundaries.

Can you construct a fourth-order accurate centered difference for d^2u/dx^2, choosing the right coefficients to multiply $u_2, u_1, u_0, u_{-1}, u_{-2}$?

9 Show that the fourth difference $\Delta^4 u/(\Delta x)^4$ with coefficients $1, -4, 6, -4, 1$ approximates d^4u/dx^4 by testing on $u = x, x^2, x^3$, and x^4:

$$\frac{\Delta^4 u}{\Delta x^4} = \frac{u_2 - 4u_1 + 6u_0 - 4u_{-1} + u_{-2}}{(\Delta x)^4} = \frac{d^4 u}{dx^4} + \text{(which leading error ?)}\,.$$

10 Multiply the first difference matrices in the order $\Delta_+\Delta_-$, instead of $\Delta_-\Delta_+$ in equation (27). Which boundary row, first or last, corresponds to the boundary condition $u = 0$? Where is the approximation to $u' = 0$?

11 Suppose we want a one-sided approximation to $\frac{du}{dx}$ with second order accuracy:

$$\frac{ru(x) + su(x - \Delta x) + tu(x - 2\Delta x)}{\Delta x} = \frac{du}{dx} \quad \text{for} \quad u = 1, x, x^2\,.$$

Substitute $u = 1, x, x^2$ to find and solve three equations for r, s, t. The corresponding difference matrix will be lower triangular. The formula is "causal."

12 Equation (7) shows the "first difference of the first difference." Why is the left side within $O(h^2)$ of $\frac{1}{h}\left[u'_{i+\frac{1}{2}} - u'_{i-\frac{1}{2}}\right]$? Why is this within $O(h^2)$ of u''_i?

Problems 13–19 solve differential equations to test global accuracy.

13 Graph the free-fixed solution $u_0, \ldots, u_8$ with $n = 7$ in Figure 1.4, in place of the existing graph with $n = 3$. You can use formula (30) or solve the 7 by 7 system. The $O(h)$ error should be cut in half, from $h = \frac{1}{4}$ to $\frac{1}{8}$.

14 (a) Solve $-u'' = 12x^2$ with free-fixed conditions $u'(0) = 0$ and $u(1) = 0$. The complete solution involves integrating $f(x) = 12x^2$ twice, plus $Cx + D$.

(b) With $h = \frac{1}{n+1}$ and $n = 3, 7, 15$, compute the discrete $u_1, \ldots, u_n$ using T_n:

$$\frac{u_{i+1} - 2u_i + u_{i-1}}{h^2} = 3(ih)^2 \quad \text{with } u_0 = 0 \text{ and } u_{n+1} = 0\,.$$

Compare u_i with the exact answer at the center point $x = ih = \frac{1}{2}$. Is the error proportional to h or h^2?

15 Plot the $u = \cos 4\pi x$ for $0 \leq x \leq 1$ and the discrete values $u_i = \cos 4\pi ih$ at the meshpoints $x = ih = \frac{i}{n+1}$. For small n those values will not catch the oscillations of $\cos \pi x$. How large is a good n? How many mesh points per oscillation?

16 Solve $-u'' = \cos 4\pi x$ with fixed-fixed conditions $u(0) = u(1) = 0$. Use K_4 and K_8 to compute $u_1, \ldots, u_n$ and plot on the same graph with $u(x)$:

$$\frac{u_{i+1} - 2u_i + u_{i-1}}{h^2} = \cos 4\pi ih \quad \text{with} \quad u_0 = u_{n+1} = 0\,.$$

17 Test the differences $\Delta_0 u = (u_{i+1} - u_{i-1})$ and $\Delta^2 u = u_{i+1} - 2u_i + u_{i-1}$ on $u(x) = e^{ax}$. Factor out e^{ax} (this is why exponentials are so useful). Expand $e^{a\Delta x} = 1 + a\Delta x + (a\Delta x)^2/2 + \cdots$ to find the leading error terms.

18 Write a finite difference approximation (using K) with $n = 4$ unknowns to

$$\frac{d^2u}{dx^2} = x \quad \text{with boundary conditions } u(0) = 0 \text{ and } u(1) = 0\,.$$

Solve for u_1, u_2, u_3, u_4. Compare them to the true solution.

19 Construct a *centered* difference approximation using K/h^2 and $\Delta_0/2h$ to

$$-\frac{d^2u}{dx^2} + \frac{du}{dx} = 1 \quad \text{with } u(0) = 0 \text{ and } u(1) = 0\,.$$

Separately use a *forward* difference $\Delta_+ U/h$ for du/dx. Notice $\Delta_0 = (\Delta_+ + \Delta_-)/2$. Solve for the centered u and uncentered U with $h = 1/5$. The true $u(x)$ is the particular solution $u = x$ plus any $A + Be^x$. Which A and B satisfy the boundary conditions? How close are u and U to $u(x)$?

20 The transpose of the centered difference Δ_0 is $-\Delta_0$ (*antisymmetric*). That is like the minus sign in integration by parts, when $f(x)g(x)$ drops to zero at $\pm\infty$:

Integration by parts $$\int_{-\infty}^{\infty} f(x)\,\frac{dg}{dx}\,dx = -\int_{-\infty}^{\infty} \frac{df}{dx}\,g(x)\,dx\,.$$

Verify the **summation by parts** $\displaystyle\sum_{-\infty}^{\infty} \boldsymbol{f_i\,(g_{i+1} - g_{i-1})} = -\sum_{-\infty}^{\infty} \boldsymbol{(f_{i+1} - f_{i-1})\,g_i}$.

Hint: Change $i + 1$ to i in $\sum f_i g_{i+1}$, and change $i - 1$ to i in $\sum f_i g_{i-1}$.

21 Use the expansion $u(h) = u(0) + hu'(0) + \frac{1}{2}h^2 u''(0) + \cdots$ with zero slope $u'(0) = 0$ and $-u'' = f(x)$ to derive the top boundary equation $\boldsymbol{u_0 - u_1 = \frac{1}{2}h^2 f(0)}$. This factor $\frac{1}{2}$ removes the $O(h)$ error from Figure 1.4: good.

1.3 ELIMINATION LEADS TO $K = LDL^{\mathrm{T}}$

This book has two themes—how to understand equations, and how to solve them. This section is about solving a system of n linear equations $Ku = f$. Our method will be **Gaussian elimination** (not determinants and not Cramer's Rule!). All software packages use elimination on positive definite systems of all sizes. MATLAB uses u = K\f (known as **backslash**), and [L, U] = lu(K) for triangular factors of K.

The **symmetric factorization** $\boldsymbol{K = LDL^{\mathrm{T}}}$ takes two extra steps beyond the solution itself. First, *elimination factors K into LU*: lower triangular L times upper triangular U. Second, the symmetry of K leads to $U = DL^{\mathrm{T}}$. The steps from K to U and back to K are by ***lower triangular matrices****—rows operating on lower rows.*

$K = LU$ and $K = LDL^{\mathrm{T}}$ are the right "matrix ways" to understand elimination. The pivots go into D. This is the most frequently used algorithm in scientific computing (billions of dollars per year) so it belongs in this book. If you met LU and LDL^{T} earlier in a linear algebra course, I hope you find this a good review.

The multipliers in L and the pivots in D have neat formulas for the special tridiagonal families K_n and T_n. Our first example is the 3 by 3 matrix $K = K_3$. It contains the nine coefficients (two of them are zero) in the linear equations $Ku = f$. The vector on the right side is not so important now, and we choose $f = (4, 0, 0)$. Then $Ku = f$ is a system of three equations in three unknowns $u = (u_1, u_2, u_3)$:

$$\mathbf{Ku = f} \qquad \begin{bmatrix} 2 & -1 & 0 \\ -1 & 2 & -1 \\ 0 & -1 & 2 \end{bmatrix} \begin{bmatrix} u_1 \\ u_2 \\ u_3 \end{bmatrix} = \begin{bmatrix} f_1 \\ f_2 \\ f_3 \end{bmatrix} \quad \text{is} \quad \begin{aligned} 2u_1 - u_2 \phantom{{}- u_3} &= 4 \\ -u_1 + 2u_2 - u_3 &= 0 \\ - u_2 + 2u_3 &= 0 \end{aligned}$$

The first step is to eliminate u_1 from the second equation. **Multiply equation 1 by $\frac{1}{2}$ and add to equation 2.** The new matrix has a zero in the 2, 1 position—where u_1 is eliminated. I have circled the **first two pivots**:

$$\begin{bmatrix} \textcircled{2} & -1 & 0 \\ 0 & \textcircled{\tfrac{3}{2}} & -1 \\ 0 & -1 & 2 \end{bmatrix} \begin{bmatrix} u_1 \\ u_2 \\ u_3 \end{bmatrix} = \begin{bmatrix} f_1 \\ f_2 + \frac{1}{2} f_1 \\ f_3 \end{bmatrix} \quad \text{is} \quad \begin{aligned} 2u_1 - u_2 \phantom{{}- u_3} &= 4 \\ \tfrac{3}{2} u_2 - u_3 &= 2 \\ - u_2 + 2u_3 &= 0 \end{aligned}$$

The next step looks at the 2 by 2 system in the last two equations. The pivot $d_2 = \frac{3}{2}$ is circled. To eliminate u_2 from the third equation, **add $\frac{2}{3}$ of the second equation.** Then the matrix has a zero in the 3, 2 position. It is now the **upper triangular** U. The three pivots $\mathbf{2}, \frac{\mathbf{3}}{\mathbf{2}}, \frac{\mathbf{4}}{\mathbf{3}}$, are on its diagonal:

$$\begin{bmatrix} \textcircled{2} & -1 & 0 \\ 0 & \textcircled{\tfrac{3}{2}} & -1 \\ 0 & 0 & \textcircled{\tfrac{4}{3}} \end{bmatrix} \begin{bmatrix} u_1 \\ u_2 \\ u_3 \end{bmatrix} = \begin{bmatrix} f_1 \\ f_2 + \frac{1}{2} f_1 \\ f_3 + \frac{2}{3} f_2 + \frac{1}{3} f_1 \end{bmatrix} \quad \text{is} \quad \begin{aligned} 2u_1 - u_2 \phantom{{}- u_3} &= 4 \\ \tfrac{3}{2} u_2 - u_3 &= 2 \\ \tfrac{4}{3} u_3 &= \tfrac{4}{3} \end{aligned} \qquad (1)$$

Forward elimination is complete. Note that all pivots and multipliers were decided by the matrix K, not the vector f. The right side changed from $f = (4, 0, 0)$ into the new $c = (4, 2, \frac{4}{3})$, and back substitution can begin. Triangular systems are quick to solve (the Thomas algorithm is at the end of this section).

Solution by back substitution. The last equation gives $u_3 = 1$. Substituting into the second equation gives $\frac{3}{2}u_2 - 1 = 2$. Therefore $u_2 = 2$. Substituting into the first equation gives $2u_1 - 2 = 4$. Therefore $u_1 = 3$ and the system is solved.

The solution vector is $u = (3, 2, 1)$. When we multiply the columns of K by those three numbers, they add up to the vector f. **I always think of a matrix-vector multiplication Ku as a combination of the columns of K.** Please look:

Combine columns for Ku
$$\begin{bmatrix} 2 & -1 & 0 \\ -1 & 2 & -1 \\ 0 & -1 & 2 \end{bmatrix} \begin{bmatrix} \mathbf{3} \\ \mathbf{2} \\ \mathbf{1} \end{bmatrix} = \mathbf{3} \begin{bmatrix} 2 \\ -1 \\ 0 \end{bmatrix} + \mathbf{2} \begin{bmatrix} -1 \\ 2 \\ -1 \end{bmatrix} + \mathbf{1} \begin{bmatrix} 0 \\ -1 \\ 2 \end{bmatrix}. \quad (2)$$

That sum is $f = (4, 0, 0)$. Solving a system $Ku = f$ is exactly the same as finding **a combination of the columns of K that produces the vector f.** *This is important.* The solution u expresses f as the "right combination" of the columns (with coefficients $3, 2, 1$). For a singular matrix there might be *no* combination that produces f, or there might be *infinitely many* combinations.

Our matrix K is invertible. When we divide $Ku = (4, 0, 0)$ by 4, the right side becomes $(1, 0, 0)$ which is the first column of I. So we are looking at the first column of $KK^{-1} = I$. We must be seeing the first column of K^{-1}. After dividing the previous $u = (3, 2, 1)$ by 4, the first column of K^{-1} must be $\frac{3}{4}, \frac{2}{4}, \frac{1}{4}$:

Column 1 of inverse
$$\begin{bmatrix} 2 & -1 & 0 \\ -1 & 2 & -1 \\ 0 & -1 & 2 \end{bmatrix} \begin{bmatrix} \frac{3}{4} & * & * \\ \frac{2}{4} & * & * \\ \frac{1}{4} & * & * \end{bmatrix} = \begin{bmatrix} 1 & * & * \\ 0 & * & * \\ 0 & * & * \end{bmatrix} = I. \quad (3)$$

If we really want K^{-1}, its columns come from $Ku =$ columns of I. So $K^{-1} = K \backslash I$.

Note about the multipliers: When we know the pivot in row j, and we know the entry to be eliminated in row i, the multiplier ℓ_{ij} is their ratio:

$$\textbf{Multiplier} \quad \ell_{ij} = \frac{\textbf{entry to eliminate} \quad (in\ row\ i)}{\textbf{pivot} \quad (in\ row\ j)}$$

The convention is to **subtract** (*not add*) ℓ_{ij} times one equation from another equation. The multiplier ℓ_{21} at our first step was $-\frac{1}{2}$ (the ratio of -1 to 2). That step added $\frac{1}{2}$ of row 1 to row 2, which is the same as subtracting $-\frac{1}{2}$ (row 1) from row 2.

Subtract ℓ_{ij} times the pivot row j from row i. Then the i, j entry is 0.

The $3, 1$ entry in the lower left corner of K was already zero. So there was nothing to eliminate and that multiplier was $\ell_{31} = 0$. The last multiplier was $\ell_{32} = -\frac{2}{3}$.

Elimination Produces $K = LU$

Now put those multipliers $\ell_{21}, \ell_{31}, \ell_{32}$ into a **lower triangular matrix** L, with ones on the diagonal. L records the steps of elimination by storing the multipliers. The upper triangular U records the final result, and here is the connection $\boldsymbol{K = LU}$:

$$L = \begin{bmatrix} 1 & 0 & 0 \\ -\frac{1}{2} & 1 & 0 \\ 0 & -\frac{2}{3} & 1 \end{bmatrix} \quad \text{times} \quad U = \begin{bmatrix} 2 & -1 & 0 \\ 0 & \frac{3}{2} & -1 \\ 0 & 0 & \frac{4}{3} \end{bmatrix} \quad \text{equals} \quad K. \tag{4}$$

The short and important and beautiful statement of Gaussian elimination is that $K = LU$. Please multiply those two matrices L and U.

The lower triangular matrix L times the upper triangular matrix U recovers the original matrix K. I think of it this way: L *reverses the elimination steps.* This takes U back to K. LU is the "matrix form" of elimination and we have to emphasize it.

> Suppose forward elimination uses the multipliers in L to change the rows of K into the rows of U (upper triangular). **Then $\boldsymbol{K}$ is factored into $\boldsymbol{L}$ times $\boldsymbol{U}$.**

Elimination is a two-step process, going forward (down) and then backward (up). Forward uses L, backward uses U. Forward elimination reached a new right side c. (The elimination steps are really multiplying by L^{-1} to solve $Lc = f$.) Back substitution on $Uu = c$ leads to the solution u. ***Then*** $c = L^{-1}f$ ***and*** $u = U^{-1}c$ ***combine into*** $u = U^{-1}L^{-1}f$ ***which is the correct*** $u = K^{-1}f$.

Go back to the example and check that $Lc = f$ produces the right vector c:

$$\boldsymbol{Lc = f} \qquad \begin{bmatrix} 1 & 0 & 0 \\ -\frac{1}{2} & 1 & 0 \\ 0 & -\frac{2}{3} & 1 \end{bmatrix} \begin{bmatrix} c_1 \\ c_2 \\ c_3 \end{bmatrix} = \begin{bmatrix} 4 \\ 0 \\ 0 \end{bmatrix} \quad \text{gives} \quad \begin{matrix} c_1 = 4 \\ c_2 = 2 \\ c_3 = \frac{4}{3} \end{matrix} \quad \text{as in (1).}$$

By keeping the right side up to date in elimination, we were solving $Lc = f$. Forward elimination changed f into c. Then back substitution quickly finds $u = (3, 2, 1)$.

You might notice that we are not using "inverse matrices" anywhere in this computation. The inverse of K is not needed. Good software for linear algebra (the LAPACK library is in the public domain) separates Gaussian elimination into a factoring step that works on K, and a solving step that works on f:

Step 1. **Factor** K into LU	$[L, U] = \mathsf{lu}(K)$ in MATLAB
Step 2. **Solve** $Ku = f$ for u	$Lc = f$ forward for c, then $Uu = c$ backward

The first step factors our 3 by 3 matrix K into triangular matrices L times U:

$$\boldsymbol{K = LU} \qquad \begin{bmatrix} 2 & -1 & 0 \\ -1 & 2 & -1 \\ 0 & -1 & 2 \end{bmatrix} = \begin{bmatrix} 1 & 0 & 0 \\ -\frac{1}{2} & 1 & 0 \\ 0 & -\frac{2}{3} & 1 \end{bmatrix} \begin{bmatrix} 2 & -1 & 0 \\ 0 & \frac{3}{2} & -1 \\ 0 & 0 & \frac{4}{3} \end{bmatrix}. \tag{5}$$

The solution step computes c (forward elimination) and then u (back substitution). MATLAB should almost never be asked for an inverse matrix. **Use the backslash command $K\backslash f$ to compute u, and not the inverse command** $\mathsf{inv}(K) * f$:

Step $1+2$ Solve $Ku = f$ by $u = K\backslash f$ (Backslash notices symmetry).

The reason for two subroutines in LAPACK is to avoid repeating the same steps on K when there is a new vector f^*. It is quite common (and desirable) to have several right sides with the same K. Then we **Factor** only once; it is the expensive part. The quick subroutine **Solve** finds the solutions $u, u^*, \ldots$ *without computing* K^{-1}. For multiple f's, put them in the columns of a matrix F. Then use K \ F.

Singular Systems

Back substitution is fast because U is triangular. It generally fails if a zero appears in the pivot. Forward elimination also fails, because a zero entry can't remove a nonzero entry below it. The official definition requires that **pivots are never zero**. If we meet a zero in the pivot position, we can *exchange rows*—hoping to move a nonzero entry up into the pivot. **An invertible matrix has a full set of pivots.**

When the column has all zeros in the pivot position and below, this is our signal that the matrix is ***singular***. It has no inverse. An example is C.

Example 1 Add -1's in the corners to get the circulant C. The first pivot is $d_1 = 2$ with multipliers $\ell_{21} = \ell_{31} = -\frac{1}{2}$. The second pivot is $d_2 = \frac{3}{2}$. But there is no third pivot:

$$C = \begin{bmatrix} \textcircled{2} & -1 & -1 \\ -1 & 2 & -1 \\ -1 & -1 & 2 \end{bmatrix} \longrightarrow \begin{bmatrix} \textcircled{2} & -1 & -1 \\ 0 & \textcircled{\tfrac{3}{2}} & -\frac{3}{2} \\ 0 & -\frac{3}{2} & \frac{3}{2} \end{bmatrix} \longrightarrow \begin{bmatrix} \textcircled{2} & -1 & -1 \\ 0 & \textcircled{\tfrac{3}{2}} & -\frac{3}{2} \\ \mathbf{0} & \mathbf{0} & \mathbf{0} \end{bmatrix} = U.$$

In the language of linear algebra, the rows of C are **linearly dependent**. Elimination found a combination of those rows (it was their sum) that produced the last row of all zeros in U. With only two pivots, C is **singular**.

Example 2 Suppose a zero appears in the second pivot position but there is a nonzero below it. Then a row exchange produces the second pivot and elimination can continue. This example is **not singular**, even with the zero appearing in the $2,2$ position:

$$\begin{bmatrix} 1 & -1 & 0 \\ -1 & 1 & -1 \\ 0 & -1 & 1 \end{bmatrix} \text{ leads to } \begin{bmatrix} 1 & -1 & 0 \\ 0 & \mathbf{0} & -1 \\ 0 & \mathbf{-1} & 1 \end{bmatrix}. \text{ Exchange rows to } U = \begin{bmatrix} 1 & -1 & 0 \\ 0 & -1 & 1 \\ 0 & 0 & -1 \end{bmatrix}.$$

Exchange rows on the right side of the equations too! The pivots become 1 and -1 and -1, and elimination succeeds. The original matrix is invertible but not positive definite. (And its determinant is *minus* the product of pivots, because of the row exchange.)

The exercises show how a *permutation matrix* P carries out this row exchange. The triangular L and U are now the factors of PA (so that $PA = LU$). The original A had no LU factorization, even though it was invertible. After the row exchange, PA has its rows in the right order for LU. We summarize the three possibilities:

Elimination on an n by n matrix A may or may not require row exchanges:

No row exchanges to get n pivots: A is invertible and $A = LU$.
Row exchanges by P to get n pivots: A is invertible and $PA = LU$.
No way to find n pivots: A is singular. There is no inverse matrix A^{-1}.

Positive definite matrices are recognized by the fact that they are symmetric and they need no row exchanges and all pivots are *positive*. We are still waiting for the meaning of this property—elimination gives a way to test for it.

Symmetry Converts $K = LU$ to $K = LDL^{\mathrm{T}}$

The factorization $K = LU$ comes directly from elimination—which produces U by the multipliers in L. This is extremely valuable, but something good was lost. The original K was symmetric, but L and U are not symmetric:

Symmetry is lost
$$K = \begin{bmatrix} 2 & -1 & 0 \\ -1 & 2 & -1 \\ 0 & -1 & 2 \end{bmatrix} = \begin{bmatrix} 1 & & \\ -\frac{1}{2} & 1 & \\ 0 & -\frac{2}{3} & 1 \end{bmatrix} \begin{bmatrix} 2 & -1 & 0 \\ & \frac{3}{2} & -1 \\ & & \frac{4}{3} \end{bmatrix} = LU\,.$$

The lower factor L has *ones* on the diagonal. The upper factor U has the *pivots*. This is unsymmetric, but the symmetry is easy to recover. Just separate the pivots into a diagonal matrix D, by dividing the rows of U by the pivots 2, $\frac{3}{2}$, and $\frac{4}{3}$:

Symmetry is recovered
$$K = \begin{bmatrix} 1 & & \\ \left(-\frac{1}{2}\right) & 1 & \\ 0 & \left(-\frac{2}{3}\right) & 1 \end{bmatrix} \begin{bmatrix} 2 & & \\ & \frac{3}{2} & \\ & & \frac{4}{3} \end{bmatrix} \begin{bmatrix} 1 & \left(-\frac{1}{2}\right) & 0 \\ & 1 & \left(-\frac{2}{3}\right) \\ & & 1 \end{bmatrix}. \tag{6}$$

Now we have it. The pivot matrix D is in the middle. The matrix on the left is still L. **The matrix on the right is the transpose of** L:

The symmetric factorization of a symmetric matrix is $K = LDL^{\mathrm{T}}$.

This triple factorization preserves the symmetry. That is important and needs to be highlighted. It applies to LDL^{T} and to every other "symmetric product" $A^{\mathrm{T}}CA$.

The product LDL^{T} is automatically a symmetric matrix, if D is diagonal. More than that, $A^{\mathrm{T}}CA$ is automatically symmetric if C is symmetric. The factor A is not necessarily square and C is not necessarily diagonal.

The reason for symmetry comes directly from matrix multiplication. The transpose of any product AB is equal to $B^{\mathrm{T}}A^{\mathrm{T}}$. The individual transposes come in the opposite order, and that is just what we want:

The transpose of LDL^{T} **is** $(L^{\mathrm{T}})^{\mathrm{T}}D^{\mathrm{T}}L^{\mathrm{T}}$. **This is** LDL^{T} **again.**

$(L^{\mathrm{T}})^{\mathrm{T}}$ is the same as L. Also $D^{\mathrm{T}} = D$ (diagonal matrices are symmetric). The displayed line says that the transpose of LDL^{T} is LDL^{T}. This is symmetry.

The same reasoning applies to $A^{\mathrm{T}}CA$. Its transpose is $A^{\mathrm{T}}C^{\mathrm{T}}(A^{\mathrm{T}})^{\mathrm{T}}$. If C is symmetric ($C = C^{\mathrm{T}}$), then this is $A^{\mathrm{T}}CA$ again. Notice the special case when the matrix in the middle is the identity matrix $C = I$:

For any rectangular matrix A, the product $A^{\mathrm{T}}A$ is square and symmetric.

We will meet these products $A^{\mathrm{T}}A$ and $A^{\mathrm{T}}CA$ many times. By assuming a little more about A and C, the product will be not only symmetric but positive definite.

The Determinant of K_n

Elimination on K begins with the three pivots $\frac{2}{1}$ and $\frac{3}{2}$ and $\frac{4}{3}$. This pattern continues. The ith pivot is $\frac{i+1}{i}$. The last pivot is $\frac{n+1}{n}$. ***The product of the pivots is the determinant***, and cancelling fractions produces the answer $n+1$:

Determinant of K_n
$$\left(\frac{2}{1}\right)\left(\frac{3}{2}\right)\left(\frac{4}{3}\right)\cdots\left(\frac{n+1}{n}\right) = \boldsymbol{n+1}\,. \tag{7}$$

The reason is that determinants always multiply: $(\det K) = (\det L)(\det U)$. The triangular matrix L has 1's on its diagonal, so $\det L = 1$. The triangular matrix U has the pivots on its diagonal, so $\det U = \textit{product of pivots} = n+1$. The LU factorization not only solves $Ku = f$, it is the quick way to compute the determinant.

There is a similar pattern for the multipliers that appear in elimination:

Multipliers
$$\ell_{21} = -\frac{1}{2} \quad \ell_{32} = -\frac{2}{3} \quad \ell_{43} = -\frac{3}{4} \quad \cdots \quad \ell_{n,n-1} = -\frac{n-1}{n}\,. \tag{8}$$

All other multipliers are zero. This is the crucial fact about elimination on a tridiagonal matrix, that L and U are *bidiagonal. If a row of K starts with p zeros (no elimination needed there), then that row of L also starts with p zeros.* If a column of K starts with q zeros, then that column of U starts with q zeros. **Zeros inside the band can unfortunately be "filled in" by elimination**. This leads to the fundamental problem of reordering the rows and columns to make the p's and q's as large as possible. For our tridiagonal matrices the ordering is already perfect.

You may not need a proof that the pivots $\frac{i+1}{i}$ and the multipliers $-\frac{i-1}{i}$ are correct. For completeness, here is row i of L multiplying columns $i-1, i$, and $i+1$ of U:

$$\begin{bmatrix} -\frac{i-1}{i} & 1 \end{bmatrix} \begin{bmatrix} \frac{i}{i-1} & -1 & 0 \\ 0 & \frac{i+1}{i} & -1 \end{bmatrix} = \begin{bmatrix} \mathbf{-1} & \mathbf{2} & \mathbf{-1} \end{bmatrix} = \text{row } i \text{ of } K\,.$$

Positive Pivots and Positive Determinants

I will repeat one note about positive definiteness (the matrix must be symmetric to start with). **It is positive definite if all n pivots are positive.** We need n nonzero pivots for invertibility, and we need n *positive* pivots (without row exchanges) for positive definiteness.

For 2 by 2 matrices $\left[\begin{smallmatrix} a & b \\ b & c \end{smallmatrix}\right]$, the first pivot is a. The only multiplier is $\ell_{21} = b/a$. Subtracting b/a times row 1 from row 2 puts the number $c - (b^2/a)$ into the second pivot. This is the same as $(ac - b^2)/a$. Please notice L and L^{T} in $K = LDL^{\mathrm{T}}$:

2 by 2 factors
$$\begin{bmatrix} a & b \\ b & c \end{bmatrix} = \begin{bmatrix} 1 & \\ b/a & 1 \end{bmatrix} \begin{bmatrix} a & \\ & \frac{ac-b^2}{a} \end{bmatrix} \begin{bmatrix} 1 & b/a \\ & 1 \end{bmatrix}. \tag{9}$$

These pivots are positive when $a > 0$ and $ac - b^2 > 0$. This is the 2 by 2 test:

$$\begin{bmatrix} a & b \\ b & c \end{bmatrix} \quad \textbf{\textit{is positive definite if and only if}}\ a > 0\ \textbf{\textit{and}}\ ac - b^2 > 0\,.$$

Out of four examples, the last three fail the test:

$$\underset{\textbf{pos def}}{\begin{bmatrix} 2 & 3 \\ 3 & 8 \end{bmatrix}} \qquad \underset{\textbf{pos semidef}}{\begin{bmatrix} 2 & 4 \\ 4 & 8 \end{bmatrix}} \qquad \underset{\textbf{indef}}{\begin{bmatrix} 2 & 6 \\ 6 & 8 \end{bmatrix}} \qquad \underset{\textbf{neg def}}{\begin{bmatrix} -2 & -3 \\ -3 & -8 \end{bmatrix}}$$

The matrix with $b = 4$ is singular (pivot missing) and positive *semidefinite*. The matrix with $b = 6$ has $ac - b^2 = -20$. That matrix is ***indefinite*** (pivots $+2$ and -10). The last matrix has $a < 0$. It is negative definite even though its determinant is positive.

Example 3 K_3 shows the key link between pivots and upper left determinants:

$$\begin{bmatrix} 2 & -1 & 0 \\ -1 & 2 & -1 \\ 0 & -1 & 2 \end{bmatrix} = \begin{bmatrix} 1 & & \\ -\frac{1}{2} & 1 & \\ 0 & -\frac{2}{3} & 1 \end{bmatrix} \begin{bmatrix} \mathbf{2} & & \\ 0 & \mathbf{\frac{3}{2}} & \\ & & \mathbf{\frac{4}{3}} \end{bmatrix} \begin{bmatrix} 1 & -\frac{1}{2} & 0 \\ & 1 & -\frac{2}{3} \\ & & 1 \end{bmatrix}.$$

The upper left determinants of K are $2, 3, 4$. **The pivots are their ratios** $2, \frac{3}{2}, \frac{4}{3}$. All upper left determinants are positive exactly when all pivots are positive.

Operation Counts

The factors L and U are *bidiagonal* when $K = LU$ is tridiagonal. Then the work of elimination is proportional to n (a few operations per row). This is very different from the number of additions and multiplications to factor a full matrix. **The leading terms are $\frac{1}{6}n^3$ with symmetry and $\frac{1}{3}n^3$ in general.** For $n = 1000$, we are comparing thousands of operations (quick) against hundreds of millions.

Between those extremes (tridiagonal versus full) are *band matrices*. There might be w nonzero diagonals above and also below the main diagonal. Each row operation needs a division for the multiplier, and w multiplications and additions. With w entries below each pivot, that makes $2w^2 + w$ to clear out each column. With n columns the overall count grows like $2w^2 n$, still only linear in n.

On the right side vector f, forward elimination and back substitution use w multiply-adds per row, plus one division. A full matrix needs n^2 multiply-adds on the right side, $[(n-1)+(n-2)+\cdots+1]$ forward and $[1+2+\cdots+(n-1)]$ backward. This is still much less than $\frac{2}{3}n^3$ total operations on the left side. Here is a table:

Operation Count (*Multiplies + adds*)	***Full***	***Banded***	***Tridiagonal***
Factor: Find L and U	$\approx \frac{2}{3}n^3$	$2w^2n + wn$	$3n$
Solve: Forward and back on f	$2n^2$	$4wn + n$	$5n$

Example 4 The Thomas algorithm solves tridiagonal $Au = f$ in $8n$ floating-point operations. A has $b_1, \ldots, b_n$ on the diagonal with $a_2, \ldots, a_n$ below and $c_1, \ldots, c_{n-1}$ above. Exchange equations i and $i+1$ if $|b_i| < |a_{i+1}|$ at step i. With no exchanges:

for i from 1 to $n-1$
$c_i \leftarrow c_i/b_i$
$f_i \leftarrow f_i/b_i$
$b_{i+1} \leftarrow b_{i+1} - a_{i+1}c_i$
$f_{i+1} \leftarrow f_{i+1} - a_{i+1}f_i$
end forward loop
$u_n \leftarrow f_n/b_n$
for i from $n-1$ to 1
$u_i \leftarrow f_i - c_i u_{i+1}$
end backward loop

Example 5 Test the commands [L, U, P] = lu(A) and P $*$ A $-$ L $*$ U on A_1, A_2, A_3.

$$A_1 = \begin{bmatrix} 0 & -1 & 1 \\ -1 & 2 & -1 \\ 1 & -1 & 0 \end{bmatrix} \quad A_2 = \begin{bmatrix} 1 & 0 & 0 \\ 2 & 3 & 0 \\ 0 & 4 & 5 \end{bmatrix} \quad A_3 = \begin{bmatrix} 1 & 2 & 3 \\ 2 & 3 & 4 \\ 3 & 4 & 5 \end{bmatrix}$$

For A_1, the permutation matrix P exchanges which rows? Always $PA = LU$.
For A_2, MATLAB exchanges rows to achieve the largest pivots column by column.
For A_3, which is *not* positive definite, rows are still exchanged: $P \neq I$ and $U \neq DL^{\mathrm{T}}$.

Problem Set 1.3

1 Extend equation (5) into a 4 by 4 factorization $K_4 = L_4 D_4 L_4^{\mathrm{T}}$. What is the determinant of K_4?

2
1. Find the inverses of the 3 by 3 matrices L and D and L^{T} in equation (5).
2. Write a formula for the ith pivot of K.
3. Check that the i, j entry of L_4^{-1} is j/i (on and below the diagonal) by multiplying $L_4 L_4^{-1}$ or $L_4^{-1} L_4$.

3
1. Enter the matrix K_5 by the MATLAB command toeplitz([2 −1 0 0 0]).
2. Compute the determinant and the inverse by det(K) and inv(K). For a neater answer compute the determinant times the inverse.
3. Find the L, D, U factors of K_5 and verify that the i, j entry of L^{-1} is j/i.

4 The vector of pivots for K_4 is $d = \left[\frac{2}{1}\ \frac{3}{2}\ \frac{4}{3}\ \frac{5}{4}\right]$. This is $d =$ (2:5)./(1:4), using MATLAB's counting vector $i : j = (i, i+1, \ldots, j)$. The extra **.** makes the division act *a component at a time.* Find ℓ in the MATLAB expression for $L =$ eye(4) − diag(ℓ, −1) and multiply $L *$ diag(d) $* L'$ to recover K_4.

5 If A has pivots 2, 7, 6 with no row exchanges, what are the pivots for the upper left 2 by 2 submatrix B (without row 3 and column 3)? Explain why.

6 How many entries can you choose freely in a 5 by 5 symmetric matrix K? How many can you choose in a 5 by 5 diagonal matrix D and lower triangular L (with ones on its diagonal)?

7 Suppose A is rectangular (m by n) and C is symmetric (m by m).

1. Transpose $A^{\mathrm{T}}CA$ to show its symmetry. What shape is this matrix?
2. Show why $A^{\mathrm{T}}A$ has no negative numbers on its diagonal.

8 Factor these symmetric matrices into $A = LDL^{\mathrm{T}}$ with the pivots in D:

$$A = \begin{bmatrix} 1 & 3 \\ 3 & 2 \end{bmatrix} \quad \text{and} \quad A = \begin{bmatrix} 1 & b \\ b & c \end{bmatrix} \quad \text{and} \quad A = \begin{bmatrix} 2 & 1 & 0 \\ 1 & 2 & 1 \\ 0 & 1 & 2 \end{bmatrix}$$

9 The **Cholesky** command $A =$ chol(K) produces an upper triangular A with $K = A^{\mathrm{T}}A$. The square roots of the pivots from D are now included on the diagonal of A (so Cholesky *fails* unless $K = K^{\mathrm{T}}$ and the pivots are positive). Try the chol command on K_3, T_3, B_3, and $B_3 +$ eps $*$ eye(3).

10 The all-ones matrix ones(4) is positive *semidefinite.* Find all its pivots (zero not allowed). Find its determinant and try eig(ones(4)). Factor it into a 4 by 1 matrix L times a 1 by 4 matrix L^{T}.

11 The matrix $K =$ ones(4) + eye(4)/100 has all 1's off the diagonal, and 1.01 down the main diagonal. Is it positive definite? Find the pivots by lu(K) and eigenvalues by eig(K). Also find its LDL^{T} factorization and inv(K).

12 The matrix $K =$pascal(4) contains the numbers from the Pascal triangle (tilted to fit symmetrically into K). Multiply its pivots to find its determinant. Factor K into LL^{T} where the lower triangular L also contains the Pascal triangle!

13 The Fibonacci matrix $\left[\begin{smallmatrix} 1 & 1 \\ 1 & 0 \end{smallmatrix}\right]$ is *indefinite.* Find its pivots. Factor it into LDL^{T}. Multiply $(1, 0)$ by this matrix 5 times, to see the first 6 Fibonacci numbers.

14 If $A = LU$, solve by hand the equation $Ax = f$ without ever finding A itself. Solve $Lc = f$ and then $Ux = c$ (then $LUx = Lc$ is the desired equation $Ax = f$). $Lc = f$ is forward elimination and $Ux = c$ is back substitution:

$$L = \begin{bmatrix} 1 & & \\ 3 & 1 & \\ 0 & 2 & 1 \end{bmatrix} \qquad U = \begin{bmatrix} 2 & 8 & 0 \\ & 3 & 5 \\ & & 7 \end{bmatrix} \qquad f = \begin{bmatrix} 0 \\ 3 \\ 6 \end{bmatrix}.$$

15 From the multiplication LS show that

$$L = \begin{bmatrix} 1 & & \\ \ell_{21} & 1 & \\ \ell_{31} & 0 & 1 \end{bmatrix} \quad \text{is the inverse of} \quad S = \begin{bmatrix} 1 & & \\ -\ell_{21} & 1 & \\ -\ell_{31} & 0 & 1 \end{bmatrix}.$$

S subtracts multiples of row 1 from lower rows. L adds them back.

16 Unlike the previous exercise, which eliminated only one column, show that

$$L = \begin{bmatrix} 1 & & \\ \ell_{21} & 1 & \\ \ell_{31} & \ell_{32} & 1 \end{bmatrix} \quad \text{is } \textit{not} \text{ the inverse of} \quad S = \begin{bmatrix} 1 & & \\ -\ell_{21} & 1 & \\ -\ell_{31} & -\ell_{32} & 1 \end{bmatrix}.$$

Write L as $L_1 L_2$ to find the correct inverse $L^{-1} = L_2^{-1} L_1^{-1}$ (notice the order):

$$L = \begin{bmatrix} 1 & & \\ \ell_{21} & 1 & \\ \ell_{31} & 0 & 1 \end{bmatrix} \begin{bmatrix} 1 & & \\ 0 & 1 & \\ 0 & \ell_{32} & 1 \end{bmatrix} \quad \text{and} \quad L^{-1} = \begin{bmatrix} 1 & & \\ 0 & 1 & \\ 0 & -\ell_{32} & 1 \end{bmatrix} \begin{bmatrix} 1 & & \\ -\ell_{21} & 1 & \\ -\ell_{31} & 0 & 1 \end{bmatrix}.$$

17 By trial and error, find examples of 2 by 2 matrices such that

1. $LU \neq UL$
2. $A^2 = -I$, with real entries in A
3. $B^2 = 0$, with no zeros in B
4. $CD = -DC$, not allowing $CD = 0$

18 Write down a 3 by 3 matrix with row 1 $-$ 2 $*$ row 2 $+$ row 3 $= 0$ and find a similar dependence of the columns—a combination of columns that gives zero.

19 Draw these equations in their *row* form (two intersecting lines) and find the solution (x, y). Then draw their *column* form by adding two vectors:

$$\begin{bmatrix} 3 & 1 \\ 0 & 1 \end{bmatrix} \begin{bmatrix} x \\ y \end{bmatrix} = \begin{bmatrix} 5 \\ 2 \end{bmatrix} \quad \text{has column form} \quad x \begin{bmatrix} 3 \\ 0 \end{bmatrix} + y \begin{bmatrix} 1 \\ 1 \end{bmatrix} = \begin{bmatrix} 5 \\ 2 \end{bmatrix}.$$

20 True or false: Every matrix A can be factored into a lower triangular L times an upper triangular U, with *nonzero diagonals*. Find L and U when possible:

$$\text{When is } A = \begin{bmatrix} 2 & 4 \\ 4 & d \end{bmatrix} = LU\,? \qquad A = \begin{bmatrix} a & b \\ c & d \end{bmatrix} = LU\,?$$

1.4 INVERSES AND DELTA FUNCTIONS

We are comparing matrix equations with differential equations. One is $Ku = f$, the other is $-u'' = f(x)$. The solutions are vectors u and functions $u(x)$. This comparison is quite remarkable when special vectors f and functions $f(x)$ are the forcing terms on the right side. With a uniform load $f(x) =$ constant, both solutions are parabolas (Section 1.2). Now comes the opposite choice with $f =$ **point load**:

In the matrix equation, take $f = \delta_j = j$th column of the identity matrix.
In the differential equation, take $f(x) = \delta(x-a) =$ **delta function** at $x = a$.

The delta function may be partly or completely new to you. It is zero except at one point. The function $\delta(x-a)$ represents a "spike" or a "point load" or an "impulse" concentrated at the single point $x = a$. The solution $u(x)$ or $u(x, a)$, where a gives the placement of the load, is the **Green's function**. When we know the Green's function for all point loads $\delta(x-a)$, we can solve $-u'' = f(x)$ for any load $f(x)$.

In the matrix equation $Ku = \delta_j$, the right side is column j of I. The solution is $u =$ column j of K^{-1}. **We are solving $KK^{-1} = I$, column by column.** So we are finding the inverse matrix, which is the "discrete Green's function." Like x and a, the discrete $(K^{-1})_{ij}$ locates *the solution at point i from a load at point j.*

The amazing fact is that the entries of K^{-1} and T^{-1} fall **exactly on the solutions $u(x)$** to the continuous problems. The figures show this, and so will the text.

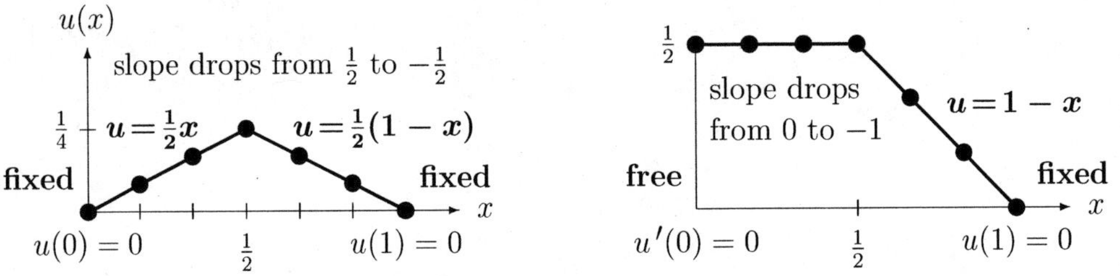

Figure 1.5: Middle columns of $h\,K_5^{-1}$ and $h\,T_5^{-1}$ lie on solutions to $-u'' = \delta(x-\frac{1}{2})$.

Concentrated Load

Figure 1.5 shows the form of $u(x)$, when the load is at the halfway point $x = \frac{1}{2}$. Away from this load, our equation is $u'' = 0$ and its solution is $u =$ straight line. The problem is to *match the two lines* (before and after $\frac{1}{2}$) with the point load.

Example 1 Solve $-u'' =$ point load with **fixed-fixed** and **free-fixed** endpoints:

$$-\frac{d^2u}{dx^2} = f(x) = \delta(x - \frac{1}{2}) \quad \text{with} \quad \begin{cases} \textbf{fixed: } u(0) = 0 \text{ and } \textbf{fixed: } u(1) = 0 \\ \textbf{free: } u'(0) = 0 \text{ and } \textbf{fixed: } u(1) = 0 \end{cases}$$

Solution In the fixed-fixed problem, the up and down lines must start and end at $u = 0$. At the load point $x = \frac{1}{2}$, the function $u(x)$ is continuous and the lines meet. **The slope drops by 1** because the delta function has "area $= 1$". To see the drop in slope, integrate both sides of $-u'' = \delta$ across $x = \frac{1}{2}$:

$$\int_{\text{left}}^{\text{right}} -\frac{d^2u}{dx^2}\,dx = \int_{\text{left}}^{\text{right}} \delta(x - \frac{1}{2})\,dx \quad \text{gives} \quad -\left(\frac{du}{dx}\right)_{\text{right}} + \left(\frac{du}{dx}\right)_{\text{left}} = 1\,. \qquad (1)$$

The fixed-fixed case has $u'_{\text{left}} = \frac{1}{2}$ and $u'_{\text{right}} = -\frac{1}{2}$. The fixed-free case has $u'_{\text{left}} = 0$ and $u'_{\text{right}} = -1$. In every case the slope drops by 1 at the unit load.

These solutions $u(x)$ are ***ramp functions***, with a corner. In the rest of the section we move the load to $x = a$ and compute the new ramps. (The fixed-fixed ramp will have slopes $1 - a$ and $-a$, always dropping by 1.) And we will find *discrete ramps* for the columns of the inverse matrices K^{-1} and T^{-1}. The entries will increase linearly, up to the diagonal of K^{-1}, then go linearly down to the end of the column.

It is remarkable to be finding exact solutions and exact inverses. We take this chance to do it. These problems are exceptionally simple and important, so why not?

Example 2 Move the point load to $x = a$. Everywhere else $u'' = 0$, so the solution is $u = Ax + B$ up to the load. It changes to $u = Cx + D$ beyond that point. Four equations (two at boundaries, two at $x = a$) determine those constants A, B, C, D:

Boundary Conditions		**Jump/No Jump Conditions at $x = a$**	
fixed $u(0) = 0$:	$B = 0$	No jump in u :	$Aa + B = Ca + D$
fixed $u(1) = 0$:	$C + D = 0$	Drop by 1 in u' :	$A = C + 1$

Substitute $B = 0$ and $D = -C$ into the first equation on the right:

$$Aa + 0 = Ca - C \quad \text{and} \quad A = C + 1 \quad \text{give slopes} \quad A = 1 - a \quad \text{and} \quad C = -a. \qquad (2)$$

Then $D = -C = a$ produces the solution in Figure 1.6. The ramp is $u = (1 - a)x$ going up and $u = a(1 - x)$ going down. On the right we show a column of K^{-1}, computed in equation (10): linear up and down.

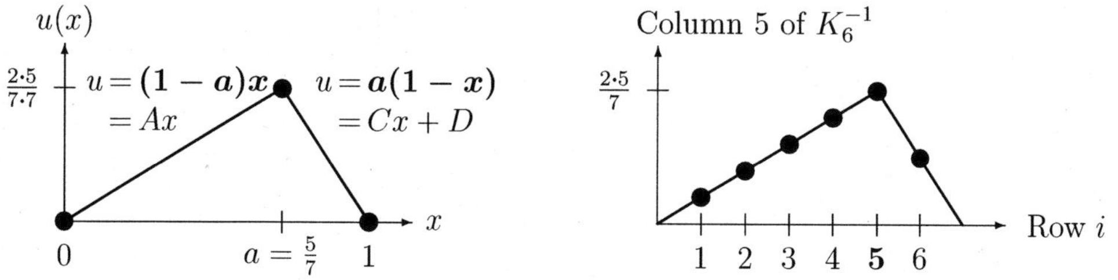

Figure 1.6: Response at x to a load at $a = \frac{5}{7}$ (fixed-fixed boundary). For the matrix K_6^{-1}, the entries in each column go linearly up and down like the true $u(x)$.

Delta Function and Green's Function

We solve $-u'' = \delta(x-a)$ again, by a slightly different method (same answer). A *particular solution* is a ramp. Then we add all solutions $Cx+D$ to $u''=0$. Example 2 used the boundary conditions *first*, and now we use them *last*.

You must recognize that $\delta(x)$ and $\delta(x-a)$ are not true functions! They are zero except at one point $x=0$ or $x=a$ where the function is "infinite"—too vague. The spike is "infinitely tall and infinitesimally thin." One definition is to say that the integral of $\delta(x)$ is the unit step function $S(x)$ in Figure 1.7. "*The area is* 1 *under the spike at* $x=0$." No true function could achieve that, but $\delta(x)$ is extremely useful.

The standard ramp function is $R=0$ up to the corner at $x=0$ and then $R=x$. Its slope dR/dx is a step function. **Its second derivative is $d^2R/dx^2 = \delta(x)$.**

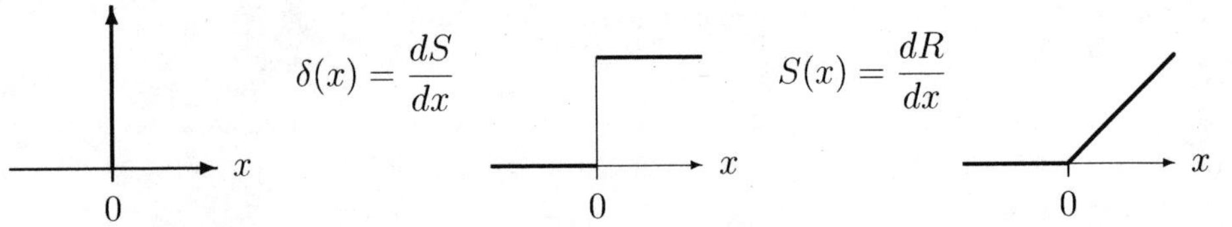

Delta function $\delta(x)$ **Step function $S(x)$** **Ramp function $R(x)$**

Figure 1.7: The integral of the delta function is the step function, so $\delta(x) = dS/dx$. The integral of the step $S(x)$ is the ramp $R(x)$, so $\delta(x) = d^2R/dx^2$.

Now shift the three graphs by a. The shifted ramp $R(x-a)$ is 0 then $x-a$. This has first derivative $S(x-a)$ and second derivative $\delta(x-a)$. In words, **the first derivative jumps by 1 at $x=a$ so the second derivative is a delta function.** Since our equation $-d^2u/dx^2 = \delta(x-a)$ has a minus sign, we want the slope to *drop* by 1. The descending ramp $-R(x-a)$ is a particular solution to $-u'' = \delta(x-a)$.

Main point We have $u''=0$ except at $x=a$. So u is a straight line on the left and right of a. *The slope of this ramp drops by* 1 *at* a, as required by $-u''=\delta(x-a)$. The downward ramp $-R(x-a)$ is one particular solution, and we can add $Cx+D$. The two constants C and D came from two integrations.

The complete solution (*particular* + *nullspace*) is a family of ramps:

Complete solution
$$-\frac{d^2u}{dx^2} = \delta(x-a) \quad \text{is solved by} \quad u(x) = -R(x-a) + Cx + D\,. \tag{3}$$

The constants C and D are determined by the boundary conditions.

$$u(0) = -R(0-a) + C\cdot 0 + D = 0. \qquad \text{Therefore } D \text{ must be zero}\,.$$

From $u(1)=0$ we learn that the other constant (in Cx) is $C = 1-a$:

$$u(1) = -R(1-a) + C\cdot 1 + D = a - 1 + C = 0. \qquad \text{Therefore } C = 1-a\,.$$

So the ramp increases with slope $1-a$ until $x=a$. Then it decreases to $u(1)=0$. When we substitute $R=0$ followed by $R=x-a$, we find the two parts:

FIXED ENDS $$u(x) = -R(x-a) + (1-a)x = \begin{cases} \boldsymbol{(1-a)x} & \text{for } x \le a \\ \boldsymbol{(1-x)a} & \text{for } x \ge a \end{cases} \tag{4}$$

The slope of $u(x)$ starts at $1-a$ and drops by 1 to $-a$. This unit drop in the slope means a delta function for $-d^2u/dx^2$, as required. The first part $(1-a)x$ gives $u(0)=0$, the second part $(1-x)a$ gives $u(1)=0$.

Please notice the symmetry between x and a in the two parts! Those are like i and j in the symmetric matrix $(K^{-1})_{ij} = (K^{-1})_{ji}$. **The response at x to a load at a equals the response at a to a load at x.** It is the "Green's function."

Free-Fixed Boundary Conditions

When the end $x=0$ becomes free, that boundary condition changes to $u'(0)=0$. This leads to $C=0$ in the complete solution $u(x) = -R(x-a) + Cx + D$:

$$\text{Set } x = 0: \quad u'(0) = 0 + C + 0. \quad \text{Therefore } C \text{ must be zero.}$$

Then $u(1) = 0$ yields the other constant $D = 1 - a$:

$$\text{Set } x = 1: \quad u(1) = -R(1-a) + D = a - 1 + D = 0. \quad \text{Therefore } D = 1 - a.$$

The solution is a constant D (zero slope) up to the load at $x=a$. Then the slope drops to -1 (descending ramp). The two-part formula for $u(x)$ is

FREE-FIXED $$u(x) = \begin{cases} \boldsymbol{1-a} & \text{for } x \le a \\ \boldsymbol{1-x} & \text{for } x \ge a \end{cases} \tag{5}$$

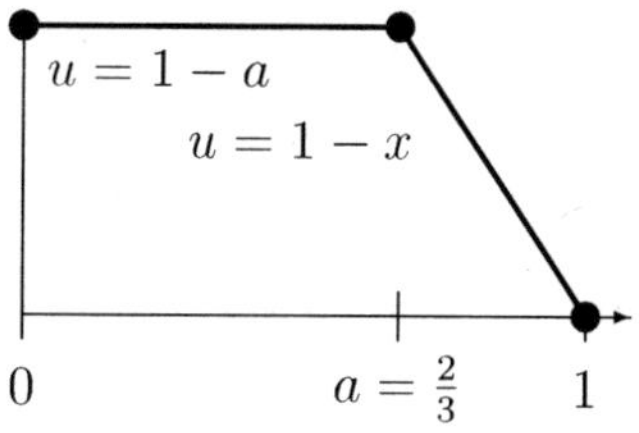

Free-Free: There is *no solution* for $f = \delta(x-a)$ when both ends are free. If we require $u'(0)=0$ and also $u'(1)=0$, those give conditions on C and D that cannot be met. A ramp can't have zero slope on both sides (and support the load). In the same way, the matrix B is singular and $BB^{-1} = I$ has no solution.

The free-free problem does have a solution when $\int f(x)\,dx = 0$. The example in problem 7 is $f(x) = \delta\left(x - \frac{1}{3}\right) - \delta\left(x - \frac{2}{3}\right)$. The problem is still singular and it has infinitely many solutions (any constant can be added to $u(x)$, without changing $u'(0) = 0$ and $u'(1) = 0$).

Discrete Vectors: Load and Step and Ramp

Those solutions $u(x)$ in (4) and (5) are the **Green's functions** $G(x,a)$ for fixed ends and free-fixed ends. They will correspond to K^{-1} and T^{-1} in the matrix equations. The matrices have second differences in place of second derivatives.

It is a pleasure to see how difference equations imitate differential equations. **The crucial equation becomes $\Delta^2 R = \delta$.** This copies $R''(x) = \delta(x)$:

The **delta vector** δ has one nonzero component $\delta_0 = 1$:	$\delta = (\ldots, 0, 0, \mathbf{1}, 0, 0, \ldots)$
The **step vector** S has components $S_i = 0$ or 1:	$S = (\ldots, 0, 0, \mathbf{1}, 1, 1, \ldots)$
The **ramp vector** R has components $R_i = 0$ or i:	$R = (\ldots, 0, 0, \mathbf{0}, 1, 2, \ldots)$

These vectors are all centered at $i = 0$. **Notice that $\Delta_- S = \delta$ but $\Delta_+ R = S$.** We need a backward Δ_- and a forward Δ_+ to get a centered second difference $\Delta^2 = \Delta_-\Delta_+$. Then $\Delta^2 R = \Delta_- S = \delta$. Matrix multiplication shows this clearly:

$$\boldsymbol{\Delta^2}\textbf{(ramp)} \qquad \begin{bmatrix} \ddots & & & & \\ & 1 & -2 & 1 & \\ & & 1 & -2 & 1 \\ & & & & \ddots \end{bmatrix} \begin{bmatrix} 0 \\ 0 \\ 1 \\ 2 \end{bmatrix} = \begin{bmatrix} 0 \\ \mathbf{1} \\ 0 \\ 0 \end{bmatrix} = \textbf{delta}. \tag{6}$$

The ramp vector R is piecewise linear. At the center point, the second difference jumps to $R_1 - 2R_0 + R_{-1} = 1$. At all other points (where the delta vector is zero) the ramp solves $\Delta^2 R = 0$. Thus $\Delta^2 R = \delta$ copies $R''(x) = \delta(x)$.

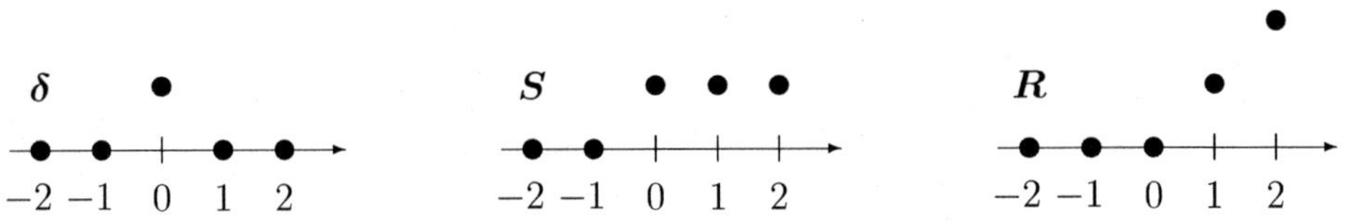

Figure 1.8: The delta vector δ and step vector S and ramp vector R. The key relations are $\boldsymbol{\delta = \Delta_- S}$ (backward) and $\boldsymbol{S = \Delta_+ R}$ (forward) and $\boldsymbol{\delta = \Delta^2 R}$ (centered).

The solutions to $d^2u/dx^2 = 0$ are linear functions $Cx + D$. The solutions to $\Delta^2 u = 0$ are "linear vectors" with $u_i = Ci + D$. The equation $u_{i+1} - 2u_i + u_{i-1} = 0$ is satisfied by constant vectors and linear vectors, since $(i+1) - 2i + (i-1) = 0$. **The complete solution to $\Delta^2 u = \delta$ is $u_{\textbf{particular}} + u_{\textbf{nullspace}}$.** Thus $u_i = R_i + Ci + D$.

I want to emphasize that this is unusually perfect. The discrete $R_i + Ci + D$ is an exact copy of the continuous solution $u(x) = R(x) + Cx + D$. We can solve $\Delta^2 u = \delta$ by **sampling the ramp** $u(x)$ at equally spaced points, without any error.

The Discrete Equations $Ku = \delta_j$ and $Tu = \delta_j$

In the differential equation, the point load and step and ramp moved to $x = a$. In the difference equation, *the load moves to component* j. The right side δ_j has components δ_{i-j}, zero except when $i = j$. Then the shifted step and shifted ramp have components S_{i-j} and R_{i-j}, also centered at j.

The fixed-ends difference equation from $-u''(x) = \delta(x-a)$ is now $-\Delta^2 u = \delta_j$:

$$-\Delta^2 u_i = -u_{i+1} + 2u_i - u_{i-1} = \begin{cases} 1 & \text{if } i = j \\ 0 & \text{if } i \neq j \end{cases} \quad \text{with } u_0 = 0 \text{ and } u_{n+1} = 0. \tag{7}$$

The left side is exactly the matrix-vector multiplication $K_n u$. The minus sign in $-\Delta^2$ changes the rows $1, -2, 1$ to their positive definite form $-1, 2, -1$. On the right side, the shifted delta vector is the jth column of the identity matrix. When the load is at meshpoint $j = 2$, **the equation is column 2 of $KK^{-1} = I$:**

$$\begin{matrix} n = 4 \\ j = 2 \end{matrix} \qquad \begin{bmatrix} 2 & -1 & 0 & 0 \\ -1 & 2 & -1 & 0 \\ 0 & -1 & 2 & -1 \\ 0 & 0 & -1 & 2 \end{bmatrix} \begin{bmatrix} u_1 \\ u_2 \\ u_3 \\ u_4 \end{bmatrix} = \begin{bmatrix} 0 \\ 1 \\ 0 \\ 0 \end{bmatrix} \begin{matrix} \\ \leftarrow j = 2 \\ \\ \\ \end{matrix} \tag{8}$$

When the right sides are the four columns of I (with $j = 1, 2, 3, 4$) the solutions are the four columns of K_4^{-1}. This inverse matrix is the discrete Green's function.

What is the solution vector u? A particular solution is the descending ramp $-R_{i-j}$, shifted by j and sign-reversed. The complete solution includes $Ci + D$, which solves $\Delta^2 u = 0$. Thus $u_i = -R_{i-j} + Ci + D$. The constants C and D are determined by the two boundary conditions $u_0 = 0$ and $u_{n+1} = 0$:

$$u_0 = -R_{0-j} + C \cdot 0 + D = 0. \qquad \text{Therefore } D \text{ must be zero} \tag{9}$$

$$u_{n+1} = -R_{n+1-j} + C(n+1) + 0 = 0. \qquad \text{Therefore } C = \frac{\boldsymbol{n+1-j}}{\boldsymbol{n+1}} = 1 - \frac{j}{n+1} \tag{10}$$

Those results are parallel to $D = 0$ and $C = 1 - a$ in the differential equation. The tilted ramp $u = -R + Ci$ in Figure 1.9 increases linearly from $u_0 = 0$. Its peak is at the position j of the point load, and the ramp descends linearly to $u_{n+1} = 0$:

$$\begin{matrix} \textbf{FIXED} \\ \textbf{ENDS} \end{matrix} \quad u_i = -R_{i-j} + C\,i = \begin{cases} \left(\frac{n+1-j}{n+1}\right) i & \text{for } i \le j \\ \left(\frac{n+1-i}{n+1}\right) j & \text{for } i \ge j \end{cases} \tag{11}$$

Those are the entries of K_n^{-1} (asked for in earlier problem sets). Above the diagonal, for $i \le j$, the ramp is zero and $u_i = Ci$. Below the diagonal, we can just exchange i and j, since we know that K_n^{-1} is symmetric. These formulas for the vector u are exactly parallel to $(1-a)x$ and $(1-x)a$ in equation (4) for the fixed-ends continuous problem.

Figure 1.9 shows a typical case with $n = 4$ and the load at $j = 2$. The formulas in (11) give $u = \left(\frac{3}{5}, \frac{6}{5}, \frac{4}{5}, \frac{2}{5}\right)$. The numbers go linearly up to $\frac{6}{5}$ (on the main diagonal of K_4^{-1}). Then $4/5$ and $2/5$ go linearly back down. The matrix equation (8) shows that this vector u should be the second column of K_4^{-1}, and it is.

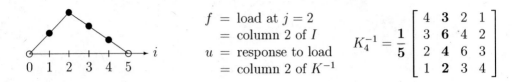

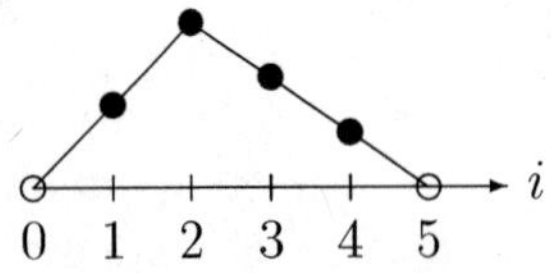

$$\begin{aligned} f &= \text{load at } j = 2 \\ &= \text{column 2 of } I \\ u &= \text{response to load} \\ &= \text{column 2 of } K^{-1} \end{aligned} \qquad K_4^{-1} = \frac{\mathbf{1}}{\mathbf{5}} \begin{bmatrix} 4 & \mathbf{3} & 2 & 1 \\ 3 & \mathbf{6} & 4 & 2 \\ 2 & \mathbf{4} & 6 & 3 \\ 1 & \mathbf{2} & 3 & 4 \end{bmatrix}$$

Figure 1.9: $K_4 u = \delta_2$ has the point load in position $j = 2$. The equation is column 2 of $K_4 K_4^{-1} = I$. The solution u is column 2 of K_4^{-1}.

The **free-fixed** discrete equation $Tu = f$ can also have $f = \delta_j$ = point load at j:

$$\textbf{Discrete} \qquad -\Delta^2 u_i = \delta_{i-j} \quad \text{with } u_1 - u_0 = 0 \text{ (zero slope) and } u_{n+1} = 0\,. \qquad (12)$$

The solution is still a ramp $u_i = -R_{i-j} + Ci + D$ with corner at j. But the constants C and D have new values because of the new boundary condition $u_1 = u_0$:

$$u_1 - u_0 = 0 + C + 0 = 0 \qquad \text{so the first constant is} \quad C = 0 \qquad (13)$$

$$u_{n+1} = -R_{n+1-j} + D = 0 \qquad \text{so the second constant is} \quad D = n + 1 - j\,. \qquad (14)$$

Those are completely analogous to $C = 0$ and $D = 1 - a$ in the continuous problem above. The solution equals D up to the point load at position j. Then the ramp descends to reach $u_{n+1} = 0$ at the other boundary. The two-part formula $-R_{i-j} + D$, before and after the point load at $i = j$, is

$$\textbf{FREE-FIXED} \qquad u_i = -R_{i-j} + (n + 1 - j) = \begin{cases} \boldsymbol{n+1-j} & \text{for } i \le j \\ \boldsymbol{n+1-i} & \text{for } i \ge j \end{cases} \qquad (15)$$

The two parts are above and below the diagonal in the matrix T^{-1}. The point loads at $j = 1, 2, 3, \ldots$ lead to columns $1, 2, 3, \ldots$ and you see $n + 1 - 1$ in the corner:

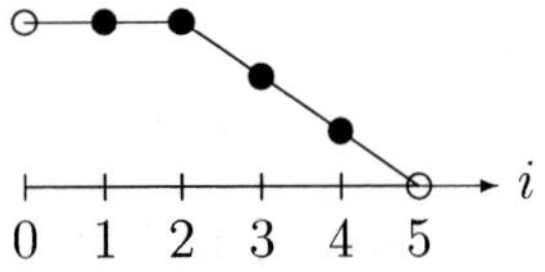

$$\begin{aligned} f &= \text{load at } j = 2 \\ &= \text{column 2 of } I \\ u &= \text{response to load} \\ &= \text{column 2 of } T^{-1} \end{aligned} \qquad T_4^{-1} = \begin{bmatrix} 4 & \mathbf{3} & 2 & 1 \\ 3 & \mathbf{3} & 2 & 1 \\ 2 & \mathbf{2} & 2 & 1 \\ 1 & \mathbf{1} & 1 & 1 \end{bmatrix}$$

Figure 1.10: $T_4 u = \delta_2$ is column 2 of $TT^{-1} = I$, so u = column 2 of T^{-1}.

This T^{-1} is the matrix that came in Section 1.2 by inverting $T = U^{\mathrm{T}}U$. Each column of T^{-1} is constant down to the main diagonal and then linear, just like $u(x) = 1 - a$ followed by $u(x) = 1 - x$ in the free-fixed Green's function $u(x, a)$.

Green's Function and the Inverse Matrix

If we can solve for point loads, we can solve for any loads. In the matrix case this is immediate (and worth seeing). *Any vector f is a combination of n point loads*:

$$f = \begin{bmatrix} f_1 \\ f_2 \\ f_3 \end{bmatrix} = f_1 \begin{bmatrix} 1 \\ 0 \\ 0 \end{bmatrix} + f_2 \begin{bmatrix} 0 \\ 1 \\ 0 \end{bmatrix} + f_3 \begin{bmatrix} 0 \\ 0 \\ 1 \end{bmatrix}. \tag{16}$$

The inverse matrix multiplies each column to combine three point load solutions:

$$K^{-1}f = f_1(\text{column 1 of } K^{-1}) + f_2(\text{column 2 of } K^{-1}) + f_3(\text{column 3 of } K^{-1}). \tag{17}$$

Matrix multiplication $u = K^{-1}f$ is perfectly chosen to combine those columns.

In the continuous case, the combination gives an *integral* not a sum. The load $f(x)$ is an integral of point loads $f(a)\delta(x-a)$. The solution $u(x)$ is an integral over all a of responses $u(x,a)$ to those loads at each point a:

$$-u'' = f(x) = \int_0^1 f(a)\delta(x-a)\,da \quad \textbf{is solved by} \quad u(x) = \int_0^1 f(a)u(x,a)\,da. \tag{18}$$

The **Green's function** $u(x,a)$ corresponds to "row x and column a" of a *continuous* K^{-1}. We will see it again. To summarize, we repeat formulas (4) and (5) for $u(x,a)$:

$$\textbf{FIXED ENDS} \quad u = \begin{cases} (1-a)x & \text{for } x \le a \\ (1-x)a & \text{for } x \ge a \end{cases} \qquad \textbf{FREE FIXED} \quad u = \begin{cases} 1-a & \text{for } x \le a \\ 1-x & \text{for } x \ge a \end{cases} \tag{19}$$

If we sample the fixed-ends solution at $x = \frac{i}{n+1}$, when the load is at $a = \frac{j}{n+1}$, then we (almost!) have the i,j entry of K_n^{-1}. The only difference between equations (11) and (19) is an extra factor of $n+1 = 1/\Delta x$. The exact analogy would be this:

$$-\frac{d^2u}{dx^2} = \delta(x) \quad \text{corresponds to} \quad \frac{K}{(\Delta x)^2}U = \left(\frac{\delta}{\Delta x}\right). \tag{20}$$

We divide K by $h^2 = (\Delta x)^2$ to approximate the second derivative. We divide δ by $h = \Delta x$ because the area should be 1. Each component of δ corresponds to a little x-interval of length Δx, so area $= 1$ requires height $= 1/\Delta x$. Then our u is $U/\Delta x$.

■ WORKED EXAMPLES ■

1.4 The "Woodbury-Sherman-Morrison formula" will find K^{-1} from T^{-1}. This formula gives the rank-one change in the inverse, when the matrix has a rank-one change in $\boldsymbol{K} = \boldsymbol{T} - \boldsymbol{u}\boldsymbol{v}^{\mathrm{T}}$. In this example the change is only $+1$ in the $1,1$ entry, coming from $T_{11} = 1 + K_{11}$. The column vectors are $v = (1, 0, \ldots 0) = -u$.

Here is one of the most useful formulas in linear algebra (it extends to $T - UV^{\mathrm{T}}$):

Woodbury-Sherman-Morrison Inverse of $K = T - uv^{\mathrm{T}}$

$$K^{-1} = T^{-1} + \frac{T^{-1}uv^{\mathrm{T}}T^{-1}}{1 - v^{\mathrm{T}}T^{-1}u} \tag{21}$$

The proof multiplies the right side by $T - uv^{\mathrm{T}}$, and simplifies to I.

Problem 1.1.7 displays $T^{-1} - K^{-1}$ when the vectors have length $n = 4$:

$$v^{\mathrm{T}}T^{-1} = \text{row 1 of } T^{-1} = \begin{bmatrix} 4 & 3 & 2 & 1 \end{bmatrix} \quad 1 - v^{\mathrm{T}}T^{-1}u = 1 + 4 = 5.$$

For any n, K^{-1} comes from the simpler T^{-1} by subtracting $w^{\mathrm{T}}w/(n+1)$ with $w =$n:−1:1.

Problem Set 1.4

1 For $-u'' = \delta(x - a)$, the solution must be linear on each side of the load. What four conditions determine A, B, C, D if $u(0) = 2$ and $u(1) = 0$?

$$u(x) = Ax + B \quad \text{for} \quad 0 \le x \le a \quad \text{and} \quad u(x) = Cx + D \quad \text{for} \quad a \le x \le 1\,.$$

2 Change Problem 1 to the free-fixed case $u'(0) = 0$ and $u(1) = 4$. Find and solve the four equations for A, B, C, D.

3 Suppose there are *two* unit loads, at the points $a = \frac{1}{3}$ and $b = \frac{2}{3}$. Solve the fixed-fixed problem in two ways: First combine the two single-load solutions. The other way is to find six conditions for A, B, C, D, E, F:

$$u(x) = Ax + B \text{ for } x \le \frac{1}{3}, \quad Cx + D \text{ for } \frac{1}{3} \le x \le \frac{2}{3}, \quad Ex + F \text{ for } x \ge \frac{2}{3}\,.$$

4 Solve the equation $-d^2u/dx^2 = \delta(x - a)$ with **fixed-free** boundary conditions $u(0) = 0$ and $u'(1) = 0$. Draw the graphs of $u(x)$ and $u'(x)$.

5 Show that the same equation with **free-free** conditions $u'(0) = 0$ and $u'(1) = 0$ has no solution. The equations for C and D cannot be solved. This corresponds to the singular matrix B_n (with $1,1$ and n,n entries both changed to 1).

6 Show that $-u'' = \delta(x - a)$ with **periodic** conditions $u(0) = u(1)$ and $u'(0) = u'(1)$ cannot be solved. Again the requirements on C and D cannot be met. This corresponds to the singular circulant matrix C_n (with $1,n$ and $n,1$ entries changed to -1).

7 A *difference* of point loads, $f(x) = \delta(x - \frac{1}{3}) - \delta(x - \frac{2}{3})$, does allow a free-free solution to $-u'' = f$. Find *infinitely many* solutions with $u'(0) = 0$ and $u'(1) = 0$.

8 The difference $f(x) = \delta(x - \frac{1}{3}) - \delta(x - \frac{2}{3})$ has zero total load, and $-u'' = f(x)$ can also be solved with periodic boundary conditions. Find a particular solution $u_{\mathbf{part}}(x)$ and then the complete solution $u_{\mathbf{part}} + u_{\mathbf{null}}$.

9 The distributed load $f(x) = 1$ is the integral of loads $\delta(x-a)$ at all points $x = a$. The free-fixed solution $u(x) = \frac{1}{2}(1-x^2)$ from Section 1.3 should then be the integral of the point-load solutions ($1-x$ for $a \le x$, and $1-a$ for $a \ge x$):

$$u(x) = \int_0^x (1-x)\,da + \int_x^1 (1-a)\,da = (1-x)x + (1-\frac{1^2}{2}) - (x - \frac{x^2}{2}) = \frac{1}{2} - \frac{1}{2}x^2.\ \text{YES!}$$

Check the fixed-fixed case $u(x) = \int_0^x (1-x)a\,da + \int_x^1 (1-a)x\,da =$ ____.

10 If you add together the columns of K^{-1} (or T^{-1}), you get a "discrete parabola" that solves the equation $Ku = f$ (or $Tu = f$) with what vector f? Do this addition for K_4^{-1} in Figure 1.9 and T_4^{-1} in Figure 1.10.

Problems 11–15 are about delta functions and their integrals and derivatives.

11 The integral of $\delta(x)$ is the step function $S(x)$. The integral of $S(x)$ is the ramp $R(x)$. Find and graph the next two integrals: the quadratic spline $Q(x)$ and the cubic spline $C(x)$. Which derivatives of $C(x)$ are continuous at $x = 0$?

12 The cubic spline $C(x)$ solves the fourth-order equation $u'''' = \delta(x)$. What is the complete solution $u(x)$ with four arbitrary constants? Choose those constants so that $u(1) = u''(1) = u(-1) = u''(-1) = 0$. This gives the bending of a uniform *simply supported beam* under a point load.

13 The defining property of the delta function $\delta(x)$ is that

$$\int_{-\infty}^{\infty} \delta(x)\, g(x)\, dx = g(0) \quad \text{for every smooth function } g(x).$$

How does this give "area = 1" under $\delta(x)$? What is $\int \delta(x-3)\, g(x)\, dx$?

14 The function $\delta(x)$ is a "weak limit" of very high, very thin square waves SW:

$$SW(x) = \frac{1}{2h} \ \text{ for } \ |x| \le h \quad \text{has} \quad \int_{-\infty}^{\infty} SW(x)\, g(x)\, dx \to g(0) \ \text{ as } \ h \to 0.$$

For a constant $g(x) = 1$ and every $g(x) = x^n$, show that $\int SW(x)g(x)\,dx \to g(0)$. We use the word "weak" because the rule depends on *test functions* $g(x)$.

15 The derivative of $\delta(x)$ is the *doublet* $\delta'(x)$. Integrate by parts to compute

$$\int_{-\infty}^{\infty} g(x)\, \delta'(x)\, dx = -\int_{-\infty}^{\infty} (?)\, \delta(x)\, dx = (??) \ \text{ for smooth } g(x).$$

1.5 EIGENVALUES AND EIGENVECTORS

This section begins with $Ax = \lambda x$. That is the equation for an eigenvector x and its eigenvalue λ. We can solve $Ax = \lambda x$ for small matrices, starting from $\det(A-\lambda I) = 0$. Possibly you know this already (it would be a horrible method for large matrices). There is no "elimination" that leads in a finite time to the exact λ and x. Since λ multiplies x, the equation $Ax = \lambda x$ is not linear.

One great success of numerical linear algebra is the development of fast and stable algorithms to compute eigenvalues (especially when A is symmetric). The command eig(A) in MATLAB produces n numbers $\lambda_1, \ldots, \lambda_n$ and not a formula. But this chapter is dealing with special matrices! For those we will find λ and x exactly.

$\boldsymbol{A = S\Lambda S^{-1}}$ **Part I**: Applying eigenvalues to A^k and $du/dt = Au$.
$\boldsymbol{K = Q\Lambda Q^{\mathrm{T}}}$ **Part II**: The eigenvalues of K_n, T_n, B_n, C_n are all $\lambda = 2 - 2\cos\theta$.

The two parts may need two lectures. The table at the end reports all we know about λ and x for important classes of matrices. The first big application of eigenvalues is to Newton's Law $Mu'' + Ku = 0$ in Section 2.2.

Part I: $Ax = \lambda x$ and $A^k x = \lambda^k x$ and Diagonalizing A

Almost every vector changes direction when it is multiplied by A. **Certain exceptional vectors $\boldsymbol{x}$ lie along the same line as $\boldsymbol{Ax}$.** Those are the eigenvectors. For an eigenvector, **$\boldsymbol{Ax}$ is a number $\boldsymbol{\lambda}$ times the original $\boldsymbol{x}$.**

The eigenvalue λ tells whether the special vector x is stretched or shrunk or reversed or left unchanged, when it is multiplied by A. We may find $\lambda = 2$ (stretching) or $\lambda = \frac{1}{2}$ (shrinking) or $\lambda = -1$ (reversing) or $\lambda = 1$ (steady state, because $Ax = x$ is unchanged). We may also find $\lambda = 0$. If the nullspace contains nonzero vectors, they have $Ax = 0x$. So the nullspace contains eigenvectors corresponding to $\lambda = 0$.

For our special matrices, we will guess x and then discover λ. For matrices in general, we find λ first. To separate λ from x, start by rewriting the basic equation:

$$\boldsymbol{Ax = \lambda x} \quad \textit{means that} \quad \boldsymbol{(A - \lambda I)x = 0}. \tag{1}$$

The matrix $A-\lambda I$ must be singular. *Its determinant must be zero.* The eigenvector x will be in the nullspace of $A-\lambda I$. The first step is to recognize that λ is an eigenvalue exactly when the shifted matrix $A - \lambda I$ is not invertible:

The number $\boldsymbol{\lambda}$ is an eigenvalue of $\boldsymbol{A}$ if and only if $\det(A - \lambda I) = 0$.

This "characteristic equation" $\det(A - \lambda I) = 0$ involves only λ, not x. The determinant of $A-\lambda I$ is a polynomial in λ of degree n. By the Fundamental Theorem of Algebra, this polynomial must have n roots $\lambda_1, \ldots, \lambda_n$. Some of those eigenvalues may be repeated and some may be complex—those cases can give us a little trouble.

Example 1 Start with the special 2 by 2 matrix $K = [2\ \ -1;\ -1\ \ 2]$. Estimate K^{100}.

Step 1 Subtract λ from the diagonal to get $K - \lambda I = \begin{bmatrix} 2-\lambda & -1 \\ -1 & 2-\lambda \end{bmatrix}$.

Step 2 *Take the determinant of this matrix.* That is $(2-\lambda)^2 - 1$ and we simplify:

$$\det(K - \lambda I) = \begin{vmatrix} 2-\lambda & -1 \\ -1 & 2-\lambda \end{vmatrix} = \lambda^2 - 4\lambda + 3\,.$$

Step 3 Factoring into $\lambda - 1$ times $\lambda - 3$, the roots are 1 and 3:

$$\lambda^2 - 4\lambda + 3 = 0 \quad \text{yields the eigenvalues} \quad \lambda_1 = 1 \quad \text{and} \quad \lambda_2 = 3\,.$$

Now find the eigenvectors by solving $(K - \lambda I)x = 0$ separately for each λ:

$$\lambda_1 = 1 \qquad K - I = \begin{bmatrix} 1 & -1 \\ -1 & 1 \end{bmatrix} \quad \text{leads to} \quad x_1 = \begin{bmatrix} 1 \\ 1 \end{bmatrix}$$

$$\lambda_2 = 3 \qquad K - 3I = \begin{bmatrix} -1 & -1 \\ -1 & -1 \end{bmatrix} \quad \text{leads to} \quad x_2 = \begin{bmatrix} 1 \\ -1 \end{bmatrix}$$

As expected, $K - I$ and $K - 3I$ are singular. Each nullspace produces a line of eigenvectors. We chose x_1 and x_2 to have nice components 1 and -1, but any multiples c_1x_1 and c_2x_2 (other than zero) would have been equally good as eigenvectors. The MATLAB choice is $c_1 = c_2 = 1/\sqrt{2}$, because then the eigenvectors have length 1 (unit vectors).

These eigenvectors of K are special (since K is). If I graph the functions $\sin \pi x$ and $\sin 2\pi x$, their samples at the two meshpoints $x = \frac{1}{3}$ and $\frac{2}{3}$ are the eigenvectors in Figure 1.11. (The functions $\sin k\pi x$ will soon lead us to the eigenvectors of K_n.)

K^{100} will grow like 3^{100} because $\lambda_{max} = 3$.

An exact formula would be

$$2K^{100} = 1^{100} \begin{bmatrix} 1 & 1 \\ 1 & 1 \end{bmatrix} + 3^{100} \begin{bmatrix} 1 & -1 \\ -1 & 1 \end{bmatrix}$$

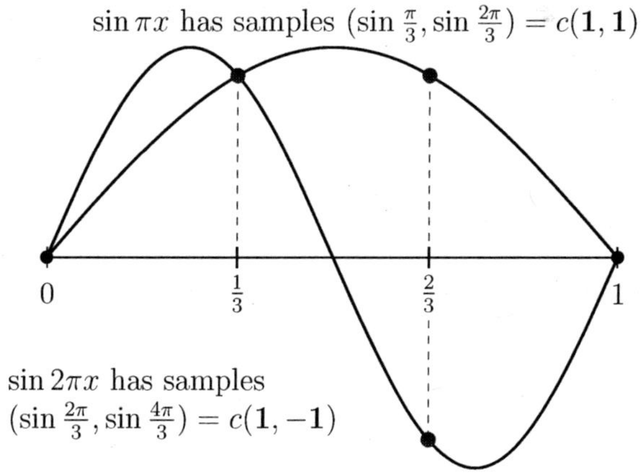

Figure 1.11: The eigenvectors of $\begin{bmatrix} 2 & -1 \\ -1 & 2 \end{bmatrix}$ lie on the graphs of $\sin \pi x$ and $\sin 2\pi x$.

Example 2 Here is a 3 by 3 singular example, the circulant matrix $C = C_3$:

$$C = \begin{bmatrix} 2 & -1 & -1 \\ -1 & 2 & -1 \\ -1 & -1 & 2 \end{bmatrix} \quad \text{and} \quad C - \lambda I = \begin{bmatrix} 2-\lambda & -1 & -1 \\ -1 & 2-\lambda & -1 \\ -1 & -1 & 2-\lambda \end{bmatrix}.$$

A little patience (3 by 3 is already requiring work) produces the determinant and its factors:

$$\det(C - \lambda I) = -\lambda^3 + 6\lambda^2 - 9\lambda = -\lambda(\lambda - 3)^2.$$

This third degree polynomial has three roots. The eigenvalues are $\lambda_1 = 0$ (singular matrix) and $\lambda_2 = 3$ and $\lambda_3 = 3$ (repeated root!). The all-ones vector $x_1 = (1,1,1)$ is in the nullspace of C, so it is an eigenvector for $\lambda_1 = 0$. We hope for *two* independent eigenvectors corresponding to the repeated eigenvalue $\lambda_2 = \lambda_3 = 3$:

$$C - 3I = \begin{bmatrix} -1 & -1 & -1 \\ -1 & -1 & -1 \\ -1 & -1 & -1 \end{bmatrix} \text{ has rank 1 (doubly singular).}$$

Elimination will zero out its last two rows. The three equations in $(C - 3I)x = 0$ are all the same equation $-x_1 - x_2 - x_3 = 0$, with a whole plane of solutions. They are all eigenvectors for $\lambda = 3$. Allow me to make this choice of eigenvectors x_2 and x_3 from that plane of solutions to $Cx = 3x$:

$$x_1 = \frac{1}{\sqrt{3}}\begin{bmatrix} 1 \\ 1 \\ 1 \end{bmatrix}, \qquad x_2 = \frac{1}{\sqrt{2}}\begin{bmatrix} 1 \\ 0 \\ -1 \end{bmatrix}, \qquad x_3 = \frac{1}{\sqrt{6}}\begin{bmatrix} 1 \\ -2 \\ 1 \end{bmatrix}.$$

With this choice, the x's are orthonormal (orthogonal unit vectors). **Every symmetric matrix has a full set of n perpendicular unit eigenvectors.**

For an n by n matrix, the determinant of $A - \lambda I$ will start with $(-\lambda)^n$. The rest of this polynomial takes more work to compute. Galois proved that an algebraic formula for the roots $\lambda_1, \ldots, \lambda_n$ is impossible for $n > 4$. (He got killed in a duel, but not about this.) That is why the eigenvalue problem needs its own special algorithms, which do *not* begin with the determinant of $A - \lambda I$.

The eigenvalue problem is harder than $Ax = b$, but there is partial good news. Two coefficients in the polynomial are easy to compute, and they give direct information about the product and sum of the roots $\lambda_1, \ldots, \lambda_n$.

The product of the n eigenvalues equals the *determinant* of A. *This is the constant term in* $\det(A - \lambda I)$:

Determinant = Product of λ's	$(\lambda_1)(\lambda_2)\cdots(\lambda_n) = \det(A)$.	(2)

The sum of the n eigenvalues equals the sum of the n diagonal entries. **The *trace*** *is the coefficient of* $(-\lambda)^{n-1}$ *in* $\det(A - \lambda I)$.

Trace = Sum of λ's	$\lambda_1 + \lambda_2 + \cdots + \lambda_n = a_{11} + a_{22} + \cdots + a_{nn}$ $= \text{sum down diagonal of } A.$	(3)

Those checks are very useful, especially the trace. They appear in Problems 20 and 21. They don't remove all the pain of computing $\det(A - \lambda I)$ and its factors. But when the computation is wrong, they generally tell us so. In our examples,

$$\boldsymbol{\lambda = 1, 3} \quad K = \begin{bmatrix} 2 & -1 \\ -1 & 2 \end{bmatrix} \qquad \text{has trace } 2 + 2 = 1 + 3 = 4.\ \det(K) = 1 \cdot 3.$$

$$\boldsymbol{\lambda = 0, 3, 3} \quad C = \begin{bmatrix} 2 & -1 & -1 \\ -1 & 2 & -1 \\ -1 & -1 & 2 \end{bmatrix} \qquad \text{has trace } 2 + 2 + 2 = 0 + 3 + 3 = 6.\ \det(C) = 0.$$

Let me note three important facts about the eigenvalue problem $Ax = \lambda x$.

1. *If A is triangular then its eigenvalues lie along its main diagonal.*

$$\text{The determinant of } \begin{bmatrix} 4 - \lambda & 3 \\ 0 & 2 - \lambda \end{bmatrix} \text{ is } (4 - \lambda)(2 - \lambda), \quad \text{so } \lambda = 4 \text{ and } \lambda = 2.$$

2. **The eigenvalues of $\boldsymbol{A^2}$ are $\boldsymbol{\lambda_1^2, \ldots, \lambda_n^2}$. The eigenvalues of $\boldsymbol{A^{-1}}$ are $\boldsymbol{1/\lambda_1, \ldots, 1/\lambda_n}$.**

$$\begin{array}{ll} \text{Multiply } Ax = \lambda x \text{ by } A. & \text{Then } A^2 x = \lambda A x = \lambda^2 x. \\ \text{Multiply } Ax = \lambda x \text{ by } A^{-1}. & \text{Then } x = \lambda A^{-1} x \text{ and } A^{-1} x = \frac{1}{\lambda} x. \end{array}$$

Eigenvectors of A are also eigenvectors of A^2 and A^{-1} (and any function of A).

3. *Eigenvalues of $A + B$ and AB are not known from eigenvalues of A and B.*

$$A = \begin{bmatrix} 0 & 1 \\ 0 & 0 \end{bmatrix} \text{ and } B = \begin{bmatrix} 0 & 0 \\ 1 & 0 \end{bmatrix} \quad \text{yield} \quad A + B = \begin{bmatrix} 0 & 1 \\ 1 & 0 \end{bmatrix} \text{ and } AB = \begin{bmatrix} 1 & 0 \\ 0 & 0 \end{bmatrix}.$$

A and B have zero eigenvalues (triangular matrices with zeros on the diagonal). But the eigenvalues of $A + B$ are 1 and -1. And AB has eigenvalues 1 and 0.

In the special case when $AB = BA$, these *commuting matrices* A and B will share eigenvectors: $Ax = \lambda x$ and $Bx = \lambda^* x$ for the same eigenvector x. Then we do have $(A + B)x = (\lambda + \lambda^*)x$ and $ABx = \lambda\lambda^* x$. Eigenvalues of A and B can now be added and multiplied. (With $B = A$, the eigenvalues of $A + A$ and A^2 are $\lambda + \lambda$ and λ^2.)

Example 3 A *Markov matrix* has no negative entries and each column adds to 1 (some authors work with row vectors and then each row adds to one):

$$\textbf{Markov matrix} \qquad A = \begin{bmatrix} .8 & .3 \\ .2 & .7 \end{bmatrix} \qquad \text{has } \lambda = 1 \text{ and } .5\,.$$

Every Markov matrix has $\lambda = 1$ as an eigenvalue ($A - I$ has dependent rows). When the trace is $.8 + .7 = 1.5$, the other eigenvalue must be $\lambda = .5$. The determinant of A must be $(\lambda_1)(\lambda_2) = .5$ and it is. The eigenvectors are $(.6, .4)$ and $(-1, 1)$.

Eigshow

A MATLAB demo (just type eigshow) displays the eigenvalue problem for a 2 by 2 matrix. Figure 1.12 starts with the vector $x = (1, 0)$. *The mouse makes this vector move around the unit circle.* At the same time the screen shows Ax, in color and also moving. Possibly Ax is ahead of x. Possibly Ax is behind x. *Sometimes Ax is parallel to x.* At that parallel moment, Ax equals λx.

$$A = \begin{bmatrix} .8 & .3 \\ .2 & .7 \end{bmatrix} \text{ has eigenvalues } \begin{matrix} \boldsymbol{\lambda_1 = 1} \\ \boldsymbol{\lambda_2 = .5} \end{matrix}$$

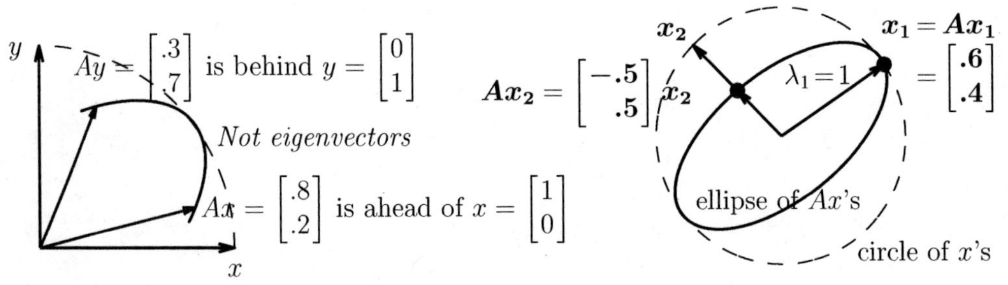

Figure 1.12: Eigshow for the Markov matrix: x_1 and x_2 line up with Ax_1 and Ax_2.

The eigenvalue λ is the length of Ax, when it is parallel to the unit eigenvector x. **On web.mit.edu/18.06 we added a voice explanation of what can happen.** The choices for A illustrate three possibilities, 0 or 1 or 2 real eigenvectors:

1. There may be *no real eigenvectors. Ax stays behind or ahead of x.* This means the eigenvalues and eigenvectors are complex (as for a rotation matrix).

2. There may be only *one* line of eigenvectors (unusual). The moving directions Ax and x meet but don't cross. This can happen only when $\lambda_1 = \lambda_2$.

3. There are *two* independent eigenvectors. This is typical! Ax crosses x at the first eigenvector x_1, and it crosses back at the second eigenvector x_2 (also at $-x_1$ and $-x_2$). The figure on the right shows those crossing directions: x is parallel to Ax. These eigenvectors are *not* perpendicular because A is not symmetric.

The Powers of a Matrix

Linear equations $Ax = b$ come from steady state problems. Eigenvalues have their greatest importance in *dynamic problems.* The solution is changing with time—growing or decaying or oscillating or approaching a steady state. We cannot use elimination (which changes the eigenvalues). But the eigenvalues and eigenvectors tell us everything.

Example 4 The two components of $u(t)$ are the US populations east and west of the Mississippi at time t. Every year, $\frac{8}{10}$ of the eastern population stays east and $\frac{2}{10}$ moves west. At the same time $\frac{7}{10}$ of the western population stays west and $\frac{3}{10}$ moves east:

$$\boldsymbol{u(t+1) = Au(t)} \qquad \begin{bmatrix} \text{east at time } t+1 \\ \text{west at time } t+1 \end{bmatrix} = \begin{bmatrix} .8 & .3 \\ .2 & .7 \end{bmatrix} \begin{bmatrix} \text{east at time } t \\ \text{west at time } t \end{bmatrix}.$$

Start with a million people in the east at $t = 0$. After one year (multiply by A), the numbers are $800{,}000$ and $200{,}000$. Nobody is created or destroyed because the columns add to 1. Populations stay positive because a Markov matrix has no negative entries. The initial state $u(0)$ is a combination of the eigenvectors $(.6, .4)$ and $(-1, 1)$:

Steady state plus transient

$$u(0) = \begin{bmatrix} 1{,}000{,}000 \\ 0 \end{bmatrix} = \begin{bmatrix} 600{,}000 \\ 400{,}000 \end{bmatrix} + \begin{bmatrix} 400{,}000 \\ -400{,}000 \end{bmatrix}.$$

After 100 steps the populations are almost exactly at the steady state:

$$u(100) = \begin{bmatrix} \mathbf{600{,}000} \\ \mathbf{400{,}000} \end{bmatrix} + \left(\frac{1}{2}\right)^{100} \begin{bmatrix} 400{,}000 \\ -400{,}000 \end{bmatrix} \quad \left(\text{and } \left(\frac{1}{2}\right)^{100} \text{ is very small}\right).$$

You can see the steady state directly from the powers A, A^2, A^3, and A^{100}:

$$\boldsymbol{A} = \begin{bmatrix} .8 & .3 \\ .2 & .7 \end{bmatrix} \quad \boldsymbol{A^2} = \begin{bmatrix} .70 & .45 \\ .30 & .55 \end{bmatrix} \quad \boldsymbol{A^3} = \begin{bmatrix} .650 & .525 \\ .350 & .475 \end{bmatrix} \quad \boldsymbol{A^{100}} = \begin{bmatrix} .6000 & .6000 \\ .4000 & .4000 \end{bmatrix}$$

Three steps are the key to using eigenvalues and eigenvectors to find $\boldsymbol{u_k = A^k u_0}$.

Step 1. Write u_0 as a combination of the eigenvectors $u_0 = a_1 x_1 + \cdots + a_n x_n$.

Step 2. Multiply each number a_j by $(\lambda_j)^k$.

Step 3. Recombine the eigenvectors into $u_k = a_1(\lambda_1)^k x_1 + \cdots + a_n(\lambda_n)^k x_n$.

In matrix language this is exactly $u_k = S\Lambda^k S^{-1} u_0$. **The matrix $\boldsymbol{S}$ has the eigenvectors in its columns. The diagonal matrix $\boldsymbol{\Lambda}$ contains the eigenvalues.** The steps give S^{-1} then Λ^k then S.

Step 1. Write $u_0 = \begin{bmatrix} x_1 & \cdots & x_n \end{bmatrix} \begin{bmatrix} a_1 \\ \vdots \\ a_n \end{bmatrix} = S\,a$, which gives $a = S^{-1} u_0$.

Step 2. Multiply $\begin{bmatrix} \lambda_1^k & & \\ & \ddots & \\ & & \lambda_n^k \end{bmatrix} \begin{bmatrix} a_1 \\ \vdots \\ a_n \end{bmatrix} = \Lambda^k a$ which gives $\Lambda^k S^{-1} u_0$.

$$\textbf{Step 3.} \quad \text{Recombine } u_k = \begin{bmatrix} & & \\ x_1 & \cdots & x_n \\ & & \end{bmatrix} \begin{bmatrix} (\lambda_1)^k a_1 \\ \vdots \\ (\lambda_n)^k a_n \end{bmatrix} = \begin{matrix} S\Lambda^k a \text{ which is} \\ \boldsymbol{u_k = S\Lambda^k S^{-1} u_0}. \end{matrix}$$

Step 2 is certainly the fastest—just n multiplications. Step 1 solves a linear system to analyze u_0 into eigenvectors. Step 3 multiplies by S to reconstruct the answer.

This process occurs over and over in applied mathematics. We see the same steps next for $du/dt = Au$, and again in Section 3.5 for A^{-1}. All of Fourier series and signal processing depends on using the eigenvectors in exactly this way (the Fast Fourier Transform makes it quick). Example 4 carried out the steps in a specific case.

Diagonalizing a Matrix

For an eigenvector x, multiplication by A just multiplies by a number: $Ax = \lambda x$. All the n by n difficulties are swept away. Instead of an interconnected system, we can follow the eigenvectors separately. It is like having a *diagonal matrix*, with no off-diagonal interconnections. The 100th power of a diagonal matrix is easy.

The matrix A turns into a diagonal matrix Λ when we use the eigenvectors properly. This is the matrix form of our key idea. Here is the one essential computation.

Suppose the n by n matrix A has n linearly independent eigenvectors $x_1, \ldots, x_n$. Those are the columns of an **eigenvector matrix** S. Then $S^{-1}AS = \Lambda$ is diagonal:

$$\textbf{Diagonalization} \qquad S^{-1}AS = \Lambda = \begin{bmatrix} \lambda_1 & & \\ & \ddots & \\ & & \lambda_n \end{bmatrix} = \begin{matrix} \textbf{eigenvalue} \\ \textbf{matrix} \end{matrix} \tag{4}$$

We use capital lambda for the eigenvalue matrix, with the small λ's on its diagonal.

Proof Multiply A times its eigenvectors $x_1, \ldots, x_n$, which are the columns of S. The first column of AS is Ax_1. That is $\lambda_1 x_1$:

$$\boldsymbol{A} \textbf{ times } \boldsymbol{S} \qquad A \begin{bmatrix} & & \\ x_1 & \cdots & x_n \\ & & \end{bmatrix} = \begin{bmatrix} & & \\ \lambda_1 x_1 & \cdots & \lambda_n x_n \\ & & \end{bmatrix}.$$

The trick is to split this matrix AS into $\boldsymbol{S}$ ***times*** $\boldsymbol{\Lambda}$:

$$\begin{bmatrix} & & \\ \lambda_1 x_1 & \cdots & \lambda_n x_n \\ & & \end{bmatrix} = \begin{bmatrix} & & \\ x_1 & \cdots & x_n \\ & & \end{bmatrix} \begin{bmatrix} \lambda_1 & & \\ & \ddots & \\ & & \lambda_n \end{bmatrix}.$$

Keep those matrices in the right order! Then λ_1 multiplies the first column x_1, as shown. We can write the diagonalization $AS = S\Lambda$ in two good ways:

$$AS = S\Lambda \quad \text{is} \quad S^{-1}AS = \Lambda \quad \text{or} \quad A = S\Lambda S^{-1}. \tag{5}$$

The matrix S has an inverse, because its columns (the eigenvectors of A) were assumed to be independent. *Without n independent eigenvectors, we cannot diagonalize A.* With no repeated eigenvalues, it is automatic that A has n independent eigenvectors.

Application to Vector Differential Equations

A single differential equation $\frac{dy}{dt} = ay$ has the general solution $y(t) = Ce^{at}$. The initial value $y(0)$ determines C. The solution $y(0)e^{at}$ decays if $a < 0$ and it grows if $a > 0$. Decay is stability, growth is instability. When a is a complex number, its *real part* determines the growth or decay. The imaginary part gives an oscillating factor $e^{i\omega t} = \cos\omega t + i\sin\omega t$.

Now consider two coupled equations, which give one vector equation:

$$\frac{d\boldsymbol{u}}{dt} = A\boldsymbol{u} \qquad \begin{aligned} dy/dt &= 2y - z \\ dz/dt &= -y + 2z \end{aligned} \qquad \text{or} \qquad \frac{d}{dt}\begin{bmatrix} y \\ z \end{bmatrix} = \begin{bmatrix} 2 & -1 \\ -1 & 2 \end{bmatrix}\begin{bmatrix} y \\ z \end{bmatrix}.$$

The solution will still involve exponentials $e^{\lambda t}$. But we no longer have a single growth rate as in e^{at}. There are *two eigenvalues* $\lambda = 1$ and $\lambda = 3$ of this matrix $A = K_2$. The solution has two exponentials e^t and e^{3t}. They multiply $x = (1,1)$ and $(1,-1)$.

The neat way to find solutions is by the eigenvectors. The *pure solutions* $e^{at}x$ are eigenvectors that grow according to their own eigenvalue 1 or 3. We combine them:

$$\boldsymbol{u}(t) = \boldsymbol{C}e^{t}\boldsymbol{x}_1 + \boldsymbol{D}e^{3t}\boldsymbol{x}_2 \quad \text{is} \quad \begin{bmatrix} y(t) \\ z(t) \end{bmatrix} = \begin{bmatrix} Ce^t + De^{3t} \\ Ce^t - De^{3t} \end{bmatrix}. \tag{6}$$

This is the complete solution. Its two constants (C and D) are determined by two initial values $y(0)$ and $z(0)$. Check first that each part $e^{\lambda t}x$ solves $\frac{du}{dt} = Au$:

$$\textbf{Each eigenvector} \quad \boldsymbol{u}(t) = e^{\lambda t}\boldsymbol{x} \quad \text{yields} \quad \frac{du}{dt} = \lambda e^{\lambda t}x = Ae^{\lambda t}x = Au\,. \tag{7}$$

The number $e^{\lambda t}$ just multiplies all components of the eigenvector x. This is the point of eigenvectors, they grow by themselves at their own rate λ. Then the complete solution $u(t)$ in (6) combines the pure modes Ce^tx_1 and $De^{3t}x_2$. The three steps for powers apply here too: **Expand $\boldsymbol{u}(0) = \boldsymbol{S}\boldsymbol{a}$, multiply each $\boldsymbol{a}_j$ by $e^{\lambda_j t}$, recombine into $\boldsymbol{u}(t) = \boldsymbol{S}e^{\Lambda t}\boldsymbol{S}^{-1}\boldsymbol{u}(0)$.**

Example 5 Suppose the initial values are $y(0) = 7$ and $z(0) = 3$. This determines the constants C and D. At the starting time $t = 0$, the growth factors $e^{\lambda t}$ are both one:

$$u(0) = C\begin{bmatrix} 1 \\ 1 \end{bmatrix} + D\begin{bmatrix} 1 \\ -1 \end{bmatrix} \quad \text{is} \quad \begin{bmatrix} 7 \\ 3 \end{bmatrix} = 5\begin{bmatrix} 1 \\ 1 \end{bmatrix} + 2\begin{bmatrix} 1 \\ -1 \end{bmatrix}.$$

We solved two equations to find $C = 5$ and $D = 2$. Then $u(t) = 5e^tx_1 + 2e^{3t}x_2$ solves the whole problem. The solution is a combination of slow growth and fast growth. Over a long time the faster e^{3t} will dominate, and the solution will line up with x_2.

Section 2.2 will explain the key equation $\boldsymbol{M}\boldsymbol{u}'' + \boldsymbol{K}\boldsymbol{u} = \boldsymbol{0}$ in much more detail. Newton's law involves acceleration (second derivative instead of first derivative). We might have two masses connected by springs. They can oscillate together, as in the first eigenvector $(1,1)$. Or they can be completely out of phase and move in opposite directions, as in the second eigenvector $(1,-1)$. The eigenvectors give the pure motions $e^{i\omega t}x$, or "normal modes." The initial conditions produce a mixture.

Symmetric Matrices and Orthonormal Eigenvectors

Our special matrices K_n and T_n and B_n and C_n are all symmetric. When A is a *symmetric matrix*, its eigenvectors are perpendicular (and the λ's are real):

Symmetric matrices have real eigenvalues and orthonormal eigenvectors.

The columns of S are these orthonormal eigenvectors $q_1, \ldots, q_n$. We use q instead of x for orthonormal vectors, and we use Q instead of S for the eigenvector matrix with those columns. *Orthonormal vectors are perpendicular unit vectors:*

$$q_i^{\mathrm{T}} q_j = \begin{cases} 0 & \text{when } i \neq j \quad (\textit{orthogonal} \text{ vectors}) \\ 1 & \text{when } i = j \quad (\textit{orthonormal} \text{ vectors}) \end{cases} \tag{8}$$

The matrix Q is easy to work with because $\boldsymbol{Q}^{\mathrm{T}}\boldsymbol{Q} = \boldsymbol{I}$. The transpose is the inverse! This repeats in matrix language that the columns of Q are orthonormal. $Q^{\mathrm{T}}Q = I$ contains all those inner products $q_i^{\mathrm{T}} q_j$ that equal 0 or 1:

Orthogonal Matrix

$$Q^{\mathrm{T}}Q = \begin{bmatrix} — q_1^{\mathrm{T}} — \\ — \cdots — \\ — q_n^{\mathrm{T}} — \end{bmatrix} \begin{bmatrix} | & | & | \\ q_1 & \vdots & q_n \\ | & | & | \end{bmatrix} = \begin{bmatrix} 1 & \cdots & 0 \\ \vdots & \ddots & \vdots \\ 0 & \cdots & 1 \end{bmatrix} = I\,. \tag{9}$$

For two orthonormal columns in three-dimensional space, Q is 3 by 2. In this rectangular case, we still have $Q^{\mathrm{T}}Q = I$ but we don't have $QQ^{\mathrm{T}} = I$. For our full set of eigenvectors, Q is square and then Q^{T} is Q^{-1}. *The diagonalization of a real symmetric matrix has $S = Q$ and $S^{-1} = Q^{\mathrm{T}}$:*

Symmetric diagonalization $\quad A = S\Lambda S^{-1} = Q\Lambda Q^{\mathrm{T}}$ with $\boldsymbol{Q}^{\mathrm{T}} = \boldsymbol{Q}^{-1}$. (10)

Notice how $Q\Lambda Q^{\mathrm{T}}$ is automatically symmetric (like LDL^{T}). These factorizations perfectly reflect the symmetry of A. The eigenvalues $\lambda_1, \ldots, \lambda_n$ are the "spectrum" of the matrix, and $A = Q\Lambda Q^{\mathrm{T}}$ is the *spectral theorem* or *principal axis theorem.*

Part II: Eigenvectors for Derivatives and Differences

A main theme of this textbook is the analogy between discrete and continuous problems (*matrix equations and differential equations*). Here we go first to differential equations. The eigenvectors of K_n and B_n and C_n and T_n will be easy because they come from cosines and sines. After dividing by $(\Delta x)^2$, the analog of $K_n y$ is $-y''$:

$$\frac{1}{(\Delta x)^2}\begin{bmatrix} 2 & -1 & & \\ -1 & 2 & -1 & \\ & \cdot & \cdot & \cdot \\ & & -1 & 2 \end{bmatrix}\begin{bmatrix} y_1 \\ y_2 \\ \cdot \\ y_n \end{bmatrix} \quad \text{is like} \quad -\frac{\boldsymbol{d^2y}}{\boldsymbol{dx^2}} \quad \text{with } y(0) = 0 \text{ and } y(1) = 0\,.$$

The second difference from $-1, 2, -1$ is like a second derivative, with signs reversed. That was the point of Section 1.2. The continuous eigenvalue problem asks for the *second derivative of $y(x)$ to be a multiple of $y(x)$.* We find cosines and sines:

$$-\frac{d^2y}{dx^2} = \lambda y(x) \text{ is solved by } y = \cos\omega x \text{ and } y = \sin\omega x \text{ with } \lambda = \omega^2. \quad (11)$$

Allowing all frequencies ω, we have too many eigenfunctions. It is the boundary conditions that pick out special frequencies $\omega = k\pi$ in $\sin\omega x$.

The eigenfunctions are $y(x) = \sin k\pi x$, because $y(0) = 0$ knocks out cosines. That condition at $x = 0$ reduces to $\sin 0 = 0$, good. The condition $y(1) = 0$ reduces to $\sin k\pi = 0$. The sine comes back to zero at π and 2π and every integer multiple of π. So $k = 1, 2, 3, \ldots$ (since $k = 0$ only produces $\sin 0x = 0$ which is useless). Substitute $y(x) = \sin k\pi x$ into (11) to find the eigenvalues $\lambda = k^2\pi^2$:

$$-\frac{d^2}{dx^2}(\sin k\pi x) = k^2\pi^2 \sin k\pi x \quad \text{so} \quad \lambda = k^2\pi^2 = \left\{\pi^2, 4\pi^2, 9\pi^2, \ldots\right\}. \quad (12)$$

We will make a similar guess (*discrete sines*) for the discrete eigenvectors of K_n.

Changing the boundary conditions gives new eigenfunctions and eigenvalues. The equation $-y'' = \lambda y$ is still solved by sines and cosines. Instead of $y = \sin k\pi x$ which is zero at both endpoints, here are the eigenfunctions $y_k(x)$ and their eigenvalues λ_k for **zero slope** and **periodic** and **mixed** conditions:

Analog of B_n	$y'(0) = 0$ and $y'(1) = 0$	$y(x) = \boldsymbol{\cos k\pi x}$	$\lambda = \boldsymbol{k^2\pi^2}$
Analog of C_n	$y(0) = y(1), y'(0) = y'(1)$	$y(x) = \boldsymbol{\sin 2\pi kx, \cos 2\pi kx}$	$\lambda = \boldsymbol{4k^2\pi^2}$
Analog of T_n	$y'(0) = 0$ and $y(1) = 0$	$y(x) = \boldsymbol{\cos (k+\tfrac{1}{2})\pi x}$	$\lambda = \boldsymbol{(k+\tfrac{1}{2})^2\pi^2}$.

Remember that B_n and C_n are singular matrices ($\lambda = 0$ is an eigenvalue). Their continuous analogs also have $\lambda = 0$, with $\cos 0x = 1$ as the eigenfunction (set $k = 0$). This constant eigenfunction $y(x) = 1$ is like the constant vector $y = (1, 1, \ldots, 1)$.

The free-fixed eigenfunctions $\cos(k + \frac{1}{2})\pi x$ start with zero slope because $\sin 0 = 0$. They end with zero height because $\cos(k + \frac{1}{2})\pi = 0$. So $y'(0) = 0$ and $y(1) = 0$. The matrix eigenvectors will use these same sines and cosines (but different λ).

Eigenvectors of K_n: Discrete Sines

Now come eigenvectors for the $-1, 2, -1$ matrices. They are **discrete sines and cosines**—try them and they work. *For all the middle rows,* $\sin j\theta$ and $\cos j\theta$ are still successful for $-y_{j-1} + 2y_j - y_{j+1} = \lambda y_j$, with **eigenvalues $\boldsymbol{\lambda = 2 - 2\cos\theta}$**:

$$-1\begin{Bmatrix}\sin(j-1)\theta \\ \cos(j-1)\theta\end{Bmatrix} + 2\begin{Bmatrix}\sin j\theta \\ \cos j\theta\end{Bmatrix} - 1\begin{Bmatrix}\sin(j+1)\theta \\ \cos(j+1)\theta\end{Bmatrix} = (2 - 2\cos\theta)\begin{Bmatrix}\sin j\theta \\ \cos j\theta\end{Bmatrix}. \quad (13)$$

The first and third sines use $\sin(a - \theta) + \sin(a + \theta) = 2\sin a\cos\theta$ with $a = j\theta$. And $2\cos\theta$ also factors from $\cos(a - \theta) + \cos(a + \theta) = 2\cos a\cos\theta$. Notice $2 - 2\cos\theta \geq 0$.

The boundary rows decide θ and everything! I will begin with K_n, which cuts off the -1 in rows 1 and n. This corresponds to $y_0 = 0$ and $y_{n+1} = 0$. (The vanished -1 would have multiplied y_0 and y_{n+1}, both zero.) The first eigenvector y_1 of K_n will sample the first continuous eigenfunction $\sin \pi x$ at the n meshpoints with $h = \frac{1}{n+1}$:

Eigenvector = Discrete Sine $\quad y_1 = (\sin \pi h, \sin 2\pi h, \ldots, \sin n\pi h) \quad (14)$

The jth component is $\sin \frac{j\pi}{n+1}$. It is zero for $j = 0$ and $j = n+1$, as desired. The angle is $\theta = \pi h = \frac{\pi}{n+1}$. In (13), $2 - 2\cos\theta \approx \theta^2$ is the smallest eigenvalue:

First eigenvalue of K_n $$\lambda_1 = 2 - 2\cos \pi h = 2 - 2\left(1 - \frac{\pi^2 h^2}{2} + \cdots\right) \approx \pi^2 h^2. \quad (15)$$

The other continuous eigenfunctions are $\sin 2\pi x$, $\sin 3\pi x$, and generally $\sin k\pi x$. It is neat for the kth discrete eigenvector to sample $\sin k\pi x$ again at $x = h, \ldots, nh$:

Eigenvectors = Discrete Sines $\quad \boldsymbol{y_k = (\sin k\pi h, \ldots, \sin nk\pi h)} \quad (16)$

All eigenvalues of K_n $\quad \boldsymbol{\lambda_k = 2 - 2\cos k\pi h,\ k = 1, \ldots, n}. \quad (17)$

The sum $\lambda_1 + \cdots + \lambda_n$ must be $2n$, because that is the sum of the 2's on the diagonal (the *trace*). The product of the λ's must be $n+1$. This probably needs an expert (not the author). For K_2 and K_3, Figure 1.13 shows the eigenvalues (symmetric around 2).

Eigenvalues $2 - 2\cos\theta$ of K_3

$\boldsymbol{\lambda_1} = 2 - 2\left(\frac{\sqrt{2}}{2}\right) = \boldsymbol{2 - \sqrt{2}}$

$\boldsymbol{\lambda_2} = 2 - 2(0) = \boldsymbol{2}$

$\boldsymbol{\lambda_3} = 2 - 2\left(-\frac{\sqrt{2}}{2}\right) = \boldsymbol{2 + \sqrt{2}}$

Trace $\lambda_1 + \lambda_2 + \lambda_3 = \boldsymbol{6}$

Determinant $\lambda_1\lambda_2\lambda_3 = \boldsymbol{4}$

For B_4 include also $\lambda_0 = 0$

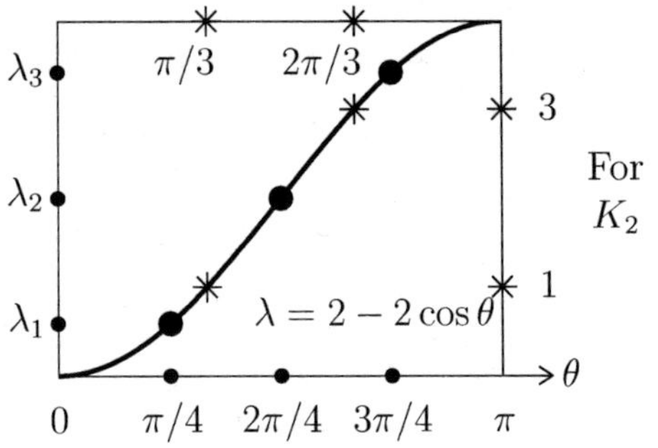

Figure 1.13: Eigenvalues $*$ of K_{n-1} interlace eigenvalues $\bullet = 2 - 2\cos\frac{k\pi}{n+1}$ of K_n.

Orthogonality *The eigenvectors of a symmetric matrix are perpendicular.* That is confirmed for the eigenvectors $(1,1)$ and $(1,-1)$ in the 2 by 2 case. The three eigenvectors (when $n = 3$ and $n+1 = 4$) are the columns of this ***sine matrix***. Each column lies on a sine curve in Figure 1.14.

Discrete Sine Transform

$$\text{DST} = \begin{bmatrix} \sin\frac{\pi}{4} & \sin\frac{2\pi}{4} & \sin\frac{3\pi}{4} \\ \sin\frac{2\pi}{4} & \sin\frac{4\pi}{4} & \sin\frac{6\pi}{4} \\ \sin\frac{3\pi}{4} & \sin\frac{6\pi}{4} & \sin\frac{9\pi}{4} \end{bmatrix} = \begin{bmatrix} \frac{1}{\sqrt{2}} & 1 & \frac{1}{\sqrt{2}} \\ 1 & 0 & -1 \\ \frac{1}{\sqrt{2}} & -1 & \frac{1}{\sqrt{2}} \end{bmatrix}. \quad (18)$$

The columns of S are orthogonal vectors, of length $\sqrt{2}$. If we divide all components by $\sqrt{2}$, the three eigenvectors become *orthonormal*. All columns will be unit vectors. The **DST** matrix becomes an orthogonal $Q = \mathbf{DST}/\sqrt{2}$, with $Q^{-1} = Q^{\mathrm{T}}$.

Section 3.5 uses the **DST** matrix in a Fast Poisson Solver for a two-dimensional difference equation $(K2D)U = F$. The columns of the matrix are displayed for $n = 5$. The code there connects our **DST** to the FFT.

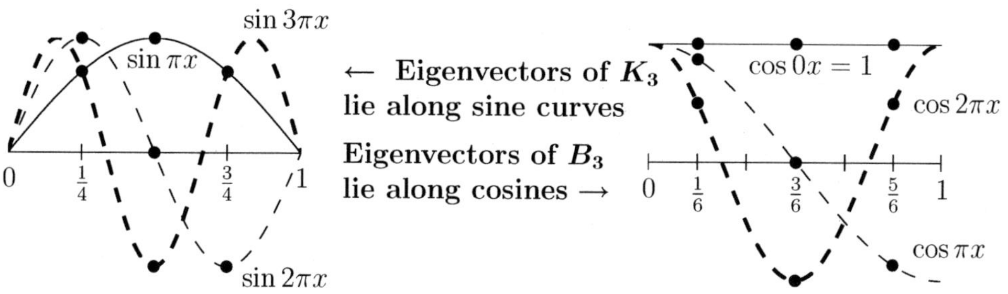

Figure 1.14: Three discrete eigenvectors fall on three continuous eigenfunctions.

Eigenvectors of B_n: Discrete Cosines

The matrices B_n correspond to zero slope at *both* ends. Remarkably, B_n has the same $n-1$ eigenvalues as K_{n-1} plus the additional eigenvalue $\lambda = 0$. (B is singular with $(1, \ldots, 1)$ in its nullspace, because its first and last rows contain $+1$ and -1.) Thus B_3 has eigenvalues $0, 1, 3$ and trace 4, agreeing with $1 + 2 + 1$ on its diagonal:

Eigenvalues of B_n
$$\lambda = 2 - 2\cos\frac{k\pi}{n}, \quad k = 0, \ldots, n-1. \tag{19}$$

Eigenvectors of B sample $\cos k\pi x$ at the n *midpoints* $x = (j - \frac{1}{2})/n$ in Figure 1.14, where eigenvectors of K sample the sines at the meshpoints $x = j/(n+1)$:

Eigenvectors of B_n
$$y_k = \left(\cos\frac{1}{2}\frac{k\pi}{n}, \cos\frac{3}{2}\frac{k\pi}{n}, \ldots, \cos\left(n - \frac{1}{2}\right)\frac{k\pi}{n}\right). \tag{20}$$

At the left end $j = 0$ and the right end $j = n+1$, those eigenvectors satisfy the required conditions $y_0 = y_1$ and $y_n = y_{n+1}$ for zero slope:

$$\cos\left(-\frac{1}{2}\frac{k\pi}{n}\right) = \cos\left(\frac{1}{2}\frac{k\pi}{n}\right) \quad \text{and} \quad \cos\left(n - \frac{1}{2}\right)\frac{k\pi}{n} = \cos\left(n + \frac{1}{2}\right)\frac{k\pi}{n}.$$

Notice that $k = 0$ gives the all-ones eigenvector $y_0 = (1, 1, \ldots, 1)$ which has eigenvalue $\lambda = 0$. This is the DC vector with zero frequency. Starting the count at zero is the useful convention in electrical engineering and signal processing.

These eigenvectors of B_n give the **Discrete Cosine Transform**. Here is the cosine matrix for $n = 3$, with the unnormalized eigenvectors of B_3 in its columns:

Discrete Cosine Transform

$$\mathrm{DCT} = \begin{bmatrix} \cos 0 & \cos \frac{1}{2}\frac{\pi}{3} & \cos \frac{1}{2}\frac{2\pi}{3} \\ \cos 0 & \cos \frac{3}{2}\frac{\pi}{3} & \cos \frac{3}{2}\frac{2\pi}{3} \\ \cos 0 & \cos \frac{5}{2}\frac{\pi}{3} & \cos \frac{5}{2}\frac{2\pi}{3} \end{bmatrix} = \begin{bmatrix} 1 & \frac{1}{2}\sqrt{3} & \frac{1}{2} \\ 1 & 0 & -1 \\ 1 & -\frac{1}{2}\sqrt{3} & \frac{1}{2} \end{bmatrix} \tag{21}$$

Eigenvectors of C_n: Powers of $w = e^{2\pi i/n}$

After sines from K_n and cosines from B_n, we come to the eigenvectors of C_n. These are *both* sines and cosines. Equivalently, they are ***complex exponentials***. They are even more important than the sine and cosine transforms, because now the eigenvectors give the **Discrete Fourier Transform**.

You can't have better eigenvectors than that. Every circulant matrix shares these eigenvectors, as we see in Chapter 4 on Fourier transforms. A circulant matrix is a "periodic matrix." It has *constant diagonals with wrap-around* (the -1's below the main diagonal of C_n wrap around to the -1 in the upper right corner). Our goal is to find the eigenvalues and eigenvectors of the matrices C_n, like C_4:

Circulant matrix (periodic)

$$C_4 = \begin{bmatrix} 2 & -1 & 0 & \mathbf{-1} \\ -1 & 2 & -1 & 0 \\ 0 & -1 & 2 & -1 \\ \mathbf{-1} & 0 & -1 & 2 \end{bmatrix}.$$

This real symmetric matrix has real orthogonal eigenvectors (discrete sines and cosines). They have full cycles like $\sin 2k\pi x$, not half cycles like $\sin k\pi x$. But the numbering gets awkward when cosines start at $k = 0$ and sines start at $k = 1$. It is better to work with the kth eigenvector as a complex exponential $e^{i\theta}$. *The eigenvector comes from sampling $y_k(x) = e^{i2\pi kx}$ at the n meshpoints which are now $x = j/n$.*

jth component of y_k $$e^{i2\pi k(j/n)} = w^{jk} \quad \text{where} \quad w = e^{2\pi i/n} = n\text{th root of } 1. \tag{22}$$

That special number $\boldsymbol{w = e^{2\pi i/n}}$ is the key to the Discrete Fourier Transform. *Its angle is* $2\pi/n$, which is an nth part of the whole way around the unit circle. The powers of w cycle around the circle and come back to $w^n = 1$:

Eigenvectors of C_n $$\boldsymbol{y_k = (1, w^k, w^{2k}, \ldots, w^{(n-1)k})} \tag{23}$$

Eigenvalues of C_n $$\boldsymbol{\lambda_k = 2 - w^k - w^{-k} = 2 - 2\cos\frac{2\pi k}{n}} \tag{24}$$

The numbering is $k = 0, 1, \ldots, n-1$. The eigenvector with $k = 0$ is the constant $y_0 = (1, 1, \ldots, 1)$. The choice $k = n$ would give the same $(1, 1, \ldots, 1)$—***nothing new, just aliasing***! The lowest eigenvalue $2 - 2\cos 0$ is $\lambda_0 = 0$. *The C_n are singular.*

The eigenvector with $k = 1$ is $y_1 = (1, w, \ldots, w^{n-1})$. ***Those components are the n roots of 1***. Figure 1.15 shows the unit circle $r = 1$ in the complex plane, with the $n = 4$ numbers $1, i, i^2, i^3$ equally spaced around the circle on the left. Those numbers are $e^0, e^{2\pi i/4}, e^{4\pi i/4}, e^{6\pi i/4}$ and ***their fourth powers are 1***.

$$\boldsymbol{Cy_1 = \lambda_1 y_1} \qquad Cy_1 = \begin{bmatrix} 2 & -1 & 0 & -1 \\ -1 & 2 & -1 & 0 \\ 0 & -1 & 2 & -1 \\ -1 & 0 & -1 & 2 \end{bmatrix} \begin{bmatrix} 1 \\ i \\ i^2 \\ i^3 \end{bmatrix} = (2 - i - i^3) \begin{bmatrix} 1 \\ i \\ i^2 \\ i^3 \end{bmatrix}. \quad (25)$$

For any n, the top row gives $2 - w - w^{n-1} = 2 - w - \overline{w}$. Notice that w^{n-1} is also the complex conjugate $\overline{w} = e^{-2\pi i/n} = 1/w$, because one more factor w will reach 1.

$$\textbf{Eigenvalue of } C \qquad \lambda_1 = 2 - w - \overline{w} = 2 - e^{2\pi i/n} - e^{-2\pi i/n} = 2 - 2\cos\frac{2\pi}{n}. \quad (26)$$

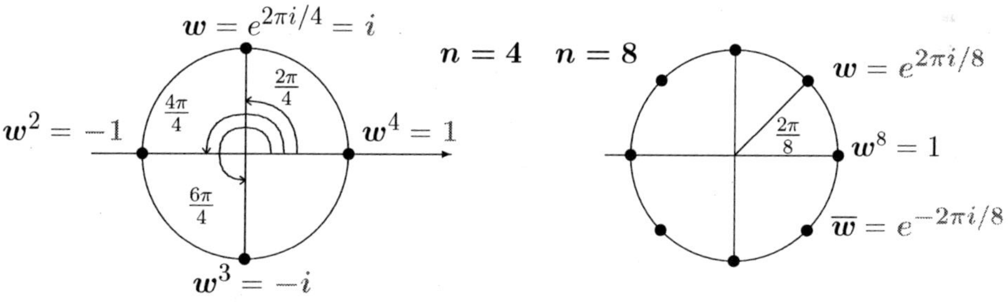

Figure 1.15: The solutions to $z^4 = 1$ are $1, i, i^2, i^3$. The 8th roots are powers of $e^{2\pi i/8}$.

Now we know the first eigenvectors $y_0 = (1, 1, 1, 1)$ and $y_1 = (1, i, i^2, i^3)$ of C_4. The eigenvalues are 0 and 2. To finish, we need the eigenvectors $y_2 = (1, i^2, i^4, i^6)$ and $y_3 = (1, i^3, i^6, i^9)$. *Their eigenvalues are* 4 *and* 2, which are $2 - 2\cos\pi$ and $2 - 2\cos\frac{3\pi}{2}$. Then the sum of the eigenvalues is $0 + 2 + 4 + 2 = 8$, agreeing with the sum of the diagonal entries (the trace $2 + 2 + 2 + 2$) of this matrix C_4.

Allow me to use letters k and n and w, rather than specific values $k = 2$ and $n = 4$ and $w = i$. It is enough to check the first row of $C_n y_k = \lambda_k y_k$:

$$\begin{bmatrix} 2 & -1 & \ldots & -1 \\ & & & \\ & & & \\ & & & \end{bmatrix} \begin{bmatrix} 1 \\ w^k \\ \vdots \\ w^{(n-1)k} \end{bmatrix} = (2 - w^k - w^{(n-1)k}) \begin{bmatrix} 1 \\ w^k \\ \vdots \\ w^{(n-1)k} \end{bmatrix}. \quad (27)$$

The other rows of $Cy = \lambda y$ are just powers of w times this first row. The eigenvectors in (23) are confirmed. Since $w^{(n-1)k} = \overline{w}^k$ we can see the good formula (24) for λ_k.

The Fourier Matrix

As always, the eigenvectors go into the columns of a matrix. Instead of the sine or cosine matrix, these eigenvectors of C_n give the **Fourier matrix** F_n. We have the **DFT** instead of the **DST** or **DCT**. For $n = 4$ the columns of F_4 are y_0, y_1, y_2, y_3:

Fourier matrix F_n

Eigenvectors of C_n

$$F_4 = \begin{bmatrix} 1 & 1 & 1 & 1 \\ 1 & i & i^2 & i^3 \\ 1 & i^2 & i^4 & i^6 \\ 1 & i^3 & i^6 & i^9 \end{bmatrix} \qquad \boldsymbol{(F_n)_{jk} = w^{jk} = e^{2\pi ijk/n}}\,.$$

The columns of the Fourier matrix are orthogonal! The inner product of two complex vectors requires that we take the complex conjugate of one of them (by convention the first one). Otherwise we would have $y_1^{\mathrm{T}} y_3 = 1 + 1 + 1 + 1 = 4$. But y_1 is truly orthogonal to y_3 because the correct product uses the conjugate $\overline{y}_1$:

Complex inner product

$$\overline{y}_1^{\mathrm{T}} y_3 = \begin{bmatrix} 1 & -i & (-i)^2 & (-i)^3 \end{bmatrix} \begin{bmatrix} 1 \\ i^3 \\ i^6 \\ i^9 \end{bmatrix} = 1 - 1 + 1 - 1 = 0\,. \qquad (28)$$

Similarly $\overline{y}_1^{\mathrm{T}} y_1 = 4$ gives the correct length $\|y_1\| = 2$ (not $y_1^{\mathrm{T}} y_1 = 0$). The matrix $\overline{F}^{\mathrm{T}} F$ of all the column inner products is $4I$. *Orthogonality of columns* reveals F^{-1}:

Orthogonal $$\overline{F}_4^{\mathrm{T}} F_4 = 4I \quad \text{so that} \quad F_4^{-1} = \tfrac{1}{4}\overline{F}_4^{\mathrm{T}} = \textbf{inverse of } \boldsymbol{F}\,. \qquad (29)$$

Always $\overline{F}_n^{\mathrm{T}} F_n = nI$. ***The inverse of F_n is $\overline{F}_n^{\mathrm{T}}/n$***. We could divide F_n by $\sqrt{n}$, which normalizes it to $U_n = F_n/\sqrt{n}$. **This normalized Fourier matrix is unitary**:

Orthonormal $$\overline{U}_n^{\mathrm{T}} U_n = \left(\overline{F}_n^{\mathrm{T}}/\sqrt{n}\right)\left(F_n/\sqrt{n}\right) = \frac{n}{n} I = I\,. \qquad (30)$$

A unitary matrix has $\overline{U}^{\mathrm{T}} U = I$ and orthonormal columns. It is the complex analog of a real orthogonal Q (which has $Q^{\mathrm{T}} Q = I$). The Fourier matrix is the most important complex matrix ever seen. F_n and F_n^{-1} produce the Discrete Fourier Transform.

Problem Set 1.5

The first nine problems are about the matrices K_n, T_n, B_n, C_n.

1 The 2 by 2 matrix K_2 in Example 1 has eigenvalues 1 and 3 in Λ. Its *unit* eigenvectors q_1 and q_2 are the columns of Q. Multiply $Q\Lambda Q^{\mathrm{T}}$ to recover K_2.

2 When you multiply the eigenvector $y = (\sin \pi h, \sin 2\pi h, \ldots)$ by K, the first row will produce a multiple of $\sin \pi h$. Find that multiplier λ by a double-angle formula for $\sin 2\pi h$:

$$(Ky)_1 = 2\sin \pi h - 1 \sin 2\pi h = \lambda \sin \pi h \qquad \text{Then } \lambda = \underline{\qquad}.$$

3 In MATLAB, construct $K = K_5$ and then its eigenvalues by $e = \mathsf{eig}(K)$. That column should be $(2-\sqrt{3}, 2-1, 2-0, 2+1, 2+\sqrt{3})$. Verify that e agrees with $2 * \mathsf{ones}(5,1) - 2 * \mathsf{cos}([1:5] * \mathsf{pi}/6)'$.

4 Continue **3** to find an eigenvector matrix Q by $[Q, E] = \mathsf{eig}(K)$. The Discrete Sine Transform $\mathbf{DST} = Q * \mathsf{diag}([-1\ \ -1\quad 1\ \ -1\quad 1])$ starts each column with a positive entry. The matrix $JK = [1:5]' * [1:5]$ has entries j times k. Verify that **DST** agrees with $\mathsf{sin}(JK * \mathsf{pi}/6)/\mathsf{sqrt}(3)$, and test $\mathbf{DST}^{\mathrm{T}} = \mathbf{DST}^{-1}$.

5 Construct $B = B_6$ and $[Q, E] = \mathsf{eig}(B)$ with $B(1,1) = 1$ and $B(6,6) = 1$. Verify that $E = \mathsf{diag}(e)$ with eigenvalues $2 * \mathsf{ones}(1,6) - 2 * \mathsf{cos}([0:5] * \mathsf{pi}/6)$ in e. How do you adjust Q to produce the (highly important) Discrete Cosine Transform with entries $\mathbf{DCT} = \mathsf{cos}([.5:5.5]' * [0:5] * \mathsf{pi}/6)/\mathsf{sqrt}(3)$?

6 The free-fixed matrix $T = T_6$ has $T(1,1) = 1$. Check that its eigenvalues are $2 - 2\cos\left[(k-\frac{1}{2})\pi/6.5\right]$. The matrix $\mathsf{cos}([.5:5.5]' * [.5:5.5] * \mathsf{pi}/6.5)/\mathsf{sqrt}(3.25)$ should contain its unit eigenvectors. Compute $Q' * Q$ and $Q' * T * Q$.

7 The columns of the Fourier matrix F_4 are eigenvectors of the circulant matrix $C = C_4$. But $[Q, E] = \mathsf{eig}(C)$ does not produce $Q = F_4$. What combinations of the columns of Q give the columns of F_4? Notice the double eigenvalue in E.

8 Show that the n eigenvalues $2 - 2\cos\frac{k\pi}{n+1}$ of K_n add to the trace $2 + \cdots + 2$.

9 K_3 and B_4 have the same nonzero eigenvalues because they come from the same 4×3 backward difference Δ_-. Show that $K_3 = \Delta_-^{\mathrm{T}}\Delta_-$ and $B_4 = \Delta_-\Delta_-^{\mathrm{T}}$. The eigenvalues of K_3 are the squared **singular values** σ^2 of Δ_- in 1.7.

Problems 10–23 are about diagonalizing A by its eigenvectors in S.

10 Factor these two matrices into $A = S\Lambda S^{-1}$. Check that $A^2 = S\Lambda^2 S^{-1}$:

$$A = \begin{bmatrix} 1 & 2 \\ 0 & 3 \end{bmatrix} \qquad \text{and} \qquad A = \begin{bmatrix} 1 & 1 \\ 2 & 2 \end{bmatrix}.$$

11 If $A = S\Lambda S^{-1}$ then $A^{-1} = (\quad)(\quad)(\quad)$. The eigenvectors of A^3 are (the same columns of S)(different vectors).

12 If A has $\lambda_1 = 2$ with eigenvector $x_1 = \left[\begin{smallmatrix}1\\0\end{smallmatrix}\right]$ and $\lambda_2 = 5$ with $x_2 = \left[\begin{smallmatrix}1\\1\end{smallmatrix}\right]$, use $S\Lambda S^{-1}$ to find A. No other matrix has the same λ's and x's.

13 Suppose $A = S\Lambda S^{-1}$. What is the eigenvalue matrix for $A + 2I$? What is the eigenvector matrix? Check that $A + 2I = (\quad)(\quad)(\quad)^{-1}$.

14 If the columns of S (n eigenvectors of A) are linearly independent, then

(a) A is invertible (b) A is diagonalizable (c) S is invertible

15 The matrix $A = \left[\begin{smallmatrix} 3 & 1 \\ 0 & 3 \end{smallmatrix}\right]$ is not diagonalizable because the rank of $A - 3I$ is ____. A only has one line of eigenvector. Which entries could you change to make A diagonalizable, with two eigenvectors?

16 $A^k = S\Lambda^k S^{-1}$ approaches the zero matrix as $k \to \infty$ if and only if every λ has absolute value less than ____. Which of these matrices has $A^k \to 0$?

$$A_1 = \begin{bmatrix} .6 & .4 \\ .4 & .6 \end{bmatrix} \quad \text{and} \quad A_2 = \begin{bmatrix} .6 & .9 \\ .1 & .6 \end{bmatrix} \quad \text{and} \quad A_3 = K_3.$$

17 Find Λ and S to diagonalize A_1 in Problem 16. What is ${A_1}^{10} u_0$ for these u_0?

$$u_0 = \begin{bmatrix} 1 \\ 1 \end{bmatrix} \quad \text{and} \quad u_0 = \begin{bmatrix} 1 \\ -1 \end{bmatrix} \quad \text{and} \quad u_0 = \begin{bmatrix} 2 \\ 0 \end{bmatrix}.$$

18 Diagonalize A and compute $S\Lambda^k S^{-1}$ to prove this formula for A^k:

$$A = \begin{bmatrix} 2 & 1 \\ 1 & 2 \end{bmatrix} \quad \text{has} \quad A^k = \frac{1}{2}\begin{bmatrix} 3^k + 1 & 3^k - 1 \\ 3^k - 1 & 3^k + 1 \end{bmatrix}$$

19 Diagonalize B and compute $S\Lambda^k S^{-1}$ to show how B^k involves 3^k and 2^k:

$$B = \begin{bmatrix} 3 & 1 \\ 0 & 2 \end{bmatrix} \quad \text{has} \quad B^k = \begin{bmatrix} 3^k & 3^k - 2^k \\ 0 & 2^k \end{bmatrix}.$$

20 Suppose that $A = S\Lambda S^{-1}$. Take determinants to prove that $\det A = \lambda_1 \lambda_2 \cdots \lambda_n =$ product of λ's. This quick proof only works when A is ____.

21 Show that trace GH = trace HG, by adding the diagonal entries of GH and HG:

$$G = \begin{bmatrix} a & b \\ c & d \end{bmatrix} \quad \text{and} \quad H = \begin{bmatrix} q & r \\ s & t \end{bmatrix}.$$

Choose $G = S$ and $H = \Lambda S^{-1}$. Then $S\Lambda S^{-1} = A$ has the same trace as $\Lambda S^{-1} S = \Lambda$, so the trace is the sum of the eigenvalues.

22 Substitute $A = S\Lambda S^{-1}$ into the product $(A - \lambda_1 I)(A - \lambda_2 I) \cdots (A - \lambda_n I)$ and explain why $(\Lambda - \lambda_1 I) \cdots (\Lambda - \lambda_n I)$ produces the zero matrix. We are substituting A for λ in the polynomial $p(\lambda) = \det(A - \lambda I)$. The ***Cayley-Hamilton Theorem*** says that $p(A)$ = *zero matrix* (true even if A is not diagonalizable).

Problems 23–26 solve first-order systems $u' = Au$ by using $Ax = \lambda x$.

23 Find λ's and x's so that $u = e^{\lambda t} x$ solves

$$\frac{du}{dt} = \begin{bmatrix} 4 & 3 \\ 0 & 1 \end{bmatrix} u.$$

What combination $u = c_1 e^{\lambda_1 t} x_1 + c_2 e^{\lambda_2 t} x_2$ starts from $u(0) = (5, -2)$?

24 Find A to change the scalar equation $y'' = 5y' + 4y$ into a vector equation for $u = (y, y')$. What are the eigenvalues of A? Find λ_1 and λ_2 also by substituting $y = e^{\lambda t}$ into $y'' = 5y' + 4y$.

$$\frac{du}{dt} = \begin{bmatrix} y' \\ y'' \end{bmatrix} = \begin{bmatrix} & \\ & \end{bmatrix} \begin{bmatrix} y \\ y' \end{bmatrix} = Au.$$

25 The rabbit and wolf populations show fast growth of rabbits (from $6r$) but loss to wolves (from $-2w$). Find A and its eigenvalues and eigenvectors:

$$\frac{dr}{dt} = 6r - 2w \qquad \text{and} \qquad \frac{dw}{dt} = 2r + w.$$

If $r(0) = w(0) = 30$ what are the populations at time t? After a long time, is the ratio of rabbits to wolves 1 to 2 or is it 2 to 1?

26 Substitute $y = e^{\lambda t}$ into $y'' = 6y' - 9y$ to show that $\lambda = 3$ is a repeated root. This is trouble; we need a second solution after e^{3t}. The matrix equation is

$$\frac{d}{dt} \begin{bmatrix} y \\ y' \end{bmatrix} = \begin{bmatrix} 0 & 1 \\ -9 & 6 \end{bmatrix} \begin{bmatrix} y \\ y' \end{bmatrix}.$$

Show that this matrix has $\lambda = 3, 3$ and only one line of eigenvectors. *Trouble here too.* Show that the second solution is $y = te^{3t}$.

27 Explain why A and A^{T} have the same eigenvalues. Show that $\lambda = 1$ is always an eigenvalue when A is a Markov matrix, because each row of A^{T} adds to 1 and the vector ____ is an eigenvector of A^{T}.

28 Find the eigenvalues and unit eigenvectors of A and T, and check the trace:

$$A = \begin{bmatrix} 1 & 1 & 1 \\ 1 & 0 & 0 \\ 1 & 0 & 0 \end{bmatrix} \qquad T = \begin{bmatrix} 1 & -1 \\ -1 & 2 \end{bmatrix}.$$

29 Here is a quick "proof" that the eigenvalues of all real matrices are real:

$$Ax = \lambda x \quad \text{gives} \quad x^{\mathrm{T}} Ax = \lambda x^{\mathrm{T}} x \quad \text{so} \quad \lambda = \frac{x^{\mathrm{T}} Ax}{x^{\mathrm{T}} x} \quad \text{is real.}$$

Find the flaw in this reasoning—a hidden assumption that is not justified.

30 Find all 2 by 2 matrices that are orthogonal and also symmetric. Which two numbers can be eigenvalues of these matrices?

31 To find the eigenfunction $y(x) = \sin k\pi x$, we could put $y = e^{ax}$ in the differential equation $-u'' = \lambda u$. Then $-a^2 e^{ax} = \lambda e^{ax}$ gives $a = i\sqrt{\lambda}$ or $a = -i\sqrt{\lambda}$. The complete solution $y(x) = Ce^{i\sqrt{\lambda}x} + De^{-i\sqrt{\lambda}x}$ has $C + D = 0$ because $y(0) = 0$. That simplifies $y(x)$ to a sine function:

$$y(x) = C(e^{i\sqrt{\lambda}x} - e^{-i\sqrt{\lambda}x}) = 2iC \sin \sqrt{\lambda}x\,.$$

$y(1) = 0$ yields $\sin \sqrt{\lambda} = 0$. Then $\sqrt{\lambda}$ must be a multiple of $k\pi$, and $\lambda = k^2\pi^2$ as before. *Repeat these steps for $y'(0) = y'(1) = 0$ and also $y'(0) = y(1) = 0$.*

32 Suppose eigshow follows x and Ax for these six matrices. How many real eigenvectors? When does Ax go around in the opposite direction from x?

$$A = \begin{bmatrix} 2 & 0 \\ 0 & 1 \end{bmatrix} \quad \begin{bmatrix} 2 & 0 \\ 0 & -1 \end{bmatrix} \quad \begin{bmatrix} 0 & 1 \\ 1 & 0 \end{bmatrix} \quad \begin{bmatrix} 0 & 1 \\ -1 & 0 \end{bmatrix} \quad \begin{bmatrix} 1 & 1 \\ 1 & 1 \end{bmatrix} \quad \begin{bmatrix} 1 & 1 \\ 0 & 1 \end{bmatrix}$$

33 **Scarymatlab** shows what can happen when roundoff destroys symmetry:

$$A = [\,1\,1\,1\,1\,1;\ 1:5\,]'; \quad B = A' * A; \quad P = A * \mathsf{inv}(B) * A'; \quad [\,Q,\ E\,] = \mathsf{eig}(P);$$

B is exactly symmetric. The projection P should be symmetric, but isn't. From $Q' * Q$ show that two eigenvectors of P fail badly to have inner product 0.

■ WORKED EXAMPLE ■

The eigenvalue problem $-u'' + x^2u = \lambda u$ for the Schrödinger equation is important in physics (**the harmonic oscillator**). The exact eigenvalues are the odd numbers $\lambda = 2n+1$. This is a beautiful example for numerical experiment (the website develops it further). One new point is that for computations, the infinite interval $(-\infty, \infty)$ is reduced to $-L \le x \le L$. The eigenfunctions decay so quickly, like $e^{-x^2/2}$, that the matrix K could be replaced by B (maybe even by the circulant C). Try harmonic$(10, 10, 8)$ and $(10, 20, 8)$ and $(5, 10, 8)$ to see how the error in $\lambda = 1$ depends on h and L.

```
function harmonic(L,n,k)                  % positive integers L,n,k
h=1/n; N=2*n*L+1;                         % N points in interval [-L,L]
K= toeplitz([2 -1 zeros(1,N-2)]);         % second difference matrix
H=K/h∧2+ diag((-L:h:L).∧2);              % diagonal matrix from x∧2
[V,F]= eig(H);                            % trideig is faster for large N
E=diag(F); E=E(1:k)                       % first k eigenvalues (near 2n+1)
j=1:k; plot(j,E);                         % choose sparse K and diag if needed
```

A tridiagonal eigenvalue code trideig is on math.mit.edu/~persson.

The exact eigenfunctions $u_n = H_n(x)e^{-x^2/2}$ come from a classical method: Substitute $u(x) = (\sum a_j x^j)e^{-x^2/2}$ into the equation $-u'' + x^2u = (2n+1)u$ and *match up each power of* x. Then a_{j+2} comes from a_j (even powers stay separate from odd powers):

$$\text{The coefficients are connected by } (j+1)(j+2)a_{j+2} = -2(n-j)a_j.$$

At $n = j$ the right side is zero, so $a_{j+2} = 0$ and the power series stops (good thing). Otherwise the series would produce a solution $u(x)$ that blows up at infinity. (The cutoff explains why $\lambda = 2n+1$ is an eigenvalue.) I am happy with this chance to show a success for the power series method, which is not truly a popular part of computational science and engineering.

The functions $H_n(x)$ turn out to be **Hermite polynomials**. The eigenvalues in physical units are $E = (n + \frac{1}{2})\hbar\omega$. That is the **quantization condition** that picks out discrete energy states for this quantum oscillator.

The hydrogen atom is a stiffer numerical test because $e^{-x^2/2}$ disappears. You can see the difference in experiments with $-u'' + \big(l(l+1)/2x^2 - 1/x\big)u = \lambda u$ on the radial line $0 \le x < \infty$. Niels Bohr discovered that $\lambda_n = c/n^2$, which Griffiths [69] highlights as "*the most important formula in all of quantum mechanics.* Bohr obtained it in 1913 by a serendipitous mixture of inapplicable classical physics and premature quantum theory..."

Now we know that Schrödinger's equation and its eigenvalues hold the key.

Matrix	***Eigenvalues***	***Eigenvectors***
Symmetric: $A^{\mathrm{T}} = A$	all λ are real	orthogonal $\boldsymbol{x}_i^{\mathrm{T}}\boldsymbol{x}_j = 0$
Orthogonal: $Q^{\mathrm{T}} = Q^{-1}$	all $\lvert\lambda\rvert = 1$	orthogonal $\overline{\boldsymbol{x}}_i^{\mathrm{T}}\boldsymbol{x}_j = 0$
Skew-symmetric: $A^{\mathrm{T}} = -A$	all λ are imaginary	orthogonal $\overline{\boldsymbol{x}}_i^{\mathrm{T}}\boldsymbol{x}_j = 0$
Complex Hermitian: $\overline{A}^{\mathrm{T}} = A$	all λ are real	orthogonal $\overline{\boldsymbol{x}}_i^{\mathrm{T}}\boldsymbol{x}_j = 0$
Positive Definite: $\boldsymbol{x}^{\mathrm{T}}A\boldsymbol{x} > 0$	all $\lambda > 0$	orthogonal
Markov: $m_{ij} > 0, \sum_{i=1}^{n} m_{ij} = 1$	$\lambda_{\max} = 1$	steady state $\boldsymbol{x} > 0$
Similar: $B = M^{-1}AM$	$\lambda(B) = \lambda(A)$	$\boldsymbol{x}(B) = M^{-1}\boldsymbol{x}(A)$
Projection: $P = P^2 = P^{\mathrm{T}}$	$\lambda = 1;\ 0$	column space; nullspace
Reflection: $I - 2\boldsymbol{u}\boldsymbol{u}^{\mathrm{T}}$	$\lambda = -1;\ 1,..,1$	$\boldsymbol{u}; \boldsymbol{u}^{\perp}$
Rank One: $\boldsymbol{u}\boldsymbol{v}^{\mathrm{T}}$	$\lambda = \boldsymbol{v}^{\mathrm{T}}\boldsymbol{u};\ 0,..,0$	$\boldsymbol{u};\ \boldsymbol{v}^{\perp}$
Inverse: A^{-1}	$1/\lambda(A)$	eigenvectors of A
Shift: $A + cI$	$\lambda(A) + c$	eigenvectors of A
Stable Powers: $A^n \to 0$	all $\lvert\lambda\rvert < 1$	
Stable Exponential: $e^{At} \to 0$	all Re $\lambda < 0$	
Cyclic: $P(1,..,n) = (2,..,n,1)$	$\lambda_k = e^{2\pi ik/n}$	$\boldsymbol{x}_k = (1, \lambda_k, \ldots, \lambda_k^{n-1})$
Toeplitz: $-1, 2, -1$ on diagonals	$\lambda_k = 2 - 2\cos\frac{k\pi}{n+1}$	$\boldsymbol{x}_k = \big(\sin\frac{k\pi}{n+1}, \sin\frac{2k\pi}{n+1}, \ldots\big)$
Diagonalizable: $S\Lambda S^{-1}$	diagonal of Λ	columns of S are independent
Symmetric: $Q\Lambda Q^{\mathrm{T}}$	diagonal of Λ (real)	columns of Q are orthonormal
Jordan: $J = M^{-1}AM$	diagonal of J	each block gives $\boldsymbol{x} = (0,..,1,..,0)$
SVD: $A = U\Sigma V^{\mathrm{T}}$	singular values in Σ	eigenvectors of $A^{\mathrm{T}}A, AA^{\mathrm{T}}$ in V, U

1.6 POSITIVE DEFINITE MATRICES

This section focuses on the meaning of "positive definite." Those words apply to square symmetric matrices with especially nice properties. They are summarized at the end of the section, and I believe we need three basic facts in order to go forward:

1. Every $K = A^{\mathrm{T}}A$ is symmetric and positive definite (or at least semidefinite).

2. If K_1 and K_2 are positive definite matrices then so is $K_1 + K_2$.

3. All pivots and all eigenvalues of a positive definite matrix are positive.

The pivots and eigenvalues have been emphasized. But those don't give the best approach to facts **1** and **2**. When we add $K_1 + K_2$, it is not easy to follow the pivots or eigenvalues in the sum. When we multiply $A^{\mathrm{T}}A$ (and later $A^{\mathrm{T}}CA$), why can't the pivots be negative? ***The key is in the energy*** $\frac{1}{2}\boldsymbol{u}^{\mathrm{T}}\boldsymbol{K}\boldsymbol{u}$. We really need an *energy-based definition of positive definiteness*, from which facts **1**, **2**, **3** will be clear.

Out of that definition will come the test for a function $P(u)$ to have a minimum. Start with a point where all partial derivatives $\partial P/\partial u_1, \partial P/\partial u_2, \ldots, \partial P/\partial u_n$ are zero. **This point is a minimum** (not a maximum or saddle point) **if the matrix of second derivatives is positive definite**. The discussion yields an algorithm that actually finds this minimum point. When $P(u)$ is a quadratic function (involving only $\frac{1}{2}K_{ii}u_i^2$ and $K_{ij}u_iu_j$ and f_iu_i) that minimum has a neat and important form:

The minimum of $P(u) = \frac{1}{2}u^{\mathrm{T}}Ku - u^{\mathrm{T}}f$ **is** $P_{\text{min}} = -\frac{1}{2}f^{\mathrm{T}}K^{-1}f$ **when** $Ku = f$.

Examples and Energy-based Definition

Three example matrices $\frac{1}{2}K, B, M$ are displayed below, to show the difference between *definite* and *semidefinite* and *indefinite.* The off-diagonal entries in these examples get larger at each step. You will see how the "energy" goes from positive (for K) to possibly zero (for B) to possibly negative (for M).

Definite	Semidefinite	Indefinite
$\frac{1}{2}\boldsymbol{K} = \begin{bmatrix} 1 & -\frac{1}{2} \\ -\frac{1}{2} & 1 \end{bmatrix}$	$\boldsymbol{B} = \begin{bmatrix} 1 & -1 \\ -1 & 1 \end{bmatrix}$	$\boldsymbol{M} = \begin{bmatrix} 1 & -3 \\ -3 & 1 \end{bmatrix}$
$u_1^2 - u_1u_2 + u_2^2$	$u_1^2 - 2u_1u_2 + u_2^2$	$u_1^2 - 6u_1u_2 + u_2^2$
Always positive	**Positive or zero**	**Positive or negative**

Below the three matrices you will see something extra. The matrices are multiplied on the left by the row vector $u^{\mathrm{T}} = [\,u_1 \;\; u_2\,]$ and on the right by the column vector u. The results $u^{\mathrm{T}}\left(\frac{1}{2}K\right)u$ and $u^{\mathrm{T}}Bu$ and $u^{\mathrm{T}}Mu$ are printed under the matrices.

With zeros off the diagonal, I is positive definite (pivots and eigenvalues all 1). When the off-diagonals reach $-\frac{1}{2}$, the matrix $\frac{1}{2}K$ is still positive definite. At -1

we hit the semidefinite matrix B (singular matrix). The matrix M with -3 off the diagonal is very indefinite (pivots and eigenvalues of both signs). It is the *size* of those off-diagonal numbers $-\frac{1}{2}, -1, -3$ that is important, not the minus signs.

Quadratics These pure quadratics like $u_1^2 - u_1u_2 + u_2^2$ contain only second degree terms. The simplest positive definite example would be $u_1^2 + u_2^2$, coming from the identity matrix I. This is positive except at $u_1 = u_2 = 0$. Every pure quadratic function comes from a symmetric matrix. When the matrix is S, the function is $u^{\mathrm{T}}Su$.

When S has an entry b on both sides of its main diagonal, those entries combine into $2b$ in the function. Here is the multiplication $u^{\mathrm{T}}Su$, when a typical 2 by 2 symmetric matrix S produces au_1^2 and $2b\,u_1u_2$ and cu_2^2:

Quadratic Function

$$u^{\mathrm{T}}Su = \begin{bmatrix} u_1 & u_2 \end{bmatrix} \begin{bmatrix} a & b \\ b & c \end{bmatrix} \begin{bmatrix} u_1 \\ u_2 \end{bmatrix} = au_1^2 + 2b\,u_1u_2 + cu_2^2 \qquad (1)$$

Notice how a and c on the diagonal multiply u_1^2 and u_2^2. The two b's multiply u_1u_2.

The numbers a, b, c will decide whether $u^{\mathrm{T}}Su$ is always positive (except at $u = 0$). This positivity of $u^{\mathrm{T}}Su$ is the requirement for S to be a "positive definite matrix."

Definition **The symmetric matrix $\boldsymbol{S}$ is *positive definite* when $\boldsymbol{u^{\mathrm{T}}Su > 0}$ for every vector $\boldsymbol{u}$ except $\boldsymbol{u = 0}$.**

The graph of $u^{\mathrm{T}}Su$ goes *upward* from zero. There is a minimum point at $u = 0$. Figure 1.16a shows $u_1^2 - u_1u_2 + u_2^2$, from $S = \frac{1}{2}K$. *Its graph is like a bowl.*

This definition makes it easy to see why the sum $K_1 + K_2$ stays positive definite (Fact **2** above). We are adding positive energies so the sum is positive. We don't need to know the pivots or eigenvalues. The sum of $u^{\mathrm{T}}K_1u$ and $u^{\mathrm{T}}K_2u$ is $u^{\mathrm{T}}(K_1 + K_2)u$. If the two pieces are positive whenever $u \neq 0$, the sum is positive too. Short proof!

In the **indefinite** case, the graph of $u^{\mathrm{T}}Mu$ goes *up and down* from the origin in Figure 1.16c. There is no minimum or maximum, and the surface has a "saddle point." If we take $u_1 = 1$ and $u_2 = 1$ then $u^{\mathrm{T}}Mu = -4$. If $u_1 = 1$ and $u_2 = 10$ then $u^{\mathrm{T}}Mu = +41$. The **semidefinite** matrix B has $u^{\mathrm{T}}Bu = (u_1 - u_2)^2$. This is positive for most u, but it is zero along the line $u_1 = u_2$.

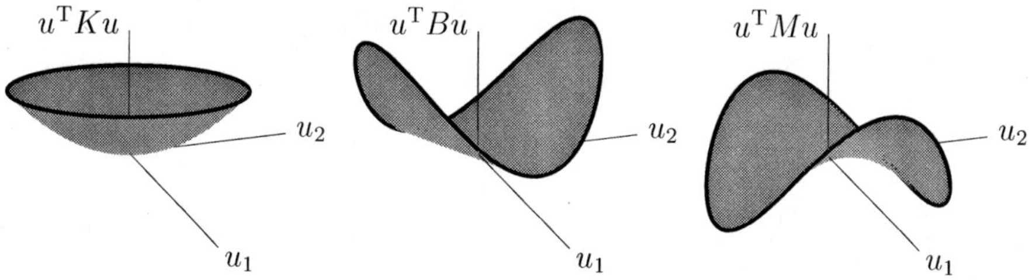

Figure 1.16: Positive definite, semidefinite, and indefinite: Bowl, trough, and saddle.

Sums of Squares

To confirm that M is indefinite, we found a vector with $u^{\mathrm{T}}Mu > 0$ and another vector with $u^{\mathrm{T}}Mu < 0$. The matrix K needs more thought. How do we show that $u^{\mathrm{T}}Ku$ stays positive? We cannot substitute every u_1, u_2 and it would not be enough to test only a few vectors. We need an expression that is *automatically positive*, like $u^{\mathrm{T}}u = u_1^2 + u_2^2$. The key is to write $u^{\mathrm{T}}Ku$ as a **sum of squares**:

$$u^{\mathrm{T}}Ku = 2u_1^2 - 2u_1u_2 + 2u_2^2 = u_1^2 + (u_1 - u_2)^2 + u_2^2 \qquad \textbf{(three squares)} \qquad (2)$$

The right side cannot be negative. It cannot be zero, except if $u_1 = 0$ and $u_2 = 0$. So **this sum of squares proves that K is a positive definite matrix.**

We could achieve the same result with *two squares* instead of three:

$$u^{\mathrm{T}}Ku = 2u_1^2 - 2u_1u_2 + 2u_2^2 = 2(u_1 - \frac{1}{2}u_2)^2 + \frac{3}{2}u_2^2 \qquad \textbf{(two squares)} \qquad (3)$$

What I notice about this sum of squares is that the coefficients 2 and $\frac{3}{2}$ are the **pivots** of K. And the number $-\frac{1}{2}$ inside the first square is the multiplier ℓ_{21}, in $K = LDL^{\mathrm{T}}$:

Two squares $$K = \begin{bmatrix} 2 & -1 \\ -1 & 2 \end{bmatrix} = \begin{bmatrix} 1 & \\ -\frac{1}{2} & 1 \end{bmatrix} \begin{bmatrix} 2 & \\ & \frac{3}{2} \end{bmatrix} \begin{bmatrix} 1 & -\frac{1}{2} \\ & 1 \end{bmatrix} = LDL^{\mathrm{T}}. \qquad (4)$$

The sum of three squares in (2) is connected to a factorization $K = A^{\mathrm{T}}A$, in which A has three rows instead of two. The three rows give the squares in $u_1^2 + (u_2 - u_1)^2 + u_2^2$:

Three squares $$K = \begin{bmatrix} 2 & -1 \\ -1 & 2 \end{bmatrix} = \begin{bmatrix} 1 & -1 & 0 \\ 0 & 1 & -1 \end{bmatrix} \begin{bmatrix} 1 & 0 \\ -1 & 1 \\ 0 & -1 \end{bmatrix} = A^{\mathrm{T}}A. \qquad (5)$$

Probably there could be a factorization $K = A^{\mathrm{T}}A$ with four squares in the sum and four rows in the matrix A. What happens if there is only *one square* in the sum?

Semidefinite $$u^{\mathrm{T}}Bu = u_1^2 - 2u_1u_2 + u_2^2 = (u_1 - u_2)^2 \qquad \textbf{(only one square).} \qquad (6)$$

The right side can never be negative. But that single term $(u_1 - u_2)^2$ could be zero! A sum of less than n squares will mean that an n by n matrix is only semidefinite.

The indefinite example $u^{\mathrm{T}}Mu$ is a *difference of squares* (mixed signs):

$$u^{\mathrm{T}}Mu = u_1^2 - 6u_1u_2 + u_2^2 = (u_1 - 3u_2)^2 - 8u_2^2 \quad \textbf{(square minus square).} \qquad (7)$$

Again the pivots 1 and -8 multiply the squares. Inside is the number $\ell_{21} = -3$ from elimination. The difference of squares is coming from $M = LDL^{\mathrm{T}}$, but the diagonal pivot matrix D is no longer all positive and M is indefinite:

Indefinite $$M = \begin{bmatrix} 1 & -3 \\ -3 & 1 \end{bmatrix} = \begin{bmatrix} 1 & \\ -3 & 1 \end{bmatrix} \begin{bmatrix} 1 & \\ & -8 \end{bmatrix} \begin{bmatrix} 1 & -3 \\ & 1 \end{bmatrix} = LDL^{\mathrm{T}}. \qquad (8)$$

The next page moves to the matrix form $u^{\mathrm{T}}A^{\mathrm{T}}Au$ for a sum of squares.

Positive Definiteness from $A^{\mathrm{T}}A$, $A^{\mathrm{T}}CA$, LDL^{T}, and $Q\Lambda Q^{\mathrm{T}}$

Now comes the key point. Those 2 by 2 examples suggest what happens for n by n positive definite matrices. K might come as A^{T} times A, for some rectangular matrix A. Or elimination factors K into LDL^{T} and $D > 0$ gives positive definiteness. Eigenvalues and eigenvectors factor K into $Q\Lambda Q^{\mathrm{T}}$, and the eigenvalue test is $\Lambda > 0$.

The matrix theory only needs a few sentences. In linear algebra, "simple is good."

$K=A^{\mathrm{T}}A$ is symmetric positive definite if and only if A has independent columns. This means that the only solution to $Au = 0$ is the zero vector $u = 0$. If there are nonzero solutions to $Au = 0$, then $A^{\mathrm{T}}A$ is positive semidefinite.

We now show that $u^{\mathrm{T}}Ku \geq 0$, when K is $A^{\mathrm{T}}A$. Just move the parentheses!

Basic trick for $A^{\mathrm{T}}A$ $$u^{\mathrm{T}}Ku = u^{\mathrm{T}}(A^{\mathrm{T}}A)u = (Au)^{\mathrm{T}}(Au) \geq 0 \qquad (9)$$

This is the length squared of Au. So $A^{\mathrm{T}}A$ is at least semidefinite.

When A has independent columns, $Au = 0$ only happens when $u = 0$. The only vector in the nullspace is the zero vector. For all other vectors $u^{\mathrm{T}}(A^{\mathrm{T}}A)u = \|Au\|^2$ is positive. So $A^{\mathrm{T}}A$ is positive definite, using the energy-based definition $u^{\mathrm{T}}Ku > 0$.

Example 1 If A has more columns than rows, then those columns are *not* independent. With dependent columns $A^{\mathrm{T}}A$ is only semidefinite. This example (the free-free matrix B_3) has three columns and two rows in A, so *dependent* columns:

3 columns of A add to zero
3 columns of $A^{\mathrm{T}}A$ add to zero
$$\begin{bmatrix} -1 & 0 \\ 1 & -1 \\ 0 & 1 \end{bmatrix} \begin{bmatrix} -1 & 1 & 0 \\ 0 & -1 & 1 \end{bmatrix} = \begin{bmatrix} 1 & -1 & 0 \\ -1 & 2 & -1 \\ 0 & -1 & 1 \end{bmatrix}.$$

This is the semidefinite case. If $Au = 0$ then certainly $A^{\mathrm{T}}Au = 0$. The rank of $A^{\mathrm{T}}A$ always equals the rank of A (its rank here is only $r = 2$). The energy $u^{\mathrm{T}}Bu$ is $(u_2 - u_1)^2 + (u_3 - u_2)^2$, with only **two squares** but $n = 3$.

It is a short step from $A^{\mathrm{T}}A$ to positive definiteness of the triple products $A^{\mathrm{T}}CA$ and LDL^{T} and $Q\Lambda Q^{\mathrm{T}}$. The middle matrices C and D and Λ are easily included.

The matrix $K = A^{\mathrm{T}}CA$ is symmetric positive definite, provided A has independent columns and the middle matrix C is symmetric positive definite.

To check positive energy in $A^{\mathrm{T}}CA$, use the same idea of moving the parentheses:

Same trick $$u^{\mathrm{T}}Ku = u^{\mathrm{T}}(A^{\mathrm{T}}CA)u = (Au)^{\mathrm{T}}C(Au) > 0\,. \qquad (10)$$

If u is not zero then Au is not zero (because A has independent columns). Then $(Au)^{\mathrm{T}}C(Au)$ is positive because C is positive definite. So $u^{\mathrm{T}}Ku > 0$: positive definite. $C = C^{\mathrm{T}}$ in the middle could be the pivot matrix D or the eigenvalue matrix Λ.

If a symmetric K has a full set of positive pivots, it is positive definite.

Reason: The diagonal pivot matrix D in LDL^{T} is positive definite. L^{T} has independent columns (1's on the diagonal and invertible). This is the special case of $A^{\mathrm{T}}CA$ with $C = D$ and $A = L^{\mathrm{T}}$. Pivots in D multiply squares in $L^{\mathrm{T}}u$ to give $u^{\mathrm{T}}Ku$:

$$\textbf{LDL}^{\mathrm{T}} \qquad \begin{bmatrix} u_1 & u_2 \end{bmatrix} \begin{bmatrix} a & b \\ b & c \end{bmatrix} \begin{bmatrix} u_1 \\ u_2 \end{bmatrix} = a\left(u_1 + \frac{b}{a}u_2\right)^2 + \left(c - \frac{b^2}{a}\right)u_2^2. \tag{11}$$

The pivots are those factors a and $c - \frac{b^2}{a}$. This is called "completing the square."

If a symmetric K has all positive eigenvalues in Λ, it is positive definite.

Reason: Use $K = Q\Lambda Q^{\mathrm{T}}$. The diagonal eigenvalue matrix Λ is positive definite. The orthogonal matrix is invertible (Q^{-1} is Q^{T}). Then the triple product $Q\Lambda Q^{\mathrm{T}}$ is positive definite. The eigenvalues in Λ multiply the squares in $Q^{\mathrm{T}}u$:

$$\boldsymbol{Q\Lambda Q}^{\mathrm{T}} \qquad \begin{bmatrix} u_1 & u_2 \end{bmatrix} \begin{bmatrix} 2 & -1 \\ -1 & 2 \end{bmatrix} \begin{bmatrix} u_1 \\ u_2 \end{bmatrix} = 3\left(\frac{u_1 - u_2}{\sqrt{2}}\right)^2 + 1\left(\frac{u_1 + u_2}{\sqrt{2}}\right)^2. \tag{12}$$

The eigenvalues are 3 and 1. The unit eigenvectors are $(1,-1)/\sqrt{2}$ and $(1,1)/\sqrt{2}$.

If there were negative pivots or negative eigenvalues, we would have a difference of squares. The matrix would be indefinite. Since $Ku = \lambda u$ leads to $u^{\mathrm{T}}Ku = \lambda u^{\mathrm{T}}u$, positive energy $u^{\mathrm{T}}Ku$ requires positive eigenvalues λ.

Review and Summary A symmetric matrix K is positive definite if it passes any of these five tests (then it passes them all). I will apply each test to the 3 by 3 second difference matrix $K =$ toeplitz([2 −1 0]).

1.	All pivots are positive	$K = LDL^{\mathrm{T}}$ with pivots $2, \frac{3}{2}, \frac{4}{3}$
2.	Upper left determinants > 0	K has determinants $2, 3, 4$
3.	All eigenvalues are positive	$K = Q\Lambda Q^{\mathrm{T}}$ with $\lambda = 2, 2+\sqrt{2}, 2-\sqrt{2}$
4.	$u^{\mathrm{T}}Ku > 0$ if $u \neq 0$	$u^{\mathrm{T}}Ku = 2(u_1 - \frac{1}{2}u_2)^2 + \frac{3}{2}(u_2 - \frac{2}{3}u_3)^2 + \frac{4}{3}{u_3}^2$
5.	$K = A^{\mathrm{T}}A$, indep. columns	A can be the Cholesky factor chol(K)

That Cholesky factorization chooses the square upper triangular $A = \sqrt{D}L^{\mathrm{T}}$. The command chol will fail unless K is positive definite, with positive pivots:

$$\begin{array}{l} \textbf{Square} \\ \boldsymbol{A^{\mathrm{T}}A = K} \\ \boldsymbol{A} = \mathsf{chol}(\boldsymbol{K}) \end{array} \quad K = \begin{bmatrix} 1.4142 & & \\ -0.7071 & 1.2247 & \\ & -0.8165 & 1.1547 \end{bmatrix} \begin{bmatrix} 1.4142 & -0.7071 & \\ & 1.2247 & -0.8165 \\ & & 1.1547 \end{bmatrix}$$

Minimum Problems in n Dimensions

Minimum problems appear everywhere in applied mathematics. Very often, $\frac{1}{2}u^{\mathrm{T}}Ku$ is the "internal energy" in the system. This energy should be positive, so K is naturally positive definite. The subject of ***optimization*** deals with minimization, to produce the best design or the most efficient schedule at the lowest cost. But the cost function $P(u)$ is not a pure quadratic $u^{\mathrm{T}}Ku$ with minimum at 0.

A key step moves the minimum away from the origin by including a linear term $-u^{\mathrm{T}}f$. **The optimization problem is to minimize $P(u)$:**

$$\textbf{\textit{Total energy}} \quad P(u) = \frac{1}{2}u^{\mathrm{T}}Ku - u^{\mathrm{T}}f = (u_1^2 - u_1u_2 + u_2^2) - u_1f_1 - u_2f_2\,. \qquad (13)$$

The partial derivatives (gradient of P) with respect to u_1 and u_2 must both be zero:

$$\textbf{Calculus gives } \boldsymbol{Ku = f} \qquad \begin{aligned} \partial P/\partial u_1 &= \;\;2u_1 - \;\;u_2 - f_1 = 0 \\ \partial P/\partial u_2 &= -u_1 + 2u_2 - f_2 = 0 \end{aligned} \qquad (14)$$

In all cases the partial derivatives of $P(u)$ are zero when $Ku = f$. This is truly a minimum point (the graph goes up) when K is positive definite. We substitute $u = K^{-1}f$ into $P(u)$ to find the minimum value of P:

$$\textbf{The minimum is} \quad P_{\text{min}} = \frac{1}{2}(K^{-1}f)^{\mathrm{T}}K(K^{-1}f) - (K^{-1}f)^{\mathrm{T}}f = -\frac{1}{2}f^{\mathrm{T}}K^{-1}f. \quad (15)$$

$P(u)$ is never below that value P_{min}. For every $P(u)$ the difference is ≥ 0:

$$\begin{aligned} P(u) - P(K^{-1}f) &= \tfrac{1}{2}u^{\mathrm{T}}Ku - u^{\mathrm{T}}f - (-\tfrac{1}{2}f^{\mathrm{T}}K^{-1}f) \\ &= \tfrac{1}{2}(u - K^{-1}f)^{\mathrm{T}}K(u - K^{-1}f) \geq 0\,. \end{aligned} \qquad (16)$$

The last result is never negative, because it has the form $\frac{1}{2}v^{\mathrm{T}}Kv$. That result is zero only when the vector $v = u - K^{-1}f$ is zero (which means $u = K^{-1}f$). So at every point except $u = K^{-1}f$, the value $P(u)$ is above the minimum value P_{min}.

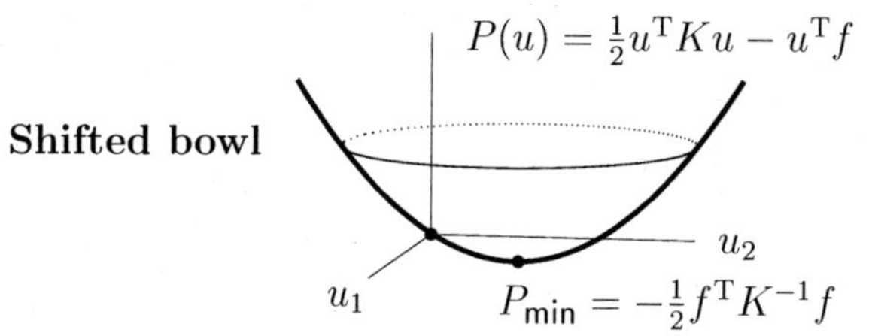

Figure 1.17: The minimum of $P(u_1, \ldots, u_n) = \frac{1}{2}u^{\mathrm{T}}Ku - u^{\mathrm{T}}f$ is at $u = K^{-1}f$.

Test for a Minimum: Positive Definite Second Derivatives

Suppose $P(u_1, \ldots, u_n)$ is not a quadratic function. Then its derivatives won't be linear functions. But to minimize $P(u)$ we still look for points where all the first derivatives (the partial derivatives) are zero:

1st derivative vector is gradient $\partial P/\partial u$
$$\frac{\partial P}{\partial u_1} = 0 \qquad \frac{\partial P}{\partial u_2} = 0 \quad \cdots \quad \frac{\partial P}{\partial u_n} = 0\,. \tag{17}$$

If those n first derivatives are all zero at the point $u^* = (u_1^*, \ldots, u_n^*)$, how do we know whether $P(u)$ has a minimum (not a maximum or saddle point) at u^*?

To confirm a minimum we look at the second derivatives. Remember the rule for an ordinary function $y(x)$ at a point where $dy/dx = 0$. This point is a minimum if $d^2y/dx^2 > 0$. The graph curves upward. The n-dimensional version of d^2y/dx^2 is the **symmetric "Hessian" matrix H of second derivatives:**

2nd derivative matrix
$$H_{ij} = \frac{\partial^2 P}{\partial u_i\, \partial u_j} = \frac{\partial^2 P}{\partial u_j\, \partial u_i} = H_{ji}\,. \tag{18}$$

The Taylor series for $P(u)$, when u is near u^*, starts with these three terms (constant, linear from gradient, and quadratic from Hessian):

Taylor series
$$P(u) = P(u^*) + (u^* - u)^{\mathrm{T}} \frac{\partial P}{\partial u}(u^*) + \frac{1}{2}(u^* - u)^{\mathrm{T}} H(u^*)(u^* - u) + \cdots \tag{19}$$

Suppose the gradient vector $\partial P/\partial u$ of the first derivatives is zero at u^*, as in (17). So the linear term is gone and the second derivatives are in control. If H is positive definite at u^*, then $(u^* - u)^{\mathrm{T}} H(u^* - u)$ carries the function upward as we leave u^*. **A positive definite $H(u^*)$ produces a minimum at $u = u^*$.**

Our quadratic functions were $P(u) = \frac{1}{2}u^{\mathrm{T}}Ku - u^{\mathrm{T}}f$. The second derivative matrix was $H = K$, the same at every point. For non-quadratic functions, H changes from point to point, and we might have several *local minima* or *local maxima.* The decision depends on H at every point u^* where the first derivatives are zero.

Here is an example with one local minimum at $(0, 0)$, even though the overall minimum is $-\infty$. The function includes a fourth power u_1^4.

Example 2 $P(u) = 2u_1^2 + 3u_2^2 - u_1^4$ has zero derivatives at $(u_1^*, u_2^*) = (0, 0)$.

Second derivatives
$$H = \begin{bmatrix} \partial^2 P/\partial u_1^2 & \partial^2 P/\partial u_1 \partial u_2 \\ \partial^2 P/\partial u_2 \partial u_1 & \partial^2 P/\partial u_2^2 \end{bmatrix} = \begin{bmatrix} 4 - 12u_1^2 & 0 \\ 0 & 6 \end{bmatrix}.$$

At the point $(0, 0)$, H is certainly positive definite. So this is a local minimum.

There are two other points where both first derivatives $4u_1 - 4u_1^3$ and $6u_2$ are zero. Those points are $u^* = (1, 0)$ and $u^* = (-1, 0)$. The second derivatives are -8 and 6 at both of those points, so H is indefinite. The graph of $P(u)$ will look like a bowl around $(0, 0)$, but $(1, 0)$ and $(-1, 0)$ are saddle points. MATLAB could draw $y = P(u_1, u_2)$.

Newton's Method for Minimization

This section may have seemed less "applied" than the rest of the book. Maybe so, but minimization is a problem with a million applications. And we need an algorithm to minimize $P(u)$, especially when this function is not a quadratic. We have to expect an *iterative method*, starting from an initial guess u^0 and improving it to u^1 and u^2 (approaching the true minimizer u^* if the algorithm is successful).

The natural idea is to **use the first and second derivatives of $P(u)$ at the current point**. Suppose we have reached u^i with coordinates $u_1^i, \ldots, u_n^i$. We need a rule to choose the next point u^{i+1}. Close to u^i, the function $P(u)$ is approximated by cutting off the Taylor series, as in (19). **Newton will minimize $P_{\text{cutoff}}(u)$.**

$$P_{\text{cutoff}}(u) = P(u^i) + (u - u^i)^{\mathrm{T}} \frac{\partial P}{\partial u} + \frac{1}{2}(u - u^i)^{\mathrm{T}} H (u - u^i)\,. \qquad (20)$$

P_{cutoff} is a quadratic function. Instead of K it has the second derivative H. Both $\partial P/\partial u$ and H are evaluated at the current point $u = u^i$ (this is the expensive part of the algorithm). The minimum of P_{cutoff} is the next guess u^{i+1}.

Newton's method to solve $\partial P/\partial u = 0$ $\quad H(u^{i+1} - u^i) = -\dfrac{\partial P}{\partial u}(u^i)\,. \qquad (21)$

For quadratics, one step gives the minimizer $u^1 = K^{-1}f$. Now $\partial P/\partial u$ and H are changing as we move to u^1 and u^i and u^{i+1}. If u^i exactly hits u^* (not too likely) then $\partial P/\partial u$ will be zero. So $u^{i+1} - u^i = 0$ and we don't move away from perfection.

Section 2.6 will return to this algorithm. We propose examples in the Problem Set below, and add one comment here. The full Newton step to u^{i+1} may be too bold, when the true minimizer u^* is far away. The terms we cut off could be too large. In that case we shorten the Newton step $u^{i+1} - u^i$, for safety, by a factor $c < 1$.

Problem Set 1.6

1 Express $u^{\mathrm{T}}Tu$ as a combination of u_1^2, u_1u_2, and u_2^2 for the free-fixed matrix

$$T = \begin{bmatrix} 1 & -1 \\ -1 & 2 \end{bmatrix}.$$

Write the answer as a sum of two squares to prove positive definiteness.

2 Express $u^{\mathrm{T}}Ku = 4{u_1}^2 + 16u_1u_2 + 26{u_2}^2$ as a sum of two squares. Then find $\text{chol}(K) = \sqrt{D}L^{\mathrm{T}}$.

$$K = \begin{bmatrix} 4 & 8 \\ 8 & 26 \end{bmatrix} = \begin{bmatrix} 1 & 0 \\ 2 & 1 \end{bmatrix} \begin{bmatrix} 4 & \\ & 10 \end{bmatrix} \begin{bmatrix} 1 & 0 \\ 2 & 1 \end{bmatrix} = \left(L\sqrt{D}\right)\left(\sqrt{D}L^{\mathrm{T}}\right).$$

3 A different A produces the circulant second-difference matrix $C = A^{\mathrm{T}}A$:

$$A = \begin{bmatrix} 1 & -1 & 0 \\ 0 & 1 & -1 \\ -1 & 0 & 1 \end{bmatrix} \quad \text{gives} \quad A^{\mathrm{T}}A = \begin{bmatrix} 2 & -1 & -1 \\ -1 & 2 & -1 \\ -1 & -1 & 2 \end{bmatrix}.$$

How can you tell from A that $C = A^{\mathrm{T}}A$ is only semidefinite? Which vectors solve $Au = 0$ and therefore $Cu = 0$? Note that chol(C) will fail.

4 Confirm that the circulant $C = A^{\mathrm{T}}A$ above is semidefinite by the pivot test. Write $u^{\mathrm{T}}Cu$ as a sum of *two squares* with the pivots as coefficients. (The eigenvalues $0, 3, 3$ give another proof that C is semidefinite.)

5 $u^{\mathrm{T}}Cu \geq 0$ means that $u_1^2 + u_2^2 + u_3^2 \geq u_1u_2 + u_2u_3 + u_3u_1$ for any u_1, u_2, u_3. A more unusual way to check this is by the Schwarz inequality $|v^{\mathrm{T}}w| \leq \|v\|\,\|w\|$:

$$|u_1u_2 + u_2u_3 + u_3u_1| \leq \sqrt{u_1^2 + u_2^2 + u_3^2}\,\sqrt{u_2^2 + u_3^2 + u_1^2}\,.$$

Which u's give *equality*? Check that $u^{\mathrm{T}}Cu = 0$ for those u.

6 For what range of numbers b is this matrix positive definite?

$$K = \begin{bmatrix} 1 & b \\ b & 4 \end{bmatrix}.$$

There are two borderline values of b when K is only semidefinite. In those cases write $u^{\mathrm{T}}Ku$ with only one square. Find the pivots if $b = 5$.

7 Is $K = A^{\mathrm{T}}A$ or $M = B^{\mathrm{T}}B$ positive definite (independent columns in A or B)?

$$A = \begin{bmatrix} 1 & 2 \\ 2 & 4 \\ 3 & 6 \end{bmatrix} \qquad B = \begin{bmatrix} 1 & 4 \\ 2 & 5 \\ 3 & 6 \end{bmatrix}$$

We know that $u^{\mathrm{T}}Mu = (Bu)^{\mathrm{T}}(Bu) = (u_1 + 4u_2)^2 + (2u_1 + 5u_2)^2 + (3u_1 + 6u_2)^2$. Show how the three squares for $u^{\mathrm{T}}Ku = (Au)^{\mathrm{T}}(Au)$ collapse into one square.

Problems 8–16 are about tests for positive definiteness.

8 Which of A_1, A_2, A_3, A_4 has two positive eigenvalues? Use the tests $a > 0$ and $ac > b^2$, don't compute the λ's. Find a vector u so that $u^{\mathrm{T}}A_1u < 0$.

$$A_1 = \begin{bmatrix} 5 & 6 \\ 6 & 7 \end{bmatrix} \quad A_2 = \begin{bmatrix} -1 & -2 \\ -2 & -5 \end{bmatrix} \quad A_3 = \begin{bmatrix} 1 & 10 \\ 10 & 100 \end{bmatrix} \quad A_4 = \begin{bmatrix} 1 & 10 \\ 10 & 101 \end{bmatrix}.$$

9 For which numbers b and c are these matrices positive definite?

$$A = \begin{bmatrix} 1 & b \\ b & 9 \end{bmatrix} \quad \text{and} \quad A = \begin{bmatrix} 2 & 4 \\ 4 & c \end{bmatrix}.$$

With the pivots in D and multiplier in L, factor each A into LDL^{T}.

10 Show that $f(x,y) = x^2 + 4xy + 3y^2$ does not have a minimum at $(0,0)$ even though it has positive coefficients. Write f as a *difference* of squares and find a point (x,y) where f is negative.

11 The function $f(x,y) = 2xy$ certainly has a saddle point and not a minimum at $(0,0)$. What symmetric matrix S produces this f? What are its eigenvalues?

12 Test the columns of A to see if $A^{\mathrm{T}}A$ will be positive definite in each case:

$$A = \begin{bmatrix} 1 & 2 \\ 0 & 3 \end{bmatrix} \quad \text{and} \quad A = \begin{bmatrix} 1 & 1 \\ 1 & 2 \\ 2 & 1 \end{bmatrix} \quad \text{and} \quad A = \begin{bmatrix} 1 & 1 & 2 \\ 1 & 2 & 1 \end{bmatrix}.$$

13 Find the 3 by 3 matrix S and its pivots, rank, eigenvalues, and determinant:

$$\begin{bmatrix} x_1 & x_2 & x_3 \end{bmatrix} \begin{bmatrix} & & \\ & S & \\ & & \end{bmatrix} \begin{bmatrix} x_1 \\ x_2 \\ x_3 \end{bmatrix} = 4(x_1 - x_2 + 2x_3)^2.$$

14 Which 3 by 3 symmetric matrices S produce these functions $f = x^{\mathrm{T}}Sx$? Why is the first matrix positive definite but not the second one?

(a) $f = 2(x_1^2 + x_2^2 + x_3^2 - x_1x_2 - x_2x_3)$

(b) $f = 2(x_1^2 + x_2^2 + x_3^2 - x_1x_2 - x_1x_3 - x_2x_3)$.

15 For what numbers c and d are A and B positive definite? Test the three upper left determinants (1 by 1, 2 by 2, 3 by 3) of each matrix:

$$A = \begin{bmatrix} c & 1 & 1 \\ 1 & c & 1 \\ 1 & 1 & c \end{bmatrix} \quad \text{and} \quad B = \begin{bmatrix} 1 & 2 & 3 \\ 2 & d & 4 \\ 3 & 4 & 5 \end{bmatrix}.$$

16 *If A is positive definite then A^{-1} is positive definite.* Best proof: The eigenvalues of A^{-1} are positive because _____. *Second proof* (only quick for 2 by 2):

$$\text{The entries of } A^{-1} = \frac{1}{ac - b^2} \begin{bmatrix} c & -b \\ -b & a \end{bmatrix} \text{ pass the determinant tests } \_\_\_\_\_.$$

17 A positive definite matrix cannot have a zero (or even worse, a negative number) on its diagonal. Show that this matrix fails to have $u^{\mathrm{T}}Au > 0$.

$$\begin{bmatrix} u_1 & u_2 & u_3 \end{bmatrix} \begin{bmatrix} 4 & 1 & 1 \\ 1 & 0 & 2 \\ 1 & 2 & 5 \end{bmatrix} \begin{bmatrix} u_1 \\ u_2 \\ u_3 \end{bmatrix} \text{ is not positive when } (u_1, u_2, u_3) = (\ ,\ ,\ ).$$

18 A diagonal entry a_{jj} of a symmetric matrix cannot be smaller than all the λ's. If it were, then $A - a_{jj}I$ would have _____ eigenvalues and would be positive definite. But $A - a_{jj}I$ has a zero on the main diagonal.

19 If all $\lambda > 0$, show that $u^{\mathrm{T}}Ku > 0$ for *every* $u \neq 0$, not just the eigenvectors x_i. Write u as a combination of eigenvectors. Why are all "cross terms" $x_i^{\mathrm{T}}x_j = 0$?

$$u^{\mathrm{T}}Ku = (c_1x_1 + \cdots + c_nx_n)^{\mathrm{T}}(c_1\lambda_1x_1 + \cdots + c_n\lambda_nx_n) = c_1^2\lambda_1x_1^{\mathrm{T}}x_1 + \cdots + c_n^2\lambda_nx_n^{\mathrm{T}}x_n > 0\,.$$

20 Without multiplying $A = \begin{bmatrix} \cos\theta & -\sin\theta \\ \sin\theta & \cos\theta \end{bmatrix} \begin{bmatrix} 2 & 0 \\ 0 & 5 \end{bmatrix} \begin{bmatrix} \cos\theta & \sin\theta \\ -\sin\theta & \cos\theta \end{bmatrix}$, find

(a) the determinant of A (b) the eigenvalues of A
(c) the eigenvectors of A (d) a reason why A is symmetric positive definite.

21 For $f_1(x,y) = \frac{1}{4}x^4 + x^2y + y^2$ and $f_2(x,y) = x^3 + xy - x$ find the second derivative (Hessian) matrices H_1 and H_2:

$$H = \begin{bmatrix} \partial^2 f/\partial x^2 & \partial^2 f/\partial x\partial y \\ \partial^2 f/\partial y\partial x & \partial^2 f/\partial y^2 \end{bmatrix}.$$

H_1 is positive definite so f_1 is concave up (= convex). Find the minimum point of f_1 and the saddle point of f_2 (look where first derivatives are zero).

22 The graph of $z = x^2 + y^2$ is a bowl opening upward. *The graph of* $z = x^2 - y^2$ *is a saddle.* The graph of $z = -x^2 - y^2$ is a bowl opening downward. What is a test on a, b, c for $z = ax^2 + 2bxy + cy^2$ to have a saddle at $(0,0)$?

23 Which values of c give a bowl and which give a saddle point for the graph of $z = 4x^2 + 12xy + cy^2$? Describe this graph at the borderline value of c.

24 Here is another way to work with the quadratic function $P(u)$. Check that

$$P(u) = \frac{1}{2}u^{\mathrm{T}}Ku - u^{\mathrm{T}}f \quad \text{equals} \quad \frac{1}{2}(u - K^{-1}f)^{\mathrm{T}}K(u - K^{-1}f) - \frac{1}{2}f^{\mathrm{T}}K^{-1}f\,.$$

The last term $-\frac{1}{2}f^{\mathrm{T}}K^{-1}f$ is P_{min}. The other (long) term on the right side is always ____. When $u = K^{-1}f$, this long term is zero so $P = P_{\mathsf{min}}$.

25 Find the first derivatives in $f = \partial P/\partial u$ and the second derivatives in the matrix H for $P(u) = u_1^2 + u_2^2 - c(u_1^2 + u_2^2)^4$. Start Newton's iteration (21) at $u^0 = (1,0)$. Which values of c give a next vector u^1 that is closer to the local minimum at $u^* = (0,0)$? Why is $(0,0)$ not a global minimum?

26 Guess the smallest 2, 2 block that makes $\left[\boldsymbol{C^{-1}} \;\; \boldsymbol{A};\; \boldsymbol{A^{\mathrm{T}}} \;\; \_\_\_\_ \right]$ semidefinite.

27 If H and K are positive definite, explain why $M = \begin{bmatrix} H & 0 \\ 0 & K \end{bmatrix}$ is positive definite but $N = \begin{bmatrix} K & K \\ K & K \end{bmatrix}$ is not. Connect the pivots and eigenvalues of M and N to the pivots and eigenvalues of H and K. How is $\mathsf{chol}(M)$ constructed from $\mathsf{chol}(H)$ and $\mathsf{chol}(K)$?

28 This "KKT matrix" has eigenvalues $\lambda_1 = 1, \lambda_2 = 2, \lambda_3 = -1$: **Saddle point**.

$$\begin{bmatrix} w_1 & w_2 & u \end{bmatrix} \begin{bmatrix} 1 & 0 & -1 \\ 0 & 1 & 1 \\ -1 & 1 & 0 \end{bmatrix} \begin{bmatrix} w_1 \\ w_2 \\ u \end{bmatrix} = w_1^2 + w_2^2 - 2uw_1 + 2uw_2.$$

Put its unit eigenvectors inside the squares and $\lambda = 1, 2, -1$ outside:

$$\text{Verify } w_1^2 + w_2^2 - 2uw_1 + 2uw_2 = \mathbf{1}(\_\_\_\_)^2 + \mathbf{2}(\_\_\_\_)^2 - \mathbf{1}(\_\_\_\_)^2.$$

The first parentheses contain $(w_1 - w_2)/\sqrt{2}$ from the eigenvector $(1, -1, 0)/\sqrt{2}$. We are using $Q\Lambda Q^{\mathrm{T}}$ instead of LDL^{T}. Still two squares minus one square.

29 (Important) Find the three pivots of that indefinite KKT matrix. Verify that the product of pivots equals the product of eigenvalues (this also equals the determinant). Now put the pivots outside the squares:

$$w_1^2 + w_2^2 - 2uw_1 + 2uw_2 = \mathbf{1}(w_1 - u)^2 + \mathbf{1}(w_2 - u)^2 - \mathbf{2}(\_\_\_\_)^2.$$

1.7 NUMERICAL LINEAR ALGEBRA: LU, QR, SVD

Applied mathematics starts from a problem and builds an equation to describe it. Scientific computing aims to solve that equation. Numerical linear algebra displays this "*build up, break down*" process in its clearest form, with matrix models:

$$Ku = f \qquad \text{or} \qquad Kx = \lambda x \qquad \text{or} \qquad Mu'' + Ku = 0\,.$$

Often the computations break K into simpler pieces. The properties of K are crucial: *symmetric* or not, *banded* or not, *sparse* or not, *well conditioned* or not. Numerical linear algebra can deal with a large class of matrices in a uniform way, without adjusting to every detail of the model. The algorithm becomes clearest when we see it as a **factorization** into triangular matrices or orthogonal matrices or very sparse matrices. We will summarize those factorizations quickly, for future use.

This chapter began with the special matrices K, T, B, C and their properties. We needed something to work with! Now we pull together the factorizations you need for more general matrices. They lead to "*norms*" and "*condition numbers*" of any A. In my experience, applications of rectangular matrices constantly lead to A^{T} and $A^{\mathrm{T}}A$.

Three Essential Factorizations

I will use the neutral letter A for the matrix we start with. It may be rectangular. If A has independent columns, then $K = A^{\mathrm{T}}A$ is symmetric positive definite. Sometimes we operate directly with A (better conditioned and more sparse) and sometimes with K (symmetric and more beautiful).

Here are the three essential factorizations, $A = LU$ and $A = QR$ and $A = U\Sigma V^{\mathrm{T}}$:

(1) Elimination reduces A to U by row operations using multipliers in L:

$$\boldsymbol{A = LU} = \textit{lower triangular} \text{ times } \textit{upper triangular}$$

(2) Orthogonalization changes the columns of A to orthonormal columns in Q:

$$\boldsymbol{A = QR} = \textit{orthonormal columns} \text{ times } \textit{upper triangular}$$

(3) Singular Value Decomposition sees every A as (rotation)(stretch)(rotation):

$$\boldsymbol{A = U\Sigma V^{\mathrm{T}}} = \textit{orthonormal columns} \times \textit{singular values} \times \textit{orthonormal rows}$$

As soon as I see that last line, I think of more to say. In the SVD, the orthonormal columns in U and V are the *left and right singular vectors* (eigenvectors of AA^{T} and $A^{\mathrm{T}}A$). Then $AV = U\Sigma$ is like the usual diagonalization $AS = S\Lambda$ by eigenvectors, but with two matrices U and V. We only have $U = V$ when $AA^{\mathrm{T}} = A^{\mathrm{T}}A$.

For a positive definite matrix K, everything comes together: U is Q and V^{T} is Q^{T}. The diagonal matrix Σ is Λ (singular values are eigenvalues). Then $K = Q\Lambda Q^{\mathrm{T}}$. The columns of Q are the principal axes = eigenvectors = singular vectors. **Matrices with orthonormal columns** play a central role in computations. Start there.

Orthogonal Matrices

The vectors $q_1, q_2, \ldots, q_n$ are *orthonormal* if all their inner products are 0 or 1:

$$q_i^{\mathrm{T}} q_j = 0 \text{ if } i \neq j \ \ \textbf{(orthogonality)} \qquad q_i^{\mathrm{T}} q_i = 1 \ \ \begin{matrix}\textbf{(normalization}\\ \textbf{to unit vectors)}\end{matrix} \tag{1}$$

Those dot products are beautifully summarized by the matrix multiplication $Q^{\mathrm{T}}Q = I$:

$$\textbf{Orthonormal } \boldsymbol{q}\textbf{'s} \qquad Q^{\mathrm{T}}Q = \begin{bmatrix} - & q_1^{\mathrm{T}} & - \\ - & q_n^{\mathrm{T}} & - \end{bmatrix} \begin{bmatrix} | & & | \\ q_1 & & q_n \\ | & & | \end{bmatrix} = \begin{bmatrix} 1 & \cdot & 0 \\ \cdot & 1 & \cdot \\ 0 & \cdot & 1 \end{bmatrix} = I. \tag{2}$$

If Q is *square*, we call it an **orthogonal matrix**. $Q^{\mathrm{T}}Q = I$ tells us immediately that

- **The inverse of an orthogonal matrix is its transpose:** $Q^{-1} = Q^{\mathrm{T}}$.
- **Multiplying a vector by Q doesn't change its length:** $\|Qx\| = \|x\|$.

Length (soon called **norm**) is preserved because $\|Qx\|^2 = x^{\mathrm{T}}Q^{\mathrm{T}}Qx = x^{\mathrm{T}}x = \|x\|^2$. This doesn't require a square matrix: $Q^{\mathrm{T}}Q = I$ for rectangular matrices too. But a two-sided inverse $Q^{-1} = Q^{\mathrm{T}}$ (so that QQ^{T} is also I) does require that Q is square. Here are three quick examples of Q: **permutations, rotations, reflections**.

Example 1 Every **permutation matrix** P has the same rows as I, but probably in a different order. P has a single 1 in every row and in every column. Multiplying Px puts the components of x in that row order. Reordering doesn't change the length. All n by n permutation matrices (there are $n!$ of them) have $P^{-1} = P^{\mathrm{T}}$.

The 1's in P^{T} hit the 1's in P to give $P^{\mathrm{T}}P = I$. Here is a 3 by 3 example of Px:

$$\begin{bmatrix} 0 & 1 & 0 \\ 0 & 0 & 1 \\ 1 & 0 & 0 \end{bmatrix} \begin{bmatrix} \mathrm{x} \\ \mathrm{y} \\ \mathrm{z} \end{bmatrix} = \begin{bmatrix} \mathrm{y} \\ \mathrm{z} \\ \mathrm{x} \end{bmatrix} \qquad P^{\mathrm{T}}P = \begin{bmatrix} 0 & 0 & 1 \\ 1 & 0 & 0 \\ 0 & 1 & 0 \end{bmatrix} \begin{bmatrix} 0 & 1 & 0 \\ 0 & 0 & 1 \\ 1 & 0 & 0 \end{bmatrix} = I \tag{3}$$

Example 2 **Rotation** changes the direction of vectors. It doesn't change lengths. Every vector just turns:

$$\textbf{Rotation matrix in the 1-3 plane} \qquad Q = \begin{bmatrix} \cos\theta & 0 & -\sin\theta \\ 0 & 1 & 0 \\ \sin\theta & 0 & \cos\theta \end{bmatrix}$$

Every orthogonal matrix Q with determinant 1 is a product of plane rotations.

Example 3 The **reflection** H takes every v to its image Hv on the other side of a plane mirror. The unit vector u (perpendicular to the mirror) is reversed into $Hu = -u$:

Reflection matrix
$\boldsymbol{u = (\cos\theta, 0, \sin\theta)}$

$$H = I - 2uu^{\mathrm{T}} = \begin{bmatrix} -\cos 2\theta & 0 & -\sin 2\theta \\ 0 & 1 & 0 \\ -\sin 2\theta & 0 & \cos 2\theta \end{bmatrix} \tag{4}$$

This "Householder reflection" has determinant -1. Both rotations and reflections have orthonormal columns, and $(I - 2uu^{\mathrm{T}})u = u - 2u$ guarantees that $Hu = -u$. Modern orthogonalization uses reflections to create the Q in $A = QR$.

Orthogonalization $A = QR$

We are given an m by n matrix A with linearly independent columns $a_1, \ldots, a_n$. Its rank is n. Those n columns are a basis for the column space of A, but not necessarily a good basis. All computations are improved by switching from the a_i to orthonormal vectors $q_1, \ldots, q_n$. There are two important ways to go from A to Q.

1. The **Gram-Schmidt algorithm** gives a simple construction of the q's from the a's. First, q_1 is the unit vector $a_1/\|a_1\|$. In reverse, $a_1 = r_{11}q_1$ with $r_{11} = \|a_1\|$. Second, *subtract from a_2 its component in the q_1 direction* (the Gram-Schmidt idea). That vector $B = a_2 - (q_1^{\mathrm{T}}a_2)q_1$ is orthogonal to q_1. Normalize B to $q_2 = B/\|B\|$. At every step, subtract from a_k its components in the settled directions $q_1, \ldots, q_{k-1}$, and normalize to find the next unit vector q_k.

Gram-Schmidt
$\boldsymbol{(m}$ **by** $\boldsymbol{n)(n}$ **by** $\boldsymbol{n)}$

$$\begin{bmatrix} \\ a_1 & a_2 \\ \\ \end{bmatrix} = \begin{bmatrix} \\ q_1 & q_2 \\ \\ \end{bmatrix} \begin{bmatrix} r_{11} & r_{12} \\ \mathbf{0} & r_{22} \end{bmatrix} \tag{5}$$

2. The **Householder algorithm** uses reflection matrices $I - 2uu^{\mathrm{T}}$. Column by column, it produces zeros in R. In this method, Q is square and R is rectangular:

Householder qr(A)
$\boldsymbol{(m}$ **by** $\boldsymbol{m)(m}$ **by** $\boldsymbol{n)}$

$$\begin{bmatrix} \\ a_1 & a_2 \\ \\ \end{bmatrix} = \begin{bmatrix} \\ q_1 & q_2 & q_3 \\ \\ \end{bmatrix} \begin{bmatrix} r_{11} & r_{12} \\ \mathbf{0} & r_{22} \\ \mathbf{0} & \mathbf{0} \end{bmatrix} \tag{6}$$

The vector q_3 comes for free! It is orthogonal to a_1, a_2 and also to q_1, q_2. This method is MATLAB's choice for qr because it is more stable than Gram-Schmidt and gives extra information. Since q_3 multiplies the zero row, it has no effect on $A = QR$. Use qr$(A, 0)$ to return to the "economy size" in (5).

Section 2.3 will give full explanations and example codes for both methods. Most linear algebra courses emphasize Gram-Schmidt, which gives an orthonormal basis $q_1, \ldots, q_r$ for the column space of A. Householder is now the method of choice, completing to an orthonormal basis $q_1, \ldots, q_m$ for the whole space $\mathbf{R}^m$.

Numerically, the great virtue of Q is its stability. When you multiply by Q, overflow and underflow will not happen. All formulas involving $A^{\mathrm{T}}A$ become simpler, since $Q^{\mathrm{T}}Q = I$. A square system $Qx = b$ will be *perfectly conditioned*, because $\|x\| = \|b\|$ and an error Δb produces an error Δx of the *same size*:

$$Q(x + \Delta x) = b + \Delta b \quad \text{gives} \quad Q(\Delta x) = \Delta b \quad \text{and} \quad \|\Delta x\| = \|\Delta b\|. \tag{7}$$

Singular Value Decomposition

This section now concentrates on the SVD, which reaches a diagonal matrix Σ. Since diagonalization involves eigenvalues, the matrices from $A = QR$ will not do the job. Most square matrices A are diagonalized by their eigenvectors $x_1, \ldots, x_n$. If x is a combination $c_1x_1 + \cdots + c_nx_n$, then A multiplies each x_i by λ_i.

In matrix language this is $Ax = S\Lambda S^{-1}x$. *Usually, the eigenvector matrix S is not orthogonal.* Eigenvectors only meet at right angles when A is special (for example symmetric). If we want to diagonalize an ordinary A by orthogonal matrices, we need *two different Q's*. They are generally called U and V, so $\boldsymbol{A = U\Sigma V^{\mathrm{T}}}$.

What is this diagonal matrix Σ? It now contains *singular values* σ_i instead of eigenvalues λ_i. To understand those σ_i, the key is always the same: **Look at** $A^{\mathrm{T}}A$.

Find V and Σ $\quad A^{\mathrm{T}}A = (U\Sigma V^{\mathrm{T}})^{\mathrm{T}}(U\Sigma V^{\mathrm{T}}) = V\Sigma^{\mathrm{T}}U^{\mathrm{T}}U\Sigma V^{\mathrm{T}} = V\Sigma^{\mathrm{T}}\Sigma V^{\mathrm{T}}$. (8)

Removing $U^{\mathrm{T}}U = I$ leaves $V(\Sigma^{\mathrm{T}}\Sigma)V^{\mathrm{T}}$. This is exactly like $K = Q\Lambda Q^{\mathrm{T}}$, *but it applies to* $K = A^{\mathrm{T}}A$. The diagonal matrix $\Sigma^{\mathrm{T}}\Sigma$ contains the numbers σ_i^2, and those are the positive eigenvalues of $A^{\mathrm{T}}A$. The orthonormal eigenvectors of $A^{\mathrm{T}}A$ are in V.

In the end we want $AV = U\Sigma$. So we must choose $\boldsymbol{u_i = Av_i/\sigma_i}$. These u_i are orthonormal eigenvectors of AA^{T}. At this point we have the "reduced" SVD, with $v_1, \ldots, v_r$ and $u_1, \ldots, u_r$ as perfect bases for the column space and row space of A. The rank r is the dimension of these spaces, and $\mathsf{svd}(A, 0)$ gives this form:

Reduced SVD from $u_i = Av_i/\sigma_i$

$$A = U_{m\times r}\Sigma_{r\times r}V^{\mathrm{T}}_{r\times n} = \begin{bmatrix} & & \\ u_1 & \cdots & u_r \\ & & \\ & & \end{bmatrix}\begin{bmatrix} \sigma_1 & & \\ & \ddots & \\ & & \sigma_r \end{bmatrix}\begin{bmatrix} & v_1^{\mathrm{T}} & \\ & \vdots & \\ & v_r^{\mathrm{T}} & \end{bmatrix} \tag{9}$$

To complete the v's, add any orthonormal basis $v_{r+1}, \ldots, v_n$ for the nullspace of A. To complete the u's, add any orthonormal basis $u_{r+1}, \ldots, u_m$ for the nullspace of A^{T}. To complete Σ to an m by n matrix, add zeros for $\mathsf{svd}(A)$ and the unreduced form:

Full SVD

$$A = U_{m\times m}\Sigma_{m\times n}V^{\mathrm{T}}_{n\times n} = \begin{bmatrix} \\ u_1 \cdots u_r \cdots u_m \\ \\ \end{bmatrix}\begin{bmatrix} \sigma_1 & & & \\ & \ddots & & \\ & & \sigma_r & \\ & & & \end{bmatrix}\begin{bmatrix} v_1^{\mathrm{T}} \\ \vdots \\ v_r^{\mathrm{T}} \\ \vdots \\ v_n^{\mathrm{T}} \end{bmatrix} \quad (10)$$

Normally we number the u_i, σ_i, v_i so that $\sigma_1 \geq \sigma_2 \geq \cdots \geq \sigma_r > 0$. Then the SVD has the wonderful property of splitting any matrix A into **rank-one pieces ordered by their size**:

Columns times rows $A = u_1\sigma_1 v_1^{\mathrm{T}}$ (largest σ_1) $+ \cdots + u_r\sigma_r v_r^{\mathrm{T}}$ (smallest σ_r) (11)

The first piece $u_1\sigma_1 v_1^{\mathrm{T}}$ is described by only $m+n+1$ numbers, not mn. Often a few pieces contain almost all the information in A (in a stable form). This isn't a fast method for image compression because computing the SVD involves eigenvalues. (Filters are faster.) The SVD is the centerpiece of matrix approximation.

The right and left singular vectors v_i and u_i are the **Karhunen-Loève bases** in engineering. A symmetric positive definite K has $v_i = u_i$: one basis.

I think of the SVD as the final step in the Fundamental Theorem of Linear Algebra. First come the *dimensions* of the four subspaces. Then their *orthogonality*. Then the *orthonormal bases* $u_1, \ldots, u_m$ *and* $v_1, \ldots, v_n$ *which diagonalize* A.

SVD

$Av_j = \sigma_j u_j$	for $j \leq r$	$A^{\mathrm{T}}u_j = \sigma_j v_j$	for $j \leq r$
$Av_j = 0$	for $j > r$	$A^{\mathrm{T}}u_j = 0$	for $j > r$

(12)

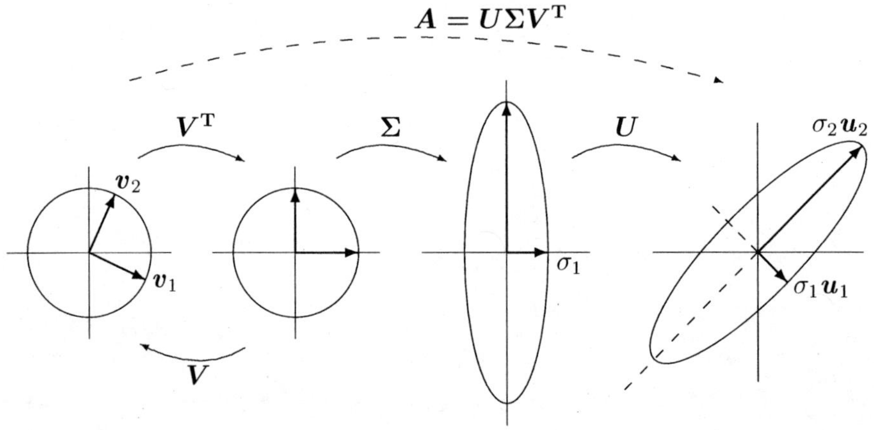

Figure 1.18: U and V are rotations and reflections. Σ stretches by $\sigma_1, \ldots, \sigma_r$.

These $u_i = Av_i/\sigma_i$ are orthonormal eigenvectors of AA^{T}. Start from $A^{\mathrm{T}}Av_i = {\sigma_i}^2 v_i$:

Multiply by v_i^{T}: $v_i^{\mathrm{T}}A^{\mathrm{T}}Av_i = {\sigma_i}^2 v_i^{\mathrm{T}}v_i$ says that $\|Av_i\| = \sigma_i$ so $\|u_i\| = 1$

Multiply by v_j^{T}: $v_j^{\mathrm{T}}A^{\mathrm{T}}Av_i = {\sigma_i}^2 v_j^{\mathrm{T}}v_i$ says that $(Av_j)\cdot(Av_i) = 0$ so $u_j^{\mathrm{T}}u_i = 0$

Multiply by A: $AA^{\mathrm{T}}Av_i = {\sigma_i}^2 Av_i$ says that $\boldsymbol{AA^{\mathrm{T}}u_i = {\sigma_i}^2 u_i}$

Here is a homemade code to create the SVD. It follows the steps above, based primarily on eig($A'*A$). The faster and more stable codes in LAPACK work directly with A. Ultimately, stability may require that very small singular values are replaced by $\sigma = 0$. The SVD identifies the dangers in $Ax = b$ (near 0 in A, very large in x).

```
% input A, output orthogonal U,V and diagonal sigma with A=U*sigma*V'
[m,n]=size(A); r=rank(A); [V,squares]=eig(A'*A);   % n by n matrices
sing=sqrt(squares(1:r,1:r));                       % r by r, singular values > 0 on diagonal
sigma=zeros(m,n); sigma(1:r,1:r)=sing;             % m by n singular value matrix
u=A*V(:,1:r)*inv(sing);                            % first r columns of U (singular vectors)
[U,R]=qr(u); U(:,1:r)=u;    % qr command completes u to an m by m U
A-U*sigma*V';               % test for zero m by n matrix (could print its norm)
```

Example 4 Find the SVD for the singular matrix $A = \begin{bmatrix} 1 & 1 \\ 7 & 7 \end{bmatrix}$.

Solution A has rank one, so there is one singular value. First comes $A^{\mathrm{T}}A$:

$$A^{\mathrm{T}}A = \begin{bmatrix} 50 & 50 \\ 50 & 50 \end{bmatrix} \text{ has } \lambda = 100 \text{ and } 0, \text{ with eigenvectors } \begin{bmatrix} v_1 & v_2 \end{bmatrix} = \frac{1}{\sqrt{2}}\begin{bmatrix} 1 & -1 \\ 1 & 1 \end{bmatrix}.$$

The singular value is $\sigma_1 = \sqrt{100} = 10$. Then $u_1 = Av_1/10 = (1,7)/\sqrt{50}$. Add in $u_2 = (-7,1)/\sqrt{50}$:

$$A = U\Sigma V^{\mathrm{T}} = \frac{1}{\sqrt{50}}\begin{bmatrix} 1 & -7 \\ 7 & 1 \end{bmatrix}\begin{bmatrix} 10 & 0 \\ 0 & 0 \end{bmatrix}\frac{1}{\sqrt{2}}\begin{bmatrix} 1 & 1 \\ -1 & 1 \end{bmatrix}.$$

Example 5 Find the SVD of the $n+1$ by n backward difference matrix Δ_-.

Solution With diagonal 1's and subdiagonal -1's in Δ_-, the products $\Delta_-^{\mathrm{T}}\Delta_-$ and $\Delta_-\Delta_-^{\mathrm{T}}$ are K_n and B_{n+1}. When $(n+1)h = \pi$, K_n has eigenvalues $\lambda = \sigma^2 = 2 - 2\cos kh$ and eigenvectors $v_k = (\sin kh, \ldots, \sin nkh)$. B_{n+1} has the same eigenvalues (plus $\lambda_{n+1} = 0$) and its eigenvectors are $u_k = \left(\cos \frac{1}{2}kh, \ldots, \cos(n + \frac{1}{2})kh\right)$ in U.

Those eigenvectors v_k and u_k fill the DST and DCT matrices. Normalized to unit length, these are the columns of V and U. The SVD is $\Delta_- = (\mathbf{DCT})\Sigma(\mathbf{DST})$. The equation $\Delta_- v_k = \sigma_k u_k$ says that *the first differences of sine vectors are cosine vectors.*

Section 1.8 will apply the SVD to Principal Component Analysis and to Model Reduction. The goal is to find a small part of the data and the model (starting with u_1 and v_1) that carries the important information.

The Pseudoinverse

By choosing good bases, A multiplies v_i in the row space to give $\sigma_i u_i$ in the column space. A^{-1} must do the opposite! If $Av = \sigma u$ then $A^{-1}u = v/\sigma$. The singular values of A^{-1} are $1/\sigma$, just as the eigenvalues of A^{-1} are $1/\lambda$. The bases are reversed. The u's are in the row space of A^{-1}, the v's are in the column space.

Until this moment we would have added "*if* A^{-1} *exists.*" Now we don't. A matrix that multiplies u_i to produce v_i/σ_i *does* exist. It is the pseudoinverse $A^+ = \text{pinv}(A)$.

Pseudoinverse $\boldsymbol{A^+ = V\Sigma^+U^{\mathrm{T}}}$ $\quad A^+u_i = \dfrac{v_i}{\sigma_i}$ for $i \le r$ and $A^+u_i = 0$ for $i > r$. (13)

The vectors $u_1, \ldots, u_r$ in the column space of A go back to the row space. The other vectors $u_{r+1}, \ldots, u_m$ are sent to zero. When we know what happens to each basis vector u_i, we know A^+. The pseudoinverse has the same rank r as A.

In the pseudoinverse Σ^+ of the diagonal matrix Σ, each σ is replaced by σ^{-1}. The product $\Sigma^+\Sigma$ is as near to the identity as we can get. So are AA^+ and A^+A:

$$\begin{aligned} AA^+ &= \text{projection matrix onto the column space of } A \\ A^+A &= \text{projection matrix onto the row space of } A \end{aligned}$$

Example 6 Find the pseudoinverse A^+ of the same rank one matrix $A = \begin{bmatrix} 1 & 1 \\ 7 & 7 \end{bmatrix}$.

Solution Since A has $\sigma_1 = 10$, the pseudoinverse $A^+ = \text{pinv}(A)$ has $1/10$.

$$A^+ = V\Sigma^+U^{\mathrm{T}} = \frac{1}{\sqrt{2}}\begin{bmatrix} 1 & -1 \\ 1 & 1 \end{bmatrix}\begin{bmatrix} 1/10 & 0 \\ 0 & 0 \end{bmatrix}\frac{1}{\sqrt{50}}\begin{bmatrix} 1 & 7 \\ -7 & 1 \end{bmatrix} = \frac{1}{100}\begin{bmatrix} 1 & 7 \\ 1 & 7 \end{bmatrix}.$$

The pseudoinverse of a rank-one matrix $A = \sigma uv^{\mathrm{T}}$ is $A^+ = vu^{\mathrm{T}}/\sigma$, also rank-one.

Always A^+b is in the row space of A (a combination of the basis $u_1, \ldots, u_r$). With $n > m$, $Ax = b$ is solvable when b is in the column space of A. Then A^+b is the shortest solution because it has no nullspace component, while $A\backslash b$ is a different "sparse solution" with $n - m$ zero components.

Condition Numbers and Norms

The *condition number* of a positive definite matrix is $c(K) = \lambda_{\max}/\lambda_{\min}$. This ratio measures the "sensitivity" of the linear system $Ku = f$. Suppose f changes by Δf because of roundoff or measurement error. Our goal is to estimate Δu (the change in the solution) . If we are serious about scientific computing, we have to control errors.

Subtract $Ku = f$ from $K(u + \Delta u) = f + \Delta f$. **The error equation is** $K(\Delta u) = \Delta f$. Since K is positive definite, $\lambda_{\min}$ gives a reliable bound on Δu:

Error bound $\quad K(\Delta u) = \Delta f \quad \text{means} \quad \Delta u = K^{-1}(\Delta f). \quad \text{Then } \|\Delta u\| \le \dfrac{\|\Delta f\|}{\lambda_{\min}(K)}.$ (14)

The top eigenvalue of K^{-1} is $1/\lambda_{\min}(K)$. Then Δu is largest in the direction of that eigenvector. The eigenvalue $\lambda_{\min}$ indicates how close K is to a singular matrix (but eigenvalues are not reliable for an unsymmetric matrix A). That single number $\lambda_{\min}$ has two serious drawbacks in measuring the *sensitivity* of $Ku = f$ or $Ax = b$.

First, if we multiply K by 1000, then u and Δu are divided by 1000. That rescaling (to make K less singular and $\lambda_{\min}$ larger) cannot change the reality of the problem. The **relative error** $\|\Delta u\|/\|u\|$ stays the same, since $1000/1000 = 1$. It is the relative changes in u and f that we should compare. Here is the key for positive definite K:

$$\text{Dividing } \|\Delta u\| \leq \frac{\|\Delta f\|}{\lambda_{\min}(K)} \text{ by } \|u\| \geq \frac{\|f\|}{\lambda_{\max}(K)} \text{ gives } \frac{\|\Delta u\|}{\|u\|} \leq \frac{\lambda_{\max}(K)}{\lambda_{\min}(K)} \frac{\|\Delta f\|}{\|f\|}.$$

In words: Δu is largest when Δf is an eigenvector for $\lambda_{\min}$. The true solution u is *smallest* when f is an eigenvector for $\lambda_{\max}$. The ratio $\lambda_{\max}/\lambda_{\min}$ produces the condition number $c(K)$, the maximum "blowup factor" in the relative error.

Condition number for positive definite K

$$c(K) = \frac{\lambda_{\max}(K)}{\lambda_{\min}(K)}$$

When A is not symmetric, the inequality $\|Ax\| \leq \lambda_{\max}(A)\|x\|$ can be false (see Figure 1.19). **Other vectors can blow up more than eigenvectors.** A triangular matrix with 1's on the diagonal might look perfectly conditioned, since $\lambda_{\max}=\lambda_{\min}=1$. We need a **norm** $\|A\|$ to measure the size of every A, and $\lambda_{\max}$ won't work.

DEFINITIONS The norm $\|A\|$ is the maximum of the ratio $\|Ax\|/\|x\|$. The condition number of A is $\|A\|$ times $\|A^{-1}\|$.

$$\textbf{Norm } \|A\| = \max_{x\neq 0} \frac{\|Ax\|}{\|x\|} \qquad \textbf{Condition number } c(A) = \|A\|\,\|A^{-1}\| \tag{15}$$

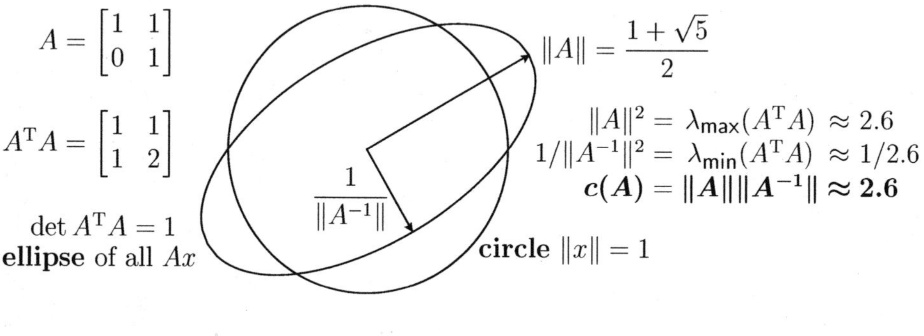

Figure 1.19: The norms of A and A^{-1} come from the longest and shortest Ax.

$\|Ax\|/\|x\|$ is never larger than $\|A\|$ (its maximum), so always $\|Ax\| \le \|A\|\,\|x\|$. For all matrices and vectors, the number $\|A\|$ meets these requirements:

$$\|Ax\| \le \|A\|\,\|x\| \quad \text{and} \quad \|AB\| \le \|A\|\,\|B\| \quad \text{and} \quad \|A+B\| \le \|A\| + \|B\|. \tag{16}$$

The norm of $1000A$ will be $1000\|A\|$. But $1000A$ has the same condition number as A.

For a positive definite matrix, the largest eigenvalue is the norm: $\|K\| = \lambda_{\text{max}}(K)$. Reason: The orthogonal matrices in $K = Q\Lambda Q^{\mathrm{T}}$ leave lengths unchanged. So $\|K\| = \|\Lambda\| = \lambda_{\text{max}}$. Similarly $\|K^{-1}\| = 1/\lambda_{\text{min}}(K)$. Then $c(K) = \lambda_{\text{max}}/\lambda_{\text{min}}$ is correct.

A very unsymmetric example has $\lambda_{\text{max}} = 0$, but the norm is $\|A\| = 2$:

$$Ax = \begin{bmatrix} 0 & 2 \\ 0 & 0 \end{bmatrix}\begin{bmatrix} 0 \\ 1 \end{bmatrix} = \begin{bmatrix} 2 \\ 0 \end{bmatrix} \quad \text{and the ratio is} \quad \frac{\|Ax\|}{\|x\|} = \frac{2}{1}.$$

This unsymmetric A leads to the symmetric $A^{\mathrm{T}}A = \left[\begin{smallmatrix} 0 & 0 \\ 0 & 4 \end{smallmatrix}\right]$. The largest eigenvalue is $\sigma_1^2 = 4$. *Its square root is the norm:* $\|A\| = 2 =$ **largest singular value.**

This singular value $\sqrt{\lambda_{\text{max}}(A^{\mathrm{T}}A)}$ is generally larger than $\lambda_{\text{max}}(A)$. Here is the great formula for $\|A\|^2$ all on one line:

Norm $$\|A\|^2 = \max \frac{\|Ax\|^2}{\|x\|^2} = \max \frac{x^{\mathrm{T}}A^{\mathrm{T}}Ax}{x^{\mathrm{T}}x} = \lambda_{\text{max}}(A^{\mathrm{T}}A) = \sigma^2_{\text{max}}. \tag{17}$$

The norm of A^{-1} is $1/\sigma_{\text{min}}$, generally larger than $1/\lambda_{\text{min}}$. The product is $c(A)$:

Condition number $$c(A) = \|A\|\|A^{-1}\| = \frac{\sigma_{\text{max}}}{\sigma_{\text{min}}}. \tag{18}$$

Here is one comment: σ_{min} tells us the distance from an invertible A to the *nearest singular matrix*. When σ_{min} changes to zero inside Σ, it is multiplied by U and V^{T} (orthogonal, preserving norms). So the norm of that smallest change in A is σ_{min}.

Example 7 For this 2 by 2 matrix A, the inverse just changes 7 to -7. Notice that $7^2 + 1^2 = 50$. The condition number $c(A) = \|A\|\,\|A^{-1}\|$ is at least $\sqrt{50}\sqrt{50} = 50$:

$$Ax = \begin{bmatrix} 1 & 7 \\ 0 & 1 \end{bmatrix}\begin{bmatrix} 0 \\ 1 \end{bmatrix} = \begin{bmatrix} 7 \\ 1 \end{bmatrix} \quad \text{has} \quad \frac{\|Ax\|}{\|x\|} = \frac{\sqrt{50}}{1} \quad \text{So } \|A\| \ge \sqrt{50}$$

$$A^{-1}x = \begin{bmatrix} 1 & -7 \\ 0 & 1 \end{bmatrix}\begin{bmatrix} 0 \\ 1 \end{bmatrix} = \begin{bmatrix} -7 \\ 1 \end{bmatrix} \quad \text{has} \quad \frac{\|A^{-1}x\|}{\|x\|} = \frac{\sqrt{50}}{1} \quad \text{So } \|A^{-1}\| \ge \sqrt{50}.$$

Suppose we intend to solve $Ax = b = \left[\begin{smallmatrix} 7 \\ 1 \end{smallmatrix}\right]$. The solution is $x = \left[\begin{smallmatrix} 0 \\ 1 \end{smallmatrix}\right]$. Move the right side by $\Delta b = \left[\begin{smallmatrix} 0 \\ .1 \end{smallmatrix}\right]$. Then x moves by $\Delta x = \left[\begin{smallmatrix} -.7 \\ .1 \end{smallmatrix}\right]$, since $A(\Delta x) = \Delta b$. The relative change in x is 50 times the relative change in b:

$$\frac{\|\Delta x\|}{\|x\|} = (.1)\sqrt{50} \quad \text{is 50 times greater than} \quad \frac{\|\Delta b\|}{\|b\|} = \frac{.1}{\sqrt{50}}.$$

Example 8 The eigenvalues of the $-1, 2, -1$ matrix are $\lambda = 2 - 2\cos\frac{\pi k}{n+1}$. Then $k = 1$ and $k = n$ give λ_{min} and λ_{max}. The condition number of K_n grows like n^2:

$$c(K) = \|K\|\,\|K^{-1}\| = \frac{\lambda_{\text{max}}}{\lambda_{\text{min}}} = \frac{2 - 2\cos\frac{n\pi}{n+1}}{2 - 2\cos\frac{\pi}{n+1}} \approx \frac{4}{\pi^2}(n+1)^2. \tag{19}$$

λ_{max} is nearly $2 - 2\cos\pi = 4$, at the top of Figure 1.13. The smallest eigenvalue uses $\cos\theta \approx 1 - \frac{1}{2}\theta^2$ from calculus, which is the same as $2 - 2\cos\theta \approx \theta^2 = (\frac{\pi}{n+1})^2$.

A rough rule for $Ax = b$ is that ***the computer loses about*** $\log c$ ***decimals to roundoff error***. MATLAB gives a warning when the condition number is large (c is not calculated exactly, the eigenvalues of $A^{\mathrm{T}}A$ would take too long). It is normal for $c(K)$ to be of order $1/(\Delta x)^2$ in approximating a second-order differential equation, agreeing with n^2 in (19). Fourth order problems have $\lambda_{\text{max}}/\lambda_{\text{min}} \approx C/(\Delta x)^4$.

Row Exchanges in $PA = LU$

Our problems might be ill conditioned or well conditioned. We can't necessarily control $c(A)$, but we don't want to make the condition worse by a bad algorithm. Since elimination is the most frequently used algorithm in scientific computing, a lot of effort has been concentrated on doing it right. **Often we reorder the rows of A.**

The main point is that *small pivots are dangerous.* To find the numbers that multiply rows, we divide by the pivots. Small pivots mean large multipliers in L. Then L (and probably U) are more ill-conditioned than A. The simplest cure is to exchange rows by P, bringing the largest possible entry up into the pivot.

The command $\mathsf{lu}(A)$ does this "*partial pivoting*" for $A = [1\ \ 2;\ \ 3\ \ 3]$. The first pivot changes from 1 to 3. **Partial pivoting avoids multipliers in L larger than** 1:

$$[\boldsymbol{P}, \boldsymbol{L}, \boldsymbol{U}] = \mathsf{lu}(\boldsymbol{A}) \qquad \boldsymbol{PA} = \begin{bmatrix} 3 & 3 \\ 1 & 2 \end{bmatrix} = L = \begin{bmatrix} 1 & 0 \\ \frac{1}{3} & 1 \end{bmatrix} \begin{bmatrix} 3 & 3 \\ 0 & 1 \end{bmatrix} = \boldsymbol{LU}$$

The product of pivots is $-\det A = +3$ since P exchanged the rows of A.

A positive definite matrix K has no need for row exchanges. Its factorization into $K = LDL^{\mathrm{T}}$ can be rewritten as $K = L\sqrt{D}\sqrt{D}L^{\mathrm{T}}$ (named after Cholesky). In this form we are seeing $K = A^{\mathrm{T}}A$ with $\boldsymbol{A} = \sqrt{\boldsymbol{D}}\boldsymbol{L}^{\mathrm{T}}$. Then we know from (17) that $\lambda_{\text{max}}(K) = \|K\| = \sigma^2_{\text{max}}(A)$ and $\lambda_{\text{min}}(K) = \sigma^2_{\text{min}}(A)$. Elimination to $A = \mathsf{chol}(K)$ does absolutely no harm to the condition number of a positive definite $K = A^{\mathrm{T}}A$:

$$\boldsymbol{A} = \mathsf{chol}(\boldsymbol{K}) \qquad c(K) = \frac{\lambda_{\text{max}}(K)}{\lambda_{\text{min}}(K)} = \left(\frac{\sigma_{\text{max}}(A)}{\sigma_{\text{min}}(A)}\right)^2 = (c(A))^2. \tag{20}$$

Usually elimination into $PA = LU$ makes $c(L)c(U)$ larger than the original $c(A)$. That price is often remarkably low—a fact that we don't fully understand.

The next chapters build models for important applications. Discrete problems lead to matrices A and A^{T} and $A^{\mathrm{T}}A$ in Chapter 2. A differential equation produces many discrete equations, as we choose finite differences or finite elements or spectral methods or a Fourier transform—or any other option in scientific computing. All these options replace calculus, one way or another, by linear algebra.

Problem Set 1.7

Problems 1–5 are about orthogonal matrices with $Q^{\mathrm{T}}Q = I$.

1 Are these pairs of vectors orthonormal or only orthogonal or only independent?

$$\text{(a)} \begin{bmatrix}1\\0\end{bmatrix} \text{ and } \begin{bmatrix}-1\\1\end{bmatrix} \qquad \text{(b)} \begin{bmatrix}.6\\.8\end{bmatrix} \text{ and } \begin{bmatrix}.4\\-.3\end{bmatrix} \qquad \text{(c)} \begin{bmatrix}\cos\theta\\\sin\theta\end{bmatrix} \text{ and } \begin{bmatrix}-\sin\theta\\\cos\theta\end{bmatrix}.$$

Change the second vector when necessary to produce orthonormal vectors.

2 Give an example of each of the following:

(a) A matrix Q that has orthonormal columns but $QQ^{\mathrm{T}} \neq I$.

(b) Two orthogonal vectors that are not linearly independent.

(c) An orthonormal basis for $\mathbf{R}^4$, where every component is $\frac{1}{2}$ or $-\frac{1}{2}$.

3 If Q_1 and Q_2 are orthogonal matrices, show that their product Q_1Q_2 is also an orthogonal matrix. (Use $Q^{\mathrm{T}}Q = I$.)

4 Orthonormal vectors are automatically linearly independent. Two proofs:

(a) Vector proof: When $c_1q_1 + c_2q_2 + c_3q_3 = 0$, what dot product leads to $c_1 = 0$? Similarly $c_2 = 0$ and $c_3 = 0$. Thus the q's are independent.

(b) Matrix proof: Show that $Qx = 0$ leads to $x = 0$. Since Q may be rectangular, you can use Q^{T} but not Q^{-1}.

5 If a_1, a_2, a_3 is a basis for $\mathbf{R}^3$, any vector b can be written as

$$b = x_1a_1 + x_2a_2 + x_3a_3 \qquad \text{or} \qquad \begin{bmatrix} & & \\ a_1 & a_2 & a_3 \\ & & \end{bmatrix}\begin{bmatrix}x_1\\x_2\\x_3\end{bmatrix} = b.$$

(a) Suppose the a's are orthonormal. Show that $x_1 = a_1^{\mathrm{T}}b$.

(b) Suppose the a's are orthogonal. Show that $x_1 = a_1^{\mathrm{T}}b/a_1^{\mathrm{T}}a_1$.

(c) If the a's are independent, x_1 is the first component of ____ times b.

Problems 6–14 and 31 are about norms and condition numbers.

6 Figure 1.18 displays any matrix A as rotation times stretching times rotation:

$$A = U\Sigma V^{\mathrm{T}} = \begin{bmatrix} \cos\alpha & -\sin\alpha \\ \sin\alpha & \cos\alpha \end{bmatrix} \begin{bmatrix} \sigma_1 & \\ & \sigma_2 \end{bmatrix} \begin{bmatrix} \cos\theta & \sin\theta \\ -\sin\theta & \cos\theta \end{bmatrix} \quad (21)$$

The count of four parameters $\alpha, \sigma_1, \sigma_2, \theta$ agrees with the count of four entries a_{11}, a_{12}, a_{21}, a_{22}. When A is symmetric and $a_{12} = a_{21}$, the count drops to three because $\alpha = \theta$ and we only need one Q. The determinant of A in (21) is $\sigma_1\sigma_2$. For $\det A < 0$, add a reflection. In Figure 1.19, verify $\lambda_{\mathsf{max}}(A^{\mathrm{T}}A) = \frac{1}{2}(3+\sqrt{5})$ and its square root $\|A\| = \frac{1}{2}(1+\sqrt{5})$.

7 Find by hand the norms λ_{max} and condition numbers $\lambda_{\mathsf{max}}/\lambda_{\mathsf{min}}$ of these positive definite matrices:

$$\begin{bmatrix} 3 & 0 \\ 0 & 2 \end{bmatrix} \quad \begin{bmatrix} 2 & 1 \\ 1 & 2 \end{bmatrix} \quad \begin{bmatrix} 3 & 1 \\ 1 & 1 \end{bmatrix}.$$

8 Compute the norms and condition numbers from the square roots of $\lambda\left(A^{\mathrm{T}}A\right)$:

$$\begin{bmatrix} 1 & 7 \\ 1 & 1 \end{bmatrix} \quad \begin{bmatrix} 1 & 1 \\ 0 & 0 \end{bmatrix} \quad \begin{bmatrix} 1 & 1 \\ -1 & 1 \end{bmatrix}.$$

9 Explain these two inequalities from the definitions of the norms $\|A\|$ and $\|B\|$:

$$\|ABx\| \le \|A\|\,\|Bx\| \le \|A\|\,\|B\|\,\|x\|.$$

From the ratio that gives $\|AB\|$, deduce that $\|AB\| \le \|A\|\,\|B\|$. This fact is the key to using matrix norms.

10 Use $\|AB\| \le \|A\|\,\|B\|$ to prove that the condition number of any matrix A is at least 1. Show that an orthogonal Q has $c(Q) = 1$.

11 If λ is any eigenvalue of A, explain why $|\lambda| \le \|A\|$. Start from $Ax = \lambda x$.

12 The "*spectral radius*" $\rho(A) = |\lambda_{\mathsf{max}}|$ is the largest absolute value of the eigenvalues. Show with 2 by 2 examples that $\rho(A+B) \le \rho(A) + \rho(B)$ and $\rho(AB) \le \rho(A)\rho(B)$ can both be *false*. The spectral radius is not acceptable as a norm.

13 Estimate the condition number of the ill-conditioned matrix $A = \left[\begin{smallmatrix} 1 & 1 \\ 1 & 1.0001 \end{smallmatrix}\right]$.

14 The "ℓ^1 norm" and the "ℓ^∞ norm" of $x = (x_1, \ldots, x_n)$ are

$$\|x\|_1 = |x_1| + \cdots + |x_n| \quad \text{and} \quad \|x\|_\infty = \max_{1\le i\le n} |x_i|.$$

Compute the norms $\|x\|$ and $\|x\|_1$ and $\|x\|_\infty$ of these two vectors in $\mathbf{R}^5$:

$$x = (1, 1, 1, 1, 1) \qquad x = (.1, .7, .3, .4, .5).$$

Problems 15–22 are about the Singular Value Decomposition.

15 Suppose $A = U\Sigma V^{\mathrm{T}}$ and a vector x is a combination $c_1v_1 + \cdots + c_nv_n$ of the columns of V. Then Ax is what combination of the columns $u_1, \ldots, u_n$ of U?

16 Compute $A^{\mathrm{T}}A$ and AA^{T} and their eigenvalues $\sigma_1^2, 0$. Then complete the SVD:

$$A = \begin{bmatrix} 1 & 4 \\ 2 & 8 \end{bmatrix} = \begin{bmatrix} u_1 & u_2 \end{bmatrix} \begin{bmatrix} \sigma_1 & \\ & 0 \end{bmatrix} \begin{bmatrix} v_1 & v_2 \end{bmatrix}^{\mathrm{T}}.$$

17 Find the eigenvalues and unit eigenvectors of $A^{\mathrm{T}}A$ and AA^{T} for the Fibonacci matrix, and construct its SVD:

$$A = \begin{bmatrix} 1 & 1 \\ 1 & 0 \end{bmatrix}$$

18 Compute $A^{\mathrm{T}}A$ and AA^{T} and their eigenvalues and unit eigenvectors for

$$A = \begin{bmatrix} 1 & 1 & 0 \\ 0 & 1 & 1 \end{bmatrix}.$$

Multiply the three matrices $U\Sigma V^{\mathrm{T}}$ to recover A.

19 Explain how the SVD expresses the matrix A as the sum of r rank one matrices:

$$U\Sigma V^{\mathrm{T}} = \text{columns} \times \text{rows} \quad A = \sigma_1 u_1 v_1^{\mathrm{T}} + \cdots + \sigma_r u_r v_r^{\mathrm{T}} \quad \text{when } A \text{ has rank } r.$$

20 Suppose $u_1, \ldots, u_n$ and $v_1, \ldots, v_n$ are orthonormal bases for $\mathbf{R}^n$. Which matrix transforms each v_j into u_j to give $Av_1 = u_1, \ldots, Av_n = u_n$? What are the σ's?

21 Suppose A is invertible (with $\sigma_1 > \sigma_2 > 0$). Change A by as small a matrix as possible to produce a singular matrix A_0. Hint: U and V do not change:

$$A = \begin{bmatrix} u_1 & u_2 \end{bmatrix} \begin{bmatrix} \sigma_1 & \\ & \sigma_2 \end{bmatrix} \begin{bmatrix} v_1 & v_2 \end{bmatrix}^{\mathrm{T}}$$

22 (a) If A changes to $4A$, what is the change in the SVD?

(b) What is the SVD for A^{T} and for A^{-1}?

(c) Why doesn't the SVD for $A + I$ just use $\Sigma + I$?

Problems 23–27 are about $A = LU$ and $K = LDL^{\mathrm{T}}$ and $A = QR$.

23 For $K = \left[\begin{smallmatrix}1 & 2\\ 2 & 5\end{smallmatrix}\right]$, why does $\mathsf{lu}(K)$ not give factors with $K = LU$? Which pivots are chosen instead of 1 and 1? Try $A = \mathsf{chol}(K)$ to find the factor $A = L\sqrt{D}$ with no row exchange.

24 What multiple of $a = \left[\begin{smallmatrix}1\\ 1\end{smallmatrix}\right]$ should be subtracted from $b = \left[\begin{smallmatrix}4\\ 0\end{smallmatrix}\right]$ to make the result B orthogonal to a? Sketch a figure to show a, b, and B.

25 Complete the Gram-Schmidt process in Problem 24 by computing $q_1 = a/\|a\|$ and $q_2 = B/\|B\|$ and factoring into QR:

$$\begin{bmatrix}1 & 4\\ 1 & 0\end{bmatrix} = \begin{bmatrix}q_1 & q_2\end{bmatrix}\begin{bmatrix}\|a\| & ?\\ 0 & \|B\|\end{bmatrix}.$$

26 (MATLAB) Factor $[Q, R] = \mathsf{qr}(A)$ for $A = \mathsf{eye}(4) - \mathsf{diag}([1\ \ 1\ \ 1], -1)$. Can you renormalize the orthogonal columns of Q to get nice integer components?

27 For $n = 3$ and $n = 4$, find the QR factors of the special tridiagonal matrices T and K and B from $\mathsf{qr}(T)$ and $\mathsf{qr}(K)$ and $\mathsf{qr}(B)$. Can you see a pattern?

28 What condition number do you compute for K_9 and T_9, using the eig command to find $\lambda_{\mathsf{max}}/\lambda_{\mathsf{min}}$? Compare with the estimate in equation (19).

29 For the matrix A in Example 4, how do you know that $50 < \lambda_{\mathsf{max}}(A^{\mathrm{T}}A) < 51$?

$$A = \begin{bmatrix}1 & 7\\ 0 & 1\end{bmatrix} \qquad A^{\mathrm{T}}A = \begin{bmatrix}1 & 7\\ 7 & 50\end{bmatrix}$$

30 Apply $[U, \mathsf{sigma}, V] = \mathsf{svd}(\mathsf{DIFF})$ to the 3 by 2 backward difference matrix $\mathsf{DIFF} = [1\ 0; -1\ 1; 0\ \ -1]$. Reverse signs in u_1, u_2, v_1, v_2 to recognize them as the normalized cosine and sine vectors in Example 5 with $h = \pi/3$. Which column vector is in the nullspace of $(\mathsf{DIFF})^{\mathrm{T}}$?

31 The **Frobenius norm** $\|A\|_F^2 = \sum\sum |a_{ij}|^2$ treats A as a long vector. Verify that

$$\|I\|_F = \sqrt{n} \qquad\qquad \|A + B\|_F \le \|A\|_F + \|B\|_F$$
$$\|AB\|_F \le \|A\|_F\,\|B\|_F \qquad\qquad \|A\|_F^2 = \mathrm{trace}(A^{\mathrm{T}}A)\,.$$

32 (Recommended) Using $\mathsf{pinv}(A)$ to find the pseudoinverse A^+ of the 4 by 5 forward difference A. Multiply $AA^+ = I$ and $A^+A \ne I$. Predict A^+ when A is n by $n + 1$.

1.8 BEST BASIS FROM THE SVD

This optional section could have been called "*SVD for PCA and MOR and POD.*" I don't know if you would approve of such a title. But after explaining eigenvalues and singular values, I want to show one of the ways they are used.

The eigen*vectors* of $A^{\mathrm{T}}A$ and AA^{T} are the right and left singular vectors of A. The nonzero (and equal) eigen*values* of $A^{\mathrm{T}}A$ and AA^{T} are the squares of the singular values $\sigma_i(A)$. The eigenvectors give orthonormal bases $v_1, \ldots, v_n$ and $u_1, \ldots, u_m$ in V and U. The numbers $\lambda_i(A^{\mathrm{T}}A) = \lambda_i(AA^{\mathrm{T}}) = \sigma_i^2(A)$ put those basis vectors in order of importance. Those ordered bases are highly valuable in applications:

Orthonormal bases	$A^{\mathrm{T}}Av_i = \lambda_i v_i$	$AA^{\mathrm{T}}u_i = \lambda_i u_i$	$Av_i = \sigma_i u_i$	(1)
$\boldsymbol{V^{\mathrm{T}}V = I \quad U^{\mathrm{T}}U = I}$	$A^{\mathrm{T}}A = V\Lambda V^{\mathrm{T}}$	$AA^{\mathrm{T}} = U\Lambda U^{\mathrm{T}}$	$AV = U\Sigma$	(2)

All five matrices $A, A^{\mathrm{T}}A, AA^{\mathrm{T}}, \Lambda$, and Σ have the same rank r. The last four share r positive eigenvalues $\lambda_i = \sigma_i^2$. If A is m by n, $A^{\mathrm{T}}A$ has size n and AA^{T} has size m. Then $A^{\mathrm{T}}A$ has $n-r$ zero eigenvalues and AA^{T} has $m-r$. Those zeros produce $n-r$ eigenvectors v in the nullspace of A ($\lambda = 0$), and $m-r$ u's in the nullspace of A^{T}.

Example 1 Often A is a tall thin matrix ($m > n$) with independent columns, so $r = n$:

$$A = \begin{bmatrix} 1 & 0 \\ -1 & 1 \\ 0 & -1 \end{bmatrix} \qquad A^{\mathrm{T}}A = \begin{bmatrix} 2 & -1 \\ -1 & 2 \end{bmatrix} \qquad AA^{\mathrm{T}} = \begin{bmatrix} 1 & -1 & 0 \\ -1 & 2 & -1 \\ 0 & -1 & 1 \end{bmatrix} \tag{3}$$

The matrix AA^{T} has size $m = 3$ and rank $r = 2$. The unit vector $u_3 = (1, 1, 1)/\sqrt{3}$ is in its nullspace. The point of this section is that the v's and u's are good bases for the column spaces. For a first difference matrix like A, those bases are sensational:

$v_1, \ldots, v_n =$ **discrete sines** $\quad u_1, \ldots, u_n =$ **discrete cosines** $\quad u_{n+1} = (\mathbf{1}, \ldots, \mathbf{1})/\sqrt{n}$

The extra cosine is $\cos 0$ (and $\sin 0$ is useless). The key property $\boldsymbol{Av_i = \sigma_i u_i}$ says that first differences of discrete sines are cosines. The reverse property $A^{\mathrm{T}}u_i = \sigma_i v_i$ says that first differences of discrete cosines are *minus* discrete sines. A^{T} has -1's above the diagonal and first differences are antisymmetric.

The orthogonality $V^{\mathrm{T}}V = I$ of discrete sine vectors leads to the Discrete Sine Transform. $U^{\mathrm{T}}U = I$ leads to the Discrete Cosine Transform. But this (*very optional*) section is about **data matrices**, not difference matrices.

Start by measuring m properties (m features) of n samples. The measurements could be grades in m courses, for n students. The goal is to find meaning in those mn numbers. In the absurd case when $A^{\mathrm{T}}A$ has only zeros off the diagonal after shifting to zero mean, the course grades are independent.

The success of the SVD is to find **combinations of courses** and **combinations of students** that are independent. In matrix language, $A = U\Sigma V^{\mathrm{T}}$ shows the right combinations in U and V to produce the diagonal matrix Σ.

Correlation Matrices $A^{\mathrm{T}}A$ and AA^{T}

In typical examples, A is a *matrix of measurement data*. Each of the n samples gives a column a_j of the data matrix A. Each of the m properties corresponds to a row. The n^2 dot products $a_i^{\mathrm{T}}a_j$ indicate "correlations" or "covariances" between samples:

Sample correlation matrix $\quad A^{\mathrm{T}}A \quad \text{has entries} \quad a_i^{\mathrm{T}}a_j = \text{rows times columns.} \quad (4)$

In the opposite direction, AA^{T} indicates correlations between properties (features):

Property correlation matrix
$$AA^{\mathrm{T}} = \sum_{j=1}^{n} a_j a_j^{\mathrm{T}} = \text{columns times rows.} \qquad (5)$$

Some applications focus on $A^{\mathrm{T}}A$ and others on AA^{T}. Some applications have $m > n$ and others have $m < n$. Common sense suggests that we should solve the smaller eigenvalue problem. But one more thought reveals that a good svd code will solve both eigenvalue problems at once. We get both sets of eigenvectors, v's and u's. And those right and left singular vectors have the remarkable property $Av_i = \sigma_i u_i$.

The Golub-Welsch algorithm begins by reducing A to *bidiagonal form* $B = U_1^{\mathrm{T}}AV_1$. The orthogonal U_1 and V_1 come directly from rotations to produce zeros in B (no eigenvalue problems). Then U_2 and V_2 find the singular values of B and the eigenvalues of $B^{\mathrm{T}}B$ (the same σ_i and λ_i). MATLAB has no special commands for that bidiagonal svd and tridiagonal eig, so Persson unwrapped the LAPACK subroutines.

The codes bidsvd and trideig on math.mit.edu/~persson allow you to skip U_1 and V_1 when A is already bidiagonal and $A^{\mathrm{T}}A$ is already tridiagonal (as in 1D problems).

Principal Component Analysis

The goal of principal component analysis (**PCA**) is to identify the most important properties revealed by the measurements in A. Those will be *combinations* of the original properties. Often the weights in the combination are called **loadings** and all are nonzero. We will always assume, by shifting if necessary, that this data has *mean value zero*. The variance is the critical indicator of importance, large or small, and the n samples in the data give an m by m covariance matrix:

Covariance matrix
$$\Sigma_n = \frac{1}{n-1}\left(a_1 a_1^{\mathrm{T}} + \cdots + a_n a_n^{\mathrm{T}}\right) = \frac{1}{n-1} AA^{\mathrm{T}}. \qquad (6)$$

This approximates the true covariance matrix Σ for the whole population (we are seeing only n samples). The off-diagonal entries show correlations between properties. Section 2.8 will give a short introduction to covariance matrices in statistics, which correspond perfectly to resistances in electric circuits and elasticities of springs.

Here I just mention that "correlation matrices" are often normalized to have ones on the diagonal. When some course grades are 1 to 5 and others go to 100, that rescaling is needed. But if the units are consistent, the covariance matrix (6) is the best. A statistician explains $n-1$ as the number of degrees of freedom, when one degree has already been used for zero mean.

The eigenvectors $u_1, u_2, \ldots$ of AA^{T} tell us the independent combinations of properties in order of their variance (highest to lowest). The u's are the best basis in property space $\mathbf{R}^m$. The v's are the best basis in sample space $\mathbf{R}^n$. If A is already a covariance matrix, then PCA looks at $\lambda_{\text{max}}(A)$ and its eigenvector.

Orthogonality of the u's makes the combinations independent. The mixture of properties given by u_1 has highest variance $\sigma_1^2/(n-1)$. This is the largest eigenvalue $\lambda/(n-1)$ of the sample covariance matrix $AA^{\mathrm{T}}/(n-1)$. PCA says that the optimal number to measure is $u_1^{\mathrm{T}}a$. The other combinations $u_i^{\mathrm{T}}a$ have lesser importance.

Example 2 Suppose each column of A measures the position x, y, z of a mass moving in a straight line. With exact measurements $a_i = (x_i, y_i, z_i)$, A has rank $r = 1$. After shifting to zero mean (line through origin), the constant ratios of x, y, z are given by the unit vector u_1 (eigenvector of Σ, left singular vector of A, direction cosines of the line). The perpendicular u_2 and u_3 directions show no movement, and the measurements $u_2^{\mathrm{T}}a$ and $u_3^{\mathrm{T}}a$ are zero.

Real measurements include noise. The sample covariances are not exact. The noisy A has full rank $r = 3$, but $\sigma_1 >> \sigma_2$. The data $u_2^{\mathrm{T}}a$ and $u_3^{\mathrm{T}}a$ will not be exactly zero, but the svd still tells us to measure $u_1^{\mathrm{T}}a$. By comparing $\sigma_1^2, \ldots, \sigma_n^2$ we determine how many combinations of properties are revealed by the experiment.

Principal component analysis is a fundamental technique in statistics [99], invented and used long before the SVD made it computationally feasible for large m and n.

Gene Expression Data

In bioinformatics, the SVD determines combinations of genes (***eigengenes***) that are seen together. Applications to drug testing are of enormous importance.

Determining their function is the outstanding problem of genetics. Observing frequency of appearance of mRNA is a first step, and huge quantities of data are now produced by single experiments. *Mass spectrometry* is the primary tool in proteomics, and *DNA microarrays* give the gene expression data. The back cover of this book shows a small fraction of the data that comes from a single sample (one column of A is packed into that 2D Affymetrix chip, measuring tens of thousands of genes).

This is data mining with a difference. Studies of large data sets lead to classifying, with Vector Support Machines, or clustering (Section 2.9), or ranking as in Google. The SVD produces numerical weights based on the data, and it is unsupervised. The extra feature of genetic experiments is the biological science behind them—*we want explanations of the functions of the genes*, not just counts. PCA gives a large dimension reduction for gene microarrays, but it is not the end of the analysis.

In systems biology (and eventually in medical diagnosis), the rows of A correspond to genes and the columns correspond to samples (assays). The n right singular vectors v_j are **eigengenes** (usually $n << m$). Those capture the expression profiles, and the true dimension, that is seen in the n samples.

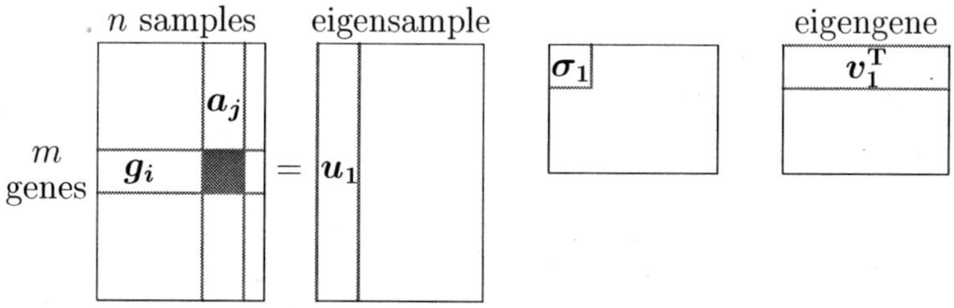

Figure 1.20: The SVD of a gene expression matrix. Its largest rank-1 piece is $\sigma_1 u_1 v_1^{\mathrm{T}}$.

Important note In fundamental applications throughout science and engineering, the singular values have an extremely useful property. **They drop almost to zero after the first r** (σ_{r+1} is small). Then r is the **effective rank** of the matrix A. The conventional rank of A may be larger, and noisy data leads to full rank.

The SVD and the QR factors from orthogonalization are "rank-revealing." A central idea of high-dimensional statistics (and dynamical systems) is to locate the low-dimensional manifold on which the important action occurs.

This is the century of data, but we try hard to reduce r.

Model Order Reduction

The goal of model order reduction (MOR) is to identify the components in a *dynamic* problem that are most important to follow. The dynamics are given by differential equations. Some components of the solution may be nearly constant, perhaps nearly zero. Our effort should go into computing the other components, that are varying with the flow. Those will be (a few) combinations of the (many) original components.

The differential equations may come from biology or control theory or physics. When they are nonlinear, we may linearize. When they are linear time-invariant, a Fourier transform moves to the frequency domain. In all cases the goal is *to reduce the order*. A **proper orthogonal decomposition** (**POD**) is based on the SVD:

Start with n snapshots $a_1, \ldots, a_n$ showing the m components of the solution
Find the largest k eigenvalues of $AA^{\mathrm{T}} = \sum a_i a_i^{\mathrm{T}}$. The eigenvectors fill $U_k = [u_1 \ldots u_k]$
The projection P_k that minimizes $\sum \|a_i - P_k a_i\|^2$ is $P_k = U_k U_k^{\mathrm{T}}$.

That projection is picking out the k most important combinations of components.

Again I emphasize that two eigenvalue problems are being solved at once. The eigenvectors u_i of AA^{T} give the projection. The singular values match the variances

σ_i^2 in decreasing order. The **ordering** and the **orthogonality** of the basis are the key contributions of the SVD. Ultimately the goal is to reduce m differential equations to k equations.

The projection P_k acts in sample space. The samples a_i are all over that high-dimensional space. Their projections $P_k a_i$ lie in a much smaller k-dimensional subspace, spanned by $u_1, \ldots, u_k$. The projection is optimal for the n samples a_i :

Minimum variance $$\sum \|a_i - P_k a_i\|^2 = \lambda_{k+1} + \cdots + \lambda_n = \sigma_{k+1}^2 + \cdots + \sigma_n^2 \quad (7)$$

Linear algebra shows that the trace $\sum \|a_i\|^2$, from the sum of diagonal entries of $R = A^{\mathrm{T}}A$, equals the sum of all the eigenvalues σ_i^2 of R. The projection captures the top k eigenvalues, from the combinations that have the greatest variance (the most information). No k-dimensional projection can do better than that.

I need to say that Model Reduction is a much deeper subject when it works on the underlying differential equations. *The real problem is to reduce the model, not just the data.* We applied the SVD to data matrices, with output samples. Better to reduce the problem size first. A key application is to the equations of control theory, with state vector x, control u, and observations y:

State eqn $dx/dt = Ax(t) + Bu(t)$ **Observations** $y(t) = Cx(t) + Du(t)$. (8)

Our data-based approach applied to y. The state-based approach reduces the size of x. The model is smaller, faster, and much cheaper. Its key features are saved.

Control engineering models factories and whole industries. At a different scale, integrated circuits have the same need for model reduction. Section 2.5 introduces the **transfer function** $G(s)$ from input to output. The model-based problem is to reduce the degree of G (often by a **Padé approximation**, described on the cse website). The data-based problem is to reduce the size of the measurement matrix.

Limitations of the SVD

$A = U\Sigma V^{\mathrm{T}}$ produces remarkable basis vectors in the columns of U and V. But they cannot be perfect in every way. Here are two serious limitations on the SVD:

1. *U and V are not at all sparse.* Computing and using them has a significant cost. Very large matrices are expected in computational science, when they reflect "local" behavior. The neighborhood remains small even if the world is large. But orthogonal eigenvectors and singular vectors are not local. *They have small components from everywhere.*

   In processing an image, the SVD is not a top choice for compression. It gives optimal **Karhunen-Loève bases**, but their cost can be high. Good eigenvectors are computed at speeds once thought to be impossible—but local processing of pixel values is faster by the filters of Section 4.4.

The search for good decompositions was advanced by Tucker and Kruskal in mathematical psychology (measuring many attributes). Now statistics and finance regularly see dimensions like 2^{50} or 2^{100}, where the SVD is slow. Sparsity in finance means fewer transaction costs—very small loadings are useless in the applications of PCA.

2. *The SVD is "two-dimensional."* Matrix entries A_{ij} are like function values $a(x,y)$. The SVD splits A into rank one matrices $\sigma u v^{\mathrm{T}}$, like separating $a(x,y)$ into a sum of $b(x)\,c(y)$. Separation of variables is an enormous simplification when it works. But eigenvectors and the SVD have no perfect extension to tensors A_{ijkl} with four indices, or by analogy to $a(x,y,z,w)$ with four variables.

This chapter is ending with two research problems. The SVD does not even exist for a fourth-order tensor $A_{ijk\ell}$. And so many computations would be faster if the SVD bases in U and V were sparse. You will see that least squares approximations are vitally important, minimizing $\|Au-b\|^2$ for Au in a low-dimensional subspace. (This may be the number one application of linear algebra.) More and more often, u is made sparse by including a penalty term $\alpha(|u_1|+\cdots+|u_n|)$ in the minimization.

The search is on for ***sparse-fast-accurate*** approximations to the SVD.

A request No textbook can be a newspaper of fast-breaking ideas. The cse website is far better able to fill that need. Readers are invited to help in identifying important links. As I write these words, a SIAM Review article on Sparse PCA has just arrived (49:434–448, 2007). It adapts the ℓ^1 methods of Sections 4.7 and 8.6 to variance maximization. New techniques are appearing throughout computational science and engineering—this subject is alive!

When chapters end with open problems, I hope the cse page can go farther and faster than the book.

CHAPTER 2

A FRAMEWORK FOR APPLIED MATHEMATICS

2.1 EQUILIBRIUM AND THE STIFFNESS MATRIX

This chapter highlights a basic structure of this book. You will see it in a wide range of applications. This framework appears over and over again in applied mathematics (differential equations as well as matrix equations). *I look for it every time I meet a new problem.* There are generally three equations in the framework:

Three steps $e = Au$ and $w = Ce$ and $f = A^{\mathrm{T}}w$. (1)

The primary unknown is u, the force from outside is f. When we combine those three equations they give $f = A^{\mathrm{T}}w = A^{\mathrm{T}}Ce = A^{\mathrm{T}}CAu$. In matrix language, the triple product $K = A^{\mathrm{T}}CA$ connects the output u directly to the input f. As soon as these matrices A and C are identified, a new application fits into the framework.

This matrix $K = A^{\mathrm{T}}CA$ is associated with *equilibrium problems.* The system is in steady state—time is not a factor. Forces f produce movements u. *The vector of forces equals K times the vector u of displacements.* K is the **stiffness matrix** in mechanics and it reappears all over applied mathematics.

The modeling problem is to find $K = A^{\mathrm{T}}CA$. The computing problem is to solve $Ku = f$. This framework will be illustrated first in three specific examples:

1. ***A line of springs*** (the springs can be stretched or compressed): Section 2.1
3. ***Best solution of $Au = b$*** (least squares regression in statistics): Section 2.3
4. ***A network*** with flows on the edges (driven by potential differences): Section 2.4

If your own field of application is different from those three, no surprise. These are an excellent starting point; they are not the end. We will discuss other applications (chemical engineering, fluid flow, economics, control theory, and many more) as we go. We also move to *dynamical problems*—oscillation, diffusion, changing response to changing inputs. The goal is to understand A and C and the product $K = A^{\mathrm{T}}CA$.

Dynamics and Nonlinearity

$Ku = f$ is the framework of linear equilibrium. It will be extended (in fact it must be extended) in two directions. One is to escape from linearity. The other is to escape from equilibrium. The material may have a **nonlinear response**—current is not exactly proportional to voltage, and displacement is not exactly proportional to force. Ohm's Law and Hooke's Law are close approximations to the truth, but not perfect. Nonlinearity starts to be important when voltages and forces are large. We will show by example how to account for nonlinearity.

The other major extension is to **time-dependent** problems. The equations can stay linear but they become **dynamic** (not static). In our three examples, the external forces and the incoming measurements and the applied voltages can change with time. Then we find that

2. The springs are oscillating. They obey Newton's law $F = ma$: Section 2.2

5. The circuit has inductors and capacitors and alternating current: Section 2.5

7. New measurements require us to update the statistics: Section 2.8

The steady state matrix equation is $Ku = f$. For dynamic problems this becomes a differential equation in time, either first-order or second-order:

$$\frac{du}{dt} = Ku - f \qquad \text{or} \qquad M\frac{d^2u}{dt^2} + Ku = f(t)\,. \tag{2}$$

Nonlinearity and time-dependence push us to the frontiers of computational science. Chapter 3 goes forward to continuum models, where the unknown becomes a function $u(x,y)$ or $u(x,y,t)$. Our system changes to a *partial differential equation* (Ku may involve u_{xx} or u_{yy}). The computer is really stretched by nonlinear time-dependent partial differential equations. But the framework doesn't change.

A Line of Springs

Figure 2.1 shows three masses m_1, m_2, m_3 connected by a line of springs. In one case there are four springs, with top and bottom fixed. The second example has only three springs; it is fixed at the top, and the lowest mass hangs freely. The two problems are **fixed-fixed** and **fixed-free**. We want the equations for the important unknowns—the displacements of the masses and the tension in the springs:

$$\begin{aligned} \mathbf{u} &= (u_1, u_2, u_3) = \textbf{displacements of the masses} \\ \mathbf{w} &= (w_1, w_2, w_3, w_4) \;\text{ or }\; (w_1, w_2, w_3) = \textbf{tension in the springs}\,. \end{aligned}$$

For the masses, displacement is positive downwards. For the springs, tension is positive and compression is negative ($w_i < 0$). In tension, the spring is stretched and pulls the masses inward. In compression, the masses are pushed outward.

We need the elastic properties (the spring constants c_i) of each spring. This is a key change from Chapter 1! There K_n and T_n had "spring constants = 1."

Here c_i connects the stretching e_i to the force w_i. **Hooke's Law is $\boldsymbol{w_i = c_i e_i}$**, four constants c_1, c_2, c_3, c_4 for four springs. *Force* $=$ (*spring constant*)(*elongation*).

Our job is to link these one-spring equations into a vector equation $f = Ku$ for the whole system. The vector f is the force from outside. Gravity pulls down on each mass and produces $f = (m_1 g, m_2 g, m_3 g)$. At the earth's surface g is about 32 feet/ sec^2 or 9.8 meters/ sec^2, and multiplied by mass this gives force.

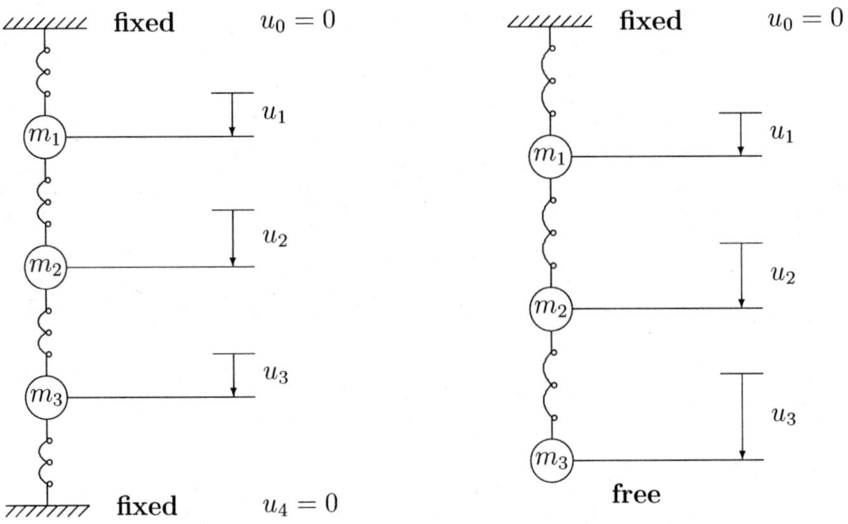

Figure 2.1: Fixed-fixed springs with $u_4 = 0$. Fixed-free with $w_4 = 0$.

Our real problem is the stiffness matrix K, connecting u to f. Two different structures, fixed-fixed and fixed-free, produce two different K's.

The best way to create K is in **three steps**, not one. Here comes the dominating framework of this chapter, seen first for a line of springs. Instead of connecting the displacements u directly to the forces f, it is much better to connect each vector to the next vector in the following list:

$$
\begin{array}{lcl}
\mathrm{u} & = & \textbf{Displacements} \text{ of } n \text{ masses} = (u_1, \cdots, u_n) \\
\mathrm{e} & = & \textbf{Elongations} \text{ of } m \text{ springs} = (e_1, \cdots, e_m) \\
\mathrm{w} & = & \textbf{Internal forces} \text{ in } m \text{ springs} = (w_1, \cdots, w_m) \\
\mathrm{f} & = & \textbf{External forces} \text{ on } n \text{ masses} = (f_1, \cdots, f_n)
\end{array}
$$

The framework that connects **u** to **e** to **w** to **f** looks like this:

Displacement **Elongation** **Internal force** **External force**	$\boxed{\mathrm{u}}$ $\quad$ $\boxed{\mathrm{f}}$ $A\downarrow$ $\quad$ $\uparrow A^{\mathrm{T}}$ $\boxed{\mathrm{e}} \xrightarrow{C} \boxed{\mathrm{w}}$	$\mathbf{e} = A\mathbf{u}$ $\mathbf{w} = C\mathbf{e}$ $\mathbf{f} = A^{\mathrm{T}}\mathbf{w}$	A is m by n C is m by m A^{T} is n by m

We will write down the matrices A and C and A^{T} for the two examples, first with fixed ends and then with the lower end free. Forgive the simplicity of these matrices, it is their form that is so important.

STEP 1: The *elongation* e is the stretching—how far the springs are extended. Originally there is no displacement and no stretching—the system is on a table. When it becomes vertical and upright, gravity acts. The masses fall by u_1, u_2, u_3. If mass 2 drops by u_2 and mass 1 drops by u_1, **the spring stretches by** $\boldsymbol{u_2 - u_1}$**:**

First spring	$e_1 = u_1$	(the top is fixed so $u_0 = 0$)
Second spring	$e_2 = u_2 - u_1$	(as in the figure)
Third spring	$e_3 = u_3 - u_2$	(as in the figure)
Fourth spring	$e_4 = \quad - u_3$	(the bottom is fixed so $u_4 = 0$)

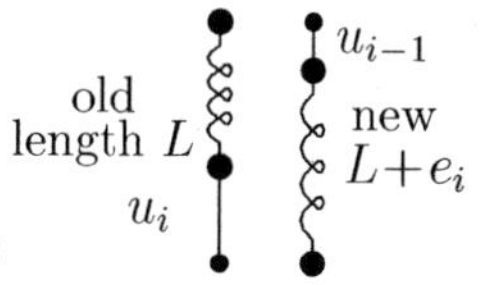

The lower end of spring i moves down by u_i. The upper end moves down by u_{i-1}. If both ends move the same distance, that spring is not stretched: $u_i = u_{i-1}$ and $e_i = 0$. Notice that the equation $\boldsymbol{e_i = u_i - u_{i-1}}$ (*the difference in displacements*) applies also at the ends, when we fix the top and bottom by $u_0 = 0$ and $u_4 = 0$.

The matrix A in those four equations is a 4 by 3 *difference matrix*. We write those four differences $u_i - u_{i-1}$ as a matrix A times a vector u. Our equation is $e = Au$:

Stretching
$\boldsymbol{e = Au}$

$$\begin{bmatrix} e_1 \\ e_2 \\ e_3 \\ e_4 \end{bmatrix} = \begin{bmatrix} 1 & 0 & 0 \\ -1 & 1 & 0 \\ 0 & -1 & 1 \\ 0 & 0 & -1 \end{bmatrix} \begin{bmatrix} u_1 \\ u_2 \\ u_3 \end{bmatrix} = \begin{bmatrix} \boldsymbol{u_1} - 0 \\ \boldsymbol{u_2 - u_1} \\ \boldsymbol{u_3 - u_2} \\ 0 - \boldsymbol{u_3} \end{bmatrix}. \tag{3}$$

In a continuous problem, the differences $e = Au$ will become $e = du/dx$. The matrix becomes a derivative! We get a differential equation instead of a matrix equation.

STEP 2: The physical equation $w = Ce$ connects the spring elongations e with the spring tensions w. *This is Hooke's Law* $w_i = c_i e_i$ *for each separate spring.* It is the "constitutive law" that depends on the material in the spring and its shape. A soft thin spring has small c, so a moderate force w can produce a large elongation e. Note again that Hooke's law is *linear*. This is nearly exact for real springs over a wide range, before the spring is overstretched and the material becomes plastic.

Since each spring has its own law, the matrix in $\boldsymbol{w = Ce}$ is a diagonal matrix C:

Hooke's Law
$\boldsymbol{w = Ce}$

$$\begin{aligned} w_1 &= c_1 e_1 \\ w_2 &= c_2 e_2 \\ w_3 &= c_3 e_3 \\ w_4 &= c_4 e_4 \end{aligned} \quad \text{is} \quad \begin{bmatrix} w_1 \\ w_2 \\ w_3 \\ w_4 \end{bmatrix} = \begin{bmatrix} \boldsymbol{c_1} & & & \\ & \boldsymbol{c_2} & & \\ & & \boldsymbol{c_3} & \\ & & & \boldsymbol{c_4} \end{bmatrix} \begin{bmatrix} e_1 \\ e_2 \\ e_3 \\ e_4 \end{bmatrix} = Ce. \tag{4}$$

Combining $e = Au$ with $w = Ce$, we now know the relation $w = CAu$ between internal spring forces w and mass displacements u.

STEP 3: Finally comes the "**balance equation.**" The internal forces w from the springs must balance the external forces f on the masses. Each mass is in equilibrium, pulled up by a spring force w_j and down by w_{j+1} plus the gravitational force f_j. Thus $w_j = w_{j+1} + f_j$ or $\boldsymbol{f_j = w_j - w_{j+1}}$:

Balance of forces $\boldsymbol{A^T w = f}$

$$\begin{aligned} f_1 &= w_1 - w_2 \\ f_2 &= w_2 - w_3 \\ f_3 &= w_3 - w_4 \end{aligned} \quad \text{and} \quad \begin{bmatrix} f_1 \\ f_2 \\ f_3 \end{bmatrix} = \begin{bmatrix} 1 & -1 & 0 & 0 \\ 0 & 1 & -1 & 0 \\ 0 & 0 & 1 & -1 \end{bmatrix} \begin{bmatrix} w_1 \\ w_2 \\ w_3 \\ w_4 \end{bmatrix}. \tag{5}$$

That matrix is A^T !! *The equation for balance of forces is* $f = A^T w$. Nature transposes the rows and columns of the $e - u$ matrix to produce the $f - w$ matrix. This is the beauty of the framework, that A^T appears along with A.

A proper author would never use two exclamation marks—I apologize. One of those marks is to call attention to the wonderful appearance of A^T (which makes K a symmetric matrix). The other is to emphasize the presence of a **balance equation**. To understand equations you have to know what to look for, and "balance" or "conservation" or "continuity" appears somehow in every model. The three equations combine into $Ku = f$, where $K = A^T CA$ is n by n:

$$\begin{matrix} m \text{ by } n \\ m \text{ by } m \\ n \text{ by } m \end{matrix} \quad \left\{ \begin{aligned} \mathbf{e} &= A\mathbf{u} \\ \mathbf{w} &= C\mathbf{e} \\ \mathbf{f} &= A^T\mathbf{w} \end{aligned} \right\} \quad \text{combine into} \quad A^T CA\mathbf{u} = \mathbf{f}. \tag{6}$$

In the language of elasticity, $e = Au$ is the **kinematic** equation (for displacement). The force balance $f = A^T w$ is the **static** equation (for equilibrium). They are connected by the **constitutive** law $w = Ce$ (from the material properties).

Stiffness Matrix and Solution

All large finite element programs spend major effort on assembling the stiffness matrix $K = A^T CA$ from smaller pieces. We do it for four springs by matrix multiplication of A^T times CA. Here is the **fixed-fixed** stiffness matrix K:

$$K = \begin{bmatrix} 1 & -1 & 0 & 0 \\ 0 & 1 & -1 & 0 \\ 0 & 0 & 1 & -1 \end{bmatrix} \begin{bmatrix} c_1 & 0 & 0 \\ -c_2 & c_2 & 0 \\ 0 & -c_3 & c_3 \\ 0 & 0 & -c_4 \end{bmatrix} = \begin{bmatrix} \mathbf{c_1 + c_2} & \mathbf{-c_2} & \mathbf{0} \\ \mathbf{-c_2} & \mathbf{c_2 + c_3} & \mathbf{-c_3} \\ \mathbf{0} & \mathbf{-c_3} & \mathbf{c_3 + c_4} \end{bmatrix} \tag{7}$$

Important note: Suppose all springs are identical with $c_1 = c_2 = c_3 = c_4 = 1$. Then C is the identity matrix: $C = I$. The stiffness matrix reduces to $K = A^T A$. By substituting all $c_i = 1$, it becomes the special matrix K_3 of Chapter 1.

Stiffness matrix with $C = I$

$$K_3 = A^{\mathrm{T}}A = \begin{bmatrix} 2 & -1 & 0 \\ -1 & 2 & -1 \\ 0 & -1 & 2 \end{bmatrix}.$$

Four identical springs, fixed at both ends, have produced our favorite matrix. A line of $n+1$ identical springs would produce K_n. The matrix is tridiagonal because each spring connects only to its two neighbors. It has constant diagonals because all springs are identical. K_n is symmetric positive definite because Nature insists on that property (by producing A and A^{T}).

$K_3 = A^{\mathrm{T}}A$ is very different from $K_3 = LL^{\mathrm{T}}$. The matrix A from four springs is 4 by 3. The matrix L from elimination is square. K is assembled from $A^{\mathrm{T}}A$, and then it is broken up into LL^{T}. One step is applied mathematics, the other is computational mathematics. Each matrix K_n is built from rectangular matrices and factored into square matrices.

May I list some properties of $K = A^{\mathrm{T}}CA$? You know almost all of them:

1. K is tridiagonal, because mass 3 is not connected to mass 1.

2. K is symmetric, because C is symmetric (and A^{T} appears with A).

3. K is positive definite, because A has **independent columns**.

4. K^{-1} is a full matrix with **all positive entries**.

That last property leads to an important fact about $u = K^{-1}f$: *If all forces act downwards* ($f_j > 0$) *then all displacements are downwards* ($u_j > 0$). Notice well that "positiveness" of a matrix is different from "positive definiteness." Here K is not positive (it has -1's) while both matrices K and K^{-1} are positive definite.

Example 1 Suppose all $c_i = c$ and $m_j = m$. Find the displacements u and forces w.

All springs are the same and all masses are the same. But all displacements and elongations and spring forces will *not* be the same. And the inverse matrix K^{-1} includes the factor $\frac{1}{c}$ because $K = A^{\mathrm{T}}CA$ includes c:

Displacements

$$u = K^{-1}f = \frac{1}{4c}\begin{bmatrix} 3 & 2 & 1 \\ 2 & 4 & 2 \\ 1 & 2 & 3 \end{bmatrix}\begin{bmatrix} mg \\ mg \\ mg \end{bmatrix} = \frac{mg}{c}\begin{bmatrix} 1.5 \\ 2.0 \\ 1.5 \end{bmatrix}$$

The displacement u_2, for the mass in the middle, is greater than u_1 and u_3. The units are correct: the force mg divided by force per unit length c gives a length u. The elongations of the springs are $e = Au$, to compute next.

Elongations $$e = Au = \begin{bmatrix} 1 & 0 & 0 \\ -1 & 1 & 0 \\ 0 & -1 & 1 \\ 0 & 0 & -1 \end{bmatrix} \frac{mg}{c} \begin{bmatrix} 1.5 \\ 2.0 \\ 1.5 \end{bmatrix} = \frac{mg}{c} \begin{bmatrix} 1.5 \\ 0.5 \\ -0.5 \\ -1.5 \end{bmatrix}.$$

Those elongations add to zero because the ends of the line are fixed. The sum $u_1 + (u_2 - u_1) + (u_3 - u_2) + (-u_3)$ is certainly zero. For each spring force w Hooke's Law just multiplies e by c. So w_1, w_2, w_3, w_4 are $\frac{3}{2}mg$, $\frac{1}{2}mg$, $-\frac{1}{2}mg$, $-\frac{3}{2}mg$. The upper two springs are stretched, the lower two springs are compressed.

Notice how u, e, w are computed in that order. We assembled $K = A^{\mathrm{T}}CA$ from rectangular matrices. To find $u = K^{-1}f$, we work with the whole matrix and not its three pieces. The rectangular matrices A and A^{T} do not have (two-sided) inverses.

Warning: *Normally you cannot write* $K^{-1} = A^{-1}C^{-1}(A^{\mathrm{T}})^{-1}$.

The matrices are mixed together by the triple product $A^{\mathrm{T}}CA$, and they cannot easily be untangled. In general, $A^{\mathrm{T}}w = f$ has many solutions. And four equations $Au = e$ would usually have no solution with three unknowns u. But $A^{\mathrm{T}}CA$ gives the correct solution to all three equations in the framework. Only when $m = n$ and the matrices are square can we go from $w = (A^{\mathrm{T}})^{-1}f$ to $e = C^{-1}w$ to $u = A^{-1}e$. We will see that now.

Fixed End and Free End

Remove the fourth spring. All matrices become 3 by 3. The pattern does not change! The matrix A loses its fourth row (there is no e_4). Then A^{T} loses its fourth column (there is no w_4). The stiffness matrix becomes a product of square matrices:

$$A^{\mathrm{T}}CA = \begin{bmatrix} 1 & -1 & 0 \\ 0 & 1 & -1 \\ 0 & 0 & 1 \end{bmatrix} \begin{bmatrix} c_1 & & \\ & c_2 & \\ & & c_3 \end{bmatrix} \begin{bmatrix} 1 & 0 & 0 \\ -1 & 1 & 0 \\ 0 & -1 & 1 \end{bmatrix}.$$

The missing column and row both multiplied the missing c_4. So the quickest way to find the new $A^{\mathrm{T}}CA$ is to set $c_4 = 0$ in the old stiffness matrix:

FIXED
FREE

$$A^{\mathrm{T}}CA = \begin{bmatrix} \boldsymbol{c_1 + c_2} & \boldsymbol{-c_2} & \mathbf{0} \\ \boldsymbol{-c_2} & \boldsymbol{c_2 + c_3} & \boldsymbol{-c_3} \\ \mathbf{0} & \boldsymbol{-c_3} & \boldsymbol{c_3} \end{bmatrix}. \tag{8}$$

You recognize this matrix in the standard case when $c_1 = c_2 = c_3 = 1$. It is the familiar -1, 2, -1 tridiagonal matrix, except the last entry is $c_3 = 1$ instead of $c_3 + c_4 = 2$. Compared with T_3 in Chapter 1, the ends are reversed to give the **hanging matrix** H_3. This corresponds to a second difference matrix with $u_0 = 0$ at one end but $u_4 = u_3$ at the other end. The spring at the bottom is free.

Example 2 All $c_i = c$ and all $m_j = m$ in the fixed-free hanging line of springs. Then

$$A^{\mathrm{T}}CA = c\begin{bmatrix} 2 & -1 & 0 \\ -1 & 2 & -1 \\ 0 & -1 & 1 \end{bmatrix} \quad \text{and} \quad (A^{\mathrm{T}}CA)^{-1} = \frac{1}{c}\begin{bmatrix} 1 & 1 & 1 \\ 1 & 2 & 2 \\ 1 & 2 & 3 \end{bmatrix}.$$

The displacements $u = K^{-1}f$ change from the fixed-fixed example because K has changed:

Displacements
$$u = (A^{\mathrm{T}}CA)^{-1}f = \frac{1}{c}\begin{bmatrix} 1 & 1 & 1 \\ 1 & 2 & 2 \\ 1 & 2 & 3 \end{bmatrix}\begin{bmatrix} mg \\ mg \\ mg \end{bmatrix} = \frac{mg}{c}\begin{bmatrix} \mathbf{3} \\ \mathbf{5} \\ \mathbf{6} \end{bmatrix}.$$

In this fixed-free case, those displacements $3, 5, 6$ are greater than $1.5, 2.0, 1.5$. The number 3 appears in the first displacement u_1 because all three masses are pulling the first spring down. The next mass has an additional displacement $(3 + 2 = 5)$ from the two masses below it. The third mass drops even more $(3 + 2 + 1 = 6)$. The elongations $e = Au$ in the three springs display those numbers 3, 2, 1:

Elongations
$$e = \begin{bmatrix} 1 & 0 & 0 \\ -1 & 1 & 0 \\ 0 & -1 & 1 \end{bmatrix}\frac{mg}{c}\begin{bmatrix} 3 \\ 5 \\ 6 \end{bmatrix} = \frac{mg}{c}\begin{bmatrix} \mathbf{3} \\ \mathbf{2} \\ \mathbf{1} \end{bmatrix}.$$

Multiplying by c, the forces in the three springs are $w_1 = 3mg$ and $w_2 = 2mg$ and $w_3 = mg$. The first spring has three masses below it, the second spring has two, the third spring has one. All springs are now stretched.

The special point of a square matrix A is that those internal forces w can be found directly from the external forces f. The balance equation $A^{\mathrm{T}}w = f$ determines w immediately and uniquely, because $m = n$ and A^{T} is square and invertible:

Spring forces
$$w = (A^{\mathrm{T}})^{-1}f \text{ is } \begin{bmatrix} 1 & 1 & 1 \\ 0 & 1 & 1 \\ 0 & 0 & 1 \end{bmatrix}\begin{bmatrix} mg \\ mg \\ mg \end{bmatrix} = \begin{bmatrix} \mathbf{3}mg \\ \mathbf{2}mg \\ \mathbf{1}mg \end{bmatrix} \quad \begin{matrix} \text{3 masses below} \\ \text{2 masses below} \\ \text{1 mass: free end} \end{matrix}$$

Then e comes from $C^{-1}w$ and u comes from $A^{-1}e$. In this "*determinate*" case $m = n$, we are allowed to write $(A^{\mathrm{T}}CA)^{-1} = A^{-1}C^{-1}(A^{\mathrm{T}})^{-1}$.

Remark 1 When the displacement at the top is fixed by $u_0 = 0$, it requires a force to keep it that way. This is an external *reaction force* f_0, holding up the line of springs. This reaction force is not given in advance. It is part of the output, from force balance at the top. The first spring is pulling down with internal force $w_1 = 3mg$. The reaction $f_0 = -3mg$ pulls upward to balance it. A structural engineer needs to know the reaction forces, to be sure the support will hold and the structure won't collapse.

Example 3 A **FREE-FREE** line of springs has no supports. This means trouble in A and K (spring 1 is gone). The matrix A is 2 by 3, short and wide. Here is $e = Au$:

$$\textbf{Unstable} \qquad \begin{bmatrix} e_2 \\ e_3 \end{bmatrix} = \begin{bmatrix} u_2 - u_1 \\ u_3 - u_2 \end{bmatrix} = \begin{bmatrix} -1 & 1 & 0 \\ 0 & -1 & 1 \end{bmatrix} \begin{bmatrix} u_1 \\ u_2 \\ u_3 \end{bmatrix}. \tag{9}$$

Now there is a nonzero solution to $Au = 0$. **The masses can move with no stretching of the springs**. The whole line can shift by $u = (1, 1, 1)$ and this still leaves $e = (0, 0)$. The columns of A are *dependent* and the vector $(1, 1, 1)$ is in the nullspace:

$$\textbf{Rigid motion } \boldsymbol{u} = \begin{bmatrix} 1 \\ 1 \\ 1 \end{bmatrix} \qquad Au = \begin{bmatrix} -1 & 1 & 0 \\ 0 & -1 & 1 \end{bmatrix} \begin{bmatrix} 1 \\ 1 \\ 1 \end{bmatrix} = \begin{bmatrix} 0 \\ 0 \end{bmatrix} = e\,. \tag{10}$$

In this case, $A^{\mathrm{T}}CA$ cannot be invertible. K must be **singular**, because $Au = 0$ certainly leads to $\boldsymbol{A^{\mathrm{T}}CAu = 0}$. The stiffness matrix $A^{\mathrm{T}}CA$ is still square and symmetric, but it is only *positive semidefinite* (like B in Chapter 1, with both ends free):

$$\begin{matrix}\textbf{Singular} \\ \boldsymbol{A^{\mathrm{T}}CA}\end{matrix} \quad \begin{bmatrix} -1 & 0 \\ 1 & -1 \\ 0 & 1 \end{bmatrix} \begin{bmatrix} c_2 & \\ & c_3 \end{bmatrix} \begin{bmatrix} -1 & 1 & 0 \\ 0 & -1 & 1 \end{bmatrix} = \begin{bmatrix} c_2 & -c_2 & 0 \\ -c_2 & c_2 + c_3 & -c_3 \\ 0 & -c_3 & c_3 \end{bmatrix}. \tag{11}$$

The pivots will be c_2 and c_3 and *no third pivot.* Two eigenvalues will be positive but the vector $(1, 1, 1)$ will be an eigenvector for $\lambda = 0$. The matrix is not invertible and we can solve $A^{\mathrm{T}}CAu = f$ only for special vectors f. The external forces have to add to zero, $f_1 + f_2 + f_3 = 0$. Otherwise the whole line of springs (with both ends free) will take off like a rocket.

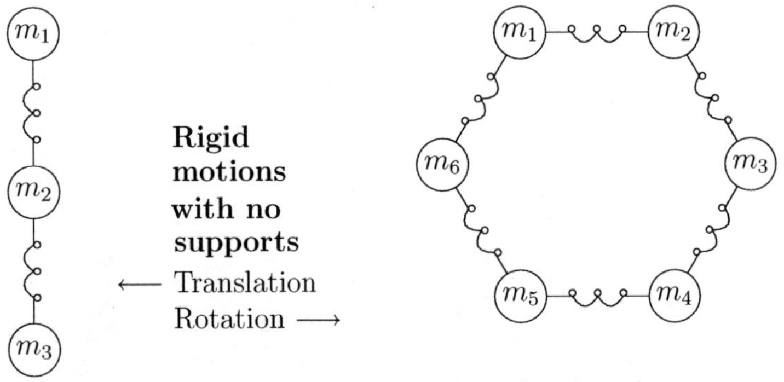

Figure 2.2: The free-free line of springs can move without stretching so $Au = 0$ has nonzero solutions $u = (c, c, c)$. Then $A^{\mathrm{T}}CA$ is singular (also for the "circle" of springs).

Problem 4 pulls the top up and the bottom down, with balancing forces -1 and 1. We can solve $A^{\mathrm{T}}CAu = (-1, 0, 1)$ even though the system is singular. A circle of springs (when K is the circulant matrix C with wrap-around in Chapter 1) is also singular.

Minimum Principles

There are two ways to describe the laws of mechanics, **by equations and also by minimum principles**. One of our goals is to explain the connections. For masses and springs, we started with equations for e, w, and u (to reach $Ku = f$). That was more direct than a minimum principle. But Section 1.6 described the minimization that leads to $Ku = f$, and that was exactly the minimum principle we want:

Minimize the total potential energy P $\quad P(u) = \dfrac{1}{2}u^{\mathrm{T}}Ku - u^{\mathrm{T}}f\,.$

Nature minimizes energy. The springs stretch (or compress) as gravity pulls the masses down. Stretching increases the internal energy $\frac{1}{2}e^{\mathrm{T}}Ce = \frac{1}{2}u^{\mathrm{T}}Ku$. The masses lose potential energy by $f^{\mathrm{T}}u$ (force times displacement is the work done by gravity). Equilibrium comes when a little more displacement Δu gives $\Delta P = 0$, energy gain = energy loss. $\Delta P = 0$ is the "equation of virtual work," where P is smallest.

Rewriting $P(u)$ shows why $u = K^{-1}f$ is minimizing, and $P_{\text{min}} = -\frac{1}{2}f^{\mathrm{T}}K^{-1}f$:

$$P(u) = \frac{1}{2}u^{\mathrm{T}}Ku - u^{\mathrm{T}}f = \frac{1}{2}(u - K^{-1}f)^{\mathrm{T}}K(u - K^{-1}f) - \frac{1}{2}f^{\mathrm{T}}K^{-1}f\,. \qquad (12)$$

At the minimum $u - K^{-1}f = 0$. At first I was surprised that $P_{\text{min}} = -\frac{1}{2}f^{\mathrm{T}}K^{-1}f = -\frac{1}{2}f^{\mathrm{T}}u$ is negative. Now I realize that the masses lost potential energy when they were displaced. (Interesting that exactly half of that loss is stored in the springs as $\frac{1}{2}u^{\mathrm{T}}Ku = \frac{1}{2}u^{\mathrm{T}}f$. The other half must have gone into the Earth, a large mass that moved a very short distance.) In the next section about oscillation, the moving masses exchange potential energy for kinetic energy and back again.

Our point is that minimum principles are an alternative to equations. Sometimes they come first, as in least squares (Section 2.3 will minimize the squared error). Sometimes the equations $Ku = f$ come first. In continuous time, the energy $P(u)$ will be an integral and minimizing leads to a differential equation for u. Always the model problem is the first and best application of ordinary calculus:

$$\text{Minimize } P(u) \text{ by solving } \frac{dP}{du} = 0 \text{ or gradient } (P) = 0 \text{ or first variation } \frac{\delta P}{\delta u} = 0.$$

When $P(u)$ is not quadratic, its derivative is not linear. A **nonlinear stiffness equation $A^{\mathrm{T}}C(Au) = f$ has a function $w = C(e)$, not just a multiplication.**

An Inverted Pendulum

For pleasure, we describe a problem that is much less stable—*because the mass is at the top.* The system stays upright when the mass m is small. As the mass increases, we "bifurcate" into a new stable equilibrium at a tipping angle θ^*. Figure 2.3 shows the old and new positions, with a "rotational spring" adding strength to the thin support. It is like a tomato plant that is staked up but still tips over part way. The mass increases to m, $\theta = 0$ becomes unstable, and we find the new stable angle θ^*.

The equilibrium position comes from force balance; at the same time it minimizes the potential energy. In all the stable problems of this chapter, that energy includes a positive definite quadratic $\frac{1}{2}u^{\mathrm{T}}Ku$. In this very different problem, *loss of stability comes with loss of positive definiteness.* The indicator is $d^2P/d\theta^2$.

The potential energy $P(\theta)$ is partly in the mass at height $L\cos\theta$, and partly in the spring (stretched or compressed). Equilibrium is at the minimum of $P(\theta)$:

Energy $\quad P = \frac{1}{2}c\,\theta^2 + mgL\cos\theta \quad\quad \frac{dP}{d\theta} = c\,\theta - mgL\sin\theta = 0 \quad$ (13)

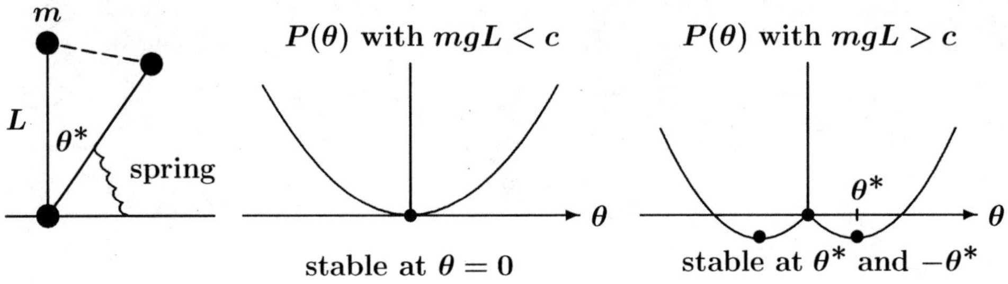

Figure 2.3: The mass tips over to the stable angle θ^* when $mgL > c$.

That equation $dP/d\theta = 0$ always has the solution $\theta = 0$. The first question is whether this vertical solution is stable. Stability is decided by the *second derivative*:

Stability/instability $\quad \dfrac{d^2P}{d\theta^2} = c - mgL\,\cos\theta > 0$ for stability $\quad$ (14)

This is positive at $\theta = 0$ provided $c > mgL$. Then the spring is strong enough to keep the system upright. When m or L increases, we pass the critical bifurcation point $c = mgL$ and the vertical position $\theta = 0$ becomes unstable. The graphs in Figure 2.3 show how $\theta = 0$ changes from a global minimum of $P(\theta)$ to a local *maximum.* The system has to look for a new minimum, which equation (15) finds at $\theta = \theta^*$:

New equilibrium $\quad mgL\,\sin\theta^* = c\,\theta^* \quad\quad P''(\theta^*) > 0 \quad$ (15)

In Figure 2.4, the line $mgL\,\theta/c$ meets the curve $\sin\theta$ at this new equilibrium θ^*. The second figure shows how θ^* moves away from zero (the pendulum begins to tip over) when that ratio $\lambda = mgL/c$ passes $\lambda = 1$. The "pitchfork" in that middle figure is very typical of bifurcations.

The last figure shows a straight line pitchfork, when the equation is $Ax = \lambda x$. For most $\lambda's$ the only solution is $x = 0$. When λ is an eigenvalue of A, nonzero solutions (the eigenvectors) suddenly appear. They disappear when λ passes the eigenvalue, where the inverted pendulum tips further over. Maybe it would be possible to slide a mass up a thin rod, increasing the effective length L. Then watch the rod begin to tip.

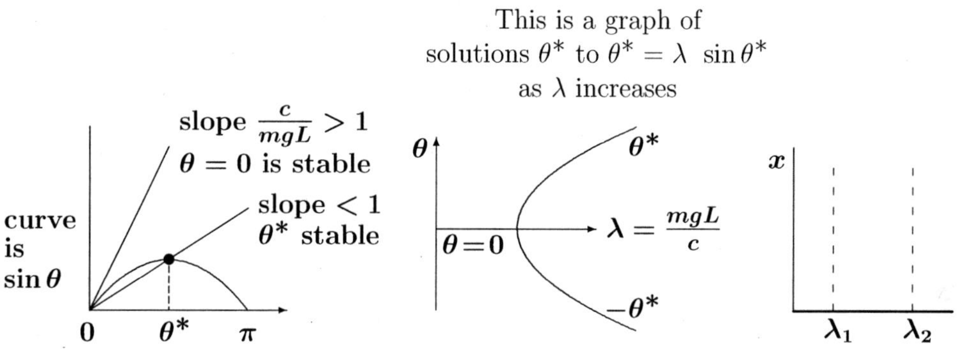

Figure 2.4: Solutions of $\dfrac{dP}{d\theta} = 0$ as mL increases. Bifurcation at λ, as in $Ax = \lambda x$.

Problem Set 2.1

1 The formula for K^{-1} involves *division by the determinant of* K (which must not be zero). In the fixed-fixed case, the 3 by 3 determinant in (7) is

$$\begin{aligned}\det K &= (c_1+c_2)(c_2+c_3)(c_3+c_4) - c_2^2(c_3+c_4) - c_3^2(c_1+c_2)\\ &= c_1c_2c_3 + c_1c_3c_4 + c_1c_2c_4 + c_2c_3c_4\,.\end{aligned}$$

Find the determinant of $A^{\mathrm{T}}CA$ in the 3-spring case (8) with the third mass hanging free (maybe set $c_4 = 0$). Also find the determinant in the free-free case (11).

2 The numerators in K^{-1} are the 2 by 2 subdeterminants of K. These are called the *cofactors* of K, after they are given + and − signs alternately. For the first row of K^{-1} we remove the first column of K, and find the 2 by 2 determinants from columns 2 and 3. Delete row 1 then row 2 then row 3 of K:

$$\text{Cofactors are} \begin{vmatrix} c_2+c_3 & -c_3 \\ -c_3 & c_3+c_4 \end{vmatrix} \text{ and } -\begin{vmatrix} -c_2 & 0 \\ -c_3 & c_3+c_4 \end{vmatrix} \text{ and } \begin{vmatrix} -c_2 & 0 \\ c_2+c_3 & -c_3 \end{vmatrix}.$$

The first row of K^{-1} has $\dfrac{1}{\det K}\begin{bmatrix} c_2c_3+c_2c_4+c_3c_4 & c_2c_3+c_2c_4 & c_2c_3 \end{bmatrix}$

Find row 2 and then 3 of K^{-1} by removing columns 2 and then 3 of K. Compute the 2 by 2 determinants, with rows 1 or 2 or 3 removed. Then alternate signs by $(-1)^{i+j}$. The inverse K^{-1} should be symmetric and all positive.

3 Find $(A^{\mathrm{T}}CA)^{-1}$ in the fixed-free example by multiplying $A^{-1}C^{-1}(A^{\mathrm{T}})^{-1}$. Check the special case with all $c_i = 1$ and $C = I$.

4 In the free-free case when $A^{\mathrm{T}}CA$ in (11) is singular, add the three equations $A^{\mathrm{T}}CAu = f$ to show that we need $f_1 + f_2 + f_3 = 0$. Find a solution to $A^{\mathrm{T}}CAu = f$ when the forces $f = (-1, 0, 1)$ balance themselves. Find all solutions!

5 In the fixed-fixed case, what are the reaction forces on the top of spring 1 and on the bottom of spring 4? They should balance the total force $3mg$ from gravity, pulling down on the three masses.

6 With $c_1 = c_3 = 1$ in the fixed-free case, suppose you strengthen spring 2. Find $K = A^{\mathrm{T}}CA$ for $c_2 = 10$ and $c_2 = 100$. Compute $u = K^{-1}f$ with equal masses $f = (1, 1, 1)$.

7 With $c_1 = c_3 = c_4 = 1$ in the fixed-fixed case, weaken spring 2 in the limit to $c_2 = 0$. Does $K = A^{\mathrm{T}}CA$ remain invertible? Solve $Ku = f = (1, 1, 1)$ and explain the answer physically.

8 For one free-free spring only, show that $K = c\begin{bmatrix} 1 & -1 \\ -1 & 1 \end{bmatrix} =$ "element matrix."

(a) Assemble K's for springs 2 and 3 into equation (11) for $K_{\text{free-free}}$.

(b) Now include K for spring 1 (top fixed) to reach $K_{\text{fixed-free}}$ in (8)

(c) Now place K for spring 4 (bottom fixed) to reach $K_{\text{fixed-fixed}}$ in (7).

9 When $P'(\theta^*) = 0$ for the inverted pendulum, show that $P''(\theta^*) > 0$ which makes θ^* stable. In other words: $\lambda \sin\theta^* = \theta^*$ in (13) gives $\lambda\cos\theta^* < 1$ in (14). For proof, show that $F(\theta) = \theta\cos\theta/\sin\theta$ decreases from $F(0) = 1$ because its derivative is negative. Then $F(\theta^*) = \lambda\cos\theta^* < 1$.

10 The stiffness matrix is $K = A^{\mathrm{T}}CA = D - W =$ diagonal − off-diagonal. It has row sums ≥ 0 and $W \geq 0$. Show that K^{-1} has *positive entries* by checking this identity (the infinite series converges to K^{-1} and all its terms are ≥ 0):

$$KK^{-1} = (D - W)(D^{-1} + D^{-1}WD^{-1} + D^{-1}WD^{-1}WD^{-1} + \cdots) = I.$$

2.2 OSCILLATION BY NEWTON'S LAW

This section is about the most important equation in mechanics. It is Newton's Law $F = ma$. We have n masses $m_1, \ldots, m_n$ that obey this law, force = mass times acceleration. Their displacements $u_1(t), \ldots, u_n(t)$ are changing with time, but not at anywhere near the speed of light (we hope). The acceleration of each mass is $a = d^2u/dt^2$ (also written u_{tt} or u'' or $\ddot{u}$). We need the forces F.

Compare $F = ma$ with the previous section about equilibrium. There, the masses didn't move ($a = 0$). Each mass was in balance between external forces f and spring forces Ku. That balance $F = f - Ku = 0$ is now gone and the masses are in motion. When $f = 0$, and all forces come from the springs, we have $\boldsymbol{Mu'' = -Ku}$.

Friction and damping would involve the velocities du/dt. So would flow problems (and many applications involve flows). This section has only u_{tt} and not u_t. *Without damping or external forces, the springs will oscillate forever.* The total of the kinetic energies $\frac{1}{2}mu_t^2$ of the masses and stored energies $\frac{1}{2}ce^2$ of the springs must be constant.

When the differential equations are coupled, of course we use matrices. The vector of n displacements will be $u(t)$, and the masses go into a diagonal **mass matrix** M:

Displacements $u(t)$
Mass matrix M

$$u(t) = \begin{bmatrix} u_1(t) \\ \vdots \\ u_n(t) \end{bmatrix} \quad \text{and} \quad M = \begin{bmatrix} m_1 & & \\ & \ddots & \\ & & m_n \end{bmatrix}.$$

The vector of n external forces on the masses is $f(t)$. When $Ku = f$, we are in equilibrium: no oscillation. The force in $F = ma$ is the difference $F = f - Ku$.

Newton's Law $F = ma$ $\quad f - Ku = Mu_{tt} \quad$ or $\quad \boldsymbol{Mu_{tt} + Ku = f}$. $\quad$ (1)

We do not have to repeat the same steps for every new application. This is the point of the framework! Once you have found A and C and $K = A^{\mathrm{T}}CA$ and M, *the system takes over.* The basic equation $Mu'' + Ku = 0$ is conservative, with $f = 0$. We will solve it exactly using eigenvalues and eigenvectors of $M^{-1}K$.

In reality, large problems are solved by finite differences with time steps $\boldsymbol{\Delta t}$. A key issue in scientific computing is the choice between "explicit and implicit." Explicit methods tell us directly the new $Mu(t + \Delta t)$. Implicit methods also involve $Ku(t+\Delta t)$. A coupled system has to be solved at each step for $u(t+\Delta t)$, but the implicit methods have extra stability and they allow a larger Δt.

This section describes the two leading methods, with computed examples:

Explicit Leapfrog Method (short fast steps) (chosen for molecular dynamics)

Implicit Trapezoidal Rule (larger slower steps) (chosen for finite elements)

We plan to solve a mass-spring example $Mu'' + Ku = 0$ in three ways:

$$\textbf{Example} \quad \begin{bmatrix} 9 & 0 \\ 0 & 1 \end{bmatrix} \begin{bmatrix} u'' \end{bmatrix} + \begin{bmatrix} 81 & -6 \\ -6 & 6 \end{bmatrix} \begin{bmatrix} u \end{bmatrix} = \begin{bmatrix} 0 \\ 0 \end{bmatrix} \text{ with } u(0) = \begin{bmatrix} 1 \\ 0 \end{bmatrix} \text{ and } u'(0) = \begin{bmatrix} 0 \\ 0 \end{bmatrix}$$

There will be codes for the eigenvector solution (normal modes) and the leapfrog and trapezoidal methods. Sections 2.5 and 2.6 introduce *damping* and *nonlinearity*, working also with the parallel problems of circuit analysis.

One Mass and One Spring

Start with one mass m hanging from one spring (with spring constant c). The top is fixed. When the mass moves down by a distance $u(t)$, the spring pulls it back up with force $-cu(t)$. The minus sign is because the spring force has opposite direction from the displacement. Newton's law is force = (mass) (acceleration) = $m\,u''$:

$$\textbf{One unknown} \qquad m\frac{d^2u}{dt^2} + cu = 0 \quad \text{with} \quad u(0) \quad \text{and} \quad u'(0) \quad \text{given.} \qquad (2)$$

Note that we are speaking about *movement away from equilibrium*. Gravity is already accounted for. If you want the complete displacement (from no stretching at all), you would add mg to the right side and mg/c to the solution—this is the constant value of u in equilibrium. We measure from equilibrium instead of from absolute zero.

The solution $u(t)$ combines a cosine and sine (a second order equation has two solutions). By themselves, $\cos t$ and $\sin t$ satisfy $u'' + u = 0$, when $m = 1$ and $c = 1$. equation (2) needs c/m from the second derivative, so multiply t by the square root:

$$\textbf{Oscillating solution} \qquad u(t) = A\cos\sqrt{\frac{c}{m}}\,t + B\sin\sqrt{\frac{c}{m}}\,t\,. \qquad (3)$$

At $t = 0$ the displacement is $u(0) = A$. Taking derivatives in (3), the velocity at $t = 0$ is $\sqrt{\frac{c}{m}}\,B = u'(0)$. The initial conditions determine $\boldsymbol{A = u(0)}$ and $\boldsymbol{B = \sqrt{\frac{m}{c}}u'(0)}$. **The oscillation frequency is** $\boldsymbol{\omega = \sqrt{\frac{c}{m}}}$. A small mass on a hard spring vibrates quickly, like an electron. A large mass hanging from a soft spring oscillates slowly, like a heavy ball on a rubber band.

The potential energy in the single spring is $\frac{1}{2}cu^2$. The kinetic energy of the single mass is $\frac{1}{2}m(u')^2$. For more springs and masses, the potential energy becomes $\frac{1}{2}e^{\mathrm{T}}Ce$ and the kinetic energy is $\frac{1}{2}(u')^{\mathrm{T}}Mu'$. The total energy (kinetic plus potential) is constant, equal to the total energy at the start:

$$\textbf{Conserved energy} \quad \frac{1}{2}m\,(u'(t))^2 + \frac{1}{2}c\,(u(t))^2 = \frac{1}{2}m\,(u'(0))^2 + \frac{1}{2}c\,(u(0))^2\,. \qquad (4)$$

For one spring, the derivative of this total energy is $mu'u'' + cuu'$. This is u' times $mu'' + cu = 0$, so the derivative is zero and the energy doesn't change.

Key Example: Motion Around a Circle

The simplest and best example is $\boldsymbol{u''+u=0}$. One solution is $u=\cos t$. The velocity is $v=u'=-\sin t$ and certainly $u^2+v^2=\cos^2 t+\sin^2 t=1$. The exact solution travels around that constant energy circle in the u, v plane (the *phase plane*).

Let me try four finite difference methods. I will write $u''+u=0$ as two equations $\boldsymbol{u'=v}$ and $\boldsymbol{v'=-u}$. All four methods replace u' by $(U_{n+1}-U_n)/h$, and v' similarly. The crucial choice is *where to evaluate* the right sides v and $-u$.

Both Euler methods quickly leave the circle in Figure 2.5, because of low accuracy. The growth matrices G_F and G_B at each time step $h=\Delta t$ are officially stable, but the $O(h)$ errors are unacceptable. The eigenvalues λ of G produce growth or decay:

Forward Euler	$U_{n+1}=U_n+h\boldsymbol{V_n}$ $V_{n+1}=V_n-h\boldsymbol{U_n}$	$G_F=\begin{bmatrix}1 & h\\ -h & 1\end{bmatrix}$	$\lambda=1+ih, 1-ih$ $\boldsymbol{\lvert\lambda\rvert>1}$ **(growth)**
Backward Euler	$U_{n+1}=U_n+h\boldsymbol{V_{n+1}}$ $V_{n+1}=V_n-h\boldsymbol{U_{n+1}}$	$G_B=\begin{bmatrix}1 & -h\\ h & 1\end{bmatrix}^{-1}$	$\lambda=(1\pm ih)/(1+h^2)$ $\boldsymbol{\lvert\lambda\rvert<1}$ **(decay)**

Each step multiplies (U_n, V_n) by G to find the next (U_{n+1}, V_{n+1}). Notice that 32 steps don't return to the x axis at $t=2\pi$. That is phase error.

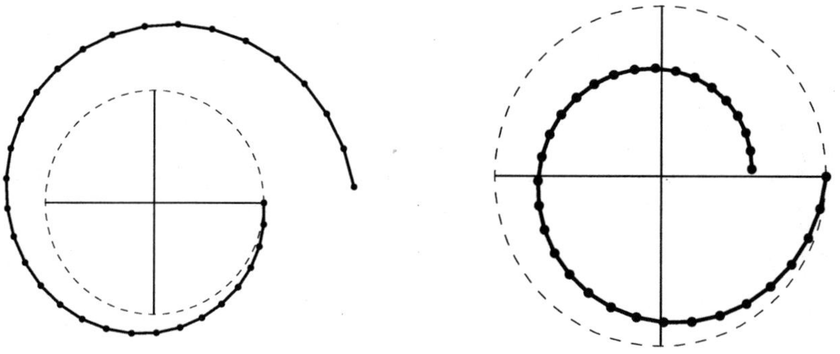

Figure 2.5: Euler spirals out, Backward Euler spirals in, $h=\dfrac{2\pi}{32}$, $\begin{bmatrix}U\\ V\end{bmatrix}_n=\boldsymbol{G^n}\begin{bmatrix}1\\ 0\end{bmatrix}$.

Second-order accuracy will make a big difference. The **trapezoidal method** is centered at $n+\frac{1}{2}$. Every (U_n, V_n) stays exactly on the circle (a small phase error in the double bullet at $(1,0)$). Energy is conserved because G_T is an orthogonal matrix.

Trapezoidal Method	$U_{n+1}=U_n+h\boldsymbol{(V_n+V_{n+1})}/2$ $V_{n+1}=V_n-h\boldsymbol{(U_n+U_{n+1})}/2$	$G_T=\begin{bmatrix}1 & -\frac{h}{2}\\ \frac{h}{2} & 1\end{bmatrix}^{-1}\begin{bmatrix}1 & \frac{h}{2}\\ -\frac{h}{2} & 1\end{bmatrix}$	$\det(G_T)=1$ $\boldsymbol{\lvert\lambda_1\rvert=\lvert\lambda_2\rvert=1}$

The **leapfrog method** also has $|\lambda| = 1$ for $h \leq 2$. But G_L is not an orthogonal matrix and the orbit follows an ellipse in Figure 2.6. The ellipse comes closer to the circle as $h \to 0$, and leapfrog has a giant advantage: **it is explicit**. From $U_{n+1} = U_n + h\,V_n$ we know $V_{n+1} = V_n - h\,U_{n+1} = \boldsymbol{V_n - h^2 V_n - h\,U_n}$:

Leapfrog Method $\quad U_{n+1} = U_n + h\,\boldsymbol{V_n}$, $\quad V_{n+1} = V_n - h\,\boldsymbol{U_{n+1}}$

$$G_L = \begin{bmatrix} 1 & h \\ -h & 1-h^2 \end{bmatrix} \qquad \lambda = e^{i\theta},\ e^{-i\theta} \text{ for } h \leq 2 \qquad \boldsymbol{\cos\theta = 1 - \tfrac{1}{2}h^2 \geq -1}$$

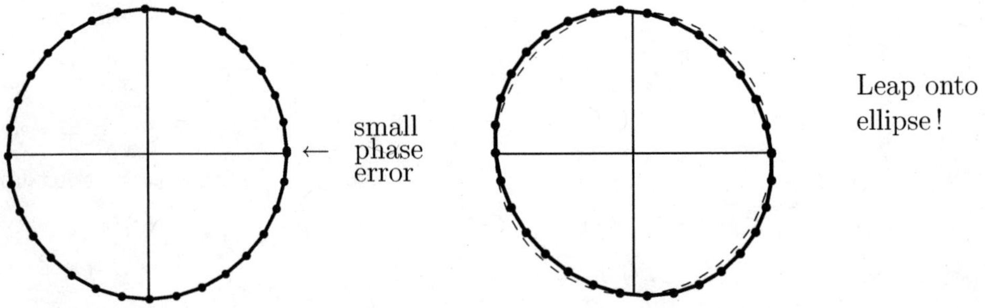

Figure 2.6: Trapezoidal (implicit) conserves energy. Leapfrog (explicit) conserves area.

Important new word: The determinants of G_T and G_L are 1. The trapezoidal and leapfrog methods are "**symplectic**." Multiplication by G_T and G_L preserves areas in the phase plane. All the triangles from $(0,0)$ to (U_n, V_n) to (U_{n+1}, V_{n+1}) have the same area. *Equal areas in equal times*, as in Kepler's Second Law for planets. This property is fundamental for success in long-time integration.

Equal areas are especially clear in the six triangles in Figure 2.7. This special case has $h = 1$ and $\theta = 2\pi/6$ and $e^{6i\theta} = 1$. Then $G^6 = I$ and $(\boldsymbol{U_6}, \boldsymbol{V_6}) = (\boldsymbol{U_0}, \boldsymbol{V_0})$. For each N, Problem 2 shows that the time step $h = 2\sin(\pi/N)$ gives $G^N = I$.

The jagged figure has $h{=}1.3$. This large time step is still stable and the points (U_n, V_n) lie on an ellipse. But stability isn't everything; the accuracy is terrible. I intended to show $h = 2.01$ beyond the stability limit, but the graph left the page.

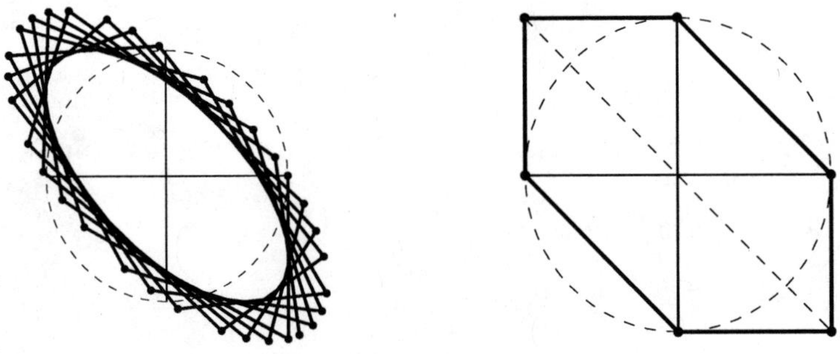

Figure 2.7: 32 leapfrog steps with $\Delta t = h = 1.3$; six steps with $h = 1$ (**equal areas**).

Line of Masses and Springs

The framework $\boldsymbol{u} \to \boldsymbol{e} \to \boldsymbol{w} \to \boldsymbol{f}$ does not change much when the displacement $u(t)$ is measured from equilibrium. But the force balance looks different. That includes Newton's inertia term $(mass)(acceleration)$ along with any applied force $f(t)$:

$$\begin{array}{llcll} \text{oscillations} & u_1(t), \ldots, u_n(t) & & \text{force balance} & Mu'' + Ku = f(t) \\ & \quad \boldsymbol{A} \big\downarrow & & & \quad \big\uparrow \boldsymbol{A}^{\mathrm{T}} \\ \text{elongations} & e_1(t), \ldots, e_m(t) & \xrightarrow{\ \boldsymbol{C}\ } & \text{spring forces} & w_1(t), \ldots, w_m(t) \end{array}$$

The all-important matrix K is still $A^{\mathrm{T}}CA$. We will first discuss $Mu'' + Ku = 0$, assuming no applied force. We need $2n$ solutions (one constant C for each) to match the starting vector $u(0)$ and the n initial velocities in $u'(0)$. Those $2n$ solutions will come from eigenvectors x! **Try the solutions $\boldsymbol{u} = (\cos \omega t)\boldsymbol{x}$ and $(\sin \omega t)\boldsymbol{x}$.**

$$Mu'' + Ku = M(-\omega^2 \cos \omega t)x + K(\cos \omega t)x = 0 \quad \text{gives} \quad \boldsymbol{Kx = \omega^2 Mx}. \tag{5}$$

The eigenvalue is $\lambda = \omega^2$. The matrix with eigenvector x is $M^{-1}K$ (*not symmetric*):

$$Kx = \omega^2 Mx \quad \text{means} \quad M^{-1}Kx = \lambda x. \tag{6}$$

Unsymmetric if $m_1 \neq m_2$

$$M^{-1}K = \begin{bmatrix} m_1^{-1} & 0 \\ 0 & m_2^{-1} \end{bmatrix} \begin{bmatrix} k_{11} & k_{12} \\ k_{12} & k_{22} \end{bmatrix} \qquad \begin{array}{l} \text{Row 1 contains } k_{12}/m_1 \\ \text{Row 2 contains } k_{12}/m_2 \end{array}$$

$M^{-1}K$ is a product of positive definite matrices, but I won't call it positive definite. It would fit a wider definition of positive definiteness, but safer to insist on symmetry. Still the good properties of a symmetric K continue to be good for $M^{-1}K$:

1. The eigenvalues λ_i of $M^{-1}K$ are still real and positive: $\boldsymbol{\lambda_i > 0}$.

2. The eigenvectors x_i can be chosen orthogonal, even orthonormal, but the inner product now involves M. Orthogonality is now $\boldsymbol{x^{\mathrm{T}}My = 0}$.

This is easy to prove if you look at the matrix $M^{-\frac{1}{2}}KM^{-\frac{1}{2}}$. That matrix is symmetric and positive definite (like K), when we split M^{-1} symmetrically. So the triple product has real positive eigenvalues λ_i and orthonormal eigenvectors y_i:

Symmetrized

$$\left(M^{-\frac{1}{2}}KM^{-\frac{1}{2}}\right) y_i = \lambda_i y_i \quad \text{with} \quad y_i^{\mathrm{T}} y_j = \delta_{ij} = \begin{cases} 1 & i = j \\ 0 & i \neq j \end{cases} \tag{7}$$

Substitute $y_i = M^{\frac{1}{2}}x_i$ to reach $M^{-\frac{1}{2}}Kx_i = \lambda_i M^{\frac{1}{2}}x_i$. Then multiply by $M^{-\frac{1}{2}}$:

M-orthogonality

$$(M^{-1}K)\,x_i = \lambda_i x_i \quad \text{and} \quad \delta_{ij} = x_i^{\mathrm{T}} M x_j = y_i^{\mathrm{T}} y_j. \tag{8}$$

The eigenvalues did not change, whether M^{-1} is on one side or $M^{-\frac{1}{2}}$ is on both sides. The eigenvectors do change. The y_i are orthogonal and the x_i are "M-*orthogonal*." Now comes the general solution vector $u(t)$ to the equation $Mu'' + Ku = 0$.

The solution combines the eigenvectors x_i of $M^{-1}K$ with $\cos\omega_i t$ and also $\sin\omega_i t$:

General solution $$u(t) = \sum_{i=1}^{n} \left(A_i \cos\sqrt{\lambda_i}\,t + B_i \sin\sqrt{\lambda_i}\,t\right) x_i\,. \qquad (9)$$

Each term is a *pure oscillation* at a fixed frequency $\omega_i = \sqrt{\lambda_i}$. All λ_i are positive. At $t = 0$ we have $u(0) = \sum A_i x_i$ (expansion in eigenvectors) and $u'(0) = \sum B_i\sqrt{\lambda_i}\,x_i$. A straightforward MATLAB code finds this $u(t)$ from eig(K, M):

```
% inputs M, K, uzero, vzero, t
[vectors, values] = eig(K, M); eigen = diag(values); % solve Kx = λMx
A = vectors\uzero; B = (vectors * sqrt(values))\vzero;
coeffs = A. * cos(t * sqrt(eigen)) + B. * sin(t * sqrt(eigen));
u = vectors * coeffs; % solution (9) at time t to Mu'' + Ku = 0
```

Example 1 Two equal masses $m_1 = m_2$ and three identical springs: *Both ends fixed.* The 2 by 2 mass matrix is just $M = mI$. The 2 by 2 stiffness matrix is also familiar:

Fixed-fixed $$K = c\begin{bmatrix} 2 & -1 \\ -1 & 2 \end{bmatrix} \quad \text{and} \quad M^{-1}K = \frac{c}{m}\begin{bmatrix} 2 & -1 \\ -1 & 2 \end{bmatrix}.$$

The eigenvalues are $\lambda_1 = c/m$ and $\lambda_2 = 3c/m$. The eigenvectors are $x_1 = (1, 1)$ and $x_2 = (1, -1)$. They are orthogonal for the M-inner product. But here $M = mI$ and $M^{-1}K$ is symmetric, so they are orthogonal in the usual way and $x_1^{\mathrm{T}} x_2 = 0$. Substitute λ's and x's into (9), and the solution is a combination of the **normal modes** x_1 and x_2:

$$u(t) = \left(A_1 \cos\sqrt{\frac{c}{m}}\,t + B_1 \sin\sqrt{\frac{c}{m}}\,t\right)\begin{bmatrix} 1 \\ 1 \end{bmatrix} + \left(A_2 \cos\sqrt{\frac{3c}{m}}\,t + B_2 \sin\sqrt{\frac{3c}{m}}\,t\right)\begin{bmatrix} 1 \\ -1 \end{bmatrix}.$$

Figure 2.8 shows these two pure oscillations on the left. The masses move together in $x_1 = (1, 1)$. If they *start* together at $u_1(0) = u_2(0)$ and $u_1'(0) = u_2'(0)$, then they oscillate together forever. The eigenvector $x_2 = (1, -1)$ moves the masses in opposite directions, faster because λ_2 has the factor 3.

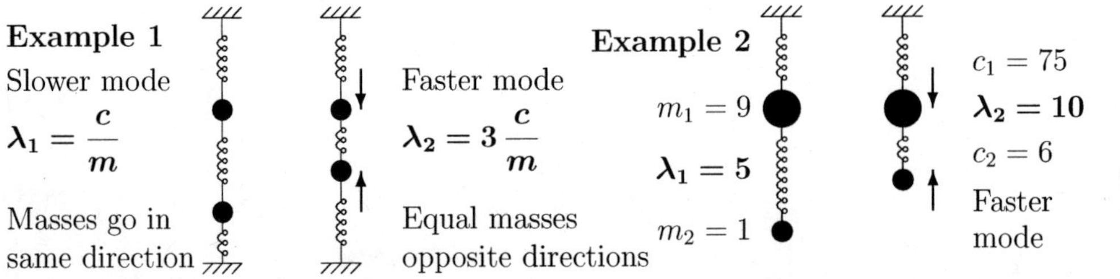

Figure 2.8: Eigenvectors $\begin{bmatrix} 1 \\ 1 \end{bmatrix}$ and $\begin{bmatrix} 1 \\ -1 \end{bmatrix}$ for equal masses, $\begin{bmatrix} 1 \\ 6 \end{bmatrix}$ and $\begin{bmatrix} 2 \\ -3 \end{bmatrix}$ for $m_1 \neq m_2$.

Example 2 Masses $m_1 = 9$ and $m_2 = 1$ with $c_1 = 75$ and $c_2 = 6$: *Lower end free.*

Now $c_1 = 75$ and $c_2 = 6$ go into $K = A^{\mathrm{T}}CA$. The last row adds to zero (free end):

Fixed-free $$M = \begin{bmatrix} 9 & 0 \\ 0 & 1 \end{bmatrix} \quad \text{and} \quad K = \begin{bmatrix} 75+6 & -6 \\ -6 & 6 \end{bmatrix}.$$

The eigenvalues $\lambda_1 = 5$ and $\lambda_2 = 10$ come from $M^{-1}K$ (notice the non-symmetry):

$$M^{-1}K = \begin{bmatrix} \frac{81}{9} & -\frac{6}{9} \\ -6 & 6 \end{bmatrix} \quad \text{leads to} \quad \det\left(M^{-1}K - \lambda I\right) = \lambda^2 - 15\lambda + 50 = 0\,.$$

The eigenvectors $(\mathbf{1}, \mathbf{6})$ and $(\mathbf{2}, \mathbf{-3})$ are not orthogonal because $M^{-1}K$ is not symmetric. The rule is that $x_1^{\mathrm{T}} M x_2 = 0$. Here $(1)(9)(2) + (6)(1)(-3) = 0$. Both normal modes x_1 and x_2 in Figure 2.8b now have larger displacements for the smaller mass. Starting from rest at $(1, 0)$ (no sine terms), the solution is again a combination of two **normal modes**:

$$u(t) = \left(\frac{1}{5}\cos\sqrt{5}\,t + 0\sin\sqrt{5}\,t\right)\begin{bmatrix} 1 \\ 6 \end{bmatrix} + \left(\frac{2}{5}\cos\sqrt{10}\,t + 0\sin\sqrt{10}\,t\right)\begin{bmatrix} 2 \\ -3 \end{bmatrix}.$$

Please notice: The mass matrix M is *not diagonal* in the finite element method (Section 3.6), when "Galerkin's method" discretizes the differential equation. The matrices M^{-1} and $M^{-1}K$ become full. But eig(K, M) is still successful.

Standing Waves and Traveling Waves

The oscillations become interesting (even worth a movie) with more masses. The point is that *a sum of standing waves* (up and down, staying in place) *produces a traveling wave.* A surfer rides the wave in to shore, but the water stays in the ocean.

A standing wave has *one* normal mode x_i. The n masses share the same λ_i:

Standing wave $$u(t) = (A_i \cos\sqrt{\lambda_i}\,t + B_i \sin\sqrt{\lambda_i}\,t)\, x_i\,.$$

We see the wave better when the springs are horizontal and the masses go up and down (Figure 2.9a). Notice the special points in between with no movement. We are just looking at an eigenvector of $M^{-1}K$.

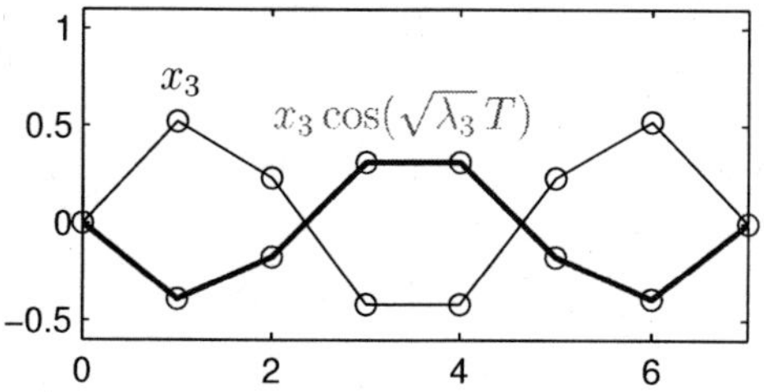

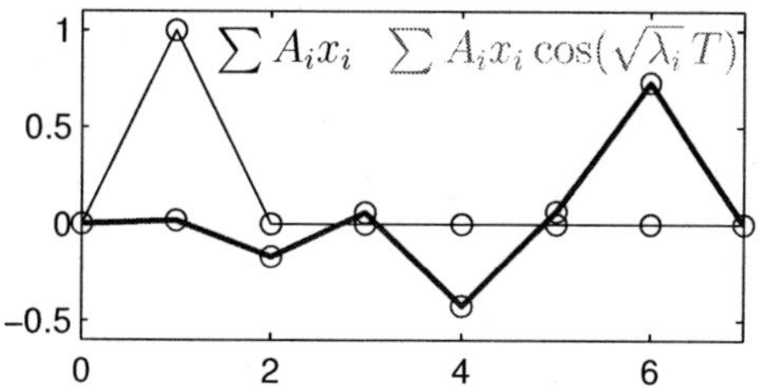

Figure 2.9: Standing wave (one eigenvector) and traveling wave (all eigenvectors).

A **traveling wave** can start at the left end (zeros elsewhere). Eigenvectors go up and down at different frequencies. All down the line, masses pick up energy and lose it and recover it. (Figure 2.9b becomes a movie on math.mit.edu/cse.) Observers see a wave travel down the line of springs, and reflect back at the other end (free or fixed). The energy is conserved (no damping) so the motion never dies out.

For equal masses m and equal spring constants c, the central equation becomes $mIu'' + cKu = 0$. The eigenvectors of our $-1, 2, -1$ second difference matrix K are discrete sines. The displacements involve the products $\sin(\sqrt{\lambda_k}\, t)\sin(k\pi jh)$.

Important A violin string is the limiting case of more masses ($n \to \infty$). The discrete jh becomes a continuous variable x. The normal modes become $\sin\left(\sqrt{c/m}\, t\right)$ $\sin(k\pi x)$, an infinite sequence of harmonics. Notice the **separation of variables** t and x. The discrete $mIu'' + cKu = 0$ becomes the **wave equation** $mu_{tt} - cu_{xx} = 0$ of Section 6.6.

Total Energy is Conserved

The kinetic energy of a mass is $\frac{1}{2}mv^2$, when its velocity is $v = du/dt$. The kinetic energy of a system of n masses is just the sum of n separate energies:

Kinetic energy $$\frac{1}{2}m_1 v_1^2 + \cdots + \frac{1}{2}m_n v_n^2 = \frac{1}{2}\left(\frac{du}{dt}\right)^{\mathrm{T}} M \left(\frac{du}{dt}\right). \tag{10}$$

The potential energy in a spring is $\frac{1}{2}ce^2$, when its elongation is e. The potential energy in m springs is $\frac{1}{2}(c_1e_1^2 + \cdots + c_m e_m^2) = \frac{1}{2}e^{\mathrm{T}}Ce$. Then $e = Au$ brings in K:

Potential energy $$\frac{1}{2}e^{\mathrm{T}}Ce = \frac{1}{2}(Au)^{\mathrm{T}}C(Au) = \frac{1}{2}u^{\mathrm{T}}Ku\,. \tag{11}$$

An oscillation with no applied force $f(t)$ conserves the total energy = "*Hamiltonian.*"

Conservation $Mu'' + Ku = 0$ leads to $$\frac{d}{dt}(\textbf{Kinetic} + \textbf{Potential}) = 0\,. \tag{12}$$

Proof The ordinary derivative of a product u_iv_i has two terms, $u_iv_i' + u_i'v_i$. The derivative of $u^{\mathrm{T}}v = u_1v_1 + \cdots + u_nv_n$ is the sum of n ordinary derivatives:

Derivative of dot product $$\frac{d}{dt}u^{\mathrm{T}}v = \sum_{i=1}^{n}(u_iv_i' + u_i'v_i) = u^{\mathrm{T}}v' + (u')^{\mathrm{T}}v. \tag{13}$$

Apply this to the energies $\mathbf{KE} = \frac{1}{2}\left(\frac{du}{dt}\right)^{\mathrm{T}}M\left(\frac{du}{dt}\right)$ and $\mathbf{PE} = \frac{1}{2}u^{\mathrm{T}}Ku$:

$$\frac{d}{dt}\mathbf{KE} = \frac{1}{2}\left(\frac{du}{dt}\right)^{\mathrm{T}} M \left(\frac{d^2u}{dt^2}\right) + \frac{1}{2}\left(\frac{d^2u}{dt^2}\right)^{\mathrm{T}} M \left(\frac{du}{dt}\right) \tag{14}$$

$$\frac{d}{dt}\mathbf{PE} = \frac{1}{2}\left(\frac{du}{dt}\right)^{\mathrm{T}} Ku + \frac{1}{2}u^{\mathrm{T}}K\left(\frac{du}{dt}\right) \tag{15}$$

The first terms on the right add to zero since $Mu'' + Ku = 0$. So do the second terms. Therefore the left sides add to zero: **total energy KE + PE is conserved**. This is an excellent check on our codes.

Example 2 continued Suppose the masses $m_1 = 9$ and $m_2 = 1$ start from rest, so $v(0) = u'(0) = (0, 0)$. The sine coefficients are $B_1 = B_2 = 0$. The first mass is displaced so $u(0) = (1, 0)$. The energy is $\frac{1}{2}u^{\mathrm{T}}Ku = \frac{1}{2}(81)$, all potential energy at the start.

Applied Force and Resonance

Forcing terms $f(t) = (f_1(t), \ldots, f_n(t))$ come from outside,like pushing a child on a swing (or pushing n children on connected swings). Very often, all components of $f(t)$ are oscillating at the same *frequency* ω_0. Then we can solve $Ku'' + Mu = f_0 \cos \omega_0 t$. The oscillation will involve ω_0 as well as the n *natural frequencies* $\omega_i = \sqrt{\lambda_i}$ from the eigenvalues of $M^{-1}K$.

There is a critical case of **resonance**, when formulas break down. The forcing frequency equals a natural frequency, which can be good or bad. If we push a swing, we want it to go higher—so we match $\omega_0^2 = \lambda_1$. If we walk on a narrow bridge, we do *not* want it to oscillate—a good designer chooses λ's that stay far from ω_0. The Millennium Bridge in London looked safe, but a sideways mode was overlooked.

Here are solutions to $mu'' + cu = \cos \omega_0 t$, when ω_0 is *near* the natural frequency $\lambda = \sqrt{c/m}$ and when $w_0 = \lambda$ exactly:

Near resonance $u(t) = \dfrac{\cos \lambda t - \cos \omega_0 t}{m(\omega_0^2 - \lambda^2)}$ **Resonance** $u(t) = \dfrac{t \sin \omega_0 t}{2m\omega_0}$. (16)

Near resonance, the movie on the website shows large displacements because $\omega_0^2 - \lambda^2$ is close to zero. At resonance, the movie has to stop because $u(t)$ is blowing up.

Explicit Finite Differences

Large codes can find eigenvalues and eigenvectors in $Kx = \lambda Mx$. But the workhorse of computational engineering has **finite differences in time**. We begin with equal time steps Δt, and a centered second difference to replace u_{tt}. Notice KU at time t:

Leapfrog method with $\Delta^2 U/(\Delta t)^2$ $M\big[U(t+\Delta t) - 2U(t) + U(t-\Delta t)\big] + (\Delta t)^2 KU(t) = (\Delta t)^2 f(t)$

$U(t)$ is the approximation to $u(t)$. The centered time difference "leaps over" the forces $KU(t)$ and $f(t)$ to give $U(t + \Delta t)$. It is natural to write U_n for $U(n\Delta t)$. Then the new MU_{n+1} comes explicitly from the known U_n and U_{n-1}. Rewrite leapfrog:

Explicit $$MU_{n+1} = \big[2M - (\Delta t)^2 K\big]U_n - MU_{n-1} + (\Delta t)^2 f_n\,. \qquad (17)$$

The starting value U_0 is specified by $u(0)$. One step later, U_1 also comes from the initial conditions: we can take $U_1 = u(0) + \Delta t\, u'(0)$, or do better. Then $U_2, U_3, \ldots$ come quickly from the explicit leapfrog equation (also called Störmer's method).

```
function u = leapfrog(n)            % n time steps to t = 2π for u'' + 9u = 0
dt = 2*pi/n; uold = 0; u = 3*dt;    % Starting values u(0) = 0 and u(dt) = 3 * dt
for i = 2:n
   unew = 2*u-uold-9*dt^2*u;        % Leapfrog formula with u_{n+1} - 2u_n + u_{n-1}
   uold = u; u = unew;              % Update u's for the next time step
end
u                                   % u_n approximates u(2π) = sin(6π) = 0
C = n^2 * u                         % Second-order methods have leading error C/n^2
```

In practice, most computations work with *first differences.* By introducing the velocity $v(t)$, the differential equation $Mu'' + Ku = f$ becomes a first-order system:

First-order $$Mv'(t) + Ku(t) = f(t) \quad \text{and} \quad u'(t) = v(t). \tag{18}$$

A "staggered" difference equation involves $V_{n+1/2}$ at $(n+\frac{1}{2})\Delta t$. Centering the two first-order equations at staggered points produces a system equivalent to leapfrog:

First-order leapfrog $$M\left(V_{n+\frac{1}{2}} - V_{n-\frac{1}{2}}\right) + \Delta t\, KU_n = \Delta t\, f_n \qquad U_{n+1} - U_n = \Delta t\, V_{n+\frac{1}{2}}. \tag{19}$$

To see the equivalence, subtract the equation $U_n - U_{n-1} = \Delta t\, V_{n-\frac{1}{2}}$ at the previous time to find $U_{n+1} - 2U_n + U_{n-1} = \Delta t(V_{n+\frac{1}{2}} - V_{n-\frac{1}{2}})$. Substitute into the first equation and (19) becomes (17). The first-order system is better numerically.

In molecular dynamics, discussed below, leapfrog is the "Verlet method". The first order system (19) is a version of "velocity Verlet".

Stability and Instability

Stability places an essential limitation on the size of the step Δt. To confirm that the stability condition is serious, we take 100 steps in a simple code for $Mu'' + Ku = 0$. With step size $\Delta t = .64$ in Example 2, the output is an explosion. That time step is just above the stability limit $\Delta t \le 2/\sqrt{10} = .632$. The slightly smaller step $\Delta t = .63$ has no explosion, but the output is totally inaccurate. The code divides Δt by 2 until the $(\Delta t)^2$ accuracy is dominant. Then smaller steps reduce the error by 4.

Why is the stability limit between .63 and .64? Starting from $Kx = \lambda Mx$, look for leapfrog's growth factor in the discrete normal mode $U(n\,\Delta t) = G^n x$:

$$(G^{n+1} - 2G^n + G^{n-1})x + (\Delta t)^2 \lambda\, G^n x = 0 \quad \text{and} \quad \boldsymbol{G^2 - (2 - \lambda(\Delta t)^2)G + 1 = 0}. \tag{20}$$

We cancelled G^{n-1}, leaving a quadratic equation with two roots. Their sum is that coefficient $2 - \lambda(\Delta t)^2$. If this number is below -2, one of the roots is below -1 and the leapfrog solution $G^n x$ will grow exponentially. Example 2 has $\lambda = 5$ and 10:

Stability condition $$-2 \le 2 - 10(\Delta t)^2 \quad \text{or} \quad \boldsymbol{(\Delta t)^2 \le \frac{4}{10}}. \tag{21}$$

Then $(.63)^2 = .3969$ gives a stable but very inaccurate U, and $(.64)^2 = .4096$ is a total disaster. Every stable Δt has $|G| = 1$ exactly, so leapfrog has no damping.

For a single mass with $mu''+cu=0$, Problem 17 finds the condition $\boldsymbol{\Delta t \le 2\sqrt{m/c}}$. Stability is a serious problem for explicit methods, studied in detail in Chapter 6.

Implicit Trapezoidal Rule

Large finite element codes need more stability than leapfrog offers. The way to remove limitations on Δt is to move stiffness terms to the new time level $t + \Delta t$. Since K is not a diagonal matrix, this produces a system of N equations for the N components of $U(t + \Delta t)$. The time step is larger and safer but also more expensive.

The model for an implicit method is the trapezoidal rule $\frac{1}{2}(new + old)$:

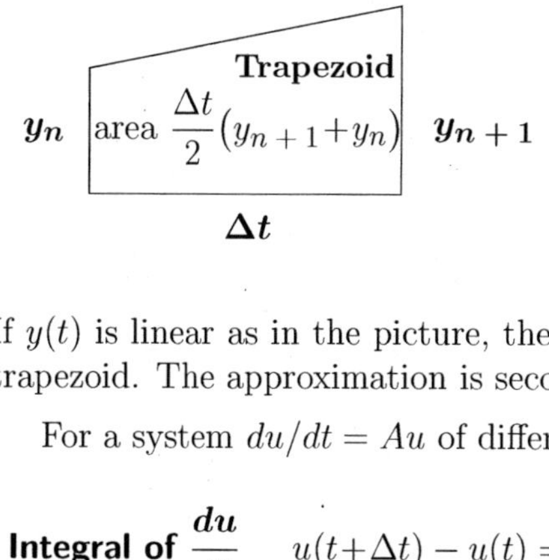

$$\int_t^{t+\Delta t} y\,dt \approx \frac{\boldsymbol{\Delta t}}{\boldsymbol{2}}\big(\boldsymbol{y(t+\Delta t) + y(t)}\big). \tag{22}$$

If $y(t)$ is linear as in the picture, the rule gives the correct integral—the area of the trapezoid. The approximation is second-order (because centered at the halfstep).

For a system $du/dt = Au$ of differential equations, put du/dt for y in (22):

Integral of $\frac{du}{dt}$ $$u(t+\Delta t) - u(t) = \int_t^{t+\Delta t} \frac{du}{dt}\,dt \approx \frac{\Delta t}{2}\big(Au(t+\Delta t) + Au(t)\big). \tag{23}$$

When U_n approximates $u(t)$, this is $U_{n+1} - U_n = \Delta t\,(AU_{n+1} + AU_n)/2$. That equation has many names: Trapezoidal = Crank-Nicolson = Newmark = BDF2:

Trapezoidal rule for $u' = Au$ $$\left(I - \frac{\Delta t}{2}A\right)U_{n+1} = \left(I + \frac{\Delta t}{2}A\right)U_n. \tag{24}$$

When A is fixed, we can factor $I - \frac{\Delta t}{2}A$ into LU once and for all. In other problems, especially for large displacements, A depends on U (nonlinear equation). An iteration will be needed and the natural choice is some form of Newton's method. This comes in Section 2.6, and here we pursue the key question of stability.

Equation (23) is a system $U_{n+1} = GU_n$ with growth matrix G. You need to see two cases, when the eigenvalues of A are *negative* or *imaginary*:

Negative $\boldsymbol{\lambda(A) < 0}$ $$G = \left(I - \frac{\Delta t}{2}A\right)^{-1}\left(I + \frac{\Delta t}{2}A\right) \text{ has eigenvalues } \left|\frac{1+\frac{\Delta t}{2}\lambda}{1-\frac{\Delta t}{2}\lambda}\right| < 1 \quad (25)$$

Imaginary $\boldsymbol{\lambda(A) = i\theta}$ $$G \text{ is barely stable: } \left|\frac{1+\frac{\Delta t}{2}i\theta}{1-\frac{\Delta t}{2}i\theta}\right| = 1 \text{ and } \|U_{n+1}\| = \|U_n\| \quad (26)$$

Negative eigenvalues of A come from diffusion (stable). Imaginary eigenvalues come from oscillation. Damping and viscosity push the real part of λ in the negative (stable) direction. The stability region for the trapezoidal rule is the half-plane $\operatorname{Re}\lambda(A) \leq 0$:

Eigenvalues $$|\boldsymbol{\lambda(G)}| \leq \mathbf{1} \quad \text{if and only if} \quad \mathbf{Re}\,\boldsymbol{\lambda(A)} \leq \mathbf{0}. \quad (27)$$

Second Order Equations

To develop a trapezoidal rule for $Mu'' + Ku = 0$, introduce the velocity $v = u'$. The equation becomes $Mv' + Ku = 0$ or $v' = -M^{-1}Ku$. All approximations are centered at the half-step, for stability and second-order accuracy:

Trapezoidal rule for	$V_{n+1} - V_n = -\Delta t M^{-1}K(U_{n+1} + U_n)/2$	(28)
$\boldsymbol{v' = -M^{-1}Ku,\ u' = v}$	$U_{n+1} - U_n = \Delta t(V_{n+1} + V_n)/2$	(29)

A very direct proof of stability shows that energy is conserved. Multiply (28) by $(V_{n+1}+V_n)^{\mathrm{T}}M$ and multiply (29) by $(U_{n+1}+U_n)^{\mathrm{T}}K$. Use $M^{\mathrm{T}} = M$ and $K^{\mathrm{T}} = K$:

$$V_{n+1}^{\mathrm{T}}MV_{n+1} - V_n^{\mathrm{T}}MV_n = -\Delta t(V_{n+1} + V_n)^{\mathrm{T}}K(U_{n+1} + U_n)/2 \quad (30)$$

$$U_{n+1}^{\mathrm{T}}KU_{n+1} - U_n^{\mathrm{T}}KU_n = \Delta t(U_{n+1} + U_n)^{\mathrm{T}}K(V_{n+1} + V_n)/2 \quad (31)$$

Add (30) and (31) to see that energy is unchanged at time $n+1$:

Energy identity $$V_{n+1}^{\mathrm{T}}MV_{n+1} + U_{n+1}^{\mathrm{T}}KU_{n+1} = V_n^{\mathrm{T}}MV_n + U_n^{\mathrm{T}}KU_n\,. \quad (32)$$

This identity gives an excellent check on the code. Compare V_n, U_n with V_0, U_0.

The new V_{n+1}, U_{n+1} come from the old V_n, U_n by block matrices in (28) and (29):

Block form $$\begin{bmatrix} I & \Delta t M^{-1}K/2 \\ -\Delta t I/2 & I \end{bmatrix}\begin{bmatrix} V_{n+1} \\ U_{n+1} \end{bmatrix} = \begin{bmatrix} I & -\Delta t M^{-1}K/2 \\ \Delta t I/2 & I \end{bmatrix}\begin{bmatrix} V_n \\ U_n \end{bmatrix} \quad (33)$$

If you multiply both sides by the block matrix on the right, the result is surprising. The off-diagonal blocks on the left become zero. Both diagonal blocks contain $B = I + (\Delta t)^2 M^{-1}K/4$. This is the matrix that has to be inverted at each step:

Trapezoidal rule
Alternate form $$\begin{bmatrix} B & 0 \\ 0 & B \end{bmatrix}\begin{bmatrix} V_{n+1} \\ U_{n+1} \end{bmatrix} = \begin{bmatrix} I & -\Delta t M^{-1}K/2 \\ \Delta t I/2 & I \end{bmatrix}^{\mathbf{2}}\begin{bmatrix} V_n \\ U_n \end{bmatrix}. \quad (34)$$

The eigenvalues of B are $1 + (\Delta t)^2\lambda/4$, safely larger than 1. Introducing $B^{-1} = H$ leads to an unconventional but short code for $Mu'' + Ku = 0$ (trapezoidal rule).

```
% inputs M, K, dt, n, V, U (initial values)
energy0 = V' * M * V + U' * K * U ; H = inv(M + K * dt * dt/4) * M ;
for i = 1 : n % multiply (U, V) twice by block matrix, then by H = B^-1
    W= V - dt * inv(M) * K * U/2 ;      U = U + dt * V/2 ;
    V = W - dt * inv(M) * K * U/2 ;     U = U + dt * W/2 ;
    V = H * V ; U = H * U ;
end % compute the energy change at T = n * dt
change = V' * M * V + U' * K * U - energy0 % change = 0, same energy
[U, V] % output U(T) and V(T)
```

Molecular Dynamics

For molecular dynamics, Newton's Law becomes $\boldsymbol{u}'' + \boldsymbol{F}(\boldsymbol{u}) = \mathbf{0}$. The force F depends nonlinearly on the position u. In fact F is the derivative or the gradient of a potential energy $V(u)$. When $V = \frac{1}{2}u^{\mathrm{T}}Ku$ for a constant matrix K, we are back to the normalized linear model $F(u) = Ku$. In these pages, K depends on u.

This is **computational chemistry,** a subject that requires fast computers for long times. It studies very fast vibrations. The goal is not the same as astronomy, which follows a single trajectory with high accuracy. Astronomers care about one planet, but chemists don't care about one atom! They average over millions of orbits and they live with errors in timing (phase errors) along those orbits.

What astronomers and chemists cannot accept is a steady loss of energy for the sake of stability. Numerical damping is the savior of many computations in fluid dynamics, but it would bring a planet close to the Sun. The right choice for long-time integration is a symplectic method, and the favorite in molecular dynamics is **leapfrog-Verlet**. We write it as "Velocity Verlet" or "velocity centered leapfrog" with $V_{n+\frac{1}{2}}$ = normal leapfrog value and V_{n+1} = saved value after the complete step:

Velocity Verlet $\Delta t \leq 2/\lambda_{\max}(F')$: **stable** $(\Delta t)^2$ **accuracy**	$\begin{aligned} V_{n+\frac{1}{2}} &= V_n - \tfrac{1}{2}\Delta t\, F(U_n) \\ U_{n+1} &= U_n + \Delta t\, V_{n+\frac{1}{2}} \\ V_{n+1} &= V_{n+\frac{1}{2}} - \tfrac{1}{2}\Delta t\, F(U_{n+1}) \end{aligned}$	(35)

Long-time Integration

If you try to follow the Earth's orbit over many years, using Euler's explicit method $U_{n+1} = U_n + \Delta t\, f(U_n)$, you will soon be out beyond Pluto. These pages are about symplectic methods that maintain periodic motion, close to the correct orbits but not necessarily with the correct period. The Lotka-Volterra model from mathematical biology and ecology is an excellent nonlinear example with periodic solutions.

Example 3 **The Lotka-Volterra model** with populations u and v (*predator* and *prey*)

$$\begin{aligned} u' &= u(v-b) & &\text{Predator increases with more prey } v \\ v' &= v(a-u) & &\text{Prey decreases with more predators } u \end{aligned}$$

The system is in equilibrium when $u = a$ and $v = b$ (a critical point where $u' = v' = 0$). If $u_0 < a$ at the start, the prey v will begin to increase ($v' > 0$). Then the predators u increase by feeding on the prey. When u passes a, the prey population v starts to decrease. Then the predators decrease below a and the cycle starts again. To find this closed periodic orbit, combine the two equations and integrate:

$$\frac{u'}{u}(a-u) = \frac{v'}{v}(v-b) \quad \text{gives} \quad a \log u - u = v + b \log v + C. \tag{36}$$

The constant C is determined by u_0 and v_0. The solution $u(t), v(t)$ stays on its own curve in Figure 2.10, which is drawn in the u–v plane (the *phase plane*). This curve shows *where* the populations go but not *when*. For the timing we compute $u(t)$ and $v(t)$.

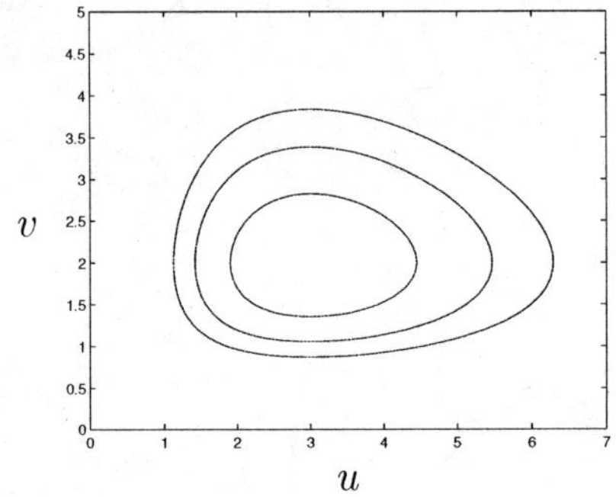

Figure 2.10: The predator u is in periodic equilibrium with the prey v.

Symplectic methods preserve phase plane areas, and this section ends with four options. We already know most of them. The system of equations is $u' = f(u)$.

1 Implicit midpoint rule $$U_{n+1} = U_n + \Delta t\, f\left(\frac{U_n + U_{n+1}}{2}\right) \tag{37}$$

2 Trapezoidal rule $$U_{n+1} = U_n + \frac{\Delta t}{2}\left(f(U_n) + f(U_{n+1})\right) \tag{38}$$

For a partitioned system $u' = g(u, v)$, $v' = h(u, v)$ like Lotka-Volterra, we can treat u by backward Euler (implicit) and then v by forward Euler:

3 Partitioned Euler $$U_{n+1} = U_n + \Delta t\, g(U_{n+1}, V_n) \tag{39a}$$

$$V_{n+1} = V_n + \Delta t\, h(U_{n+1}, V_n) \tag{39b}$$

A specially important partitioned system is $u' = v$ and $v' = -F(u)$. This reduces to $u'' + F(u) = 0$, for which the Störmer-Verlet-leapfrog method (35) was created.

What we now add is that Verlet is a composition of even simpler Euler methods, because the implicit step is actually explicit when $u' = g(v) = v$ depends only on v:

4 **Verlet for $2\,\Delta t$** (Partitioned Euler)(Partitioned Euler reversing U, V)

This "composition idea" imitates our symmetric matrix $A^{\mathrm{T}}A$ (now A is nonlinear). In fact $A^{\mathrm{T}}A$ will be midpoint or trapezoidal, when A is forward or backward Euler.

Finally, the test for a (nonlinear) 2 by 2 symplectic method is straightforward:

$$\begin{aligned} U_{n+1} &= G(U_n, V_n) \\ V_{n+1} &= H(U_n, V_n) \end{aligned} \quad \textbf{is symplectic if} \quad \frac{\partial G}{\partial U}\frac{\partial H}{\partial V} - \frac{\partial G}{\partial V}\frac{\partial H}{\partial U} = 1. \qquad (40)$$

The cse website displays the oscillations (normal modes) of a line of equal masses or a circle of masses. Each pure oscillation comes from an eigenvector of K or T or B or C. With $n = 4$ masses in a circle, the eigenvectors of C_4 are $(1,1,1,1)$ and $(1,0,-1,0)$ and $(0,1,0,-1)$ and $(1,-1,-1,1)$. That fourth one is the fastest, with two pairs of masses going in opposite directions. The pictures are worth seeing!

Problem Set 2.2

Problems 1-8 are about the four ways to draw circles (G_F, G_B, G_T, G_L).

1 The leapfrog matrix for $u''+u=0$ is $G_L = \begin{bmatrix} 1 & h \\ -h & 1-h^2 \end{bmatrix}$ with eigenvalues λ_1, λ_2.

(a) From the trace $\lambda_1 + \lambda_2 = e^{i\theta} + e^{-i\theta}$, find $\cos\theta = 1 - \frac{1}{2}h^2$ for $h \le 2$.

(b) At $h = 2$ find the eigenvalues and all eigenvectors of G_L.

(c) At $h = 3$ find the eigenvalues and verify $\lambda_1\lambda_2 = 1$ but $|\lambda_{\text{max}}| > 1$.

2 In Problem 1, $\cos\theta = 1 - \frac{1}{2}h^2$ turns into $h = 2\sin(\theta/2)$ by a half-angle formula. Then $\theta = 2\pi/N$ and $h = 2\sin(\pi/N)$ lead to $\cos N\theta = \cos 2\pi = 1$. In this special case (U_N, V_N) returns to (U_0, V_0) and $G^N = I$.

For $N = 3$ and 4, plot the N points $(U_n, V_n) = G^n(1,0)$. Check the *equal areas* of the 3 and 4 triangles from $(0,0)$ to (U_n, V_n) to (U_{n+1}, V_{n+1}).

3 (Big challenge) I have no idea of the axes of the inner ellipse in Figure 2.7.

4 The leapfrog ellipse in Figure 2.6 has half-axes σ_1 and σ_2, the square roots of the eigenvalues of $G_L^{\mathrm{T}}G_L$. Show that this matrix has determinant 1 (so $\sigma_1\sigma_2 = 1$) and trace $2 + h^4$ (which is $\sigma_1^2 + \sigma_2^2$, the sum of the eigenvalues):

Ellipse close to circle $\quad (\sigma_1 - \sigma_2)^2 = \sigma_1^2 + \sigma_2^2 - 2 = h^4 \quad$ and $\quad \sigma_{\text{max}} - \sigma_{\text{min}} = h^2.$

5 The matrix in this question is skew-symmetric ($A^{\mathrm{T}} = -A$):

$$\frac{du}{dt} = \begin{bmatrix} 0 & c & -b \\ -c & 0 & a \\ b & -a & 0 \end{bmatrix} u \quad \text{or} \quad \begin{aligned} u_1' &= cu_2 - bu_3 \\ u_2' &= au_3 - cu_1 \\ u_3' &= bu_1 - au_2. \end{aligned}$$

(a) The derivative of $\|u(t)\|^2 = u_1^2 + u_2^2 + u_3^2$ is $2u_1u_1' + 2u_2u_2' + 2u_3u_3'$. Substitute u_1', u_2', u_3' to get *derivative* = *zero*. Then $\|u(t)\|^2 = \|u(0)\|^2$.

(b) In matrix language, $Q = e^{At}$ is *orthogonal*. Prove that $Q^{\mathrm{T}} = e^{-At}$ from the series $Q = e^{At} = I + At + (At)^2/2! + \cdots$. Then $Q^{\mathrm{T}}Q = e^{-At}e^{At} = I$.

6 The trapezoidal rule conserves the energy $\|u\|^2$ when $u' = Au$ and $A^{\mathrm{T}} = -A$. *Multiply* (24) *by* $U_{n+1} + U_n$. *Show that* $\|U_{n+1}\|^2 = \|U_n\|^2$. The growth matrix $G_T = (I - A\Delta t/2)^{-1}(I + A\Delta t/2)$ is orthogonal like e^{At} if $A^{\mathrm{T}} = -A$.

$$\boldsymbol{u' = Au} \textbf{ conserves } \|\boldsymbol{u}\|^2 \quad \frac{d}{dt}(u, u) = (u', u) + (u, u') = ((A + A^{\mathrm{T}})u, u) = 0.$$

7 The trapezoidal rule has no energy error but a small phase error. The 32 steps with $h = 2\pi/32$ don't give a perfect 1. Compute λ^{32} and its angle θ when $\lambda = (1 + i\frac{h}{2})/(1 - i\frac{h}{2})$.

Which low power of h is wrong when you compare λ with e^{ih}?

8 Forward Euler multiplies the energy by $1 + h^2$ at every step:

$$\textbf{Energy} \quad U_{n+1}^2 + V_{n+1}^2 = (U_n + hV_n)^2 + (\qquad\qquad)^2 = (1 + h^2)(U_n^2 + V_n^2).$$

Compute $(1+h^2)^{32}$ for $h = 2\pi/32$. Is it true or not that $(1+h^2)^{2\pi/h}$ approaches 1 as $h \to 0$? If true, Euler does converge slowly. Show that a backward Euler step *divides* the energy $U_n^2 + V_n^2$ by $1 + h^2$.

9 The "*ma*" in Newton's Law has three steps $d/dt\,(m(u,t)\,du/dt)$. When the mass is constant, this is mu''. But Einstein found that mass increases with velocity. A low-speed example: Suppose rain falls into an open train at rate $r = dm/dt$. What force F will keep the train at constant velocity v? (Here $ma = 0$ but $F \neq 0$.)

10 In equation (16), show that the resonance is the limit of the near resonance formula as ω_0 approaches λ. L'Hôpital's Rule f'/g', for the limit as f/g approaches 0/0, is needed after all these years!

11 The "*Hamiltonian*" is the total energy $H = \frac{1}{2}p^{\mathrm{T}}M^{-1}p + \frac{1}{2}u^{\mathrm{T}}Ku$ for oscillating linear springs and masses. The position u and momentum p (instead of the velocity u') are Hamilton's preferred unknowns. From Hamilton's equations $p' = -\partial H/\partial u$ and $u' = \partial H/\partial p$, derive Newton's Law $Mu'' + Ku = 0$.

12 Show that $H(p,u) = \textit{constant}$ is a first integral for Hamilton's equations:

Chain rule $$\frac{dH}{dt} = \frac{\partial H}{\partial p}\frac{dp}{dt} + \frac{\partial H}{\partial u}\frac{du}{dt} = \_\_\_\_ + \_\_\_\_ = 0.$$

Great scientists hoped for a second integral, to complete the solution. We now know this is impossible for three attracting bodies. Pluto's orbit is chaotic.

13 The sun and one planet have $H = \frac{1}{2}p_1^2 + \frac{1}{2}p_2^2 - (u_1^2 + u_2^2)^{-1/2}$ by the law of gravity. From $p_i' = -\partial H/\partial u_i$ and $u_i' = \partial H/\partial p_i$ show that the area $A(t) = u_1 p_2 - u_2 p_1$ in the u-p plane has $dA/dt = 0$.

This is Kepler's Second Law: the line from sun to planet sweeps out area at a constant rate. Newton discovered Verlet's method in 1687 when he gave a geometric proof of this law (*Principia* Book I). "Gravitation is symplectic."

14 In the Lotka-Volterra example, $a \log u + b \log v - u - v$ stays constant. With $p = \log u$ and $q = \log v$, this constant is $H = ap + bq - e^p - e^q$. Show that Hamilton's $p' = -\partial H/\partial q$ and $q' = \partial H/\partial p$ are exactly the Lotka-Volterra equations. In logarithmic scale, area is preserved in the predator-prey plane.

15 The linear step $U_{n+1} = a\,U_n + b\,V_n$, $V_{n+1} = c\,U_n + d\,V_n$ is symplectic by the test (40) when $\_\_\_\_ = 1$. What matrix G has determinant 1? Then triangle areas stay the same:

$$\det \begin{bmatrix} U_{n+1} & U_{n+2} \\ V_{n+1} & V_{n+2} \end{bmatrix} = (\det G)\ \det \begin{bmatrix} U_n & U_{n+1} \\ V_n & V_{n+1} \end{bmatrix}.$$

16 Show that nonlinear leapfrog also passes the test $\dfrac{\partial G}{\partial U}\dfrac{\partial H}{\partial V} - \dfrac{\partial G}{\partial V}\dfrac{\partial H}{\partial U} = 1.$

$$\begin{aligned} U_{n+1} &= G(U_n, V_n) &&= U_n + hV_n \\ V_{n+1} &= H(U_n, V_n) &&= V_n + hF(U_{n+1}) = V_n + hF(U_n + hV_n). \end{aligned}$$

17 For one equation $mu'' + cu = 0$, write down the leapfrog equations for U_{n+1} and V_{n+1}. Find the growth matrix G and the sum of its eigenvalues (the trace $G_{11} + G_{22}$). Show that $(\Delta t)^2 \le 4m/c$ is the stability test for trace ≥ -2.

18 Graph the difference $\cos 9t - \cos 11t$. You should see a fast oscillation inside a slow $2 \sin t$ envelope, because this difference (an undamped forced oscillation) equals $2 \sin 10t \sin t$.

2.3 LEAST SQUARES FOR RECTANGULAR MATRICES

This section starts again with a linear system $Au = b$, but there is a big difference from $Ku = f$. The matrix K is square and invertible. In contrast, the matrix A is rectangular: more equations than unknowns ($\boldsymbol{m > n}$). The equations $Au = b$ have **no solution** and A^{-1} does not exist. We have to find the **best solution $\widehat{u}$ when the system $Au = b$ is overdetermined**: too many equations.

Unsolvable equations are absolutely normal, when we try to fit m measurements by a small number n of parameters (linear regression in statistics). We might have $m = 100$ points that nearly fall on a straight line. But a line $C + Dx$ has only $n = 2$ parameters C and D. An exact fit means solving 100 equations with 2 unknowns. The closest line should be more reliable as m increases beyond 100 (more measurements). But $Au = b$ is less likely to be exactly solvable, as we try to fit more points.

Example 1 Suppose we measure $b = 1, 9, 9, 21$ at the four positions $x = 0, 1, 3, 4$. If a straight line $C + Dx$ passed through all four points (which I doubt), then the two unknowns $u = (C, D)$ would solve four equations $Au = b$:

Line through 4 points: unsolvable

$$\begin{aligned} C + 0D &= 1 \\ C + 1D &= 9 \\ C + 3D &= 9 \\ C + 4D &= 21 \end{aligned} \quad \text{or} \quad \begin{bmatrix} 1 & 0 \\ 1 & 1 \\ 1 & 3 \\ 1 & 4 \end{bmatrix} \begin{bmatrix} C \\ D \end{bmatrix} = \begin{bmatrix} 1 \\ 9 \\ 9 \\ 21 \end{bmatrix}. \tag{1}$$

Those equations have no solution. The vector b on the right is not a combination of the two column vectors $(1, 1, 1, 1)$ and $(0, 1, 3, 4)$. The first equation gives $C = 1$, then the second equation gives $D = 8$, then the other equations fail by a lot. This line $1 + 8x$ through the first two points is almost certainly not the best line.

The four equations in $Au = b$ will have errors e_1, e_2, e_3, e_4. Right now one equation is not more reliable than another. So we minimize the sum $e_1^2 + e_2^2 + e_3^2 + e_4^2$ which is $e^{\mathrm{T}}e$. Since the residual error is $e = b - Au$ (right side minus left side), we are minimizing the total squared error $E = (b - Au)^{\mathrm{T}}(b - Au) =$ (**sum of squares**):

Total squared error $\boldsymbol{E = \|e\|^2 = \|b - Au\|^2}$

$$E = (1 - C - 0D)^2 + (9 - C - 1D)^2 + (9 - C - 3D)^2 + (21 - C - 4D)^2.$$

Our rule will be the **principle of least squares**. The vector $e = b - Au$ gives the errors in the m equations. We choose $\widehat{u}$ (in this case $\widehat{C}$ and $\widehat{D}$) so that this error is as small as possible, and here we measure the error by $\|e\|^2 = e_1^2 + \cdots + e_m^2 = E$.

If A has independent columns, then $A^{\mathrm{T}}A$ is invertible. **The normal equations will produce $\widehat{u}$.** If A has dependent columns (or almost dependent, so its condition number is large), the QR factorization is much safer. Least squares is a projection of b onto the columns of A.

Summary The (unweighted) least squares method chooses $\widehat{u}$ to minimize $\|e\|^2$.

Least Squares **Minimize** $\|\boldsymbol{b} - \boldsymbol{A}\boldsymbol{u}\|^2 = (\boldsymbol{b} - \boldsymbol{A}\boldsymbol{u})^{\mathrm{T}}(\boldsymbol{b} - \boldsymbol{A}\boldsymbol{u})$.

We can use pure linear algebra to find the best $\widehat{u}$, or pure calculus. No statistics are involved at this point. We are treating all m measurements as independent and equally reliable. I will give away the answer immediately (the equation for $\widehat{u}$), and then explain it in two ways. **The least squares estimate for $\boldsymbol{u}$ is the solution $\widehat{\boldsymbol{u}}$ of the square symmetric system using $\boldsymbol{A}^{\mathrm{T}}\boldsymbol{A}$:**

"Normal equation" $\boldsymbol{A}^{\mathrm{T}}\boldsymbol{A}\widehat{\boldsymbol{u}} = \boldsymbol{A}^{\mathrm{T}}\boldsymbol{b}$. (2)

In short, multiply the unsolvable equations $Au = b$ by A^{T}. Solve $A^{\mathrm{T}}A\widehat{u} = A^{\mathrm{T}}b$.

Example 1 (completed) The normal equation $A^{\mathrm{T}}A\widehat{u} = A^{\mathrm{T}}b$ in equation (2) is

$$\begin{bmatrix} 1 & 1 & 1 & 1 \\ 0 & 1 & 3 & 4 \end{bmatrix} \begin{bmatrix} 1 & 0 \\ 1 & 1 \\ 1 & 3 \\ 1 & 4 \end{bmatrix} \begin{bmatrix} \widehat{C} \\ \widehat{D} \end{bmatrix} = \begin{bmatrix} 1 & 1 & 1 & 1 \\ 0 & 1 & 3 & 4 \end{bmatrix} \begin{bmatrix} 1 \\ 9 \\ 9 \\ 21 \end{bmatrix}.$$

After multiplication this matrix $A^{\mathrm{T}}A$ is square and symmetric and positive definite:

$$\boldsymbol{A}^{\mathrm{T}}\boldsymbol{A}\widehat{\boldsymbol{u}} = \boldsymbol{A}^{\mathrm{T}}\boldsymbol{b} \qquad \begin{bmatrix} 4 & 8 \\ 8 & 26 \end{bmatrix} \begin{bmatrix} \widehat{C} \\ \widehat{D} \end{bmatrix} = \begin{bmatrix} 40 \\ 120 \end{bmatrix} \quad \text{gives} \quad \begin{bmatrix} \widehat{C} \\ \widehat{D} \end{bmatrix} = \begin{bmatrix} 2 \\ 4 \end{bmatrix}. \qquad (3)$$

At $x = 0, 1, 3, 4$ this best line $2 + 4x$ in Figure 2.11 has heights $p = 2, 6, 14, 18$. The minimum error $b - p$ is $e = (-1, 3, -5, 3)$. The picture on the right is the "linear algebra way" to see least squares. We project b to p in the column space of A (you see how p is perpendicular to the error vector e). Then $A\widehat{u} = p$ has the best right side p. The solution $\widehat{u} = (\widehat{C}, \widehat{D}) = (2, 4)$ is the best choice of C and D.

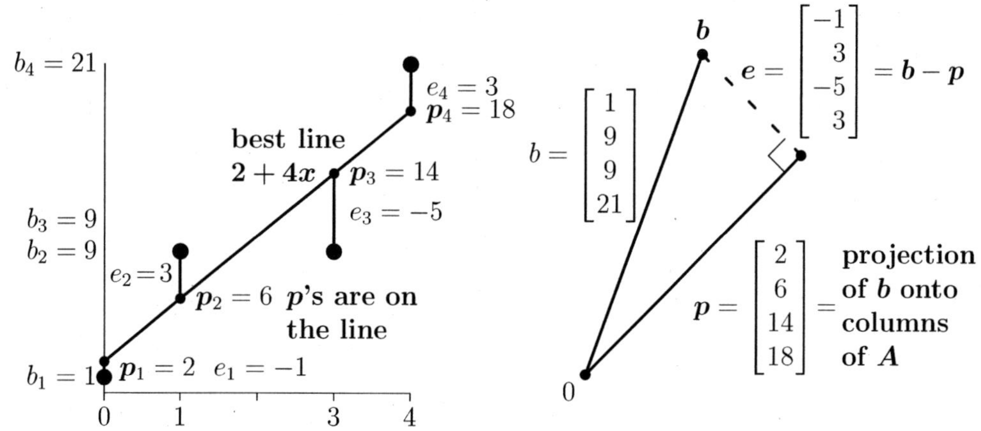

Figure 2.11: The total error is $e^{\mathrm{T}}e = 1+9+25+9 = 44$. Other lines have more error.

Underdetermined Equations and Sparsity

Before continuing with least squares, allow me to mention recent developments. I can introduce them by discussing the opposite situation when the matrix A has $m << n$. Then we have far fewer measurements (samples in b) than descriptive parameters (unknowns in u). Instead of expecting no solution to an overdetermined $Au = b$ (and choosing a best $\widehat{u}$ for $m > n$ equations), the underdetermined $Au = b$ has **infinitely many solutions**. What rule should govern the new choice u^*?

You would think that this century of data never leaves us with too few samples. But the fantastically active areas of gene expression analysis and bioinformatics present this problem all the time. We have 30,000 genes, and maybe samples from 20 patients. The great puzzle (very unsolved as I write this in 2007) is to discover which genes are responsible for the good or bad outcomes observed in those patients.

A very similar problem appears in **sparse sensing**. A signal or an image is sampled only a few times, far fewer than the number of bits in the signal. How can we possibly reconstruct an accurate signal? This is closely related to **sparse compression**. How can we represent images by storing only a few bits, and still reconstruct their essential features with high probability (although never 100 %)?

Part of the answer is that the sum of squares norm (Euclidean norm) is not appropriate. That $\boldsymbol{\ell^2}$ ***norm*** led to the pseudoinverse A^+ in Section 1.7, but A^+b is generally a poor u^*. In the gene expression problem, we are looking for a few responsible genes. A vector A^+b that involves all 30,000 genes in very small amounts is perfectly useless. Small is good in ℓ^2, because of the squaring, but zero is much better in many applications. We want a lot of zeros in u^*, *with a few nonzeros in the right positions.* The norm that is dominating the new developments is the $\boldsymbol{\ell^1}$ ***norm***:

ℓ^1 and L^1 norm $\quad \|u\|_1 = |u_1| + \cdots + |u_n| \quad$ and $\quad \|u(x)\|_1 = \int |u(x)|\, dx. \qquad (4)$

I emphasize also the ℓ^1 and L^1 norms of the difference Δu and derivative $u'(x)$:

Total variation $\quad \|u\|_V = |u_2 - u_1| + \cdots + |u_n - u_{n-1}| \quad$ and $\quad \|u(x)\|_V = \int |u'(x)|\, dx. \qquad (5)$

Minimizing $\|u\|_V$ removes oscillations that don't cost much in ℓ^2 or L^2. Section 4.7 shows how these norms are used to compress signals and produce good images.

Historically, the ℓ^1 norm appeared in statistics because of outliers b_i with large errors. Minimizing $||Au - b||^2$ gave too much importance to those b_i. To fit data that includes significant noise, robust regression prefers to avoid squaring large $(Au - b)_i$. It is curious that now (to achieve sparsity) we avoid squaring small u's.

There is a computational cost in any move from ℓ^2 to ℓ^1. The normal equation $A^TA\widehat{u} = A^Tb$ for the best ℓ^2 solution is linear. An ℓ^1 penalty makes it *piecewise* linear, with exponentially many pieces. **The problem is to identify which components of the best $\boldsymbol{u^*}$ are nonzero.** This is the task of linear programming, to find the right m nonzeros among the n components of u. The binomial coefficient $\binom{n}{m} = n!/m!\,(n-m)!$ counts the possible combinations. For $m = 20$ samples and $n = 30{,}000$ genes, this is a daunting number that I won't even estimate.

Section 8.6 describes two ways to compute u^*: the simplex method and the interior-point methods. Interior-point is a "primal-dual algorithm" that uses Newton's method of Section 2.6 on the nonlinear optimality equations in Section 8.6.

To summarize: Energy minimization is a fundamental principle and it leads to ℓ^2. That principle dominates this book. Minimization with sparsity leads to ℓ^1.

This idea is at the heart of the intense efforts, and the host of proposed algorithms, to improve data compression and sampling. Surprisingly, the best sampling is by inner products with random vectors. Coherence will defeat the plan of reconstructing full images from sparse data. I notice sparsity appearing also in biomechanics: If many muscles are available to support a load, do a few of them actually do the job? The same question could be asked for human society: If m jobs have $n >> m$ available workers, do m or n of them actually do the work?

Least Squares by Calculus

Suppose we have only one unknown u but two equations. Thus $n = 1$ but $m = 2$ (probably no solution). One unknown means only one column in A:

$$\boldsymbol{Au = b} \qquad \begin{aligned} a_1 u &= b_1 \\ a_2 u &= b_2 \end{aligned} \qquad \text{or} \qquad \begin{bmatrix} a_1 \\ a_2 \end{bmatrix} u = \begin{bmatrix} b_1 \\ b_2 \end{bmatrix}.$$

The matrix A is 2 by 1. The squared error $e^{\mathrm{T}}e$ is the sum of two terms:

Sum of squares

$$E(u) = (a_1 u - b_1)^2 + (a_2 u - b_2)^2\,. \tag{6}$$

The graph of $E(u)$ is a parabola. Its bottom point is at the least squares solution $\widehat{u}$. The minimum error occurs when $dE/du = 0$:

Equation for $\widehat{u}$

$$\frac{dE}{du} = 2a_1\,(a_1\widehat{u} - b_1) + 2a_2\,(a_2\widehat{u} - b_2) = 0\,. \tag{7}$$

Canceling the 2's leaves $(a_1^2 + a_2^2)\,\widehat{u} = (a_1 b_1 + a_2 b_2)$. The left side is $a_1^2 + a_2^2 = A^{\mathrm{T}}A$. The right side is now $a_1 b_1 + a_2 b_2 = A^{\mathrm{T}}b$. Calculus has found $A^{\mathrm{T}}A\widehat{u} = A^{\mathrm{T}}b$:

$$\begin{bmatrix} a_1 & a_2 \end{bmatrix} \begin{bmatrix} a_1 \\ a_2 \end{bmatrix} \widehat{u} = \begin{bmatrix} a_1 & a_2 \end{bmatrix} \begin{bmatrix} b_1 \\ b_2 \end{bmatrix} \quad \text{produces} \quad \widehat{u} = \frac{\boldsymbol{a}^{\mathrm{T}}\boldsymbol{b}}{\boldsymbol{a}^{\mathrm{T}}\boldsymbol{a}} = \frac{a_1 b_1 + a_2 b_2}{a_1^2 + a_2^2}\,. \tag{8}$$

Example 2 The special case $a_1 = a_2 = 1$ has two measurements $u = b_1$ and $u = b_2$ of the same quantity (like pulse rate or blood pressure). The matrix has $A^{\mathrm{T}} = [1 \quad 1]$. To minimize $(u - b_1)^2 + (u - b_2)^2$, the best $\widehat{u}$ is just the average measurement:

$$\text{If} \quad a_1 = a_2 = 1 \quad \text{then} \quad A^{\mathrm{T}}A = 2 \quad \text{and} \quad A^{\mathrm{T}}b = b_1 + b_2 \quad \text{and} \quad \widehat{u} = \frac{b_1 + b_2}{2}.$$

The average $\widehat{u}$ between b_1 and b_2 makes the sum of squared distances smallest.

For m equations $Au = b$ in n unknowns, we need matrix notation. The squared errors add to $E = \|b - Au\|^2 = \|Au - b\|^2$. In (6) this was $(a_1u - b_1)^2 + (a_2u - b_2)^2$. Now we separate the quadratic term $\|Au\|^2 = u^{\mathrm{T}}A^{\mathrm{T}}Au$ from the linear terms and the constant term $b^{\mathrm{T}}b$, to see the general case:

Error squared $$E(u) = u^{\mathrm{T}}A^{\mathrm{T}}Au - (Au)^{\mathrm{T}}b - b^{\mathrm{T}}(Au) + b^{\mathrm{T}}b. \tag{9}$$

The term $(Au)^{\mathrm{T}}b$ is the same as $b^{\mathrm{T}}(Au)$; either vector can come first, making $2u^{\mathrm{T}}A^{\mathrm{T}}b$. Write $\boldsymbol{K} = \boldsymbol{A^{\mathrm{T}}A}$ in the quadratic term, and $\boldsymbol{f} = \boldsymbol{A^{\mathrm{T}}b}$ in the linear term:

Minimize $u^{\mathrm{T}}A^{\mathrm{T}}Au - 2u^{\mathrm{T}}A^{\mathrm{T}}b + b^{\mathrm{T}}b$ which is $\boldsymbol{u^{\mathrm{T}}Ku - 2u^{\mathrm{T}}f} + b^{\mathrm{T}}b$.

The constant term $b^{\mathrm{T}}b$ doesn't affect the minimization. The minimizing $\widehat{u}$ solves $K\widehat{u} = f$, which is $A^{\mathrm{T}}A\widehat{u} = A^{\mathrm{T}}b$. When $K = A^{\mathrm{T}}A$ is positive definite we know that $\widehat{u}$ yields a minimum in Figure 2.12 and not a maximum or a saddle point. For two variables $u = (u_1, u_2)$, we can see $K\widehat{u} = f$ by calculus:

$$\begin{aligned}&\text{Minimize} \quad \left(k_{11}u_1^2 + k_{12}u_1u_2 + k_{21}u_2u_1 + k_{22}u_2^2\right) - 2\left(u_1f_1 + u_2f_2\right) + b^{\mathrm{T}}b \\ &u_1 \text{ derivative is zero:} \quad 2(k_{11}\widehat{u}_1 + k_{12}\widehat{u}_2 - f_1) = 0 \\ &u_2 \text{ derivative is zero:} \quad 2(k_{21}\widehat{u}_1 + k_{22}\widehat{u}_2 - f_2) = 0\end{aligned} \qquad \text{which is } \boldsymbol{K\widehat{u} = f}.$$

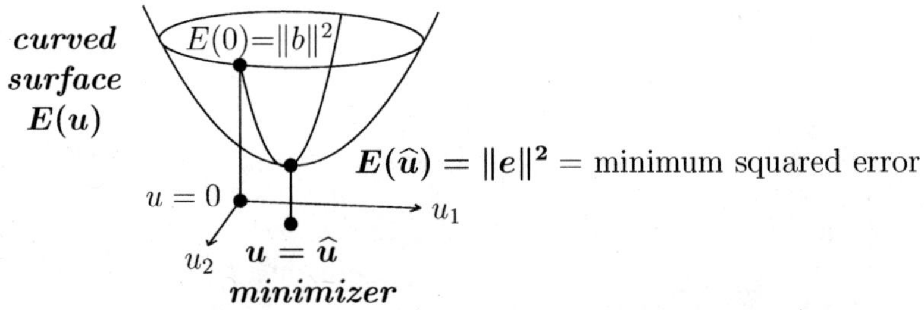

Figure 2.12: The graph of $E(u) = \|b - Au\|^2$ is a bowl opening upward. The lowest point occurs at $\widehat{u} = (A^{\mathrm{T}}A)^{-1}A^{\mathrm{T}}b$. There $E(\widehat{u}) = \|e\|^2 = \|b\|^2 - \|A\widehat{u}\|^2$.

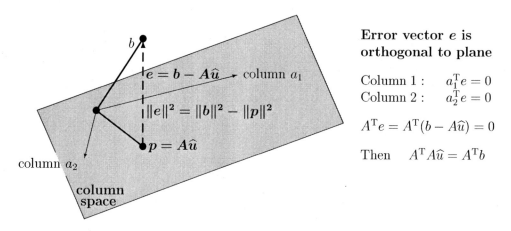

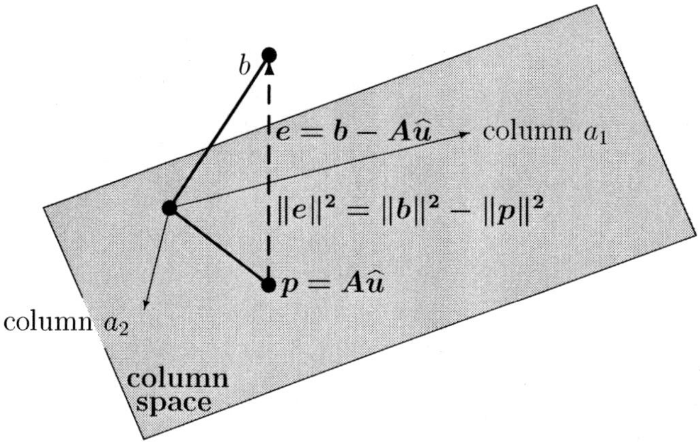

Error vector e is orthogonal to plane

Column 1 : $a_1^{\mathrm{T}} e = 0$
Column 2 : $a_2^{\mathrm{T}} e = 0$

$A^{\mathrm{T}} e = A^{\mathrm{T}}(b - A\widehat{u}) = 0$

Then $A^{\mathrm{T}} A\widehat{u} = A^{\mathrm{T}} b$

Figure 2.13: The projection p is the nearest point to b in the column space of A. The perpendicular error $e = b - A\widehat{u}$ has $A^{\mathrm{T}}e = 0$. Then $A^{\mathrm{T}}A\widehat{u} = A^{\mathrm{T}}b$.

Least Squares by Linear Algebra

In the linear algebra picture, b is in m-dimensional space. The impossible equation $Au = b$ is trying to write b as a combination of the n columns of A. But those columns only give an n-dimensional plane inside the much larger m-dimensional space. The vector b is not likely to lie in that plane, so $Au = b$ is not likely to be solvable. **The least squares choice $A\widehat{u}$ is the point in the plane that is nearest to b.**

Here is the one-line proof from Section 1.6 that the total error E in equation (9) has its minimum when $\widehat{u} = K^{-1}f = (A^{\mathrm{T}}A)^{-1}A^{\mathrm{T}}b$. Rewrite $E(u)$ in a special way:

$$u^{\mathrm{T}}Ku - 2u^{\mathrm{T}}f + b^{\mathrm{T}}b = \left(u - K^{-1}f\right)^{\mathrm{T}} K \left(u - K^{-1}f\right) - f^{\mathrm{T}}K^{-1}f + b^{\mathrm{T}}b\,. \tag{10}$$

The right side is smallest when its first term is zero, because that term is never negative. So the minimizer is $\widehat{u} = K^{-1}f$. Then E reduces to the last two terms: $E_{\mathsf{min}} = -f^{\mathrm{T}}K^{-1}f + b^{\mathrm{T}}b$, which is also the bottom height in the calculus picture:

$$E_{\mathsf{min}} = E(\widehat{u}) = (b - A\widehat{u})^{\mathrm{T}}(b - A\widehat{u}) = b^{\mathrm{T}}b - b^{\mathrm{T}}A(A^{\mathrm{T}}A)^{-1}A^{\mathrm{T}}b\,. \tag{11}$$

Figure 2.13 has the error $e = b - A\widehat{u}$ in its correct place. This error is not zero ($Au = b$ has no solution) unless perfect measurements put b in the column space. **The best $A\widehat{u}$ is the projection p.** This is the part of b that we can account for, by the columns of A. The residual error $e = b - A\widehat{u}$ is the part we can't account for.

The picture shows the key to the projection $A\widehat{u}$. Now we need the equation.

The error vector $e = b - A\widehat{u}$ is perpendicular to the column space. The n dot products of e with the columns of A are all zero, which gives n equations $A^{\mathrm{T}}e = 0$:

Perpendicularity $\begin{bmatrix} (\text{column } 1)^{\mathrm{T}} \\ \vdots \\ (\text{column } n)^{\mathrm{T}} \end{bmatrix} \begin{bmatrix} \\ e \\ \\ \end{bmatrix} = \begin{bmatrix} 0 \\ \vdots \\ 0 \end{bmatrix}$ or $\boldsymbol{A^{\mathrm{T}}e = 0}$.

This geometry equation $A^{\mathrm{T}}e = 0$ finds $\widehat{u}$. The projection is $p = A\widehat{u}$ (the combination of columns that is closest to b). We reach again the normal equation for $\widehat{u}$:

Linear algebra $\quad A^{\mathrm{T}}e = A^{\mathrm{T}}(b - A\widehat{u}) = 0 \quad \text{gives} \quad A^{\mathrm{T}}A\widehat{u} = A^{\mathrm{T}}b. \qquad (12)$

Changing from the minimum in calculus to the projection in linear algebra gives the right triangle with sides b, p, e. The perpendicular vector e hits the column space at the nearest point $p = A\widehat{u}$. This is the *projection of b onto the column space*:

Projection $\quad \widehat{u} = (A^{\mathrm{T}}A)^{-1}A^{\mathrm{T}}b \quad p = A\widehat{u} = \left[\boldsymbol{A(A^{\mathrm{T}}A)^{-1}A^{\mathrm{T}}}\right] b = \boldsymbol{P}b. \qquad (13)$

The system $Au = b$ had no solution. The system $Au = p$ has one solution $\widehat{u}$. We are making the smallest adjustment from b to p that puts us in the column space. The measurements are inconsistent in $Au = b$, but consistent in $A\widehat{u} = p$.

The **projection matrix** $P = A(A^{\mathrm{T}}A)^{-1}A^{\mathrm{T}}$ is symmetric. It has the special property $\boldsymbol{P^2 = P}$, because two projections give the same result as one projection. P is m by m but its rank is only n. All three factors in $A(A^{\mathrm{T}}A)^{-1}A^{\mathrm{T}}$ have rank n.

Example 3 A plane is overdetermined by trying to pass through four points in space. Find the closest plane $b = C + Dx + Ey$ (choose the best three parameters $\widehat{C}, \widehat{D}, \widehat{E}$).

Solution Four unsolvable equations $Au = b$ aim to reach height b_i above (x_i, y_i). They have no solution $u = (C, D, E)$. The normal equation $A^{\mathrm{T}}A\widehat{u} = A^{\mathrm{T}}b$ gives the best $\widehat{u} = \widehat{C}, \widehat{D}, \widehat{E})$ and the closest plane in Figure 2.14.

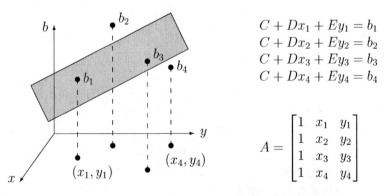

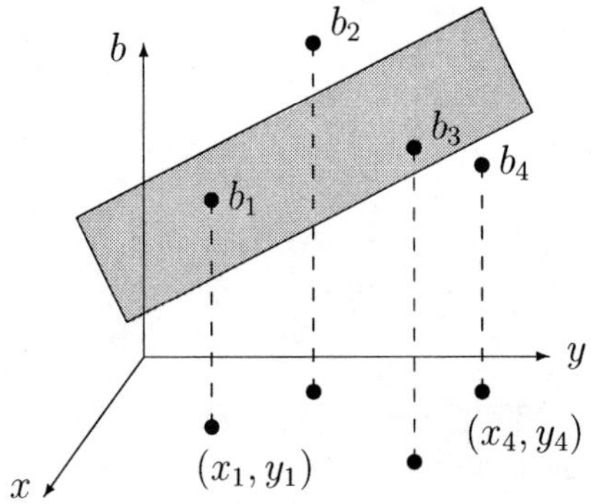

$$\begin{aligned} C + Dx_1 + Ey_1 &= b_1 \\ C + Dx_2 + Ey_2 &= b_2 \\ C + Dx_3 + Ey_3 &= b_3 \\ C + Dx_4 + Ey_4 &= b_4 \end{aligned}$$

$$A = \begin{bmatrix} 1 & x_1 & y_1 \\ 1 & x_2 & y_2 \\ 1 & x_3 & y_3 \\ 1 & x_4 & y_4 \end{bmatrix}$$

Figure 2.14: The equation $A^{\mathrm{T}}A\widehat{u} = A^{\mathrm{T}}b$ gives $\widehat{u} = (\widehat{C}, \widehat{D}, \widehat{E})$ and the closest plane.

Example 4 Suppose we are tracking a satellite or monitoring the net worth of a company. (There is uncertainty in both.) Let us accept $u_0 = 0$ as an accurate starting value, in kilometers and dollars. We measure the *changes* $u_1 - u_0, u_2 - u_1, u_3 - u_2$ between times t_0 and t_1, then t_1 and t_2, then t_2 and t_3. The measurements give

$$\begin{aligned} u_1 - u_0 &= b_1 \quad \text{(with variance } \sigma_1^2 = 1/c_1) \\ u_2 - u_1 &= b_2 \quad \text{(with variance } \sigma_2^2 = 1/c_2) \\ u_3 - u_2 &= b_3 \quad \text{(with variance } \sigma_3^2 = 1/c_3) \end{aligned}$$

It would not be surprising if c_i is proportional to the time interval $t_{i+1} - t_i$ (greater accuracy over a short time interval). For the 3 by 3 system we don't need least squares:

$$\begin{bmatrix} 1 & 0 & 0 \\ -1 & 1 & 0 \\ 0 & -1 & 1 \end{bmatrix} \begin{bmatrix} u_1 \\ u_2 \\ u_3 \end{bmatrix} = \begin{bmatrix} b_1 \\ b_2 \\ b_3 \end{bmatrix} \quad \text{gives} \quad \begin{aligned} u_1 &= b_1 \\ u_2 &= b_1 + b_2 \\ u_3 &= b_1 + b_2 + b_3 \end{aligned} \tag{14}$$

Now add a measurement b_4 of u_3 (with variance $\sigma_4^2 = 1/c_4$). This adds a fourth row to A, and $Au = b$ becomes rectangular. We use weighted least squares:

$$A = \begin{bmatrix} 1 & 0 & 0 \\ -1 & 1 & 0 \\ 0 & -1 & 1 \\ 0 & 0 & 1 \end{bmatrix} \quad A^{\mathrm{T}}A = \begin{bmatrix} 2 & -1 & 0 \\ -1 & 2 & -1 \\ 0 & -1 & 2 \end{bmatrix} \quad A^{\mathrm{T}}CA = \begin{bmatrix} c_1 + c_2 & -c_2 & 0 \\ -c_2 & c_2 + c_3 & -c_3 \\ 0 & -c_3 & c_3 + c_4 \end{bmatrix}$$

Please notice $A^{\mathrm{T}}A$, which is our **fixed-fixed** matrix K_3. The matrix $A^{\mathrm{T}}CA$ already appeared in Section 2.1, for a line of four springs. This example connects least squares to physics, and it leads to *recursive least squares* and the *Kalman filter*:

How can we update the old u to the new $\widehat{u}$ which accounts for b_4?

Adding a new row to A only changes $A^{\mathrm{T}}CA$ in its last row and column. We want to compute the new $\widehat{u}$ from $A^{\mathrm{T}}CA$ (now including $c_4 = 1/\sigma_4^2$) without repeating the work already finished using b_1, b_2, b_3. Section 2.8 will update $\widehat{u}$ by **recursive least squares**.

Computational Least Squares

We stay with the basic question in numerical linear algebra: ***How to compute $\widehat{u}$?***

So far you have only seen one way: Solve the normal equations by elimination. That requires forming $A^{\mathrm{T}}A$ or $A^{\mathrm{T}}CA$, and most people do it. But the condition number of $A^{\mathrm{T}}A$ is the *square* of the condition number of A in Section 1.7. Working with $A^{\mathrm{T}}A$ can make an unstable problem very unstable.

When stability is in doubt, experts recommend a different computation of $\widehat{u}$: *orthogonalize the columns.* ***The rectangular matrix A is split into QR.***

$A = QR$ has a matriz Q with orthonormal columns times an upper triangular matrix R. Then $A^{\mathrm{T}}A\widehat{u} = A^{\mathrm{T}}b$ reduces to a much simpler equation, because $\boldsymbol{Q}^{\mathrm{T}}\boldsymbol{Q} = \boldsymbol{I}$:

$$(QR)^{\mathrm{T}}QR\widehat{u} = (QR)^{\mathrm{T}}b \quad \text{is} \quad R^{\mathrm{T}}R\widehat{u} = R^{\mathrm{T}}Q^{\mathrm{T}}b \quad \text{and then} \quad \boldsymbol{R\widehat{u}} = \boldsymbol{Q^{\mathrm{T}}b}. \tag{15}$$

We multiply $Q^{\mathrm{T}}b$ (this is very stable). Then back-substitution with R is very simple. For full matrices, producing Q and R takes twice as long as the mn^2 steps to form $A^{\mathrm{T}}A$. That extra cost gives a more reliable solution.

One way to compute Q and R is by **Gram-Schmidt** (*modified*). The orthonormal columns $q_1, \ldots, q_n$ come from the columns $a_1, \ldots, a_n$ of A. Here is how Gram and Schmidt might do it in MATLAB. Start with $[m, n] = \text{size}(A); Q = \text{zeros}(m, n);$ $R = \text{zeros}(n, n);$ to initialize the matrices, then go a column at a time:

```
for j = 1:n                         % Gram-Schmidt orthogonalization
  v = A(:,j);                       % v begins as column j of A
  for i = 1:j-1                     % columns up to j-1, already settled in Q
    R(i,j) = Q(:,i)'*A(:,j);        % modify A(:,j) to v for more accuracy
    v = v-R(i,j)*Q(:,i);            % subtract the projection (q_i^T a_j)q_i = (q_i^T v)q_i
  end                               % v is now perpendicular to all of q_1,...,q_{j-1}
  R(j,j) = norm(v);
  Q(:,j) = v/R(j,j);                % normalize v to be the next unit vector q_j
end
```

If you undo the last step and the middle steps, you find column j:

$$R(j,j)q_j = (v \textit{ minus its projections}) = (\text{column } j \text{ of } A) - \sum_{i=1}^{j-1} R(i,j)q_i\,. \tag{16}$$

Moving the sum to the far left, this is column j in the multiplication $A = QR$.

That crucial change from a_j to v in line 4 gives "*modified Gram-Schmidt.*" In exact arithmetic, the number $R(i,j) = q_i^{\mathrm{T}}a_j$ is the same as $q_i^{\mathrm{T}}v$. (The current v has subtracted from a_j its projections onto earlier $q_1, \ldots, q_{i-1}$. But the new q_i is orthogonal to those directions.) In real arithmetic this orthogonality is not perfect, and computations show a difference in Q. Everybody uses v at that step in the code.

Example 5 A is 2 by 2. The columns of Q, normalized by $\frac{1}{5}$, are q_1 and q_2:

$$A = \begin{bmatrix} 4 & -2 \\ 3 & 1 \end{bmatrix} = \frac{1}{5}\begin{bmatrix} 4 & -3 \\ 3 & 4 \end{bmatrix}\begin{bmatrix} 5 & -1 \\ 0 & 2 \end{bmatrix} = QR\,. \tag{17}$$

Starting with the columns a_1 and a_2 of A, Gram-Schmidt normalizes a_1 to q_1. Then it subtracts from a_2 its projection in the direction of q_1. Here are the steps to the q's:

$$a_1 = \begin{bmatrix} 4 \\ 3 \end{bmatrix} \quad q_1 = \frac{1}{5}\begin{bmatrix} 4 \\ 3 \end{bmatrix} \quad a_2 = \begin{bmatrix} -2 \\ 1 \end{bmatrix} \quad \boldsymbol{v} = \boldsymbol{a_2} - (\boldsymbol{q_1^{\mathrm{T}}a_2})\boldsymbol{q_1} = \frac{1}{5}\begin{bmatrix} -6 \\ 8 \end{bmatrix} \quad q_2 = \frac{1}{5}\begin{bmatrix} -3 \\ 4 \end{bmatrix}$$

Along the way, we divided by $\|a_1\| = 5$ and $\|v\| = 2$. Then 5 and 2 go on the diagonal of R, and $q_1^{\mathrm{T}} a_2 = -1$ is $R(1,2)$. The left side of Figure 2.15 shows every vector.

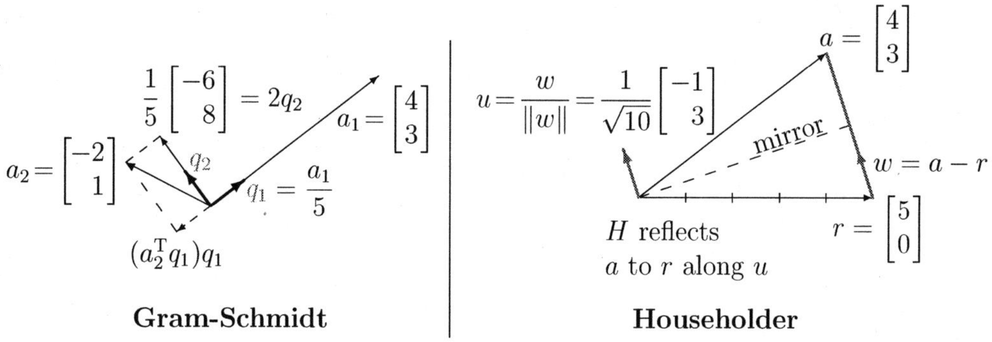

Figure 2.15: Gram-Schmidt finds q_1 then q_2. Householder finds r first then u.

Householder Reflectors in Q

MATLAB finds $[Q, R] = \mathsf{qr}(A)$ in a new way that Gram and Schmidt never thought of. It is more like elimination, where row operations reach an upper triangular U. Now the goal is R. **We produce zeros below the diagonal of R by "*reflection matrices*."** At the end, the orthogonal matrix Q is the product of those reflectors.

The reflection matrices H have Householder's special form $\boldsymbol{H = I - 2uu^{\mathrm{T}}}$. Here u is a unit vector $w/\|w\|$, chosen to produce the zeros in equation (19) below. Notice that H is automatically symmetric and also orthogonal ($H^{\mathrm{T}}H$ is I):

$$H^{\mathrm{T}}H = (I - 2uu^{\mathrm{T}})(I - 2uu^{\mathrm{T}}) = I - 4uu^{\mathrm{T}} + 4uu^{\mathrm{T}} = I \quad \text{because} \quad u^{\mathrm{T}}u = 1. \qquad (18)$$

H reflects u into $-u$, because $(I - 2uu^{\mathrm{T}})u = u - 2u$. All vectors x perpendicular to u are unchanged by H, because $(I - 2uu^{\mathrm{T}})x = x - 0$. So H reflects every vector like $x + cu$ to its image $x - cu$ on the other side of that mirror perpendicular to u.

How does H produce zeros below the diagonal of R? Look at the first column of A, reflected to column $r_1 = H_1 a_1$ of R. We must keep $\|r_1\| = \|a_1\|$, since $H^{\mathrm{T}}H = I$:

H creates 3 zeros in r

$$H_1 a_1 = \begin{bmatrix}\|a_1\|\\0\\0\\0\end{bmatrix} \quad \text{or} \quad \begin{bmatrix}-\|a_1\|\\0\\0\\0\end{bmatrix} = r_1 = \text{column 1 of } R. \qquad (19)$$

Figure 2.15 shows the unit vector u_1 in the direction of $\boldsymbol{w_1 = a_1 - r_1}$. MATLAB chooses between $+\|a_1\|$ and $-\|a_1\|$. By storing u_1 it knows H_1.

Example 6 For the same 2 by 2 matrix A in (17), the first column $(4, 3)$ can be reflected to the first column $r_1 = (5, 0)$. That zero in r_1 makes R upper triangular.

$$a_1 = \begin{bmatrix}4\\3\end{bmatrix} \quad r_1 = \begin{bmatrix}5\\0\end{bmatrix} \quad w_1 = \begin{bmatrix}-1\\3\end{bmatrix} \quad u_1 = \frac{1}{\sqrt{10}}\begin{bmatrix}-1\\3\end{bmatrix} \quad H_1 = I - 2u_1u_1^{\mathrm{T}} = \frac{1}{5}\begin{bmatrix}4 & 3\\3 & -4\end{bmatrix}$$

The next step finds the next column r_2 of R. Where equation (19) needed 3 zeros in r_1, we just need 2 zeros in r_2. We only work *on and below the diagonal of HA*. The Householder code starts step k with *column k* of the current A. It looks at the lower part a on and below the diagonal. It finds w and the unit vector u (upper part zero) for the next reflector H_k. Multiplying by H_k gives $n-k$ zeros in column k of the next A, which is turning into R.

The u's are saved in a matrix U, to remember all the reflectors $H_1, \ldots, H_n$ that go into Q. We never multiply matrices to form Q! When we need $Q^{\mathrm{T}}b$ in the simplified normal equation $R\widehat{u} = Q^{\mathrm{T}}b$, the n reflectors are applied in reverse order to b. Here is the commented code to construct the orthogonal U and upper triangular R:

```
function [U, R] = house(A)  % Produce R from Householder reflectors saved in U

[m, n] = size(A); U = zeros(m, n);
for k = 1:n
  w = A(k:m, k);             % start with column k of current A, from diagonal down
  w(1) = w(1)- norm(w);      % subtract (||w||, 0, ..., 0) from a = w. New w = a-r
  u = w/norm(w);             % normalize to unit vector u in the kth reflector H_k
  U(k:m, k) = u;             % save u in U to know the H's that produce Q
  A(k:m, k:n) = A(k:m, k:n)-2*u*(u'*A(k:m, k:n)); % multiply current A by H_k
end
R = triu(A(:, 1:n));         % square R from nonzeros on and above diagonal of final A
```

I thank Per-Olof Persson for the Gram-Schmidt and Householder codes (and others!).

The Singular Value Decomposition in Section 1.7 factors A into $U\Sigma V^{\mathrm{T}}$. Here U and V are orthogonal matrices ($U^{\mathrm{T}} = U^{-1}$ and $V^{\mathrm{T}} = V^{-1}$). Then $A^{\mathrm{T}}A = V\Sigma^{\mathrm{T}}\Sigma V^{\mathrm{T}}$. This leads to a formula for $\widehat{u}$ that is the most stable of all:

$$V\Sigma^{\mathrm{T}}\Sigma V^{\mathrm{T}}\widehat{u} = V\Sigma^{\mathrm{T}}U^{\mathrm{T}}b \longrightarrow V^{\mathrm{T}}\widehat{u} = (\Sigma^{\mathrm{T}}\Sigma)^{-1}\Sigma^{\mathrm{T}}U^{\mathrm{T}}b \longrightarrow \boldsymbol{\widehat{u} = V\Sigma^{+}U^{\mathrm{T}}b}. \qquad (20)$$

That matrix Σ^{+} has $1/\sigma_1, \ldots, 1/\sigma_n$ on its main diagonal and zeros elsewhere. An important advantage is that we can monitor the singular values $\sigma_1 \geq \ldots \geq \sigma_n > 0$. $A^{\mathrm{T}}A$ is ill-conditioned when σ_n is small. If σ_n is *extremely* small, remove it.

The operation count for the SVD is often comparable to QR. Here Σ^{+} is the "***pseudoinverse***" of Σ, and $V\Sigma^{+}U^{\mathrm{T}}$ in (20) is the pseudoinverse of A. **That is the neatest formula for the least squares solution of $\boldsymbol{Au = b}$, overdetermined or underdetermined: $\boldsymbol{\widehat{u} = A^{+}b = V\Sigma^{+}U^{\mathrm{T}}b}$.**

Weighted Least Squares

Section 2.8 will use statistical information about the measurement errors e. This is the "noise" in the system, and the true equation is $Au = b - e$. Typically, the errors e_i (plus and minus) average to zero. *Each "expected error" is* $\mathrm{E}[e_i] = 0$. Otherwise the zero point on the ith meter should be reset. But the average of e_i^2, which can't be negative, is almost certainly *not* zero. This average $\mathrm{E}\left[e_i^2\right]$ is the ***variance*** $\boldsymbol{\sigma_i^2}$.

Now we can bring in C, the **weighting matrix**. A small variance σ_i^2 implies that the measurement b_i is more reliable. We weight that equation more heavily by choosing $c_i = 1/\sigma_i^2$. When the errors e_i are not independent (next section), the "covariances" $\mathrm{E}\left[e_i e_j\right]$ also enter the *inverse* of C. We are now minimizing the weighted error $e^{\mathrm{T}}Ce$, where unweighted least squares ($C = I$) just minimizes $e^{\mathrm{T}}e$.

The best $\widehat{u}$, taking these weights into account, comes from $\boldsymbol{A^{\mathrm{T}}CA\widehat{u} = A^{\mathrm{T}}Cb}$. Our three-matrix framework fits perfectly. We learn the best $\widehat{u}$, and we also learn *the statistics of* $\widehat{u} - u$. **How reliable is** $\boldsymbol{\widehat{u} = (A^{\mathrm{T}}CA)^{-1}A^{\mathrm{T}}Cb}$? This step comes in Section 2.8, where the errors e_i need not be independent. **The matrix of variances and covariances**, *in the outputs* $\widehat{u}$, **turns out to be** $\boldsymbol{(A^{\mathrm{T}}CA)^{-1}}$.

Problem Set 2.3

1 Suppose $Au = b$ has m equations $a_i u = b_i$ in *one unknown* u. For the sum of squares $E(u) = (a_1 u - b_1)^2 + \cdots + (a_m u - b_m)^2$, find the minimizing $\widehat{u}$ by calculus. Then use linear algebra to form $A^{\mathrm{T}}A\widehat{u} = A^{\mathrm{T}}b$ with one column in A, and reach the same $\widehat{u}$.

2 Suppose $Au = b$ has a solution u. Show that $\widehat{u} = u$. When is $\widehat{u}$ unique?

3 A QR experiment on the Vandermonde matrix $V =$ fliplr(vander(0 : 49)/49) is proposed by Trefethen-Bau [159]. $A = V(:, 1{:}12)$ and $b = \cos(0{:}.08{:}3.92)$ have $m = 50$ and $n = 12$. In format long compute $\widehat{u}$ in multiple ways (MATLAB's svd(A) is another way). How many correct digits does each method yield?

1. Directly from the normal equations by $A^{\mathrm{T}}A\backslash(A^{\mathrm{T}}b)$
2. From the unmodified Gram-Schmidt codes by $R\backslash(Q^{\mathrm{T}}b)$
3. From the modified Gram-Schmidt code
4. From the Householder code using 12 columns of Q and 12 rows of R
5. From MATLAB's $A\backslash b$ and MATLAB's qr (which uses Householder)

4 From the columns a_1 and a_2 of $[2\ \ 2\ \ 1;\ -1\ \ 2\ \ 2]'$, follow the steps of Gram-Schmidt to create orthonormal columns q_1 and q_2. What is R?

5 For the same first column a_1, follow the Householder steps to construct r_1, w_1, u_1, and H_1. The second column of $H_1 A$ still needs work, on and below the diagonal (call those two components a_2). Follow the same steps to construct r_2, w_2, u_2, and H_2 (with first row $1, 0, 0$). Then find $H_2 H_1 A = Q^{-1}A =$ upper triangular R.

6 For stability, MATLAB chooses the sign in (15) *opposite* to the sign of $a(1)$. Our example with $a = (4, 3)$ changes to $r = (\mathbf{-5}, 0)$ and $w = a - r = (9, 3)$. Find $u = w/\|w\|$ and $H = I - 2uu^{\mathrm{T}}$ and check that HA is upper triangular.

7 With $b = (4,1,0,1)$ at the points $x = (0,1,2,3)$, set up and solve the normal equation for the coefficients $\widehat{u} = (C, D)$ in the nearest line $C + Dx$. Start with the four equations $Au = b$ that would be solvable if the points fell on a line.

8 In Problem 7, find the projection $p = A\widehat{u}$. Check that those four values do lie on the line $C + Dx$. Compute the error $e = b - p$ and verify that $A^{\mathrm{T}}e = 0$.

9 (Problem 7 by calculus) Write down $E = \|b - Au\|^2$ as a sum of four squares—the last one is $(1 - C - 3D)^2$. Find the derivative equations $\partial E/\partial C = 0$ and $\partial E/\partial D = 0$. Divide by 2 to obtain the normal equation $A^{\mathrm{T}}A\widehat{u} = A^{\mathrm{T}}b$.

10 Find the height of the best *horizontal* line to fit $b = (4,1,0,1)$. Use the 4 by 1 matrix in the unsolvable equations $C = 4, C = 1, C = 0, C = 1$.

11 In Problem 7, the average of the four x's is $\overline{x} = \frac{1}{4}(0 + 1 + 2 + 3) = 1.5$. The average of the four b's is $\overline{b} = \frac{1}{4}(4+1+0+1) = 1.5$ (by chance). Verify that the best line $b = C + Dx$ goes through this center point $(1.5, 1.5)$. How does the first equation in $A^{\mathrm{T}}A\widehat{u} = A^{\mathrm{T}}b$ lead to that fact $C + D\overline{x} = \overline{b}$?

12 For the closest parabola $C + Dx + Ex^2$ to the same four points, write down the unsolvable equations $Au = b$ for $u = (C, D, E)$. Set up the normal equation for $\widehat{u}$. If you fit the best cubic $C + Dx + Ex^2 + Fx^3$ to those four points (thought experiment), what is the error vector e?

13 Factor the 4 by 3 matrix A created in Problem 12 by $[Q, R] = \mathsf{qr}(A)$. Solve $R\,\widehat{u} = Q^{\mathrm{T}}b$ in equation (15), and verify that $\widehat{u}$ solves the full normal equation $A^{\mathrm{T}}A\widehat{u} = A^{\mathrm{T}}b$. Compute the error vector $e = b - A\widehat{u}$ and compare $\|e\|^2$ for this quadratic $C + Dx + Ex^2$ to $\|e\|^2 = 4$ for the best line.

Problems 14–17 introduce key ideas of statistics—the basis for least squares.

14 (Recommended) This problem projects $b = (b_1, \ldots, b_m)$ onto the line through $a = (1, \ldots, 1)$. We solve m equations $au = b$ in 1 unknown (by least squares).

(a) Solve $a^{\mathrm{T}}a\widehat{u} = a^{\mathrm{T}}b$ to show that $\widehat{u}$ is the *mean* (the average) of the b's.

(b) Find $e = b - a\widehat{u}$ and the *variance* $\|e\|^2$ and the *standard deviation* $\|e\|$.

(c) The horizontal line $\widehat{b} = 3$ is closest to $b = (1, 2, 6)$. Check that $p = (3, 3, 3)$ is perpendicular to e and find the projection matrix $P = A(A^{\mathrm{T}}A)^{-1}A^{\mathrm{T}}$.

15 First assumption behind least squares: Each measurement error has ***mean zero***. Multiply the 8 error vectors $b - Au = (\pm 1, \pm 1, \pm 1)$ by $(A^{\mathrm{T}}A)^{-1}A^{\mathrm{T}}$ to show that the 8 vectors $\widehat{u} - u$ also average to zero. The estimate $\widehat{u}$ is *unbiased.*

16 Second assumption behind least squares: The m errors e_i are independent with variance σ^2, so $\mathrm{E}[(b - A\widehat{u})(b - A\widehat{u})^{\mathrm{T}}] = \sigma^2 I$. Multiply on the left by $(A^{\mathrm{T}}A)^{-1}A^{\mathrm{T}}$ and on the right by $A(A^{\mathrm{T}}A)^{-1}$ to show that $\mathrm{E}[(\widehat{u} - u)(\widehat{u} - u)^{\mathrm{T}}]$ is $\sigma^2(A^{\mathrm{T}}A)^{-1}$. This is the ***covariance matrix*** for the error in $\widehat{u}$.

17 A doctor takes 4 readings of your heart rate. The best solution to $u = b_1, u = b_2, u = b_3, u = b_4$ is the average $\widehat{u}$ of $b_1, \ldots, b_4$. The matrix A is a column of 1's. Problem 16 gives the expected error $(\widehat{u} - u)^2$ as $\sigma^2(A^T A)^{-1} =$ ____. By averaging, the variance drops from σ^2 to $\sigma^2/4$.

18 If you know the average $\widehat{u}_9$ of 9 numbers $b_1, \ldots, b_9$, how can you quickly find the average $\widehat{u}_{10}$ with one more number b_{10}? The idea of *recursive* least squares is to avoid adding 10 numbers. What coefficient correctly gives $\widehat{u}_{10}$?

$$\widehat{u}_{10} = \tfrac{1}{10} b_{10} + \underline{\qquad} \widehat{u}_9 = \tfrac{1}{10}(b_1 + \cdots + b_{10}).$$

19 Write down three equations for the line $b = C + Dt$ to go through $b = 7$ at $t = -1$, $b = 7$ at $t = 1$, and $b = 21$ at $t = 2$. Find the least squares solution $\widehat{u} = (C, D)$ and draw the closest line.

20 Find the projection $p = A\widehat{u}$ in Problem 19. This gives the three heights of the closest line. Show that the error vector is $e = (2, -6, 4)$.

21 Suppose the measurements at $t = -1, 1, 2$ are the errors $2, -6, 4$ in Problem 20. Compute $\widehat{u}$ and the closest line to these new measurements. Explain the answer: $b = (2, -6, 4)$ is perpendicular to ____ so the projection is $p = 0$.

22 Suppose the measurements at $t = -1, 1, 2$ are $b = (5, 13, 17)$. Compute $\widehat{u}$ and the closest line and e. The error is $e = 0$ because this b is ____.

23 Find the best line $C + Dt$ to fit $b = 4, 2, -1, 0, 0$ at times $t = -2, -1, 0, 1, 2$.

24 Find the *plane* that gives the best fit to the 4 values $b = (0, 1, 3, 4)$ at the corners $(1, 0)$ and $(0, 1)$ and $(-1, 0)$ and $(0, -1)$ of a square. The equations $C + Dx + Ey = b$ at those 4 points are $Au = b$ with 3 unknowns $u = (C, D, E)$. At the center $(0, 0)$ of the square, show that $C + Dx + Ey =$ average of the b's.

25 Multiplying $A^T A$ seems to need n^2 inner products, but symmetry cuts this in half to leave mn^2 operations in all. Explain where the Gram-Schmidt code uses $2mn^2$ operations. (So does the Householder code.)

26 The Householder matrices in Q are *square*. So that factorization $A = QR$ is $(m \text{ by } m)(m \text{ by } n)$ where Gram-Schmidt is reduced to $(m \text{ by } n)(n \text{ by } n)$.

$$(QR)_{\text{householder}} = \begin{bmatrix} Q_{\text{GS}} & Q_{\text{null}} \end{bmatrix} \begin{bmatrix} R_{\text{GS}} \\ \text{zero} \end{bmatrix} = \begin{bmatrix} \qquad & Q_{\text{null}} \end{bmatrix} \begin{bmatrix} \qquad \end{bmatrix}.$$

The Gram-Schmidt columns in Q_{GS} are an orthonormal basis for ____. The $m - n$ columns in Q_{null} are an orthonormal basis for ____.

2.4 GRAPH MODELS AND KIRCHHOFF'S LAWS

This section will develop the most important model in applied mathematics. We begin with a **graph**, consisting of **n nodes connected** (or not) **by m edges**. Those connections are recorded in an m by n "*incidence matrix*" A. In row j of A, the nonzeros -1 and 1 indicate which two nodes are connected by the jth edge.

A line of springs is a special case. Then A is a first difference matrix, and $A^{\mathrm{T}}A$ is a second difference matrix (it has -1, 2, -1 on the inside rows). I can name right away the key matrices for any graph, starting with the "Laplacian" $A^{\mathrm{T}}A$:

Graph Laplacian $\quad A^{\mathrm{T}}A = D - W = \text{(diagonal)} - \text{(off-diagonal)} \quad (1)$

W is the **adjacency matrix** and D is the **degree matrix**. The number w_{ij} tells whether nodes i and j are connected by an edge. The number d_{jj} tells how many edges meet node j. For four springs, $A^{\mathrm{T}}A$ is the free-free second difference matrix B_4:

$$A^{\mathrm{T}}A = \begin{bmatrix} 1 & -1 & & \\ -1 & 2 & -1 & \\ & -1 & 2 & -1 \\ & & -1 & 1 \end{bmatrix} \qquad W = \begin{bmatrix} 0 & 1 & & \\ 1 & 0 & 1 & \\ & 1 & 0 & 1 \\ & & 1 & 0 \end{bmatrix} \qquad D = \begin{bmatrix} 1 & & & \\ & 2 & & \\ & & 2 & \\ & & & 1 \end{bmatrix}$$

Laplacian **Adjacency** **Degrees**

For other graphs the edges are no longer in a line, and $A^{\mathrm{T}}A$ is no longer tridiagonal.

You will expect $A^{\mathrm{T}}CA$ to appear, when C is a diagonal matrix of m weights:

Weighted Laplacian $\quad \boldsymbol{A^{\mathrm{T}}CA = D - W} = \text{(node weight matrix)} - \text{(edge weight matrix)} \quad (2)$

If three edges in a line have weights a, b, c in C, those numbers enter W and D:

$$\boldsymbol{A^{\mathrm{T}}CA} = \begin{bmatrix} a & -a & & \\ -a & a+b & -b & \\ & -b & b+c & -c \\ & & -c & c \end{bmatrix} \quad \boldsymbol{W} = \begin{bmatrix} 0 & a & & \\ a & 0 & b & \\ & b & 0 & c \\ & & c & 0 \end{bmatrix} \quad \boldsymbol{D} = \begin{bmatrix} a & & & \\ & a+b & & \\ & & b+c & \\ & & & c \end{bmatrix}$$

Weighted Laplacian **Edge weights** **Node weights**

Notice especially the sums along every row of these matrices:

Row sums of W are in D **Row sums of $A^{\mathrm{T}}A$ and $A^{\mathrm{T}}CA$ are zero**

Those zero row sums put $(1, 1, 1, 1)$ into the nullspace of A and $A^{\mathrm{T}}A$ and $A^{\mathrm{T}}CA$. These are great matrices to work with. This section creates the matrices; Section $*$ 2.9 on Graph Cuts and Gene Clustering uses the eigenvalues.

The graph in Figure 2.16 shows $m = 6$ edges connecting $n = 4$ nodes. This is a *complete graph* (all possible edges). It is also a *directed graph* (each edge has a direction arrow). Those arrows will determine the signs in the incidence matrix A, but they don't affect $A^{\mathrm{T}}A$ or $A^{\mathrm{T}}CA$. For this graph model, our framework can have three equations or two or one:

$$\begin{aligned} e &= b - Au \\ w &= Ce \\ f &= A^{\mathrm{T}}w \end{aligned} \qquad \begin{bmatrix} C^{-1} & A \\ A^{\mathrm{T}} & 0 \end{bmatrix} \begin{bmatrix} w \\ u \end{bmatrix} = \begin{bmatrix} b \\ f \end{bmatrix} \qquad A^{\mathrm{T}}CAu = A^{\mathrm{T}}Cb - f \tag{3}$$

These equations will soon extend to finite differences and finite elements for differential equations. I think of (3) as the *"fundamental problem of scientific computing."*

The Incidence Matrix

The incidence matrix A has $m = 6$ rows and $n = 4$ columns. Each row corresponds to an edge in the graph, and each column corresponds to a node. We do have to number the edges and nodes, and also choose directions for the arrows, in order to construct A. But the numbering and edge directions are arbitrary. Flows can travel both ways, and a different choice of arrows will not change the reality of the model.

The entries -1 and 1 in each row of A give a record of the corresponding edge:

Row 1 The first edge leaves node 1 and goes to node 2.
The first row has -1 in column 1 and $+1$ in column 2.

Row 5 is typical. Edge 5 leaves node 2 (by -1 in column 2), and it enters node 4 ($+1$ in column 4). We chose arrows from lower-numbered nodes to higher-numbered nodes, for simplicity. Then the -1 comes before the $+1$ in each row. In all cases, you can write down A immediately by looking at the graph. The graph and the matrix have the same information.

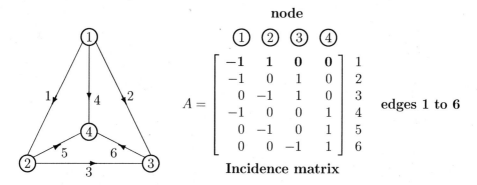

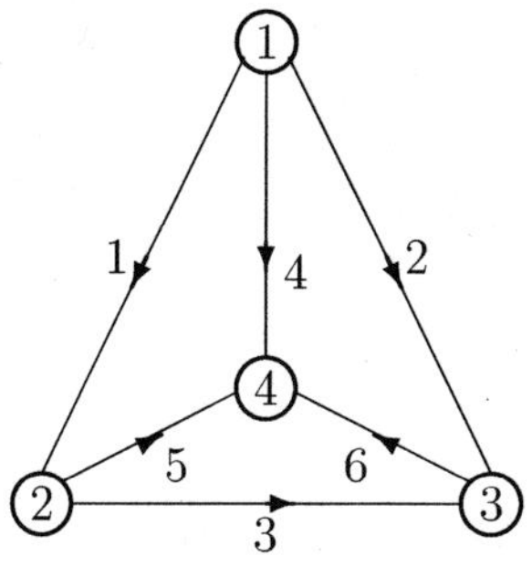

node

① ② ③ ④

$$A = \begin{bmatrix} \mathbf{-1} & \mathbf{1} & \mathbf{0} & \mathbf{0} \\ -1 & 0 & 1 & 0 \\ 0 & -1 & 1 & 0 \\ -1 & 0 & 0 & 1 \\ 0 & -1 & 0 & 1 \\ 0 & 0 & -1 & 1 \end{bmatrix} \begin{matrix} 1 \\ 2 \\ 3 \\ 4 \\ 5 \\ 6 \end{matrix} \quad \textbf{edges 1 to 6}$$

Incidence matrix

Figure 2.16: Complete graph with $m = 6$ edges and $n = 4$ nodes. A is 6 by 4.

Our second example is a subgraph of the first. It has the same four nodes but only three edges 1, 3, and 6. Its incidence matrix is 3 by 4. Removing three edges from the graph just removes three rows from the incidence matrix.

This graph is a **tree**. It has *no closed loops.* The tree has only $m = n - 1$ edges, the minimum to connect all n nodes. The rows of A are linearly independent! A complete graph has the maximum number of edges $m = \frac{1}{2}n(n-1)$, to connect every pair of nodes. Other subgraphs are also trees; the three edges $1, 2, 4$ come out from one node. (The six edges contain a total of 16 trees.) The rank of A_{tree} is $r = 3$.

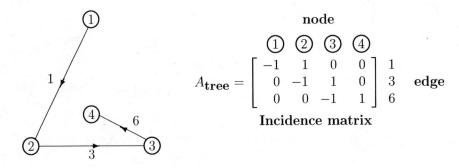

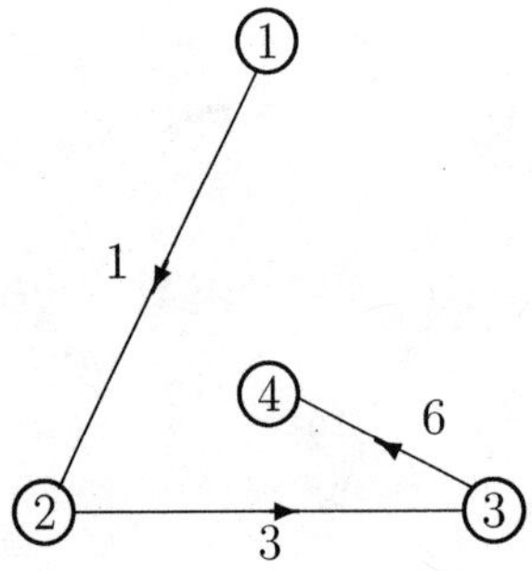

node

$$A_{\mathsf{tree}} = \begin{array}{c} \text{①} \;\; \text{②} \;\; \text{③} \;\; \text{④} \\ \begin{bmatrix} -1 & 1 & 0 & 0 \\ 0 & -1 & 1 & 0 \\ 0 & 0 & -1 & 1 \end{bmatrix} \end{array} \begin{array}{c} 1 \\ 3 \\ 6 \end{array} \quad \textbf{edge}$$

Incidence matrix

Figure 2.17: A tree has no loops. With 4 nodes it has 3 edges.

The matrix A has two purposes. It gives a record of all connections in the graph (it is a topology matrix). At the same time, we can multiply A times a vector u. The matrix can *act.* When A multiplies u, you see it as a *difference matrix*:

Differences across edges

$$Au = \begin{bmatrix} -1 & 1 & 0 & 0 \\ -1 & 0 & 1 & 0 \\ 0 & -1 & 1 & 0 \\ -1 & 0 & 0 & 1 \\ 0 & -1 & 0 & 1 \\ 0 & 0 & -1 & 1 \end{bmatrix} \begin{bmatrix} u_1 \\ u_2 \\ u_3 \\ u_4 \end{bmatrix} = \begin{bmatrix} u_2 - u_1 \\ u_3 - u_1 \\ u_3 - u_2 \\ u_4 - u_1 \\ u_4 - u_2 \\ u_4 - u_3 \end{bmatrix}. \tag{4}$$

The numbers u_1, u_2, u_3, u_4 could represent the heights of the nodes, or the pressures at the nodes, or the voltages at the nodes. Most often they are simply called **potentials**. Then the vector Au contains the "potential difference" across each edge:

$$u = \begin{cases} \text{heights} \\ \text{pressures} \\ \text{voltages} \\ \text{potentials} \end{cases} \qquad Au = \begin{cases} \text{height differences} \\ \text{pressure differences} \\ \text{voltage differences} \\ \text{potential differences} \end{cases}$$

This model of nodes and edges is everywhere. The main point is that the n-component node vector u leads to an m-component edge vector Au.

The Nullspace of A

The nullspace of A contains the vectors that solve $Au = 0$. When the columns of A are independent, the only solution is $u = 0$ and the nullspace contains only that one "zero vector." Otherwise the nullspace might be a line of u's, or a plane, depending on how many combinations of the columns of A lead to $Au = 0$.

For incidence matrices, **the nullspace is a line**. Constant vectors solve $Au = 0$:

$$u = \begin{bmatrix} 1 \\ 1 \\ 1 \\ 1 \end{bmatrix} \quad \text{and any} \quad u = \begin{bmatrix} C \\ C \\ C \\ C \end{bmatrix} \quad \text{will satisfy} \quad Au = 0\,. \tag{5}$$

In every row of Au, $-C$ is canceled by $+C$ and we get $Au = 0$. More intuitively, we see Au as a vector of differences. When the components of u are all equal to C, every difference is zero in Au. Thus $u = (C, C, C, C)$ is a vector in the nullspace of A. This applies to the complete graph and the tree example and all connected graphs. $A^{\mathrm{T}}A$ has the same nullspace as A, containing the constant vectors.

The word "connected" means that each pair of nodes is connected by a path of edges. The graph does not break up into two or more separate pieces. If it did break up, the vector u could be all ones in the first piece and all zeros in the other pieces. This would still have differences $Au = 0$ across all existing edges; it would be in the nullspace. The dimension of the nullspace $N(A)$ is the number of separate pieces, and we always assume that this number is *one*: a connected graph.

The rank of A is $r = n - 1$. Any $n - 1$ columns of the incidence matrix are linearly independent. But the n columns are linearly dependent: their sum is the zero column. We will have to remove one column (**ground one node**) to produce independent columns in A. Then $A^{\mathrm{T}}A$ is invertible (and positive definite). We can only solve for the $n - 1$ potentials after one node is grounded: say $u_4 = 0$.

Looking ahead For m currents and $n-1$ voltages, we will need $m+n-1$ equations. We have Ohm's Law on m edges (involving A) and Kirchhoff's Law at $n - 1$ nodes (involving A^{T}). The right sides are voltage sources (batteries $b_1, \ldots, b_m$) and current sources f. Here is the framework and the all-important block matrix (**KKT matrix**):

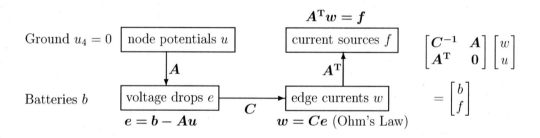

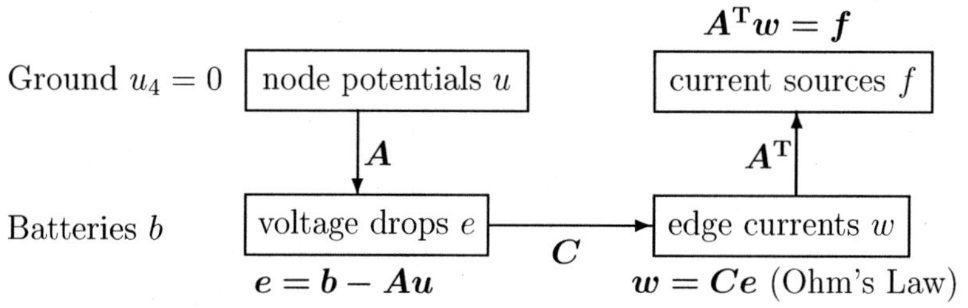

$$\begin{bmatrix} \boldsymbol{C}^{-1} & \boldsymbol{A} \\ \boldsymbol{A}^{\mathrm{T}} & \boldsymbol{0} \end{bmatrix} \begin{bmatrix} w \\ u \end{bmatrix} = \begin{bmatrix} b \\ f \end{bmatrix}$$

Kirchhoff's Current Law $A^{\mathrm{T}}w = 0$

$A^{\mathrm{T}}w = 0$ enforces zero net flow into every node: **Flow in equals flow out**. These are the balance equations for the currents $w_1, \ldots, w_m$ along the edges. There are n equations in $A^{\mathrm{T}}w = 0$, one for each node. We are looking for currents that "balance themselves" without any current sources from outside. The nullspace of A^{T} is more interesting than the line of constant vectors in the nullspace of A.

$A^{\mathrm{T}}w = 0$ is **Kirchhoff's Current Law (KCL)**. It is crucial for our framework that transposing A produces the correct statement $A^{\mathrm{T}}w = 0$ of Kirchhoff's Law.

$$A^{\mathrm{T}} = \begin{bmatrix} -1 & -1 & 0 & -1 & 0 & 0 \\ 1 & 0 & -1 & 0 & -1 & 0 \\ 0 & 1 & 1 & 0 & 0 & -1 \\ 0 & 0 & 0 & 1 & 1 & 1 \end{bmatrix} \qquad \begin{aligned} -w_1 - w_2 - w_4 &= 0 \quad \text{at node } 1 \\ w_1 - w_3 - w_5 &= 0 \quad 2 \\ w_2 + w_3 - w_6 &= 0 \quad 3 \\ w_4 + w_5 + w_6 &= 0 \quad 4 \end{aligned} \qquad (6)$$

The plus and minus signs in the equations are consistent with the arrows. At node 1, all arrows go outward (the flows w_1, w_2, w_4 can go either way!). Kirchhoff's Law says that those flows add to zero (no net flow). But the four equations are *not independent.* **If we add the equations, everything cancels to give 0 = 0.** The rows of A^{T} add to the zero row—because the columns of A add to the zero column.

When we remove column 4 of A (by grounding node 4) this removes row 4 of A^{T}. That fourth equation $w_4 + w_5 + w_6 = 0$ comes from the other three equations. So $A^{\mathrm{T}}w = 0$ has $n - 1 = 3$ independent equations in $m = 6$ unknowns $w_1, \ldots, w_6$. We expect $6 - 3 = 3$ independent solutions. ***This is*** $\boldsymbol{m - (n-1)}$.

What are the solutions to $A^{\mathrm{T}}w = 0$? Which flows on the six edges balance at every node? It is certainly possible to solve by elimination, but fortunately there is a direct way to visualize a flow that "balances itself."

Suppose one unit of flow goes around a closed loop. Let the flow be zero on all other edges not in the loop. Kirchhoff's Law is satisfied by this loop flow w:

Loop flow

$$w_i = \begin{cases} +1 & \text{when edge } i \text{ is in the loop, in the arrow direction} \\ -1 & \text{when edge } i \text{ is in the loop; flow against the arrow} \\ 0 & \text{when edge } i \text{ is not in the loop} \end{cases} \qquad (7)$$

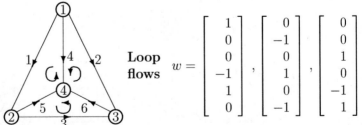

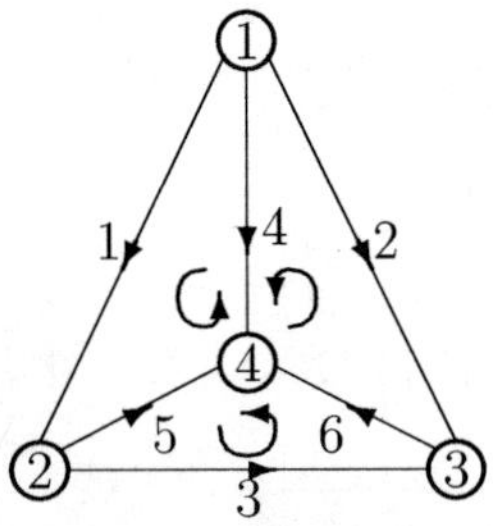

Loop flows $w = \begin{bmatrix} 1 \\ 0 \\ 0 \\ -1 \\ 1 \\ 0 \end{bmatrix}, \begin{bmatrix} 0 \\ -1 \\ 0 \\ 1 \\ 0 \\ -1 \end{bmatrix}, \begin{bmatrix} 0 \\ 0 \\ 1 \\ 0 \\ -1 \\ 1 \end{bmatrix}$

Figure 2.18: Three independent loop flows solve Kirchhoff's Current Law $A^{\mathrm{T}}w = 0$.

The loop of nodes $1-2-4-1$ in Figure 2.18 consists of edge 1 then edge 5 then *backward* on edge 4. Thus $w_1 = 1$, $w_5 = 1$, $w_4 = -1$ solves Kirchhoff's Current Law. Two independent solutions come from the other two small loops in the graph.

The graph has other loops! One possibility is the big loop around the outside, from nodes $1-2-3-1$. This gives the solution $w_{\text{big}} = (1,-1,1,0,0,0)$. *That is the sum of the three w's from the small loops.* The three small loops give a *basis* for the nullspace of A^{T}. The Fundamental Theorem of Linear Algebra confirms that **the dimension of the nullspace** (number of basis vectors) is $6-3=3$:

Number of independent solutions = (Number of unknowns) − (Rank).

There are six unknowns $w_1, \ldots, w_6$ (six columns in A^{T}). There are three independent equations, counted by the rank. Apparently $A^{\mathrm{T}}w = 0$ gives four equations, but they add to $0 = 0$. Three equations for six unknowns leaves a three-dimensional nullspace.

The tree has no loops at all. The only flow in a tree that satisfies KCL is a zero flow. A^{T} has three columns, and they are independent (rank $= 3$). So this nullspace has dimension $3-3=0$. It contains only the single point $(w_1, w_2, w_3) = (0,0,0)$.

If a connected graph has n nodes, then A and A^{T} have rank $n-1$. Therefore $A^{\mathrm{T}}w = 0$ has $m-(n-1)$ independent solutions coming from loops:

Dimension of nullspace = Number of independent loops $= \boldsymbol{m - n + 1}$.

When the graph lies in a plane (like our examples) the small loops are easy to count. This count gives a linear algebra proof of ***Euler's Formula*** for every plane graph:

(Number of nodes) − (Number of edges) + (Number of loops) = 1 (8)

A triangle has (3 nodes)−(3 edges)+(1 loop). Our six-edge graph has $4-6+3=1$. On a seven-node tree, Euler's Formula would give $7-6+0=1$. All graphs lead to the same answer $(n)-(m)+(m-n+1)=1$.

Kirchhoff's Voltage Law The twin laws of circuit theory are KCL and KVL, current law and voltage law. The voltage law says that *the sum of voltage drops* e_i *around every closed loop is zero.* We now put this into matrix language: $\boldsymbol{e} = \boldsymbol{A}\boldsymbol{u}$.

When w gives flow around a loop ($w_i = \pm 1$), the product $e^{\mathrm{T}}w$ is the sum of voltage drops on that loop. So the voltage law is $e^{\mathrm{T}}w = 0$. The Fundamental Theorem of Linear Algebra says that if e is perpendicular to the nullspace of A^{T}, then e is in the column space of A. Thus e must be a combination $e = Au$ of the columns of A.

Here is the point. If $A^{\mathrm{T}}w = 0$ is in the framework, then $e = Au$ must be there too. The voltage law says that the "potentials" $u_1, \ldots, u_n$ *must exist.* ***The twin laws assure that*** A ***and*** A^{T} ***will both appear.*** We discovered A^{T} when we wrote out the balance equation, but Kirchhoff knew that it would be there waiting for us.

The Graph Laplacian Matrix $A^{\mathrm{T}}A$

The incidence matrix A is rectangular (m by n). You expect the network equations to produce $A^{\mathrm{T}}A$ and eventually $A^{\mathrm{T}}CA$. These matrices are square (n by n) and symmetric and very important. $A^{\mathrm{T}}A$ is also a pleasure to calculate.

For the complete graph with four nodes, multiplying $A^{\mathrm{T}}A$ gives 3's and -1's:

$$\begin{bmatrix} -1 & -1 & 0 & -1 & 0 & 0 \\ 1 & 0 & -1 & 0 & -1 & 0 \\ 0 & 1 & 1 & 0 & 0 & -1 \\ 0 & 0 & 0 & 1 & 1 & 1 \end{bmatrix} \begin{bmatrix} -1 & 1 & 0 & 0 \\ -1 & 0 & 1 & 0 \\ 0 & -1 & 1 & 0 \\ -1 & 0 & 0 & 1 \\ 0 & -1 & 0 & 1 \\ 0 & 0 & -1 & 1 \end{bmatrix} = \begin{bmatrix} \mathbf{3} & -1 & -1 & -1 \\ -1 & \mathbf{3} & -1 & -1 \\ -1 & -1 & \mathbf{3} & -1 \\ -1 & -1 & -1 & \mathbf{3} \end{bmatrix} \tag{9}$$

The columns still add to produce the zero column. The all-ones vector $u = (1,1,1,1)$ is in the nullspace of $A^{\mathrm{T}}A$. This must be true, because $Au = 0$ gives $A^{\mathrm{T}}Au = 0$. The matrix $A^{\mathrm{T}}A$ always has the same rank and nullspace as A. Here the rank is $r = 3$ and the nullspace is the line of constant vectors.

The numbers in $A^{\mathrm{T}}A$ follow a neat pattern. Its diagonal is the **degree matrix** D. Here the degrees are $3,3,3,3$. The off-diagonal part of $A^{\mathrm{T}}A$ is $-W$. Here the **adjacency matrix** W has all possible 1's, because the graph has all possible edges.

On the diagonal $\quad (A^{\mathrm{T}}A)_{jj} = \text{degree} = \text{number of edges meeting at node } j.$

Row 4 of A^{T} and column 4 of A are $(0,0,0,1,1,1)$. They multiply to give $(A^{\mathrm{T}}A)_{44} = 3$. But column 4 overlaps column $3 = (0,1,1,0,0,-1)$ in a single -1:

Off the diagonal $\quad (A^{\mathrm{T}}A)_{jk} = \begin{cases} -1 & \text{if nodes } j \text{ and } k \text{ share an edge} \\ 0 & \text{if no edge goes between those nodes.} \end{cases}$

For the complete graph, every off-diagonal entry in $A^{\mathrm{T}}A$ is -1. All edges are present. But the tree has missing edges, which produce zeros in the graph Laplacian $A^{\mathrm{T}}A$:

$$(A^{\mathrm{T}}A)_{\mathsf{tree}} = \begin{bmatrix} \mathbf{1} & -1 & 0 & 0 \\ -1 & \mathbf{2} & -1 & 0 \\ 0 & -1 & \mathbf{2} & -1 \\ 0 & 0 & -1 & \mathbf{1} \end{bmatrix} = D - W \qquad \begin{array}{l} \text{The zeros show} \\ \text{3 edges removed} \\ \text{in Figure 2.17} \end{array} \tag{10}$$

The middle nodes in Figure 2.17 have two edges. The outer nodes only have one edge, so those diagonal entries are 1. The off-diagonals show 0's for missing edges. Our $-1, 2, -1$ matrix B_4 appears because this tree is really a line of four nodes.

When node 4 is grounded, which fixes $u_4 = 0$, the last row and column disappear from $A^{\mathrm{T}}A$. Then $(A^{\mathrm{T}}A)_{\mathsf{reduced}}$ becomes invertible (it is exactly the matrix T_3).

In many applications another potential is fixed, say $u_1 = V$ volts. Then row 1 and column 1 also disappear, since u_1 is known. That number V will turn up on the *right side* of the equations. Currents still balance. Since u_1 multiplied column 1, moving it to the right side will produce $-V$ times column 1:

Fixed voltage $u_1 = V$
3 identical resistors

$$\begin{aligned} 2u_2 - u_3 &= V \\ -u_2 + 2u_3 &= 0 \end{aligned} \qquad (11)$$

This tree is like a line of springs. The grounded node 4 is like a fixed end $u_4 = 0$. ***The potential $u_1 = V$ is like a nonzero fixed displacement.*** All springs are equally stretched and all edges carry the same current, and (11) is easy to solve:

Potentials at nodes

$$(u_1, u_2, u_3, u_4) = (V, \frac{2}{3}V, \frac{1}{3}V, 0) \qquad (12)$$

Question What is $A^{\mathrm{T}}A$ for the tree with edges 1, 2, 4 all coming out of node 1?

$$(A^{\mathrm{T}}A)_{\text{tree}} = \begin{bmatrix} \mathbf{3} & -1 & -1 & -1 \\ -1 & \mathbf{1} & 0 & 0 \\ -1 & 0 & \mathbf{1} & 0 \\ -1 & 0 & 0 & \mathbf{1} \end{bmatrix} = D - W$$

3 edges to node 1
1 edge to nodes 2, 3, 4

Important: $A^{\mathrm{T}}A$ is positive *semidefinite* but not positive definite. The determinant is zero; $A^{\mathrm{T}}A$ is not invertible. We have to remove a column of A (*ground a node*). That removes a row and column of $A^{\mathrm{T}}A$, and then $(A^{\mathrm{T}}A)_{\text{reduced}}$ is invertible.

Inputs b, f and Matrices A, C, A^{T}

A ***network*** has nodes and edges, and it also assigns numbers $c_1, \ldots, c_m$ to those edges. Thus the network starts with a graph, and its incidence matrix A. The m numbers go into a diagonal matrix C. These positive numbers are the *conductances*, and they give the flow law for each edge. Hooke's Law becomes Ohm's Law:

Ohm's Law $w_i = c_i e_i$	**Edge current = (Conductance) × (Voltage drop)**

Important! *Voltage drops e_i are measured across the resistors.* Those drops make the current flow. Some or all of the edges can include batteries (voltage sources). We have separated out edge 2 in Figure 2.19 to see the sign convention in $e = b - Au$.

As in least squares, b is a given vector ($b = 0$ means no batteries). A enters with a *minus sign* because the flow is from higher potential to lower potential. The minus sign on A also appears in heat flow and fluid flow: from higher temperature to lower temperature, from higher pressure to lower pressure.

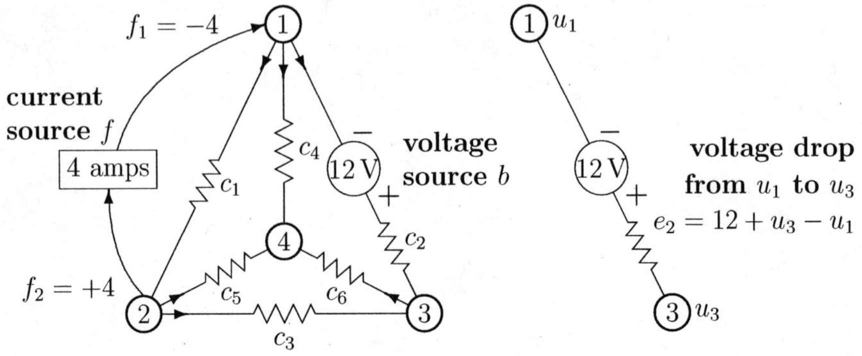

Figure 2.19: The network has conductances c_i, batteries b_i, and current sources f_j.

Assembling the Matrix $K = A^{\mathrm{T}}CA$

The **weighted Laplacian matrix** $K = A^{\mathrm{T}}_{n \times m} C_{m \times m} A_{m \times n}$ is still n by n. When C was I and all $c_i = 1$, the unweighted $A^{\mathrm{T}}A$ came from counting edges into nodes. Now we include the numbers c_i that are assigned to those edges. Row 4 of A^{T} and column 4 of A are $(0,0,0,1,1,1)$ for the complete graph. *When C is in the middle, the multiplication produces* $c_4 + c_5 + c_6$. This will be K_{44}, in the bottom corner of the **conductance matrix** $K = A^{\mathrm{T}}CA = D - W$:

On the diagonal K_{jj} = sum of weights c_i on the edges meeting at node j

The off-diagonals of $A^{\mathrm{T}}A$ are -1 or 0, edge or no edge. Then $A^{\mathrm{T}}CA$ gives $-c_i$ or 0:

Off the diagonal $$K_{jk} = \begin{cases} -c_i & \text{if edge } i \text{ connects nodes } j \text{ and } k \\ 0 & \text{if no edge goes between those nodes} \end{cases} \qquad (13)$$

Not grounded
Not invertible
$\boldsymbol{K = D - W}$

$$K = \begin{bmatrix} c_1+c_2+c_4 & -c_1 & -c_2 & -c_4 \\ -c_1 & c_1+c_3+c_5 & -c_3 & -c_5 \\ -c_2 & -c_3 & c_2+c_3+c_6 & -c_6 \\ -c_4 & -c_5 & -c_6 & c_4+c_5+c_6 \end{bmatrix} \qquad (14)$$

Grounding node 4 removes row 4 and column 4. Then K_{reduced} becomes invertible.

May I mention how K can be "*assembled*" from small matrices? Each edge of the network contributes a 2 by 2 matrix to be placed into K. If we look at the tree, its edges $1, 3, 6$ contribute **three element matrices** K_1, K_3, K_6:

$$K_{\text{tree}} \textbf{ from } \begin{bmatrix} c_1 & -c_1 \\ -c_1 & c_1 \end{bmatrix} ++ \begin{bmatrix} c_3 & -c_3 \\ -c_3 & c_3 \end{bmatrix} ++ \begin{bmatrix} c_6 & -c_6 \\ -c_6 & c_6 \end{bmatrix}. \qquad (15)$$

The typical element matrix K_3 comes from the 3rd column of A^{T} times c_3 times the 3rd row of A. Matrix multiplication can be done this way (*columns times rows*):

$$\boldsymbol{A^{\mathrm{T}}CA = \textit{assembly of } K_i = \sum (\textit{column } i \textit{ of } A^{\mathrm{T}})(c_i)(\textit{row } i \textit{ of } A).} \qquad (16)$$

The element matrices K_i are actually full-size, 4 by 4. But only the 2 by 2 parts shown in (15) are nonzero. The double plus signs in (15) mean that K_i has to be *placed correctly into* K. Here the pieces are assembled into $K = A^{\mathrm{T}}CA$ for the tree:

Line of edges
Tridiagonal K

$$\mathbf{K}_{\mathbf{tree}} = \begin{bmatrix} c_1 & -c_1 & 0 & 0 \\ -c_1 & c_1 + \mathbf{c_3} & -\mathbf{c_3} & 0 \\ 0 & -\mathbf{c_3} & \mathbf{c_3} + c_6 & -c_6 \\ 0 & 0 & -c_6 & c_6 \end{bmatrix}. \tag{17}$$

K is singular because $u = (1, 1, 1, 1)$ is in its nullspace. When all $c_i = 1$, this is the $-1, 2, -1$ matrix $B_4 = A^{\mathrm{T}}A$. When node 4 is grounded, $A^{\mathrm{T}}A$ becomes T_3 (invertible!).

Example 1 Suppose all the conductances in Figure 2.19 are $c_i = 1$. Exceptionally we can solve this system by hand. *Look first at the* 4*-amp current source in* f. That current has to return from node 1 to node 2. Consider three paths from node 1 to node 2:

$$\begin{array}{llcll} \text{Edge 1 (node 1 directly to node 2)}: & \text{conductance} & = & 1 & \\ \text{Edges 2 and 3 in series (via node 3)}: & \text{conductance} & = & (1+1)^{-1} & = 0.5 \\ \text{Edges 4 and 5 in series (via node 4)}: & \text{conductance} & = & (1+1)^{-1} & = 0.5 \end{array}$$

These three paths are in parallel. Their total conductance is $1 + \frac{1}{2} + \frac{1}{2} = 2$. The four amps of current will travel down those paths in the ratio 2 to 1 to 1. Following the arrows,

$$w_1 = 2 \quad w_2 = 1 \quad w_3 = -1 \quad w_4 = 1 \quad w_5 = -1 \quad w_6 = 0 \quad \text{(by symmetry)}.$$

Those six currents satisfy the balance equations $A^{\mathrm{T}}w = f$. The potential drop between node 1 and node 2 is total current/total conductance $= 4/2 = u_1 - u_2$:

Voltages $\quad u_1 = 1 \quad u_2 = -1 \quad u_3 = 0$ (by symmetry) and $u_4 = 0$ (grounded).

The systematic way to find those currents w and potentials u is from $A^{\mathrm{T}}w = f$ and $w = Ce$ and $e = b - Au$. With $e = C^{-1}w$, the voltage equation becomes $C^{-1}w + Au = b$. Column 4 of A is removed by $u_4 = 0$. For the six currents and three voltages, we have Ohm's Law on six edges and Kirchhoff's Law at nodes 1, 2, 3:

$$\begin{array}{rcr} w_1/c_1 + u_2 - u_1 & = & 0 \\ w_2/c_2 + u_3 - u_1 & = & 12 \\ w_3/c_3 + u_3 - u_2 & = & 0 \\ w_4/c_4 \qquad - u_1 & = & 0 \\ w_5/c_5 \qquad - u_2 & = & 0 \\ w_6/c_6 \qquad - u_3 & = & 0 \\ -w_1 - w_2 - w_4 & = & -4 \\ w_1 - w_3 - w_5 & = & +4 \\ w_2 + w_3 - w_6 & = & 0 \end{array} \qquad \left[\begin{array}{cccccc|ccc} 1/c_1 & & & & & & -1 & 1 & 0 \\ & \cdot & & & & & -1 & 0 & 1 \\ & & \cdot & & & & 0 & -1 & 1 \\ & & & \cdot & & & -1 & 0 & 0 \\ & & & & \cdot & & 0 & -1 & 0 \\ & & & & & 1/c_6 & 0 & 0 & -1 \\ \hline -1 & -1 & 0 & -1 & 0 & 0 & 0 & 0 & 0 \\ 1 & 0 & -1 & 0 & -1 & 0 & 0 & 0 & 0 \\ 0 & 1 & 1 & 0 & 0 & -1 & 0 & 0 & 0 \end{array}\right] \begin{bmatrix} w_1 \\ w_2 \\ \cdot \\ \cdot \\ \cdot \\ w_6 \\ u_1 \\ u_2 \\ u_3 \end{bmatrix} \tag{18}$$

Notice the -4 and $+4$ adding to zero as required. Our solutions above account for this 4-amp current source. Problem 11 will account for the 12-volt battery. By addition we account for both, and solve the full system (18) with all conductances $c_i = 1$.

The Saddle Point KKT Matrix

The "KKT" matrix in (18) **is absolutely fundamental to applied mathematics.** It appears in network equilibrium problems (like this one). It also appears in optimization problems (maximum or minimum with constraints). It has a square symmetric block C^{-1} in one corner and a square zero block. The other blocks A and A^{T} make it symmetric. Its size is $m+n-1=6+4-1$, when one node is grounded:

$$\begin{bmatrix} C^{-1} & A \\ A^{\mathrm{T}} & 0 \end{bmatrix} \begin{bmatrix} w \\ u \end{bmatrix} = \begin{bmatrix} b \\ f \end{bmatrix} \quad \text{becomes} \quad A^{\mathrm{T}}CAu = A^{\mathrm{T}}Cb - f. \tag{19}$$

We reached $K = A^{\mathrm{T}}CA$ when we eliminated w. Multiply the first equation by $A^{\mathrm{T}}C$ and subtract from $A^{\mathrm{T}}w = f$. This gives our one equation for u.

Is this block matrix invertible? **Yes**, from grounding. *Is it positive definite?* **No.** The zero block on the diagonal rules out positive definiteness. It is true that the first m pivots (which depend only on C^{-1}) are all positive. But those steps will put $-A^{\mathrm{T}}CA$ into the $(2,2)$ block, and this has n negative pivots. **We have a saddle point:**

$$\begin{matrix} m \text{ rows} \\ n \text{ rows} \end{matrix} \begin{bmatrix} C^{-1} & A \\ A^{\mathrm{T}} & 0 \end{bmatrix} \longrightarrow \begin{bmatrix} C^{-1} & A \\ 0 & -A^{\mathrm{T}}CA \end{bmatrix} \qquad \begin{matrix} \text{Solve } A^{\mathrm{T}}CAu = A^{\mathrm{T}}Cb - f \\ \text{Then } w = C(b - Au) \end{matrix}$$

Every area of applied mathematics has its own interpretation of A, C, b and f. Certainly different letters are often used, and some problems change the $(1,2)$ block from A to $-A$. (Springs and masses had $e = Au$, which is $C^{-1}w - Au = 0$.) Least squares brought the minus sign into $b - Au$, and now we see it again in networks. The flow is from higher potential to lower potential, and in fluid mechanics from higher pressure to lower pressure. We will see this same framework for differential equations, provided there are no convection or damping terms. This Karush-Kuhn-Tucker matrix reappears in Section 8.1.

How to solve the equations? For problems of moderate size, we give a direct answer: Use elimination on the matrix $K = A^{\mathrm{T}}CA$. The backslash command K\ in MATLAB will be adequate. But applications in 3D can produce really large systems. Then elimination has to be improved by reordering the unknowns (the KLU code by Tim Davis is tuned for networks). Chapter 7 also explains "incomplete LU" and the (preconditioned) conjugate gradient method.

The problem for now is to create the model and understand $K = A^{\mathrm{T}}CA$, the conductance matrix (weighted Laplacian matrix) for the graph and the network.

■ WORKED EXAMPLE ■

2.5 A For a complete graph with n nodes and edges between all pairs, compute

(1) $A^{\mathrm{T}}A$ **(2)** $K = (A^{\mathrm{T}}A)_{\text{reduced}}$ **(3)** K^{-1} **(4)** eigenvalues of K **(5)** $\det(K)$

Solution Every node has $n-1$ edges, connecting to all other nodes. So all diagonal entries of $A^{\mathrm{T}}A$ are $n-1$, and all off-diagonal entries are -1. That unreduced matrix $A^{\mathrm{T}}A$ is n by n and singular. When a node is grounded to reach the reduced matrix K, we lose a row and column of $A^{\mathrm{T}}A$. The size of K_{reduced} becomes $n-1$:

$$K_{\text{reduced}} = \begin{bmatrix} n{-}1 & -1 & \cdot & -1 \\ -1 & n{-}1 & \cdot & -1 \\ \cdot & \cdot & \cdot & \cdot \\ -1 & -1 & \cdot & n{-}1 \end{bmatrix} \quad \text{has} \quad K^{-1} = \frac{1}{n}\begin{bmatrix} 2 & 1 & \cdot & 1 \\ 1 & 2 & \cdot & 1 \\ \cdot & \cdot & \cdot & \cdot \\ 1 & 1 & \cdot & 2 \end{bmatrix}. \tag{20}$$

It is unusual to discover such a neat K^{-1}, but you can quickly check $KK^{-1} = I$.

The $n-1$ eigenvalues of K are $\lambda = 1, n, \ldots, n$. This comes from knowing the eigenvalues of the all-ones matrix $E = \text{ones}(n-1)$. Its trace is a sum of 1's:

E has trace $n-1$. Its rank is 1. *Its eigenvalues must be* $n-1, 0, \ldots, 0$.

Then $K = nI - E$ has first eigenvalue $n - (n-1) = 1$. The other $n-2$ eigenvalues of K are $n - 0 = n$. The determinant of K is the product of its $n-1$ eigenvalues:

Determinant $(1)(n)\cdots(n) = n^{n-2}$ **Trace** $n(n-2) + 1 = (n-1)^2$ (21)

Our complete graph with $n = 4$ nodes and 6 edges has a 3 by 3 matrix K_{reduced}:

$$K = \begin{bmatrix} 3 & -1 & -1 \\ -1 & 3 & -1 \\ -1 & -1 & 3 \end{bmatrix} \qquad K^{-1} = \frac{1}{4}\begin{bmatrix} 2 & 1 & 1 \\ 1 & 2 & 1 \\ 1 & 1 & 2 \end{bmatrix} \qquad \begin{aligned} &\boldsymbol{\lambda(K) = 1, 4, 4} \\ &\textbf{trace } \boldsymbol{(K) = 9} \\ &\textbf{det}\boldsymbol{(K) = 4^2 = 16}. \end{aligned} \tag{22}$$

Most remarkably, there are 16 spanning trees (each with 4 nodes) in the graph. **For any connected graph, the determinant of a reduced $A^{\mathrm{T}}A$ counts the spanning trees.** The word "spanning" means that the tree reaches all nodes.

Eigenvectors of K
Not normalized

$$\begin{bmatrix} 1 & 1/2 & 1/3 \\ -1 & 1/2 & 1/3 \\ 0 & -1 & 1/3 \end{bmatrix} \tag{23}$$

Problem Set 2.4

1 What are the incidence matrices $A_{\textsf{triangle}}$ and $A_{\textsf{square}}$ for these graphs? Find $A^{\mathrm{T}}A$.

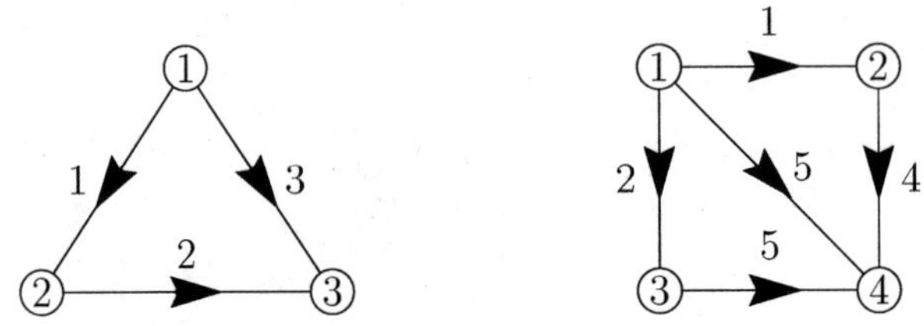

2 Find all vectors in the nullspaces of $A_{\textsf{triangle}}$ and its transpose.

3 Find one solution to $A_{\textsf{square}}u = 0$. Find two solutions to $(A_{\textsf{square}})^{\mathrm{T}}w = 0$.

4 Imagine a 9 by 9 square grid (like graph paper) with $n = 100$ nodes.

(a) How many edges will there be? The ratio m/n is nearly ____.

(b) Add edges on the diagonals of slope $+1$ in each grid square. Find the new edge count m. The new ratio m/n is nearly ____.

5 For every connected graph, explain why the *only* solutions to $Au = 0$ are the constant vectors $u = (C, \ldots, C)$. How do you know that $u_j = u_k$ when the nodes are not connected directly by an edge?

6 The sum down the main diagonal of a matrix is the *trace*. For the complete graph and the tree, the traces of $A^{\mathrm{T}}A$ are $3+3+3+3 = 12$ and $1+2+2+1 = 6$. Why is the trace of $A^{\mathrm{T}}A$ always $2m$ for any graph with m edges?

7 What is $K = A^{\mathrm{T}}CA$ for the four-node tree with all three edges into node 4? Ground a node to find the reduced (invertible) K and $\det K$.

8 Show how the six "element matrices" for the complete graph are assembled into $A^{\mathrm{T}}CA$ in (14). Each 2 by 2 element matrix comes from one of the edges:

Element matrix for edge i connecting nodes j and k
$$K_i = \begin{bmatrix} c_i & -c_i \\ -c_i & c_i \end{bmatrix} \begin{matrix} \text{row } j \\ \text{row } k \end{matrix}$$

With all $c_i = 1$, assembly should give $(A^{\mathrm{T}}A)_{jj} = 3$ and $(A^{\mathrm{T}}A)_{jk} = -1$ in (9).

9 (Recommended) If a tree has five nodes in a line (four edges), answer the questions in Worked Example 2.5 A.

10 If a line of three resistors has conductances $1, 4, 9$, what is $K = A^{\mathrm{T}}CA$ and what is $\det(K_{\textsf{reduced}})$? Find the eigenvalues from $\textsf{eig}(K)$.

11 For the 12 volt battery in equation (18), with all $c_i = 1$, find u and w by imagining the voltages in the network or by direct solution.

12 Check $KK^{-1} = I$ in equation (20). How do you know K is positive definite?

13 Determine all trees for the two graphs in Problem 1 (triangle and square).

14 The **adjacency matrix** has $w_{ij} = 1$ when nodes i and j are connected by an edge; otherwise $w_{ij} = 0$ (including $w_{ii} = 0$). Show how (column i of A) $\cdot$ (column j of A) in the Laplacian matrix $A^{\mathrm{T}}A$ produces $-w_{ij}$.

15 Find the $n-1$ eigenvalues of K^{-1} in (20), knowing that the all-ones matrix E has $\lambda = n-1, 0, \ldots, 0$. Check your answer with $\lambda = 1, n, \ldots, n$ for K.

16 Write down the edges in each of the 16 spanning trees within Figure 2.16. This tree count matches $\det(A^{\mathrm{T}}A)$ in (22) because of the Cauchy-Binet formula for the determinant of $A^{\mathrm{T}}_{n\times m} \times A_{m\times n}$: $\det(A^{\mathrm{T}}A) =$ sum of $\det(S^{\mathrm{T}}S)$ for all $n \times n$ submatrices S of A. An incidence matrix has $\det(S^{\mathrm{T}}S) = 1$ or 0 (the subgraph is a tree or not). So the sum counts the spanning trees in any graph.

17 A 3 by 3 square grid has $n = 9$ nodes and $m = 12$ edges. Number nodes by rows.

(a) How many zeros among the 81 entries of $A^{\mathrm{T}}A$?

(b) Write down its main diagonal D (the degree matrix).

(c) Why does the middle row have $d_{55} = 4$ and four -1's in $-W$? Second differences in 2D come from the *continuous Laplacian* $-\partial^2/\partial x^2 - \partial^2/\partial y^2$.

The Laplacian matrix $L = A^{\mathrm{T}}A$ for an N by N grid is created by kron.
B = toeplitz([2 -1 zeros(1, $N-2$)]); $B(1,1) = 1$; $B(N,N) = 1$;
L = kron(B, eye(N)) + kron(eye(N), B); % Section 3.5 explains kron.

18 For $N = 3$, send a current $f = 1$ from node $(1,1)$ to $(3,3)$. Ground the $(3,3)$ node by $K = L(1:8, 1:8)$. Solve the 8 equations $Ku = f$ to find the voltage $u(1,1)$. This is the "grid resistance" between the far corners.

19 For $N = 4$, the $(2,2)$ node is grounded by $L(6,:) = [\,]$; $L(:,6) = [\,]$; $K = L$. Send current $f = 1$ into the $(3,3)$ node. Solve $Ku = f$ for the voltage $u(3,3)$, which gives the grid resistance between those diagonal neighbors (nodes 6 and 11 renumbered 10).

20 Repeat Problem 19 for $N = 10$ and nodes 45 and 56: the neighbors $(5,5)$ and $(6,6)$. The resistance between diagonal neighbors on an infinite grid is $2/\pi$.

21 (Recommended) Nodes 55 and 56 are neighbors near the center of a 10 by 10 grid. Ground node 56 as in Problem 19, by removing row 56 and column 56 of L. Set $f_{55} = 1$. Solve $Ku = f$ for the grid resistance between those neighbors.

22 Guess the resistance between closest neighbors on an infinite grid ($N \to \infty$).

2.5 NETWORKS AND TRANSFER FUNCTIONS

The standard *RLC* circuit allows capacitors and inductors as well as resistors. The algebraic equations for u and w become differential equations for voltages $V_i(t)$ and currents $I_j(t)$. The transients decay with time as the resistors dissipate energy.

Of great importance in many applications is a **sinusoidal forcing term** with fixed frequency ω. A typical voltage can be written as $V\cos\omega t = \text{Re}(Ve^{i\omega t})$. These alternating voltages produce alternating currents. The dependence on time of every current has the same $e^{i\omega t}$. All unknowns are now *complex numbers*.

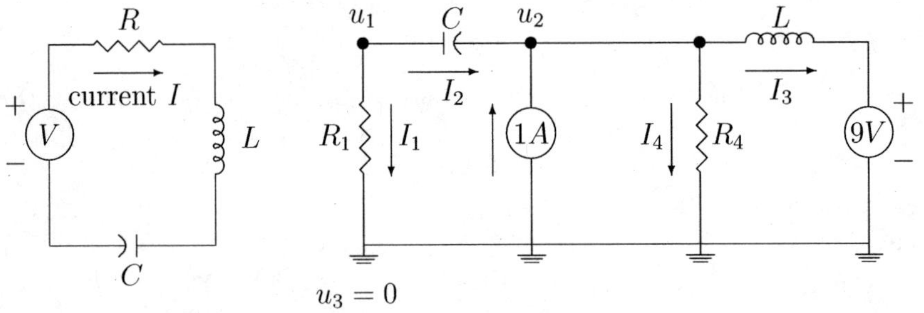

Figure 2.20: A single *RLC* loop. A small *RLC* circuit, grounded by $u_3 = 0$.

The circuit becomes as simple to analyze as before, after real resistances R change to ***complex impedances*** Z. To find Z we look at the equation for one *RLC* loop. If the inductance is L and the capacitance is C, then $\boldsymbol{V = L\,dI/dt}$ for the first and $\boldsymbol{I = C\,dV/dt}$ for the second. The voltage drops V in inductance, resistance, and capacitance ($V = \int I\,dt/C$) combine to give the loop equation for the current:

Voltage V
Current I

$$L\frac{dI}{dt} + RI + \frac{1}{C}\int I dt = \text{Re}(Ve^{i\omega t}). \tag{1}$$

Substituting $I = \text{Re}(We^{i\omega t})$ produces $i\omega$ in the derivative and $1/i\omega$ in the integral:

Loop equation for W

$$\left(i\omega L + R + \frac{1}{i\omega C}\right) We^{i\omega t} = Ve^{i\omega t}.$$

Cancel $e^{i\omega t}$, which is possible because every term has frequency ω:

Complex impedance Z

$$V = WZ \quad \text{with} \quad Z = i\omega L + R + \frac{1}{i\omega C}. \tag{2}$$

This is Ohm's law $V = IR$, with R made complex. For one loop in Figure 2.20 there is nothing more to do. The current is the real part of $(V/Z)e^{i\omega t}$. The change from R to Z produced an impedance of magnitude $|Z|$:

$|Z| \geq |R|$

$$|Z| = \left|R + i\left(\omega L - \frac{1}{\omega C}\right)\right| = \left(R^2 + \left(\omega L - \frac{1}{\omega C}\right)^2\right)^{1/2} \tag{3}$$

The capacitor and inductor reduce the flow, except at one ω when L cancels C:

$$\textbf{Real impedance } Z = R \qquad \omega L = \frac{1}{wC} \quad \text{and} \quad \omega = \sqrt{\frac{1}{LC}}. \tag{4}$$

This is what happens when you tune a radio. You are adjusting the capacitance C to match the frequency you want. At that resonant frequency, given by (4), the impedance is smallest and you can hear the signal (after it is amplified). Other frequencies will be received too, but their impedance $|Z|$ is much larger.

The capacitor and inductor also change the *phase* by an angle θ:

$$\textbf{Phase change} \qquad I = \operatorname{Re}\left(\frac{V}{Z}e^{i\omega t}\right) = \operatorname{Re}\left(\frac{V}{|Z|}e^{i(\omega t - \theta)}\right). \tag{5}$$

The cycles are advanced or retarded depending on θ. If the circuit contains only resistors then $\theta = 0$. If the circuit contains *no* resistors, then Z is a pure imaginary number (from $i\omega L$ and $-i/\omega C$). Its phase angle is $\pi/2$ or $3\pi/2$.

For a more general RLC circuit, we go back to the basic framework. Each voltage source and current source, together with each potential and current, is represented by a complex number. After the (periodic) equilibrium equations are solved, the actual time-varying currents include $e^{i\omega t}$. The coefficient matrix is still $A^{\mathrm{T}}CA$, with a complex diagonal matrix C whose entries are the "***admittances***" $1/Z$.

Example 1 Two resistances are changed to a capacitance C and an inductance L in Figure 2.20. The 4 by 2 connectivity matrix A is unchanged. But the diagonal of C^{-1} contains impedances instead of resistances:

$$\begin{bmatrix} C^{-1} & A \\ A^{\mathrm{T}} & 0 \end{bmatrix}\begin{bmatrix} W \\ V \end{bmatrix} = \left[\begin{array}{cccc:cc} R_1 & & & & -1 & 0 \\ & (i\omega C)^{-1} & & & -1 & 1 \\ & & i\omega L & & 0 & -1 \\ & & & R_4 & 0 & -1 \\ \hdashline -1 & -1 & 0 & 0 & 0 & 0 \\ 0 & 1 & -1 & -1 & 0 & 0 \end{array}\right]\left[\begin{array}{c} W_1 \\ W_2 \\ W_3 \\ W_4 \\ \hdashline V_1 \\ V_2 \end{array}\right] = \begin{bmatrix} b \\ f \end{bmatrix} \tag{6}$$

Along with batteries b we could have ***transistors***, which are nonlinear voltage sources. Their strength depends on the voltages at their terminals. In other words, a transistor is a "voltage-dependent" voltage source. It makes Kirchhoff's laws nonlinear (and a diode makes Ohm's law nonlinear). An operational amplifier (*op-amp)* is an active circuit element (RLC is passive). The voltage difference $v_1 - v_2$ is multiplied by the *gain* A to give the output v_{out}. This leads to "modified nodal analysis" in the widely-used code SPICE.

Time Domain versus Frequency Domain

Hidden in the start of this section were two key decisions for the formulation of network theory. One of them came immediately in the step from equation (1) to (2):

Equation (1) is in the **time domain**. The unknowns are in **state space**.

Equation (2) is in the **frequency domain**. It includes a **transfer function**.

The link from (1) to (2) is a transform. For an initial-value problem this will be a ***Laplace transform***. The simplicity of equation (2) shows the value of working in the frequency domain (especially for small networks). This section introduces the Laplace transform by using its rules on a few functions. We reach a fundamental concept in modern engineering: the **transfer function** connecting input to output.

Transforming differential equations to algebra is beautiful (and very insightful) when it works. Transient responses and stability are clearest in the frequency domain. But its applicability is limited to **linear time-invariant equations**. Fourier transforms will have the same limitation to linear space-invariant equations. For nonlinear equations and time-varying systems, **state space** is far more convenient. That formulation in the time domain embraces nonzero initial conditions, and also multiple input-multiple output systems. Software like SPICE for general circuit analysis usually succeeds best in state space.

Looking ahead, Section 5.3 studies the Laplace transform and its inverse. This needs the complex analysis in Section 5.1. Here we apply the transform to typical examples of very small networks. **The poles of the transfer function become eigenvalues in linear algebra**. Later we move up to the state space equations at the heart of control theory, and Kalman's (A, B, C, D) representation:

State equation $$x' = Ax + Bu \tag{7}$$

Observation equation $$y = Cx + Du \tag{8}$$

The other crucial decision is the choice between loop equations for the current, and nodal equations for the voltage. The loop equations use the Voltage Law and the nodal equations use the Current Law. This book consistently works with the potential u and the Current Law. We now discuss that choice, and stay with it.

Loop Equations versus Nodal Equations

I must pause to say something mysterious but important. It was natural to describe a simple RLC loop by equation (1). A small network with two loops would similarly lead to two coupled "loop equations." But notice well: **Section 2.4 described a large network by its nodes and not by its loops**.

The loop description is based on Kirchhoff's Voltage Law: *Add voltage drops.* The node description is based on his Current Law: *Add currents into nodes.* The circuit simulation community seems to have made its choice: **Nodal analysis.** The finite element community made the same choice: The **displacement method.** The $A^{\mathrm{T}}CA$ framework is dominant, based on C = conductances or admittances, with currents $w = C(e)$. The unknowns u are the voltages and the displacements.

The alternative $N^{\mathrm{T}}ZN$ formulation goes "the other way" around the framework. The middle step is based on Z = resistance or impedance and $e = C^{-1}(w) = Z(w)$. The unknowns are currents (or stresses). The simplicity of A compared to N gave the victory (we believe) to nodal analysis and the displacement method.

The nodal method uses *edges* in the graph, the mesh method uses *loops*. Flow around each loop satisfies the Current Law $A^{\mathrm{T}}w = 0$. ***Loop flows describe the nullspace of*** $\boldsymbol{A^{\mathrm{T}}}$. In matrix language $\boldsymbol{A^{\mathrm{T}}N}$ = ***zero matrix*** (discrete div curl = 0). When A has n columns from n ungrounded nodes, N has $m-n$ columns from $m-n$ loops. In hand calculations we prefer the smaller of n and $m-n$ (with one loop, that method wins). But who does hand calculations now? The verdict in the SPICE codes is that nodal analysis is simpler to organize for realistic networks.

Computational mechanics faced the same choice and reached the same conclusion. The displacement method and stress method are again dual. One way, the primary unknown is u, and force balance $A^{\mathrm{T}}w = f$ is the constraint. The other way, $A^{\mathrm{T}}w = 0$ is solved for a complete set of self-stresses (plus a particular w that balances f). Thus the stress method is again a ***nullspace method***, directly solving the balance law.

This nullspace computation appears in Section 8.2 on constrained optimization (by solving $Bu = d$ with the qr command). Section 8.5 introduces a *mixed method* (with both u and w as unknowns). That **saddle point or primal-dual method** is a winner in optimization, when the constraints include inequalities.

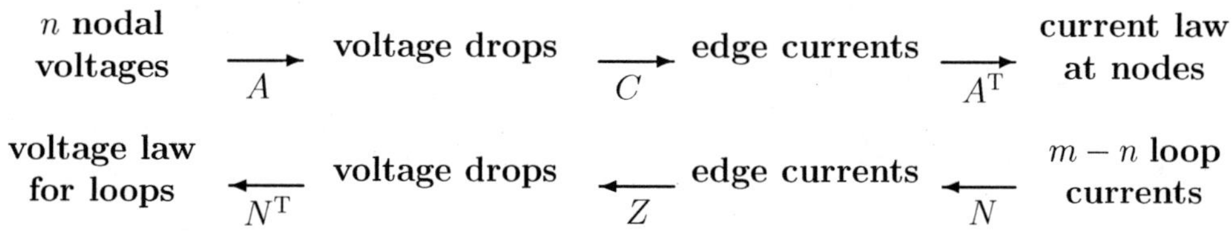
n nodal voltages
A
voltage drops
C
edge currents
A^T
current law at nodes
voltage law for loops
N^T
voltage drops
Z
edge currents
N
m − n loop currents

Impedances and Admittances

The variable "s" has not yet appeared in this book, but soon will. The differential equation in the time domain becomes an **algebraic equation in the frequency domain**. The all-important **transfer function** is a function of s. The full Laplace transform and its inversion in Chapter 5 need complex analysis with $s = \sigma + i\omega$. Briefly: The Laplace transform is for one-sided initial-value problems ($0 \le t < \infty$). The Fourier transform applies to two-sided boundary-value problems ($-\infty < x < \infty$). Frequency analysis is a tremendous simplification for linear time-invariance.

Return for a moment to the simple RLC loop, for two reasons. First, I will use the frequency variable $s = i\omega$ instead of the time variable t. Second, I will compare loop analysis with nodal analysis (Voltage Law with Current Law).

Figure 2.21 shows the loop with impedances R, Ls, and $1/Cs$ taken from this table. Columns 1 and 3 are functions of t. Columns 2 and 4 are transformed to s. The impedances are $Z(s) = V(s)/I(s)$. The admittances in the last column are the reciprocals $Y(s) = I(s)/V(s)$. The excellent book by Nise [118] will be our guide.

Capacitor	$V = \frac{1}{C}\int_0^t I\,dt$	$\frac{1}{Cs}$	$I = C\frac{dV}{dt}$	Cs
Resistor	$V = RI$	R	$I = V/R$	$1/R$
Inductor	$V = L\frac{dI}{dt}$	Ls	$I = \frac{1}{L}\int_0^t V\,dt$	$\frac{1}{Ls}$

Notation Circuit analysis prefers $e^{j\omega t}$ with $\boldsymbol{j} = \sqrt{-1}$. Then $s = j\omega$ replaces $s = i\omega$. This frees the letter i to represent current. Let me compare u, e, w in this book (covering many applications) with the usual $i(t)$ for current and $v(t)$ for voltage:

$$\textbf{Standard} \qquad s = j\omega \quad \text{and} \quad i(t) = \text{Re}[I(s)e^{st}] \quad \text{and} \quad v(t) = \text{Re}[V(s)e^{st}]. \qquad (9)$$

The letter s indicates a Laplace transform. In this section $\boldsymbol{s = i\omega}$ comes from the single driving frequency in the voltage source. In Section 5.3, $s = \sigma + i\omega$ becomes a complex variable, and the time dependence includes a whole range of frequencies.

One Loop by Transform Methods

Figure 2.21 shows the voltage drop V_C across the capacitor. ***The problem is to relate $V_C(s)$ to the input voltage $V(s)$ by the transfer function.***

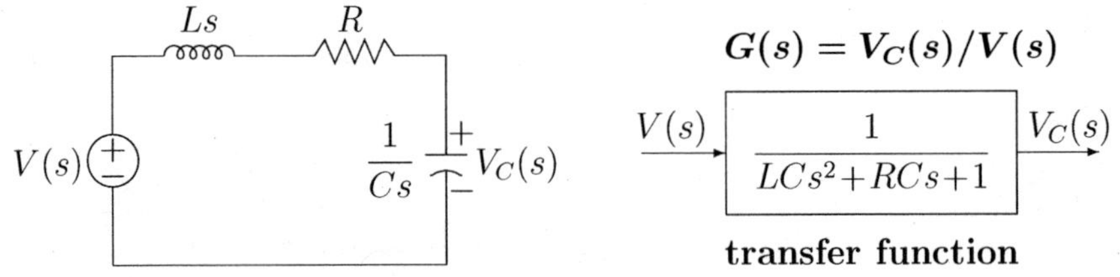

Figure 2.21: Laplace-transformed loop and its block diagram with transfer function.

The loop current I is the unknown in the Voltage Law (1). The transformed loop equation is (2). The transformed capacitor equation for V_C comes from the table:

$$\textbf{Transformed equations} \qquad \left(Ls + R + \frac{1}{Cs}\right) I(s) = V(s) \text{ and } V_C(s) = \frac{I(s)}{Cs}. \qquad (10)$$

Eliminating I produces the transfer function from the input V to the response V_C:

Transfer function is $G = V_C/V$

$$\left(Ls + R + \frac{1}{Cs}\right) Cs\, V_C(s) = V(s). \tag{11}$$

The transfer function $G(s)$ in the block diagram divides $V_C(s)$ by $LCs^2 + RCs + 1$.

Nise obtains the same transfer function by **nodal analysis** (preferred). Place a node at the capacitor, and apply the Current Law. The current flowing through the capacitor balances the current flowing through the resistor and inductor:

Current Law: Multiply by $R + Ls$
Then $(LCs^2 + RCs + 1)V_C(s) = V(s)$

$$\frac{V_C(s)}{1/Cs} + \frac{V_C(s) - V(s)}{R + Ls} = 0. \tag{12}$$

Note that the largest application area for MathWorks is simulation and control of electrical and mechanical systems (extended to problems in all fields of engineering). The SIMULINK package combines block diagrams into complete networks.

Mesh Analysis and Nodal Analysis: Two Loops

Nise [118] also gives an example with two loops and two equations. The transformed network in Figure 2.22 has the transfer function $I_2(s)/V(s)$ in the block diagram. This comes first from the Voltage Law around each of the loops:

Analysis of two loops

$$\begin{aligned} (R_1 + Ls)\, I_1(s) - Ls\, I_2(s) &= V(s) \\ -Ls\, I_1(s) + \left(Ls + R_2 + \frac{1}{Cs}\right) I_2(s) &= 0 \end{aligned} \tag{13}$$

Elimination (or Cramer's Rule) will solve this 2 by 2 system to find $I_2(s)/V(s)$. But nodal analysis is really better for large networks, and SPICE would make that choice. This example happens to have $m - n = 2$ and also $n = 2$:

Analysis at two nodes

$$\begin{aligned} (V_1 - V)/R_1 + V_1/Ls + (V_1 - V_2)/R_2 &= 0 \\ CsV_2 + (V_2 - V_1)/R_2 &= 0 \end{aligned} \tag{14}$$

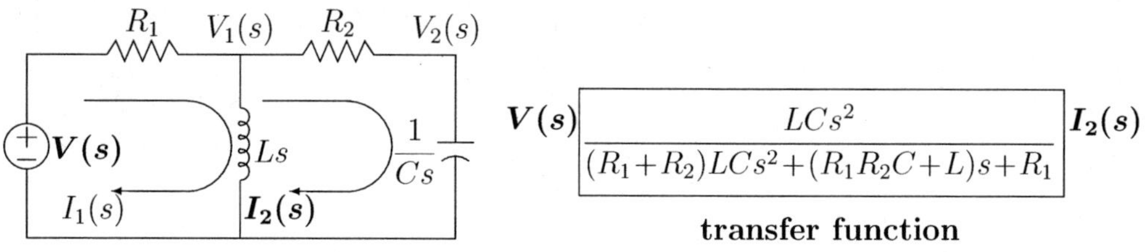

Figure 2.22: A two-loop network and its block diagram with transfer function.

Those resistances might be replaced by conductances $c_1 = 1/R_1$ and $c_2 = 1/R_2$. Impedances Z change to admittances $1/Z$ in nodal analysis. The two approaches have parallel descriptions, but nodal analysis is recognized as the winner:

Loop analysis		Nodal analysis	
1	Replace elements by impedances	1′	Replace elements by admittances
2	Apply the Voltage Law around loops	2′	Apply the Current Law at nodes
3	Solve for the loop currents	3′	Solve for the nodal voltages

This is Euler's formula in Section 2.4 proved by geometry or by the dimensions of subspaces (test it for a triangle).

For linear time-invariant networks, we now emphasize the importance of the ***poles of the transfer function***. Poles give the exponents, when solving differential equations in the time domain. In nonlinear or time-varying modern network theory, the state-space approach is the overwhelming choice.

Transient Response and Poles of the Transfer Function

The solutions to matrix equations have two parts: a **particular solution** to $Au_p = b$ plus any **nullspace solution** to the homogeneous equation $Au_n = 0$. The solutions to linear differential equations similarly have two parts: a **forced response** (the *steady state*, independent of initial values) plus a **natural response** (the *transient*, from the homogeneous equation and the initial values). When the system starts with a step function input at $t = 0$, this solution $u_p(t) + u_n(t)$ is the step response.

Our goal is to identify the **exponents** in the transient solution as the **poles** in the transfer function. This is not a mystery. Every course on differential equations begins with constant coefficients. The equation is LTI (linear time-invariant) and the solutions are combinations of exponentials. We substitute $u(t) = e^{st}$ into the homogeneous equation ($u(t) = ve^{st}$ for a system of equations), and then cancel e^{st} from every term. This leaves a polynomial equation for s. For systems it leaves an eigenvalue-eigenvector equation for s and v. That polynomial is exactly the one that appears in the one-loop example, where its reciprocal is the transfer function:

Differential equation	$LCu'' + RCu' + u = 0$	**Polynomial equation**	$LCs^2 + RCs + 1 = 0$	(15)

The *zeros* s_1 and s_2 of the polynomial P are the *poles* of the transfer function G. That function $G = 1/P$ becomes infinite at s_1 and s_2. The circuit designer chooses R, L, and C to produce the desired exponents in $e^{s_1 t}$ and $e^{s_2 t}$ with the least cost.

With $R = 0$ (no damping), $s^2 = -1/LC$ has pure imaginary solutions $s = i\omega$. The poles are on the imaginary axis. The transients are pure oscillations with $\cos \omega t$ and $\sin \omega t$, as in the harmonic oscillator $Mu'' + Ku = 0$.

With damping from R, the exponents s_1 and s_2 (the poles of the transfer function) are *complex numbers*. Add dashpots (viscous dampers D) to the spring-mass system, and the eigenvalues become complex solutions of $\det(Ms^2 + Ds + K) = 0$. We expect the dampers to dissipate energy and the eigenvalues to have $\operatorname{Re} s < 0$: **stability**.

Thus damped systems give quadratic eigenvalue problems! The scalar case is $ms^2 + ds + k = 0$ for a mass-damper-spring and $Ls^2 + Rs + 1/C = 0$ for one loop.

The solutions come next, to show the difference between underdamping (roots still complex) and overdamping (real negative roots). For a large system, it goes without saying that we would never compute the coefficients of $\det(Ms^2 + Ds + K)$ and then try to find the roots of that polynomial: *A computational crime.*

Quadratic eigenvalue problems $(M\lambda^2 + D\lambda + K)v = 0$, can be solved by polyeig. A survey is in [154]. Frequency domain versions of SPICE include eigenvalue solvers.

Underdamping and Overdamping

The roots of a quadratic have a famous formula. We want to follow those two roots s_1 and s_2 as the middle coefficient due to damping increases from zero. The roots go from complex conjugate numbers (*underdamping*) to real negative numbers (*overdamping*). At the moment of transition they are equal numbers $s_1 = s_2 < 0$ (*critical damping*).

The path of the roots is the **root locus**, drawn in Figure 2.23. The figure also shows the parallels between an RLC loop and a mass-spring with damper (both systems in series). For a rotational system the mass becomes the *moment of inertia.* The driving force from a motor is a *torque*, and the displacement becomes an *angle.* We are staying with one degree of freedom (scalars not matrices).

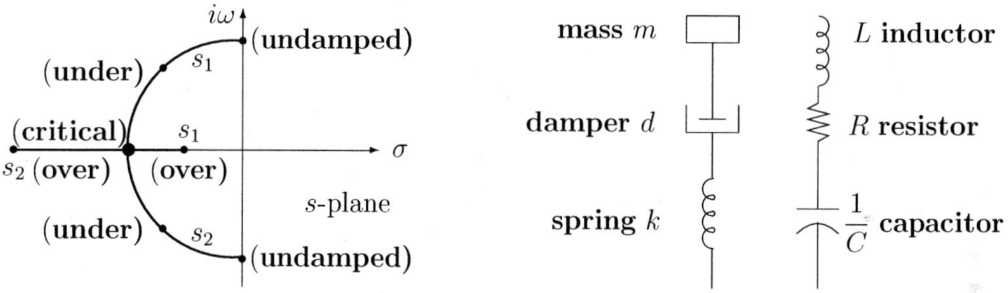

Figure 2.23: The roots s_1, s_2 become real as the damping from d or R increases.

The quadratic formula reveals this transition from oscillation to decay:

$ms^2 + ds + k = 0$	$d^2 < 4km$	$\overline{s_2} = s_1$	**underdamping**
$s = \dfrac{-d \pm \sqrt{d^2 - 4km}}{2m}$	$d^2 = 4km$	$s_2 = s_1 < 0$	**critical damping**
	$d^2 > 4km$	$s_2 < s_1 < 0$	**overdamping**

This is all about the natural response (transient). A forcing term $f(t)$ produces a forced response (steady state). When a constant force is turned on at $t = 0$, we solve the differential equation with that step function $f(t)$ and zero initial conditions.

Step response $u(t)$ $\quad mu'' + du' + ku = 1 \quad \text{for} \quad t > 0,\ u(0) = u'(0) = 0. \quad (16)$

Solution $\quad u(t) = u_{\text{particular}} + u_{\text{nullspace}} = u_{\text{steady}} + u_{\text{transient}}$

The step response is $\dfrac{1}{k} + Ae^{s_1 t} + Be^{s_2 t} = \text{constant} + \text{oscillation-decay}.$

Example 2 Suppose $m = k = 1$ and the damping coefficient d increases from zero. The quadratic equation is $s^2 + ds + 1 = 0$. Factoring into $(s - s_1)(s - s_2)$, the roots multiply to give $s_1 s_2 = 1$. They add to give $s_1 + s_2 = -d$. In this key example, we now plot those roots at four values $d = 0, 1, 2$ and 2.05 of the damping coefficient.

$s^2 + 1 = 0$	$s^2 + \mathbf{s} + 1 = 0$	$s^2 + \mathbf{2s} + 1 = 0$	$s^2 + \mathbf{2.05s} + 1 = 0$

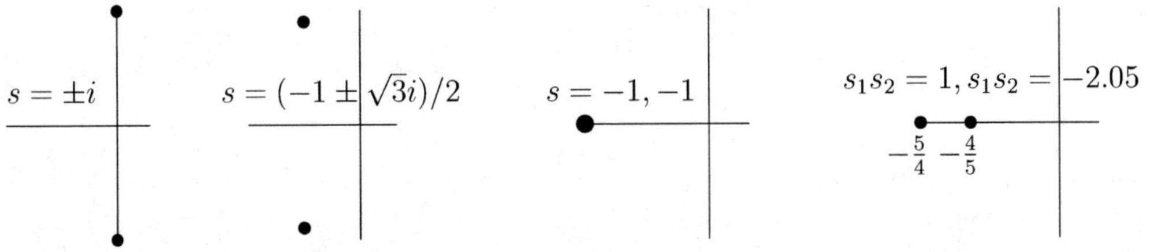

Undamped **Underdamped** **Critically damped** **Overdamped**

The coefficients A and B in the transient response are found from $u(0) = u'(0) = 0$. The graphs in Figure 2.24 show the four step responses with increasing d.

A useful measure of decay/oscillation is the **damping ratio**, defined as $d/2\sqrt{km}$. This is a natural time divided by a decay time. (Notice in $e^{-aT} = 1$ how a has the units of 1/time.) A designer also wants to know the **rise time** in the last two graphs. By convention this is the time from $u = .1$ to $u = .9$ when $u(\infty) = 1$.

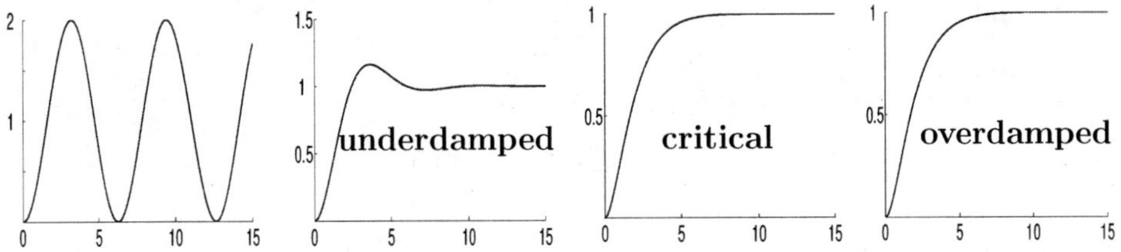

Figure 2.24: Step responses $u(t)$ = transients plus steady state ($u(\infty) = 1$).

Let me review the overdamped equation (fourth example) in detail. The equation is $u'' + 2.05\,u' + u = 1$ for $t \geq 0$. The steady-state forced solution is $u = 1$. To find the transient solutions, set $u = e^{st}$ in the unforced equation $u'' + 2.05\,u' + u = 0$. This produces $s^2 + 2.05\,s + 1 = 0$, and we find $s_1 = -0.8$ and $s_2 = -1.25$:

$$s^2 + 2.05s + 1 = \left(s + \frac{4}{5}\right)\left(s + \frac{5}{4}\right) = 0 \text{ has } s_1 = -\frac{4}{5} \text{ and } s_2 = -\frac{5}{4} \text{ since } .8 + 1.25 = 2.05.$$

The nullspace (homogeneous) solutions are combinations of those exponentials e^{st}.

Complete solution $\quad u'' + 2.05u' + u = 1$ is solved by $u(t) = 1 + Ae^{-4t/5} + Be^{-5t/4}$. (17)

The initial conditions determine A and B and $u(t)$. Here $u(0) = u'(0) = 0$:

$$u(0) = 1 + A + B = 0 \text{ and } u'(0) = -\frac{4}{5}A - \frac{5}{4}B = 0 \text{ give } A = -\frac{25}{9} \text{ and } B = \frac{16}{9}.$$

The Laplace Transform

Notice that after finding s_1 and s_2, we went back to the time domain for $u(t)$. **The Laplace transform can solve the whole problem in the frequency domain.** We will find the transform $U(s)$, including the constants A and B. Then the very last step is an inverse transform from $U(s)$ to $u(t)$. Start with the forward transform:

Laplace transform of $u(t)$
$$U(s) = \int_0^\infty u(t)\, e^{-st}\, dt \qquad (18)$$

Solving $u'' + 2.05\,u' + u = 1$ requires only the transform $U = 1/(a+s)$ of $u = e^{-at}$:

Key transform
$$U(s) = \int_0^\infty e^{-at}\, e^{-st}\, dt = \int_0^\infty e^{-(a+s)t}\, dt = \left[\frac{e^{-(a+s)t}}{-(a+s)}\right]_0^\infty = \frac{\mathbf{1}}{\boldsymbol{a+s}}. \qquad (19)$$

In the special case $a = 0$, the step function is $e^{-0t} = 1$ and the transform is $1/s$.

The other requirement is to connect the transforms of u' and u'' to $U(s)$:

Key rule The transform of $u'(t)$ is $s\,U(s) - u(0)$. (20)

That rule comes from integration by parts (remember $\int u'v + uv' = uv$):

$$\int_0^\infty u'(t)e^{-st}\, dt = -\int_0^\infty u(t)(e^{-st})'\, dt + \Big[u(t)e^{-st}\Big]_0^\infty = s\,U(s) - u(0).$$

Applying the rule again to u' gives the Laplace transform of the next derivative u'':

Transform of $u''(t)$ $\quad s\big[\textit{transform of } u'\big] - u'(0) = \boldsymbol{s^2\,U(s) - su(0) - u'(0)}.$

Our example has $u(0) = u'(0) = 0$. Now use linearity of the integral (18) that defined $U(s)$. The transform of a sum $u'' + 2.05\,u' + u = 1$ is the **sum of the transforms**:

$$U(s) = \begin{pmatrix}\text{input}\\\text{transform}\end{pmatrix}\begin{pmatrix}\text{transfer}\\\text{function}\end{pmatrix} \qquad \begin{aligned} &s^2U(s) + 2.05\,s\,U(s) + U(s) = 1/s \\ &U(s) = \left(\frac{1}{s}\right)\left(\frac{1}{s^2 + 2.05\,s + 1}\right)\end{aligned} \qquad (21)$$

The Algebra of Partial Fractions

We have the solution, but it is in the frequency domain. The equation for $u(t)$ was transformed and solved for $U(s)$. The final step is always to invert the transform and reconstruct $u(t)$. To take that inverse step to $u(t)$, write $U(s)$ as a combination of **three transforms that we already know**:

Partial fractions
$$U(s) = \frac{1}{s(s^2 + 2.05\,s + 1)} = \frac{1}{s\left(s + \frac{4}{5}\right)\left(s + \frac{5}{4}\right)} = \frac{1}{s} + \frac{A}{s + \frac{4}{5}} + \frac{B}{s + \frac{5}{4}}. \qquad (22)$$

Those are the same coefficients A and B that gave $u(t) = 1 + Ae^{s_1 t} + Be^{s_2 t}$ in the time-domain. To find A and B, we could use the ilaplace command in MATLAB's

Symbolic Toolbox, from Maple. We could also apply the Laplace inversion formula from Section 5.3 (an integral in the complex plane, not needed here). Or use ordinary algebra to find $A = -25/9$ and $B = 16/9$ that match $U(s)$ in the partial fractions:

Multiply by $s+\frac{4}{5}$ and set $s=-\frac{4}{5}$ $\quad \dfrac{1}{\left(-\frac{4}{5}\right)\left(-\frac{4}{5}+\frac{5}{4}\right)} = \dfrac{1}{\left(-\frac{4}{5}+\frac{9}{20}\right)} = -\dfrac{25}{9} = 0 + A + 0$

Similarly we multiply (22) by $\left(s+\frac{5}{4}\right)$ and set $s = -\frac{5}{4}$ to find $16/9 = 0 + 0 + B$.

The final (inverse) step is to recognize the three fractions as Laplace transforms:

$$\boldsymbol{U(s)} = \frac{1}{s} + \frac{-25/9}{s+\frac{4}{5}} + \frac{16/9}{s+\frac{5}{4}} \quad \text{comes from} \quad \boldsymbol{u(t)} = 1 - \frac{25}{9}e^{-4t/5} + \frac{16}{9}e^{-5t/4}. \qquad (23)$$

This is the overdamped solution whose graph (drawn above) rises steadily to $u(\infty)=1$.

Key idea The exponentials Ae^{st} involve the **poles** s_1, s_2 and their **residues** A, B.

Five Transforms and Five Rules

The underdamped $u(t)$ oscillates as it decays. It includes $e^{-\sigma t}\cos\omega t$ and $e^{-\sigma t}\sin\omega t$. The critically damped solution with a double pole includes e^{-t} and also te^{-t}. To find those solutions in the frequency domain, and to invert to $u(t)$ in the time domain, we need a list of transforms and rules. All functions start at $t = 0^-$, so the impulse $\delta(t)$ is safely captured at $t = 0$ with transform $U(s) = \int \delta(t)e^{-st}\,dt = 1$.

Transforms

$\delta(t)$	$\longrightarrow$	1
e^{-at}	$\longrightarrow$	$\dfrac{1}{s+a}$
$\cos\omega t$	$\longrightarrow$	$\dfrac{s}{s^2+\omega^2}$
$\sin\omega t$	$\longrightarrow$	$\dfrac{\omega}{s^2+\omega^2}$
t^n	$\longrightarrow$	$\dfrac{n!}{s^{n+1}}$

Rules

$u(t)+v(t)$	$\longrightarrow$	$U(s)+V(s)$
du/dt	$\longrightarrow$	$s\,U(s)-u(0)$
d^2u/dt^2	$\longrightarrow$	$s^2\,U(s)-s\,u(0)-u'(0)$
$e^{-at}u(t)$	$\longrightarrow$	$U(s+a)$
$u(t-T)$	$\longrightarrow$	$e^{-sT}\,U(s)$ for $T \geq 0$

By splitting $U(s)$ into simple pieces (partial fractions), we recognize $u(t)$ for each piece in the list of transforms. This plan will succeed for the other three examples: undamped, critically damped, and underdamped. The step function $f(t) = 1$ (for $t > 0$) contributes the input transfer function $1/s$. For a more general forcing function $f(t)$, we need the longer list of transforms in Section 5.3 and the general formula for the *inverse Laplace transform*—going beyond ratios of polynomials.

Example 3 (undamped) Solve $u''+u = 1$ by Laplace transforms with $u(0) = u'(0) = 0$.

Solution Transform the equation to $s^2U(s) + U(s) = 1/s$. Solve for $U(s)$ and invert:

$$U(s) = \frac{1}{s(s^2+1)} = \frac{1}{s} - \frac{s}{s^2+1} \text{ is the transform of } u(t) = \mathbf{1 - \cos t} \text{ with } \omega = 1.$$

Example 4 (critical) Solve $u'' + 2u' + u = 1$ by finding $U(s)$ and inverting to $u(t)$.

$$\frac{1}{s(s^2+2s+1)} = \frac{1}{s} - \frac{1}{s+1} - \frac{1}{(s+1)^2} \text{ is the transform of } u(t) = \mathbf{1 - e^{-t} - te^{-t}}.$$

Notice the second solution te^{-t} when the root $s = -1$ is repeated. This is critical damping, when the complex roots meet before splitting into separate real roots. The inverse transform of $1/(s+1)^2$ used the last transform $t \to 1/s^2$ in the table together with Rule 4 to change s to $s+1$ and t to te^{-t}.

Example 5 (underdamped) Solve $u'' + u' + u = 1$ to see oscillation with decay in e^{st}.

$$U(s) = \frac{1}{s(s^2+s+1)} = \frac{1}{s} - \frac{s+1}{s^2+s+1} = \frac{1}{s} + \frac{1}{s_1 - s_2}\left[\frac{1-s_1}{s+s_1} - \frac{1-s_2}{s+s_2}\right]. \quad (24)$$

Here the roots of $s^2 + s + 1 = (s+s_1)(s+s_2)$ are $s_1 = -\frac{1}{2} + \frac{\sqrt{3}}{2}i$ and $s_2 = -\frac{1}{2} - \frac{\sqrt{3}}{2}i$. Those complex roots offer two possibilities in partial fractions: keep $s^2 + 2s + 1$ with a linear factor $s+1$ in the numerator as above, or split into $A/(s+s_1) + B/(s+s_2)$ with constants in two numerators. A third way is to get help from ilaplace.

The linear/quadratic option (preferred) aims to recognize the transforms of $\cos\omega t$ and $\sin\omega t$ in the list. Our denominator is $s^2 + s + 1 = \left(s + \frac{1}{2}\right)^2 + \frac{3}{4}$. Rule 4 shifts by $a = \frac{1}{2}$ to $s^2 + \frac{3}{4}$. This brings the factor $e^{-t/2}$ into $u(t)$. Then we recognize $\omega^2 = \frac{3}{4}$:

$$\begin{aligned} \frac{s+1}{s^2+s+1} &= \frac{s+\frac{1}{2}}{\left(s+\frac{1}{2}\right)^2 + \frac{3}{4}} + \frac{\frac{1}{2}}{\left(s+\frac{1}{2}\right)^2 + \frac{3}{4}} && \to \left(\text{shift } s + \tfrac{1}{2} \text{ to } s\right) \\ &= \text{shift of } \frac{s}{s^2+\omega^2} + \frac{1/2}{s^2+\omega^2} && \to e^{-t/2}\left(\cos\omega t + \frac{1}{\sqrt{3}}\sin\omega t\right). \end{aligned} \quad (25)$$

Amazingly and happily, this agrees with the solution in the underdamped graph.

Problem Set 2.5

Problems 1-9 solve $u'' + du' + 4u = 1$ in the frequency domain with zero initial conditions $u(0) = u'(0) = 0$. Then $U(s)$ is transformed back to $u(t)$.

1 (**No damping**) Transform $u'' + 4u = 1$ to $s^2 U(s) + 4U(s) = 1/s$ and solve for $U(s)$. Write $U(s)$ as the sum of two fractions as in Example 3. From the table of transforms identify $u(t)$.

2 (**Critical damping**) Transform $u'' + 4u' + 4u = 1$ to $(s^2 + 4s + 4)\,U(s) = 1/s$ and identify the transfer function $G(s)$ for this problem. Note that $1/s$ from the forcing term is not included in $G(s)$. Since $s^2 + 4s + 4$ has a double root at $s = -2$, the transfer function has a double ____. Write $U(s)$ as the sum of three fractions as in Example 4.

3 Continue Problem 2 to identify the inverse transforms for those three fractions and find $u(t)$. The exceptional term $1/(s+2)^2$ is the transform of te^{-2t}, the second solution to $u'' + 4u' + 4u = 0$

which has a repeated root $s = -2$. Substitute te^{-2t} directly into that equation, to confirm this solution.

4 (**Overdamping**) Transform $u'' + 5u' + 4u = 1$ to $(s^2 + 5s + 4)\,U(s) = 1/s$. Factor that quadratic to find the two poles of the transfer function. Express $U(s)$ as the sum of $1/s$ and $A/(s+1)$ and $B/(s+4)$, to find $u(t)$.

5 As the damping coefficient $d = 5$ is reduced to its critical value $d = 4$, how do the two zeros of $s^2 + ds + 4$ move to the double zero at $s = -2$?

(a) Plot each zero as a function of d for $d = 5 : -.1 : 4$ or $d = 5 : -.01 : 4$.

(b) Solve $s^2 + (4 + \epsilon)s + 4 = 0$ to find the leading term in the roots as $\epsilon \to 0$.

6 (**Underdamping**) Transform $u'' + 2u' + 4u = 1$ to $(s^2 + 2s + 4)U(s) = 1/s$. Find the complex conjugate roots of that quadratic. What will be the decay rate a in the factor e^{-at} in the solution $u(t)$? What will be the frequency ω in the oscillating factors $\cos \omega t$ and $\sin \omega t$ in that solution?

7 Continuing Problem 6, write $U(s) = 1/s(s^2 + 2s + 4)$ as the sum of $1/s$ and $(As + B)/(s^2 + 2s + 4)$. To invert that last transform, write

$$\frac{As + B}{s^2 + 2s + 4} = \frac{A(s+1)}{(s+1)^2 + 3} + \frac{B - A}{(s+1)^2 + 3} = \text{shift to } \frac{As}{s^2 + 3} + \frac{B - A}{s^2 + 3}.$$

That shift produces the e^{-at} factor in $u(t)$. Invert the shifted terms to find the oscillating factors $A \cos \omega t$ and $C \sin \omega t$.

8 Continuing Problem 6, graph $u(t)$ and locate its maximum u_{max} above $u = 1$. Challenge: Plot together the graphs of $u(t)$ for $d = 2 : .5 : 4$. Find u_{max} and t_{max} for each d (note $u_{\mathsf{max}} = 1$ and $t_{\mathsf{max}} = +\infty$ for the critical $d = 4$).

9 With *negative damping* $d = -5$, transform $u'' - 5u' + 4u = 1$ to find $U(s)$. Write $U(s)$ as $1/s + A/(s-1) + B/(s-4)$ and invert to find $u(t)$. The change from Problem 4 with $d = +5$ is that now the solution _____ as $t \to \infty$.

10 Solve the unforced equation $u'' + 4u = 0$ with initial conditions $u(0) = u'(0) = 1$ by finding the Laplace transform $U(s)$. The table shows how $u(0)$ and $u'(0)$ give the source terms that no longer come from the forcing term. Write $U(s)$ as $A/(s-2i) + B/(s+2i)$ and identify $u(t) = Ae^{2it} + Be^{-2it}$.

11 Continuing Problem 10, write $u(t)$ as a combination of $\cos 2t$ and $\sin 2t$. From the table, verify that its transform agrees with $U(s)$ in Problem 10.

12 The critically damped equation $u'' + 4u' + 4u = 0$ has double root $s = -2$. Find the combination $u(t)$ of e^{-2t} and te^{-2t} that satisfies the initial conditions $u(0) = 4$ and $u'(0) = 8$. Verify that the transform of this $u(t)$ from the table agrees with the transform $U(s)$ found directly from $u'' + 4u' + 4u = 0$.

Problems 13-15 ask for *RLC* impedances, transfer functions, and responses.

13 The single loop in Figure 2.20 with $L = 0$ (no inductor) leads to transfer functions as in equations (10) and (11):

$$\frac{I(s)}{V(s)} = \frac{1}{R + \frac{1}{Cs}} \quad \text{and} \quad \frac{V_C(s)}{V(s)} = \frac{1}{RCs + 1}.$$

What is the impedance Z in this loop? The *first-order* equation $Ru' + u/C = 0$ is satisfied by what exponential $u = e^{-at}$? Identify the decay rate $s = -a$ as the pole of the transfer function.

14 For positive values of R, L, and C find the poles of the transfer function $1/(LCs^2 + RCs + 1)$. What are the limit values of those poles as $L \to 0$?

15 An RLC loop (in *series*) has impedance $Z = Ls + R + (Cs)^{-1}$ and admittance $Y = 1/Z$. What are Y and Z if the three elements are connected in *parallel*? (You add admittances in parallel.)

16 A line of springs is now an *RLC line* or a *spring-mass-dashpot line*:

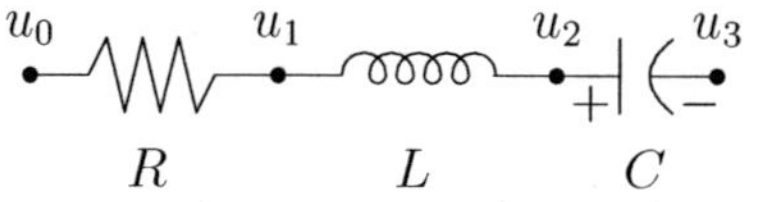

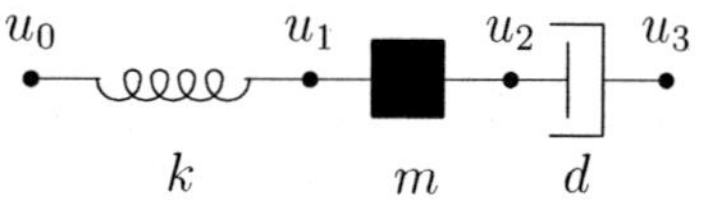

The first equations will be $e_1 = u_1 - u_0 = RI(t)$ from Ohm's Law and $e = w(t)/k$ from Hooke's Law. Find the differential equations for e_2 and e_3 in the RLC line. The current $I(t)$ is the same at each node (current balance).

17 Example 3.1 in Nise [118] gives the state space equations (time not frequency) for the current $I_R(t)$ in this network. Explain the three equations.

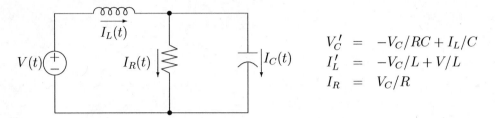

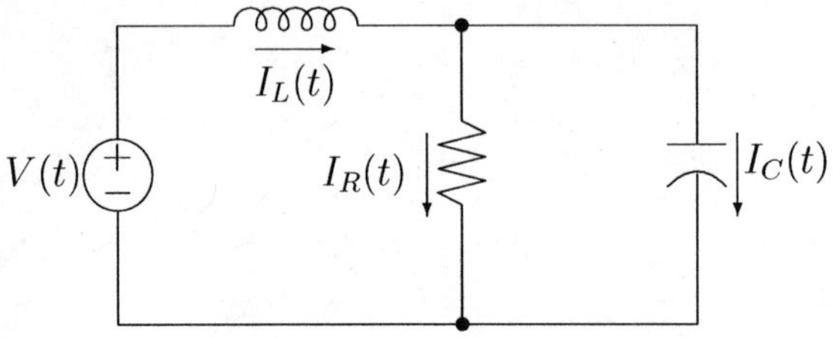

$$\begin{aligned} V_C' &= -V_C/RC + I_L/C \\ I_L' &= -V_C/L + V/L \\ I_R &= V_C/R \end{aligned}$$

18 (Recommended) Identify in Problem 17 the state variables x, the input u, the output y, and the matrices A, B, C, D in the **state equation** $x' = Ax + Bu$ and the **output equation** $y = Cx + Du$.

19 In mechanics, the position $u(t)$ and velocity $v(t)$ of the masses are natural state variables. Draw a line of dashpot d, mass m_1, spring k, mass m_2, force $f(t)$, with the left end fixed. Explain these state equations (Nise, page 143):

$$\begin{bmatrix} u_1' \\ v_1' \\ u_2' \\ v_2' \end{bmatrix} = \begin{bmatrix} 0 & 1 & 0 & 0 \\ -k/m_1 & -d/m_1 & k/m_1 & 0 \\ 0 & 0 & 0 & 1 \\ k/m_2 & 0 & -k/m_2 & 0 \end{bmatrix} \begin{bmatrix} u_1 \\ v_1 \\ u_2 \\ v_2 \end{bmatrix} + \begin{bmatrix} 0 \\ 0 \\ 0 \\ 1/m_2 \end{bmatrix} f(t).$$

20 (Highly recommended) With zero initial conditions and constant matrices A, B, C, D transform the state equation $x' = Ax + Bu$ and the output equation $y = Cx + Du$ to frequency domain equations for $X(s)$ and $Y(s)$. Solve first for $X(s)$ and substitute into $Y = CX + DU$ to find $Y(s) = \left[\textit{transfer matrix}\right] U(s)$. Your formula involves $(sI - A)^{-1}$, so the eigenvalues of A are the poles of the transfer function $T(s)$, which is *the determinant of the transfer matrix.*

21 Find $(sI - A)^{-1}$, the 1 by 1 transfer matrix, and its poles $-1, -2, -3$:

$$A = \begin{bmatrix} 0 & 1 & 0 \\ 0 & 0 & 1 \\ -6 & -11 & -6 \end{bmatrix} \quad B = \begin{bmatrix} 1 \\ 0 \\ 0 \end{bmatrix} \quad C = \begin{bmatrix} 1 & 0 & 0 \end{bmatrix} \quad D = \begin{bmatrix} 0 \end{bmatrix}.$$

22 Find the current around the basic RLC loop if $R = 3$, $\omega L = 5$, and $\omega C = 1$. Put the voltage and current on a (sinusoidal) graph. What is their difference in phase? With $R_1 = C = L = R_4 = 1$ in the circuit of Figure 2.20, at the start of this section, set up the equilibrium system (6) and eliminate W.

23 Suppose $Ax = b$ involves complex matrices and vectors: $A = A_1 + iA_2$ and $b = b_1 + ib_2$, with solution $x = x_1 + ix_2$. By taking the real and imaginary parts of $Ax = b$, find $2n$ real equations for the $2n$ real unknowns x_1 and x_2.

2.6 NONLINEAR PROBLEMS

The reader knows that nature is not linear. Our equations $Ku = f$ and $Mu''+Ku = 0$ are excellent approximations in many problems, but they are not the whole truth. Transistors in networks, large displacements in mechanics, the motions of fluids, the laws of biology—all those applications and many more require us to solve nonlinear equations. *Newton's method is the key* (with a whole range of variations).

May I start with the basic model of n equations in n unknowns:

Nonlinear system $\quad g(u) = 0 \quad g_1(u_1, \ldots, u_n) = 0 \ldots g_n(u_1, \ldots, u_n) = 0 \qquad (1)$

A linear system would have $g(u) = Ku - f$. The right side is included in $g(u)$.

We expect to solve $g(u) = 0$ by starting from an initial guess u^0. At each iteration we improve u^k to u^{k+1}. In a good case we can compute all the first derivatives:

Jacobian matrix J $\qquad J_{ij} = \dfrac{\partial g_i}{\partial u_j} = n$ by n matrix of derivatives $\qquad (2)$

This allows a linear approximation to $g(u)$ around the point $u^0 = (u_1^0, \ldots, u_n^0)$:

Linear approximation $\qquad g(u) \approx g_{\text{cutoff}} = g(u^0) + J(u^0)(u - u^0). \qquad (3)$

Newton's method chooses the vector $u = u^1$ that produces $g_{\text{cutoff}}(u^1) = 0$. This is a linear equation with that coefficient matrix $J(u^0)$. Each iteration uses the updated Jacobian matrix J of derivatives at u^k to find the next u^{k+1}:

Newton's Method $J\,\Delta u = -g$ $\qquad J(u^k)(u^{k+1} - u^k) = -g(u^k). \qquad (4)$

Here is an example of Newton's method for $g(u) = u^2 - 9$, with root $u^* = 3$ and Jacobian $J(u) = g' = 2u$. I will start at $u^0 = 10/3$ where the Jacobian is $20/3$.

Newton's method updates to $J^k = 2u^k$ at each step. The ***modified Newton method*** stays with the original derivative $J^0 = 2u^0 = 20/3$. The errors $|u^k - 3|$ show a very big difference between quadratic and linear convergence.

$$\mathbf{2u^k}(u^{k+1} - u^k) = 9 - (u^k)^2 \qquad\qquad \mathbf{2u^0}(u^{k+1} - u^k) = 9 - (u^k)^2$$

		Error $\lvert u^k - 3\rvert$
Newton	$k = 0$	.33333333333333
	$k = 1$	.01666666666667
	$k = 2$	.00004604051565
	$k = 3$	.00000000035328
	$k = 4$	.00000000000000

		Error $\lvert u^k - 3\rvert$
Modified	0	.33333333333333
	1	.01666666666667
	2	.00162500000000
	3	.00016210390625
	4	.00001620644897

Newton **squares the error** at every step, which doubles the number of correct digits:

Newton $\quad u^{k+1} - 3 \approx \dfrac{1}{6}(u^k - 3)^2 \qquad$ **Modified** $\quad u^{k+1} - 3 \approx \left(1 - \dfrac{3}{u^0}\right)(u^k - 3) \quad (5)$

Problem 2 shows that Newton's equation (4) averages u^k with $9/u^k$ to find the next u^{k+1}. The starting choice $u^0 = 0$ with $J = 0$ would be a disaster (flat tangent).

Modified Newton multiplies the error by a number $c \approx 1 - (3/u^0) = 1/10$. This c is close to zero when u^0 is close to $u^* = 3$ in Figure 2.25. But $u^0 = 1$ gives $c = -2$ and divergence (the error doubles at every step). The great advantage for complicated problems is to compute the Jacobian $J^0 = J(u^0)$ only once. Newton's method $\boldsymbol{J^k \, \Delta u^k = -g(u^k)}$ is terrific, but two major difficulties can arise:

1. It may be impractical to compute exactly each $J^k = J(u^k)$ and each Δu^k.

2. The full Newton step $\Delta u^k = u^{k+1} - u^k$ may be dangerously large.

Those produce changes in a pure Newton method that we describe in these pages. Often these changes lead to a "fixed-point iteration" $u^{k+1} = H(u^k)$. This gives linear convergence (no longer quadratic). Equation (7) will find the error reduction factor c.

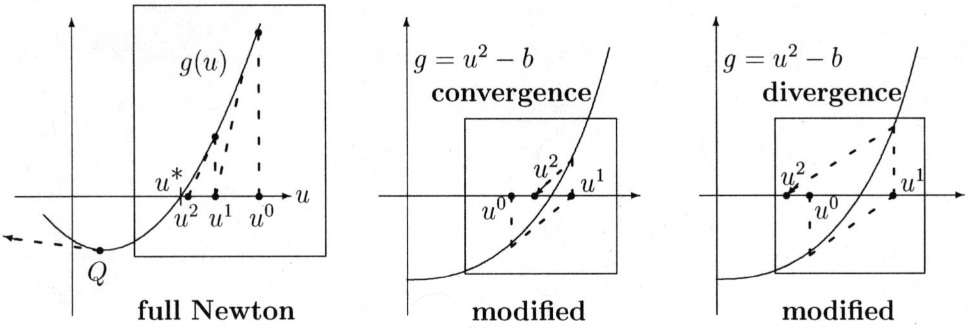

Figure 2.25: Newton follows tangents, modified Newton stays with the first slope.

Fixed Point Iterations

Newton's method computes $u^{k+1} = u^k - J(u^k)^{-1} g(u^k)$. Modified Newton changes $J(u^k)$ to the fixed matrix $J^0 = J(u^0)$. At every step we are substituting the current approximation u^k into a function $H(u)$ to find the next u^{k+1}. This is **iteration**:

Iteration for Modified Newton $\quad \boldsymbol{u^{k+1} = H(u^k)} \quad$ with $\quad H(u) = u - (J^0)^{-1} g(u) \qquad (6)$

When the u^k approach a limit u^*, we have a **fixed point** $u^* = H(u^*)$.

The equation $g(u) = 0$ is equivalent to $u = H(u)$. Modified Newton has been rewritten as a **fixed point iteration** $u^{k+1} = H(u^k)$. The new error multiplies the old error $e^k = u^* - u^k$ by a factor close to c:

Error reduction factor **$c = H'(u^*)$ = slope** $\quad u^* - u^{k+1} = H(u^*) - H(u^k) \approx \boldsymbol{H'(u^*)}(u^* - u^k). \qquad (7)$

This is the error equation $e^{k+1} \approx ce^k$ with $c = H'(u^*)$. It produces linear convergence unless $c = 0$ (the convergence is faster when c is smaller). Newton achieved $c = 0$ by his choice $H_{\text{Newton}} = u - J^{-1}(u)g(u)$. Then $e^{k+1} \approx C(e^k)^2$: quadratic convergence.

Example 1 $H = u-(J^0)^{-1}g(u)$ has the Jacobian $H'(u^*) = I-(J^0)^{-1}J(u^*)$. Modified Newton succeeds when J^0 is near $J(u^*)$. Then $c = H'(u^*)$ is small and the modification is almost exact. But $c = H' > 1$ will give failure, if J^0 has opposite sign to $J(u^*)$.

Example 2 Newton's method itself has $H_{\text{Newton}} = u - J^{-1}(u)g(u)$. At the point where $g(u^*) = 0$, its Jacobian is $H'_{\text{Newton}}(u^*) = I - J^{-1}J = 0$. That is the key idea of Newton's method, to adjust H so the linear term in the convergence rate is $c = 0$.

Many other iterations have been invented (bisection, secant method, chord method, Aitken, regular falsi, Dekker-Brent, and more). We could discount those as limited to scalar problems, while computational science works with long vectors. That argument is weak, because normally a search direction d^k is chosen at each step. The unknown in $g\,(u^k + \alpha d^k) = 0$ is only the number α. This is a "***line search.***"

Our escape from excessive detail here is the fact that most readers will look for a MATLAB command like fzero (or roots, when $g(u)$ is a polynomial). Those commands are not Newton-based and fzero is not robust even in solving $u^2 - 1 = 0$:

```
g = @(u)  u^2-1;
u = fzero (g, 10);          % output is u = 1 starting from u^0 = 10
u = fzero (g, 11);          % output is NaN: divergence from u^0 = 11
```

Notice the convenient $@(u)$ definition of $g(u)$. This notation seems to be replacing inline('u^2−1'). The roots command for a polynomial $g(u)$ constructs a "companion matrix" C whose eigenvalues satisfy $g(\lambda) = 0$. Then it computes eig(C).

Surprisingly, MATLAB's more flexible algorithm fsolve is currently restricted to the Optimization Toolbox. The options in fsolve(@g,u0, opts) are described online in **help desk**. Octave and netlib offer free Newton solvers.

We will create a simple Newton code, allowing n equations $g(u) = 0$. The scalar equation $\sin(u) = 0$ is a small but revealing test: very fast convergence.

```
g = @(u) sin(u); J = @(u) cos(u); u = 1;     % start at u^0 = 1
for i = 1 : 10                                % try 10 iterations
    u = u - J(u)\g(u); end                    % Newton's iteration
format long [u, g(u)];                        % squaring of errors
```

The code quickly finds $u^* = 0$ with tolerance $|\sin(u^*)| < 10^{-8}$. A better code would also include a convergence test on Δu. Experiments with different u^0 converge to other solutions of $\sin(u) = 0$, very irregularly:

$u^0 = 5$ leads to $u^* = 3\pi$ $\quad$ $u^0 = 6$ leads to $u^* = 2\pi$ $\quad$ $u^0 = 1.5$ leads to ____?

Variations on Newton's Method

If u^0 is close to u^*, and we know the derivatives in J, and we can accurately and quickly solve each $J(u^k)\Delta u^k = -g(u^k)$, then Newton's method is a success. But scientific computing must deal with the reality that those assumptions don't hold.

One idea is to update the derivatives in $J(u^k)$, but not at every step. I mention five other variations, to provide key words for your future reference.

We must decide the **size**, the **accuracy**, and the **direction** of each step.

1. **Damped Newton** reduces the step to $\alpha\,\Delta u^k$ when a full step is unsafe. We stay inside a "*trust region*" where the linear approximation to $g(u) = 0$ is reliable. As u^k approaches u^*, the damping factor α becomes safe to remove.

2. **Continuation methods** solve simpler problems $g^{(1)}(u) = 0$, $g^{(2)}(u) = 0$, ... by using the computed solution to each problem as starting vector in the next problem. Typically a large source term is introduced in small steps to avoid divergence. *Source-stepping* is well described on ocw.mit.edu (Course 6.336). Eventually the full source is included in the true problem $g(u) = g^{(N)}(u) = 0$. These "homotopy methods" are useful in many nonlinear problems.

3. **Inexact Newton** is fully acceptable when the linear system $J\Delta u = -g$ is large and expensive. The inner iteration for each Δu^k stops early. Frequently this iteration (for example by *conjugate gradients*) uses the Krylov subspaces of Chapter 7. This **Newton-Krylov** method works at each step with a sparse J.

4. **Nonlinear conjugate gradients** finds the new direction d^k by combining the locally steep direction $-g(u^k)$ and the previous d^{k-1}. The *stepsize* is separate:

Nonlinear conjugate gradients using α^k, β^k	Direction $d^k = -g(u^k) + \beta d^{k-1}$ Line search $u^{k+1} = u^k + \alpha d^k$	(8)

A favorite choice is $\beta = (g^k)^{\mathrm{T}}(g^k - g^{k-1})/(g^{k-1})^{\mathrm{T}}g^{k-1}$, because of its remarkable properties in the linear case $g = Au - b$. The code in Section 7.4 implements conjugate gradients for large sparse positive definite linear systems.

5. **Quasi-Newton** is an important possibility for large systems. Each step adjusts the approximation to J, but not by computing new derivatives of g. That is often too expensive, even once at the start or by finite differences around each u^k. A quasi-Newton "BFGS update" to J uses only information gained from evaluating $g(u^k)$. The low rank update is chosen to make the approximate J consistent with the true $J(u^k)$ in the most recent step direction $\Delta u = u^k - u^{k-1}$:

Quasi-Newton equation $\qquad (J^{k-1} + \textit{update})\,(\Delta u) = g(u^k) - g(u^{k-1}). \qquad (9)$

Minimizing $P(u)$

Many problems arrive at n equations by minimizing one function $P(u_1, \ldots, u_n)$. The equations are $g_i(u) = \partial P/\partial u_i = 0$. Now the first derivatives of the g's are the *second* derivatives of P. We have three generations of functions of $u_1, \ldots, u_n$:

One parent P to minimize	$P(u_1, \ldots, u_n)$
Gradient vector g of n children	$g_i(u) = \partial P/\partial u_i = 0$
Matrix J of n^2 grandchildren	$J_{ij}(u) = \dfrac{\partial g_i}{\partial u_j} = \dfrac{\partial^2 P}{\partial u_i \partial u_j}$

The n^3 great-grandchildren go into a tensor, but we stop at the Jacobian matrix J. The first derivatives of the g's give the **Hessian matrix** (second derivatives) for P. Its special new feature is **symmetry**: $J = J^{\mathrm{T}}$ because $\partial^2 P/\partial u_i\, \partial u_j = \partial^2 P \,/\, \partial u_j\, \partial u_i$. Every symmetric Jacobian comes from one parent P, as discussed in [76, p.186].

The Taylor series uses three generations P, g, J to approximate $P(u)$ near u^0:

$$P(u) \approx P_{\text{cutoff}}(u) = P(u^0) + (u - u^0)^{\mathrm{T}} g(u^0) + \frac{1}{2}(u - u_0)^{\mathrm{T}} J(u^0)(u - u^0). \qquad (10)$$

Minimizing that right side P_{cutoff} brings back Newton's method for the next $u = u^1$:

Derivative of $P_{\text{cutoff}}(u)$ $$g(u^0) + J(u^0)(u^1 - u^0) = 0. \qquad (11)$$

This equation was the last step in Section 1.6. Positive definiteness of J ensures that $g(u) = 0$ gives a minimum of P, not a maximum or saddle point. The all-important stopping test can now be based on the decrease in $P(u)$. Similarly P can decide each one-dimensional search along d^k. Then u^{k+1} minimizes $P\big(u^k + \alpha d^k\big)$.

Steepest Descent

At first, the gradient of P seems like the best direction to move to a minimum. $P(u)$ is falling most rapidly in the negative gradient direction $-g(u)$. This choice doesn't need the matrix J. But **steepest descent along $-g$ is not a success.**

The descent is like a skier who can't turn. The first step ends at u^1, the lowest contour in Figure 2.26. The gradient g^1 perpendicular to that contour $P =$ constant fixes the next step direction. But straight steps can't adjust to changes in g.

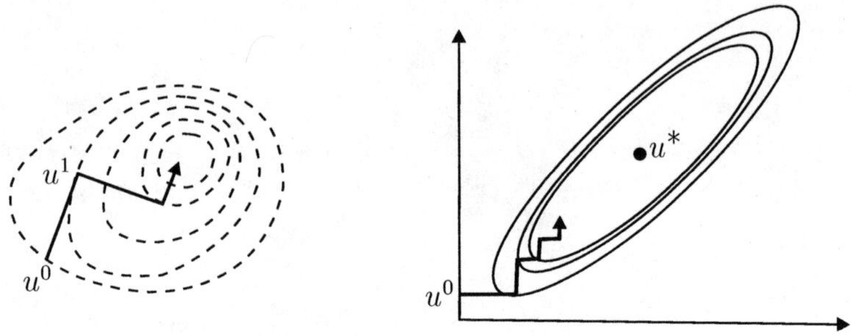

descending the contours of P entering a narrow valley

Figure 2.26: Steepest descent is narrow-minded. The gradient doesn't point to u^*.

When the graph of $P(u)$ is a narrow valley, the result is a lot of short steps across the valley. The goal is a long step in a better direction. Even in this simple example with minimum at $u^* = (0,1)$, the gradient search is too slow:

Example 3 Minimize $P(u_1, u_2) = 2u_1^2 - 2u_1u_2 + u_2^2 + 2u_1 - 2u_2$ by steepest descent. Starting at $u^0 = (0,0)$, the gradient is $g^0 = (\partial P/\partial u_1, \partial P/\partial u_2) = (2,-2)$. In the downhill direction (not the best), the minimum of P is at $u^1 = -g^0/5$. At that point the gradient is $g^1 = (-2,-2)/5$. The best second step reaches $u^2 = (0,4)/5$.

The original distance from (0,0) to $u^* = (0,1)$ was 1. The new distance is $1/5$. After two more steps it is $1/25$. The convergence rate is $1/\sqrt{5}$, very poor for two simple linear equations $g(u) = Au - b = 0$. Without using J, Newton's squaring is lost.

To repeat: The **conjugate gradient method** chooses a much better search direction. Then u^k converges to u^* while steepest descent is still crossing the valley.

Implicit Difference Equations

A key to success with Newton's method is a good initial guess u^0. A close start allows quadratic convergence to u^*. This goal is achieved for implicit difference equations, which solve a nonlinear system for the new U_{n+1} at each time step. *Reason*: U_n at the previous time $n\,\Delta t$ is already quite close. A simple predictor provides a u^0 that is even closer to $u^* = U_{n+1}$, and we expect very few iterations.

Writing finite difference codes for large nonlinear systems $u' = f(u,t)$ has become a job for professionals. You may become one; I never will. But we all have to choose a code, and it is fascinating to see how each one answers two fundamental questions:

1 What is the integrator? **2 What is the solver?**

The integrator gives the time step from U_n to U_{n+1}. The solver is inside that step. An implicit method needs a nonlinear solver to find U_{n+1}. A large Jacobian matrix also needs a linear solver, because $J\,\Delta u = -g$ can easily take most of the computing time. In a nutshell, those are the crucial decisions.

This section focuses on nonlinear solvers (Newton or fixed point iteration). Chapter 7 will be about linear solvers (direct or iterative). Section 6.2 describes families of integrators, starting with Euler and leapfrog and the trapezoidal rule. I am hoping you might be interested in very brief comments on a few codes:

1. General-purpose solvers like ode45 and ode15s for $u' = f(u,t)$.

2. Finite element codes like ABAQUS and ADINA.

3. Electronics codes like SPICE and PISCES and SUNDIALS for $F(u', u, t) = 0$.

A code like ode45 doesn't know what equation it will solve. The code must allow variable order and variable stepsize. It adapts to each new problem by estimating the accuracy (the local truncation error) at every time step. If the differential equation is **stiff**, with widely varying time scales, the difference method must be implicit. Otherwise a fast scale e^{-1000t} will force a small time step. The slower scale $u_2' = -3u_2$ will be agonizingly slow, even though e^{-3t} is far more important.

The letter s in the codename ode15s signals an implicit method for stiff equations. Each time step is a nonlinear equation involving $f_{n+1} = f(U_{n+1}, t_{n+1})$ for the components of U_{n+1}. The order of accuracy varies from 1 to 5.

The Reality of Computational Engineering

An everyday problem like a car crash is an enormous challenge to finite element simulation. For a frontal impact, here is typical data for today's best codes:

1/10 second crash time needs 10^5 explicit time steps

5 million variables need 30 hours on 8 CPU's

A key word was *explicit*. This is essential for fast dynamics. *Contact problems are truly difficult*—large deformations in the car body, rigid motion by the engine block, tires meeting the road with friction along an unknown surface. Those large deformations (plus the failure of spot welds) make the crash problem highly nonlinear.

An explicit integrator for $MU'' = F(U)$ centers the velocity $V = U'$:

Nonlinear $F(U)$ $$V_{n+\frac{1}{2}} - V_{n-\frac{1}{2}} = \frac{1}{2}(\Delta t_{n+1} + \Delta t_n) M^{-1} F(U_n) \qquad U_{n+1} - U_n = \Delta t_{n+1} V_{n+\frac{1}{2}} \qquad (12)$$

The hard work is to update the external and internal forces F during the crash. A diagonal M (lumped masses) avoids the full matrix M^{-1} that the finite element method will produce in Section 3.6.

A smaller but still important crash is a *dropped cell phone*. Impacts are so fast and nonlinear, and the phone is essentially elastic—it has to accept the shock and keep working. (A less sophisticated code for the car crash can dissipate energy. Dropped calls are EE problems.)

The next category of nonlinear equations is **quasi-static**. This is typical in assembling cars, not destroying them. The process is slow, acceleration is neglected, and the steps Δt are larger. Time becomes a parameter (*artificial time*) instead of an independent variable.

Slow dynamics have fully implicit difference methods. (Surprisingly, an earthquake can count as slow.) Steps of 1 second compare to 1 millisecond for quasi-static and 1 microsecond for fast dynamics. An offshore oil rig has inertia, and nonlinearity, and enormous Jacobian matrices in Newton's method.

The integrator needs enough numerical dissipation to maintain stability. Trapezoidal moves toward backward Euler to remove high-frequency ringing (often coming from a change in Δt). ABAQUS chooses the Hilber-Hughes-Tayler integrator [11] for slow dynamics. The energy dissipation in typical problems is below 1%.

We will analyze a newer split-step method below, because this is a textbook and suggestions are cheap—but I never forget the long experience and the engineering judgment that make a nonlinear code run reliably for 30 hours.

Trapezoidal, Backward Differences, and Split Steps

The earliest dynamics codes used a predictor without a corrector—nonlinear failure. Now the workhorse is the trapezoidal method with some variant of Newton as the nonlinear solver. **TR** is stable until you push it too far.

1. The trapezoidal growth factor in $U_{n+1} = GU_n$ has $|G| \leq 1$ whenever $u' = au$ has $|e^{-at}| \leq 1$. This ***A-stability*** means that Re $a \leq 0$ guarantees $|G| \leq 1$:

Trapezoidal A-stable
$$U_{n+1} - \frac{\Delta t}{2} f(U_{n+1}) = U_n + \frac{\Delta t}{2} f(U_n) \qquad G = \frac{1 + a\,\Delta t/2}{1 - a\,\Delta t/2} \tag{13}$$

An imaginary number $a = i\omega$, with oscillation $e^{i\omega t}$ in the true solution, gives $|G| = 1$ exactly. The method is simple and its A-stability looks secure, but in too many nonlinear problems that is simply false. $|G| = 1$ can be too dangerous for large ω.

2. For greater stability, each time step can reach back to the previous U_{n-1}:

Backward differences Second order BDF2
$$\frac{U_{n+1} - U_n}{\Delta t} + \frac{U_{n+1} - 2U_n + U_{n-1}}{2\,\Delta t} = f(U_{n+1}) \tag{14}$$

Now $|G| < 1$ for the equation $u' = i\omega u$. Solutions that should conserve energy ($|e^{i\omega t}| = 1$) will actually lose energy. But nonlinearity of those oscillations will not disrupt stability of the discrete problem. In applying finite elements to structures, second-order accuracy is often sufficient and higher-order can be uselessly expensive.

3. Split steps Every user is torn between TR and BDF2, dangerously trying to conserve energy or cautiously dissipating it. A split step offers a compromise: Compute $U_{n+\frac{1}{2}}$ from U_n by **TR**. Compute U_{n+1} from $U_{n+\frac{1}{2}}$ and U_n by **BDF2**.

The cse website shows success on a nonlinear pendulum and on convection-diffusion-reaction. (The reaction term multiplies $u_1 u_2$.) This split step idea also brings the possibility of *unequal steps*. The family of PISCES codes, for VLSI networks and device modeling, moved from $\frac{1}{2}\Delta t$ to $c\,\Delta t$ for the trapezoidal part:

TR + BDF2 $c\Delta t, (1-c)\Delta t$	$\dfrac{U_{n+c} - U_n}{c\,\Delta t} = \dfrac{f_{n+c} + f_n}{2}$	$AU_{n+1} - BU_{n+c} + CU_n = (1-c)\Delta t\, f_{n+1}$	(15)

Second order accuracy in the BDF part leads to $A = 2 - c$, $B = 1/c$, $C = (1-c)^2/c$.

The choice $c = 2 - \sqrt{2}$ happens to have special properties [9]. Computing the Jacobian matrix is normally the expensive part of Newton's method. Here the BDF Jacobian will be A times the TR Jacobian, provided A times $c\,\Delta t/2$ agrees with $(1-c)\Delta t$. This produces the magic choice $c = 2 - \sqrt{2}$, and the two Jacobians only differ by the factor $A = \sqrt{2}$. So the extra safety of BDF comes at a small extra price.

At least academically (in this textbook), $c = 2 - \sqrt{2}$ has three big advantages:

(1) The TR and BDF2 steps have effectively the same Jacobian matrix.

(2) Any other choice of $c\,\Delta t$ and $(1-c)\Delta t$ gives larger local error for $u' = au$.

(3) This choice yields the largest set of stable complex values $-a\,\Delta t$, with $|G| \le 1$.

Properties (1) and (2) are at the end of the Problem Set, based on algebra. Property (3) is clearest from a graph on the website, showing the points where $|G| \le 1$. That region grows as BDF2 is more heavily used and c decreases. But for small c, the backward difference sees U_{n+c} very close to U_n and stability begins to suffer. You are seeing a typical problem of code development in this basic example.

Nonlinear Circuit Simulation

Everyone who works with circuit simulation knows the SPICE code in some form. The original Berkeley SPICE provides free access to C code. The newer commercial versions have improved interfaces, and new solution methods. It is fascinating that the older IBM code ASTAP uses a block equation for voltages u and currents w, exactly as in our saddle-point matrix $S = [C^{-1}\ A;\ A^{\mathrm{T}}\ 0]$. SPICE eliminates w to work with the admittance matrix $A^{\mathrm{T}}CA$, now complex.

The problem is also nonlinear. Transistors will be present (by the thousands). Voltage drops $Ee^{i\omega t}$ are connected to currents $Ye^{i\omega t}$ by a nonlinear law $Y = C(E)$. The voltage drops come from potentials $Ve^{i\omega t}$ by an incidence matrix A in $E = AV$.

Circuit equations	$A^{\mathrm{T}}C(AV) = \text{sources}$	Jacobian matrix $J = A^{\mathrm{T}}C'A$

In mechanics, that Jacobian is the **tangent stiffness matrix**. It is the stiffness matrix K evaluated using the slope C' at a particular point on the stress-strain curve $w = C(e)$. This Jacobian matrix is what Newton's method needs at each iteration. In circuit simulation, the corresponding name for $J = A^{\mathrm{T}}C'A$ could be *tangent conductance matrix* or **tangent admittance matrix**.

Section 2.4 analyzed resistive circuits and DC currents. Time-dependent circuits with inductors and capacitors and AC currents came in 2.5. The codes for nonlinear devices are mostly protected, held secret from any author however innocent. Among the exceptions are SPICE at Berkeley and its high-performance descendant XYCE at Sandia. We can compare those two in a very quick and informal way:

Linear solvers SPICE models circuits of moderate size. XYCE now has KLU from Tim Davis, for optimizing its direct linear solver on large circuits. XYCE also includes Krylov iteration methods (Section 7.4) for very large sparse systems.

Integrators At the low end, SPICE has TR and similar options (not split steps). At the high end, XYCE solves differential-algebraic equations by calling SUNDIALS.

This is no criticism of Berkeley SPICE, which had the foresight to lead circuit simulation into a new era. Now the website www.llnl.gov/CASC/sundials shows how an ODE-DAE-sensitivity analysis software package can be well organized:

CVODE	Nonstiff ODE's by Adams methods 1 to 12	Stiff ODE's by BDF1 to 5
IDA	Differential-algebraic $F(u', u, t) = 0$ by variable-order variable-coefficient	
CVODES	Sensitivities $\partial u/\partial p$ for $u' = f(u, t, p)$	Adjoint methods for $\partial g(u)/\partial p$
KINSOL	Inexact Newton using CG/GMRES for large algebraic systems	

The sensitivity problem (dependence of u on parameters p) is the subject of Section 8.7. Conjugate gradients and GMRES are explained in 7.3. Here we introduce differential-algebraic equations, which need and deserve more space than we can give. You will see the main point about a singular Jacobian matrix $\partial F/\partial u'$.

Constraints and DAE's

If a ball is rolling inside a sphere, that is a constrained mechanical system. The equations of motion turn into a **differential-algebraic equation** for the position u_1, u_2, u_3. The constraint $g(u) = 0$ is built in by a Lagrange multiplier ℓ:

Differential equations $\quad mu_1'' = -2\ell u_1, \quad mu_2'' = -2\ell u_2, \quad mu_3'' = -2\ell u_3 - mg$

Algebraic equation $g(u) = 0$ $\quad u_1^2 + u_2^2 + u_3^2 = R^2$

The multiplier ℓ will be the force that keeps the ball on the sphere. Now we are seeing an algebraic constraint $g(u) = 0$ in dynamics. By introducing velocities as three more unknowns, we get six first-order ODE's within seven DAE's.

In that example, the two types of equations are well separated. Generally they are mixed together into $\boldsymbol{F(u', u, t) = 0}$. The partial derivatives of the n components of F with respect to the n components of u' form a Jacobian matrix J'. When this Jacobian is nonsingular, the equations $F(u', u, t) = 0$ can be solved to give the ODE's $u' = f(u, t)$. When J' is singular (its last row is zero from $\partial g(u)/\partial u'$), we are working with a DAE.

Petzold developed the DASSL package for DAE's, replacing u' by a backward difference of U. The integrator in SUNDIALS uses the BDF formulas of Section 6.2. This section concentrates on the nonlinear aspect of each implicit time step:

Modified Newton (out of date Jacobian) with direct solver for $J\Delta u = -g$

Inexact Newton (updating J by matrix-free products) with an iterative solver.

Large problems always bring that step from direct elimination to inexact iterations.

Heart Fibrillation: Alternating Between Twin Limits

Fixed-point iteration can have consequences for fibrillation of the heart. Our example is the iteration to solve $\boldsymbol{u = au - au^2}$. One solution is $u^* = 0$:

The equation is $(a-1)u = au^2$ and the second solution is $u^{**} = (a-1)/a$.

We want to find u^* or u^{**} by iteration, starting with $0 < u^0 < 1$:

Quadratic model $$u^{k+1} = H(u^k) = au^k - a(u^k)^2 \tag{16}$$

The convergence of u^k depends on a. For $a > 3$ we will fail to converge:

1 If $0 \le a \le 1$ the iterations converge to $u^* = 0$

2 If $1 \le a < 3$ the iterations converge to $u^{**} = (a-1)/a$

3 If $3 < a \le 4$ the iterations u^k don't converge *but they don't blow up*

Remember the convergence factor c in the error equation $e^{k+1} \approx c\,e^k$. That factor is the derivative $\boldsymbol{H'(u) = a - 2au}$, evaluated at the limit point u^* or u^{**}. We find $|c| < 1$ in cases **1** and **2**, which explains their convergence:

1 If $0 \le a \le 1$ then $c = H'(u^*) = \boldsymbol{a}$ at the limit $u^* = 0$

2 If $1 \le a \le 3$ then $c = H'(u^{**}) = \boldsymbol{2 - a}$ at the limit u^{**}

3 If $3 < a \le 4$ then both $c = a$ and $c = 2 - a$ have $\boldsymbol{|c| > 1}$

Example 4 Suppose $a = 2.5$. Then $u^{**} = \dfrac{1.5}{2.5} = \dfrac{3}{5}$ and $c = a - 2au^{**} = -\dfrac{1}{2}$.

Error $$\boldsymbol{e^{k+1}} = u - u^{k+1} = a(u - u^k) - a(u^2 - (u^k)^2) \approx c\,\boldsymbol{e^k}. \tag{17}$$

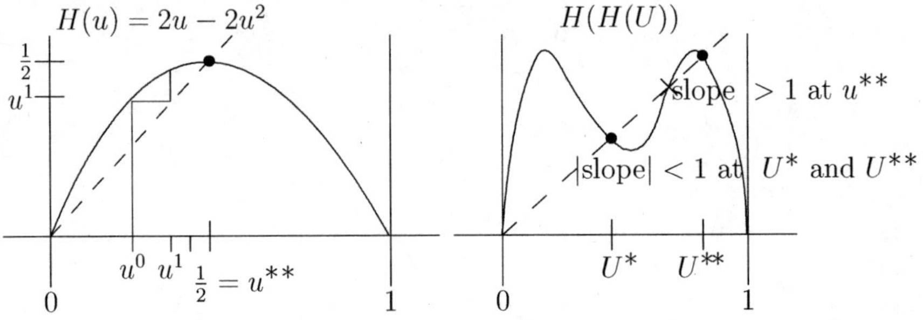

Figure 2.27: Convergence to u^{**} for $a = 2$. **Twin limits appear for $a = 3.4$.**

The interesting case is when $3 < a < 4$. Convergence is impossible because $H'(u^*) = a$ and $H'(u^{**}) = 2 - a$. Both have $|H'| > 1$. But a new convergence is possible, to **twin limits U^* and U^{**}**. Those numbers are not solutions to $u = H(u)$, they are solutions to $\boldsymbol{U = H\big(H(U)\big)}$. This is the equation with stable twin limits that connects to fibrillation of the heart. Let me explain.

If $U^* = H\big(H(U^*)\big)$, this means that two iterations will bring us from U^* back to U^*. The first iteration will produce $U^{**} = H(U^*)$. The next iteration returns to $U^* = H(U^{**}) = H\big(H(U^*)\big)$. A third iteration will go back to U^{**}.

This is what happens in the heart condition called "*alternans*." The timing of the heart's electrical activity goes wrong. If the crucial *AV* (atrioventricular) node receives the beating impulse too soon, it can't establish a steady heartbeat. The heart needs the right time delay to allow the ventricle to fill. Fibrillation will start, when the timing of the impulse alternates between too soon and too late.

Unfortunately this alternans mode can become stable. Then fibrillation continues too long, with not good results. Going through airports I see "Defibrillator" written on mysterious doors. Those machines give the heart a big shock to reset the timing. If you have one implanted in your chest, it monitors the heartbeat to detect alternans. The shock needs a big current, your heart is healthier if you can find another way.

Why is alternans stable? The twin limits solve $U^* = H\big(H(U^*)\big)$. So the derivative of $H\big(H(U)\big)$ is in control of stability. Use the chain rule:

Convergence factor C at U^*	$H\big(H(U)\big)$ has slope	$C = H'\big(H(U)\big)H'(U) = H'(U^{**})H'(U^*)$.	(18)

In our example, $U = H\big(H(U)\big)$ is fourth degree: $U = a(aU - aU^2) - a(aU - aU^2)^2$. The graph in Figure 2.27 shows how |slope| < 1 at the new solutions U^* and U^{**}. The iteration now produces an **alternating limit**. The numbers u^k approach $U^*, U^{**}, U^*, U^{**}, \ldots$ and the beat goes on, with bad and possibly fatal timing.

Christini and Collins proposed a control theory solution, not yet tested on humans. They delay or advance the heartbeat by a suitable time λ. **The system is directed to the unstable fixed point u^***, where the timing is good and the ventricle fills properly. Then a low-current device could stop the fibrillation.

Period Doubling and Chaos

As a increases beyond 3.45, the alternating limit also becomes unstable: $C > 1$. The next thing to appear is a *stable 4-cycle*, which solves $\boldsymbol{u} = H(H(H(H(\boldsymbol{u}))))$. Now $u^{k+1} = H(u^k)$ cycles between $\boldsymbol{u}$ and $H(\boldsymbol{u})$ and $H(H(\boldsymbol{u}))$ and $H(H(H(\boldsymbol{u})))$, and back to $\boldsymbol{u}$. But this also becomes unstable as a increases. In fact the stability intervals for a get shorter as the cycle period doubles from 2 to 4 to 8 and onward.

The ratio of interval lengths is **Feigenbaum's number** $\delta = 4.669\ldots$ that might appear in turbulence. The stability intervals for periods $2, 4, 8, \ldots$ end just before $a = 3.57$. What happens for $3.57 < a < 4$ is partly chaotic and partly stable. Long periods always appear in a special order. The cover of my earlier text [141] shows the limits as a increases toward 4. The possibilities are quite fantastic.

Chaos was seen in differential equations by the great meteorologist Ed Lorenz. Mandelbrot moved to the complex plane, to model the fractal boundaries of clouds and coastlines. *The Beauty of Fractals* is a book with amazing images, and the cse website provides a further guide. We hope the defibrillation succeeds.

Problem Set 2.6

1 The Newton code in this section solves $\sin u = 0$ by $u^{k+1} = u^k - \sin u^k / \cos u^k$. Which solutions $u^* = n\pi$ come from which intervals of starting points u^0? Start the iterations from N equally spaced points $u^0 = (1 : N)\,\pi/N$.

2 Show that Newton's method for $u^2 - a = 0$ finds u^{k+1} as the average of u^k and a/u^k. Connect the new error $u^{k+1} - \sqrt{a}$ to the square of the old error $u^k - \sqrt{a}$:

$$u^{k+1} - \sqrt{a} = \frac{1}{2}\left(u^k + \frac{a}{u^k}\right) - \sqrt{a} = \left(u^k - \sqrt{a}\right)^2 / 2u^k.$$

3 Test fzero and roots and our Newton method on a high-degree polynomial $g(u) = (u-1)\cdots(u-N)$ with roots $u^* = 1, \ldots, N$. For what N do the answers from roots become complex numbers (totally wrong)?

4 The simplest *fixed point iteration* for $g(u) = 0$ is $u^{k+1} = H(u^k) = u^k - g(u^k)$:

If $g(u) = au - b$, start from $u^0 = 1$ to find u^1, u^2, and every u^k.
For which values of a does u^k converge to the correct solution $u^* = b/a$?

5 With $g(u) = Au - b$ in the vector case, show that Newton's method converges in *one step*: $u^1 = A^{-1}b$. The fixed point iteration $u^{k+1} = H(u^k) = u^k - (Au^k - b)$ has $H' = I - A$. Its convergence factor c is the maximum eigenvalue $|1 - \lambda(A)|$.

Why is $c > 1$ for $A = K = (-1,\ 2,\ -1$ matrix) but $c < 1$ for $A = K/2$?

6 Plot the graph of $g(u) = ue^{-u}$. Draw two steps of Newton's method, following the tangent line at u^0 (and then u^1) to the points u^1 (and then u^2) where the line crosses the axis. Start from $u^0 = \frac{1}{2}$ and also from $u^0 = 1$.

7 Write a 2 by 2 Newton code for $g_1 = u_1^3 - u_2 = 0$ and $g_2 = u_2^3 - u_1 = 0$. Those two equations have three real solutions $(1, 1)$, $(0, 0)$, $(-1, -1)$.

Can you draw the (*fractal*) basins of attraction in color? Those are the four regions of starting points (u_1^0, u_2^0) that lead to the three solutions and to infinity.

8 $P_N(z) = 1 + z + \cdots + z^N/N!$ comes from truncating the series for e^z. Solve $P_N(z) = 0$ for $N = 20, 40, \cdots$ using roots and plot the solutions $z = u + iv$. Try Newton's method on the two real equations $\operatorname{Re} P_N(u, v) = \operatorname{Im} P_N(u, v) = 0$.

9 Find the Jacobian $\partial g_i / \partial u_j$ for $g_1 = u_1 + \sin u_2 = 0$, $g_2 = u_1 \cos u_2 + u_2 = 0$. If J is symmetric, find a function $P(u)$ that has gradient $g(u)$.

10 In steepest descent, u^{k+1} minimizes $P(u^k - \alpha\, g(u^k))$. Apply to $P(u)$ in Problem 9 with $u^0 = (2, 1)$. What is the convergence rate, based on $\lambda_{\text{max}}(J)$ at (u_1^*, u_2^*)?

Problems 11-13 lead to fractals and the Mandelbrot set and chaos.

11 What are the solutions to $u = 2u - 2u^2 = H(u)$? Starting the fixed-point iteration $u^{k+1} = H(u^k)$ from $u^0 = 1/4$, what is the limit u^* and what is the convergence rate $c = H'(u^*)$?

12 For $H(u) = au - au^2$ test the behavior of $u^{k+1} = H(u^k)$ when $a > 3$:

For $a = 3.2$ the even u^{2k} and odd u^{2k+1} have different limits (**period 2**)

For $a = 3.46$ there are four limits coming from u^{4k}, u^{4k+1}, u^{4k+2}, u^{4k+3}

For $a =$? there are eight different limits

For $a =$?? < 4 the u^k become *chaotic*.

13 The **Mandelbrot set** M contains all complex numbers c for which the fixed-point iterations $u^{k+1} = (u^k)^2 + c$ stay bounded (from $u_0 = 0$). The fractal boundary of M is beautiful. Plot 100 c's inside M near that boundary.

14 If $f' = \partial f / \partial u$, the Jacobians in the split steps (15) are

$$J_{\mathbf{TR}} = I - c\Delta t f'/2 \qquad J_{\mathbf{BDF}} = I - (1-c)\Delta t f'/A$$

Show that $J_{\mathbf{TR}} = J_{\mathbf{BDF}}$ when $c = 2 - \sqrt{2}$ (the optimal c).

15 For $u' = au$ find U_{n+c} and then U_{n+1} in the split-step method (15) with $a\,\Delta t = z$. The growth factor in $U_{n+1} = GU_n$ is (linear in z)/(quadratic in z). *Challenge*: What is the coefficient of z^3 in the local error $e^z - G(z)$? Can you show that $c = 2 - \sqrt{2}$ minimizes this coefficient?

2.7 STRUCTURES IN EQUILIBRIUM

I hope this section is enjoyable. Trusses are new examples of the $A^{\mathrm{T}}CA$ framework, when the line of springs becomes two-dimensional. One new feature is that A can have a larger nullspace than $(c, c, \ldots, c)$. If other vectors solve $Au = 0$, they are "**collapse mechanisms**" and the structure is unstable (the matrix $A^{\mathrm{T}}CA$ is singular). The neat part of the section is to find these mechanisms in specific examples.

A three-dimensional "space truss" is like a jungle gym that children climb on. That would have $3N$ forces and displacements (three at each node). For simplicity we stay in a plane with flat children. This section is still fun.

A truss is built from elastic bars (Figure 2.28). The connections are pin joints, where the bars can turn freely. The internal forces $w_1, \ldots, w_m$ are only *along* the bars. Unlike beams, the bars do not bend; unlike plates, they are one-dimensional; unlike shells, they are simple and straight. In this section the bars lie in a plane.

Suppose the truss has m bars and N nodes. **There are two displacements** u^{H} **and** u^{V} (horizontal and vertical) **at each free node**. The fixed nodes have a total of r known displacements. The vector u has $n = 2N - r$ unknown displacements.

In the same way there are **two forces** f^{H} and f^{V} at each free node. The vector f of known applied forces has $n = 2N - r$ components. The remaining r forces (reactions at the supports) maintain the r fixed displacements. The plane trusses in Figure 2.28 have $n = 4$ unknown displacements and known forces, at the two upper nodes. They have $r = 4$ zero displacements and unknown reactions at the supports.

Known	$\boldsymbol{f_j^{\mathrm{H}}}$ **and** $\boldsymbol{f_j^{\mathrm{V}}}$	=	*horizontal and vertical forces* applied at node j
Unknown	$\boldsymbol{u_j^{\mathrm{H}}}$ **and** $\boldsymbol{u_j^{\mathrm{V}}}$	=	*horizontal and vertical displacements* at node j.

The m by n matrix A has a row for each bar and *two* columns for each of those nodes.

The number of bars in Figure 2.28 goes from $m = 5$ to 4 to 3, and the trusses behave very differently. For graphs and networks m was never below n. Now the shape of A is not so certain. We start with small trusses and build up.

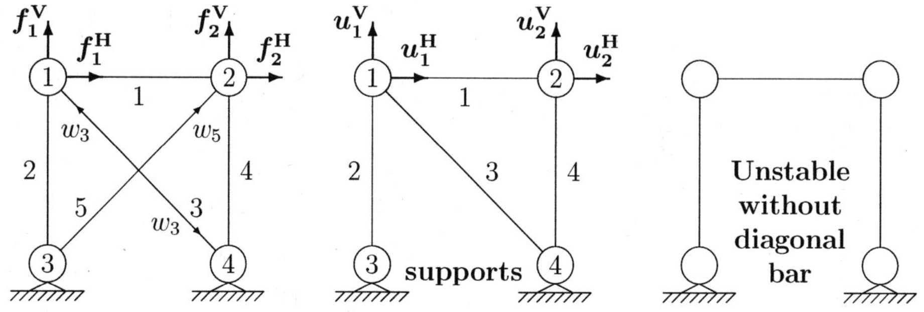

Figure 2.28: Trusses with $m = 5, 4, 3$ bars and $n = 4$ displacements $u_1^{\mathrm{H}}, u_1^{\mathrm{V}}, u_2^{\mathrm{H}}, u_2^{\mathrm{V}}$.

Stable and Unstable Trusses

Stable trusses can withstand all forces f, they will not collapse. The matrix A has full column rank n. For an unstable truss, $\text{rank}(A) < n$ and $A^{\mathrm{T}}CA$ is singular. We will describe stability and instability even before we construct the matrix A!

Stable truss The n columns of A are **independent**

1. The only solution to $Au=0$ is $u=0$ (**any displacement produces stretching**)

2. The force balance equation $A^{\mathrm{T}}w = f$ can be solved for every f

Example 1 The second truss has $m = n = 4$. A and A^{T} are square matrices. This does not make them automatically invertible (Example $3'$ will be unstable even with $m > n$). We have to test either A or A^{T}, by constructing the matrix or by studying the truss:

> Bar 4 can balance any f_2^{V}. The force in bar 1 is $f_2^{\mathrm{H}} - f_1^{\mathrm{H}}$. The force in bar 3 comes from horizontal balance at node 1. Then bar 2 gives vertical balance.

We could also check that $Au = 0$ (no stretch) only happens if $u = 0$ (no displacement). You will be surprised how much can be learned without constructing A.

The first truss (5 bars) is also stable. The third truss is unstable (large displacements from small forces). This is a bad thing in a bridge, but maybe not in a car. Linear algebra describes instability two ways, when $Au = 0$ and $A^{\mathrm{T}}w = f$ go wrong:

Unstable truss The n columns of A are **dependent**

1. $e = Au = 0$ has a nonzero solution: displacements with no stretching

2. $A^{\mathrm{T}}w = f$ is not solvable for every f: some forces can't be balanced

Example 2 Take away the supports, so A is 4 by 8. Suddenly the trusses can move. We have $n = 8$ displacements (H and V at 4 nodes x_i, y_i) and three ***rigid motions***:

> Horizontal translation: move right by $u = (1,0,1,0,1,0,1,0)$
>
> Vertical translation: move up by $u = (0,1,0,1,0,1,0,1)$
>
> Rotation around node 3: $u = (1,0,1,-1,0,0,0,-1) = (y_1, -x_1, y_2, -x_2, \ldots)$

By my count $n - m = 8 - 4 = 4$. There must be a fourth motion (a mechanism).

If we put back the supports at node 3, that stops the two translations. Rigid rotation around node 3 would still be allowed. Notice that $u_3^{\mathrm{H}} = u_3^{\mathrm{V}} = 0$ in the rotation above.

Two types of unstable trusses

Rigid motion	The truss translates and/or rotates as a whole
Mechanism	The truss deforms—change of shape without any stretching

Example 3 The third truss in Figure 2.28 has $m = 3$ bars. Rigid motion is not possible, because of the supports, but there must be a mechanism: Three equations $Au = 0$ must have a nonzero solution, because $n = 4$. The truss can deform without any stretching, and in this example it can lean to the right or left:

Mechanism $e = Au = 0$ **Unstable** $\quad u = \begin{bmatrix} 1 \\ 0 \\ 1 \\ 0 \end{bmatrix}$

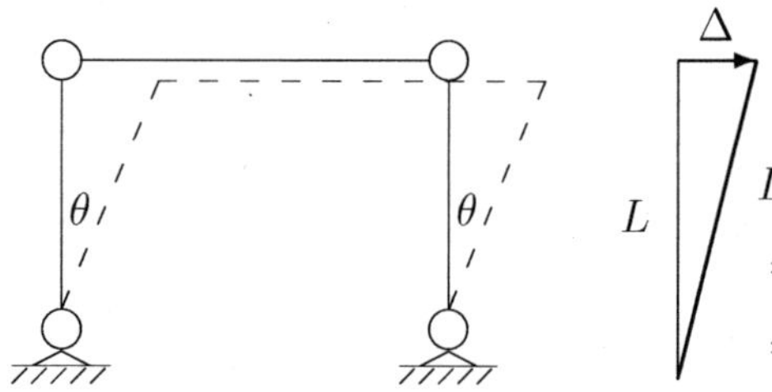

$$L_{\text{new}} = \sqrt{L^2 + \Delta^2} = L + \frac{\Delta^2}{2L} + \cdots = L \text{ to first order}$$

Three bar forces (w_1, w_2, w_3) cannot balance all four applied forces f_1^{H}, f_1^{V}, f_2^{H}, f_2^{V}. In fact w_1 can balance f_1^{V} and w_3 can balance f_2^{V}. But if $f_1^{\mathrm{H}} + f_2^{\mathrm{H}} > 0$, those forces will push the truss over. Bar 2 can only give horizontal balance when $f_1^{\mathrm{H}} + f_2^{\mathrm{H}} = 0$.

Notice that the acceptable force vector $f = (f_1^{\mathrm{H}}, 0, -f_1^{\mathrm{H}}, 0)$ is perpendicular to the mechanism vector $u = (1, 0, 1, 0)$. The force is not activating the mechanism. So for this special pair of forces $f_2^{\mathrm{H}} = -f_1^{\mathrm{H}}$, the unstable truss doesn't collapse.

Important comment If you look at the drawing of the mechanism, you will say that there are small vertical displacements u_1^{V} and u_2^{V}. I will say no, those displacements are zero. This is because I am thinking linearly, and those vertical displacements are *second-order*. Suppose the angle is θ, and the bar length is 1. The new position of node 1 is $(\sin\theta, \cos\theta)$. The displacement from the starting position $(0, 1)$ is u:

Exact displacement $\qquad u_1^{\mathrm{H}} = \sin\theta$ and $u_1^{\mathrm{V}} = \cos\theta - 1$

To first order $u = (\theta, 0)$ $\qquad \sin\theta \approx \theta$ and $\cos\theta - 1 \approx -\frac{1}{2}\theta^2 = \textbf{zero}$. $\qquad (1)$

Ours is a theory of *small displacements*. It was misleading to write $u = (1, 0, 1, 0)$ for the mechanism. The movement is only $u = (\theta, 0, \theta, 0)$ to first order, neglecting θ^2.

The linear equation $Au = 0$ will be solved even by $u = (1000, 0, 1000, 0)$. But the physical interpretation should stay with small f and small u. This justifies linear equations $e = Au$ and $A^{\mathrm{T}}w = f$, for the stretching and the force balance. In constructing A, you will see how all geometric nonlinearity is ignored.

Example 3′ We could add a truss with many bars on top of this third example. It would be no trouble to reach $m > n$ for the combined truss. But that truss would have the same collapse mechanism—all free nodes moving to the right. So $m > n$ does *not* guarantee n independent columns of A, and stability.

The Construction of A

We expect to see A and A^{T} in our framework, with Hooke's Law in between.

$$\boxed{\text{movements } u} \xrightarrow{A} \boxed{\text{elongations } e} \xrightarrow{C} \boxed{\text{bar forces } w} \xrightarrow{A^{\mathrm{T}}} \boxed{\text{force balance } A^{\mathrm{T}}w = f}$$

Each row of A comes from the stretching of a bar ($e = Au$ is the change of length). The n columns of A come from force balance at the nodes (two columns per node, from H and V forces). We will find the matrix A both ways.

Instead of two nonzero entries in each row, $+1$ and -1, we now expect four. They will be $\pm\cos\theta$ and $\pm\sin\theta$, where θ is the slope angle of the bar. (The row still adds to zero.) For a horizontal or vertical bar we are back to ± 1, since $\sin\theta$ or $\cos\theta$ is zero. If an end is fixed, that row of A only has two nonzeros from the free end.

Suppose the ends of a bar are moved: ***How much does the bar stretch***? If its original length is L and its angle is θ, then before stretching it extends $L\cos\theta$ horizontally and $L\sin\theta$ vertically. When its ends are moved, the new length is $L+e$ with **stretching** e. Add (horizontal)^2+ (vertical)^2, then take the square root:

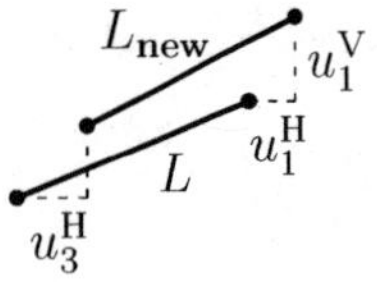

$$\begin{aligned} L_{\mathbf{new}}^2 &= (L\cos\theta + u_1^{\mathrm{H}} - u_3^{\mathrm{H}})^2 + (L\sin\theta + u_1^{\mathrm{V}} - u_3^{\mathrm{V}})^2 \\ &= L^2 + 2L(u_1^{\mathrm{H}}\cos\theta + u_1^{\mathrm{V}}\sin\theta - u_3^{\mathrm{H}}\cos\theta - u_3^{\mathrm{V}}\sin\theta) + \cdots \\ L_{\mathbf{new}} &\approx L + (\boldsymbol{u_1^{\mathrm{H}}\cos\theta + u_1^{\mathrm{V}}\sin\theta - u_3^{\mathrm{H}}\cos\theta - u_3^{\mathrm{V}}\sin\theta}) \\ &= L + \boldsymbol{e} \end{aligned}$$

$$\textbf{Row of } \boldsymbol{A} \;=\; \begin{bmatrix} \cos\theta & \sin\theta & 0 & 0 & -\cos\theta & -\sin\theta & 0 & \ldots & 0 \end{bmatrix}$$
$$\qquad\qquad\quad \boldsymbol{u_1^{\mathrm{H}}} \quad \boldsymbol{u_1^{\mathrm{V}}} \quad u_2^{\mathrm{H}} \quad u_2^{\mathrm{V}} \quad \boldsymbol{u_3^{\mathrm{H}}} \quad \boldsymbol{u_3^{\mathrm{V}}} \quad u_4^{\mathrm{H}} \quad \ldots \quad u_N^{\mathrm{V}}$$

A horizontal motion will not stretch the bar: $[\text{ Row }][\, u_{\text{rigid}}^{\mathrm{H}} \,] = \cos\theta - \cos\theta = 0$. Similarly a vertical motion has $[\text{ Row }][\, u_{\text{rigid}}^{\mathrm{V}} \,] = \sin\theta - \sin\theta = 0$ in the even-numbered columns. Also a rotation produces no stretching. The nodes will move in a direction perpendicular to $(\cos\theta, \sin\theta)$. Then $[\text{ Row }][\, u_{\text{rigid}}^{\text{turn}} \,] = 0$.

A pure stretching is produced by $u_1^{\mathrm{H}} = \cos\theta$, $u_1^{\mathrm{V}} = \sin\theta$, $u_3^{\mathrm{H}} = u_3^{\mathrm{V}} = 0$. This is a unit elongation $[\text{ Row }][\, u_{\text{stretch}} \,] = \cos^2\theta + \sin^2\theta = 1$. So the four nonzero entries in the row come correctly from testing three rigid motions and u_{stretch}.

Small deformations (much smaller than in the Figure!) can ignore the u^2/L corrections. The nonzero entries in this row are $\pm\cos\theta, \pm\sin\theta$. In 3D the six entries will be $\pm\cos\theta_1, \pm\cos\theta_2, \pm\cos\theta_3$—the cosines that give the direction of the bar.

The Construction of A^{T}

The relation $e = Au$ between bar elongations and node displacements is the ***compatibility equation***. The transpose of A must appear in the ***equilibrium equation***. That is the balance $A^{\mathrm{T}}w = f$ between internal forces w in the bars and applied forces f at the nodes. Since each node is in equilibrium, the net force on it—both horizontal and vertical—must be zero. The balance of horizontal forces gives

Row of $A^{\mathrm{T}}w = f$ $$-w_1 \cos\theta_1 - w_2 \cos\theta_2 - w_3 \cos\theta_3 = f^{\mathrm{H}}. \quad (2)$$

There will be another force balance for the vertical components, with a row of sines in A^{T}. Some find A^{T} from this force balance, others find A from displacements.

Plus and minus signs Everybody asks for a simple rule. Note that $a_{ij} > 0$ when a positive displacement u_j *stretches* bar i. For the signs in A, I imagine the movement u^{H} or u^{V} and ask if the bar is stretched or compressed.

We check the signs in (2). A positive w_1 means that bar 1 is in tension; it is pulling on the joint. The slope angle of bar 1 is $\theta = \theta_1 - \pi$, so the term $-w_1 \cos\theta$ is $w_1 \cos\theta_1$. It comes from the same matrix entry $+\cos\theta_1$ as the term in $e = Au$.

For $e = Au$ we look at each bar. For A^{T} we look at each node.

Finally there is $w = Ce$, the constitutive law. This connects the force w_i in each bar with its elongation e_i. C is a diagonal matrix, m by m, with the elastic constants c_i of the bars on its diagonal. This is the "material matrix," and Hooke's law $w = Ce$ completes the path from the displacements u to the applied forces f:

Stiffness matrix $$f = A^{\mathrm{T}}w = A^{\mathrm{T}}Ce = A^{\mathrm{T}}CAu \quad \text{or} \quad \boldsymbol{f} = \boldsymbol{Ku}. \quad (3)$$

Note Equilibrium also holds at the supports! It has the same form as $A^{\mathrm{T}}w = f$, except that it comes from the r columns of the original A_0 that were dropped to produce A. *After we know* w, the r extra equations in $A_0^{\mathrm{T}}w = f$ give the r reaction forces supplied by the supports (in order to fix the r displacements).

Examples of A and A^{T} and $K = A^{\mathrm{T}}CA$

In creating A for the next trusses in Figure 2.29, I want to make an important point about $K = A^{\mathrm{T}}CA$. Matrix multiplication can be done in two ways:

Row times column This gives each entry $K_{ij} =$ (row i of A^{T})(column j of CA)

Column times row This gives a matrix k_i for each bar. Then $K = k_1 + \cdots + k_m$.

Stiffness matrix for bar i $$k_i = (\text{column } i \text{ of } A^{\mathrm{T}})\, c_i\, (\text{row } i \text{ of } A)$$

K is actually assembled as the sum of the k_i, one bar at a time. The k_i are ***element stiffness matrices***. Since the rows of A (and columns of A^{T}) have at most four nonzeros, $\pm\cos\theta$ and $\pm\sin\theta$, each k_i has at most 16 nonzeros:

$$\begin{bmatrix} \cos\theta \\ \sin\theta \\ -\cos\theta \\ -\sin\theta \end{bmatrix} \begin{bmatrix} c_1 \end{bmatrix} \begin{bmatrix} \cos\theta & \sin\theta & -\cos\theta & -\sin\theta \end{bmatrix} = \begin{array}{l}\textbf{element matrix } \boldsymbol{k_1} \\ \textbf{nonzero entries only}\end{array}$$

In large problems we may not even compute k_i until the elimination process needs one of its nonzeros. This is ***frontal elimination***, where a front of active elements leaves behind the fully eliminated elements and moves toward the untouched elements. In each example, I will write K as $A^{\mathrm{T}}CA$ and also as $k_1 + \cdots + k_m$.

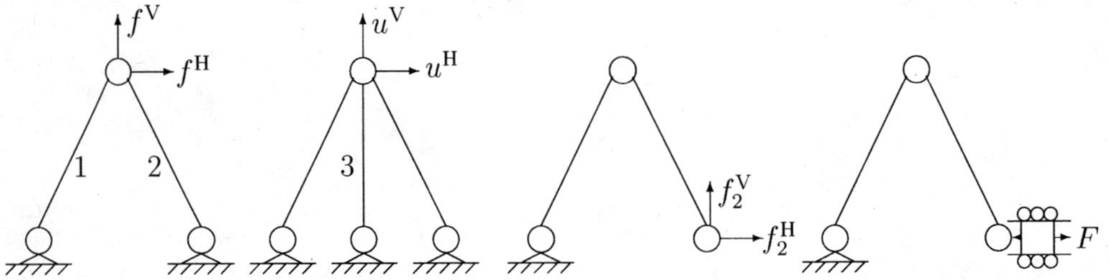

Figure 2.29: Stable: Determinate and indeterminate. Unstable: Rigid and mechanism.

Example 4 The first truss in Figure 2.29 has $m = 2$ bars and $n = 2$ unknown displacements. If the angles θ are $\pm 45°$ then $\cos\theta$ and $\sin\theta$ are $\pm 1/\sqrt{2}$. Force balance $A^{\mathrm{T}}w = f$ tells us those signs (the matrix is 2 by 2 because of the supports):

$$\boldsymbol{A^{\mathrm{T}}w = f} \quad \frac{w_1}{\sqrt{2}} - \frac{w_2}{\sqrt{2}} = f^{\mathrm{H}} \quad \text{and} \quad \frac{w_1}{\sqrt{2}} + \frac{w_2}{\sqrt{2}} = f^{\mathrm{V}} \quad \boldsymbol{A^{\mathrm{T}}} = \frac{\mathbf{1}}{\sqrt{\mathbf{2}}} \begin{bmatrix} \mathbf{1} & \mathbf{-1} \\ \mathbf{1} & \mathbf{1} \end{bmatrix}$$

The stretching equation $e = Au$ will move that minus sign to A_{21}:

$$\boldsymbol{e = Au} \quad e_1 = \frac{u^{\mathrm{H}}}{\sqrt{2}} + \frac{u^{\mathrm{V}}}{\sqrt{2}} \quad \text{and} \quad e_2 = -\frac{u^{\mathrm{H}}}{\sqrt{2}} + \frac{u^{\mathrm{V}}}{\sqrt{2}} \quad \boldsymbol{A} = \frac{\mathbf{1}}{\sqrt{\mathbf{2}}} \begin{bmatrix} \mathbf{1} & \mathbf{1} \\ \mathbf{-1} & \mathbf{1} \end{bmatrix}$$

A is square and invertible, so $A^{\mathrm{T}}w = f$ determines w. Then Hooke's Law gives $e = C^{-1}w$. Then $Au = e$ determines u, without forming $A^{\mathrm{T}}CA$ at all.

In this *determinate case* (square matrices), u is $(A^{-1})(C^{-1})(A^{\mathrm{T}})^{-1}f$ and those separate inverses exist. Here is $A^{\mathrm{T}}CA$, multiplied **row-column** and **column-row**:

$$K = \begin{bmatrix} 1/\sqrt{2} & -1/\sqrt{2} \\ 1/\sqrt{2} & 1/\sqrt{2} \end{bmatrix} \begin{bmatrix} c_1 & 0 \\ 0 & c_2 \end{bmatrix} \begin{bmatrix} 1/\sqrt{2} & 1/\sqrt{2} \\ -1/\sqrt{2} & 1/\sqrt{2} \end{bmatrix} = \frac{1}{2} \begin{bmatrix} c_1 + c_2 & c_1 - c_2 \\ c_1 - c_2 & c_1 + c_2 \end{bmatrix}$$

Matrices for bars 1 and 2
Each *k* is (column) (*c*) (row)

$$K = k_1 + k_2 = \frac{c_1}{2} \begin{bmatrix} 1 & 1 \\ 1 & 1 \end{bmatrix} + \frac{c_2}{2} \begin{bmatrix} 1 & -1 \\ -1 & 1 \end{bmatrix} \tag{4}$$

Example 5 The third bar in Figure 2.29 makes A rectangular (3 by 2). The vertical force balance includes w_3 from that middle bar. Now two balance equations cannot determine three bar forces (Indeterminate). But combined with the three equations $e = Au$ we can determine three w's and two u's. The matrix $K = A^{\mathrm{T}}CA$ gives everything at once:

$$\begin{bmatrix} 1/\sqrt{2} & -1/\sqrt{2} & 0 \\ 1/\sqrt{2} & 1/\sqrt{2} & 1 \end{bmatrix} \begin{bmatrix} c_1 & & \\ & c_2 & \\ & & c_3 \end{bmatrix} \begin{bmatrix} 1/\sqrt{2} & 1/\sqrt{2} \\ -1/\sqrt{2} & 1/\sqrt{2} \\ 0 & 1 \end{bmatrix} = \begin{bmatrix} \frac{c_1+c_2}{2} & \frac{c_1-c_2}{2} \\ \frac{c_1-c_2}{2} & \frac{c_1+c_2}{2} + c_3 \end{bmatrix}$$

$$\textbf{Columns times rows} \quad k_1 + k_2 + k_3 = \frac{c_1}{2}\begin{bmatrix} 1 & 1 \\ 1 & 1 \end{bmatrix} + \frac{c_2}{2}\begin{bmatrix} 1 & -1 \\ -1 & 1 \end{bmatrix} + c_3\begin{bmatrix} 0 & 0 \\ 0 & 1 \end{bmatrix} \qquad (5)$$

Those bar matrices (element matrices) only have rank 1 because a column multiplies a row. For large n, the nonzeros will be surrounded by many zeros. We only compute the nonzeros, and a list of **local-to-global indices** tells us where to put them in the big matrix K. *The stiffness matrix is "assembled" from* $k_1 + \cdots + k_m$.

Example 6 The new unsupported node in Figure 2.29(c) makes $n = 4$. But the 2 by 4 matrix A can only have rank 2. The four columns of A are dependent and there must be nonzero solutions to $Au = 0$. *Actually there are* $4 - 2$ *solutions*:

One is a rigid motion: The whole truss rotates around the fixed node.

Another solution is a mechanism: Bar 2 swings around the top node.

Bar 1 has a fixed end, so k_1 has extra zeros. All sines and cosines are $\pm 1/\sqrt{2}$:

$$K = k_1 + k_2 = \frac{c_1}{2}\begin{bmatrix} 1 & 1 & 0 & 0 \\ 1 & 1 & 0 & 0 \\ 0 & 0 & 0 & 0 \\ 0 & 0 & 0 & 0 \end{bmatrix} + \frac{c_2}{2}\begin{bmatrix} 1 & -1 & -1 & 1 \\ -1 & 1 & 1 & -1 \\ -1 & 1 & 1 & -1 \\ 1 & -1 & -1 & 1 \end{bmatrix}. \qquad (6)$$

Example 7 The roller support in Figure 2.29(d) only stops vertical movement. The truss has $n = 3$ balance equations $A^{\mathrm{T}}w = f$, and only $m = 2$ bar forces w_1 and w_2:

$$w_1 \cos\phi - w_2 \cos\theta = 0 \qquad w_1 \sin\phi - w_2 \sin\theta = 0 \qquad w_2 \cos\theta = F. \qquad (7)$$

If the applied force F at the roller (or slider) is nonzero, the truss must move. And when it moves, it does not stay rigid. There are enough supports ($r = 3$) to prevent rigid motion, so *the truss will change shape*. As F pulls back and forth, bar 1 turns around the fixed node (translation into rotation!). This deformation is a ***mechanism***.

Remark 2 The $2N$ by $2N$ stiffness matrix (unreduced and singular) is assembled from the k_i for all bars. Good codes do this first! Rigid motions and mechanisms give $K_{\textbf{unreduced}}\, u = 0$. Then the supports remove r rows of A^{T} and r columns of A to leave $K_{\textbf{reduced}}$ of size $2N - r$. For a stable truss, this reduced K is invertible.

Remark 3 With only three reactive forces, $r = 3$, they can be calculated directly from the applied forces f—without knowing the bar forces w. The reactions combine with f to prevent rigid motions, which gives three equations: zero horizontal force, zero vertical force, and zero moment.

Remark 4 In continuum mechanics the strain ε is dimensionless and the stress σ is force per unit area. These match our elongation e and internal force w after dividing by the length and cross-sectional area of the bar: $\boldsymbol{\varepsilon = e/L}$ **and** $\boldsymbol{\sigma = w/A}$.

Then the constant in Hooke's law $\sigma = E\varepsilon$ depends only on the material, and not on the shape of the bar. E is *Young's modulus*, with the units of stress. For each separate bar it gives the elastic constant in $w = ce$:

$$\boldsymbol{\sigma = E\varepsilon} \textbf{ with Young's modulus} \qquad c = \frac{w}{e} = \frac{\sigma A}{\varepsilon L} = \frac{EA}{L}. \tag{8}$$

The most beautiful examples of trusses are the "tensegrity structures" of Buckminster Fuller. Every bar is in tension, and a mechanism is barely prevented.

Tree Houses and Collapse Mechanisms

The special interest in this truss problem is the possibility of collapse. After removing the r columns that correspond to fixed displacements, are the remaining n columns independent? In principle, elimination will decide if every column has a pivot. (If so, A has full column rank. Its columns are independent.) Dependent columns give a solution to $Au = 0$—a *collapse mechanism* u in the nullspace of A.

For the unsupported truss in Figure 2.30, the matrix A will be 8 by 14. Then the supports give $u_6^{\mathrm{H}} = u_6^{\mathrm{V}} = u_7^{\mathrm{H}} = u_7^{\mathrm{V}} = 0$. Four columns of A are removed and the matrix becomes 8 by 10. In both cases A has more columns than rows, so there must be solutions to $e = Au = 0$. These are the **rigid motions** and the **mechanisms**, the best part of this section.

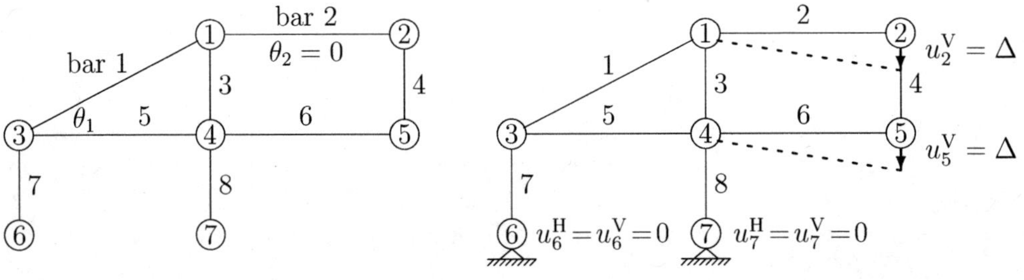

Figure 2.30: The unsupported tree house has $m = 8$ bars and $2N = 14$ forces. Then $Au = 0$ allows 3 rigid motions and 3 mechanisms. The supports leave $n = 10$: no rigid motions and $10 - 8 = 2$ mechanisms. Mechanism **1** (*no stretching*) is shown.

You can often find mechanisms directly from the truss. Ask yourself, ***could the nodes move without stretching the bars***? That will be a deformation u with no bar extension, $e = Au = 0$. It is first order movement with no first order stretching. The truss is unstable. The stiffness matrix $K = A^{\mathrm{T}}CA$ will be singular ($Au = 0$ produces $Ku = 0$), even if the truss has enough supports to prevent rigid motion.

Please look at the supported truss on the right in Figure 2.30. How could that truss move with no stretching? Since A is 8 by 10, there must be (at least) $10 - 8 = 2$ independent vectors u that give $Au = 0$. The supports prevent rigid motion.

A mechanism has rigid motions of each bar (so every $e_i = 0$) but **not** *the same motion in every bar.* I can see two outstanding deformations (and all combinations):

1. The right side of the truss collapses: $u_2^{\mathrm{V}} = u_5^{\mathrm{V}} \neq 0$. All other movements u are zero (to first order). Bars 2 and 6 rotate, and bar 4 falls with no stretching.

2. The whole truss moves to the right, except $u_6^{\mathrm{H}} = u_7^{\mathrm{H}} = 0$ at the supports. All vertical displacements are zero (to first order). Bars 7 and 8 rotate.

Now return to the unsupported truss in Figure 2.30, when A is 8 by 14. There must be (at least) $14 - 8 = 6$ solutions to $Au = 0$. We already know mechanisms **1** and **2**. There are three rigid motions (since no supports). What is one more independent solution to $e = Au = 0$, completing the picture for the unsupported truss?

3. Bar 7 swings freely. *It can rotate around node* 3 ($u_6^{\mathrm{H}} = 1$). Of course, bar 8 could also swing around node 4 ($u_7^{\mathrm{H}} = 1$). This will not give a seventh independent solution to $Au = 0$, since their sum with $u_6^{\mathrm{H}} = u_7^{\mathrm{H}} = 1$ equals a rigid horizontal motion of the whole truss *minus* mechanism **2** for nodes 1 to 5.

New Example The 9-bar truss in Figure 2.31 presents a more delicate problem. How many mechanisms and what are they? The new bar gives one new row in A, which is 9 by 10. There must be one mechanism (not so easy to see). It has to combine the original mechanisms **1** and **2**, because the first eight rows of $Au = 0$ hold as before. *Some combination* of those mechanisms ($u_2^{\mathrm{V}} = u_5^{\mathrm{V}}$ and $u_1^{\mathrm{H}} = u_2^{\mathrm{H}} = u_3^{\mathrm{H}} = u_4^{\mathrm{H}} = u_5^{\mathrm{H}}$) surely will be perpendicular to the new row of A, produced by bar 9.

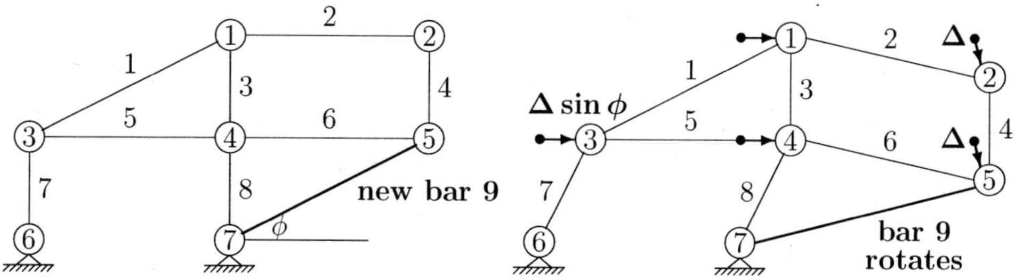

Figure 2.31: The same tree house has a new bar. A is 9 by 10 with **one mechanism**.

The new bar 9 can only rotate. Node 5 will move by Δ perpendicular to that bar, with $u_5^{\mathrm{H}} = \Delta \sin\phi$ and $u_5^{\mathrm{V}} = -\Delta\cos\phi$. All the other u_j^{H} are also $\Delta\sin\phi$ (mechanism **2**). And $u_2^{\mathrm{V}} = u_5^{\mathrm{V}}$ in mechanism **1**. The truss is collapsing.

I could imagine hammering up the original truss in Figure 2.30 for the kids, and sending them up into the tree house. As it begins to collapse, I would quickly put in bar 9 (Figure 2.31). Not enough bars, the kids still fall. They are condemned by linear algebra, since A is 9 by 10.

I believe the truss has no more independent mechanisms. Actually I am sure. A becomes 10 by 10, and it is invertible. The truss is now stable, and the stiffness matrix $K = A^{\mathrm{T}}CA$ will be invertible and positive definite (sum of ten k_i). *Because A is square, we are in the determinate case*: $K^{-1} = (A^{-1})(C^{-1})(A^{\mathrm{T}})^{-1}$ is correct. The ten bar forces w are directly determined by the ten balance equations $A^{\mathrm{T}}w = f$:

Determinate case $$w = (A^{\mathrm{T}})^{-1}f \quad \text{and} \quad e = C^{-1}w \quad \text{and} \quad u = A^{-1}e\,. \qquad (9)$$

Generating a Triangular Mesh

A basic problem in computer graphics and finite elements is geometric: **To cover a region by nearly uniform triangles**. Those triangles provide a "*mesh*" over the region. We compute at the corners of the triangles, and maybe also edge midpoints. Those computations are more accurate when the angles are close to 60°. Thin triangles (with angles near 0° or 180°) are dangerous.

It is not so simple to generate a good mesh. We have two decisions to make:

1 The choice of **nodes** (well spaced and reaching the boundary)

2 The choice of **edges** (this gives the "topology" of the mesh)

Reaching the boundary is fundamental, to use the boundary conditions. We can start with an absolutely regular 60° mesh inside the region. Somehow those meshpoints must be pushed out toward the boundary. If we move only the outer nodes, the triangles near the boundary will be terrible. We are aiming for a mesh like Figure 2.32.

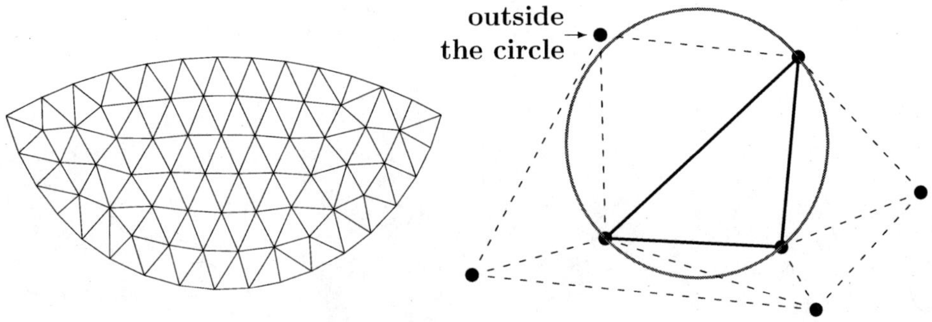

Figure 2.32: A nearly regular mesh, obeying Delaunay's "empty circle" rule.

Per-Olof Persson provided a short MATLAB code for mesh generation, with a link on math.mit.edu/cse. The key idea is to think of the mesh as a plane truss! *He replaces Hooke's Law* $w = ce$ *on each edge by a nonlinear function* $w = c(e)$. Starting from the regular mesh (inside and too small), *all forces push nodes outward.* No compression is allowed, as the algorithm moves the nodes to a final position.

Goal: **The edge forces add to zero at each interior node** $(A^{\mathrm{T}}w = 0)$.

At every iteration, the unbalanced edge forces move the nodes. If a node goes outside the region, it is projected back to the boundary. The boundary provides a *reaction force*, pushing inward on that node, which is included in the force balance. The algorithm stops when the nodes are hardly moving and the mesh fills the region.

I have to add four comments to help users of this code:

1. Each time the nodes are moved, we call a *Delaunay subroutine* to choose new edges. The topology can change (mostly it doesn't). The code delaunay.m makes the unique choice of edges so that for any triangle, the circle through the corners has no meshpoint inside (Figure 2.32 shows the empty circle).

2. The user describes the region by its *distance function* and not by equations for the boundary curves. The distance to the boundary is $d > 0$ outside the region and $d < 0$ inside. Then the boundary is the "level set" where $d = 0$. The code evaluates $d(P)$ only at meshpoints P. We don't require a formula for $d(x, y)$.

3. We want good triangles but not always uniform sizes. Close to corners or sharp curves on the boundary, smaller triangles will give more accuracy. The user can specify an *element size function* that varies over the region.

4. The force function $w = c(e)$ should *not be linear*. The user can specify a length L_0 slightly greater than most edges can reach (without leaving the region). One choice of the stress-strain law to prevent negative forces is $w = \max\,\{ce, 0\}$. This nonlinear $w = C(e)$ changes our framework to $A^{\mathrm{T}}C(Au) = f$.

Applied Linear Algebra

The basic framework of equilibrium leads to the positive definite matrix $A^{\mathrm{T}}CA$. Each application has its special features, but please don't miss the common thread.

Mechanics	Statistics	Networks
$u =$ displacements	$\widehat{u} =$ best parameters	$u =$ voltages at nodes
$e = Au$ (elongations)	$e = b - A\widehat{u}$ (errors)	$e = b - Au$ (voltage drops)
$w = Ce$ (Hooke's law)	$w = Ce$ (weight $c_i = 1/\sigma_i^2$)	$w = Ce$ (Ohm's law)
$f = A^{\mathrm{T}}w$ (force balance)	$0 = A^{\mathrm{T}}w$ (projection)	$f = A^{\mathrm{T}}w$ (Kirchhoff)
$\boldsymbol{A^{\mathrm{T}}CAu = f}$	$\boldsymbol{A^{\mathrm{T}}CA\widehat{u} = A^{\mathrm{T}}Cb}$	$\boldsymbol{A^{\mathrm{T}}CAu = A^{\mathrm{T}}Cb - f}$

In mechanics, the source terms are external forces f. The least squares problem has observations b. The network problem can have both f and b, current sources and voltage sources. Notice that b enters the framework early, while f enters at the end. Therefore b is acted on by C and A^{T} before $A^{\mathrm{T}}Cb$ catches up to f. The network equation has $-f$ because current flows from higher to lower potential.

$K = A^{\mathrm{T}}CA$ is *symmetric positive definite* provided A has independent columns. (If $Au = 0$ then $Ku = 0$ and we have a singular matrix K, positive semidefinite.) Each positive definite matrix is directly associated with a minimization:

Minimize the quadratic function $\quad P(u) = \frac{1}{2}(b - Au)^{\mathrm{T}}C(b - Au) - u^{\mathrm{T}}f$

Symmetry is assured because every matrix of second derivatives is symmetric:

$$\frac{\partial^2 P}{\partial u_i \partial u_j} = \frac{\partial^2 P}{\partial u_j \partial u_i} \quad \text{means that} \quad (A^{\mathrm{T}}CA)_{ij} = (A^{\mathrm{T}}CA)_{ji}\,. \tag{10}$$

Positive definiteness ensures a *unique minimum*: $u^{\mathrm{T}}Ku > 0$ except at $u = 0$. The graph of $\frac{1}{2}u^{\mathrm{T}}Ku$ is a "bowl" resting on the origin. The same bowl is shifted by source terms f and b. In mechanics, the minimizer is moved to $u = K^{-1}f$. In the third figure (statistics) the equation is $A^{\mathrm{T}}CAu = A^{\mathrm{T}}Cb$. The bowl is the same in all cases because the second derivative matrix is always $K = A^{\mathrm{T}}CA$.

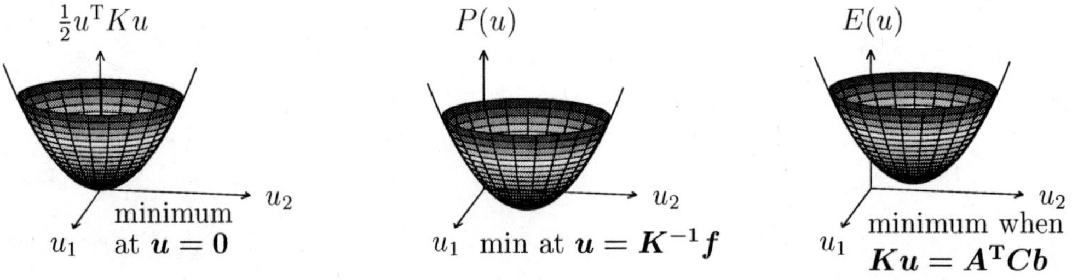

Figure 2.33: Low points of $\frac{1}{2}u^{\mathrm{T}}Ku$ and $\frac{1}{2}u^{\mathrm{T}}Ku - u^{\mathrm{T}}f$ and $\frac{1}{2}(b - Au)^{\mathrm{T}}C(b - Au)$.

It is very helpful to write $u^{\mathrm{T}}Ku$ as $(Au)^{\mathrm{T}}C(Au)$. Mechanics has $e = Au$ so *the energy in the springs is* $\frac{1}{2}e^{\mathrm{T}}Ce$. The linear part is $u^{\mathrm{T}}f$:

Work $\quad \boldsymbol{u^{\mathrm{T}}f} = u_1 f_1 + \cdots + u_n f_n =$ displacement times force. (11)

Thus $P(u) = \frac{1}{2}e^{\mathrm{T}}Ce - u^{\mathrm{T}}f$ represents internal energy minus external work. Nature chooses the displacements that make $P(u)$ a minimum (which happens at $Ku = f$).

In the least squares problem, nature is replaced by statisticians. They minimize the covariance matrix of the error in $\widehat{u}$. In the network problem, $e^{\mathrm{T}}Ce$ gives the heat loss and $u^{\mathrm{T}}f$ is the power (voltage times current source). Minimizing $P(u)$ leads to *the same equations* that we found directly from the laws of circuit theory.

One final point, that mechanics illustrates well. Each minimum principle comes with a dual principle—a different problem that yields the same answer. The dual of minimum potential energy $P(u)$ is *minimum complementary energy* $Q(w)$:

Dual Problem: Choose w to minimize $Q(w) = \frac{1}{2}w^{\mathrm{T}}C^{-1}w$ subject to $A^{\mathrm{T}}w = f$.

Those constraints $A^{\mathrm{T}}w = f$ bring the u's as *Lagrange multipliers* in Section 8.1.

Problem Set 2.7

1 Truss A doesn't look safe to me. How many independent solutions to $Au = 0$? Draw them and also find the solutions $u = (u_1^{\mathrm{H}}, u_1^{\mathrm{V}}, \ldots, u_4^{\mathrm{H}}, u_4^{\mathrm{V}})$. What shapes are A and $A^{\mathrm{T}}A$? What are their first rows?

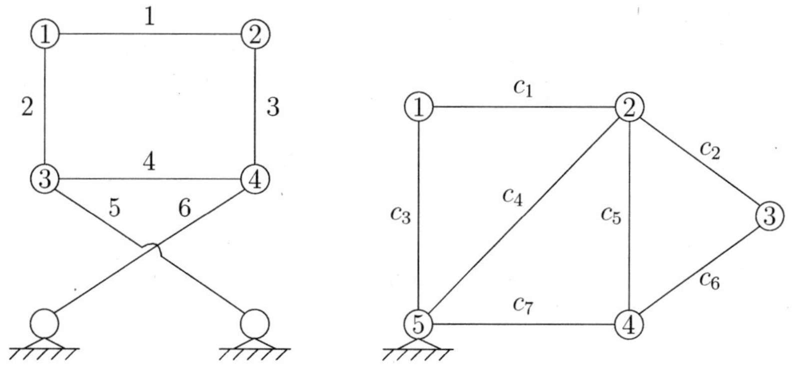

Truss A **Truss B**

2 Truss B has 7 bars and $n = 2N - r = 10 - 2$ unknown displacements. What motion solves $Au = 0$? By adding one bar, can A become square and invertible? Write out row 2 of A (for bar 2 at a 45° angle). What is the third equation in $A^{\mathrm{T}}w = f$ with right side f_2^{H}?

3 Truss C is a square, no supports. Find $8 - 4$ independent solutions to $Au = 0$. Find 4 sets of f's so that $A^{\mathrm{T}}w = f$ has a solution. Check that $u^{\mathrm{T}}f = 0$ for these four u's and f's. *The force f must not activate the instabilities u.*

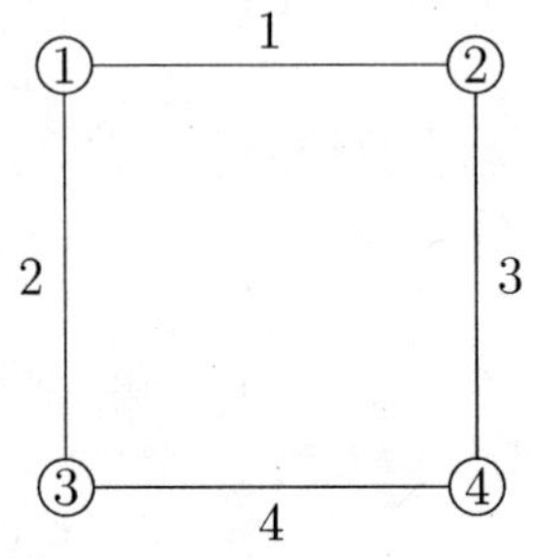

Truss C

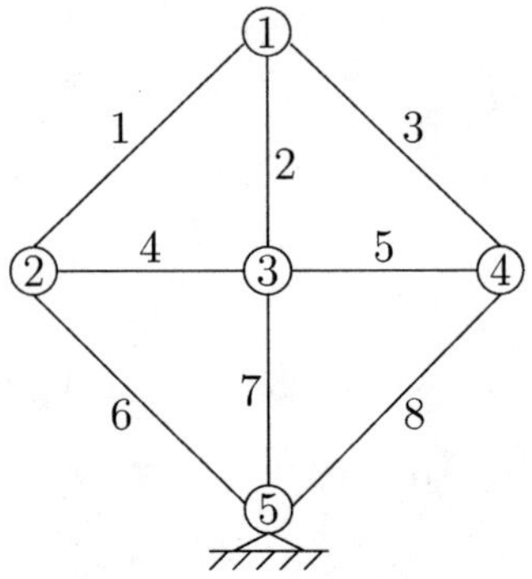

Truss D

4 Truss D has how many rows and columns in the matrix A? Find column 1, with 8 elongations from

a small displacement u_1^{H}. Draw a nonzero solution to $Au = 0$. Why will $A^{\mathrm{T}}w = 0$ have a nonzero solution (8 bar forces in balance)?

5 Truss E has 8 bars and 5 unsupported joints. Draw a complete set of mechanisms. Is $A^{\mathrm{T}}A$ positive definite? Semidefinite? Not required to compute $A^{\mathrm{T}}A$.

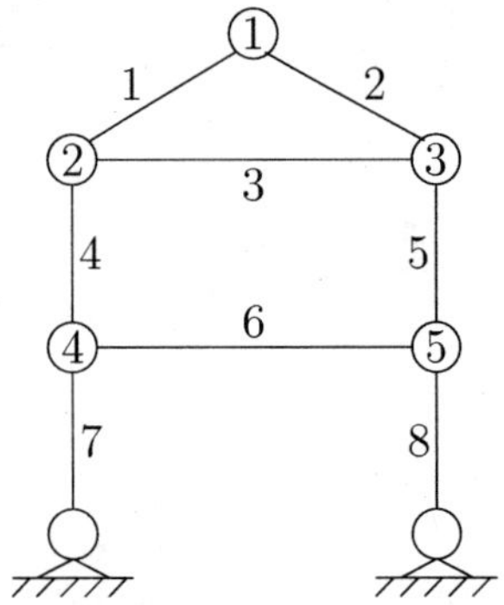

Truss E

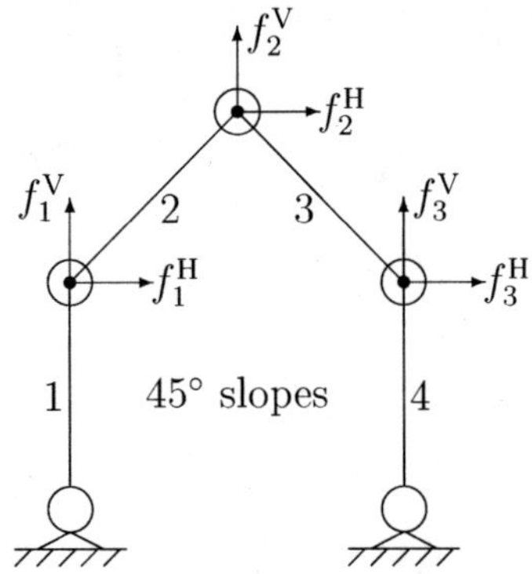

Truss F

6 Truss F has how many mechanisms? Describe them with a picture or a solution to $Au = 0$. Draw in just enough bars to make the truss stable. How many solutions does $A^{\mathrm{T}}w = f$ now have?

7 Suppose a *space truss* has the shape of a cube. The four joints at the base are fixed, the upper joints have 3 displacements and 3 forces each. Why is A an 8 by 12 matrix? Describe four independent mechanisms of the cube.

8 Sketch a six-sided truss with fixed supports at two opposite vertices. Will one diagonal crossbar between free nodes make it stable, or what is the mechanism? What are m and n? What if a second crossbar is added?

9 Suppose a truss consists of *one bar* at an angle θ with the horizontal. Sketch forces f_1 and f_2 at the upper end, acting in the positive x and y directions, and corresponding forces f_3 and f_4 at the lower end. Write down the 1 by 4 matrix A_0, the 4 by 1 matrix A_0^{T}, and the 4 by 4 matrix $A_0^{\mathrm{T}} C A_0$. This is the element matrix. For which forces can the equation $A_0^{\mathrm{T}} y = f$ be solved?

10 There are three rigid motions for a plane truss (horizontal, vertical, rotation around $(0,0)$). Why is rotation around another center point not a fourth? **Describe six rigid motions in 3D for a space truss.**

11 Where could you place a tenth bar to make Figure 2.31 stable?

12 Sketch a six-sided truss with fixed supports at two opposite vertices. Will one diagonal crossbar between free nodes make it stable, or what is the mechanism? What are m and n? What if a second crossbar is added?

13 The "stiffness coefficients" k_{ij} in K give the forces f_i corresponding to a unit displacement $u_j = 1$, since $Ku = f$. What are the "flexibility coefficients" that give the displacements u_i caused by a unit force $f_j = 1$? Are they $1/k_{ij}$?

14 For the 4-bar truss in Figure 2.28, find the element stiffness matrix k_i for each bar and assemble into K.

15 Write a code for the cse website that produces a 4 by 4 element matrix k_i for each bar. Assemble K from the k_i and test for stability. Inputs are $c = (c_1, \ldots, c_m)$, an N by 2 list of joint coordinates x_i, y_i, an m by 2 list of bars (two joint numbers), and an r by 2 list of fixed displacements.

2.8 COVARIANCES AND RECURSIVE LEAST SQUARES

Part of scientific computing is statistical computing. When outputs $\widehat{u}$ come from inputs b, ***we must estimate the reliability of*** $\widehat{\boldsymbol{u}}$. Reliability is measured by variances and covariances. The ***covariance matrix*** $\boldsymbol{P}$ has variances on the diagonal and covariances off the diagonal. The reliability of $\widehat{u}$ depends on the reliability of the input b, measured by *its* covariance matrix $\boldsymbol{\Sigma}$.

The covariance $\boldsymbol{P}$ **has the beautiful formula** $(\boldsymbol{A^{\mathrm{T}}CA})^{-1} = (\boldsymbol{A^{\mathrm{T}}\Sigma^{-1}A})^{-1}$. This matrix shows how reliable (small P) or unreliable (large P) the estimated $\widehat{u}$ will be. Notice that P does not depend on a specific b (the experimental data). It only depends on A and Σ (the experimental *setup*). The knowledge of P tells, in advance of any particular observations b, how good the experiment should be.

This is the "century of data." Reliability is a central scientific problem. This section goes more deeply into least squares, after Section 2.3 prepared the way with $A^{\mathrm{T}}A\widehat{u} = A^{\mathrm{T}}b$. When you see the $A^{\mathrm{T}}CA$ framework and the recursive algorithms that lead to $\widehat{u}$, they will connect statistics to other parts of applied mathematics. The analysis of reliability is the crucial link between experiment and simulation.

First we explain mean and variance and covariance. Then we show why the weighting matrix C (the middle step in our framework) should be the inverse of the input covariance matrix Σ. Finally we ask how to use new inputs b_{new} without repeating calculations already done on b_{old}. This is **recursive least squares** when we are adding new equations in $Au \approx b$. If the state u and its statistics are changing at each step i, the recursion for $\widehat{u}_i$ and P_i becomes the famous **Kalman filter**.

Mean and Variance

I want to write the unsolvable equation $Au = b$ as a true equation (with noise):

Observation equations $$Au = b - e = b - \textbf{noise}\,. \tag{1}$$

In applications, we don't know the measurement errors e. (If we did, we would include them in b.) But we may know something about the probabilities of different noise levels—we may know the *probability distribution of* e. That information will tell us the right weights to assign to the equations (equal weights if the errors e have the same distribution). We can also find the distribution of errors in the output $\widehat{u}$. Important!

Suppose we are estimating a child's age in years, with errors -1 or 0 or $+1$. If those errors have equal probabilities $\frac{1}{3}, \frac{1}{3}, \frac{1}{3}$, then the average error (the **mean** or **expected value**) is zero:

$$\textbf{mean} = \mathrm{E}\,[e] = \frac{1}{3}(-1) + \frac{1}{3}(0) + \frac{1}{3}(1) = 0. \tag{2}$$

The expected value $\sum \boldsymbol{p_i e_i}$ **combines all possible errors multiplied by their probabilities** $\boldsymbol{p_i}$ (which add to 1). Often we have $\mathrm{E}\,[e_i] = 0$: **zero mean.**

A nonzero mean can be subtracted from b_i to "reset the meter." The measurements do include errors, but they are *not biased* to one side or the other.

To deal with the *size of those errors* (and not their sign) we look at e^2. When squared errors are weighted by their probabilities to give the average value of e^2, this is the **variance** σ^2. When the mean is $\mathrm{E}[e] = 0$, the variance is $\mathrm{E}[e^2]$:

Variance $$\sigma^2 = \mathrm{E}[e^2] = \frac{1}{3}(-1)^2 + \frac{1}{3}(0)^2 + \frac{1}{3}(1)^2 = \frac{2}{3}. \qquad (3)$$

Notice that σ^2 has nothing to do with the actual measurements b_i, which were random samples from our population of all possible children and ages. We know averages, we don't know individuals. If the mean of e were not zero, we would have computed σ^2 by squaring the distance $e - \mathrm{E}[e]$ **from the mean**:

Suppose we estimate the ages of 100 children. The total error $e_{\mathsf{sum}} = e_1 + \cdots + e_{100}$ is now between -100 and 100. But e_{sum} is not likely to reach 100 (meaning that every error is $+1$), which has very small probability $(\frac{1}{3})^{100}$. The mean of e_{sum} will still be zero. ***The variance of*** $\boldsymbol{e_{\mathsf{sum}}}$ ***will be*** $\mathbf{100\,\sigma^2}$:

Check for $m = 2$ children: $e_{\mathsf{sum}} = -2$ or -1 or 0 or -1 or -2

Probabilities appear in $\left(\frac{1}{3} + \frac{1}{3} + \frac{1}{3}\right)^2 = \frac{\mathbf{1}}{\mathbf{9}} + \frac{\mathbf{2}}{\mathbf{9}} + \frac{\mathbf{3}}{\mathbf{9}} + \frac{\mathbf{2}}{\mathbf{9}} + \frac{\mathbf{1}}{\mathbf{9}}$ (adding to 1)

Variance $= \frac{\mathbf{1}}{\mathbf{9}}(-2)^2 + \frac{\mathbf{2}}{\mathbf{9}}(-1)^2 + \frac{\mathbf{3}}{\mathbf{9}}(0)^2 + \frac{\mathbf{2}}{\mathbf{9}}(1)^2 + \frac{\mathbf{1}}{\mathbf{9}}(2^2) = \frac{12}{9} = 2\left(\frac{2}{3}\right) = \mathbf{2\sigma^2}$.

Central Limit Theorem

For m children, the combined error e_{sum} is between $-m$ and m. It has its own probability distribution computable from $(\frac{1}{3} + \frac{1}{3} + \frac{1}{3})^m$. **Its variance is** $\boldsymbol{m\sigma^2}$. So the natural scaling is to divide by $\sqrt{m}$ and look at $\boldsymbol{x = e_{\mathsf{sum}}/\sqrt{m}}$. This has mean zero and variance fixed at σ^2. As $m \to \infty$, what are the probabilities for different x?

The answer is in the **central limit theorem**. The probability distribution for x approaches (as $m \to \infty$) a **normal distribution** $p(x)$ with variance σ^2:

Normal distribution $$p(x) = \frac{1}{\sqrt{2\pi}\,\sigma} e^{-x^2/2\sigma^2} \quad \text{with} \quad \int_{-\infty}^{\infty} p(x)\,dx = 1. \qquad (4)$$

Then $p(x)dx$ gives the chance that a random sample falls between x and $x + dx$. Since the sample falls somewhere, the integral over all chances is 1. The graph of $p(x)$ is the famous bell-shaped curve in Figure 2.34. The integral of $p(x)$ is $F(x)$.

The integral $F(x)$ is the **cumulative probability**. It allows all errors up to x. Its derivative $p(x)$ is the ***probability density function***. This *p.d.f.* gives the frequency that a sample will fall near x. Errors below x have probability $F(x)$ and errors below $x + dx$ have probability $F(x + dx)$. Errors in between have probability $p(x)\,dx$:

$$F(x + dx) - F(x) = p(x)dx \quad \text{and thus} \quad p(x) = \frac{dF}{dx}.$$

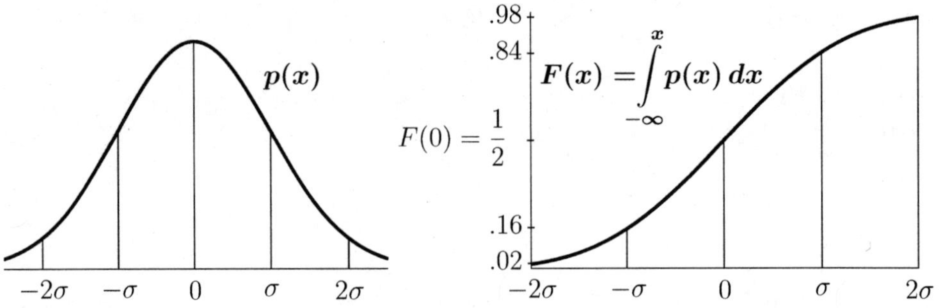

Figure 2.34: The normal (Gaussian) distribution $p(x)$ and its integral $F(x)$.

For this particular $p(x)$ there is no simple expression for $F(x)$. That integral is connected to the "*error function*" and carefully tabulated. There is one integral we can do exactly—the variance! Integration by parts succeeds on $(x)(xe^{-x^2/2\sigma^2})$:

$$\textbf{Variance of } p(x) \qquad \int_{-\infty}^{\infty} x^2\, p(x)\, dx = \frac{1}{\sqrt{2\pi}\,\sigma} \int_{-\infty}^{\infty} x^2\, e^{-x^2/2\sigma^2}\, dx = \sigma^2 . \qquad (5)$$

The variance σ measures the **width of the bell-shaped curve**, for a normal distribution. This indicates the noise level—the sizes of the errors. The right side of Figure 2.34 shows the probability $.84 - .16 = .68$ that a random sample from a normal Gaussian distribution is less than σ away from the mean. "Two thirds of the samples are within one standard deviation σ of the mean."

Probability Distributions

1. Uniform 2. Binomial 3. Poisson 4. Normal (Gaussian) 5. Chi-square. Those are five important probability distributions. Examples 1 and 4 (box-shaped graph and bell-shaped graph) have *continuous* variables. The height of the curve is the **probability density** $p(x)$. The chance that a sample falls between x and $x+dx$ is $p(x)dx$. For the mean, each error is weighted by its probability, in the integral $\mu = \mathrm{E}[e] = \int p(x)e(x)\,dx$. Symmetry around zero guarantees that $\mathrm{E}[e] = 0$. Those errors have **mean zero**. Examples 2, 3, 5 have $\mu > 0$.

Example 2 counts how often we expect M heads in N fair coin flips. Now M is a *discrete* random variable. The probabilities $p_0, \ldots, p_N$ for $M = 0, \ldots, N$ add to 1. The **expectation** $\mathrm{E}[M]$ (the average **number of heads**) is the mean value $N/2$. The ***strong law of large numbers*** says the probability is zero that M/N will go infinitely often outside any fixed interval around $\frac{1}{2}$, as we continue to flip the coin. (The *weak law* only says that the probability for M/N to be outside approaches 0.)

$$\textbf{\textit{We don't expect }} M \to \frac{N}{2} \text{ (\textit{common mistake}).} \quad \textbf{\textit{We do expect }} \frac{M}{N} \to \frac{1}{2}.$$

1. **Uniform distribution:** Suppose each measurement is rounded to the nearest integer. All numbers between 6.5 and 7.5 give $b = 7$. The error e lies between $-.5$ and $.5$. All errors in this interval are equally likely (this explains the words ***uniform distribution***). The probability that e falls between .1 and .3 is .2:

$\boldsymbol{p(x) = 1}$	Probability that $x <$ error $< x + dx$ is dx for $\boldsymbol{\lvert x\rvert \le \frac{1}{2}}$
$\boldsymbol{\int p(x)\, dx}$	Total probability that $-\frac{1}{2} < e < \frac{1}{2}$ is $\int_{-\frac{1}{2}}^{\frac{1}{2}} dx = \mathbf{1}$
Mean $\boldsymbol{m}$	Expected value of the error $\mathrm{E}[e] = \int_{-\frac{1}{2}}^{\frac{1}{2}} xp(x)\, dx = \mathbf{0}$
Variance $\boldsymbol{\sigma^2}$	Expected value of *squared* error $= \int_{-\frac{1}{2}}^{\frac{1}{2}} x^2\, p(x)\, dx = \mathbf{\frac{1}{12}}$.

2. **Binomial distribution:** For each flip of a fair coin, the probability of heads is $\frac{1}{2}$. For $N = 3$ flips, the probability of heads every time is $\left(\frac{1}{2}\right)^3 = \frac{1}{8}$. The probability of heads twice and tails once is $\frac{3}{8}$, from three sequences THH and HTH and HHT. These numbers $\frac{1}{8}$ and $\frac{3}{8}$ are pieces of $\left(\frac{1}{2} + \frac{1}{2}\right)^3 = 1$:

Total probability
$$\left(\frac{1}{2}\right)^3 + 3\left(\frac{1}{2}\right)^3 + 3\left(\frac{1}{2}\right)^3 + \left(\frac{1}{2}\right)^3 = \frac{1}{8} + \frac{3}{8} + \frac{3}{8} + \frac{1}{8} = 1\,.$$

The average number of heads is $\frac{12}{8} = 1.5$, using those probabilities as weights:

3 flips
$$\textbf{mean} = (3 \text{ heads})\,\frac{1}{8} + (2 \text{ heads})\,\frac{3}{8} + (1 \text{ head})\,\frac{3}{8} + 0 = \frac{12}{8}\,.$$

What is the probability of M heads in N flips? Again we look at the terms in $\left(\frac{1}{2} + \frac{1}{2}\right)^N$. The chance p_M of seeing M heads and $N - M$ tails involves the **binomial coefficient** $\binom{M}{N} =$ "N choose M" that gamblers know and love:

Binomial distribution
$$p_M = \frac{1}{2^N}\binom{M}{N} = \frac{1}{2^N}\,\frac{N!}{M!(N-M)!}\,.$$

The total probability is $p_0 + \cdots + p_N = \left(\frac{1}{2} + \frac{1}{2}\right)^N = 1$. The expected number of heads is $0p_0 + 1p_1 + \cdots + Np_N$. This sum is $N/2$ from common sense.

Since the mean is $N/2$, we work with the *squared distance from the mean.* Its expected value (squared distance times probability) is the **variance** σ^2:

Variance
$$\sigma^2 = \left(0 - \frac{N}{2}\right)^2 p_0 + \left(1 - \frac{N}{2}\right)^2 p_1 + \cdots + \left(N - \frac{N}{2}\right)^2 p_N\,.$$

This turns out to be $\sigma^2 = N/4$. The ***standard deviation*** is its square root $\sigma = \sqrt{N}/2$. This measures the spread around the mean.

An unfair coin has probability p of heads and $q = 1 - p$ of tails. ***The mean number of heads in N flips is p times N.*** Those flips are "**Bernoulli trials.**"

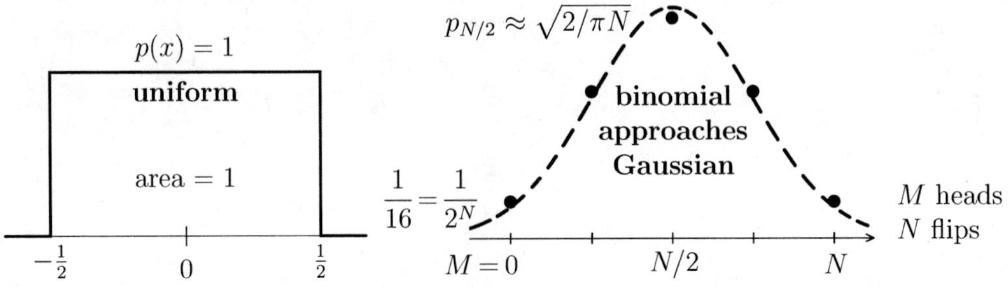

Figure 2.35: Uniform probability between $-\frac{1}{2}$ and $\frac{1}{2}$. The binomial probabilities $p = (1,\ 4,\ 6,\ 4,\ 1)/16$ adding to 1 come from $\binom{M}{N}/2^N$. For large N, this approaches a Gaussian distribution of variance $\sigma^2 = N/4$ and height $1/(\sqrt{2\pi}\,\sigma) = \sqrt{2/\pi N}$.

3. **Poisson distribution:**

Suppose the coin is very unfair (p *is small*) but we flip it very often (N *is large*). The expected number of heads is $\lambda = pN$. *Keep that number* λ *fixed as* $p \to 0$ *and* $N \to \infty$. What are the "Poisson probabilities" $p_0, p_1, p_2, \ldots$ of seeing $0, 1, 2, \ldots$ heads in this limiting case of a very lopsided binomial distribution? This is the probability theory of fairly rare events.

Probability of 0 heads $$(1-p)^N = \left(1 - \frac{\lambda}{N}\right)^N \longrightarrow e^{-\lambda} = p_0\,. \qquad (6)$$

That limit is one of the most important in calculus, I hope you recognize it. More often you see plus signs in $(1 + (\lambda/N))^N \to e^\lambda$. This comes from interest at λ per cent, compounded N times in a year. At the end of the year one dollar becomes e^λ dollars, in the limit $N \to \infty$ of continuous compounding. Daily compounding with $N = 365$ and $\lambda = .1$ would come very close to $e^\lambda = 1.10517$:

$$\left(1 + \frac{.1}{365}\right)^{365} = 1.10516 \quad \text{and in our case} \quad \left(1 - \frac{.1}{365}\right)^{365} \approx \mathbf{e^{-.1}}\,. \qquad (7)$$

Maybe our negative bank is charging fees (typical!) instead of offering interest.

Now compute the probability p_1 of seeing heads *once* in N flips, with $p = \lambda/N$:

Probability of 1 head $$Np(1-p)^{N-1} = \lambda\left(1 - \frac{\lambda}{N}\right)^{N-1} \longrightarrow \lambda e^{-\lambda} = p_1\,. \qquad (8)$$

The chance of heads followed by $N-1$ tails is $p(1-p)^{N-1}$. But there were N places for heads to appear, so we multiplied by N above.

If we look for **two heads** followed by $N-2$ tails, the chance in that order is $p^2(1-p)^{N-2}$. Now the two heads could appear in $\binom{N}{2} = N(N-1)/2$ pairs of places:

2 heads $$\frac{N(N-1)}{2}p^2(1-p)^{N-2} = \frac{pN(pN-p)}{2}\left(1 - \frac{\lambda}{N}\right)^{N-2} \longrightarrow \frac{\lambda^2}{2}e^{-\lambda} = p_2\,.$$

The pattern for k heads is similar. The binomial coefficient $\left[\begin{smallmatrix} N \\ k \end{smallmatrix}\right]$ times p^k approaches $\lambda^k/k!$ as N increases. ***Then*** $\boldsymbol{p_k = \lambda^k e^{-\lambda}/k!}$ ***and the sum over all possibilities is*** $\boldsymbol{\sum p_k = 1}$:

Poisson probabilities $$p_k = \frac{\lambda^k}{k!} e^{\lambda} \quad \text{and} \quad \sum_{k=0}^{\infty} \frac{\lambda^k}{k!} e^{-\lambda} = e^{\lambda} e^{-\lambda} = 1\,. \tag{9}$$

Example 1 (from Feller [51]) Among $N = 500$ people, what is the probability that k birthdays will fall on May 1? For each person the chance $p = 1/365$ is small.

Poisson will look at $\lambda = pN = 500/365 \approx 1.37$. Then his approximation to the exact binomial distribution involves $e^{-\lambda} = .254\ldots$ which is p_0 (no birthdays on May 1):

$$p_0{=}.254 \quad p_1{=}.348 \quad p_2{=}.239 \quad p_3{=}.109 \quad p_4{=}.037 \quad p_5{=}.010 \quad p_6{=}.002 \quad \text{add to } .999\,.$$

With probability $3/4$, May 1 is someone's birthday. The probability that two of the 500 have the *same* birthday is exactly 1! With 100 people that probability is ____.

As always, we want the **mean and variance** of the distribution. Both are λ:

Poisson mean $$\mu = 0 + \lambda e^{-\lambda} + 2\,\frac{\lambda^2}{2!}\,e^{-\lambda} + 3\,\frac{\lambda^3}{3!}\,e^{-\lambda} + \cdots = \lambda e^{-\lambda}\left(\sum_0^{\infty} \frac{\lambda^n}{n!}\right) = \boldsymbol{\lambda}$$

Poisson variance $$\sigma^2 = \left(0 + \lambda e^{-\lambda} + 2^2\,\frac{\lambda^2}{2!}\,e^{-\lambda} + 3^2\,\frac{\lambda^3}{3!}\,e^{-\lambda} + \cdots\right) - \mu^2 = \boldsymbol{\lambda} \tag{10}$$

Variance is always $\sigma^2 = \sum k^2 p_k - \mu^2$. That sum is inside the parentheses in (10):

$$\sum k^2 p_k = \lambda e^{-\lambda}\left(1 + 2\lambda + 3\,\frac{\lambda^2}{2!} + \cdots\right) = \lambda e^{-\lambda}\,\frac{d}{d\lambda}\left(\lambda e^{\lambda}\right) = \lambda^2 + \lambda\,. \tag{11}$$

For an unfair coin, the binomial mean is pN and the variance is pqN. Those are exact, before Poisson's limit $pN \to \lambda$. Then both numbers become λ, because $q = 1 - p$. Feller states that the three principal distributions are binomial, normal, and Poisson.

Poisson probabilities apply to infrequent events counted over a time $\boldsymbol{T}$**.** Many measurements lead to Poisson. If the expected number of events in unit time is λ, then the expected number in time T is λT. The probabilities of $0, 1$, or 2 events are $e^{-\lambda T}, \lambda T e^{-\lambda T}, \frac{1}{2}\lambda^2 T^2 e^{-\lambda T}$. The reason lies in two important assumptions on the experiment:

1. No change in the conditions over time (**time-invariance**)

2. No dependence between separate time periods (**interval-independence**).

The chance of an event in a small time interval Δt is $p = \lambda \Delta t$. The possibility of two or more successes within Δt is so remote that we can neglect it. Assumptions 1 and 2 make the number of successes in $N = T/\Delta t$ independent small intervals (independent!) into a binomial problem, with $pN = (\lambda \Delta t)(T/\Delta t) = \lambda T$. In the limit as $\Delta t \to 0$ and $N \to \infty$, binomial becomes Poisson.

4. **Normal distribution:** This "**Gaussian**" distribution is the most important of all. It always appears when we combine a large number of identical and independent samples (like coin flips). Normalize the head count M by measuring from the mean $N/2$ and dividing by the standard deviation $\sigma = \sqrt{N}/2$:

$$\textbf{Normalized count of heads} \qquad x = \frac{1}{\sigma}(M - \text{mean}) = \frac{2}{\sqrt{N}}\left(M - \frac{N}{2}\right).$$

As N increases, the possible outcomes x begin to fill in the whole line from $-\infty$ to ∞. The *Central Limit Theorem* says that the probabilities for these random variables x approach a Gaussian distribution. The probability that the normalized count falls in the small interval between x and $x + dx$ is $p(x)\,dx$:

$$\textbf{Standard normal} \qquad p(x) = \frac{1}{\sqrt{2\pi}}\,e^{-x^2/2} \text{ with total probability } \int_{-\infty}^{\infty} p(x)\,dx = 1. \tag{12}$$

The factor $\sqrt{2\pi}$ ensures that the total probability equals one. The graph of $e^{-x^2/2}$ is the famous bell-shaped curve. By symmetry, the mean value is $\int x\,p(x)\,dx = 0$. MATLAB's randn uses this normal distribution, where rand (without the n) gives numbers uniformly distributed on $[0, 1]$. *The variance is* $\int x^2\,p(x)\,dx = 1$.

$$\textbf{Variance} = 1 \ \textbf{(by parts)} \quad \frac{1}{\sqrt{2\pi}}\int_{-\infty}^{\infty}(-x)(-x)e^{-x^2/2}\,dx = \left.\frac{-xe^{-x^2/2}}{\sqrt{2\pi}}\right|_{-\infty}^{\infty} + \int_{-\infty}^{\infty} p(x)\,dx = 0 + 1$$

This "standard" normal distribution $p(x)$, with mean $\mu = 0$ and variance $\sigma^2 = 1$, is written $\mathbf{N(0,1)}$. It was produced by normalizing the head count. A non-standard distribution $\mathrm{N}(\mu, \sigma)$ is centered at its mean μ, and the "width of the bell" is σ:

$$p(x) = \frac{1}{\sigma\sqrt{2\pi}}e^{-(x-\mu)/2\sigma^2} \quad \text{has} \quad \int x\,p(x)\,dx = \mu \quad \text{and} \quad \int (x-\mu)^2\,p(x)\,dx = \sigma^2.$$

When you read the results of a poll, the newspaper always gives the mean value μ. Very often it also reports the interval from $\mu - 2\sigma$ to $\mu + 2\sigma$. The probability is about 95% that the sample lies in this range. Figure 2.34 (where $\sigma = 1$) shows that about 95% of the area under $p(x)$ lies between -2σ and $+2\sigma$. That area is shown by $F(x)$, the integral of $p(x)$. The definite integral $F(2) - F(-2)$ is close to 0.95.

5. **Chi-squared (χ^2) distribution:** Start with n independent samples $x_1, \ldots, x_n$ from a standard normal distribution (standard means that $\mu = 0$ and $\sigma^2 = 1$). Then the χ^2 variable S is the **sum of squares**.

$$\textbf{Chi-squared} \qquad S_n = \chi_n^2 = x_1^2 + x_2^2 + \cdots + x_n^2. \tag{13}$$

χ_n is the distance from the origin to the point $(x_1, \ldots, x_n)$. *It depends on* n.

$n=1$ When x_1^2 is below a value S, that puts x_1 between $-\sqrt{S}$ and $\sqrt{S}$. The probability is an integral of $p(x_1)$ between those limits. Take the derivative of this cumulative probability to find the probability density $p(S)$:

$$\sqrt{2\pi}\,\boldsymbol{p(S)} = \frac{d}{dS}\int_{-\sqrt{S}}^{\sqrt{S}} e^{-x^2/2}\,dx = e^{-S/2}\frac{d(\sqrt{S})}{dS} - e^{-S/2}\frac{d(-\sqrt{S})}{dS} = \frac{\mathbf{1}}{\sqrt{\boldsymbol{S}}}\boldsymbol{e^{-S/2}}. \quad (14)$$

This starts at $S=0$ since $\chi^2 \geq 0$. Its integral is $\int_0^\infty e^{-S/2}\,dx/\sqrt{2\pi S}$, which is 1.

$n=2$ The probability $F(R)$ that $x_1^2+x_2^2 \leq R^2$ is a double integral over that circle:

$$\left(\frac{1}{\sqrt{2\pi}}\right)^2 \iint e^{-x_1^2/2}e^{-x_2^2/2}\,dx\,dy = \frac{1}{2\pi}\int_0^{2\pi}\int_0^{R} e^{-r^2/2}r\,dr\,d\theta = 1-e^{-R^2/2}. \quad (15)$$

At $S=R^2$, the derivative of this F gives the probability density for $S=x_1^2+x_2^2$:

$$p_2(S) = \frac{d}{dS}\left(1-e^{-S/2}\right) = \boldsymbol{\tfrac{1}{2}e^{-S/2}} \quad \text{and} \quad \int_0^\infty \tfrac{1}{2}e^{-S/2}\,dS = 1. \quad (16)$$

For all n the density $p_n(S)$ of $S=\chi_n^2$ involves the Gamma function $\Gamma(n)=(n-1)!$.

Probability density $$p_n(S) = \frac{1}{2^{n/2}\Gamma(n/2)}S^{(n/2)-1}e^{-S/2}, \quad S \geq 0. \quad (17)$$

The mean is n (sum of the n means). The variance is $2n$. As $n\to\infty$, the distribution of the *average* χ_n^2/n must follow the Central Limit Theorem like everybody else. It approaches the normal distribution with mean 1 and variance $2/n$.

The Covariance Matrix

Now run n different experiments at once. They might be independent, or there might be some correlation between them. Each measurement x is now a *vector* with n components. Those are the outputs x_i from the n experiments.

If we measure distances from the means μ_i, each error $e_i = x_i - \mu_i$ has *mean zero*. If two errors e_i and e_j are *independent* (no relation between them), their product e_ie_j also has mean zero. But if the measurements are by the same observer at nearly the same time, the errors e_i and e_j could tend to have the same sign or the same size. ***The errors in the n experiments could be correlated.*** The average of the product e_ie_j, weighted by its probability p_{ij}, is the *covariance* $\sigma_{ij} = \sum\sum p_{ij}e_ie_j$. The average of e_i^2 is the variance σ_i^2:

Covariance $$\boldsymbol{\sigma_{ij} = \sigma_{ji} = \mathrm{E}[e_ie_j] = \textbf{expected value of } (e_i \textbf{ times } e_j).} \quad (18)$$

This is the (i,j) and (j,i) entry of the ***covariance matrix*** $\boldsymbol{\Sigma}$. The (i,i) entry is σ_i^2.

One way to estimate this number σ_{ij} is to run the experiment many times. An opinion poll might find that the replies from a wife and husband are correlated. Could be positive, could be negative. Replies might tend to be the same (covariance > 0) or possibly opposite (covariance < 0). It is an important and nontrivial problem to estimate the variances and covariances from the data.

If each experiment is run N times, the output vectors $x^1, x^2, \ldots, x^N$ provide *sample means* $\overline{\mu}_i$ *and variances* $\overline{\sigma}_i^2$ *and covariances* $\overline{\sigma}_{ij}$. These are a natural choice (but open for discussion) when we don't know the true μ_i and σ_i^2 and σ_{ij}:

Sample values
$$\overline{\boldsymbol{\mu}}_i = \frac{x_i^1 + \cdots + x_i^N}{N} \qquad \overline{\boldsymbol{\sigma}}_{ij} = \frac{\text{sum of } \left(x_i^k - \overline{\mu}_i\right)\left(x_j^k - \overline{\mu}_j\right)}{N-1}. \tag{19}$$

Notice the division by $N - 1$, when one degree of freedom is used in $\overline{\mu}$.

Suppose $p_{12}(x, y)$ is the *joint distribution* of two errors e_1 and e_2. This gives the probability that e_1 lies near x and e_2 lies near y. Then a double integral over all x and y gives the covariance of e_1 and e_2:

Covariance in continuous case
$$\sigma_{12} = \iint xy\, p_{12}(x, y)\, dx\, dy\,. \tag{20}$$

For *independent* errors, $p_{12}(x, y)$ is the product $p_1(x)p_2(y)$. Then the integral is $\sigma_{12} = 0$:

Independence
$$\sigma_{12} = \iint xy\, p_1(x)p_2(y)\, dx\, dy = \int x p_1(x)\, dx \int y p_2(y)\, dy = (0)(0).$$

Σ becomes a diagonal matrix, when e's are independent.

The diagonal entries of Σ are the variances σ^2. Those are the averages of e_i^2, necessarily positive. There is a neat way to put all variances and covariances into one matrix formula, using the column vector e times the row e^{T} (**Σ is symmetric**):

Covariance matrix
$$\boldsymbol{\Sigma} = \mathrm{E}[\boldsymbol{e}\boldsymbol{e}^{\mathrm{T}}] = \mathrm{E}\begin{bmatrix} e_1^2 & e_1e_2 & \cdots & e_1e_m \\ & & \cdots & \\ e_me_1 & e_me_2 & \cdots & e_m^2 \end{bmatrix}. \tag{21}$$

The average value of that product ee^{T} is Σ. This matrix is always symmetric and almost always positive definite! It is semidefinite when a fixed combination of the errors is zero all the time. That indicates a poor experiment, which we exclude.

The "correlation coefficient" $\sigma_{ij}/\sigma_i\sigma_j$ is dimensionless. The diagonal entries of the correlation matrix are $\sigma^2/\sigma^2 = 1$. Off-diagonals are ≤ 1. The concepts of "autocorrelation" and "power spectral density" are in many applications. These will employ Fourier techniques in Section 4.5.

We now show that the choice $C = \Sigma^{-1}$ minimizes the expected error in $\widehat{u}$.

The Weighting Matrix $C = \Sigma^{-1}$

The normal equation for any choice of C produces $\widehat{u} = Lb$:

$$\textbf{Weighted } \widehat{u} \qquad A^{\mathrm{T}}CA\widehat{u} = A^{\mathrm{T}}Cb \quad \text{gives} \quad \widehat{u} = (A^{\mathrm{T}}CA)^{-1}A^{\mathrm{T}}Cb = \boldsymbol{Lb}. \tag{22}$$

Notice that L times A, which is $(A^{\mathrm{T}}CA)^{-1}A^{\mathrm{T}}C$ times A, always gives $\boldsymbol{LA = I}$.

We want the covariance matrix (all the variances and covariances) for the error vector $u - \widehat{u}$. This is the *output* error (in our estimates), when $e = b - Au$ is the input error (in our measurements). Since $LA = I$ and $\widehat{u} = Lb$, this output error is $-Le$:

$$\textbf{Output error} \qquad u - \widehat{u} = LAu - Lb = L(Au - b) = -Le. \tag{23}$$

In equation (21), the matrix ee^{T} produced all the products e_ie_j. Similarly we multiply a column $u - \widehat{u}$ times its transpose to get an n by n matrix. The **covariance matrix** P for the error $u - \widehat{u}$ is the average value (expected value) of $(u - \widehat{u})(u - \widehat{u})^{\mathrm{T}}$:

$$\textbf{Covariance} \quad \boldsymbol{P} = \mathrm{E}\left[(u - \widehat{u})(u - \widehat{u})^{\mathrm{T}}\right] = \mathrm{E}\left[Lee^{\mathrm{T}}L^{\mathrm{T}}\right] = L\mathrm{E}\left[ee^{\mathrm{T}}\right]L^{\mathrm{T}} = \boldsymbol{L\Sigma L^{\mathrm{T}}}. \tag{24}$$

This is our key equation. The second step uses (23). The only new step was to bring the constant matrices L and L^{T} outside the sums or integrals for the expected value $\mathrm{E}\left[ee^{\mathrm{T}}\right]$. That is standard procedure, and it is called "propagation of variance." Now we are ready to minimize P, by choosing the best C in this matrix L.

> $\boldsymbol{P = L\Sigma L^{\mathrm{T}}}$ ***is as small as possible when the matrix used in*** $\boldsymbol{L}$ ***is*** $\boldsymbol{C = \Sigma^{-1}}$.
> **This gives the best linear unbiased estimate** $\widehat{\boldsymbol{u}}$ **(BLUE).**
>
> $$\textbf{Output covariances} \qquad \boldsymbol{P = \mathrm{E}\left[(u - \widehat{u})(u - \widehat{u})^{\mathrm{T}}\right] = \left(A^{\mathrm{T}}\Sigma^{-1}A\right)^{-1}}. \tag{25}$$

To check P, use $C = \Sigma^{-1}$ in the matrix L in (22). This choice gives a special L^*:

$$P = L^*\Sigma L^{*\mathrm{T}} = \left[(A^{\mathrm{T}}\Sigma^{-1}A)^{-1}A^{\mathrm{T}}\Sigma^{-1}\right]\Sigma\left[\Sigma^{-1}A(A^{\mathrm{T}}\Sigma^{-1}A)^{-1}\right] = (A^{\mathrm{T}}\Sigma^{-1}A)^{-1}. \tag{26}$$

A different choice of C gives a different L. To show that the change produces a larger covariance matrix P, write $L = L^* + (L - L^*)$. We still have $LA = I$ and $L^*A = I$, so $(L - L^*)A = 0$. Compute $P = L\Sigma L^{\mathrm{T}}$ for this different choice:

$$P = L^*\Sigma L^{*\mathrm{T}} + (L - L^*)\Sigma L^{*\mathrm{T}} + L^*\Sigma(L - L^*)^{\mathrm{T}} + (L - L^*)\Sigma(L - L^*)^{\mathrm{T}}. \tag{27}$$

The middle terms in (27) are transposes of one another, and they are both zero:

$$(L - L^*)\Sigma\left[\Sigma^{-1}A(A^{\mathrm{T}}\Sigma^{-1}A)^{-1}\right] = (\boldsymbol{LA} - \boldsymbol{L^*A})(A^{\mathrm{T}}\Sigma^{-1}A)^{-1} = 0. \tag{28}$$

The last term in (27) is positive semidefinite. That term is zero and P is smallest when $L = L^*$, now proved to be the best. Then the matrix $P^{-1} = A^{\mathrm{T}}\Sigma^{-1}A$ is called the **information matrix**. It goes up as Σ goes down (better observations). It also goes up as the experiment continues. Adding new rows to A increases $A^{\mathrm{T}}\Sigma^{-1}A$.

Note We can obtain $\Sigma = I$ (*whiten the noise*) by a change of variables. Factor Σ^{-1} into $W^{\mathrm{T}}W$. The normalized errors $\epsilon = We = W(b - Au)$ have $\Sigma = I$:

$$\textbf{Normalized covariance} \qquad \mathrm{E}\left[\epsilon\epsilon^{\mathrm{T}}\right] = W\,\mathrm{E}\left[ee^{\mathrm{T}}\right]W^{\mathrm{T}} = W\,\Sigma\,W^{\mathrm{T}} = \boldsymbol{I}.$$

This weighting returns us to white noise, $\sigma_i^2 = 1$ and $\sigma_{ij} = 0$. *Ordinary least squares.*

Recursive Least Squares by Example

Example 2 Suppose we have computed the average $\widehat{u}_{99}$ of 99 numbers $b_1, \ldots, b_{99}$. A new number b_{100} arrives. How can we find the new average $\widehat{u}_{100}$ of the 100 b's *without adding the first* 99 *all over again* (plus b_{100})? We want to use only $\widehat{u}_{99}$ and b_{100}.

Solution Here is the right combination $\widehat{u}_{100}$ of old and new, expressed two ways:

$$\textbf{New average} \qquad \widehat{u}_{100} = \frac{99}{100}\widehat{u}_{99} + \frac{1}{100}b_{100} = \boldsymbol{\widehat{u}_{99}} + \frac{\mathbf{1}}{\mathbf{100}}(\boldsymbol{b_{100}} - \boldsymbol{\widehat{u}_{99}}). \tag{29}$$

That first term $\frac{99}{100}\widehat{u}_{99}$ is $\frac{99}{100}$ times $\frac{1}{99}$ times $b_1 + b_2 + \cdots + b_{99}$. Canceling 99's, this is $\frac{1}{100}$ times the sum of 99 b's (without adding them again!). Adding the extra $\frac{1}{100}b_{100}$ gives the sum of all b's, divided by 100. This is the correct average of 100 b's.

I prefer the second form of the recursive formula (29). The right side is an **update of** $\boldsymbol{\widehat{u}_{99}}$, by a multiple of the **innovation** $\boldsymbol{b_{100} - \widehat{u}_{99}}$. That innovation tells how much "new information" is in b_{100}. When b_{100} equals the old average, the innovation is zero. In that case the updated $\widehat{u}_{100}$ is the old $\widehat{u}_{99}$, and correction = prediction.

The innovation is multiplied in the update formula (29) by $\frac{1}{100}$. This ***gain factor*** makes the formula correct. To see the gain factor for $Au = b$, start from the least squares solution $\widehat{u}_{\text{old}}$ to an equation $A_{\text{old}}u = b_{\text{old}}$. *New information arrives.* There are new measurements b_{new} and new rows of A.

$$\textbf{Combined system } \boldsymbol{Au = b} \qquad \begin{bmatrix} A_{\text{old}} \\ A_{\text{new}} \end{bmatrix} \begin{bmatrix} u \end{bmatrix} = \begin{bmatrix} b_{\text{old}} \\ b_{\text{new}} \end{bmatrix} \quad \text{leads to } \widehat{u}_{\text{new}}. \tag{30}$$

The estimate $\widehat{u}_{\text{new}}$ comes from this whole system $Au = b$. The data in b_{old} still contributes to $\widehat{u}_{\text{new}}$. But we don't want to do the same calculation twice.

Question *Can we update $\widehat{u}_{\text{old}}$ to $\widehat{u}_{\text{new}}$, by using only A_{new} and b_{new}?*

Answer Since $A^{\mathrm{T}} = \begin{bmatrix} A_{\text{old}}^{\mathrm{T}} & A_{\text{new}}^{\mathrm{T}} \end{bmatrix}$, we need $A^{\mathrm{T}}A$ in the normal equation:

$$\textbf{Update} \qquad \boldsymbol{A^{\mathrm{T}}A = A_{\text{old}}^{\mathrm{T}}A_{\text{old}} + A_{\text{new}}^{\mathrm{T}}A_{\text{new}}} = \textbf{(known)} + \textbf{(new)}. \tag{31}$$

On the right side of the normal equation is $A^{\mathrm{T}}b$, also involving old and new:

$$A^{\mathrm{T}}b = A_{\text{old}}^{\mathrm{T}}b_{\text{old}} + A_{\text{new}}^{\mathrm{T}}b_{\text{new}} = A_{\text{old}}^{\mathrm{T}}A_{\text{old}}\widehat{u}_{\text{old}} + A_{\text{new}}^{\mathrm{T}}b_{\text{new}}. \tag{32}$$

Substitute $A^{\mathrm{T}}A - A_{\text{new}}^{\mathrm{T}}A_{\text{new}}$ for $A_{\text{old}}^{\mathrm{T}}A_{\text{old}}$. Then multiply $A^{\mathrm{T}}b$ by $(A^{\mathrm{T}}A)^{-1}$ for $\widehat{u}_{\text{new}}$:

$$\widehat{u}_{\text{new}} = (A^{\mathrm{T}}A)^{-1}\left[(A^{\mathrm{T}}A - A_{\text{new}}^{\mathrm{T}}A_{\text{new}})\,\widehat{u}_{\text{old}} + A_{\text{new}}^{\mathrm{T}}b_{\text{new}}\right].$$

Our update formula simplifies that line to produce the new $\widehat{u}$ from the old:

$$\textbf{Recursive least squares} \qquad \boldsymbol{\widehat{u}_{\text{new}} = \widehat{u}_{\text{old}} + (A^{\mathrm{T}}A)^{-1}A_{\text{new}}^{\mathrm{T}}(b_{\text{new}} - A_{\text{new}}\widehat{u}_{\text{old}})}. \tag{33}$$

That last term $b_{\text{new}} - A_{\text{new}}\widehat{u}_{\text{old}}$ is the **innovation.** It is the error in our prediction of the measurements b_{new}. If this error is zero, the data b_{new} is exactly consistent with the old estimate. That case gives no reason to change, so in that case $\widehat{u}_{\text{new}} = \widehat{u}_{\text{old}}$.

In general the innovation $b_{\text{new}} - A_{\text{new}}\widehat{u}_{\text{old}}$ is not zero. Then (33) multiplies by the ***gain matrix*** $\boldsymbol{G = (A^{\mathrm{T}}A)^{-1}A^{\mathrm{T}}_{\text{new}}}$ to find the change in $\widehat{u}$. The gain matrix is the "amplifier" and it is often denoted by K (for Kalman). Since this book already uses K so often, the letter G will appear even in Kalman's own filter.

Notice that $A^{\mathrm{T}}A$ and $\widehat{u}$ in the updates (31) and (33) have size n, smaller than m.

Example 3 (completed) The average $\widehat{u}_{99} = \frac{1}{99}(b_1 + \cdots + b_{99})$ is the least squares solution to 99 equations in one unknown. The 99 by 1 matrix A_{old} is all ones:

$$\begin{bmatrix} 1 \\ \vdots \\ 1 \end{bmatrix} u = \begin{bmatrix} b_1 \\ \vdots \\ b_{99} \end{bmatrix} \qquad A^{\mathrm{T}}_{\text{old}}A_{\text{old}}\widehat{u}_{\text{old}} = A^{\mathrm{T}}_{\text{old}}b_{\text{old}} \quad \text{is} \quad 99\,\widehat{u}_{\text{old}} = b_1 + \cdots + b_{99}\,.$$

The 100th equation is $u = b_{100} = b_{\text{new}}$. The new row is $A_{\text{new}} = [\,1\,]$. Check everything:

(31) updates $\boldsymbol{A^{\mathrm{T}}A}$ $\qquad A^{\mathrm{T}}A = 99\,(\text{old}) + 1\,(\text{new}) = 100$

(33) updates $\boldsymbol{\widehat{u}}$ $\qquad \widehat{u}_{100} = \widehat{u}_{99} + \dfrac{1}{100}(b_{\text{new}} - A_{\text{new}}\widehat{u}_{\text{old}}) = \widehat{u}_{99} + \dfrac{1}{100}(b_{100} - \widehat{u}_{99})$

That update formula matches equation (29). The gain G is $(A^{\mathrm{T}}A)^{-1}A_{\text{new}} = \frac{1}{100}$.

Important You might think that $A^{\mathrm{T}}A = 100$ is only a useful step on the way to $\widehat{u}_{100}$. Not at all. In least squares, $A^{\mathrm{T}}A$ (and its inverse) can be more significant than the solution itself! When we include the weighting matrix $C = \Sigma^{-1}$, the update equation (31) gives $A^{\mathrm{T}}CA$. We already know why we want this matrix:

The inverse of $\boldsymbol{A^{\mathrm{T}}CA = A^{\mathrm{T}}\Sigma^{-1}A}$ measures the reliability $\boldsymbol{P}$ of $\boldsymbol{\widehat{u}}$.

In the example of 100 equations, the b_i were equally reliable. They had the same variance σ^2. Their sum has variance $100\sigma^2$. The weighting matrix is $C = I/\sigma^2$ (as we chose when $\sigma^2 = 1$). Then the inverse of $A^{\mathrm{T}}CA = 100/\sigma^2$ correctly measures the reliability of their average $\widehat{u}_{100}$.

If 100 samples have the same $\boldsymbol{\sigma^2}$, their average has variance $\boldsymbol{\sigma^2/100}$.

Recursive least squares updates the matrix $P = (A^{\mathrm{T}}\Sigma^{-1}A)^{-1}$ while it is updating $\widehat{u}$.

Kalman Filter by Example

The Kalman filter applies to ***time-varying least squares***. The state u is changing. In discrete time, we produce an estimate $\widehat{u}_i$ at each time $t = i$. Earlier measurements still give information about this current state, so those b's are included in computing $\widehat{u}_i$. They might count less, but they still count.

Example 4 Stay with one unknown u, your heart rate. The doctor measures it as b_1, and then later as b_2. If there is no reason to expect change, the best estimate $\widehat{u}$ will be the average $\frac{1}{2}(b_1 + b_2)$. But if pulse rates are expected to slow down with age, a "state equation" will express *the expected change c_1 over that time interval*:

$$\textbf{State equation} \qquad u_2 - u_1 = c_1 \quad + \text{ error } \epsilon_1 . \tag{34}$$

Now we have three equations for two states u_1 and u_2. They are linked by (34):

$$\textbf{Observations and state equations} \qquad \begin{aligned} u_1 \qquad &= b_1 \\ -u_1 + u_2 &= c_1 \\ u_2 &= b_2 \end{aligned} \quad \text{is} \quad \begin{bmatrix} A_{\text{old}} \\ A_{\text{state}} \\ A_{\text{new}} \end{bmatrix} \begin{bmatrix} u_{\text{old}} \\ u_{\text{new}} \end{bmatrix} = \begin{bmatrix} b_{\text{old}} \\ c_{\text{state}} \\ b_{\text{new}} \end{bmatrix} . \tag{35}$$

Important There are errors in all three equations. The state equation is not exact, because our hearts don't all slow down the same way. The state error ϵ_1 in (34) has its own variance v_1^2. We do assume that the errors e_1, ϵ_1, e_2 are independent, which makes a recursive computation (the Kalman filter) possible.

The state u_i is often a *vector*, with components like position and velocity (think of tracking a space satellite, or GPS in a moving vehicle). Then (34) predicts new positions u_{i+1} from old u_i. In general there will be covariance matrices Σ_i and V_i for the measurement errors in b_i and the state equation errors in $u_{i+1} = F_i u_i + c_i$.

Solution The (weighted) least squares principle for (35) still gives $\widehat{u}_1$ and $\widehat{u}_2$:

$$\text{Minimize} \quad E = \frac{1}{\sigma_1^2}(b_1 - u_1)^2 + \frac{1}{v_1^2}(c_1 + u_1 - u_2)^2 + \frac{1}{\sigma_2^2}(b_2 - u_2)^2 . \tag{36}$$

The weighted normal equations $A^{\mathrm{T}}CA = A^{\mathrm{T}}Cb$ will have $C^{-1} = \operatorname{diag}(\sigma_1^2, v_1^2, \sigma_2^2)$:

$$\begin{matrix} \textbf{With } \boldsymbol{C = I} \\ \boldsymbol{\sigma_1 = \sigma_2 = v_1 = 1} \end{matrix} \qquad \begin{bmatrix} 2 & -1 \\ -1 & 2 \end{bmatrix} \begin{bmatrix} \widehat{u}_1 \\ \widehat{u}_2 \end{bmatrix} = \begin{bmatrix} b_1 - c_1 \\ b_2 + c_1 \end{bmatrix} \quad \text{gives} \quad \begin{aligned} \widehat{u}_1 &= \tfrac{1}{3}(2b_1 + b_2 - c_1) \\ \boldsymbol{\widehat{u}_2} &= \boldsymbol{\tfrac{1}{3}(b_1 + 2b_2 + c_1)} \end{aligned} \tag{37}$$

The latest estimate $\widehat{u}_2$ gives a heavier weight $\frac{2}{3}$ to the latest measurement b_2.

Now compute recursively. *The key point is that $A^{\mathrm{T}}CA$ is a tridiagonal matrix.* (It will be *block* tridiagonal when the state u is a vector.) Measurement equations $A_i u_i = b_i$ are connected by state equations $u_{i+1} = F_i u_i + c_i$. Forward elimination on the tridiagonal matrix $A^{\mathrm{T}}CA$ is always a recursion for a multiplier and a pivot. Then back-substitution is a second recursion, backward in time.

Key fact By itself, the forward recursion finds the best estimate of $\widehat{u}_{i|i}$ based on measurements and state equations *up to and including time $t = i$*. Very often an estimate $\widehat{u}_{n|n}$ of the final state is all we want! Then forget about back-substitution.

The back-substitution step adjusts the earlier $\widehat{u}_{i|i}$ to account for *later* measurements and state equations, after time i. Going back in this way is called "smoothing." It produces the correct solutions $\widehat{u}_{i|n}$ to the normal equations $A^{\mathrm{T}}CA\widehat{u} = A^{\mathrm{T}}Cb$.

Even the forward recursion to find $\widehat{u}_{i|i}$ is a two-step process. The previous $\widehat{u}_{i-1|i-1}$ uses all information through time $i-1$. *The next state equation gives a* ***prediction****. Then the measurement b_i adds a* ***correction***. Together Kalman's filter produces $\widehat{u}_{i|i}$:

Prediction	$\widehat{\boldsymbol{u}}_{i\|i-1} = \boldsymbol{F}_{i-1}\widehat{\boldsymbol{u}}_{i-1\|i-1} + \boldsymbol{c}_i$	(38)
Correction	$\widehat{\boldsymbol{u}}_{i\|i} = \widehat{\boldsymbol{u}}_{i\|i-1} + \boldsymbol{G}_i(\boldsymbol{b}_i - \boldsymbol{A}_i\,\widehat{\boldsymbol{u}}_{i\|i-1})$	(39)

That correction is written as an update using the **gain matrix G_i**. The new data are c_i and b_i. We are solving the complete system $Au = b$ by least squares, adding in one equation at a time.

As in recursive least squares, there is something more to compute—the reliability of these estimates $\widehat{u}_{i|i}$. The latest covariance matrix $P_{i|i} = (A^{\mathrm{T}}CA)_i^{-1}$ is updated recursively too! Each Kalman filter step adds a (block) row to A and C, and a (block) column to A^{T} and C. The prediction-correction steps compute $P_{i|i-1}$ and $P_{i|i}$, the variances of the errors in $\widehat{u}_{i|i-1}$ and $\widehat{u}_{i|i}$.

It is fair to say that the Kalman filter formulas get complicated, even if the plan is straightforward. All authors try to find a clear way to derive the matrix equations for $\widehat{u}_{i|i}$ and $P_{i|i}$. (There are multiple forms that give numerically different recursions. They all use variations of the Woodbury-Morrison **matrix inversion lemma** in Problem 14.) **Square-root filters** using LDL^{T} or QR were developed to reduce numerical instability when variances become very small or very large. We refer to [100] among many possible descriptions of the Kalman filter. Our own presentation in [143] went so far as to quote a reader who "just asks for the damn formula."

The essential point is that the covariance matrices $P_{i|i}$ have the same size as the states u_i. That size is independent of the number m_i of measurements at step i. If we are updating the best fit by a straight line, our matrices remain 2 by 2.

Example 4 (heart rates) Find P and $\widehat{u}$ recursively, with $C = I$ (unit variances):

Start from $u_1 = b_1$ $\quad A_{1|1} = [1]$ gives $P_{1|1} = (A^{\mathrm{T}}A)^{-1}_{1|1} = [1]$

Add $u_2 - u_1 = c_1$ $\quad A_{2|1} = \begin{bmatrix} 1 & 0 \\ -1 & 1 \end{bmatrix}$ and $(A^{\mathrm{T}}A)^{-1}_{2|1} = \begin{bmatrix} 1 & 1 \\ 1 & \mathbf{2} \end{bmatrix}$ give $P_{2|1} = \mathbf{2}$

Include $u_2 = b_2$ $\quad A_{2|2} = \begin{bmatrix} 1 & 0 \\ -1 & 1 \\ 0 & 1 \end{bmatrix}$ and $(A^{\mathrm{T}}A)^{-1}_{2|2} = \dfrac{\mathbf{1}}{\mathbf{3}}\begin{bmatrix} 2 & 1 \\ 1 & \mathbf{2} \end{bmatrix}$ give $P_{2|2} = \dfrac{\mathbf{2}}{\mathbf{3}}$

The first estimate is $\widehat{u}_{1|1} = b_1$ (not smoothed!). The next prediction is $\widehat{u}_{2|1} = b_1 + c_2$, using the state equation. The correction is $\frac{1}{3}(b_1 + 2b_2 + c_1)$, using the final $A_{2|2}$.

Those variances $P_{2|1} = 2$ and $P_{2|2} = \frac{2}{3}$ are the last entries in $(A^{\mathrm{T}}A)^{-1}_{2|1}$ and $(A^{\mathrm{T}}A)^{-1}_{2|2}$. Vectors u_i lead to *block* pivots P^{-1}. Here 2 and $\frac{2}{3}$ are also seen as the sum of squares of coefficients in $b_1 + c_1$ and $\frac{1}{3}(b_1 + 2b_2 + c_1)$.

Back-substitution (smoothing) adjusts $\widehat{u}_{1|1} = b_1$ to $\widehat{u}_1 = \frac{1}{3}(2b_1 + b_2 - c_1)$ as in (37).

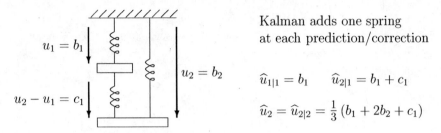

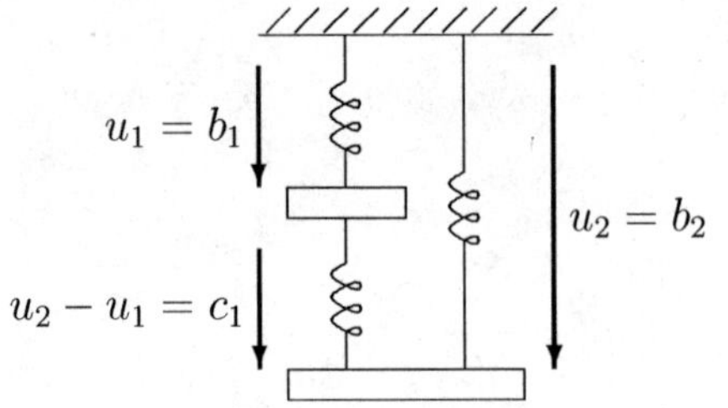

Kalman adds one spring at each prediction/correction

$\widehat{u}_{1|1} = b_1 \qquad \widehat{u}_{2|1} = b_1 + c_1$

$\widehat{u}_2 = \widehat{u}_{2|2} = \frac{1}{3}(b_1 + 2b_2 + c_1)$

Figure 2.36: Mass-spring equivalent of the observation and state equations (35).

Problem Set 2.8

1 After $N = 4$ coin flips (binomial distribution) what are the five probabilities $p_0, \ldots, p_4$ of $M = 0, \ldots, 4$ heads? Find the mean $\overline{M} = \sum M\, p_M$. Show that the variance $\sigma^2 = \sum (M - \overline{M})^2 p_M$ agrees with $N/4 = 1$.

2 (a) At the center of Figure 2.35 with $N = 4$ and $\sigma^2 = N/4 = 1$, check that the actual height $p_2 = \frac{6}{16}$ is a little below the Gaussian $p(x) = 1/\sqrt{2\pi}\,\sigma$.

(b) The center of the Gaussian with $\sigma = \sqrt{N}/2$ has height $\sqrt{2/\pi N}$. Using *Stirling's approximation to* $N!$ *and* $(N/2)!$, show that the middle binomial coefficient $p_{N/2}$ approaches that height:

$$\left(\boldsymbol{M = \frac{N}{2}}\right) \qquad p_{N/2} = \frac{N!}{[(N/2)!]^2} \approx \frac{(N/e)^N\sqrt{2\pi N}}{[(N/2e)^{N/2}\sqrt{\pi N}]^2} = \underline{\quad ? \quad}$$

3 The variance $\sigma^2 = \sum (n - \overline{n}) p_n$ is computed around the mean $\overline{n} = \sum n\, p_n$. Show that this σ^2 equals $(\sum n^2 p_n) - \overline{n}^2$.

4 Imagine a line of masses $p_0, \ldots, p_n$ at the points $x = 0, \ldots, n$. Explain how the mean $\mathrm{E}[x]$ corresponds to the center of mass, and the variance σ^2 is the moment of inertia (around what point?).

5 Start with r *independent* random variables $X_1, \ldots, X_r$ with variances $\sigma_1^2, \ldots, \sigma_r^2$. Show that the sum $X = X_1 + \cdots + X_r$ has variance $\sigma_1^2 + \cdots + \sigma_r^2$.

6 One flip of a weighted coin has $M = 1$ (heads) with probability p and $M = 0$ (tails) with probability $q = 1 - p$. What are the mean $\overline{M}$ and the variance σ^2? What are the mean and variance for the number M of heads after N coin flips?

7 What would you change in Example 2 if every number is *rounded down* to the nearest integer? The distribution of e is still uniform, but on what interval of e's? What is the mean m? What is the variance around the mean $\int (x - m)^2 dx$?

8 The random variable X has mean $\int X p(X)\, dX = \mu$. Its variance σ^2 is $\int (X-\mu)^2 p(X)\, dX$. Note that we square distances *from the mean.*

(a) Show that the new variable $Y = aX + b$ has mean $a\mu + b$.

(b) Show that the variance of Y is $a^2\sigma^2$.

9 Suppose X is a vector of random variables, each with mean zero, and $Y = LX$ is related to X by a fixed matrix L (m by n). Derive from (21) the "Law of Covariance Propagation" which brings L and L^{T} outside:

$$\Sigma_Y = L\,\Sigma_X\, L^{\mathrm{T}} \quad \text{or} \quad \mathrm{E}\left[YY^{\mathrm{T}}\right] = L\,\mathrm{E}\left[XX^{\mathrm{T}}\right] L^{\mathrm{T}}.$$

Problems 10-13 give experience with a small-size Kalman filter.

10 Extend the matrix A in (35) to 5 by 3 with $u_3 - u_2 = c_2$ and a new measurement $u_3 = b_3$. With unit variances in $C = I$, solve $A^{\mathrm{T}}A\widehat{u} = A^{\mathrm{T}}b$ for the best estimates $\widehat{u}_1, \widehat{u}_2, \widehat{u}_3$.

11 In Problem 10, continue the Kalman recursion from $\widehat{u}_{2|2}$ in the text to predict $\widehat{u}_{3|2}$ and correct to $\widehat{u}_{3|3}$. As in (37), find their variances $P_{3|2}$ and $P_{3|3}$ from the last entries in $(A^{\mathrm{T}}A)^{-1}_{3|2}$ and $(A^{\mathrm{T}}A)^{-1}$.

12 In this Kalman example, the determinants of $A^{\mathrm{T}}A$ come from the Fibonacci numbers $1, 1, 2, 3, 5, 8, \ldots$ as new rows are added to A. Find the three pivots of $(A^{\mathrm{T}}A)_{3|3}$ as *ratios of Fibonacci numbers*:

$$A^{\mathrm{T}}A = \begin{bmatrix} 2 & -1 & 0 \\ -1 & 3 & -1 \\ 0 & -1 & 2 \end{bmatrix} = LDL^{\mathrm{T}} \quad \text{with pivots in } D.$$

13 For $\sigma_1^2 = \sigma_2^2 = 1$ and any v_1^2 in (36), the covariance matrix is $\Sigma = \mathsf{diag}(1, v_1^2, 1)$. Solve $A^{\mathrm{T}}\Sigma^{-1}A\widehat{u} = A^{\mathrm{T}}\Sigma^{-1}b$. What are the limiting values of $\widehat{u}_i$, as $v_1 \to 0$?

14 M^{-1} shows the change in A^{-1} (useful to know) when a matrix is subtracted from A. Direct multiplication gives $MM^{-1} = I$. I recommend doing #3:

1 $M = I - uv$ and $M^{-1} = I + uv/(1 - vu)$
2 $M = A - uv$ and $M^{-1} = A^{-1} + A^{-1}uvA^{-1}/(1 - vA^{-1}u)$
3 $M = I - UV$ and $M^{-1} = I_n + U(I_m - VU)^{-1}V$
4 $M = A - UW^{-1}V$ and $M^{-1} = A^{-1} + A^{-1}U(W - VA^{-1}U)^{-1}VA^{-1}$

The **Woodbury-Morrison formula 4** is the "matrix inversion lemma" in engineering. The four identities come from the 1,1 block when inverting these matrices (v is 1 by n, u is n by 1, V is m by n, U is n by m, $m \le n$):

$$\begin{bmatrix} I & u \\ v & 1 \end{bmatrix} \qquad \begin{bmatrix} A & u \\ v & 1 \end{bmatrix} \qquad \begin{bmatrix} I_n & U \\ V & I_m \end{bmatrix} \qquad \begin{bmatrix} A & U \\ V & W \end{bmatrix}$$

15 From Figure 2.34, the chance that a sample from the normal distribution lies more than 2σ from the mean is about .4 or .5. Give an exact formula using the error function.

16 Show how $S = x^2$ changes the Gaussian $\int p(x)\,dx = 1$ into the chi-square $\int p_1(S)\,dS = 1$ (*not* $\frac{1}{2}$):

$$\int_{-\infty}^{\infty} \frac{1}{\sqrt{2\pi}} e^{-x^2/2}\,dx = 1 \quad \text{becomes} \quad \int_{0}^{\infty} \frac{1}{\sqrt{2\pi S}} e^{-S/2}\,dS = 1\,.$$

17 Suppose the outcomes $x_i \geq 0$ occur with probabilities $p_i > 0$ (and $\sum p_i = 1$). Markov's inequality says that for any $\lambda > 0$,

$$\text{Prob}\,[x \geq \lambda] \leq \frac{\mu}{\lambda} \quad \text{since} \quad \mu = \sum p_i x_i \geq \lambda \sum_{x_i \geq \lambda} p_i\,. \quad \text{Explain that step.}$$

Chebyshev's inequality is $\text{Prob}\,[|x-\mu| \geq \lambda] = \text{Prob}\,[|x-\mu|^2 \geq \lambda^2] \leq \sigma^2/\lambda^2$. This is Markov's inequality with λ changed to λ^2 and x_i changed to $(x_i - \mu)^2$.

∗ 2.9 GRAPH CUTS AND GENE CLUSTERING

This section has an extraordinary number ∗2.9, because it is not an ordinary section. The theory and algorithms and applications are far from attaining steady state. The one certainty is that the problems are important. Often they are best expressed in the language of *graphs* (the nodes and edges and incidence matrix A and "graph Laplacian" $A^{\mathrm{T}}CA = D - W$ of Section 2.4). This section could fit into the final chapter on optimization, but I am unwilling to bury the exciting problems of clustering where you won't see them. Here is a first application.

A DNA microarray measures the expression levels of thousands of genes in a single experiment. That produces one long column in a matrix G. For convenience this column may be placed in a rectangular array. It can be visualized in color (as on the back cover of this book). G is a tall thin matrix, because samples from 20 patients give 20 columns and thousands of rows.

A key step in understanding this data set is to *cluster the genes* that show highly correlated (and sometimes anti-correlated!) expression levels. Those genes may lie in the same cellular pathway. The great achievement of the Human Genome project was to tell us the pieces in the puzzle of life: the rows of G. We now face the greater problem of fitting those pieces together to produce *function*: such as creating proteins.

Three Methods for Partitioning

Out of many applications, we start with this one: **to break a graph in two pieces**. We are aiming for two clusters of nodes, with these objectives:

1. Each piece should contain roughly half of the nodes.

2. The number of edges between the pieces should be small.

For load balancing in high performance computing, we are assigning equal work to two processors (with small communication between them). We are breaking a social network into two distinct groups. We are segmenting an image. We are reordering rows and columns of a matrix to make off-diagonal blocks sparse.

Many algorithms have been and will be invented for this partitioning problem. I will focus on three successful methods that extend to more difficult problems: **Spectral clustering** (Fiedler vector), **minimum normalized cut**, **weighted *k*-means**.

I. Find the **Fiedler vector** z that solves $A^{\mathrm{T}}CAz = \lambda Dz$. The matrix $A^{\mathrm{T}}CA$ is the graph Laplacian (among many other meanings). Its diagonal D contains the total weights on edges into each of the nodes. *D normalizes the Laplacian.*

The eigenvector for $\lambda_1 = 0$ is $(1, \ldots, 1)$. The Fiedler eigenvector has $\lambda = \lambda_2$. Its positive and negative components can indicate the two clusters of nodes.

II. Find the **minimum normalized cut** that separates the nodes in two clusters P and Q. The unnormalized measure of a cut is the sum of edge weights w_{ij} across that cut. Those edges connect a node in P to a node outside P:

Weight across cut $$\mathit{links}(P) = \sum w_{ij} \quad \text{for } i \text{ in } P \text{ and } j \text{ not in } P. \qquad (1)$$

By this measure, a minimum cut could have no nodes in P. *We normalize by the sizes of P and Q.* The weights are involved, so these are weighted sizes:

Size of cluster $$\mathit{size}(P) = \sum w_{ij} \quad \text{for } i \text{ in } P. \qquad (2)$$

Note that an edge inside P is counted twice, as w_{ij} and w_{ji}. The unweighted size would just count the nodes, and lead to "ratio cut." Here we divide weight across the cut by the weighted sizes of P and Q, to normalize *Ncut*:

Normalized cut weight $$Ncut(P, Q) = \frac{links(P)}{size(P)} + \frac{links(Q)}{size(Q)}. \qquad (3)$$

Minimizing $Ncut(P, Q)$ gives a good partitioning of the graph, as Shi and Malik found in their outstanding paper [137]. That application was to segmentation of images. They uncovered the crucial connection to the normalized Laplacian L.

The definition of *Ncut* extends from two clusters of nodes to k clusters $P_1, \ldots, P_k$:

Normalized k-cut $$Ncut(P_1, \ldots, P_k) = \sum_{i=1}^{k} \frac{links(P_i)}{size(P_i)} \qquad (4)$$

We are coming close to **k-means clustering**. Start with $k = 2$ clusters (P and Q).

III. Represent the nodes as vectors $a_1, \ldots, a_n$. Separate them into two clusters:

2-means clustering
c_P, c_Q = centroids
$$\text{Minimize } E = \sum_{i \text{ in } P} ||a_i - c_P||^2 + \sum_{i \text{ in } Q} ||a_i - c_Q||^2 \qquad (5)$$

The *centroid* c_P of a set of vectors is its *mean* or *average*. Divide the sum of all vectors in P by the number of vectors in P. Thus $c_P = (\sum a_i)/|P|$.

The vector a_i may or may not represent the physical location of node i. So the clustering objective E is not restricted to Euclidean distance. The more general **kernel k-means** algorithm works entirely with a kernel matrix K that assigns inner products $K_{ij} = a_i^{\mathrm{T}} a_j$. Distances and means are computed from a weighted K.

The distance measure E will also be weighted, to improve the clusters P and Q.

The Normalized Laplacian Matrix

The first step to L is $A^{\mathrm{T}}A$ (A = incidence matrix of the graph, m by n). Off the diagonal, the i, j entry of $A^{\mathrm{T}}A$ is -1 if an edge connects nodes i and j. The diagonal entries make all row sums zero. Then $(A^{\mathrm{T}}A)_{ii}$ = number of edges into node i = degree of node i. Before any weighting, $A^{\mathrm{T}}A$ = *degree matrix – adjacency matrix*.

The edge weights in C can be conductances or spring constants or edge lengths. They appear on and off the diagonal of $\boldsymbol{A^{\mathrm{T}}CA = D - W}$ = **node weight matrix – edge weight matrix**. Off the diagonal, the entries of $-W$ are minus the weights w_{ij}. The diagonal entries d_i still make all row sums zero: $D = \mathsf{diag}(\mathsf{sum}(W))$.

The all-ones vector $\mathbf{1} = \mathsf{ones}(n, 1)$ is in the nullspace of $A^{\mathrm{T}}CA$, because $A\mathbf{1} = 0$. Each row of A has 1 and -1. Equivalently, $D\mathbf{1}$ cancels $W\mathbf{1}$ (row sums are zero). The next eigenvector is like the lowest vibration mode of a drum, with $\lambda_2 > 0$.

For the **normalized weighted Laplacian**, multiply $A^{\mathrm{T}}CA$ on the left and right by $D^{-1/2}$, preserving symmetry. Row i and column j are divided by $\sqrt{d_i}$ and $\sqrt{d_j}$, so the i, j entry of $A^{\mathrm{T}}CA$ is divided by $\sqrt{d_i d_j}$. The diagonal entries of L are $d_i/d_i = 1$:

Normalized Laplacian L
Normalized weights n_{ij}

$$L = D^{-1/2}\,A^{\mathrm{T}}CA\,D^{-1/2} = I - N \qquad n_{ij} = \frac{w_{ij}}{\sqrt{d_i d_j}} \tag{6}$$

A triangle graph has $n = 3$ nodes and $m = 3$ edge weights $c_1, c_2, c_3 = w_{12}, w_{13}, w_{23}$:

$$\boldsymbol{A^{\mathrm{T}}CA} = \begin{bmatrix} d_1 & -w_{12} & -w_{13} \\ -w_{21} & d_2 & -w_{23} \\ -w_{31} & -w_{32} & d_3 \end{bmatrix} \quad \begin{matrix} d_1 = w_{12} + w_{13} \\ d_2 = w_{21} + w_{23} \\ d_3 = w_{31} + w_{32} \end{matrix} \quad \boldsymbol{L} = \begin{bmatrix} 1 & -n_{12} & -n_{13} \\ -n_{21} & 1 & -n_{23} \\ -n_{31} & -n_{32} & 1 \end{bmatrix} \tag{7}$$

$$\boldsymbol{D - W} \qquad\qquad \boldsymbol{D^{-1/2}A^{\mathrm{T}}CA\,D^{-1/2}}$$

The normalized Laplacian $L = I - N$ is like a *correlation matrix* in statistics, with unit diagonal. Three of its properties are crucial for clustering:

1. L is symmetric positive definite: orthogonal eigenvectors, all eigenvalues $\lambda \geq 0$.

2. The eigenvector for $\lambda = 0$ is $\boldsymbol{u} = (\sqrt{d_1}, \ldots, \sqrt{d_n})$. Then $L\boldsymbol{u} = D^{-1/2}A^{\mathrm{T}}CA\mathbf{1} = 0$.

3. The next eigenvector $\boldsymbol{v}$ of L minimizes the **Rayleigh quotient** on a subspace:

First nonzero eigenvalue of L
Minimize subject to $x^{\mathrm{T}}u = 0$

$$\min \frac{x^{\mathrm{T}}Lx}{x^{\mathrm{T}}x} = \frac{v^{\mathrm{T}}Lv}{v^{\mathrm{T}}v} = \lambda \text{ at } x = v \tag{8}$$

The quotient $x^{\mathrm{T}}Lx/x^{\mathrm{T}}x$ gives an upper bound for λ_2, for any x orthogonal to the first eigenvector $\boldsymbol{u} = D^{1/2}\mathbf{1}$. A good lower bound on λ_2 is more difficult to find.

Normalized versus Unnormalized

The algorithms of clustering could use the unnormalized matrix $A^{\mathrm{T}}CA$. But L usually gives better results. The connection between them is $Lv = D^{-1/2}A^{\mathrm{T}}CAD^{-1/2}v = \lambda v$. With $z = D^{-1/2}v$ this has the simple and important form $A^{\mathrm{T}}CAz = \lambda Dz$:

Normalized Fiedler vector $\boldsymbol{z}$ $\quad A^{\mathrm{T}}CA\boldsymbol{z} = \lambda D\boldsymbol{z} \quad \text{with} \quad \mathbf{1}^{\mathrm{T}}D\boldsymbol{z} = 0$ (9)

For this "generalized" eigenvalue problem, the eigenvector for $\lambda = 0$ is $\mathbf{1} = \text{ones}(n, 1)$. The next eigenvector $\boldsymbol{z}$ is D-orthogonal to $\mathbf{1}$, which means $\mathbf{1}^{\mathrm{T}}D\boldsymbol{z} = 0$ (Section 2.2). By changing x to $D^{1/2}y$, the Rayleigh quotient will find that second eigenvector $\boldsymbol{z}$:

Same eigenvalue λ_2
Fiedler $\boldsymbol{z} = D^{-1/2}\boldsymbol{v}$

$$\min_{\mathbf{1}^{\mathrm{T}}D\boldsymbol{y}=0} \frac{y^{\mathrm{T}}A^{\mathrm{T}}CAy}{y^{\mathrm{T}}Dy} = \frac{\sum\sum w_{ij}(y_i - y_j)^2}{\sum d_i\, y_i^2} = \lambda_2 \text{ at } y = z. \quad (10)$$

In Ay, the incidence matrix A gives the differences $y_i - y_j$. C multiplies them by w_{ij}.

The first eigenvector of $D^{-1}A^{\mathrm{T}}CA$ is $\mathbf{1}$, with $\lambda = 0$. The next eigenvector is $\boldsymbol{z}$.

Note *Some authors call $\boldsymbol{v}$ the Fiedler vector*. We prefer to work with $\boldsymbol{z} = D^{-1/2}\boldsymbol{v}$. Then $A^{\mathrm{T}}CA\boldsymbol{z} = \lambda_2 D\boldsymbol{z}$. Experiments seem to give similar clusters from $\boldsymbol{v}$ and $\boldsymbol{z}$. Those weighted degrees d_i (the sum of edge weights into node i) have normalized the ordinary $A^{\mathrm{T}}CA$ eigenvalue problem, to improve the partition.

Example 1 A 20-node graph has two 10-node clusters P and Q (to find from z).

The following code creates edges within P and within Q, with probability 0.7. Edges between nodes in P and Q have smaller probability 0.1. All edges have weights $w_{ij} = 1$, so $C = I$. P and Q are obvious from the graph but not from its adjacency matrix W.

With $G = A^{\mathrm{T}}A$, the eigenvalue command $[V, E] = \text{eig}(G, D)$ solves $A^{\mathrm{T}}Ax = \lambda Dx$. Sorting the λ's leads to λ_2 and its Fiedler vector z. The third graph shows how the components of z fall into two clusters (plus and minus), to give a good reordering.

```
N = 10; W = zeros(2*N, 2*N);                % Generate 2N nodes in two clusters
rand('state', 100)                          % rand repeats to give the same graph
for i = 1:2*N-1
   for j = i+1:2*N
      p = 0.7-0.6 * mod(j-i, 2);            % p = 0.1 when j - i is odd, 0.7 else
      W(i, j) = rand < p;                   % Insert edges with probability p
   end                                      % The weights are w_ij = 1 (or zero)
end                                         % So far W is strictly upper triangular
W = W + W'; D = diag(sum(W));               % Adjacency matrix W, degrees in D
G = D-W; [V, E] = eig(G, D);                % Eigenvalues of Gx = λDx in E
[a, b] = sort(diag(E)); z = V(:, b(2));     % Fiedler eigenvector z for λ2
plot(sort(z), '.-');                        % Show groups of Fiedler components
```

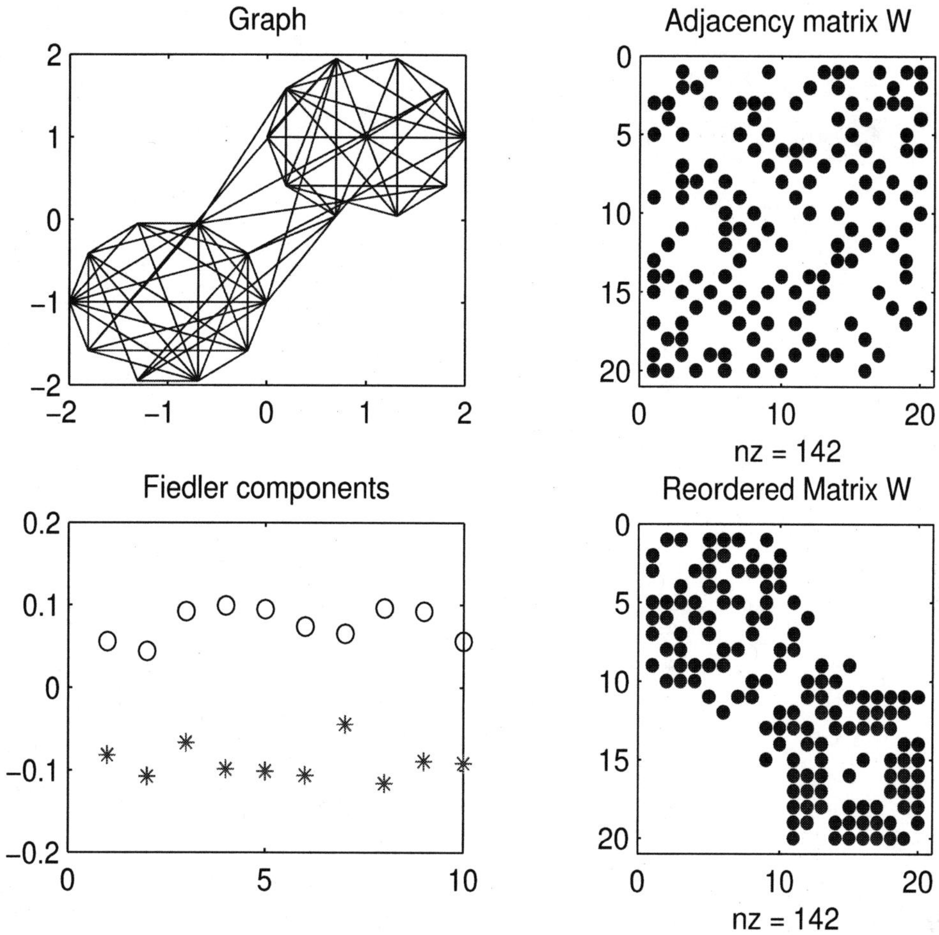


```
theta = [1:N] * 2 * pi/N; x = zeros(2*N, 1); y = x;   % Angles to plot graph
x(1:2:2*N-1) = cos(theta)-1; x(2:2:2*N) = cos(theta)+1;
y(1:2:2*N-1) = sin(theta)-1; y(2:2:2*N) = sin(theta)+1;
subplot(2, 2, 1), gplot(W, [x, y]), title ('Graph')          % First of four plots
subplot(2, 2, 2), spy(W), title ('Adjacency matrix W')      % Clusters unclear in W
subplot(2, 2, 3), plot(z(1:2:2*N-1), 'ko'), hold on         % z separates clusters
plot(z(2:2:2*N), 'r*'), hold off, title ('Fiedler components')
[c, d] = sort(z); subplot(2, 2, 4), spy(W(d, d)), title ('Reordered Matrix W')
```

Why would we solve an eigenvalue problem $Lv = \lambda v$ (usually expensive) as a first step in reordering a linear system $Ax = b$? One answer is that we don't need an accurate eigenvector v. A "hierarchical" *multilevel method* clumps nodes together to give a smaller L and a satisfactory v. The fastest k-means algorithms coarsen the graph level by level, and then adjust the coarse clustering during the refinement phase. This approach can use only $O(n)$ memory for multilevel cuts in large data sets.

Application to Microarray Data

Microarray data comes as a matrix M from m genes and n samples. Its entries m_{ij} record the activity (expression level) of gene i in sample j. The n by n weight matrix $M^{\mathrm{T}}M$ measures the similarity between samples (the nodes in a complete graph).

The off-diagonal entries of $M^{\mathrm{T}}M$ enter W. The row sums of W go into D. Then $D - W$ is the weighted Laplacian matrix $A^{\mathrm{T}}CA$. We solve $A^{\mathrm{T}}CAz = \lambda Dz$.

The valuable paper [88] by Higham, Kalna, and Kibble ends with a report of tests on three data sets. Those involve leukemia ($m = 5000$ genes, $n = 38$ patients), brain tumors ($m = 7129$, $n = 40$), and lymphoma. "The normalized spectral algorithm is far superior to the unnormalized version at revealing biologically relevant information."

The experiments also show how the *next eigenvector after Fiedler* helps to produce $k = 3$ clusters. The k lowest eigenvalues provide eigenvectors to identify k clusters.

Cuts Connected to Eigenvectors

How is the graph cut separating P from Q related to the Fiedler eigenvector in $A^{\mathrm{T}}CAz = \lambda Dz$? The crucial link comes from comparing $Ncut(P,Q)$ in (5) with the Rayleigh quotient $y^{\mathrm{T}}A^{\mathrm{T}}CAy/y^{\mathrm{T}}Dy$ in (10). The perfect indicator of a cut would be a vector y with all components equal to p or $-q$ (two values only):

Two values Node i goes in P if $y_i = p$ Node i goes in Q if $y_i = -q$

$\mathbf{1}^{\mathrm{T}}Dy$ will multiply one group of d_i by p and the other group by $-q$. The first d_i add to $size(P)$ = sum of w_{ij} (i in P) = sum of d_i (i in P). The second group of d_i adds to $size(Q)$. **The constraint $\mathbf{1}^{\mathrm{T}}\boldsymbol{Dy} = 0$ becomes $\boldsymbol{p}\ \boldsymbol{size}(\boldsymbol{P}) = \boldsymbol{q}\ \boldsymbol{size}(\boldsymbol{Q})$.**

When we substitute this y into the Rayleigh quotient, we get exactly $Ncut(P,Q)$! The differences $y_i - y_j$ are zero inside P and Q. They are $p + q$ across the cut:

Numerator $$y^{\mathrm{T}}A^{\mathrm{T}}CAy = \sum\sum w_{ij}\,(y_i - y_j)^2 = (p+q)^2\, links(P,Q) \qquad (11)$$

Denominator $$y^{\mathrm{T}}Dy = p^2\, size(P) + q^2\, size(Q) = p\,(p\, size(P)) + q\,(p\, size(P)). \qquad (12)$$

That last step used $p\ size(P) = q\ size(Q)$. Cancel $p + q$ in the quotient:

Rayleigh quotient $$\frac{(p+q)\ links(P,Q)}{p\ size(P)} = \frac{p\ links(P,Q)}{p\ size(P)} + \frac{q\ links(P,Q)}{q\ size(Q)} = Ncut(P,Q). \qquad (13)$$

The $Ncut$ problem is the same as the eigenvalue problem, with the extra constraint that y has only two values. (This problem is NP-hard because there are so many choices of P and Q.) The Fiedler vector z will not satisfy this two-value condition. But its components in that specially good example clearly separated into two groups. Clustering by z is a success if we can make it efficient.

Clustering by k-means

The most basic problem begins with a set of n points $(a_1, \ldots, a_n)$ in d-dimensional space. The goal is to partition them into k clusters. Those clusters $P_1, \ldots P_k$ have centroids $c_1, \ldots, c_k$. Each centroid c_j minimizes the total distance $D_j = \sum d(c_j, a)$ to points a in the cluster P_j. When the distances between points are the squared lengths $\|x - a\|^2$, the centroid is the mean (the average) of those n_j points:

Centroid of P_j $\quad c_j$ minimizes $D_j(x) = \sum\limits_{a \text{ in } P_j} d(x, a) \qquad c_j = \dfrac{\text{sum of } a\text{'s}}{\text{number of } a\text{'s}}$ if $d = \|x - a\|^2$

The goal is to find the partition $P_1, \ldots, P_k$ with minimum total distance to centroids:

Clustering $\quad$ Minimize $D = D_1 + \cdots + D_k = \sum d(c_j, a_i)$ for a_i in P_j. $\quad (14)$

Key idea Each partition $P_1, \ldots, P_k$ produces k centroids (step 1). **Each set of centroids produces a partition** (step 2). That step moves a into P_j if c_j is the closest centroid to a. (In case of equally close centroids, choose one arbitrarily.) The classical "*batch k-means algorithm*" iterates from a partition to its centroids to a new partition:

1. Find the centroids c_j of the (old) partition $P_1, \ldots, P_k$.
2. Find the (new) partition that puts a in P_j if $d(c_j, a) \le d(c_i, a)$ for all i.

Each step reduces the total distance D. We reset the centroids c_j for each P_j, and then we improve to new P_j around those c_j. Since D decreases at both steps, the k-means algorithm converges (but not necessarily to the global minimum).

Unfortunately, it is hard to know much about the limiting P_j. Many non-optimal partitions can give local minima. Better partitions come from weighted distances.

Step 1 is the more expensive, to compute all the distances $d(c_j, a)$. The complexity is normally $O(n^2)$ per iteration. When the algorithm is extended below to kernel k-means, generating a kernel matrix K from the data can cost $O(n^2 d)$. Step 2 is the "Voronoidal idea" of finding the set closest to each of the centroids. This code allows a first comparison of k-means with spectral clustering.

The cse page has a k-means code from Brian Kulis and Inderjit Dhillon. On the 20-node graph in the Fiedler example above, it finds the best partition. The multilevel code coarsens to 11 and then 6 supernodes, clusters that small base graph, and propagates back. In this example the merging and the refinement steps are all correct.

Weights and Kernels

When we introduce weights in the distances, they appear in the centroids:

Distances $d(x, a_i) = w_i \, \|x - a_i\|^2$ **Centroid of P_j** $c_j = \dfrac{\sum w_i \, a_i}{\sum w_i}$ (a_i in P_j) (15)

The weighted distance $D_j = \sum w_i \, \|x - a_i\|^2$ is minimized by $x = c_j$ in step 1. To reduce the total $D = D_1 + \cdots + D_k$, step 2 resets the partitions. Each a_i goes with the closest centroid. Then iterate step 1 (new centroids) and step 2 (new P_j).

A key point is that distances to centroids only require dot products $a_i \cdot a_j$:

Each i in P_j $\|c_j - a_i\|^2 = c_j \cdot c_j - 2c_j \cdot a_i + a_i \cdot a_i$ [take c_j from (15)] (16)

Introduce the weighted kernel matrix K with entries $a_i \cdot a_\ell$. (Remember that the vectors a_i need not be actual positions in space. Each application can map the nodes of the graph to vectors a_i in a linear or *nonlinear* way, by its own rule.) When the nodes are points x_i in input space, their representing vectors $a_i = \phi(x_i)$ can be points in a high-dimensional *feature space*. Three kernels are commonly used:

In vision	**Polynomial**	$K_{i\ell} = (x_i \cdot x_\ell + c)^d$
In statistics	**Gaussian**	$K_{i\ell} = \exp(-\|x_i - x_\ell\|^2/2\sigma^2)$
In neural networks	**Sigmoid**	$K_{i\ell} = \tanh(c\, x_i \cdot x_\ell + \theta)$

The distance in (16) needs only the kernel matrix because of the centroid formula (15):

Sum over nodes in P_j $$\sum \|c_j - a_i\|^2 = \frac{\sum\sum w_i w_\ell K_{i\ell}}{\left(\sum w_i\right)^2} - 2\,\frac{\sum w_i K_{i\ell}}{\sum w_i} + K_{ii}. \quad (17)$$

The **kernel batch k-means algorithm** uses K to compute this distance.

Note Weighted k-means minimization can also be expressed as a graph cut problem. Then it has an equivalent eigenvalue form. One difference is that weights w_i are now associated to *nodes* a_i (instead of edges), so the diagonal matrix W is n by n.

The matrix that enters will be $W^{1/2}\, K\, W^{1/2}$. Dhillon shows the equivalence to an eigenvalue problem that is again constrained to k values (like p and $-q$ above). Relaxing that constraint brings back Fiedler eigenvectors and spectral clustering.

Multilevel Clustering

For large data sets, with many nodes a_i, k-means (alternating steps 1 and 2) and eig$(A^{\mathrm{T}}CA, D)$ will both be expensive. We mention two approaches that create a sequence of manageable problems. **Random sampling** finds the best partition for a sample of the nodes. Then use its centroids to partition all nodes, by assignment to the nearest centroid. This sampling approach has become a major research direction, aiming to prove that with high probability the partition is good.

Dhillon's graclus code uses the **multilevel approach** established by METIS: graph coarsening, then clustering at the base level, and then refinement. Coarsening forms supernodes with superweights (the sum of edge weights). Visiting nodes in a random order, find the heaviest edge from and to an unmerged node, and merge those two nodes. (Normalized version: the heaviest edge maximizes $w_{ij}/d_i + w_{ij}/d_j$.) Supernodes grow larger at each level of coarsening. Stop with $5k$ supernodes.

For the small supergraph at base level, spectral clustering or recursive 2-means will be sufficiently fast. **This multilevel approach is like algebraic multigrid** in Section 7.3, when the graph of points a_i is not a 2D or 3D mesh.

In refinement, the supernodes at level L are initial clusters for level $L-1$. That step can use weighted kernel k-means (precomputing cluster weights). *Incremental* k-means moves from a poor local minimum by swapping individual nodes.

Applications

The reason for this starred section 2.9 is the wide variety of applications (these are the last discrete problems before starting differential equations). Here is a collection that goes far beyond clustering. This part of applied mathematics is growing very quickly—new algorithms, applications, theory, and certainly journals and books. My thought is that you will want to see a few key words from multiple areas, and know about the key idea of clustering.

1. Learning theory, training sets, neural networks, Hidden Markov Models

2. Classification, regression, pattern recognition, Support Vector Machines, VC dimension, supervised or unsupervised

3. Statistical learning, maximum likelihood, Bayesian statistics, spatial statistics, kriging, time series, ARMA models, stationary process, prediction

4. Social networks, small world networks, six degrees of separation, organization theory, probability distributions with heavy tails

5. Data mining, document indexing, semantic indexing, word-document matrix, image retrieval, kernel-based learning, Nystrom method, low rank approximation

6. Bioinformatics, microarray data, systems biology, protein homology detection

7. Cheminformatics, drug design, ligand binding, pairwise similarity, decision trees

8. Information theory, vector quantization, rate distortion theory, loss function, Bregman divergences

9. Image segmentation, computer vision, texture, min cut, normalized cuts

10. Predictive control, feedback samples, robotics, adaptive control, Riccati and Sylvester and Lyapunov equations.

Nonnegative Matrix Factorization

For linear algebra, the SVD is a perfect way to highlight basis vectors in order of their importance. But those principal components can be impossible to recognize. The data might be images or documents, with nonnegative entries. Then a **nonnegative factorization**, with no plus-minus cancellation, produces recognizable features.

A symmetric nonnegative factorization of G is VV^{T} with all $V_{ij} \geq 0$. Clearly this requires $G_{ij} \geq 0$ and also $x^{\mathrm{T}}Gx = \|V^{\mathrm{T}}x\|^2 \geq 0$. The matrix G must be *positive* as well as *positive semidefinite* (those are very different). This approach would be wonderful if those two conditions on G were sufficient to factor $G = VV^{\mathrm{T}}$ with $V \geq 0$.

That "theorem" is not true. The matrix $G = \mathsf{toeplitz}([1 + \mathsf{sqrt}(5)\ 2\ 0\ 0\ 2])$ shows by example that $G = VV^{\mathrm{T}}$ may be impossible with $V \geq 0$. The idea of **nonnegative matrix factorization (NMF)** is to come as close as possible. We minimize the difference $M = G - VV^{\mathrm{T}}$ in the Frobenius norm $\|M\|_F^2 = \sum\sum M_{ij}^2 = \mathsf{trace}(M^{\mathrm{T}}M)$.

In applications, G is the kernel matrix K. It is still the Gram matrix or pairwise similarity matrix of inner products $K_{ij} = a_i \cdot a_j$. Each a_i in high-dimensional feature space is a (*nonlinear*) function of node i in input space. We only need the kernel K, not that function from i to a_i. This is the strong point of kernels.

We express clustering in terms of V. The jth cluster P_j is identified by a unit-length **indicator vector** v_j. Its ith component is $1/\sqrt{|P_j|}$ if a_i is in cluster P_j, otherwise zero. Multiply the data matrix A by v_j to pick out the columns a_i in cluster P_j. The sum $\sum \|c_j - a_i\|^2$ of their distances to the centroid is D_j, and we choose V to minimize the total distance over all clusters:

Cluster distance $\quad D_j = \sum \|a_i\|^2 - \sum\sum a_i^{\mathrm{T}} a_\ell / |P_j| \quad$ **Total** $\quad \sum D_j = \|A\|_F^2 - \|AV\|_F^2 \qquad (18)$

Since clusters are disjoint, the nonzeros in v_j and v_ℓ don't overlap. The columns of V are orthonormal and $V^{\mathrm{T}}V = I$. For example the columns might be $v_1 = (1,1,0,0)/\sqrt{2}$ and $v_2 = (0,0,1,1)/\sqrt{2}$. The first term $\|A\|_F^2 = \sum\sum a_{ij}^2$ is given by the data. **The k-means objective is to maximize** $\|AV\|_F^2$, which minimizes (18).

Key point For k-means, the columns v_j of V take only two values $1/\sqrt{|P_j|}$ and 0, with $V^{\mathrm{T}}V = I$. If we relax to require only $V^{\mathrm{T}}V = I$, we have principal component analysis (PCA). If we relax to $V \geq 0$, we are close to nonnegative matrix factorization (NMF). *We are always maximizing* $\|AV\|_F^2$, which equals the trace of $V^{\mathrm{T}}A^{\mathrm{T}}AV$.

The new book [40] will be a central reference for NMF in data mining.

Pairwise Closeness

A long line of closely spaced points will (up to now) not stay in the same cluster. The ends of the line are not close. To avoid cutting the line into two clusters, measure the distance $d(P,Q)$ between clusters by the distance between *nearest points.* Then maximize the distance between pairs of clusters—a different clustering rule:

Choose $P_1,\ldots,P_k$ to maximize D^* $\quad D^* = \min d(P_i,P_j) = \min d(a_i,a_j)$. (19)

Think of a line of points and one separate point q. Those are now the best two clusters P and Q. If the line is cut, the distance between clusters will be very small.

There is a **greedy algorithm** to find the cluster that maximizes D^*. It starts with n clusters, *one point in each.* At each step, the two nearest clusters are combined into one. After $n-k$ steps, you have k clusters with maximum separation.

Example 2 The $n = 4$ points are $a = 1, 2, 4, 8$.

The first step puts 1 and 2 in the same cluster. The best three clusters $\{1,2\},\{4\},\{8\}$ are separated by $2, 4$, and 6. The smallest distance $D^* = 2$ between $k = 3$ clusters is a maximum. If you had put 1 and 2 in different clusters, then D^* would drop to 1.

The second step "agglomerates" the nearest clusters $\{1,2\}$ and $\{4\}$ into one cluster. The best $k = 2$ clusters are $\{1,2,4\}$ and $\{8\}$. Their distance $D^* = 4$ is a maximum.

The point of a "greedy algorithm" is to proceed step by step without undoing any steps later. You don't have to look ahead, the future comes out right. For the original rule, minimizing total distance D between points and centroids, there is no way to take $n-k$ steps that will never need to be undone.

Problem Set ∗ 2.9

1 If the graph is a line of 4 nodes, and all weights are 1 ($C = I$), the best cut is down the middle. Find this cut from the $\pm$ components of the Fiedler vector z:

$$A^{\mathrm{T}}CA\,z = \begin{bmatrix} 1 & -1 & & \\ -1 & 2 & -1 & \\ & -1 & 2 & -1 \\ & & -1 & 1 \end{bmatrix}\begin{bmatrix} z_1 \\ z_2 \\ z_3 \\ z_4 \end{bmatrix} = \lambda_2 \begin{bmatrix} 1 & & & \\ & 2 & & \\ & & 2 & \\ & & & 1 \end{bmatrix}\begin{bmatrix} z_1 \\ z_2 \\ z_3 \\ z_4 \end{bmatrix} = \lambda_2 D z.$$

Here $\lambda_2 = \frac{1}{2}$. Solve for z by hand, and check $[1\ \ 1\ \ 1\ \ 1]\,Dz = 0$.

2 For the same 4-node tree, compute *links*(P) and *size*(P) and *Ncut*(P,Q) for the cut down the middle.

3 Starting from the same four points $1,2,3,4$ find the centroids c_P and c_Q and the total distance D for the partition $P = \{1,2\}$ and $Q = \{3,4\}$. The k-means algorithm will not change this partition when it assigns the four points to nearest centroids.

4 Start the k-means algorithm with the partition $P = \{1,2,4\}$ and $Q = \{3\}$. Find the two centroids and reassign points to the nearest centroid.

5 For the partition $P = \{1,2,3\}$ and $Q = \{4\}$, the centroids are $c_P = 2$ and $c_Q = 4$. Resolving a tie the wrong way leaves this partition with no improvement. But find its total distance D.

6 If the graph is a 2 by 4 mesh of 8 nodes, with weights $C = I$, use $\mathsf{eig}(A^{\mathrm{T}}A, D)$ to find the Fiedler vector z. The incidence matrix A is 10 by 8 and $D = \mathsf{diag}(\mathsf{diag}(A^{\mathrm{T}}A))$. What partition comes from the $\pm$ components of z?

7 Use the Fiedler code with probabilities narrowed from $p = 0.1$ and 0.7 to $p = 0.5$ and 0.6. Compute z and plot the graph and its partition.

Problems 8-12 are about the graph with $n = 5$ nodes $(0,0)$, $(1,0)$, $(3,0)$, $(0,4)$, $(0,8)$. Distances between nodes (the edge lengths) are normal distances like 1 and 2 and $\sqrt{3^2+4^2}$.

8 Which clusters P and Q maximize the minimum distance D^* between them?

9 Find those best clusters by the *greedy algorithm*. Start with five clusters, and combine the two closest clusters. What are the best k clusters for $k = 4, 3, 2$?

10 The **minimum spanning tree** is the shortest group of edges that connects all nodes. There will be $n-1$ edges and no loops; otherwise the total length would not be minimal. Several greedy algorithms will find that shortest tree:

(Dijkstra's algorithm) Start with any node like $(0,0)$. At each step, include the shortest edge that connects a new node to the partial tree already created.

11 The minimum spanning tree can also be found by *greedy inclusion*. With the edges in increasing order of length, keep each edge unless it completes a loop. Apply this algorithm to the 5-node graph.

12 Find the minimum spanning tree for the 5-node graph. Delete the largest edge in that tree to find the best four clusters. Then delete the next largest to find the best three clusters. This gives another greedy algorithm to maximize D^* in (19), the distance between clusters.

CHAPTER 3

BOUNDARY VALUE PROBLEMS

3.1 DIFFERENTIAL EQUATIONS AND FINITE ELEMENTS

This section introduces differential equations $-d/dx(c\,du/dx) = f(x)$ on a line. **The difference matrix A in $A^{\mathrm{T}}CA$ is changed to a first derivative d/dx.** The problem is continuous instead of discrete, with boundary conditions at $x = 0$ and $x = 1$. We are going beyond the model problems $-u'' = 1$ and $-u'' = \delta(x-a)$.

The differential equation allows an exact solution $u(x)$, by integrating twice. This gives practice with delta functions in $f(x)$ and jump functions for $c(x)$. And the numerical approximation $U(x)$ will bring something new and important. **In addition to finite differences we will explain and use finite elements.**

Second-Order Equations

Probably the reader has studied differential equations. That is good but not essential. The basic course has one very practical message, when the differential equation is linear and its coefficients are constant. A key example is $mu'' + ku = 0$, and the messsage is to expect solutions with the simple form $Ae^{\lambda x}$:

Constant coefficients	*Look for solutions* $u(x) = A\,e^{\lambda x}$. *Solve for* λ.

Substituting $u(x) = A\,e^{\lambda x}$ turns $mu'' + ku = 0$ into pure algebra: $m\lambda^2 + k = 0$. When the highest derivative is d^2u/dx^2, which equals $\lambda^2 Ae^{\lambda x}$, we get a quadratic equation with two roots λ_1 and λ_2 (and $Ae^{\lambda x}$ cancels out). Provided $\lambda_1 \neq \lambda_2$, the solution with no forcing term will be a **combination of pure exponentials**:

$$u(x) = Ae^{\lambda_1 x} + Be^{\lambda_2 x} \quad \text{with arbitrary constants } A \text{ and } B.$$

A and B are determined by two initial conditions for an initial-value problem, or two boundary conditions for a boundary-value problem. So far all good.

The equations of applied mathematics are not random examples. They arise from real problems, they express important principles, and we can find a pattern. That will be our first point, before solving the differential equations.

How does the framework of $K = A^{\mathrm{T}} CA$ extend to differential equations?

In our first example, A becomes d/dx. Its "transpose" becomes −d/dx. Multiplication by the numbers $c_1, \ldots, c_m$ changes into multiplication by $c(x)$. We have a differential equation for $u(x)$, with boundary conditions on u or $w = c\, du/dx$:

$$\boldsymbol{A^{\mathrm{T}}CAu = f} \textbf{ with } \boldsymbol{A = \frac{d}{dx}} \qquad -\frac{d}{dx}\left(c(x)\frac{du}{dx}\right) = f(x) \qquad \begin{array}{l}\textbf{Fixed: } \boldsymbol{u(0) = 0} \\ \textbf{Free: } \boldsymbol{w(1) = 0}\end{array} \tag{1}$$

The external force is often constant or periodic, as in $f(x) = 1$ or $f(x) = \cos\omega x$. The force could act *at one point* (a point load) or *at one instant of time* (an impulse). This spike is modeled by a ***delta function***. It is a mixture of all frequencies and all cosines. They cancel each other except at one point $x = a$: $f(x) = \delta(x - a)$.

I believe you will enjoy working with delta functions. The solutions are clean and explicit, not complicated integrals. As a function, $\delta(x)$ is hard to believe in—a very extreme limit. The width of the spike goes to zero and the height goes to infinity and the area stays fixed at 1. You will say that this can't happen, and I have to agree. It is the rules for integrating with $\delta(x - a)$ that put these non-functions onto a firm mathematical foundation. ***The integral of*** $\boldsymbol{v(x)\,\delta(x - a)}$ ***is*** $\boldsymbol{v(a)}$.

We mention four more limiting cases, because *applied mathematics is extremely interested in zero and infinity.* Maybe ordinary examples like $u'' - 3u' + 2u = 8$ are too boring, when $\lambda = 1, 2$ and $u(x) = Ae^x + Be^{2x} + 4$. Often we are close to dividing by zero, where the solution method breaks down. Boundary layers are studied in the problem set, stiff equations in Section 6.2, and resonance in Section 2.2:

$\boldsymbol{\lambda \to \infty}$:	Boundary layers	$\boldsymbol{\lambda_2 \to \lambda_1}$:	Second solution $xe^{\lambda x}$
$\boldsymbol{\lambda \to -\infty}$:	Stiff equations	$\boldsymbol{f(t) \to \cos\lambda_1 t}$:	Resonance

The full technical details of all these possibilities are not for this book (examples teach a lot). Often the important questions are not *at* the limit, where the solution takes a new form. The difficulty is *close to the limit.* The old form is correct but we are losing control of it. A transition is needed to the new form.

Finally, and most important for scientific computing, we explain ***finite elements.*** This is a fantastic opportunity to show the "weak form" of the equation:

$$\textbf{Weak form} \qquad \int c(x)\,\frac{du}{dx}\,\frac{dv}{dx}\,dx = \int f(x)\,v(x)\,dx \text{ for every admissible } v(x)$$

The $A^{\mathrm{T}}CA$ Framework for a Hanging Bar

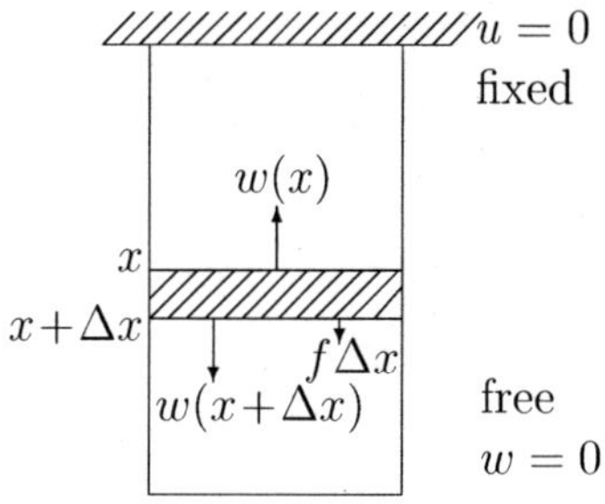

The forces on a hanging bar are its own weight, and possibly additional weights. The bar stretches like a line of springs. The point that begins at distance x along the unstretched bar moves down to $x + u(x)$. Our goal is to find this displacement $u(x)$.

The top at $x = 0$ is ***fixed***: therefore $\boldsymbol{u(0) = 0}$. The bottom at $x = 1$ is ***free***. The internal force at that point must be zero because no external force will balance it. Thus $\boldsymbol{w(1) = 0}$. These are the boundary conditions for a **fixed-free bar**.

Note that the bottom end actually moves down to $x = 1 + u(1)$. Nevertheless the boundary condition is written at $x = 1$. The reason is that *displacements* $u(x)$ *are assumed small.* Large displacements lead to serious nonlinearity and we are not ready to take that road.

There is still an unknown $e(x)$ between $u(x)$ and $w(x)$. This is the *"strain"* in the bar, the elongation per unit length. It is a local quantity, defined right at the point x. Remember that the ith spring was stretched by $u_i - u_{i-1}$, the difference in displacement of its ends. *Now the difference becomes a derivative*:

Stretching: Step 1 $\quad e(x) = A\,u(x) = \dfrac{du}{dx} \quad \text{with } u(0) = 0. \qquad (2)$

That boundary condition (on u not w!) is part of the definition of A.

The second step is Hooke's law $w = c\,e$, the material property or constitutive law. It is a linear relation of stress to strain, or internal force $w(x)$ to stretching $e(x)$:

Hooke's Law: Step 2 $\quad w(x) = c(x)\,e(x) = c(x)\dfrac{du}{dx}\,. \qquad (3)$

For a uniform bar, $c(x)$ is a constant. For a tapered bar, $c(x)$ varies gradually. At a point where the material of the bar suddenly changes, the function $c(x)$ will have a jump. *The product* $w(x) = c(x)\,u'(x)$ *will not jump.* The force balance at that point demands that $w(x)$ must be continuous. The jump in $c(x)$ must be compensated by a jump in $e(x) = du/dx$. Only a point load $\delta(x - x_0)$ produces a discontinuity in $w(x)$.

The third step is **force balance**. The figure shows a small piece of the bar, with thickness Δx. The internal forces are $w(x)$ upwards and $w(x + \Delta x)$ downwards. The external force is the integral of $f(x)$ across that little piece. In the absence of delta functions, this integral is approximately $f(x)\Delta x$. That piece is in equilibrium.

$$w(x) = w(x + \Delta x) + f(x)\Delta x \qquad \text{or} \qquad -\left[\frac{w(x + \Delta x) - w(x)}{\Delta x}\right] = f(x)\,.$$

The derivative of w appears as Δx approaches zero:

> **Force balance: Step 3** $\quad A^{\mathrm{T}} w = -\dfrac{dw}{dx} = f(x) \quad$ with $w(1) = 0.$ $\qquad$ (4)

The notation T (for transpose) is still being used, even when A is no longer a matrix. Strictly speaking we should change to a new word like "*adjoint*" with a new symbol. But this book emphasizes the analogies between matrix equations and differential equations. $A^{\mathrm{T}} = -d/dx$ is the "**transpose**" of $A = d/dx$: still to explain.

The differential equation combines A and C and A^{T} into $K = A^{\mathrm{T}}CA$:

> **Boundary value problem** $\quad Ku = -\dfrac{d}{dx}\left(c(x)\dfrac{du}{dx}\right) = f(x) \qquad \begin{array}{l} u(0) \;\;\;= 0 \\ c(1)u'(1) \;= 0 \end{array}$

$u(0) = 0$ | displacement $u(x)$ | $\qquad\qquad \boldsymbol{K = A^{\mathrm{T}}CA}$ $\qquad$ | external force per unit length $f(x)$ |

$\downarrow$ $\qquad\qquad\qquad\qquad\qquad\qquad\qquad\qquad\qquad\qquad\qquad\qquad\qquad\qquad \uparrow$

$\quad$ **strain-displacement** $\qquad\qquad\qquad\qquad\qquad\qquad\qquad$ **force balance**

$\boldsymbol{e(x) = Au(x) = du/dx} \qquad\qquad\qquad\qquad \boldsymbol{f(x) = A^{\mathrm{T}}w(x) = -dw/dx}$

$\downarrow$ $\qquad\qquad\qquad\qquad\qquad\qquad\qquad\qquad\qquad\qquad\qquad\qquad\qquad\qquad \uparrow$

| strain = elongation $e(x)$ | $\quad$ **stress-strain law** $\quad$ | internal stress $w(x)$ | $w(1) = 0$

$$\boldsymbol{w(x) = C\overrightarrow{e(x)} = c(x)e(x)}$$

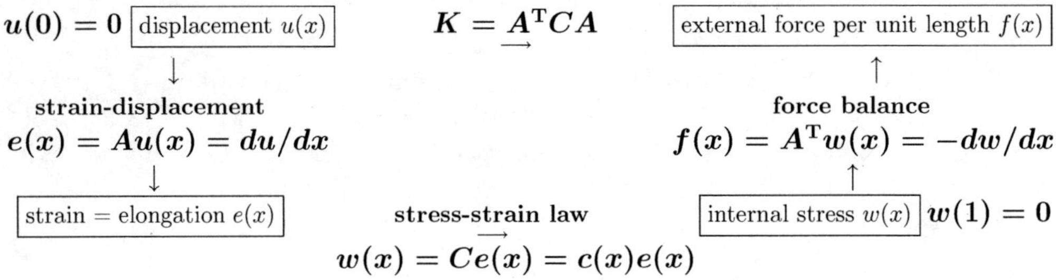

Figure 3.1: The three-step framework $A^{\mathrm{T}}CAu = f$ with stress-strain law $w = Ce$.

General Solution and Examples

To solve $-(cu')' = f$, which is $-dw/dx = f(x)$, integrate both sides once:

> **Internal force (stress)** $\qquad c(x)\dfrac{du}{dx} = w(x) = -\displaystyle\int_0^x f(s)\,ds + C.$ $\qquad$ (5)

If the end $x = 1$ is free, $w(1) = 0$, we can find C from $-\int_0^1 f(s)\,ds + C = 0$:

> **Internal force** $\quad \boldsymbol{w(x) = -\displaystyle\int_0^x f(s)\,ds + \int_0^1 f(s)\,ds = \int_x^1 f(s)\,ds}$ $\qquad$ (6)

The last formula (for a free end only) has a simple meaning: *The internal force w at the point x balances the total applied force f below that point.* That total force is the integral of the load from x to 1.

Now solve $c(x)\,du/dx = w(x)$ by integrating once more.

Displacement $$\frac{du}{dx} = \frac{w(x)}{c(x)} \quad \text{and} \quad \int_0^x \frac{w(s)}{c(s)}\,ds = u(x) \tag{7}$$

The boundary condition $u(0) = 0$ was built in by starting the integration at $x = 0$. If the end $x = 1$ is fixed, $u(1) = 0$, this now determines the constant C in (5).

Example 1 Suppose $f(x)$ and $c(x)$ are *constants*. A uniform bar is hanging under its own weight. The force per unit length is $f_0 = \rho g$ (ρ = mass per unit length). The integrals (6) and (7) are easy, but notice the boundary conditions:

$$\boldsymbol{w(x)} = \int_x^1 f_0\,ds = \boldsymbol{(1-x)f_0} \qquad \boldsymbol{u(x)} = \int_0^x \frac{(1-s)f_0}{c}\,ds = \left(\boldsymbol{x} - \frac{\mathbf{1}}{\mathbf{2}}\boldsymbol{x}^2\right)\frac{\boldsymbol{f_0}}{\boldsymbol{c}}. \tag{8}$$

The linear function $w(x)$ equals the total weight below x. The graph of the displacement $u(x)$ is a parabola. It ends with zero slope because $w(1) = 0$.

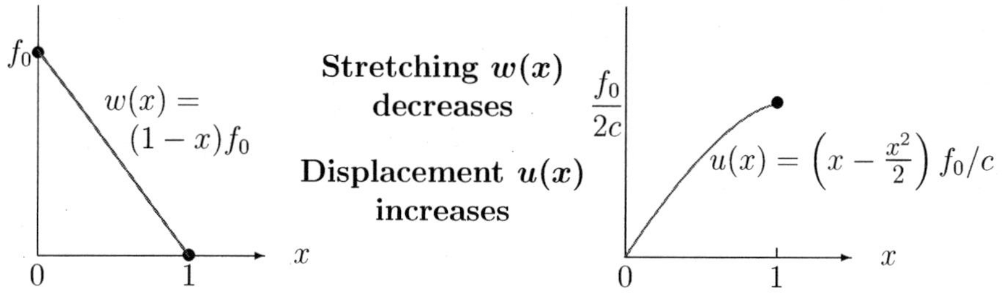

Figure 3.2: Internal force $w(x)$ and displacement $u(x)$ for constant f_0 and c.

Example 2 $c(x) = f(x) = 2 - x$ with fixed ends $u(0) = u(1) = 0$. Find $w(x)$ and $u(x)$.

Solution The first step integrates $f(x)$ with an undetermined constant C:

Internal force (stress) $$w(x) = -\int_0^x (2-s)ds = \frac{(2-x)^2}{2} + C \tag{9}$$

Now divide $w(x)$ by $c(x) = 2 - x$ and integrate again with $u(0) = 0$:

$$u(x) = \int_0^x \left[\frac{2-x}{2} + \frac{C}{2-x}\right] dx = -\frac{(2-x)^2}{4} + 1 - C\log(2-x) + C\log 2 \tag{10}$$

Then $u(1) = 0$ gives $C = -3/(4\log 2)$. This solution is in the code on the website. When the end $x = 1$ is free, $w(1) = 0$ gives $C = 1/4$ already in (9).

Free versus fixed With $w(1) = 0$, $A^{\mathrm{T}}w = f$ determines w immediately. With $u(1) = 0$, we find w after we find u. We must work with $A^{\mathrm{T}}CA$ all at once. For trusses, an invertible A^{T} was called *statically determinate*. Fixed-free bars have this property. Fixed-fixed bars are like rectangular matrices, *statically indeterminate*.

Comment This $c(x) = 2 - x$ comes from a tapered bar, whose width decreases from 2 to 1. The force $f(x)$ from its weight does the same. **Suppose instead that $c(x) = f(x) = 1 - x$.** Now $c(1) = f(1) = 0$, the bar tapers to a point, and $u(x)$ will involve $\log(1 - x)$ instead of $\log(2 - x)$. When we set $x = 1$, this logarithm is infinite. Maybe it is impossible to support the bar when it ends at a single point?

Point Loads and Delta Functions

The third example has the entire load f_0 concentrated at the point $x = x_0$:

Point load $\quad f(x) = f_0\,\delta(x - x_0) = \{\text{zero for } x \neq x_0 \text{ but its integral is } f_0\}$ (11)

Integrate this delta function to find the internal force above and below x_0:

Jump in force $$w(x) = \int_x^1 f_0\,\delta(s - x_0)\,ds = \left\{ \begin{matrix} f_0 & \text{if} & x < x_0 \\ 0 & \text{if} & x > x_0 \end{matrix} \right\}. \quad (12)$$

Below the point load, the internal force is $w = 0$. The lower part of the bar hangs free. *Above the point load,* the internal force is $w = f_0$. The upper part of the bar is uniformly stressed. The graph of $w(x)$ in Figure 3.3 shows a *step function.* **This is what we expect from the integral of a delta function.**

Notice the two-part formula for the solution $w(x)$. Its integral gives a two-part formula for $u(x)$. One formula applies above the load, the other gives the displacement below the load. That lower part of the bar has constant displacement because the whole piece below the load just moves downward:

Ramp in $u(x)$ $$u(x) = \int_0^x \frac{w(s)}{c}\,ds = \left\{ \begin{matrix} f_0 x/c & \text{if} & x \le x_0 \\ f_0 x_0/c & \text{if} & x \ge x_0 \end{matrix} \right\}. \quad (13)$$

The uniform stretching in the top part gives a linearly increasing displacement. The zero stretching in the lower part gives $u(x) =$ constant. Since the bar doesn't split, $u(x)$ is continuous. Both parts must give the *same value for $u(x_0)$.*

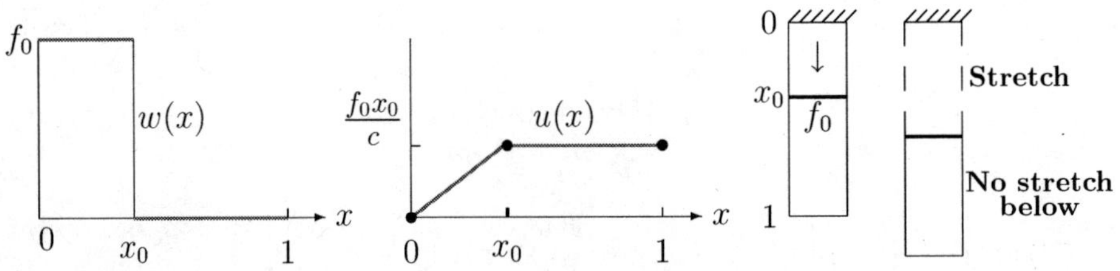

Figure 3.3: Piecewise constant $w(x)$ and piecewise linear $u(x)$ from point load at x_0.

The Transpose of $A = d/dx$

Why is the transpose of $A = d/dx$ given by $A^{\mathrm{T}} = A^* = -d/dx$? What are correct boundary conditions on A and A^{T}? We quietly allow ourselves to say "transpose" and write A^{T}, even if we have derivatives instead of matrices.

For a matrix $(A^{\mathrm{T}})_{ij} = A_{ji}$. For the transpose of $A = d/dx$, we will compare with difference matrices and then go deeper:

Difference matrices Transpose of A_- is $-A_+$

$$A = \begin{bmatrix} 1 & & & \\ -1 & 1 & & \\ & -1 & 1 & \\ & & -1 & 1 \end{bmatrix} \qquad A^{\mathrm{T}} = \begin{bmatrix} 1 & -1 & & \\ & 1 & -1 & \\ & & 1 & -1 \\ & & & 1 \end{bmatrix} \tag{14}$$

The -1's went across the diagonal to produce $-A_+$. But there is a better definition of A^{T}. The underlying physics is the connection of energy $e^{\mathrm{T}}w$ to work $u^{\mathrm{T}}f$. The mathematical reason is this requirement for inner products:

$A^{\mathrm{T}}w$ is defined by $\quad (Au)^{\mathrm{T}}w = u^{\mathrm{T}}(A^{\mathrm{T}}w) \quad$ ***for every u and w*** $\quad$ (15)

To extend that rule to $A = d/dx$, we need the *inner product of functions*. Instead of the sum in $e^{\mathrm{T}}w = e_1w_1 + \cdots + e_mw_m$, the continuous case has an integral:

Inner product of functions

$$(e, w) = \int_0^1 e(x)\, w(x)\, dx \tag{16}$$

Functions are "orthogonal" when $(e, w) = 0$. For example $\sin \pi x$ and $\sin 2\pi x$ are orthogonal (crucial for Fourier series). Those are the first eigenfunctions of $-d^2/dx^2$. The transpose of $A = d/dx$ must follow the rule (15), with inner product = integral:

$$(Au, w) = \int_0^1 \frac{du}{dx}\, w(x)\, dx = \int_0^1 u(x) \left(\frac{d}{dx}\right)^{\mathrm{T}} w(x)\, dx \text{ for every } u \text{ and } w. \tag{17}$$

That is asking for **integration by parts**, one of the central formulas of calculus:

Integration by parts

$$\int_0^1 \frac{du}{dx} w(x) dx = \int_0^1 u(x) \left(-\frac{dw}{dx}\right) dx + \Big[u(x)w(x)\Big]_{x=0}^{x=1} \tag{18}$$

The left side is $(Au)^{\mathrm{T}}w$. So the right side tells us that $A^{\mathrm{T}}w = -dw/dx$. More than that, it tells us the boundary conditions on A^{T} needed for $[uw]_0^1 = 0$:

If A has boundary condition $u(0)=0$, A^{T} *must have* $w(1) = 0$. (19a)

If A has boundary conditions $u(0)=u(1)=0$, A^{T} *has no conditions.* (19b)

If A has no boundary conditions, A^{T} *has two conditions* $w(0)=w(1)=0$. (19c)

In two dimensions, the inner product will be a double integral $\iint e(x,y)\, w(x,y)\, dx\, dy$. Then $(Au)^{\mathrm{T}}w = (u, A^{\mathrm{T}}w)$ will become the Gauss-Green formula, which is integration by parts in 2D. The boundary term $[u\,w]$ moves up to a line integral of $u\,w \cdot n$.

Galerkin's Method

This is an important moment—the beginning of finite elements! Introducing them into our one-dimensional problem gives a perfect start. Finite differences were based on the *strong form* of the differential equation, which is $-d/dx(c\, du/dx) = f(x)$. ***Finite elements are based on the "weak form" with test functions $v(x)$:***

Weak form $$\int_0^1 c(x)\,\frac{du}{dx}\,\frac{dv}{dx}\,dx = \int_0^1 f(x)\,v(x)\,dx \quad \text{for all } v(x). \tag{20}$$

This integrated form comes from multiplying both sides of the strong form by $v(x)$. Integrate the left side by parts, to move one derivative onto v:

By parts $$\int_0^1 -\frac{d}{dx}\left(c\,\frac{du}{dx}\right) v(x)\,dx = \int_0^1 c(x)\,\frac{du}{dx}\,\frac{dv}{dx}\,dx \;-\; \left[c(x)\,\frac{du}{dx}\,v(x)\right]_{x=0}^{x=1} \tag{21}$$

In our fixed-free example, the end $x = 1$ has $w(1) = c(1)\,u'(1) = 0$. At the fixed end $x = 0$, we require $\boldsymbol{v(0) = 0}$. This *admissibility condition on* $v(x)$ removes the integrated term from equation (21). So we have the neat weak form (20).

In a fixed-fixed problem, with no boundary condition on w, admissibility requires $v(0) = 0$ and $v(1) = 0$. In the language of mechanics, $v(x)$ is a virtual displacement added to the correct $u(x)$. Then the weak form says that "virtual displacements do no work." ***Galerkin's method discretizes the weak form.***

Galerkin's Method Choose n trial functions $\boldsymbol{\phi_1(x), \ldots, \phi_n(x)}$. Finite elements will be specially simple choices. Look for $U(x)$ as a combination of the ϕ's:

Combination of trial functions $$U(x) = U_1\,\phi_1(x) + \cdots + U_n\,\phi_n(x). \tag{22}$$

To discretize $v(x)$, choose n admissible "test functions" $V_1(x), \ldots, V_n(x)$. Frequently they are the same as the ϕ's. Substituting $U(x)$ for $u(x)$ in the weak form (20), each test function $V_i(x)$ gives one equation involving the numbers $U_1, \ldots, U_n$:

Equation i for $U_1, \ldots, U_n$ $$\int_0^1 c(x)\left(\sum_1^n U_j\,\frac{d\phi_j}{dx}\right)\frac{dV_i}{dx}\,dx = \int_0^1 f(x)\,V_i(x)\,dx\,. \tag{23}$$

These n equations are $KU = F$. The n components of F are those integrals on the right side of (23). The number K_{ij} multiplies U_j in equation i:

KU = F $$K_{ij} = \int_0^1 c(x)\,\frac{dV_i}{dx}\,\frac{d\phi_j}{dx}\,dx \quad \text{and} \quad F_i = \int_0^1 f(x)\,V_i(x)\,dx\,. \tag{24}$$

When the test V_i are the same as the trial ϕ_i (often true), K_{ij} is the same as K_{ji}. The stiffness matrix K is then symmetric. We will see that K is positive definite.

Notice a good point. When $f(x) = \delta(x-a)$ is a point load, the vector F doesn't use its values $f(x_i)$ at the meshpoints. We are happy to integrate a delta function: $\int \delta(x-a)\,V_i(x)\,dx = V_i(a)$. Similarly if $c(x)$ has a jump (when the bar material changes), that step function $c(x)$ is no problem in the integral for K_{ij}. *But we could not allow* $\phi_i(x) = V_i(x) =$ *step function*! The derivatives $\phi_i' = V_i'$ would be delta functions and their product δ^2 would have an infinite integral: not admissible.

Construction of the Finite Element Method

1. Choose the ϕ_i and V_i: one unknown for each ϕ, one equation for each V.

2. Compute exact or approximate integrals (24). If all $\phi_i = V_i$ then $K_{ij} = K_{ji}$.

3. The weak form becomes $KU = F$. The FEM approximation is $\sum U_i\,\phi_i(x)$.

Linear Finite Elements

As examples, I will choose the hat functions ϕ_1, ϕ_2, ϕ_3 in Figure 3.4. Those will also be the test functions V_1, V_2, V_3. The functions are *local*—they are zero outside intervals of length $2h$, $2h$, h. There is no overlap between ϕ_1 and the half-hat ϕ_3, which makes the integral zero: $K_{13} = K_{31} = 0$. Our stiffness matrix K will be *tridiagonal.*

At $x = h$, only the first trial function ϕ_1 is nonzero. So its coefficient U_1 equals the approximation $U(x)$ at that point. The right figure shows that each of the coefficients U_1, U_2, U_3 is also a mesh value of $U(x)$: very convenient.

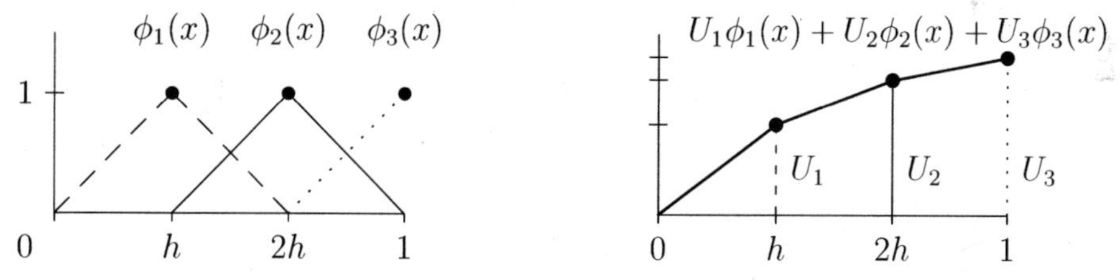

Figure 3.4: Hat functions ϕ_1, ϕ_2, half-hat ϕ_3, and a combination (piecewise linear).

We will apply these linear elements to three fixed-free examples:

1. $-u'' = 1$ has $c(x) = 1$ and $f(x) = 1$ and $w(x) = 1 - x$ and $u(x) = x - \frac{1}{2}x^2$

2. $-\dfrac{d}{dx}\left(c(x)\,\dfrac{du}{dx}\right) = \delta\left(x - \frac{1}{2}\right)$ when $c(x)$ jumps from 2 to 4 at $x = \frac{1}{3}$

3. Any acceptable $c(x)$ and $f(x)$, using numerical integration for K and F.

Example 3 The complete solution to $-u'' = 1$ is $u(x) = A + Bx - \frac{1}{2}x^2$ (nullspace plus particular solution). $A = 0$ and $B = 1$ are determined by $u(0) = 0$ and $u'(1) = 0$. Then $\boldsymbol{u(x) = x - \frac{1}{2}x^2}$. The piecewise linear $U(x)$ will approximate this parabola.

To compute U_1, U_2, U_3 we need the vector F and matrix K with $f(x) = c(x) = 1$. Remember that the test functions V_1, V_2, V_3 are two hats and a half-hat, with $h = \frac{1}{3}$.

Areas $\quad F_1 = \int V_1\,dx = \frac{1}{3} \quad F_2 = \int V_2\,dx = \frac{1}{3} \quad F_3 = \int V_3\,dx = \frac{1}{6}$ **(half)**

With $c(x) = 1$, the stiffness matrix has $K_{ij} = \int V_i'\phi_j'\,dx$. Those slopes are constant:

Slopes $\phi' = V'$ are 3 and -3

$$K_{11} = \int_0^1 \left(\frac{dV_1}{dx}\right)^2 dx = \int_0^{2/3} 9\,dx = \mathbf{6} \quad K_{22} = \mathbf{6} \quad K_{33} = \mathbf{3}$$

Multiply slopes $V_i'\phi_j'$

$$K_{12} = \int_{1/3}^{2/3} (3)(-3)\,dx = \mathbf{-3} \quad K_{23} = \mathbf{-3} \quad K_{13} = \mathbf{0}\ \textbf{(no overlap)}$$

Now the finite element equation $KU = F$ is solved for the three mesh values in U:

KU = F

$$\begin{bmatrix} 6 & -3 & 0 \\ -3 & 6 & -3 \\ 0 & -3 & 3 \end{bmatrix} \begin{bmatrix} U_1 \\ U_2 \\ U_3 \end{bmatrix} = \begin{bmatrix} 1/3 \\ 1/3 \\ 1/6 \end{bmatrix} \text{ gives } \begin{bmatrix} U_1 \\ U_2 \\ U_3 \end{bmatrix} = \begin{bmatrix} 5/18 \\ 4/9 \\ 1/2 \end{bmatrix}. \tag{25}$$

All three values U_1, U_2, U_3 agree exactly with $u(x) = x - \frac{1}{2}x^2$ at the meshpoints.

Comparison with Finite Differences

You may remember that the U_i in Section 1.2 were *not exact* for the free-fixed problem. Figure 1.4 showed the $O(h)$ errors coming from the difference equation $Tu = f$. The Worked Example gave $O(h^2)$ by improving the equation at the free boundary, where the right side was multiplied by $\frac{1}{2}$ to keep second-order accuracy.

Here the free boundary is at the other end $x = 1$. ***Finite elements have automatically chosen*** $\boldsymbol{F_3 = \frac{1}{6}}$, where $F_1 = F_2 = \frac{1}{3}$. The crucial factor $\frac{1}{2}$ came from the half-hat, without special planning. Second-order accuracy was saved. For the parabola $u(x) = x - \frac{1}{2}x^2$, that means perfect accuracy in (25).

Comparing finite elements with finite differences, a factor h has moved into F:

$$KU = F \quad \text{is like} \quad \frac{1}{h}\left(-\Delta^2 U\right) = hf \quad \text{instead of} \quad \frac{1}{h^2}\left(-\Delta^2 U\right) = f\,.$$

The finite difference code on page 244 creates $K = A^{\mathrm{T}}CA$ from backward differences in A and midpoint values of $c(x)$ in C. K is still tridiagonal.

Example 4 **Point load $f(x) = \delta(x - \frac{1}{2})$ and $c = 2$ jumps to $c = 4$ at $x = \frac{1}{3}$.**

Solution The differential equation $A^{\mathrm{T}}CAu = f$ splits into $A^{\mathrm{T}}w = f$ and $CAu = w$:

$$\mathbf{A^Tw = f} \qquad -\frac{dw}{dx} = \delta(x - \tfrac{1}{2}) \quad \text{with} \quad w(1) = 0 \qquad \boldsymbol{w(x)} = \begin{cases} \mathbf{1} & \text{for } \boldsymbol{x} < \frac{\mathbf{1}}{\mathbf{2}} \\ \mathbf{0} & \text{for } \boldsymbol{x} > \frac{\mathbf{1}}{\mathbf{2}} \end{cases}$$

The force $w(x)$ is constant on each half of the bar, and changes by 1 at the point load. From this $w(x)$ we find $u(x)$ by one more integration (*watching the jump in c!*):

$$\mathbf{CAu = w} \qquad c(x)\frac{du}{dx} = w(x) \quad \text{with} \quad u(0) = 0 \qquad \boldsymbol{u(x)} = \int_0^{\boldsymbol{x}} \frac{\boldsymbol{w(x)}}{\boldsymbol{c(x)}}\, \boldsymbol{dx}$$

That integral of $\frac{1}{2}, \frac{1}{4}, \frac{0}{4}$ has three parts—to $x = \frac{1}{3}$, to $x = \frac{1}{2}$, and finally to $x = 1$:

$$u(x) = \int_0^x \frac{dx}{2} = \frac{\boldsymbol{x}}{\mathbf{2}} \qquad u(x) = \frac{1}{6} + \int_{1/3}^x \frac{dx}{4} = \frac{\mathbf{1}}{\mathbf{12}} + \frac{\boldsymbol{x}}{\mathbf{4}} \qquad u(x) = \frac{1}{12} + \frac{1}{8} + \int_{1/2}^x 0\, dx = \frac{\mathbf{5}}{\mathbf{24}}$$

Now use finite elements. The integral for F_i still has $V_i(x) =$ hat function:

$$F_1 = \int_0^1 \delta(x-\tfrac{1}{2})V_1(x)\,dx = \tfrac{\mathbf{1}}{\mathbf{2}} \qquad F_2 = \int_0^1 \delta(x-\tfrac{1}{2})V_2(x)\,dx = \tfrac{\mathbf{1}}{\mathbf{2}} \qquad F_3 = \mathbf{0} \text{ (no load)}.$$

The load centered between the first two meshpoints is shared by $F_1 = F_2 = \frac{1}{2}$. In the matrix K, the integral of $c\,V_i'V_j'$ (constant!) includes the jump from $c = 2$ to $c = 4$:

$$K_{11} = \frac{1}{3}(2 \cdot 9) + \frac{1}{3}(4 \cdot 9) = \mathbf{18} \qquad K_{12} = K_{21} = \frac{1}{3} \cdot 4(-9) = \mathbf{-12} \qquad K_{13} = K_{31} = \mathbf{0}$$

$$K_{22} = \frac{1}{3}(4 \cdot 9) = \mathbf{24} \qquad K_{23} = K_{32} = \frac{1}{3} \cdot 4(-9) = \mathbf{-12} \qquad K_{33} = \frac{1}{3}(4 \cdot 9) = \mathbf{12}$$

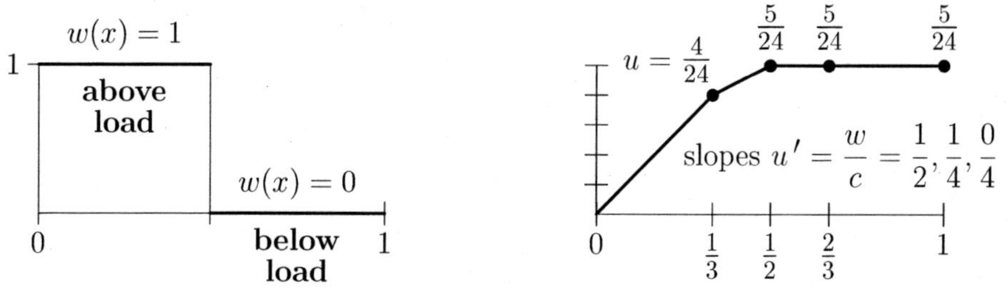

Figure 3.5: Jump in $w(x)$ from load at $x = \frac{1}{2}$. Corners in $u(x)$ at $\frac{1}{3}$ and $\frac{1}{2}$.

The finite element equation $KU = F$ produces exact meshpoint values U_1, U_2, U_3:

$$\textbf{KU} = \textbf{F} \qquad \begin{bmatrix} 18 & -12 & 0 \\ -12 & 24 & -12 \\ 0 & -12 & 12 \end{bmatrix} \begin{bmatrix} U_1 \\ U_2 \\ U_3 \end{bmatrix} = \begin{bmatrix} 1/2 \\ 1/2 \\ 0 \end{bmatrix} \text{ gives } \begin{bmatrix} U_1 \\ U_2 \\ U_3 \end{bmatrix} = \begin{bmatrix} 4/24 \\ 5/24 \\ 5/24 \end{bmatrix}. \quad (26)$$

U_1, U_2, U_3 still match the true solution $u(x)$ at the meshpoints in Figure 3.5. Inside the middle interval, $u(x)$ has a corner at $x = \frac{1}{2}$ but $U(x)$ has no corner—it stays linear. This is a case of "*superconvergence*" at the meshpoints. Probably it helped that the jump in $c(x)$ was exactly at a meshpoint $x = \frac{1}{3}$.

Example 5 Allow any $c(x)$ and $f(x)$, using numerical integration for K and F.

Solution For the integrals $F_i = \int f(x)\, V_i\, dx$ and $K_{ij} = \int c(x)\, \phi_i' V_j'\, dx$, we now introduce **numerical integration**. This is fast, and as accurate as we want. We can use values at the midpoints $\frac{1}{6}, \frac{3}{6}, \frac{5}{6}$ (where all $V_i = \frac{1}{2}$) to approximate the integrals over the three separate mesh intervals. *Integrate element by element*:

Midpoint $\frac{1}{6}$ of the first interval $$\int_0^{1/3} f(x)\, V_1(x)\, dx \approx \frac{1}{3} \cdot f\left(\frac{1}{6}\right) \cdot \frac{1}{2}$$

Similarly the midpoint values at $\frac{3}{6}$ and $\frac{5}{6}$ give approximations to the components F_2 and F_3. This integration rule is adequate for linear elements (it is exact for a uniform load $f(x) = $ constant).

$$\int_{1/3}^{2/3} f(x)\, V_1(x)\, dx \approx \frac{1}{3} \cdot f\left(\frac{3}{6}\right) \cdot \frac{1}{2} \qquad \int_{1/3}^{2/3} f(x)\, V_2(x)\, dx \approx \frac{1}{3} \cdot f\left(\frac{3}{6}\right) \cdot \frac{1}{2}$$

$$\int_{2/3}^{1} f(x)\, V_2(x)\, dx \approx \frac{1}{3} \cdot f\left(\frac{5}{6}\right) \cdot \frac{1}{2} \qquad \int_{2/3}^{1} f(x)\, V_3(x)\, dx \approx \frac{1}{3} \cdot f\left(\frac{5}{6}\right) \cdot \frac{1}{2}$$

The integrals from V_1 add to F_1. The next two add to F_2. The last one is F_3.

Similarly the integral K_{11} is the sum of two pieces (from two intervals):

$$\int_0^{1/3} c(x)\, \phi_1' V_1'\, dx \approx \frac{1}{3} \cdot c\left(\frac{1}{6}\right) \cdot 9 \quad \text{plus} \quad \int_{1/3}^{2/3} c(x)\, \phi_1' V_1'\, dx \approx \frac{1}{3} \cdot c\left(\frac{3}{6}\right) \cdot 9$$

My point is to work with "element integrals" and soon "element stiffness matrices." Those don't need equally spaced meshpoints! Finite differences become painful when the mesh spacing changes (second differences need a new formula), but finite elements just take one interval at a time, in the construction of K and f.

This will be seen again in the double integrals over triangles in Section 3.6. The **geometric flexibility of finite elements** is really appreciated in two dimensions—compared to the inflexibility of a finite difference grid.

More Accurate Finite Elements

Linear elements can give second-order accuracy in $u(x)$, and first-order in $u'(x)$. The approximations $U(x)$ and $U'(x)$ are piecewise linear and piecewise constant. If an engineering problem needs 1% accuracy, many meshpoints may be required (especially in two or three dimensions). Instead of refining the mesh, a better and less expensive way to reduce error is to *increase the degree of the finite elements.*

We move from linear to quadratic elements, quite easily. Keep the three hat functions and add three parabolas ϕ_4, ϕ_5, ϕ_6 as "*bubble functions.*" Each bubble in Figure 3.6 stays inside a mesh interval, so it overlaps only two hat functions.

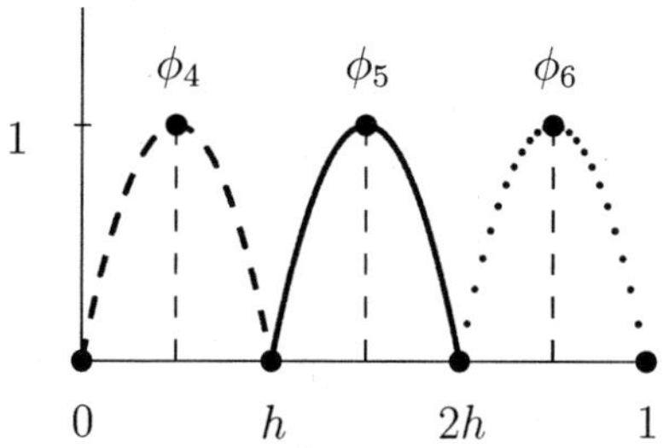

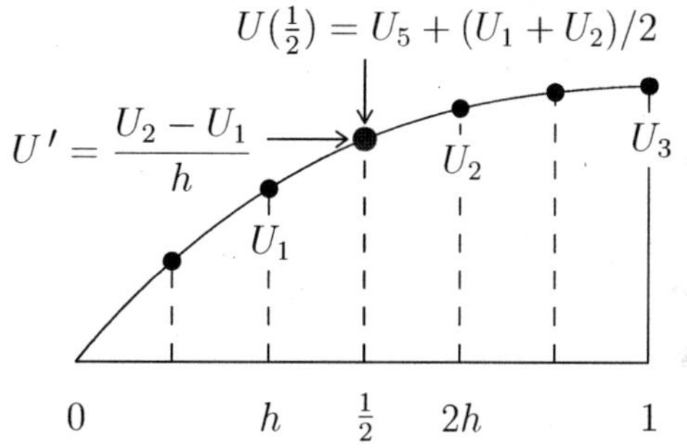

Figure 3.6: Add bubble functions for a piecewise quadratic $U(x) = U_1\phi_1 + \cdots + U_6\phi_6$.

The slope $U'(x)$ is now piecewise linear. It is not continuous at the meshpoints (because U has three separate parabolas). But we may expect improvements in the finite element errors to $|u(x) - U(x)| = O(h^3)$ and $|u'(x) - U'(x)| = O(h^2)$. High accuracy is achieved without the very fine mesh required by linear elements.

We take another step toward integrating over one element at a time, which is how the major codes organize the assembly of K and F. At the center of the middle element, Figure 3.6 shows $U(\frac{1}{2})$ and $U'(\frac{1}{2})$. *Note that* $\phi_5' = 0$ *at that midpoint* $x = \frac{1}{2}$. **The midpoint rule would give zero**: not good enough!

The order of the integration rule has to move up with the degree of the polynomial functions. In this case Simpson's 3-point rule with weights $\frac{1}{6}, \frac{4}{6}, \frac{1}{6}$ does well:

$$\textbf{Simpson} \quad \int_h^{2h} c(x)\,(\phi_5')^2\,dx \approx \tfrac{h}{6}\,c(h)\,(\phi_5'(h))^2 + \tfrac{4h}{6}\,c\left(\tfrac{3h}{2}\right)(\mathbf{0}) + \tfrac{h}{6}\,c(2h)\,(\phi_5'(2h))^2.$$

Every finite element system (ABAQUS, ADINA, ANSYS, FEMLAB, ...) has a library of elements and integration rules to choose from. The next 1D element in the library is almost sure to be piecewise cubic. For a cubic bubble function inside each element, the nine trial functions $\phi_i(x)$ will have jumps in slope (like the bubbles in Figure 3.6). The next section will create better piecewise cubics with *continuous slopes.* These are very good elements.

Problem Set 3.1

1 For a bar with constant c but with decreasing $f = 1 - x$, find $w(x)$ and $u(x)$ as in equations (9-10). Solve with $w(1) = 0$ and also with $u(1) = 0$.

2 For a hanging bar with constant f but weakening elasticity $c(x) = 1 - x$, find the displacement $u(x)$. The first step $w = (1 - x)f$ is the same as in (8), but there will be stretching even at $x = 1$ where there is no force. (The condition is $w = c\,du/dx = 0$ at the free end, and $c = 0$ allows $du/dx \neq 0$).

3 With the bar free at both ends, what condition on $f(x)$ allows $-\frac{dw}{dx} = f(x)$ with $w(0) = w(1) = 0$ to have a solution? (Integrate both sides of the equation from 0 to 1.) This corresponds in the discrete case to solving $A^{\mathrm{T}}w = f$. There is no solution for most f, because the rows of A^{T} add to zero.

4 Find the displacement for an exponential force, $-u'' = e^x$ with $u(0) = u(1) = 0$. Note that $A + Bx$ can be added to any particular solution. A and B can be adjusted to fit the boundary conditions $u(0) = u(1) = 0$.

5 Suppose the force f is constant but the elastic constant c jumps from $c = 1$ for $x \leq \frac{1}{2}$ to $c = 2$ for $x > \frac{1}{2}$. Solve $-dw/dx = f$ with $w(1) = 0$ as before, and then solve $c\,du/dx = w$ with $u(0) = 0$. Even if c jumps, the combination $w = c\,du/dx$ remains smooth.

6 Find the exponentials $u = e^{ax}$ that satisfy $-u'' + 5u' - 4u = 0$ and the combination that has $u(0) = 4$ and $u(1) = 4e$.

7 What is the general solution to $-u'' + pu' = 0$ with constant p? Notice that pu' corresponds to adding a skew-symmetric matrix to $A^{\mathrm{T}}CA$. This illustrates the difference between diffusion and convection. Convection is not symmetric.

8 With $u(0) = 0$ and $w(1) = 0$, the solution to $-u'' = 1$ is $u(x) = x - \frac{1}{2}x^2$. Solve the perturbed equation $-u'' + pu' = 1$. Then substitute $u = x - \frac{1}{2}x^2 + pv(x)$ and keep only the terms that are linear in p, to find the equation for v. This is a "regular perturbation" for small p.

9 The solution to $-cu'' + u' = 1$ is $u = d_1 + d_2 e^{x/c} + x$. Find d_1 and d_2 if $u(0) = u(1) = 0$, and find their limits as $c \to 0$. The limit of u should satisfy $U' = 1$. Which boundary condition does it keep and which end has a boundary layer (very fast change in u, a "singular perturbation").

10 Use three hat functions, with $h = \frac{1}{4}$, to solve $-u'' = 2$ with $u(0) = u(1) = 0$. Verify that the approximation U matches $u = x - x^2$ at the nodes.

11 Solve $-u'' = x$ with $u(0) = u(1) = 0$. Here $u(x)$ is cubic. Then solve approximately with two hat functions and $h = \frac{1}{3}$. Where is the largest error?

12 What is the mass matrix $M_{ij} = \int V_i V_j \, dx$ for the three hat functions?

13 The product rule gives the derivative of $w(x)$ times $v(x)$

$$\frac{d}{dx}\left(w(x)\,v(x)\right) = \frac{dw}{dx}\,v(x) + w(x)\,\frac{dv}{dx}\,.$$

Integrate both sides from 0 to 1, to find the usual rule for *integration by parts*. Then set $w(x) = c(x)\,du/dx$ to produce equation (21) and the weak form.

14 Use Simpson's $\frac{1}{6}, \frac{4}{6}, \frac{1}{6}$ rule to find the area under the bubble function $\phi_5 = V_5$ in Figure 3.6. This is easier than integrating a quadratic function by calculus:

$$\text{Area under } \phi_5 = \int_h^{2h} \phi_5(x)\,dx = \tfrac{h}{6}\phi_5(h) + \tfrac{4h}{6}\phi_5(\tfrac{3h}{2}) + \tfrac{h}{6}\phi_5(2h).$$

15 Find a formula for the second bubble function $\phi_5(x)$ in Figure 3.6. It is a parabola of height 1 with zeros at $x = h$ and $x = 2h$. Then compute the slopes ϕ_5' at those endpoints, and use Simpson's Rule which is exact with $c(x) = 1$:

$$K_{55} = \int_h^{2h} \left(\phi_5'\right)^2 dx = \tfrac{h}{6}\left(\phi_5'(h)\right)^2 + \tfrac{4h}{6}\left(\phi_5'(\tfrac{3h}{2})\right)^2 + \tfrac{h}{6}\left(\phi_5'(2h)\right)^2.$$

16 K is *positive definite* with any trial-test functions $(\phi_1, \ldots, \phi_n) = (V_1, \ldots, V_n)$. We assume that the slopes $\phi_1', \ldots, \phi_n'$ are independent: then $\boldsymbol{U}^{\mathrm{T}}\boldsymbol{K}\boldsymbol{U} > \mathbf{0}$.

$$\sum_i \sum_j U_i K_{ij} U_j = \sum_i \sum_j \int_0^1 c(x) U_i \phi_i' U_j \phi_j' \, dx = \int_0^1 c(x) \left(\sum_i U_i \phi_i'\right)^2 dx > 0.$$

With $a_i = U_i \phi_i'$ that expressed $\sum \sum a_i \, a_j$ as $\left(\sum a_i\right)^2$. Why is this true?

17 Combinations $U(x)$ of the linear and parabolic trial functions $\phi_1, \ldots, \phi_6$ are parabolas $C + Dx + Ex^2$ on each interval $\left[0, \frac{1}{3}\right], \left[\frac{1}{3}, \frac{2}{3}\right], \left[\frac{2}{3}, 1\right]$.

Why is $U(x)$ continuous at the nodes $\frac{1}{3}$ and $\frac{2}{3}$? Is the slope dU/dx continuous ? $U(0) = 0$ leaves two parameters in $Dx + Ex^2$ on $\left[0, \frac{1}{3}\right]$. Then continuity leaves two more in the other intervals. Total 6, the number of quadratic elements.

18 For a fixed-free hanging bar, $u'(1) = 0$ is a *natural boundary condition* that trial and test functions need not satisfy. To the N hat functions ϕ_i at interior meshpoints, add the "half-hat" that goes up to $U_{N+1} = 1$ at the endpoint $x = 1 = (N+1)h$. This $\phi_{N+1} = V_{N+1}$ has a *nonzero slope* $1/h$.

(a) The N by N stiffness matrix K for $-u_{xx}$ now has an extra row and column. How does the new last row of K_{N+1} represent $u'(1) = 0$?

(b) For constant load, find the new last component $F_{N+1} = \int f_0 \, V_{N+1} \, dx$. Solve $K_{N+1} U = F$ and compare U with the true mesh values of $f_0(x - \frac{1}{2}x^2)$.

Notes on the Dirac delta function $\boldsymbol{\delta(x)}$ (unit impulse at $x = 0$)
Its integral from $-\infty$ to x is a *step function*: jump from 0 to 1 at $x = 0$
Second integral is a *ramp function* ($= x$ for $x > 0$; solution to $u'' = \delta$)
Third integral is a *quadratic spline* ($= \frac{1}{2}x^2$ for $x > 0$; jump in second derivative)
Fourth integral is a *cubic spline* ($= \frac{1}{6}x^3$ for $x > 0$; solution to $u'''' = \delta$)
Its derivative δ' is a doublet with $\int f(x)\,\delta'(x)\,dx = -f'(0)$
Delta function $\delta(x)\delta(y)$ in two dimensions: $\iint f(x,y)\,\delta(x)\delta(y)\,dx\,dy = f(0,0)$
Defining property: $\int v(x)\,\delta(x)\,dx = v(0)$ for every smooth function v.

Notes on finite differences in one dimension

The equation $-(cu')' = f$ can be approximated by finite differences. The backward difference matrix $A = A_-$ is the Toeplitz matrix in the code. Notice the simplicity of $K = A' * C * A$ when midpoint values of $c(x)$ go into the diagonal matrix C. Linear finite elements with the midpoint rule gives the same K. We expect $O(h^2)$ accuracy.

```
n=4; h=1/(n+1); x=(1:n)'*h; f=2*ones(n,1)-x;  % f(x) = 2-x at n interior nodes
mid=(.5:(n+.5))'*h; c=2*ones(n+1,1)-mid; C=diag(c); % c(x)=2-x at n+1 midpts
A=toeplitz([1 -1 zeros(1,n-1)],[1 zeros(1,n-1)]);   % n + 1 by n back differences
K=A'*C*A/h^2;                   % stiffness matrix has c_left + c_right on its diagonal
U=K\f                        % U_0 = 0 and U_{n+1} = 0 to match u(0) = 0 and u(1) = 0
uexact=(-f.^2 + ones(n,1) + 3*log(f)/log(2))/4;   error = uexact-U
```

$$A^{\mathrm{T}}CA = \begin{bmatrix} c\left(\frac{h}{2}\right) + c\left(\frac{3h}{2}\right) & -c\left(\frac{3h}{2}\right) & \\ -c\left(\frac{3h}{2}\right) & c\left(\frac{3h}{2}\right) + c\left(\frac{5h}{2}\right) & -c\left(\frac{5h}{2}\right) \\ & -c\left(\frac{5h}{2}\right) & \cdot \end{bmatrix} \quad \text{is like} \quad \begin{bmatrix} c_1 + c_2 & -c_2 & \\ -c_2 & c_2 + c_3 & -c_3 \\ & -c_3 & \cdot \end{bmatrix}.$$

3.2 CUBIC SPLINES AND FOURTH-ORDER EQUATIONS

This section moves up to fourth-order equations and third-degree polynomials. The equations come from *bending* instead of stretching. The cubic polynomials come from point loads. Where $u'' = \delta(x)$ produced a jump in the slope u', the new equation $u'''' = \delta(x)$ produces a jump in the third derivative u'''. Then $u(x)$ is a much smoother function: $u'''' = 0$ gives cubics, just as $u'' = 0$ gives $A + Bx$.

$$\frac{\boldsymbol{d^4u}}{\boldsymbol{dx^4}} = \boldsymbol{\delta(x)} \qquad u(x) = \begin{cases} A + Bx + Cx^2 + dx^3 & \text{for } x \le 0 \\ A + Bx + Cx^2 + Dx^3 & \text{for } x \ge 0 \end{cases} \qquad D = d + \frac{1}{6} \tag{1}$$

Piecewise cubics have applications that go far beyond the mechanics of bending. Above all, they are used for approximation of functions from point values $u(x_i)$. This section will explain **cubic splines** and **cubic finite elements**:

Cubic splines	u, u', u'' are continuous and u''' jumps as above.
Cubic finite elements	u and u' are continuous, u'' and u''' jump.

The splines have one free parameter per node, the finite elements have two. By using piecewise cubics for approximation, the error drops to order $h^4 = (\Delta x)^4$. This is a huge improvement on the $(\Delta x)^2$ error for linear approximation.

Cubic finite elements are the first step after the linear and parabolic elements in Section 3.1. Then the new $A = d^2/dx^2$ leads to fourth-order equations and splines.

Cubic Finite Elements

A linear function is determined by its values U_i and U_{i+1} at the endpoints of an interval. *A cubic needs four values.* The four coefficients of $a + bx + cx^2 + dx^3$ are determined by the endpoint displacements U_i^d, U_{i+1}^d and the endpoint slopes U_i^s, U_{i+1}^s.

Example 1 With $U_i^d = 1$ and $U_i^s = U_{i+1}^d = U_{i+1}^s = 0$, the cubic $\phi_i^d(x)$ is in Figure 3.7.

Example 2 With $U_i^s = 1$ and $U_i^d = U_{i+1}^d = U_{i+1}^s = 0$, the cubic $\phi_i^s(x)$ is in Figure 3.7.

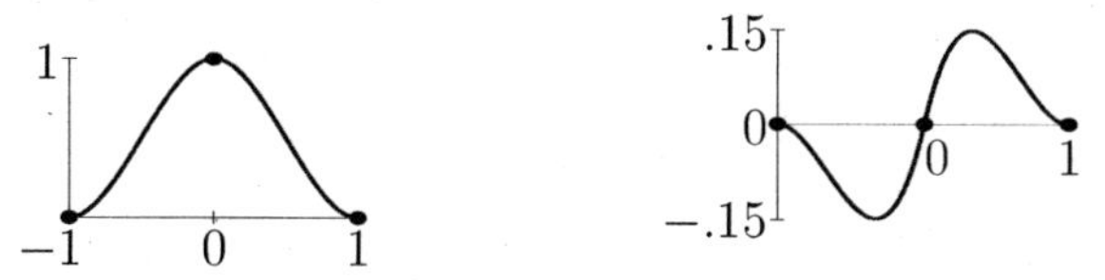

$(|X| - 1)^2(2|X| + 1)$ $\qquad$ $(|X| - 1)^2 * X$, $X = (x - ih)/h$

Figure 3.7: Displacement trial function ϕ_i^d and slope function ϕ_i^s: Two elements/node.

The previous section had a row of hat functions $\phi_1, \ldots, \phi_N$. Their peaks were at the meshpoints $x = h, \ldots, Nh$ with $Nh = 1$. Now we have a row of rounded hats $\phi_1^d, \ldots, \phi_N^d$. And we also have a row of slope functions $\phi_1^s, \ldots, \phi_N^s$ (unit slope at the center). The finite element approximation $U(x)$ is a combination of these $2N$ trial functions (called Hermite cubics). In fact it is the "best" combination:

Finite element solution
$$U(x) = U_1^d\phi_1^d(x) + U_1^s\phi_1^s(x) + \cdots + U_N^d\phi_N^d(x) + U_N^s\phi_N^s(x). \qquad (2)$$

This solution will come from the weak form of the differential equation. Since we have $2N$ trial functions ϕ, we need $2N$ test functions V. Normally these V's will be the same as the ϕ's, to preserve symmetry of the matrix K. For unsymmetric problems with first derivative advection terms, where finite differences are one-sided (upwind), we might choose different V's.

By choosing the heights U_i^d, U_{i+1}^d and the slopes U_i^s; U_{i+1}^s, we can match any cubic over an interval. Since the neighboring intervals end with the same height and slope, the overall piecewise cubic will have *continuous height and slope.* This describes our trial space, apart from boundary conditions.

$\boldsymbol{u(0) = 0}$: Include the slope function ϕ_0^s in (2)
$\boldsymbol{u(0) = u'(0) = 0}$: Don't include ϕ_0^s

The first case has $2N+1$ unknowns, The second case has $2N$. This gives the size of $KU = F$. We keep the final "half-functions" ϕ_N^d and ϕ_N^s because the end $x = 1$ is assumed free. No boundary conditions are imposed on u at that end. Natural conditions (Neumann conditions on w) are not imposed on the trial functions.

Please notice the small but important equation $X = (x - ih)/h$ in Figure 3.7. This connects the global coordinate x to the "local" coordinate X. The local coordinate gives the cubic $(1-X)^2(1+2X)$ on a standard interval $0 \le X \le 1$. We can do integrations on the standard interval of length 1, and rescale to the actual x-interval of length h. This local-global mapping is a basic step in finite element codes.

To reach $KU = F$, substitute the trial function $U(x)$ into the weak form of $-(cu')' = f(x)$. Integrate with each of the test functions $V_i^d = \phi_i^d$ and $V_i^s = \phi_i^s$:

Weak form
$$\int_0^1 c(x)\,\frac{dU}{dx}\,\frac{dV}{dx}\,dx = \int_0^1 f(x)\,V(x)\,dx \quad \text{for each } V(x). \qquad (3)$$

As always, the integral on the left side leads to the matrix entries K_{ij} when $U = \phi_j$ and $V = \phi_j$. Both dU/dx and dV/dx are quadratic polynomials in each interval (derivatives of cubics). We recommend numerical integration, and add three remarks.

1. These trial and test functions can still be used when the weak form for $u'''' = f$ integrates **second derivatives** d^2U/dx^2 times d^2V/dx^2. Those will have jumps at the nodes (no delta functions, because slopes are continuous). Hat functions could *not* be used in bending problems, because then we are multiplying delta functions in U'' and V''. The integral of δ^2 is infinite.

Multiplying delta functions and ignoring infinities is a **variational crime** [144]. This has been known to happen in two dimensions, where continuous slopes are harder to achieve. Sometimes the crime is justified, when a "patch test" confirms that $KU = F$ is luckily consistent with the differential equation.

2. The error $u(x) - U(x)$ is of order h^4, because the trial space includes cubics. $U(x)$ could match the Taylor series of $u(x)$ in each interval, until the x^4 term produces an h^4 error. Similarly $u'(x) - U'(x)$ is $O(h^3)$. The actual $U(x)$ from finite elements does not match the Taylor series, because it is based on integrals (the weak form). $\boldsymbol{U(x)}$ **gives the smallest possible error in the energy.**

Section 8.4 will show that the error $\int c(u' - U')^2 dx$ is minimized. In the "energy inner product," $U(x)$ is the *projection* of the true $u(x)$ onto the trial space. The finite element method finds the U that is closest (in energy) to u.

3. In practice, the integrals in (3) are computed separately over each interval $[ih, (i+1)h]$. On that interval only four trial functions are nonzero: ϕ_i^d, ϕ_i^s, ϕ_{i+1}^d, ϕ_{i+1}^s. Similarly only four test functions are nonzero. This produces 16 integrals in $\int c\, U'V'$, which go into the 4 by 4 **element stiffness matrix** K_i.

It is important to see how those element matrices assemble into the global stiffness matrix K. Since ϕ_i^d and ϕ_i^s also contribute to the previous element matrix K_{i-1}, there will be a 2 by 2 overlap in K and 6 nonzeros per row:

Assembled stiffness matrix $K =$

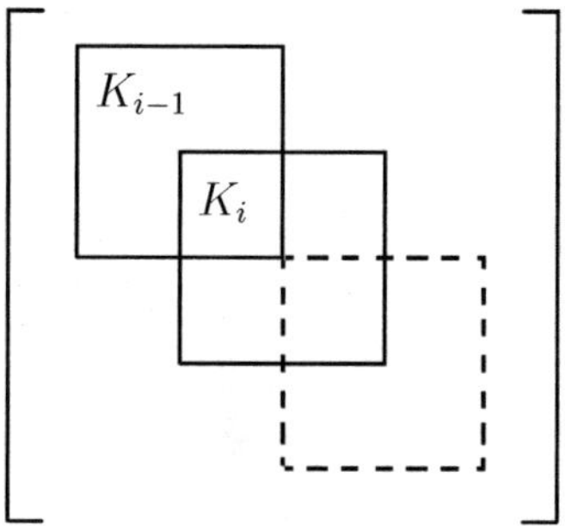

ϕ_{i-1}^d and ϕ_{i-1}^s

ϕ_i^d and ϕ_i^s

ϕ_{i+1}^d and ϕ_{i+1}^s

Fourth-Order Equations: Beam Bending

We turn from an elastic rod to a beam. The difference is that ***the beam bends.*** This bending produces internal forces that try to straighten it. The restoring force is no longer governed by the stretching, but by the ***curvature.*** The displacement u and load f, previously in the direction of the rod, are now *perpendicular* to the beam.

Mathematically the difference is in A. For stretching we had $Au = du/dx$; for bending it will be $\boldsymbol{Au = d^2u/dx^2}$. This is the leading term in the curvature. If it is zero then u is linear and the beam is straight. Otherwise there is a *bending moment* $M = CAu$, or $M = cu''$. The balance between the restoring force and the applied force f will give $M'' = f(x)$, the equation of equilibrium. You recognize that M is taking the place of w; the material constant c is the bending stiffness.

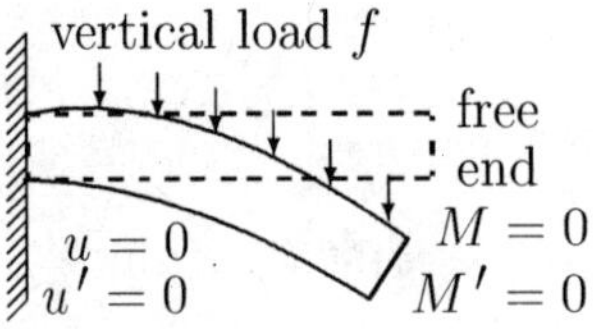

displacement u **balance** $M'' = f$

curvature $e = u''$ moment $M = cu''$

Figure 3.8: Bending a cantilever beam by perpendicular force: $(cu'')'' = f(x)$.

We might make a similar comparison in two dimension between a plate and an elastic membrane. When the plate is bent, it fights back. When a membrane is bent, it doesn't care. Its only forces are "in the plane," resisting stretching. A combination of the two is called a shell, in which membrane forces mix with bending moments and eighth-order equations appear. In fact the success of eggshells lies exactly in this possibility, to balance a perpendicular applied forces by an in-plane internal force. The shell stretches a little, and doesn't break.

The mathematics of beam theory will fit directly into our framework. We expect A^{T} to be d^2/dx^2, with a plus sign, since somewhere there will be two integrations by parts. The square of $(d/dx)^{\mathrm{T}} = -d/dx$ should be $(d^2/dx^2)^{\mathrm{T}} = d^2/dx^2$. The second derivative is formally symmetric, like its discrete approximation in the $-1, 2, -1$ matrix. This symmetry is destroyed at the endpoints (the corners of the matrix) when u and M have different boundary conditions.

$A^{\mathrm{T}}CA$ for a beam $e = Au = u''$ $M = ce$ $f = A^{\mathrm{T}}M = M''$

The rule for homogeneous (zero) boundary conditions is that (Au, M) should equal $(u, A^{\mathrm{T}}M)$. To compare these inner products we integrate both sides by parts. Each side becomes $-\int u'M'dx$, and they are equal when the boundary terms cancel:

$$\int_0^1 \frac{d^2u}{dx^2}\, M\, dx = \int_0^1 u\, \frac{d^2M}{dx^2}\, dx \quad \text{when} \quad \left[M\,\frac{du}{dx} - u\,\frac{dM}{dx} \right]_{x=0}^{x=1} = 0. \tag{4}$$

There are four important combinations which make this expression zero:

(1) **Simply supported end:** $u = 0$ and $M = 0$ (see equation (5))

(2) **Clamped (fixed) end:** $u = 0$ and $\dfrac{du}{dx} = 0$ (see Figure 3.8)

(3) **Free end:** $M = 0$ and $\dfrac{dM}{dx} = 0$ (see Figure 3.8)

(4) **Sliding clamped end:** $\dfrac{du}{dx} = 0$ and $\dfrac{dM}{dx} = 0$ (this seems to be rare)

If one of these combinations is present at each end, the integrated term (4) will vanish and we have correct boundary conditions. The conditions on u come from A, and the conditions on M come from A^{T}. The combination $M = du/dx = 0$ is not allowed. It gives no control of $u\, dM/dx$, the last term in (4).

A **simply supported beam** has no displacement and no bending moment:

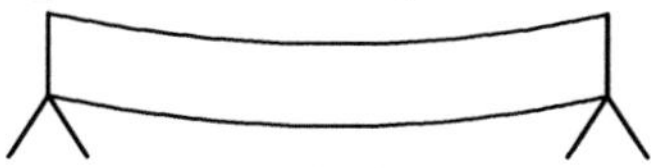

$$Au = \frac{d^2u}{dx^2} \quad \text{with} \quad u(0) = u(1) = 0$$
$$A^{\mathrm{T}}M = \frac{d^2M}{dx^2} \quad \text{with} \quad M(0) = M(1) = 0 \tag{5}$$

The differential equation can be written as a single equation $A^{\mathrm{T}}CAu = f$, or as a pair of equations for u and M:

Bending $$\frac{d^2}{dx^2}\left(c\,\frac{d^2u}{dx^2}\right) = f(x) \quad \text{or} \quad M = c\,\frac{d^2u}{dx^2} \text{ and } \frac{d^2M}{dx^2} = f. \tag{6}$$

With uniform load $f = 1$ and constant bending stiffness $c = 1$, the solution will be a fourth-degree polynomial. A particular solution is $u(x) = x^4/24$:

Uniform beam with $u'''' = 1$ $$u(x) = \frac{x^4}{24} + A + Bx + Cx^2 + Dx^3. \tag{7}$$

The weak form multiplies the strong form (6) by a test function $v(x)$ and integrates:

Weak form (unsymmetric) $$\int_0^1 \frac{d^2}{dx^2}\left(c\,\frac{d^2u}{dx^2}\right) v(x)\,dx = \int_0^1 f(x)\,v(x)\,dx. \tag{8}$$

Two integrations by parts use the essential boundary conditions on $u(x)$ and $v(x)$:

Weak form (symmetric) $$\int_0^1 c(x)\,\frac{d^2u}{dx^2}\,\frac{d^2v}{dx^2}\,dx = \int_0^1 f(x)\,v(x)\,dx. \tag{9}$$

Then the finite element method replaces u and v by cubic elements ϕ and V. This produces discrete $KU = F$. The approximation to $u(x)$ is $U(x)$ in equation (2).

Cubic Splines for Interpolation

Interpolation is the problem of choosing a function $y(x)$ that fits n measurements $y_1, \ldots, y_n$ at n points $x_1, \ldots, x_n$. This is an **exact fit** $y(x_i) = y_i$, not least squares. The function $y(x)$ could be a polynomial of high degree. Or it could be a piecewise polynomial (different in each interval, for example linear):

$$y(x) = a_0 + a_1x + \cdots + a_{n-1}x^{n-1} \quad \text{or} \quad y(x) = y_i\frac{x - x_{i+1}}{x_i - x_{i+1}} + y_{i+1}\frac{x - x_i}{x_{i+1} - x_i}. \tag{10}$$

High degree polynomials are not stable! If you interpolate two many values, the polynomial will oscillate wildly in between (Figure 5.1). This method is only useful for the best functions (analytic functions) and the best nodes x_i. Section 5.4 uses Chebyshev nodes successfully.

Interpolation by linear pieces is entirely stable. But the accuracy is poor, and the slope jumps from one piece to the next. The idea of **splines** is to use cubic pieces with good accuracy $O(h^4)$, and to achieve *continuous slopes and second derivatives.*

Figure 3.9 shows an output from the spline command in MATLAB . There are $n = 5$ interpolation points. In principle, the cubic spline has four free parameters for $a + bx + cx^2 + dx^3$ in the first interval. Then at each of the $n-2$ interior nodes, there is only one parameter—the jump in the third derivative y'''. This gives $n+2$ available parameters, with n conditions $y(x_i) = Y_i$. We need two more boundary conditions in addition to the end values y_1 and y_n.

Continuity Conditions

The spline cannot be computed one interval at a time. At the endpoints of interval i, we only know the heights y_i and y_{i+1}. We are not given the slopes s_i and s_{i+1}. The continuity of y'' at the interior nodes must provide the $n-2$ extra equations we need.

This condition on y'' will couple all the data in equation (11). A change in any input y_i will change the spline far away from the node x_i. Fortunately the size of the change decays exponentially and spline computations are very stable.

At three nodes x_{i-1}, x_i, x_{i+1}, suppose the heights are y_{i-1}, y_i, y_{i+1} and the slopes are s_{i-1}, s_i, s_{i+1}. Those numbers determine one cubic on the left of x_i and another cubic on the right of x_i. The cubics will have the same height y_i and slope s_i at the middle node, because both cubics use those numbers. A spline must also have the *same second derivative* y'' from both sides. This is one condition on the heights and slopes at each interior node. Problem 12 finds that condition:

Continuity of y'' at x_i
$$3y_{i+1} - 3y_{i-1} = h(s_{i+1} + 4s_i + s_{i-1}). \qquad (11)$$

Let me count again, thinking of the y_i and s_i as $2n$ numbers that determine the cubic piece in each interval. The $2n$ equations come from $y(x_i) = y_i$ (n equations), plus the continuity (11) of y'' ($n-2$ equations), plus two more equations in the first and last intervals. The choice made by spline is to clamp the ends: slopes $\boldsymbol{s_1 = s_n = 0}$. The Spline Toolbox offers a different choice called "not-a-knot", when the spline fits the halfway (piecewise linear) values:

Not-a-knot
$$y\left(\frac{x_1 + x_2}{2}\right) = \frac{y_1 + y_2}{2} \quad \text{and} \quad y\left(\frac{x_{n-1} + x_n}{2}\right) = \frac{y_{n-1} + y_n}{2}. \qquad (12)$$

Either way, two extra conditions produce the correct total for a spline $y(x)$. This solves a problem (in 1D) that appears very frequently in scientific computing.

B-Splines

There is an attractive basis for the whole $(n+2)$-dimensional space of splines—piecewise cubics with u, u', u'' continuous. The basis functions are called **B-splines**. They are *uniform* B-splines because we are assuming equally spaced nodes.

A typical B-spline is shown in Figure 3.9. It is nonzero in only four intervals. This is the smallest distance over which a spline can rise from zero and return to zero. We have $B(x) = x^3/6$ in the first interval, so that B, B', B'' are all zero at $x = 0$ as required (and B''' jumps from 0 to 1). This rounded corner at $x = 0$ gives the cubic as the fourth integral of the delta function $\delta(x)$:

Step	**Ramp**	**Quadratic ramp**	**Cubic ramp**	
1	x	$\dfrac{x^2}{2}$	$\dfrac{x^3}{6}$	for $x > 0$

The heights of $B(x)$ at the nodes are $(0, 1, 4, 1, 0)/6$. The slopes are $(0, 1, 0, -1, 0)/2$. Those y_i and s_i satisfy (11) so B'' is continuous. The jumps in B''' are $1, -4, 6, -4, 1$.

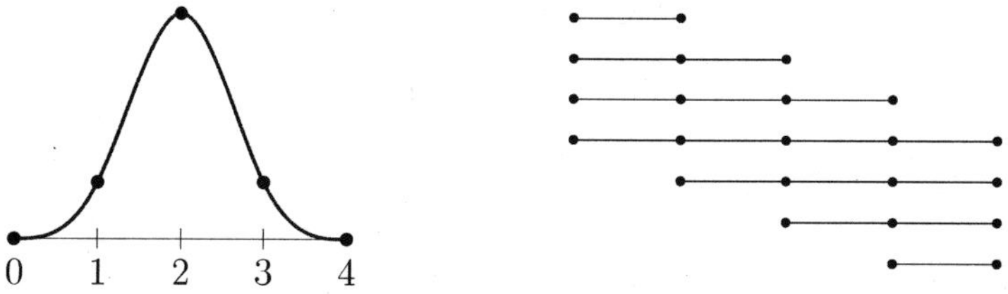

Figure 3.9: The uniform cubic B-Spline. Five nodes contain $n + 2 = 7$ shifts of $B(x)$.

This B-spline produces the $n + 2$ basis functions just by shifting its graph. The second part of Figure 3.9 shows $n = 5$ nodes and $n + 2 = 7$ shifts of $B(x)$, all with nonzero pieces between x_1 and x_5. Any cubic spline is a combination of those shifts:

Basis for all splines on $[0, 4]$

$$y(x) = c_3 \, B(x - 3) + \cdots + c_0 \, B(x) + \cdots + c_{-3} \, B(x + 3). \qquad (13)$$

The spline command gives a stable computation of the spline with heights $y_1, \ldots, y_n$ and clamped ends $s_1 = 0$ and $s_n = 0$. From $y = (0, 1, 4, 1, 0)/6$ we recover the B-spline:

```
x = 0:4; y = [0 1 4 1 0]/6; yB = spline(x,[0 y 0]);
xx = linspace(0,4,101); plot(x,y,'o',xx,ppval(yB,xx),'-');
```

Note Physically, splines come from bending a long thin beam to give it the correct heights at the interpolation points (also called knots). Think of rings at those points, and the beam going through the rings. At all other points the force is zero, the beam is free to choose its own shape, and the solution to $d^4u/dx^4 = 0$ is an ordinary cubic. At each node the ring imparts a point load.

The name "spline" came from naval architects. I was surprised to learn from my class that actual splines are still used (perhaps naval engineers don't trust MATLAB).

Finite Differences for $(cu'')'' = f(x)$

For simple geometries, finite differences can compete with finite elements. The 1D interval is simple. From $1, -2, 1$ second differences we can easily create $\Delta^4 u$:

Fourth difference $\Delta^4 u/(\Delta x)^4$

$$\Delta^2\Delta^2 u \text{ gives } (\Delta^4 u)_i = u_{i+2} - 4u_{i+1} + 6u_i - 4u_{i-1} + u_{i-2}. \qquad (14)$$

A fourth difference matrix has *five* nonzero diagonals. Its first and last two rows will be decided by the two boundary conditions at each end. When $u = 0$ and also $w = cu'' = 0$ at both ends, A and A^{T} will be the special $1, -2, 1$ matrix $-K$. That minus sign disappears for $A^{\mathrm{T}}A = K^2$ at $x = h, 2h, \ldots, 1-h$:

Simply supported beam

$$\frac{d^4}{dx^4} \approx \frac{1}{h^4}\begin{bmatrix} -2 & 1 & & & \\ 1 & -2 & 1 & & \\ & \mathbf{1} & \mathbf{-2} & \mathbf{1} & \\ & & 1 & -2 & 1 \\ & & & 1 & -2 \end{bmatrix}^{\mathbf{2}} = \frac{1}{h^4}\begin{bmatrix} 5 & -4 & 1 & & \\ -4 & 6 & -4 & 1 & \\ \mathbf{1} & \mathbf{-4} & \mathbf{6} & \mathbf{-4} & \mathbf{1} \\ & 1 & -4 & 6 & -4 \\ & & 1 & -4 & 5 \end{bmatrix}.$$

A cantilevered beam is clamped at one end ($u(0) = u'(0) = 0$) and free at the other end ($w(1) = w'(1) = 0$). The same $1, -4, 6, -4, 1$ will appear on the interior rows. But the boundary rows in Problem 11 are changed.

This fixed-free beam is statically determinate. $A^{\mathrm{T}}w = f$ gives w directly without $A^{\mathrm{T}}CA$. In the differential equation, the boundary conditions $w(1) = w'(1) = 0$ allow us to solve $w'' = f(x)$ by two integrations. Then $u''(x) = w(x)/c(x)$ has two more integrations with $u(0) = u'(0) = 0$. In this case the fourth-order equation is solved in two second-order steps.

Problem Set 3.2

1 For a cantilevered beam with $u(0) = u'(0) = 0$ and $M(1) = M'(1) = 0$, solve $u''''(x) = \delta(x - \frac{1}{2})$ for a midpoint load in two steps: $M'' = \delta(x - \frac{1}{2})$ and $u'' = M(x)$.

2 A cantilevered beam of length 2 has $u(-1) = u'(-1) = 0$ at the new left endpoint $x = -1$, and $u''(1) = u'''(1) = 0$ at the right endpoint. Solve $u'''' = \delta(x)$ for a point load at the center $x = 0$. The two-part solution in equation (1) has A, B, C, D to determine from the four boundary conditions.

3 For a built-in beam with $u = u' = 0$ at both ends $x = -1$ and $x = 1$, solve $u'''' = \delta(x)$ by determining A, B, C, D in equation (1) from the four boundary conditions.

4 For a simply supported beam with $u = u'' = 0$ at both ends $x = -1$ and $x = 1$, solve $u'''' = \delta(x)$ by determining A, B, C, D in equation (1).

Problems 5-12 use the 8 cubic finite elements $\phi_0^d(x), \phi_3^s(x), \ldots, \phi_3^d(x), \phi_3^s(x)$ based at the meshpoints $x = 0, \frac{1}{3}, \frac{2}{3}, 1$.

5 Which ϕ's are dropped because of essential boundary conditions for $-u'' = f$?

(a) **Fixed-fixed**: $u(0) = u(1) = 0$.

(b) **Fixed-free**: $u(0) = 0, u'(1) = 0$.

6 Which ϕ's are dropped because of essential boundary conditions for $u'''' = f$?

(a) **Built-in beam**: $u = u' = 0$ at both ends.

(b) **Simply supported beam**: $u = u'' = 0$ at both ends.

(c) **Cantilevered beam**: $u(0) = u'(0) = u''(1) = u'''(1) = 0$.

7 A cubic $a + bx + cx^2 + dx^3$ has four parameters in the first interval $[0, \frac{1}{3}]$. If the slope is continuous ("$\boldsymbol{C^1}$ **cubic**") when it meets the next piece at $x = \frac{1}{3}$, that cubic has ____ parameters. Then the same at $x = \frac{2}{3}$ for a total of ____ parameters.

8 Find the second derivatives of the four cubic elements $\phi_0^d(x)$, ϕ_0^s, $\phi_1^d(x)$, $\phi_1^s(x)$ on the first interval $[0, \frac{1}{3}]$.

9 The **element stiffness matrix** K_e for u'''' on the first interval $[0, \frac{1}{3}]$ is 4 by 4. Find its 16 entries by integrating each product $\phi'' V''$ using the second derivatives from Problem 8. The V's and $\phi'(s)$ are the same, so those integrals (linear times linear) can be found directly or by Simpson's Rule with weights $\frac{1}{18}, \frac{4}{18}, \frac{1}{18}$ at $x = 0, \frac{1}{6}, \frac{1}{3}$.

10 With the same 4 by 4 element stiffness matrix K_e from Problem 9 for each of the three intervals $[0, \frac{1}{3}]$, $[\frac{1}{3}, \frac{2}{3}]$, $[\frac{2}{3}, 1]$, assemble into the 8 by 8 global stiffness matrix K as in Remark 3.

11 The global matrix K from Problem 10 is singular. Now add boundary conditions:

(a) **Built-in beam**: Remove row and column 1, 2, 7, 8 for $u = u' = 0$.

(b) **Simply supported beam**: Remove row and column 1, 7 for ϕ_0^d, ϕ_3^d because $u(0) = u(1) = 0$. Why are the conditions $u''(0) = u''(1) = 0$ *not imposed*?

(c) **Cantilevered beam**: Which rows and columns to remove?

12 Find these second derivatives from the formulas in Figure 3.7 for $X \geq 0$:

$$(\phi^d)'' = -6 \text{ and } (\phi^s)'' = -4 \text{ at } X = 0, (\phi^d)'' = 6 \text{ and } (\phi^s)'' = 2 \text{ at } X = 1.$$

Then the piecewise cubic $U(x)$ in (2) has these derivatives at $x = ih$:

$$\text{From } x \geq ih \quad h^2 U''_{\text{right}} = -6U_i^d + 6U_{i+1}^d - 4hU_i^s - 2hU_{i+1}^s$$

$$\text{From } x \leq ih \quad h^2 U''_{\text{left}} = -6U_i^d + 6U_{i-1}^d + 4hU_i^s + 2hU_{i-1}^s$$

Splines have $U''_{\text{left}} = U''_{\text{right}}$. Show how this gives equation (11).

13 Find the cubic $B(x)$ for the B-spline between $x = 1$ and $x = 2$.

14 The Cox-de Boor recursion formula starts with the box function of degree $d = 0$. This is the constant B-spline with $B_{0,0}(x) = 1$ for $x_0 \le x \le x_1$. Then each degree d comes from the previous degree $d - 1$ [37, page 131]. The key properties follow from the recursion and you can prove this directly from Figure 3.9: $B(x) + B(x-1) + B(x+1) + \cdots = 1$.

15 The section ends with the fourth difference matrix Δ^4 for a simply supported beam. Change -2 to -1 in the first and last entries of Δ^2, and then square to find the singular matrix Δ^4 (with no supports).

16 Suppose you change -2 to -1 only in the first entry of Δ^2. What boundary conditions now correspond to $(\Delta^2)^2$?

17 Use the spline command to interpolate the function $f(x) = 1/(1+x^2)$ at 10 and then 20 equally spaced points on the interval $0 \le x \le 1$. Plot $f(x)$ and the two interpolating splines for $0 \le x \le 0.2$.

18 Find the largest of the errors at the 9 and 19 midpoints in Problem 17. Does this show an $O(h^4)$ interpolation error for cubics?

19 The *hat function* has $f(x) = \{x \text{ and } 1-x \text{ meeting at } x = \frac{1}{2}\}$. Use the spline command to interpolate $f(x)$ with $\Delta x = \frac{1}{3}$, and $\frac{1}{9}$. Plot the two interpolating splines on the same graph. Are the errors of order $(\Delta x)^4$ at $x = \frac{1}{2}$?

20 The *step function* has $f(x) = 0$ for $x < \frac{1}{2}$ and $f(x) = 1$ for $x > \frac{1}{2}$. Plot the interpolates from spline for $\Delta x = \frac{1}{3}$ and $\Delta x = \frac{1}{9}$. For the middle value $f(\frac{1}{2}) = \frac{1}{2}$, are the errors of order $(\Delta x)^4$?

3.3 GRADIENT AND DIVERGENCE

This section leads up to Laplace's equation $u_{xx} + u_{yy} = 0$. That equation is built from two operations, the **gradient** of u and the **divergence** of $\operatorname{grad} u$. Together those produce $\operatorname{div}(\operatorname{grad} u) = 0$, which is Laplace's equation. These pages are about the two pieces $v = \operatorname{grad} u$ and $\operatorname{div} w = 0$. The next sections solve Laplace's equation by complex variables and Fourier series and finite differences and finite elements.

The gradient and divergence will at first come separately. The beautiful parallels between them will be collected in a table that is the key to vector calculus. Then we describe the Gauss-Green formula that connects gradient with divergence. The formula shows that $(\textbf{gradient})^{\text{T}} = -\textbf{divergence}$. This is integration by parts in two dimensions, producing the analog of $(d/dx)^{\text{T}} = -d/dx$. As always, the boundary conditions apply to u (for $A = $ gradient) or to w (for $A^{\text{T}} = -$divergence): not both.

$$\textbf{gradient} = \begin{bmatrix} \dfrac{\partial}{\partial x} \\[2mm] \dfrac{\partial}{\partial y} \end{bmatrix} \qquad \textbf{grad } u = \begin{bmatrix} \dfrac{\partial u}{\partial x} \\[2mm] \dfrac{\partial u}{\partial y} \end{bmatrix} \qquad \textbf{divergence} = \begin{bmatrix} \dfrac{\partial}{\partial x} & \dfrac{\partial}{\partial y} \end{bmatrix}$$

$$\textbf{div}\,(w_1, w_2) = \dfrac{\partial w_1}{\partial x} + \dfrac{\partial w_2}{\partial y}$$

The gradient of a scalar u is a vector v. The divergence of a vector w is a scalar f. Those give the first and last steps in our framework, $\boldsymbol{v = \textbf{grad } u}$ and $\boldsymbol{-\textbf{div } w = f}$. In between is multiplication by $c(x, y)$, and **Laplace's equation has $c = 1$:**

potential $u(x, y)$ $\qquad\qquad\qquad\qquad$ **source $f(x, y) = -\operatorname{div} w$**

$$\begin{array}{c|c|c}
\begin{array}{l} \text{boundary} \\ \text{condition} \\ u = u_0(x, y) \end{array} \Big\downarrow & A = \operatorname{grad} \qquad\qquad A^{\text{T}} = -\operatorname{div} & \Big\uparrow \begin{array}{l} \text{boundary} \\ \text{condition} \\ w \cdot n = F_0(x, y) \end{array}
\end{array}$$

$$\textbf{velocity } v(x, y) = (v_1, v_2) \xrightarrow[\;\;C\;\;]{w = cv} \textbf{flow rate } w(x, y) = (w_1, w_2)$$

When there is a nonzero source $f(x, y)$, $A^{\text{T}} C A u = f$ becomes **Poisson's equation**. When $f = 0$ and the density $c(x, y)$ is constant, $A^{\text{T}} A u = 0$ is Laplace's equation:

Poisson equation $\qquad -\operatorname{div}(c \operatorname{grad} u) = -\dfrac{\partial}{\partial x}\left(c\dfrac{\partial u}{\partial x}\right) - \dfrac{\partial}{\partial y}\left(c\dfrac{\partial u}{\partial y}\right) = f(x, y) \qquad (1)$

Laplace equation $\qquad \operatorname{div} \operatorname{grad} u = \nabla \cdot \nabla u = \nabla^2 u = \dfrac{\partial^2 u}{\partial x^2} + \dfrac{\partial^2 u}{\partial y^2} = 0. \qquad (2)$

Boundary conditions: At each point (x, y) of the boundary we know u *or* $w \cdot n$:

1. The potential $u = u_0(x, y)$ is given (this is a **Dirichlet condition**)

2. The flow rate $w \cdot n = F_0(x, y)$ is given (this is a **Neumann condition**)

Zero values of u_0 or F_0 correspond to fixed or free endpoints in one dimension. Notice that we don't give both components of w!

Outward flow rate $$w \cdot n = (c \ \operatorname{grad} u) \cdot n = c \frac{\partial u}{\partial n} = F_0 . \qquad (3)$$

This section has two chief goals. We want to understand the operators $A =$ gradient and $A^{\mathrm{T}} = -$ divergence. What do they mean separately and why are they transposes? We can explain three key ideas before we start.

1. The gradient extends the derivative du/dx to a two-variable function $u(x, y)$. For the derivative of u in the direction of any unit vector (n_1, n_2) we only need the partial derivatives in $\operatorname{grad} u = (\partial u/\partial x, \partial u/\partial y)$:

   Derivative in direction n $$\frac{\partial u}{\partial n} = \frac{\partial u}{\partial x} n_1 + \frac{\partial u}{\partial y} n_2 = (\operatorname{grad} u) \cdot n . \qquad (4)$$

   The direction of the gradient vector is **perpendicular to the level curves** $u(x, y) =$ constant. Along that curve, u is not changing and the component of $\operatorname{grad} u$ is zero. Perpendicular to a level curve, u is changing fastest (steepest descent or steepest increase). That "normal direction" is $n = \operatorname{grad} u / |\operatorname{grad} u|$, a unit vector in the gradient direction. Then $\partial u/\partial n = (\operatorname{grad} u) \cdot n = |\operatorname{grad} u|$ for fastest increase.

2. A zero divergence is the continuous analogue of Kirchhoff's Current Law: ***Flow in equals flow out.*** The matrix equation $A^{\mathrm{T}} w = 0$ becomes the differential equation $\operatorname{div} w = 0$. This is incompressible flow with no sources and no sinks.

   Divergence-free $$\operatorname{div} w = \nabla \cdot w = \frac{\partial w_1}{\partial x} + \frac{\partial w_2}{\partial y} = 0 . \qquad (5)$$

3. Laplace's equation $u_{xx} + u_{yy} = 0$ or $\operatorname{div} \operatorname{grad} u = 0$ has polynomial solutions that are easy to find. The first examples are $u = 1$ and $u = x$ and $u = y$. An example of second degree is $u = 2xy$. If we want to include x^2, we have to balance it with ____. After that blank is filled in, we have two first-degree solutions (x and y) and two second-degree solutions ($2xy$ and $x^2 - y^2$).

   This is the great pattern to continue, *a pair of solutions for each polynomial degree.* Surprisingly the key is in the complex variable $x + iy$. The solutions to Laplace's equation are "real parts" and "imaginary parts" of complex functions $f(x+iy)$. This idea of using $x+iy$ is developed in Section 3.4. Its magic doesn't work in three dimensions, for $u_{xx} + u_{yy} + u_{zz} = 0$.

There are no surprises in the $A^{\mathrm{T}}CA$ framework, except for the notations ∇ and $\nabla \cdot$ and ∇^2 (or Δ) for the gradient and divergence and Laplacian. The gradient $\nabla = (\partial/\partial x, \partial/\partial y)$ is called "del"—I think it is a nickname for delta—and the Laplacian is sometimes "del squared."

Gradients and Irrotational Velocity Fields

In a network, the potential differences are $e = Au$. A linear algebraist would say: e must be in the column space of A. Kirchhoff would say: *The sum of potential differences around any loop must be zero.* His "voltage law" is clear when the nodes $1, 2, 3$ are in a loop, because $(u_2 - u_1) + (u_3 - u_2) + (u_1 - u_3)$ is automatically zero.

In the continuous case, A is the gradient. We are writing $v = Au$ instead of $e = Au$, because we are thinking of velocity (fluid mechanics) instead of strains and stresses (solid mechanics). In physics, the gradient of potential is force. What are all the velocity vectors $v = (\partial u/\partial x, \partial u/\partial y)$ that come from potentials $u(x, y)$?

We are looking for a **continuous form of Kirchhoff's Voltage Law**. The law has a derivative form (at each point) and an integral form (around every loop).

The gradient $(\partial u/\partial x, \partial u/\partial y) = v$ of a potential $u(x, y)$ is an *irrotational* velocity field grad $u = v(x, y) = (v_1, v_2)$:

Zero vorticity $\qquad \dfrac{\partial v_2}{\partial x} - \dfrac{\partial v_1}{\partial y} = 0$ at each point $\qquad$ (6)

Zero circulation $\qquad \displaystyle\int v_1\, dx + v_2\, dy = 0$ around every loop $\qquad$ (7)

Either of those conditions ensures that the vector field v is a gradient. The link between them is Stokes' Theorem, connecting line integrals around a loop to double integrals over the region inside the loop:

Circulation around a loop is the integral of vorticity

$$\int_C v_1\, dx + v_2\, dy = \iint_R \left(\frac{\partial v_2}{\partial x} - \frac{\partial v_1}{\partial y} \right) dx\, dy\,. \tag{8}$$

So zero vorticity (on the right side) means zero circulation (on the left side). Zero vorticity is "no rotation." This is easy to verify whenever v is a gradient:

$$\text{If} \quad v_1 = \frac{\partial u}{\partial x} \quad \text{and} \quad v_2 = \frac{\partial u}{\partial y} \quad \text{then} \quad \frac{\partial v_2}{\partial x} - \frac{\partial v_1}{\partial y} = \boldsymbol{\frac{\partial^2 u}{\partial x \partial y} - \frac{\partial^2 u}{\partial y \partial x} = 0}\,. \tag{9}$$

The mixed derivatives u_{yx} and u_{xy} are equal! Vector calculus uses that fundamental rule over and over. At the end of this section we move to three dimensions. Then there are three conditions for any gradient $v_1 = \partial u/\partial x, v_2 = \partial u/\partial y, v_3 = \partial u/\partial z$:

curl $v = 0$

$$\frac{\partial v_3}{\partial y} - \frac{\partial v_2}{\partial z} = 0 \qquad \frac{\partial v_1}{\partial z} - \frac{\partial v_3}{\partial x} = 0 \qquad \frac{\partial v_2}{\partial x} - \frac{\partial v_1}{\partial y} = 0\,. \tag{10}$$

A gradient field has zero vorticity: curl $v = 0$. This is one of the great identities of vector calculus: curl grad $u = 0$ for every function $u(x, y)$ and $u(x, y, z)$. **For the plane field $(v_1(x, y), v_2(x, y), 0)$, curl $v = 0$ becomes $\partial v_2/\partial x = \partial v_1/\partial y$.**

Example 1 These velocity fields v and V are gradients of potentials u and U:

$$\textbf{Plane gradient fields} \quad v(x,y) = (2x, 2y) \quad \text{and} \quad V(x,y) = (2x, -2y)\,.$$

The zero vorticity test $\partial v_1/\partial y = \partial v_2/\partial x$ is easily passed. With $v_1 = 2x$, the left side is $\partial v_1/\partial y = 0$. With $v_2 = 2y$, the right side is $\partial v_2/\partial x = 0$. The velocity field $V = (2x, -2y)$ passes the test just as easily. Therefore v and V are gradients.

To find the potential u from v, integrate the first component $\partial u/\partial x$ of the gradient:

$$\frac{\partial u}{\partial x} = v_1 = 2x \quad \text{so} \quad u = x^2 + \text{function } F(y)\,.$$

The second component $\partial u/\partial y = v_2$ requires $\partial u/\partial y = 2y$. Substituting $u = x^2 + F(y)$, that function of y must be $y^2 + C$. There will always be an arbitrary constant C in the potential $u(x,y)$, because the gradient of every constant C is zero. We set $C = 0$ to have a specific potential $u = x^2 + y^2$. Similarly $\operatorname{grad} U = V$ for $U = x^2 - y^2$:

$$\operatorname{grad}(x^2 + y^2) = (2x, 2y) = v \qquad \operatorname{grad}(x^2 - y^2) = (2x, -2y) = V$$

The only difference is a minus sign on $2y$, but that will change Laplace to Poisson. The function $u = x^2 + y^2$ does *not* satisfy Laplace's equation, but $U = x^2 - y^2$ does. The outward flow $v = (2x, 2y)$ does not have zero divergence, but $V = (2x, -2y)$ does.

$$u_{xx} + u_{yy} = 4 \quad \text{(Poisson with source 4)} \quad \text{and} \quad U_{xx} + U_{yy} = 0 \quad \text{(Laplace)}.$$

We want to draw these velocity fields v and V. There is a vector at every point (we show a few points). The velocity $v = (2x, 2y)$ is radially outward in Figure 3.10 with magnitude $|v| = 2\sqrt{x^2 + y^2}$ (the *speed*). The velocity $V = (2x, -2y)$ has the same magnitude but a key change in direction.

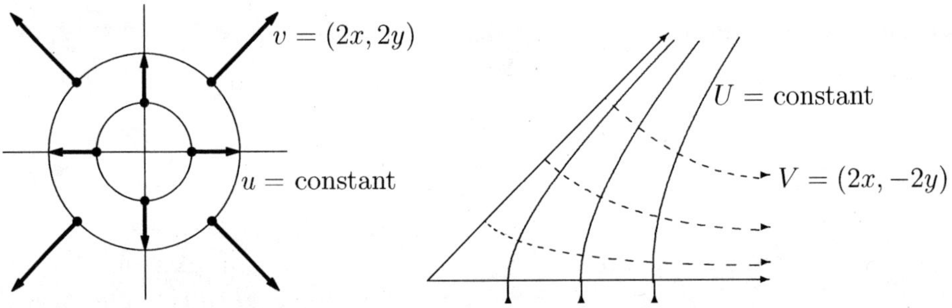

Figure 3.10: The velocity fields $v = (2x, 2y)$ and $V = (2x, -2y)$ are perpendicular to the equipotential curves $u = x^2 + y^2 = c$ (circles) and $U = x^2 - y^2 = c$ (hyperbolas).

Those curves in Figure 3.10 are graphs of $u =$ constant and $U =$ constant. Since the potential is constant, these are **equipotential curves**. Key point: **The velocity vector is always perpendicular to the equipotential curves.**

I think of equipotential curves $u =$ constant as the contour lines on a map. The contours connect points that have the same height (same potential). They are **level curves**. If you are climbing a mountain, the steepest way up is perpendicular to the level curves. That is the gradient direction.

Example 2 The vector field $w = (2y, -2x)$ is not a gradient.

The zero vorticity test $\partial w_1/\partial y = \partial w_2/\partial x$ is failed since $2 \neq -2$. And if we try to find a potential function u, we get stuck:

Failure $\quad \dfrac{\partial u}{\partial x} = 2y$ gives $u = 2xy + F(y)$ but then $\dfrac{\partial u}{\partial y} \neq -2x$.

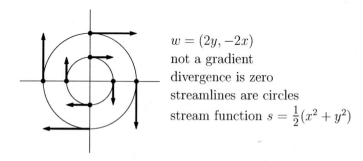

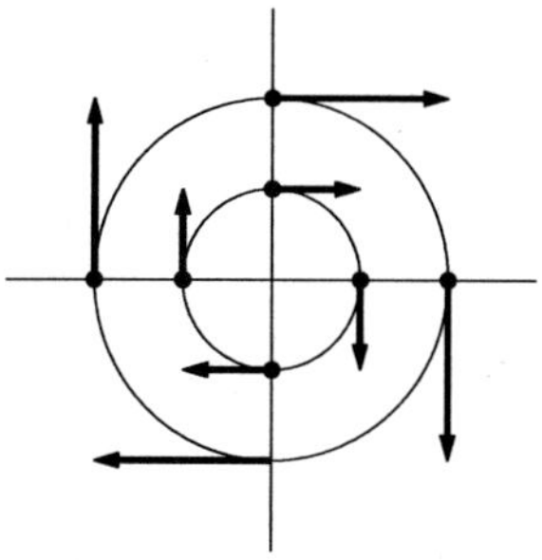

$w = (2y, -2x)$
not a gradient
divergence is zero
streamlines are circles
stream function $s = \frac{1}{2}(x^2 + y^2)$

Figure 3.11: $w = (2y, -2x)$ is tangent to the circles: rotation field, not a gradient.

The Divergence

We turn from Kirchhoff's Voltage Law (no rotation) to Kirchhoff's Current Law (flow in equals flow out). For the incidence matrix of a network, this took us to $A^{\mathrm{T}}w = 0$. With derivatives we can see in a formal way that $(\text{gradient})^{\mathrm{T}} = -\text{divergence}$:

$$A = \begin{bmatrix} \partial/\partial x \\ \partial/\partial y \end{bmatrix} \quad \text{leads to} \quad A^{\mathrm{T}} = \left[(\partial/\partial x)^{\mathrm{T}} \quad (\partial/\partial y)^{\mathrm{T}} \right] = -\begin{bmatrix} \dfrac{\partial}{\partial x} & \dfrac{\partial}{\partial y} \end{bmatrix}. \tag{11}$$

This suggests the right answer but it's not much of a proof. We need to see this "transpose" more deeply, both mathematically and physically. And we need to include boundary conditions, because those are part of A and A^{T}.

Start with the physical statement: Flow in equals flow out. This current law also has a **derivative form** (at each point) and an **integral form** (around every loop).

The flow vector $w = (w_1(x, y), w_2(x, y))$ is source-free if mass is conserved:

Zero divergence $\quad \operatorname{div} w = \dfrac{\partial w_1}{\partial x} + \dfrac{\partial w_2}{\partial y} = 0$ at each point $\quad$ (12)

Zero flux $\quad \displaystyle\int w_1\, dy - w_2\, dx = 0$ through every loop $\quad$ (13)

Important: For the circulation (flow around the loop) we integrated the **tangential component** $v \cdot t\, ds = v_1\, dx + v_2\, dy$. For the flux (through the loop) we integrate the **normal component** $w \cdot n\, ds = w_1\, dy - w_2\, dx$. The symbol s measures length along the curve. It is the shape of the curve (not v or w) that decides ds and t and n:

$$\boldsymbol{ds} = \sqrt{(dx)^2+(dy)^2} \quad \boldsymbol{t\,ds} = (dx, dy) \quad \boldsymbol{n\,ds} = (dy, -dx) \quad \int ds = \textbf{length} \tag{14}$$

The link between derivative and integral forms was Stokes' Theorem (8) for the circulation. Here it is the Divergence Theorem for the flux. This important identity applies to any $w = (w_1, w_2)$. Both sides are zero when mass is conserved:

Divergence Theorem $$\int_C w_1 dy - w_2 dx = \iint_R \operatorname{div} w\, dx\, dy\,. \tag{15}$$

Example 3 We can use the same three vector fields as before:

Find the divergence $\quad v = (2x, 2y) \quad V = (2x, -2y) \quad w = (2y, -2x)$

The first one has divergence $\frac{\partial}{\partial x}(2x) + \frac{\partial}{\partial y}(2y) = 4 =$ source. **Mass is not conserved.** We need a uniform source (like steady rain) to produce this flow field. The flux going out of any region R is balanced by rain landing inside R:

$$\textbf{flux} = \iint \operatorname{div}(2x, 2y)\, dx\, dy = \iint 4\, dx\, dy = (4)\,(\text{area of } R) = \textbf{total rain}. \tag{16}$$

The fields V and w have zero divergence. They are source-free. *Mass is conserved.*

I am going to push further, and define the **stream function**. Whenever the vorticity is zero, there is a potential function $u(x, y)$. **Whenever the divergence is zero,** $\operatorname{div} w = 0$, **there is a stream function** $s(x, y)$:

Stream function $s(x, y)$ $$w_1 = \frac{\partial s}{\partial y} \quad \text{and} \quad w_2 = -\frac{\partial s}{\partial x}\,. \tag{17}$$

For $V = (2x, -2y)$, those equations are satisfied by $s = 2xy$.

You can see why equation (17) for the stream function is consistent with zero divergence. Again the key is the automatic identity between derivatives s_{yx} and s_{xy}:

$$\begin{array}{l}\textbf{div } \boldsymbol{w} = \mathbf{0} \\ \boldsymbol{w} = \textbf{curl } \boldsymbol{s}\end{array} \qquad \frac{\partial w_1}{\partial x} + \frac{\partial w_2}{\partial y} = \frac{\partial^2 \boldsymbol{s}}{\partial \boldsymbol{x} \partial \boldsymbol{y}} - \frac{\partial^2 \boldsymbol{s}}{\partial \boldsymbol{y} \partial \boldsymbol{x}} = \mathbf{0}. \tag{18}$$

There can only be a stream function when the divergence is zero.

Physically, the curves $s(x, y) = c$ are the **streamlines**. The flow travels along those streamlines. The stream function for $w = (2y, -2x)$ is $s = x^2 + y^2$. The curves $x^2 + y^2 = c$ are circles around the origin. Flow traveling around these circles is source-free. But there is rotation so Laplace's equation fails. The example $v = (2x, 2y)$ was a gradient but not source-free; $w = (2y, -2x)$ is source-free but not a gradient.

The best flows combine both properties, so they obey Laplace's equation. There is a potential function $u(x,y)$ and a stream function $s(x,y)$. There are equipotential curves $u(x,y)=c$ and streamlines $s(x,y)=c$. The flow is *parallel* to the streamlines and *perpendicular* to the equipotentials. So those two families of curves are perpendicular to each other, as you see in Figure 3.12.

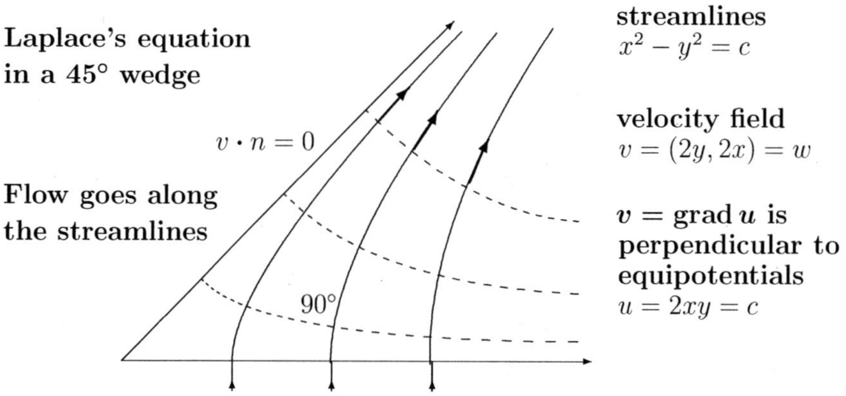

Figure 3.12: The velocity field $(2y,2x)$ is irrotational and also source-free: $\operatorname{div} v = 0$. The equipotentials and streamlines are perpendicular. All curves are hyperbolas!

The Divergence Theorem

What is the meaning of the divergence? To Kirchhoff, it is (flow out minus flow in) at each node. By adding those net flows at all nodes, we get a balance equation for the whole network. The Divergence Theorem integrates instead of adding, to yield a balance equation for the whole region : *Total source in = total flux out.*

Divergence Theorem
$$\iint\limits_R (\operatorname{div} w)\,dx\,dy = \int\limits_B (w \cdot n)\,ds = \int\limits_B (w_1\,dy - w_2\,dx)\,. \quad (19)$$

Suppose $\operatorname{div} w = 0$ at all points: no source or sink. Then the left side will be zero for every region R. So the integral around the boundary B is also zero. That integral of the outward flow $w \cdot n$ is the **flux through the boundary** (out minus in).

Figure 3.13 shows the flux $w \cdot n\,ds$ through a boundary segment of length ds. That flux is the product of "flow rate out" times ds. The flow rate out is the normal component $w \cdot n$ (the other component of w is along the boundary, not out). So the flux is $w \cdot n\,ds = w_1\,dy - w_2\,dx$, which we integrate around the boundary B.

Suppose we look only at the horizontal component w_1 of the flow (set $w_2 = 0$ as in Figure 3.13.) Then the statement of the Divergence Theorem becomes clearer:

Horizontal flow
$\boldsymbol{w = (w_1(x, y), 0)}$

$$\iint\limits_R \frac{\partial w_1}{\partial x}\, dx\, dy = \int\limits_B w_1\, dy\,. \tag{20}$$

On each line across R, the x-integral of $\partial w_1/\partial x$ is ordinary one-dimensional calculus. That integral equals $w_1(\textbf{right}) - w_1(\textbf{left})$. Then the y-integral of $w_1(\textbf{right})$ produces $\int w_1\, dy$ up the right side of the boundary B. Since dy is negative down the left side of B, that part of $\int w_1\, dy$ matches the minus sign on $w_1(\textbf{left})$.

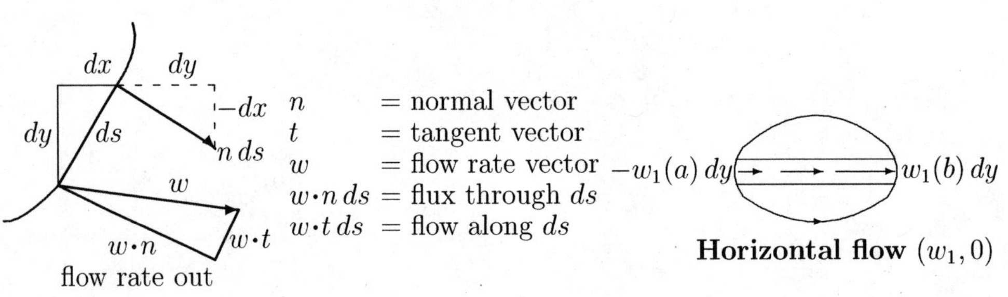

Figure 3.13: The integral of $w \cdot n\, ds = (w_1, w_2) \cdot (dy, -dx) = w_1\, dy - w_2\, dx$ is the flux. In case $w_2 = 0$, this $\oint w_1\, dy$ equals $\iint \partial w_1/\partial x\, dx\, dy$: 1D calculus on each strip.

The same reasoning for $w_2(x, y)$ leads to $\iint (\partial w_2/\partial y)\, dy\, dx = -\int w_2\, dx$. (Going around B, dx is negative along the top!) Add the w_1 and w_2 parts to prove (19). I hope this very informal proof shows how the Divergence Theorem with $w \cdot n$ is the multidimensional version of the Fundamental Theorem of Calculus:

Divergence Theorem in 1D

$$\int_a^b \frac{dw}{dx}\, dx = w(b) - w(a). \tag{21}$$

We don't notice the normal vector n in one dimension, but it is there. At the end $x = b$, the outward direction n is to the right (out of the interval). This gives $+w(b)$. At the end $x = a$, n points to the left (also outward). That gives $-w(a)$.

The Gauss-Green Formula

We come back to the question, why is $A^{\mathrm{T}} = -\operatorname{div}$ the "adjoint" of $A = \operatorname{grad}$? We need a continuous form of $(Au)^{\mathrm{T}} w = u^{\mathrm{T}}(A^{\mathrm{T}} w)$. Those inner products become double integrals. Let me write all the components so you see the integration by parts:

$$\iint_R \left(\frac{\partial u}{\partial x} w_1 + \frac{\partial u}{\partial y} w_2\right) dx\, dy = -\iint_R \left(u \frac{\partial w_1}{\partial x} + u \frac{\partial w_2}{\partial y}\right) dx\, dy + \int_C u(w_1 dy - w_2\, dx). \tag{22}$$

Applying the Divergence Theorem to $u\, w$, that is $\iint \operatorname{div}(u\, w) dx\, dy = \int u w \cdot n\, ds$.

The x derivative is removed from u and applied to w_1. The y derivative is applied to w_2. Better to use vector notation and recognize the gradient and divergence:

Gauss-Green $$\iint_R (\operatorname{grad} u) \cdot w \, dx \, dy = \iint_R u(-\operatorname{div} w) \, dx \, dy + \int_C u \, w \cdot n \, ds. \quad (23)$$

To see the connection with the Divergence Theorem, you need the divergence of uw:

$$\frac{\partial}{\partial x}(uw_1) + \frac{\partial}{\partial y}(uw_2) = \left(\frac{\partial u}{\partial x} w_1 + \frac{\partial u}{\partial y} w_2\right) + u\left(\frac{\partial w_1}{\partial x} + \frac{\partial w_2}{\partial y}\right) = (\operatorname{grad} u) \cdot w + u \operatorname{div} w. \quad (24)$$

Now the Divergence Theorem for uw is exactly the Gauss-Green identity (23).

Div Grad Curl in 3D

The gradient and divergence extend directly from two dimensions to three:

Gradient $$\operatorname{grad} u = \nabla u = \begin{bmatrix} \partial/\partial x \\ \partial/\partial y \\ \partial/\partial z \end{bmatrix} u = \begin{bmatrix} \partial u/\partial x \\ \partial u/\partial y \\ \partial z/\partial z \end{bmatrix} \quad (25)$$

Divergence $$\operatorname{div} w = \nabla \cdot w = \begin{bmatrix} \frac{\partial}{\partial x} & \frac{\partial}{\partial y} & \frac{\partial}{\partial z} \end{bmatrix} \begin{bmatrix} w_1 \\ w_2 \\ w_3 \end{bmatrix} = \frac{\partial w_1}{\partial x} + \frac{\partial w_2}{\partial y} + \frac{\partial w_3}{\partial z} \quad (26)$$

$u = u(x, y, z)$ is a scalar and $w = w(x, y, z)$ is a vector. The key questions are still about the equations $v = \operatorname{grad} u$ and $\operatorname{div} w = 0$. We are looking at those separately, before combining them into Laplace's equation $\operatorname{div} \operatorname{grad} u = u_{xx} + u_{yy} + u_{zz} = 0$.

1. **Gradient fields** Which vector fields $v(x, y, z)$ are gradients? If $v = (v_1, v_2, v_3)$ $= \operatorname{grad} u$ then the integral around a closed loop (with $Q = P$) will be zero:

   Line integral = work $$= \int_P^Q v_1 \, dx + v_2 \, dy + v_3 \, dz = u(Q) - u(P) \quad (27)$$

2. **Divergence-free fields** Which vector fields $w(x, y, z)$ have zero divergence? If $\operatorname{div} w = 0$ then *flux = zero*:

Flux through closed surface
Divergence theorem in 3D $$\iint w \cdot n \, dS = \iiint \operatorname{div} w \, dx \, dy \, dz \quad (28)$$

$\operatorname{div} w = 0$ is the continuous analog of Kirchhoff's Current Law. *No source or sink.*

We want a test on v, to know if $v_1 = \partial u/\partial x$ and $v_2 = \partial u/\partial y$ and $v_3 = \partial u/\partial z$ have a solution u (usually they don't). The test comes from **equality of the cross derivatives**. In 2D, $\partial^2 u/\partial x \partial y = \partial^2 u/\partial y \partial x$ produced one requirement $\partial v_2/\partial x = \partial v_1/\partial y$. In 3D there are three cross derivatives and three requirements on v:

Test for gradients $$v = \operatorname{grad} u \qquad \frac{\partial v_2}{\partial x} = \frac{\partial v_1}{\partial y}, \; \frac{\partial v_3}{\partial y} = \frac{\partial v_2}{\partial z}, \; \frac{\partial v_1}{\partial z} = \frac{\partial v_3}{\partial x} \qquad \textbf{curl}\, \boldsymbol{v} = 0.$$

The second question looks at $\operatorname{div} w = 0$. In 2D, this was $\partial w_1/\partial x + \partial w_2/\partial y = 0$. The solutions had the form $w_1 = \partial s/\partial y$ and $w_2 = -\partial s/\partial x$. There was one identity $\partial^2 s/\partial x \partial y = \partial^2 s/\partial y \partial x$. The stream function $s(x, y)$ was a scalar.

In 3D we have three cross derivatives and three identities. The stream function $S(x, y, z)$ is a **vector potential** (s_1, s_2, s_3). 2D fits into 3D when those components are $(0, 0, s)$. The three identities combine into the vector identity $\textbf{div curl}\, \boldsymbol{S} \equiv \mathbf{0}$. Here is the curl of $S = (s_1, s_2, s_3)$:

$$\operatorname{curl} S = \nabla \times S = \begin{bmatrix} 0 & -\dfrac{\partial}{\partial z} & \dfrac{\partial}{\partial y} \\ \dfrac{\partial}{\partial z} & 0 & -\dfrac{\partial}{\partial x} \\ -\dfrac{\partial}{\partial y} & \dfrac{\partial}{\partial x} & 0 \end{bmatrix} \begin{bmatrix} s_1 \\ s_2 \\ s_3 \end{bmatrix} = \begin{bmatrix} \dfrac{\partial s_3}{\partial y} - \dfrac{\partial s_2}{\partial z} \\ \dfrac{\partial s_1}{\partial z} - \dfrac{\partial s_3}{\partial x} \\ \dfrac{\partial s_2}{\partial x} - \dfrac{\partial s_1}{\partial y} \end{bmatrix}. \tag{29}$$

The solutions to $\operatorname{div} w = 0$ are "vorticity fields" $w = \operatorname{curl} S$. If $\operatorname{div} w = 0$ in a volume without holes, then w is the curl of some 3D field $S = (s_1, s_2, s_3)$. The key identity (twin of $\operatorname{curl} \operatorname{grad} u = 0$) adds the x, y, z derivatives of the components of $\operatorname{curl} S$:

div curl $\boldsymbol{S} = 0$ because three pairs of cross derivatives cancel

$$\frac{\partial}{\partial x}\left(\frac{\partial s_3}{\partial y} - \frac{\partial s_2}{\partial z}\right) + \frac{\partial}{\partial y}\left(\frac{\partial s_1}{\partial z} - \frac{\partial s_3}{\partial x}\right) + \frac{\partial}{\partial z}\left(\frac{\partial s_2}{\partial x} - \frac{\partial s_1}{\partial y}\right) \text{ is identically } 0. \tag{30}$$

A gradient field comes from a potential: $v = \operatorname{grad} u$ when $\operatorname{curl} v = 0$.

A source-free field comes from a stream function: $\operatorname{div} w = 0$ when $w = \operatorname{curl} S$.

The identity **div curl** $= 0$ is the "transpose" of **curl grad** $= 0$.

That last statement comes from $(\text{grad})^{\mathrm{T}} = -\operatorname{div}$ and $(\text{curl})^{\mathrm{T}} = \text{curl}$.

Example 4 Is $v = (yz, xz, xy)$ a gradient field? Yes, it is the gradient of $u = xyz$. Is v also divergence-free? Yes, its divergence is $0 + 0 + 0$. Then $\operatorname{div} v = \operatorname{div} \operatorname{grad} u = 0$, and $u = xyz$ solves Laplace's equation $u_{xx} + u_{yy} + u_{zz} = 0$.

The vector potential $S = \frac{1}{2}(y^2 z, z^2 x, x^2 y)$ has $v = \operatorname{curl} S$ (to verify directly). But notice something new in 3D: Any gradient field can be added to S without changing $\operatorname{curl} S$ (because $\operatorname{curl} \operatorname{grad} u = 0$). This is a "gauge transformation." In 2D we could only add a constant to $s(x, y)$.

Example 5 Suppose (v_1, v_2, v_3) is a **rotation field.** The flow goes around a fixed axis. Then $\operatorname{curl} v$ is *not zero.* In fact $\operatorname{curl} v$ points in the direction of the rotation axis. So v is not the gradient of any potential u. If a particle is pushed around the axis (take this v to be a force field) then it picks up energy. The work integral (27) is not zero.

The rotation field does have zero divergence. In 2D it was $v = (-y, x)$.

Example 6 The **radial field** $v = (x, y, z)$ is the gradient of $u = \frac{1}{2}(x^2 + y^2 + z^2)$. But this field has divergence $1 + 1 + 1 = 3$. In other words $\operatorname{div}\operatorname{grad} u = u_{xx} + u_{yy} + u_{zz} = 3$.

We have Poisson's equation with source $f = 3$. The flux out of any closed surface S is 3 times the volume V inside. Suppose that surface is the sphere $x^2 + y^2 + z^2 = R^2$:

$$\boldsymbol{V = \frac{4}{3}\pi R^3} \quad \text{Flux} \iint v \cdot n \, dS = \iint R \, dS \quad \textbf{Check}\,(\boldsymbol{R})\,(\textbf{area}) = \boldsymbol{4\pi R^3 = 3V}$$

Here is a table to bring together the principal facts of vector calculus. In two dimensions, the equipotentials and streamlines are perpendicular. But the underlying ideas are parallel.

Gradient and Divergence
Plane Vector Fields $\boldsymbol{v(x,y)}$ and $\boldsymbol{w(x,y)}$

$\boldsymbol{v = \textbf{grad}\, u = \nabla u}$	$\boldsymbol{\textbf{div}\, w = \nabla \cdot w = 0}$
Potential $\boldsymbol{u}$ $v_1 = \dfrac{\partial u}{\partial x}, v_2 = \dfrac{\partial u}{\partial y}$	**Stream function $\boldsymbol{s}$** $w_1 = \dfrac{\partial s}{\partial y}, w_2 = -\dfrac{\partial s}{\partial x}$
Test on v: $\operatorname{curl} v = \dfrac{\partial v_2}{\partial x} - \dfrac{\partial v_1}{\partial y} = 0$	Test on w: $\operatorname{div} w = \dfrac{\partial w_1}{\partial x} + \dfrac{\partial w_2}{\partial y} = 0$
Irrotational flow: zero vorticity	Solenoidal flow: zero source
Net circulation around loops is zero:	Net flux through loops is zero:
$\oint v_{\text{tangent}}\, ds = \int v_1\, dx + v_2\, dy = 0$	$\oint w_{\text{normal}}\, ds = \int w_1\, dy - w_2\, dx = 0$
Continuous form of the Voltage Law	Continuous form of the Current Law
Equipotentials: $u(x, y) = \text{constant}$	**Streamlines:** $s(x, y) = \text{constant}$
v is perpendicular to equipotentials	w is tangent to streamlines

Gauss-Green $$\iint w \cdot \operatorname{grad} u \, dx\, dy = \iint u(-\operatorname{div} w)\, dx\, dy + \int u\, w \cdot n \, ds \qquad (31)$$

$\boldsymbol{A^{\mathrm{T}} = (\textbf{grad})^{\mathrm{T}} = -\,\textbf{div}}$ **from integration by parts** $(Au)^{\mathrm{T}} w = u^{\mathrm{T}}(A^{\mathrm{T}} w)$ (32)

Divergence Theorem when $\boldsymbol{u = 1}$ $$\iint (\operatorname{div} w)\, dx\, dy = \oint w \cdot n \, ds \qquad (33)$$

Problem Set 3.3

1 For uniform flow $v=(1,0)=w$, what are the equipotentials and streamlines? For a flow field $w=(0,x)$ what are the streamlines? (Solve for s, there is no u.)

2 Show that this *shear flow* $w=(0,x)$ is not a gradient field. But the streamlines are straight vertical lines, parallel to w. How can there be any rotation when the flow is all upward or downward?

3 *Discrete Divergence Theorem* The flows out of nodes 1, 2, 4 are w_1+w_3 and ____ and ____. The sum of those three "divergences" is the total flow ____ across the dashed line.

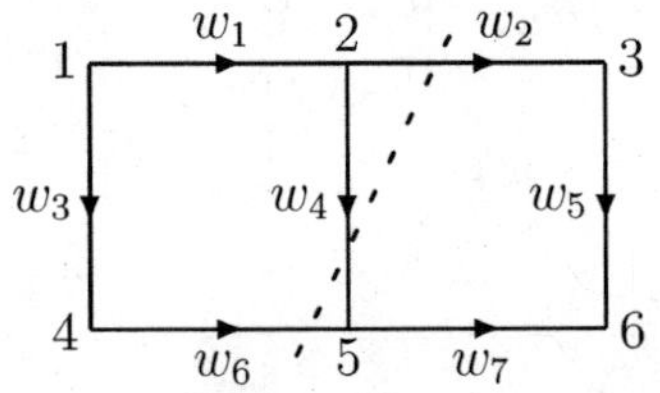

4 *Discrete Stokes Theorem* The circulation around the left rectangle is $w_3+w_6-w_4-w_1$. Add to the circulation around the right rectangle to get the circulation around the large rectangle. (The continuous Stokes Theorem is a foundation of modern calculus.)

5 In Stokes' law (8), let $v_1=-y$ and $v_2=0$ to show that the area of S equals the line integral $-\int_C y\,dx$. Find the area of an ellipse ($x=a\cos t$, $y=b\sin t$, $x^2/a^2+y^2/b^2=1$, $0\le t\le 2\pi$).

6 By computing curl v, show that $v=(y^2,x^2)$ is not the gradient of any function u but that $v=(y^2,2xy)$ is such a gradient—and find u.

7 From div w, show that $w=(x^2,y^2)$ does not have the form $(\partial s/\partial y,-\partial s/\partial x)$ for any function s. Show that $w=(y^2,x^2)$ does have that form, and find the stream function s.

8 If $u=x^2$ in the square $S=\{-1<x,y<1\}$, compute both sides when $w=$ grad u:

$$\textbf{Divergence Theorem}\quad \iint_S \operatorname{div}\operatorname{grad} u\,dx\,dy=\int_C n\cdot\operatorname{grad} u\,ds.$$

9 The curves $u(x,y)=$ constant are orthogonal to the family $s(x,y)=$ constant if grad u is perpendicular to grad s. These gradient vectors are at right angles to the curves, which can be equipotentials and streamlines. Construct $s(x,y)$ and verify $(\operatorname{grad} u)^{\mathrm{T}}(\operatorname{grad} s)=0$:

(a) $u(x,y)=y$: equipotentials are parallel horizontal lines

(b) $u(x,y) = x - y$: equipotentials are parallel 45° lines

(c) $u(x,y) = \log(x^2 + y^2)^{1/2}$: equipotentials are concentric circles.

10 Which u and s correspond to $v = (u_x, u_y) = (2xy, x^2 - y^2)$? Sketch the equipotentials and streamlines for flow into a 30° wedge (Figure 3.12 was 45°). Show that $v \cdot n = 0$ on the upper boundary $y = x/\sqrt{3}$.

11 In the 2D Divergence Theorem, change w_1 to v_2 and w_2 to $-v_1$ for Stokes:

Vorticity inside
Circulation around $$\iint \left(\frac{\partial v_2}{\partial x} - \frac{\partial v_1}{\partial y}\right) dx\, dy = \int v_1\, dx + v_2\, dy.$$

Compute both sides when $v = (0, x)$, and also when $v = \operatorname{grad} u = (u_x, u_y)$.

12 Verify that $\operatorname{curl} v = 0$ when $v = (x(y^2+z^2), y(x^2+z^2), z(x^2+y^2))$. This v must be the gradient of some $u(x,y,z)$. What is u?

13 (a) A *plane field* has the form $v = \big(v_1(x,y),\ v_2(x,y),\ 0\big)$. Find the three components of $\operatorname{curl} v$. The curl of a plane field points in which direction?

(b) Suppose $u = u(x,y)$ depends only on x and y. Find the three components of the plane field $v = \operatorname{grad} u$. Show that the three components of $\operatorname{curl}(\operatorname{grad} u) = 0$ give the two-dimensional form (6): zero vorticity.

14 Suppose $S(x,y,z)$ has the special form $S = (0, 0, s(x,y))$. Find the three components of $\operatorname{curl} S$. Check that the identity $\operatorname{div}(\operatorname{curl} S) = 0$ reduces to (18).

15 The *position field* is just $R = (x,y,z)$. Find its divergence and its curl. The direction and magnitude of the flow field $w = (x,y,z)$ are ____. What source term $f(x,y,z)$ is needed to maintain this flow?

16 A *rotation field* is the cross product of the axis $A = (a_1, a_2, a_3)$ with $R = (x,y,z)$:

Rotation field $$v(x,y,z) = A \times R = (a_2 z - a_3 y,\ a_3 x - a_1 z,\ a_1 y - a_2 x).$$

Show that $\operatorname{curl} v = 2a$ and $\operatorname{div} v = 0$. Is v a gradient field? Is v a vorticity field and what is the stream function S? What choice of the rotation axis A gives rotation in the $x - y$ plane, so v is a plane field?

17 Suppose w is a vorticity field $w = \operatorname{curl} S$. Why can you add any gradient field $v = \operatorname{grad} u$ to S, and still have the same $w = \operatorname{curl}(S + v)$? The three equations $w = \operatorname{curl} S$ only determine $S = (s_1, s_2, s_3)$ up to the addition of any $\operatorname{grad} u$.

18 The curl operator is not invertible. Its nullspace contains all gradient fields $v = \operatorname{grad} u$. Take the "determinant" of the 3 by 3 curl matrix in (29) to show that formally $\det(\operatorname{curl}) = 0$. Find two "vector potentials" S_1 and S_2 whose curl is $(2x, 3y, -5z)$.

19 Find $S = (0, 0, s_3)$ such that $\operatorname{curl} S = (y, x^2, 0)$.

20 In three dimensions, why is $\operatorname{div} \operatorname{curl} \operatorname{grad} u$ automatically zero in two ways?

21 For $u(x,y,z)$ and vector fields $v(x,y,z)$ and $w(x,y,z)$, verify these identities:

(a) $\operatorname{div}(uw) = (\operatorname{grad} u) \cdot w + u(\operatorname{div} w)$

(b) $\operatorname{curl}(uw) = (\operatorname{grad} u) \times w + u(\operatorname{curl} w)$

(c) $\operatorname{div}(v \times w) = w \cdot (\operatorname{curl} v) - v \cdot (\operatorname{curl} w)$

(d) $\operatorname{div}(\operatorname{grad} w) = \operatorname{grad}(\operatorname{div} w) - \operatorname{curl}(\operatorname{curl} w)$ (3 components $\operatorname{div}(\operatorname{grad} w_1), \ldots$)

Problems 22–24 use the three-dimensional version of the Gauss-Green formula. This is the **Gauss Law** $(\operatorname{grad} u, w) = (u, -\operatorname{div} w)$ plus $\iint uw \cdot n\, dS$. Formally this identity produces $(\mathbf{grad})^{\mathrm{T}} = -\,\mathbf{div}$ and $(\mathbf{curl})^{\mathrm{T}} = \mathbf{curl}$.

22 By choosing $u = 1$, write down the Divergence Theorem in V. For $(w_1, w_2, w_3) = (y, z, x)$, compute both sides of the Divergence Theorem for $V =$ unit cube.

23 Looking at the 3 by 3 matrix for curl, why does it equal its adjoint (transpose)? Write out the terms in $\iiint (s \cdot \text{curl } v) dV = \iiint (v \cdot \text{curl } s) dV$ when $v = s = 0$ on the surface S of the volume V.

24 (a) If $\operatorname{curl} v = 0$ and $\operatorname{div} w = 0$ in a three-dimensional volume V, with $w \cdot n = 0$ on the boundary, show that v and w are orthogonal: $\iiint v^{\mathrm{T}} w \, dV = 0$.

(b) How could an arbitrary vector field $f(x,y,z)$ be split into $v + w$?

25 Choose u and w in Green's formula to prove $\iint (\psi_{xx} + \psi_{yy})\, dx\, dy = \int \partial\psi/\partial n \, ds$.

26 With $w = \operatorname{grad} v$ in Green's formula show that

$$\iint (u\nabla^2 v + \nabla u \cdot \nabla v) dx\, dy = \int u \frac{\partial v}{\partial n} ds$$

$$\iint (u\nabla^2 v - v\nabla^2 u) dx\, dy = \int \left(u\frac{\partial v}{\partial n} - v\frac{\partial u}{\partial n} \right) ds$$

27 If A is the gradient and C^{-1} is the curl, the saddle point matrix in our framework includes all three of the key operators in vector calculus:

$$M = \begin{bmatrix} C^{-1} & A \\ A^{\mathrm{T}} & 0 \end{bmatrix} = \begin{bmatrix} \text{curl} & \text{grad} \\ -\,\text{div} & 0 \end{bmatrix} = \begin{bmatrix} 0 & -\partial/\partial z & \partial/\partial y & \partial/\partial x \\ \partial/\partial z & 0 & -\partial/\partial x & \partial/\partial y \\ -\partial/\partial y & \partial/\partial x & 0 & \partial/\partial z \\ -\partial/\partial x & -\partial/\partial y & -\partial/\partial z & 0 \end{bmatrix}$$

Show that M^2 is diagonal! It is $-\Delta^2 I$, and the multiplication verifies the useful identity $\operatorname{curl}\operatorname{curl} - \operatorname{grad}\operatorname{div} = -\Delta^2$, as well as $\operatorname{curl}\operatorname{grad} = 0$ and $\operatorname{div}\operatorname{curl} = 0$.

28 Suppose $v = (v_1, v_2, v_3)$ is a gradient field $(\partial u/\partial x,\ \partial u/\partial y,\ \partial u/\partial z)$. The identity $u_{xy} = u_{yx}$ says that $\partial v_2/\partial x = \partial v_1/\partial y$. Write down the other two cross-derivative identities (assuming derivatives exist). Show that they give $\mathbf{curl}\,(\mathbf{grad}\, \boldsymbol{u}) = \mathbf{0}$ **for every function** $\boldsymbol{u(x, y, z)}$. All gradient fields are curl-free.

3.4 LAPLACE'S EQUATION

This section begins with a list of solutions to Laplace's equation $u_{xx} + u_{yy} = 0$. One remarkable point: *those solutions come in pairs.* With every solution $u(x,y)$ will come another solution (we call it $s(x,y)$). One pair can be mentioned right away:

Laplace's equation is solved by $u(x,y) = x^2 - y^2$ and $s(x,y) = 2xy$.

It is quick to check that $u_{xx} = 2$ and $u_{yy} = -2$ add to zero. The particular example $2xy$ has $s_{xx} = 0$ and $s_{yy} = 0$. It is easy to find a simpler pair $u = x$ and $s = y$. With work we can find a cubic pair (start with x^3 and subtract $3xy^2$ so that Laplace's equation has $u_{xx} = 6x$ and $u_{yy} = -6x$). When each u and s is expressed in polar coordinates, using $x = r\cos\theta$ and $y = r\sin\theta$, the pattern starts to appear:

$u(x,y)$	$s(x,y)$	$u(r,\theta)$	$s(r,\theta)$
x	y	$r\cos\theta$	$r\sin\theta$
$x^2 - y^2$	$2xy$	$r^2\cos 2\theta$	$r^2\sin 2\theta$
$x^3 - 3xy^2$	$3x^2y - y^3$	$r^3\cos 3\theta$	$r^3\sin 3\theta$
...	...	...	...

When the potential is u, the stream function is s. When the temperature is u, varying over a region, heat flows along the streamlines $s =$ constant. The link from u to s is called the Hilbert transform. The first step is to complete this list of polynomials.

I am going to jump to the key insight because I don't know any better way to introduce it. That insight involves the **complex variable $z = x + iy$**. The solutions x and y of degree 1 are the real and imaginary parts of z. More important, the solutions of degree 2 come from $(x+iy)^2 = (x^2 - y^2) + i(2xy)$. This was the first time we used $i^2 = -1$. We hope that the degree 3 solutions are the real and imaginary parts of $z^3 = (x+iy)^3$. *They are.* The step into the unknown comes at degree 4:

$$u_4(x,y) + is_4(x,y) = \boldsymbol{(x+iy)^4} = (x^4 - 6x^2y^2 + y^4) + i(4x^3y - 4xy^3)\,.$$

By direct calculation, this does add a new pair of Laplace solutions u_4 and s_4.

The crucial step is $z^n = (x+iy)^n$. Its x- and y-derivatives are $n(x+iy)^{n-1}$ and $in(x+iy)^{n-1}$. The "chain rule" contributes that factor i, from the y-derivative of $x + iy$. Then the second y-derivative contributes another factor i, and $i^2 = -1$ gives the minus sign that Laplace's equation is hoping for:

$$\frac{\partial^2}{\partial x^2}(x+iy)^n + \frac{\partial^2}{\partial y^2}(x+iy)^n = n(n-1)(x+iy)^{n-2} + i^2 n(n-1)(x+iy)^{n-2} = 0\,. \quad (1)$$

In a moment we will convert the solutions $u_n = \mathrm{Re}(x+iy)^n$ and $s_n = \mathrm{Im}(x+iy)^n$ to polar coordinates as $\boldsymbol{u_n = r^n \cos n\theta}$ and $\boldsymbol{s_n = r^n \sin n\theta}$.

Important: *The reasoning that led to equation* (1) *is not limited to the particular functions* $z^n = (x+iy)^n$. We could choose any nice function $f(z) = f(x+iy)$, not just powers z^n, and the chain rule still contributes the same $i^2 = -1$:

$$\frac{\partial^2}{\partial x^2} f(x+iy) + \frac{\partial^2}{\partial y^2} f(x+iy) = f''(x+iy) + i^2 f''(x+iy) = 0\,. \tag{2}$$

That equation is very formal, let me reach this conclusion in another way. We know that any superposition of solutions to Laplace's equation (a linear equation) is again a solution. So we may take any combination of $1, z, z^2, \ldots$ with coefficients $c_0, c_1, c_2, \ldots$ as long as the sum converges. Section 5.1 will study this convergence:

Analytic function $$f(x+iy) = f(z) = c_0 + c_1 z + \cdots = \sum_{n=0}^{\infty} c_n z^n\,. \tag{3}$$

Then the real and imaginary parts of $f(z)$ are real solutions to Laplace's equation:

Harmonic functions $u(x,y) = \text{Re}[f(x+iy)]$ $s(x,y) = \text{Im}[f(x+iy)]$ (4)

Notice the words "analytic function" of z and "harmonic functions" of x and y. The analytic function f is complex, the harmonic functions u and s are both real. Inside any $x-y$ region where the power series in (3) converges, $u(x,y)$ and $s(x,y)$ both solve Laplace's equation. In fact (no proof here) we have in this way found all solutions around the center point $z=0$.

Example 1 One power series that converges everywhere is the exponential series, with $1/n!$ as the nth coefficient c_n:

Series for e^z $$\sum_{n=0}^{\infty} \frac{z^n}{n!} = e^z = e^{x+iy} = e^x e^{iy}\,. \tag{5}$$

Use Euler's great identity $e^{iy} = \cos y + i \sin y$ to separate the real and imaginary parts:

$$e^x(\cos y + i\sin y) \quad \text{produces} \quad u(x,y) = e^x \cos y \quad \text{and} \quad s(x,y) = e^x \sin y\,. \tag{6}$$

We check that $u_{yy} = -u_{xx}$. Laplace's equation is satisfied by both parts of e^z.

Example 2 The function $f(z) = 1/z$ can't be a convergent power series around $z=0$, because it blows up at that point. But at all other points $1/z$ is analytic:

$\boldsymbol{u+is}$ $$\frac{1}{z} = \frac{1}{x+iy} = \frac{1}{x+iy}\frac{x-iy}{x-iy} = \left(\frac{x}{x^2+y^2}\right) + i\left(\frac{-y}{x^2+y^2}\right). \tag{7}$$

Of course those solutions u and s both have problems at $z=0$ which is $x=y=0$.

The Cauchy-Riemann Equations

The potential u and stream function s are closely linked. Physically, the flow velocity $v = \operatorname{grad} u$ is along the streamlines $s =$ constant. Geometrically, the equipotentials $u =$ constant are perpendicular to those streamlines. Mathematically, u and s both come from the same analytic function $f(x+iy) = u(x,y) + is(x,y)$.

The direct connection between u and s comes quickly from first derivatives:

$$\frac{\partial}{\partial y} f(x+iy) = i\frac{\partial}{\partial x} f(x+iy) \text{ by the chain rule. This is } \frac{\partial}{\partial y}(u+is) = i\frac{\partial}{\partial x}(u+is).$$

Match the imaginary parts on both sides, and then match the real parts:

Cauchy-Riemann equations
$$\frac{\partial u}{\partial x} = \frac{\partial s}{\partial y} \quad \text{and} \quad \frac{\partial u}{\partial y} = -\frac{\partial s}{\partial x} \qquad (8)$$

These two equations give the perfect connection between $u(x,y)$ and $s(x,y)$:

Streamlines perpendicular to equipotentials
$$\frac{\partial u}{\partial x}\frac{\partial s}{\partial x} + \frac{\partial u}{\partial y}\frac{\partial s}{\partial y} = \frac{\partial u}{\partial x}\left(-\frac{\partial u}{\partial y}\right) + \frac{\partial u}{\partial y}\left(\frac{\partial u}{\partial x}\right) = 0\,. \qquad (9)$$

Thus $\operatorname{grad} s$ is a 90° rotation of $\operatorname{grad} u$. The derivative of u *across a curve* equals the derivative of s *along the curve*. Suppose we integrate along a curve connecting a point P to another point Q. The integral of $\partial u/\partial n$ is the flow going through the curve. The integral of the derivative of s is $s_{\text{end}} - s_{\text{start}} = s(Q) - s(P)$:

The change $s(Q) - s(P)$ measures the flow passing between P and Q.

Finally we have a physical meaning for the stream function! Streamlines pass through any and every curve from P to Q. The total flow between the points is $s(Q) - s(P)$.

Polar Coordinates: Laplace's Equation in a Circle

Our polynomials $\operatorname{Re}[(x+iy)^n]$ and $\operatorname{Im}[(x+iy)^n]$ are simple for $n = 1$ and 2. They begin to look awkward by $n = 4$. That is because x and y are the wrong coordinates for taking powers of $z = x + iy$. Polar coordinates are much better, where $x = r\cos\theta$ and $y = r\sin\theta$. The combination $z = x + iy$ is fantastic when written as $re^{i\theta}$:

Polar coordinates
$$\boldsymbol{x + iy} = r\cos\theta + ir\sin\theta = r(\cos\theta + i\sin\theta) = \boldsymbol{re^{i\theta}}. \qquad (10)$$

Those coordinates are shown in Figure 3.14. Immediately we can find and split z^n:

Powers of z
$$(re^{i\theta})^n = r^n e^{in\theta} = \boldsymbol{r^n \cos n\theta + ir^n \sin n\theta}. \qquad (11)$$

The real part $u = r^n \cos n\theta$ and the imaginary part $s = r^n \sin n\theta$ are the polynomial solutions to Laplace's equation. Their combinations give all solutions around $r = 0$:

Complete solution $$u(r,\theta) = \sum_{n=0}^{\infty} (a_n r^n \cos n\theta + b_n r^n \sin n\theta). \qquad (12)$$

To be really efficient, we should convert the Laplace equation to polar coordinates:

Laplace's equation in r, θ $$\frac{\partial^2 u}{\partial r^2} + \frac{1}{r}\frac{\partial u}{\partial r} + \frac{1}{r^2}\frac{\partial^2 u}{\partial \theta^2} = 0. \qquad (13)$$

Substitute $u = r^n \cos n\theta$ to get $r^{n-2} \cos n\theta$ times $[n(n-1) + n - n^2] = 0$.

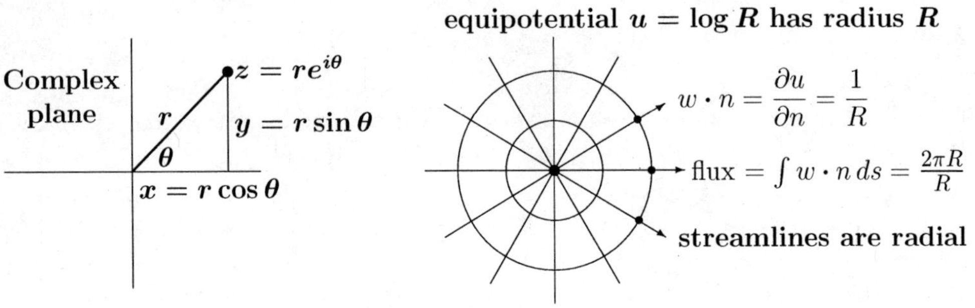

Figure 3.14: The x, y and r, θ coordinates of z. Flux 2π from a point source $2\pi\delta$.

Example 3 The logarithm of $z = re^{i\theta}$ becomes a sum of two simple logarithms:

Radial flow $$\log z = \log r + i\theta \quad \text{so that} \quad \boldsymbol{u = \log r} \quad \text{and} \quad \boldsymbol{s = \theta}\,. \qquad (14)$$

This is a very useful pair of solutions to Laplace's equation (except at the center point $z = 0$, where the logarithm is infinite). The equipotentials $\log r = c$ are circles around the origin. The streamlines are the rays $\theta = c$ going out from the origin, perpendicular to the circles. The flow is leaving from a point source $\delta(x, y)$ at the center.

The magnitude of that source is the flux through any circle of radius R. The flux must be the same for all circles (all R) because there are no other sources:

$$\textbf{Flux} = \int_{r=R} w \cdot n\, ds = \int_0^{2\pi} \left(\frac{\partial u}{\partial n}\right)(R\,d\theta) = \int_0^{2\pi} \frac{1}{R} R\,d\theta = 2\pi\,. \qquad (15)$$

The function $u = \log r = \log\sqrt{x^2 + y^2} = \frac{1}{2}\log(x^2 + y^2)$ satisfies Poisson's equation with the point source $f = 2\pi\delta$. That $\delta(x, y)$ is a *two-dimensional delta function*:

$\delta(x, y)$ in $2D$ $$\iint \delta\, dx\, dy = 1 \qquad \iint F(x, y)\,\delta(x, y)\, dx\, dy = F(0, 0). \qquad (16)$$

Since $r = 0$ is special for the potential $u = \log r$, it must also be special for the stream function $s = \theta$. At $r = 0$, the angle θ is not defined. Watching θ as we circle the origin (so $P = Q$), θ increases by $s(Q) - s(P) = 2\pi$. This equals the flux.

In the language used earlier, **$(\log r)/2\pi$ is the Green's function** for Laplace's equation with a unit source at $r = 0$. The gradient of $\log r$ is $v = w = (x/r^2, y/r^2)$. The Green's function for $u_{xx} + u_{yy} + u_{zz} = \delta(x, y, z)$ in three dimensions is $u = 1/4\pi r$.

Example 4 *We can solve Laplace's equation when the boundary is a circle*:

Laplace solution $$u(r, \theta) = \sum_{n=0}^{\infty} (a_n r^n \cos n\theta + b_n r^n \sin n\theta). \tag{17}$$

On the circle $r = 1$, this solution can match any boundary condition $u(1, \theta) = u_0(\theta)$:

Boundary condition on u $$u_0(\theta) = \sum_{n=0}^{\infty} (a_n \cos n\theta + b_n \sin n\theta). \tag{18}$$

This is the **Fourier series** for the boundary function $u_0(\theta)$. The general formulas for a_n and b_n will come in Section 4.1. Here we choose $u_0 = 1$ on the top half of the circle and $u_0 = -1$ on the bottom half (two jumps on the circle).

The only nonzero Fourier coefficients of this odd function are $b_n = 4/\pi n$ for odd n. The solution inside the circle is smooth (no jump inside). Substitute b_n into (17):

Zero along the x axis $$u(r, \theta) = \frac{4}{\pi}\left(\frac{r \sin \theta}{1} + \frac{r^3 \sin 3\theta}{3} + \cdots\right)$$

Poisson's Equation in a Square

In a circle we separate r from θ. In a square we separate x from y. An example will show how this solves Poisson's equation by an infinite series, when the boundary condition is $u = 0$ on the unit square. Then we can compare this solution (truncating the series after N^2 terms) with the upcoming finite difference and finite element solutions. Those involve N by N grids, so they also produce N^2 numbers.

To work with $-u_{xx} - u_{yy}$ in a unit square, **the key is the eigenvectors** $u_{mn}(x, y)$:

$$u_{mn} = (\sin m\pi x)(\sin n\pi y) \quad \text{gives} \quad -u_{xx} - u_{yy} = (m^2 + n^2)\pi^2 u = \lambda_{mn} u. \tag{19}$$

Using these eigenvectors, the solution of $-u_{xx} - u_{yy} = f(x, y)$ has three steps:

1. Write $f(x, y)$ as a combination $f = \sum\sum b_{mn} u_{mn}$ of the eigenvectors.

2. Divide each coefficient b_{mn} by the eigenvalue $\lambda_{mn} = (m^2 + n^2)\pi^2$.

3. The solution is $u(x, y) = \displaystyle\sum_{m=1}^{\infty}\sum_{n=1}^{\infty} \frac{b_{mn}}{\lambda_{mn}} (\sin m\pi x)(\sin n\pi y)$.

Certainly $u(x, y) = 0$ on the boundary of the square: $\sin m\pi x = 0$ if $x = 0$ or 1, and $\sin n\pi y = 0$ if $y = 0$ or 1. This infinite series is computationally effective when the coefficients b_{mn} decay quickly and can be computed quickly. Example 5 with $f(x, y) = 1$ will be both good and bad: a simple formula for b_{mn} but slow decay.

Example 5 Solve $-u_{xx} - u_{yy} = 1$ with $u = 0$ on the boundary of the unit square.

Solution When the eigenvectors $u_{mn}(x, y)$ are sines, the series $f = 1 = \sum\sum b_{mn}\, u_{mn}$ is a **double Fourier sine series**. This function f separates into 1 times 1:

Sine series in 2D $$f(x,y) = 1 = \left(\sum_{\text{odd } m} \frac{4 \sin m\pi x}{m\pi}\right)\left(\sum_{\text{odd } n} \frac{4 \sin n\pi y}{n\pi}\right). \tag{20}$$

Step 2 divides each $b_{mn} = 16/mn\pi^2$ by $\lambda_{mn} = (m^2 + n^2)\pi^2$. The solution is the sine series with coefficients b_{mn}/λ_{mn}. Here is a quick code poisson.m to compute the center value $u(\frac{1}{2}, \frac{1}{2})$, truncating the infinite series at $m = n = N$. The error is the size $1/N^3$ of the next terms, which alternate in sign (or they would add to a larger error $1/N^2$). This rate of decay $1/N^3$ is normal when $u_{xx} + u_{yy}$ has a jump at the boundary.

```
function u = poisson(x, y)                   % Evaluation points x = [ ] and y = [ ]
N = 39; u = zeros(size(x));                  % size = 1,1 for evaluation at 1 point
if nargin == 1                               % Only x coordinates so 1D problem
   for k = 1:2:N                             % Add N terms in the 1D sine series
      u = u + 2^2/pi^3/k^3 * sin(k*pi*x); end
% xx = 0:.01:1; yy = poisson(xx); plot(xx, yy) to plot u in 1D (2D is below)

elseif nargin == 2                           % x and y coordinates so 2D problem
   for i = 1:2:N                             % -u_xx - u_yy = 1 in unit square
     for j = 1:2:N                           % Add N^2 terms in the 2D sine series
        u = u + 2^4/pi^4/(i*j)/(i^2+j^2) * sin(i*pi*x).* sin(j*pi*y);
     end; end; end                           % 3D would have (i*j*k)/(i^2+j^2+k^2)
% [xx, yy] = meshgrid(0:.1:1, 0:.1:1); zz = poisson(xx, yy); contourf(xx, yy, zz)
```

This section is about analytical solutions of Laplace's equation. We concentrate on two classical methods: **Fourier series and conformal mapping**. The reader understands that those methods work best for special geometries. They are among the important tools of science and engineering, even if their applications are limited. A computational course will emphasize finite elements and finite differences—but Fourier and Riemann and Cauchy will never disappear.

Let me first summarize the special solutions in two dimensions, coming from $f(x+iy)$ and the beautiful relation of $u(x,y)$ to $s(x,y)$: real and imaginary parts.

Laplace's equation $\Delta u = 0$ when $(v_1, v_2) = (w_1, w_2)$

1. **Equipotentials** $u(x,y) = c$ are perpendicular to **streamlines** $s(x,y) = C$

2. **Laplace's equation** $\operatorname{div}(\operatorname{grad} u) = \dfrac{\partial}{\partial x}\left(\dfrac{\partial u}{\partial x}\right) + \dfrac{\partial}{\partial y}\left(\dfrac{\partial u}{\partial y}\right) = \nabla \cdot \nabla u = 0$

3. **Cauchy-Riemann equations** $\dfrac{\partial u}{\partial x} = \dfrac{\partial s}{\partial y}$ and $\dfrac{\partial u}{\partial y} = -\dfrac{\partial s}{\partial x}$ connect u to s

4. **Laplace's equation** also holds for s: $\dfrac{\partial^2 s}{\partial x^2} + \dfrac{\partial^2 s}{\partial y^2} = -\dfrac{\partial^2 u}{\partial x \partial y} + \dfrac{\partial^2 u}{\partial y \partial x} = 0$

5. **Zero vorticity** and **zero source**: Ideal potential flow or heat flow

6. **Complex variable** (2D only) $\quad u(x,y) + is(x,y)$ is a function of $z = x + iy$

$$u + is = (x^2 - y^2) + i(2xy) = (x+iy)^2 = r^2 e^{2i\theta} = r^2 \cos 2\theta + ir^2 \sin 2\theta$$

7. $\boldsymbol{A^{\mathrm{T}}CAu} = -\operatorname{div}(c(x,y)\operatorname{grad} u) = -\dfrac{\partial}{\partial x}\left(c\dfrac{\partial u}{\partial x}\right) - \dfrac{\partial}{\partial y}\left(c\dfrac{\partial u}{\partial y}\right) = f(x,y)$

Conformal Mapping

What to do when the boundary is not circular? A key idea is to change variables. If the boundary becomes a circle in the new variables X and Y, equations (17)–(18) give a Fourier series solution. Then change $U(X,Y)$ back to find the solution $u(x,y)$.

This seems extremely hopeful, to improve the boundary without spoiling Laplace's equation. It is remarkable that the $x+iy$ trick for the solution can combine with an $X+iY$ trick for the change of variables. We will explain the idea and give examples, without any hope of exhausting this beautiful subject.

A change from x, y to X, Y based on an analytic function $F(z)$ is a **conformal mapping**: A region in the x-y plane has a new shape in the X-Y plane.

Conformal mapping $$F(x+iy) = X(x,y) + iY(x,y)\,. \tag{21}$$

If $U(X,Y)$ solves Laplace's equation in these X,Y variables, the corresponding $u(x,y)$ solves Laplace's equation in the x,y variables. Why? Any solution $U(X,Y)$ is the real part of some function $f(X+iY)$. We are not losing our magic combination, because (21) gives $X+iY$ as a function F of the original $x+iy$:

$$u(x,y) = U(X(x,y), Y(x,y)) = \operatorname{Re} f(X+iY) = \operatorname{Re} f(F(x+iy))\,. \tag{22}$$

So u is the real part of $\boldsymbol{f(F(z))}$. This u automatically satisfies Laplace's equation.

Example 6 The squaring function $F(z) = z^2$ doubles the angle θ. It spreads the points z in the top half of the unit circle to cover the whole circle (which is the boundary we wanted). The new variables from $Z = z^2$ are $X = x^2 - y^2$ and $Y = 2xy$:

Semicircle to circle $$(x + iy)^2 = x^2 - y^2 + 2ixy = X + iY\,. \tag{23}$$

X and Y solve Laplace's equation in x, y. And $U = \text{Re}(X+iY)^n$ solves $U_{XX}+U_{YY} = 0$. So the function $u = \text{Re}\, f(F(z)) = \text{Re}(x + iy)^{2n}$ must solve $u_{xx} + u_{yy} = 0$.

There is one danger in conformal mapping, and this example runs right into it. The mapping from X, Y back to x, y involves $(dF/dz)^{-1}$. **The derivative dF/dz should not be zero.** In our example $F = z^2$ has derivative $2z$. So $z = 0$ is in trouble. At that point angles are doubled and Laplace's equation is not preserved.

How does this trouble appear in mapping a semicircle to a circle? The semicircle is closed up by the line from $x = -1$ to $x = 1$. That segment was part of the original boundary. When $z \to z^2$ changes a semicircle into a circle, we get a "crack" from $(0, 0)$ out to $(1, 0)$. The crack tip is at the origin—the bad point where $dF/dz = 0$.

Actually we can live with a bad point on the boundary (not in the interior). The point $re^{i\theta}$ goes to $r^2e^{2i\theta}$. Since θ is doubled, rays from the origin are rotated into other rays. Circles of radius r are taken into circles of radius r^2.

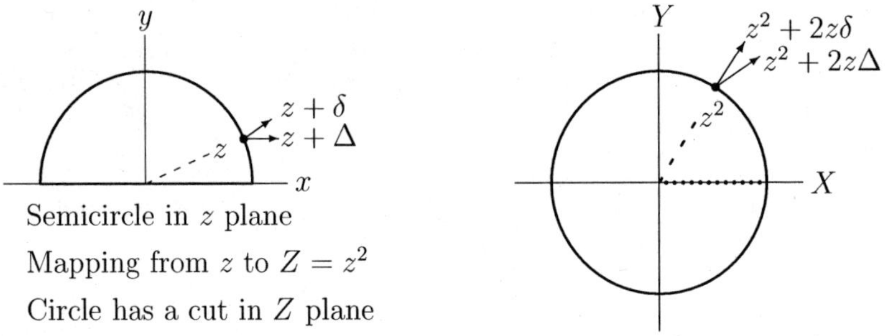

Figure 3.15: Conformal mapping to $z^2 = X + iY = (x + iy)^2$. **Angles preserved**.

Conformal mappings have an extra property, which seems in this case unbelievable. They also ***preserve angles***. Somehow, while doubling every θ, the angle between lines is not changed! Figure 3.15 shows $z + \Delta$ going to $z^2 + 2\Delta$ and $z + \delta$ going to $z^2 + 2z\delta$. The small segments Δ and δ, whose squares we ignore, are multiplied by the same number $2z$—**which rotates both segments by the same angle**.

Question Why not use the mapping that doubles θ without squaring r? That takes the 45° wedge to the 90° wedge, and it takes $re^{i\theta}$ to $re^{2i\theta}$. It looks simple but it has a terrible flaw: It is *not conformal*. The special combinations $x + iy$ and $re^{i\theta}$ are not preserved. Therefore this map will not not produce Laplace's equation in X, Y.

The little triangle is twice as big in the second figure, but its angle is not changed. The amplification factor is $|2z|$, from the derivative of z^2. The straight line to $z + \Delta$ is curved in the Z-plane, because of Δ^2. But the rays meet at the same angle.

At the origin you will not believe that angles are preserved; and you are right. The $45°$ angle in Figure 3.16 is undeniably doubled to $90°$. The mapping is not conformal at that point, where the derivative of z^2 is $2z = 0$.

Example 7 The map from z to z^2 simplifies Laplace's equation in the wedge. Suppose $u = 0$ on the x-axis and $\partial u/\partial n = 0$ perpendicular to the $45°$ line. Since the x-axis goes to the X-axis when z is squared, the first condition looks the same: $U = 0$ on the line $Y = 0$. Since points on the $45°$ line go to points on the Y-axis, and right angles remain right angles (*because angles are preserved*), the condition on that axis is $\partial U/\partial n = \partial U/\partial X = 0$. The solution in the new coordinates is just $U = cY$.

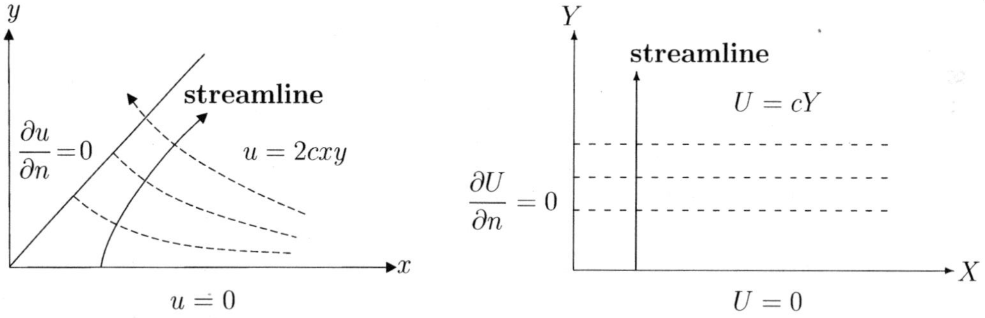

Figure 3.16: The solution $U = cY$ to Laplace's equation gives $u = 2cxy$.

Returning to the x-y plane, $U = cY$ becomes $u = 2cxy$. This satisfies Laplace's equation, and it vanishes on the line $y = 0$. The stream function is $s = c(y^2 - x^2)$. Check that the derivative of $u = 2cxy$ perpendicular to the $45°$ line $y = x$ is $\partial u/\partial n = 0$:

$$\frac{\partial u}{\partial n} = n_1 \frac{\partial u}{\partial x} + n_2 \frac{\partial u}{\partial y} = \left(\frac{-1}{\sqrt{2}}\right) 2cy + \left(\frac{1}{\sqrt{2}}\right) 2cx = 0 \quad \text{on} \quad y = x\,.$$

Perpendicular X and Y give perpendicular hyperbolas $u = C$ and $s = C$.

According to Riemann's Mapping Theorem, every region without holes (except the entire x-y plane) can be mapped conformally onto every other such region. In principle, we can always make the boundary into a circle or a straight line. The difficulty is to do it in practice. For a boundary composed of circular arcs or line segments, a "*Schwarz-Christoffel map*" can be computed by the SC Toolbox.

We want to describe three important mappings. The last one $Z = \frac{1}{2}(z + z^{-1})$ is the key to computational complex analysis (integration and the spectral method in Section 5.4). Remarkably, it also produces a fairly realistic airfoil. But the reality of computational aerodynamics is in three dimensions and not in conformal mapping.

Important Conformal Mappings

1. $Z = e^z = e^{x+iy} = e^x e^{iy}$ **Infinite strip $0 \le y \le \pi$ to upper half plane**

Watch the boundary lines $y = 0$ and $y = \pi$ of the strip. For $y = 0$, $Z = e^x$ gives the *positive* x-axis. For $y = \pi$, $Z = -e^x$ gives the *negative* x-axis. Each horizontal line $y =$ constant is mapped to the ray at angle y in the half-plane $Y = \text{Im } Z \ge 0$.

This conformal mapping allows us to solve Laplace's equation in a half-plane (comparatively easy to do) and then change the geometry to an infinite channel.

2. $Z = (az+b)/(cz+d)$ **Circles to circles, $z = 0$ to new center $Z = b/d$**

If we decide where three points should go, the constants a, b, c, d (real or complex) are determined. The inverse map from Z back to z is also *linear fractional*:

Solve for $z = F^{-1}(Z)$ $\quad Z = \dfrac{az+b}{cz+d}$ leads to $z = \dfrac{-dZ+b}{cZ-a}$ (24)

A straight line is a special case of a circle. The radius is infinite and the center is at infinity, but it is still a circle. Here are particular choices of a, b, c, d:

(a) $Z = az + b$: All circles are shifted by b and expanded or contracted by a.

(b) $Z = 1/z$: The outside of the unit circle $|z| = 1$ goes to the inside of $|Z| = 1$. **The plane is inverted.** The circle of radius r around the origin becomes a circle of radius $1/r$. Flows outside a circle become flows inside.

(c) $Z = (z - z_0)/(\overline{z_0}z - 1)$: $z_0 = x_0 + iy_0$ is any point in the circle and $\overline{z_0} = x_0 - iy_0$. **The circle $|z| = 1$ goes to the circle $|Z| = 1$, and $z = z_0$ goes to $Z = 0$.**

$$\text{If } |z| = 1 \text{ then } |Z| = \frac{|z - z_0|}{|\overline{z}||\overline{z_0}z - 1|} = \frac{|z - z_0|}{|\overline{z_0} - \overline{z}|} = 1.$$

(d) $Z = (1+z)/(1-z)$ **Unit circle $|z| = 1$ to imaginary axis $Z = iY$**

$$z = e^{i\theta} \text{ gives } Z = \frac{1 + e^{i\theta}}{1 - e^{i\theta}}\,\frac{1 - e^{-i\theta}}{1 - e^{-i\theta}} = \frac{2i\sin\theta}{2 - 2\cos\theta} = iY. \qquad (25)$$

3. $Z = \frac{1}{2}\left(z + \frac{1}{z}\right)$ **Circle $|z| = r$ to ellipse, circle $|z| = 1$ to $-1 \le Z \le 1$**

This mapping has a remarkable property. For $z = e^{i\theta}$ on the unit circle, $\boldsymbol{Z}$ **is** $\boldsymbol{\cos\theta}$:

Joukowsky $Z = \frac{1}{2}\left(e^{i\theta} + e^{-i\theta}\right) = \frac{1}{2}(\cos\theta + i\sin\theta + \cos\theta - i\sin\theta) = \cos\theta.$ (26)

The cosine stays between -1 and 1. Points from $|z| > 1$ fill the rest of the Z plane. So do the points from $|z| < 1$. Two values of z are mapped to the same Z.

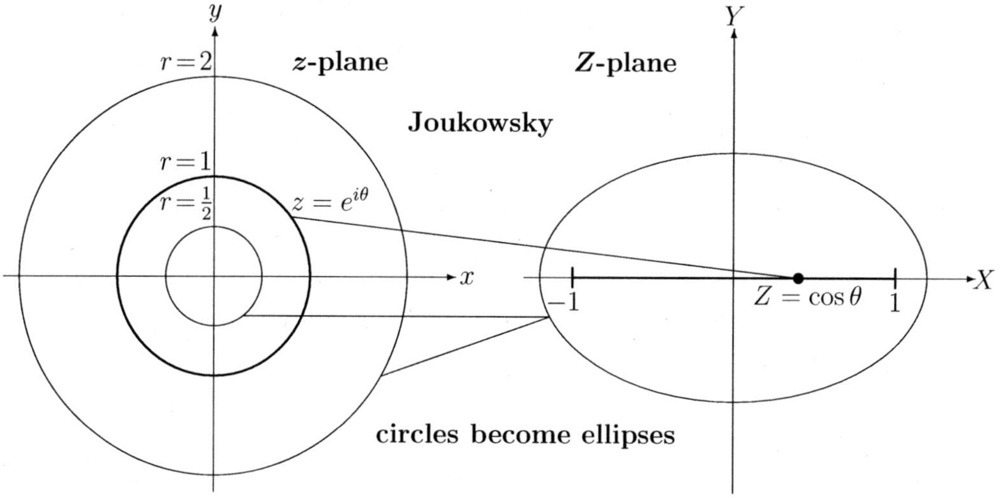

Figure 3.17: The 2 to 1 map from z to $Z = \frac{1}{2}(z + z^{-1})$. Circle $|z| = 1$ to $-1 \le Z \le 1$.

Best of all are the curved lines in the z-plane that become straight in the Z-plane. Those curves are the ***lines of flow around a circle*** in Figure 3.18. If we add a third dimension coming out of the page, they are the ***streamlines*** around a circular cylinder.

The boundary condition $\partial u/\partial n = 0$ prevents flow into the circle, which is a solid obstacle. In the Z-plane this becomes so simple you have to smile: $\partial U/\partial Y = 0$ for $-1 \le Z \le 1$. If $U = aX$ then the stream function is $S = aY$. The constant a is fixed by the velocity at infinity, where the flow is uniform and horizontal.

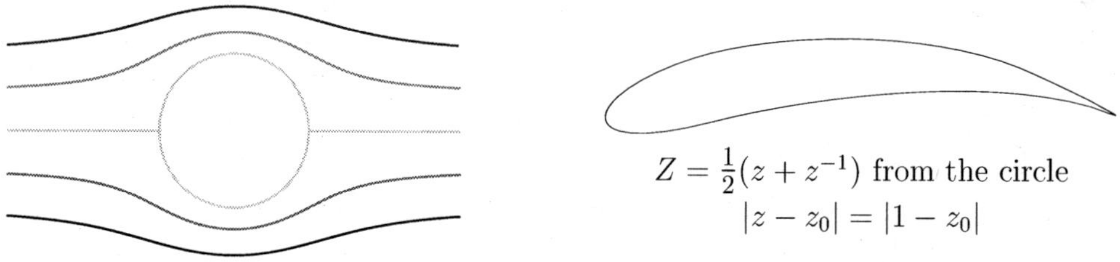

Figure 3.18: Streamlines $Y = y - \frac{y}{x^2+y^2} = c$. Airfoil from an off-center circle.

To go back to the z-plane we take real and imaginary parts of $Z = \frac{1}{2}(z + z^{-1})$:

$$Z = \frac{1}{2}\left(x + iy + \frac{1}{x+iy}\right) \quad X = \frac{1}{2}\left(x + \frac{x}{x^2+y^2}\right) \quad Y = \frac{1}{2}\left(y - \frac{y}{x^2+y^2}\right). \tag{27}$$

Aerodynamics and Design

The streamlines in Figure 3.18 are the curves $Y = c$. Equipotentials would be $X = c$. They stay at right angles because the map from z to Z is conformal. Of course most airfoils are not circles. A true airfoil can have a cross-section like Figure 3.18b, with a sharp trailing edge at $Z = 1$. What is really amazing is that this shape comes from a circle by the same conformal mapping. The circle must go through $z = 1$ to produce the singularity at $Z = 1$, but the center is moved away from the origin. The streamlines around the circle now go around the airfoil.

To map the airfoil onto the line segment from -1 to 1 we actually use three mappings: from the airfoil to the circle in Figure 3.18, then from that circle to the unit circle, and finally from the unit circle to a line in Figure 3.17.

I am afraid there is one more practical point. As it is, this plane will not fly. It needs *circulation* around the airfoil to create lift. The potential needs an extra term $k\theta$, where $\theta(x, y)$ is the usual angle from the origin to the point (x, y). Since θ is constant on rays, $\partial\theta/\partial n = 0$ on the circle. At infinity $\partial\theta/\partial x = \partial\theta/\partial y = 0$.

The potential $u = k\theta$ is not single-valued, since θ increases by 2π as we travel around the origin. That is the source of circulation, which lifts the plane:

New term has real part $k\theta$
$$Z = \frac{1}{2}\left(z + \frac{1}{z}\right) - ik \log z. \tag{28}$$

Applied to an airfoil, which k does the actual solution choose? Kutta and Joukowsky guessed correctly: The circulation adjusts itself to make the velocity finite at the trailing edge. The lifting force $-2\pi\rho V k$ depends on the density ρ, the velocity V at infinity, and the circulation k. This is our ultimate example of a conformal mapping.

For fluids, Laplace's equation comes from steady irrotational incompressible flow. This is "potential flow." For the flight of an airplane, air is not incompressible (and the flight may not be so steady). However one case of crucial importance to aircraft designers can be reduced to Laplace's equation. Linearize around a given flow field:

$$M = \textbf{Mach number} = \frac{\text{plane velocity}}{\text{sound speed}} \qquad (1 - M^2)\frac{\partial^2 u}{\partial x^2} + \frac{\partial^2 u}{\partial y^2} = 0 \tag{29}$$

If $M > 1$ the flow is supersonic and we reach the wave equation instead of Laplace. If $M < 1$ the flow is subsonic, and by rescaling x—the distance in the flight direction—the constant coefficient $1 - M^2$ disappears to leave Laplace's equation.

It is almost true that the battles between Boeing and Airbus depend on numerical simulations (and on politics). The designer changes shape to increase the ratio of lift to drag. **Design is an inverse problem.** This requires many forward solutions. It pays to compute sensitivities: solve an adjoint problem for $d(\textit{output})/d(\textit{input})$.

Problem Set 3.4

1 When $u = \operatorname{grad} v$ in Green's formula, this produces "Green's first identity":

$$\iint u\,\Delta u\,dx\,dy = -\iint |\operatorname{grad}\ u|^2\,dx\,dy + \int u\,(\operatorname{grad}\ u)\cdot n\,ds.$$

If u satisfies Laplace's equation, and $u = 0$ at all boundary points, deduce that $u = 0$. If the boundary condition is Neumann's $(\operatorname{grad}\ u)\cdot n = 0$, deduce that $u =$ constant. These are the *uniqueness theorems* for Laplace's equation.

2 Solve Poisson's equation $u_{xx} + u_{yy} = 4$ by trial and error if $u = 0$ on the circle $x^2 + y^2 = 1$.

3 Find a quadratic solution to Laplace's equation if $u = 0$ on the axes $x = 0$ and $y = 0$ and $u = 3$ on the curve $xy = 1$.

4 Show that $u = r\cos\theta + r^{-1}\cos\theta$ solves Laplace's equation (13), and express u in terms of x and y. Find $v = (u_x, u_y)$ and verify that $v\cdot n = 0$ on the circle $x^2 + y^2 = 1$. This is the velocity of flow past a circle in Figure 3.18.

5 Show that $u = \log r$ and $U = \log r^2$ satisfy Laplace's equation. What are $u + is$ and $U + iS$? Check the Cauchy-Riemann equations for U and S.

6 For each r, the points $Z = \frac{1}{2}(z + z^{-1}) = \frac{1}{2}(re^{i\theta} + r^{-1}e^{-i\theta})$ lie on an ellipse.

Proof Separate Z into $X+iY$ with $2X = (r+r^{-1})\cos\theta$ and $2Y = (r-r^{-1})\sin\theta$:

$$\frac{4X^2}{(r+r^{-1})^2} + \frac{4Y^2}{(r-r^{-1})^2} = \cos^2\theta + \sin^2\theta = 1 \quad \text{produces an } X - Y \text{ ellipse.}$$

Why do the circles $|z| = r$ and $|z| = r^{-1}$ produce the same ellipse?

7 Show that Joukowsky's $Z = \frac{1}{2}(z + z^{-1})$ maps a ray $\theta =$ constant to a hyperbola in the Z-plane. Draw the hyperbola for the ray $\theta = \pi/4$.

8 For $Z = 1/z$, give an example of a z-line that maps to a Z-circle and a z-circle that maps to a Z-line. Challenge: Every circle $|z - z_0| = 1$ maps to a circle in Z.

9 Find a fractional mapping $Z = (az + b)/(cz + d)$ and its inverse $z(Z)$ that maps the upper half-plane $\operatorname{Im} z > 0$ to the unit disk $|Z| < 1$.

10 Find a conformal mapping $Z(z)$ from $\operatorname{Im} z > 0$ to the half-plane $\operatorname{Re} Z > 0$. Find a different $Z(z)$ from $\operatorname{Im} z > 0$ to the quarter-plane $\operatorname{Im} Z > 0$, $\operatorname{Re} Z > 0$.

11 Show that the upper half-plane $\operatorname{Im} z > 0$ maps to the half-strip $Y > 0$ and $|X| < \pi/2$, if $Z = \sin^{-1}(z)$. First try $z = i$ by solving $\sin(X + iY) = i$.

12 Why is the mapping $Z = \overline{z}$ to the complex conjugate of z not conformal?

13 Where is the vertical line $x = \text{Re}\, z = -2$ mapped in the Z-plane if $Z = i/z$? Find a function $Z(z)$ that maps $|z| < 1$ to $|Z| > 2$, inside to outside. Find a function $Z(z)$ that maps $|z| < 1$ to the shifted $|Z - i| < 2$.

14 Substitute $Z = (az+b)/(cz+d)$ into a second mapping $w = (AZ+B)/(CZ+D)$ to show that $w(Z(z))$ is again a linear fractional transformation.

15 A linear fractional transformation $Z = (az + b)/(cz + d)$ has four complex parameters a, b, c, d. We require $ad - bc \neq 0$ and can rescale so that $ad - bc = 1$. Any three points z_1, z_2, z_3 can map to Z_1, Z_2, Z_3 by solving this equation for Z:

$$(Z_1 - Z)(Z_3 - Z_2)(z_1 - z_2)(z_3 - z) = (Z_1 - Z_2)(Z_3 - Z)(z_1 - z)(z_3 - z_2).$$

Find the function $Z(z)$ that maps $z = 0, 1, i$ to $Z_1 = 1, Z_2 = 2, Z_3 = 3$.

16 For $z = 1/z$, a large z means a small Z, and $z = 1$ goes to $Z = 1$. The vertical line $x = 1$ goes to a circle $|Z - \underline{\ ?\ }| \leq \underline{\ ?\ }$ that contains $Z = 0$ and 1.

17 Verify that $u_k(x, y) = \sin(\pi kx)\sinh(\pi ky)/\sinh(\pi k)$ solves Laplace's equation for $k = 1, 2, \ldots$ Its boundary values on the unit square are $u_0 = \sin(\pi kx)$ along $y = 1$ and $u_0 = 0$ on the three lower edges. Recall $\sinh z = (e^z - e^{-z})/2$.

18 Suppose $u_0 = \sum b_k \sin(\pi kx)$ along the top edge $y = 1$ of the unit square and $u_0 = 0$ on the other three edges. By linearity $u(x, y) = \boldsymbol{\sum b_k u_k(x, y)}$ solves Laplace's equation with those boundary values, taking u_k from Problem 17.

What is the solution if $u_0 = \sum B_k \sin(\pi kx)$ along the *bottom edge* $y = 0$ and zero on the other three edges? Again you will see a sinh function.

Note Problem 18 gives a fast algorithm for Laplace's equation on a square. If all four corner values of u_0 are zero, *solve separately on each side and add.* (Reverse x and y for the vertical sides.) If the corner values are not zero, match them with the simple solution $U = A + Bx + Cy + Dxy$.

The fast algorithm will find the solution $u - U$ with boundary values $u_0 - U_0$ (zero at the corners to give a sine series on each edge). This is a *spectral method* of full accuracy, not finite differences of h^2 accuracy. We don't have a "Fast Sinh Transform" to compute $\sum b_k u_k(x, y)$, but I recommend this algorithm.

19 Use the comment in the Poisson code to graph the solution to $-u_{xx} - u_{yy} = 1$.

20 The **Helmholtz operator** $Hu = -u_{xx} - u_{yy} - k^2 u$ has what eigenvalues? The eigenfunctions are $(\sin m\pi x)$ $(\sin n\pi y)$. Revise the Poisson code to solve $Hu = 1$ by a Helmholtz code. Compute $u(\frac{1}{2}, \frac{1}{2})$ for different k increasing to $\sqrt{2}\pi$.

3.5   FINITE DIFFERENCES AND FAST POISSON SOLVERS

It is extremely unusual to use eigenvectors to solve a linear system $KU = F$. Above all, the matrix S containing the eigenvectors of K must be especially fast to work with. Both S and S^{-1} are required, because $K^{-1} = S\Lambda^{-1}S^{-1}$. The eigenvalue matrices Λ and Λ^{-1} are diagonal, so that middle step is quick.

For Poisson's equation $-u_{xx} - u_{yy} = f(x, y)$ in a square, the derivatives are replaced by second differences. K *becomes* $K2D$. The eigenvectors are discrete sines in the columns of S. Then the Fast Sine Transform rapidly multiplies by S^{-1} and S: A fast solver. At the end, we discuss $B2D$ for a Neumann condition $\partial u/\partial n = 0$.

On a square mesh those differences have $-1, 2, -1$ in the x-direction and $-1, 2, -1$ in the y-direction (divided by h^2, where $h =$ meshwidth). Figure 3.19 shows how the second differences combine into a "5-*point molecule*" for the discrete Laplacian. Boundary values $u = u_0(x, y)$ are assumed to be given along the sides of a unit square.

The regular mesh has N interior points in each direction ($N = 5$ in the figure). In this case there are $n = N^2 = 25$ unknown mesh values U_{ij}. When the molecule is centered at position (i, j), the discrete Poisson equation gives a row of $(K2D) U = F$:

$$(\boldsymbol{K}\textbf{2D})U = F \qquad 4U_{ij} - U_{i,j-1} - U_{i-1,j} - U_{i+1,j} - U_{i,j+1} = h^2 f(ih, jh) \qquad (1)$$

The inside rows of $K2D$ have five nonzero entries $4, -1, -1, -1, -1$. When (i, j) is next to a boundary point of the square, the known value u_0 at that neighboring boundary point moves to the right side of equation (1). It becomes part of the vector F, and an entry -1 drops out of the corresponding row of K. So $K2D$ has five nonzeros on inside rows, and fewer nonzeros on next-to-boundary rows.

Inside row of $K2D$

$$[\ldots \; -1 \; 0 \; 0 \; 0 \; -1 \; 4 \; -1 \; 0 \; 0 \; 0 \; -1 \; \ldots]$$

$$\qquad \uparrow \qquad\qquad \uparrow \quad\; \uparrow \qquad\quad \uparrow$$
$$\quad South \quad\; West \;\; East \quad\; North$$

$$K2D =$$

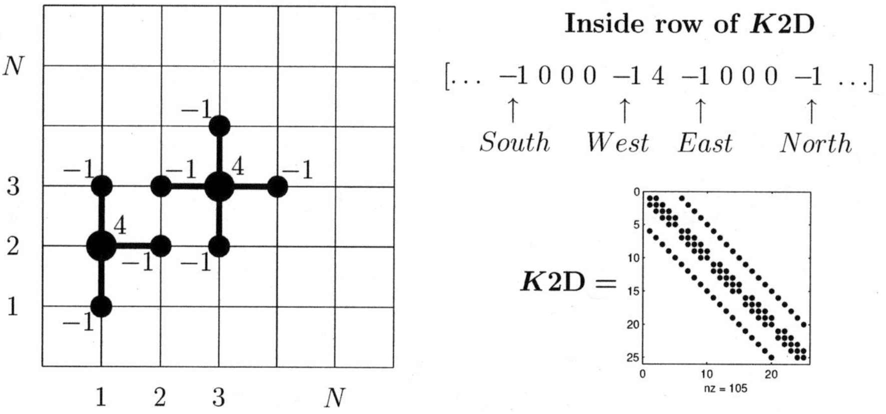

Figure 3.19: 5-point molecules at inside points (fewer -1's next to boundary).

This matrix $K2D$ is sparse. Using blocks of size N, we can create the 2D matrix from the familiar N by N second difference matrix K. Number the nodes of the square a row at a time (this "natural numbering" is not necessarily best). Then the -1's for the neighbors above and below are N *positions away* from the main diagonal of $K2D$. The 2D matrix is *block tridiagonal with tridiagonal blocks*:

$$K = \begin{bmatrix} 2 & -1 & & \\ -1 & 2 & -1 & \\ & \cdot & \cdot & \cdot \\ & & -1 & 2 \end{bmatrix} \qquad \mathbf{K2D} = \begin{bmatrix} K+2I & -I & & \\ -I & K+2I & -I & \\ & \cdot & \cdot & \cdot \\ & & -I & K+2I \end{bmatrix} \tag{2}$$

Size N   **Size $n = N^2$**   **Bandwidth $w = N$**

Time N   **Space $nw = N^3$**   **Time $nw^2 = N^4$**

That matrix $K2D$ has 4's down the main diagonal from equation (1). Its bandwidth $w = N$ is the distance from the main diagonal to the nonzeros in $-I$. Many of the spaces in between are filled during elimination! This is discussed in Section 7.1.

Kronecker product One good way to create $K2D$ from K and I is by the kron command. When A and B have size N by N, the matrix $\mathsf{kron}(A, B)$ is N^2 by N^2. *Each number A_{ij} is replaced by the block $A_{ij}B$.*

To take second differences in all rows at the same time, $\mathsf{kron}(I, K)$ produces a block diagonal matrix of K's. The identity matrix diag(1,...,1) grows into the matrix diag(K, ..., K). In the y-direction, I and K are reversed: $\mathsf{kron}(K, I)$ changes from -1 and 2 and -1 to $-I$ and $2I$ and $-I$ (dealing with a column of meshpoints at a time). Add those x and y second differences:

$$\mathbf{K2D} = \mathsf{kron}(I, K) + \mathsf{kron}(K, I) = \begin{bmatrix} K & & \\ & K & \\ & & \cdot \end{bmatrix} + \begin{bmatrix} 2I & -I & \cdot \\ -I & 2I & \cdot \\ \cdot & \cdot & \cdot \end{bmatrix} \tag{3}$$

This sum agrees with the 5*-point matrix in* (2). The computational question is how to work with the large matrix $K2D$. We will propose three methods for $(K2D)\,U = F$:

1. Elimination in a good order (not using the special structure of $K2D$)

2. Fast Poisson Solver (applying the FFT = Fast Fourier Transform)

3. Odd-Even Reduction (since $K2D$ is block tridiagonal).

The novelty is in the Fast Poisson Solver, which uses the known eigenvalues and eigenvectors of K and $K2D$. It is strange to solve linear equations $KU = F$ by expanding F and U in eigenvectors, but here (with sines) it is extremely successful.

Elimination and Fill-in

For most two-dimensional problems, elimination is the way to go. The matrix from a partial differential equation is sparse (like $K2D$). It is banded but the bandwidth is not so small. (Meshpoints cannot be numbered so that all five neighbors in the molecule receive nearby numbers.) This is part of the "curse of dimension."

Figure 3.19 has points $1, \ldots, N$ along the first row, then a row at a time going up the square. *The neighbors above and below point j have numbers $j - N$ and $j + N$.* Ordering by rows produces the -1's in $K2D$ that are N places away from the diagonal. The matrix $K2D$ has bandwidth N, which can be expensive.

The key point is that elimination fills in the zeros inside the band. We add row 1 (times $\frac{1}{4}$) to row 2, to eliminate the -1 in position $(2, 1)$. But the last -1 in row 1 produces a new $-\frac{1}{4}$ in row 2. A zero inside the band has disappeared. As elimination continues, virtually the whole band of multipliers in L is filled in.

In the end, L has about 5 times 25 nonzeros (this is N^3, the space to store L). **Reason for N^4 operations**: There will be about N nonzeros next to the pivot when we reach a typical row, and N nonzeros below the pivot. Row operations to remove those nonzeros will require up to N^2 multiplications, and there are N^2 pivots. The count of multiplications is about 25 times 25 (this is N^4, for elimination in 2D).

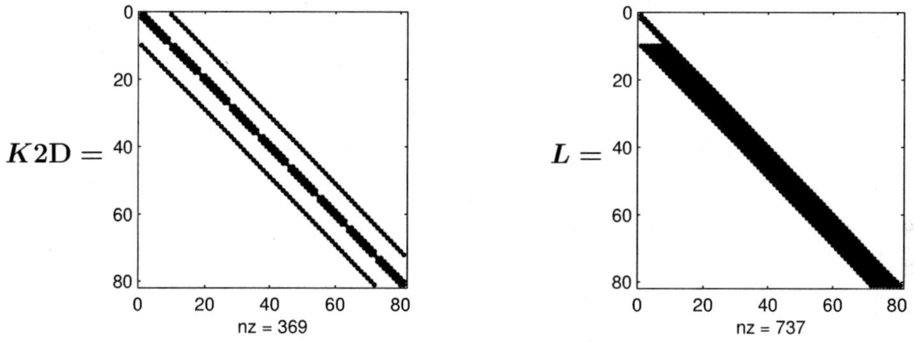

Figure 3.20: Typical rows of $K2D$ have 5 nonzeros. Elimination fills in the band.

Section 7.1 will renumber the meshpoints, to reduce the fill-in that we see in Figure 3.20. This reorders the rows of $K2D$ by a permutation matrix P, and the columns by P^{T}. The new matrix $P(K2D)P^{\mathrm{T}}$ is still symmetric, but elimination (with fill-in) proceeds in a completely different order. The MATLAB command symamd(K2D) produces a nearly optimal choice of the renumbering matrix P.

Elimination is fast in two dimensions (but a Fast Poisson Solver is faster!). In three dimensions, the matrix size is N^3 and the bandwidth is N^2. By numbering the nodes a plane at a time, vertical neighbors are N^2 nodes apart. The operation count $(\text{size})(\text{bandwidth})^{\mathbf{2}} = N^7$ becomes seriously large. Chapter 7 on *Solving Large Systems* will introduce badly needed alternatives to elimination in 3D.

Solvers Using Eigenvalues

Our matrices K and $K2D$ are extremely special. We know the eigenvalues and eigenvectors of the second-difference matrix K. The eigenvalues have the special form $\lambda = 2 - 2\cos\theta$, for equally spaced angles θ. The eigenvectors of K are discrete sines. There will be a similar pattern for $K2D$, which is formed in a neat way from K (by Kronecker product). The Poisson Solver uses those eigenvalues and eigenvectors to solve $(K2D)(U2D) = (F2D)$, faster than elimination.

Here is the idea, first in one dimension. The matrix K has eigenvalues $\lambda_1, \ldots, \lambda_N$ and eigenvectors $y_1, \ldots, y_N$. There are three steps to the solution of $KU = F$:

1. Expand F as a combination $F = a_1 y_1 + \cdots + a_N y_N$ of the eigenvectors
2. Divide each a_k by λ_k
3. Recombine eigenvectors into $U = (a_1/\lambda_1)\, y_1 + \cdots + (a_N/\lambda_N)\, y_N$.

The success of the method depends on the speed of steps 1 and 3. Step 2 is fast.

To see that U in step 3 is correct, *multiply by K*. Every eigenvector gives $Ky = \lambda y$. That cancels the λ in each denominator. Then KU agrees with F in step 1.

Now look at the calculation required in each step, using matrices. Suppose S is the **eigenvector matrix**, with the eigenvectors $y_1, \ldots, y_N$ of K in its columns. Then the coefficients $a_1, \ldots, a_N$ come by solving $Sa = F$:

$$\textbf{Step 1} \quad \textbf{Solve } \boldsymbol{Sa = F} \qquad \begin{bmatrix} & & \\ y_1 & \cdots & y_N \\ & & \end{bmatrix} \begin{bmatrix} a_1 \\ \vdots \\ a_N \end{bmatrix} = a_1 y_1 + \cdots + a_N y_N = F\,. \tag{4}$$

Thus $a = S^{-1}F$. Step 2 divides the a's by the λ's to find $\Lambda^{-1}a = \Lambda^{-1}S^{-1}F$. (The **eigenvalue matrix** Λ is just the diagonal matrix of λ's.) Step 3 uses those coefficients a_k/λ_k in recombining the eigenvectors into the solution vector $U = K^{-1}F$:

$$\textbf{Step 3} \qquad U = \begin{bmatrix} & & \\ y_1 & \cdots & y_N \\ & & \end{bmatrix} \begin{bmatrix} a_1/\lambda_1 \\ \vdots \\ a_N/\lambda_N \end{bmatrix} = \boldsymbol{S\Lambda^{-1}a = S\Lambda^{-1}S^{-1}F}\,. \tag{5}$$

The eigenvalue method is using the $K = S\Lambda S^{-1}$ factorization instead of $K = LU$.

The speed of steps 1 and 3 depends on multiplying quickly by S^{-1} and S. Those are full matrices, not sparse like K. Normally they both need N^2 operations in one dimension (where the matrix size is N). But the "**sine eigenvectors**" in S give the Discrete Sine Transform, and the *Fast Fourier Transform* executes S and S^{-1} in $N\log_2 N$ steps. In one dimension this is slower than cN from tridiagonal elimination. But in two dimensions $N^2\log_2(N^2)$ easily wins over N^4.

The Discrete Sine Transform

Column k of S contains the eigenvector y_k. The jth component of that eigenvector is $S_{jk} = \sin \frac{jk\pi}{N+1}$. For our example with $N = 5$ and $N + 1 = 6$, all the angles are multiples of $\pi/6$. Here is a list of $\sin \pi/6$, $\sin 2\pi/6, \ldots$ that will continue forever:

Sines $\frac{1}{2}, \frac{\sqrt{3}}{2}, 1, \frac{\sqrt{3}}{2}, \frac{1}{2}, 0$ **(repeat with minus signs) (repeat the 12 numbers)**

The kth column of S (kth eigenvector y_k) takes every kth number from that list:

$$y_1 = \begin{bmatrix} 1/2 \\ \sqrt{3}/2 \\ 1 \\ \sqrt{3}/2 \\ 1/2 \end{bmatrix} \quad y_2 = \begin{bmatrix} \sqrt{3}/2 \\ \sqrt{3}/2 \\ 0 \\ -\sqrt{3}/2 \\ -\sqrt{3}/2 \end{bmatrix} \quad y_3 = \begin{bmatrix} 1 \\ 0 \\ -1 \\ 0 \\ 1 \end{bmatrix} \quad y_4 = \begin{bmatrix} \sqrt{3}/2 \\ -\sqrt{3}/2 \\ 0 \\ \sqrt{3}/2 \\ -\sqrt{3}/2 \end{bmatrix} \quad y_5 = \begin{bmatrix} 1/2 \\ -\sqrt{3}/2 \\ 1 \\ -\sqrt{3}/2 \\ 1/2 \end{bmatrix}$$

Those eigenvectors are orthogonal. This is guaranteed by the symmetry of K. All eigenvectors have $\|y\|^2 = 3 = (N+1)/2$. Dividing by $\sqrt{3}$, we have *orthonormal eigenvectors*. $S/\sqrt{3}$ is the orthogonal DST matrix with $\mathrm{DST} = \mathrm{DST}^{-1} = \mathrm{DST}^{\mathrm{T}}$.

Notice that y_k has $k - 1$ changes of sign. It comes from k loops of the sine curve. The eigenvalues are increasing: $\lambda = 2 - \sqrt{3},\ 2 - 1,\ 2 - 0,\ 2 + 1,\ 2 + \sqrt{3}$. Those eigenvalues add to 10, which is the sum down the diagonal (the *trace*) of K_5. The product of the 5 eigenvalues (easiest by pairs) confirms that $\det(K_5) = 6$.

The Discrete Sine Transform is in FFTPACK. For efficient software, that is a good source. Here we connect the DST in a less efficient but simpler way to the FFT, by recognizing the sines in S as **imaginary parts** of the exponentials in a Fourier matrix F_M. The inefficiency is because the angle (0 to π for sines) extends to 2π for the exponentials $w^k = \exp(i2\pi k/M)$. Take $M = 2(N + 1)$, so the 2's cancel.

The N by N sine matrix S is a submatrix of the imaginary part of F_M:

S=imag(F(1:N,1:N))

$$\sin \frac{jk\pi}{N+1} = \mathrm{Im}\ w^{jk} = \mathrm{Im}\big(e^{i\pi jk/(N+1)}\big) \tag{6}$$

The numbering for F started at 0, so that row 0 and column 0 of F are all ones (not wanted in the sine matrix S). For the sine transform Su of an N-vector u, we extend by zeros to an M-vector v. The FFT gives fast multiplication by the complex conjugate $\overline{F}$, then we extract N components of $\overline{F}v$ for the DST which is Su:

```
v=[0; u; zeros(N+1,1)]; z = fft(v);    % Fourier transform of size M
Su = -imag(z(2:N+1));                  % Sine transform of size N
```

Fast Poisson Solvers

To extend this eigenvalue method to two dimensions, we need the eigenvalues and eigenvectors of $K2D$. Those N^2 eigenvectors are ***separable***. Each eigenvector $y_{k\ell}$ (the double index gives N^2 vectors) separates into a product of sines:

Eigenvectors $y_{k\ell}$ The (i,j) component of $y_{k\ell}$ is $\sin\dfrac{ik\pi}{N+1}\sin\dfrac{j\ell\pi}{N+1}$. (7)

When you multiply that eigenvector by $K2D$, you take its second differences in the x-direction and y-direction. The second differences of the first sine (x-direction) produce a factor $\lambda_k = 2 - 2\cos\frac{k\pi}{N+1}$. This is the eigenvalue of K in 1D. The second differences of the other sine (y-direction) produce a factor $\lambda_\ell = 2 - 2\cos\frac{\ell\pi}{N+1}$. The eigenvalue $\lambda_{k\ell}$ in two dimensions is the sum $\boldsymbol{\lambda_k + \lambda_\ell}$ of one-dimensional eigenvalues:

$$(\boldsymbol{K}\mathbf{2D})\boldsymbol{y_{k\ell}} = \boldsymbol{\lambda_{k\ell}\, y_{k\ell}} \qquad \lambda_{k\ell} = (2 - 2\cos\tfrac{k\pi}{N+1}) + (2 - 2\cos\tfrac{\ell\pi}{N+1}). \tag{8}$$

Now the solution of $\boldsymbol{K}\mathbf{2D\,U} = \mathbf{F}$ comes by a *two-dimensional sine transform*:

$$\boldsymbol{F_{i,j}} = \sum\sum a_{k\ell}\sin\frac{ik\pi}{N+1}\sin\frac{j\ell\pi}{N+1} \qquad \boldsymbol{U_{i,j}} = \sum\sum\frac{a_{k\ell}}{\lambda_{k\ell}}\sin\frac{ik\pi}{N+1}\sin\frac{j\ell\pi}{N+1} \tag{9}$$

Again we find the a's, divide by the λ's, and build U from the eigenvectors in S:

Step 1 $a = S^{-1}F$ **Step 2** $\Lambda^{-1}a = \Lambda^{-1}S^{-1}F$ **Step 3** $U = S\Lambda^{-1}S^{-1}F$

Swartztrauber [SIAM Review **19** (1977) 490] gives the operation count $2N^2\log_2 N$. This uses the Fast Sine Transform (based on the FFT) to multiply by S^{-1} and S. The Fast Fourier Transform is explained in Section 4.3.

Note We take this chance to notice the good properties of a Kronecker product $\mathsf{kron}(A,B)$. Suppose A and B have their eigenvectors in the columns of S_A and S_B. Their eigenvalues are in Λ_A and Λ_B. Then we know S and Λ for $\mathsf{kron}(A,B)$:

The eigenvectors and eigenvalues are in $\mathsf{kron}(\boldsymbol{S_A}, \boldsymbol{S_B})$ ***and*** $\mathsf{kron}(\boldsymbol{\Lambda_A}, \boldsymbol{\Lambda_B})$.

The diagonal blocks in $\mathsf{kron}(\Lambda_A, \Lambda_B)$ are entries $\lambda_k(A)$ times the diagonal matrix Λ_B. So the eigenvalues $\lambda_{k\ell}$ of the Kronecker product are just the products $\lambda_k(A)\lambda_\ell(B)$.

In our case A and B were I and K. The matrix $K2D$ added the two products $\mathsf{kron}(I,K)$ and $\mathsf{kron}(K,I)$. Normally we cannot know the eigenvectors and eigenvalues of a matrix sum—except when the matrices commute. Since all our matrices are formed from K, *these Kronecker products do commute.* (The region is a square.) This gives the separable eigenvectors and eigenvalues in (7) and (8).

Packing 2D Vectors into Matrices

Each component of F and U is linked to a meshpoint. That point is in row i and column j of the square. With such a nice ordering, we can pack the numbers F_{ij} and U_{ij} into N by N matrices FM and UM. Rows of the mesh match matrix rows.

The eigenvalues $\lambda_{k\ell}$ of $K2D$ can go similarly into a matrix LM (L stands for lambda). When F is expanded into the eigenvectors $y_{k\ell}$ of $K2D$, the coefficients $a_{k\ell}$ pack into an N by N matrix AM. For the square mesh (not for an unstructured mesh!), the three steps from F to U can be described using FM, AM, LM, UM:

FM to AM	F is a combination of eigenvectors $\sum\sum a_{k\ell}\, y_{k\ell}$ with $a_{k\ell}$ in AM
$AM./LM$	Divide each coefficient $a_{k\ell}$ by $\lambda_{k\ell}$
Find UM	Recombine the eigenvectors $y_{k\ell}$ with coefficients $a_{k\ell}/\lambda_{k\ell}$

Each step has a simple MATLAB construction. The eigenvalues go into LM:

$$L = 2 * \mathsf{ones}(1, N) - 2 * \mathsf{cos}(1\!:\!N) * \mathsf{pi}/(N+1); \quad \% \text{ row of eigenvalues of } K \text{ in 1D}$$
$$LM = \mathsf{ones}(N, 1) * L + L' * \mathsf{ones}(1, N); \quad \% \text{ matrix of eigenvalues of } K2D$$

Expanding F into eigenvectors is a 2D inverse transform. This step is dazzlingly neat as a 1D transform of each column of FM followed by a 1D transform of each row:

2D coefficients of F $$AM = \text{DST} * FM * \text{DST} \tag{10}$$

Remember that the DST matrix with factor $\sqrt{2/(N+1)}$ equals its inverse and its transpose. The forward sine transform (to recombine eigenvectors) also uses DST:

2D coefficients of U $$UM = \text{DST} * (AM./LM) * \text{DST} \tag{11}$$

The inverse of the packing operation is vec. This puts the matrix entries (by columns) into a long vector. Since our list of mesh values has been by rows, vec is applied to the transpose of UM. The solution to $(K2D)U = F$ is $U = \mathsf{vec}(UM')$.

Software for Poisson's Equation

FORTRAN software for Poisson's equation is provided by FISHPACK. The reader will know that the French word *poisson* translates into fish. The Fast Poisson Solver uses the double sine series in equation (9). The option FACR(m) begins with m steps of **cyclic reduction** before that FFT solver takes over.

We now explain cyclic reduction. In one dimension it can be repeated until the system is very small. In two dimensions, later steps of *block cyclic reduction* become expensive. The optimal m grows like $\log\log N$, with operation count $3mN^2$. For $N = 128$ to 1024, a frequent choice is $m = 2$ cyclic reduction steps before the Fast Sine Transform. In practical scientific computing with N^2 unknowns (and even more with N^3 unknowns in three dimensions), the Fast Poisson Solver is a winner.

Cyclic Odd-Even Reduction

There is an entirely different (and very simple) approach to $KU = F$. I will start in one dimension, by writing down three rows of the usual second difference equation:

$$\begin{array}{lrcl} \text{Row } i-1 & -U_{i-2} + 2U_{i-1} - U_i & & = F_{i-1} \\ \text{Row } i & -U_{i-1} + 2U_i - U_{i+1} & & = F_i \\ \text{Row } i+1 & -U_i + 2U_{i+1} - U_{i+2} & & = F_{i+1} \end{array} \qquad (12)$$

Multiply the middle equation by 2, and add. ***This eliminates*** U_{i-1} ***and*** U_{i+1}:

Odd-even reduction in 1D $\quad -U_{i-2} + 2U_i - U_{i+2} = F_{i-1} + 2F_i + F_{i+1}\,. \qquad (13)$

Now we have a **half-size system**, involving only half of the U's (with even indices). The new system (13) has the same tridiagonal form as before. When we repeat, *cyclic reduction produces a quarter-size system.* Eventually we can reduce $KU = F$ to a very small problem, and then cyclic back-substitution produces the whole solution.

How does this look in two dimensions? The big matrix $K2D$ is block triangular:

$$\boldsymbol{K2D} = \begin{bmatrix} A & -I & & \\ -I & A & -I & \\ & \cdot & \cdot & \cdot \\ & & -I & A \end{bmatrix} \quad \text{with} \quad A = K + 2I \quad \text{from equation (2)}. \qquad (14)$$

The three equations in (12) become *block equations for whole rows of N mesh values.* We are taking the unknowns $\mathbf{U}_i = (U_{i1}, \ldots, U_{iN})$ a row at a time. If we write three rows of (14), the block A replaces the number 2 in the scalar equation. The block $-I$ replaces the number -1. To reduce $(K2D)(U2D) = (F2D)$ to a half-size system, multiply the middle equation (with i even) by A and add the three block equations:

Reduction in 2D $\quad -I\mathbf{U}_{i-2} + (A^2 - 2I)\mathbf{U}_i - I\mathbf{U}_{i+2} = \mathbf{F}_{i-1} + A\mathbf{F}_i + \mathbf{F}_{i+1}\,. \qquad (15)$

The new half-size matrix is still block tridiagonal. *The diagonal blocks that were previously A in* (14) *are now* $A^2 - 2I$, with the same eigenvectors. The unknowns are the $\frac{1}{2}N^2$ values $U_{i,j}$ at meshpoints with even indices i. But $A^2 - 2I$ has *five diagonals.*

This bad point gets worse as cyclic reduction continues. At each step the bandwidth doubles. Storage and computation and roundoff error are increasing rapidly, but stable variants were developed by Buneman and Hockney. The clear explanation in [28] allows other boundary conditions and other separable equations.

Cyclic reduction is associated to a *red-black ordering.* No equation contains two red unknowns or two black unknowns (D_{black} and D_{red} are diagonal):

Red variables in black equations
Black variables in red equations

$$\begin{bmatrix} D_{\text{b}} & R \\ B & D_{\text{r}} \end{bmatrix} \begin{bmatrix} u_{\text{black}} \\ u_{\text{red}} \end{bmatrix} = \begin{bmatrix} f_{\text{black}} \\ f_{\text{red}} \end{bmatrix}$$

Neumann Conditions and $B2D$

Suppose $\partial u/\partial n = 0$ is the boundary condition on the sides of a square. In 1D, this zero slope condition $du/dx = 0$ (free end) led to the singular second difference matrix B. The corner entries B_{11} and B_{NN} are 1, not 2. A natural choice in two dimensions would seem to be $\mathsf{kron}(I, B) + \mathsf{kron}(B, I)$, but that is not right. **The correct choice for B2D replaces I by the matrix $D = \mathsf{diag}\left(\left[\frac{1}{2}\ 1\ \cdots\ 1\ \frac{1}{2}\right]\right)$.**

B2D with $N=3$
$\mathsf{kron}(\boldsymbol{D}, \boldsymbol{B}) + \mathsf{kron}(\boldsymbol{B}, \boldsymbol{D})$

$$\boldsymbol{B2D} = \begin{bmatrix} B/2 & & \\ & B & \\ & & B/2 \end{bmatrix} + \begin{bmatrix} D & -D & 0 \\ -D & 2D & -D \\ 0 & -D & D \end{bmatrix}. \qquad (16)$$

The mysterious factor $\frac{1}{2}$ appeared at a free end already in Section 1.2, in the Worked Example. Without it, the approximation was only first order accurate. In 1D and again in 2D, the right side f needs the factors $\frac{1}{2}$ at boundary points. The new aspect in 2D is $-u_{xx} = f + u_{yy}$, and u_{yy} is also multiplied by $\frac{1}{2}$ at vertical boundaries. Here are the first three rows of B2D:

First block row
$\left[\frac{B}{2} + D \ \ -D \ \ 0\right]$
corner/midpt/corner

$$\begin{bmatrix} 1 & -\frac{1}{2} & 0 & -\frac{1}{2} & 0 & 0 & 0 & 0 & 0 \\ -\frac{1}{2} & 2 & -\frac{1}{2} & 0 & -1 & 0 & 0 & 0 & 0 \\ 0 & -\frac{1}{2} & 1 & 0 & 0 & -\frac{1}{2} & 0 & 0 & 0 \end{bmatrix} \qquad (17)$$

To derive B2D systematically, Giles uses the **control volumes** inside dashed lines.

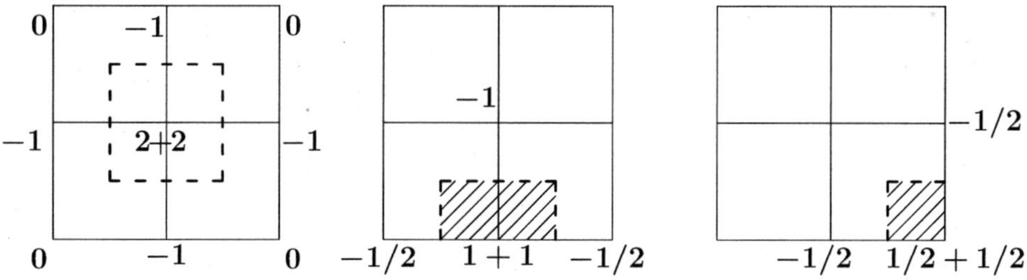

Around each control volume, the double integral of $\text{div}(\text{grad}\, u) = 0$ equals the boundary integral of $\partial u/\partial n$ (Divergence Theorem). On the sides of the control volumes, replace $\partial u/\partial n$ by differences. **The half-length sides in the two shaded regions automatically produce $\frac{1}{2}\Delta y$ or $\frac{1}{2}\Delta x$:**

Middle box / **Corner box**	$\frac{1}{2}(2U_{21} - U_{31} - U_{11}) + (U_{21} - U_{11})$	$\frac{1}{2}(U_{31} - U_{21}) + \frac{1}{2}(U_{31} - U_{32})$

Those are rows 2 and 3 of $(B2D)U$ in (17). The control volumes ensure a symmetric matrix. Fluxes cancel across internal boundaries. **This is the way to model $c_+\, \partial u/\partial n = c_-\, \partial u/\partial n$ when the conductance c has an internal jump.**

Problem Set 3.5

1 The 7-point Laplace difference equation in 3D has $+6$ along the diagonal and six -1's on interior rows. Thus $K3\text{D} = -\Delta_x^2 - \Delta_y^2 - \Delta_z^2$ has size N^3.

Create $K3\text{D}$ by the kron command from $K2\text{D}$ and $I2\text{D} = \text{kron}(I, I)$ in the x-y plane, using K and I of size N in the z-direction.

2 Factor $K3\text{D}{=}LU$ by the lu command and use spy to display the nonzeros in L.

3 In parallel with equations (7) and (8), what are the eigenvectors y_{klm} and the eigenvalues λ_{klm} of $K3\text{D}$? (Write the i, j, s component of the eigenvector.) A triple sum like (9) gives U from F.

4 Create a 3D MATLAB code (imitating 2D) to solve $(K3\text{D})U = F$.

5 The "**9-point scheme**" for Laplace's equation in 2D gives $O(h^4)$ accuracy:

$$20U_{ij}-4(U_{i+1,j}+U_{i-1,j}+U_{i,j+1}+U_{i,j-1})-(U_{i+1,j+1}+U_{i+1,j-1}+U_{i-1,j+1}+U_{i-1,j-1})=0.$$

Draw the 9-point molecule with those coefficients $20, -4,$ and -1. What is the bandwidth of $K2\text{D}9$, with N^2 meshpoints and nine diagonals?

6 The 9-point matrix seems to separate into 6 times $K2\text{D}$ minus $\Delta_x^2\ \Delta_y^2$ (that term gives -1 in the corners of the molecule). Is there a fast way to construct $K2\text{D}9$ from K and I and kron?

7 $K2\text{D}9$ has the same eigenvectors y_{kl} as $K2\text{D}$ in equation (7). Using Problem 6, what are the eigenvalues of $K2\text{D}9$? ($y = 0$ on the edges of the square.)

8 Why is the transpose of $C = \text{kron}(A, B)$ equal to $\text{kron}(A^{\text{T}}, B^{\text{T}})$? You have to transpose each block $A_{ij}B$. Why is the inverse equal to $C^{-1} = \text{kron}(A^{-1}, B^{-1})$? Multiplying C times C^{-1}, explain why the block row $[A_{11}B; \ldots; A_{1n}B]$ times the block column $[(A^{-1})_{11}B^{-1}; \ldots; (A^{-1})_{n1}B^{-1}]$ is I.

C is symmetric (or orthogonal) when A and B are symmetric (or orthogonal).

9 Why is the matrix $C = \text{kron}(A, B)$ times the matrix $D = \text{kron}(S, T)$ equal to $CD{=}\text{kron}(AS, BT)$? This needs even more patience with block multiplication.

Note Suppose S and T are eigenvector matrices for A and B. Then

$$\text{kron}(A, B)\ \text{kron}(S, T) = \text{kron}(AS, BT) = \text{kron}(S, T)\ \text{kron}(\Lambda_A, \Lambda_B).$$

This says that $CD = D\Lambda_C$. So $D = \text{kron}(S, T)$ is the eigenvector matrix for C.

10 Why is the 2D equation $(K2\text{D})U = F$ equivalent to the packed matrix equation $K * UM + UM * K = FM$, when U and F are packed into UM and FM?

11 The matrix $K + I$ has diagonals $-1, 3, -1$ to represent the one-dimensional finite difference $-\Delta^2 U + U$. Write down three rows of $(K + I)U = F$ as in (13). Use odd-even reduction to produce a half-size system like (14).

3.6 THE FINITE ELEMENT METHOD

Finite elements appeared in Sections 3.1 and 3.2, only in one dimension. They were hat functions and piecewise parabolas and cubics. The real success is in two and three dimensions, where finite differences mostly hope for a square or rectangle or cube.

Finite elements are the best way out of that box. The boundaries can be curved and the mesh can be unstructured. The steps of the method are still the same:

1. Write the equation in its **weak form**, integrated with test functions $v(x, y)$
2. **Subdivide the region** into triangles or quadrilaterals
3. Choose N simple **trial functions** $\phi_j(x, y)$ and look for $U = U_1\phi_1 + \cdots + U_N\phi_N$. The 1D hat functions $\phi(x)$ can change to 2D pyramid functions $\phi(x, y)$
4. Produce N equations $KU = F$ from **test functions** $V_1, \ldots, V_N$ (often $V_j = \phi_j$)
5. **Assemble** the stiffness matrix K and the load vector F. **Solve** $\boldsymbol{KU = F}$.

The computations are all in step 5, but the first four steps decide if the method will be efficient and accurate. The key is the appearance of *trial and test functions.*

I will explain the weak form, which is highly important in scientific computing. We are not directly forcing Laplace's equation to hold at every point. That strong form has *second* derivatives of u. The weak form in (3) has only *first* derivatives of u and also of test functions v. Integration by parts changes $-u_{xx}v$ to $u_x v_x$.

In the discrete case, for matrix equations $A^{\mathrm{T}}CAu = f$, take inner products with all vectors v. Transposing to produce (Av) is exactly like integration by parts:

$$(A^{\mathrm{T}}CAu)^{\mathrm{T}}v = f^{\mathrm{T}}v \quad \text{becomes the weak form:} \quad (CAu)^{\mathrm{T}}(Av) = f^{\mathrm{T}}v \quad \text{for every } v. \tag{1}$$

The weak form makes A^{T} disappear! In mechanics, v is any "virtual displacement" added to u. The force balance $A^{\mathrm{T}}w = f$ is hidden in the weak form as $w^{\mathrm{T}}Av = f^{\mathrm{T}}v$.

Inner products $f^{\mathrm{T}}v$ now become integrals of f times v. We are creating a pure *displacement method* involving u and v. To reach the weak form directly, **multiply the strong form by a test function $v(x, y)$ and integrate**. Integration by parts in 2D becomes the Gauss-Green formula in Section 3.3. $C = I$ puts $(Au)^{\mathrm{T}}(Av) = \iint (\operatorname{grad} u) \cdot (\operatorname{grad} v) = \iint u_x v_x + u_y v_y$ in the weak form of Laplace's equation:

$$\textbf{Multiply by } \boldsymbol{v(x,y)} \textbf{ and integrate} \qquad \iint (-u_{xx} - u_{yy})\, v(x, y)\, dx\, dy = 0$$

$$\textbf{Weak form by Green's formula} \qquad \iint (u_x v_x + u_y v_y)\, dx\, dy = \int \frac{\partial u}{\partial n}\, v\, ds \tag{2}$$

What boundary conditions are imposed on u and v? The answer is that *essential* boundary conditions are imposed, but *natural* boundary conditions are not imposed.

An essential condition is $u = u_0(x, y)$ in Laplace's equation. Then $v = 0$ is required at those same boundary points (so $u + v$ will keep the same boundary values).

A natural condition is a boundary value $w \cdot n = F_0(x, y)$. Morally, we can't impose that condition because w is gone. Allow me to proceed with essential conditions.

With $v = 0$ on the boundary of R, the last integral in (2) is zero. The weak form of Laplace's equation has the double integral of $(\text{grad}\, u) \cdot (\text{grad}\, v) = u_x v_x + u_y v_y$:

Weak form $$\iint \left(\frac{\partial u}{\partial x}\frac{\partial v}{\partial x} + \frac{\partial u}{\partial y}\frac{\partial v}{\partial y} \right) dx\, dy = 0 \quad \text{for all admissible } v(x, y)\,. \tag{3}$$

A source term $f(x, y)$ on the right side of the strong form changes Laplace to Poisson. This produces $\iint f v \, dx\, dy$ in the weak form for $-u_{xx} - u_{yy} = f(x, y)$.

The beauty of this weak form is that it involves only first derivatives. It has Au and Av instead of $A^{\mathrm{T}} Au$. We can create trial and test functions much more easily when only first derivatives are required. They can be **pyramid functions** in 2D where they were **hat functions** in 1D. The goal is a fast and accurate method, and after two examples we will move to the real thing (including a code).

Trial and Test Functions: Galerkin's Method

For a discrete approximation to the weak form, Galerkin had a simple but terrific plan. Let $U(x, y)$ be a combination of N well-chosen **trial functions** $\boldsymbol{\phi_j(x, y)}$:

Approximation $$U(x, y) = \sum_{j=1}^{N} U_j \phi_j(x, y) \quad (\text{plus } U_B(x, y) \text{ if needed})\,. \tag{4}$$

Choosing the basis functions ϕ_j is the main decision in much of scientific computing. The extra function $U_B(x, y)$ satisfies any nonzero essential conditions $U_B = u_0$ at boundary mesh points. The trial functions $\phi_1, \ldots, \phi_N$ equal *zero* on the boundary (so they could also be test functions V). For a boundary condition like $u(0) = u(1) = 0$, U_B is identically zero and not needed. ***We now have N unknown coefficients $U_1, \ldots, U_N$, and we need N equations.***

The equations come by choosing N ***test functions*** $V_1, V_2, \ldots, V_N$. Every test function V_i that we substitute into the weak form yields one equation for the U's. Replace u in the weak form (3) by $U = \sum U_j \phi_j$ and replace v by each V_i:

$$\iint \left[\left(\sum_1^N U_j \frac{\partial \phi_j}{\partial x} \right) \frac{\partial V_i}{\partial x} + \left(\sum_1^N U_j \frac{\partial \phi_j}{\partial y} \right) \frac{\partial V_i}{\partial y} \right] dx\, dy = \iint f(x, y)\, V_i(x, y)\, dx\, dy\,. \tag{5}$$

Do you see this as a linear system $KU = F$? There are N equations indexed by i. The N unknowns U_j are indexed by j. The right side of (5) gives the ith component of the load vector F. Multiplying U_j on the left side is the matrix entry K_{ij}.

Stiffness matrix $$K_{ij} = \iint \left[\frac{\partial \phi_j}{\partial x} \frac{\partial V_i}{\partial x} + \frac{\partial \phi_j}{\partial y} \frac{\partial V_i}{\partial y} \right] dx\, dy \,. \tag{6}$$

If each $V_i = \phi_i$, the matrix K is symmetric and *positive definite*. It is *sparse* provided the ϕ_j are localized ($K_{ij} = 0$ when the graphs of ϕ_j and V_i don't overlap). The right side F comes from $f(x, y)$. It also comes from nonzero boundary values $u = u_0$ (in U_B) and from any $w \cdot n = \partial u / \partial n = F_0$ in (3).

The first example will show how one pyramid function produces the usual 5-point Laplacian. The second example will show element matrices and boundary conditions. Then the "production code" will assemble $KU = F$ for any triangular mesh.

Pyramid Functions

Our key example will be Laplace's equation $u_{xx} + u_{yy} = 0$ inside a square. Boundary values are given around the whole square of side $2h$ (then the test functions have boundary values $v = 0$). The square is divided into four smaller squares with sides h, and each square is split into two triangles (Figure 3.21). Our finite element approximation $U(x, y)$ will be ***linear inside each of the eight triangles***.

Thus $U = a + bx + cy$ in each triangle. For T_1, with horizontal shading, those numbers a, b, c are determined by the values U, U_E, U_N at the corners. The East and North values U_E and U_N are known from $u_0(x, y)$. The interior value U is what we want to find. ***The full graph of $U(x, y)$ has eight plane pieces meeting along the edges.*** On the edge going out to E, the planes in T_1 and T_2 both go linearly from U to U_E. So those planes do meet, and we have a continuous roof.

We use only one test function V because we have one unknown U. The test function (our most natural choice) will also be linear in each triangle. *All boundary values of V are zero*, and we may choose the interior value $V = 1$ at $x = y = 0$. In the triangles T_1 and T_2, those values $1, 0, 0$ are matched by simple formulas:

Test function $$V(x, y) = 1 - \frac{x}{h} - \frac{y}{h} \quad \text{in } T_1 \qquad V(x, y) = 1 - \frac{x}{h} \quad \text{in } T_2 \,. \tag{7}$$

The graph of the complete $V(x, y)$ will be a six-sided pyramid over six triangles. Please pause here to visualize this piecewise linear roof. It has six plane sides sloping up to $V = 1$ at the center. The planes in two corner triangles never leave zero.

$U(x, y)$ adjusts $a + bx + cy$ to match U, U_E, U_N at the corners of T_1:

$$U + \frac{x}{h}(U_E - U) + \frac{y}{h}(U_N - U) \text{ in } T_1 \qquad U + \frac{x}{h}(U_E - U) + \frac{y}{h}(U_E - U_{SE}) \text{ in } T_2 \,. \tag{8}$$

Notice the shared slope $(U_E - U)/h$ along the horizontal edge, where $U(x, y)$ goes from U to U_E over a distance h. The six flat pieces of $U(x, y)$ safely meet.

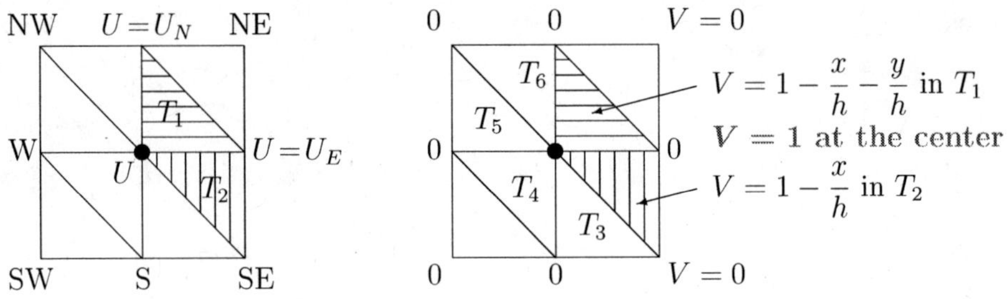

Figure 3.21: Approximation $U(x,y)$ and test pyramid $V = \phi$, linear in eight triangles.

The integral of $U_xV_x + U_yV_y$ in the weak form is easy, because *all derivatives are constants. Just multiply by the area* $\frac{1}{2}h^2$:

$$\textbf{Over } T_1 \quad \iint \left[\left(\frac{U_E-U}{h}\right)\left(-\frac{1}{h}\right) + \left(\frac{U_N-U}{h}\right)\left(-\frac{1}{h}\right)\right] dx\,dy = \tfrac{1}{2}(-U_E + 2U - U_N)$$

$$\nearrow \qquad\qquad \nearrow$$

$$\partial V/\partial x \qquad\qquad \partial V/\partial y$$

$$\searrow \qquad\qquad \searrow$$

$$\textbf{Over } T_2 \quad \iint \left[\left(\frac{U_E-U}{h}\right)\left(-\frac{1}{h}\right) + \left(\frac{U_E-U_{SE}}{h}\right)(0)\right] dx\,dy = \tfrac{1}{2}(U - U_E)\,.$$

There are four more triangles to go. We report the integrals over those triangles.

The southwest T_4 will produce $\frac{1}{2}(-U_W + 2U - U_S)$ in analogy with T_1. The triangles T_3, T_5, T_6 will produce $\frac{1}{2}(U - U_S)$ and $\frac{1}{2}(U - U_W)$ and $\frac{1}{2}(U - U_N)$ in analogy with T_2. Adding the six integrals gives one assembled equation $KU = F$:

$$\boldsymbol{KU = F} \qquad\qquad \boldsymbol{4U = U_E + U_W + U_N + U_S} \qquad\qquad (9)$$

Our goal is achieved (with one unknown U). The 1 by 1 stiffness matrix is $K = [4]$. The right side F is the sum of four boundary values. The equation says that U is the average of those boundary values! This matches a key property of the true solution: *At the center of any circle, $u(x,y)$ equals its average around the circle.*

By rewriting equation (9) you see how u_{xx} and u_{yy} are replaced by second differences, horizontal plus vertical. **This is exactly the five-point Laplacian:**

$$\textbf{Second differences} \qquad (-U_E + 2U - U_W) + (-U_N + 2U - U_S) = 0\,. \qquad (10)$$

Please remember this key example as you read about the whole finite element idea. Larger examples will show how K is assembled from *element matrices.*

Element Matrices and Element Vectors

There is a good way to compute the stiffness matrix K—one element at a time. We plan to choose each $V_i = \phi_i$. Within a single interval in 1D, or one triangle in

2D, the approximate solution U only involves two or three of the trial functions ϕ_i (the others are zero within that element). The contribution to the global matrix K will be a 2 by 2 or 3 by 3 *element matrix* K_e. When assembled into K, this matrix will overlap other element matrices from triangles that share a meshpoint.

The weak form says that K_{ij} is the integral of $(\operatorname{grad}\phi_j)\cdot(\operatorname{grad}V_i)$. We choose $V_i=\phi_i$, and $U=\Sigma U_j\phi_j$. **When you integrate $U_x^2+U_y^2$, you will see a sum of $U_iU_jK_{ij}$ which is $U^{\mathrm{T}}KU$:**

$$\iint (U_x^2+U_y^2)\,dx\,dy=\sum_{i=1}^{N}\sum_{j=1}^{N}U_iU_j\iint\left(\frac{\partial\phi_i}{\partial x}\frac{\partial\phi_j}{\partial x}+\frac{\partial\phi_i}{\partial y}\frac{\partial\phi_j}{\partial y}\right)dx\,dy\,. \tag{11}$$

The integral over the whole region is $U^{\mathrm{T}}KU$ with $U^{\mathrm{T}}=[U_1\ U_2\ \ldots\ U_N]$. The integral over a single triangle is $U^{\mathrm{T}}K_eU$. This involves only three of the U's, from the three corners of the triangle. Strictly speaking, we have an N by N matrix, but its only non-zero entries are in the 3 by 3 matrix K_e. At the end K is an assembly of the matrices K_e from all the triangles.

I am going to repeat the pyramid example for a standard 45-45-90 right triangle and then for any triangle. The three unknowns U_i, U_{i+1}, U_{i+2} are the corners of T:

$$\iint_T (U_x^2+U_y^2)\,dx\,dy=\left[\left(\frac{U_{i+1}-U_i}{h}\right)^2+\left(\frac{U_{i+2}-U_i}{h}\right)^2\right]\text{ times the area }\frac{h^2}{2} \tag{12}$$

Rewrite that answer to see K_T for the triangle in Figure 3.22:

Element matrix K_T

$$U^{\mathrm{T}}(K_T)U=\begin{bmatrix}U_i & U_{i+1} & U_{i+2}\end{bmatrix}\begin{bmatrix}1 & -\frac{1}{2} & -\frac{1}{2}\\ -\frac{1}{2} & \frac{1}{2} & 0\\ -\frac{1}{2} & 0 & \frac{1}{2}\end{bmatrix}\begin{bmatrix}U_i\\ U_{i+1}\\ U_{i+2}\end{bmatrix} \tag{13}$$

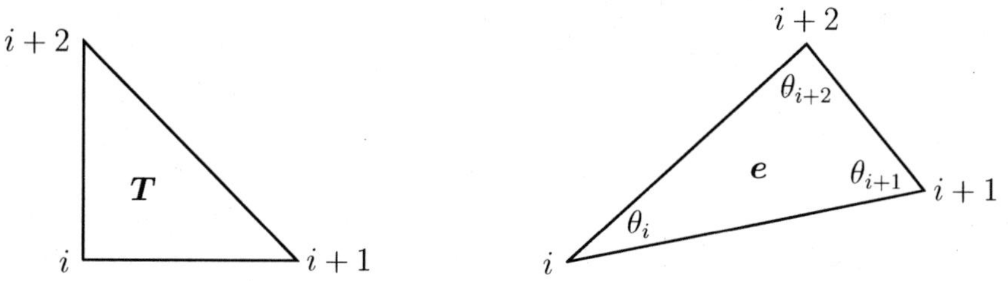

Figure 3.22: The standard triangle T (lengths 1 or h) and an arbitrary triangle e.

For the six triangles in our first example (Figure 3.21), we can assemble K by hand. Two triangles share the horizontal edge from i to E. The link from U_i to U_E is $-\frac{1}{2}$ from the triangle above and $-\frac{1}{2}$ from the triangle below. The assembled K has -1 for U_E and also for the other close neighbors U_S, U_N, U_W. The diagonal entry of K

is +4 (1's from two triangles and $\frac{1}{2}$'s from four triangles). ***The second derivatives*** u_{xx} ***and*** u_{yy} ***are replaced by second differences***:

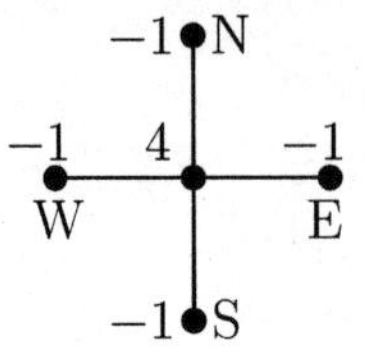

$$\begin{aligned} 4U_i - U_E - U_W - U_N - U_S &= 0 \\ (-U_E + 2U_i - U_W) + (-U_N + 2U_i - U_S) &= 0 \\ -(\text{2nd } x\text{-difference}) - (\text{2nd } y\text{-difference}) &= 0 \end{aligned} \qquad (14)$$

The element matrix K_e depends on the tangents of the corner angles. This matrix comes in Problems 4 and 14 from integrating $U_x^2 + U_y^2$ over e (the corner tangents were $\infty, 1, 1$ for the 90–45–45 triangle T, then K_T agrees with K_e):

Element matrix

$$K_e = \begin{bmatrix} c_2 + c_3 & -c_3 & -c_2 \\ -c_3 & c_1 + c_3 & -c_1 \\ -c_2 & -c_1 & c_1 + c_2 \end{bmatrix} \quad \text{with} \quad c_i = \frac{1}{2\tan\theta_i}. \qquad (15)$$

K_e is only semidefinite! The constant vector $(1, 1, 1)$ is in its nullspace. This is natural and unavoidable, because $U = 1$ at all three corners gives $U =$ constant and $\text{grad}\, U \equiv 0$ in the triangle. A fixed boundary $U = u_0$ will make K positive definite.

How do boundary values of U ***enter the equation*** $KU = F$***?*** If U is known at a meshpoint, it moves to the right side (into F). This is equivalent to the extra term $U_B(x, y)$ in (4) that matches the boundary conditions.

The load vector F comes from assembling integrals of $f(x, y)$ times U:

Element load vector F_e

$$\iint_{\text{triangle } e} f\left(\sum U_i \phi_i\right) dx\, dy = \sum U_i \iint_{\text{triangle } e} f\, \phi_i\, dx\, dy = U^{\mathrm{T}}(F_e) \qquad (16)$$

Each triangle produces a vector F_e with 3 nonzeros. On assembly, those F_e overlap. You will see how the code assembles element matrices and vectors of size 3 into global matrices K and vectors F of size N. The input includes the geometry of the mesh—the positions of nodes and the list of triangles.

We don't need a perfect integration, an approximation will do. We could look at one point P, the centroid of the triangle. For linear elements, $U(P)$ is the average $\frac{1}{3}(U_i + U_{i+1} + U_{i+2})$. So evaluate $f(x, y)$ at P and multiply by the area of e:

One-point integration

$$\iint_e f(x, y)\, U(x, y)\, dx\, dy \approx f(P)\left(\frac{U_i + U_{i+1} + U_{i+2}}{3}\right)(\text{area of } e)\,. \qquad (17)$$

Boundary Conditions Come Last

Three points about finite element codes are best explained with a one-dimensional example. Our 2D code will build from these ideas, keeping the overall plan simple:

1. K and F are assembled from element matrices K_e and load vectors F_e

2. The intervals and triangles (or quads) can have different lengths and shapes

3. To start, K and F can be constructed with *no boundary conditions.* Complete that main part first. Then for boundary nodes put I into K and u_0 into F.

The weak form of $-u'' = 1$ is $\int u_x v_x\, dx = \int 1 v\, dx$. Figure 3.23 shows *two half-hats* ϕ_0 *and* ϕ_2, because boundary conditions are being saved for later. Look below for K and Kb, F and Fb—the code operates this way in 2D.

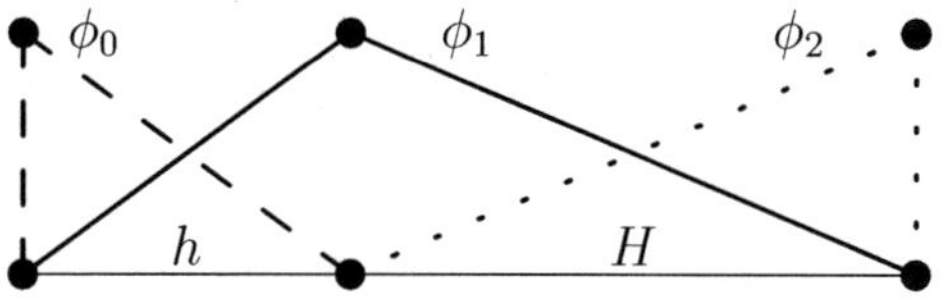

$U = U_0\phi_0 + U_1\phi_1 + U_2\phi_2$

Element matrices Kh and KH

Assemble Kh and KH into K.

Figure 3.23: A hat and two half-hats: K will be 3 by 3 and singular.

For the element matrix Kh we integrate $(dU/dx)^2$ over the first interval, 0 to h. Adjust $U = a + bx$ to $U_0 + (U_1 - U_0)x/h$, matching U_0 and U_1 at the nodes:

First interval $$\int_0^h \left(\frac{dU}{dx}\right)^2 dx = \int_0^h \left(\frac{U_1 - U_0}{h}\right)^2 dx = \frac{1}{h}(U_1 - U_0)^2 . \tag{18}$$

Write this answer using the matrix $Kh = \frac{1}{h}\left[\begin{smallmatrix} 1 & -1 \\ -1 & 1\end{smallmatrix}\right]$ and the vector $[U_0 \;\; U_1]$:

Element matrix *Kh* $$\frac{1}{h}(U_1 - U_0)^2 = \begin{bmatrix} U_0 & U_1 \end{bmatrix} \frac{1}{\boldsymbol{h}} \begin{bmatrix} 1 & -1 \\ -1 & 1 \end{bmatrix} \begin{bmatrix} U_0 \\ U_1 \end{bmatrix} . \tag{19}$$

On the second interval, with length H, the slope of U is $(U_2 - U_1)/H$:

KH $$\int_h^{h+H} \left(\frac{dU}{dx}\right)^2 dx = \frac{1}{H}(U_2 - U_1)^2 = \begin{bmatrix} U_1 & U_2 \end{bmatrix} \frac{1}{\boldsymbol{H}} \begin{bmatrix} 1 & -1 \\ -1 & 1 \end{bmatrix} \begin{bmatrix} U_1 \\ U_2 \end{bmatrix} .$$

Now assemble Kh and KH into their right places in K. They overlap:

Global matrix $$K = \begin{bmatrix} Kh & \\ & KH \end{bmatrix} = \begin{bmatrix} \frac{1}{h} & -\frac{1}{h} & 0 \\ -\frac{1}{h} & \frac{1}{h} + \frac{1}{H} & -\frac{1}{H} \\ 0 & -\frac{1}{H} & \frac{1}{H} \end{bmatrix} .$$

This matrix has the vector $(1,1,1)$ in its nullspace. If $U_0 = U_1 = U_2$ then $U =$ constant and $dU/dx \equiv 0$. Notice how the middle row of K involves both h and H:

Second difference $$\begin{bmatrix} -\frac{1}{h} & \frac{1}{h}+\frac{1}{H} & -\frac{1}{H} \end{bmatrix} \text{ times } U \text{ gives } \frac{U_1-U_0}{h} - \frac{U_2-U_1}{H}. \quad (20)$$

This is a difference of first differences, as it should be. Finite elements automatically adjust for changes in meshlength. They also handle a variable coefficient in $-(c(x)u'(x))' = f(x)$. The element matrices are multiplied by c_1 and c_2, when $c(x)$ has those values in the two intervals. (For the integrals, I would take $c(x)$ at the two midpoints.) For the first time we are taking differences without constant $c(x)$:

$$\begin{bmatrix} -\frac{c_1}{h} & \frac{c_1}{h}+\frac{c_2}{H} & -\frac{c_2}{H} \end{bmatrix} \text{ leads to } \frac{c_1(U_1-U_0)}{h} - \frac{c_2(U_2-U_1)}{h}. \quad (21)$$

Now impose an essential boundary condition $U_0 = 0$ (corresponding to $u(0) = 0$). In the boundary row and column, insert the identity matrix:

Change K to Kb $$Kb = \begin{bmatrix} 1 & 0 & 0 \\ 0 & \frac{1}{h}+\frac{1}{H} & -\frac{1}{H} \\ 0 & -\frac{1}{H} & \frac{1}{H} \end{bmatrix} \quad (22)$$

When we put $F_0 = 0$ on the right side of the equation, the solution will have $U_0 = 0$. We are keeping three equations, even if one of them is trivial. In the lower 2 by 2 submatrix you can see the usual *fixed-free matrix* $\left[\begin{smallmatrix} 2 & -1 \\ -1 & 1 \end{smallmatrix}\right]$ when $h = H$. The key point is to maintain simplicity in the logic, when the elements get more complicated.

The 3 by 1 load vector F follows the same logic. Assemble F from the element vectors Fh and FH on the intervals. Keep $f(x) = 1$ and $h + H = 1$ for simplicity:

$$\int_0^h f(x)U(x)\,dx = \int_0^h \left[U_0 + (U_1 - U_0)\frac{x}{h}\right]dx = \frac{h}{2}(U_0 + U_1) = \begin{bmatrix} U_0 & U_1 \end{bmatrix} \frac{h}{2} \begin{bmatrix} 1 \\ 1 \end{bmatrix}. \quad (23)$$

Then $Fh = \frac{h}{2}\left[\begin{smallmatrix} 1 \\ 1 \end{smallmatrix}\right]$ and $FH = \frac{H}{2}\left[\begin{smallmatrix} 1 \\ 1 \end{smallmatrix}\right]$. Place those 2 by 1 vectors correctly into F:

Assemble load vector F before boundary conditions $$F = \begin{bmatrix} Fh \\ \hline \end{bmatrix} + \begin{bmatrix} \hline FH \end{bmatrix} = \frac{1}{2}\begin{bmatrix} h \\ h+H \\ H \end{bmatrix}. \quad (24)$$

Notice that $h/2$ and $(h+H)/2$ and $H/2$ are the areas under the graphs of ϕ_0, ϕ_1, ϕ_2 (two half-hats and a full hat in Figure 3.23). To impose $U_0 = 0$ at the left endpoint, for a fixed-free bar, change the first component of F to zero in Fb.

Now solve the finite element equation $(Kb)(Ub) = (Fb)$ to find U_0, U_1, U_2:

Last step $$\begin{bmatrix} 1 & 0 & 0 \\ 0 & \frac{1}{h}+\frac{1}{H} & -\frac{1}{H} \\ 0 & -\frac{1}{H} & \frac{1}{H} \end{bmatrix} \begin{bmatrix} U_0 \\ U_1 \\ U_2 \end{bmatrix} = \frac{1}{2}\begin{bmatrix} 0 \\ 1 \\ H \end{bmatrix} \text{ gives } \begin{bmatrix} U_0 \\ U_1 \\ U_2 \end{bmatrix} = \frac{1}{2}\begin{bmatrix} 0 \\ h+hH \\ 1 \end{bmatrix}.$$

The solution to $-u'' = 1$ with fixed-free boundary conditions $u(0) = 0$ and $u'(1) = 0$ is $u(x) = x - \frac{1}{2}x^2$. *This agrees with the approximation U at the nodes!*

We end this example by highlighting the difference between an essential condition $u(0) = A$ and a natural condition $w(1) = c(1)\,u'(1) = G$:

Essential (Dirichlet) (Fixed)	1. The condition $u(0) = A$ is imposed on U (through U_B) 2. A zero condition $v(0) = 0$ is imposed on V (so $U + V = A$) 3. The integrated term $cu'v$ vanishes at $x = 0$ since $v = 0$.
Natural (Neumann) (Free)	1. No condition is imposed on $u'(1)$ or $U'(1)$ 2. No condition is imposed on $v'(1)$ or $V'(1)$ 3. The free term $cu'v = Gv(1)$ moves into the load vector F.

One last comment on the change from K (singular) to Kb (invertible) and F to Fb. Suppose the essential boundary condition is $U_0 = u(0) = A$. That number is multiplying $-1/h$ in row 2 of K, so $-A/h$ must move into the load vector Fb as A/h:

$$(\boldsymbol{Kb}) * (\boldsymbol{Ub}) = (\boldsymbol{Fb}) \quad \begin{bmatrix} 1 & 0 & 0 \\ 0 & \frac{1}{h} + \frac{1}{H} & -\frac{1}{H} \\ 0 & -\frac{1}{H} & \frac{1}{H} \end{bmatrix} \begin{bmatrix} U_0 \\ U_1 \\ U_2 \end{bmatrix} = \begin{bmatrix} A \\ \frac{1}{2}(h+H) + A/h \\ \frac{1}{2}h \end{bmatrix}. \tag{25}$$

Element Matrices in Two Dimensions

The value of finite elements for complicated shapes is better seen in two dimensions. One-dimensional examples give good practice, but intervals cannot get complicated. Figure 3.24 shows a quarter-circle divided into triangles by our distmesh code. The *graded mesh* has small triangles to provide higher accuracy at the corner where the stress is likely to be greatest. The problem becomes realistic.

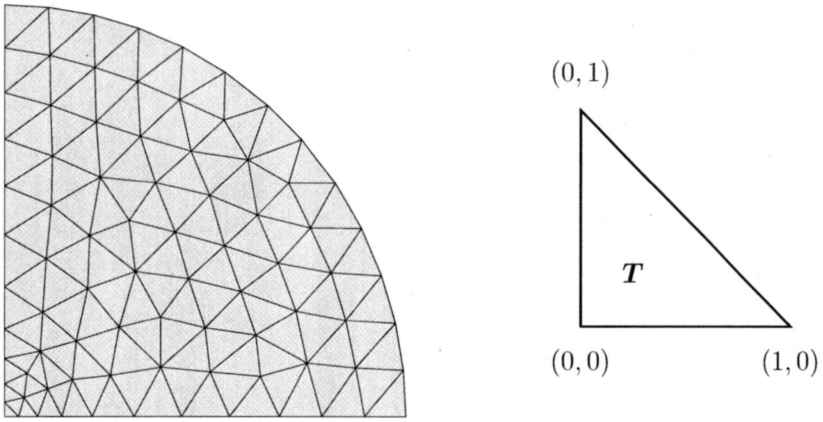

Figure 3.24: Distmesh gave 83 nodes and 129 triangles. Standard triangle T.

The trial functions have $\phi = a + bx + cy$ inside each triangle. Those coefficients a, b, c are determined by the three values 1 and 0 and 0 at the corners. For each triangle we need the coordinates of those corners. The mesh information from the user or distmesh is in two lists p and t:

p = N by 2 matrix to give x, y coordinates of all nodes 1 to N
t = T by 3 matrix of node numbers for 3 corners of T triangles

The ith row nodes = t(i,:) is a vector of the 3 node numbers for triangle i. The x, y coordinates of these nodes are in the 3 by 2 matrix p(nodes,:). We include a column of three 1's to produce a 3 by 3 position matrix P for that triangle:

Position matrix P
Standard triangle

$$P = [\text{ones(3,1), p(nodes,:)}] = \begin{bmatrix} 1 & \mathbf{0} & \mathbf{0} \\ 1 & \mathbf{1} & \mathbf{0} \\ 1 & \mathbf{0} & \mathbf{1} \end{bmatrix} \quad \begin{matrix} \text{node 1 at } (0,0) \\ \text{node 2 at } (1,0) \\ \text{node 3 at } (0,1) \end{matrix}$$

To find the coefficients in $a_i + b_i x + c_i y$ for the trial functions ϕ_1, ϕ_2, ϕ_3, the beautiful way is to *invert the position matrix P for that triangle.* Here is $PC = I$:

$C = P^{-1}$ gives the coefficients a, b, c in the three ϕ's

$$\begin{bmatrix} 1 & x_1 & y_1 \\ 1 & x_2 & y_2 \\ 1 & x_3 & y_3 \end{bmatrix} \begin{bmatrix} a_1 & a_2 & a_3 \\ b_1 & b_2 & b_3 \\ c_1 & c_2 & c_3 \end{bmatrix} = \begin{bmatrix} 1 & 0 & 0 \\ 0 & 1 & 0 \\ 0 & 0 & 1 \end{bmatrix} = I\,. \tag{26}$$

The second column of $PC = I$ gives values $0, 1, 0$ at nodes $1, 2, 3$: $\phi_2 = a_2 + b_2 x + c_2 y$. For the standard triangle, invert P above to find the coefficients a, b, c for each ϕ:

Standard triangle

$$PC = \begin{bmatrix} 1 & 0 & 0 \\ 1 & 1 & 0 \\ 1 & 0 & 1 \end{bmatrix} \begin{bmatrix} \mathbf{1} & \mathbf{0} & \mathbf{0} \\ \mathbf{-1} & \mathbf{1} & \mathbf{0} \\ \mathbf{-1} & \mathbf{0} & \mathbf{1} \end{bmatrix} = \begin{bmatrix} 1 & 0 & 0 \\ 0 & 1 & 0 \\ 0 & 0 & 1 \end{bmatrix} \quad \begin{aligned} \phi_1 &= 1 - x - y \\ \phi_2 &= x \\ \phi_3 &= y \end{aligned}$$

The derivatives of $\phi = a + bx + cy$ are b and c. Those b's and c's are in rows 2 and 3 of C, and they enter the integrals for the 3 by 3 element matrix $\boldsymbol{Ke}$:

Stiffness matrix for element e

$$(Ke)_{ij} = \iint \left(\frac{\partial \phi_i}{\partial x} \frac{\partial V_j}{\partial x} + \frac{\partial \phi_i}{\partial y} \frac{\partial V_j}{\partial y} \right) dx\, dy = (\text{area})(b_i\, b_j + c_i\, c_j)\,. \tag{27}$$

The area of the triangle is $|\det(P)|/2$. The line $\boldsymbol{Ke} = \ldots$ in our MATLAB code computes these nine integrals ($i = 1:3, j = 1:3$) for Laplace's equation. For the standard triangle, $\boldsymbol{Ke} = \boldsymbol{KT}$ is the 2D analog of the 1D element matrix $\left[\begin{smallmatrix} 1 & -1 \\ -1 & 1 \end{smallmatrix}\right]$:

Standard element matrix

$$\boldsymbol{KT} = (\text{area})(b_i\, b_j + c_i\, c_j) = \frac{1}{2} \begin{bmatrix} 2 & -1 & -1 \\ -1 & 1 & 0 \\ -1 & 0 & 1 \end{bmatrix}. \tag{28}$$

KT is a singular matrix with $(1, 1, 1)$ in its nullspace. *Reason*: $U = \phi_1 + \phi_2 + \phi_3$ has corner values $1, 1, 1$ and must be a constant $U \equiv 1$ in the triangle, with zero slopes.

When the differential equation is $-\operatorname{div}(c\,(x, y) \operatorname{grad} u) = f$, I would evaluate $c(x, y)$ at the centroid (center of gravity) of triangle e. That number multiplies $\boldsymbol{Ke}$, just as

f(centroid) multiplies the 3 by 1 element load vector $\boldsymbol{Fe}$ (see comments in the code). In fact a 3 by 3 positive definite matrix $c(x, y)$ can go between grad^{T} and grad, in the equation and code, if the material properties are orientation-dependent (anisotropic).

We owe this neat code to Per-Olof Persson. Notice how $\boldsymbol{Ke}$ is added into three rows and columns (given by nodes) of the N by N matrix K. These m-files on the website can follow a meshing code like squaregrid or distmesh, which lists the node coordinates in p and triangles in t. Here is Persson's code with comments:

```
% [p,t,b] = squaregrid(m,n)  % create grid of N = mn nodes to be listed in p
% generate mesh of T=2(m-1)(n-1) right triangles in unit square
m=11; n=11;  % includes boundary nodes, mesh spacing 1/(m-1) and 1/(n-1)
[x,y]=ndgrid((0:m-1)/(m-1),(0:n-1)/(n-1));  % matlab forms x and y lists
p=[x(:),y(:)];  % N by 2 matrix listing x,y coordinates of all N = mn nodes
t=[1,2,m+2; 1,m+2,m+1];  % 3 node numbers for two triangles in first square
t=kron(t,ones(m-1,1))+kron(ones(size(t)),(0:m-2)');
% now t lists 3 node numbers of 2(m-1) triangles in the first mesh row
t=kron(t,ones(n-1,1))+kron(ones(size(t)),(0:n-2)'*m);
% final t lists 3 node numbers of all triangles in T by 3 matrix
b=[1:m,m+1:m:m*n,2*m:m:m*n,m*n-m+2:m*n-1];  % bottom, left, right, top
% b = numbers of all 2m+2n **boundary nodes** preparing for U(b)=0

% [K,F] = assemble(p,t)  % K and F for any mesh of triangles: linear phi's
N=size(p,1);T=size(t,1);  % number of nodes, number of triangles
% p lists x,y coordinates of N nodes, t lists triangles by 3 node numbers
K=sparse(N,N);  % zero matrix in sparse format: zeros(N) would be "dense"
F=zeros(N,1);  % load vector F to hold integrals of phi's times load f(x,y)

for e=1:T  % integration over one triangular element at a time
  nodes=t(e,:);  % row of t = node numbers of the 3 corners of triangle e
  Pe=[ones(3,1),p(nodes,:)];  % 3 by 3 matrix with rows=[1 xcorner ycorner]
  Area=abs(det(Pe))/2;  % area of triangle e = half of parallelogram area
  C=inv(Pe);  % columns of C are coeffs in a + bx + cy to give phi=1,0,0 at nodes
  % now compute 3 by 3 Ke and 3 by 1 Fe for element e
  grad=C(2:3,:);Ke=Area*grad'*grad;  % element matrix from slopes b,c in grad
  Fe=Area/3;  % integral of phi over triangle is volume of pyramid: f(x,y) = 1
  % multiply Fe by f at centroid for load f(x,y): one-point quadrature!
  % centroid would be mean(p(nodes,:)) = average of 3 node coordinates
  K(nodes,nodes)=K(nodes,nodes)+Ke;  % add Ke to 9 entries of global K
  F(nodes)=F(nodes)+Fe;  % add Fe to 3 components of load vector F
end  % all T element matrices and vectors now assembled into K and F
```

To emphasize: *The element matrices overlap in the singular matrix* K. It has free (Neumann) boundary conditions, like our free-free second-difference matrix B.

A Dirichlet condition fixes $U(b) = 0$ at a set b of boundary nodes, without changing the N by N shape of K. Instead of removing rows and columns for the node numbers listed in b, we insert the identity matrix into K and zeros into F. Then $(Kb)U = (Fb)$ has a *nonsingular matrix* Kb, and the solution has $U(b) = 0$:

```
% [Kb,Fb] = dirichlet(K,F,b)  % assembled K was singular! K * ones(N,1)=0
% Implement Dirichlet boundary conditions U(b)=0 at nodes in list b
K(b,:)=0; K(:,b)=0; F(b)=0;  % put zeros in boundary rows/columns of K and F
K(b,b)=speye(length(b),length(b));  % put I into boundary submatrix of K
Kb=K; Fb=F;  % Stiffness matrix Kb (sparse format) and load vector Fb
% Solving for the vector U will produce U(b)=0 at boundary nodes
U=Kb\Fb;  % The FEM approximation is U_1 phi_1 + ... + U_N phi_N
% Plot the FEM approximation U(x,y) with values U_1 to U_N at the nodes
trisurf(t,p(:,1),p(:,2),0 * p(:,1),U,'edgecolor','k','facecolor','interp');
view(2),axis equal,colorbar
```

Quadrilateral Elements

In one dimension, we moved from linear elements $a + bx$ to quadratics and cubics. In two dimensions it is often enough to allow an xy term (Q_1 element for rectangles). Even better are the x^2, xy, y^2 terms that produce P_2 for triangles.

Bilinear Q_1 elements $U = a + bx + cy + dxy$ *on rectangles.* The four coefficients of U in each rectangle are determined by the values of U at the four corners. The element matrices are 4 by 4 (four square pyramids are now involved).

The overall function $U(x, y)$ is continuous across the small rectangles, because U is a linear function (not quadratic) along each side. Horizontal sides have $y =$ constant. Vertical sides have $x =$ constant. The two corner values determine U along the whole side (and we get the same U from both rectangles that share this side). So there are no delta functions in the derivative across the edge.

The bilinear $a + bx + cy + dxy$ in Figure 3.25 has corner values U_i, U_E, U_N, U_{NE}:

$$U(x,y) = U_i + \frac{x}{h}(U_E - U_i) + \frac{y}{h}(U_N - U_i) + \frac{xy}{h^2}(U_{NE} - U_N - U_E + U_i)\,. \qquad (29)$$

Integrating $U_x^2 + U_y^2$ over the square S gives a 4 by 4 element matrix KS. Assembling element matrices (from four squares around meshpoint i) produces a *nine-point* discrete Laplace equation. Each U_i is the average of **eight neighbors**:

$$\boldsymbol{KU = F} \qquad \frac{8}{3}U_i = \frac{1}{3}(U_E + U_W + U_N + U_S + U_{NE} + U_{SW} + U_{NW} + U_{SE})\,. \qquad (30)$$

Quadratic P_2 elements $U = a + bx + cy + dxy + ex^2 + fy^2$ *on triangles.* Those six coefficients $a, \ldots, f$ are determined by six values of U in each triangle T—at the *three corners and three midpoints* of the edges. The element matrix KT is 6 by 6.

Again U is continuous between triangles. Each edge has three nodes (two corners and the midpoint). The three values determine exactly one quadratic function U along the whole edge. So U is the same from both sides of the edge.

Since quadratics can be reproduced exactly by the trial functions, the error in $U - u$ is of *order* h^3 *instead of* h^2. This improvement is explained in Section 8.4.

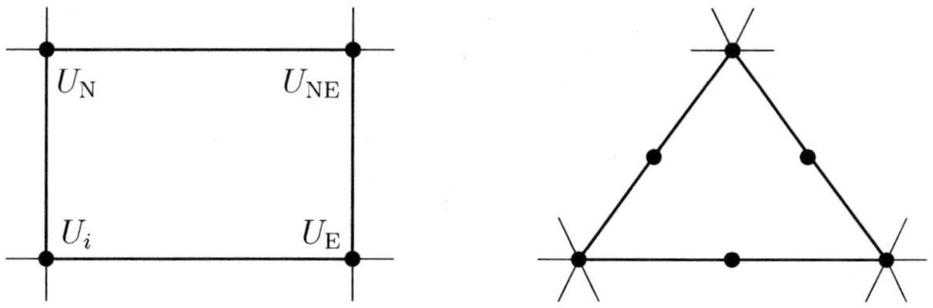

Figure 3.25: Bilinear Q_1 element $U = a + bx + cy + dxy$ matches four corner values. Six values of U determine $a + bx + cy + dxy + ex^2 + fy^2$ in a triangle (P_2 element).

Higher degree elements use more meshpoints. Ten points placed like bowling pins would give ten terms including x^3, x^2y, xy^2, y^3. Fifteen points placed like billiard balls would move to degree 4. That element may be too expensive, when Ke is 15 by 15.

We could also use slopes as unknowns (as for cubics in one dimension). The four values U, U_x, U_y, U_{xy} at the corners of rectangles would give sixteen terms in a "bicubic," going up to an x^3y^3 term. Engineers had a lot of fun creating these elements, that was a golden age. They are described in my book with George Fix: *An Analysis of the Finite Element Method* (Wellesley-Cambridge Press).

The Mass Matrix

We cannot leave finite elements without explaining the mass matrix. It comes from a term with no space derivatives, as in $-u_{xx} - u_{yy} + u = 0$. It would also come from the right side of the eigenvalue problem $-u_{xx} - u_{yy} = \lambda u$, and from the initial value problem $u_{xx} + u_{yy} = u_{tt}$. Those new terms u and u_{tt} are usually multiplied by a density ρ or a mass m. Together with K we reach a ***mass matrix*** M. When $h = 1$, the discrete form of $-u_{xx} - u_{yy} + u$ is $(K + M)U$. The discrete eigenvalue problem is $KU = \lambda MU$. The discrete wave equation is $MU'' + KU = 0$. So we often need M.

Integrating $U_x^2 + U_y^2$ led to $U^{\mathrm{T}}KU$. Integrating U^2 leads to $\sum\sum U_iU_jM_{ij}$:

$$\iint U^2\,dx\,dy = \iint\left(\sum_1^N U_i\phi_i\right)\left(\sum_1^N U_j\phi_j\right)dx\,dy = \sum_1^N\sum_1^N U_iU_j\iint \boldsymbol{\phi_i\phi_j\,dx\,dy}. \quad (31)$$

That integral of $\phi_i\phi_j$ is the mass matrix entry M_{ij}, when the trial and test functions are ϕ_i. We integrate over small triangles or rectangles, one element at a time. For a linear $U = U_1 + x(U_2 - U_1) + y(U_3 - U_1)$ in the standard triangle with $h = 1$, the element mass matrix MT is 3 by 3. The integral of $x^m y^n$ is $m!\,n!/(m+n+2)!$

Element mass matrix

$$\iint_T U^2\,dx\,dy = [U_1 \quad U_2 \quad U_3]\,\frac{1}{24}\begin{bmatrix} 2 & 1 & 1 \\ 1 & 2 & 1 \\ 1 & 1 & 2 \end{bmatrix}\begin{bmatrix} U_1 \\ U_2 \\ U_3 \end{bmatrix}. \qquad (32)$$

Linear elements (hat functions) in one dimension start with $U(x) = U_0 + (U_1 - U_0)x/h$. The element mass matrix Me on that first interval comes from integrating U^2:

Element mass matrix

$$\int_0^h \left[U_0 + (U_1 - U_0)\frac{x}{h}\right]^2 dx = U_0^2 h + 2U_0(U_1 - U_0)\frac{h}{2} + (U_1 - U_0)^2\frac{h}{3}$$
$$= [U_0 \quad U_1]\begin{bmatrix} h/3 & h/6 \\ h/6 & h/3 \end{bmatrix}\begin{bmatrix} U_0 \\ U_1 \end{bmatrix}. \qquad (33)$$

Assembling this matrix Me with next one (from h to $2h$) will double the diagonal entry to give $2h/3$. Then a typical rows of the 1D global mass matrix M (with density $P = 1$) has entries $\boldsymbol{h/6,\ 4h/6,\ h/6}$.

The mass matrix is not diagonal. This is an unpleasant fact in computing with finite elements. Any formula involving M^{-1} represents a full matrix—*not sparse.* One approach has been to replace M by a diagonal "lumped matrix". Or a well-organized code can factor M into LL^{T} (by Cholesky) and solve triangular systems.

A newer way to produce a diagonal M is called ***discontinuous Galerkin***. The finite elements are not required to be continuous. *Instead of a hat function at each node, we have a half-hat on each side*! The number of trial functions and nodal unknowns has doubled in 1D, because U_i from the left is not the same as U_i from the right. Discontinuous Galerkin is an extremely active research area [85] in 2D.

The essence of finite elements is to have a clear principle in going from continuous to discrete. Use the weak form and choose N trial functions. Select N simple test functions to get N equations for node values of the finite element approximation U.

Problem Set 3.6

1 For hat functions on intervals of length $h = 1$, find the entries of K:

$$\int \left(\frac{d\phi_j}{dx}\right)^2 dx = 2 \quad \text{and} \quad \int \frac{d\phi_j}{dx}\frac{d\phi_{j+1}}{dx}\,dx = -1.$$

2 With point load $f(x) = \delta(x - a)$ and hats V_i, find the components of the load vector: $F_i = \int f(x)\,V_i(x)\,dx$.

3 What shapes should replace triangles in 3-dimensional space for linear elements $U = a + bx + cy + dz$? Find U for a "standard shape" with $U = U_0, U_1, U_2, U_3$ at the four corners.

4 When U is linear on a triangle with corner values U_1, U_2, U_3, a calculation gives

$$\iint_e (U_x^2 + U_y^2)\,dx\,dy = \frac{1}{2}\left[\frac{(U_2-U_1)^2}{\tan\theta_3} + \frac{(U_3-U_1)^2}{\tan\theta_2} + \frac{(U_3-U_2)^2}{\tan\theta_1}\right].$$

(a) Show that this is $[U_1\ U_2\ U_3]K_e[U_1\ U_2\ U_3]^{\mathrm{T}}$ with K_e from (15).

(b) Evaluate K_e for an equilateral triangle (angles $= 60°$).

(c) Draw a grid of equilateral triangles and assemble a typical ith row of K with 7 nonzeros from the six triangles meeting at meshpoint i.

5 For the mesh of eight triangles in Figure 3.21, use Persson's code to assemble the 9 by 9 singular matrix K and the load vector F for $f(x) = 1$. Then list the 8 boundary nodes in b and reduce K to the 1 by 1 matrix Kb.

6 Solve Poisson's equation $-u_{xx} - u_{yy} = 1$ with $u = 0$ on the standard unit triangle T, using Persson's code with $h = 1/4$. Print the mesh information in the lists p and t and b (boundary node numbers). Display Kb and Fb and Ub.

7 The square $0 \le x, y \le 1$ is cut below into two triangles by the 45° line $y = x$. If $U = 1$ at the midpoint $(\frac{1}{2}, \frac{1}{2})$ of that diagonal, and $U = 0$ at all other nodes, find $U(x,y) = a + bx + cy + dx^2 + exy + fy^2$ in both triangles.

8 (a) Write the ten terms in a cubic polynomial $p(x,y)$ to match the ten nodes in the triangle below. Why does $p(x,y)$ in a neighboring triangle share the same value all along the common edge?

(b) Count the terms $1, x, y, \cdots, x^3y^3$ in a bicubic polynomial, with the exponents of x and y going separately up to 3. We can match U, U_x, U_y, U_{xy} at the four corners of a rectangle.

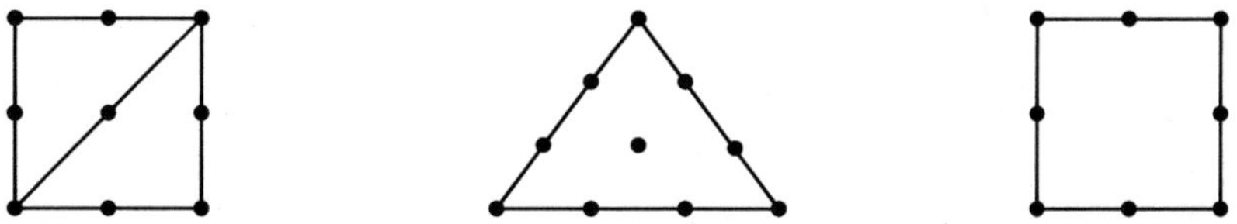

9 The square drawn above has 8 nodes rather than the usual 9 for biquadratic Q_2. Therefore we remove the x^2y^2 term and keep

$$U = a_1 + a_2x + a_3y + a_4x^2 + a_5xy + a_6y^2 + a_7x^2y + a_8xy^2.$$

Find the $\phi(x,y)$ which equals 1 at $x = y = 0$ and zero at all other nodes.

10 Suppose a square has 9 nodes—its corners, edge midpoints, and center. The rows of K will have varying numbers of nonzeros (a varying bandwidth):

(a) How many nodes are neighbors of a corner node? They lie in the four squares that meet at the corner.

(b) How many nodes are neighbors of a midpoint node?

(c) For the node at the center of the square, why is elimination permitted within the element matrix K_e before assembling it with others into K?

11 (a) If $U = a+bx+cy+dxy$ find the coefficients a, b, c, d from the four equations $U = U_1, U_2, U_3, U_4$ at the corners $(\pm 1, \pm 1)$ of a standard square.

(b) From part (a) write down the 2 by 4 gradient matrix G at the center point $P = (0,0)$. The derivatives $b + dy$ and $c + dx$ reduce there to b and c:

At the center $$\begin{bmatrix} \partial U/\partial x \\ \partial U/\partial y \end{bmatrix} = \begin{bmatrix} b \\ c \end{bmatrix} = G \begin{bmatrix} U_1 \\ U_2 \\ U_3 \\ U_4 \end{bmatrix}.$$

(c) Show that $(1,1,1,1)$ and $(1,-1,1,-1)$ are in the nullspace of G. The first comes from a constant $U = 1$ and correctly has zero energy. The second comes from an "hourglass" $U = xy$ and should have positive energy.

12 From the previous problem find the approximation $K_e = 4G^{\mathrm{T}}G$ for the Q_1 bilinear element on the square of area 4. Compare with the correct K_e found by integrating $(b+dy)^2 + (c+dx)^2$ analytically.

13 If $U = a+bx+cy$ on the triangle below, find b and c from the equations $U = U_1$, $U = U_2$, $U = U_3$ at the nodes. Show that the gradient matrix G is

$$\begin{bmatrix} b \\ c \end{bmatrix} = GU = \begin{bmatrix} -\dfrac{1}{L} & \dfrac{1}{L} & 0 \\ \dfrac{d}{Lh} - \dfrac{1}{h} & -\dfrac{d}{Lh} & \dfrac{1}{h} \end{bmatrix} \begin{bmatrix} U_1 \\ U_2 \\ U_3 \end{bmatrix}.$$

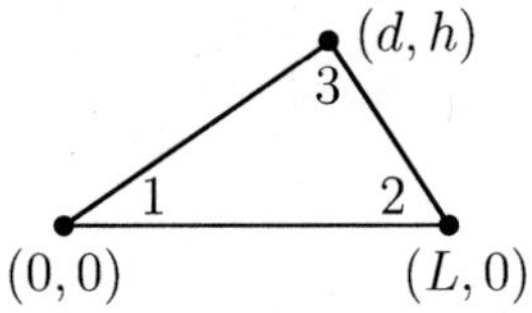

14 (a) For the previous matrix multiply $G^{\mathrm{T}}G$ by the area $Lh/2$ to find the element stiffness matrix K_e. For the standard triangle T reduce it to (28).

(b) Show that the off-diagonal entries agree with $c_1 = (2\tan\theta_1)^{-1}$ predicted in (15). The tangents of θ_1 and θ_2 can be read from the figure, and

$$\tan\theta_3 = -\tan(\theta_1 + \theta_2) = \frac{\tan\theta_1 + \tan\theta_2}{\tan\theta_1 \tan\theta_2 - 1}.$$

15 Show that the numerical integration using the centroid in (16) is exactly correct if f is a constant. Is it exact if $f = x$?

16 Find the eigenvalues of $KU = \lambda MU$, if

$$K = \begin{bmatrix} 2 & -1 \\ -1 & 2 \end{bmatrix} \quad \text{and} \quad M = \begin{bmatrix} 1 & 0 \\ 0 & 2 \end{bmatrix}.$$

This gives the oscillation frequencies for two unequal masses in a line of springs.

17 If the symmetric matrices K and M are not positive definite, $KU = \lambda MU$ may not have real eigenvalues. Construct a 2 by 2 example.

18 For two hat functions on the unit interval, with $U(0) = U(1) = 0$ and stepsize $h = \frac{1}{3}$, assemble K and M:

$$K = \begin{bmatrix} 6 & -3 \\ -3 & 6 \end{bmatrix} \quad \text{and} \quad M = \frac{1}{18}\begin{bmatrix} 4 & 1 \\ 1 & 4 \end{bmatrix}.$$

Find the lowest eigenvalue of $KU = \lambda MU$ and compare with the true eigenvalue π^2 (the eigenfunction is $u = \sin \pi x$) of $-u'' = \lambda u$.

19 The finite element form of $-u'' + u$ is $K/h^2 + M$—the sum of the stiffness and mass matrices. Find the approximation U_1 at the midpoint $x = \frac{1}{2}$, using two hat functions when $-u'' + u = 1$. What is the exact solution $u(x)$?

20 The standard $\boldsymbol{Q}_1$ element in the unit square has four trial functions $\phi_i = (1-X)(1-Y), X(1-Y), XY, (1-X)Y$ for the corner nodes. Show that the element mass matrix of inner products $\iint \phi_i \phi_j \, dx \, dy$ is $M_e =$ toeplitz([4 2 1 2]/36).

21 Using the four ϕ_i in Problem 3, an *isoparametric* change of variables takes the corners of the unit square to the corners (x_i, y_i) of any quadrilateral (*quad*):

$$x(X,Y) = \sum x_i \phi_i(X,Y) \quad \text{and} \quad y(X,Y) = \sum y_i \phi_i(X,Y).$$

Which corner of the quadrilateral comes from $(X,Y) = (1,1)$ on the square?

22 The standard $\boldsymbol{Q}_1$ brick element in 3D has nodes at the 8 corners of the unit cube. What are the eight trial functions ϕ_i (equal to zero at 7 nodes)? They use the eight terms $1, X, Y, Z, XY, XZ, YZ, XYZ$.

3.7 ELASTICITY AND SOLID MECHANICS

This optional section moves from elastic bars and beams to elastic solids. The $A^{\mathrm{T}}CA$ framework still applies in three dimensions. We will see the basic equations of continuum mechanics without every detail (but certainly with examples).

The displacement u becomes a vector $u_1(x_1, x_2, x_3)$, $u_2(x_1, x_2, x_3)$, $u_3(x_1, x_2, x_3)$. The strain e and the stress σ (which earlier was w) become 3 by 3 **symmetric matrices**. Then equilibrium is a balance $A^{\mathrm{T}}\sigma = f$ between internal and external forces. Often those external forces (f_1, f_2, f_3) inside the body are zero. Then the displacement is produced by surface forces (nonzero boundary conditions on σ).

Our goal is to understand the three relations $\boldsymbol{e} = \boldsymbol{Au}$ and $\boldsymbol{\sigma} = \boldsymbol{Ce}$ and $\boldsymbol{f} = \boldsymbol{A}^{\mathrm{T}}\boldsymbol{w}$. Thay connect the vectors u and f to the symmetric matrices e and σ. All three equations will here be *linear* (small displacements, small strains). The equation $e = Au$ only involves first derivatives of u (it extends the stretching $e = du/dx$ to 3D). Hooke's Law $\sigma = Ce$ involves material constants (preferably just two).

A linear relation $\sigma = Ce$ between 3 by 3 matrices with components e_{ij} and σ_{kl} would conceivably allow $9^2 = 81$ coefficients $C_{ijkl}(x)$. Very fortunately that won't happen here, because of our assumptions:

(1) The material is *uniform* (no dependence on the position x)
(2) The material is *isotropic* (no dependence on direction)

A material composed of parallel fibers would be "anisotropic." It has strength in the fiber direction and weakness in the perpendicular directions. But isotropic materials are described by only **two coefficients** in Hooke's Law, for the following reason:

(3) e and σ have the *same principal directions* (same orthogonal eigenvectors).

Hooke's Law can multiply e by a constant, normally written 2μ. It can also add a multiple of I (no change in the eigenvectors). To maintain rotational invariance, that multiple is a constant λ times the trace of e (the sum of principal strains, which are the eigenvalues of e). Those "Lamé constants" produce the constitutive law $\sigma = Ce$:

Hooke's Law with μ and λ $\qquad \sigma = 2\mu e + \lambda(e_{11} + e_{22} + e_{33})I \qquad (1)$

Four Examples

To understand the matrices e and σ, four particular displacements $u(x)$ are extremely helpful. The first is a rigid motion (translation by a vector t plus rotation through an angle θ). This motion produces no internal strains or stresses:

1. Rigid motion
$$\begin{bmatrix} u_1 \\ u_2 \\ u_3 \end{bmatrix} = \begin{bmatrix} \cos\theta & -\sin\theta & 0 \\ \sin\theta & \cos\theta & 0 \\ 0 & 0 & 0 \end{bmatrix} \begin{bmatrix} x_1 \\ x_2 \\ x_3 \end{bmatrix} + \begin{bmatrix} t_1 \\ t_2 \\ t_3 \end{bmatrix} \quad \text{has} \quad \begin{aligned} e &= 0 \\ \sigma &= 0 \\ f &= 0 \end{aligned}$$

The second example does produce stress. For a material at the bottom of the ocean, the forces on the surface are radially inward (*hydrostatic pressure*). Then the displacements are radially inward (pure compression):

2. Compression $(u_1, u_2, u_3) = \alpha(x_1, x_2, x_3)$ has $e = \alpha I$ and $\sigma = 2\mu\alpha I + 3\lambda\alpha I$. That diagonal stress matrix σ means that there is no shear. If we imagine a small plane inside the material, perpendicular to the x_1 direction, the only internal force is normal to the plane. This is σ_{11}, the force per unit area. Since σ is a multiple of I, this stress acts normally to *all* planes in the material.

Example 3 is the opposite—a **shear stress** on a box that is centered at $x = 0$. The top of the box is pushed in the positive x_1 direction, the bottom is pushed in the negative x_1 direction. All movement is along x_1, and it is *proportional to the height* x_3.

3. Simple shear $u = \begin{bmatrix} x_3 \\ 0 \\ 0 \end{bmatrix}$ and $e = \frac{1}{2}\begin{bmatrix} 0 & 0 & 1 \\ 0 & 0 & 0 \\ 1 & 0 & 0 \end{bmatrix}$ and $\sigma = 2\mu e$ (the trace of e is zero).

This shows that the strain e is not just the matrix J of first derivatives of u. That "Jacobian matrix" would have $J_{13} = \partial u_1/\partial x_3 = 1$ and $J_{31} = \partial u_3/\partial x_1 = 0$. **The strain is the symmetric part** $\boldsymbol{e = \frac{1}{2}(J + J^{\mathrm{T}})}$. The antisymmetric part $\frac{1}{2}(J - J^{\mathrm{T}})$ produces no length change (to first order) and therefore no strain.

The fourth example is the most valuable of all, because it involves both of the material constants μ and λ. It comes from pulling a uniform bar. That tension will produce displacement $u_1 = \alpha x_1$ and stretching $e_{11} = \alpha$ in the direction of the bar (x_1 direction). The key difference between 1D elasticity and 3D elasticity is that **the bar contracts in the $\boldsymbol{x_2}$ and $\boldsymbol{x_3}$ directions: $\boldsymbol{b < 0}$.**

In those transverse directions, a tension test will show $u_2 = bx_2$ and $u_3 = bx_3$. There are no shear forces, so e and σ are diagonal matrices (but interesting).

4. **Tension in one direction produces compression in two directions.**

$$e = \begin{bmatrix} a & & \\ & b & \\ & & b \end{bmatrix} \quad \text{and} \quad \sigma = \begin{bmatrix} \sigma_{11} & & \\ & 0 & \\ & & 0 \end{bmatrix} = 2\mu e + \lambda(a + 2b)I. \tag{2}$$

Those two zeros in σ mean that $2\mu b + \lambda(a + 2b) = 0$. Solve for $-b/a$:

Poisson's ratio $$\nu = \frac{\textbf{contraction}}{\textbf{extension}} = -\frac{b}{a} = \frac{\lambda}{2(\mu + \lambda)}. \tag{3}$$

This ratio reveals the change in volume when the bar is stretched. A bar of length L and cross-sectional area A now has length $(1+a)L$ and area $(1+b)^2 A$. To first order, $1 + a$ times $(1 + b)^2$ is $1 + a + 2b$. So there is no volume change when $a + 2b = 0$ and in that case Poisson's ratio is $\nu = -b/a = 0.5$. A typical material has $\nu = 0.3$ and it does lose volume when stretched.

The other experimental constant in the tension test is Young's modulus E:

Young's modulus $$Ee_{11} = \sigma_{11} \quad \text{and} \quad Ee_{22} = Ee_{33} = -\nu\sigma_{11}. \tag{4}$$

Now the $1,1$ entry in Hooke's Law connects the number E to λ and μ:

$$Ee_{11} = (2\mu+\lambda)e_{11}+2\lambda e_{33} \text{ and } e_{33} = -\nu e_{11} = \frac{\lambda e_{11}}{2(\mu+\lambda)} \text{ lead to } E = \frac{\mu(2\mu+3\lambda)}{\mu+\lambda}. \tag{5}$$

When the tension experiment gives E and ν, Problem 9 will solve for λ and μ.

Strain from Displacement

We turn next to $e = Au$. For an elastic rod A is d/dx. Now three displacements u_1, u_2, u_3 have derivatives in three directions x_1, x_2, x_3. However the strain is not just the Jacobian matrix with entries $\partial u_i/\partial x_j$. (That entry J_{ij} is abbreviated to $u_{i,j}$ with a comma.) The change in position is $\boldsymbol{du} = \boldsymbol{J dx}$ by the chain rule: the first component is $du_1 = u_{1,1}\,dx_1 + u_{1,2}\,dx_2 + u_{1,3}\,dx_3$. But **stretching involves changes in length, not just changes in position**. Rotation doesn't change length.

Strain matrix $e = \dfrac{J+J^{\mathrm{T}}}{2}$ **Elongation** $\boldsymbol{e = Au}$ $$e_{ij} = \frac{1}{2}\left(\frac{\partial u_i}{\partial x_j} + \frac{\partial u_j}{\partial x_i}\right) \tag{6}$$

If two points start out separated by Δx, then after displacement they are separated by $\Delta x + \Delta u \approx \Delta x + J\Delta x$: A strain from $J + J^{\mathrm{T}}$ and a rotation from $J - J^{\mathrm{T}}$:

Stretch plus rotation $$J\Delta x = \frac{1}{2}(J + J^{\mathrm{T}})\,\Delta x + \frac{1}{2}(J - J^{\mathrm{T}})\,\Delta x. \tag{7}$$

The stretch gives the length change because $\Delta x^{\mathrm{T}}(J - J^{\mathrm{T}})\,\Delta x = 0$ for rotation:

Length change $$|\Delta x + J\Delta x|^2 = |\Delta x|^2 + \Delta x^{\mathrm{T}}(J + J^{\mathrm{T}})\,\Delta x + \cdots \tag{8}$$

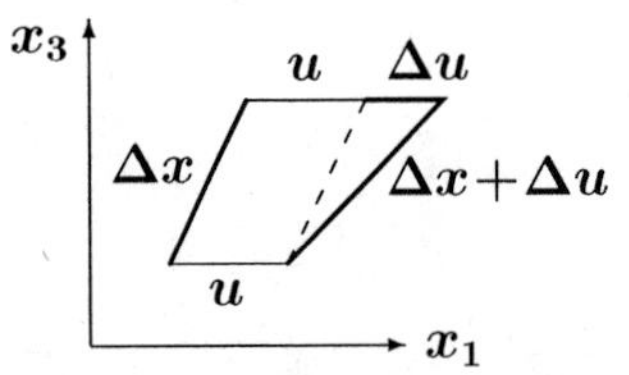

$$\Delta u = (\Delta x_3, 0, 0)$$
$$|\Delta x + \Delta u|^2 = (\Delta x_1 + \Delta x_3)^2 + (\Delta x_2)^2 + (\Delta x_3)^2$$
$$2\Delta x_1\,\Delta x_3 = \Delta x^{\mathrm{T}}(J + J^{\mathrm{T}})\,\Delta x = \Delta x^{\mathrm{T}}\begin{bmatrix} 0 & 0 & 1 \\ 0 & 0 & 0 \\ 1 & 0 & 0 \end{bmatrix}\Delta x$$

Figure 3.26: Length change from simple shear (top slides further than bottom).

Figure 3.26 shows Δx and Δu for the simple shear $u_1 = x_3$. The strain $\frac{1}{2}(J + J^{\mathrm{T}})$ has $e_{13} = e_{31} = \frac{1}{2}$. For this large deformation, the second-order term from $J^{\mathrm{T}}J$ (the Cauchy-Green tensor) could not be ignored. A better example has $u_1 = \alpha x_3$, $\alpha << 1$.

Stress and Force

The force balance $\boldsymbol{f} = \boldsymbol{A}^{\mathrm{T}}\boldsymbol{\sigma} = -\,\mathbf{div}\,\boldsymbol{\sigma}$ completes the equations of equilibrium. (Dynamics adds an acceleration term mu''.) To identify A^{T}, recall the two ways that led to $\text{grad}^{\mathrm{T}} = -\,\text{div}$. One was mathematical, through Green's formula for integration by parts. The other was a physical conservation law. A third approach finds A^{T} through the principle of virtual work: At equilibrium, the work $u^{\mathrm{T}}f$ of the external forces in any virtual displacement equals the work $e^{\mathrm{T}}\sigma$ of the internal stresses. The key step is still integration by parts and $(Au)^{\mathrm{T}}\sigma = u^{\mathrm{T}}(A^{\mathrm{T}}\sigma)$.

Green's formula will have a boundary term which we explain in advance. For fluids it contained $w \cdot n$, the flow rate through the boundary. For solids it contains $\sigma^{\mathrm{T}}n$, the stress matrix times the unit normal vector. That product is a vector, called the ***surface traction***. It gives the force from inside the body on each piece of the surface. It is again a mixture of shear, pushing the boundary to the side, and extension or compression, pushing the boundary out or in. The extensional part is $n^{\mathrm{T}}\sigma^{\mathrm{T}}n$, the "normal component of the normal component" of stress. All components of $\sigma^{\mathrm{T}}n$ must be in balance across every interface, including the boundary surface S between the body and the outside world.

The boundary conditions will specify $\sigma^{\mathrm{T}}n = F$ or else the displacement $u = u_0$. When u_0 is given, a force is required to maintain that displacement—the reaction force (*surface traction*) at the supports. When F is given, the boundary displacement u is the Lagrange multiplier for the constraint $\sigma^{\mathrm{T}}n = F$. You will see how $u^{\mathrm{T}}\sigma^{\mathrm{T}}n$ replaces $uw \cdot n$ when Green's formula moves up to matrices. This boundary term is zero if either $u = 0$ or $\sigma^{\mathrm{T}}n = 0$ in each component:

Integration by parts $$\iiint e^{\mathrm{T}}\sigma\, dV = -\iiint u^{\mathrm{T}}\,\text{div}\,\sigma\, dV + \iint u^{\mathrm{T}}\sigma^{\mathrm{T}}n\, dS. \qquad (9)$$

The derivatives of u (within e) become derivatives of σ. The matrix inner product $e^{\mathrm{T}}\sigma$ is the sum of all nine terms $e_{ij}\sigma_{ij}$. The left side of (9) is the inner product of Au with σ. Therefore the volume integral on the right must be the inner product of u with $A^{\mathrm{T}}\sigma$, and this identifies the transpose of A:

Force balance $$A^{\mathrm{T}}\sigma = -\,\text{div}\,\sigma = -\begin{bmatrix} \dfrac{\partial\sigma_{11}}{\partial x_1} + \dfrac{\partial\sigma_{12}}{\partial x_2} + \dfrac{\partial\sigma_{13}}{\partial x_3} \\[2ex] \dfrac{\partial\sigma_{21}}{\partial x_1} + \dfrac{\partial\sigma_{22}}{\partial x_2} + \dfrac{\partial\sigma_{23}}{\partial x_3} \\[2ex] \dfrac{\partial\sigma_{31}}{\partial x_1} + \dfrac{\partial\sigma_{32}}{\partial x_2} + \dfrac{\partial\sigma_{33}}{\partial x_3} \end{bmatrix} = \begin{bmatrix} f_1 \\[2ex] f_2 \\[2ex] f_3 \end{bmatrix}. \qquad (10)$$

The Torsion of a Rod

This example is good because most of the strain and stress components are zero. It starts with a vertical rod, whose cross-section need not be a circle. By putting your hands on the top and bottom, and twisting the top while holding the bottom, all cross-sections will turn. The boundary conditions on the sides are $\sigma^{\mathrm{T}} n = 0$: no force. On the top and bottom there is no *vertical* force: $\sigma_{33} = 0$. The other conditions are $u_1 = u_2 = 0$ on the bottom and $u_1 = -\theta x_2 h$, $u_2 = \theta x_1 h$ on the top—where h is the height (the x_3 component) and θ is the twist angle.

The turning of cross-sections will increase linearly with their height x_3:

Turn and warp $$u_1 = -\theta x_2 x_3, \quad u_2 = \theta x_1 x_3, \quad u_3 = w(x_1, x_2). \tag{11}$$

The *warping function* w is identical for all cross-sections, which start flat but become warped as they turn. Their movement out of the plane is w, still to be determined. The strains and stresses are symmetric matrices:

$$e = Au = \begin{bmatrix} 0 & 0 & \frac{1}{2}(\partial w/\partial x_1 - \theta x_2) \\ 0 & 0 & \frac{1}{2}(\partial w/\partial x_2 + \theta x_1) \\ - & - & 0 \end{bmatrix} \qquad \sigma = Ce = 2\mu e$$

On the sides, where $n = (n_1, n_2, 0)$ points outwards, multiplying by σ^{T} gives zero automatically in two components. The only serious boundary condition is

$$(\sigma^{\mathrm{T}} n)_3 = \mu \left(\frac{\partial w}{\partial x_1} - \theta x_2 \right) n_1 + \mu \left(\frac{\partial w}{\partial x_2} + \theta x_1 \right) n_2 = 0. \tag{12}$$

The equilibrium equations $\operatorname{div} \sigma = f = 0$ are similar. The first two are automatic, and the third reduces to Laplace's equation by discarding $\partial x_2/\partial x_1 = 0 = \partial x_1/\partial x_2$:

$$\frac{\partial}{\partial x_1} \left(\frac{\partial w}{\partial x_1} - \theta x_2 \right) + \frac{\partial}{\partial x_2} \left(\frac{\partial w}{\partial x_2} + \theta x_1 \right) + \frac{\partial}{\partial x_3} 0 = w_{,11} + w_{,22} = 0. \tag{13}$$

Final remark The strain e and the stress σ are tensors. Properly speaking, u and f are tensors. And more important, **A and C and A^{T} are tensors**. They are linear transformations, and what earns them the name "tensor" is that they have an intrinsic geometrical definition—not dependent on the coordinate system.

The statement $u = x_2$ has no meaning until the coordinates are known; x_2 is not a tensor. The formula $e = \operatorname{grad} u$ does have a meaning; the gradient is a tensor. It is true that to *compute* the gradient we need coordinates—if they are rectangular, as you and I immediately assumed they were for $u = x_2$, then $\operatorname{grad} u = (0, 1, 0)$. But if they were cylindrical coordinates, and x_2 is actually θ, the gradient can go forward in that system—and it involves $1/r$. The gradient and divergence look different for different coordinate systems; but in themselves, they do not change.

A and C and A^{T} were written in rectangular coordinates, but a tensor analyst is prepared for other systems. A rotation of axes gives the test that a tensor must pass, to verify its ***invariance under coordinate transformations***. The theory of relativity includes moving coordinate changes, so Einstein had to go further. He needed curvilinear coordinates and the Schwarz-Christoffel symbols that come with derivatives. That would carry us pretty far, and not with the speed of light, but we do mention three more tensors. One is the curl; the second is the Laplacian div grad; the third computes acceleration from velocity. It involves $v \cdot \nabla$, which is $\sum v_i \, \partial/\partial x_i$ in rectangular coordinates, and it will be seen in Section 6.7 as basic for fluids.

Problem Set 3.7

1 Pure shear has displacement $u = (\alpha x_2, \alpha x_1, 0)$. Draw the unit square before and after displacement. Find the symmetric strain matrix e from the derivatives of u. This is the same constant strain as in simple shear (Example 3 in the text) and only the boundary conditions can tell the difference.

2 Find the eigenvectors of e in Problem 1 (the principal strains). Explain how the shear $u = (\alpha x_2, \alpha x_1, 0)$ is a combination of pure stretching in these principal directions. Every strain matrix $e = Q\Lambda Q^{\mathrm{T}}$ is a 3-way stretch in the direction of its eigenvectors.

3 What are the boundary conditions on the square for simple shear and pure shear (Problem 1)? Since e and σ are constant, the body force is $f = 0$ as usual.

4 A rigid motion combines a constant displacement u_0 (a translation of the whole body) and a pure rotation: $u = u_0 + \omega \times r$. Find the strain Au.

5 From the laws (1)-(6)-(10) find the strain and stress and external force for each of the following displacements:

(a) $u = (\lambda_1 x_1, \lambda_2 x_2, \lambda_3 x_3)$ (stretching)

(b) $u = (-x_2 v(x_1), v(x_1), 0)$ (bending of a beam)

(c) $u = (\partial\varphi/\partial x_1, \partial\varphi/\partial x_2, \partial\varphi/\partial x_3)$ (displacement potential)

6 The principle of virtual work applies to any "virtual displacement" v:

$$\iiint v^{\mathrm{T}} f \, dV + \iint v^{\mathrm{T}} F \, dS = \iiint (Av)^{\mathrm{T}} \sigma \, dV$$

It is the weak form of the equilibrium equation; the perturbation v is required to be zero where $u = u_0$ is prescribed. Use formula (9) for integration by parts to reach the strong form $\operatorname{div} \sigma + f = 0$ in V, $\sigma^{\mathrm{T}} n = F$ on S.

7 In two-dimensional flow the continuity equation $\operatorname{div} w = 0$ was solved by means of a stream function: $w = (\partial s/\partial y, -\partial s/\partial x)$ is divergence-free for any s. In two-dimensional elasticity show that $\operatorname{div} \sigma = 0$ is solved by an Airy stress function:

$$\sigma = \begin{bmatrix} \dfrac{\partial^2 A}{\partial y^2} & -\dfrac{\partial^2 A}{\partial x \partial y} & 0 \\ -\dfrac{\partial^2 A}{\partial x \partial y} & \dfrac{\partial^2 A}{\partial x^2} & 0 \\ 0 & 0 & 0 \end{bmatrix} \quad \text{has } \operatorname{div} \sigma = 0 \text{ for any } A(x,y).$$

8 Verify that the elasticity equation $A^{\mathrm{T}}CAu = f$ can be rewritten as

$$\mu \text{ curl curl } u - (\lambda + 2\mu) \text{ grad div } u = f.$$

9 Find μ and λ from Young's modulus E and Poisson's ratio ν:

$$E = \frac{\mu(2\mu + 3\lambda)}{\mu + \lambda} \text{ and } \nu = \frac{\lambda}{2(\mu + \lambda)} \text{ give } 2\mu = \frac{E}{1 + \nu} \text{ and } \lambda = \frac{vE}{(1 + \nu)(1 - 2\nu)}.$$

10 (More important than the above) Invert the isotropic stress-strain relation $\sigma = 2\mu e + \lambda(\operatorname{tr} e)I$ to find the strain from the stress: $e = C^{-1}\sigma$. Show first that the trace of σ is $(2\mu + 3\lambda)$, (trace of e). Then substitute for tr e to find

$$e = \frac{1}{2\mu}\sigma - \frac{\lambda}{2\mu + 3\lambda} (\operatorname{tr} \sigma)I.$$

11 Show that the strain energy $\frac{1}{2}e^{\mathrm{T}}Ce$ is $\mu\Sigma\Sigma e_{ij}^2 + \frac{1}{2}\lambda(\operatorname{tr} e)^2$. From the previous exercise find the complementary energy $\frac{1}{2}\sigma^{\mathrm{T}}C^{-1}\sigma$.

12 What minimum principles govern equilibrium continuum mechanics?

13 In the torsion of a *circular* rod show that $\nabla w \cdot n = \theta(x_2 n_1 - x_1 n_2)$ is zero around the side—where n points radially outward. The warping is $w = 0$ everywhere.

14 For a rod with the square cross-section $-1 \le x_1, x_2 \le 1$ find $F = \theta(x_2 n_1 - x_1 n_2)$ on each of the four sides and verify that $\int F\, ds = 0$.

15 For an infinitely long rod with fixed boundary, suppose all internal forces and displacements are in the x_3-direction, but are independent of the distance x_3 along that axis: $u = (0, 0, u_3(x_1, x_2))$. Find the strains, the stresses, the equilibrium equation $A^{\mathrm{T}}CAu = f$, and the boundary condition, all in terms of u_3.

16 For the displacement $u = (x, xy, xyz)$, find the matrix J with entries $\partial u_i/\partial x_j$. Split J into a symmetric strain part e and a skew-symmetric rotational part.

CHAPTER 4

FOURIER SERIES AND INTEGRALS

4.1 FOURIER SERIES FOR PERIODIC FUNCTIONS

This section explains three Fourier series: **sines, cosines, and exponentials e^{ikx}**. Square waves (1 or 0 or -1) are great examples, with delta functions in the derivative. We look at a spike, a step function, and a ramp—and smoother functions too.

Start with $\sin x$. It has period 2π since $\sin(x+2\pi) = \sin x$. It is an odd function since $\sin(-x) = -\sin x$, and it vanishes at $x = 0$ and $x = \pi$. Every function $\sin nx$ has those three properties, and Fourier looked at *infinite combinations of the sines*:

Fourier sine series $$S(x) = b_1 \sin x + b_2 \sin 2x + b_3 \sin 3x + \cdots = \sum_{n=1}^{\infty} b_n \sin nx \qquad (1)$$

If the numbers $b_1, b_2, \ldots$ drop off quickly enough (we are foreshadowing the importance of the decay rate) then the sum $S(x)$ will inherit all three properties:

Periodic $S(x+2\pi) = S(x)$ **Odd** $S(-x) = -S(x)$ $S(0) = S(\pi) = 0$

200 years ago, Fourier startled the mathematicians in France by suggesting that *any function* $S(x)$ with those properties could be expressed as an infinite series of sines. This idea started an enormous development of Fourier series. Our first step is to compute from $S(x)$ the number b_k that multiplies $\sin kx$.

Suppose $S(x) = \sum b_n \sin nx$. *Multiply both sides by* $\sin kx$. *Integrate from* 0 *to* π:

$$\int_0^{\pi} S(x) \sin kx \, dx = \int_0^{\pi} b_1 \sin x \sin kx \, dx + \cdots + \int_0^{\pi} \boldsymbol{b_k \sin kx \, \sin kx \, dx} + \cdots \qquad (2)$$

On the right side, all integrals are zero except the highlighted one with $n = k$. This property of "**orthogonality**" will dominate the whole chapter. The sines make $90°$ angles in function space, when their inner products are integrals from 0 to π:

Orthogonality $$\int_0^{\pi} \sin nx \, \sin kx \, dx = 0 \quad \text{if} \quad n \neq k\,. \qquad (3)$$

Zero comes quickly if we integrate $\int \cos mx\, dx = \left[\frac{\sin mx}{m}\right]_0^\pi = 0 - 0$. So we use this:

Product of sines $$\sin nx \, \sin kx = \frac{1}{2}\cos(n-k)x - \frac{1}{2}\cos(n+k)x\,. \qquad (4)$$

Integrating $\cos mx$ with $m = n - k$ and $m = n + k$ proves orthogonality of the sines.

The exception is when $n = k$. Then we are integrating $(\sin kx)^2 = \frac{1}{2} - \frac{1}{2}\cos 2kx$:

$$\int_0^\pi \sin kx \, \sin kx \, dx = \int_0^\pi \frac{1}{2}\, dx - \int_0^\pi \frac{1}{2}\cos 2kx \, dx = \frac{\pi}{2}\,. \qquad (5)$$

The highlighted term in equation (2) is $\boldsymbol{b_k \pi/2}$. Multiply both sides of (2) by $2/\pi$:

Sine coefficients **$S(-x) = -S(x)$** $$b_k = \frac{2}{\pi}\int_0^\pi S(x)\sin kx\, dx = \frac{1}{\pi}\int_{-\pi}^{\pi} S(x)\sin kx\, dx. \qquad (6)$$

Notice that $S(x)\sin kx$ is *even* (equal integrals from $-\pi$ to 0 and from 0 to π).

I will go immediately to the most important example of a Fourier sine series. $S(x)$ is an **odd square wave** with $SW(x) = 1$ for $0 < x < \pi$. It is drawn in Figure 4.1 as an odd function (with period 2π) that vanishes at $x = 0$ and $x = \pi$.

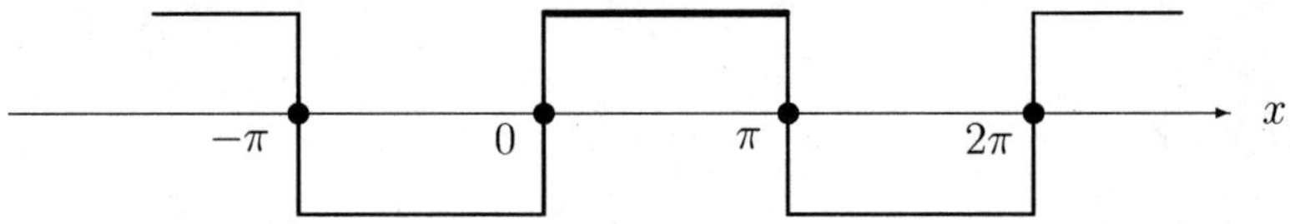

Figure 4.1: The odd square wave with $SW(x + 2\pi) = SW(x) = \{1 \text{ or } 0 \text{ or } -1\}$.

Example 1 Find the Fourier sine coefficients b_k of the square wave $SW(x)$.

Solution For $k = 1, 2, \ldots$ use the first formula (6) with $S(x) = 1$ between 0 and π:

$$b_k = \frac{2}{\pi}\int_0^\pi \sin kx\, dx = \frac{2}{\pi}\left[\frac{-\cos kx}{k}\right]_0^\pi = \frac{2}{\pi}\left\{\frac{\mathbf{2}}{\mathbf{1}}, \frac{0}{2}, \frac{\mathbf{2}}{\mathbf{3}}, \frac{0}{4}, \frac{\mathbf{2}}{\mathbf{5}}, \frac{0}{6}, \ldots\right\} \qquad (7)$$

The even-numbered coefficients b_{2k} are all zero because $\cos 2k\pi = \cos 0 = 1$. The odd-numbered coefficients $b_k = 4/\pi k$ decrease at the rate $1/k$. We will see that same $1/k$ decay rate for all functions formed from *smooth pieces and jumps*.

Put those coefficients $4/\pi k$ and zero into the Fourier sine series for $SW(x)$:

Square wave $$\boldsymbol{SW(x)} = \frac{4}{\pi}\left[\frac{\sin x}{\mathbf{1}} + \frac{\sin 3x}{\mathbf{3}} + \frac{\sin 5x}{\mathbf{5}} + \frac{\sin 7x}{\mathbf{7}} + \cdots\right] \qquad (8)$$

Figure 4.2 graphs this sum after one term, then two terms, and then five terms. You can see the all-important **Gibbs phenomenon** appearing as these "partial sums" include more terms. Away from the jumps, we safely approach $SW(x) = 1$ or -1. At $x = \pi/2$, the series gives a beautiful alternating formula for the number π:

$$1 = \frac{4}{\pi}\left[\frac{1}{1} - \frac{1}{3} + \frac{1}{5} - \frac{1}{7} + \cdots\right] \quad \text{so that} \quad \boldsymbol{\pi = 4\left[\frac{1}{1} - \frac{1}{3} + \frac{1}{5} - \frac{1}{7} + \cdots\right]}. \tag{9}$$

The Gibbs phenomenon is the overshoot that moves closer and closer to the jumps. Its height approaches $1.18\ldots$ and it does not decrease with more terms of the series! Overshoot is the one greatest obstacle to calculation of all discontinuous functions (like shock waves in fluid flow). We try hard to avoid Gibbs but sometimes we can't.

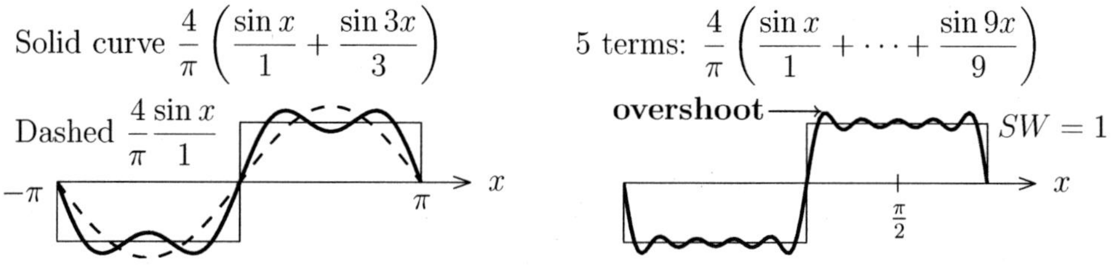

Figure 4.2: **Gibbs phenomenon**: Partial sums $\sum_1^N b_n \sin nx$ overshoot near jumps.

Fourier Coefficients are Best

Let me look again at the first term $b_1 \sin x = (4/\pi)\sin x$. This is the **closest possible approximation** to the square wave SW, by any multiple of $\sin x$ (closest in the least squares sense). To see this optimal property of the Fourier coefficients, minimize the error over all b_1:

$$\text{The error is} \int_0^\pi (SW - b_1 \sin x)^2\,dx \quad \text{The } b_1 \text{ derivative is } -2\int_0^\pi (SW - b_1 \sin x)\sin x\,dx.$$

The integral of $\sin^2 x$ is $\pi/2$. So the derivative is zero when $b_1 = (2/\pi)\int_0^\pi S(x)\sin x\,dx$. This is exactly equation (6) for the Fourier coefficient.

Each $b_k \sin kx$ is as close as possible to SW ⊛. We can find the coefficients b_k one at a time, *because the sines are orthogonal.* The square wave has $b_2 = 0$ because all other multiples of $\sin 2x$ increase the error. Term by term, we are "projecting the function onto each axis $\sin kx$."

Fourier Cosine Series

The cosine series applies to *even functions* with $C(-x) = C(x)$:

$$\textbf{Cosine series} \quad C(x) = a_0 + a_1 \cos x + a_2 \cos 2x + \cdots = a_0 + \sum_{n=1}^{\infty} a_n \cos nx. \tag{10}$$

Every cosine has period 2π. Figure 4.3 shows two even functions, the **repeating ramp** $RR(x)$ and the **up-down train** $UD(x)$ of delta functions. That sawtooth ramp RR is the integral of the square wave. The delta functions in UD give the derivative of the square wave. (For sines, the integral and derivative are cosines.) RR and UD will be valuable examples, one smoother than SW, one less smooth.

First we find formulas for the cosine coefficients a_0 and a_k. The constant term a_0 is the *average value* of the function $C(x)$:

a_0 = Average
$$a_0 = \frac{1}{\pi}\int_0^\pi C(x)\,dx = \frac{1}{2\pi}\int_{-\pi}^\pi C(x)\,dx. \tag{11}$$

I just integrated every term in the cosine series (10) from 0 to π. On the right side, the integral of a_0 is $a_0\pi$ (divide both sides by π). All other integrals are zero:

$$\int_0^\pi \cos nx\,dx = \left[\frac{\sin nx}{n}\right]_0^\pi = 0 - 0 = 0. \tag{12}$$

In words, the constant function 1 is orthogonal to $\cos nx$ over the interval $[0, \pi]$.

The other cosine coefficients a_k come from the *orthogonality of cosines.* As with sines, we multiply both sides of (10) by $\cos kx$ and integrate from 0 to π:

$$\int_0^\pi C(x)\cos kx\,dx = \int_0^\pi a_0\cos kx\,dx + \int_0^\pi a_1\cos x\cos kx\,dx + \cdots + \int_0^\pi \boldsymbol{a_k(\cos kx)^2\,dx} + \cdots$$

You know what is coming. On the right side, only the highlighted term can be nonzero. Problem 4.1.1 proves this by an identity for $\cos nx\cos kx$—now (4) has a plus sign. The bold nonzero term is $\boldsymbol{a_k\pi/2}$ and we multiply both sides by $2/\pi$:

Cosine coefficients
$C(-x) = C(x)$
$$a_k = \frac{2}{\pi}\int_0^\pi C(x)\cos kx\,dx = \frac{1}{\pi}\int_{-\pi}^\pi C(x)\cos kx\,dx\,. \tag{13}$$

Again the integral over a full period from $-\pi$ to π (also 0 to 2π) is just doubled.

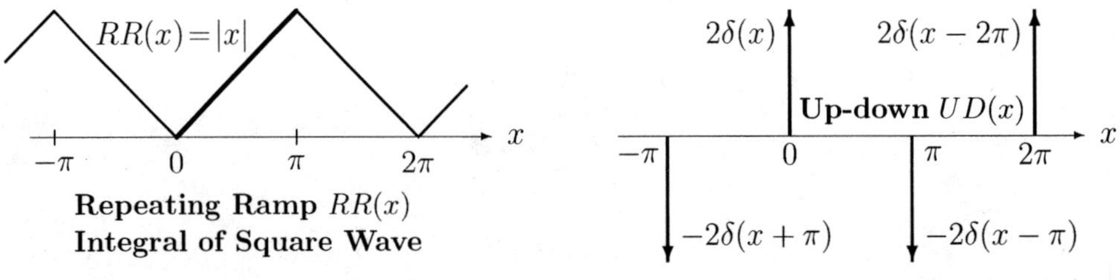

Figure 4.3: The repeating ramp RR and the up-down UD (periodic spikes) are even. The derivative of RR is the odd square wave SW. **The derivative of SW is UD.**

Example 2 Find the cosine coefficients of the ramp $RR(x)$ and the up-down $UD(x)$.

Solution The simplest way is to start with the sine series for the square wave:

$$SW(x) = \frac{4}{\pi}\left[\frac{\sin x}{1} + \frac{\sin 3x}{3} + \frac{\sin 5x}{5} + \frac{\sin 7x}{7} + \cdots\right].$$

Take the derivative of every term to produce cosines in the up-down delta function:

Up-down series $$UD(x) = \frac{4}{\pi}\left[\cos x + \cos 3x + \cos 5x + \cos 7x + \cdots\right]. \tag{14}$$

Those coefficients don't decay at all. The terms in the series don't approach zero, so officially the series cannot converge. Nevertheless it is somehow correct and important. Unofficially this sum of cosines has all 1's at $x = 0$ and all -1's at $x = \pi$. Then $+\infty$ and $-\infty$ are consistent with $2\delta(x)$ and $-2\delta(x-\pi)$. The true way to recognize $\delta(x)$ is by the test $\int \delta(x) f(x)\, dx = f(0)$ and Example 3 will do this.

For the repeating ramp, we integrate the square wave series for $SW(x)$ and add the average ramp height $a_0 = \pi/2$, halfway from 0 to π:

Ramp series $$\boldsymbol{RR(x)} = \frac{\pi}{2} - \frac{\pi}{4}\left[\frac{\cos x}{\mathbf{1^2}} + \frac{\cos 3x}{\mathbf{3^2}} + \frac{\cos 5x}{\mathbf{5^2}} + \frac{\cos 7x}{\mathbf{7^2}} + \cdots\right]. \tag{15}$$

The constant of integration is a_0. *Those coefficients a_k drop off like $1/k^2$.* They could be computed directly from formula (13) using $\int x \cos kx\, dx$, but this requires an integration by parts (or a table of integrals or an appeal to *Mathematica* or *Maple*). It was much easier to integrate every sine separately in $SW(x)$, which makes clear the crucial point: Each "degree of smoothness" in the function is reflected in a faster decay rate of its Fourier coefficients a_k and b_k.

No decay	**Delta** functions (with spikes)
$1/k$ decay	**Step** functions (with jumps)
$1/k^2$ decay	**Ramp** functions (with corners)
$1/k^4$ decay	**Spline** functions (jumps in f''')
r^k decay with $r < 1$	**Analytic** functions like $1/(2 - \cos x)$

Each integration divides the kth coefficient by k. So the decay rate has an extra $1/k$. The "Riemann-Lebesgue lemma" says that a_k and b_k approach zero for any continuous function (in fact whenever $\int |f(x)| dx$ is finite). Analytic functions achieve a new level of smoothness—they can be differentiated forever. Their Fourier series and Taylor series in Chapter 5 converge **exponentially fast**.

The poles of $1/(2 - \cos x)$ will be complex solutions of $\cos x = 2$. Its Fourier series converges quickly because r^k decays faster than any power $1/k^p$. Analytic functions are ideal for computations—the Gibbs phenomenon will never appear.

Now we go back to $\delta(x)$ for what could be the most important example of all.

Example 3 Find the (cosine) coefficients of the *delta function* $\delta(x)$, made 2π-periodic.

Solution The spike occurs at the start of the interval $[0, \pi]$ so safer to integrate from $-\pi$ to π. We find $a_0 = 1/2\pi$ and the other $a_k = 1/\pi$ (cosines because $\delta(x)$ is even):

$$\textbf{Average}\quad a_0 = \frac{1}{2\pi}\int_{-\pi}^{\pi} \delta(x)\,dx = \frac{\mathbf{1}}{\mathbf{2\pi}} \qquad \textbf{Cosines}\quad a_k = \frac{1}{\pi}\int_{-\pi}^{\pi} \delta(x)\cos kx\,dx = \frac{\mathbf{1}}{\boldsymbol{\pi}}$$

Then the series for the delta function has all cosines in equal amounts:

$$\textbf{Delta function}\qquad \delta(x) = \frac{1}{2\pi} + \frac{1}{\pi}\left[\cos x + \cos 2x + \cos 3x + \cdots\right]. \tag{16}$$

Again this series cannot truly converge (its terms don't approach zero). But we can graph the sum after $\cos 5x$ and after $\cos 10x$. Figure 4.4 shows how these "partial sums" are doing their best to approach $\delta(x)$. They oscillate faster and faster away from $x = 0$.

Actually there is a neat formula for the partial sum $\delta_N(x)$ that stops at $\cos Nx$. Start by writing each term $2\cos\theta$ as $e^{i\theta} + e^{-i\theta}$:

$$\delta_N = \frac{1}{2\pi}\left[1 + 2\cos x + \cdots + 2\cos Nx\right] = \frac{1}{2\pi}\left[1 + e^{ix} + e^{-ix} + \cdots + e^{iNx} + e^{-iNx}\right].$$

This is a geometric progression that starts from e^{-iNx} and ends at e^{iNx}. We have powers of the same factor e^{ix}. The sum of a geometric series is known:

$$\begin{array}{l}\textbf{Partial sum}\\ \textbf{up to } \cos Nx\end{array}\qquad \delta_N(x) = \frac{1}{2\pi}\,\frac{e^{i(N+\frac{1}{2})x} - e^{-i(N+\frac{1}{2})x}}{e^{ix/2} - e^{-ix/2}} = \frac{1}{2\pi}\,\frac{\sin(N+\frac{1}{2})x}{\sin\frac{1}{2}x}. \tag{17}$$

This is the function graphed in Figure 4.4. We claim that for any N the area underneath $\delta_N(x)$ is 1. (Each cosine integrated from $-\pi$ to π gives zero. The integral of $1/2\pi$ is 1.) The central "lobe" in the graph ends when $\sin(N + \frac{1}{2})x$ comes down to zero, and that happens when $(N + \frac{1}{2})x = \pm\pi$. I think the area under that lobe (marked by bullets) approaches the same number $1.18\ldots$ that appears in the Gibbs phenomenon.

In what way does $\delta_N(x)$ approach $\delta(x)$? The terms $\cos nx$ in the series jump around at each point $x \neq 0$, not approaching zero. At $x = \pi$ we see $\frac{1}{2\pi}[1 - 2 + 2 - 2 + \cdots]$ and the sum is $1/2\pi$ or $-1/2\pi$. The bumps in the partial sums don't get smaller than $1/2\pi$. The right test for the delta function $\delta(x)$ is to multiply by a smooth $f(x) = \sum a_k \cos kx$ and integrate, because *we only know* $\delta(x)$ *from its integrals* $\int \delta(x)f(x)\,dx = f(0)$:

$$\begin{array}{l}\textbf{Weak convergence}\\ \textbf{of } \delta_N(x) \textbf{ to } \delta(x)\end{array}\qquad \int_{-\pi}^{\pi} \boldsymbol{\delta_N(x) f(x)\,dx = a_0 + \cdots + a_N \to f(0)}\,. \tag{18}$$

In this integrated sense (*weak sense*) the sums $\delta_N(x)$ do approach the delta function! The convergence of $a_0 + \cdots + a_N$ is the statement that at $x = 0$ the Fourier series of a smooth $f(x) = \sum a_k \cos kx$ converges to the number $f(0)$.

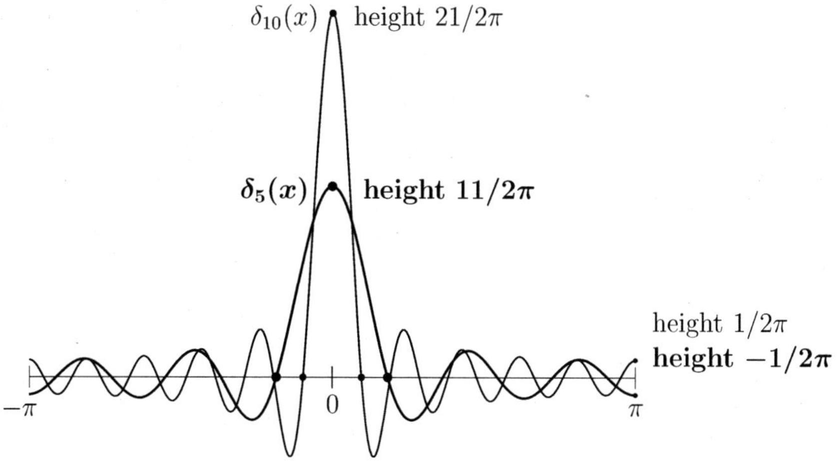

Figure 4.4: The sums $\delta_N(x) = (1 + 2\cos x + \cdots + 2\cos Nx)/2\pi$ try to approach $\delta(x)$.

Complete Series: Sines and Cosines

Over the half-period $[0, \pi]$, the sines are not orthogonal to all the cosines. In fact the integral of $\sin x$ times 1 is not zero. So for functions $F(x)$ that are not odd or even, we move to the complete series (sines plus cosines) on the full interval. Since our functions are periodic, that "full interval" can be $[-\pi, \pi]$ or $[0, 2\pi]$:

Complete Fourier series
$$F(x) = a_0 + \sum_{n=1}^{\infty} a_n \cos nx + \sum_{n=1}^{\infty} b_n \sin nx\,. \tag{19}$$

On every "2π interval" all sines and cosines are mutually orthogonal. We find the Fourier coefficients a_k and b_k in the usual way: **Multiply** (19) **by** 1 **and** $\cos kx$ **and** $\sin kx$, **and integrate both sides from** $-\pi$ **to** π:

$$\boldsymbol{a_0} = \frac{1}{2\pi}\int_{-\pi}^{\pi} F(x)\,dx \quad \boldsymbol{a_k} = \frac{1}{\pi}\int_{-\pi}^{\pi} F(x)\cos kx\,dx \quad \boldsymbol{b_k} = \frac{1}{\pi}\int_{-\pi}^{\pi} F(x)\sin x\,dx. \tag{20}$$

Orthogonality kills off infinitely many integrals and leaves only the one we want.

Another approach is to split $F(x) = C(x) + S(x)$ into an even part and an odd part. Then we can use the earlier cosine and sine formulas. The two parts are

$$C(x) = F_{\mathbf{even}}(x) = \frac{F(x) + F(-x)}{2} \qquad S(x) = F_{\mathbf{odd}}(x) = \frac{F(x) - F(-x)}{2}. \tag{21}$$

The even part gives the a's and the odd part gives the b's. Test on a short square pulse from $x = 0$ to $x = h$—this one-sided function is not odd or even.

Example 4 Find the a's and b's if $F(x) = \textbf{square pulse} = \begin{cases} \mathbf{1} & \text{for } 0 < x < h \\ \mathbf{0} & \text{for } h < x < 2\pi \end{cases}$

Solution The integrals for a_0 and a_k and b_k stop at $x = h$ where $F(x)$ drops to zero. The coefficients decay like $1/k$ because of the jump at $x = 0$ and the drop at $x = h$:

Coefficients of square pulse $\qquad a_0 = \frac{1}{2\pi}\int_0^h 1\,dx = \frac{\mathbf{h}}{\mathbf{2\pi}} = \textbf{average}$

$$a_k = \frac{1}{\pi}\int_0^h \cos kx\,dx = \frac{\sin kh}{\pi k} \qquad b_k = \frac{1}{\pi}\int_0^h \sin kx\,dx = \frac{1-\cos kh}{\pi k}. \tag{22}$$

If we divide $F(x)$ by h, its graph is a tall thin rectangle: height $\frac{1}{h}$, base h, and area $= 1$.

When h approaches zero, $F(x)/h$ is squeezed into a very thin interval. *The tall rectangle approaches (weakly) the delta function $\delta(x)$.* The average height is area$/2\pi = 1/2\pi$. Its other coefficients a_k/h and b_k/h approach $1/\pi$ and 0, already known for $\delta(x)$:

$$\frac{\boldsymbol{F(x)}}{\boldsymbol{h}} \to \boldsymbol{\delta(x)} \qquad \frac{a_k}{h} = \frac{1}{\pi}\frac{\sin kh}{kh} \to \frac{1}{\pi} \quad \text{and} \quad \frac{b_k}{h} = \frac{1-\cos kh}{\pi kh} \to 0 \text{ as } h \to 0. \tag{23}$$

When the function has a jump, its Fourier series picks the halfway point. This example would converge to $F(0) = \frac{1}{2}$ and $F(h) = \frac{1}{2}$, halfway up and halfway down.

The Fourier series converges to $F(x)$ at each point where the function is smooth. This is a highly developed theory, and Carleson won the 2006 Abel Prize by proving convergence for every x except a set of measure zero. If the function has finite energy $\int |F(x)|^2\,dx$, he showed that the Fourier series converges "almost everywhere."

Energy in Function = Energy in Coefficients

There is an extremely important equation (***the energy identity***) that comes from integrating $(F(x))^2$. When we square the Fourier series of $F(x)$, and integrate from $-\pi$ to π, all the "cross terms" drop out. The only nonzero integrals come from 1^2 and $\cos^2 kx$ and $\sin^2 kx$, multiplied by a_0^2 and a_k^2 and b_k^2:

$$\textbf{Energy in } \boldsymbol{F(x)} = \int_{-\pi}^{\pi}\left(a_0 + \sum a_k \cos kx + \sum b_k \sin kx\right)^2 dx$$
$$\int_{-\pi}^{\pi}(F(x))^2 dx = 2\pi a_0^2 + \pi\left(a_1^2 + b_1^2 + a_2^2 + b_2^2 + \cdots\right). \tag{24}$$

The energy in $F(x)$ equals the energy in the coefficients. The left side is like the length squared of a vector, except *the vector is a function.* The right side comes from an infinitely long vector of a's and b's. The lengths are equal, which says that the Fourier transform from function to vector is like an orthogonal matrix. Normalized by constants $\sqrt{2\pi}$ and $\sqrt{\pi}$, we have an *orthonormal basis in function space.*

What is this function space? It is like ordinary 3-dimensional space, except the "vectors" are functions. Their length $\|f\|$ comes from integrating instead of adding: $\|f\|^2 = \int |f(x)|^2 dx$. These functions fill **Hilbert space**. The rules of geometry hold:

Length $\|f\|^2 = (f, f)$ comes from the inner product $(f, g) = \int f(x)g(x)\,dx$
Orthogonal functions $(f, g) = 0$ produce a right triangle: $\|f + g\|^2 = \|f\|^2 + \|g\|^2$

I have tried to draw Hilbert space in Figure 4.5. It has infinitely many axes. *The energy identity* (24) *is exactly the Pythagoras Law in infinite-dimensional space.*

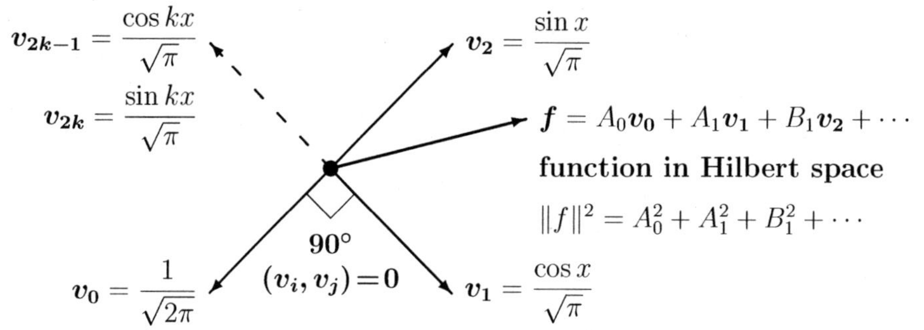

Figure 4.5: The Fourier series is a combination of orthonormal v's (sines and cosines).

Complex Exponentials $c_k e^{ikx}$

This is a small step and we have to take it. In place of separate formulas for a_0 and a_k and b_k, we will have *one formula* for all the complex coefficients c_k. And the function $F(x)$ might be complex (as in quantum mechanics). The Discrete Fourier Transform will be much simpler when we use N complex exponentials for a vector. We practice in advance with the complex infinite series for a 2π-periodic function:

Complex Fourier series $$F(x) = c_0 + c_1 e^{ix} + c_{-1} e^{-ix} + \cdots = \sum_{n=-\infty}^{\infty} c_n e^{inx} \quad (25)$$

If every $c_n = c_{-n}$, we can combine e^{inx} with e^{-inx} into $2\cos nx$. Then (25) is the cosine series for an even function. If every $c_n = -c_{-n}$, we use $e^{inx} - e^{-inx} = 2i\sin nx$. Then (25) is the sine series for an odd function and the c's are pure imaginary.

To find c_k, multiply (25) by e^{-ikx} (not e^{ikx}) **and integrate from $-\pi$ to π:**

$$\int_{-\pi}^{\pi} F(x)e^{-ikx}dx = \int_{-\pi}^{\pi} c_0 e^{-ikx}dx + \int_{-\pi}^{\pi} c_1 e^{ix}e^{-ikx}dx + \cdots + \int_{-\pi}^{\pi} \boldsymbol{c_k e^{ikx} e^{-ikx} dx} + \cdots$$

The complex exponentials are orthogonal. Every integral on the right side is zero, except for the highlighted term (when $n = k$ and $e^{ikx}e^{-ikx} = 1$). The integral of 1 is 2π. That surviving term gives the formula for c_k:

Fourier coefficients $$\int_{-\pi}^{\pi} F(x)e^{-ikx}\,dx = 2\pi c_k \quad \text{for } k = 0, \pm 1, \ldots \quad (26)$$

Notice that $c_0 = a_0$ is still the average of $F(x)$, because $e^0 = 1$. The orthogonality of e^{inx} and e^{ikx} is checked by integrating, as always. But the complex inner product (F, G) takes the *complex conjugate* $\overline{G}$ *of* G. Before integrating, change e^{ikx} to e^{-ikx}:

Complex inner product **Orthogonality of e^{inx} and e^{ikx}**

$$(F,G) = \int_{-\pi}^{\pi} F(x)\overline{G(x)}\,dx \qquad \int_{-\pi}^{\pi} e^{i(n-k)x}\,dx = \left[\frac{e^{i(n-k)x}}{i(n-k)}\right]_{-\pi}^{\pi} = 0\,. \tag{27}$$

Example 5 Add the complex series for $1/(2-e^{ix})$ and $1/(2-e^{-ix})$. These geometric series have exponentially fast decay from $1/2^k$. The functions are analytic.

$$\left(\frac{1}{2} + \frac{e^{ix}}{4} + \frac{e^{2ix}}{8} + \cdots\right) + \left(\frac{1}{2} + \frac{e^{-ix}}{4} + \frac{e^{-2ix}}{8} + \cdots\right) = 1 + \frac{\cos x}{2} + \frac{\cos 2x}{4} + \frac{\cos 3x}{8} + \cdots$$

When we add those functions, we get a real analytic function:

$$\frac{1}{2-e^{ix}} + \frac{1}{2-e^{-ix}} = \frac{(2-e^{-ix}) + (2-e^{ix})}{(2-e^{ix})(2-e^{-ix})} = \frac{4-2\cos x}{5-4\cos x} \tag{28}$$

This ratio is the infinitely smooth function whose cosine coefficients are $1/2^k$.

Example 6 Find c_k for the 2π-periodic shifted pulse $F(x) = \begin{cases} 1 & \text{for } s \le x \le s+h \\ 0 & \text{elsewhere in } [-\pi,\pi] \end{cases}$

Solution The integrals (26) from $-\pi$ to π become integrals from s to $s+h$:

$$c_k = \frac{1}{2\pi}\int_s^{s+h} 1 \cdot e^{-ikx}\,dx = \frac{1}{2\pi}\left[\frac{e^{-ikx}}{-ik}\right]_s^{s+h} = \boldsymbol{e^{-iks}}\left(\frac{1-e^{-ikh}}{2\pi ik}\right). \tag{29}$$

Notice above all the simple effect of the shift by s. It "modulates" each c_k by e^{-iks}. The energy is unchanged, the integral of $|F|^2$ just shifts, and all $|e^{-iks}| = 1$:

$$\textbf{Shift } F(x) \text{ to } F(x-s) \longleftrightarrow \textbf{Multiply } c_k \text{ by } e^{-iks}. \tag{30}$$

Example 7 **Centered pulse** with shift $s = -h/2$. The square pulse becomes centered around $x = 0$. This even function equals 1 on the interval from $-h/2$ to $h/2$:

Centered by $s = -\frac{h}{2}$ $\qquad c_k = e^{ikh/2}\dfrac{1-e^{-ikh}}{2\pi ik} = \dfrac{\mathbf{1}}{\mathbf{2\pi}}\dfrac{\sin(\boldsymbol{kh/2})}{\boldsymbol{k/2}}.$

Divide by h for a tall pulse. The ratio of $\sin(kh/2)$ to $kh/2$ is the **sinc function**:

Tall pulse $\qquad \dfrac{F_{\text{centered}}}{h} = \dfrac{1}{2\pi}\displaystyle\sum_{-\infty}^{\infty} \operatorname{sinc}\left(\frac{kh}{2}\right) e^{ikx} = \begin{cases} 1/h & \text{for } -h/2 \le x \le h/2 \\ 0 & \text{elsewhere in } [-\pi,\pi] \end{cases}$

That division by h produces area $= 1$. **Every coefficient approaches $\frac{1}{2\pi}$ as $h \to 0$.** The Fourier series for the tall thin pulse again approaches the Fourier series for $\delta(x)$.

Hilbert space can contain vectors $c = (c_0, c_1, c_{-1}, c_2, c_{-2}, \cdots)$ instead of functions $F(x)$. The length of c is $2\pi \sum |c_k|^2 = \int |F|^2 dx$. The function space is often denoted by L^2 and the vector space is ℓ^2. The energy identity is trivial (but deep). Integrating the Fourier series for $F(x)$ times $\overline{F(x)}$, orthogonality kills every $c_n\overline{c_k}$ for $n \neq k$. This leaves the $c_k\overline{c_k} = |c_k|^2$:

$$\int_{-\pi}^{\pi} |F(x)|^2 dx = \int_{-\pi}^{\pi} \left(\sum c_n e^{inx}\right)\left(\sum \overline{c_k} e^{-ikx}\right) dx = 2\pi(|c_0|^2 + |c_1|^2 + |c_{-1}|^2 + \cdots). \quad (31)$$

This is Plancherel's identity: The energy in x-space equals the energy in k-space.

Finally I want to emphasize the three big rules for operating on $F(x) = \sum c_k e^{ikx}$:

1. **The derivative** $\dfrac{dF}{dx}$ **has Fourier coefficients** ikc_k (energy moves to high k).

2. **The integral of** $F(x)$ **has Fourier coefficients** $\dfrac{c_k}{ik}$, $k \neq 0$ (faster decay).

3. **The shift to** $F(x-s)$ **has Fourier coefficients** $e^{-iks}c_k$ (no change in energy).

Application: Laplace's Equation in a Circle

Our first application is to Laplace's equation. The idea is to construct $u(x,y)$ as an infinite series, choosing its coefficients to match $u_0(x,y)$ along the boundary. Everything depends on the shape of the boundary, and we take a circle of radius 1.

Begin with the simple solutions 1, $r\cos\theta$, $r\sin\theta$, $r^2\cos 2\theta$, $r^2\sin 2\theta$, ... to Laplace's equation. Combinations of these special solutions give all solutions in the circle:

$$u(r,\theta) = a_0 + a_1 r\cos\theta + b_1 r\sin\theta + a_2 r^2\cos 2\theta + b_2 r^2 \sin 2\theta + \cdots \quad (32)$$

It remains to choose the constants a_k and b_k to make $u = u_0$ on the boundary. For a circle $u_0(\theta)$ is periodic, since θ and $\theta + 2\pi$ give the same point:

$$\text{Set } r = 1 \qquad u_0(\theta) = a_0 + a_1\cos\theta + b_1\sin\theta + a_2\cos 2\theta + b_2\sin 2\theta + \cdots \quad (33)$$

This is exactly the Fourier series for u_0. **The constants a_k and b_k must be the Fourier coefficients of** $u_0(\theta)$. Thus the problem is completely solved, if an infinite series (32) is acceptable as the solution.

Example 8 **Point source** $u_0 = \delta(\theta)$ at $\theta = 0$ The whole boundary is held at $u_0 = 0$, except for the source at $x = 1$, $y = 0$. Find the temperature $u(r,\theta)$ inside.

$$\textbf{Fourier series for } \delta \qquad u_0(\theta) = \frac{1}{2\pi} + \frac{1}{\pi}(\cos\theta + \cos 2\theta + \cos 3\theta + \cdots) = \frac{1}{2\pi}\sum_{-\infty}^{\infty} e^{in\theta}$$

Inside the circle, each $\cos n\theta$ is multiplied by r^n:

Infinite series for u $$u(r,\theta) = \frac{1}{2\pi} + \frac{1}{\pi}(r\cos\theta + r^2\cos 2\theta + r^3\cos 3\theta + \cdots) \quad (34)$$

Poisson managed to sum this infinite series! It involves a series of powers of $re^{i\theta}$. So we know the response at every (r,θ) to the point source at $r = 1$, $\theta = 0$:

Temperature inside circle $$u(r,\theta) = \frac{1}{2\pi}\frac{1-r^2}{1+r^2-2r\cos\theta} \quad (35)$$

At the center $r = 0$, this produces the average of $u_0 = \delta(\theta)$ which is $a_0 = 1/2\pi$. On the boundary $r = 1$, this produces $u = 0$ except at the point source where $\cos 0 = 1$:

On the ray $\theta = 0$ $$u(r,\theta) = \frac{1}{2\pi}\frac{1-r^2}{1+r^2-2r} = \frac{1}{2\pi}\frac{1+r}{1-r}. \quad (36)$$

As r approaches 1, the solution becomes infinite as the point source requires.

Example 9 Solve for any boundary values $u_0(\theta)$ by integrating over point sources.

When the point source swings around to angle φ, the solution (35) changes from θ to $\theta - \varphi$. Integrate this "Green's function" to solve in the circle:

Poisson's formula $$u(r,\theta) = \frac{1}{2\pi}\int_{-\pi}^{\pi} u_0(\varphi)\,\frac{1-r^2}{1+r^2-2r\cos(\theta-\varphi)}\,d\varphi \quad (37)$$

Ar $r = 0$ the fraction disappears and u is the average $\int u_0(\varphi)d\varphi/2\pi$. The steady state temperature at the center is the average temperature around the circle.

Poisson's formula illustrates a key idea. Think of any $u_0(\theta)$ as a circle of point sources. The source at angle $\varphi = \theta$ produces the solution inside the integral (37). Integrating around the circle adds up the responses to all sources and gives the response to $u_0(\theta)$.

Example 10 $u_0(\theta) = 1$ on the top half of the circle and $u_0 = -1$ on the bottom half.

Solution The boundary values are the square wave $SW(\theta)$. Its sine series is in (8):

Square wave for $u_0(\theta)$ $$SW(\theta) = \frac{4}{\pi}\left[\frac{\sin\theta}{1} + \frac{\sin 3\theta}{3} + \frac{\sin 5\theta}{5} + \cdots\right] \quad (38)$$

Inside the circle, multiplying by r, r^2, r^3,... gives fast decay of high frequencies:

Rapid decay inside $$u(r,\theta) = \frac{4}{\pi}\left[\frac{r\sin\theta}{1} + \frac{r^3\sin 3\theta}{3} + \frac{r^5\sin 5\theta}{5} + \cdots\right] \quad (39)$$

Laplace's equation has smooth solutions, even when $u_0(\theta)$ is not smooth.

■ WORKED EXAMPLE ■

A hot metal bar is moved into a freezer (zero temperature). The sides of the bar are coated so that heat only escapes at the ends. *What is the temperature $u(x,t)$ along the bar at time t?* It will approach $u=0$ as all the heat leaves the bar.

Solution The heat equation is $u_t = u_{xx}$. At $t=0$ the whole bar is at a constant temperature, say $u=1$. The ends of the bar are at zero temperature for all time $t>0$. This is an **initial-boundary value problem**:

Heat equation $\quad u_t = u_{xx}$ with $u(x,0)=1$ and $u(0,t)=u(\pi,t)=0.$ (40)

Those zero boundary conditions suggest a sine series. Its coefficients depend on t:

Series solution of the heat equation $$u(x,t) = \sum_{1}^{\infty} b_n(t) \sin nx. \qquad (41)$$

The form of the solution shows **separation of variables**. In a comment below, we look for products $A(x)\,B(t)$ that solve the heat equation and the boundary conditions. What we reach is exactly $A(x) = \sin nx$ and the series solution (41).

Two steps remain. First, choose each $b_n(t) \sin nx$ to satisfy the heat equation:

Substitute into $u_t = u_{xx}$ $\quad b_n'(t) \sin nx = -n^2 b_n(t) \sin nx \quad b_n(t) = e^{-n^2 t} b_n(0).$

Notice $b_n' = -n^2 b_n$. Now determine each $b_n(0)$ from the initial condition $u(x,0)=1$ on $(0,\pi)$. Those numbers are the Fourier sine coefficients of $SW(x)$ in equation (38):

Box function/square wave $\quad \sum_{1}^{\infty} b_n(0) \sin nx = 1 \quad b_n(0) = \dfrac{4}{\pi n}$ for odd n

This completes the series solution of the initial-boundary value problem:

Bar temperature $$u(x,t) = \sum_{\text{odd } n} \frac{4}{\pi n} e^{-n^2 t} \sin nx. \qquad (42)$$

For large n (high frequencies) the decay of $e^{-n^2 t}$ is very fast. The dominant term $(4/\pi)e^{-t} \sin x$ for large times will come from $n=1$. This is typical of the heat equation and all diffusion, that the solution (the temperature profile) becomes very smooth as t increases.

Numerical difficulty I regret any bad news in such a beautiful solution. To compute $u(x,t)$, we would probably truncate the series in (42) to N terms. When that finite series is graphed on the website, serious bumps appear in $u_N(x,t)$. You ask if there is a physical reason but there isn't. The solution should have maximum temperature at the midpoint $x=\pi/2$, and decay smoothly to zero at the ends of the bar.

Those unphysical bumps are precisely the **Gibbs phenomenon**. The initial $u(x,0)$ is 1 on $(0,\pi)$ but its odd reflection is -1 on $(-\pi,0)$. That jump has produced the slow $4/\pi n$ decay of the coefficients, with Gibbs oscillations near $x=0$ and $x=\pi$. The sine series for $u(x,t)$ is not a success numerically. Would finite differences help?

Separation of variables We found $b_n(t)$ as the coefficient of an eigenfunction $\sin nx$. Another good approach is to put $u = A(x)\,B(t)$ directly into $u_t = u_{xx}$:

$$\textbf{Separation} \quad A(x)\,B'(t) = A''(x)\,B(t) \text{ requires } \frac{A''(x)}{A(x)} = \frac{B'(t)}{B(t)} = \textbf{constant}. \quad (43)$$

A''/A is constant in space, B'/B is constant in time, and they are equal:

$$\frac{A''}{A} = -\lambda \text{ gives } A = \sin\sqrt{\lambda}\,x \text{ and } \cos\sqrt{\lambda}\,x \qquad \frac{B'}{B} = -\lambda \text{ gives } B = e^{-\lambda t}$$

The products $AB = e^{-\lambda t}\sin\sqrt{\lambda}\,x$ and $e^{-\lambda t}\cos\sqrt{\lambda}\,x$ solve the heat equation for any number λ. But the boundary condition $u(0,t)=0$ eliminates the cosines. Then $u(\pi,t)=0$ requires $\lambda = n^2 = 1,4,9,\ldots$ to have $\sin\sqrt{\lambda}\,\pi = 0$. Separation of variables has recovered the functions in the series solution (42).

Finally $u(x,0)=1$ determines the numbers $4/\pi n$ for odd n. We find zero for even n because $\sin nx$ has $n/2$ positive loops and $n/2$ negative loops. For odd n, the extra positive loop is a fraction $1/n$ of all loops, giving slow decay of the coefficients.

Heat bath (the opposite problem) The solution on the website is $1-u(x,t)$, because it solves a different problem. **The bar is initially frozen at** $U(x,0)=0$. It is placed into a heat bath at the fixed temperature $U=1$ (or $U=T_0$). The new unknown is U and its boundary conditions are no longer zero.

The heat equation and its boundary conditions are solved first by $U_B(x,t)$. In this example $U_B \equiv 1$ is constant. Then the difference $V = U - U_B$ has zero boundary values, and its initial values are $V=-1$. Now the eigenfunction method (or separation of variables) solves for V. (The series in (42) is multiplied by -1 to account for $V(x,0)=-1$.) Adding back U_B solves the heat bath problem: $U = U_B + V = 1 - u(x,t)$.

Here $U_B \equiv 1$ is the *steady state* solution at $t=\infty$, and V is the *transient* solution. The transient starts at $V=-1$ and decays quickly to $V=0$.

Heat bath at one end The website problem is different in another way too. The Dirichlet condition $u(\pi,t)=1$ is replaced by the Neumann condition $u'(1,t)=0$. Only the left end is in the heat bath. Heat flows down the metal bar and out at the far end, now located at $x=1$. How does the solution change for fixed-free?

Again $U_B = 1$ is a steady state. The boundary conditions apply to $V = 1 - U_B$:

$$\textbf{Fixed-free eigenfunctions} \quad \boxed{V(0)=0 \text{ and } V'(1)=0} \text{ lead to } \boxed{A(x) = \sin\left(n+\frac{1}{2}\right)\pi x.} \quad (44)$$

Those eigenfunctions give a new form for the sum of $B_n(t)\,A_n(x)$:

Fixed-free solution $$V(x,t) = \sum_{\text{odd } n} B_n(0)\, e^{-(n+\frac{1}{2})^2\pi^2 t} \sin\left(n + \frac{1}{2}\right)\pi x. \qquad (45)$$

All frequencies shift by $\frac{1}{2}$ and multiply by π, because $A'' = -\lambda A$ has a free end at $x = 1$. The crucial question is: **Does orthogonality still hold for** these new eigenfunctions $\sin\left(n+\frac{1}{2}\right)\pi x$ **on** $[0,1]$? The answer is *yes* because this fixed-free "Sturm–Liouville problem" $A'' = -\lambda A$ is still symmetric.

Summary The series solutions all succeed but the truncated series all fail. We can see the overall behavior of $u(x,t)$ and $V(x,t)$. But their exact values close to the jumps are not computed well until we improve on Gibbs.

We could have solved the fixed-free problem on $[0,1]$ with the fixed-fixed solution on $[0,2]$. That solution will be symmetric around $x = 1$ so its slope there is zero. Then rescaling x by 2π changes $\sin(n+\frac{1}{2})\pi x$ into $\sin(2n+1)x$. I hope you like the graphics created by Aslan Kasimov on the cse website.

Problem Set 4.1

1 Find the Fourier series on $-\pi \le x \le \pi$ for

(a) $f(x) = \sin^3 x$, an odd function

(b) $f(x) = |\sin x|$, an even function

(c) $f(x) = x$

(d) $f(x) = e^x$, using the complex form of the series.

What are the even and odd parts of $f(x) = e^x$ and $f(x) = e^{ix}$?

2 From Parseval's formula the square wave sine coefficients satisfy

$$\pi(b_1^2 + b_2^2 + \cdots) = \int_{-\pi}^{\pi} |f(x)|^2\, dx = \int_{-\pi}^{\pi} 1\, dx = 2\pi.$$

Dirive the remarkable sum $\pi^2 = 8(1 + \frac{1}{9} + \frac{1}{25} + \cdots)$.

3 If a square pulse is centered at $x = 0$ to give

$$f(x) = 1 \quad \text{for} \quad |x| < \frac{\pi}{2},\ f(x) = 0 \quad \text{for} \quad \frac{\pi}{2} < |x| < \pi,$$

draw its graph and find its Fourier coefficients a_k and b_k.

4 Suppose f has period T instead of $2x$, so that $f(x) = f(x+T)$. Its graph from $-T/2$ to $T/2$ is repeated on each successive interval and its real and complex Fourier series are

$$f(x) = a_0 + a_1 \cos\frac{2\pi x}{T} + b_1 \sin\frac{2\pi x}{T} + \cdots = \sum_{-\infty}^{\infty} c_k\, e^{ik2\pi x/T}$$

Multiplying by the right functions and integrating from $-T/2$ to $T/2$, find a_k, b_k, and c_k.

5 Plot the first three partial sums and the function itself:

$$x(\pi - x) = \frac{8}{\pi}\left(\frac{\sin x}{1} + \frac{\sin 3x}{27} + \frac{\sin 5x}{125} + \cdots\right), 0 < x < \pi.$$

Why is $1/k^3$ the decay rate for this function? What is the second derivative?

6 What constant function is closest in the least square sense to $f = \cos^2 x$? What multiple of $\cos x$ is closest to $f = \cos^3 x$?

7 Sketch the 2π-periodic half wave with $f(x) = \sin x$ for $0 < x < \pi$ and $f(x) = 0$ for $-\pi < x < 0$. Find its Fourier series.

8 (a) Find the lengths of the vectors $u = (1, \frac{1}{2}, \frac{1}{4}, \frac{1}{8}, \ldots)$ and $v = (1, \frac{1}{3}, \frac{1}{9}, \ldots)$ in Hilbert space and test the Schwarz inequality $|u^{\mathrm{T}}v|^2 \leq (u^{\mathrm{T}}u)(v^{\mathrm{T}}v)$.

(b) For the functions $f = 1 + \frac{1}{2}e^{ix} + \frac{1}{4}e^{2ix} + \cdots$ and $g = 1 + \frac{1}{3}e^{ix} + \frac{1}{9}e^{2ix} + \cdots$ use part (a) to find the numerical value of each term in

$$\left|\int_{-\pi}^{\pi} \overline{f}(x)\, g(x)\, dx\right|^2 \leq \int_{-\pi}^{\pi} |f(x)|^2\, dx \int_{-\pi}^{\pi} |g(x)|^2\, dx.$$

Substitute for f and g and use orthogonality (or Parseval).

9 Find the solution to Laplace's equation with $u_0 = \theta$ on the boundary. Why is this the imaginary part of $2(z - z^2/2 + z^3/3 \cdots) = 2\log(1+z)$? Confirm that on the unit circle $z = e^{i\theta}$, the imaginary part of $2\log(1+z)$ agrees with θ.

10 If the boundary condition for Laplace's equation is $u_0 = 1$ for $0 < \theta < \pi$ and $u_0 = 0$ for $-\pi < \theta < 0$, find the Fourier series solution $u(r, \theta)$ inside the unit circle. What is u at the origin?

11 With boundary values $u_0(\theta) = 1 + \frac{1}{2}e^{i\theta} + \frac{1}{4}e^{2i\theta} + \cdots$, what is the Fourier series solution to Laplace's equation in the circle? Sum the series.

12 (a) Verify that the fraction in Poisson's formula satisfies Laplace's equation.

(b) What is the response $u(r, \theta)$ to an impulse at the point $(0, 1)$, at the angle $\varphi = \pi/2$?

(c) If $u_0(\varphi) = 1$ in the quarter-circle $0 < \varphi < \pi/2$ and $u_0 = 0$ elsewhere, show that at points on the horizontal axis (and especially at the origin)

$$u(r, 0) = \frac{1}{2} + \frac{1}{2\pi}\tan^{-1}\left(\frac{1 - r^2}{-2r}\right) \quad \text{by using}$$

$$\int \frac{d\varphi}{b + c\cos\varphi} = \frac{1}{\sqrt{b^2 - c^2}}\tan^{-1}\left(\frac{\sqrt{b^2 - c^2}\,\sin\varphi}{c + b\cos\varphi}\right).$$

13 When the centered square pulse in Example 7 has width $h = \pi$, find

(a) its energy $\int |F(x)|^2\, dx$ by direct integration

(b) its Fourier coefficients c_k as specific numbers

(c) the sum in the energy identity (31) or (24)

If $h = 2\pi$, why is $c_0 = 1$ the only nonzero coefficient? What is $F(x)$?

14 In Example 5, $F(x) = 1 + (\cos x)/2 + \cdots + (\cos nx)/2^n + \cdots$ is infinitely smooth:

(a) If you take 10 derivatives, what is the Fourier series of $d^{10}F/dx^{10}$?

(b) Does that series still converge quickly? Compare n^{10} with 2^n for n^{1024}.

15 (*A touch of complex analysis*) The analytic function in Example 5 blows up when $4\cos x = 5$. This cannot happen for real x, but equation (28) shows blowup if $e^{ix} = 2$ or $\frac{1}{2}$. In that case we have *poles at* $x = \pm i \log 2$. Why are there also poles at all the complex numbers $x = \pm i \log 2 + 2\pi n$?

16 (*A second touch*) Change 2's to 3's so that equation (28) has $1/(3 - e^{ix}) + 1/(3 - e^{-ix})$. Complete that equation to find the function that gives fast decay at the rate $1/3^k$.

17 (*For complex professors only*) Change those 2's and 3's to 1's:

$$\frac{1}{1-e^{ix}} + \frac{1}{1-e^{-ix}} = \frac{(1-e^{-ix}) + (1-e^{ix})}{(1-e^{ix})(1-e^{-ix})} = \frac{2 - e^{ix} - e^{-ix}}{2 - e^{ix} - e^{-ix}} = 1\,.$$

A constant! What happened to the pole at $e^{ix} = 1$? Where is the dangerous series $(1 + e^{ix} + \cdots) + (1 + e^{-ix} + \cdots) = 2 + 2\cos x + \cdots$ involving $\delta(x)$?

18 Following the Worked Example, solve the heat equation $u_t = u_{xx}$ from a point source $u(x, 0) = \delta(x)$ with free boundary conditions $u'(\pi, t) = u'(-\pi, t) = 0$. Use the infinite cosine series for $\delta(x)$ with time decay factors $b_n(t)$.

4.2 CHEBYSHEV, LEGENDRE, AND BESSEL

The sines and cosines are orthogonal on $[-\pi, \pi]$, but not by accident. Those zeros in a table of definite integrals are not lucky chances. The real reason for this orthogonality is that $\sin kx$ and $\cos kx$ are the *eigenfunctions of a symmetric operator.* So are the exponentials e^{ikx}, when d^2/dx^2 has periodic boundary conditions.

Symmetric operators have orthogonal eigenfunctions. This section looks at the eigenfunctions of other symmetric operators. They give new and important families of orthogonal functions, named after their discoverers.

Two-dimensional Fourier Series

In 2D, the Laplacian is $L = \partial^2/\partial x^2 + \partial^2/\partial y^2$. The orthogonal functions are $e^{inx}e^{imy}$ (every e^{inx} times every e^{imy}). Those are eigenfunctions of L since $Le^{inx}e^{imy}$ produces $(-n^2 - m^2)e^{inx}e^{imy}$. We have **separation of variables** (x is separated from y):

Double Fourier series $$F(x,y) = \sum_{n=-\infty}^{\infty} \sum_{m=-\infty}^{\infty} c_{nm}\, e^{inx} e^{imy}\,. \qquad (1)$$

These functions are periodic in x and also in y: $F(x+2\pi, y) = F(x, y+2\pi) = F(x,y)$. We check that $e^{inx}e^{imy}$ is orthogonal to $e^{ikx}e^{i\ell y}$ on a square $-\pi \le x \le \pi, -\pi \le y \le \pi$. The double integral separates into x and y integrals that we know are zero:

Orthogonality $$\int_{-\pi}^{\pi}\int_{-\pi}^{\pi} \left(e^{inx}e^{imy}\right)\left(e^{-ikx}e^{-i\ell y}\right) dx\, dy = 0 \quad \text{unless} \quad \begin{matrix} n = k \\ m = \ell \end{matrix} \qquad (2)$$

The Fourier coefficient $c_{k\ell}$ comes from multiplying the series (1) by $e^{-ikx}e^{-i\ell y}$ and integrating over the square. One term survives and the formula looks familiar:

Double Fourier coefficients $$c_{k\ell} = \left(\frac{1}{2\pi}\right)^2 \int_{-\pi}^{\pi}\int_{-\pi}^{\pi} F(x,y)\, e^{-ikx}e^{-i\ell y}\, dx\, dy\,. \qquad (3)$$

The two-dimensional delta function $\delta(x)\delta(y)$ (made periodic) has all $c_{k\ell} = (1/2\pi)^2$.

Separating x from y simplifies the calculation of $c_{k\ell}$. The integral of $F(x,y)e^{-ikx}dx$ is a one-dimensional transform for each y. The result depends on y and k. Then multiply by $e^{-i\ell y}$ and integrate between $y = -\pi$ and $y = \pi$, to find $c_{k\ell}$.

I see this separation of variables in processing a square image. The x-transform goes along each row of pixels. Then the output is ordered by columns, and the y-transform goes down each column. *The two-dimensional transform is computed by one-dimensional software.* In practice the pixels are equally spaced and the computer is adding instead of integrating—the Discrete Fourier Transform in the next section is a sum at N equally spaced points. The DFT in 2D has N^2 points.

A Delta Puzzle

The two-dimensional $\delta(x)\delta(y)$ is concentrated at $(0,0)$. It is defined by integration:

Delta in 2D $$\int_{-\pi}^{\pi}\int_{-\pi}^{\pi} \delta(x)\delta(y)\, G(x,y)\, dx\, dy = G(0,0) \quad \text{for any smooth } G(x,y)\,. \tag{4}$$

Choosing $G \equiv 1$ confirms "area $= 1$" under the spike. Choosing $G = e^{-ikx}e^{-i\ell y}$ confirms that all Fourier coefficients $c_{k\ell}$ are $1/4\pi^2$ for $\delta(x)\delta(y)$, since $G(0,0)=1$:

Delta function $$\delta(x)\delta(y) = \left(\sum \frac{e^{ikx}}{2\pi}\right)\left(\sum \frac{e^{i\ell y}}{2\pi}\right) = \frac{1}{4\pi^2}\sum\sum e^{ikx}e^{i\ell y}\,. \tag{5}$$

Now try a *vertical line of spikes* $F(x,y) = \delta(x)$. They go up the y-axis, where $x = 0$. Every horizontal x-integral crosses that line at $x = 0$, and picks out $G(0,y)$:

Line of spikes $\delta(x)$ $$\int_{-\pi}^{\pi}\int_{-\pi}^{\pi} \delta(x)\, G(x,y)\, dx\, dy = \int_{-\pi}^{\pi} G(0,y)\, dy\,. \tag{6}$$

Choosing $G \equiv 1$ gives "area $= 2\pi$" under this line of spikes. The line has length 2π. Integrating $\delta(x)\, e^{-ikx}e^{-i\ell y}$ gives $c_{k\ell} = 0$ when $\ell \neq 0$, since $\int_{-\pi}^{\pi} e^{-i\ell y}\, dy = 0$. So the two-dimensional series for $F(x,y) = \delta(x)$ is really one-dimensional. So far no puzzle:

Spikes along $x = 0$ $$\delta(x) = \sum_{\ell}\sum_{k} c_{k\ell}e^{-ikx}e^{-i\ell y} = \sum_{k}\left(\frac{1}{2\pi}\right)e^{-ikx}\,. \tag{7}$$

The puzzle comes for a diagonal line of spikes $\boldsymbol{\delta(x+y)}$. Let me ask, what is the area under the spikes along the line $x + y = 0$? This line runs from $x = -\pi, y = \pi$ diagonally down to the opposite corner $x = \pi, y = -\pi$. Its length is 2π times $\sqrt{2}$. For a "unit delta" I am now expecting area $= 2\pi\sqrt{2}$. But I don't see that $\sqrt{2}$ in the double integral. Each x-integral just meets a spike at $x = -y$:

$\sqrt{2}$ disappears $$\textbf{Area} = \int_{-\pi}^{\pi}\left[\int_{-\pi}^{\pi} \delta(x+y)\, dx\right] dy = \int_{-\pi}^{\pi} 1\, dy = 2\pi\,. \tag{8}$$

But the area under a finite diagonal pulse (width h and height $1/h$) does include the $\sqrt{2}$ factor. It stays there as $h \to 0$. Diagonal lines must be thicker than I thought!

Maybe I should change variables in (8) to $X = x + y$. After many suggestions from students and faculty, this is what I believe (for now):

> *Everybody is right.* The function $\delta(x+y)$ has area 2π. Its Fourier series, including the parallel spikes $\delta(x + y - 2\pi n)$ to be periodic, is $\frac{1}{2\pi}\sum e^{ik(x+y)}$. But this is not the unit spike I thought it was. The unit spike along the diagonal is a different function $\delta((x+y)/\sqrt{2})$. That one has area $2\pi\sqrt{2}$.

Dividing $x + y$ by $\sqrt{2}$ leads me to think about $\delta(2x)$. Its values are "zero or infinity" but actually **$\boldsymbol{\delta(2x)}$ is half of $\boldsymbol{\delta(x)}$**! For delta functions, the right way to understand $\delta(2x)$ is by integration with a smooth function G. Set $2x = t$:

$$\boldsymbol{\delta(2x) = \tfrac{1}{2}\delta(x)} \qquad \int_{-\infty}^{\infty} \delta(2x)G(x)\,dx = \int_{-\infty}^{\infty} \delta(t)G(t/2)\,dt/2 = \frac{1}{2}\,G(0)\,. \qquad (9)$$

The area under $\delta(2x)$ is $\frac{1}{2}$. Multiplied by any $G(x)$, this half-width spike produces $\frac{1}{2}G(0)$ in integration. Similarly $\delta((x+y)/\sqrt{2}) = \sqrt{2}\,\delta(x+y)$.

In three dimensions we could have a point spike $\delta(x)\delta(y)\delta(z)$, or a line of spikes $\delta(x)\delta(y)$ along the z-axis, or a horizontal plane $x = y = 0$ of one-dimensional spikes $\delta(z)$. Physically, those represent a point source f or a line source or a plane source. They can all appear in Poisson's equation $u_{xx} + u_{yy} + u_{zz} = f(x, y, z)$.

Chebyshev Polynomials

Start with the cosines 1, $\cos\theta$, $\cos 2\theta$, $\cos 3\theta, \ldots$ and ***change from*** $\boldsymbol{\cos\theta}$ ***to*** $\boldsymbol{x}$. The first Chebyshev polynomials are $T_0 = 1$ and $T_1 = x$. The next polynomials T_2 and T_3 come from identities for $\cos 2\theta$ and $\cos 3\theta$:

$$\boldsymbol{x = \cos\theta} \qquad \begin{aligned} \cos 2\theta &= 2\cos^2\theta - 1 \\ \cos 3\theta &= 4\cos^3\theta - 3\cos\theta \end{aligned} \qquad \begin{aligned} T_2(x) &= \boldsymbol{2x^2 - 1} \\ T_3(x) &= \boldsymbol{4x^3 - 3x} \end{aligned}$$

These $T_k(x)$ are certain to be important, because the cosines are so important. There is a neat way to find T_{k+1} from the previous T_k and T_{k-1}, by using cosines:

Cosine identity	$\cos(k{+}1)\theta + \cos(k{-}1)\theta = 2\cos\theta\cos k\theta$	(10)
Chebyshev recursion	$\boldsymbol{T_{k+1}(x) + T_{k-1}(x) = 2\,x\,T_k(x)}$	(11)

Figure 4.6 shows the even polynomials $T_2(x)$ and $T_4(x) = 2xT_3(x) - T_2(x) = \cos 4\theta$ (four zeros).

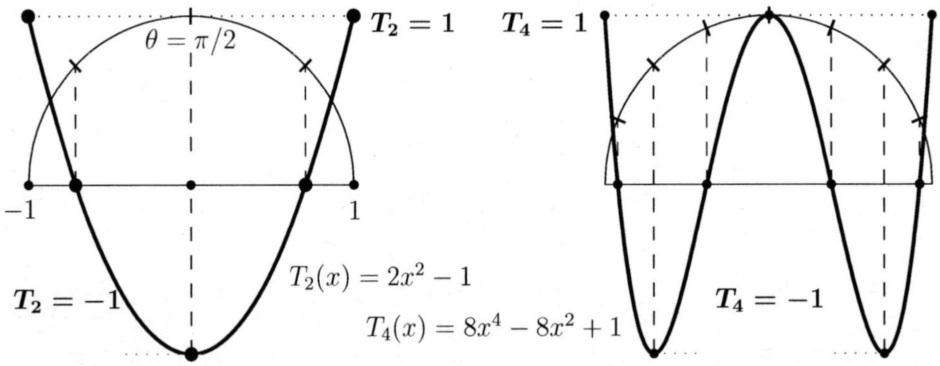

Figure 4.6: Chebyshev polynomials oscillate between 1 and -1 (because cosines do).

The quick formula $T_k(x) = \cos k\theta = \cos(k \cos^{-1} x)$ looks a little awkward because it involves the *arc cosine* (inverse to the cosine function):

Chebyshev polynomials $\quad x = \cos\theta \text{ and } \theta = \cos^{-1} x \qquad T_k(x) = \cos k\theta = \cos(k\cos^{-1} x)\,. \quad (12)$

The cosine of $k\theta$ reaches top and bottom at the $k+1$ angles $\theta = 2\pi j/k$. Those angles give $\cos k\theta = \cos 2\pi j = \pm 1$. On the x-axis, those are the ***Chebyshev points*** where $T_k(x)$ has its maximum $+1$ or its minimum -1:

Chebyshev points $\quad x_j = \cos\dfrac{2\pi j}{k} \quad \text{for} \quad j = 0, 1, \ldots, k \quad (13)$

These points will play a central role in Section 5.4 on computational complex analysis. Evaluating a function $f(x)$ at the Chebyshev points is the same as evaluating $f(\cos\theta)$ at the equally spaced angles $\theta = 2\pi j/k$. These calculations use the Fast Fourier Transform to give an exponential convergence rate at top numerical speed.

The **zeros of the Chebyshev polynomials** lie between the Chebyshev points. We know that $\cos k\theta = 0$ when $k\theta$ is an odd multiple of $\pi/2$. Figure 4.7 shows those angles $\theta_1, \ldots, \theta_k$ equally spaced around a unit semicircle. To keep the correspondence $x = \cos\theta$, we just take the x-coordinates by dropping perpendicular lines. Those lines meet the x-axis at the zeros $x_1, \ldots, x_k$ of the Chebyshev polynomials:

Zeros of $T_k(x)$

$$\cos k\theta = 0 \quad \text{if} \quad k\theta = (2j-1)\frac{\pi}{2}$$

$$T_k(x_j) = 0 \quad \text{if} \quad x_j = \cos\theta_j = \cos\left[\frac{2j-1}{2}\,\frac{\pi}{k}\right]. \qquad (14)$$

Notice the spacing of Chebyshev points and zeros along the interval $-1 \le x \le 1$. More space at the center, more densely packed near the ends. This irregular spacing is infinitely better than equal spacing, if we want to fit a polynomial through the points.

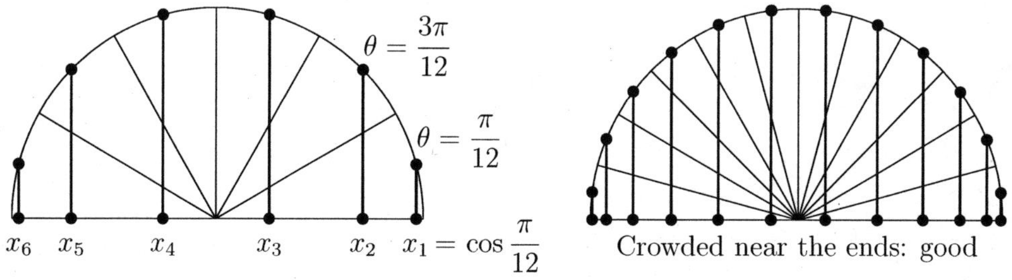

Figure 4.7: The six solutions $x = \cos\theta$ of $T_6(x) = \cos 6\theta = 0$. Twelve for $T_{12}(x)$.

Are the Chebyshev polynomials orthogonal over $-1 \le x \le 1$? The answer is "yes" but only if you include their **weight function** $1/\sqrt{1-x^2}$ in the integral.

Weighted Orthogonality

The Chebyshev weight $w(x) = 1/\sqrt{1-x^2}$ comes from $dx = -\sin\theta\, d\theta = -\sqrt{1-x^2}\, d\theta$:

Weighted orthogonality $$\int_{-1}^{1} T_n(x)T_k(x)\frac{dx}{\sqrt{1-x^2}} = \int_0^{\pi} \cos n\theta \cos k\theta\, d\theta = 0\,. \tag{15}$$

The sines and cosines had weight function $w(x) = 1$. The Chebyshev polynomials have $w(x) = 1/\sqrt{1-x^2}$. There are Bessel functions on $[0,1]$ with $w(x) = x$ and Laguerre polynomials on $[0,\infty)$ with $w(x) = e^{-x}$ and Hermite polynomials on $(-\infty,\infty)$ with $w(x) = e^{-x^2/2}$. These weights are *never negative.* For all of those orthogonal functions, the coefficients in $F(x) = \sum c_k T_k(x)$ are found the same way:

Multiply $F(x) = c_0T_0(x) + c_1T_1(x) + \cdots$ *by* $T_k(x)$ *and also* $w(x)$*. Then integrate:*

$$\int F(x)T_k(x)w(x)\,dx = \int c_0T_0(x)T_k(x)w(x)\,dx + \cdots + \int \boldsymbol{c_k(T_k(x))^2 w(x)\,dx} + \cdots$$

On the right side only the boldface term survives, as in Fourier series. There T_k was $\cos kx$, the weight was $w(x) = 1$, and the integral from $-\pi$ to π was π times c_k. For any orthogonal functions, division leaves the formula for c_k:

Orthogonal $T_k(x)$ Weight $w(x)$ **Coefficients** $$c_k = \frac{\int F(x)T_k(x)w(x)\,dx}{\int (T_k(x))^2 w(x)\,dx}$$

The positive weight $w(x)$ is like the positive definite mass matrix in $Ku = \lambda Mu$. The eigenvectors u_k are orthogonal when weighted by M: for example $u_1^{\mathrm{T}}Mu_2 = 0$. In the continuous case, the $T_k(x)$ are **eigenfunctions** and $\int T_k(x)T_n(x)w(x)\,dx = 0$.

The eigenvalue problem could be Chebyshev's or Legendre's or Bessel's equation, with weight $w = 1/\sqrt{1-x^2}$ or $w = 1$ or $w = x$. The Chebyshev polynomials are seen as eigenfunctions, by changing from the cosines in $-d^2u/d\theta^2 = \lambda u$:

Chebyshev equation $$-\frac{d}{dx}\left(\frac{1}{w}\frac{dT}{dx}\right) = \lambda\, w(x)T(x)\,. \tag{16}$$

That operator on the left looks to me like $A^{\mathrm{T}}CA$. This is a continuous $KT = \lambda MT$.

Legendre Polynomials

The direct way to the Legendre polynomials $P_n(x)$ is to start with $1, x, x^2, \ldots$ on the interval $[-1,1]$ with weight $w(x) = 1$. Those functions are *not orthogonal.* The integral of 1 times x is $\int_{-1}^{1} x\,dx = 0$, but the integral of 1 times x^2 is $\int_{-1}^{1} x^2\,dx = \frac{2}{3}$. The **Gram-Schmidt idea** will produce orthogonal functions out of $1, x$, and x^2:

Subtract from x^2 *its component* $\frac{1}{3}$ *in the direction of* 1. *Then* $\int_{-1}^{1}(x^2 - \frac{1}{3})\,1\,dx = 0$.

This Legendre polynomial $P_2(x) = x^2 - \frac{1}{3}$ is also orthogonal to the odd $P_1(x) = x$.

For $P_3(x)$, subtract from x^3 its component $\frac{3}{5}x$ in the direction of $P_1(x) = x$. Then $\int (x^3 - \frac{3}{5}x)\, x\, dx = 0$. Gram-Schmidt subtracts from each new x^n the right multiples of $P_0(x), \ldots, P_{n-1}(x)$. The convention is that every $P_n(x)$ equals 1 at $x = 1$, so we rescale P_2 and P_3 to their final form $\frac{1}{2}(3x^2 - 1)$ and $\frac{1}{2}(5x^3 - 3x)$.

I cannot miss telling you the beautiful formula and *three-term recurrence* for $P_n(x)$:

Rodrigues formula $$P_n(x) = \frac{1}{2^n n!} \frac{d^n}{dx^n} (x^2 - 1)^n \qquad (17)$$

Three-term recurrence $$P_n(x) = \frac{2n-1}{n}\, x\, P_{n-1}(x) - \frac{n-1}{n} P_{n-2}(x) \qquad (18)$$

The key point about (18) is *automatic orthogonality* to all lower-degree polynomials. Gram-Schmidt stops early, which makes the calculations very efficient. The right side has $\int x\, P_{n-1} P_{n-3}\, dx = 0$, because x times P_{n-3} only has degree $n-2$. Therefore $x P_{n-3}$ is orthogonal to P_{n-1}, and so is P_{n-2}. Then P_n from (18) is orthogonal to P_{n-3}.

The same three term recurrence appears in the discrete case, when Arnoldi orthogonalizes $b, Ab, \ldots, A^{n-1}b$ in Section 7.4. The orthogonal vectors lead to the "conjugate gradient method." For Legendre, $b \equiv 1$ and A is multiplication by x.

Bessel Functions

For a square, the right coordinate system is x, y. A double Fourier series with $e^{inx}e^{imy}$ is perfect. On a circle, polar coordinates r, θ are much better. If $u(r, \theta)$ depends only on the angle θ, sines and cosines are good. But if u depends on r *only* (the quite common case of radial symmetry) then new functions are needed.

The best example is a circular drum. If you strike it, it oscillates. Its motion contains a mixture of "pure" oscillations at single frequencies. The goal is to discover those natural frequencies (eigenvalues) of the drum and the shapes (eigenfunctions) of the drumhead. The problem is governed by Laplace's equation in polar coordinates:

Laplace equation in r, θ $$\frac{\partial^2 u}{\partial r^2} + \frac{1}{r}\frac{\partial u}{\partial r} + \frac{1}{r^2}\frac{\partial^2 u}{\partial \theta^2} = -\lambda u\,. \qquad (19)$$

The boundary condition is $u = 0$ at $r = 1$; the outside of the drum is fastened. The natural idea is to separate r from θ, and to look for eigenfunctions of the special form $u = A(\theta)B(r)$. This is **separation of variables**. It needs an exceptional geometry, and the circle is exceptional. Separation of variables will reach an ordinary differential equation for $A(\theta)$ and another one for $B(r)$.

Substitute $u = A(\theta)B(r)$ $$AB'' + \frac{1}{r}AB' + \frac{1}{r^2}A''B = -\lambda AB\,. \qquad (20)$$

Now multiply by r^2 and divide by AB. *The key point is to separate r from θ:*

Separated variables $$\frac{r^2B'' + rB' + \lambda r^2 B}{B} = -\frac{A''(\theta)}{A(\theta)} = \textit{constant}\,. \qquad (21)$$

The left side depends only on r. But $A''(\theta)/A(\theta)$ is independent of r. *Both sides must be constant.* If the constant is n^2, then on the right $A'' = -n^2 A$. This gives $A(\theta)$ as $\sin n\theta$ and $\cos n\theta$. Especially it requires n to be an integer. The solution must have the same value at $\theta = 0$ and $\theta = 2\pi$, since those are the same points on the circle.

The left side of (21) now gives an ordinary differential equation for $B = B_n(r)$:

Bessel's equation $$r^2 B'' + rB' + \lambda r^2 B = n^2 B, \quad \text{with } B(1) = 0\,. \tag{22}$$

The eigenfunctions $u = A(\theta)B(r)$ of the Laplacian will be $\sin n\theta B_n(r)$ and $\cos n\theta B_n(r)$.

Solving Bessel's equation (22) is not easy. The direct approach looks for an infinite series $B(r) = \sum c_m r^m$. This technique can fill a whole chapter, which I frankly think is unreasonable (you could find it on the web). We construct only one power series, in the radially symmetric case $n = 0$ with no dependence on θ, to see what a Bessel function looks like. Substitute $\boldsymbol{B = \sum c_m r^m}$ into $r^2 B'' + rB' + \lambda r^2 B = 0$:

$$\sum c_m m(m-1) r^m + \sum c_m m r^m + \lambda \sum c_m r^{m+2} = 0\,. \tag{23}$$

The third sum multiplies r^m by λc_{m-2}. *Compare the coefficients of each* r^m:

c_m from c_{m-2} $$c_m m(m-1) + c_m m + \lambda c_{m-2} = 0\,. \tag{24}$$

In other words $m^2 c_m = -\lambda c_{m-2}$. Suppose $c_0 = 1$. This recursion gives $c_2 = -\lambda/2^2$. Then c_4 is $-\lambda/4^2$ times c_2. Each step gives one more coefficient in the series for B:

Bessel function $$B(r) = c_0 + c_2 r^2 + \cdots = 1 - \frac{\lambda r^2}{2^2} + \frac{\lambda^2 r^4}{2^2 4^2} - \frac{\lambda^3 r^6}{2^2 4^2 6^2} + \cdots \tag{25}$$

This is a Bessel function of order $n = 0$. Its standard notation is $B = \boldsymbol{J_0(\sqrt{\lambda}\, r)}$. The eigenvalues λ come from $J_0(\sqrt{\lambda}) = 0$ at the boundary $r = 1$. The best way to appreciate these functions is by comparison with the cosine, whose behavior we know:

$$\cos(\sqrt{\lambda}) = 1 - \frac{\lambda}{2!} + \frac{\lambda^2}{4!} - \frac{\lambda^3}{6!} + \cdots \quad \text{and} \quad J_0(\sqrt{\lambda}) = 1 - \frac{\lambda}{2^2} + \frac{\lambda^2}{2^2 4^2} - \frac{\lambda^3}{2^2 4^2 6^2} + \cdots \tag{26}$$

The zeros of the cosine, although you couldn't tell it from the series, have constant spacing π. The zeros of $J_0(\sqrt{\lambda})$ occur at $\sqrt{\lambda} \approx 2.4, 5.5, 8.65, 11.8, \ldots$ and their spacing converges rapidly to π (fortunately for our ears). The function $J_0(r)$ approaches a damped cosine $\sqrt{2/\pi r}\cos(r - \pi/4)$, with its amplitude slowly decreasing.

You must see the analogy between the Bessel function and the cosine. $B(r)$ comes from the oscillations of a circular drum; for $C(x) = \cos(k - \frac{1}{2})\pi x$ the drum is square. The circular drum is oscillating radially, as in Figure 4.8. The center of the circle and the left side of the square have zero slope (a free edge). $B(r)$ and $C(x)$ are eigenfunctions of Laplace's equation (with θ and y separated away):

$$-\frac{d}{dr}\left(r\frac{dB}{dr}\right) = \lambda r B \quad \text{and} \quad -\frac{d^2 C}{dx^2} = \lambda C\,. \tag{27}$$

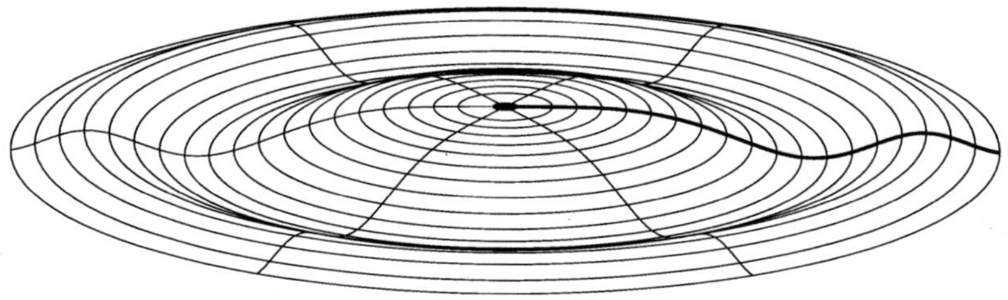

Figure 4.8: Bessel's $J_0(\sqrt{\lambda_3}\,r)$ shows the 3rd radial eigenfunction ($n = 0$) of a drum.

The first eigenfunction B drops from 1 to 0, like the cosine. $B(\sqrt{\lambda_2}\,r)$ crosses zero and comes up again. The kth eigenfunction, like the kth cosine, has k arches (Figure 4.8 shows $k = 3$). Each pure oscillation has its own frequency.

These are eigenfunctions of a symmetric problem. *Orthogonality must hold.* The Bessel functions $B_k(r) = J_0(\sqrt{\lambda_k}r)$ are orthogonal over a unit circle:

Orthogonality with $w = r$ $$\int_0^{2\pi}\int_0^1 B_k(r)B_l(r)\,r\,dr\,d\theta = 0 \quad \text{if} \quad k \neq l\,. \tag{28}$$

The cosines are orthogonal (with $w = 1$) over a unit square:

$$\int_0^1\int_0^1 \cos(k - \tfrac{1}{2})\pi x\,\cos(l - \tfrac{1}{2})\pi x\,dx\,dy = 0 \quad \text{if} \quad k \neq l\,. \tag{29}$$

The θ integral and the y integral make no difference and can be ignored. The boundary conditions are identical, zero slope at the left endpoint 0 and zero value at the right endpoint 1. The difference for Bessel is the weighting factor $w = r$ in (28).

In closing we describe the other oscillations of a circular drum. If $A(\theta) = \cos n\theta$ then new Bessel functions will appear. Equation (22) has a solution which is finite at $r = 0$. That is the *Bessel function of order n.* (All other solutions blow up at $r = 0$; they involve Bessel functions of the second kind.) For every positive λ the solution is rescaled to $J_n(\sqrt{\lambda}r)$. The boundary condition $J_n(\sqrt{\lambda}) = 0$ at $r = 1$ picks out the eigenvalues. The products $A(\theta)B(r) = \cos n\theta J_n(\sqrt{\lambda_k}r)$ and $\sin n\theta J_n(\sqrt{\lambda_k}r)$ are the eigenfunctions of the drum in its pure oscillations.

The question "***Can you hear the shape of a drum?***" was unsolved for a long time. Do the Laplace eigenvalues determine the shape of a region? The answer turned out to be ***no***. Different shapes have the same λ's, and sound the same.

Along the "nodal lines" the drum does not move. Those are like the zeros of the sine function, where a violin string is still. For $A(\theta)B(r)$, there is a nodal line from the center whenever $A = 0$ and a nodal circle whenever $B = 0$. Figure 4.9 shows where the drumhead is still. The oscillations $A(\theta)B(r)e^{i\sqrt{\lambda}t}$ solve the wave equation.

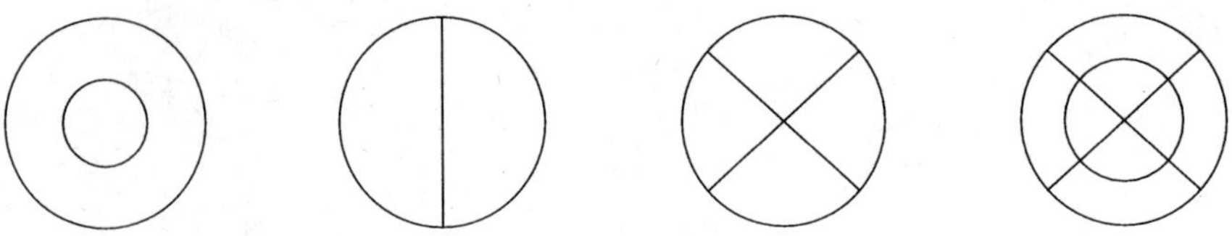

$n = 0$	$n = 1$	$n = 2$	$n = 2$
$k = 2$	$k = 1$	$k = 1$	$k = 2$

Figure 4.9: Nodal lines of a circular drum = zero lines of $A(\theta)B(r)$.

Problem Set 4.2

1 Find the double Fourier coefficients c_{mn} of these periodic functions $F(x, y)$:

(a) $F = \text{quarter square} = \begin{cases} 1 \text{ for } 0 \leq x \leq \pi,\ 0 \leq y \leq \pi \\ 0 \text{ if } -\pi < x < 0 \text{ or } -\pi < y < 0 \end{cases}$

(b) $F = \text{checkerboard} = \begin{cases} 1 \text{ if } xy \geq 0 & -\pi < x \leq \pi \\ 0 \text{ if } xy < 0 & -\pi < y \leq \pi \end{cases}$

2 Which functions $S(x, y)$ will have double sine series $\sum\sum b_{mn} \sin mx \sin ny$? State the orthogonality of those basis functions $\sin mx \sin ny$ (on what square?).

3 Find a formula for the coefficients b_{mn} in the double sine series.

4 Which functions $C(x, y)$ will have double cosine series $\sum\sum a_{mn} \cos mx \cos ny$? Show that this basis $\cos mx \cos ny$ is orthogonal on $[0, \pi]^2$.

5 Find a formula for the coefficients a_{mn} in the double cosine series. What is the coefficient a_{00} in the constant term?

6 Every $F(x) = C(x) + S(x) = \frac{1}{2}(F(x) + F(-x)) + \frac{1}{2}(F(x) - F(-x))$ is even plus odd. Split the function $F(x, y)$ similarly into $C(x, y) + S(x, y) +$ (two odd-even pieces). Those pieces use $\sin mx \cos ny$ and $\cos mx \sin ny$.

7 What is the double Fourier series of $\delta(x + y)$, the diagonal line of spikes?

8 Expand $F(x) = x^4$ as a combination of Chebyshev polynomials.

9 Estimate the distance from $x = 1$ to the next Chebyshev point $x = \cos(2\pi/k)$.

10 Chebyshev's $T_n(x)$ is a determinant from our second-difference matrix T:

$$T_n(x) = \det \begin{bmatrix} x & -1 & & \\ -1 & 2x & -1 & \\ & -1 & 2x & \cdot \\ & & \cdot & \cdot \end{bmatrix} \qquad \begin{aligned} T_1(x) &= x \\ T_2(x) &= 2x^2 - 1 \\ T_3(x) &= 4x^3 - 4x \end{aligned}$$

Including the next $-1, 2x, -1$ will give $T_4 = 2xT_3 - T_2$ from the rules for determinants. Explain why the determinant always has the same recursion $T_{n+1} = 2xT_n - T_{n-1}$ as the Chebyshev polynomial, so they are equal.

11 Chebyshev's $U_{n-1}(x)$ is a determinant from our second-difference matrix K:

$$U_{n-1}(x) = \frac{\sin n\theta}{\sin \theta} = \det \begin{bmatrix} 2x & -1 & \\ -1 & 2x & \cdot \\ & \cdot & \cdot \end{bmatrix} \qquad \begin{aligned} U_1(x) &= 2x \\ U_2(x) &= 4x^2 - 1 \end{aligned}$$

The recursion from the dots is still $U_{n+1} = 2xU_n - U_{n-1}$ but with a new start U_1, U_2. Show that $U_3(x) = 0$ at $x = \left\{\cos\frac{\pi}{4}, \cos\frac{2\pi}{4}, \cos\frac{3\pi}{4}\right\} = \left\{\frac{1}{\sqrt{2}}, 0, -\frac{1}{\sqrt{2}}\right\}$. How are the eigenvalues λ of K related to the zeros of $U_n(x)$?

12 Expand the determinant for T_n along row 1 and column 1 to get matrices (cofactors) of sizes $n-1$ and $n-2$, to show that $T_n(x) = xU_{n-1}(x) - U_{n-2}(x)$.

13 With $x = \cos\theta$ and $dx = -\sin\theta\, d\theta$, the derivative of $T_n(x) = \cos n\theta$ is $n\, U_{n-1}$:

$$T_n'(x) = -n \sin n\theta \frac{d\theta}{dx} = n \frac{\sin n\theta}{\sin\theta} = n\, U_{n-1}(x) = \text{second kind Chebyshev.}$$

Why are the extreme values of T_n at the zeros of U_{n-1}?

14 From its recursion, U_n starts with $2^n x^n$. Find the first term in T_n.

15 From the three-term recurrence (18), find the Legendre polynomial $P_4(x)$ when $P_2 = (3x^2-1)/2$ and $P_3 = (5x^3-3x)/2$. Which powers have $\int x^k\, P_4(x)\, dx = 0$?

16 Use *integration by parts* on the interval $-1 \le x \le 1$ to show that the third derivative of $(x^2-1)^3$ is orthogonal to the derivative of (x^2-1), coming from Rodrigues formula (17).

17 If $L_1 = x - a$ is orthogonal to $L_0 = 1$ with weight $w(x) = e^{-x}$ on $0 \le x < \infty$, what is a in that Laguerre polynomial $L_1(x)$?

18 If $H_2 = x^2 - b$ is orthogonal to 1 and x with weight e^{-x^2} on $-\infty < x < \infty$, what is b in that Hermite polynomial $H_2(x)$?

19 The polynomials $1, x, y, x^2 - y^2, 2xy, \ldots$ solve Laplace's equation in 2D. Find five combinations of $x^2, y^2, z^2, xy, xz, yz$ that satisfy $u_{xx} + u_{yy} + u_{zz} = 0$. With spherical polynomials of all degrees we can match $u = u_0$ on a sphere.

20 A Sturm-Liouville eigenvalue problem is $(pu')' + qu + \lambda wu = 0$. Multiply the equation for u_1 (with $\lambda = \lambda_1$) by u_2. Multiply the equation for u_2 by u_1 and subtract. With zero boundary conditions integrate $u_2(pu_1')'$ and $u_1(pu_2')'$ by parts to show *weighted orthogonality* $\int u_1 u_2 \, w \, dx = 0$ (if $\lambda_2 \neq \lambda_1$).

21 Fit the Bessel equation (22) into the framework of a Sturm-Liouville equation $(pu')' + qu + \lambda wu = 0$. What are p, q, and w? What are they for the Legendre equation $(1 - x^2)P'' - 2xP' + \lambda P = 0$?

22 The cosine series has $n!$ when the Bessel series has $2^2 4^2 \cdots n^2$. Write the latter as $2^n[(n/2)!]^2$ and use Stirling's formula $n! \approx \sqrt{2\pi n}\, n^n e^{-n}$ to show that the ratio of these coefficients approaches $\sqrt{\pi n/2}$. They have the same alternating signs.

23 Substitute $B = \sum c_m r^m$ into Bessel's equation and show from the analogue of (24) that λc_{m-2} must equal $(n^2 - m^2)c_m$. This recursion starts from $c_n = 1$ and successively finds $c_{n+2} = \lambda/(n^2 - (n+2)^2), c_{n+4}, \ldots$ as the coefficients in a *Bessel function of order* n:

$$B_n(r) = r^n \left[1 + \frac{\lambda r^2}{n^2 - (n+2)^2} + \frac{\lambda^2 r^2}{(n^2 - (n+2)^2)(n^2 - (n+4)^2)} + \cdots\right]$$

$$= \frac{n!}{2^n} \sum_{k=0}^{\infty} \frac{(-1)^k \, (\sqrt{\lambda}/2)^{2k+n}}{k! \, (k+n)!}.$$

24 Explain why the third Bessel function $J_0(\sqrt{\lambda_3}\, r)$ is zero at $r = \sqrt{\lambda_1/\lambda_3}, \sqrt{\lambda_2/\lambda_3}, 1$.

25 Show that the first Legendre polynomials $P_0 = 1, P_1 = \cos\varphi, P_2 = \cos^2\varphi - \frac{1}{3}$ are eigenfunctions of Laplace's equation $(wu_\varphi)_\varphi + w^{-1}u_{\theta\theta} = \lambda wu$ with $w = \sin\varphi$ on the surface of a sphere. Find the eigenvalues λ of these *spherical harmonics*. These $P_n(\cos\varphi)$ are the eigenfunctions that don't depend on longitude.

26 Where are the drum's nodal lines in Figure 4.9 if $n = 1, k = 2$ or $n = 2, k = 3$?

Table of Special Functions: Weighted Orthogonality, Recursion Formula, Differential Equation, and Series

Legendre Polynomial $P_n(x)$ with $w=1$ on $-1 \le x \le 1$ $\quad \int_{-1}^{1} P_m(x)P_n(x)\,dx=0$

$(n+1)P_{n+1} = (2n+1)xP_n - nP_{n-1}$ and $(1-x^2)P_n'' - 2xP_n' + n(n+1)P_n = 0$

$$P_n(x) = \sum_{k=0}^{[n/2]} (-1)^k \binom{-\frac{1}{2}}{n-k}\binom{n-k}{k}(2x)^{n-k} = \frac{1}{2^n n!}\left(\frac{d}{dx}\right)^n (x^2-1)^n$$

Chebyshev Polynomial $T_n(x)$ $= \cos n\theta$, with $x = \cos\theta$ and $w = 1/\sqrt{1-x^2}$

$T_{n+1} = 2xT_n - T_{n-1}$ and $(1-x^2)T_n'' - xT_n' + n^2T_n = 0$

$\int_{-1}^{1} T_m(x)\,T_n(x)\,dx/\sqrt{1-x^2} = \int_{-\pi}^{\pi} \cos m\theta \cos n\theta\, d\theta = 0$

$$T_n(x) = \frac{n}{2}\sum_{k=0}^{[n/2]} \frac{(-1)^k (n-k-1)!}{k!\,(n-2k)!}(2x)^{n-2k}$$

Bessel Function $J_p(x)$ with weight $w = x$ on $0 \le x \le 1$

$xJ_{p+1} = 2pJ_p - xJ_{p-1}$ and $x^2J_p'' + xJ_p' + (x^2 - p^2)J_p = 0$

$\int_0^1 x\,J_p(r_m x)\,J_p(r_n x)\,dx = 0$ if $J_p(r_m) = J_p(r_n) = 0$

$$J_p(x) = \frac{\Gamma(p+1)}{2^p}\sum_{k=0}^{\infty}\frac{(-1)^k (x/2)^{2k+p}}{k!\,\Gamma(k+p+1)}$$

Laguerre Polynomial $L_n(x)$ with weight $w = e^{-x}$ on $0 \le x < \infty$

$(n+1)L_{n+1} = (2n+1-x)L_n - nL_{n-1}$ and $xL_{n+1}'' + (1-x)L_n' + nL_n = 0$

$$L_n(x) = \sum_{k=0}^{n}\frac{(-1)^k\, n!}{(k!)^2(n-k)!}x^k \qquad \int_0^\infty e^{-x}L_m(x)L_n(x)\,dx = 0$$

Hermite Polynomial $H_n(x)$ with weight $w = e^{-x^2}$ on $-\infty < x < \infty$

$H_{n+1} = 2xH_n - 2nH_{n-1}$ and $H_n'' - 2xH_n' + 2nH_n = 0$

$$H_n(x) = \sum_{k=1}^{[n/2]}\frac{(-1)^k\, n!}{k!\,(n-2k)!}(2x)^{n-2k} \qquad \int_{-\infty}^{\infty} e^{-x^2}H_m(x)H_n(x)\,dx = 0$$

Gamma Function $\Gamma(n+1) = n\Gamma(n)$ leading to $\Gamma(n+1) = n!$

$\Gamma(n) = \int_0^\infty e^{-x}x^{n-1}\,dx$ gives $\Gamma(1) = 0! = 1$ and $\Gamma(\frac{1}{2}) = \sqrt{\pi}$

$\Gamma(n+1) = n! \approx \sqrt{2\pi n}\left(\frac{n}{e}\right)^n$ (Stirling's factorial formula for large n)

Binomial Numbers $\binom{n}{m} = \frac{n!}{m!\,(n-m)!} =$ "n choose m" $= \frac{\Gamma(n+1)}{\Gamma(m+1)\,\Gamma(n-m+1)}$

Binomial Theorem $(a+b)^n = \sum_{m=0} \binom{n}{m} a^{n-m} b^m$ (infinite series unless $n = 1, 2, \ldots$)

4.3 DISCRETE FOURIER TRANSFORM AND THE FFT

This section moves from functions $F(x)$ and infinite series to vectors $(f_0, \ldots, f_{N-1})$ and finite series. The vectors have N components and the series have N terms. The exponential e^{ikx} is still basic, but now x only takes N different values. Those values $x = 0, 2\pi/N, 4\pi/N, \ldots$ have equal spacing $2\pi/N$. This means that the N numbers e^{ix} are the powers of a totally important complex number $\boldsymbol{w = \exp(i2\pi/N)}$:

Powers of w	$e^{i0} = 1 = w^0$	$e^{i2\pi/N} = w$	$e^{i4\pi/N} = w^2$	...	w^{N-1}

The **Discrete Fourier Transform (DFT)** deals entirely with those powers of w. Notice that the Nth power w^N cycles back to $e^{2\pi i N/N} = 1$.

The DFT and the inverse DFT are multiplications by the Fourier matrix F_N and its inverse matrix F_N^{-1}. The **Fast Fourier Transform (FFT)** is a brilliant way to multiply quickly. When a matrix has N^2 entries, an ordinary matrix-vector product uses N^2 multiplications. The Fast Fourier Transform uses only N times $\frac{1}{2}\log_2 N$ multiplications. It is the most valuable numerical algorithm in my lifetime, changing (1024)(1024) into (1024)(5). Whole industries have been speeded up by this one idea.

Roots of Unity and the Fourier Matrix

Quadratic equations have two roots (or a double root). Equations of degree n have n roots (counting repetitions). This is the Fundamental Theorem of Algebra, and to make it true we must allow complex roots. This section is about the very special equation $z^N = 1$. ***The solutions $z = 1, w, \ldots, w^{N-1}$ are the "Nth roots of unity".*** They are N evenly spaced points around the unit circle in the complex plane.

Figure 4.10 shows the eight solutions to $z^8 = 1$. Their spacing is $\frac{1}{8}(360°) = 45°$. The first root is at 45° or $\theta = 2\pi/8$ radians. ***It is the complex number $w = e^{i2\pi/8}$.*** We call this number w_8 to emphasize that it is an 8th root. You could write it as $\cos\frac{2\pi}{8} + i\sin\frac{2\pi}{8}$, but don't do it. Powers of w are best in the form $e^{i\theta}$, because we work only with the angle.

The seven other 8th roots around the circle are $w^2, w^3, \ldots, w^8$, and that last one is $w^8 = 1$. The next to last root w^7 is the same as the complex conjugate $\overline{w} = e^{-i2\pi/8}$. (Multiply $\overline{w}$ by w to get $e^0 = 1$, so $\overline{w}$ is also w^{-1}.) The powers of $\overline{w}$ just go backward around the circle (clockwise). You will see them in the inverse Fourier matrix.

For the fourth roots of 1, the separation angle is $2\pi/4$ or 90°. The number $e^{2\pi i/4} = \cos\frac{\pi}{2} + i\sin\frac{\pi}{2}$ is nothing but i. The four roots are i, $i^2 = -1$, $i^3 = -i$, and $i^4 = 1$.

The idea behind the FFT is to go from an 8 by 8 Fourier matrix (powers of w_8) to a 4 by 4 matrix (powers of $w_4 = i$). By exploiting the connections of F_4 and F_8 and F_{16} and beyond, multiplication by F_{1024} is very quick. ***The key connection for the Fast Fourier Transform is the simple fact that $(w_8)^2 = w_4$.***

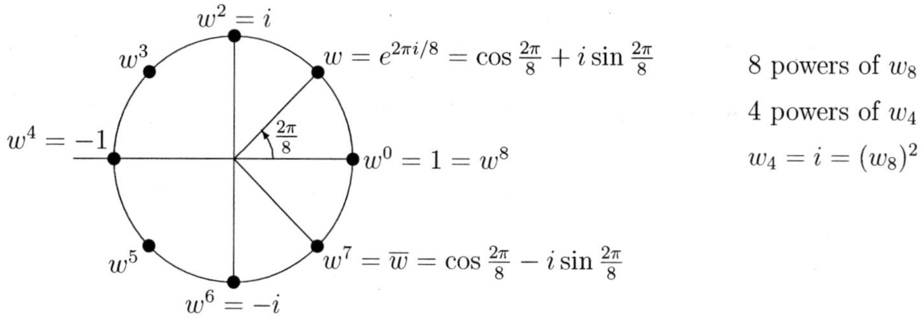

Figure 4.10: The eight solutions to $z^8 = 1$ are $1, w, w^2, \ldots, w^7$ with $w = (1+i)/\sqrt{2}$.

Here is the **Fourier matrix** F_N for $N = 4$. Each entry is a power of $w_4 = i$:

Fourier matrix
$$F_4 = \begin{bmatrix} 1 & 1 & 1 & 1 \\ 1 & w & w^2 & w^3 \\ 1 & w^2 & w^4 & w^6 \\ 1 & w^3 & w^6 & w^9 \end{bmatrix} = \begin{bmatrix} 1 & 1 & 1 & 1 \\ 1 & i & i^2 & i^3 \\ 1 & i^2 & i^4 & i^6 \\ 1 & i^3 & i^6 & i^9 \end{bmatrix}.$$

Those four columns are orthogonal! Columns 0 and 1 have zero inner product:

$$(\textbf{column 0})^{\mathrm{T}}(\textbf{column 1}) = w^0 + w^1 + w^2 + w^3 = \mathbf{0}\,.\ \text{This is } 1 + i + i^2 + i^3 = 0\,. \quad (1)$$

We are adding four equally spaced points in Figure 4.10, and *each pair of opposite points cancels* (i^2 cancels 1 and i^3 cancels i). For the 8 by 8 Fourier matrix, we would be adding all eight points in the figure. The sum $1 + w + \cdots + w^7$ is again zero.

Now look at columns 1 and 3 (remember that the numbering starts at zero). Their ordinary inner product looks like 4, which we don't want:

$$1 \cdot 1 + i \cdot i^3 + i^2 \cdot i^6 + i^3 \cdot i^9 = \mathbf{1 + 1 + 1 + 1} \qquad \textbf{\textit{but this is wrong.}}$$

These are complex vectors, not real vectors. The correct inner product must take the **complex conjugate** of one vector (change i to $-i$). Now we see orthogonality:

$$(\overline{\textbf{col 1}})^{\mathrm{T}}(\textbf{col 3}) = 1 \cdot 1 + (-i) \cdot i^3 + (-i)^2 \cdot i^6 + (-i)^3 \cdot i^9 = \mathbf{1 - 1 + 1 - 1 = 0}\,. \quad (2)$$

The correct inner product of every column with itself is $1 + 1 + 1 + 1 = 4$:

$$\|\text{Column } 1\|^2 = (\overline{\text{col } 1})^{\mathrm{T}}(\text{col } 1) = 1 \cdot 1 + (-i) \cdot i + (-i)^2 \cdot i^2 + (-i)^3 \cdot i^3 = 4\,. \quad (3)$$

The columns of F_4 are not unit vectors. They all have length $\sqrt{4} = 2$, so $\frac{1}{2}F_4$ has **orthonormal columns**. Multiplying $\frac{1}{2}\overline{F}_4$ times $\frac{1}{2}F_4$ (row times column) produces I.

The inverse of F_4 is the matrix with $\overline{F}_4$ on the left (including both factors $\frac{1}{2}$):

$$\frac{1}{2}\begin{bmatrix} 1 & 1 & 1 & 1 \\ 1 & (-i) & (-i)^2 & (-i)^3 \\ 1 & (-i)^2 & (-i)^4 & (-i)^6 \\ 1 & (-i)^3 & (-i)^6 & (-i)^9 \end{bmatrix} \frac{1}{2}\begin{bmatrix} 1 & 1 & 1 & 1 \\ 1 & i & i^2 & i^3 \\ 1 & i^2 & i^4 & i^6 \\ 1 & i^3 & i^6 & i^9 \end{bmatrix} = \begin{bmatrix} 1 & 0 & 0 & 0 \\ 0 & 1 & 0 & 0 \\ 0 & 0 & 1 & 0 \\ 0 & 0 & 0 & 1 \end{bmatrix} = I. \qquad (4)$$

Thus F_4^{-1} is $\frac{1}{4}\overline{F}_4^{\mathrm{T}}$, also written $\frac{1}{4}F_4^*$. Here is the general rule for F_N:

The columns of $\frac{1}{\sqrt{N}}F_N$ ***are orthonormal. Their inner products produce*** I.

$$\left(\frac{1}{\sqrt{N}}\overline{F}_N^{\mathrm{T}}\right)\left(\frac{1}{\sqrt{N}}F_N\right) = I \text{ **means that the inverse is** } F_N^{-1} = \frac{1}{N}\overline{F}_N^{\mathrm{T}} = \frac{1}{N}F_N^* \qquad (5)$$

The Fourier matrix is symmetric, so transposing has no effect. The inverse matrix just divides by N and replaces i by $-i$, which changes every $w = \exp(i2\pi/N)$ into $\omega = \overline{w} = \exp(-i2\pi/N)$. For every N, the Fourier matrix contains the powers $(w_N)^{jk}$:

Fourier Matrix

$$F_N = \begin{bmatrix} 1 & 1 & 1 & \cdot & 1 \\ 1 & w & w^2 & \cdot & w^{N-1} \\ 1 & w^2 & w^4 & \cdot & w^{2(N-1)} \\ \cdot & \cdot & \cdot & \cdot & \cdot \\ 1 & w^{N-1} & w^{2(N-1)} & \cdot & w^{(N-1)^2} \end{bmatrix} \begin{matrix} \longleftarrow \textbf{row 0} \\ \\ \textbf{with } \mathbf{F_{jk} = w^{jk}} \\ \\ \longleftarrow \textbf{row N} - \mathbf{1} \end{matrix} \qquad (6)$$

This matrix is the key to the Discrete Fourier Transform. Its special patterns give the fast DFT, which is the FFT. The row and column numbers j and k go from 0 to $N-1$. ***The entry in row*** j, ***column*** k ***is*** $w^{jk} = \exp(ijk\,2\pi/N)$.

Fourier matrix in MATLAB $\quad j = 0 : N-1; \;\; k = j\,'; \;\; F = w.\hat{}(k * j);$

Important note. Many authors prefer to work with $\omega = e^{-2\pi i/N}$, which is the *complex conjugate* of our w. (They often use the Greek omega, and I will do that to keep the two options separate.) With this choice, their DFT matrix contains powers of ω not w. It is conj(F) = complex conjugate of our F.

This is a completely reasonable choice! MATLAB uses $\omega = e^{-2\pi i/N}$. The DFT matrix fft(eye(N)) contains powers of this number $\omega = \overline{w}$. In our notation that matrix is $\overline{F}$. **The Fourier matrix with** w**'s reconstructs** f **from** c. **The matrix** $\overline{F}$ **with** ω**'s transforms** f **to** c, **so we call it the DFT matrix**:

DFT matrix $= \overline{F}$ $\qquad \overline{F}_{jk} = \omega^{jk} = e^{-2\pi ijk/N} =$ fft(eye(N))

The factor $1/N$ in F^{-1} is like the earlier $1/2\pi$. We include it in $c = F_N^{-1}f = \frac{1}{N}\overline{F}f$.

The Discrete Fourier Transform

The Fourier matrices F_N and F_N^{-1} produce the Discrete Fourier Transform and its inverse. Functions with infinite series turn into vectors $f_0, \ldots, f_{N-1}$ with finite sums:

$$F(x) = \sum_{-\infty}^{\infty} c_k e^{ikx} \quad \textbf{becomes} \quad f_j = \sum_{k=0}^{N-1} c_k w^{jk} \quad \textbf{which is} \quad f = F_N c. \tag{7}$$

In the other direction, an integral with e^{-ikx} becomes a sum with $\overline{w}^{jk} = e^{-ikj2\pi/N}$:

$$c_k = \frac{1}{2\pi}\int_0^{2\pi} F(x)e^{-ikx}\,dx \quad \textbf{becomes} \quad c_k = \frac{1}{N}\sum_{j=0}^{N-1} f_j \overline{w}^{jk} \quad \textbf{which is} \quad c = F_N^{-1} f \tag{8}$$

The power w^{jk} is the same as e^{ikx} at the jth point $x_j = j2\pi/N$. At those N points, we reconstruct $f_0, \ldots, f_{N-1}$ by combining the N columns of the Fourier matrix. Previously we reconstructed functions $F(x)$ at all points by an infinite sum.

The zeroth coefficient c_0 is always the average of f. Here $c_0 = (f_0 + \cdots + f_{N-1})/N$.

Example 1 The **Discrete Delta Function** is $\delta = (1, 0, 0, 0)$. For functions, the Fourier coefficients of the spike $\delta(x)$ are all equal. Here the coefficients $c = F_4^{-1}\delta$ are all $\frac{1}{N} = \frac{1}{4}$:

$$\begin{bmatrix} c_0 \\ c_1 \\ c_2 \\ c_3 \end{bmatrix} = \frac{1}{4}\begin{bmatrix} 1 & 1 & 1 & 1 \\ 1 & (-i) & (-i)^2 & (-i)^3 \\ 1 & (-i)^2 & (-i)^4 & (-i)^6 \\ 1 & (-i)^3 & (-i)^6 & (-i)^9 \end{bmatrix}\begin{bmatrix} 1 \\ 0 \\ 0 \\ 0 \end{bmatrix} = \frac{1}{4}\begin{bmatrix} 1 \\ 1 \\ 1 \\ 1 \end{bmatrix}. \tag{9}$$

To reconstruct $f = (1, 0, 0, 0)$ from its transform $c = (\frac{1}{4}, \frac{1}{4}, \frac{1}{4}, \frac{1}{4})$, multiply F times c. Notice again how all rows except the zeroth row of F add to zero:

$$Fc = \begin{bmatrix} f_0 \\ f_1 \\ f_2 \\ f_3 \end{bmatrix} = \begin{bmatrix} 1 & 1 & 1 & 1 \\ 1 & i & i^2 & i^3 \\ 1 & i^2 & i^4 & i^6 \\ 1 & i^3 & i^6 & i^9 \end{bmatrix} \frac{1}{4} \begin{bmatrix} 1 \\ 1 \\ 1 \\ 1 \end{bmatrix} = \begin{bmatrix} 1 \\ 0 \\ 0 \\ 0 \end{bmatrix}. \tag{10}$$

Example 2 The **constant vector** $f = (1, 1, 1, 1)$ produces $c =$ delta vector $= (1, 0, 0, 0)$. This reverses the previous example without $1/N$. We mention that f and c are both "even". What does it mean for vectors to be even or odd? **Think cyclically**.

Symmetry or antisymmetry is across the zero position. **The entry in the -1 position is by definition the entry in the $N - 1$ position.** We are working "mod N" or "mod 4" so that $-1 \equiv 3$ and $-2 \equiv 2$. In this mod 4 arithmetic $2 + 2 \equiv 0$, because w^2 times w^2 is w^0. In the mod N world, f_{-k} is f_{N-k}:

$$\textbf{Even vector } \boldsymbol{f}\text{:} \qquad f_k = f_{N-k} \quad \text{as in } (f_0, f_1, f_2, f_1) \tag{11}$$

$$\textbf{Odd vector } \boldsymbol{f}\text{:} \qquad f_k = -f_{N-k} \quad \text{as in } (0, f_1, 0, -f_1) \tag{12}$$

Example 3 The **discrete sine** $f = (0, 1, 0, -1)$ is an odd vector. Its Fourier coefficients c_k are pure imaginary, as in $\sin x = \frac{1}{2i}e^{ix} - \frac{1}{2i}e^{-ix}$. In fact we still get $\frac{1}{2i}$ and $-\frac{1}{2i}$:

$$c = F_4^{-1}f = \frac{1}{4}\begin{bmatrix} 1 & 1 & 1 & 1 \\ 1 & (-i) & (-i)^2 & (-i)^3 \\ 1 & (-i)^2 & (-i)^4 & (-i)^6 \\ 1 & (-i)^3 & (-i)^6 & (-i)^9 \end{bmatrix}\begin{bmatrix} 0 \\ 1 \\ 0 \\ -1 \end{bmatrix} = \begin{bmatrix} 0 \\ 1/2i \\ 0 \\ -1/2i \end{bmatrix}. \tag{13}$$

Odd inputs f produce pure imaginary Fourier coefficients $c_k = a_k + ib_k = ib_k$.

The Discrete Cosine Transform (**DCT**) is the key to **JPEG compression**. All .jpeg files were created from 8×8 DCT's, until wavelets arrived in the JPEG2000 standard. Cosines give a symmetric extension at the ends of vectors, like starting with a function from 0 to π and reflecting it to be even: $C(-x) = C(x)$. *No jump is created at the reflection points.* Compression of data and images and video is so important that we come back to it in Section 4.7.

One Step of the Fast Fourier Transform

To reconstruct f we want to multiply F_N times $\mathbf{c}$ as quickly as possible. The matrix has N^2 entries, so normally we would need N^2 separate multiplications. You might think it is impossible to do better. (Since F_N has no zero entries, no multiplications can be skipped.) By using the special pattern w^{jk} for its entries, F_N can be factored in a way that produces many zeros. This is the **FFT**.

The key idea is to connect F_N ***with the half-size Fourier matrix*** $F_{N/2}$. Assume that N is a power of 2 (say $N = 2^{10} = 1024$). We will connect F_{1024} to F_{512}—or rather to ***two copies*** of F_{512}. When $N = 4$, we connect F_4 to $[\,F_2\ 0\ ;\ 0\ F_2\,]$:

$$F_4 = \begin{bmatrix} 1 & 1 & 1 & 1 \\ 1 & i & i^2 & i^3 \\ 1 & i^2 & i^4 & i^6 \\ 1 & i^3 & i^6 & i^9 \end{bmatrix} \quad \text{and} \quad \begin{bmatrix} F_2 & 0 \\ 0 & F_2 \end{bmatrix} = \begin{bmatrix} 1 & 1 & & \\ 1 & i^2 & & \\ & & 1 & 1 \\ & & 1 & i^2 \end{bmatrix}.$$

On the left is F_4, with no zeros. On the right is a matrix that is half zero. The work is cut in half. But wait, those matrices are not the same. The block matrix with F_2's is only one piece of the factorization of F_4. The other pieces have many zeros:

$$\textbf{Key idea} \qquad F_4 = \begin{bmatrix} 1 & & 1 & \\ & 1 & & i \\ 1 & & -1 & \\ & 1 & & -i \end{bmatrix}\begin{bmatrix} 1 & 1 & & \\ 1 & i^2 & & \\ & & 1 & 1 \\ & & 1 & i^2 \end{bmatrix}\begin{bmatrix} 1 & & & \\ & & 1 & \\ & 1 & & \\ & & & 1 \end{bmatrix}. \tag{14}$$

The permutation matrix on the right puts c_0 and c_2 (evens) ahead of c_1 and c_3 (odds). The middle matrix performs separate half-size transforms on those evens and odds. The matrix at the left combines the two half-size outputs, in a way that produces the correct full-size output $\mathbf{f} = F_4\mathbf{c}$. You could multiply those three matrices to see F_4.

The same idea applies when $N = 1024$ and $M = \frac{1}{2}N = 512$. The number w is $e^{2\pi i/1024}$. It is at the angle $\theta = 2\pi/1024$ on the unit circle. The Fourier matrix F_{1024} is full of powers of w. The first stage of the FFT is the great factorization discovered by Cooley and Tukey (and foreshadowed in 1805 by Gauss):

FFT (Step 1) $$F_{1024} = \begin{bmatrix} I_{512} & D_{512} \\ I_{512} & -D_{512} \end{bmatrix} \begin{bmatrix} F_{512} & \\ & F_{512} \end{bmatrix} \begin{bmatrix} \text{even-odd} \\ \text{permutation} \end{bmatrix} \tag{15}$$

I_{512} is the identity matrix. D_{512} is the diagonal matrix with entries $(1, w, \ldots, w^{511})$ using w_{1024}. The two copies of F_{512} are what we expected. Don't forget that they use the 512th root of unity, which is nothing but $(w_{1024})^2$. The even-odd permutation matrix separates the incoming vector $\mathbf{c}$ into $\mathbf{c}' = (c_0, c_2, \ldots, c_{1022})$ and $\mathbf{c}'' = (c_1, c_3, \ldots, c_{1023})$.

Here are the algebra formulas which express this neat FFT factorization of F_N:

(FFT) Set $M = \frac{1}{2}N$. The components of $\mathbf{f} = F_N\mathbf{c}$ are combinations of the half-size transforms $\mathbf{f}' = F_M\mathbf{c}'$ and $\mathbf{f}'' = F_M\mathbf{c}''$. Equation (15) shows $I\mathbf{f}' + D\mathbf{f}''$ and $I\mathbf{f}' - D\mathbf{f}''$:

$$\begin{array}{llcll} \textbf{First half} & \mathbf{f}_j & = & \mathbf{f}'_j + (w_N)^j\mathbf{f}''_j, & j = 0, \ldots, M-1 \\ \textbf{Second half} & \mathbf{f}_{j+M} & = & \mathbf{f}'_j - (w_N)^j\mathbf{f}''_j, & j = 0, \ldots, M-1 \end{array} \tag{16}$$

Thus each FFT step has three parts: split $\mathbf{c}$ into $\mathbf{c}'$ and $\mathbf{c}''$, transform them separately by F_M into $\mathbf{f}'$ and $\mathbf{f}''$, and reconstruct $\mathbf{f}$ from equation (16). N must be even!

The algebra of (16) is a splitting into even numbers $2k$ and odd $2k+1$, with $w = w_N$:

Even/Odd $$f_j = \sum_0^{N-1} w^{jk}c_k = \sum_0^{M-1} w^{2jk}c_{2k} + \sum_0^{M-1} w^{j(2k+1)}c_{2k+1} \text{ with } M = \tfrac{1}{2}N. \tag{17}$$

The even c's go into $c' = (c_0, c_2, \ldots)$ and the odd c's go into $c'' = (c_1, c_3, \ldots)$. Then come the transforms F_Mc' and F_Mc''. The key is $\boldsymbol{w_N^2 = w_M}$. This gives $w_N^{2jk} = w_M^{jk}$.

Rewrite $$f_j = \sum w_M^{jk}c'_k + (w_N)^j \sum w_M^{jk}c''_k = f'_j + (w_N)^j f''_j. \tag{18}$$

For $j \geq M$, the minus sign in (16) comes from factoring out $(w_N)^M = -1$.

MATLAB easily separates even c's from odd c's and multiplies by w_N^j. We use conj(F) or equivalently MATLAB's inverse transform ifft, because fft is based on $\omega = \overline{w} = e^{-2\pi i/N}$. Problem 2 shows that F and conj(F) are linked by permuting rows.

FFT Step from N to $N/2$ in MATLAB

```
f' = ifft (c(0 : 2 : N − 2)) ∗ N/2;
f'' = ifft (c(1 : 2 : N − 1)) ∗ N/2;
d = w.^(0 : N/2 − 1)';
f = [f' + d. ∗ f''; f' − d. ∗ f''];
```

The flow graph shows c' and c'' going through the half-size F_2. Those steps are called "*butterflies*," from their shape. Then the outputs f' and f'' are combined (multiplying f'' by $1, i$ and also by $-1, -i$) to produce $f = F_4c$.

Flow Graph
c to f
$N = 4$
$M = 2$

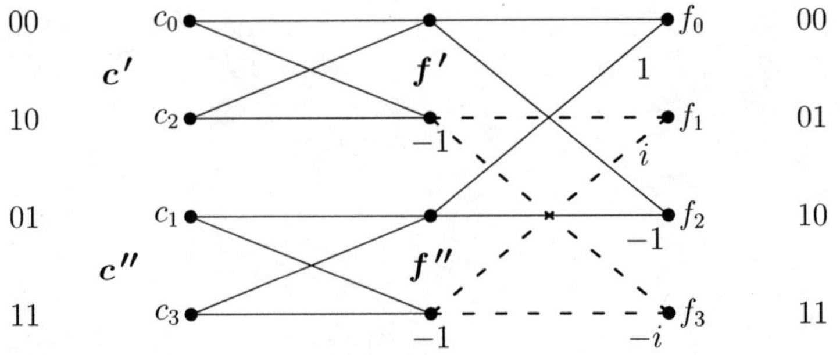

This reduction from F_N to two F_M's almost cuts the work in half—you see the zeros in the matrix factorization (15). That reduction is good but not great. The full idea of the FFT is much more powerful. It saves much more time than 50%.

The Full FFT by Recursion

If you have read this far, you have probably guessed what comes next. We reduced F_N to $F_{N/2}$. ***Keep going to*** $F_{N/4}$. The two copies of F_{512} lead to four copies of F_{256}. Then 256 leads to 128. *That is recursion.* It is a basic principle of many fast algorithms. Here is the second stage with $F = F_{256}$ and $D = \text{diag}\,(1, w_{512}, \ldots, (w_{512})^{255})$:

$$\begin{bmatrix} F_{512} & 0 \\ 0 & F_{512} \end{bmatrix} = \begin{bmatrix} I & D & & \\ I & -D & & \\ & & I & D \\ & & I & -D \end{bmatrix} \begin{bmatrix} F & & & \\ & F & & \\ & & F & \\ & & & F \end{bmatrix} \begin{bmatrix} \text{pick } 0,4,8,\cdots \\ \text{pick } 2,6,10,\cdots \\ \text{pick } 1,5,9,\cdots \\ \text{pick } 3,7,11,\cdots \end{bmatrix}.$$

We can count the individual multiplications, to see how much is saved. Before the FFT was invented, the count was $N^2 = (1024)^2$. This is about a million multiplications. I am not saying that they take a long time. The cost becomes large when we have many, many transforms to do—which is typical. Then the saving is also large:

The final count for size $N = 2^L$ ***is reduced from*** N^2 ***to*** $\frac{1}{2}NL$.

The number $N = 1024$ is 2^{10}, so $L = 10$. The original count of $(1024)^2$ is reduced to $(5)(1024)$. The saving is a factor of 200, because a million is reduced to five thousand. That is why the FFT has revolutionized signal processing.

Here is the reasoning behind $\frac{1}{2}NL$. There are L levels, going from $N = 2^L$ down to $N = 1$. Each level has $\frac{1}{2}N$ multiplications from diagonal D, to reassemble the half-size outputs. This yields the final count $\frac{1}{2}NL$, which is $\frac{1}{2}N\log_2 N$.

Exactly the same idea gives a fast inverse transform. The matrix F_N^{-1} contains powers of the conjugate $\overline{w}$. We just replace w by $\overline{w}$ in the diagonal matrix D, and in formula (16). At the end, divide by N.

One last note about this remarkable algorithm. There is an amazing rule for the order that the c's enter the butterflies, after all L of the odd-even permutations. Write the numbers 0 to $N-1$ in base 2. *Reverse the order of their bits (binary digits).* The complete flow graph shows the bit-reversed order at the start, then $L = \log_2 N$ recursion steps. The final output is F_N times $\mathbf{c}$.

The fastest FFT will be adapted to the processor and cache capacities of each specific computer. There will naturally be differences from a textbook description, but the idea of recursion is still crucial. For free software that automatically adjusts, we highly recommend the website fftw.org.

Problem Set 4.3

1 Multiply the three matrices in equation (14) and compare with F. In which six entries do you need to know that $i^2 = -1$? This is $(w_4)^2 = w_2$. If $M = N/2$, why is $(w_N)^M = -1$?

2 *Why is row i of $\overline{F}$ the same as row $N - i$ of F* (numbered from 0 to $N - 1$)?

3 From Problem 2, find the 4 by 4 permutation matrix P so that $F = P\overline{F}$. Check that $P^2 = I$ so that $P = P^{-1}$. Then from $\overline{F}F = 4I$ show that $P = F^2/4$. It is amazing that $P^2 = F^4/16 = I$! Four transforms of c bring back $16\,c$.

Note For all N, F^2/N is a symmetric permutation matrix P. It has the rows of I in the order $1, N, N-1, \ldots, 2$. Then $P = \left[\begin{smallmatrix} 1 & 0 \\ 0 & J \end{smallmatrix}\right] = I([1, N\!:\!-1\!:\!2], :)$ for the *reverse identity* J. From $P^2 = I$ we find (surprisingly!) that $F^4 = N^2 I$. The key facts about P and F and their eigenvalues are on the cse website.

4 Invert the three factors in equation (14) to find a fast factorization of F^{-1}.

5 F is symmetric. Transpose equation (14) to find a new Fast Fourier Transform!

6 All entries in the factorization of F_6 involve powers of w = sixth root of 1:

$$F_6 = \begin{bmatrix} I & D \\ I & -D \end{bmatrix} \begin{bmatrix} F_3 & \\ & F_3 \end{bmatrix} \begin{bmatrix} & P & \end{bmatrix}.$$

Write down these factors with $1, w, w^2$ in D and powers of w^2 in F_3. Multiply!

7 By analogy with the discrete sine $(0, 1, 0, -1)$ what is the discrete cosine vector $(N = 4)$? What is its transform?

8 Put the vector $c = (1, 0, 1, 0)$ through the three steps of the FFT to find $y = Fc$. Do the same for $c = (0, 1, 0, 1)$.

9 Compute $y = F_8 c$ by the three FFT steps for $c = (1, 0, 1, 0, 1, 0, 1, 0)$. Repeat the computation for $c = (0, 1, 0, 1, 0, 1, 0, 1)$.

10 If $w = e^{2\pi i/64}$ then w^2 and $\sqrt{w}$ are among the ____ and ____ roots of 1.

11 (a) Draw all the sixth roots of 1 on the unit circle. Prove they add to zero.

(b) What are the three cube roots of 1? Do they also add to zero?

Problems 12–14 give an important speedup for the transform of real f's.

12 If the vector f is *real*, show that its transform c has the crucial property $\overline{c}_{N-k} = c_k$. This is the analog of $\overline{c}_{-k} = c_k$ for Fourier series $f(x) = \sum c_k e^{ikx}$. Start from

$$c_{N-k} = \frac{1}{N} \sum_{j=0}^{N-1} f_j w^{j(N-k)}. \quad \text{Use } w^N = 1, w^{-1} = \overline{w}, \overline{f}_j = f_j, \text{ to find } \overline{c}_{N-k}.$$

13 The DFT of *two real vectors* f and g comes from one complex DFT of $h = f + ig$. From the transform b of h, show that the transforms c and d of f and g are

$$c_k = \frac{1}{2}(b_k + \overline{b}_{N-k}) \quad \text{and} \quad d_k = \frac{i}{2}(\overline{b}_{N-k} - b_k).$$

14 To speed up the DFT of *one real vector* f, separate it into half-length vectors $f_{\mathbf{even}}$ and $f_{\mathbf{odd}}$. From $h = f_{\mathbf{even}} + i f_{\mathbf{odd}}$ find its M-point transform b (for $M = \frac{1}{2}N$). Then form the transforms c and d of $f_{\mathbf{even}}$ and $f_{\mathbf{odd}}$ as in Problem 13. Use equation (17) to construct the transform $\widehat{f}$ from c and d.

Note For real f, this reduces the number $\frac{1}{2}N \log_2 N$ of *complex* multiplications by $\frac{1}{2}$. Each complex $(a + ib)(c + id)$ requires only three real multiplications (not 4) with an extra addition.

15 The columns of the Fourier matrix F are the *eigenvectors* of the *cyclic* (not odd-even) permutation P. Multiply PF to find the eigenvalues λ_1 to λ_4 of P:

$$\begin{bmatrix} 0 & 1 & 0 & 0 \\ 0 & 0 & 1 & 0 \\ 0 & 0 & 0 & 1 \\ 1 & 0 & 0 & 0 \end{bmatrix} \begin{bmatrix} 1 & 1 & 1 & 1 \\ 1 & i & i^2 & i^3 \\ 1 & i^2 & i^4 & i^6 \\ 1 & i^3 & i^6 & i^9 \end{bmatrix} = \begin{bmatrix} 1 & 1 & 1 & 1 \\ 1 & i & i^2 & i^3 \\ 1 & i^2 & i^4 & i^6 \\ 1 & i^3 & i^6 & i^9 \end{bmatrix} \begin{bmatrix} \lambda_1 & & & \\ & \lambda_2 & & \\ & & \lambda_3 & \\ & & & \lambda_4 \end{bmatrix}.$$

This is $PF = F\Lambda$ or $P = F\Lambda F^{-1}$. The eigenvector matrix for P is F.

16 The equation $\det(P - \lambda I) = 0$ reduces to $\lambda^4 = 1$. Again the eigenvalues of P are ____. Which permutation matrix has eigenvalues = cube roots of 1?

17 Two eigenvectors of this "circulant matrix" C are $(1, 1, 1, 1)$ and $(1, i, i^2, i^3)$. Multiply these vectors by C to find the two eigenvalues λ_0 and λ_1:

$$\textbf{Circulant matrix} \quad \begin{bmatrix} c_0 & c_1 & c_2 & c_3 \\ c_3 & c_0 & c_1 & c_2 \\ c_2 & c_3 & c_0 & c_1 \\ c_1 & c_2 & c_3 & c_0 \end{bmatrix} \quad \text{has} \quad C \begin{bmatrix} 1 \\ 1 \\ 1 \\ 1 \end{bmatrix} = \lambda_0 \begin{bmatrix} 1 \\ 1 \\ 1 \\ 1 \end{bmatrix}.$$

Notice that $C = c_0 I + c_1 P + c_2 P^2 + c_3 P^3$ with the cyclic permutation P in Problem 15. Therefore $C = F(c_0 I + c_1 \Lambda + c_2 \Lambda^2 + c_3 \Lambda^3) F^{-1}$. That matrix in parentheses is diagonal. It contains the ____ of C.

18 Find the eigenvalues of the cyclic $-1, 2, -1$ matrix from $2I - \Lambda - \Lambda^3$ in Problem 17. The -1's in the corners make the second difference matrix periodic:

$$C = \begin{bmatrix} 2 & -1 & 0 & -1 \\ -1 & 2 & -1 & 0 \\ 0 & -1 & 2 & -1 \\ -1 & 0 & -1 & 2 \end{bmatrix} \quad \text{has } (c_0, c_1, c_2, c_3) = (2, -1, 0, -1)\,.$$

19 An even vector $c = (a, b, d, b)$ produces a ____ circulant matrix. Its eigenvalues are real. An odd vector $c = (0, e, 0, -e)$ produces a ____ circulant matrix with imaginary eigenvalues.

20 To multiply $C = FEF^{-1}$ times a vector x, we can multiply $F(E(F^{-1}x))$. The direct Cx uses n^2 separate multiplications. The Fourier matrices F and F^{-1} and the eigenvalue matrix E use only $n \log_2 n + n$ multiplications. How many of those come from E, how many from F, and how many from F^{-1}?

21 How can you quickly compute these four components of Fc if you know $c_0 + c_2$, $c_0 - c_2$, $c_1 + c_3$, $c_1 - c_3$? You are finding the Fast Fourier Transform!

$$Fc = \begin{bmatrix} c_0 & + & c_1 & + & c_2 & + & c_3 \\ c_0 & + & ic_1 & + & i^2c_2 & + & i^3c_3 \\ c_0 & + & i^2c_1 & + & i^4c_2 & + & i^6c_3 \\ c_0 & + & i^3c_1 & + & i^6c_2 & + & i^9c_3 \end{bmatrix}.$$

4.4 CONVOLUTION AND SIGNAL PROCESSING

Convolution answers a question that we unavoidably ask. When $\sum c_k e^{ikx}$ multiplies $\sum d_k e^{ikx}$ (call those functions $f(x)$ and $g(x)$), **what are the Fourier coefficients of** $f(x)g(x)$? The answer is not $c_k d_k$. Those are *not* the coefficients of $h(x) = f(x)g(x)$. The correct coefficients of $(\sum c_k e^{ikx})(\sum d_k e^{ikx})$ come from *"convolving"* the vector of c's with the vector of d's. That convolution is written $\boldsymbol{c} * \boldsymbol{d}$.

Before I explain convolution, let me ask a second question. **What function does have the Fourier coefficients $\boldsymbol{c_k d_k}$?** This time we are multiplying in "transform space." In that case we should convolve $f(x)$ with $g(x)$ in "x-space." **Multiplication in one domain is convolution in the other domain**:

Convolution Rules	The multiplication $\boldsymbol{f(x)g(x)}$ has Fourier coefficients $\boldsymbol{c * d}$ Multiplying $2\pi \boldsymbol{c_k d_k}$ gives the coefficients of $\boldsymbol{f(x) * g(x)}$

Our job is to define those convolutions $c * d$ and $f * g$, and to see how useful they are.

The same convolution rules hold for the discrete N-point transforms. Those are easy to show by examples, because the sums are finite. The new twist is that the discrete convolutions have to be "cyclic", so we write $c \circledast d$. All the sums have N terms, because higher powers of w fold back into lower powers. They circle around. *N is the same as 0 because $w^N = w^0 = 1$.*

The vectors c and d and $c \circledast d$ all have N components. I will start with N-point examples because they are easier to see. We just multiply polynomials. *Cyclically.*

Example 1 What are the coefficients of $f(w) = 1 + 2w + 4w^2$ times $g(w) = 3 + 5w^2$ if $w^3 = 1$? This is **cyclic convolution** with $N = 3$.

$$\begin{array}{ll} \textbf{Non-cyclic} & (1+2w+4w^2)(3+0w+5w^2) = 3 + 6w + 17w^2 + 10w^3 + 20w^4 \\ \textbf{Cyclic} & (1+2w+4w^2)(3+0w+5w^2) = \underline{\quad} + \underline{\quad} w + \underline{\quad} w^2 . \end{array} \tag{1}$$

The w^2 term comes from 1 times $5w^2$, and $2w$ times $0w$, and $4w^2$ times 3: Total $\boldsymbol{17w^2}$.

The w term comes from $2w$ times 3, and $4w^2$ times $5w^2$ (because $w^4 = w$): Total $\boldsymbol{26w}$.

The constant term is $(1)(3) + (2)(5) + (4)(0)$ (because $(w)(w^2) = 1$): Total **13**.

$$\textbf{Cyclic Convolution} \qquad c \circledast d = (1,2,4) \circledast (3,0,5) = (13, 26, 17) . \tag{2}$$

Underneath this example is third-grade multiplication! For $w = 10$ the multiplication is $f = 421$ times $g = 503$. But teachers could get disturbed when 17 appears and you don't carry 1. That is just a difference of opinion. The serious reaction is when you say that w^3 counts the same as 1. The cyclic answer is 13 plus $26w$ plus $17w^2$.

Compare cyclic $c \circledast d$ with non-cyclic $c * d$. Read from right to left because $w = 10$:

$$
\begin{array}{ccccc}
 & & 4 & 2 & 1 \\
 & & 5 & 0 & 3 \\
\hline
 & & 12 & 6 & 3 \\
 & \mathbf{0} & 0 & 0 & \\
\mathbf{20} & \mathbf{10} & 5 & & \\
\hline
20 & 10 & 17 & 6 & 3
\end{array}
\qquad
\begin{array}{c}
\textbf{non-cyclic} \\
\text{right to left} \\
\boldsymbol{c * d}
\end{array}
\qquad\qquad
\begin{array}{ccc}
4 & 2 & 1 \\
5 & 0 & 3 \\
\hline
12 & 6 & 3 \\
0 & 0 & \mathbf{0} \\
5 & \mathbf{20} & \mathbf{10} \\
\hline
17 & 26 & 13
\end{array}
\qquad
\begin{array}{c}
\textbf{cyclic} \\
\text{right to left} \\
\boldsymbol{c \circledast d}
\end{array}
$$

That product $3 + 60 + 1700 + 10000 + 200000$ is the correct answer for 421 times 503. If it gets marked wrong for not carrying, don't forget that the life of teachers (and professors) is not easy. Just when we thought we understood multiplication...

Example 2 Multiply $f(x) = 1 + 2e^{ix} + 4e^{2ix}$ times $g(x) = 3 + 5e^{2ix}$. The answer is $3 + 6e^{ix} + 17e^{2ix} + 10e^{3ix} + 20e^{4ix}$. This shows **non-cyclic convolution**.

The e^{2ix} coefficient in $f(x)g(x)$ is the same $(4)(3) + (2)(0) + (1)(5) = 17$ as before. Now there is also $10e^{3ix} + 20e^{4ix}$ and the cyclic property $w^3 = 1$ is gone.

Non-cyclic Convolution $\quad c * d = (1, 2, 4) * (3, 0, 5) = (3, 6, 17, 10, 20)\,. \qquad (3)$

This non-cyclic convolution is produced by MATLAB's **conv** command:

$$c = [\ 1 \quad 2 \quad 4\ ];\ \ d = [\ 3 \quad 0 \quad 5\ ];\ \ \mathbf{conv}(c, d) \ \text{ produces } \ c * d\,.$$

If c has length L and d has length N, then $\mathbf{conv}(c, d)$ has length $L + N - 1$.

Equation (5) will show that the nth component of $c * d$ is $\sum \boldsymbol{c_k d_{n-k}}$.

These subscripts k and $n - k$ add to n. We are collecting **all pairs** $\boldsymbol{c_k w^k}$ **and** $\boldsymbol{d_{n-k} w^{n-k}}$ **whose product yields** $\boldsymbol{w^n}$. This eye-catching $k + (n - k) = n$ is the mark of a convolution.

Cyclic convolution has no MATLAB command. But $c \circledast d$ is easy to construct by folding back the non-cyclic part. Now c and d and $c \circledast d$ have the same length N:

$$
\begin{array}{rcll}
q & = & [\ \mathsf{conv}(c, d) \quad 0\ ]; & \%\ \text{The extra zero gives length } 2N \\
\mathbf{cconv} & = & q(1:N) + q(N+1:N+N)\,; & \%\ \mathbf{cconv} = c \circledast d \text{ has length } N
\end{array}
$$

The nth component of $c \circledast d$ is still a sum of $c_k d_l$, but now $k + l = n \ (mod\ N) =$ remainder after dividing by N. That expression ***mod N*** is the cyclic part, coming from $w^N = 1$. So $\mathbf{1 + 2 = 0(}\boldsymbol{mod}\ \mathbf{3)}$. Here are convolution and cyclic convolution:

Discrete convolution $\quad (c * d)_n = \sum c_k d_{n-k} \qquad (c \circledast d)_n = \sum c_k d_l \text{ for } k + l = n (mod\ N) \qquad (4)$

Infinite Convolution

Convolution still applies when $f(x)$ and $g(x)$ and $f(x)g(x)$ have infinitely many terms. We are ready to see the rule for $c * d$, when $\sum c_k e^{ikx}$ multiplies $\sum d_l e^{ilx}$. *What is the coefficient of e^{inx} in the result?*

1. e^{inx} comes from multiplying e^{ikx} times e^{ilx} when $k + l = n$.
2. The product $(c_k e^{ikx})(d_l e^{ilx})$ equals $c_k d_l e^{inx}$ when $k + l = n$.
3. The e^{inx} term in $f(x)g(x)$ contains ***every product $c_k d_l$ in which $l = n - k$.***

Add these products $c_k d_l = c_k d_{n-k}$ to find the coefficient of e^{inx}. Convolution combines all products $c_k d_{n-k}$ whose indices add to n:

Infinite Convolution The nth component of $c * d$ is $\displaystyle\sum_{k=-\infty}^{\infty} c_k d_{n-k}$. (5)

Example 3 The "identity vector" δ in convolution has exactly one nonzero coefficient $\delta_0 = 1$. Then δ gives the Fourier coefficients of the unit function $f(x) = 1$. Multiplying $f(x) = 1$ times $g(x)$ gives $g(x)$, so convolving $\delta * d$ gives d:

$$\boldsymbol{\delta} * \boldsymbol{d} = (\ldots, 0, 1, 0, \ldots) * (\ldots, d_{-1}, d_0, d_1, \ldots) = \boldsymbol{d}\,. \tag{6}$$

The only term in $\sum \delta_k d_{n-k}$ is $\delta_0 d_n$. That term is d_n. So $\delta * d$ recovers d.

Example 4 The **autocorrelation** of a vector c is the convolution of c with its "flip" or "conjugate transpose" or "time reversal" $d(n) = \overline{c(-n)}$. The real signal $c = (1, 2, 4)$ has $d_0 = 1$ and $d_{-1} = 2$ and $d_{-2} = 4$. The convolution $c * d$ is the autocorrelation of c:

Autocorrelation $(\ldots, 1, 2, 4, \ldots) * (\ldots, 4, 2, 1, \ldots) = (\ldots, 4, 10, 21, 10, 4, \ldots)$. (7)

The dots all represent zeros. The autocorrelation $4, 10, 21, 10, 4$ is symmetric around the zero position. To be honest, I did not actually use the convolution formula $\sum c_k d_{n-k}$. It is easier to multiply $f(x) = \sum c_k e^{ikx}$ times its conjugate $\overline{f(x)} = \sum \bar{c}_k e^{-ikx} = \sum d_k e^{ikx}$:

$$\underset{\displaystyle c_0 \quad\;\; c_1 \qquad\quad c_2}{\overset{\displaystyle \boldsymbol{f(x)}}{(1 + 2e^{ix} + 4e^{2ix})}}\;\underset{\displaystyle d_{-2} \qquad d_{-1} \;\; d_0}{\overset{\displaystyle \overline{\boldsymbol{f(x)}}}{(4e^{-2ix} + 2e^{-ix} + 1)}} = \underset{\text{autocorrelation of } c}{\overset{\displaystyle |\boldsymbol{f(x)}|^2}{4e^{-2ix} + 10e^{-ix} + 21 + 10e^{ix} + 4e^{2ix}}} \tag{8}$$

This answer $f(x)\overline{f(x)}$ (often written $f(x)f^*(x)$) is always real, and never negative.

Note The autocorrelation $f(t) * \overline{f(-t)}$ is extremely important. Its transform is $|c_k|^2$ (discrete case) or $|\widehat{f}(k)|^2$ (continuous case). That transform is never negative. This is the **power spectral density** that appears in Section 4.5.

In MATLAB, the autocorrelation of c is conv(c, fliplr(c)). The left-right flip produces the correct $d(n) = c(-n)$. When the vector c is complex, use conj(fliplr(c)).

Convolution of Functions

Reverse the process and multiply c_k times d_k. Now the numbers $2\pi c_k d_k$ are the coefficients of the convolution $f(x) * g(x)$. This is a 2π-periodic convolution because $f(x)$ and $g(x)$ are periodic. Instead of the sum of $c_k d_{n-k}$ in convolving coefficients, we have the integral of $f(t)g(x-t)$ in convolving functions.

Please notice: *The indices k and $n-k$ add to n. Similarly t and $x-t$ add to x:*

Convolution of Periodic Functions $$(f * g)(x) = \int_0^{2\pi} f(t)\, g(x-t)\, dt\,. \qquad (9)$$

Example 5 Convolve $f(x) = \sin x$ with itself. Check $2\pi c_k d_k$ in the convolution rule.

Solution The convolution $(\sin x) * (\sin x)$ is $\int_0^{2\pi} \sin t \sin(x-t) dt$. Separate $\sin(x-t)$ into $\sin x \cos t - \cos x \sin t$. The integral produces (to my surprise) $-\pi \cos x$:

$$(\sin x) * (\sin x) = \sin x \int_0^{2\pi} \sin t \cos t\, dt - \cos x \int_0^{2\pi} \sin^2 t\, dt = -\pi \cos x\,.$$

For $(\sin x) * (\sin x)$, the convolution rule has $c_k = d_k$. The coefficients of $\sin x = \frac{1}{2i}(e^{ix} - e^{-ix})$ are $\frac{1}{2i}$ and $-\frac{1}{2i}$. Square them to get $-\frac{1}{4}$ and multiply by 2π. Then $2\pi c_k d_k = -\frac{\pi}{2}$ gives the correct coefficients of $-\pi \cos x = -\frac{\pi}{2}(e^{ix} + e^{-ix})$.

Note that *autocorrelation* would convolve $f(x) = \sin x$ with $f(-x) = -\sin x$. The result is $+\pi \cos x$. Its coefficients $+\frac{\pi}{2}$ are now positive because they are $2\pi |c_k|^2$.

Example 6 If $I(x)$ is the integral of $f(x)$ and $D(x)$ is the derivative of $g(x)$, show that $\boldsymbol{I * D = f * g}$. *Give the reason in x-space and also in k-space.* This is my favorite.

Solution In k-space, $I * D = f * g$ is quick from the rules for integrals and derivatives. The integral $I(x)$ has coefficients $\boldsymbol{c_k / ik}$ and the derivative $D(x)$ has coefficients $\boldsymbol{ik\, d_k}$. Multiplying those coefficients, ik cancels $1/ik$. The same $c_k d_k$ appears for $I * D$ and $f * g$. Actually we should require $c_0 = 0$, to avoid dividing by $k = 0$.

In x-space, we use integration by parts (a great rule). The integral of $f(t)$ is $I(t)$. The derivative of $g(x-t)$ is *minus* $D(x-t)$. Since our functions are periodic, the integrated term $I(t)g(x-t)$ is the same at 0 and 2π. It vanishes to leave $f * g = I * D$.

After those examples, we confirm that $\boldsymbol{f * g}$ ***has coefficients*** $\boldsymbol{2\pi c_k d_k}$. First,

$$\int_0^{2\pi} (f * g)(x) e^{-ikx} dx = \int_0^{2\pi} \left[\int_0^{2\pi} f(t) g(x-t) e^{-ik[t+(x-t)]}\, dt \right] dx\,. \qquad (10)$$

With the x-integral first, bring out $f(t)e^{-ikt}$. This separates (10) into two integrals:

$$\int_0^{2\pi} f(t) e^{-ikt} dt \int_0^{2\pi} g(x-t) e^{-ik(x-t)} dx \quad \text{which is} \quad (2\pi c_k)(2\pi d_k)\,. \qquad (11)$$

In that last integral we substituted s for $x-t$. The new limits $s=0-t$ and $s=2\pi-t$ still cover a full period, and the integral is $2\pi d_k$. Dividing (10) and (11) by 2π gives the function / coefficient convolution rule: ***The coefficients of $f*g$ are $2\pi c_k d_k$.***

Cyclic Convolution Rules

This section began with the cyclic convolution $(1,2,4)\circledast(3,0,5)=(13,26,17)$. Those are the coefficients in $fg=(1+2w+4w^2)(3+5w^2)=(13+26w+17w^2)$ when $w^3=1$. A useful check is to set $w=1$. Adding each set of coefficients gives $(7)(8)=(56)$.

The discrete convolution rule connects this cyclic convolution $c\circledast d$ with a multiplication of function values $f_j g_j$. Please keep the vectors f and g in j-space separate from c and d in k-space. The convolution rule *does not say* that $c_k \circledast d_k$ equals $f_k g_k$!

The correct rule for $c\circledast d$ transforms the vector with components $f_j g_j$ back into k-space. Writing $f=Fc$ and $g=Fd$ produces an identity that is true for all vectors. In MATLAB, the entry by entry product $(f_0 g_0,\ldots,f_{N-1}g_{N-1})$ is the N-vector $f\,.\!*\,g$. The dot removes summation and leaves N separate components $f_j g_j$. Of course $*$ in MATLAB does *not* mean convolution, and components are numbered 1 to N:

Cyclic Convolution: Multiply in j-space $\quad c\circledast d \text{ is } F^{-1}((Fc)\,.\!*\,(Fd)) \qquad (12)$

In MATLAB, this is $N*\text{fft}(\text{ifft}(c)\,.\!*\,\text{ifft}(d))$.

Suppose the convolution is $f\circledast g$. This is a **multiplication in k-space**. Possibly the reason for no cyclic convolution command in MATLAB is the simplicity of this one-line code for cconv(f,g). It copies (12) with ifft and fft reversed:

$$c=\text{fft}(f); \quad d=\text{fft}(g); \quad cd=c\,.\!*\,d; \quad f\circledast g=\text{ifft}(cd); \qquad (13)$$

Combined into one command this cconv is $\text{ifft}(\text{fft}(f)\,.\!*\,\text{fft}(g))$. The factor N disappears when we do it this way, multiplying in k-space.

I have to say that the convolution rule is more bad news for the third-grade teacher. Long multiplication is being taught the slow way (as all third-graders have suspected). When we multiply N-digit numbers, we are doing N^2 separate multiplications for the convolution. *This is inefficient.* Three FFT's make convolution much faster.

One more thing. We may want $c*d$ and the FFT is producing the cyclic $c\circledast d$. To fix that, add $N-1$ zeros to c and d so that cyclic and non-cyclic convolution involve exactly the same multiplications. If c and d have length N, $c*d$ has length $2N-1$:

$$C=[\;c\;\;\text{zeros}(1,N-1)\;];\quad D=[\;d\;\;\text{zeros}(1,N-1)\;];\quad \text{then } c*d \text{ is } C\circledast D. \qquad (14)$$

For $N=2$, this $c*d$ is $(c_0,c_1,0)\circledast(d_0,d_1,0)=(c_0d_0,\,c_0d_1+c_1d_0,\,c_1d_1)=C\circledast D$.

Convolution by Matrices

You have the essential ideas of $c * d$ and $c \circledast d$—their link to multiplication allows us to convolve quickly. I want to look again at those sums $\sum c_k d_{n-k}$, to see a matrix C multiplying a vector d. Convolution is linear so there has to be a matrix.

In the cyclic case, C is a **circulant matrix** C_N. The non-cyclic case has an infinite **constant-diagonal matrix** C_∞ (called a *Toeplitz matrix*). Here are those convolution matrices, cyclic C_N and non-cyclic C_∞, with the c's in every row and column. Notice how the diagonals wrap around in C_N:

Circulant matrix $$C_N d = \begin{bmatrix} c_0 & c_{N-1} & \cdot & \cdot & c_1 \\ c_1 & c_0 & c_{N-1} & \cdot & c_2 \\ c_2 & c_1 & c_0 & \cdot & \cdot \\ \cdot & \cdot & c_1 & c_0 & \cdot \\ c_{N-1} & \cdot & c_2 & c_1 & c_0 \end{bmatrix} \begin{bmatrix} d_0 \\ d_1 \\ \cdot \\ \cdot \\ d_{N-1} \end{bmatrix} = c \circledast d \qquad (15)$$

Toeplitz matrix $$C_\infty d = \begin{bmatrix} \cdot & \cdot & c_{-2} & \cdot & \cdot \\ \cdot & c_0 & c_{-1} & c_{-2} & \cdot \\ c_2 & c_1 & c_0 & c_{-1} & c_{-2} \\ \cdot & c_2 & c_1 & c_0 & \cdot \\ \cdot & \cdot & c_2 & \cdot & \cdot \end{bmatrix} \begin{bmatrix} \cdot \\ d_{-1} \\ d_0 \\ d_1 \\ \cdot \end{bmatrix} = c * d \qquad (16)$$

For the circulant C_N, the all-important polynomial is $C(w) = c_0 + c_1 w + \cdots + c_{N-1} w^{N-1}$. Multiplying by $D(w)$ shows $c \circledast d$ when $w^N = 1$. For the infinite matrix, $C_\infty d$ is multiplying infinite Fourier series: w becomes e^{ix} and all $|w| = 1$ are included. Section 4.6 will show that the matrices are invertible if and only if $C(w) \neq 0$ (the inverse has to divide by C). They are positive definite if and only if $C(w) > 0$. In this case $C(w) = |F(w)|^2$ and c is the autocorrelation of f as in (8). For the matrices, this is the Cholesky factorization $C = F^{\mathrm{T}} F$.

Processing a Signal by a Filter

Filtering (the key step in signal and image processing) is a convolution. One example is a running average A (*lowpass filter*). The second difference matrix $D = K/4$ is a *highpass filter*. For now we are pretending that the signal has no start and no end. With a long signal, like the audio on a CD, endpoint errors are not a serious problem. So we use the infinite matrix, not the finite wrap-around circulant matrix.

The "second average" filter A has centered coefficients $\frac{1}{4}, \frac{2}{4}, \frac{1}{4}$ that add to 1:

Output at time n = average of three inputs $$y_n = \frac{1}{4} x_{n-1} + \frac{2}{4} x_n + \frac{1}{4} x_{n+1}.$$

In matrix notation $y = a * x$ is $y = Ax$. The filter matrix A is "Toeplitz":

Averaging filter is a convolution $a = \frac{1}{4}(.,1,2,1,.)$

$$\begin{bmatrix} \cdot \\ y_0 \\ y_1 \\ y_2 \\ \cdot \end{bmatrix} = \frac{1}{4}\begin{bmatrix} \cdot & \cdot & & & \\ 1 & 2 & 1 & & \\ & 1 & 2 & 1 & \\ & & 1 & 2 & \cdot \\ & & & \cdot & \cdot \end{bmatrix}\begin{bmatrix} x_{-1} \\ x_0 \\ x_1 \\ x_2 \\ \cdot \end{bmatrix} = Ax = a * x. \qquad (17)$$

When the input is $\boldsymbol{x}_{\mathbf{low}} = (.,1,1,1,1,.)$, the output is $y = x$. This zero frequency DC component passes unchanged through the filter, which is **lowpass**. The highest frequency input is the alternating vector $\boldsymbol{x}_{\mathbf{high}} = (.,1,-1,1,-1,.)$. In that case the output is $y = (0,0,0,0)$, and the highest frequency $\omega = \pi$ is stopped.

A lowpass filter like A will remove noise from the signal (since random noise tends to be high frequency). But filtering also blurs significant details in the input x. The big problem of signal processing is to choose the best filter.

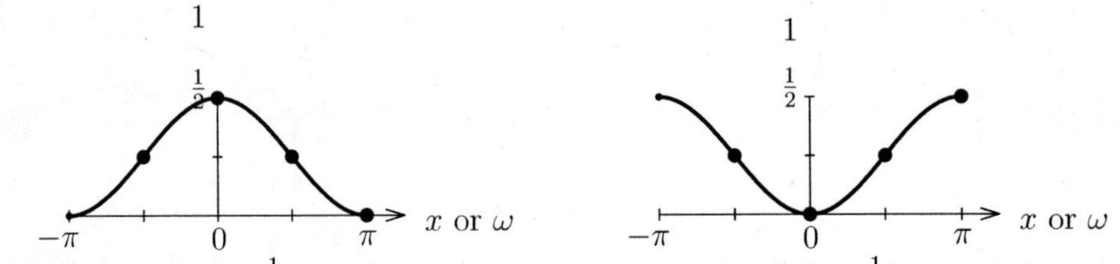

Figure 4.11: Frequency responses of the second average filter A and second difference filter D. The highpass response $D(\omega)$ is the lowpass response $A(\omega)$ shifted by π.

Frequency response $A(\omega) = \frac{1}{4}e^{-i\omega} + \frac{2}{4} + \frac{1}{4}e^{i\omega} = \frac{1}{2}(1+\cos\omega)$ $\quad \begin{matrix} A(0) = 1 \\ A(\pi) = 0 \end{matrix}$ (18)

Figure 4.11 is a graph of the frequency response $A(\omega)$, which is also written $A(e^{i\omega})$. The second graph shows the frequency response to a highpass filter $D = K/4$.

Highpass filter is $D = K/4$

$$D = \frac{1}{4}\begin{bmatrix} \cdot & \cdot & & & \\ -1 & 2 & -1 & & \\ & -1 & 2 & -1 & \\ & & -1 & 2 & -1 \\ & & & \cdot & \cdot \end{bmatrix} \qquad \text{Output } y = Dx = d * x.$$

Now the lowest frequency $\omega = 0$ (the DC term) is stopped by the filter. The all-ones input $x(n) = 1$ produces a zero output $y(n) = 0$. The highest frequency $\omega = \pi$ is passed: the alternating input $x(n) = (-1)^n$ has $Dx = x$ with eigenvalue 1. The frequencies between 0 and π have eigenvalues $D(\omega)$ between 0 and 1 in Figure 4.11b:

Highpass response $$D(\omega) = -\frac{1}{4}e^{-i\omega} + \frac{1}{2} - \frac{1}{4}e^{i\omega} = \frac{1}{2}(1 - \cos\,\omega). \qquad (19)$$

All pure frequencies $-\pi \leq \omega \leq \pi$ give eigenvectors with components $x(n) = e^{-i\omega n}$. The extreme low frequency $\omega = 0$ gave $x(n) = 1$, and the highest frequency $\omega = \pi$ gave $x(n) = (-1)^n$. The key to understanding filters is to see the response $y(n)$ or y_n or $y[n]$ to the pure input $x(n) = e^{-i\omega n}$. That response is just $A(\omega)e^{-i\omega n}$.

Better Filters

The truth is that the filters A and D are not very sharp. The purpose of a filter is to preserve a band of frequencies and destroy another band. Figure 4.11 only goes gradually between 1 and 0. The response $I(\omega)$ from an **ideal lowpass filter** is exactly 1 or 0. But we can't achieve that ideal with a finite number of filter coefficients. Figure 4.12 shows a nearly ideal FIR filter.

The vector a is called the **impulse response**, since $a * \delta = a$. Its entries are the Fourier coefficients of $A(\omega) = \sum a_n e^{-i\omega n}$. The filter is **FIR** when it has *finite* impulse response—only $d + 1$ nonzero coefficients a_n. The ideal lowpass filter is **IIR** because the Fourier coefficients of the box function $A(\omega)$ come from the sinc function.

Which polynomial to choose? If we chop off the ideal filter, the result is not good! Truncating the Fourier series for the box function produces *large overshoot* in the Gibbs phenomenon. That truncation minimizes the energy in the error (mean square error), but the maximum error and the oscillations are unacceptable.

A popular choice is an **equiripple filter**. The oscillations in the frequency response $A(\omega)$ all have the same height (or depth) in Figure 4.12. If we try to reduce the error at one of those maximum points, other errors would become larger. **A polynomial of degree d cannot change sign at $d+2$ successive points. When the error has $d + 2$ equal ripples, the maximum error is minimized.**

The command firpm (previously remez) will design this equiripple symmetric filter of length $30 + 1$. The passband-stopband interval is $.49 \leq f \leq .51$. The Signal Processing Toolbox normalizes by $f = \omega/\pi \leq 1$ (help firpm specifies the inputs).

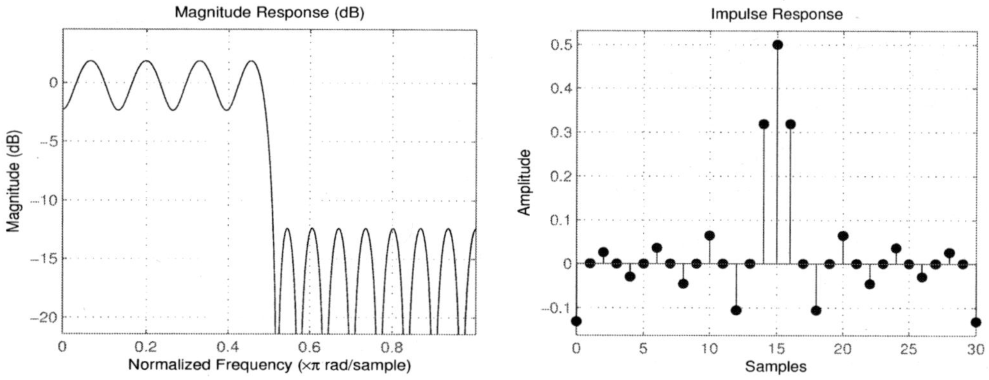

Figure 4.12: $A(\omega)$ and $a =$ firpm(30, [0, .49, .51, 1], [1 1 0 0]). Use fvtool(a).

Finite Length Signals

The key point for this book is that *filters are convolutions*: needed constantly. We are seeing the second difference matrices in a new context, as highpass filters. A is an infinite matrix when the signals $x(n)$ and $y(n)$ extend over $-\infty < n < \infty$. If we want to work with finite length signals, one way is to assume *wraparound*. The signal becomes periodic. The infinite Toeplitz matrices giving $a * x$ and $d * x$ become N by N **circulant matrices** giving $a \circledast x$ and $d \circledast x$:

Periodic signals
Circulant matrices
Cyclic convolution

$$A = \frac{1}{4}\begin{bmatrix} 2 & 1 & 0 & 1 \\ 1 & 2 & 1 & 0 \\ 0 & 1 & 2 & 1 \\ 1 & 0 & 1 & 2 \end{bmatrix} \quad \text{and} \quad D = \frac{1}{4}\begin{bmatrix} 2 & -1 & 0 & -1 \\ -1 & 2 & -1 & 0 \\ 0 & -1 & 2 & -1 \\ -1 & 0 & -1 & 2 \end{bmatrix} \tag{20}$$

The right side of Figure 4.11 shows the frequency response function $D(e^{i\omega})$ for this second difference (*highpass*) filter, at the four frequencies $\omega = 0, \pm\pi/2, \pi$:

$$D(e^{i\omega}) = -\frac{1}{4}e^{-i\omega} + \frac{2}{4} - \frac{1}{4}e^{i\omega} = \frac{1}{2}(1 - \cos\omega) \quad \text{has values} \quad \lambda = 0, \frac{1}{2}, \frac{1}{2}, 1. \tag{21}$$

The lowest frequency $\omega = 0$ corresponds to the DC input $x = (1,1,1,1)$. This is killed by the filter ($\lambda = 0$ because $2 - 1 - 1 = 0$). The second differences of a constant are zero. The highest frequency $\omega = \pi$ corresponds to the AC input $x = (1,-1,1,-1)$ which is passed by the filter, $Dx = x$. In between, the inputs $(1, i, -1, -i)$ and $(1, -i, -1, i)$ at $\omega = \pm\frac{\pi}{2}$ have outputs multiplied by $\lambda = \frac{1}{2}$. The discrete cosine $(1, 0, -1, 0)$ and discrete sine $(0, 1, 0, -1)$ are combinations of those eigenvectors of D.

The eigenvalues of D are the discrete transform of the filter coefficients:

$$\text{Eigenvalues } \mathsf{eig}(D) = 0, \tfrac{1}{2}, 1, \tfrac{1}{2} \overset{\textbf{transform}}{\longleftrightarrow} \text{coefficients } d_k = \tfrac{2}{4}, -\tfrac{1}{4}, 0, -\tfrac{1}{4}.$$

It is not surprising that signal processing theory is mostly in the *frequency domain.* The response function tells us everything. The filter could even be implemented by the convolution rule. But here we would certainly compute Cx and Dx directly from x, with a circuit composed of multipliers and adders and delays.

We end with a light-hearted puzzle involving these two particular filters.

Puzzle. The matrices A and D illustrate a strange possibility in linear algebra. They have the *same eigenvalues and eigenvectors*, but they are not the same matrix. This seems incredible, since both matrices factor into $S\Lambda S^{-1}$ (with S = eigenvector matrix and Λ = eigenvalue matrix). How can A and D be different matrices?

The trick is in the ordering. The eigenvector $(1,1,1,1)$ goes with the eigenvalue $\lambda = 1$ of A and $\lambda = 0$ of D. The oscillating eigenvector $(1,-1,1,-1)$ has the opposite eigenvalues. *The columns of F^{-1} (also of F) are the eigenvectors for all circulants,* explained in Section 4.6. But Λ can have the eigenvalues $1, \frac{1}{2}, \frac{1}{2}, 0$ in different orders.

Worked Example: Convolution of Probabilities

Suppose p_i is the probability that a random variable equals i ($p_i \geq 0$ and $\sum p_i = 1$). *For the sum* $i+j$ of two independent samples, what is the probability c_k that $i+j = k$? For two dice, what is the probability c_7 of rolling a 7, when each $p_i = \frac{1}{6}$?

Solution 1 The sample i followed by j will appear with probability $p_i p_j$. The result $i + j = k$ is the union of mutually exclusive events (sample i followed by $j = k - i$). That probability is $p_i p_{k-i}$. Combining all the ways to add to k yields a **convolution:**

Probability of $i + j = k$ $$c_k = \sum p_i\, p_{k-i} \quad \text{or} \quad c = p * p. \tag{22}$$

For each of the dice, the probability of $i = 1, 2, \ldots, 6$ is $p_i = 1/6$. For two dice, the probability of rolling $k = 12$ is $\frac{1}{36}$. For $k = 11$ it is $\frac{2}{36}$, from 5 + 6 and 6 + 5. Two dice produce $k = 2, 3, \ldots, 12$ with probabilities $\boldsymbol{p} * \boldsymbol{p} = \boldsymbol{c}$ (box $*$ box = hat):

$$\frac{1}{6}(1,1,1,1,1,1) * \frac{1}{6}(1,1,1,1,1,1) = \frac{1}{36}(1,2,3,4,5,6,5,4,3,2,1). \tag{23}$$

Solution 2 The "**generating function**" is $P(z) = (z + z^2 + \cdots + z^6)/6$, the polynomial with coefficients p_i. For two dice the generating function is $\boldsymbol{P^2(z)}$.

This is $C(z) = \frac{1}{36}z^2 + \frac{2}{36}z^3 + \cdots + \frac{1}{36}z^{12}$ (coefficients c_k times powers z^k), by the convolution rule for (23). Multiply P times P when you convolve p with p.

Repeated Trials: Binomial and Poisson

Binomial probabilities come from n coin flips. The chance of heads is p on each flip. The chance b_i of i heads in n flips comes from convolving n copies of $(1 - p, p)$:

Binomial $b_i = \binom{n}{i} p^i (1-p)^{n-i}$ from $(1-p, p) * \cdots * (1-p, p)$

Generating function $\boldsymbol{B(z) = (pz + 1 - p)^n}$

The factor $pz + 1 - p$ is the simple generator for one trial (probability p and $1 - p$ of events 1 and 0). By taking the nth power, b_i is the correct probability for the sum of n independent samples: convolution rule! Differentiating $B(z)$ at $z = 1$ gives the mean np (expected number of heads in n flips). Now try the Poisson distribution:

Poisson probabilities $p_i = e^{-\lambda}\, \lambda^i / i!$

Generating function $\boldsymbol{P(z)} = \sum p_i z^i = e^{-\lambda} \sum \lambda^i z^i / i! = \boldsymbol{e^{-\lambda} e^{\lambda z}}$

Squaring that generating function, $P^2 = e^{-2\lambda} e^{2\lambda z}$ is correct for the sum of two Poisson samples. So the sum is still Poisson with parameter 2λ. And differentiating $P(z)$ at $z = 1$ gives mean $= \lambda$ for each sample.

The central limit theorem looks at the sum of n samples as $n \to \infty$. It tells us that the (scaled) limit of many convolutions is Gaussian.

Problem Set 4.4

1 (from age 7) **When you multiply numbers you are convolving their digits.** We have to "carry" numbers in actual multiplication, while convolution leaves them in the same decimal place. What is t?

$$(12)(15) = (180) \quad \text{but} \quad (\ldots,1,2,\ldots) * (\ldots,1,5,\ldots) = (\ldots,1,7,t,\ldots)\,.$$

2 Check the cyclic convolution rule $F(c \circledast d) = (Fc)\,.\!*\,(Fd)$ directly for $N = 2$:

$$F = \begin{bmatrix} 1 & 1 \\ 1 & -1 \end{bmatrix} \quad Fc = \begin{bmatrix} c_0 + c_1 \\ c_0 - c_1 \end{bmatrix} \quad Fd = \begin{bmatrix} d_0 + d_1 \\ d_0 - d_1 \end{bmatrix} \quad c \circledast d = \begin{bmatrix} c_0 d_0 + c_1 d_1 \\ c_0 d_1 + c_1 d_0 \end{bmatrix}$$

3 Factor the 2 by 2 circulant $C = \left[\begin{smallmatrix} c_0 & c_1 \\ c_1 & c_0 \end{smallmatrix}\right]$ into $F^{-1}\mathsf{diag}(Fc)F$ from Problem 2.

4 The right side of (12) shows the fast way to convolve. Three fast transforms will compute Fc and Fd and transform back by F^{-1}. For $N = 128, 1024, 8192$ create random vectors c and d. Compare tic; cconv(c, d); toc; with this FFT way.

5 Write the steps to prove the Cyclic Convolution Rule (13) following this outline: $F(c \circledast d)$ has entries $\sum(\sum c_n d_{k-n})w^{jk}$. The inner sum on n produces $c \circledast d$ and the outer sum on k multiplies by F. Write w^{jk} as w^{jn} times $w^{j(k-n)}$. When you sum first on k and last on n, the double sum splits into $\sum c_n w^{jn} \sum d_k w^{jk}$.

6 What is the identity vector δ_N in cyclic convolution? It gives $\delta_N \circledast d = d$.

7 Which vectors s and s_N give ***one-step delays***, noncyclic and cyclic?

$$s * (\ldots, d_0, d_1, \ldots) = (\ldots, d_{-1}, d_0, \ldots) \text{ and } s_N \circledast (d_0, \ldots, d_{N-1}) = (d_{N-1}, d_0, \ldots).$$

8 (a) Compute directly the convolution $f \circledast f$ (cyclic convolution with $N = 6$) when $f = (0,0,0,1,0,0)$. Connect $(f_0, \ldots, f_5)$ with $f_0 + f_1 w + \cdots + f_5 w^5$.

(b) What is the Discrete Transform $c = (c_0, c_1, c_2, c_3, c_4, c_5)$ of this f?

(c) Compute $f \circledast f$ by using c in "transform space" and transforming back.

9 Multiplying $C_\infty D_\infty$ will convolve $c * d$ and multiply $(\sum c_k e^{ikx})(\sum d_k e^{ikx})$. If $D = C^{\mathrm{T}}$ is real, this is an **autocorrelation** of c leading to $|c_k e^{ikx}|^2 > 0$. For $c = 1,3,4$ show directly that the diagonals of $CC^{\mathrm{T}} = C^{\mathrm{T}}C$ (positive definite) agree with $(1,3,4) * (4,3,1) = (4,10,21,10,4)$ in equation (8).

10 The chance of grade $i = (70, 80, 90, 100)$ on one quiz is $p = (.3, .4, .2, .1)$. What are the probabilities c_k for the sum of two grades to be $k = (140, 150, \ldots, 200)$? You need to convolve $c = p * p$ or multiply 3421 by 3421 (without carrying).

11 What is the expected value (mean m) for the grade on that quiz? The generating function is $P(z) = .3z^{70} + .4z^{80} + .2z^{90} + .1z^{100}$. Show that $m = p'(1)$.

12 What is the mean M for the total grade on two quizzes, with those probabilities c_k? I expect $M = 2m$. The derivative of $(P(z))^2$ is $2P(z)P'(z) = (2)(1)(m)$ at $z = 1$.

13 With 9 coefficients, which firpm filter is closest to ideal in Figure 4.12?

4.5 FOURIER INTEGRALS

A Fourier series is perfect for a 2π-periodic function. The only frequencies in $\sum c_k e^{ikx}$ are whole numbers k. *When $f(x)$ is not periodic, all frequencies k are allowed.* That sum has to be replaced by an integral $\int \widehat{f}(k)e^{ikx}\,dk$ over $-\infty < k < \infty$.

The **Fourier transform** $\widehat{f}(k)$ measures the presence of e^{ikx} in the function $f(x)$. In changing from c_k to $\widehat{f}(k)$, you will see how the important things survive.

I can write the integral transforms by analogy with the formulas of Fourier series:

Transform $f(x)$ to $\widehat{f}(k)$

$$c_k = \frac{1}{2\pi}\int_{-\pi}^{\pi} f(x)e^{-ikx}\,dx \quad \text{becomes} \quad \widehat{f}(k) = \int_{-\infty}^{\infty} f(x)e^{-ikx}\,dx \qquad (1)$$

Reconstruction $\widehat{f}(k)$ to $f(x)$

$$f(x) = \sum_{k=-\infty}^{\infty} c_k e^{-ikx} \quad \text{becomes} \quad f(x) = \frac{1}{2\pi}\int_{-\infty}^{\infty} \widehat{f}(k)e^{ikx}\,dk \qquad (2)$$

The analysis step (1) finds the density $\widehat{f}(k)$ of each pure oscillation e^{ikx}, inside $f(x)$. The synthesis step (2) combines all those oscillations $\widehat{f}(k)e^{ikx}$, to reconstruct $f(x)$.

At the zero frequency $k = 0$, notice $\widehat{f}(0) = \int_{-\infty}^{\infty} f(x)\,dx$. This is the area under the graph of $f(x)$. Thus $\widehat{f}(0)$ compares with the *average value* c_0 in a Fourier series.

We expect the graph of $|f(x)|$ to enclose a finite area. In applications $f(x)$ might drop off as quickly as e^{-x} or e^{-x^2}. It might have a "heavy tail" and decay like a power of $1/x$. **The smoothness of $f(x)$ controls the dropoff in the transform $\widehat{f}(k)$.** We approach this subject by examples—here are the first five.

Five Essential Transforms

Example 1 The transform of $f(x) =$ **delta function** $= \delta(x)$ is a constant (no decay):

$$\widehat{f}(k) = \widehat{\delta}(k) = \int_{-\infty}^{\infty} \delta(x)\,e^{-ikx}\,dx = 1 \quad \text{for all frequencies } k\,. \qquad (3)$$

The integral picks out the value 1 of e^{-ikx}, at the "spike point" $x = 0$.

Example 2 The transform of a **centered square pulse** is a **sinc function** of k:

Square pulse

$$f(x) = \left\{ \begin{matrix} 1 & -L \le x \le L \\ 0 & |x| > L \end{matrix} \right\} = \text{box function}$$

The integral from $-\infty$ to ∞ reduces to an easy integral from $-L$ to L. Notice $\widehat{f}(0) = 2L$:

$2L$ sinc kL

$$\widehat{f}(k) = \int_{-L}^{L} e^{-ikx}\,dx = \frac{e^{-ikL} - e^{ikL}}{-ik} = \frac{2\sin kL}{k} \qquad (4)$$

Example 3 The transform of a **one-sided decaying pulse** is $1/(a+ik)$:

Exponential decay $$f(x) = \left\{ \begin{matrix} e^{-ax} & x \geq 0 \\ 0 & x < 0 \end{matrix} \right\}$$

Now the integral is from 0 to ∞, and we integrate $e^{-(a+ik)x}$. The area is $\widehat{f}(0) = \frac{1}{a}$:

Pole at $k = -ia$ $$\widehat{f}(k) = \int_0^\infty e^{-ax} e^{-ikx}\, dx = \left[\frac{e^{-(a+ik)x}}{-(a+ik)} \right]_0^\infty = \frac{1}{a+ik}. \qquad (5)$$

We are assuming $a > 0$ (for decay). It is somehow very pleasant to use $e^{-a\infty} = 0$. This transform $1/(a+ik)$ drops off slowly, like $1/k$, because $f(x)$ has a jump at $x = 0$.

Example 4 An **even decaying pulse** has an even transform $\widehat{f}(k) = 2a/(a^2+k^2)$:

Two-sided pulse $$f(x) = e^{-a|x|} = \left\{ \begin{matrix} e^{-ax} & \text{for } x \geq 0 \\ e^{ax} & \text{for } x \leq 0 \end{matrix} \right\}$$

One-sided + one-sided $$\widehat{f}(k) = \frac{1}{a+ik} + \frac{1}{a-ik} = \frac{2a}{a^2+k^2}. \qquad (6)$$

We are adding two one-sided pulses, so add their transforms. The even pulse in Figure 4.13 has no jump at $x = 0$. But the slope drops from a to $-a$, so $\widehat{f}(k)$ decays like $2a/k^2$.

Real even functions $f(x) = f(-x)$ still lead to cosines. For the Fourier integral that means $\widehat{f}(k) = \widehat{f}(-k)$, since $\cos kx = (e^{ikx} + e^{-ikx})/2$. Real odd functions lead to sines, and $\widehat{f}(k)$ is imaginary and odd in Example 6.

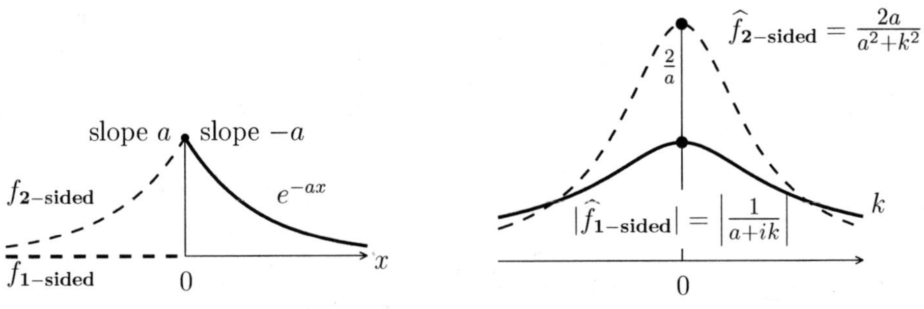

Figure 4.13: The one-sided pulse has a jump at $x = 0$, and slow $1/k$ decay in $\widehat{f}(k)$. The two-sided pulse has a corner at $x = 0$, and faster $1/k^2$ decay in $2a/(a^2+k^2)$.

Example 5 The transform of $f(x) =$ **constant function** $= 1$ is a delta $\widehat{f}(k) = 2\pi\delta(k)$.

This is a dangerous example, because $f(x) = 1$ encloses infinite area. I see it best as the limiting case $a \to 0$ in Example 4. Certainly $e^{-a|x|}$ approaches 1 as the decay rate a goes to zero. For all frequencies $k \neq 0$, the limit of $\widehat{f}(k) = 2a/(a^2+k^2)$ is $\widehat{f}(k) = 0$.

At the frequency $k = 0$ we need a delta function times 2π to recover $f(x) = 1$:

$$\text{Equation (2) reconstructs} \quad e^{-a|x|} = \frac{1}{2\pi}\int_{-\infty}^{\infty} \frac{2a}{a^2+k^2} e^{ikx}\,dk \tag{7}$$

$$\text{As } a \to 0 \text{ this becomes} \quad 1 = \frac{1}{2\pi}\int_{-\infty}^{\infty} 2\pi\delta(k)e^{ikx}\,dk \tag{8}$$

To understand equations (1) and (2), start with the Fourier series. Key idea: *Use a period T much larger than 2π.* The function $f_T(x)$ is chosen to agree with $f(x)$ from $-T/2$ to $T/2$, and then continue with period T. As $T \to \infty$ the Fourier series for f_T should approach (with the right scaling) the Fourier integral.

When the period is T instead of 2π the coefficient c_k of e^{iKx} comes from $f_T(x)$:

$$\textbf{Period } T \textbf{ with } K = k\frac{2\pi}{T} \qquad c_k = \frac{1}{T}\int_{-T/2}^{T/2} f_T(x)e^{-iKx}\,dx \tag{9}$$

The exponentials e^{iKx} have the right period T. They combine to reproduce $f_T(x)$:

$$\textbf{Fourier series with period } T \quad f_T(x) = \sum_{k=-\infty}^{\infty} c_k e^{iKx} = \sum_{k=-\infty}^{\infty} \frac{1}{T}\left[\int_{-T/2}^{T/2} f_T(x)e^{-iKx}\,dx\right] e^{iKx}. \tag{10}$$

As T gets larger, the function $f_T(x)$ agrees with $f(x)$ over a longer interval. **The sum from $k = -\infty$ to ∞ approaches an integral**. Each step in the sum changes k by 1, so K changes by $2\pi/T$; that is ΔK. We replace $1/T$ by $\Delta K/2\pi$. As $T \to \infty$, the sum in (10) becomes an integral with respect to K, and f_T approaches f:

$$\textbf{Transform to } \widehat{f}(k) \textbf{ Then recover } f(x) \quad f(x) = \int_{K=-\infty}^{\infty}\left[\int_{x=-\infty}^{\infty} f(x)e^{-iKx}\,dx\right] e^{iKx}\frac{dK}{2\pi}. \tag{11}$$

We are free to change the "dummy variable" from K back to k. The integral inside the brackets is (1), producing $\widehat{f}(k)$. The outer integral that reconstructs $f(x)$ is (2).

Derivatives, Integrals, and Shifts: The Key Rules

The transform of df/dx follows a simple rule. For Fourier series, ik multiplies c_k:

$$\text{The derivative of} \quad f(x) = \sum_{-\infty}^{\infty} c_k e^{ikx} \quad \text{leads to} \quad \frac{df}{dx} = \sum_{-\infty}^{\infty} ikc_k e^{ikx}.$$

For Fourier integrals the transform of df/dx is $ik\widehat{f}(k)$:

$$f(x) = \frac{1}{2\pi}\int_{-\infty}^{\infty} \widehat{f}(k)e^{ikx}\,dk \quad \text{leads to} \quad \frac{df}{dx} = \frac{1}{2\pi}\int_{-\infty}^{\infty} ik\widehat{f}(k)e^{ikx}\,dk.$$

The underlying reason is that e^{ikx} is an eigenfunction of d/dx with eigenvalue ik. Fourier's formulas simply express $f(x)$ as a linear combination of these eigenfunctions:

$$\frac{d}{dx}e^{ikx} = ike^{ikx}. \tag{12}$$

The rule for indefinite integrals is the opposite. Since integration is the inverse of differentiation, we *divide* by ik instead of multiplying. **The transform of the integral is $\widehat{f}(k)/ik$.** There is one exception: $k = 0$ is ruled out. For the integral of $f(x)$ to approach zero as $|x| \to \infty$, we need $\widehat{f}(0) = \int_{-\infty}^{\infty} f(x)\,dx = 0$.

A third operation on $f(x)$ is a *shift of the graph.* For $f(x-d)$, the graph moves a distance d to the right. **The Fourier transform of $f(x-d)$ is $\widehat{f}(k)$ times e^{-ikd}:**

$$\textbf{Shift of } f(x) \quad \int_{-\infty}^{\infty} e^{-ikx} f(x-d)\,dx = \int_{-\infty}^{\infty} e^{-ik(y+d)} f(y)\,dy = e^{-ikd}\widehat{f}(k)\,. \tag{13}$$

This is especially clear for the delta function $\delta(x)$, which has $\widehat{\delta}(k) = 1$. Moving the impulse to $x = d$ multiplies the transform by e^{-ikd}. And multiplying $f(x)$ by an exponential e^{+ikd} will shift its transform! We summarize the four key rules:

Rule 1 Transform of	df/dx	$ik\widehat{f}(k)$	Increase high frequencies
Rule 2 Transform of	$\int_{-\infty}^{x} f(x)\,dx$	$\widehat{f}(k)/ik$	Decrease high frequencies
Rule 3 Transform of	$f(x-d)$	$e^{-ikd}\widehat{f}(k)$	Shift of f changes phase of $\widehat{f}$
Rule 4 Transform of	$e^{ixc}f(x)$	$\widehat{f}(k-c)$	Phase change of f shifts $\widehat{f}$

Example 6 The derivative of the two-sided pulse in Example 4 is an *odd pulse*:

$$\frac{d}{dx}\left\{\begin{array}{ll} e^{-ax} & \text{for } x \geq 0 \\ e^{ax} & \text{for } x \leq 0 \end{array}\right\} = \left\{\begin{array}{ll} -ae^{-ax} & \text{for } x > 0 \\ +ae^{ax} & \text{for } x < 0 \end{array}\right\} = \textbf{odd pulse} \text{ (times } -a).$$

The transform of this df/dx must be $ik\widehat{f}(k) = 2ika/(a^2+k^2)$. Check by Example 3!

$$\textbf{Transform of odd pulse} \quad (-a)\left(\frac{1}{a+ik} - \frac{1}{a-ik}\right) = \frac{(-a)(-2ik)}{(a+ik)(a-ik)} = \frac{2ika}{a^2+k^2}\,.$$

The drop of $2a$ in df/dx at $x = 0$ produces this slower $2a/k$ decay in the transform.

Example 7 The box function (square pulse) in Example 2 has $\widehat{f}(k) = (e^{ikL} - e^{-ikL})/ik$. The derivative of the box function is $\delta(x+L) - \delta(x-L)$, with a spike at $x = -L$ where the box jumps to 1, minus a spike at $x = L$ where it jumps back to 0. *Check*: Those spikes transform by **Rule 3** to $e^{ikL} - e^{-ikL}$. This agrees with $ik\widehat{f}(k)$ from **Rule 1**.

The hat function needs *two derivatives* to produce delta functions from ramps:

$$\textbf{Hat Function} \quad H(x) = \left\{\begin{array}{ll} 1+x & \text{for } -1 \leq x \leq 0 \\ 1-x & \text{for } \quad 0 \leq x \leq 1 \end{array}\right\} \quad H'(x) = \left\{\begin{array}{r} 1 \\ -1 \end{array}\right\}$$

The slope $H'(x)$ has jumps of $+1, -2, +1$ and the second derivative has three spikes. By **Rule 3**, the transform of this H'' is $e^{ik} - 2 + e^{-ik} = 2\cos k - 2$. Then use **Rule 2**:

$$\textbf{Transform of hat function} = \frac{\text{Transform of } H''}{(ik)^2} = \frac{2-2\cos k}{k^2}\,. \tag{14}$$

Example 8 The **bell-shaped Gaussian** $f(x) = e^{-x^2/2}$ transforms to $\widehat{f}(k) = \sqrt{2\pi}e^{-k^2/2}$

This is a fascinating and important example. The function $f(x)$ is infinitely smooth, and $\widehat{f}(k)$ decreases rapidly. At the same time $f(x)$ decreases rapidly and $\widehat{f}(k)$ is infinitely smooth. To find $\widehat{f}(k)$, use the fact that df/dx = derivative of $e^{-x^2/2} = -xf(x)$:

$$
\begin{aligned}
ik\widehat{f}(k) &= \int_{-\infty}^{\infty} -xe^{-x^2/2}e^{-ikx}\,dx \qquad \text{(transform of } \frac{df}{dx} \text{ by } \textbf{Rule 1}\text{)} \\
&= \frac{1}{i}\frac{d}{dk}\int_{-\infty}^{\infty} e^{-x^2/2}e^{-ikx}\,dx = \frac{1}{i}\frac{d}{dk}\widehat{f}(k)\,.
\end{aligned}
$$

Thus $\widehat{f}(k)$ solves the same equation $d\widehat{f}/dk = -k\widehat{f}(k)$ that $f(x)$ solved! This equation must have the same solution multiplied by some constant: $\widehat{f}(k) = Ce^{-k^2/2}$. The constant $C = \sqrt{2\pi}$ is determined at $k = 0$ by the known integral $\widehat{f}(0) = \int e^{-x^2/2}\,dx = \sqrt{2\pi}$.

This example leads to the most important probability distribution $p(x) = e^{-(x-m)^2/2\sigma^2}$, divided by $\sqrt{2\pi}\sigma$ so $\int p(x)\,dx = \widehat{p}(0)$ = total probability $= 1$. Shifting the center to the mean value m multiplies $\widehat{p}(k)$ by e^{-ikm} (this is **Rule 3**). Rescaling x to x/σ rescales k to σk (this is Problem 9). *The normal distribution has* $\widehat{p}(k) = e^{-ikm}e^{-\sigma^2k^2/2}$.

When all derivatives of $f(x)$ are smooth, all of their transforms $(ik)^n\widehat{f}(k)$ decay rapidly for large k. Reversing the roles, a rapidly decreasing $f(x)$ corresponds to a smooth $\widehat{f}(k)$. The one-sided pulse e^{-ax} is rapidly decaying but not smooth (at $x = 0$). Its transform $1/(a + ik)$ is smooth but not rapidly decreasing.

The bell-shaped Gaussian $e^{-x^2/2}$ and its transform $\sqrt{2\pi}\,e^{-k^2/2}$ illustrate how both $f(x)$ and $\widehat{f}(k)$ can decrease smoothly and rapidly. Heisenberg's Uncertainty Principle sets a limit; all these Gaussians reach it.

Green's Functions

With these rules for derivatives we can solve differential equations (when they have constant coefficients and no problems from boundaries). Here is an example:

Equation in x
$$-\frac{d^2u}{dx^2} + a^2u = h(x) \quad \text{for } -\infty < x < \infty\,. \tag{15}$$

There are three steps. Step 1 is to take the Fourier transform of each term:

Equation in k
$$-(ik)^2\,\widehat{u}(k) + a^2\,\widehat{u}(k) = \widehat{h}(k) \quad \text{for each } k\,. \tag{16}$$

Step 2 is to find the transform $\widehat{u}(k)$ of the solution (just divide):

Solution in k
$$\widehat{u}(k) = \frac{\widehat{h}(k)}{a^2 + k^2}\,. \tag{17}$$

Step 3 (the hard step) inverts this transform $\widehat{u}(k)$ to construct the solution $u(x)$.

The most important right side is a *delta function*: $h(x) = \delta(x)$. Its transform is $\widehat{\delta}(k) = 1$. Then $\widehat{u}(k) = 1/(a^2 + k^2)$ and we saw this transform in Example 4. The solution with $h(x) = \delta(x)$ is the **Green's function**. I will write $G(x)$ instead of $u(x)$:

Green's function $\quad G(x) = \dfrac{1}{2a} e^{-a|x|} = \text{even decaying pulse divided by } 2a\,. \quad (18)$

In engineering, $G(x)$ is the ***impulse response*** (the response at x to an impulse at 0). In mathematics, $G(x)$ is the ***fundamental solution*** of the differential equation. The fraction $\widehat{G}(k) = 1/(a^2 + k^2)$ is the ***transfer function*** for each frequency k.

Check. Two derivatives of e^{-ax} (and also e^{ax}) give $-G'' + a^2G = 0$. So equation (15) is correct away from $x = 0$. At that point the slope $G'(x)$ is $a/2a$ from the left and $-a/2a$ from the right. Therefore $-G''$ is the unit delta function $\delta(x)$, as required.

Convolution with Green's Function

Using this Green's function $G(x)$, we can solve the differential equation for any right side $h(x)$. From (17), we have a multiplication $\widehat{G}(k)\widehat{h}(k)$ in frequency space:

Multiply in frequency domain $\quad \widehat{u}(k) = \dfrac{\widehat{h}(k)}{a^2 + k^2} = \widehat{G}(k)\widehat{h}(k)\,. \quad (19)$

What function has this transform? The answer is not $G(x)h(x)$! The solution $u(x)$ to (15) is not the product but the ***convolution*** of $G(x)$ and $h(x)$. It combines all the responses at x to impulses $h(y)$ at every y, by integrating $G(x - y)h(y)$:

Convolution $G(x) * h(x)$ is the analogue of $\sum G_{j-k}h_k$. The sum becomes an integral:

Solution = Convolution $\quad u(x) = \displaystyle\int_{y=-\infty}^{\infty} G(x - y)h(y)\, dy = G(x) * h(x)\,. \quad (20)$

The Fourier transform of $u(x)$ is $\widehat{u}(k) = \widehat{G}(k)\widehat{h}(k)$. This is the ***convolution rule.***

Example 9 Solve equation (15) with $h(x) = \delta(x - d) =$ **point load at** d. The transform is $\widehat{h}(k) = e^{-ikd}$. Then $\widehat{u}(k) = e^{-ikd}/(a^2 + k^2)$. We can find $u(x)$ in three ways:

(1) If $\widehat{u}(k)$ is multiplied by e^{-ikd} then $u(x)$ is shifted by d: $u(x) = G(x - d)$.

(2) Convolution gives $u(x) = G(x) * h(x) = \displaystyle\int G(x - y)\delta(y - d)\, dy = G(x - d)$.

(3) When $h(x)$ is shifted by d, so is the solution! Constant coefficients are shift-invariant.

This is very different from Laplace's equation in a circle. There the Green's function has to change as the impulse moves toward the boundary. Here there is no boundary. The entire problem shifts by d. It is like Laplace's equation in free space, where the Green's function is $1/4\pi r$—and r is the distance from the impulse. **Our problem is shift-invariant**.

A direct proof of the convolution rule $\widehat{u} = \widehat{G}\,\widehat{h}$ starts with the formula for $\widehat{u}(k)$:

$$\widehat{u}(k) = \int_{-\infty}^{\infty} e^{-ikx} u(x)\,dx = \int_{x=-\infty}^{\infty} \int_{y=-\infty}^{\infty} e^{-ik(x-y)} e^{-iky} G(x-y) h(y)\,dy\,dx\,.$$

On the right, move e^{-iky} and $h(y)$ outside the x integral. Then change variables from $x - y$ to z. The two integrals are $\widehat{h}(k)$ and $\widehat{G}(k)$ as desired:

Convolution Rule: Integrals
$$\widehat{u}(k) = \int_{y=-\infty}^{\infty} e^{-iky} h(y)\,dy \int_{z=-\infty}^{\infty} e^{-ikz} G(z)\,dz = \widehat{h}(k)\widehat{G}(k)\,. \qquad (21)$$

Example 10 The convolution **Box $*$ Box** gives a hat function! The convolution integral in x-space is not fun to do. But multiplication (squaring) in k-space is great. Take $L = \frac{1}{2}$ in Example 2 to get the hat $H(x)$ in Example 7:

$$\widehat{H}(k) = \left(\frac{e^{ik/2} - e^{-ik/2}}{ik} \right)^2 = \frac{e^{ik} - 2 + e^{-ik}}{-k^2} = \frac{2 - 2\cos k}{k^2}\,. \qquad (22)$$

Example 11 The convolution of two bell-shaped Gaussian functions $e^{-x^2/2\sigma}$ and $e^{-x^2/2\tau}$ is still bell-shaped. I could have used σ^2 and τ^2, but this way **we just add σ and τ**:

Convolution of Gaussians
$$\frac{1}{\sqrt{2\pi\sigma}} e^{-x^2/2\sigma} * \frac{1}{\sqrt{2\pi\tau}} e^{-x^2/2\tau} = \frac{1}{\sqrt{2\pi(\sigma+\tau)}} e^{-x^2/2(\sigma+\tau)}\,. \qquad (23)$$

The convolution integral is computable, but multiplication is a lot easier:

Multiply transforms
$$(e^{-\sigma k^2/2})(e^{-\tau k^2/2}) = e^{-(\sigma+\tau)k^2/2}\,. \qquad (24)$$

Transforming back to x-space gives the Gaussian in (23), with $\sigma + \tau$ going into the denominator. The constants in (23) give "total probability = integral = 1."

Example 1 in Section 6.4 describes another proof by solving the heat equation $u_t = u_{xx}$. The solution at time 2σ starting from $u = \delta(x)$ is the first Gaussian. The second Gaussian takes us onward to $T = 2\sigma + 2\tau$. The third Gaussian gets to T in one step. All Gaussians give equality in Heisenberg's inequality.

Example 12 The graph of $e^{-x^2/2\sigma}$ gets *narrower* as σ goes to zero. Divided by $\sqrt{2\pi\sigma}$, it also gets *higher*. The area under the curve (the integral) stays at 1.

The limit as σ approaches zero is the delta function. You might say, what else could it be? With $-x^2/2\sigma$ in the exponent, the pointwise limit as $\sigma \to 0$ is certainly zero (except at $x = 0$). The integral stays at 1, because we divide by $\sqrt{2\pi\sigma}$. So the higher and narrower bells approach an infinite spike at $x = 0$. This is confirmed by the Fourier transforms: $e^{-\sigma k^2/2} \to 1$ as $\sigma \to 0$.

The Energy Equation

The energy in $f(x)$ equals the energy in its Fourier coefficients. In Fourier series, the length of $f(x)$ in the Hilbert function space L^2 equals the length of the vector c in the Hilbert vector space ℓ^2. The equation was Parseval's:

Energy in Fourier series
$$\int_{-\pi}^{\pi} |f(x)|^2\,dx = 2\pi \sum_{-\infty}^{\infty} |c_k|^2 . \tag{25}$$

That was proved in Section 4.1 by multiplying $(\sum c_k e^{ikx})\,(\sum \overline{c}_k e^{-ikx})$ and integrating. Now we state a similar energy equation for the Fourier *integral* pair $f(x)$ and $\widehat{f}(k)$.

Energy in Fourier integrals
$$\int_{-\infty}^{\infty} |f(x)|^2\,dx = \frac{1}{2\pi}\int_{-\infty}^{\infty} |\widehat{f}(k)|^2\,dk . \tag{26}$$

In the same way, inner products of $f(x)$ and $g(x)$ transform to inner products:

Inner products
$$\int_{-\infty}^{\infty} f(x)\overline{g(x)}\,dx = \frac{1}{2\pi}\int_{-\infty}^{\infty} \widehat{f}(k)\overline{\widehat{g}(k)}\,dk . \tag{27}$$

Example 13 The one-sided decaying pulse $f(x) = e^{-x}$ on $0 \le x < \infty$ has energy $\frac{1}{2}$:

$$\int_{-\infty}^{\infty} |f(x)|^2\,dx = \int_0^{\infty} e^{-2x}\,dx = \frac{1}{2} .$$

Its transform $\widehat{f}(k)$ has the same energy, after we multiply by 2π:

$$\int_{-\infty}^{\infty} \left|\frac{1}{1+ik}\right|^2 dk = \int_{-\infty}^{\infty} \frac{dk}{1+k^2} = \left[\tan^{-1} k\right]_{-\infty}^{\infty} = \pi .$$

Rescaling The factor 2π in the transform can be moved. If $\widehat{f}(k)$ is divided by $\sqrt{2\pi}$, call this new transform $F(k)$. After squaring, 2π disappears in the energy equation. This "symmetrized" transform is like an orthogonal matrix with $Q^{\mathrm{T}}Q = I$:

Energy in F = energy in f
$$F^{\mathrm{T}}F = f^{\mathrm{T}}Q^{\mathrm{T}}Qf = f^{\mathrm{T}}f .$$

More correctly, the Fourier transform preserves the length of every *complex* vector:

$$\overline{F}^{\mathrm{T}}F = \overline{f}^{\mathrm{T}}f \text{ corresponds to } \int |F(k)|^2\,dk = \int |f(x)|^2\,dx .$$

This complex symmetrized Fourier transform is unitary, as in $\overline{Q}^{\mathrm{T}}Q = I$:

$$F(k) = Qf = \frac{1}{\sqrt{2\pi}}\int e^{-ikx} f(x)\,dx \quad\text{and}\quad f(x) = \overline{Q}^{\mathrm{T}}F = \frac{1}{\sqrt{2\pi}}\int e^{ikx}F(k)\,dk . \tag{28}$$

Heisenberg's Uncertainty Principle

Heisenberg dealt with position and momentum in quantum mechanics. As one is measured more exactly, the other becomes less exact. There is a similar "product of uncertainty" for phase and amplitude of oscillations—and also time and energy.

Here the uncertainty principle involves $f(x)$ and $\widehat{f}(k)$. *If one is concentrated in a narrow band, the other fills a wide band.* An impulse $\delta(x)$ of zero width has a transform $\widehat{\delta}(k) = 1$ of infinite width. Probability suggests that the square root σ of the variance (normalized by the energy in f) is the right measure of width:

Widths σ_x and σ_k $$\sigma_x^2 = \frac{\int x^2 (f(x))^2\,dx}{\int (f(x))^2\,dx} \qquad \sigma_k^2 = \frac{\int k^2 |\widehat{f}(k)|^2\,dk}{\int |\widehat{f}(k)|^2\,dk}\,.$$

All integrals go from $-\infty$ to ∞, and the uncertainty principle is quick to state.

Heisenberg's Uncertainty Principle *Every function has* $\sigma_x \sigma_k \geq \frac{1}{2}$.

The cosine of the angle between $xf(x)$ and $f'(x)$ is at most one, even in Hilbert space. The Schwarz inequality $|a^{\mathrm{T}}b|^2 \leq (a^{\mathrm{T}}a)(b^{\mathrm{T}}b)$ becomes

$$\left| \int x f(x) f'(x)\,dx \right|^2 \leq \left(\int (xf(x))^2\,dx \right) \left(\int (f'(x))^2\,dx \right). \tag{29}$$

Since $f(x)f'(x)$ is the derivative of $\frac{1}{2}(f(x))^2$, integrate the left side by parts:

$$\int x f(x) f'(x)\,dx = \left[x \frac{(f(x))^2}{2} \right]_{-\infty}^{\infty} - \int \frac{(f(x))^2}{2}\,dx\,. \tag{30}$$

The integrated term is zero at $\pm\infty$ whenever the bandwidths are finite.

Plancherel's energy equation allows us to switch $\int (f(x))^2\,dx$ and $\int (f'(x))^2\,dx$ to $\int |\widehat{f}(k)|^2\,dk$ and $\int |k\widehat{f}(k)|^2\,dk$. The factors 2π cancel when we combine (29) and (30):

$$\left(\int \frac{(f(x))^2}{2}\,dx \right) \left(\int \frac{|\widehat{f}(k)|^2}{2}\,dk \right) \leq \left(\int (xf(x))^2\,dx \right) \left(\int |k\widehat{f}(k)|^2\,dk \right). \tag{31}$$

Taking square roots, this is the uncertainty principle $\sigma_x \sigma_k \geq \frac{1}{2}$.

Second proof Quantum mechanics associates position with multiplication $xf(x)$. Momentum corresponds to differentiation df/dx (in other words with $ik\widehat{f}(k)$). These operations $Bf = xf$ and $Af = df/dx$ do not commute:

$$\frac{d}{dx}(xf(x)) - x\frac{d}{dx}f(x) = f(x) \quad \text{means that} \quad \boldsymbol{AB - BA = I}.$$

The uncertainty principle for $\|Af\|$ times $\|Bf\|$ is again the Schwarz inequality:

Heisenberg inequality $$\|f\|^2 = |f^{\mathrm{T}}(AB - BA)f| \leq 2\,\|Af\|\,\|Bf\|\,. \tag{32}$$

Autocorrelation and Power Spectral Density

The autocorrelation of a vector is $f(n) * \overline{f(-n)}$. The autocorrelation of a function is $f(t) * \overline{f(-t)}$. We are using t instead of x, because the most important applications are to communications and electronics and power.

By the Convolution Rule, the transform of that convolution is $\widehat{f}(k)$ times its complex conjugate. That product is $|\widehat{f}(k)|^2$, the **power spectral density** of $f(t)$.

Autocorrelation $R(t)$
Power Spectral Density

$$R(t) = \int_{-\infty}^{\infty} f(s)\overline{f(t-s)}\,ds \qquad G(k) = \widehat{R}(k) = |\widehat{f}(k)|^2. \tag{33}$$

One advantage is $G \geq 0$. The key advantage is the energy identity (now for *power*):

$$\textbf{Power} = \int_{-\infty}^{\infty} |f(t)|^2\,dt = \frac{1}{2\pi}\int_{-\infty}^{\infty} |\widehat{f}(k)|^2\,dk = \frac{1}{2\pi}\int_{-\infty}^{\infty} G(k)\,dk. \tag{34}$$

$G(k)$ is the density of power at frequency k in the spectrum. Hence the name PSD.

Real signals come with noise. A sinusoidal waveform is never perfect, it shows rapid, random, usually small perturbations. The signal-to-noise ratio measures their importance. Since the noise is a random variable, we find its expected power from its probability distribution:

White noise has $G(k) = \text{constant}$ $\qquad$ **$1/f$ noise** has $G(k) = \text{constant}/k^{\alpha}$ $\qquad$ (35)

The independent jumps of many electrons approach white noise (thermal noise). There is no correlation between jumps so the autocorrelation R is a delta function and G is a constant function. But $1/f$ noise is everywhere too: economic data, traffic flow, flicker noise in metals and semiconductors. *Notice*: $R =$ constant and $R = 1/k$ have infinite integrals. It is the **average power** that stays finite for time-invariant (stationary) noise distributions.

The fundamental nonstationary process is a **random walk**.

Example 14 A random walk $x(t)$ can jump by 1 or -1 at each time step Δt.

This random walk is like counting the difference "heads minus tails" in a sequence of coin flips. This is carefully studied in probability [ ]. The limit as $\Delta t \to 0$ is a Wiener process or **Brownian motion**, which we meet in Section 6.5 as a model for stock prices.

The jump distribution can be binomial (± 1) or uniform or Gaussian or other. The *independence* of successive jumps is the key: *we can add spectral densities.* Each jump contributes a step function to $x(t)$, and its Fourier transform (from jump time to final time) is a sinc function. The sum of squares of those sinc functions gives $G(k) \approx 1/k^2$ for $k\,\Delta t >> 1$. So these random jumps are $1/f$ noise.

Periodic Components over Infinite Time

By separating Fourier series (periodic in time) from Fourier integrals (infinite time), the two transforms c_k and $\widehat{f}(k)$ are clear. But in reality, $f(t)$ could have *periodic components over infinite time.* The simplest example $f(t) = \cos \omega t = (e^{i\omega t} + e^{-i\omega t})/2$ has two inconvenient difficulties for Fourier analysis:

1 $f(t) = \cos \omega t$ does not approach zero **2** $\widehat{f}(k)$ has delta functions at $k = \pm\omega$

The power P and autocorrelation R and power spectral density G all have problems over infinite time. We need to work with *average power* over $0 \le t \le T$. On a finite interval with finite power, Parseval's identity connects $f(t)$ to its transform $\widehat{f}(T,k)$:

Average Power

$$\overline{P}(T) = \frac{1}{T}\int_0^T |f(t)|^2\, dt = \int_{-\infty}^{\infty} \frac{|\widehat{f}(T,k)|^2}{T}\, dk = \int_{-\infty}^{\infty} G(T,k)\, dk. \quad (36)$$

That identity indicates our plan: *Let* $T \to \infty$. A sharp eye might catch the difficulty: *The k-integrals also have* $k \to \infty$. Interchanging two infinite limits is not safe.

A similar problem was hidden (we didn't mention it) in the inversion formula from $\widehat{f}(k)$ to $f(x)$. The Fourier series over longer and longer intervals has coefficients c_k in (9), now called $\widehat{f}(T,k)$. In the energy identity (26) for Fourier integrals, $\int |\widehat{f}(k)|^2\, dk$ also has an infinite integral for $\widehat{f}(k)$ inside that infinite integral over k.

Exchanging limits is justified for the nicest functions $f(t)$ and $\widehat{f}(k)$, smooth and decaying. Then definitions are extended, as we know from $\int \delta(x)\, dx = 1$. Here the extension is to $\widehat{R} = G$, transform of autocorrelation equals power spectral density. Start with the identity (36) for average power, which is a useful measure in itself; $G(T,k)$ is a *periodogram.* Then work with the integral of G, always safer than G:

Wiener-Khintchine

$$F(k) = \lim_{T\to\infty} \int_{-\infty}^{k} G(T,\omega)\, d\omega \text{ is the transform of } R(t) = \int_{-\infty}^{\infty} e^{ikt}\, dF(k). \quad (37)$$

This "Stieltjes integral" allows steps in F, as in $\int \delta(x)\, dx = \int dF = 1$.

Summary of Fourier Integrals

1. Transform and inverse transform (1)-(2)
2. Transforms of $\delta(x)$, square pulse, decaying pulse, and Gaussian
3. Rules for derivatives, integrals, and shifts
4. Constant-coefficient equations solved by convolution (20)
5. Energy identity (26) for $f(x)$ and $\widehat{f}(k)$. Application to autocorrelation and $|\widehat{f}(k)|^2$

Problem Set 4.5

1 Find the transform $\widehat{g}(k)$ of the odd two-sided pulse $g(x)$:

$$g(x) = -e^{ax} \quad \text{for } x < 0\,, \quad g(x) = e^{-ax} \quad \text{for } x > 0\,.$$

The decay rate of $\widehat{g}(k)$ is ____. There is a ____ in $g(x)$.

2 Find the Fourier transforms (with $f(x) = 0$ outside the ranges given) of

(a) $f(x) = 1$ for $0 < x < L$

(b) $f(x) = 1$ for $x > 0$ and $f(x) = -1$ for $x < 0$ (set $a = 0$ in Problem 1)

(c) $f(x) = \int_0^1 e^{ikx} dk$

(d) the double sine wave $f(x) = \sin x$ for $0 \le x \le 4\pi$

3 Find the inverse transforms of

(a) $\widehat{f}(k) = \delta(k)$

(b) $\widehat{f}(k) = e^{-|k|}$ (please separate $k < 0$ from $k > 0$).

4 Apply Plancherel's formula $2\pi \int |f(x)|^2\, dx = \int |\widehat{f}(k)|^2\, dk$ to

(1) the square pulse $f(x) = 1$ for $-1 < x < 1$, to find $\displaystyle\int_{-\infty}^{\infty} \frac{\sin^2 t}{t^2}\, dt$

(2) the even decaying pulse, to find $\displaystyle\int_{-\infty}^{\infty} \frac{dt}{(a^2+t^2)^2}$.

Problems 5-9 involve $f(x) = e^{-x^2/2}$. Its transform is $\widehat{f}(k) = \sqrt{2\pi}e^{-k^2/2}$, by Example 8 and also by Cauchy's theorem on complex integration (x to $x + ik$):

$$\widehat{f}(k) = \int_{-\infty}^{\infty} e^{-x^2/2} e^{-ikx}\, dx = e^{-k^2/2} \int_{-\infty}^{\infty} e^{-(x+ik)^2/2}\, dx = \sqrt{2\pi}\, e^{-k^2/2}\,.$$

5 Verify Plancherel's energy equation for $\delta(x)$ and $e^{-x^2/2}$. Infinite energy allowed.

6 What are the half-widths σ_x and σ_k of the bell-shaped function $f(x) = e^{-x^2/2}$ and its transform? Show that equality holds in the uncertainty principle.

7 What is the transform of $xe^{-x^2/2}$ by the derivative rule? What about $x^2e^{-x^2/2}$?

8 Suppose g is a stretched version of f, $g(x) = f(ax)$. Show that $\widehat{g}(k) = a^{-1}\widehat{f}(k/a)$. Illustrate with the even pulse $f(x) = e^{-|x|}$.

9 Use the previous exercise to find the transform of $g(x) = e^{-a^2x^2/2}$. Then show that $e^{-x^2/2} * e^{-x^2/2} = \sqrt{\pi}\, e^{-x^2/4}$, transforming the left side by the convolution rule (20) and the right side by the choice $a^2 = \frac{1}{2}$.

10 The decaying pulse $f(x) = e^{-ax}$ has derivative $df/dx = -ae^{-ax}$ (and 0 for $x < 0$). Why isn't the transform of df/dx just $-a\widehat{f}(k)$ instead of $ik\widehat{f}(k)$?

11 Find $\widehat{u}(k)$ for a point load at d by taking Fourier transforms:

$$\frac{du}{dx} + au = \delta(x - d)$$

By inverse transform (or direct solution) find the Green's function $u(x) = G(x, d)$.

12 Take Fourier transforms of this unusual equation to find $\widehat{u}(k)$ and then $u(x)$:

$$(\text{integral of } u(x)) - (\text{derivative of } u(x)) = \delta(x)\,.$$

13 The convolution $f(x) * f(-x)$ of a decaying pulse (Ex. 3) and ascending pulse is an autocorrelation:

$$C(x) = \int_{-\infty}^{\infty} f(x-y)f(-y)\,dy \text{ with transform } \widehat{C}(k) = \frac{1}{a+ik}\frac{1}{a-ik} = \frac{1}{a^2+k^2}\,.$$

Find $C(x)$ from this transform, and also by computing the integral.

14 The hat function Box $*$ Box has transform $2(1 - \cos k)/k^2$ in Examples 7 and 10. Use the convolution rule for $S(x) = \text{Hat} * \text{Hat}$ to find $\widehat{S}(k)$. Show from $(ik)^4\widehat{S}(k)$ that the fourth derivative of $S(x)$ is a combination of spikes at $x = -2, -1, 0, 1, 2$. Since this fourth derivative is zero at all other points, $S(x) = \text{Hat} * \text{Hat} = \text{Box} * \text{Box} * \text{Box} * \text{Box}$ is *piecewise cubic*, with 5 jumps in its third derivative. $S(x)$ is the famous ***cubic B-spline*** for $-2 \le x \le 2$.

15 Show that the Fourier transform of $g(x)h(x)$ is the convolution $\widehat{g}(k) * \widehat{h}(k)/2\pi$ by repeating the proof of the convolution rule—but with e^{+ikx} to produce the inverse transform.

16 The derivative $\delta'(x)$ of the delta function is the *doublet*. It is a "distribution" concentrated at $x = 0$. Integration by parts picks out not $f(0)$ but $-f'(0)$:

$$\int f(x)\delta'(x)\,dx = -\int f'(x)\delta(x)\,dx = -f'(0).$$

(a) Why should the Fourier transform of the doublet $\delta'(x)$ be ik?

(b) What does the inverse formula (2) give for $\int ke^{ikx}\,dk$?

(c) Exchanging k and x, what is the Fourier transform of $f(x) = x$?

17 Suppose g is the mirror image of f, $g(x) = f(-x)$. Show from (1) that $\widehat{g}(k) = \widehat{f}(-k)$. If $f(x)$ is real, show that $\widehat{f}(-k)$ is the conjugate of $\widehat{f}(k)$.

18 If $f(x)$ is an even function, the integrals for $x > 0$ and $x < 0$ combine into

$$\begin{aligned} \widehat{f}(k) &= \int_{-\infty}^{\infty} f(x)e^{-ikx}\,dx &= 2\int_0^{\infty} f(x)\cos kx\,dx \\ f(x) &= \frac{1}{2\pi}\int_{-\infty}^{\infty} \widehat{f}(k)e^{ikx}\,dk &= \frac{1}{\pi}\int_0^{\infty} \widehat{f}(k)\cos kx\,dk \end{aligned}$$

Find $\widehat{f}(k)$ in this way for the even decaying pulse $e^{-a|x|}$. What are the corresponding formulas for sine transforms when $f(x)$ is odd?

19 If $f(x)$ is a line of equally spaced delta functions explain why $\widehat{f}(k)$ is too:

$$\text{The transform of } f(x) = \sum_{n=-\infty}^{\infty} \delta(x - 2\pi n) \text{ is } \widehat{f}(k) = \sum_{n=-\infty}^{\infty} \delta(k - n)\,.$$

20 (a) Why is $F(x) = \sum_{n=-\infty}^{\infty} f(x + 2\pi n)$ a 2π-periodic function?

(b) Show that its Fourier coefficient $c_k = \frac{1}{2\pi}\int_{-\pi}^{\pi} F(x)e^{-ikx}\,dx$ equals $\widehat{f}(k)/2\pi$.

(c) From $F(x) = \sum c_k e^{ikx}$ at $x = 0$ find ***Poisson's summation formula***:

$$\sum_{n=-\infty}^{\infty} f(2\pi n) = \frac{1}{2\pi}\sum_{k=-\infty}^{\infty} \widehat{f}(k)\,.$$

21 $u(x) = 1$ is an eigenfunction for convolution with any $g(x)$. Find the eigenvalue.

22 Take Fourier transforms in $G''''(x) - 2G''(x) + G(x) = \delta(x)$ to find the transform $\widehat{G}(k)$ of the Green's function. How would it be possible to find $G(x)$?

23 What is $\delta * \delta$?

24 What is $\widehat{f}(k)$ if $f(x) = e^{5x}$ for $x \le 0$, $f(x) = e^{-3x}$ for $x \ge 0$? Find the function $f(x)$ whose Fourier transform is $\widehat{f}(k) = e^{-|k|}$.

25 Propose a two-dimensional Fourier transform, from $f(x,y)$ to $\widehat{f}(k_1,k_2)$. Given $\widehat{f}(k_1,k_2)$, what integral like (2) will invert the transform and recover $f(x,y)$?

26 Find the 2D Fourier transform $\widehat{f}(k_1,k_2)$ of $e^{-(x^2+y^2)/2}$.

Challenge: Find the 2D transform of $e^{-Q/2}$ by diagonalizing the matrix in $Q = ax^2 + 2bxy + cy^2$.

4.6 DECONVOLUTION AND INTEGRAL EQUATIONS

In explaining $f * g$ and $c \circledast d$, we were given the inputs. From functions f and g, or from vectors c and d, we found the convolution. **Deconvolution goes backward.** The unknown function $U(x)$ or the unknown vector u is *inside* the convolution (non-cyclic or cyclic). Let me reveal the key idea before the important examples.

We are now given the output $B(x) = G(x) * U(x)$ or $b = c \circledast u$. We know the kernel function $G(x)$ or kernel vector c. The problem is to solve for $U(x)$ or u.

The equation $G(x) * U(x) = B(x)$ looks complicated in x-space (convolution produces an integral equation). In the frequency domain, that convolution becomes a multiplication. And the inverse of multiplication is division:

$$\boldsymbol{G * U = B} \quad \text{becomes} \quad \boldsymbol{\widehat{G}\widehat{U} = \widehat{B}} \quad \text{which gives} \quad \boldsymbol{\widehat{U} = \widehat{B}/\widehat{G}}. \tag{1}$$

The last step is to transform $\widehat{U}$ back to x-space, to find the solution $U(x)$.

May I say that this is the same three-step solution that all transform methods use? With the Fourier transform, the basis functions are e^{ikx}:

1. Expand the given $B(x)$ as a combination of eigenfunctions e^{ikx} times $\widehat{B}(k)$.

2. Divide each $\widehat{B}(k)$ by the known eigenvalue $\widehat{G}(k)$.

3. Reconstruct $U(x)$ from its Fourier transform $\widehat{U} = \widehat{B}/\widehat{G}$.

The convolution $G * U$ has eigenfunctions e^{ikx} and eigenvalues $\widehat{G}(k)$. This section is solving the simplest and most beautiful linear equations of applied mathematics: shift-invariant, time-invariant, constant-coefficient (those are equivalent here).

Point-Spread Functions

Along with examples of the convolution rule, I have to tell you about applications. You see convolutions (literally) in a telescope. *A star looks blurred.* The true signal (the star) is practically a point source $\delta(x, y)$ at $(0, 0)$. The blur is the **point-spread function $\boldsymbol{G(x, y)}$**. That is the response at (x, y) to a delta function input at $(0, 0)$.

If the point source is moved to (t, s), then the blurred output $G(x - t, y - s)$ moves with it. This is *shift invariance*, extremely important. If the input is an integral that combines point sources of strength $U(t, s)$, then the output is an integral that combines blurred points $G(x - t, y - s)$ multiplied by U:

$$U(t,s) = \begin{matrix}\textbf{light density of}\\ \textbf{input at } \boldsymbol{(t,s)}\end{matrix} \qquad \iint U(t,s)\, G(x-t, y-s)\, dt\, ds = \begin{matrix}\textbf{light density of}\\ \textbf{output at } \boldsymbol{(x,y)}\end{matrix} \tag{2}$$

The telescope has convolved the input U and its built-in point-spread function, to produce the output $G * U$. We need **deconvolution** to find the input U.

All sorts of imaging instruments present this same problem: Find the input from its convolution with G. Solving this problem is crucial for computed tomography (CT scanners won the Nobel Prize for Medicine in 1979). The company that makes the scanner measures its point-spread function G, once and for all. The same problem appears in magnetic resonance imaging (MRI) and in sensors carried on satellites.

Notice that a perfect convolution requires *shift-invariance and linearity.* Usually there are imperfections, especially near the edge of the field of vision. The telescope example involves two dimensions and Fourier integrals. Start in one dimension.

Example 1 Suppose a point source $\delta(x)$ spreads into a hat function $G(x) = 1 - |x|$ with area 1. Why is there a difficulty to recover an unknown distributed source $U(x)$ from the output $B = G * U$?

Solution Deconvolution in frequency space divides $\widehat{B}(k)$ by $\widehat{G}(k)$. This is only safe when $\widehat{G}(k)$ is never zero. A nonzero transform is the test for an invertible convolution.

The transform of the hat function $G(x)$ was computed in the previous section. The second derivative of the hat is $G'' = \delta(x+1) - 2\,\delta(x) + \delta(x-1)$, so we divide its transform $e^{ikx} - 2 + e^{-ikx}$ by $(ik)^2$:

Transform of the hat function
$$\widehat{G}(k) = \frac{2 - 2\cos k}{k^2}. \tag{3}$$

The difficulty is that $\widehat{G}(k) = 0$ when k is a nonzero multiple of 2π. (At $k = 0$ we have $\widehat{G}(0) = 1 =$ area under the hat.) If we divide by zero in $\widehat{U} = \widehat{B}/\widehat{G}$, we normally get an unacceptable transform $\widehat{U}$. This signals that our convolution equation $G * U = B$ is **ill-posed**. This often happens for integral equations:

Integral equation of the first kind
$$G * U = \int_{-\infty}^{\infty} G(x-t)\,U(t)\,dt = B(x) \tag{4}$$

If $U(k) = e^{ikx}$, the integral produces $\widehat{G}(k)e^{ikx}$. Thus $\widehat{G}(k)$ is an eigenvalue of convolution by G. Invertibility always requires nonzero eigenvalues.

I will mention a modification that makes the integral equation **well-posed**, when we start from $\widehat{G}(k) \geq 0$. Add any positive multiple of $U(x)$ to the left side:

Integral equation of the second kind
$$\alpha\,U(x) + \int_{-\infty}^{\infty} G(x-t)\,U(t)\,dt = B(x). \tag{5}$$

Now the transform is $\alpha + \widehat{G}(k)$, never zero. The solution U comes safely from the division $\widehat{B}/(\alpha + \widehat{G})$, followed by an inverse transform. This is like adding αI to a positive semidefinite circulant matrix C, to make it positive definite.

In a telescope, invertibility might come from a different point-spread function G (not a hat). Or the problem may truly be singular. It is impossible to recover complete information about the body when a scanner only looks in N directions. It integrates your density along rays in each direction, and some shapes are invisible (like Stealth aircraft). Spiral CT gives a more complete picture.

Note In **blind deconvolution**, G is not known. The equation $G * U = B$ may change to minimization of $\|G * U - B\|^2 + \alpha\|u\|_{\mathsf{TV}}$. Section 4.7 explains that total variation (TV) term and 8.2 returns to ill-posed equations. **Inverse problems** try to recover the differential equation from its solutions. Or they solve $Au = b$ when $A^{\mathrm{T}}A$ is singular. The adjustment by α is a stabilizing **penalty term** to produce $A^{\mathrm{T}}A + \alpha I$.

Integral equations are not necessarily in a shift-invariant convolution form:

Integral equation: 1st kind [2nd kind]
$$[\alpha\, U(x)] + \int G(x,t)\, U(t)\, dt = B(x). \tag{6}$$

In convolutions, $G\,(x,t)$ depends only on the difference $x - t$ (as for Toeplitz matrices G_{i-j} with constant diagonals). The sum of $x - t$ and t on the left side is x on the right side—the reliable indicator of a convolution. For kernels like $G = xt$, *no convolution.*

Deconvolution by Matrices

Example 2 (Discrete deconvolution) For $C =$ **circulant matrix**, solve $Cu = b$.

This example immediately makes a key point. *Multiplying by the matrix C is the same as cyclic convolution with its zeroth column c.* For the second-difference circulant matrix C from Section 1.1, we can write the four equations as $Cu = b$ or $c \circledast u = b$:

Circulant $Cu =$ convolution $c \circledast u$
$(2, -1, 0, -1) \circledast (u_0, u_1, u_2, u_3)$
$$Cu = \begin{bmatrix} 2 & -1 & 0 & -1 \\ -1 & 2 & -1 & 0 \\ 0 & -1 & 2 & -1 \\ -1 & 0 & -1 & 2 \end{bmatrix} \begin{bmatrix} u_0 \\ u_1 \\ u_2 \\ u_3 \end{bmatrix} \tag{7}$$

This special matrix C is singular. The all-ones vector $(1,1,1,1)$ is in its nullspace, with zero eigenvalue. C^{-1} does not exist, because the eigenvalues of C are 0, 2, 4, 2.

It will be extremely valuable to see how deconvolution fails in this example. Dividing $\widehat{b}$ by $\widehat{c}$ (component by component) is impossible because one component of $\widehat{c}$ is zero. That vector $\widehat{c} = (0,2,4,2)$ contains the eigenvalues of C:

Discrete transform of c
$$\begin{bmatrix} 1 & 1 & 1 & 1 \\ 1 & i & i^2 & i^3 \\ 1 & i^2 & i^4 & i^6 \\ 1 & i^3 & i^6 & i^9 \end{bmatrix} \begin{bmatrix} 2 \\ -1 \\ 0 \\ -1 \end{bmatrix} = \begin{bmatrix} \mathbf{0} \\ 2 \\ 4 \\ 2 \end{bmatrix} = \widehat{c}. \tag{8}$$

The eigenvectors of C are the columns of the Fourier matrix! The first eigenvalue is zero, and its eigenvector is the column $(1,1,1,1)$. The four eigenvalues add to 8, which is the correct trace of C (sum of four 2's on the diagonal).

While those matrices are in front of us, let me verify $\boldsymbol{CF} = \boldsymbol{F\Lambda}$:

Eigenvectors $\boldsymbol{v}, \boldsymbol{w}, \boldsymbol{y}, \boldsymbol{z}$ are columns of $\boldsymbol{F}$
$$\begin{bmatrix} 2 & -1 & 0 & -1 \\ -1 & 2 & -1 & 0 \\ 0 & -1 & 2 & -1 \\ -1 & 0 & -1 & 2 \end{bmatrix} \underset{\boldsymbol{v}\quad \boldsymbol{w}\quad \boldsymbol{y}\quad \boldsymbol{z}}{\begin{bmatrix} 1 & 1 & 1 & 1 \\ 1 & i & i^2 & i^3 \\ 1 & i^2 & i^4 & i^6 \\ 1 & i^3 & i^6 & i^9 \end{bmatrix}} = \underset{\boldsymbol{c} \circledast \boldsymbol{v} \quad \cdots \quad \boldsymbol{c} \circledast \boldsymbol{z}}{\begin{bmatrix} 0\boldsymbol{v} & 2\boldsymbol{w} & 4\boldsymbol{y} & 2\boldsymbol{z} \end{bmatrix}}. \tag{9}$$

The Fourier matrix F is the eigenvector matrix for every circulant matrix.

Example 3 Adding I, the circulant matrix $C+I$ is invertible. Deconvolution succeeds for $c=(3,-1,0,-1)$. The eigenvalues are increased by 1 to $1,3,5,3$:

$$(\boldsymbol{C}+\boldsymbol{I})\,\boldsymbol{u}=\boldsymbol{b} \qquad \begin{bmatrix} 3 & -1 & 0 & -1 \\ -1 & 3 & -1 & 0 \\ 0 & -1 & 3 & -1 \\ -1 & 0 & -1 & 3 \end{bmatrix} \begin{bmatrix} u_0 \\ u_1 \\ u_2 \\ u_3 \end{bmatrix} = \begin{bmatrix} 4 \\ 0 \\ 0 \\ 0 \end{bmatrix}. \tag{10}$$

The four columns v,w,y,z are still eigenvectors of $C+I$. The right side $b=(4,0,0,0)$ is the sum $v+w+y+z$ of all four eigenvectors. This just says that the discrete transform is $\widehat{b}=(1,1,1,1)$. Deconvolution divides by the eigenvalues of C to construct the solution u:

$$u=\frac{1}{\mathbf{1}}v+\frac{1}{\mathbf{3}}w+\frac{1}{\mathbf{5}}y+\frac{1}{\mathbf{3}}z=\frac{1}{15}(18,12,8,12). \quad \text{This is} \quad \boldsymbol{u}=\boldsymbol{F\Lambda^{-1}F^{-1}b}. \tag{11}$$

Every circulant matrix has the form $C=F\Lambda F^{-1}$. The eigenvalues in Λ come from $\widehat{c}$. The Fourier eigenvectors in F show the three steps of $u=C^{-1}b=F\Lambda^{-1}F^{-1}b$:

$\boldsymbol{F^{-1}b}$ **finds** $\boldsymbol{\widehat{b}}$ $\qquad$ $\boldsymbol{\Lambda^{-1}}$ **gives** $\boldsymbol{\widehat{u}=\widehat{b}/\widehat{c}}$ $\qquad$ $\boldsymbol{F\widehat{u}}$ **reconstructs** $\boldsymbol{u}$

Thus deconvolution solves $Cu=c\circledast u=b$ with FFT speed:

bhat = fft(b); **chat = fft(c)**; **uhat = bhat./chat**; **u = ifft(uhat)**. (12)

Deconvolution for Infinite Matrices

Circulant matrices have periodic boundary conditions to give cyclic convolution $c\circledast u$. Infinite Toeplitz matrices give non-cyclic convolution $C_\infty u=c*u$. Then the job of non-cyclic deconvolution is to solve $c*u=b$.

In the language of signal processing, we are inverting a filter. Its impulse response is $c*\delta=c$. The inverse of an infinite Toeplitz matrix (constant diagonals, time-invariant) will be another Toeplitz matrix. But there is a big difference: If C_∞ is a **banded matrix** from an **FIR filter** (finite impulse response c), then C_∞^{-1} is a **full matrix** from an **IIR filter** (infinite impulse response).

If $C(\omega)=\sum c_k e^{i\omega k}$ is a polynomial, $1/C(\omega)$ is not a polynomial. The only exception is a useless one-coefficient filter. So deconvolution (discrete case or continuous case) does not preserve a band structure.

Example 4 The second difference matrix K_∞ is only semidefinite. Change to $C_\infty=2K_\infty+I$, whose coefficients $-2,5,-2$ are the autocorrelation $(-1,2,0)*(0,2,-1)$:

$$C_\infty=\begin{bmatrix} \cdot & \cdot & & & \\ -2 & 5 & -2 & & \\ & -2 & 5 & -2 & \\ & & & \cdot & \cdot \end{bmatrix} = \begin{bmatrix} \cdot & & & \\ \cdot & 2 & & \\ & -1 & 2 & \\ & & -1 & \cdot \end{bmatrix} \begin{bmatrix} \cdot & & & \\ & 2 & -1 & \\ & & 2 & -1 \\ & & & \cdot \end{bmatrix} = L_\infty U_\infty. \tag{13}$$

A tridiagonal C_∞ has bidiagonal factors. Look at matrices or polynomials:

$$\boldsymbol{C(\omega) = L(\omega)U(\omega)} \quad -2e^{i\omega} + 5 - 2e^{-i\omega} = (2 - e^{i\omega})(2 - e^{-i\omega}) = |2 - e^{i\omega}|^2. \qquad (14)$$

Positive definiteness of the matrix C_∞ is positivity of the polynomial $C_\infty(\omega)$. Then this 3-term frequency response has a *spectral factorization* (14) into $|A(\omega)|^2$. But the inverse matrix is full!

$$C_\infty^{-1} = U_\infty^{-1} L_\infty^{-1} = \begin{bmatrix} \cdot & \frac{1}{4} & \frac{1}{8} & \frac{1}{16} \\ & \frac{1}{2} & \frac{1}{4} & \frac{1}{8} \\ & & \frac{1}{2} & \frac{1}{4} \\ & & & \cdot \end{bmatrix} \begin{bmatrix} \cdot & & & \\ \frac{1}{4} & \frac{1}{2} & & \\ \frac{1}{8} & \frac{1}{4} & \frac{1}{2} & \\ \frac{1}{16} & \frac{1}{8} & \frac{1}{4} & \cdot \end{bmatrix} \qquad (15)$$

Those triangular inverses come from $1/(2 - e^{i\omega}) = \frac{1}{2} + \frac{1}{4}e^{i\omega} + \frac{1}{8}e^{2i\omega} + \cdots$ and they are not polynomials. Their product $1/C(\omega)$ is not a polynomial. *But all these matrices are still convolutions.*

Convolution	$c * u = b$	**Divide by $C(\omega)$**	$D(\omega) = 1/C(\omega)$	
Toeplitz matrix	$C_\infty u = b$	**Toeplitz inverse**	$D_\infty = (C_\infty)^{-1}$	(16)
Frequency space	$C(\omega)U(\omega) = B(\omega)$	**Deconvolution**	$U(\omega) = B(\omega)/C(\omega)$	

Triangular Matrices and Causal Filters

The Toeplitz matrix L_∞ is **lower triangular** when the filter $\ell = (\ell_0, \ell_1, \ldots)$ is **causal.** The past affects the future, but the future has no effect on the past. There is a time arrow, and cause comes before effect.

An upper triangular matrix U_∞ is anticausal. A banded Toeplitz matrix is a product $L_\infty U_\infty$, found by factoring the polynomials. ***The inverse will exist if $C(\omega) \neq 0$ for all ω.*** But here is a disturbing point. The lower triangular inverse from $1/L(\omega)$ might be an **unbounded matrix**:

$$\frac{1}{L(\omega)} = \frac{1}{1 - 3e^{-i\omega}} \quad L_\infty = \begin{bmatrix} \cdot & & & \\ -3 & 1 & & \\ & -3 & 1 & \\ & & -3 & 1 \end{bmatrix} \quad L_\infty^{-1} = \begin{bmatrix} \cdot & & & \\ 3 & 1 & & \\ 9 & 3 & 1 & \\ 27 & 9 & 3 & 1 \end{bmatrix} \qquad (17)$$

For triangular matrices, causal or anticausal, there is a stronger condition when the inverse matrix is required to be bounded and still triangular. These are *one-sided* problems, changing from $-\infty < x < \infty$ to $0 \leq t < \infty$. *The Laplace transform replaces the Fourier transform.*

A bounded lower triangular inverse of L_∞ still depends on the zeros of $L(\omega)$. But now the test forbids $3 - e^{-i\omega} = 0$ or $z = 1/3$. $L(z)$ must have no zeros with $|z| \leq 1$ and $U(z)$ must have no zeros with $|z| \geq 1$. This stronger test comes in Section 5.3 on the Laplace transform.

Deconvolution in Two Dimensions

Our first example of deconvolution (for a telescope) was in 2D. Equation (2) was a double integral and $G*U$ was a 2D convolution. The computed examples went back to 1D, but not for any deep reason—only for simplicity. The two-dimensional problem needs double Fourier series or double Fourier integrals, but the principle stays the same:

$$G(x,y) * U(x,y) = B(x,y) \qquad \widehat{G}(\omega,\theta)\,\widehat{U}(\omega,\theta) = \widehat{B}(\omega,\theta) \qquad \widehat{U} = \widehat{B}/\widehat{G}\,. \tag{18}$$

The convolution rule is still all-important. But there can be a considerable difference in the algebra, from 1D to 2D. In one dimension, factorization is the key to explicit formulas. By computing the zeros of a polynomial $C(\omega)$, we get linear factors with easy inverses. That won't happen for $C(\omega,\theta) = \sum\sum c_{k\ell}e^{-ik\omega}e^{-i\ell\theta}$, except in the special case that we always hope for and very often construct:

Separation of variables	$C(\omega,\theta) = C_1(\omega)\,C_2(\theta)$	$1/C = (1/C_1)(1/C_2)$	(19)
Tensor products from 1D	$C = \text{kron}(C_1, C_2)$	$C^{-1} = \text{kron}(C_1^{-1}, C_2^{-1})$	

This reduces the possibilities in 2D, but it makes the solution infinitely simpler.

Problem Set 4.6

1 Solve this *cyclic convolution* equation for the vector d. (I would transform the convolution to multiplication.) Notice that $c = (5, 0, 0, 0) - (1, 1, 1, 1)$.

$$\textbf{Deconvolution} \quad c \circledast d = (4, -1, -1, -1) \circledast (d_0, d_1, d_2, d_3) = (1, 0, 0, 0).$$

2 There is no solution d if c changes to $C = (3, -1, -1, -1)$. Find the discrete transform of this C. Then find a nonzero D so that $C \circledast D = (0, 0, 0, 0)$.

3 These cyclic permutations are inverses. What are their eigenvalues?

$$C = \begin{bmatrix} 0 & 0 & 0 & 1 \\ 1 & 0 & 0 & 0 \\ 0 & 1 & 0 & 0 \\ 0 & 0 & 1 & 0 \end{bmatrix} \qquad D = \begin{bmatrix} 0 & 1 & 0 & 0 \\ 0 & 0 & 1 & 0 \\ 0 & 0 & 0 & 1 \\ 1 & 0 & 0 & 0 \end{bmatrix}.$$

4 If that cyclic delay C extends to a doubly infinite C_∞ (a non-cyclic delay), show that D_∞ (a non-cyclic advance) is still its inverse. For which complex numbers λ is $C_\infty - \lambda I$ not invertible? Use the test $e^{-i\omega} - \lambda \neq 0$ for all ω.

5 Now suppose C_+ is a *singly infinite* delay (lower triangular with 1's on the subdiagonal, *not invertible*). For which complex numbers λ is C_+ not invertible?

6 For singly infinite triangular Toeplitz matrices, show that U_+L_+ *stays Toeplitz but* L_+U_+ *does not.* The **Wiener Hopf method** for $A_+u_+ = b_+$ factors $A(z) = U(z)L(z)$ and $A_+ = U_+L_+$.

7 What is the inverse of the 1D Gaussian convolution $G * U = \int e^{-s^2/2} U(x-3)\, ds$? What is a 2D Gaussian convolution $G(x,y) * U(x,y)$ and its inverse?

4.7 WAVELETS AND SIGNAL PROCESSING

A key idea of wavelets is to separate the incoming signal into *averages* (smooth parts) and *differences* (rough parts). Let me take the inputs two at a time, with no overlap, to get the simplest wavelet transform. This "2-point DFT" is named after Haar:

Haar wavelet $x = x_1, x_2, x_3, x_4 \longrightarrow$ **averages** $y = \dfrac{x_2 + x_1}{2}$ and $\dfrac{x_4 + x_3}{2}$ **differences** $z = \dfrac{x_2 - x_1}{2}$ and $\dfrac{x_4 - x_3}{2}$

I will describe the inverse transform, the next iteration, and then the purpose.

First point You could quickly recover the four x's from the two y's and two z's. Addition would give x_2 and x_4. Subtraction would give x_1 and x_3. This **inverse transform** uses the same operations (plus and minus) as the forward transform.

Second point We could **iterate** by taking averages and differences of the y's:

Next scale $y = \dfrac{x_2 + x_1}{2}$ and $\dfrac{x_4 + x_3}{2} \longrightarrow$ **average** $yy = \dfrac{x_4 + x_3 + x_2 + x_1}{4}$ **difference** $zy = \dfrac{x_4 + x_3 - x_2 - x_1}{4}$

From yy and zy we quickly recover the two y's. Then with the two z's we recover all four x's. The information is always there, but we have changed to a "wavelet basis." In matrix language, the transform is just multiplying x by an invertible matrix A. The inverse transform (to reconstruct x) multiplies by a synthesis matrix $S = A^{-1}$.

Third point A key application of wavelet transforms is in **compression**. Signals and images and videos come with more bits than we can hear or see. High Definition TV and medical imaging by MR produce enormous bit streams (an image is 8 bits per pixel, 24 for color, with millions of pixels). We can't drop small x's and leave blanks in the picture. But we can drop small z's without a significant loss. Compression comes between the transforms A and S:

Input signal x $\xrightarrow{A}$ **Wavelet transform** $\begin{bmatrix} y \\ z \end{bmatrix} \longrightarrow$ ***Compressed transform*** $\begin{bmatrix} \hat{y} \\ \hat{z} \end{bmatrix} \xrightarrow{S = A^{-1}}$ **Output signal $\hat{x}$**

Compression is nonlinear and lossy. The transforms are linear and lossless. Wavelet theory concentrates on finding transforms that keep this overall structure, but use more refined filters. The Haar filter coefficients are $\frac{1}{2}, \frac{1}{2}$ for "running averages" and $\frac{1}{2}, -\frac{1}{2}$ for "running differences." Better filters in A will have more coefficients (a favorite pair is 9/7), carefully chosen to keep the inverse transform simple and fast.

Signals and Images

This section has two purposes. One is to develop the wavelet transform. Haar's averages and differences are a first step—they opened the door to better discrete wavelet transforms. The DWT creates the wavelet coefficients from *filters*, not from formulas like $c_k = \sum f_j w^{-jk}$. The key is to build the transform from easily invertible pieces.

Our second purpose is to represent signals and images (often medical images) in a **sparse and piecewise smooth way**. Sparsity means few coefficients, to control cost and storage and transmission rate. Smoothness means close approximation to natural images. "**Piecewise**" is our recognition that **the edges in those images are highly important**. This is where Fourier falls down. Even in one dimension, the Gibbs phenomenon and the slow $1/k$ decay of coefficients lead to ringing and smearing at a jump in $f(t)$.

An $\boldsymbol{\ell^1}$ **penalty term** discourages a crowd of small coefficients. A **total variation penalty term** (ℓ^1 norm of the gradient) discourages oscillations. Get the jump over with and stay smooth on both sides. Section 8.6 will return to the algorithms and the duality theory behind sparse and smooth compression. This section motivates the energy minimizations that are transforming JPEG and discrete cosines into better codecs. Here are four steps in $f \approx \sum c_k \phi_k$:

1. Linear transform	Use the first n coefficients (Fourier, wavelet,...)
2. Nonlinear transform	Use the largest n coefficients (a form of basis pursuit)
3. Sparse transform	Minimize $\|f - \sum c_k\phi_k\|_2^2 + \alpha \sum \|c_k\|$ (the LASSO idea)
4. Smooth transform	Minimize $\|f - \sum c_k\phi_k\|^2 + \alpha \|\sum c_k\phi_k\|_{\text{TV}}$ (total variation)

Fourier versus Wavelets

So much of mathematics involves the representation of functions—**the choice of basis**. A central example in pure and applied mathematics is the Fourier series. Its discrete version is computed by the Fast Fourier Transform, the most important algorithm of the 20th century. The Fourier basis is terrific—no basis will ever be so useful—but it is imperfect. Sines and cosines are global instead of local, and they give poor approximation at a jump (Gibbs phenomenon).

Four properties we want are: *local basis, easily refined, fast to compute, good approximation by a few terms.* Splines and finite elements achieve the first three, but removing terms will leave blank intervals. Wavelets permit compression of data—which is needed in so many applications where the volume of data is overwhelming.

To compare wavelets with sines and cosines, we need functions and not vectors. From discrete time, we move into the parallel world of continuous time. A lowpass filter like $\frac{1}{2}, \frac{1}{2}$ leads to the ***scaling function*** $\phi(t)$. A highpass filter like $\frac{1}{2}, -\frac{1}{2}$ leads to the ***wavelet*** $w(t)$. For a half-length vector like y, the parallel in the continuous case is to ***compress the t-axis***. We now meet $\phi(2t)$, which squeezes the graph of $\phi(t)$:

Averages lead to Haar scaling function ϕ	$\boldsymbol{\phi(t) = \phi(2t) + \phi(2t-1)}$	(1)
Differences lead to the Haar wavelet w	$\boldsymbol{w(t) = \phi(2t) - \phi(2t-1)}$	(2)

That two-scale "refinement equation" asks $\phi(t)$ to be the sum of its compression $\phi(2t)$ and the shifted compression $\phi(2t-1)$. The solution is the ***box function*** in Figure 4.14. Then the wavelet $w(t)$ is the difference of the two "half-boxes."

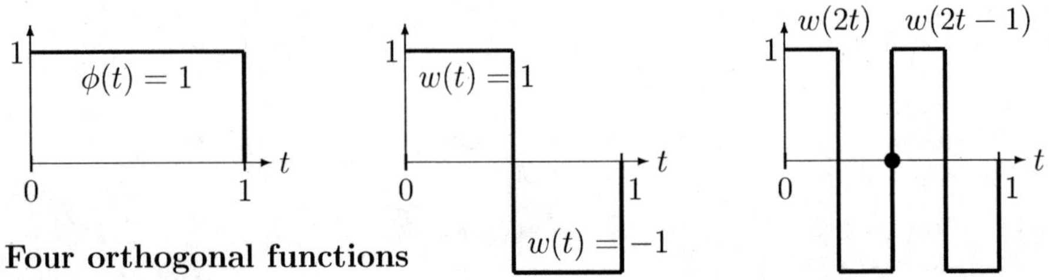

Figure 4.14: **Box function $\boldsymbol{\phi(t)}$. Haar wavelet $\boldsymbol{w(t)}$.** Rescaled $w(2t)$ and $w(2t-1)$.

Scaling functions give averages, and wavelets give details. When details are not significant, they can be compressed away to leave a smoothed signal. The image processing standard JPEG2000 chose filter pairs known as "9/7" and "5/3" from the count of coefficients. The coefficients decide the quality of the wavelet basis.

Wavelets are not perfect, and we are already seeing new ideas beyond these. To represent a face, or a signature, or the gravitational potential, we need basis functions that match particular inputs. When a video on the web stops because of congestion, you know that a more efficient representation is needed (and will be found).

Time-Frequency Multiscale Analysis

Overall, the purpose of wavelets is to represent signals in **time and frequency**. The Fourier description is entirely in the frequency domain. To know *when* something happened (such as a jump) the transform $\widehat{f}(k)$ has to be inverted to $f(t)$. The "short-time Fourier transform" operates on a sequence of windows of $f(t)$, to preserve part of the time information—but not optimally.

Wavelets capture high frequencies over short times (quick pulses). They see low frequencies over longer times. The building blocks are functions $w_{jk}(t) = w(2^j t - k)$, where j decides the scale ($w(2t)$ doubles all frequencies) and k decides the position ($w(t-k)$ shifts all time points). Those wavelet basis functions are LEGO blocks (Figure 4.15) in the Haar case of up-and-down square waves. New and smarter wavelets use better filters (short fast convolutions) on intervals that overlap. The construction takes patience but the purpose is clear: to combine higher accuracy with computational speed (of the inverse too).

At each scale, a lowpass filter captures averages and a highpass filter captures details. The details generally have low energy. Compression assigns them very few bits. The averages $y(n)$ contain most of the energy. By downsampling to $y(2n)$, we rescale the time. Then the lowpass and highpass filters are applied again, to capture averages and details at the coarser scale in Figure 4.15b. Those are **subband filters**.

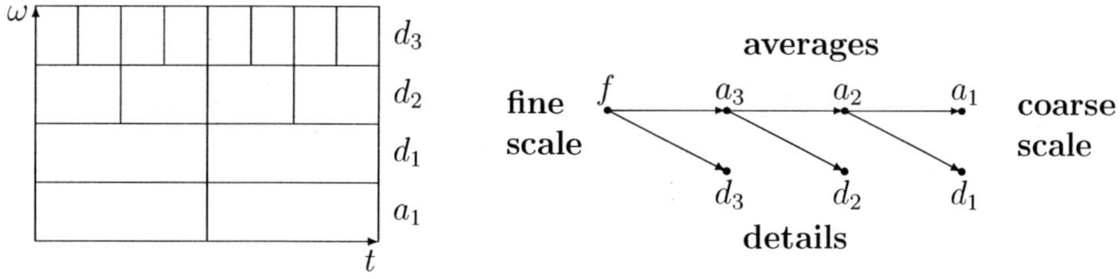

Figure 4.15: Time-frequency LEGO blocks: averages + details at time scales 2^j.

You could compare this time-frequency picture with musical notation. Time goes forward as you read the music. Frequency goes from low C to middle C to high C. Haar wavelets could be played with two fingers, left hand for averages and right hand for details. A chord gives you several frequencies, and $F(t,\omega)$ can contain *all* frequencies. But we have to point out what makes this subject difficult: *$F(t,\omega)$ is redundant.* If we know $f(t)$, we know everything. This is a deep topic [72], with uncertainty principles and Weyl-Heisenberg groups and fascinating transforms.

Altogether this multirate filter bank produces a **Discrete Wavelet Transform** (DWT). The inverse transform (IDWT) reassembles a_j from averages a_{j-1} and details d_{j-1}. This inverse process also uses a lowpass-highpass filter pair. Short filters are cheap, symmetric filters look best, orthogonal filters preserve energy, longer filters give sharp frequency cutoffs. We can't have all those properties at once!

Wavelet Basis and Refinement Equation

A wavelet basis is created from $w(t)$ by rescaling its graph (compressing by $2, 4, 8, \ldots$) and then shifting along the t axis to cover more intervals:

Rescaled by 2^j and shifted by k $$w_{jk}(t) = 2^{j/2} w(2^j t - k)\,. \tag{3}$$

The rescaled function $w(2^j t)$ is zero (unlike cosines) after an interval of length $2^{-j}N$. A fundamental property of all wavelets, like Haar's up-down $w(t)$, is *zero mean*:

Average value zero $$\int_{-\infty}^{\infty} w(t)\,dt = 0 \quad \text{and then} \quad \int_{-\infty}^{\infty} w_{jk}(t)\,dt = 0\,. \tag{4}$$

Thus the wavelets are orthogonal to the constant function 1. To approximate functions with nonzero integral, the scaling function $\phi(t)$ and its translates $\phi(t-k)$ are added to the basis. The continuous time expansion of $f(t)$ includes all ϕ and w:

Wavelet series $$f(t) = \sum_{k=-\infty}^{\infty} a_k \phi(t-k) + \sum_{k=-\infty}^{\infty} \sum_{j=0}^{\infty} b_{jk} w_{jk}(t)\,. \tag{5}$$

This series (parallel to Fourier) indicates the key ideas of the wavelet basis:

1. All basis functions are now localized in time (compact support).
2. The scaling functions $\phi(t-k)$ produce an "averaged" or "smoothed" signal.
3. Wavelets $w_{jk}(t)$ fill in the multiscale details at all scales $j = 0, 1, 2, \ldots$.

Low frequencies are associated with $\phi(t)$ and high frequencies with $w(t)$. Since a typical signal is smooth or at least piecewise smooth, *most of the information is carried by the scaling functions.* The simplest form of wavelet compression is to delete the wavelet part and destroy the fine details (we still recognize the image).

To separate signal from noise, "thresholding" keeps coefficients a_k and b_{jk} that are larger than a specified value. A more subtle compression algorithm replaces each a_k and b_{jk} by a binary number (the smallest coefficients are replaced by zero). After this "quantization," the binary numbers are easy to save and transmit.

The key point is that $\phi(t)$ *is a combination of the rescaled functions* $\phi(2t-k)$:

Refinement equation $$\phi(t) \;=\; 2\textstyle\sum_{k=0}^{N} h(k)\phi(2t-k)\,. \tag{6}$$

This is the most important equation in wavelet theory. The filter coefficients $h(k)$ are the only numbers that are needed and used to implement a wavelet basis, along with the corresponding numbers $g(k)$ in the *wavelet equation*:

Wavelet equation $$w(t) \;=\; 2\textstyle\sum_{k=0}^{M} g(k)\phi(2t-k)\,. \tag{7}$$

The $h(k)$ are the coefficients in a lowpass filter, and the $g(k)$ are the coefficients in a highpass filter. This connects filter banks to wavelets. The choice of these numbers determines $\phi(t)$ and $w(t)$. This pattern is called ***multiresolution analysis***.

Analysis and synthesis can have different filter pairs, producing two ϕ-w *pairs.* One pair determines the coefficients a_k and b_{jk} in the series (5); this is the analysis step. The other pair yields $\phi(t)$ and $w(t)$ from (6) and (7); this is the synthesis step. We can interpret (6) and (7) as statements about three spaces of functions:

Coarse averages	$\boldsymbol{V_0}$ = all combinations of $\phi(t-k)$	
Coarse details	$\boldsymbol{W_0}$ = all combinations of $w(t-k)$	(8)
Finer scale	$\boldsymbol{V_1}$ = all combinations of $\phi(2t-k)$	

By equations (6) and (7), $\boldsymbol{V_0}$ and $\boldsymbol{W_0}$ are contained in $\boldsymbol{V_1}$. **We want** $\boldsymbol{V_0}+\boldsymbol{W_0} = \boldsymbol{V_1}$.

The wavelet transform is a change of basis, to separate averages from details (y's and z's from x's). Fine signals in $\boldsymbol{V_1}$ split into pieces in $\boldsymbol{V_0}$ and $\boldsymbol{W_0}$. Then recursively, $\boldsymbol{V_1} + \boldsymbol{W_1} = \boldsymbol{V_2}$. Wavelets give scale + time; Fourier gives frequency.

Example After the box function, the simplest $\phi(t)$ comes from the filter $(1, 2, 1)/4$. $\phi(t)$ is the **hat function**. Figure 4.16 shows $\phi(t)$ as a combination of three half-hats. The wavelet $w(t)$ would be the combination of half-hats in (7), with mean zero from $g(k)$.

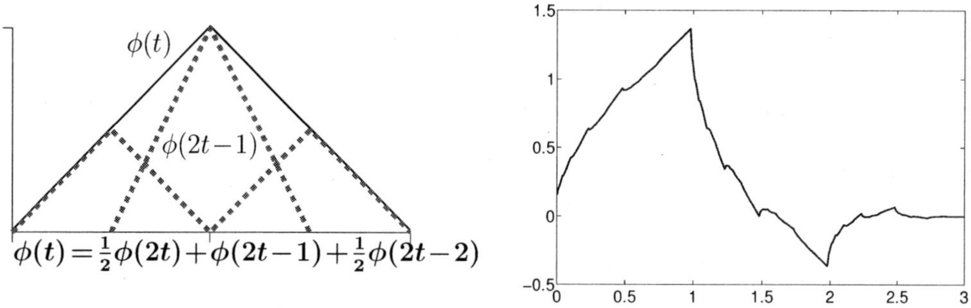

Figure 4.16: Scaling functions from lowpass filters $(1, 2, 1)/4$ and Daubechies (14).

The filter $(1, 4, 6, 4, 1)/16$ leads to a cubic B-spline (hats are linear B-splines). In fact splines are almost *the only simple solutions* to (6). The right side of Figure 4.16 is much more typical of $\phi(t)$. The **cascade algorithm** solves equation (6)—substitute $\phi^{(i)}(t)$ into the right side $\sum 2h(k)\phi^{(i)}(2t-k)$ to find $\phi^{(i+1)}(t)$. The code is on the cse site.

```
h = [1 + sqrt(3), 3 + sqrt(3), 3-sqrt(3), 1-sqrt(3)]/8; n = length(h)-1;
tsplit = 100; tt = 0:1/tsplit:n; ntt = length(tt); phi = double(tt < 1);
while 1                          % Iterate until convergence or divergence
  phinew = 0 * phi;
  for j = 1:ntt
    for k = 0:n
      index = 2 * j-k * tsplit + 1;
      if index >= 1 & index <= n * tsplit + 1
        phinew(j) = phinew(j) + 2 * h(k + 1) * phi(index);
      end
    end
  end
  plot(tt, phinew), pause(1e-1)
  if max(abs(phinew)) > 100, error('divergence'); end
  if max(abs(phinew-phi)) < 1e-3, break; end
  phi = phinew;
end
```

Filter Banks

The fundamental step is the choice of filter coefficients $h(k)$ and $g(k)$. They determine all the properties (good or bad) of the wavelets. We illustrate with the eight numbers in a very important 5/3 filter bank (notice the symmetry of each filter):

Lowpass coefficients	$h(0), h(1), h(2), h(3), h(4) = \mathbf{-1, 2, 6, 2, -1}$ (divide by 8)
Highpass coefficients	$g(0), g(1), g(2) = \mathbf{1, -2, 1}$ (divide by 4)

A filter is a **discrete convolution** acting on the inputs $x(n) = (\ldots, x(0), x(1), \ldots)$:

Filter pair
$$y(n) = \sum_{k=0}^{4} h(k)x(n-k) \quad \text{and} \quad z(n) = \sum_{k=0}^{2} g(k)x(n-k). \tag{9}$$

The input $x = (\ldots, 1, 1, 1, \ldots)$ is unchanged by the lowpass filter, since $\sum h(k) = 1$. This constant signal is stopped by the highpass filter since $\sum g(k) = 0$.

The fastest oscillation $x = (\ldots, 1, -1, 1, -1, \ldots)$ sees the opposite effects. It is stopped by the lowpass filter ($\sum(-1)^k h(k) = 0$) and passed by the highpass filter ($\sum (-1)^k g(k) = 1$). Filtering a pure frequency input $x(n) = e^{in\omega}$ multiplies those inputs by $H(\omega)$ and $G(\omega)$, and those are the response functions to know:

Frequency responses
$$H(\omega) = \sum h(k)e^{-ik\omega} \qquad G(\omega) = \sum g(k)e^{-ik\omega} \tag{10}$$

For the all-ones vector, $H = 1$ and $G = 0$ at $\omega = 0$. The oscillating vector $x(n) = (-1)^n = e^{in\pi}$ has opposite responses $H(\pi) = 0$ and $G(\pi) = 1$. *The multiplicity of this* "zero at π" *is a crucial property for the wavelet construction.* In the 5/3 example, $H(\omega)$ in Figure 4.17 has a double zero at $\omega = \pi$ because $(1 + e^{-i\omega})^2$ divides $H(\omega)$. Similarly $G(\omega) = (1 - e^{-i\omega})^2$ has a double zero at $\omega = 0$.

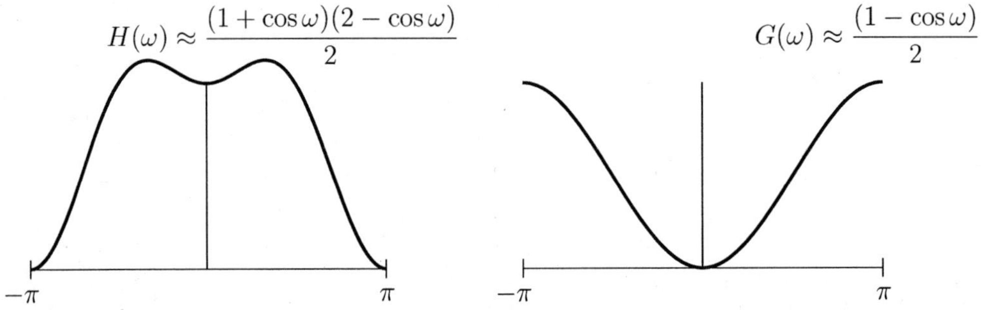

Figure 4.17: Frequency response functions, lowpass $H(\omega)$ and highpass $G(\omega)$.

The two filters combine into a ***filter bank*** (the wavelet transform!). The input is x, the filters give generalized averages y and differences z. To achieve an equal number of outputs and inputs, we ***downsample*** y ***and*** z. By keeping only their even-numbered components $y(2n)$ and $z(2n)$, their length is cut in half. The Haar transform dropped $x_3 \pm x_2$. The block diagram shows filtering and downsampling:

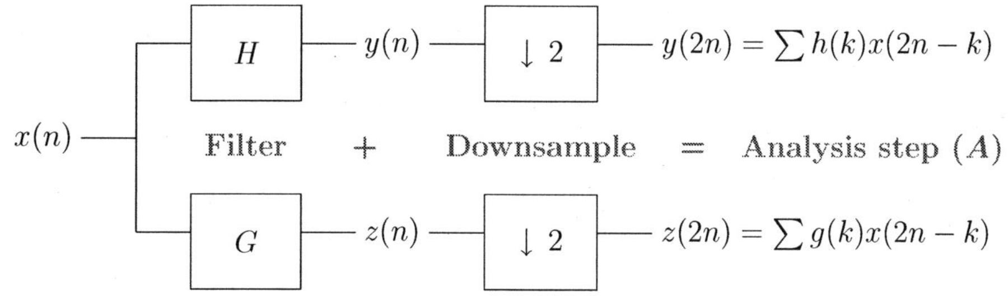

Figure 4.18: The discrete wavelet transform (**DWT**) separates averages and details.

In matrix language, the *wavelet transform* is a multiplication Ax with a *double shift* in the rows of A (from the downsampling step that removes odd-numbered rows):

DWT matrix $$A = \begin{bmatrix} (\downarrow 2)\, H \\ (\downarrow 2)\, G \end{bmatrix} = \begin{bmatrix} -1 & 2 & 6 & 2 & -1 & & & \\ & & -1 & 2 & 6 & 2 & -1 & \\ & & & & \cdot & \cdot & \cdot & \cdot \;\cdot \\ 0 & 1 & -2 & 1 & 0 & & & \\ & & 0 & 1 & -2 & 1 & 0 & \\ & & & & \cdot & \cdot & \cdot & \cdot \;\cdot \end{bmatrix}.$$

An ordinary filter has rows shifted by one, not two. H and G are constant-diagonal Toeplitz matrices, before $\downarrow 2$. For long signals $x(n)$, the model has $-\infty < n < \infty$. Matrices are doubly infinite. For a finite-length input we could assume periodicity, and loop around. Extending $x(n)$ in a symmetric way at each end (Problem 2) is better than the wraparound (cyclic convolution) in S below.

With 1024 samples $x(n)$, the rows still have only five or three nonzeros. Ax is computed in 4 times 1024 multiplications and additions. The DWT is fast. Even with iteration **the transform is $O(N)$**, because signals get shorter and $\frac{1}{2} + \frac{1}{4} + \cdots = 1$.

Perfect Reconstruction

So far the two filters $h(k)$ and $g(k)$ have been separate—no connection. But their interrelation makes everything work. To display this connection we put a second pair of filters into the *columns* of a matrix S, again with double shifts. These "synthesis" filters f and e come from *alternating the signs in the first pair* g and h. Because the choice was good, ***S is the inverse of A***. I will use wraparound to make S finite:

Synthesis $$A^{-1} = S = \frac{1}{16}\begin{bmatrix} 0 & 0 & 2 & 2 & 0 & 2 \\ 1 & 0 & 1 & -6 & 1 & 1 \\ 2 & 0 & 0 & 2 & 2 & 0 \\ 1 & 1 & 0 & 1 & -6 & 1 \\ 0 & 2 & 0 & 0 & 2 & 2 \\ 0 & 1 & 1 & 1 & 1 & -6 \end{bmatrix}$$ **Lowpass $(1, 2, 1)$** **Highpass $(1, 2, -6, 2, 1)$**

S produces the **inverse wavelet transform**. A direct calculation verifies $AS = I$. The inverse transform is as fast as A. It is not usual for a sparse matrix A to have a sparse inverse S, but the wavelet construction makes this happen.

The columns of S are the wavelet basis vectors f and e (discrete ϕ's and w's). Multiplying by A produces the coefficients Ax in the discrete wavelet transform. Then SAx reconstructs x because $SA = I$:

Perfect reconstruction
$$x = S(Ax) = \sum (\text{basis vectors in } S)(\text{coefficients in } Ax). \quad (11)$$

It is useful to see the block form of the synthesis bank S, the inverse wavelet transform:

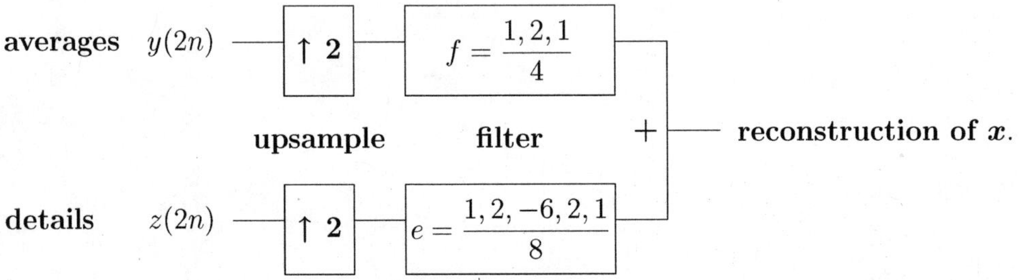

The *upsampling* step $(\uparrow 2)y$ gives the full-length vector $(\ldots, y(0), 0,\ y(2), 0, \ldots)$. The final output from SAx is a delay to $x(n-\ell)$ because the filters are "causal." This means that the coefficients are $h(0), \ldots, h(4)$ rather than $h(-2), \ldots, h(2)$. Then SA can have 1's on diagonal ℓ (an ℓ step delay) instead of diagonal 0.

What condition on the filters, two in analysis and two in synthesis, ensures that $S = A^{-1}$? The top half of A and the left half of S have lowpass filters h and f:

Lowpass
$$\frac{1}{16}(-1, 2, 6, 2, -1) * (1, 2, 1) = \frac{1}{16}(\mathbf{-1, 0, 9, 16, 9, 0, -1}) = \boldsymbol{p}. \quad (12)$$

This convolution is a multiplication of frequency responses $H(\omega)$ and $F(\omega)$:

$$\left(\sum h(k)e^{-ik\omega}\right)\left(\sum f(k)e^{-ik\omega}\right) = \frac{1}{16}\left(-1 + 9e^{-i2\omega} + 16e^{-i3\omega} + 9e^{-i4\omega} - e^{-i6\omega}\right). \quad (13)$$

Multiplying row zero of A times column zero of S produces the coefficient $\frac{1}{16}(16) = 1$. With the double shift in rows of A and columns of S, the key to perfection is this:

$\boldsymbol{AS = I}$ **The product of lowpass responses $\boldsymbol{H(\omega)\,F(\omega)}$ must have only one odd power (like $\boldsymbol{e^{-i3\omega}}$).**

This condition also assures that the highpass product is correct. The last rows of A (with $1, -2, 1$) times the last columns of S (with $1, 2, -6, 2, 1$) look like (12) and (13), but with signs of even powers reversed. When we combine lowpass and highpass, they cancel. Only the odd term survives, to give one diagonal in AS.

The construction of good filter banks A and S now reduces to three quick steps:

1. Choose a symmetric filter p like (12), with $P(\omega) = \sum p(k)e^{-ik\omega}$.

2. Factor $P(\omega)$ into $H(\omega)\,F(\omega)$ to get lowpass filters $h(k)$ and $f(k)$.

3. Reverse order and alternate signs to get highpass coefficients $e(k)$ and $g(k)$.

Orthogonal Filters and Wavelets

A filter bank is **orthogonal** when $S = A^{\mathrm{T}}$. Then we have $A^{\mathrm{T}}A = I$ in discrete time. The continuous-time functions $\phi(t)$ and $w(t)$ use those filter coefficients and inherit orthogonality. All functions in the wavelet expansion (5) will be orthogonal. (We only know this from the construction—there are no simple formulas for $\phi(t)$ and $w(t)$!) Then wavelets compete with Fourier on this property too.

The key to $S = A^{\mathrm{T}}$ is a "spectral factorization" $P(\omega) = H(\omega)\overline{H(\omega)} = |H(\omega)|^2$. For the filter $p(k)$ in (12), this factorization of (13) leads to the orthogonal wavelets discovered by Ingrid Daubechies. Her $H(\omega)$ and $\overline{H(\omega)}$ have these neat coefficients:

Daubechies 4/4
orthogonal $S = A^{\mathrm{T}}$

$$h = (1+\sqrt{3}, 3+\sqrt{3}, 3-\sqrt{3}, 1-\sqrt{3})/8$$
$$g = (1-\sqrt{3}, -3+\sqrt{3}, 3+\sqrt{3}, -1-\sqrt{3})/8 \qquad (14)$$

Orthogonal filter banks have special importance (but not total importance). The rows of A are the columns of S, so the inverse is also the transpose: $S = A^{-1} = A^{\mathrm{T}}$. The product polynomial P is factored specially into $|H(e^{-i\omega})|^2$.

For image processing, symmetry is more important than orthogonality and we choose 5/3 or 9/7. Orthogonal filters lead to *one* pair $\phi(t)$ and $w(t)$, orthogonal to their own translates. Otherwise four filters h, g, f, e give two scaling functions and wavelets [145]. The analysis $\phi(t)$ and $w(t)$ are "**biorthogonal**" to the synthesis functions. Biorthogonality is what we always see in the rows of one matrix and the columns of its inverse:

Biorthogonality $\quad AA^{-1} = I \quad$ means $\quad (\text{row } i \text{ of } A) \cdot (\text{column } j \text{ of } A^{-1}) = \delta_{ij}\,.$

Those even-numbered zeros in p lead to orthogonality of the wavelet bases at all scales (analysis functions times synthesis functions). This is the magic of wavelets:

$$\int_{-\infty}^{\infty} \phi_A(t) w_S\,(2^j t - k)\,dt = \int_{-\infty}^{\infty} \phi_S(t) w_A(2^j t - k)\,dt = 0 \quad \text{for all } k \text{ and } j \qquad (15)$$

$$\int_{-\infty}^{\infty} \phi_A(t) \phi_S(t-k)\,dt = \int_{-\infty}^{\infty} w_A(t) w_S(2^j t - k)\,dt = \delta_{0j}\,. \qquad (16)$$

Sparse Compression

Sines and cosines capture smooth signals. The wavelet transform saves small-scale features. When wavelets are tied to an x-y grid, *ridgelets* and *curvelets* avoid staircasing along edges. In the end we have a **dictionary** of trial functions ϕ_i. They are not independent, and "basis" is not the right word. How can we quickly find an approximation (with few terms) to an input signal s, from a highly redundant and non-orthogonal dictionary of functions?

Here is a greedy approach and an optimization approach [160]:

1. **Orthogonal Matching Pursuit**. At step k, include the ϕ_k that has largest inner product with the current residual $r = s - (c_1\phi_1 + \cdots + c_{k-1}\phi_{k-1})$. Those c's at step $k-1$ were chosen to minimize $\|r\|$.

2. **Basis Pursuit Denoising.** Minimize $\frac{1}{2}\|s - \sum c_i\phi_i\|^2 + L\sum|c_i|$. That ℓ^1 penalty term forces fewer nonzero coeffecients c_i as L is increased. This approach has seen tremendous development. Perhaps the best way to see the sparsifying effect of $L\sum|c_i|$ is by a simple example.

An Example of Sparse Solutions

For two equations $Ax = b$ in three unknowns, the complete solution is $x_{\text{part}} + x_{\text{null}}$:

$$\begin{bmatrix} -1 & 1 & 0 \\ 0 & -1 & 1 \end{bmatrix}\begin{bmatrix} u \\ v \\ w \end{bmatrix} = \begin{bmatrix} 1 \\ 4 \end{bmatrix} \quad \text{is solved by} \quad x = \begin{bmatrix} u \\ v \\ w \end{bmatrix} = \begin{bmatrix} 0 \\ 1 \\ 5 \end{bmatrix} + \begin{bmatrix} c \\ c \\ c \end{bmatrix}. \qquad (17)$$

That particular $x = (0, 1, 5)$ is one of the solutions with two nonzeros. MATLAB's $x = \texttt{A\b} = (-5, -4, 0)$ is another (with a larger ℓ^1 norm). The LASSO solution $x = (-1, 0, 4)$ has smallest ℓ^1 norm $\|x\| = 5$.

The smallest ℓ^2 norm comes from the pseudoinverse of A, but that solution $x^+ = \texttt{pinv}(A) * b = (-2, -1, 3)$ is not sparse at all. (Remember that x^+ is orthogonal to $y = (1, 1, 1)$ in the nullspace of A.) Our goal is **more sparsity**, not less.

To reach *one* nonzero in x, we must give up exact solutions to $Ax = b$. For noisy measurements b, this is totally acceptable. A minimization with penalty term $L\|x\|_1$ is successful:

Basis Pursuit Denoising Minimize $\frac{1}{2}\|Ax - b\|^2 + L(|u| + |v| + |w|)$ (18)

Solution with $L = 2$	$x = (u, v, w) = (\mathbf{0}, \mathbf{0}, \mathbf{3})$	**very sparse**
Solution with $L = 8$	$x = (u, v, w) = (\mathbf{0}, \mathbf{0}, \mathbf{0})$	**fully sparse**

For every L the minimizer is $x = (-(1 - L/2)_+, 0, (4 - L/2)_+)$. The components of x fall to zero and stay there. When L reaches $\|A^{\mathrm{T}}b\|_1 = 8$, the fully sparse $x = 0$ is optimal and the penalty is too heavy.

From ℓ^0 to ℓ^1

The reader may ask why the ℓ^1 norm appears, when the true measure of sparsity is the **number of nonzeros** in x. This "cardinality" of x is its ℓ^0 norm $\|x\|_0$. Our real problem is $Ax = b$ (noiseless case) with minimum $\|x\|_0$, which means maximum sparsity. For fixed cost L and noise in b, we want to minimize $\frac{1}{2}\|Ax - b\|^2 + L\|x\|_0$. Why is $\|x\|_0$ replaced by $\|x\|_1$?

That **counting norm** is important in applications: the number of nonzeros in a fieter, or branches in a network of pipelines, or bars in a truss, or stocks in a portfolio. But minimizing a count is exponentially difficult (**NP-hard**).

There is a sudden change in $\|x\|_0$ and a gradual change in $\|x\|_1$. Integer (Boolean) problems are hard, fractional (convex) problems are easier.

A packing problem with large boxes is simpler when you subdivide the boxes. The mathematical equivalent is to subdivide each nonzero x_i into pieces of size $< \epsilon$ and count again:

$\|\boldsymbol{x}\|_0$ **counts large pieces** $\quad$ $\|x_\epsilon\|_0$ counts pieces $< \epsilon$ $\quad$ $\boldsymbol{\epsilon\|x_\epsilon\|_0}$ **approaches** $\|\boldsymbol{x}\|_1$

It is **convexity** that makes minimization simple in Section 8.6. The absolute value $|x|$ is convex (its slope never decreases). The one-zero cardinality of x is *not convex* (it drops from 1 to 0 at $x = 0$). In the same way, $\|x\|_1$ is the best convex replacement for the counting norm $\|x\|_0$.

The remarkable discovery in this century is that the ℓ^1 solution almost always has nonzeros in the right places! That statement is probabilistic, not deterministic. Suppose we know that $Ax = b$ has a sparse solution x_S with only S nonzero components (so $\|x\|_0 = S$). To find that x_S we solve an ℓ^1 problem:

Linear programming $\quad$ x^* minimizes $\|x\|_1$ subject to $Ax = b$. $\quad$ (19)

The analysis of Donoho, Candès, Romberg, Tao... shows that $\boldsymbol{x^* = x_S}$ **with high probability provided** $\boldsymbol{m > S \log n}$. No need to sample more, no use to sample less. When sensors are expensive, $m << n$ is attractive in many applications. But the sampling must be suitably incoherent, reflected in the m by n matrix A:

- m random Fourier coefficients out of n
- 1024 pixels along 22 rays out of $(1024)^2$ pixels in an MR scan

That $50:1$ reduction still aims to locate the nonzeros in the image. In some way it is overcoming the *Nyquist condition* that applies to band-limited functions: at least two samples within the shortest wavelength. One goal is an analog-to-digital converter that can cope with very high bandwidth. When Nyquist requires 1 gigahertz as the sampling rate, random sampling may be the only way.

One feature to notice for NP-hard problems in general. *A fast algorithm can be close to correct with high probability.* It can't be exact every time, some level of danger has to be accepted.

The Total Variation Norm

Denoising is a fundamental problem in computational image processing. The goal is to preserve important features which the human visual system detects (the edges, the texture, the regularity). All successful models take advantage of the regularity of natural images and the irregularity of noise. Variational methods can **allow for discontinuities but disfavor oscillations**, by minimizing the right energy.

The L^1 norm of the gradient measures the variation in $u(x, y)$:

Total variation $$\|u\|_{\mathrm{TV}} = \iint |\operatorname{grad} u|\, dx\, dy = \sup_{|w|\le 1} \iint u \operatorname{div} w\, dx\, dy. \qquad (20)$$

To see this TV norm in action, suppose an image is black on the left side, white on the right side, and pixels are missing in between. How do we "inpaint" to minimize the TV norm?

The best u is monotonic, because oscillations will be punished by $\iint |\operatorname{grad} u|\, dx\, dy$. Here that u jumps from 0 to 1 across an edge. Its TV norm is the **length of the edge**. (I think of $\operatorname{grad} u$ as a line of delta functions along the edge. Integrating gives the length. The dual definition in (20) avoids delta functions and yields the same answer.) So minimization not only accepts the edge, it aims to make it short (therefore smooth). Three comments:

1. Minimizing $\iint |\operatorname{grad} u|^2\, dx\, dy$ gives a gradual ramp, not a jump. The minimizer now solves Laplace's equation. It is far from a delta function, which has infinite energy in this root mean square norm.

2. The ramp $u = x$ (from $x = 0$ to 1) is also a minimizer in this example. The integral of $\operatorname{grad} u = (1, 0)$ for that unit ramp equals the integral of $\operatorname{grad} u = (\delta(x), 0)$. *The TV norm is convex but not strictly convex.* It is possible (as in linear programming) to have multiple minimizers. When $\|u\|_{\mathrm{TV}}$ is combined with the L^2 norm, this won't happen.

3. An early success by Osher, who pioneered the TV norm in imaging, was to restore a very noisy image in a criminal case. Medical imaging is now the major application, detecting tumors instead of thieves.

Image Compression and Restoration

Imaging science is today's name for a classical problem: to represent images accurately and process them quickly. This is part of applied mathematics, but the reader may feel that "science" is becoming an overused word. The science of electromagnetism has fundamental laws (Maxwell's equations). The TV norm also connects to a partial differential equation (for minimal surfaces). But now human parameters enter too. Perhaps "engineering science" is a useful description, emphasizing that this subject combines depth with practical importance. The fundamental problem, to understand the statistics of natural images, is still unsolved.

Compression depends on the choice of a good basis. Cosines were the long-time leader in **jpeg**. Wavelets became the choice of JPEG 2000, to reduce blocking artifacts. But the other enemy is ringing (false oscillation), which tends to increase as basis functions get longer. We look for a successful compromise between fitting the data $g(x, y)$ and preserving the (piecewise) smoothness of natural images. One way is to insert that compromise into the minimization:

Total variation restoration Minimize $\frac{1}{2}\iint |u-g|^2 dx\, dy + \alpha \iint |\operatorname{grad} u|\, dx\, dy$ (21)

Duality plays a crucial role in forming the optimality equations (Section 8.6). The duality of u and w, displacements and forces, voltages and currents, has been a powerful idea throughout this book. It still has more to reveal, but first we turn back to classical mathematics and $f(x+iy)$—complex analysis and its applications.

Problem Set 4.7

1 For $h = \frac{1}{2}, \frac{1}{2}$ Haar's equations (6)-(7) have unusually simple solutions:

$$\phi(t) = \phi(2t) + \phi(2t-1) = \text{box} + \text{box} = \text{scaling function}$$

$$w(t) = \phi(2t) - \phi(2t-1) = \text{box} - \text{box} = \text{wavelet}$$

Draw the sum and difference of these two half-boxes $\phi(2t)$ and $\phi(2t-1)$. Show that all wavelets $w(2^j t - k)$ are orthogonal to $\phi(t)$.

2 The Daubechies polynomial $p(z) = -1 + 9z^2 + 16z^3 + 9z^4 - z^6$ from (12) has $p(-1) = 0$. Show that $(z+1)^4$ divides $p(z)$, so there are *four roots* at $z = -1$. Find the other two roots z_5 and z_6, from $p(z)/(z+1)^4$.

3 What cubic has the roots $-1, -1$, and z_5? Connect its coefficients to h or g in (14) for Daubechies 4/4.

4 What quartic has the roots $-1, -1, z_5$ and z_6? Connect it to equation (12) and the symmetric 5/3 filters.

5 Create a 2/6 filter bank whose two lowpass coefficients are Haar's $h = \frac{1}{2}, \frac{1}{2}$. The six highpass coefficients come from dividing $p(z)/\frac{1}{2}(z-1)$ which has degree 5.

6 Show that the hat function $H(t)$ solves the refinement equation (6) with lowpass coefficients $h = (1, 2, 1)/4$.

7 Show that the cubic B-spline $S(t) = H(t) * H(t)$ from Section 3.2 solves the refinement equation (6) for $h = (1, 2, 1) * (1, 2, 1)/16$. (You could use the cascade code on the cse site to draw $S(t)$.)

8
$$A_6 = \begin{bmatrix} -1 & 2 & 6 & 2 & -1 & 0 \\ -1 & 0 & -1 & 2 & 6 & 2 \\ 6 & 2 & -1 & 0 & -1 & 2 \\ 0 & 1 & -2 & 1 & 0 & 0 \\ 0 & 0 & 0 & 1 & -2 & 1 \\ -2 & 1 & 0 & 0 & 0 & 1 \end{bmatrix}.$$

is a circulant matrix?
is a block (2 by 2) circulant?
has what inverse by MATLAB?
extends to which matrix A_8?

9 The *ideal lowpass filter* h has $H(\omega) = \sum h(k)e^{-ik\omega} = 1$ for $|\omega| \le \pi/2$ (zero for $\pi/2 < |\omega| < \pi$). What are the coefficients $h(k)$? What highpass coefficients $g(k)$ give $G = 1 - H$?

10 Upsampling a signal $x(n)$ inserts zeros into $u = (\uparrow 2)x$, by the rule $u(2n+1) = 0$ and $u(2n) = x(n)$. Show that $U(\omega) = X(2\omega)$.

11 For a 2D image $x(m,n)$ instead of a 1D signal $x(n)$, Haar's 2D filter produces which averages $y(m,n)$? There are now *three differences*, z_H (horizontal) and z_V (vertical) and z_{HV}. What are those four outputs from a checkerboard input $x(m,n) = 1$ or 0 ($m+n$ even or odd)?

12 Apply the cascade code on the **cse** site to find $\phi(t)$ for $h = (-1, 2, 6, 2, -1)/8$.

13 (Solution unknown) In the example with $A = [-1\ 1\ 0; 0\ -1\ 1]$ and $b = [1; 4]$, use the ℓ^0 norm (number of nonzero components) directly in $\frac{1}{2}||Ax - b||^2 + L||x||_0$. Minimize for increasing L.

14 With one equation, minimize $\frac{1}{2}(u + 2v + 3w - 6)^2 + L(|u| + |v| + |w|)$. At what value of L does $(0,0,0)$ become the minimizer?

15 What is the TV norm of $u(x,y)$ if $u = 1$ in the unit disc $x^2 + y^2 \le 1$ (zero elsewhere)? What is $||u||_{\text{TV}}$ for $u = (\sin 2\pi x)(\sin 2\pi y)$ in the unit square?

CHAPTER 5

ANALYTIC FUNCTIONS

5.1 TAYLOR SERIES AND COMPLEX INTEGRATION

This chapter is about the best functions. We start with e^x and $\sin x$ and ratios of polynomials like $1/(1+x^2)$. Those and many more are attractive as functions of x (a real variable). The complex e^z and $\sin z$ and $1/(1+z^2)$ look even better. These are **analytic functions** of the variable $z = x + iy$. They deserve our attention.

How to recognize an analytic function? Its Taylor series is an excellent guide. Around the center point $z = 0$, the powers are $z^n = (x+iy)^n$ and not just x^n:

$$\boldsymbol{e^z} = 1 + \frac{z}{1!} + \frac{z^2}{2!} + \cdots \qquad \mathbf{sin}\, \boldsymbol{z} = \frac{z}{1!} - \frac{z^3}{3!} + \frac{z^5}{5!} - \cdots \qquad \frac{\mathbf{1}}{\mathbf{1} + \boldsymbol{z}^{\mathbf{2}}} = 1 - z^2 + z^4 - \cdots \tag{1}$$

The Taylor series is constructed to match all derivatives of the function at the center point. For e^z the nth derivative is e^z. At the center point $z = 0$, every derivative equals 1. In the series, z^n has derivative $n\,z^{n-1}$ and then $n(n-1)z^{n-2}$. The nth derivative is the constant $n(n-1)\cdots(1) = n!$ and all further derivatives are zero. *Conclusion*: To match the derivatives $1, 1, 1, \ldots$ of e^z we should *divide each* z^n *by* $n!$ *in the Taylor series.* The coefficient a_n of z^n is $1/n!$:

Taylor series for e^z around $z = 0$ $\qquad e^z = \displaystyle\sum_{n=0}^{\infty} a_n z^n = \sum_{n=0}^{\infty} \frac{z^n}{n!}$ $\qquad$ (2)

Matching the nth derivative by $a_n = f^{(n)}(0)/n!$ is purely formal. *What makes the function analytic is that the series actually adds up to* e^z. This series converges for all z, so that e^z is analytic everywhere (no singularities at finite z).

We have *action at a distance.* The derivatives at $z = 0$ predict $f(z)$ far away from that point. If $f(z) = 1$ in a neighborhood of $z = 0$, then $f(z) = 1$ everywhere.

The derivatives of $\sin z$ are $\cos z, -\sin z, -\cos z$ (then $\sin z$ again). At $z = 0$ their values are $0, 1, -0, -1$ (then repeat). To match those numbers with the derivatives from $1, z, z^2, z^3$, divide by $n!$ as before. Then the Taylor series for $\sin z$ starts with $z/1$ and $-z^3/6$, and every even power has coefficient $a_n = 0$.

Singularities Prevent Convergence

For $1/(1+z^2)$ we see a big change. The series $1 - z^2 + z^4 - z^6 + \cdots$ only converges if $|z| < 1$. If $|z| \geq 1$, the terms don't go toward zero, which leaves no chance of convergence. And $1/(1+z^2)$ is not analytic at the two "*poles*" $z = i$ and $z = -i$. Those are **singularities** where $1 + z^2 = 0$ and the function becomes $1/0$.

Complex analysis connects the failure of the series to the singularities of the function. Power series $\sum a_n(z - z_0)^n$ always converge inside circles around the center point z_0. Those circles of convergence reach out to the nearest singularity, where *convergence has to stop*:

$$f(z) = \sum a_n z^n \textit{ converges for } |z| < R \iff f(z) \textit{ is analytic for } |z| < R.$$

$1 - z^2 + z^4 - \cdots$ has "radius of convergence" $R = 1$ around $z = 0$. Convergence of the series gives analyticity in the unit circle. But this $f(z)$ is perfectly analytic at $z = 2$ and $z = 10$ and $z = 10i$. **We now move the center point away from** $z = 0$.

A new center point z_0 will lead to circles of convergence around z_0 (*when* $f(z)$ *is analytic in those circles*). The series has powers $(z - z_0)^n$ instead of z^n. Certainly $(z-z_0)^n$ has zero derivatives at z_0, except that its nth derivative is $n!$. Then $a_n(z-z_0)^n$ matches the nth derivative $f^{(n)}(z_0)$, *now computed at* z_0, when the Taylor series coefficient is $f^{(n)}(z_0)/n! = a_n$:

Taylor series around z_0

$$f(z) = f(z_0) + f'(z_0)(z - z_0) + \cdots = \sum_{n=0}^{\infty} \frac{f^{(n)}(z_0)}{n!}(z - z_0)^n \quad (3)$$

Question If $z_0 = 10i$, the series for $1/(1+z^2)$ converges in what disc $|z - 10i| < R$?

Answer $R = 9$ because the nearest singularity to $z_0 = 10i$ is the pole at $z = i$. The series around $z_0 = 1$ will converge out to $|z - 1| = \sqrt{2}$. Figure 5.1 shows why.

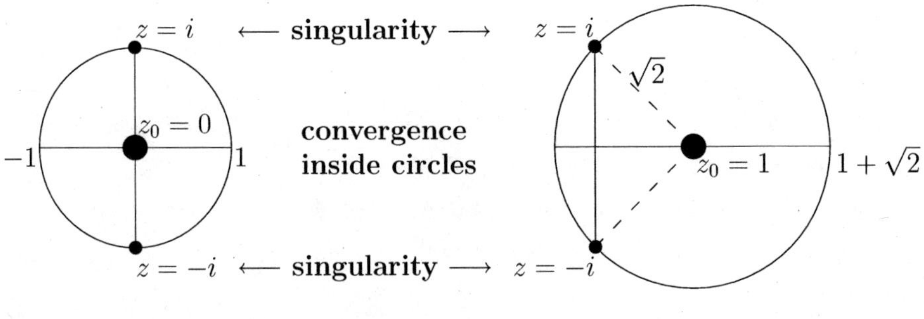

Figure 5.1: Taylor series for $1/(1+z^2)$ converge inside circles reaching to $z = \pm\, i$.

Computing with Analytic Functions

You see that these first pages are dominated by ***circles***. Derivatives at z_0 control $f(z)$ away from z_0. Soon we compute those derivatives by integrating around a circle (Cauchy's Integral Formula). The integrals will come quickly and accurately from the Fast Fourier Transform, which specializes in circles. **Scientific computing becomes exponentially fast when functions are analytic.**

Let me point ahead to other codes in Section 5.4. I think first of integration and differentiation and interpolation. The reason for success is that **polynomials are exponentially close to analytic functions**. You might guess that the exponent depends on the location of the singularities. Even for a real $f(x)$ on an interval $-1 \leq x \leq 1$, its complex extension $f(z)$ is the function in control.

Many courses explain analytic functions, but they don't compute with them. The type of polynomial is based on the location of the problem (*point, circle, interval*):

Point	Powers $(x - x_0)^n$	**Taylor**
Circle	Exponentials e^{ikx}	**Fourier**
Interval	Polynomials $T_n(x)$	**Chebyshev**

The first step is to understand the complex singularities of $f(z)$, *especially poles*. Integrating a/z on a circle around the pole at $z = 0$ gives $2\pi ia$. That special integral will be the key—it comes from the "residue" of $f(z)$ at its pole, which is a. When we want $f(z_0)$, we create a pole and integrate $f(z)/(z - z_0)$. When we want derivatives $f^{(n)}(z_0)$, we create a higher order pole and integrate $f(z)/(z - z_0)^{n+1}$.

The central and beautiful fact of complex analysis is Cauchy's Theorem, which allows us to escape instantly and completely from circles. "*The integral of every analytic $f(z)$ around any closed path is zero.*" This leads to very remarkable integrals. Paths can be deformed into circles when the function is analytic in the space between.

The Complex Derivative

Six examples will highlight analytic functions and their singularities. Convergence of the infinite series is the Weierstrass test. Riemann's test is that $f(z)$ must have a derivative $f'(z)$, the same in all complex directions. *Key point*: $f(z)$ is analytic (satisfying Weierstrass) exactly when $f(z)$ is "holomorphic" (satisfying Riemann). The first example fails both tests.

Example 1 The function $f(x + iy) = x$ is not analytic or holomorphic. This function $\boldsymbol{f(z) = \mathrm{Re}\, z = x}$ has different derivatives 1 and 0 in the real and imaginary directions:

Real Δx
Complex $i\Delta y$

$$\frac{f(z+\Delta x) - f(z)}{\Delta x} = \frac{x + \Delta x - x}{\Delta x} \qquad \frac{f(z+i\Delta y) - f(z)}{i\Delta y} = \frac{x - x}{i\Delta y}$$

A Taylor series can't even start because we don't have a derivative $f'(z_0)$. Its terms can't stay real, so a complex series can't represent a real function.

Similarly $u(x, y) = x^2 - y^2$ is not analytic. It is not a combination of powers of $x + iy$. It is the *real part* of the analytic function $z^2 = (x + iy)^2$. The real part $u(x, y)$ and the imaginary part $s(x, y)$ of an analytic $f(z)$ are **harmonic functions.**

Riemann's test that $f'(z)$ must be the same in the real and imaginary directions led in Section 3.3 to the key connections between the two real harmonic functions u and s. They both satisfy Laplace's equation (from $u_{xx} = s_{yx} = s_{xy} = -u_{yy}$).

Cauchy-Riemann equations $$\frac{\partial u}{\partial x} = \frac{\partial s}{\partial y} \quad \text{and} \quad \frac{\partial u}{\partial y} = -\frac{\partial s}{\partial x} \tag{4}$$

Weierstrass is valuable too, because df/dz comes term by term from the series:

$$\text{The derivative of } \sin z = z - \frac{z^3}{3!} + \frac{z^5}{5!} - \cdots \quad \text{is } \cos z = 1 - \frac{z^2}{2!} + \frac{z^4}{4!} - \cdots$$

Poles and Laurent Series

Example 2 The function $f(z) = 1/(1 + z^2)$ fails to be analytic at $z = i$ and $z = -i$. Since $1 + z^2 = 0$ at those points, the magnitude $|f(z)|$ blows up at these poles. Those are singularities of the simplest kind: **simple poles. When multiplying $(z - z_0)f(z)$ removes a singularity, the point z_0 is a simple pole.**

$$z = i \text{ is a simple pole because } (z - i)f(z) = \frac{z - i}{1 + z^2} = \frac{1}{z + i} \text{ is analytic there.}$$

When $f(z)$ is analytic, does $f(z)/z$ have a simple pole at $z = 0$? This is true if $f(0) \neq 0$. Dividing by z creates the pole, then multiplying by z removes it. For $f(z) = \sin z$ with $f(0) = 0$, we would have to divide by z^2 to create a pole because $(\sin z)/z$ is analytic.

Example 3 $\dfrac{1}{z - 1}$ and $\dfrac{e^z}{z - 1}$ have simple poles at $z = 1$. Not $\dfrac{e^z - e}{z - 1}$ because $e^1 = e$.

Example 4 $\dfrac{7}{z^2}$ and $\dfrac{\sin z}{z^3}$ have **double poles** at $z = 0$. To remove, multiply by $(z - 0)^2$.

With a pole at z_0, the Taylor series fails. But if we allow **negative powers** of $z - z_0$, a "Laurent series" can correctly represent $f(z)$ in an annulus (a ring):

Laurent series $f(z) = \displaystyle\sum_{n=-\infty}^{\infty} a_n (z - z_0)^n$ converges in a ring $0 < |z - z_0| < R$.

For a pole of order N, the most negative power will be $(z - z_0)^{-N}$. The simple pole of $e^z/z = (1 + z + \cdots)/z$ has one negative power $1/z$. For an essential singularity, the negative powers won't stop:

Laurent series for $|z| > 0$ $$e^{-1/z^2} = 1 - \frac{1}{z^2} + \frac{1}{2!\,z^4} - \frac{1}{3!\,z^6} + \cdots \tag{5}$$

Example 5 The function $f(z) = e^{-1/z^2}$ has an **essential singularity** at $z = 0$.

Approaching zero along the real axis, $f(x) = e^{-1/x^2}$ goes quickly to zero. All derivatives of $f(x)$ are also zero! This is an infinitely differentiable real function that is not the sum of its Taylor series $0 + 0x + 0x^2 + \cdots$. This shows that e^{-1/z^2} is not analytic at 0.

You see a bigger problem if you come down the imaginary axis. Approaching zero from this direction, $f(iy) = e^{+1/y^2}$ blows up. Actually e^{-1/z^2} is analytic except at $z = 0$.

Branch Points

Example 6 The square root function $f(z) = z^{1/2}$ has a **branch point** at $z = 0$. Away from $z = 0$, the square root has two values. There is one Taylor series around $z_0 = 4$ starting with $\sqrt{4} = 2$, and another series starting with $\sqrt{4} = -2$. Those series converge inside the circle of radius $R = 4$ that reaches the singularity of $\sqrt{z}$ at $z = 0$.

This example produces a **Riemann surface**. Its two sheets meet at the branch point $z = 0$. We don't intend to study Riemann surfaces, but by circling around $z = 0$ you can guess that you end up on the other sheet. The function $\log z$ has infinitely many sheets, because every time you go around $z = 0$ you add $2\pi i$ to the logarithm. The imaginary part of $\log(re^{i\theta})$ is θ, which increases by 2π.

Integral of z^n Around a Circle

Here is another form of "action at a distance." Suppose $f(z)$ is analytic on and inside a circle. From $f(z)$ on the circle, we can recover its derivatives at the center. There is one special integral (around a simple pole) that makes everything succeed:

Integral of $\frac{1}{z}$ or $\frac{1}{z - z_0}$

$$\int_{|z|=r} \frac{dz}{z} = 2\pi i \qquad \int_{|z-z_0|=r} \frac{dz}{z - z_0} = 2\pi i \tag{6}$$

The first integral comes directly from $z = re^{i\theta}$ on the circle from $\theta = 0$ to 2π:

Set $z = re^{i\theta}$

$$\int_{|z|=r} \frac{dz}{z} = \int_0^{2\pi} \frac{ir\,e^{i\theta}\,d\theta}{r\,e^{i\theta}} = \int_0^{2\pi} i\,d\theta = 2\pi i\,. \tag{7}$$

The integral around z_0 is the same when $z = z_0 + r\,e^{i\theta}$. We could also use $\log z$:

Same integral

$$\int \frac{dz}{z} = \Big[\log z\Big]_{\text{start}}^{\text{end}} = (\log r + 2\pi i) - (\log r) = 2\pi i\,.$$

A key example for Laplace's equation was this integral in its real form—truly important. There we had a point source at $(x, y) = (0, 0)$. The potential was $u(x, y) = \log r$, the real part of $\log z$. By the Divergence Theorem, the flux through every circle $|z| = r$ is 2π. This matches the change in the stream function $s(x, y) = \theta$.

It is the multiple values of θ at the same point $re^{i\theta}$ that produce a nonzero answer. A single-valued $F(z)$ would have $F(\text{end}) - F(\text{start}) = 0$. Zero is the normal answer on a closed loop! Cauchy's great theorem has no $1/z$ pole and the integral is zero.

This discussion pushes us to integrate other poles $1/z^2, 1/z^3, \cdots$ (now we get 0):

Integral of z^n, $n \neq -1$
$$\int_{|z|=r} z^n\, dz = \left[\frac{z^{n+1}}{n+1}\right]_{\text{start}}^{\text{end}} = 0\,. \qquad (8)$$

That becomes a real integration for positive powers too, when we set $z = r\,e^{i\theta}$:

Integral over θ
$$\int_0^{2\pi} (re^{i\theta})^n\, ire^{i\theta}\, d\theta = \left[\frac{ir^{n+1}e^{i(n+1)\theta}}{n+1}\right]_0^{2\pi} = 0 \quad \text{Notice } n+1 \neq 0.$$

Cauchy's Integral Formula

The constant term in the Taylor series is the central value $a_0 = f(0)$. To produce $f(0)$, ***divide $f(z)$ by z and integrate around a circle $|z| = r$***. You have created a pole for a_0/z, unless $a_0 = 0$. The other Taylor series terms $a_1 z + a_2 z^2 + \cdots$ are also divided by z, but their integrals are all zero by (8). The integral of the complete $f(z)/z$ is the integral of that singular part a_0/z, which is $2\pi i\, a_0$.

The same idea applies to any Taylor series $f(z) = a_0 + a_1(z - z_0) + \cdots$ around any center point z_0. ***Divide by $z - z_0$ and integrate***. All integrals are zero except the first one, for $a_0/(z - z_0)$. That produces $2\pi i\, a_0$ in the special integral (6). Creating a pole and integrating gives Cauchy's Integral Formula for $a_0 = f(z_0)$:

Cauchy's Integral Formula on circles around any z_0
$$\frac{1}{2\pi i} \int_{|z-z_0|=r} \frac{f(z)}{z - z_0}\, dz = f(z_0)\,. \qquad (9)$$

Example 7 Integrating a complicated function like $f(z)/(z-3) = e^{10/(1+z^2)}/(z-3)$ has become simple. By creating a pole at $z_0 = 3$, we get $2\pi i\, f(3)$:

$$\int_C \frac{f(z)}{z-3}\, dz = 2\pi i\, f(3) = 2\pi i\, e^{10/10} = 2\pi i\, e.$$

Notice what makes this easy. The integral goes on a *simple closed path* (start = end). The path goes one time around, counterclockwise. The function $e^{10/(1+z^2)}$ stays analytic inside the path. We must not enclose the singularities at $z = i$ and $z = -i$.

A matrix form of (9) is $\int f(z)(zI - A)^{-1} dz = 2\pi i\, f(A)$. The integral must enclose all eigenvalues of A. For $f(z) = e^{zt}$ we get $f(A) = e^{At}$, a highly important matrix function; see section 5.3 and Higham's book [90].

Derivatives *at* z_0 come from integrals *around* z_0 (when f is analytic). To find the nth derivative of $f(z)$ at $z = 0$ or $z = z_0$, ***divide by z^{n+1} or $(z - z_0)^{n+1}$***. Every term in the series has zero integral around the center by (8), *with one exception.* The nth power $a_n z^n$ is divided by z^{n+1}, and ***its integral picks out*** $\boldsymbol{2\pi i\, a_n}$.

That number a_n is $n!$ times the nth derivative of $f(z)$, which is $f^{(n)}(0)$ or $f^{(n)}(z_0)$:

Cauchy's Integral Formula for the nth derivative

$$\frac{n!}{2\pi i} \int_{|z-z_0|=r} \frac{f(z)}{(z-z_0)^{n+1}}\, dz = f^{(n)}(z_0)\,. \tag{10}$$

Example 8 The third derivative of $\sin z$ is -1 at $z = 0$. Divide $\sin z$ by z^4:

Watch $\boldsymbol{\dfrac{1}{z}}$ $$\frac{3!}{2\pi i}\int \left(\frac{z}{z^4} - \frac{\boldsymbol{z^3}}{\boldsymbol{3!\,z^4}} + \frac{z^5}{5!\,z^4} - \cdots\right) dz = \frac{1}{2\pi i}\int -\frac{1}{z}\, dz = -1.$$

Up to now, all paths have been circles. Cauchy's Theorem will soon change that.

Computing Derivatives by the FFT

The derivatives at the center point $z = 0$ are equal to integrals around a circle. We may choose any radius r such that $f(z)$ is analytic inside and on the circle $|z| = r$. The integral is closely approximated by a sum at equally spaced points. (This is the trapezoidal rule, with low accuracy on an interval $a \le x \le b$ but very high accuracy around a circle. It is periodicity that produces exponential accuracy.) For sums of equally spaced values around a circle, the FFT is perfect.

The N-point FFT computes N sums at once. It yields approximate values for all the numbers $f(0), f'(0), \ldots, f^{(N-1)}(0)$. Lower derivatives will be the most accurate, and the computation is extremely stable (because the FFT is stable). "The principal difficulties encountered in numerical differentiation simply disappear." This code could use $N = 64$ points with a real FFT since $f(x) = e^x$ stays real.

```
f = @(x) exp(x);                  % f(x) = e^x has f^(n)(0) = 1 and a_n = 1/n!
z = exp(2*i*pi*(0:N-1)'/N);       % N equally spaced points on |z| = 1
a = fft(f(z)/N);                  % FFT gives a_0 to a_{N-1} with high accuracy
a = real(a);                      % Those coefficients are real by symmetry
disp([a 1./gamma(1:N)'])          % Display computed and exact a_n = 1/n!
```

The computed coefficients a include errors from *aliasing.* The $(n + kN)$th power of each z is identical to the nth power, because every evaluation point has $z^N = 1$:

Aliases included in a $$\text{Computed } a_j = \text{Exact } a_j + a_{j+N} + a_{j+2N} + \cdots \tag{11}$$

Those errors from later coefficients (higher derivatives) drop off quickly when $f(z)$ is analytic in a larger circle than $|z| = 1$. Very small errors for e^z (analytic everywhere).

Cauchy's Theorem

Cauchy studied integration of analytic functions $f(z)$ around simple closed paths. When the path is a circle around $z = 0$, we can integrate every term of its Taylor series $a_0 + a_1 z + \cdots$. ***The integral around the circle is zero***:

Cauchy's Theorem around a circle
$$\int_{|z|=r} f(z)\,dz = \int (a_0 + a_1 z + \cdots)\,dz = 0 + 0 + \cdots = 0. \quad (12)$$

Another approach uses the term-by-term integral $g(z) = a_0 z + \frac{1}{2} a_1 z^2 + \cdots$. This series for $g(z) = \int f(z)dz$ converges in the same circle. The Fundamental Theorem of Calculus gives zero, because the starting point is also the endpoint:

Complex integration $z_1 = z_2$ for closed path
$$\int_{z_1}^{z_2} f(z)\,dz = g(z_2) - g(z_1) \;\text{ and }\; \int_{|z|=r} f(z)\,dz = 0\,. \quad (13)$$

What happens when the path C is not a circle? Complex analysts can create very complicated paths (on which Cauchy's Theorem would still be true). It is enough to consider smooth curves joined at a finite number of corners, like a square or a semicircle. Always the path C must be closed. The region inside has no holes!

Cauchy's Theorem $\int_C f(z)\,dz = 0$ **if $f(z)$ is analytic on and inside C.** (14)

I can suggest two approaches to (14) that look good. Probably they convince you and me that $\int f(z)\,dz = 0$. A fully rigorous proof takes more than a reasonable space, and we indicate a third approach. It is unfinished but you will see the point.

First approach Construct an antiderivative with $g'(z) = f(z)$, as for a circle. The Fundamental Theorem of Calculus says that $\int g'(z)\,dz = g(\textbf{end}) - g(\textbf{start})$. This is $\int f(z)\,dz = 0$ provided $g(z)$ comes back to the same value.

It is analyticity of $f(z)$ *inside the path* C that makes $g(z)$ single-valued. That was the key point for $f(z) = 1/z$, when the integral $g(z) = \log z$ is *not* single-valued. The integral of $1/z$ around the origin is $2\pi i$, not zero.

In the analytic case, the integral of $f(z)$ from z_1 to z_2 *does not depend on the path.* Two paths give the same answer, if $f(z)$ is analytic between them. Going forward on one path and back on the other, the integral on the closed path is zero.

Second approach Integrate separately the real and imaginary parts of $f(z)\,dz$:

$$\int f(z)\,dz = \int (u + i\,s)(dx + i\,dy) = \int (u\,dx - s\,dy) + i \int (u\,dy + s\,dx)\,. \quad (15)$$

Green's formula in 3.3 gives double integrals. Then Cauchy-Riemann gives zero:

$$\int_C (u\,dy + s\,dx) = \iint_R \left(\frac{\partial u}{\partial x} - \frac{\partial s}{\partial y}\right) dx\,dy = \iint_R 0\,dx\,dy = 0 \quad (16)$$

$$\int_C (u\,dx - s\,dy) = \iint_R \left(-\frac{\partial s}{\partial x} - \frac{\partial u}{\partial y}\right) dx\,dy = \iint_R 0\,dx\,dy = 0 \quad (17)$$

This was Cauchy's proof. The technical hitch is to show that $f'(z)$ is continuous.

Third approach In very small triangles, $f(z_0)+f'(z_0)(z-z_0)$ is close to $f(z)$. The error is below $\epsilon|z-z_0|$ because f' exists. The key step is to prove this with the same ϵ for all the triangles. Then fill any polygon by these small triangles, with sides in common. The integrals of $f(z)$ cancel along shared sides, to give $|\int f(z)\,dz| < C\epsilon$ around the large polygon. This approach escapes from a circle to any polygon [127], and even constructs an antiderivative $g(z)$. Finally $\int f(z)\,dz = 0$.

Changing the Path

Let me start on the most important application of Cauchy's Theorem. It is useful for *functions with poles* (not analytic). We no longer expect $\int f(z)\,dz = 0$, when the path of integration goes around a pole. Integrating $1/z$ and $1/z^2$ on circles around $z=0$ gave the answers $2\pi i$ and 0. Now we can integrate on any path around that pole, ***by changing the path to a circle***. Cauchy makes this possible.

Why can we change paths? Apply Cauchy's Theorem $\int f(z)\,dz = 0$ around the space between the two paths—the original curve C and the circle(s). If there are several poles inside C we will have circles around each of them. Cauchy's Theorem applies to paths without holes, so we add connectors from C in Figure 5.2.

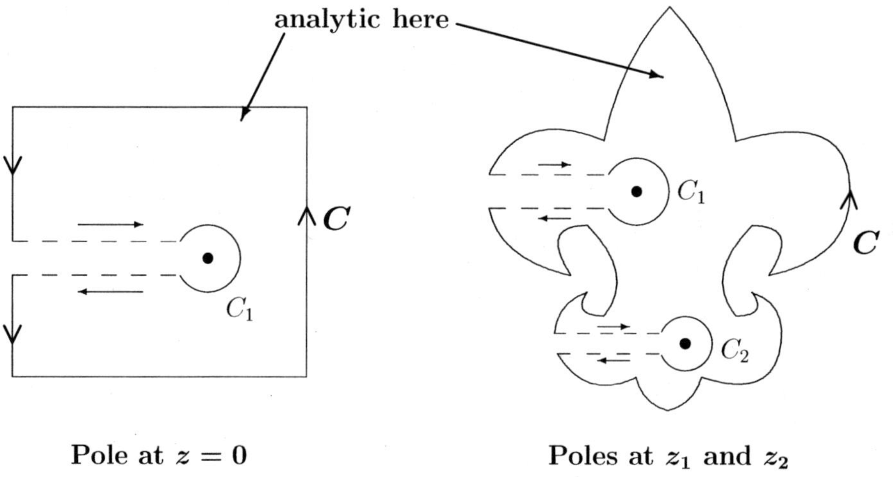

Figure 5.2: $\int_C f(z)\,dz$ equals the sum of integrals around all poles inside C.

The integrals in and out along the connectors cancel, as those dashed lines get closer. Inside the deformed path, and outside the small circles, $f(z)$ is analytic. The integral is zero by Cauchy's Theorem. This deformed path is going the wrong way (clockwise) on the circles $C_1, \ldots, C_N$ around the poles. So the integral around C minus the integrals around the poles is zero. We are back to circles.

Contour change from C to circles $C_1, \ldots, C_N$ $f(z)$ is analytic between	$$\int_C f(z)\,dz = \int_{C_1} f(z)\,dz + \cdots + \int_{C_N} f(z)\,dz\,. \quad (18)$$

Residues and Contour Integration

If there is a pole of order m at $z = z_0$, then $f(z)$ has a Laurent expansion starting with $a_{-m}/(z-z_0)^m$. When we integrate every term in the series, and the path encloses no other singularities, *only the integral of $a_{-1}/(z-z_0)$ survives*:

$$f(z) = \frac{a_{-m}}{(z-z_0)^m} + \cdots + \frac{a_{-1}}{z-z_0} + \sum_0^\infty a_n (z-z_0)^n \quad \text{has} \quad \int \boldsymbol{f(z)\,dz = 2\pi i\, a_{-1}}\,. \quad (19)$$

This key number a_{-1} is the "residue" of $f(z)$ at its pole z_0. If $f(z)$ has other poles, it will have residues at those poles. The residue at a double pole could be zero, as for $1/z^2$. The residue could be nonzero, as for $1/z + 1/z^2$. If we integrate around several poles, we *add the residues*—because the path C can change as in Figure 5.2 into a small circle around each pole.

Residue Theorem Poles at $z_1, \ldots, z_N$	$$\int_C f(z)\,dz = 2\pi i \sum_{j=1}^N (\text{Residue of } f(z) \text{ at } z_j)\,. \quad (20)$$

Example 9 Integrate $f(z) = 1/(1+z^2)$ along a small square around $z = i$.

Solution Since $1/(1+z^2)$ has a simple pole at $z_0 = i$, the only negative power around that point will be $a_{-1}/(z-i)$. Integrating on a square or a circle makes no difference by "change of path." **The residue at the simple pole $z = i$ will be** $a_{-1} = \lim_{z\to i}(z-i)f(z) = \mathbf{1/2i}$. Then the integral around $z = i$ is $(2\pi i)(1/2i) = \pi$.

We know two ways to see that this residue of $1/(1+z^2)$ is $a_{-1} = 1/2i$ at $z = i$:

Divide out pole
$$a_{-1} = \lim_{z\to i} \frac{z-i}{1+z^2} = \lim_{z\to i} \frac{1}{z+i} = \frac{1}{2i} \quad (21)$$

l'Hôpital's ratio of derivatives
$$a_{-1} = \lim_{z\to i} \frac{z-i}{1+z^2} = \lim_{z\to i} \frac{1}{2z} = \frac{1}{2i} \quad (22)$$

Example 10 Change the small square to the large semicircle in Figure 5.3. That path still encloses the one pole at $z = i$. As the semicircle radius R increases toward infinity, compute a real integral from $-\infty$ to ∞:

Integral along the real axis
$$\int_{x=-\infty}^{\infty} \frac{dx}{1+x^2} = 2\pi i \left(\frac{1}{2i}\right) = \pi\,. \quad (23)$$

Solution The bottom of the semicircle has $z = x$, and the circular part has $z = Re^{i\theta}$. *On that circular part, the integral goes to zero as $R \to \infty$.* This is the key point to prove, and it leaves the real integral (23) equal to $2\pi i(\text{Residue}) = \pi$.

We estimate the integral along the circular part $z = Re^{i\theta}$ by "maximum M of $|f(z)|$ times path length $L = \pi R$:"

Circular part $$\int \left|\frac{dz}{1+z^2}\right| = \int_0^\pi \left|\frac{iRe^{i\theta}\,d\theta}{1+R^2e^{2i\theta}}\right| \le \frac{\pi R}{R^2-1} \to 0 \quad \text{as } R\to\infty. \tag{24}$$

Choosing the path and estimating the integral are the key steps in contour integration:

Estimating integrals $$\left|\int_{z_1}^{z_2} f(z)\,dz\right| \le (\max|f(z)|)\int_{z_1}^{z_2}|dz|. \tag{25}$$

Here is a Fourier transform using the same semicircle. It only succeeds for $k \ge 0$.

Example 11 Show that the transform of $1/(1+x^2)$ is a decaying pulse:

From Fourier integrals $$\int_{-\infty}^{\infty} \frac{e^{ikx}dx}{\pi(1+x^2)} = e^{-k} \quad \text{for } k \ge 0. \tag{26}$$

Solution $f(z) = e^{ikz}/\pi(1+z^2)$ still has one pole at $z = i$ inside the semicircle:

Residue at $z = i$ $$\lim_{z\to i} \frac{(z-i)e^{ikz}}{\pi(1+z^2)} = \lim_{z\to i}\frac{e^{ikz}}{\pi(z+i)} = \frac{e^{-k}}{2\pi i}.$$

Multiplying by $2\pi i$ gives the desired answer e^{-k} for the integral along the real axis $z = x$. On the circular part, the new factor has $|e^{ikz}| \le 1$ which doesn't change the estimate:

Semicircle with $y \ge 0$ $$\left|e^{ik(x+iy)}\right| = e^{-ky} \le 1 \text{ and again } \frac{R}{R^2-1} \to 0.$$

Remark If $k < 0$ then the estimate completely fails. The factor e^{ikz} will be exponentially *large* at $z = iR$. ***Change to a semicircle below the real axis*!** Then $z = -i$ is the pole inside this new semicircle and we need that new residue:

Residue at $z = -i$ $$\lim_{z\to -i} \frac{(z+i)e^{ikz}}{\pi(1+z^2)} = \lim_{z\to -i}\frac{e^{ikz}}{\pi(z-i)} = \frac{e^{k}}{-2\pi i}. \tag{27}$$

Multiplying by $2\pi i$ gives the integral around the lower semicircle. The circular part goes to zero because $k < 0$ (now e^{ikz} is exponentially *small* at $z = -iR$). But notice, the path travels backward along the flat top of that lower semicircle. So reversing the sign produces the integral. The even pulse decays in the negative direction too:

For $k < 0$ $$\int_{-\infty}^{\infty} \frac{e^{ikx}\,dx}{\pi(1+x^2)} = -2\pi i\left(\frac{e^k}{-2\pi i}\right) = e^k. \tag{28}$$

The Fourier integral in Section 4.5 computed the transform of that two-sided pulse. At that time we could not invert the transform. Now complex analysis integrates along the whole line (not part of the line, that is still impossible).

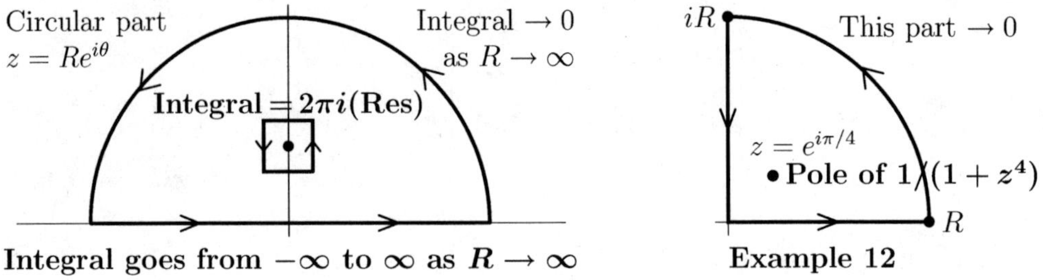

Figure 5.3: Small paths and large paths around a pole. Real integral as $R \to \infty$

Example 12 Compute $I = \displaystyle\int_0^\infty \frac{dx}{1+x^4}$ when $f(z) = \dfrac{1}{1+z^4}$ has four simple poles.

Solution The poles are at the roots of $z^4 = -1 = e^{\pi i} = e^{3\pi i}$. Their positions are $z_1 = e^{i\pi/4}$ and $z_2 = e^{3i\pi/4}$ above the real axis (angles 45° and 135°) and $z_3 = -z_1$ and $z_4 = -z_2$ below the axis. For the same upper semicircle, we add the residues at z_1 and z_2 and multiply by $2\pi i$. The real part of this path gives the integral from $-\infty$ to ∞, which is $2I$. Then divide by 2.

Another possibility is the quarter-circle path in Figure 5.3. This contains only one pole at $z_1 = e^{i\pi/4}$. Now the imaginary axis has $z = iy$ and $z^4 = y^4$:

Downwards $$\int_{iR}^0 \frac{dz}{1+z^4} = \int_R^0 \frac{i\,dy}{1+y^4} = -i\int_0^R \frac{dy}{1+y^4} \longrightarrow -iI \text{ as } R \to \infty.$$

On the circular part, $z = Re^{i\theta}$ gives $|1+z^4| \geq R^4 - 1$. The integral on that part is less than its length $\pi R/2$ divided by $R^4 - 1$. This goes to zero as $R \to \infty$, leaving two straight parts (the positive real axis $x > 0$ and imaginary axis $y > 0$):

$$(1-i)I = 2\pi i(\text{Residue}) = \frac{2\pi i}{4e^{3\pi i/4}} = \frac{2\pi}{4}\,e^{-\pi i/4} = \frac{\pi}{2}\left(\frac{1-i}{\sqrt{2}}\right) \text{ gives } \boldsymbol{I = \frac{\pi}{2\sqrt{2}}}. \quad (29)$$

That residue $1/4e^{3\pi i/4} = 1/4z_1^3$ came from l'Hôpital's Rule for $(z - z_1)f(z)$. When that limit is 0/0, we change to a *ratio of derivatives*:

l'Hôpital = $\dfrac{\textbf{Derivative}}{\textbf{Derivative}}$ $$\lim_{z\to z_1} \frac{z - z_1}{1+z^4} = \lim_{z\to z_1} \frac{1}{4z_1^3} = \frac{1}{4e^{3\pi i/4}}.$$

Direct division would also be possible, leaving $1/(z^3 + z^2 z_1 + z z_1^2 + z_1^3)$. This approaches $1/4z_1^3$ but l'Hôpital's way is easier. It leads to a valuable rule for the residue of any ratio $f(z) = n(z)/d(z)$ at any simple pole where $d(z_0) = 0$.

The pole is simple if $d'(z_0) \neq 0$ and $n(z_0) \neq 0$. L'Hôpital goes to derivatives:

$$\textbf{Residue of } \frac{n(z)}{d(z)} \qquad \lim_{z\to z_0} \frac{(z-z_0)\,n(z)}{d(z)} = \lim_{z\to z_0} \frac{n(z)}{d(z)/(z-z_0)} = \frac{n(z_0)}{d'(z_0)} \qquad (30)$$

Our example had $n(z) = 1$ and $d(z) = 1 + z^4$. The residue is $1/4z^3$ at each pole.

Puzzle I was tempted to set $x = iy$ in the original integral $I = \int_0^\infty dx/(1+x^4)$ in Example 12. Then $dx = i\,dy$ and the integral changes to iI. If that change is allowed, the false equality $I = iI$ would lead to the false conclusion that $I = 0$.

Changing x to iy has completely altered the path in the complex plane. You need to verify that on the circular part connecting the two straight parts, the integral goes to zero. And you must account for the residues at all poles trapped inside.

Our final examples change $\cos\theta$ to $\frac{1}{2}(e^{i\theta} + e^{-i\theta})$. Instead of a real integral, we go around the unit circle and use residues.

Example 13 Compute $J = \displaystyle\int_0^{2\pi} \cos^2\theta\, d\theta = \pi$ and $K = \displaystyle\int_0^{2\pi} \frac{d\theta}{20 + 2\cos\theta} = \frac{\pi}{\sqrt{99}}$.

Solution On the unit circle, $z = e^{i\theta}$ leads to $\cos\theta = \frac{1}{2}(z + \frac{1}{z})$ and $d\theta = dz/iz$:

$$\textbf{Around a circle} \qquad J = \int \frac{1}{4}\left(z + \frac{1}{z}\right)^2 \frac{dz}{iz} \quad \text{and} \quad K = \int \frac{dz}{iz(20 + z + z^{-1})}.$$

We can find J directly or by its residue $1/2i$ multiplying $2\pi i$:

$$\textbf{Notice } 1/2iz \qquad J = \int \left(\frac{z^2}{4iz} + \frac{1}{2iz} + \frac{1}{4iz^3}\right) dz = 0 + \frac{2\pi i}{2i} + 0 = \pi\,.$$

The poles for K have $20z + z^2 + 1 = 0$. They are $z_1 = -10 + \sqrt{99}$ inside the unit circle and $z_2 = -10 - \sqrt{99}$ outside (not counted). Use the residue formula (30) with $n(z) = 1$:

$$\textbf{Residue of } 1/i(20z + z^2 + 1) \qquad \frac{n(z_1)}{d'(z_1)} = \frac{1}{i(20 + 2z_1)} = \frac{1}{i\,2\sqrt{99}}\,.$$

Multiplying by $2\pi i$ gives the integral $K = \pi/\sqrt{99}$.

Other integrals have higher order poles, or logarithms and roots with branch points. When a singularity falls on the real axis, a tiny semicircle avoids it. The problems include more of these remarkable contour integrals. But here is a thought.

I cannot convince myself that this amazing art, magic as it is, deserves a giant part in a course that emphasizes scientific computing. Still I couldn't leave it out.

Problem Set 5.1

Problems 1-7 are about Taylor series and circles of convergence.

1 Find the Taylor series $\sum a_n z^n$ and its radius of convergence, for

(a) $\dfrac{2}{2z+1}$ (b) $\dfrac{1+iz}{1-iz}$ (c) $\dfrac{1}{(1+z)^2}$ (d) $\dfrac{\sin z}{z}$

2 Find two terms of the Taylor series $\sum a_n(z-1)^n$ for the same four functions.

3 Suppose that $a_{n+1}/a_n \to \frac{1}{3}$ as $n \to \infty$. Explain why $f(z) = \sum a_n z^n$ has radius of convergence $R = 3$. (Prove convergence if $|z| < 3$.) Explain why $f'(z) = \sum n a_n z^{n-1}$ also has radius of convergence $R = 3$.

4 Explain why $\int f(z)\,dz = \sum a_n z^{n+1}/(n+1)$ also has radius of convergence $R = 3$. Give an example of an $f(z)$ whose Taylor series around $z = 0$ has $R = 3$.

5 Find the radius of convergence of the Taylor series around z_0 for $1/z^{10}$.

6 Suppose L is the largest limit point of the numbers $|a_n|^{1/n}$ (allowing $L = \infty$). If $|z| > 1/L$ explain why the terms $a_n z^n$ of the Taylor series do not go to zero. Then z is outside the circle of convergence.

7 Suppose $|z| < 1/L$ in Problem 6. For any number x between $L|z| < x < 1$, explain why $|a_n z^n| < Cx^n$ for some constant C. Then the Taylor series $\sum a_n z^n$ converges by comparison with $\sum Cx^n = C/(1-x)$.

Conclusion *The Taylor series has radius of convergence exactly* $1/L$.

Problems 8-26 are about complex integration and residues.

8 (a) Compute $\int dz/z^2$ around the circle $z = re^{i\theta}$, $0 \le \theta \le 2\pi$.
(b) Despite the pole at $z = 0$ this integral is zero. What is the residue of $1/z^2$?
(c) Why is $\int dz/z^2$ also zero around circles that are not centered at the origin?

9 If $f(z) = z^2$ on the circle $z = a + re^{i\theta}$ around the point a, substitute directly into Cauchy's integral formula (10) and show that it correctly gives $f(a) = a^2$. What is the average value of e^z around the unit circle?

10 Compute the following integrals:
(a) $\int dz/z$ from 1 to i, the short way and long way on the circle $z = e^{i\theta}$
(b) $\int x\,dz$ around the unit circle, where $x = \cos\theta$ and $z = e^{i\theta}$, or $x = \frac{1}{2}(z+z^{-1})$.

11 Find the location of the poles, and the residues, for

(a) $\dfrac{1}{z^2-4}$ (b) $\dfrac{z^2}{z-3}$ (c) $\dfrac{1}{(z^2-1)^2}$ (d) $\dfrac{e^z}{z^3}$ (e) $\dfrac{1}{1-e^z}$ (f) $\dfrac{1}{\sin z}$

12 Evaluate the following integrals around the unit circle:

$$\text{(a)} \int \frac{dz}{z^2 - 2z} \quad \text{(b)} \int \frac{e^z\, dz}{z^2} \quad \text{(c)} \int \frac{dz}{\sin z}$$

13 By complex integration compute these real integrals:

$$\text{(a)} \int_0^{2\pi} (\cos\theta)^6\, d\theta \quad \text{(b)} \int_0^{2\pi} \frac{d\theta}{a + \cos\theta},\ a > 1 \quad \text{(c)} \int_0^{2\pi} \cos^3\theta\, d\theta$$

14 Find the poles above the real axis and evaluate these integrals:

$$\text{(a)} \int_{-\infty}^{\infty} \frac{dx}{(1+x^2)^2} \quad \text{(b)} \int_{-\infty}^{\infty} \frac{dx}{4+x^2} \quad \text{(c)} \int_{-\infty}^{\infty} \frac{dx}{x^2 - 2x + 3}$$

15 Find all poles, branch points, and essential singularities of eight functions:

$$\text{(a)} \frac{1}{z^4 - 1} \quad \text{(b)} \frac{1}{\sin^2 z} \quad \text{(c)} \frac{1}{e^z - 1} \quad \text{(d)} \log(1-z)$$

$$\text{(e)} \sqrt{4 - z^2} \quad \text{(f)} z\log z \quad \text{(g)} e^{2/z} \quad \text{(h)} e^z/z^e$$

To include $z = \infty$, set $w = 1/z$ and study $w = 0$. Thus $z^3 = 1/w^3$ has a triple pole at $z = \infty$.

16 The two residues of $f(z) = 1/(1+z^2)$ are $1/2i$ and $-1/2i$, adding to zero. Cauchy's Theorem makes the integral around $|z| = R$ the same for every R. Why is the integral zero?

17 $(1 = -1)$ Where does l'Hôpital's Rule go wrong for limits as $x \to \infty$?

$$1 = \lim \frac{x - \sin x^2}{x + \sin x^2} = \lim \frac{1 - 2x\cos x^2}{1 + 2x\cos x^2} = \lim \frac{1/x - 2\cos x^2}{1/x + 2\cos x^2} = -1.$$

18 Follow Example 13 with $\cos\theta = \frac{1}{2}(e^{i\theta} + e^{-i\theta}) = \frac{1}{2}(z + z^{-1})$ to find

$$\int_0^{2\pi} \frac{\sin^2\theta}{5 + 4\cos\theta}\, d\theta = \frac{\pi}{4}.$$

19 Change $d\theta/(1 + a\cos\theta)$ to $dz/\underline{\ ?\ }$ by substituting $z = e^{i\theta}$. If $0 \le a < 1$, where is the pole in the unit circle? Confirm $\int_0^{2\pi} d\theta/(1 + a\cos\theta) = 2\pi/\sqrt{1-a^2}$.

20 Find the order m of each pole ($m = 1$: simple pole) and the residue:

$$\text{(a)} \frac{z-2}{z(z-1)} \quad \text{(b)} \frac{z-2}{z^2} \quad \text{(c)} \frac{z}{\sin \pi z} \quad \text{(d)} \frac{1 - e^{iz}}{z^3}$$

21 Estimate these integrals by $ML =$ (maximum of $|f(z)|$) (length of path):

$$\text{(a)}\ \left|\int_{|z+1|=2}\frac{dz}{z}\right| \le 4\pi \qquad \text{(b)}\ \left|\int_{|z-i|=1}\frac{dz}{1+z^2}\right| \le 2\pi$$

Then compute the residues and the actual integrals.

22 If C is the diamond path with corners at $1, i, -1, -i$, find a bound ML for

$$\text{(a)}\ \left|\int_C z^n\,dz\right| \qquad \text{(b)}\ \left|\int_C e^{iz}\,dz\right|.$$

23 Explain Jordan's inequality $\sin\theta \ge 2\theta/\pi$ by drawing the curve $y = \sin\theta$ and the line $y = 2\theta/\pi$ from $\theta = 0$ to $\theta = \pi/2$. Integrate on a semicircle $z = Re^{i\theta}$:

Small integral for large R
$$\int_{\theta=0}^{\pi}\left|\frac{e^{iz}\,dz}{z}\right| = \int e^{-R\sin\theta}\,d\theta \le \int e^{-2R\theta/\pi} < \frac{\pi}{2R}$$

The usual $|e^{iz}| \le 1$ only bounds this integral by π (no use as $R \to \infty$).

24 $\sin z/z$ has no poles but the integral from $x = -\infty$ to ∞ is not zero. *Reason*: $\sin z/z$ is ____ along an upper semicircle of radius R. *Solution*: Change to e^{iz}/z and use Problem 23 (small integral along the semicircle). *New problem*: e^{iz}/z has a pole at $z = 0$. *New solution*: Follow a small semicircle around that pole. *Final question*: Why does the residue 1 of e^{iz}/z only count as $\frac{1}{2}$?

$$\int_0^{\infty}\frac{\sin x}{x}\,dx = \frac{\pi}{2} \quad \text{because} \quad \operatorname{Im}\int_{-\infty}^{\infty}\frac{e^{iz}}{z}dz = \operatorname{Im}\left(\frac{2\pi i}{2}\right) = \pi.$$

25 The integral of $\sin^2 x/x^2$ is surprisingly also $\pi/2$. Again $\sin^2 z$ is way too large on the semicircle. The solution this time is to work with $1 - e^{2iz}$. Its real part is $1 - \cos 2x = 2\sin^2 x$ when $z = x$ is real.

(a) Show that $(1 - e^{2iz})/z^2$ has residue $-2i$ at $z = 0$ (this only counts half).
(b) Explain the steps in the final answer:

$$\int_0^{\infty}\frac{\sin^2 x}{x^2}\,dx = \frac{1}{4} \quad \text{because} \quad \operatorname{Re}\int_{-\infty}^{\infty}\frac{1 - e^{2ix}}{x^2}\,dx = \frac{2\pi i(-2i)}{8} = \frac{\pi}{2}.$$

Again the residue $-2i$ *only counts half* for a small semicircle around $z = 0$.

26 Example 13 found $\int_0^{2\pi}\cos^2\theta\,d\theta$. Use the same method to find $\int_0^{2\pi}\cos^4\theta\,d\theta$.

5.2 FAMOUS FUNCTIONS AND GREAT THEOREMS

This section will look different from all the others. Analytic functions are quite beautiful, and I hope to capture part of that beauty in a few pages. My idea is to present outstanding properties of these functions, *without proof.* The proofs are beautiful too, but this way you can sit back and enjoy an overview. This section is written for your pleasure, and mine.

Over and over you will see the same assumption: ***$f(z)$ is analytic inside and on a simple closed curve C.*** The values of $f(z)$ on C decide its values inside C. If f is zero on C, it is zero inside. If $|f(z)| \leq M$ on C, this bound continues inside. Cauchy's Theorem is the centerpiece of complex analysis, that the integral of $f(z)$ around C is certain to be zero.

The beauty of this subject also lies in special, particular, often famous functions. A lover of complex analysis will know those functions intimately. Like you, I am an admirer who is acquainted but not that well. We begin by looking at just two of those special analytic functions, the exponential e^z and Riemann's zeta function $\zeta(z)$.

Exponential

The exponential function $e^z = 1 + z + z^2/2 + z^3/6 + \cdots$ is analytic (for all z except $z = \infty$). This series converges for every z. The good properties 1–6 lead to $e^{z+2\pi i} = e^z$. This makes difficulty in 7 for the inverse function $\log z$.

1. The derivative of e^z is e^z, and $e^0 = 1$. (Take the derivative term by term.)

2. The derivative of $e^{-z}e^z$ is zero (product rule). Then $e^z e^{-z} = 1$ and $e^z \neq 0$.

3. $e^z e^w = e^{z+w}$ (the outstanding fact about exponentials).

4. $e^{iy} = \left(1 - \dfrac{y^2}{2!} + \cdots\right) + i\left(y - \dfrac{y^3}{3!} + \cdots\right) = \cos y + i \sin y.$

5. If y is real then $|e^{iy}| = 1$. If x is also real then $|e^{x+iy}| = e^x$.

6. $e^{2\pi i} = 1$. Then $e^{z+2\pi i} = e^z$ and $\cos(y + 2\pi) = \cos y$ and $\sin(y + 2\pi) = \sin y$.

7. The inverse function from $e^{\log z} = z$ is $\log z = \log|z| + i\theta$, *not defined at* $z = 0$. The logarithm has infinitely many values differing by $2\pi i$. To keep one value with $-\pi < \theta < \pi$, we can forbid the curve C to cross the negative real axis. Then $\log z$ is analytic in the "cut plane" and $\log(1+z) = z - z^2/2 + z^3/3 - \cdots$.

Zeta function

The Riemann zeta function is $\zeta(z) = 1 + 1/2^z + 1/3^z + \cdots$. This series converges when $\operatorname{Re} z > 1$ because $|n^z| = n^{\operatorname{Re} z}$. By "analytic continuation" described below, we can reach all points except $z = 1$ (where $\zeta(z)$ has a simple pole of residue 1).

The ***Riemann Hypothesis*** is about the solutions to $\zeta(z) = 0$. In 1859, Riemann conjectured that every non-real solution has $\mathbf{Re}\, z = \frac{1}{2}$. For calculations of the first 10^{13} zeros $x + iy$ see dtc.umn.edu/~odlyzko. *Every one of those zeros has* $x = \frac{1}{2}$. Their distribution has mysterious connections with random matrices. After recent great successes like Fermat's Last Theorem, studying the zeros of the zeta-function seems even harder and deeper. The Riemann Hypothesis is the outstanding open problem in mathematics.

The ***Prime Number Theorem*** is the fundamental fact about the growth of $p(x)$, the number of primes $\leq x$. That jump function is not analytic. But complex analysis gives an amazing proof that the density of primes decreases like $(\log x)/x$:

Prime Number Theorem $\quad \dfrac{p(x)\,\log x}{x}$ approaches 1 as $x \to \infty$.

The zeta function is closely connected to the irregular (but not totally irregular!) distribution of the prime numbers. A new theorem recently proved: There are progressions $x, x+k, \ldots, x+nk$ of all lengths $n+1$ among the prime numbers.

Great Theorems of Complex Analysis

The next pages come from the opposite side of mathematics. They are general rather than specific. The "great theorems" apply to a class of functions instead of one function. The functions are all analytic except for singularities, and this property has very remarkable consequences. The theorems are collected into seven groups:

Series Poles Integrals Bounds Zeros Functions Mappings

Series

S1 Taylor Series Around each z_0, an analytic $f(z)$ is given by a power series

$$f(z) = \sum_{n=0}^{\infty} a_n (z - z_0)^n = a_0 + a_1(z - z_0) + \cdots \quad \text{with } a_n = \frac{f^{(n)}(z_0)}{n!}$$

The series around z_0 converges inside a circle reaching the singularity nearest to z_0.

S2 Radius of Convergence $\sum a_n (z - z_0)^n$ converges for $|z - z_0| < \frac{1}{L}$, $L = \limsup |a_n|^{1/n}$

$$a_n = 2^n \text{ has } L = 2,\ R = \frac{1}{2} \qquad \sum 2^n z^n = \frac{1}{1 - 2z} \text{ converges for } |2z| < 1 \text{ or } |z| < \frac{1}{2}$$

The "lim sup" is the largest limit point L of nth roots $|a_n|^{1/n}$. The radius is $R = \frac{1}{L}$.

S3 Laurent Series Suppose $f(z)$ is analytic inside a ring $R_1 < |z - z_0| < R_2$

$$\text{Then } f(z) = \sum_{-\infty}^{\infty} a_n (z - z_0)^n \text{ converges in the ring with } a_n = \frac{1}{2\pi i} \int \frac{f(z)\,dz}{(z - z_0)^{n+1}} \quad (1)$$

Negative powers of $z - z_0$ come from inner singularities where $|z - z_0| \leq R_1$.

S4 Energy Identity Suppose $f(z) = \sum a_n z^n$ is analytic in the unit disc $|z| \leq 1$

Energy
$$\frac{1}{2\pi} \int_0^{2\pi} |f(e^{i\theta})|^2 d\theta = |a_0|^2 + |a_1|^2 + \cdots = \sum_0^{\infty} |a_n|^2$$

The energy in the function = the energy in the coefficients (Section 4.1).

Poles

P1 Pole or Essential Singularity If $\sum_{-\infty}^{\infty} a_n (z - z_0)^n$ converges for $0 < |z - z_0| < R$

z_0 is a pole of order m if $\boldsymbol{a_{-m} \neq 0}$ and $a_{-n} = 0$ for all $n > m$

z_0 is an essential singularity $\boldsymbol{a_{-m} \neq 0}$ for infinitely many $m \geq 0$

Negative powers in this Laurent series describe the singularity at z_0.

P2 Residue The residue at a pole z_0 is $a_{-1} = \dfrac{1}{2\pi i} \displaystyle\int f(z)\,dz$ integrated around z_0

$$\text{The residue at } z_0 \text{ of } f(z) = \frac{A}{z - z_0} + \frac{B}{(z - z_0)^2} + \frac{C}{z - z_1} \text{ is } A$$

The residue of $\dfrac{n(z)}{d(z)}$ at a **simple pole** is $a_{-1} = \lim_{z \to z_0} (z - z_0) f(z) = \dfrac{n(z_0)}{d'(z_0)}$.

P3 Poles Only Suppose $f(z)$ is analytic except for poles, and $f(z) \to 0$ for $|z| \to \infty$

$$\text{Then } f(z) = \textit{rational function } \frac{n(z)}{d(z)} = \frac{\text{polynomial of degree } N}{\text{polynomial of degree } D} \quad (N < D) \quad (2)$$

Functions with only poles inside C are *meromorphic* in that region.

P4 Partial Fractions Suppose $f(z)$ is rational as in (2) with simple poles at $z_1, \ldots, z_d$

$$\text{Then } f(z) = \frac{A_1}{z - z_1} + \cdots + \frac{A_d}{z - z_d} \quad \text{with residues } A_1, \ldots, A_d \quad (3)$$

For a pole at z_1 of order m, Laurent gives m terms $c_{-1}/(z - z_1) + \cdots + c_{-m}/(z - z_1)^m$.

P5 Picard's Theorem Suppose z_0 is an isolated essential singularity of $f(z)$

Then $f(z)$ *takes all values* (except possibly one) in each ring $0 < |z - z_0| < \epsilon$

In every ring around $z = 0$, $f(z) = e^{1/z}$ takes all nonzero values except 0 ($e^{1/z} \neq 0$).

P6 Branch Point Compute $f(z_0 + re^{i\theta})$ around a small circle (θ from 0 to 2π)

z_0 is a **branch point** of $f(z)$ if the values at $\theta = 0$ and 2π are different

The functions $\log(z - z_0)$ and $(z - z_0)^\alpha$ (α not integer) have branch points at $z = z_0$.

Integrals

I1 Simple Closed Curve $C(t) = (x(t), y(t))$ has continuous $x(t), y(t)$ for $0 \leq t \leq T$

Closed $C(T) = C(0)$ **Simple** $C(t_1) \neq C(t_2)$ if $0 \leq t_1 < t_2 < T$ (no crossing)

C is **piecewise smooth** when $C'(t)$ is continuous for $0 \leq t \leq t_1, \ldots, t_N \leq t \leq T$.

I2 Jordan Curve Theorem A simple closed curve C has an inside and an outside

Complement of C = union of "inside" and "out" (disjoint connected open sets)

This is a difficult theorem to prove for very general curves C.

I3 Cauchy's Theorem Suppose $f(z)$ is analytic inside and on a closed curve C

Integral = zero	$\int_C f(z)\,dz = 0$	**On a circle in C**	$\int_0^{2\pi} f(z_0 + re^{i\theta})e^{i\theta}\,d\theta = 0$

When f is analytic except at z_0, **Integral around C = Integral around circle.**

I4 Cauchy's Integral Formula Suppose $f(z)$ is analytic inside and on C

Point z_0 inside C	$f(z_0) = \dfrac{1}{2\pi i}\displaystyle\int_C \frac{f(z)}{z - z_0}\,dz$	and	$\dfrac{d^n f}{dz^n}(z_0) = \dfrac{n!}{2\pi i}\displaystyle\int_C \frac{f(z)\,dz}{(z - z_0)^{n+1}}$

Derivatives at z_0 are known from values on C (FFT code in Section 5.1).

I5 Residue Theorem $f(z)$ is analytic on and inside C except for poles $z_1, \ldots, z_N$

Add residues
$$\int_C f(z)\,dz = 2\pi i\big[\text{Residue at } z_1 + \cdots + \text{Residue at } z_N\big] \tag{4}$$

The path C deforms to N small circles around the poles, using Cauchy's Theorem.

I6 Estimation of Integrals Suppose $|f(z)| \le M$ along a curved path of length L

Open or closed integration path $$\left| \int_{\text{path}} f(z)\, dz \right| \le ML \qquad (5)$$

For example $|\int dz/z| \le \frac{1}{r}(2\pi r) = 2\pi$ around the circle $|z| = r$. *This integral is* $2\pi i$.

Bounds

B1 Liouville's Theorem If $|f(z)| \le M$ for all z (analytic f) then $f(z) =$ *constant*

$$\text{If } f(z) = \sum a_n z^n \text{ then } |a_n| = \left| \int_{|z|=R} \frac{f(z)\, dz}{z^{n+1}\, 2\pi} \right| \le \frac{M}{R^n} \quad \text{(estimation theorem)}$$

This holds for any large radius R. So every $a_n = 0$ (except for the constant a_0).

B2 Mean Value Suppose $f(z) = \sum a_n (z - z_0)^n$ is analytic in the disc $|z - z_0| \le r$

At the center $$a_0 = f(z_0) = \frac{1}{2\pi} \int_0^{2\pi} f(z_0 + re^{i\theta}) d\theta = \textbf{average around circle}$$

The same is true for solutions $u(x, y) = \operatorname{Re} f$ and $s(x, y) = \operatorname{Im} f$ to Laplace's equation.

B3 Maximum Modulus Theorem $f(z)$ is analytic inside C and continuous out to C

The maximum of $|f(z)|$ occurs at z_0 inside C only if $f(z) =$ *constant*

The Average Value Theorem forces $f =$ constant on circles around every z_0.

B4 Schwarz Lemma Suppose $f(z)$ is analytic for $|z| \le R$ and $f(0)$ is *zero*

Bound on smaller circles $$\max |f(re^{i\theta})| \le \frac{r}{R} \max |f(Re^{i\theta})|$$

This is the maximum modulus theorem applied to the function $f(z)/z$.

Zeros

Z1 Fundamental Theorem of Algebra A polynomial $p(z)$ of degree n has n roots

$$\text{If } p(z) \text{ has no root then } \left| \frac{1}{p(z)} \right| \le \text{constant. So } p(z) = \text{constant by Liouville}$$

With a first root z_1, repeat for $\dfrac{p(z)}{z - z_1}$ (degree $n - 1$) to find a root z_2. End at z_n.

Z2 Counting Zeros Suppose $f(z)$ is analytic inside and on C, and $f(z) \neq 0$ on C

$$\frac{1}{2\pi i}\int_C \frac{f'(z)}{f(z)}\,dz = \text{number of zeros (counting multiplicity) inside } C$$

The integral is $\log f(z)$. This changes by $2\pi i$ around any simple zero of $f(z)$.

Z3 Rouché's Theorem Suppose $|f(z)| > |g(z)|$ on C (f and g analytic inside and on C)

Then f and $f - g$ have the **same number of zeros** inside the curve C

If $|g(z)| < 1$ on the circle $|z| = 1$, then $g(z) = z$ at *one* z inside. Take $f(z) = z$.

Functions

F1 Derivatives If $f(z)$ is analytic inside C, so are its derivatives $f'(z), f''(z), \ldots$

$$f'(z) = \sum_{n=1}^{\infty} n\,a_n(z - z_0)^{n-1} = a_1 + 2a_2(z - z_0) + \cdots \quad \text{converges in the same circle}$$

$f(z)$ is the derivative of $g(z) = \sum a_n(z - z_0)^{n+1}/(n+1)$, also analytic inside C.

F2 Holomorphic Function $f(z)$ must be **differentiable** inside $|z - z_0| < r$

$$\text{Differentiable at } z \text{ means } \frac{f(z + \Delta z) - f(z)}{\Delta z} \to f'(z) \text{ for all } complex\ \Delta z \to 0$$

Then $f(z)$ is "holomorphic" in the open disc $|z - z_0| < r$ (r can be small).

F3 Cauchy-Riemann If $f(x + iy) = u(x, y) + i\,s(x, y)$ is holomorphic in a disc

$$\text{Then } \boxed{\frac{\partial u}{\partial x} = \frac{\partial s}{\partial y} \text{ and } \frac{\partial u}{\partial y} = -\frac{\partial s}{\partial x}} \text{ in the open disc} \qquad (6)$$

Those real functions u and s are *harmonic*: They satisfy Laplace's equation.

F4 Holomorphic = Analytic Suppose $f(z)$ is holomorphic in the open disc $|z - z_0| < r$

Then $f(z_0) + f'(z_0)(z - z_0) + \frac{1}{2!} f''(z_0)(z - z_0)^2 + \cdots$ converges to $f(z)$ in the disc

This convergent Taylor series $\sum a_n(z - z_0)^n$ makes $f(z)$ analytic in the disc.

F5 Uniqueness Theorem Suppose $f(z) = g(z)$ at infinitely many points inside C

Same function If f and g are analytic inside and on C, then $f(z) = g(z)$ in C

Note $e^{1/z} = 1 = e^{-1/z}$ at all points $z = 1/2\pi in \to 0$. But $e^{1/z}$ is not analytic at 0.

F6 Inverse Function Theorem $f(z)$ is analytic in C and $f(z_1) = f(z_2)$ *only if* $z_1 = z_2$

The inverse function defined by $f^{-1}(f(z)) = z$ is analytic at all points $f(z)$

The derivative of $f^{-1}(w)$ at $w = f(z)$ is $1/f'(z)$ by the chain rule for $f^{-1}(f(z)) = z$.

F7 Analytic Continuation f_1, f_2 analytic in overlapping discs $|z - z_1| < r_1$, $|z - z_2| < r_2$

If $f_1(z) = f_2(z)$ in the overlap, they produce one analytic $f(z)$ in the union

When $f_1 = \sum a_n(z - z_1)^n$ in a disc containing z_2, $\sum A_n(z - z_2)^n$ may converge further.

Mappings

M1 Conformal Mapping $f(z)$ is analytic on rays $re^{i\alpha}$ and $re^{i\beta}$ in to $z = 0$, and $f'(0) \neq 0$

Conformal The curves $f(re^{i\alpha})$ and $f(re^{i\beta})$ make the same angle $\alpha - \beta$ as the rays

Near the center, $f(z) - f(0) \approx z\, f'(0)$ rotates every ray by a fixed angle from $f'(0)$.

M2 Change of Variables Lemma If $w = f(z)$ and $h = g(w)$ are analytic, so is $g(f(z))$

Analytic $g(f(z))$ $\quad f(z) = \dfrac{z-1}{z+1} \quad g(w) = \sin w \quad g(f(z)) = \sin\left(\dfrac{z-1}{z+1}\right)$

Here $|f| < 1$ if $\operatorname{Re} z > 0$: g analytic for $|w| < 1$ makes $g(f(z))$ analytic for $\operatorname{Re} z > 0$.

M3 Riemann Mapping Theorem G is simply connected (not the whole complex plane)

There is a **conformal 1–1 map** $w = f(z)$ from open set G onto the disc $|w| < 1$

Since $f'(z) \neq 0$ and $f(z_1) \neq f(z_2)$, $z = f^{-1}(w)$ is conformal from $|w| < 1$ back to G.

M4 Schwarz-Christoffel Map A conformal map w takes a polygon onto the disc $|z| \leq 1$

Schwarz-Christoffel w has the special form $\displaystyle\int (z - z_1)^{-k_1} \cdots (z - z_N)^{-k_N}\, dz$

The SC Toolbox computes $z_1, \ldots, z_n$ from the polygon corners $w_1, \ldots, w_n$.

5.3 THE LAPLACE TRANSFORM AND z-TRANSFORM

The Fourier transform can solve boundary-value problems. The Laplace transform is used for initial-value problems. Both are based on exponentials (e^{ikx} and e^{st}). They both hope for constant coefficients in differential equations. And they succeed for the same reason, that exponentials are eigenfunctions of d/dx and d/dt:

$$\frac{d}{dx}e^{ikx} = ike^{ikx} \quad \text{and} \quad \frac{d}{dt}e^{st} = se^{st} \tag{1}$$

Differentiation transforms to multiplication by ik or s. Fourier has $-\infty < x < \infty$, Laplace has $0 \le t < \infty$. The Laplace transform must account for any jump at $t = 0$. Compare ik in the Fourier transform to s in the Laplace transform:

Fourier Transform	$\widehat{f}(k) = \int_{-\infty}^{\infty} f(x)\, e^{-ikx}\, dx$	Laplace Transform	$F(s) = \int_{0}^{\infty} f(t)\, e^{-st}\, dt$ (2)

I will compute immediately the most important Laplace transform of all:

$$\textbf{e}^{at} \textbf{ transforms to } \frac{\mathbf{1}}{\boldsymbol{s-a}} \qquad F(s) = \int_0^\infty e^{at}e^{-st}dt = \left[\frac{e^{(a-s)t}}{a-s}\right]_0^\infty = \frac{\mathbf{1}}{\boldsymbol{s-a}}. \tag{3}$$

The exponent a in $f(t)$ becomes the **pole** *in the transform $F(s)$.* This is where complex variables enter. The real part of a is the growth or decay rate, and the imaginary part of a gives oscillations. The easy integral (3) gives four important transforms for 1, e^{-ct}, $\cos\omega t = (e^{i\omega t} + e^{-i\omega t})/2$, and $\sin\omega t = (e^{i\omega t} - e^{-i\omega t})/2i$:

$a = zero$ $\quad f(t) = \mathbf{1}$ $\quad$ gives $F(s) = \dfrac{\mathbf{1}}{\boldsymbol{s}}$ $\quad$ for a unit step function

$a = -c$ $\quad f(t) = \boldsymbol{e^{-ct}}$ $\quad$ gives $F(s) = \dfrac{\mathbf{1}}{\boldsymbol{s+c}}$ $\quad$ for transient decay

$a = i\omega, -i\omega$ $\quad f(t) = \boldsymbol{\cos\omega t}$ $\quad$ gives $F(s) = \dfrac{1}{2}\left(\dfrac{1}{s-i\omega} + \dfrac{1}{s+i\omega}\right) = \dfrac{\boldsymbol{s}}{\boldsymbol{s^2+\omega^2}}$

$a = i\omega, -i\omega$ $\quad f(t) = \boldsymbol{\sin\omega t}$ $\quad$ gives $F(s) = \dfrac{1}{2i}\left(\dfrac{1}{s-i\omega} - \dfrac{1}{s+i\omega}\right) = \dfrac{\boldsymbol{\omega}}{\boldsymbol{s^2+\omega^2}}$

Notice immediately: The transform of $f = 1$ is not a delta function. The decay rate is $a = 0$ and the pole of $F(s) = 1/s$ is at $s = 0$. The move from Fourier changes a full line to a **half line** $0 \le t < \infty$. The step function $f(t) = 1$ *jumps* at $t = 0$.

By applying nine rules, we will have the most important transforms. Let me get the rules straight, before their applications. Section 2.5 solved the damped equation $mu'' + du' + ku = 1$, and now we allow any force $f(t)$. At the end comes the inverse Laplace transform. For this complex integral we add residues at poles.

The first rules connect d/dt and d/ds with multiplication by s or t. Take the derivative $-dF/ds$ in (2) to see the Laplace transform of $tf(t)$. The step function transforms to $F = 1/s$, so its integral the ramp function transforms to $1/s^2$ (by Rule 4 and also Rule 1). Similarly te^{at} transforms to a double pole $1/(s-a)^2$.

1.	**Multiplied by t**	$tf(t)$	transforms to	$-dF/ds$
2.	**Derivative**	df/dt	transforms to	$sF(s) - f(0)$
3.	**Two derivatives**	d^2f/dt^2	transforms to	$s[sF(s) - f(0)] - f'(0)$
4.	**Integral**	$\int_0^t f(x)\,dx$	transforms to	$F(s)/s$

Suddenly $f(0)$ enters Rule 2. This will be crucial in solving initial-value problems by Laplace transform. The transform of df/dt comes from integration by parts:

$$\int_0^\infty \frac{df}{dt} e^{-st}\,dt = \int_0^\infty f(t)\,\frac{d}{dt}(e^{-st})\,dt + \Big[f(t)\,e^{-st}\Big]_0^\infty = \boldsymbol{sF(s) - f(0)}. \quad (4)$$

The remaining rules include shifts to $f(t-T)$ or $F(s-S)$. For Fourier, those produce multiplications by e^{-ikT} and e^{ixS}. Laplace needs $T \geq 0$, because a shift to the left would lose part of the graph. We multiply F or f by e^{-sT} or e^{St}:

5.	**Shift in f**	$f(t-T)$	transforms to	$e^{-sT}F(s)$
6.	**Shift in F**	$e^{St}f(t)$	transforms to	$F(s-S)$
7.	**Rescale**	$f(t/r)$	transforms to	$rF(rs)$
8.	**Convolution**	$\int_0^t f(T)g(t-T)\,dT$	transforms to	$F(s)G(s)$
9.	**Delta function**	$\delta(t-T)$	transforms to	e^{-sT}

Examples and Applications

Example 1 When $f(t)$ has growth rates a and c, its transform $F(s)$ has two poles:

Poles a and c
Residues A and C

$$f(t) = Ae^{at} + Ce^{ct} \quad \text{transforms to} \quad \frac{A}{s-a} + \frac{C}{s-c}.$$

Example 2 Solve $u'' + 4u = 0$ starting from position $u(0)$ and velocity $u'(0)$.

Solution $u'' + 4u = 0$ becomes $s^2U(s) - su(0) - u'(0) + 4U(s) = 0$.

Step 2 solves this algebra problem for each s separately:

$$(s^2+4)U(s) = su(0) + u'(0) \quad \text{gives} \quad U(s) = \frac{s}{s^2+4}u(0) + \frac{1}{s^2+4}u'(0).$$

The table identifies those fractions as the transforms of $\cos 2t$ and $\frac{1}{2}\sin 2t$:

$$u(t) = u(0)\,(\cos 2t) + u'(0)\left(\tfrac{1}{2}\sin 2t\right).$$

To emphasize: The poles of U at $s = 2i$ and $s = -2i$ give the frequency $\omega = 2$ in $u(t)$.

Example 3 Solve $mu'' + cu' + ku = \delta(t-T)$ with $u(0) = u'(0) = 0$.

The delayed impulse $\delta(t-T)$ transforms to e^{-sT}. Transform u'', u', and u:

$$(ms^2 + cs + k)U(s) = e^{-sT} \quad \text{gives} \quad U(s) = \frac{Ae^{-sT}}{s-a} + \frac{Ce^{-sT}}{s-c}. \tag{5}$$

Factoring that quadratic into $m(s-a)(s-c)$ produced the poles a and c of the transform. This splits the transfer function (one fraction) into two "partial fractions:"

Transfer function
Partial fractions

$$\frac{1}{ms^2 + cs + k} = \frac{A}{s-a} + \frac{C}{s-c}. \tag{6}$$

After multiplying by e^{-sT}, these are the transforms of exponentials that start at T:

Solution $\quad u(t) = Ae^{a(t-T)} + Ce^{c(t-T)} \quad$ (and $u(t) = 0$ for $t < T$). (7)

Example 4 $mv'' + cv' + kv = f(t)$ gives $(ms^2 + cs + k)V(s) = F(s)$ if $v_0 = v_0' = 0$.

Solution The Laplace transform $F(s)$ appears on the right side. Using (6), we multiply this $F(s)$ by $A/(s-a)$ and $C/(s-c)$. This is the moment for the convolution rule:

$$F(s)\left(\frac{A}{s-a}\right) \quad \text{is the transform of} \quad f(t) * Ae^{at} = \int_0^t f(T)\, Ae^{a(t-T)}\, dT. \tag{8}$$

Multiplying $F(s)$ by $C/(s-c)$ brings another convolution integral $f(t) * Ce^{ct}$. Then addition gives the neat result $\boldsymbol{v(t) = f(t) * u(t)}$, where $u(t)$ solved Example 3.

You have to look again at $v = f * u$. The impulse $\delta(t-T)$ at time T starts two exponentials $e^{a(t-T)}$ and $e^{c(t-T)}$. Those impulse responses in (7) are like Green's functions. The force at time instant T starts the response $u(t-T)$, multiplied by $f(T)$. So the solution in (8) is *a combination (an integral) of those responses*:

f = convolution of impulses $\quad f(t) = \int_0^t f(T)\delta(t-T)\, dT = f * \delta \quad$ (9)

v = convolution of responses $\quad v(t) = \int_0^t f(T)u(t-T)\, dT = f * u \quad$ (10)

That convolution (10) gives the output $v(t)$ from the input $f(t)$. In transform space, it is a multiplication $V(s) = F(s)\,G(s)$ by the **transfer function** $G(s)$.

For RLC networks and two or three poles, this algebraic equation is simplified by "partial fractions." Beyond that point the calculations are inhuman. The real value of transforms is insight into analysis and design. One example is a **feedback loop**, intended to reduce distortion and control the system.

A Feedback Loop

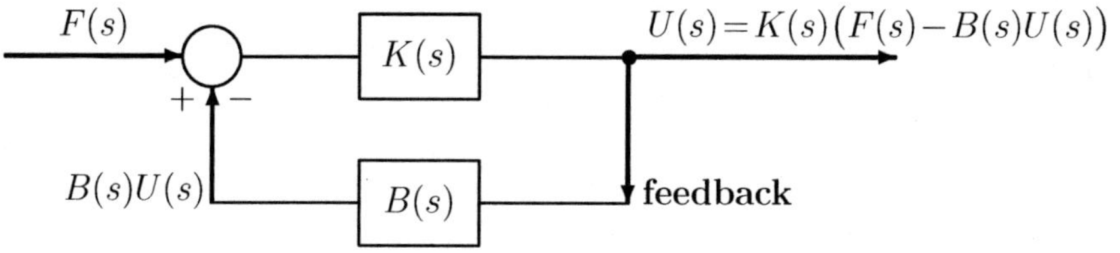

The input to the system is F. The transfer function G becomes $K/(1+BK)$:

Output with feedback $\quad U = K(F - BU) \quad$ leads to $\quad U = \dfrac{K}{1+BK}F. \quad (11)$

The K block is an active element. Standing alone, it might have an amplification factor (a *gain*) of $K = 10$. With feedback $B = 0.1$ we can add a pre-amplifier to have $K = 1000$. Because of the feedback, the transfer function is barely changed:

$BK >> 1$ gives $G \approx 1/B$ $\quad G = \dfrac{K}{1+BK} = \dfrac{1000}{1+(0.1)1000} \approx 9.9 \quad (12)$

The new system is insensitive to aging and degeneration in the amplifier. If K is reduced to 500, then G slips only to 9.8. Notice that $BK << 1$ gives $G \approx K$.

There is also *positive feedback*, in which BK reinforces the input F. This detects fluctuations. It encourages friends, while negative feedback controls them:

Positive feedback $\quad G = \dfrac{K}{1-BK}$ gives $G \to \infty$ when $BK \to 1. \quad (13)$

The Inverse Laplace Transform

For Fourier, we gave the inverse transform at the same time as the forward transform. For Laplace, we couldn't do this. The forward transform is on the *half-line* $t \geq 0$. The inverse Laplace transform runs up the **edge of a half-plane**. The integral goes up the imaginary axis $\sigma = 0$, or up a parallel line ($s = \sigma - i\infty$ to $s = \sigma + i\infty$):

Inverse Laplace Transform $\quad f(t) = \dfrac{1}{2\pi i}\displaystyle\int_{\sigma - i\infty}^{\sigma + i\infty} F(s)e^{st}\,ds \quad (14)$

All poles and other singularities of $F(s)$ must be to the left of that vertical line of integration. I will integrate around the large semicircle C in Figure 5.4. When $F(s)$ has only poles $a_1, \ldots, a_N$, they lie inside C. Then the inverse transform $f(t)$ comes directly from the Residue Theorem in Section 5.1 (integration around poles):

N poles of $F(s)$ $\quad f(t) = \displaystyle\sum_{i=1}^{N}\Big(\text{Residue of } F(s)e^{st} \text{ at } s = a_i\Big). \quad (15)$

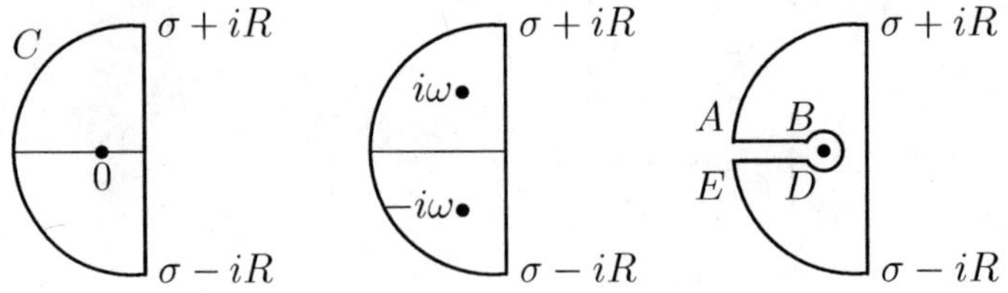

Figure 5.4: Integration paths for $F(s)e^{st}$ around poles and a branch point.

Let me do three examples. The first two are already on our list of transforms.

Example 5 Find the inverse transform of $F(s) = 1/s^3$.

Solution e^{st}/s^3 has a pole of order 3 at $s = 0$. The residue $f(t)$ is multiplying $1/s$:

$$F(s)e^{st} = \frac{e^{st}}{s^3} = \frac{1 + st + s^2t^2/2 + \cdots}{s^3} \quad \text{has residue} \quad f(t) = \frac{t^2}{2}.$$

Example 6 Find the inverse transform of $F(s) = \dfrac{s}{s^2+\omega^2}$.

Solution With poles at $i\omega$ and $-i\omega$, partial fractions will display the two residues:

$$\frac{se^{st}}{s^2+\omega^2} = \frac{1}{2}\left(\frac{e^{st}}{s-i\omega} + \frac{e^{st}}{s+i\omega}\right) \quad \text{gives} \quad f(t) = \frac{1}{2}\left(e^{i\omega t} + e^{-i\omega t}\right) = \cos\omega t.$$

Example 7 $F(s) = 1/\sqrt{s}$ with $\sqrt{s} = \sqrt{|s|}e^{i\theta/2}$. Find the inverse transform $f(t)$.

Here we have a more serious problem in complex integration. The square root function has a **branch point** at $s = 0$. Circling around that point is not allowed. We have to adjust the complex inversion integral (14) for $f(t)$, to avoid crossing the cut along the real half-line $-\infty < s \le 0$. Figure 5.4c shows the contour we need in the s-plane.

The integral is zero because $1/\sqrt{s}$ is analytic (and single-valued!) on and inside C. The integrals along the two quarter-circles both go to zero as $R \to \infty$. Here we need a better estimate than ML $= (\max|e^{st}/\sqrt{s}|)$ (length of path) $\approx (e^{\sigma t}/\sqrt{R})(\pi R)$. In fact e^{st} is extremely small when $\operatorname{Re} s << 0$ on the quarter-circles, by Jordan's inequality $\sin\theta \ge 2\theta/\pi$ in Problem 5.1.23. This leaves the integral forward on AB and back on DE after circling the branch point. As $R \to \infty$, AB and DE connect 0 to $-\infty$.

The AB direction has $\sqrt{s} = i\sqrt{x}$ $(x > 0)$. After circling the branch point, the DE direction has the other square root $\sqrt{s} = -i\sqrt{x}$. So the two integrals combine, and we can integrate by substituting y^2 for xt to reach a Gaussian:

Inverse transform for $F(s) = 1/\sqrt{s}$

$$f(t) = \frac{-2}{2\pi i}\int_0^\infty \frac{e^{-xt}dx}{i\sqrt{x}} = \frac{2}{\pi\sqrt{t}}\int_0^\infty e^{-y^2}\,dy = \frac{1}{\sqrt{\pi t}}. \qquad (16)$$

Example 8 We could invert the series for $F(s)$ using $t^n \leftrightarrow \left(\dfrac{d}{ds}\right)^n \dfrac{1}{s} = \dfrac{n!}{s^{n+1}}$:

$$\textbf{Laurent series in } s \quad F(s) = \sum_0^\infty \frac{c_n}{s^{n+1}} \qquad \textbf{Taylor series in } t \quad f(t) = \sum_0^\infty \frac{c_n t^n}{n!} \tag{17}$$

With a geometric series for F and an exponential series for f, this shows again that $F(s) = 1/(s+a)$ comes from $f(t) = e^{-at}$. The pole at $s = -a$ gives the decay rate of f.

Please notice what complex analysis has achieved: The first example for Fourier integrals was the one-sided decaying pulse $f(x) = e^{-ax}$, with $f = 0$ for negative x. Its Fourier transform is $\widehat{f}(k) = 1/(a+ik)$. But we could not then invert $\widehat{f}(k)$ to $f(x)$. Complex integration made this possible by using the residue at one pole.

Numerical inversion of the Laplace transform takes full advantage of Cauchy's Theorem, to move most of the integration path to $\text{Re}(s) << 0$ where e^{st} is very small. The path can be a parabola opening to the left [168]. It must enclose all singularities of $F(s)$, which should be near the negative real axis. By symmetry (when $F(s)$ is real for real s), N evaluations produce a midpoint rule with $2N$ values. André Weideman modified the cotangent contour proposed by Talbot, and tuned the constants a, b, c, d to get the best error exponent in $e^{-2.7}N$. Doubling N squares the error. $N = 14$ usually comes close to full precision in MATLAB.

```
function f = inverselaplace(F, t, N)          % Find f(t) by numerical inversion, t > 0
a = -1.2244 * N/t; b = 1.0035 * N/t; c = 0.5272; d = 0.6407;  % tuned parameters
theta = (2 * [0:N-1]+1) * pi/(2 * N);                % equispaced angles
s = a + b * (theta .* cot(d * theta) + c * i * theta);        % modified contour
D = b * (cot(d * theta) - d * theta .* csc(d * theta).^2 + c * i); % D = ds/dtheta
f = imag(sum(exp(s * t) .* F(s) .* D))/N;             % f(t) = midpoint sum
% example F = @(s) exp(-sqrt(s)); f = inverselaplace(F, 1, 8) in Problem 30
```

Linear Control Theory

A system of equations $dx/dt = Ax(t)$ has a matrix A instead of a scalar a. The solution is $e^{At}x(0)$ instead of $e^{at}x(0)$. The Laplace transform of e^{At} produces the transfer function $\int e^{At}e^{-st}\,dt = (sI - A)^{-1}$, which is the matrix form of $1/(s-a)$.

$$\textbf{Matrix exponential} \quad e^{At} = \sum_0^\infty \frac{t^k}{k!}A^k \quad \text{transforms to} \quad \sum_0^\infty \frac{A^k}{s^{k+1}} = (sI - A)^{-1}. \tag{18}$$

Every control engineer looks at the poles of $(sI - A)^{-1}$. That matrix blows up when s is an *eigenvalue* λ of A (then $sI - A$ is singular). The residues $x_i x_i^{\mathrm{T}}$ at the poles $\lambda_1, \ldots, \lambda_n$ involve the eigenvectors $x_1, \ldots, x_n$. So the crucial properties of A appear when we transform $x(t) = e^{At}x(0)$ into $X(s) = (sI - A)^{-1}X(0)$.

Control theory studies this **state variable** $x(t)$ when the system is driven by $\boldsymbol{m}$ **control variables** $\boldsymbol{u(t)}$. A matrix B couples the controls to n internal states x:

State equation $$\frac{dx}{dt} = Ax(t) + Bu(t) \quad (A \text{ is } n \text{ by } n,\ B \text{ is } n \text{ by } m) \tag{19}$$

Starting from $x(0) = 0$, the transform of this equation is $sX(s) = AX(s) + BU(s)$. Solving for X, the transfer function appears in $X(s) = (sI - A)^{-1}BU(s)$. But there is one more step, because we only observe r outputs $y(t) = Cx(t)$ and not the whole state $x(t)$. This output equation transforms to $Y(s) = CX(s)$:

m inputs u
r outputs y $$Y(s) = CX(s) = C(sI - A)^{-1}BU(s) = G(s)U(s) \tag{20}$$

This r by m matrix $G(s) = C(sI - A)^{-1}B$ is the transfer function in control theory. It tells us what the system can do. In many cases, we are building the system to have a desired input-output function $G(s)$. Then the problem is to design A, B, C. Notice that a change to $\widetilde{A} = S^{-1}AS$ and $\widetilde{B} = S^{-1}B$ and $\widetilde{C} = CS$ leaves $\widetilde{G} = G$:

Equivalence $$\widetilde{G} = \widetilde{C}(sI - \widetilde{A})^{-1}\widetilde{B} = C(sI - A)^{-1}B = G. \tag{21}$$

The transfer functions G and $\widetilde{G}$ look the same to the observer. Mathematically, this was just a change of variables in x, u, y. So in designing the system (realizing the transfer function), we can choose a convenient S.

Realization of a Transfer Function

The good systems (which we want to design) are **controllable and observable**. Controllability means that we can get from any internal state $x(0)$ to any final $x(T)$ with a suitable control $u(t)$. So controllability depends on A and B in (19).

The dual requirement is observability. This means that we can discover $x(0)$ by observing the outputs $y(t)$ up to time T. So observability depends on A and C. Problems 28 and 29 find the rank conditions on A, B, C for controllability and observability. A design satisfying these conditions is a **minimal realization**. This design does not use more control variables u and observation variables y (inputs and outputs) than the desired transfer function $G(s)$ requires.

The main point is to work with the Laplace transform. Instead of solving a differential equation, we solve an algebra problem: Choose A, B, C to realize a given transfer function $G(s) = C(sI - A)^{-1}B$. In the nicest case, for diagonal A, the matrix G has simple poles $\lambda_1, \ldots, \lambda_n$. Its residues as $s \to \lambda_i$ are rank one matrices:

Residues of G $$\frac{G(s)}{s - \lambda_i} \longrightarrow (\textbf{column vector } c_i)\ (\textbf{row vector } b_i^{\mathrm{T}}). \tag{22}$$

Suppose C has columns c_i and B has rows b_i^{T}, and $A = \Lambda = \operatorname{diag}(\lambda_1, \ldots, \lambda_n)$. Then we have a realization of G:

$$\textbf{(column)(diagonal)(row)} \qquad G(s) = C(sI - \Lambda)^{-1}B = \sum_{i=1}^{n} \frac{c_i b_i^{\mathrm{T}}}{s - \lambda_i}. \qquad (23)$$

Problem 28 confirms that A, B is controllable and A, C is observable.

Example 9 Choose A, B, C so that $G = 1/(s+1)(s+2)$. This has $n = 2$ poles.

The negative poles $\lambda = -1$ and -2 give a stable system to design. The residues of G at -1 and -2 are 1 and -1. Choose $c_1 = c_2 = b_1 = 1$ and $b_2 = -1$.

The z-Transform

The z-transform is like a "Laplace series" but those words are never used. Compare Fourier to Laplace. The continuous transforms apply on the whole line and half line. A Fourier series connects a doubly infinite sequence c_k to a function $\sum c_k e^{ik\theta}$ on the unit circle. A z-transform connects a **singly infinite sequence** u_k (only the integers $k = 0, 1, 2, \ldots$) to a function $U(z)$ defined *on and outside* that circle $|z| = 1$:

$$\textbf{z-transform of } \boldsymbol{u = (u_0, u_1, u_2, \ldots)} \qquad U(z) = u_0 + u_1/z + u_2/z^2 + \ldots \qquad (24)$$

Negative powers $1/z^n$ are good outside the circle. They explode inside at $z = 0$. The sum of $u_n z^{-n}$ corresponds to the integral of $u(t)e^{-st}$, and $|z| = |e^{st}| \geq 1$.

Laplace is about **causal** operators. Initial-value problems go **forward in time**. Cause comes before effect, and lower triangular matrices are causal. A component of u does not appear in earlier components of $f = Lu$. Watch how u_2 shows first in f_2:

$$L(z)U(z) = F(z) \qquad \begin{bmatrix} \ell_0 & & & \\ \ell_1 & \ell_0 & & \\ \ell_2 & \ell_1 & \ell_0 & \\ \cdot & \cdot & \cdot & \cdot \end{bmatrix} \begin{bmatrix} u_0 \\ u_1 \\ u_2 \\ \cdot \end{bmatrix} = \begin{bmatrix} \ell_0 u_0 \\ \ell_1 u_0 + \ell_0 u_1 \\ \ell_2 u_0 + \ell_1 u_1 + \boldsymbol{\ell_0 u_2} \\ \cdots \end{bmatrix} = \begin{bmatrix} f_0 \\ f_1 \\ f_2 \\ \cdot \end{bmatrix}$$

This is discrete convolution $\ell * u = f$, turning into multiplication $L(z)U(z) = F(z)$. The matrix L is Toeplitz (constant diagonals starting at row zero), as well as lower triangular. When does L have a lower triangular inverse? For finite matrices, L is invertible unless $\ell_0 = 0$. For infinite matrices, try $\ell_0 = 1$ and $\ell_1 = -2$:

$$\begin{bmatrix} 1 & & & & \\ -2 & 1 & & & \\ 0 & -2 & 1 & & \\ 0 & 0 & -2 & 1 & \\ \cdot & \cdot & \cdot & \cdot & \cdot \end{bmatrix}^{\boldsymbol{-1}} = \begin{bmatrix} 1 & & & & \\ 2 & 1 & & & \\ 4 & 2 & 1 & & \\ 8 & 4 & 2 & 1 & \\ \cdot & \cdot & \cdot & \cdot & \cdot \end{bmatrix} \quad \text{is not a bounded matrix!}$$

This corresponds to an equation $u_n - 2u_{n-1} = f_n$ with $u_0 = 0$. It is causal because $u_1 = f_1$ and $u_2 = 2f_1 + f_2$ and $u_3 = 4f_1 + 2f_2 + f_3$. But an impulse $f = (1, 0, 0, \ldots)$

is producing an unbounded response $u = (1, 2, 4, \ldots)$. We look for a reason in the z-transform $L(z) = 1 - (2/z)$ of the column vector $\ell = (1, -2, 0, 0, \ldots)$:

The triangular L^{-1} is not bounded when $L(z)$ has a root with $|z| \geq 1$.

Let me say this another way. Solutions $u = (1, A, A^2, \ldots)$ to a difference equation are stable when $|A| < 1$. Solutions $u(t) = e^{at}$ to a differential equation are stable when Re $a < 0$. The unit circle $|A| = 1$ corresponds to the imaginary axis $a = i\omega$:

Decay of A^n and e^{at}	**Oscillation**	**Explosion**
$\lvert A\rvert < 1$ and Re $a < 0$	$\lvert A\rvert = 1$ and $a = i\omega$	$\lvert A\rvert > 1$ and Re $a > 0$

I have given only this one example, but I pray you will see the point. Convolution with the sequence $\ell_0, \ell_1, \ldots$ is multiplication by the z-transform $L(z)$. The matrix equation $Lu = f$ is a convolution $\ell * u = f$ and a multiplication $L(z)U(z) = F(z)$. Solving $Lu = f$ is **deconvolution** in the discrete time domain and *division* in the z-domain. Section 4.6 explains why Fourier looks at $|z| = 1$ and Laplace at $|z| \geq 1$.

$$\boldsymbol{L(z)U(z) = F(z)} \qquad U(z) = \frac{F(z)}{L(z)} \quad \text{needs} \quad L(z) \neq 0 \text{ for } |z| \geq 1. \tag{25}$$

Examples and Rules

The z-transform rules are like the Laplace transform rules, with differences and powers replacing derivatives and exponentials. Here are three examples and five rules.

Powers	$u = (1, A, A^2, \ldots)$	$U(z) = 1 + \frac{A}{z} + \frac{A^2}{z^2} + \cdots = \frac{z}{z - A}$
Delta	$u = (1, 0, 0, \ldots)$	$U(z) = 1$ because $A = 0$
Ones	$u = (1, 1, 1, \ldots)$	$U(z) = z/(z-1)$ because $A = 1$

Delay (shift right)	$(0, u_0, u_1, \ldots)$	$U(z)/z$
Advance (shift left)	$(u_1, u_2, u_3, \ldots)$	$z(U(z) - u_0)$
Expand (upsample)	$(u_0, 0, u_1, 0, \ldots)$	$U(z^2)$
Compress (downsample)	$(u_0, u_2, u_4, \ldots)$	$\frac{1}{2}U(\sqrt{z}) + \frac{1}{2}U(-\sqrt{z})$
Convolve ($w = u * v$)	$(u_0v_0, u_0v_1 + u_1v_0, \ldots)$	$W(z) = U(z)V(z)$

Example 10 The analog of du/dt is $\Delta u = (u_1 - u_0, u_2 - u_1, \ldots) = u_{\text{advance}} - u$:

Transform of Δu $$\sum_0^\infty (u_{n+1} - u_n) z^{-n} = \sum_0^\infty u_n (z^{1-n} - z^{-n}) - u_0 z = (z-1)U(z) - u_0 z$$

Example 11 Solve the difference equation $u_{n+2} - \frac{1}{4} u_n = 0$ from $u_0 = 1$ and $u_1 = 0$.

Solution I see four ways to find the sequence $u = \left(1, 0, \frac{1}{4}, 0, \frac{1}{16}, \ldots\right)$:

1. Multiply u at each double step by $\frac{1}{4}$. Separate even n from odd n.

2. Substitute $u_n = A^n$ in the difference equation. Find two roots $A = \frac{1}{2}$ and $-\frac{1}{2}$ from $A^{n+2} = \frac{1}{4}A^n$. Match the initial conditions by $u_n = C\left(\frac{1}{2}\right)^n + D\left(-\frac{1}{2}\right)^n$.

3. Convert the second-order equation $u_{n+2} = \frac{1}{4}u_n$ into a first-order system:

$$\begin{bmatrix} u \\ v \end{bmatrix}_{n+1} = \begin{bmatrix} 0 & 1 \\ \frac{1}{4} & 0 \end{bmatrix} \begin{bmatrix} u \\ v \end{bmatrix}_n \quad \text{with eigenvalues } \frac{1}{2} \text{ and } -\frac{1}{2}.$$

4. Use Example 10 to find $z^2 U(z) - z^2 u_0 - z u_1 - \frac{1}{4} U(z) = 0$. Invert $U(z)$ to u_n:

$$U(z) = \frac{z^2}{z^2 - \frac{1}{4}} = \frac{1}{2}\left(\frac{z}{z - \frac{1}{2}} + \frac{z}{z + \frac{1}{2}}\right) \text{ comes from } u = \frac{1}{2}\left(1, \frac{1}{2}, \frac{1}{4}, \ldots\right) + \frac{1}{2}\left(1, -\frac{1}{2}, \frac{1}{4}, \ldots\right).$$

The Cobweb Model in Economics

Economics is causal. Prices at time t affect the demand d and the supply s at times $T \geq t$. When the price p is increased, demand goes down to $d_0 - ap$ and supply goes up to $s_0 + bp$. Do supply and demand move toward equilibrium or not, if it takes a month for the supply to react to the new price p_{n+1}?

$$d_{n+1} = d_0 - a\,p_{n+1} \text{ (immediate reaction) but } s_{n+1} = s_0 + b\,p_n \text{ (delayed).} \qquad (26)$$

The cobwebs in Figure 5.5 follow this graphically. At a low price, the demand d_1 is high but the next supply s_2 is low. Then d_2 is low when the price p_2 is high. The middle figure suggests convergence of the cobweb when $b < a$. In the third figure, supply overreacts to price change ($b > a$) and the cobweb grows outward.

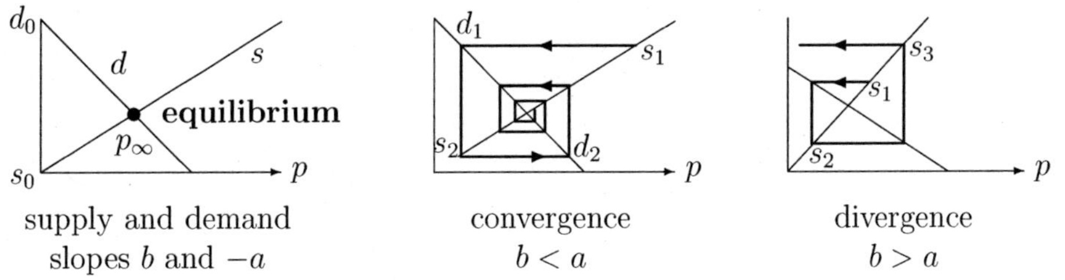

Figure 5.5: The cobweb model for supply and demand can spiral in or out.

We could solve the demand = supply equation by z-transform:

$$a\,p_{n+1} + b\,p_n = d_0 - s_0 \quad \text{or} \quad a\,z(P(z) - p_0) + b\,P(z) = (d_0 - s_0)z/(z-1). \qquad (27)$$

A direct solution is easier, since the homogeneous equation is $a\,p_{n+1} = -b\,p_n$:

Solution $$p_n = p_{\text{steady}} + p_{\text{transient}} = p_\infty + C\left(-\frac{b}{a}\right)^n. \qquad (28)$$

Use C to match p_0. The transient decays when $b < a$, and producers are less price sensitive than consumers. The unstable cobweb with $b > a$ goes out of control.

Suppose the prices are adjusted by the government and not by the laws of supply and demand. This becomes a problem in **discrete time control theory**. The state is $x = (s, d)$ and the control is $u = p$:

State equation $$\begin{bmatrix} s \\ d \end{bmatrix}_{n+1} = A\begin{bmatrix} s \\ d \end{bmatrix}_n + Bp_n$$ **Output equation** $$y_n = C\begin{bmatrix} s \\ d \end{bmatrix}_n = s_n - d_n \qquad (29)$$

The government aims for $y = 0$ by regulating the price. Take the z-transform:

$$\begin{bmatrix} z\,S(z) \\ z\,D(z) \end{bmatrix} = A\begin{bmatrix} S(z) \\ D(z) \end{bmatrix} + BP(z) \text{ and } Y(z) = C\begin{bmatrix} S(z) \\ D(z) \end{bmatrix} = S(z) - D(z) \qquad (30)$$

The transfer function in $Y(z) = G(z)P(z)$ is $G(z) = C(zI - A)^{-1}B$, from eliminating S and D. **Optimal control** would aim for $y = 0$ using the least control.

The Inverse z-Transform

We are given $U(z)$ and we want the sequence $(u_0, u_1, u_2, \ldots)$. If we know the Laurent series for $U(z)$, then the u_n are just the coefficients. Cauchy's integral formula for those coefficients is the inverse formula for the z-transform:

Coefficients $$U(z) = u_0 + \frac{u_1}{z} + \frac{u_2}{z^2} + \cdots \qquad u_n = \frac{1}{2\pi i}\int_C U(z)z^{n-1}\,dz \qquad (31)$$

When C is the circle $|z| = R$, the spectral method will choose N equally spaced points $z_k = Re^{2\pi ik/N}$ around the circle. Approximate the integral (31) by a sum of $U(z_k)z_k^{n-1}$. This is an inverse Discrete Fourier Transform! So the first N approximate u_n come quickly from the inverse FFT of N values of $U(z)$ on a circle:

```
N = 32; R = 2; k = [0:N-1]; theta = 2 * pi * k/N;      % N points on circle |z|=R
U = @(z) (1./z)./(1-1./z).^2;                          % Inverse transform of U(z) is u_n=n
% Also try U=@(z) (1./z).* (1 + 1./z)./(1-1./z).^3     % U inverts to u_n=n^2
z = R * exp(i * theta); u = (R.^k).* ifft(U(z));       % Find u by sum around |z|=R
```

Problem Set 5.3

1 Find the Laplace transform $U(s)$ of each $u(t)$, and the poles of $U(s)$:

(a) $u = 1 + t$ (b) $u = t\cos\omega t$ (c) $u = \cos(\omega t - \theta)$
(d) $u = \cos^2 t$ (e) $u = 1 - e^{-t}$ (f) $u = te^{-t}\sin\omega t$

2 Find the Laplace transform of $u(t)$ following the table of rules:

(a) $u=1$ for $t \le 1, u=0$ elsewhere (b) $u=$ next integer above t (c) $u=t\delta(t)$

3 *Inverse Laplace Transform*: Find the function $u(t)$ from its transform $U(s)$:

(a) $\dfrac{1}{s-2\pi i}$ (b) $\dfrac{s+1}{s^2+1}$ (c) $\dfrac{1}{(s-1)(s-2)}$
(d) e^{-s} (e) $e^{-s}/(s-a)$ (f) $U(s) = s$

4 Solve $u'' + u = 0$ from $u(0)$ and $u'(0)$ by expressing $U(s)$ as a combination of $s/(s^2+1)$ and $1/(s^2+1)$. Find the inverse transform $u(t)$ from the table.

5 Solve $u'' + 2u' + 2u = \delta$ starting from $u(0) = 0$ and $u'(0) = 1$ by Laplace transform. Find the poles and partial fractions for $U(s)$ or search directly in the table for $u(t)$.

6 Solve the following initial-value problems by Laplace transform:

(a) $u' + u = e^{i\omega t}, u(0) = 8$ (b) $u'' - u = e^t, u(0) = 0, u'(0) = 0$
(c) $u' + u = e^{-t}, u(0) = 2$ (d) $u'' + u = 6t, u(0) = 0, u'(0) = 0$
(e) $u' - i\omega u = \delta(t), u(0) = 0$ (f) $mu'' + cu' + ku = 0, u(0) = 1, u'(0) = 0$

7 Show that a passive response $G = 1/(s^2 + s + 1)$ is a **positive-real** function: Re $G \ge 0$ when Re $s \ge 0$.

8 The transform of e^{At} is $(sI - A)^{-1}$. Compute that transfer function when $A = [1\ 1;\ 1\ 1]$. Compare its poles to the eigenvalues of A.

9 If du/dt decays exponentially, use its transform to show that

(i) $sU(s) \to u(0)$ as $s \to \infty$ (ii) $sU(s) \to u(\infty)$ as $s \to 0$.

10 Transform Bessel's time-varying equation $tu'' + u' + tu = 0$ to find a first-order equation for U. By separating variables or by direct substitution find $U(s) = C/\sqrt{1+s^2}$, the Laplace transform of the Bessel function $J_0(t)$.

11 Find the Laplace transforms of (a) a single arch of $u = \sin \pi t$ and (b) a short ramp $u = t$. First graph both functions, which are zero beyond $t = 1$.

12 Find the Laplace transforms of the rectified sine wave $u = |\sin \pi t|$ and the sawtooth function $S(t) =$ fractional part of t. This is Problem 11 extended to all positive t; use the shift rule and $1 + x + x^2 + \cdots = (1-x)^{-1}$.

13 Your acceleration $v' = c(v^* - v)$ depends on the velocity v^* of the car ahead:

(a) Find the ratio of Laplace transforms $V^*(s)/V(s)$ (the transfer function)

(b) If that car has $v^* = t$ find your velocity $v(t)$ starting from $v(0) = 0$.

14 A line of cars has $v_n' = c[v_{n-1}(t-T) - v_n(t-T)]$ with $v_0(t) = \cos\omega t$ in front.

(a) Find the growth factor $A = 1/(1 + i\omega e^{i\omega T}/c)$ in oscillation $v_n = A^n e^{i\omega t}$.

(b) Show that $|A| < 1$ and the amplitudes are safely decreasing if $cT < \frac{1}{2}$.

(c) If $cT > \frac{1}{2}$ show that $|A| > 1$ (dangerous) for small ω. (Use $\sin\theta < \theta$.) Human reaction time is $T \geq 1$ sec and aggressiveness is $c = 0.4$/sec. Danger is pretty close. Probably drivers adjust to be barely safe.

15 The *Pontryagin maximum principle* says that the optimal control is "bang-bang." It only takes on the extreme values permitted by the constraints.

(a) With maximum acceleration A and deceleration $-A$, how should you travel from rest at $x = 0$ to rest at $x = 1$ in the minimum possible time?

(b) If the maximum braking is $-B$, find the optimal dx/dt and minimum time.

Problems 16-25 involve the z-transform and difference equations.

16 Transform a shifted $v = (0, 1, A, A^2, \ldots)$ and downsampled $w = (1, A^2, A^4, \ldots)$.

17 Find the z-transforms $U(z)$ of these sequences $(u_0, u_1, u_2, \ldots)$:

(a) $u_n = (-1)^n$ (b) $(0, 0, 1, 0, 0, 1, \ldots)$ (c) $u_n = \sin n\theta$ (d) $(u_2, u_3, u_4, \ldots)$

18 (a) By writing $U(z) = \dfrac{2}{z^2-1}$ as $\dfrac{1}{z-1} - \dfrac{1}{z+1}$, find $u = (u_0, u_1, u_2, \ldots)$.

(b) By writing $V(z) = \dfrac{2i}{z^2+1}$ as $\dfrac{1}{z-i} + \dfrac{1}{z+i}$, find $v = (v_0, v_1, v_2, \ldots)$

19 Use the z-transform convolution rule with $u = v$ to find w_0, w_1, w_2, w_3:

(a) $w(z) = 1/z^2$ (this is $1/z$ times $1/z$)

(b) $w(z) = 1/(z-2)^2$ (this is $1/(z-2)$ times $1/(z-2)$)

(c) $w(z) = 1/z^2(z-2)^2$ (this is $1/z(z-2)$ times $1/z(z-2)$)

20 The Fibonacci numbers have $u_{n+2} = u_{n+1} + u_n$ with $u_0 = 0, u_1 = 1$. Find $U(z)$ by the shift rule. From $U(z)$ find a formula for Fibonacci's u_n.

21 Solve the following difference equations by the z-transform:

(a) $u_{n+1} - 2u_n = 0,\ u_0 = 5$ (b) $u_{n+2} - 3u_{n+1} + 2u_n = 0,\ u_0 = 1, u_1 = 0$

(c) $u_{n+1} - u_n = 2^n,\ u_0 = 0$ (d) $u_{n+1} - nu_n - u_n = 0,\ u_0 = 1$

22 Show that $p_{n+1} - Ap_n = f_{n+1}$ is solved by $p_n = \sum_{k=1}^{n} A^{n-k} f_k$ if $p_0 = 0$, since f_k is carried $n-k$ steps. Find the analogous solution to $u' - au = f(t)$.

23 Suppose you have k chips, the house has $N-k$, and at each play you have a 5/11 chance of winning a chip. What is your probability u_k of breaking the bank before it breaks you? Certainly $u_0 = 0$ (no chance) and $u_N = 1$.

(a) Explain why $u_k = \frac{5}{11} u_{k+1} + \frac{6}{11} u_{k-1}$.

(b) Find λ in $u_k = C\lambda^k + D$. Choose C and D to match $u_0 = 0$ and $u_N = 1$.

(c) If you start with $k = 100$ out of $N = 1000$ chips, your chance $(5/6)^{900}$ is almost zero. Is it better to start with 1 superchip out of $N = 10$?

24 (Genetics) The frequency of a recessive gene in generations k and $k+1$ satisfies $u_{k+1} = u_k/(1+u_k)$ if receiving the gene from both parents prevents reproduction.

(a) Verify that $u_k = u_0/(1 + ku_0)$ satisfies the equation.

(b) Write $u_{k+1} = u_k/(1+u_k)$ as an equation for $v_k = 1/u_k$ to find that solution.

(c) If the gene frequency starts at $u_0 = \frac{1}{2}$, which generation has $u_k = \frac{1}{100}$?

25 Transform the scalar control system $x_{k+1} = ax_k + bu_k$, $y_k = cx_u$ to $Y(z) = [bc/(z-a)]U(z)$. What sequence of y's has that transform $G(z) = bc/(z-a)$?

26 Write four statements for Fourier that are parallel to these four for Laplace:

Half-line $t \geq 0$ Transients e^{at} Re $a \leq 0$ Input $f(t)$ affects later $u(t)$

27 Suppose $f(t) = 0$ for $t < 0$. What is the condition on $f(0)$ so that the Fourier transform $\widehat{f}(k)$ and the Laplace transform $F(s)$ are the same when $s = ik$?

28 The tests on A, B for *controllability* and on A, C for *observability* are

$$\text{rank}[B \;\; AB \;\; \ldots \;\; A^{n-1}B] = n \qquad \text{rank}[C \;\; CA \;\; \ldots \;\; CA^{n-1}] = n.$$

Show that Example 9, with A, B, C given by (23), is controllable and observable.

29 Equation (29) is controllable if it can reach any state (s, d) in finite time from (s_0, d_0). If B is an eigenvector of A, show that (29) is *not controllable*. The test in Problem 28 is not passed when $m = 1$ and $AB = \lambda B$.

30 Test the inverselaplace code on $F(s) = e^{-\sqrt{s}}$. This is the Laplace transform of the function $f(t) = e^{-1/4t}/\sqrt{4\pi t^3}$. Try $N = 2, 4, 8$ at $t = 0.5, 1, 1.5, 2$.

31 Test the inverse z-transform code on $U(z) = (z - \pi i)^{-1}$. How many reliable u_n?

5.4 SPECTRAL METHODS OF EXPONENTIAL ACCURACY

We come to an essential theme of this chapter. ***Polynomials can approximate analytic functions exponentially well.*** We have always known that a linear approximation $f(h) \approx f(0) + h\, f'(0)$ has $O(h^2)$ accuracy. When h is divided by 2, the error is very nearly divided by 4. This is a success for many calculations in scientific computing, while first-order $O(h)$ methods are generally poor. And if $f(x)$ has N derivatives, an N-term approximation improves the accuracy to $O(h^N)$.

The question to ask is: ***What accuracy is possible as $N \to \infty$ (not $h \to 0$)?***

This new question involves the numbers hidden inside $O(h^N)$. Those numbers are controlled by the derivatives of f. The error in $f(0) + h\, f'(0)$ is $\frac{1}{2}h^2 f''(x)$ at some point x between 0 and h. With N terms, the error looks like the first missing term $h^N f^{(N)}(x)/N!$ and this is the key.

The number $f^{(N)}(0)/N!$ is exactly the Taylor series coefficient a_N. For analytic functions, and *only for analytic functions*, those coefficients from Nth derivatives have bounds $|a_N| \le M/r^N = Me^{-N \log r}$. *Conclusion*: Nth-order methods give exponential accuracy as $N \to \infty$ if the singularities of $f(z)$ allow $r > 1$.

For approximation near $x = 0$, we look at $f(z)$ in circles around $z = 0$. For integration or interpolation on an interval $-1 \le x \le 1$, complex analysis will look on *ellipses* around that interval. Even for real calculations with real functions $f(x)$, the complex function $f(z)$ is in control. **Spectral methods** (infinite order) **can give spectral accuracy** (exponentially small errors) **when $f(z)$ is analytic.**

The function $1/(1 + 25x^2)$ is infinitely smooth for real x. But its complex poles dominate many computations. Runge's classical example interpolates at equally spaced points. The poles at $z = 5i$ and $z = -5i$ produce disaster at the edges of Figure 5.6. Much better to work with unequally spaced points! The Chebyshev points $x_j = \cos(j\pi/N)$ give an exponential success, and complex analysis will show why.

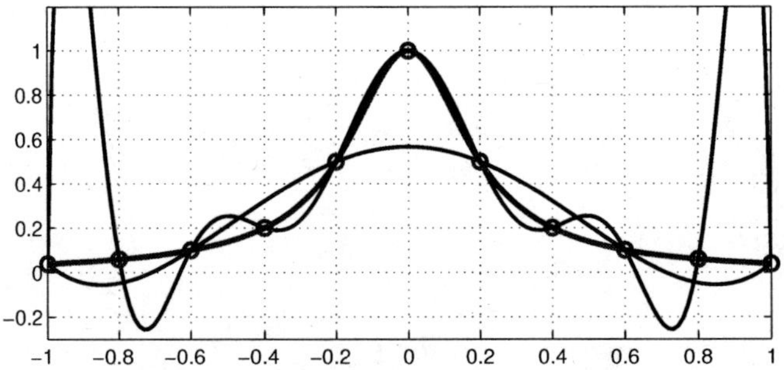

Figure 5.6: Runge's interpolation of $1/(1 + 25x^2)$ by polynomials of degree 5 and 10.

Vandermonde Matrix for Interpolation

The polynomial $p(x) = a_0 + a_1 x + \cdots + a_n x^n$ has $n+1$ coefficients. We can choose those coefficients a_j to match (interpolate) any $n+1$ function values $y_0, \ldots, y_n$ at any $n+1$ points $x_0, \ldots, x_n$. Each interpolation point gives a linear equation for the a's:

$$
\begin{array}{ll}
p(x_0) = y_0 \\
\quad \cdots \\
\quad \cdots \\
p(x_n) = y_n
\end{array}
\quad
\begin{array}{l}
a_0 + a_1 x_0 + \cdots + a_n x_0^n = y_0 \\
\qquad\qquad \cdots \\
\qquad\qquad \cdots \\
a_0 + a_1 x_n + \cdots + a_n x_n^n = y_n
\end{array}
\quad
\begin{bmatrix} 1 & x_0 & \cdots & x_0^n \\ 1 & x_1 & \cdots & x_1^n \\ & & \cdots & \\ 1 & x_n & \cdots & x_n^n \end{bmatrix}
\begin{bmatrix} a_0 \\ a_1 \\ \cdot \\ a_n \end{bmatrix}
=
\begin{bmatrix} y_0 \\ y_1 \\ \cdot \\ y_n \end{bmatrix}
\quad (1)
$$

That is a **Vandermonde matrix V**. Its determinant is the product of the differences $x_j - x_i$ between interpolation points. Check the linear and quadratic cases $n = 1$ and 2:

$$
\det \begin{bmatrix} 1 & x_0 \\ 1 & x_1 \end{bmatrix} = x_1 - x_0
\quad
\det \begin{bmatrix} 1 & x_0 & x_0^2 \\ 1 & x_1 & x_1^2 \\ 1 & x_2 & x_2^2 \end{bmatrix} = (x_1 - x_0)(x_2 - x_0)(x_2 - x_1). \quad (2)
$$

If two x's are the same, then two rows of V are the same and $\det V = 0$. If the x's are all different, the determinant is not zero and V is invertible. Then **Lagrange interpolation** in (1) gives a unique polynomial $p(x)$ through $n+1$ points (x_i, y_i).

Scientific computing always has a further question. **How should we compute $p(x)$?** I have to say immediately, watch out for equation (1)! The Vandermonde matrix V can be very badly conditioned. The columns of V are often a poor basis, and Section 7.4 will confirm this warning. The command polyfit (which works with this matrix V) has to use special care. Problem 5 pushes polyfit until it breaks.

Here we look for a better way to compute the interpolating $p(x)$. We can often choose the points $x_0, \ldots, x_n$ as well as the algorithm. May I ask those two questions explicitly, and give my (not completely expert) advice:

1.   Which interpolation points x_j ?   ***Choose the Chebyshev points*** $\cos \dfrac{j\pi}{n}$.

2.   Which algorithm to compute $p(x)$?   ***Choose the barycentric formula (9).***

The algorithm must be as stable as possible (depending on the x_j) and also *fast*. We will accept $O(n^2)$ steps to find $q_0, \ldots, q_n$ in (9). Evaluating $p(x)$ at a new point x_{n+1}, or updating $p(x)$ to make x_{n+1} an interpolation point, should only take $O(n)$ steps. You will see that formula (9) does not use the coefficients $a_0, \ldots, a_n$.

This section is greatly influenced by the ideas and publications of Nick Trefethen. He and I in turn owe special thanks to my adviser Peter Henrici and his books.

The Lagrange Formula

Suppose first that all interpolation values are $y_i = 0$ except $y_j = p(x_j) = 1$:

$$\begin{matrix} \boldsymbol{p(x_i) = 0} & \boldsymbol{i \neq j} \\ \boldsymbol{p(x_j) = 1} & \boldsymbol{i = j} \end{matrix} \qquad p(x) = \boldsymbol{\ell_j(x)} = \frac{(x-x_0)\cdots\cancel{(x-x_j)}\cdots(x-x_n)}{(x_j-x_0)\cdots\cancel{(x_j-x_j)}\cdots(x_j-x_n)}. \tag{3}$$

The factor $(x - x_j)$ is removed to leave a polynomial of degree n. Its n zeros are at the points $x_0, \ldots, x_n$ except x_j. The matching numbers in the denominator ensure that $\ell_j(x) = 1$ when $x = x_j$.

By linearity, the interpolating $p(x)$ at $n+1$ points is a combination of these $\ell_j(x)$:

Lagrange formula $\quad p(x) = y_0\,\ell_0(x) + \cdots + y_n\,\ell_n(x) \quad$ has $\quad p(x_j) = y_j\,. \qquad (4)$

This is the neatest form for $p(x)$, but numerically it looks bad. An evaluation of $p(x)$ takes $O(n^2)$ steps ($O(n)$ for each of the ℓ_j). A new point x_{n+1} needs new $\ell_j(x)$. Often (4) has been replaced by a "divided difference formula" found by Newton. A less famous "barycentric formula" has advantages that we hope to show.

The Barycentric Formula

The key polynomial for interpolation is Lagrange's $L(x)$ with $n+1$ zeros:

Zero at every x_j $\qquad L(x) = (x-x_0)(x-x_1)\cdots(x-x_n)\,. \qquad (5)$

Numerators in (3) cancel one factor of L. The denominators in (3) are *derivatives*:

Numerator of $\ell_j(x)$ $\quad \dfrac{L(x)}{x - x_j} \qquad$ **Denominator of $\ell_j(x)$** $\quad L'(x_j) \qquad$ **Weight** $\quad q_j = \dfrac{1}{L'(x_j)} \qquad (6)$

Multiply the numerator $L(x)/(x - x_j)$ by the "weight" q_j to give $\ell_j(x)$. Since all numerators share the factor $L(x)$, that factor comes outside the sum:

$$p(x) = y_0\,\ell_0(x) + \cdots + y_n\,\ell_n(x) = L(x)\left(\frac{q_0\,y_0}{x-x_0} + \cdots + \frac{q_n\,y_n}{x-x_n}\right). \tag{7}$$

When all $y_j = 1$, the polynomial that interpolates is just the constant $p(x) = 1$:

Interpolate all 1's $\quad 1 = \ell_0(x) + \cdots + \ell_n(x) = L(x)\left(\dfrac{q_0}{x-x_0} + \cdots + \dfrac{q_n}{x-x_n}\right). \qquad (8)$

When we divide (7) by (8), $L(x)$ cancels. The denominator looks like the numerator:

Barycentric formula $\quad p(x) = \dfrac{q_0 y_0/(x-x_0) + \cdots + q_n y_n/(x-x_n)}{q_0/(x-x_0) + \cdots + q_n/(x-x_n)}\,. \qquad (9)$

An evaluation of $p(x)$ takes $2n$ additions, together with $n+1$ subtractions $x - x_j$ and multiplications (by $y's$) and divisions (by $x - x_j$). One final division makes $5n + 4$. If there is a common factor in all the weights q_j, it can be cancelled.

Updating $p(x)$ is also fast, for a new interpolation point x_{n+1}. The n old weights q_j have one new factor each. The one new weight q_{n+1} has n factors. So this is $O(n)$.

Precomputation of the weights $q_0, \ldots, q_n$ does take $O(n^2)$ operations. Starting from $d_0^{(0)} = 1$, n updates produce the denominators $d_0^{(n)}, \ldots, d_n^{(n)}$. Then we know the weights $q_j^{(n)} = 1/d_j^{(n)}$. The recursion is for $j = 1 : n$

Update j known denominators by $\quad \boldsymbol{d_i^{(j)} = (x_i - x_j)\, d_i^{(j-1)}}$

Compute one new denominator by $\quad \boldsymbol{d_j^{(j)} = (x_j - x_0)\cdots(x_j - x_{j-1})}$

Chebyshev Points and Weights

A good barycentric formula is no use with a bad choice of interpolation points x_j. Spacing those points equally along an interval is a bad choice. The ratio of largest weight to smallest weight grows like $n!$ and the Vandermonde matrix V is very ill-conditioned (large ratio of singular values). And polynomials of high degree should not be expressed by their coefficients: $x(x-1)\cdots(x-20)$ is Wilkinson's famous example, when a tiny change in the coefficient of x^{19} suddenly produces complex roots. Equal spacing of nodes looks attractive, but it is unstable.

The Chebyshev points are much better. **Suppose our interval is $-1 \le x \le 1$.** Choose the $n+1$ points where the polynomials $T_n(x) = \cos n\theta = \cos(n \cos^{-1} x)$ reach $+1$ and -1. The roots of those Chebyshev polynomials come between these x_j:

$$\boldsymbol{n+1} \textbf{ points } x_j = \cos \frac{j\pi}{n} \quad \text{interlace } n \text{ roots } \cos\left(j + \frac{1}{2}\right)\frac{\pi}{n} \quad \text{in Figure 4.7.} \tag{10}$$

Those x_j are roots of the Chebyshev polynomial $U_{n-1} = T_n'/n$ of the second kind:

$$U_{n-1} = \frac{\sin n\theta}{\sin \theta} = 0 \text{ at } \theta = \frac{j\pi}{n} \text{ which is } x_j = \cos \frac{j\pi}{n} \quad (\text{plus } x_0 = 1 \text{ and } x_n = -1). \tag{11}$$

The points x_j (and also the roots) have the crucial property of clustering near the endpoints -1 and $+1$. Their density near x is proportional to $1/\sqrt{1-x^2}$. The same density appears when point charges on a wire repel each other with force $= 1/\text{distance}$. The Chebyshev *roots* are naturally associated with the second-difference matrix K, and the *points* are associated with the matrix T.

An extra bonus for interpolation is that the weights q_j have incredibly simple formulas. Each weight has n factors $x_j - x_i$, but still $\boldsymbol{q_j = C(-1)^j}$, times $\frac{1}{2}$ if $j = 0$ or n. The constant C cancels out to simplify the barycentric formula (9).

Here is the Berrut-Trefethen code to evaluate $p(x)$ at N equally spaced points xx. Always $p(x)$ interpolates $f(x)$ at the Chebyshev points $x_j = \cos(j\pi/n)$ for even n.

```
x = cos(pi * (0 : n)'/n);  y = feval(x);  q = [.5; (-1).^((1 : n)'); .5];  % weights
xx = linspace(-1, 1, N)';  numer = zeros(N, 1);  denom = zeros(N, 1);
for j = 1:(n + 1)
   diff = xx - x(j);  ratio = q(j)./diff;        % find q_j/(xx - x_j) for all xx
   numer = numer + ratio * y(j);                 % sum q_k y_k/(xx - x_k) to k = j
   denom = denom + ratio;                        % sum q_k/(xx - x_k) to k = j
end                          % numer and denom now include all terms in formula (9)
yy = numer./denom;           % N values yy = p(xx) of the interpolating polynomial
plot(x, y, '.', xx, yy, '-')
```

When the point sets x and xx overlap and diff has a zero component, ratio will contain NaN (*not a number*). Two new lines will assign $p(xx)$ its correct value $f(x)$:

After diff $= xx - x(j)$; **insert** exact(diff $== 0) = j$; % $==$ denotes equality

After $yy =$ numer./denom; **insert** $jj =$ find(exact); $yy(jj) =$ feval(exact(jj));

The direct MATLAB command for evaluating $p(xx)$ uses $yy =$ polyval(polyfit).

Exponential Accuracy

The fast interpolation algorithm allows the degree n to double at low cost. The points $\cos(j\pi/n)$ will appear again for $2n$, so function values feval(x) can be reused. The maximum difference $|f(xx) - p(xx)|$ on the interval $-1 \le xx \le 1$ is bounded by C/n^q if $f(x)$ has q derivatives. This is **polynomial convergence**. We are looking for **exponential convergence** at the faster rate $C/r^n = Ce^{-n \log r}$ with $r > 1$.

Exponential accuracy requires f to be an *analytic function*. Of course r depends on the location of its singularities. The function $1/(1+z^2)$ has poles at $z = \pm i$, and you might expect $r = 1$ as the cutoff: not so good. **The true cutoff is $r = \sqrt{2}+1$.** It is not circles around $z = 0$ that determine the rate r for Chebyshev interpolation. Instead r comes from an ellipse around the whole interval $-1 \le x \le 1$.

The exponent r The ellipse $(x/a)^2 + (y/b)^2 = 1$ has foci at ± 1 when $a^2 - b^2 = 1$. If f is analytic on and inside this ellipse, then $|f - p| \le C/r^n$ with $r = a + b$.

The ellipse $(x/\sqrt{2})^2 + y^2 = 1$ goes through the poles $\pm i$ (which have $x = 0, y = \pm 1$). That ellipse has $a + b = \sqrt{2} + 1$. This value of r is *not quite* achieved, because a pole is *on* the ellipse. But every smaller value of r is achieved, and $\sqrt{2}+1$ is the cutoff.

This is for Chebyshev interpolation. The ellipses appear in Section 3.4 from the Joukowsky map $Z = \frac{1}{2}(z + z^{-1})$, which connects circles in the z-plane to ellipses in the Z-plane. An analytic $f(Z)$ in the ellipse leads to an analytic $F(z)$ in the circle.

Spectral Methods

Earlier methods had a fixed order of accuracy $O(h^p)$. A **spectral method** is a sequence of approximations that give higher and higher p. To improve the accuracy of a second difference $[u(x+h)-2u(x)+u(x-h)]/h^2$, the standard *h-method* would reduce h. A spectral *p-method* uses more terms to get more accurate formulas.

Spectral formulas can get complicated, and they are successful on nice problems. Fortunately, real applications do often produce equations with constant coefficients. The domains are rectangles and circles and boxes. The FFT allows key computations to move to transform space, where differences and derivatives become multiplications.

We will describe spectral methods for these problems of scientific computing:

Numerical integration (called quadrature) and **numerical differentiation**

Solving differential equations (spectral collocation and spectral elements).

In each case the principle is the same: *Replace functions by polynomials of high degree. Integrate or differentiate those polynomials.*

Numerical Integration

Numerical quadrature approximates an integral by a sum at $n+1$ evaluation points:

Weights w_j
Nodes x_j

$$I = \int_{-1}^{1} f(x)\,dx \quad \text{is replaced by} \quad I_n = \sum_{j=0}^{n} w_j\, f(x_j). \tag{12}$$

The weights are chosen so that I_n equals I when $f(x)$ is a polynomial of degree n. The $n+1$ coefficients in f lead to $n+1$ linear equations for the weights $w_0, \ldots, w_n$.

Everything depends on the choice of nodes $x_0, \ldots, x_n$. If those are equally spaced between -1 and 1, we have a **Newton-Cotes formula**. If the nodes are chosen to give $I = I_n$ for all polynomials of degree $2n+1$, we have a **Gauss formula**. These rules are correct when $f(x)$ is a cubic (so $n=2$ for Newton, $n=1$ for Gauss):

$$\textbf{Newton-Cotes} \quad \frac{1}{3}f(-1)+\frac{4}{3}f(0)+\frac{1}{3}f(1) \qquad\qquad \textbf{Gauss} \quad f\left(-\frac{1}{\sqrt{3}}\right)+f\left(\frac{1}{\sqrt{3}}\right)$$

Both formulas give the correct $I = 2$ for $f(x) = 1$ and $I = 2/3$ for $f(x) = x^2$ (integrated from -1 to 1). The integrals of x and x^3 are $I = 0$ because the function is odd and the integration rules are even. These methods are fourth order because the first wrong integral is for $f(x) = x^4$:

$$\int_{-1}^{1} x^4\,dx = \frac{1}{5} \quad \text{but} \quad \frac{1}{3}(1)+0+\frac{1}{3}(1) = \frac{2}{3} \quad \text{and} \quad \left(\frac{-1}{\sqrt{3}}\right)^4 + \left(\frac{1}{\sqrt{3}}\right)^4 = \frac{2}{9}. \tag{13}$$

Newton-Cotes formulas extend to all higher orders, but we are not going there. Equal spacing is a disaster for high-order interpolation and integration. Those low-order weights $\frac{1}{3}, \frac{4}{3}, \frac{1}{3}$ do have a special place in scientific computing, because they lead to **Simpson's Rule**. Divide the interval $[-1,1]$ into N pieces of width $2h = 2/N$, and use the low-order rule on each piece. The weights where a piece ends and a new piece starts combine into $\frac{1}{3}+\frac{1}{3}=\frac{2}{3}$, to give Simpson's pattern $1,4,2,4,2,\ldots,2,4,1$:

$$I_N = \tfrac{1}{3}h\Big[f(-1)+4f(-1+h)+2f(-1+2h)+\cdots+2f(1-2h)+4f(1-h)+f(1)\Big].$$

For $f(x)=1$ this is $I_N = 6N(h/3) = 2$. The formula is simple, and it gives moderate accuracy. Breaking the integral into pieces is a good idea for high-order methods too, especially when the function itself breaks into smooth pieces:

If $f(x)$ is piecewise smooth, integrate over each piece and add.

Gauss is taken as the gold standard with the highest accuracy. His nodes x_j are the zeros of the *Legendre polynomials* starting with $x, x^2-\frac{1}{3}, x^3-\frac{3}{5}x$. Those evaluation points are the eigenvalues of a special tridiagonal matrix L. The weights w_j are 2 (squares of first components of the eigenvectors). The theory is beautiful and the computations are efficient. Trefethen's Golub-Welsch code creates the w_j and x_j.

```
b = 1/2 * sqrt(1 - (2 * (1 : n)).^(-2));    % off-diagonal entries of Legendre's L
L = diag(b, 1) + diag(b, -1);               % symmetric tridiagonal L of size n + 1
[V, X] = eig(L);                            % eigenvectors in V, eigenvalues in X
x = diag(X);  [x, j] = sort(x);             % Gauss nodes x_j are eigenvalues of L
w = 2 * V(1, j).^2;                         % the weights w_j are all positive
I = w * f(x);                               % exact quadrature for degree 2n + 1
```

The Legendre polynomial $P_{n+1}(x)$ has zeros at those points $x_0,\ldots,x_n$. That P_{n+1} is orthogonal to all polynomials $q(x)$ of degree $\le n$. This is why Gauss gets extra accuracy ($I(f) = I_n(f)$ *for any polynomial* $f(x)$ *of degree* $2n+1$). To see that doubled accuracy, divide $f(x)$ by $P_{n+1}(x)$ to get a quotient $q(x)$ and a remainder $r(x)$:

Degree $2n+1$ $\quad f(x) = P_{n+1}(x)\,q(x) + r(x)\quad$ with degree $q \le n$ and degree $r \le n$.

The term $P_{n+1}(x)\,q(x)$ has exact integral zero (because P_{n+1} is orthogonal to any q of degree n). Gauss quadrature on this term also gives zero (because $P_{n+1}(x_j) = 0$ by the choice of the nodes). This leaves the quadrature formula for $r(x)$:

$$I = \int_{-1}^{1} f(x)\,dx = \int_{-1}^{1} r(x)\,dx \quad \text{equals} \quad I_n = \sum w_j f(x_j) = \sum w_j r(x_j) \tag{14}$$

because the weights w_j are chosen to give $I = I_n$ for degree $r \le n$. So $I(f) = I_n(f)$.

These Gauss nodes x_j have increased density near the ends -1 and 1, like the points $\cos(\pi j/n)$. But the simple weights $(-1)^j$ in Chebyshev interpolation allow us to use the FFT in approximating the integral. This "Chebyshev quadrature" was proposed in 1960 by Clenshaw and Curtis, and their names are still used.

Cosine Transform and Clenshaw-Curtis Quadrature

Now the first line of code chooses the nodes $x_j = \cos(\pi j/n)$. We interpolate $f(x)$ by a polynomial $p(x)$ at those nodes, and the Clenshaw-Curtis $I_n(f)$ is the integral of $p(x)$. The earlier interpolation code evaluated $p(xx)$ at other points. To compute only at the Chebyshev points x_j, the FFT gives a better way:

Change x to $\cos\theta$

$$I = \int_{-1}^{1} f(x)\,dx = \int_{0}^{\pi} f(\cos\theta)\sin\theta\,d\theta\,. \tag{15}$$

The cosine series is the even part of the Fourier series. It expresses the even 2π-periodic function $F(\theta) = f(\cos\theta)$ as a sum of cosines. Each integral of $\cos k\theta\ \sin\theta$ is zero for odd k and $\mathbf{2/(1-k^2)}$ for even k, and we add those integrals:

$$F(\theta) = f(\cos\theta) = \sum_{k=0}^{\infty} a_k \cos k\theta \quad\text{has}\quad \int_{-1}^{1} F(\theta)\,\sin\theta\,d\theta = \sum_{\text{even } k} \frac{2a_k}{1-k^2}\,. \tag{16}$$

This is the exact integral I. Computations use the **Discrete Cosine Transform.** $F(\theta)$ is sampled at the $n+1$ equally spaced points $\theta = j\pi/n$ (Chebyshev points in the x variable). The DCT returns coefficients A_k that include the correct a_k and all its aliases among the higher cosine coefficients. This is the price of sampling, and C-C quadrature uses these A_k. The symbol $\sum''$ means half-weight for $k=0$ and n:

Clenshaw-Curtis

$$I \approx I_n = \sum_{\text{even } k}^{n}{}'' \frac{2A_k}{1-k^2}\,. \tag{17}$$

You will see that sum $w * A$ at the end of the code. Notice that the real DCT is here computed from the complex FFT. It was Gentleman who saw this connection that makes Clenshaw-Curtis so quick. A dct command would be faster but in 2007 this is only in the Signal Processing Toolbox (the DCT and IDCT are described at the end of Section 1.5). For inputs that are real and even, the cosine transform is also real and even—so the complex FFT loses a potential factor of 4 in efficiency.

```
x = cos(pi*(0:n)'/n); fx = feval(f,x)/(2*n);        % f(x) at Chebyshev points
g = real(fft(fx([1:n+1  n:-1:2])));                 % the FFT gives garbled a_k's
A = [g(1); g(2:n)+g(2*n:-1:n+2); g(n+1)];           % cosine coefficients for Σ''
w = 0*x'; w(1:2:end) = 2./(1-(0:2:n).^2);           % integrals = weights for (17)
I = w*A;  % Clenshaw-Curtis quadrature is exact when f has degree n+1
```

How does this answer compare with Gauss? The difference in order of accuracy ($n+1$ versus $2n+1$) seems not so visible in practice. Experiments in [158] show a significant difference only for analytic functions $f(x)$, which are integrated with great accuracy by both formulas. For less smooth functions, Trefethen has shown that the Clenshaw-Curtis error decreases at a $1/(2n)^k$ rate comparable to Gauss:

C-C error estimate

$$|I - I_n| \le \frac{64\|f^{(k)}\|_T}{15\pi k(2n+1-k)^k}\,. \tag{18}$$

Good aliasing at the Chebyshev points allows $1/(2n)^k$ to replace the expected $1/n^k$. *The cosines of* $(n+p)\theta$ *and* $(n-p)\theta$ *are equal at every* $\theta = j\pi/n$. Then if $p \le n$, quadrature gives the same answer for both cosines—exact for $\cos((n-p)\theta)$ and wrong only by $O(p/n^3)$ for $\cos((n+p)\theta)$:

Aliasing error $$I - I_n = \frac{2}{1-(n+p)^2} - \frac{2}{1-(n-p)^2} \le \frac{Cp}{n^3}. \qquad (19)$$

A 51-point C-C quadrature has errors near .0006 and .006 for the 60th and 90th Chebyshev polynomials. Gauss integrates those exactly since $2n+1$ is 101. But the Gauss error to integrate $T_{102}(x)$ jumps to -1.6.

Notice the error bound (18) for functions $f(x)$ with k derivatives. The Fourier coefficients decrease like $\max|f^{(k)}(x)|/n^{k+1}$. The linear hat function has $k=1$, even though $f'(x)$ has jumps. Those jumps are delta functions in f'' and they prevent $k=2$. Functions that are smooth but not analytic typically produce a ***polynomial convergence rate*** $\boldsymbol{h^{k+1} = 1/n^{k+1}}$ in scientific computing.

Here the increased density near -1 and 1 from $x = \cos\theta$ changes the max norm to $\|f^{(k)}\|_T =$ integral of $|f^{(k+1)}(x)/\sqrt{1-x^2}|$. A jump is allowed at the endpoints.

The great advantage for Clenshaw-Curtis is the speed of the transform. We can use thousands (even millions) of evaluation points. The stability of the FFT, and the fact that all weights w_k have the same sign, guarantee the numerical stability of I_n. The difference $I_{2n} - I_n$ gives a simple and realistic estimate of accuracy.

Spectral Differentiation: Equally Spaced Nodes

Estimating derivatives of $u(x)$ from discrete samples is a fundamental (and difficult) problem. Noise in u is highly amplified in u'. Here is our plan:

Fit the samples of u **by a smooth function** $p(x)$.

Use $p'(x)$ **and** $p''(x)$ **to approximate** $u'(x)$ **and** $u''(x)$.

We begin with infinitely many samples: impractical. Then we make the function periodic. On the next pages they are nonperiodic, with Chebyshev nodes. Section 8.2 will return to this tough and ill-posed and important problem of numerical derivatives (velocity from position).

The centered difference $(u(x+h) - u(x-h))/2h$ approximates $u'(x)$ with h^2 accuracy. It uses only two values of u. By using four values u_{-2}, u_{-1}, u_1, u_2 with coefficients $1, -8, 8, -1$ divided by $12h$, the accuracy jumps to $O(h^4)$. There must be formulas using six and eight values to reach orders h^6 and h^8. *Spectral methods achieve infinite order* (exact for all polynomials) *by increasing the number of values* u_i. For equally spaced samples $u_j = u(x+jh)$, the coefficients become $\pm 1/jh$:

Spectral difference formula with infinitely many nodes $$u'(x) \approx \frac{u_1 - u_{-1}}{h} - \frac{u_2 - u_{-2}}{2h} + \frac{u_3 - u_{-3}}{3h} - \cdots \qquad (20)$$

When $u(x) = x$, this formula produces $2-2+2-2+\cdots$. The partial sums $2, 0, 2, 0, \ldots$ oscillate around the correct slope $u'(x) = 1$.

Evidently we are not going to use this infinite formula in practice. It comes from Shannon's Sampling Theorem in Section 4.5. Shannon used the sinc function to interpolate the delta vector. The numbers in formula (20) are its derivatives:

Derivatives at meshpoints
$$\frac{d}{dx}\left(\operatorname{sinc}\frac{\pi x}{h}\right) = \frac{d}{dx}\,\frac{\sin(\pi x/h)}{\pi x/h} = \frac{(-1)^j}{jh} \quad \text{at } x = jh\,,\; j \neq 0\,. \tag{21}$$

For a more practical spectral difference formula, make all functions periodic. Take an even number $N = 2\pi/h$ of meshpoints. **The periodic sinc function psinc(x) interpolates the periodic delta vector at N points with spacing h:**

Periodic sinc
$$\operatorname{psinc}(x) = \frac{1}{N}\sum_{-N/2}^{N/2}{}'' e^{ikx} = \frac{\sin(\pi x/h)}{(2\pi/h)\tan(x/2)} = \begin{cases} 1 & \text{at } x = 0, \pm Nh, \ldots \\ 0 & \text{at } x = h, .., (N-1)h \end{cases}$$

Like sinc(x), this psinc(x) is band-limited. It has only the frequencies $|k| \leq N/2$. (The symbol $\sum''$ again means half-weight for the first and last terms.) Combining shifts of psinc(x) will interpolate any N-periodic vector $(u_0, \ldots, u_{N-1})$:

Periodic Shannon interpolation
$$p(x) = \sum_{j=0}^{N-1} u_j \operatorname{psinc}(x - jh)\,. \tag{22}$$

The derivatives of this $p(x)$ give periodic spectral differentiation. All we need is derivatives of psinc(x) at meshpoints $x = jh$. As an even function, the slope of psinc at $x = 0$ is zero. The analog of the previous $(-1)^j/jh$ is periodic:

$$\frac{d}{dx}\operatorname{psinc}(x) = \tfrac{1}{2}(-1)^j/\tan(jh/2) \quad \text{at } x = jh,\; j \neq 0, N, \ldots \tag{23}$$

Substituting (23) into (22) gives the derivatives $p'(x)$ at the meshpoints $x = jh$. A similar formula gives second derivatives $p''(jh)$. Since all is linear, N by N matrices DP and $DP^{(2)}$ must be multiplying the N samples of u:

Derivatives at meshpoints
$$p(jh) = u_j \;\text{ gives }\; p'(jh) = DP\,u_j \text{ and } p''(jh) = DP^{(2)}u_j. \tag{24}$$

Those periodic spectral differentiation matrices DP and $DP^{(2)}$ will be circulants. Their diagonals cycle so that each entry is repeated N times. Here are the entries of DP and $DP^{(2)}$ for $N = 6$ and $h = 2\pi/6$, with two of the six cyclic diagonals:

$$\begin{bmatrix} 0 & -1/2\tan(2h/2) & & & & \\ & 0 \quad 1/2\tan(h/2) & * & & & \\ & 0 & & * & & \\ & -1/2\tan(h/2) & 0 & & * & \\ * & 1/2\tan(2h/2) & & 0 & & \\ & * \quad -1/2\tan(3h/2) & & & & 0 \end{bmatrix} \qquad \begin{bmatrix} * & -1/2\sin^2(2h/2) & & & \\ & * \quad 1/2\sin^2(h/2) & * & & \\ & -(h^2+2\pi^2)/6h^2 & & * & \\ & -1/2\sin^2(h/2) & * & & * \\ * & 1/2\sin^2(2h/2) & & * & \\ & * \quad -1/2\sin^2(3h/2) & & & * \end{bmatrix}$$

A 2-line code (N *even*) creates the matrix DP on the left from its first column:

```
c = [0 .5 * (−1).^(1 : N−1)./tan((1 : N−1) * pi/N)]′;  % first column of DP
DP = toeplitz(c, c([1 N:−1:2]));  % periodic spectral differentiation
```

Since DP is a circulant matrix, DPu is a convolution. Problem (13) allows you to choose direct multiplication DPu or ifft(fft(c). * fft(u)) using the FFT.

Spectral Differentiation: Chebyshev Nodes

Spectral methods solve differential equations to very high accuracy when they succeed. If the equations and boundary conditions are periodic, equally spaced points are suitable. When $u(x)$ is not periodic, those formulas are poor near the endpoints.

The Chebyshev points $x_j = \cos(j\pi/h)$ are infinitely better. In this section I could say that those $N+1$ points are spectrally better. The differentiation matrix DC at these points is constructed on the usual principle of **spectral collocation**:

Interpolate $u(x_j)$ by $p(x_j)$. Then $p'(x_j)$ are the components of DCu.

When $N = 1$, the points are $x_0 = 1$ and $x_1 = -1$. Interpolation gives a straight line:

$$p(x) = \ell_0(x)u_0 + \ell_1(x)u_1 = \frac{1+x}{2}u_0 + \frac{1-x}{2}u_1 \qquad p'(x) = \frac{1}{2}(u_0 - u_1)$$

When $N = 2$, the points are $x_0 = 1, x_1 = 0, x_2 = -1$. Interpolation gives a parabola:

$$p(x) = \frac{x(x+1)}{2}u_0 + (1-x^2)u_1 + \frac{x(x-1)}{2}u_2 \qquad p'(x) = \left(x+\tfrac{1}{2}\right)u_0 - 2xu_1 + \left(x-\tfrac{1}{2}\right)u_2$$

The values $p'(x_j)$ go into row j of DC. They multiply the u's to approximate $u'(x_j)$:

$$DC_1\,u = \frac{1}{2}\begin{bmatrix} 1 & -1 \\ 1 & -1 \end{bmatrix}\begin{bmatrix} u_0 \\ u_1 \end{bmatrix} \quad \text{and} \quad DC_2\,u = \frac{1}{2}\begin{bmatrix} 3 & -4 & 1 \\ 1 & 0 & -1 \\ -1 & 4 & -3 \end{bmatrix}\begin{bmatrix} u_0 \\ u_1 \\ u_2 \end{bmatrix}. \tag{25}$$

The rows of every DC add to zero because $u = (1, \ldots, 1)$ must give derivative = zero. The middle row of DC_2 gives the second-order centered difference. The first and third rows of DC_2 are also second-order accurate, for *one-sided differences* (useful formulas). All three rows of $(DC_2)^2$ give $1, -2, 1$, which is $p''(x)$ for the parabola. The point of DC_N is to provide spectral accuracy $O(h^N)$ by using $N+1$ values of u.

```
function [DC, x] = chebdiff(N)  % DC = differentiation matrix on Chebyshev grid
x = cos(pi*(0 : N)/N)′;  c = [2; ones(N − 1, 1); 2] .*(−1).^(0 : N)′;
X = repmat(x, 1, N + 1);  dX = X − X′;
DC = (c * (1./c)′)./(dX + (eye(N + 1)));    % off-diagonal entries of DC
DC = DC − diag(sum(DC′));                   % rows of DC = DC_N add to zero
```

Spectral Methods for Differential Equations

Spectral methods are the numerical execution of classical "separation of variables" leading to infinite series solutions. Often the functions are sines and cosines in x, multiplied by exponentials in t. Those formulas dominated the subject before finite differences and finite elements became quick in practice. With fast computers the special formulas fell behind, because they are inflexible—often limited to constant coefficient equations in a square or circle or box or sphere.

These old methods have made a comeback. We will use them in Section 6.1 to see the differences between $u_t = u_x$ and $u_t = u_{xx}$ and $u_t = u_{xxx}$. Special solutions jump out, when we look at $u = e^{-i\omega t}e^{ikx}$. And in practice, the FFT can make spectral methods blazingly fast when the eigenfunctions come from Fourier. (The word *spectrum* refers to the set of eigenvalues.) The FFT normally works with equally spaced points, although the C library on math.uni-luebeck.de/potts/nfft has been created to allow unequal spacing.

The key point of this section has been the need for more meshpoints near the boundary. Chebyshev defeats Fourier, when we insist on stable computations that include boundary conditions. So the next pages will create "differentiation matrices" that can preserve the exponential accuracy of the classical series solutions. We lose the extreme simplicity of $(e^{ikx})' = ike^{ikx}$. And we can't achieve the flexibility of finite elements. But Chebyshev spectral methods, aiming to reach exponential accuracy, are finding a useful place.

Example 1 Solve $u'' = 12x^2$ by spectral Chebyshev with $u(1) = u(-1) = 0$. The true solution is $u(x) = (x^4 - 1)$.

Solution Replace d^2/dx^2 by the squared matrix DC^2. Remove the first and last rows and columns to impose $U(-1) = U(1) = 0$. Since the DC code started at zero, we need the smaller matrix $A = DC$^2 (2:end−1, 2:end−1).

This is **spectral collocation**. The equation $U'' = 12x^2$ is exactly satisfied at the Chebyshev points x_j. The right side of $AU = F$ must be $F =$ cos^2 (pi$*(1 : N-1)/N$).

Problem 16 tests for $U = u = x^4 - 1$ at the Chebyshev points.

Example 2 Solve the nonlinear $u'' = e^u$ by spectral Chebyshev with $u(1) = u(-1) = 0$.

Solution Now the discrete equation is $AU = F(U)$. We can iterate $AU^{i+1} = F(U^i)$ or use Newton's method, because the derivatives in the Jacobian matrix $J = A - F'(U)$ are easy to compute: $F(U) = U.*U$ gives $F'(U) = $ diag$(2*U)$.

Example 3 The eigenvalues of $u'' = \lambda u$ with $u(1) = u(-1) = 0$ are $\lambda = -k^2\pi^2/4$. Compare with eig(A).

Solution Trefethen emphasizes the value of this example. With $N = 36$ he finds 15 very good eigenvalues and about 6 more that are reasonable. "Eigenvalue 25 is accurate to only one digit, however, and eigenvalue 30 is wrong by a factor of 3." This is also typical of finite difference and finite element eigenvalues, that the errors $\lambda_k - \lambda_{k,N}$ increase quickly with k. Only a fraction (for A it is $2/\pi$) of the N computed eigenvalues are reliable.

The reason lies in the eigenfunctions $u_k(x) = \sin(k\pi(x+1)/2)$. Those oscillate faster as k increases. The standard error bounds involve derivatives of $u_k(x)$, and therefore powers of k. More directly, **the mesh is not fine enough to resolve the oscillations in $\sin(15\pi(x+1))$**. With $N = 36$, the mesh near the center $x = 0$ does not have two points per wavelength. So it cannot see the wave. The top eigenvalues of A grow like N^4, much too fast.

For the Laplacian in 2D, the collocation matrix is $A2D = \text{kron}(I, A) + \text{kron}(A, I)$. Remember that A is a full matrix for spectral accuracy. Then $\text{kron}(I, A)$ has full blocks on its diagonal. More important, $\text{kron}(A, I)$ has a multiple of I *in all* N^2 *blocks*. But spectral accuracy allows much smaller matrices $A2D$ than finite differences, while achieving the same quality of solution. Furthermore the spectral method produces a polynomial that can be evaluated at any point x, not just a finite difference approximation U at the meshpoints.

For our spectral collocation, *the matrix A is not symmetric*. We see this in (20) for DC. Spectral Galerkin changes $U'' = \lambda U$ into the same integrated form (weak form) that led to finite element equations. We don't have $U'' = \lambda U$ at meshpoints (collocation is also called **pseudospectral**). We do have $-\int U'V'\,dx = \lambda \int UV\,dx$ for suitable test functions V. Those integrals are computed by Gauss quadrature at Legendre points or by Clenshaw-Curtis at Chebyshev points.

Collocation or Galerkin, which to choose? Many authors feel that Galerkin is the more reliable and effective, and proofs are easier. (Spectral methods can be delicate but they offer such wonderful accuracy.) The textbooks [30, 53, 157, and others] help to complete a picture that we can only sketch. I will mention the words "spectral elements" and "mortar elements" as links to a large and growing literature.

Historically, that literature includes early ideas of Lanczos (1938). The rapid development came after Orszag's 1971 paper in the Journal of Fluid Mechanics, looking for the Reynolds number at the onset of turbulence in parallel flow. The other two leading technologies for differential equations had already been established:

1950s: Finite difference methods
1960s: Finite element methods
1970s: Spectral methods

Our sampling of key applications needs to include initial-value problems. For simplicity we choose $u_t = u_x$ and $u_t = u_{xx}$. The spatial discretization could have equal spacing with DP (periodic case, by spectral Fourier) or Chebyshev spacing with DC (non-periodic case on $[-1, 1]$). The time discretization can use the leapfrog or trapezoidal method of Section 2.2. Runge-Kutta and whole families of explicit and implicit and stiff methods are just ahead in Section 6.2.

Example 4 Solve $u_t = u_x$ and $u_t = u_{xx}$ starting from a square wave $u(x,0) = \text{sign}(x)$ on $-1 \le x \le 1$.

Solution Periodic boundary conditions for $u_t = u_x$ lead to $U_t = DP\,U$, with the circulant matrix DP in (24). The true solution to the equation is $u\,(x,t) = \text{sign}(x+t)$, a square wave that travels to the left (and reappears at the right boundary $x = 1$ by periodicity). A spectral method can successfully handle the jumps in the square wave, even though it is specially designed for analytic functions.

Zero boundary conditions for $u_t = u_{xx}$ lead to $U_t = AU$. Here A is still the squared Chebyshev differentiation DC^2 with all its boundary entries removed. The true solution to the heat equation $u_t = u_{xx}$ shows very fast decay from e^{-k^2t} of all the high frequencies:

$$u(x,0) = \textbf{square wave} \text{ in Section 4.1} = \frac{\sin \pi x}{1} - \frac{\sin 3\pi x}{3} + \frac{\sin 5\pi x}{5} - \cdots \tag{26}$$

$$u(x,t) = \textbf{exact solution} = \frac{e^{-\pi^2 t}\sin \pi x}{1} - \frac{e^{-9\pi^2 t}\sin 3\pi x}{3} + \frac{e^{-25\pi^2 t}\sin 5\pi x}{5} - \cdots \tag{27}$$

The solution of $U_t = AU$ (discrete in x) has the same $e^{-\lambda t}$ decay from the eigenvalues. The early eigenvectors of A are close to $\sin k\pi x$ and also λ is close to $-k^2\pi^2$, so $U - u$ is small. But when the time discretization enters, especially for the explicit leapfrog method, the size of Δt becomes a serious problem.

This stability problem is the subject of Chapter 6. Let me only say that it is worse for Chebyshev than Fourier, because the meshpoints are crowded near the endpoints of $[-1,1]$. The limits on Δt come from the top eigenvalues of DP and A, which are $O(N)$ and $O(N^4)$. Explicit methods are attractive for $u_t = u_x$ but certainly not for $u_t = u_{xx}$ with spectral Chebyshev, and those top eigenvalues show why:

$$\text{(Fourier for } u_x) \quad \boldsymbol{\Delta t} \le \frac{\boldsymbol{C}}{\boldsymbol{N}} \qquad \text{(Chebyshev for } u_{xx}) \quad \boldsymbol{\Delta t} \le \frac{\boldsymbol{C}}{\boldsymbol{N^4}}.$$

I will spare you the wild oscillations that come from large time steps. Implicit methods will avoid them. Notice that we are using the Method of Lines by going first to $U_t = DP\,u$ and $U_t = AU$, and then separately to finite differences in time.

The Method of Lines is quite efficient. Choose a space discretization by finite differences or finite elements or a spectral method. Then call a time-differencing code like ode45 or ode15s, designed by experts to achieve a desired accuracy even for stiff problems like $U_t = AU$. All this is coming immediately in Chapter 6.

Problem Set 5.4

Problems 1-3 establish properties of the Chebyshev polynomials.

1 Integrate $T_n(x)$ by using $\cos n\theta \sin\theta = \frac{1}{2}[\sin(n-1)\theta - \sin(n+1)\theta]$ for even n:

$$\int_{-1}^{1} T_n(x)\,dx = \int_0^{\pi} \cos n\theta \sin\theta \; d\theta = \frac{1}{2}\left[\frac{-2}{n-1} - \frac{-2}{n+1}\right] = \frac{2}{1-n^2} \text{ in (16).}$$

2 The "**generating function**" $G(x,u) = \sum_0^{\infty} T_n(x)\, u^n$ encodes all the Chebyshev polynomials in an important way. Take the real part of $\sum e^{in\theta}\, u^n$:

$$\operatorname{Re}\left(\sum_0^{\infty} e^{in\theta}\, u^n\right) = \operatorname{Re}\left(\frac{1}{1-ue^{i\theta}}\right) \stackrel{?}{=} \frac{1-u\,\cos\theta}{1-2u\,\cos\theta+u^2} = \frac{1-ux}{1-2ux+u^2} = G.$$

3 What is $T_m(T_n(x))$?

4 Test MATLAB's command $a =$ polyfit(x, y, N) to interpolate $y = e^x$ at $N+1$ equally spaced points $x = (0 : N)/N$. At what value of N does this computation of the coefficients in $p_N(x) = a_0 + \cdots + a_N x^N$ break down?

5 In Problem 4, graph the interpolating polynomials $p_N(x)$ using polyval(polyfit). At which N does the instability of equally-spaced interpolation make $p_N(x)$ useless?

6 Repeat Problems 4 and 5 for interpolation at the Chebyshev points $\cos(j\pi/N)$: polyfit is worse for the coefficients, but polyval gives a better polynomial p_N.

7 For larger N, does the barycentric code in the text give a better $p_N(x)$ than polyval(polyfit), using values of $y = 1/(1+x^2)$ at the Chebyshev nodes?

8 Compute these integrals (and errors) using the Gauss quadrature code:

(a) $\displaystyle\int_{-1}^{1} x^{2N+2}\, dx,\; N = 1, 3, 5$ (b) $\displaystyle\int_{-1}^{1} \frac{dx}{\sqrt{1-x^2}},\; N = 3, 7, 11$

9 Compute the same integrals using the Clenshaw-Curtis code (same N). Then compare for $N = 1024$.

10 For the periodic $f(x) = 1/(5+4\cos\pi x)$ on $[-1,1]$, find the differences between Gauss and Clenshaw-Curtis and the ordinary trapezoidal rule for 10 points:

$$I_{\text{trap}}(f) = \frac{2}{10}\left[\frac{1}{2}f(-1) + f(-.8) + \cdots + f(.8) + \frac{1}{2}f(1)\right].$$

11 What are the periodic spectral differentiation matrices DP and $DP^{(2)}$ (from the code or directly) for $N = 2$?

12 For $u(x) = \sin k\pi x$ compare the exact derivative at $x = \frac{1}{2}$ with the result from $DP\,u$ for large $k = 100$ and 1000. Try small $N = 6$ and large $N = 1024$ and $N = 4096$ using the matrix DP directly or the convolution rule ifft (fft (c).$*$ fft(u)).

13 With the MATLAB code for the 6-point spectral differentiation matrix DP, verify that $(DP)^2$ is the circulant matrix in displayed above the code.

14 Apply periodic spectral differentiation to the smooth $p(x) = \exp(\sin(x))$ to reproduce the figures on page 22 of [157].

15 Apply Chebyshev differentiation $DC_2\,u$ in equation (25) to the powers $u = 1, x, x^2, \ldots$ until the answer is wrong.

16 Use the chebdiff code to find DC_4. Test $DC_4\,u$ on $u = 1, x, x^2, \ldots$ until the answer is wrong, remembering that it gives u' at the Chebyshev points.

17 Example 1 in the text solves $u'' = 12x^2$ by spectral collocation using DC^2. Find the errors $U - u$ at the Chebyshev points for $N = 2, 3, 4$ when $u = x^4 - 1$.

18 Example 2 has $u'' = e^u$ with $u(1) = u(-1) = 0$. The discrete matrix A is $(DC_N)^2$ with first and last rows and columns removed.

(a) Solve the one equation $AU = F(U)$ by hand using $(DC_2)^2$ from (25).

(b) Solve $AU = F(U)$ using $(DC_4)^2$ by iterating $AU^{i+1} = F(U^i)$ with $U^0 = 0$.

19 Example 3 approximates $u'' = \lambda u$ by $AU = \Lambda U$. Plot the errors $\lambda_k - \Lambda_k$ for $k = 1, \ldots, 10$ using DC_{12} and DC_{20} to create A.

CHAPTER 6

INITIAL VALUE PROBLEMS

6.1 INTRODUCTION

Laplace's equation does not succeed as an initial-value problem. If you march forward from $t = 0$ with $u_{tt} + u_{xx} = 0$, almost every solution will explode. The easiest solutions to follow are pure exponentials $\boldsymbol{u = e^{-i\omega t}e^{ikx}}$, with t separated from x:

$$\textbf{Substitute } u = e^{-i\omega t}e^{ikx} : \qquad (-\omega^2 - k^2)e^{-i\omega t}e^{ikx} = 0 \tag{1}$$

This produces $\omega^2 = -k^2$ and $\omega = \pm ik$. The two solutions become $u = e^{-kt}e^{ikx}$ and $\boldsymbol{u = e^{kt}e^{ikx}}$. I have highlighted the exploding solution. A high k oscillation in x produces exponential growth e^{kt}, unless a boundary condition rules out this explosion.

This chapter deals with initial-value problems. The test that we just conducted (which Laplace failed) connects ω to k. This k–ω relation gives the behavior $e^{-i\omega t}$ in time for each frequency e^{ikx} in space. Fourier can assemble very general functions from those oscillations e^{ikx}, so the relation of ω to k is crucial—especially for linear equations with constant coefficients.

Here are five important equations that we will see again. In every case I will substitute $u = e^{-i\omega t}e^{ikx}$ and find the "dispersion relation" of ω to k:

- **Wave equation** : $u_{tt} = c^2 u_{xx}$ — $\omega = \pm ck$, conservative
- **Heat equation** : $u_t = u_{xx}$ — $\omega = -ik^2$, dissipative
- **Convection-diffusion** : $u_t = cu_x + u_{xx}$ — $\omega = -ck - ik^2$, dissipative
- **Schrödinger equation** : $iu_t = u_{xx}$ — $\omega = -k^2$, dispersive
- **Airy equation** : $u_t = u_{xxx}$ — $\omega = k^3$, dispersive

These equations will get most of our attention, together with their variable coefficient forms (c depends on x) and their *nonlinear forms* (c depends on u). Wave motion is absolutely fundamental in mechanics and physics and biology and engineering.

To emphasize those five examples, let me write $e^{-i\omega t}$ explicitly in each case:

$$|e^{ickt}| = 1 \quad e^{-k^2 t} \to 0 \quad e^{ickt - k^2 t} \to 0 \quad |e^{ik^2 t}| = 1 \quad |e^{-ik^3 t}| = 1 \tag{2}$$

The dissipative equations lose energy (first of all in high frequencies). The oscillations in the initial value $u(x,0)$ are smoothed out. Convection-diffusion carries that initial value along like a wave with velocity c, while it is smoothed. The Navier-Stokes equations have the same competition between wave motion and dissipation, but the waves are nonlinear $\big(c = c(u)\big)$ and often they get steeper. This nonlinear struggle between *global smoothing and local shocks* (controlled by the Reynolds number) makes fluid dynamics fascinating and difficult.

The $G - k$ Relation for Finite Differences

All these features will reappear for finite differences. And one new, potentially devastating possibility enters also: *numerical instability.* The difference equation has its own ω–k relation. It will partly copy the continuous case (for small k), but the difference equation can go off on its own for large k. Here is an example for the heat equation $u_t = u_{xx}$, using a forward time difference of the approximation U. The second difference matrix $-K$ produces $U(x+\Delta x,t) - 2U(x,t) + U(x-\Delta x,t)$:

Finite difference heat equation $$\frac{U(x,t+\Delta t) - U(x,t)}{\Delta t} = -\frac{KU(x,t)}{(\Delta x)^2} \tag{3}$$

Again we test pure exponentials e^{ikx}. The time dependence involves a **one-step growth factor** $G(k)$. This factor will be close to the true $e^{-i\omega\Delta t}$ for a single time step at a low frequency k, but G looks different for high frequencies. Substitute $U = G^n e^{ikx}$ into the difference equation (3) to find the growth factor G:

$$\boldsymbol{U(x,n\Delta t) = G^n e^{ikx}} \qquad \left(\frac{G-1}{\Delta t}\right)U = \left(\frac{2\cos k\Delta x - 2}{(\Delta x)^2}\right)U \tag{4}$$

Conclusion: G depends strongly on the mesh ratio $R = \Delta t/(\Delta x)^2$:

Growth factor $$G = 1 + R\,(2\cos k\Delta x - 2) \tag{5}$$

The size of G will tell us the **stability of the method:** $|G| > 1$ makes G^n grow too fast. Suppose $k\Delta x = \pi$ and $\cos k\Delta x = -1$. Then if $R > \frac{1}{2}$ the finite difference equation is unstable: $|G| > 1$. This test solution $U = G^n e^{ikx}$ will explode:

Instability $$\text{If } R = \frac{\Delta t}{(\Delta x)^2} > \frac{1}{2} \quad \text{then} \quad G = 1 + R(-4) \text{ is below } -1. \tag{6}$$

That stability condition $R \le \frac{1}{2}$ strongly limits Δt. If Δx is small (for good accuracy), then Δt must be below $\frac{1}{2}(\Delta x)^2$ for stability. We need a more stable difference approximation. Its construction is a key idea in this chapter.

Stable or not, G is consistent with the correct $e^{-k^2\Delta t}$ when k is small (low frequency, smooth function). Then $\theta = k\Delta x$ is a small angle and $2\cos\theta - 2 \approx -\theta^2$:

Consistency $$G \approx 1 + \frac{\Delta t}{(\Delta x)^2}(-k^2(\Delta x)^2) = 1 - k^2\Delta t \approx e^{-k^2\Delta t}. \tag{7}$$

Fourier Solution Formula

When an equation has constant coefficients, and no boundary conditions enter, the solution $u(x,t)$ is a combination of these pure exponentials $e^{-i\omega t}e^{ikx}$. This is the goal of Fourier analysis: **Write $u(x,0)$ as a combination of exponentials $\widehat{u}(k,0)\,e^{ikx}$ and follow each exponential.** Those solutions $e^{-i\omega t}e^{ikx}$ recombine into $u(x,t)$:

Fourier solution $$u(x,t) = \int_{k=-\infty}^{\infty} e^{-i\omega t}e^{ikx}\,\widehat{u}(k,0)dk \quad \text{with } \omega = \omega(k). \tag{8}$$

Example 1 To see the effects of dissipation and dispersion, solve three equations:

- $u_t = u_x$ ($\omega = -k$, the solutions $e^{ik(x+t)}$ just move to the left)
- $u_t = u_{xx}$ ($\omega = -ik^2$, energy dissipates because of e^{-k^2t})
- $u_t = u_{xxx}$ ($\omega = k^3$, constant energy, frequencies disperse because of e^{-ik^3t})

The initial condition $u(x,0)$ will be the same for all three. We choose a periodic box function, equal to 1 for $|x| \le \frac{\pi}{2}$. Its Fourier coefficients are:

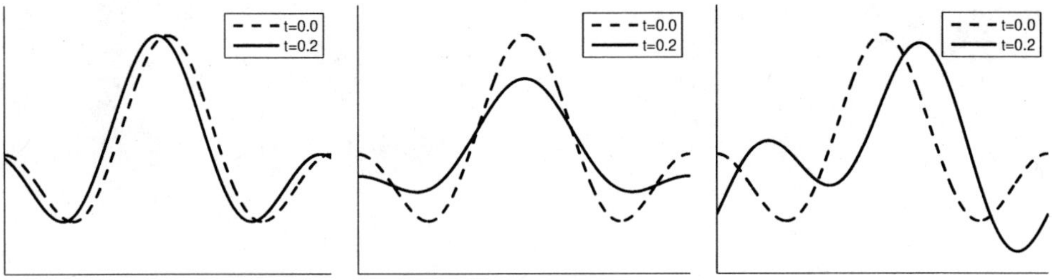

Figure 6.1: Solutions to $u_t = u_x$, $u_t = u_{xx}$, $u_t = u_{xxx}$ all starting from $u(x,0) = \cos x + \cos 2x$. The higher frequency moves faster with u_{xxx} and decays faster with u_{xx}.

The solution to $u_t = u_x$ is a one-way wave. Starting from any $u(x,0)$, Section 6.3 will show that $u(x,t)$ moves left with no change in shape (until it reaches a boundary). For the diffusion equation $u_t = u_{xx}$, the integral in Fourier's formula (8) involves the "error function"—impossible in closed form, but carefully tabulated because it appears so often.

For $u_t = u_{xxx}$ we meet the "Airy function", not so famous but illustrating perfectly the concept of **dispersion**: **Different frequencies travel at different speeds.** So the Fourier pieces disperse, as the third graph shows in Figure 6.1.

Here is a code that allows you to experiment with other c in $u(x,0) = \sum_0^n c_k e^{ikx}$. For $n = 3$ or 5 you see each wave; $n = 40$ shows the box.

```
n = 40;                                              % number of Fourier terms
c = [.5 2/pi * i.^(0:n-2)./(1:n-1).* mod(1:n-1,2)];  % half of the c_k are zero
x = linspace(-pi, pi, 1000);                         % 1000 equally spaced points
u0 = real(c * exp(i * (0:n-1)' * x));                % approximate box function
for t = 0:.01:1;
  clf
  for xderiv = 1:3                                   % number of x derivatives
    subplot(2,2,xderiv)
    ct = c.* exp((i * (0:n-1)).^xderiv * t);         % coefficients c_k e^{-iωt} in u
    plot(x, u0,'c:', x, real(ct * exp(i * (0:n-1)' * x)),'r-')
    axis([-pi pi -.5 1.5])
    title(sprintf('u_t = u_{%dx}', xderiv))
  end
  drawnow
end
```

Duhamel's Formula Includes Sources

A source term $f(x,t)$ enters at time t. That input begins to grow or decay in the same way that $u(x,0)$ grows or decays. By a later time T, **the source $f(x,t)$ has evolved over time $T-t$.** Then the solution of our linear problem $u_t = Lu + f(x,t)$ just adds up the results at time T from all the sources $f(x,t)$ at earlier times $t < T$:

Duhamel's Formula
Inputs $u(x,0)$ and f

$$u(x,T) = e^{LT}u(x,0) + \int_0^T e^{L(T-t)} f(x,t)\, dt \tag{9}$$

Each input $f(x,t)$ has time $T-t$ remaining, in which to grow or decay with $e^{L(T-t)}$.

There has to be a Duhamel formula for difference equations. Now the source term F_n enters at time $t = n\Delta t$. This input evolves (along with everybody else) to time $T = N\Delta t$, over $N-n$ steps. Let me choose S for the growth operator over one time step (S multiplies every e^{ikx} by its own growth factor G).

Copying the idea of Duhamel's formula, we add all the results at time $T = N\Delta t$:

Discrete sources F_n

$$U_n = SU_{n-1} + F_n \quad \text{is solved by} \quad U_N = S^N U_0 + \sum_{n=1}^{N} S^{N-n} F_n. \tag{10}$$

The important point is not the notation but the idea: *enter and then grow.* That will be the crucial idea in proving convergence $U \to u$ as $\Delta t \to 0$. *If stability holds, the errors that enter will not grow.* The powers of S (and every G) stay bounded.

The Helmholtz Equation

The next step allows two space dimensions x and y. The exponential solution becomes $u(x,y,t)\,e^{-i\omega t} = e^{ikx}\,e^{iny}$. Substituting into the wave equation $u_{tt} = u_{xx} + u_{yy}$, the $\omega - k - n$ relation is $\boldsymbol{\omega^2 = k^2 + n^2}$. Notice the crucial difference between the wave equation and Laplace's equation in (1): **The number ω is now real.**

The wave equation conserves energy because $|e^{-i\omega t}| = 1$. Its solution has a Fourier transform formula like (8) that integrates over k and n (this is a 2D transform). These are waves in free space with no boundaries.

The true problems of science and engineering have boundary conditions! Fourier carries us part of the way, but its simplicity is eventually defeated. The question is what to do next, when spectral methods with pure exponentials are not available. This chapter replaces differential equations by difference equations, but let me keep the simplicity of $e^{-i\omega t}$ as long as I can. That separates out the time variable.

Substitute $u = e^{-i\omega t}\,v(x,y)$ **into** $u_{tt} = u_{xx} + u_{yy}$ **and cancel** $e^{-i\omega t}$:

Helmholtz equation $\quad -\omega^2 v = v_{xx} + v_{yy}$ (with boundary conditions on v). (11)

This is Laplace's equation with an extra linear term. That term might look harmless, but it makes Helmholtz far more difficult. The immediate reason is that *positive definiteness is lost*. Let me bring all terms to the left side, and write $(K2\mathrm{D})v$ for the positive definite part (with minus signs on second derivatives):

$$-v_{xx} - v_{yy} - \omega^2 v = 0 \quad \text{is} \quad (\boldsymbol{K}\mathbf{2D} - \boldsymbol{\omega^2 I})\,v = 0. \tag{12}$$

Here $K2\mathrm{D}$ can be the continuous Laplacian $-\partial^2/\partial x^2 - \partial^2/\partial y^2$, or one of its finite difference or finite element approximations. Boundary conditions are included. The difficulty is that **all the eigenvalues $\boldsymbol{\lambda \geq 0}$ of $\boldsymbol{K}$2D are shifted to $\boldsymbol{\lambda - \omega^2}$.**

For high frequencies ω, this shift will produce very negative eigenvalues. In physics, the eigenfunctions are "bound states." We are not truly ready to deal with this loss of positive definiteness, and numerical methods for the Helmholtz equation are never easy. Software packages like ANSOFT and COMSOL will solve Helmholtz by finite element methods (elimination is preferred, iterative methods are less effective for indefinite systems).

Often we give up the simplicity of $e^{-i\omega t}$ and approach the wave equation directly by finite differences. A stable method computes good solutions (taking shorter steps and extra time for large ω). The next section begins with ordinary differential equations $u' = f(u,t)$, and the stability of finite difference methods.

6.2 FINITE DIFFERENCE METHODS

We don't plan to study highly complicated nonlinear differential equations. Our first goal is to see why a difference method is successful (or not). The crucial questions of **stability and accuracy** can be clearly understood for linear equations. Then we can construct difference approximations to a great variety of practical problems.

Another property we need is **computational speed**. That depends partly on the complexity of the equation $u' = f(u,t)$. Often we measure speed by the number of times that $f(u,t)$ has to be computed in each time step (that number could be one). When we turn to *implicit* methods and *predictor-corrector* methods, to improve stability, the cost per step goes up but we gain speed with a larger step Δt.

This chapter begins with basic methods (forward Euler, backward Euler) and then improves. Each time, we test stability on $u' = a\,u$. When a is negative, Δt is often limited by $-a\,\Delta t \le C$. This has an immediate effect: the equation with $a = -99$ requires a much smaller Δt than $a = -1$. Let me organize the equations as scalar and vector, nonlinear f in general, or linear with constant coefficients a and A:

1 equation	$u' = f(u,t)$	$u' = au$	$a \approx \partial f/\partial u$	stable $a \le 0$
N equations	$u_i' = f_i(u,t)$	$u' = Au$	$A_{ij} \approx \partial f_i/\partial u_j$	$\mathrm{Re}\,\lambda(A) \le 0$

Good codes will increase the accuracy (and keep stability) far beyond the $O(\Delta t)$ error in Euler's methods. You can rely on freely available software like ode45 to make these two crucial decisions (change to ode15s for stiff equations and implicit methods):

1. Choose an accurate difference method (and change the formula adaptively)

2. Choose a stable time step (and change Δt adaptively).

We will introduce **Runge-Kutta, backward differences, and Adams multistep methods.** We find the stability limits on Δt, and the order of accuracy p. The Euler methods have $p = 1$ (usually too inaccurate) and then comes $p = 2$.

Stiff Differential Equations

First we call attention to one extra question: ***Is the equation stiff ?*** Let me begin with a made-up example to introduce stiffness and its effects:

$$v(t) = \underset{\substack{\uparrow \\ \text{controls decay}}}{e^{-t}} + \underset{\substack{\uparrow \\ \text{controls } \Delta t}}{e^{-99t}}$$

The step Δt is 99 times smaller because of e^{-99t}, even when this term is decaying quickly in $v(t)$

Those decay rates -1 and -99 are the eigenvalues of A in the next example.

Two different time scales $$\frac{d}{dt}\begin{bmatrix} v \\ w \end{bmatrix} = \begin{bmatrix} -50 & 49 \\ 49 & -50 \end{bmatrix}\begin{bmatrix} v \\ w \end{bmatrix} \quad \text{with} \quad \begin{bmatrix} v(0) \\ w(0) \end{bmatrix} = \begin{bmatrix} 2 \\ 0 \end{bmatrix}. \tag{1}$$

The solution has $v(t) = e^{-t} + e^{-99t}$ and $w(t) = e^{-t} - e^{-99t}$. The time scales are different by a factor of 99 (the condition number of A). **The solution will decay at the slow time scale of e^{-t}, but computing e^{-99t} may require a very small Δt for stability.** It is frustrating to have Δt controlled by the component that is decaying so fast.

Any explicit method will have a requirement like $99\Delta t \leq C$. We will see how this happens and how the implicit stiff solvers ode15s and ode23t can avoid it.

Trefethen [156] points to four applications where stiffness comes with the problem:

1. Chemical kinetics (reactions go at very different speeds)

2. Control theory (probably the largest application area for MATLAB)

3. Circuit simulation (components respond at widely different time scales)

4. Method of Lines (large systems come from partial differential equations).

Example 1 The N by N second difference matrix K produces a large stiff system:

Method of Lines $$\frac{du}{dt} = \frac{-Ku}{(\Delta x)^2} \quad \text{has} \quad \frac{du_i}{dt} = \frac{u_{i+1} - 2u_i + u_{i-1}}{(\Delta x)^2}. \tag{2}$$

This comes from the heat equation $\partial u/\partial t = \partial^2 u/\partial x^2$, by discretizing only the space derivative. Equation (1) had eigenvalues -1 and -99. Now $-K$ has N eigenvalues, but the difficulty is essentially the same. The most negative eigenvalue here is about $a = -4/(\Delta x)^2$. So a small Δx (for accuracy) will require a *very small* Δt (for stability).

This "semidiscrete" method of lines is an important idea. Discretizing the space variables first produces a large system that can be given to an ODE solver. (We have ordinary differential equations in time.) If it wants to, that solver can vary the time step Δt and even the discretization formula as $u(t)$ speeds up or slows down.

The method of lines splits the approximation of a PDE into two parts. Finite differences/finite elements in earlier chapters produce the first part (discrete in space). The upcoming stability-accuracy analysis applies to the second part (discrete in time). This idea is very simple and useful, even if it misses some good methods later in this chapter that take full advantage of space-time. For the heat equation $u_t = u_{xx}$, the useful fact $u_{tt} = u_{xxxx}$ allows us to cancel space errors with time errors—which we won't notice when we discretize space separately from time.

Forward Euler and Backward Euler

The equation $u' = f(u,t)$ starts from an initial value $u(0)$. The key point is that the rate of change u' is determined by the current state u at any moment t. This model of reality, where all the history is contained in the current state $u(t)$, is a tremendous success throughout science and engineering. (It makes calculus almost as important as linear algebra.) But for a computer, continuous time has to change to discrete time. One differential equation allows many difference equations.

The simplest method (Euler is pronounced "Oiler") uses a forward difference:

Forward Euler $\quad \dfrac{\boldsymbol{U_{n+1}-U_n}}{\boldsymbol{\Delta t}} = \boldsymbol{f(U_n, t_n)} \quad$ is $\quad U_{n+1} = U_n + \Delta t\, f_n\,. \qquad (3)$

Over each Δt interval, the slope of U doesn't change. Figure 6.2 shows how the correct solution to $u' = au$ follows a smooth curve, while $U(t)$ is only piecewise linear. A better method (higher accuracy) will stay much closer to the curve by using more information than the one slope $f_n = f(U_n, t_n)$ at the start of the step.

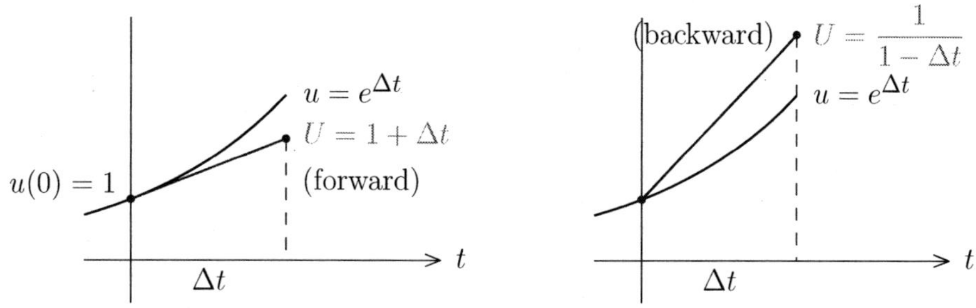

Figure 6.2: Forward Euler and Backward Euler for $u' = u$. One-step errors $\approx \frac{1}{2}(\Delta t)^2$.

Backward Euler comes from using f_{n+1} *at the end of the step*, when $t = t_{n+1}$:

Backward Euler $\quad \dfrac{\boldsymbol{U_{n+1}-U_n}}{\boldsymbol{\Delta t}} = \boldsymbol{f(U_{n+1}, t_{n+1})} \quad$ is $\quad U_{n+1} - \Delta t\, f_{n+1} = U_n\,. \qquad (4)$

This is an ***implicit method***. To find U_{n+1}, we have to solve equation (4). When f is linear in u, we are solving a linear system at each step (and the cost is low if the matrix is tridiagonal, like $I - \Delta t\, K$ in Example 2). Section 2.6 introduced iterations like Newton's method or predictor-corrector in the nonlinear case.

The first example to study is the linear scalar equation $u' = au$. Compare forward and backward Euler, for one step and for n steps:

Forward $\quad U_{n+1} = (1 + a\,\Delta t)U_n \quad$ leads to $\quad \boldsymbol{U_n = (1 + a\,\Delta t)^n U_0}\,. \qquad (5)$

Backward $\quad (1 - a\,\Delta t)U_{n+1} = U_n \quad$ leads to $\quad \boldsymbol{U_n = (1 - a\,\Delta t)^{-n} U_0}\,. \qquad (6)$

Forward Euler is like compound interest, at the rate a. Each step starts with U_n and adds the interest $a\,\Delta t\, U_n$. As the stepsize Δt goes to zero and we need $T/\Delta t$ steps to reach time T, this discrete compounding approaches continuous compounding. The discrete solution U_n approaches the continuous solution of $u' = au$:

$$\textbf{Convergence} \qquad (1 + a\,\Delta t)^{T/\Delta t} \ \text{ approaches } \ e^{aT} \ \text{ as } \ \Delta t \to 0\,.$$

This is the convergence of U to u that we will prove below, more generally. It holds for backward Euler too, because $(1 - a\,\Delta t)^{-1} = 1 + a\Delta t +$ higher order terms.

The stability question arises for very negative a. The true solution $e^{-at}u(0)$ is extremely stable, approaching zero. (If this is your own money, you should change banks and get $a > 0$.) Backward Euler will be stable because it divides by $1 - a\,\Delta t$ (which is greater than 1 when a is negative). **Forward Euler will explode if $1 + a\,\Delta t$ is smaller than -1, because its powers grow exponentially**:

Instability $\quad 1 + a\,\Delta t < -1 \quad \text{when} \quad a\,\Delta t < -2$ (7)

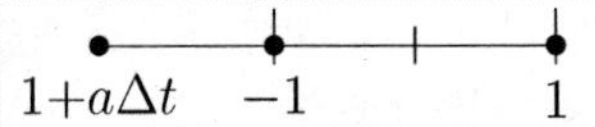

That is a pretty sharp borderline between stability and instability, at $-a\,\Delta t = 2$. For $u' = -20u$ which has $a = -20$, the borderline is $\Delta t = \frac{2}{20} = \frac{1}{10}$. Compare the results at time $T = 2$ from $\Delta t = \frac{1}{11}$ (22 steps) and $\Delta t = \frac{1}{9}$ (18 steps):

$$\textbf{Stable } \Delta t = \frac{1}{11} \qquad (1 + a\,\Delta t)^{22} = \left(-\frac{9}{11}\right)^{22} \approx .012$$

$$\textbf{Unstable } \Delta t = \frac{1}{9} \qquad (1 + a\,\Delta t)^{18} = \left(-\frac{11}{9}\right)^{18} \approx \mathbf{37.043}$$

I would describe backward Euler as absolutely stable (**A-stable**) because it is stable whenever the equation $u' = au$ is stable (Re $a < 0$). Only an implicit method can be A-stable. Forward Euler is **conditionally stable** because it succeeds as $\Delta t \to 0$. For small enough Δt, it is on the stable side of the borderline.

In this example, a *good quality approximation* requires more than stability (even $\Delta t = \frac{1}{11}$ is too big). Those powers of $-\frac{9}{11}$ alternate in sign, while e^{-20t} stays positive. The spiral on the book cover shows Euler's U_n leaving the true circle.

Accuracy and Convergence

Since forward and backward differences are *first order accurate*, it is no surprise that the errors from forward and backward Euler are $O(\Delta t)$. This error $e = u - U$ is measured at a fixed time T. As Δt decreases, so does the new error added at each step. But the number of steps to reach that time increases, keeping $n\,\Delta t = T$.

To see why the error $u(T) - U(T)$ is $O(\Delta t)$, the key is **stability. Earlier errors don't increase as they are carried forward to time T.** Forward Euler is the simplest difference equation, so it is the perfect example to follow through first. The next sections will apply the same idea to partial differential equations.

Euler's forward difference equation for $u' = f(u,t) = au$ is

$$U_{n+1} = U_n + \Delta t\, f(U_n, t_n) = U_n + a\,\Delta t\, U_n\,. \qquad (8)$$

The true solution at time $n\,\Delta t$ satisfies (8) except for a **discretization error DE**:

Exact $$u_{n+1} = u_n + \Delta t\, u_n' + \mathrm{DE} = u_n + a\,\Delta t\, u_n + \mathrm{DE}_{n+1}\,. \qquad (9)$$

That error DE is of order $(\Delta t)^2$ because the second-order term is missing (it should be $\frac{1}{2}(\Delta t)^2 u_n''$, but Euler didn't keep it). Subtracting (8) from (9) gives a difference equation for the error $e = u - U$, propagating forward in time:

Error equation $$e_{n+1} = e_n + a\,\Delta t\, e_n + \mathrm{DE}_{n+1}. \qquad (10)$$

You could think of this one-step error DE_{n+1} as a deposit like $(\Delta t)^2$ into your account. Once the deposit is made, it will grow or decay according to the error equation. To reach time $T = N\,\Delta t$, each error DE_k at step k has $N - k$ more steps to go:

Solve (10) $$e_N = (1 + a\,\Delta t)^{N-1}\,\mathrm{DE}_1 + \cdots + (1 + a\,\Delta t)^{N-k}\,\mathrm{DE}_k + \cdots + \mathrm{DE}_N \qquad (11)$$

Now stability plays its part. If a is negative, and $1 + a\,\Delta t$ *does not go below* -1, those powers are all less than 1 (in absolute value). If a is positive, those powers of $1 + a\,\Delta t$ are all less than $(e^{a\,\Delta t})^N = e^{aT}$. The error e_N has N terms in (11), and every term is less than $c(\Delta t)^2$ for a fixed constant c:

Overall error $$\boldsymbol{|e_N| = |u_N - U_N| \le N\,c\,(\Delta t)^2 = c\,T\,\Delta t\,.} \qquad (12)$$

The errors along the way, of size $(\Delta t)^2$, combined after $N = T/\Delta t$ steps into an accumulated Δt error. This depended on stability—the local errors didn't explode.

The error growth follows the difference equation in (10), not the differential equation. The stiff example with $a\,\Delta t = (-20)(\frac{1}{9})$ gave a large $1 + a\,\Delta t$, even when $e^{a\,\Delta t}$ was small. We still call Forward Euler a **stable method**, because as soon as Δt is small enough the danger has passed. Backward Euler also gives $|e_N| = O(\Delta t)$. The problem with these first-order methods is their low accuracy.

The local discretization error DE tells us the accuracy. For Euler that error $\mathrm{DE} \approx \frac{1}{2}(\Delta t)^2 u''$ is the first term that Euler misses in the Taylor series for $u(t + \Delta t)$. Better methods will capture that term exactly, and miss on a higher-order term. We find DE by comparing $u(t + \Delta t)$ with U_{n+1}, assuming $u(t)$ agrees with U_n. The error shows the first power $(\Delta t)^{p+1}$ that the method gets wrong:

Local discretization error $$\mathrm{DE} \approx c(\Delta t)^{p+1}\frac{d^{p+1}u}{dt^{p+1}}\,. \qquad (13)$$

The method decides c and $p + 1$. With stability, $T/\Delta t$ steps give a global error of order $(\Delta t)^p$. The derivative of u shows whether a specific problem is hard or easy.

Error estimates with powers of Δt or Δx appear everywhere in numerical analysis. The $1, -2, 1$ second difference has error $\frac{1}{12}(\Delta x)^4 u''''$. Partial differential equations (Laplace, wave, heat) produce similar terms. For nonlinear equations, the key is in the subtraction of (8) from (9). Then $f(U,t)$ is subtracted from $f(u,t)$. A one-sided **Lipschitz bound L** on $\partial f/\partial u$ replaces the number a in the error equation (10):

$$f(u,t) - f(U,t) \le L(u-U) \quad \text{gives} \quad e_{n+1} \le (1 + L\Delta t)\, e_n + \mathrm{DE}_{n+1}\,. \tag{14}$$

Second-Order Methods

To increase the accuracy, we could center the equation at the midpoint $(n+\frac{1}{2})\Delta t$. Averaging $f_n = f(U_n, t_n)$ and $f_{n+1} = f(U_{n+1}, t_{n+1})$ gives a *second-order method.* Section 2.2 experimented with this implicit trapezoidal rule, developed in ode23t:

Trapezoidal rule/Crank-Nicolson
$$\frac{\boldsymbol{U_{n+1} - U_n}}{\boldsymbol{\Delta t}} = \frac{\mathbf{1}}{\mathbf{2}}(\boldsymbol{f_{n+1} + f_n})\,. \tag{15}$$

Now $U_{n+1} - \frac{1}{2}\,\Delta t\, f_{n+1} = U_n + \frac{1}{2}\,\Delta t\, f_n$. For our model $u' = f(u) = au$, this is

$$(1 - \frac{1}{2}a\,\Delta t)\,U_{n+1} = (1 + \frac{1}{2}a\,\Delta t)\,U_n \quad \text{which gives} \quad U_{n+1} = \left(\frac{1+\frac{1}{2}a\,\Delta t}{1-\frac{1}{2}a\,\Delta t}\right)U_n\,. \tag{16}$$

The true solution has $u_{n+1} = e^{a\Delta t}u_n$. Problem 1 will find DE $\approx c(\Delta t)^{\mathbf{3}}$. Equation (15) is stable for $\mathrm{Re}\, a \le 0$. So $N = T/\Delta t$ steps produce $|e_N| = |u_N - U_N| \le cT(\Delta t)^{\mathbf{2}}$.

How to improve forward Euler and still keep it explicit? We don't want U_{n+1} on the right side of the equation, but we are happy with U_{n-1} (from the previous step). Here is a combination that gives second-order accuracy in a **two-step method**:

"Adams-Bashforth"
$$\frac{\boldsymbol{U_{n+1} - U_n}}{\boldsymbol{\Delta t}} = \frac{\mathbf{3}}{\mathbf{2}}\boldsymbol{f(U_n, t_n)} - \frac{\mathbf{1}}{\mathbf{2}}\boldsymbol{f(U_{n-1}, t_{n-1})}\,. \tag{17}$$

Remember that $f(U_{n-1}, t_{n-1})$ is already computed in the previous step, going from $n-1$ to n. So this **explicit multistep method** requires no extra work, and improves the accuracy. To see how $\frac{1}{2}(\Delta t)^2 u''$ comes out correctly, write u' for f:

$$\frac{3}{2}u_n' - \frac{1}{2}u_{n-1}' \approx \frac{3}{2}u_n' - \frac{1}{2}(u_n' - \Delta t\, u_n'') = u_n' + \frac{1}{2}\Delta t\, u_n''\,. \tag{18}$$

Multiplied by Δt in (17), that new term $\frac{1}{2}(\Delta t)^2 u_n''$ is exactly what Euler missed. *Each extra term in the difference equation can increase the accuracy* (power of Δt) *by* 1.

A third possibility uses the already computed value U_{n-1} (instead of the slope f_{n-1}). With $\frac{3}{2}, -\frac{4}{2}, \frac{1}{2}$ chosen for second-order accuracy, we get an implicit **backward difference method** (solve for U_{n+1} at each step). This is the useful BDF2.

Backward differences/BDF2 $$\frac{3U_{n+1} - 4U_n + U_{n-1}}{2\Delta t} = f(U_{n+1}, t_{n+1})\,. \quad (19)$$

What about stability? The trapezoidal method (15) is stable even for stiff equations, when a is very negative: $1 - \frac{1}{2}a\,\Delta t$ (left side) will be larger than $1 + \frac{1}{2}a\,\Delta t$ (right side). (19) is even more stable and accurate. The Adams method (17) will be stable if Δt is small enough, but there is always a limit on Δt for explicit systems.

Here is a quick way to find the stability limit $-a\,\Delta t \le C$ in (17) when a is real. The limit occurs when the growth factor is exactly $G = -1$. ***Set*** $U_{n+1} = -1$ ***and*** $U_n = 1$ ***and*** $U_{n-1} = -1$ ***in (17). Solve for a when*** $f(u,t) = au$:

Stability limit in (17) $$\frac{-2}{\Delta t} = \frac{3}{2}a + \frac{1}{2}a \quad \text{gives} \quad a\,\Delta t = -1\,. \quad \text{So} \quad C = 1\,. \quad (20)$$

We now have three second-order methods (15)–(17)–(19), all definitely useful. The reader might suggest including both U_{n-1} and f_{n-1} to increase the accuracy to third order. Sadly, this method is violently unstable (Problem 5). We may extend (19) by older values of U in backward differences, or extend (17) by older $f(U)$. But including both U and $f(U)$ for extreme accuracy produces instability for all Δt.

Multistep Methods: Explicit and Implicit

By using p earlier values of U, the accuracy can be increased to order p. Backward Euler has $p = 1$, and BDF2 in (19) has $p = 2$. Each ∇U is $U(t) - U(t - \Delta t)$:

Backward differences $$\left(\nabla + \frac{1}{2}\nabla^2 + \cdots + \frac{1}{p}\nabla^p\right) U_{n+1} = \Delta t\, f(U_{n+1}, t_{n+1})\,. \quad (21)$$

MATLAB's stiff code `ode15s` varies from $p = 1$ to $p = 5$ depending on the local error.

The alternative is to use older values of $f(U,t)$ instead of U. *Explicit comes first*:

Adams-Bashforth $$U_{n+1} - U_n = \Delta t(b_1 f_n + \cdots + b_p f_{n-p+1}) \quad (22)$$

The table shows the numbers b up to $p = 4$, starting with Euler for $p = 1$.

order of accuracy	b_1	b_2	b_3	b_4	limit on $-a\Delta t$ for stability	constant c in error DE
$p = 1$	1				2	1/2
$p = 2$	3/2	−1/2			1	5/12
$p = 3$	23/12	−16/12	5/12		6/11	3/8
$p = 4$	55/24	−59/24	37/24	−9/24	3/10	251/720

The fourth-order method is often a good choice, although astronomers go above $p = 8$.

The local error DE $\approx c(\Delta t)^{p+1}u^{(p+1)}$ is a problem of step control. Whether that error is amplified by later time steps is a problem of stability control.

Implicit "Adams-Moulton" methods have an extra term $c_0 f_{n+1}$ at the new time, to add one extra order of accuracy (and stability). The A-stable trapezoidal rule has $c_0 = c_1 = \frac{1}{2}$ with $p = 2$:

order of accuracy	c_0	c_1	c_2	c_3	limit on $-a\Delta t$ for stability	constant c in error DE
$p = 1$	1				∞ A-stable	$-1/2$
$p = 2$	1/2	1/2			∞ A-stable	$-1/12$
$p = 3$	5/12	8/12	$-1/12$		6	$-1/24$
$p = 4$	9/24	19/24	$-5/24$	1/24	3	$-19/720$

Every row of b's and c's adds to 1, so $u' = 1$ is solved exactly by all methods.

You see that the error constants and stability are all in favor of implicit methods. So is the user, except when solving for U_{n+1} becomes expensive. Then there is a simple and successful ***predictor-corrector*** method, or else ***Newton's method***.

Predictor-Corrector

P: Use the explicit formula to *predict* a new U^*_{n+1}
E: Use U^*_{n+1} to *evaluate* the right side f^*_{n+1}
C: Use f^*_{n+1} in the implicit formula to *correct* to a new U_{n+1}.

The stability is much improved if another E step evaluates f_{n+1} with the corrected U_{n+1}. Frequently one or two corrections are enough. By comparing the predicted U^*_{n+1} and corrected U_{n+1} the code can estimate the local error. Change Δt if this error is too large or too small (this favors Runge-Kutta, which easily changes Δt):

Local error estimate $$\text{DE} \approx \frac{c}{c^* - c}(U_{n+1} - U^*_{n+1}) \tag{23}$$

Here c^* and c are the error constants in the tables for the predictor and corrector.

Implicit methods often have a **Newton loop** inside each time step, to compute U_{n+1}. The kth iteration in the Newton loop is a linear system, with the Jacobian matrix $A_{ij} = \partial f_i/\partial u_j$ evaluated at the latest approximation $U^{(k)}_{n+1}$ with $t = t_{n+1}$.

Here is the kth iteration to solve $U_{n+1} - c_0 f(U_{n+1}, t_{n+1}) =$ (known old values):

Newton iteration $$(I - c_0 A^{(k)})\,\Delta U_{n+1} = c_0 f(U^{(k)}_{n+1}, t_{n+1}) + (\text{known})\,. \tag{24}$$

For nonlinear $f(u)$, Newton's rapid convergence squares the error at each step (when it gets close). The price is a new evaluation of $f(u)$ and its matrix $A^{(k)}$ of derivatives. Section 2.6 has an extended discussion of Newton's method and its many variations. A predictor gives an excellent start $U^{(0)}_{n+1}$, then $\Delta U = U^{(1)}_{n+1} - U^{(0)}_{n+1}$ comes from (24).

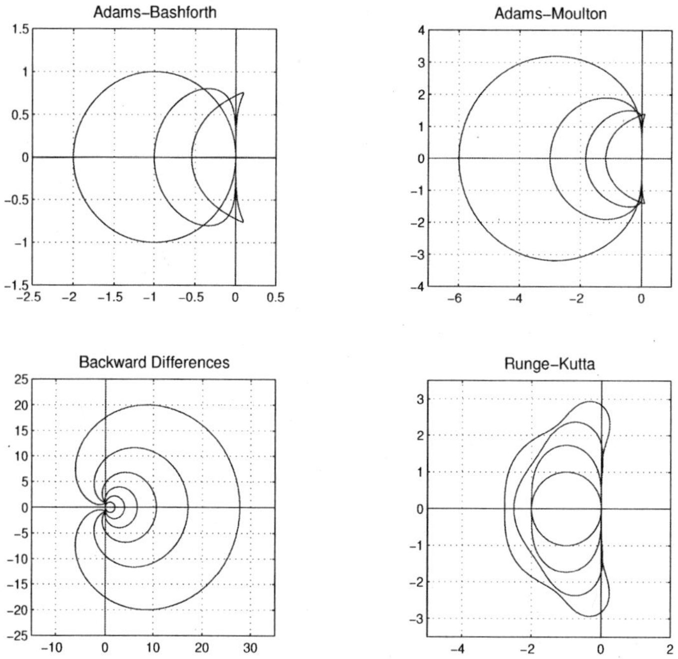

Figure 6.3: Stability regions $|G| \le 1$ for popular methods (stability.m on the cse site). Explicit methods are stable for $a\,\Delta t$ **inside** the curves; implicit methods **outside**.

Runge-Kutta Methods

If evaluations of $f(u,t)$ are not too expensive, ***Runge-Kutta methods*** are highly competitive (and self-starting). Runge-Kutta of orders 4 and 5 is the basis for ode45. These are *compound* one-step methods, using Euler's $U_n + \Delta t\, f_n$ ***inside f***:

Simplified Runge-Kutta
$$\frac{U_{n+1} - U_n}{\Delta t} = \frac{1}{2}\big[f_n + \boldsymbol{f}(U_n + \Delta t\, \boldsymbol{f}_n, t_{n+1})\big]. \tag{25}$$

You see the compounding of f. For $u' = au$ the growth factor G captures $(\Delta t)^2$:

$$u_{n+1} = u_n + \frac{1}{2}\Delta t\big[au_n + a(u_n + \Delta t\, au_n)\big] = \big(1 + a\Delta t + \frac{1}{2}a^2\Delta t^2\big)u_n = G\, u_n\,. \tag{26}$$

Comparing with the exact growth $e^{a\,\Delta t}$, this confirms second-order accuracy. Stability hits a limit at $a\Delta t = -2$ where $G = 1$. **Now let $a\,\Delta t = z$ be complex**:

Stability limit for RK2
$$|G| = \big|1 + z + \frac{1}{2}\,z^2\big| = 1 \quad \text{for } z = a + ib$$

The stability limit is a closed curve in the complex plane through $z = a\,\Delta t = -2$. Figure 6.3 shows all the numbers z (eigenvalues in the matrix case) at which $|G| \le 1$.

The famous version of Runge-Kutta is compounded *four times* and achieves $p = 4$:

Fourth-order Runge-Kutta $$\frac{U_{n+1} - U_n}{\Delta t} = \frac{1}{3}(\boldsymbol{k}_1 + 2\boldsymbol{k}_2 + 2\boldsymbol{k}_3 + \boldsymbol{k}_4) \qquad (27)$$

$$\boldsymbol{k}_1 = f(U_n, t_n)/2 \qquad \boldsymbol{k}_3 = f(U_n + \Delta t\, \boldsymbol{k}_2, t_{n+1/2})/2$$
$$\boldsymbol{k}_2 = f(U_n + \Delta t\, \boldsymbol{k}_1, t_{n+1/2})/2 \qquad \boldsymbol{k}_4 = f(U_n + 2\Delta t\, \boldsymbol{k}_3, t_{n+1})/2$$

For this one-step method, no special starting instructions are necessary. It is simple to change Δt as you go. The growth factor reproduces $e^{a\Delta t}$ through $\frac{1}{24}\, a^4(\Delta t)^4$. The error constant is the next coefficient $\frac{1}{120}$. Among highly accurate methods, Runge-Kutta is especially easy to code and run—probably the easiest there is.

The stability threshold $-a\,\Delta t < 2.78$ is genuine, at the left edge of the Runge-Kutta figure. Solve $u' = -100u + 100\sin t$ which has $a = -100$. Starting from $u(0) = 0$, here is Runge-Kutta at time $t = 3$:

$\boldsymbol{U_{120} = 0.151 = u(3)}$	**with** $\boldsymbol{\Delta t = 3/120}$	$-a\Delta t = \mathbf{2.5}$	(28)
$\boldsymbol{U_{100} = 670{,}000{,}000{,}000}$	**with** $\boldsymbol{\Delta t = 3/100}$	$-a\Delta t = \mathbf{3.0}$	

Section 2.6 mentioned a split-step trapezoidal/BDF2 combination and described SUNDIALS as a valuable code for **differential-algebraic equations**—when there are constraints $g(u) = 0$.

Problem Set 6.2

1 The one-step error in the trapezoidal rule (15) comes from the difference

$$e^{a\Delta t} - \left[\frac{1 + (a\Delta t/2)}{1 - (a\Delta t/2)}\right] = e^{a\Delta t} - \left[\left(1 + \frac{a\Delta t}{2}\right)\left(1 + \frac{a\Delta t}{2} + \left(\frac{a\Delta t}{2}\right)^2 + \cdots\right)\right]$$

This involves the two series that all of mathematics needs: the exponential series for $e^{a\Delta t}$ and the geometric series $1 + x + x^2 + \cdots$ for $1/(1 - x)$.

Multiply inside the brackets to produce the correct $\frac{1}{2}(a\Delta t)^2$. Show that the $(a\Delta t)^3$ term is wrong by $c = \frac{1}{12}$. Then the error is DE $\approx \frac{1}{12}(\Delta t)^3\, u'''$.

2 For the backward difference error in (19), expand $\frac{1}{2}(3e^{a\Delta t} - 4 + e^{-a\Delta t}) - a\Delta t\, e^{a\Delta t}$ into a series in $a\Delta t$. Show that the leading error is $-\frac{1}{3}(a\Delta t)^3$ so that $c = -\frac{1}{3}$.

3 We find $c = -\frac{1}{2}$ for the local error DE $\approx -\frac{1}{2}(\Delta t)^2 u''$ in *backward Euler*:

$$(u_{n+1} - u_n) - \Delta t\, u'_{n+1} \approx \left(\Delta t\, u'_n + \frac{(\Delta t)^2}{2}\, u''_n\right) - \Delta t(u'_n + \Delta t\, u''_n) \approx -\frac{(\Delta t)^2}{2}\, u''_n.$$

This shows no error when u is linear and u'' is zero (Euler's approximation of constant slope becomes true). For $u' = u$ with $u_0 = 1$, find the exact error in u_1.

4 Try Runge-Kutta on $u' = -100u + 100 \sin t$ with $\Delta t = -.0275$ and $-.028$. Those are close to the stability limit $-.0278$.

5 Find the coefficients that make $AU_{n+1} + BU_n + CU_{n-1} = Df_n + Ef_{n-1}$ *third order* accurate for $u' = f(u) = au$. But show that $Az^2 + Bz + C = 0$ has a root with $|z| > 1$: exponential instability.

6 Solve these predator-prey equations for small c and large c:

$$v' = v - v^2 - bvw \quad \text{and} \quad w' = w - w^2 + cvw.$$

7 (Epidemics) If $v(t)$ people are healthy and $w(t)$ are infected, explain the terms in these equations and find w_{max} numerically in terms of $v(0)$:

$$v' = -avw \quad \text{and} \quad w' = avw - bw.$$

8 Solve $u' = -Ku$ starting from the delta vector $u(0) = [\mathsf{zeros}(N,1); 1; \mathsf{zeros}(N,1)]$. For large sizes $n = 2N+1 = 201$ and 2001 compare as many methods as possible for accuracy and for time step Δt:

Backward Euler BDF2 Runge-Kutta ode45 ode15s

9 The solution to $u' = f(t)$ is just the integral of $f(t)$. Show that Runge-Kutta in (27) reduces to Simpson's integration rule (4th order accuracy):

$$\int_0^{\Delta t} f(t)\, dt = \frac{\Delta t}{6}\left[f(0) + 4f\left(\frac{\Delta t}{2}\right) + f(\Delta t)\right].$$

10 The semidiscrete form of $\partial u/\partial t = \partial^2 u/\partial x^2$ is a system of ordinary differential equations. Periodic boundary conditions produce the $-1, 2, -1$ circulant matrix C in $u' = -n^2 Cu$. Starting from $u(0) = (1:n)/n$ test these methods for their stability limits with $n = 11$ and $n = 101$, and find the steady state $u(\infty)$ for large t:

Forward Euler Runge-Kutta Trapezoidal (15) Adams-Bashforth (17)

6.3 ACCURACY AND STABILITY FOR $u_t = c\,u_x$

This section begins a major topic in scientific computing: **Initial-value problems for partial differential equations**. Naturally we start with linear equations that involve only one space dimension x (and time t). The exact solution is $u(x,t)$ and its discrete approximation on a space-time grid has the form $U_{j,n} = U(j\Delta x, n\Delta t)$. We want to know if U is near u—how close they are and how stable U is.

Begin with the simplest wave equation (first-order, linear, constant coefficient):

One-way wave equation $$\frac{\partial u}{\partial t} = c\,\frac{\partial u}{\partial x}. \qquad (1)$$

We are given $u(x,0)$ at time $t=0$. We want to find $u(x,t)$ for all $t>0$. For simplicity, these functions are defined on the whole line $-\infty < x < \infty$. There are no difficulties with boundaries (where waves could change direction and bounce back).

The solution $u(x,t)$ will have the typical feature of *hyperbolic equations*: *signals travel at finite speed.* Unlike the second-order wave equation $u_{tt} = c^2 u_{xx}$, this first-order equation $u_t = c\,u_x$ sends signals in one direction only.

Solution for $u(x,0) = e^{ikx}$

Throughout this chapter I will solve for a pure exponential $u(x,0) = e^{ikx}$. **At every time t, the solution remains a multiple Ge^{ikx}.** The growth factor G will depend on the frequency k and the time t, but different frequencies do not mix. Substituting $u = G(k,t)\,e^{ikx}$ into $u_t = c\,u_x$ yields a simple ordinary differential equation for G, because we can cancel e^{ikx}. The derivative of e^{ikx} produces the factor ik:

$$u_t = c\,u_x \quad \text{is} \quad \frac{dG}{dt}e^{ikx} = ikc\,Ge^{ikx} \quad \text{or} \quad \frac{dG}{dt} = ikc\,G. \qquad (2)$$

The growth factor is $G(k,t) = e^{ikct}$. The initial value is $G=1$.

$$\textbf{An exponential solution to } \frac{\partial u}{\partial t} = c\,\frac{\partial u}{\partial x} \text{ is } u(x,t) = e^{ikct}e^{ikx} = \boldsymbol{e^{ik(x+ct)}}. \qquad (3)$$

Immediately we see two important features of this solution:

1. The growth factor $G = e^{ikct}$ has absolute value $|G| = 1$.

2. The initial function e^{ikx} moves to the left with fixed velocity c, to $e^{ik(x+ct)}$.

The initial value at the origin is $u(0,0) = e^{ik0} = 1$. This value $u = 1$ appears at all points on the line $x + ct = 0$. **The initial data propagates along the characteristic lines $x + ct =$ *constant*,** in Figure 6.4. Right now we know this fact for the special solutions $e^{ik(x+ct)}$. Soon we will know it for all solutions.

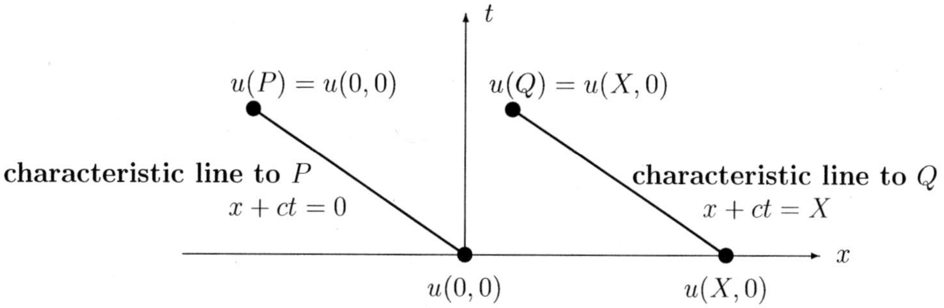

Figure 6.4: The solution $u(x,t)$ moves left with speed c, along characteristic lines.

Figure 6.4 shows the travel path of the solution in the x-t plane (we are introducing the characteristic lines). Figure 6.5 will graph the solution itself at times 0 and t. That step function combines exponentials $e^{ik(x+ct)}$ for different frequencies k. By linearity we can add those solutions to match starting values $u(x,0)$.

Every $u(x,0)$ Moves Left at Constant Speed

In almost all partial differential equations, the solution changes shape as it travels. Here the shape stays the same. All pure exponentials travel at the same velocity c, so *every* initial function moves with that velocity. We can write down the solution:

General solution $\quad \dfrac{\partial u}{\partial t} = c\,\dfrac{\partial u}{\partial x}$ is solved by $\boldsymbol{u(x,t) = u(x+ct,0)}\,. \qquad (4)$

The solution is a function only of $x+ct$. That makes it constant along characteristic lines, where $x+ct$ is constant. This dependence on $x+ct$ also makes it satisfy the equation $u_t = c\,u_x$, by the chain rule. If we take $u = (x+ct)^n$ as an example, the extra factor c appears in $\partial u/\partial t$:

$$\frac{\partial u}{\partial x} = n\,(x+ct)^{n-1} \quad \text{and} \quad \frac{\partial u}{\partial t} = cn\,(x+ct)^{n-1} \quad \text{which is} \quad c\,\frac{\partial u}{\partial x}\,.$$

A Taylor series person would combine those powers (different n) to produce a large family of solutions. A Fourier series person combines exponentials (different k) to produce an even larger family. In fact *all* solutions are functions of $x+ct$ alone.

Here are two important initial functions—a light flashes or a dam breaks.

Example 1 $\;u(x,0) =$ delta function $\delta(x) =$ **flash of light** at $x=0, t=0$

By our formula (4), the solution is $u(x,t) = \delta(x+ct)$. The light flash reaches the point $x=-c$ at the time $t=1$. It reaches $x=-2c$ at the time $t=2$. The impulse is traveling to the left at speed $|dx/dt| = c$. In this example all frequencies k are present in equal amounts, because the Fourier transform of a delta function is a constant.

Notice that a point goes dark again as soon as the flash passes through. This is the Huygens Principle in 1 and 3 dimensions. If we lived in two or four dimensions, the wave would not pass all at once and we wouldn't see clearly.

Example 2 $u(x,0) =$ step function $S(x) =$ **wall of water** at $x = 0, t = 0$

The solution $S(x+ct)$ is the moving step function in Figure 6.5. The wall of water travels to the left (*one-way wave*). At time t, the "tsunami" reaches the point $x = -ct$. The flash of light will get there first, because its speed c is greater than the tsunami speed. That is why a warning is possible for an approaching tsunami.

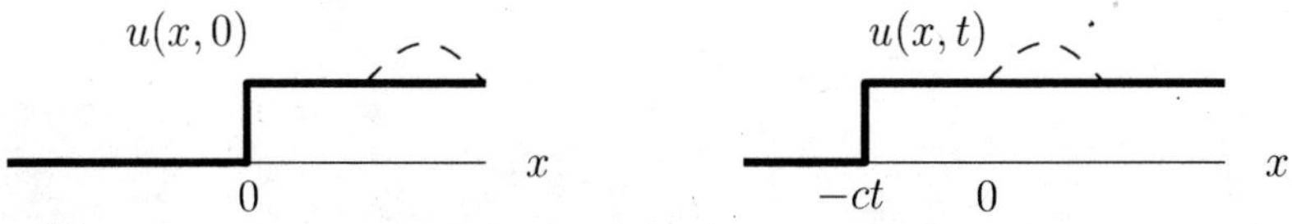

initial profile $S(x)$ at $t = 0$ later profile $S(x + ct)$ at time t

Figure 6.5: The wall travels left with velocity c (all waves e^{ikx} do too).

An actual tsunami is described by the nonlinear "shallow water equations" that give the shape of the surface. The feature of *finite speed* still holds.

Finite Difference Methods for $u_t = c\, u_x$

The one-way wave equation is a perfect example for creating and testing finite difference approximations. We can replace $\partial u/\partial t$ by a forward difference with step Δt. *Conditionally stable* means that Δt is restricted; the key ratio will be $r = c\,\Delta t/\Delta x$. Here are four choices for the discrete form of $\partial u/\partial x$ at meshpoint $i\Delta x$:

1. **Forward** $= \dfrac{U_{i+1} - U_i}{\Delta x} =$ **upwind**: Low accuracy, stable for $0 \le r \le 1$

2. **Centered** $= \dfrac{U_{i+1} - U_{i-1}}{2\Delta x}$: Unstable after a few steps as we will prove!

3. **Lax-Friedrichs**: (20) has low accuracy, stable for $-1 \le r \le 1$

4. **Lax-Wendroff**: (14) has extra accuracy, stable for $-1 \le r \le 1$.

The list doesn't end there. We have reached a central problem of scientific computing, to construct approximations that are *stable* and *accurate* and *fast*. That topic can't be developed on one page, especially when we move to nonlinear equations.

The need for a time-step restriction was noticed by Courant, Friedrichs, and Lewy.

When the space difference reaches only to $x + \Delta x$, there is an automatic restriction:

CFL requirement for stability $\quad \boldsymbol{r = c\,\dfrac{\Delta t}{\Delta x} \le 1.}$ (5)

That number $c\,\Delta t/\Delta x$ is often called the ***Courant number***. (It was really Lewy who recognized that $r \le 1$ is necessary for stability and convergence.) The reasoning is straightforward, based on using the initial value that controls $u(x,t)$:

> The true solution at (x,t) equals the initial value $u(x+ct,0)$. Taking n discrete steps to reach $t = n\,\Delta t$ uses information on the initial values as far out as $x + n\,\Delta x$. If $x + ct$ is further than $x + n\,\Delta x$, the method can't work:

CFL condition $\quad x + ct \le x + n\,\Delta x \quad$ or $\quad c\,n\,\Delta t \le n\,\Delta x \quad$ or $\quad r = c\dfrac{\Delta t}{\Delta x} \le 1.$ (6)

If the difference equation uses $U(x+2\Delta x, t)$, then CFL relaxes to $r \le 2$.

A particular finite difference equation might require a tighter restriction on Δt for stability. It might even be unstable for all ratios r (we hope not). The only route to *unconditional stability* for all Δt is an *implicit method*, which computes x-differences at the new time $t + \Delta t$. This will be useful later for diffusion terms like u_{xx}. For advection terms (first derivatives), explicit methods with a CFL limitation are usually accepted because a much larger Δt would lose accuracy as well as stability.

To repeat, if $r > 1$ then the upwind finite difference solution at x, t does not use initial value information near the correct point $x^* = x + ct$. Hopeless.

Accuracy of the Upwind Difference Equation

Linear problems with constant coefficients are the ones to understand first. Exactly as for differential equations, we can follow each pure exponential e^{ikx}. After a single time step, there will be a growth factor in $U(x,\Delta t) = Ge^{ikx}$. That growth factor $G(k,\Delta t,\Delta x)$ may have magnitude $|G| < 1$ or $|G| > 1$. This will control stability or instability. The **order of accuracy** (if we compute in the k-ω domain) comes from *comparing G with the true factor $e^{ikc\Delta t}$ from the differential equation.*

We now determine that the order of accuracy is $p = 1$ for the *upwind method.*

Forward differences $\quad \dfrac{U(x,t+\Delta t) - U(x,t)}{\Delta t} = c\,\dfrac{U(x+\Delta x,t) - U(x,t)}{\Delta x}.$ (7)

We will test the accuracy in the x-t domain and then the k-ω domain. Either way we use Taylor series to check the leading terms. Substituting the true solution $u(x,t)$ in place of $U(x,t)$, its forward differences are

Time $\quad \dfrac{1}{\Delta t}\left[u(x,t+\Delta t) - u(x,t)\right] = u_t + \dfrac{1}{2}\Delta t\,u_{tt} + \cdots$ (8)

Space $\quad \dfrac{c}{\Delta x}\left[u(x+\Delta x,t) - u(x,t)\right] = c\,u_x + \dfrac{1}{2}c\,\Delta x\,u_{xx} + \cdots$ (9)

On the right side, $u_t = c\,u_x$ is good. One more derivative gives $u_{tt} = c\,u_{xt} = c^2\,u_{xx}$. Notice c^2. Then $\Delta t\,u_{tt}$ matches $c\,\Delta x\,u_{xx}$ *only in the special case* $c\,\Delta t = \Delta x$ $(r = 1)$:

$$\frac{1}{2}\Delta t\,c^2\,u_{xx} \quad \text{equals} \quad \frac{1}{2}c\,\Delta x\,u_{xx} \quad \text{only if} \quad r = \frac{c\,\Delta t}{\Delta x} = 1.$$

For any ratio $r \neq 1$, the difference between (8) and (9) has a ***first-order error***. Let me show this also in the k-ω Fourier picture and then improve to second-order.

Fix the ratio $r = c\,\Delta t/\Delta x$ as $\Delta x \to 0$ and $\Delta t \to 0$. In the difference equation (7), write each new value at time $t + \Delta t$ as a combination of two old values of U:

Difference equation $\quad U(x, t + \Delta t) = (\mathbf{1} - \boldsymbol{r})\,U(x, t) + \boldsymbol{r}\,U(x + \Delta x, t)\,. \qquad (10)$

Starting from $U(x, 0) = e^{ikx}$ we quickly find the growth factor $\boldsymbol{G}$ at time Δt:

After 1 step $\quad (1 - r)e^{ikx} + r\,e^{ik(x+\Delta x)} = \left[\mathbf{1} - \boldsymbol{r} + \boldsymbol{r}\,\boldsymbol{e^{ik\Delta x}}\right] e^{ikx} = \boldsymbol{G}\,e^{ikx}\,. \qquad (11)$

To test the accuracy, compare this $G = G_{\mathbf{approx}}$ to the exact growth factor $e^{ick\Delta t}$. Use the power series $1 + x + x^2/2! + \cdots$ for any e^x:

$$\begin{aligned} G_{\mathbf{approx}} &= \mathbf{1} - \boldsymbol{r} + \boldsymbol{r}\,\boldsymbol{e^{ik\Delta x}} = (1 - r) + r + r(ik\Delta x) + \frac{1}{2}r\,(ik\Delta x)^2 + \cdots \\ G_{\mathbf{exact}} &= \boldsymbol{e^{ick\Delta t}} = \boldsymbol{e^{irk\Delta x}} = 1 + irk\Delta x + \frac{1}{2}(irk\Delta x)^2 + \cdots \end{aligned} \qquad (12)$$

The first terms 1 and $irk\Delta x$ agree as expected. The method is ***consistent*** with $u_t = c\,u_x$. The next terms do *not* agree unless $r = r^2$:

Compare $\frac{1}{2}r(ik\Delta x)^2$ with $\frac{1}{2}r^2(ik\Delta x)^2$. **Single-step error of order $(k\Delta t)^2$.** (13)

After $1/\Delta t$ steps, those errors of order $k^2(\Delta t)^2$ give a final error $O(k^2\Delta t)$. Forward differences are only first order accurate, and so is the whole method.

The special case $r = 1$ means $c\,\Delta t = \Delta x$. *The difference equation is exactly correct.* The true and approximate solutions at $(x, \Delta t)$ are both $u(x + \Delta x, 0)$. We are *on the characteristic line* in Figure 6.4. This is an interesting special case (the golden Δt is hard to repeat in scientific computing when c varies).

Conclusion $\quad$ Except when $r = r^2$, ***the upwind method is first-order accurate.***

Higher Accuracy for Lax-Wendroff

To upgrade the accuracy, center the differences. Lax-Wendroff matches the $\frac{1}{2}\Delta t\, u_{tt}$ error in the time difference by a space difference that gives $\frac{1}{2}\Delta t\, c^2 u_{xx}$.

Lax-Wendroff method $$\frac{U(x,t+\Delta t)-U(x,t)}{\Delta t} = \qquad (14)$$

$$c\,\frac{U(x+\Delta x,t)-U(x-\Delta x,t)}{2\Delta x} + \frac{\Delta t}{2}c^2\left(\frac{U(x+\Delta x,t)-2U(x,t)+U(x-\Delta x,t)}{(\Delta x)^2}\right)$$

Substituting the true solution, that second difference produces $\frac{1}{2}c^2\Delta t\, u_{xx}$ plus higher order terms. This cancels the $\frac{1}{2}\Delta t\, u_{tt}$ error term in the time difference, computed in equation (8). (Remember $u_{tt} = cu_{xt} = c^2 u_{xx}$. The centered difference has no Δx term.) Thus Lax-Wendroff has **second-order accuracy**.

To see this in the k-ω frequency domain, rewrite the LW difference equation (14):

$$U(x,t+\Delta t) = (1-r^2)U(x,t) + \frac{1}{2}(r^2+r)U(x+\Delta x,t) + \frac{1}{2}(r^2-r)U(x-\Delta x,t)\,. \qquad (15)$$

Substitute $U(x,t) = e^{ikx}$ to find the one-step growth factor G at time $t+\Delta t$:

Growth factor for LW $$G = (1-r^2) + \frac{1}{2}(r^2+r)e^{ik\Delta x} + \frac{1}{2}(r^2-r)e^{-ik\Delta x}.$$

Expand $e^{ik\Delta x}$ and $e^{-ik\Delta x}$ in powers of $ik\,\Delta x$, to compare G with G_{exact} in (12):

Compare with $e^{irk\Delta x}$ $$G = 1 + r(ik\Delta x) + \tfrac{1}{2}r^2(ik\Delta x)^2 + O(k\Delta x)^3 \qquad (16)$$

The first three terms agree. The one-step error is of order $(k\Delta x)^3$. After $1/\Delta t$ steps the second-order accuracy of Lax-Wendroff is confirmed.

Figure 6.6 shows the improvement in accuracy. For a first-order method, the "wall of water" is smeared out. High frequencies have growth factors $|G(k)|$ much smaller than 1. There is too much dissipation. For the first-order Lax-Friedrichs method, the dissipation is even worse (Problem 2). The Lax-Wendroff method stays much closer to the jump. But it's not perfect—those oscillations are not good.

Remark Second-order methods cannot have all coefficients positive (Problem 4). Lax-Wendroff has $r^2 < |r|$. The negative coefficient produces the oscillations.

Greater accuracy is achievable by including more terms in the difference equation. If we go from the three terms in Lax-Wendroff to five terms, we can reach fourth-order accuracy. If we use *all* values $U(j\Delta x, n\Delta t)$ at every time step, we can achieve **spectral accuracy**. Then the error decreases faster than any power of Δx, provided $u(x,t)$ is smooth. Section 5.4 gave a separate discussion of this **spectral method**.

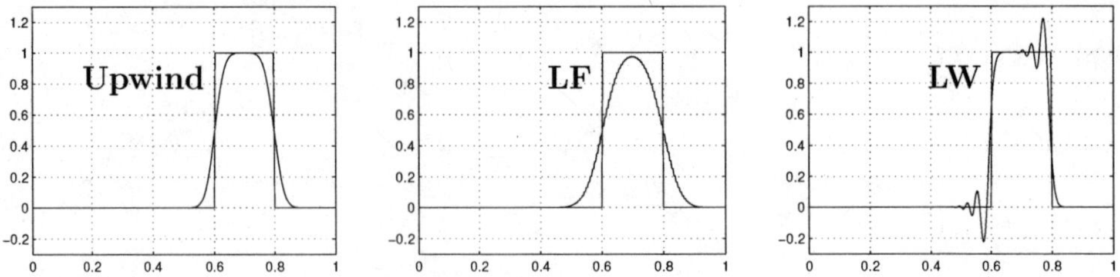

Figure 6.6: Three approximations to a sharp signal show smearing and oscillation.

For an ideal difference equation, we only want dissipation *very close to the shock*. This can avoid oscillation without losing accuracy. A lot of thought has gone into high resolution methods (Section 6.6), to capture shock waves cleanly.

Stability of the Four Finite Difference Methods

Accuracy requires G to stay close to the true $e^{ick\Delta t}$. Stability requires G to stay **inside the unit circle**. If $|G|>1$ at frequency k, the solution $G^n e^{ikx}$ will blow up.

We now check $|G| \leq 1$, in the four methods. CFL was only a necessary condition!

1. Forward differences in space and time: $\Delta U/\Delta t = c\,\Delta U/\Delta x$ (upwind).

Equation (11) was $G = 1 - r + re^{ik\Delta x}$. If the Courant number is $0 \leq r \leq 1$, then $1-r$ and r will be positive. The triangle inequality gives $|G| \leq 1$:

Stability for $0 \leq r \leq 1$ $$|G| \leq |1-r| + |re^{ik\Delta x}| = 1 - r + r = 1\,. \tag{17}$$

This sufficient condition $0 \leq c\,\Delta t/\Delta x \leq 1$ agrees with the CFL necessary condition $U(x, n\Delta t)$ depends on the initial values between x and $x + n\Delta x$. That **domain of dependence** must include the point $x + cn\Delta t$. (Otherwise, changing the initial value at the point $x + cn\Delta t$ would change the true solution u but not the approximation U.) Then $0 \leq cn\Delta t \leq n\Delta x$ means that $0 \leq r \leq 1$.

Figure 6.7 shows G in the stable case $r = \frac{2}{3}$ and the unstable case $r = \frac{4}{3}$ (when Δt is too large). As k varies, and $e^{ik\Delta x}$ goes around a unit circle, the complex number $G = 1 - r + re^{ik\Delta x}$ goes in a circle of radius r. The center is $1 - r$. Always $G = 1$ at zero frequency (constant solution, no growth).

2. Forward difference in time, centered difference in space.

This combination is never stable! The shorthand $U_{j,n}$ will stand for $U(j\Delta x, n\Delta t)$:

$$\frac{U_{j,n+1} - U_{j,n}}{\Delta t} = c\,\frac{U_{j+1,n} - U_{j-1,n}}{2\Delta x} \quad \text{or} \quad U_{j,n+1} = U_{j,n} + \frac{r}{2}\left(U_{j+1,n} - U_{j-1,n}\right). \tag{18}$$

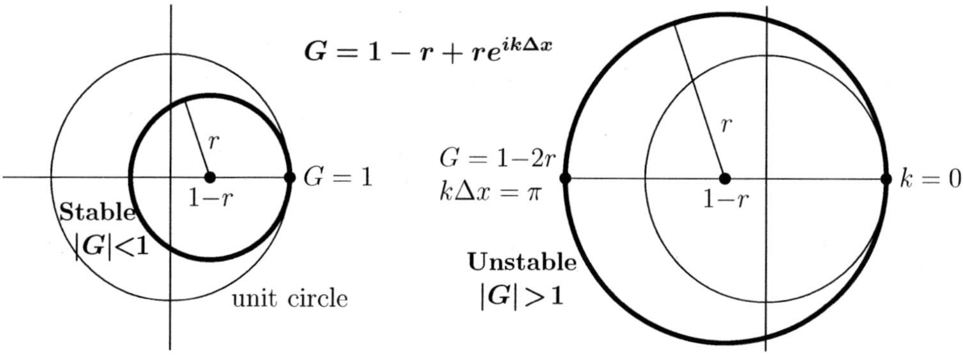

Figure 6.7: The upwind (forward difference) method is stable for $r = \frac{2}{3}$ but not $\frac{4}{3}$.

Those coefficients 1 and $r/2$ and $-r/2$ go into the growth factor G, when the solution is a pure exponential and e^{ikx} is factored out:

Unstable: $|G| > 1$

$$G = 1 + \frac{r}{2}e^{ik\Delta x} - \frac{r}{2}e^{-ik\Delta x} = \mathbf{1 + ir \sin k\Delta x}\,. \tag{19}$$

The real part is 1. The magnitude is $|G| \geq 1$. Its graph is on the left side of Figure 6.8.

3. Lax-Friedrichs recovers stability for centered differences by changing the time difference. Replace $U_{j,n}$ by the average $\frac{1}{2}(U_{j+1,n} + U_{j-1,n})$ of its neighbors:

Lax-Friedrichs

$$\frac{U_{j,n+1} - \frac{1}{2}(U_{j+1,n} + U_{j-1,n})}{\Delta t} = c\,\frac{U_{j+1,n} - U_{j-1,n}}{2\Delta x}. \tag{20}$$

Two old values $U_{j+1,n}$ and $U_{j-1,n}$ produce each new value $U_{j,n+1}$. Moving terms to the right-hand side, the coefficients are $\frac{1}{2}(1+r)$ and $\frac{1}{2}(1-r)$. The growth factor is

$$G = \frac{1+r}{2}\,e^{ik\Delta x} + \frac{1-r}{2}\,e^{-ik\Delta x} = \mathbf{\cos k\Delta x + ir \sin k\Delta x}\,. \tag{21}$$

The absolute value is $|G|^2 = (\cos k\Delta x)^2 + r^2(\sin k\Delta x)^2$. In Figure 6.8, $|G| \leq 1$ when $r^2 \leq 1$. This stability condition agrees again with the CFL condition.

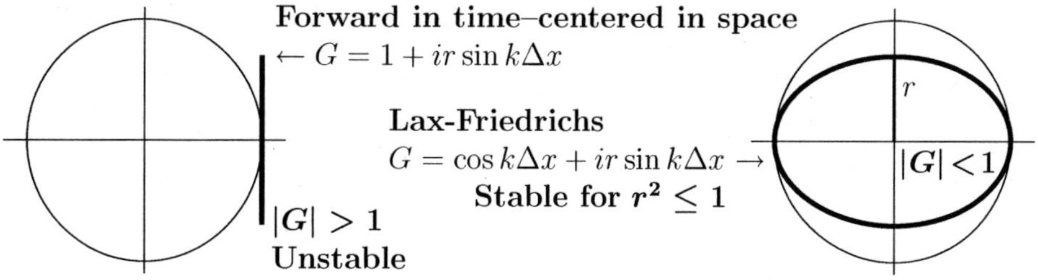

Figure 6.8: Equation (18) is unstable for all r. Equation (20) is stable for $r^2 \leq 1$.

Notice that c and r can be negative. The wave can go either way. This will be useful for the two-way wave equation, but the accuracy is still first-order. The

Lax-Friedrichs G matches the next term in the exact growth factor only if $r^2 = 1$:

$$G_{\mathbf{LF}} = \cos k\Delta x + ir \sin k\Delta x = 1 + irk\Delta x - \tfrac{1}{2}(k\Delta x)^2 + \cdots \tag{22}$$
$$G_{\text{exact}} = e^{irk\Delta x} = 1 + irk\,\Delta x + \tfrac{1}{2}i^2 r^2 (k\,\Delta x)^2 + \cdots$$

In the exceptional cases $r = 1$ and $r = -1$, G agrees with G_{exact}. Staying exactly on the characteristic line, $U_{j,n+1}$ matches the true $u(j\Delta x, t + \Delta t)$. For $r^2 < 1$, Lax-Friedrichs has an important advantage and disadvantage:

$U_{j,n+1}$ is a **positive** combination of old values. But accuracy is only **first-order**.

4. Lax-Wendroff is stable for $-1 \le r \le 1$.

The LW difference equation combines $U_{j,n}$ and $U_{j-1,n}$ and $U_{j+1,n}$ to compute $U_{j,n+1}$:

Lax-Wendroff $$G = (1 - r^2) + \frac{1}{2}(r^2 + r)e^{ik\Delta x} + \frac{1}{2}(r^2 - r)e^{-ik\Delta x}. \tag{23}$$

This is $G = 1 - r^2 + r^2 \cos k\Delta x + ir \sin k\Delta x$. At the dangerous frequency $k\Delta x = \pi$, the growth factor is $1 - 2r^2$. That stays above -1 if $r^2 \le 1$.

Problem 5 shows that $|G| \le 1$ for every $k\Delta x$. **Lax-Wendroff is stable whenever the CFL condition $r^2 \le 1$ is satisfied.** The wave can go either way (or both ways) since c can be negative. LW is the most accurate of these five methods.

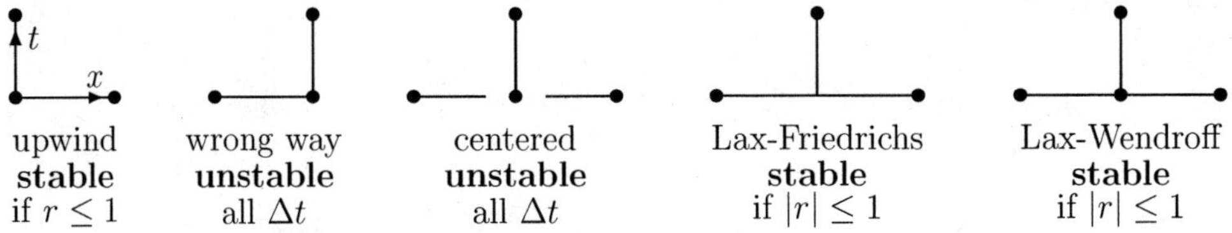

5. The centered methods of maximum accuracy are stable for $-1 \le r \le 1$.

Lax-Wendroff uses three values at time level n for accuracy two. For every even $p = 2q$, there are $p+1$ coefficients $a_{-q}, \ldots, a_q$ so that the difference equation $U_{j,n+1} = \sum a_m U_{j+m,n}$ has accuracy p. Matching $G = \sum a_m e^{imk\Delta x}$ with the exact factor $e^{ikc\Delta t} = e^{ikr\Delta x}$ gives $p+1$ equations $\sum a_m m^j = r^j$ for the a's.

Using all those values, the CFL condition allows the possibility of stability out to $-q \le c\,\Delta t/\Delta x \le q$. The actual requirement is $-1 \le r \le 1$.

Equivalence of Stability and Convergence

Does the discrete solution U approach the true solution u as $\Delta t \to 0$? The expected answer is yes. But there are two requirements for convergence, and one of them—*stability*—is by no means automatic. The other requirement is *consistency*—the discrete problem must approximate the correct continuous problem. The fact that these two properties are sufficient for convergence, and also *necessary* for convergence, is the ***fundamental theorem of numerical analysis***:

Lax equivalence theorem	Stability is equivalent to convergence, for a consistent approximation to a well-posed linear problem.

Lax proved the equivalence theorem for initial-value problems. The rate of convergence is given in (26). The theorem is equally true for boundary-value problems, and for the approximation of functions, and for the approximation of integrals. It applies to every discretization, when the given problem $Lu = f$ is replaced by $L_h U_h = f_h$. Assuming the inputs f and f_h are close, we will prove that u and U_h are close—provided L_h is stable. The key points of the proof take only a few lines when the equation is linear, and you will see the essence of this fundamental theorem.

Suppose f is changed to f_h and L is replaced by L_h. The requirements are

Consistent $f_h \to f$ and $L_h u \to Lu$ for smooth solutions u.

Well-posed The inverse of L is bounded: $\|u\| = \|L^{-1}f\| \le C\|f\|$.

Stable The inverses L_h^{-1} remain uniformly bounded: $\|L_h^{-1}f_h\| \le C\|f_h\|$.

Under those conditions, the approximation $U_h = L_h^{-1}f_h$ will approach u as h goes to zero. We subtract and add $L_h^{-1}Lu = L_h^{-1}f$ when u is smooth:

Convergence $$u - U_h = L_h^{-1}(L_h u - Lu) + L_h^{-1}(f - f_h) \to 0. \qquad (24)$$

Consistency controls the quantities in parentheses (they go to zero). Stability controls the operators L_h^{-1} that act on them. Well-posedness controls the approximation of all solutions by smooth solutions. Then always U_h converges to u.

If stability fails, there will be an input for which the approximations $U_h = L_h^{-1}f$ are not bounded. The "*uniform boundedness theorem*" *produces this bad* f, from the inputs f_h on which instability gives $\|L_h^{-1}f_h\| \to \infty$. Convergence fails for this f.

A perfect equivalence theorem goes a little further, after careful definitions:

$$\textbf{Consistency + Stability} \iff \textbf{Well-posedness + Convergence}.$$

Our effort will now concentrate on initial-value problems, to estimate the convergence rate (the error in $u - U_h$). The parameter h becomes Δt. We take n steps.

The Rate of Convergence

Consistency means that the error at each time step goes to zero as the mesh is refined. Our Taylor series estimates have done more: **The order of accuracy gives the rate** that this one-step error goes to zero. The problem is to extend this local rate to a global rate of convergence, accumulating the errors over n time steps.

Let me write S for a single finite difference step, so $\boldsymbol{U(t+\Delta t) = S\,U(t)}$. The exact solution step will be $\boldsymbol{u(t+\Delta t) = R\,u(t)}$. Then consistency means that Su is close to Ru, and the order of accuracy p tells how close:

Accuracy of discretization	$\|Su - Ru\| \le C_1(\Delta t)^{p+1}$ for smooth solutions u.
Well-posed problem	$\|R^n u\| \le C_2\|u\|$ for $n\,\Delta t \le T$.
Stable approximations	$\|S^n U\| \le C_3\|U\|$ for $n\,\Delta t \le T$.

The difference between $U = S^n u(0)$ and the true $u = R^n u(0)$ is $(S^n - R^n)u(0)$. The key idea is a "telescoping identity" that involves n single-step differences $S - R$:

$$S^n - R^n = S^{n-1}(S-R) + S^{n-2}(S-R)R + \cdots + (S-R)R^{n-1}\,. \qquad (25)$$

Each of those n terms has a clear meaning. First, a power R^k carries $u(0)$ to the true solution $u(k\,\Delta t)$. For smooth solutions $(S-R)u(k\,\Delta t)$ gives the error at step k of order $(\Delta t)^{p+1}$. Then powers of S carry that one-step error forward to time $n\Delta t$. By stability, the powers of S amplify the error by no more than C_3. There are $n \le T/\Delta t$ steps. **The final rate of convergence for smooth solutions is $(\Delta t)^p$:**

$$\|U(n\,\Delta t) - u(n\,\Delta t)\| = \|(S^n - R^n)u(0)\| \le C_1C_2C_3\frac{T}{\Delta t}(\Delta t)^{p+1} = C\,T(\Delta t)^p\,. \qquad (26)$$

Notice how smoothness was needed in the Taylor series (8) and (9), when Δt and Δx multiplied u_{tt} and u_{xx}. That first-order accuracy would not apply if u or u_t or u_x had a jump. Still the order of accuracy p gives a practical estimate of the overall approximation error $u - U$. The problem of scientific computing is to get beyond $p = 1$ while maintaining stability and speed.

Problem Set 6.3

1 Integrate $u_t = c\,u_x$ from $-\infty$ to ∞ to prove that mass is conserved: $dM/dt = 0$. Multiply by u and integrate $uu_t = c\,uu_x$ to prove that energy is also conserved:

$$M(t) = \int_{-\infty}^{\infty} u(x,t)\,dx \quad\text{and}\quad E(t) = \tfrac{1}{2}\int_{-\infty}^{\infty}(u(x,t))^2\,dx \quad \text{stay constant in time.}$$

2 Substitute the true $u(x,t)$ into the Lax-Friedrichs method (21) and use $u_t = cu_x$ and $u_{tt} = c^2u_{xx}$ to find the coefficient of the *numerical dissipation* u_{xx}.

3 The growth factor for $U_{j,n+1} = \sum a_m U_{j+m,n}$ is $G = \sum a_m e^{imk\Delta x}$. Expand each term in powers of Δx to show *consistency* with $G_{\text{exact}} = e^{ick\Delta t}$ (first-order accuracy at least) when $\sum a_m = 1$ and $\sum m a_m = c\,\Delta t/\Delta x = r$.

4 Second-order accuracy requires $\sum m^2 a_m = r^2$. Check Lax-Wendroff which has $a_0 = 1 - r^2, a_1 = \frac{1}{2}(r^2 + r), a_{-1} = \frac{1}{2}(r^2 - r)$. *If every* $a_m \geq 0$, the Schwarz inequality $(\sum m\sqrt{a_m}\sqrt{a_m})^2 \leq (\sum m^2 a_m)(\sum a_m)$ becomes $r^2 = r^2$. This equality only happens if $m\sqrt{a_m} = (\text{constant})\sqrt{a_m}$. *Second-order is impossible with* $a_m \geq 0$, unless there is only one term $U_{j,n+1} = U_{j+m,n}$.

5 The Lax-Wendroff method has $G = 1 - r^2 + r^2 \cos k\Delta x + ir \sin kx$. Square the real and imaginary parts to get (eventually!) $|G|^2 = 1 - (r^2 - r^4)(1 - \cos k\Delta x)^2$. Prove the stability of Lax-Wendroff, that $|G|^2 \leq 1$ if $r^2 \leq 1$.

6 Suppose the coefficients in a linear differential equation change as t changes. The one-step solution operators become S_k and R_k, for the step from $k\,\Delta t$ to $(k+1)\Delta t$. After n steps, products replace the powers S^n and R^n in U and u:

$$U(n\,\Delta t) = S_{n-1}S_{n-2}\ldots S_1 S_0\, u(0) \quad \text{and} \quad u(n\,\Delta t) = R_{n-1}R_{n-2}\ldots R_1 R_0\, u(0)\,.$$

Change the telescoping formula (25) *to produce this* $U - u$. Which parts are controlled by stability? Which parts are controlled by well-posedness (the stability of the differential equation)? Consistency still controls $S_k - R_k$.

7 Even an unstable method will converge to the true solution $u = e^{ickt}e^{ikx}$ for *each separate frequency* k. Consistency assures that the single-step growth factor G is $1 + ick\,\Delta t + O(\Delta t)^2$. Then G^n converges for $\Delta t = t/n$:

$$G^n = \left(1 + \frac{ickt}{n} + O(\frac{1}{n^2})\right)^n \longrightarrow e^{ickt} \quad \text{even if} \quad |G| > 1.$$

How can we have convergence for each e^{ikx} and divergence for $u(x,0) = \sum c_k e^{ikx}$? *Answer* A high frequency $k = \pi/\Delta x$ in the sum has not begun its convergence. In the completely unstable equation (18), what is $|G^n| = |1 + ir \sin \pi|^n$?

8 The upwind method with $r > 1$ is unstable because the CFL condition fails. By Problem 7, it does converge to $e^{ik(x+ct)}$ even using values of $u(x,0) = e^{ikx}$ *that do not reach as far as* $x + ct$. The method must be finding a "correct" extrapolation of e^{ikx}. But show that convergence fails for $u(x,0) = \delta(x)$.

9 Lax-Friedrichs replaces $U_{j,n}$ in the time difference by $\frac{1}{2}(U_{j+1,n} + U_{j-1,n})$. Subtract $U_{j,n}$ to show that the improved stability for Lax-Friedrichs comes from a second difference (numerical viscosity).

Problems 10-14 are about Airy's dispersive wave equation $u_t = u_{xxx}$.

10 A *centered* third difference Δ_c^3 has coefficients $1, -2, 0, 2, -1$. Test on e^{ikx} to see how $\Delta_c^3\, e^{ikx}$ has the correct factor $(ik\Delta x)^3 = (i\theta)^3$:

$$e^{i2\theta} - 2e^{i\theta} + 2e^{-i\theta} - e^{-i2\theta} = i\sin 2\theta - 2i\sin\theta = 2i\sin\theta(\cos\theta - 1) \approx (i\theta)^3.$$

(a) Show that $(U_{j,n+1} - U_{j,n})/\Delta t = \Delta_c^3 U/(\Delta x)^3$ is **unstable**.

(b) Lax-Friedrichs changes $U_{j,n}$ to $\frac{1}{2}(U_{j+1,n} + U_{j-1,n})$. Prove $|G| \le 1$ for $r \le 1/4$:

L-F growth factor $G(\theta) = \cos\theta + 2ir\sin\theta(\cos\theta - 1)$ with $r = \Delta t/(\Delta x)^3$.

11 An uncentered difference $\Delta^3 U$ needs only four values of U, with coefficients $1, -3, 3, -1$. If $\Delta_t U = r\,\Delta^3 U$ is fully upwind or fully downwind, prove instability:

$$G = 1 \pm r(e^{i\theta} - 1)^3 \text{ cannot have } |G| \le 1 \text{ for small } \theta = k\,\Delta x.$$

12 Typical solutions to $u_t = u_{xxx}$ are $\sin(x - t)$ and $\sin(2x - 8t)$. *The wind goes left to right.* Prove stability for $r \le 1/4$ when $\Delta^3 U$ is two-thirds upwind:

$$\Delta_t U = r(U_{j+1,n} - 3U_{j,n} + 3U_{j-1,n} - U_{j-2,n}) \text{ has } G = 1 + re^{-2i\theta}(e^{i\theta} - 1)^3.$$

Write $e^{i\theta/2}G$ in terms of $\cos(\theta/2)$ and $\sin(\theta/2)$. Show $(\operatorname{Re} G)^2 + (\operatorname{Im} G)^2 \le 1$.

13 For $u_t = u_{xxx}$ on the interval $0 \le x \le 1$, Problem 12 indicates a need for *two* boundary conditions at $x = 0$ and *one* condition at $x = 1$. This was not obvious. But show that the energy $E = \int u^2\, dx$ does decay when $u(1) = u(0) = u'(0) = 0$:

$$\text{Integrate } uu_t = uu_{xxx} = \frac{d}{dx}\left(uu_{xx} - \frac{1}{2}u_x^2\right) \text{ from } x = 0 \text{ to } 1 \text{ for } dE/dt.$$

14 Solve $u_t = u_{xxx}$ on $0 \le x \le 1$ with $u(x,0) = x^2(1 - x)$, using the stable method in Problem 12. The boundary conditions are $U_{0,n} = U_{1,n} = U_{10,n} = 0$ with $\Delta x = 1/10$.

15 Which differential equation is well-posed, $u_t = u_{xxxx}$ or $u_t = -u_{xxxx}$? Which difference equation is stable, $\Delta_t U = r\,\Delta_x^4 U$ or $\Delta_t U = -r\,\Delta_x^4 U$? Centering Δ^4 with coefficients $1, -4, 6, -4, 1$, find the stability limit on $r = \Delta t/(\Delta x)^4$.

6.4 WAVE EQUATIONS AND STAGGERED LEAPFROG

This section focuses on the ***second-order wave equation*** $\boldsymbol{u_{tt} = c^2 u_{xx}}$. We find the exact solution $u(x,t)$. Accuracy and stability are confirmed for the leapfrog method (centered second differences in t and x). This two-step method requires that we rethink the growth factor G, which was clear for a single step. The result will be $p = 2$ for the order of accuracy, and $c\Delta t/\Delta x \le 1$ for stability.

It is useful to write $u_{tt} = c^2 u_{xx}$ as a *first-order system* $\partial v/\partial t = A\,\partial v/\partial x$. The components v_1 and v_2 of the vector unknown can be $\partial u/\partial t$ and $c\,\partial u/\partial x$. Then we are back to a single-step growth factor, but G is now a 2 by 2 matrix.

Second-order accuracy extends to this system $v_t = Av_x$ if we use a ***staggered mesh***. The mesh for v_2 lies in between the mesh for v_1. This has become the standard method in acoustics and electromagnetics (solving Maxwell's equations). The physical laws relating the electric field $\boldsymbol{E}$ and the magnetic field $\boldsymbol{H}$ are beautifully copied by the difference equations on a staggered mesh. That mesh becomes especially important in more space dimensions (x-y and x-y-z), and in finite volume methods.

This section goes beyond the one-way wave equation in at least five ways:

1. ***Characteristic lines*** $x + ct = C_{\text{left}}$ and $x - ct = C_{\text{right}}$ go through each (x,t).
2. ***Leapfrog methods*** involve three time levels $t + \Delta t$, t, and $t - \Delta t$.
3. ***First-order systems*** have vector unknowns $v(x,t)$ and growth matrices G.
4. ***Staggered grids*** give the much-used FDTD method for Maxwell's equations.
5. ***More space dimensions*** lead to new CFL and vN stability conditions on Δt.

The Structure of Wave Equations

This introduction can take one more quick step, to see what the wave equations of physics actually look like. When A became $\frac{d}{dx}$ in Chapter 3, $K = A^{\mathrm{T}}CA$ became $-\frac{d}{dx}\left(c(x)\frac{d}{dx}\right)$. Now we write down three wave equations that involve $\partial/\partial x$ and $\partial/\partial t$:

Density ρ, Stiffness k
$$\frac{\partial}{\partial t}\left(\rho\frac{\partial u}{\partial t}\right) - \frac{\partial}{\partial x}\left(k\frac{\partial u}{\partial x}\right) = 0 \qquad (1)$$

Capacitance C, Inductance L
$$\frac{\partial}{\partial t}\left(C\frac{\partial V}{\partial t}\right) - \frac{\partial}{\partial x}\left(\frac{1}{L}\frac{\partial V}{\partial x}\right) = 0 \qquad (2)$$

Permeability μ, Permittivity ε
$$\frac{\partial}{\partial t}\left(\mu\frac{\partial u}{\partial t}\right) - \frac{\partial}{\partial x}\left(\frac{1}{\varepsilon}\frac{\partial u}{\partial x}\right) = 0 \qquad (3)$$

The first equation gives oscillations in a hanging bar. The second gives the voltage along a transmission line. The third describes electromagnetic propagation through a dielectric medium. You see $A^{\mathrm{T}}CA$ in all the space derivatives. And you see a similar form in the time derivatives. Both parts stay symmetric, as in $Mu'' + Ku = 0$.

Solution of the Wave Equation

Exactly as for the one-way equation $u_t = cu_x$, we solve $u_{tt} = c^2 u_{xx}$ for each exponential e^{ikx}. That allows us to ***separate the variables into*** $\boldsymbol{u(x,t) = G(t)e^{ikx}}$:

Constant speed c
Wave number k

$$\frac{\partial^2 u}{\partial t^2} = c^2 \frac{\partial^2 u}{\partial x^2} \quad \text{becomes} \quad \frac{d^2 G}{dt^2}\, e^{ikx} = i^2 c^2 k^2 G\, e^{ikx} . \qquad (4)$$

Thus $G_{tt} = i^2 c^2 k^2 G$. This second-order equation has two solutions, $G_{\text{left}} = e^{ickt}$ and $G_{\text{right}} = e^{-ickt}$. So there are two waves with velocities c and $-c$:

Traveling waves $\quad \boldsymbol{u_{\text{left}}(x,t) = e^{ik(x+ct)}} \quad \boldsymbol{u_{\text{right}}(x,t) = e^{ik(x-ct)}}$. $\qquad$ (5)

Combinations of left-going waves $e^{ik(x+ct)}$ will give a general function $F_1(x + ct)$. Combinations of $e^{ik(x-ct)}$ give $F_2(x - ct)$. The complete solution includes both:

$$\boldsymbol{u(x,t) = u_{\text{left}}(x,t) + u_{\text{right}}(x,t) = F_1(x+ct) + F_2(x-ct)} . \qquad (6)$$

We need those two functions to match an initial shape $u(x,0)$ and velocity $u_t(x,0)$:

$$\textbf{At } t = 0 \quad u(x,0) = F_1(x) + F_2(x) \quad \text{and} \quad u_t(x,0) = c\,F_1'(x) - c\,F_2'(x) . \qquad (7)$$

Solving for F_1 and F_2 gives the unique solution that matches $u(x,0)$ and $u_t(x,0)$:

$$\textbf{Solution} \quad u(x,t) = \frac{u(x+ct,0) + u(x-ct,0)}{2} + \frac{1}{2c}\int_{x-ct}^{x+ct} u_t(x,0)\,dx . \qquad (8)$$

The "domain of dependence" goes backward to the initial values from $x - ct$ to $x + ct$.

Example 1 A step function $S(x)$ (*wall of water*) will travel along both characteristics:

Two half-walls
$\boldsymbol{u(x,0) = S(x)}$

$$u(x,t) = \frac{1}{2}S(x+ct) + \frac{1}{2}S(x-ct) = \left\{0 \text{ or } \frac{1}{2} \text{ or } 1\right\} .$$

By time t, the initial jump at $x = 0$ gives $u = \frac{1}{2}$ between $x = -ct$ and $x = ct$. That is the "domain of influence" of $x = 0, t = 0$, going forward in Figure 6.9.

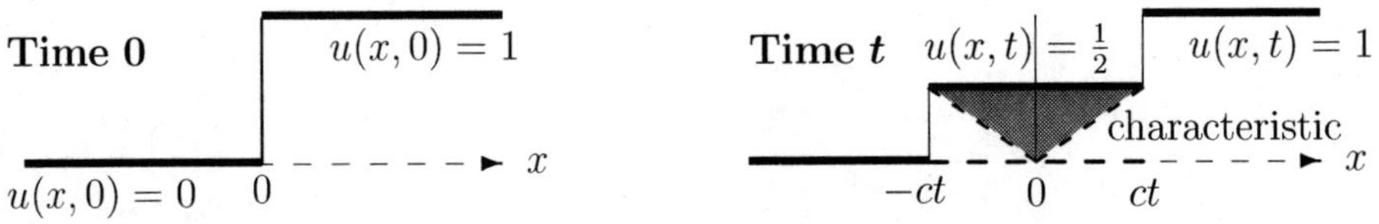

Figure 6.9: Half of a step function goes each way, when $u_t(x,0) = 0$.

The Semidiscrete Wave Equation

Let me start by discretizing only the space derivative u_{xx}. The second difference $U_{j+1} - 2U_j + U_{j-1}$ is the natural choice, divided by $(\Delta x)^2$. For the approximations $U_j(t)$ at the meshpoints $x = j\Delta x$, we have a *family of ODEs* in the time direction. This is the **method of lines**, discrete in space but continuous in time:

Semidiscrete equation $$U_j'' = \frac{c^2}{(\Delta x)^2}(U_{j+1} - 2U_j + U_{j-1}). \qquad (9)$$

Again we follow every exponential, looking for $U_j(t) = G(t)e^{ikj\Delta x}$. Substitute into (9) and cancel the common factor $e^{ikj\Delta x}$. Instead of $G_{tt} = -c^2k^2G$ we have new speeds:

Growth equation $$G_{tt} = \frac{c^2}{(\Delta x)^2}(e^{ik\Delta x} - 2 + e^{-ik\Delta x})G = -\frac{c^2}{(\Delta x)^2}(2 - 2\cos k\Delta x)G. \qquad (10)$$

The correct right side $-c^2k^2G$ is changed to $-c^2F^2k^2G$. This factor F^2 turns up so often that we need to recognize it. Use $2 - 2\cos\theta = 4\sin^2(\theta/2)$:

Phase factor $\boldsymbol{F = \mathrm{sinc}(k\Delta x/2)}$ $$F^2 = \frac{2 - 2\cos k\Delta x}{k^2(\Delta x)^2} = \frac{4\sin^2(k\Delta x/2)}{k^2(\Delta x)^2} = \left(\frac{\sin(k\Delta x/2)}{k\Delta x/2}\right)^2. \qquad (11)$$

The *sinc function* is defined as $\sin\theta$ divided by θ. When $\theta = k\Delta x/2$ is small, F is $1 + O(\theta^2)$. Then equation (10) is close to the correct $G_{tt} = -c^2k^2G$.

For every $k\Delta x$, that growth equation (10) has two exponential solutions:

Semidiscrete growth $G_{tt} = -c^2F^2k^2G$ gives $\boldsymbol{G(t) = e^{\pm icFkt}}$. (12)

Notice that F depends on k. Different frequencies e^{ikx} are traveling at different "phase velocities" $cF(k)$. This is ***dispersion***: a pulse breaks into separate waves. The "*group velocity*" is the derivative of $cF(k)k$ with respect to k. This gives the speed of a group of waves [169]: often more important.

The semidiscrete form suggests a good algorithm for the wave equation with boundary conditions (say $u = 0$ along the lines $x = 0$ and $x = \pi$). If $h = \Delta x = \frac{\pi}{n+1}$, this interval has n interior meshpoints. The n by n second difference matrix is the special K from earlier chapters (but now we have $-K$):

Semidiscrete with boundaries $$U''(t) = -c^2\,KU/(\Delta x)^2. \qquad (13)$$

This is just the equation $MU'' + KU = 0$ of oscillating springs in Section 2.2.

The n eigenvalues of K are positive numbers $2 - 2\cos k\Delta x$. The only change from the equation on an infinite line is that k takes only the values $1, 2, \ldots, n$. The oscillations go on forever as in (12), the energy is conserved, and now the waves bounce back from the boundaries instead of continuing out to $x = \pm\infty$.

Leapfrog from Centered Differences

A fully discrete method also approximates u_{tt} by a centered difference. The time difference "*leaps over*" the space difference at $t = n\Delta t$:

Leapfrog method $$\frac{U_{j,n+1} - 2U_{j,n} + U_{j,n-1}}{(\Delta t)^2} = c^2 \frac{U_{j+1,n} - 2U_{j,n} + U_{j-1,n}}{(\Delta x)^2}. \qquad (14)$$

This has two key differences from the 5-point molecule for $u_{xx} + u_{yy} = 0$ (Laplace). First, $u_{tt} - c^2 u_{xx} = 0$ has a minus sign. Second, we have two conditions at $t = 0$ and no conditions at a later time. We are marching forward in time (marching with Laplace's equation would be totally unstable). A separate calculation for the first time step computes $U_{j,1}$ from the initial shape $u(x, 0)$ and the velocity $u_t(x, 0)$.

Leapfrog is normally second-order. Substitute the true $u(x, t)$ into (14), and use its Taylor series. For second differences, the errors involve $(\Delta t)^2$ and $(\Delta x)^2$:

Second-order $$u_{tt} + \frac{1}{12}(\Delta t)^2 u_{tttt} + \cdots = c^2\left(u_{xx} + \frac{1}{12}(\Delta x)^2 u_{xxxx} + \cdots\right). \qquad (15)$$

In this case $u_{tttt} = c^2 u_{xxtt} = c^2 u_{ttxx} = c^4 u_{xxxx}$. The two sides of (15) differ by

Local discretization error $$\frac{1}{12}[(\Delta t)^2 c^4 - (\Delta x)^2 c^2] u_{xxxx} + \cdots \qquad (16)$$

Again $c\Delta t = \Delta x$ is the golden time step that follows the characteristic exactly. The two triangles in Figure 6.10 become exactly the same in this borderline case $r = 1$. The CFL reasoning shows instability for $r > 1$. We now show that $r \leq 1$ is stable.

Stability of the Leapfrog Method

A difference equation must use the initial conditions that determine $u(x, t)$, to have a chance of converging. **The domain of dependence for U must include the domain of dependence for u.** The slopes must have $\Delta t/\Delta x \leq 1/c$. So this Courant-Friedrichs-Lewy condition is necessary; we next show it is sufficient.

CFL stability condition The leapfrog method requires $r = c\,\Delta t/\Delta x \leq 1$.

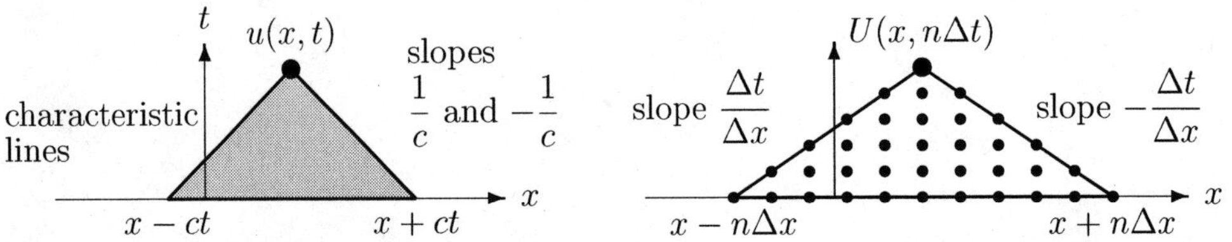

Figure 6.10: Domains of dependence: u from wave equation and U from leapfrog.

For a double-step difference equation, we still look for pure solutions $U(x, n\Delta t) = G^n e^{ikx}$, separating time from space. In the leapfrog equation (14) this gives

$$\left[\frac{G^{n+1} - 2G^n + G^{n-1}}{(\Delta t)^2}\right] e^{ikx} = c^2 G^n \left[\frac{e^{ik\Delta x} - 2 + e^{-ik\Delta x}}{(\Delta x)^2}\right] e^{ikx}.$$

Set $r = c\Delta t/\Delta x$ and cancel $G^{n-1}e^{ikx}$. This leaves a quadratic equation for G:

$$G^2 - 2G + 1 = r^2 G\,(2\cos k\Delta x - 2)\,. \qquad (17)$$

The two-step leapfrog equation allows two G's (of course!). For stability, both must satisfy $|G| \le 1$ for all frequencies k. Rewrite equation (17) as $G^2 - 2\,[\,a\,]\,G + 1 = 0$:

Growth factor equation $\quad G^2 - 2\,[1 - r^2 + r^2\cos k\Delta x]\,G + 1 = 0\,. \qquad (18)$

The roots of $G^2 - 2\,[\,a\,]\,G + 1 = 0$ are $G = a \pm \sqrt{a^2 - 1}$. Stability depends on that square root giving an imaginary number, when $[\,a\,]^2 = [1 - r^2 + r^2\cos k\Delta x]^2 \le 1$:

$$\text{If } \ a^2 \le 1 \ \text{ then } \ G = a \pm i\sqrt{1 - a^2} \ \text{ has } \ |G|^2 = a^2 + (1 - a^2) = 1\,.$$

The CFL condition $r \le 1$ does produce $a^2 \le 1$. The leapfrog method is stable:

Stability $\quad$ If $r \le 1$ then $|a| = |1 - r^2 + r^2\cos k\Delta x| \le (1 - r^2) + r^2 = 1\,. \qquad (19)$

An unstable $r > 1$ would produce $|a| = |1 - 2r^2| > 1$ at the dangerous $k\Delta x = \pi$. Then both G's are real, and their product is 1, and one of them has $|G| > 1$.

Note 1 $\quad$ Suppose $r = 1$ so that $\boldsymbol{c\,\Delta t = \Delta x}$. This "golden ratio" has perfect accuracy (in outer space...). The middle terms $-2U_{j,n}$ and $-2r^2U_{j,n}$ cancel in the leapfrog equation (14), leaving a complete leap over the center point when $r = 1$:

Exact leapfrog ($r = 1$) $\quad U_{j,n+1} + U_{j,n-1} = U_{j+1,n} + U_{j-1,n}\,. \qquad (20)$

This difference equation is satisfied by $u(x,t)$, because it is satisfied by all waves $U(x + ct)$ and $U(x - ct)$. Take $U_{j,n} = U(j\Delta x + cn\Delta t)$ and use $c\,\Delta t = \Delta x$:

$$\begin{array}{lll} U_{j,n+1} = U_{j+1,n} & \text{because both are equal to} & U(j\Delta x + cn\Delta t + \Delta x) \\ U_{j,n-1} = U_{j-1,n} & \text{because both are equal to} & U(j\Delta x + cn\Delta t - \Delta x) \end{array}$$

So (20) is exactly satisfied by traveling waves $U(x + ct)$, and similarly by $U(x - ct)$.

Note 2 $\quad$ You could also apply leapfrog to the *one-way* equation $u_t = c\,u_x$:

One-way leapfrog $\quad U_{j,n+1} - U_{j,n-1} = r(U_{j+1,n} - U_{j-1,n})\,. \qquad (21)$

Now the growth factor equation is $G^2 - 2(ir\sin k\Delta x)G - 1 = 0$. In the stable case (still $r = c\,\Delta t/\Delta x \le 1$), one growth factor G_1 is sensible but G_2 is strange:

$$G_1 = e^{ir\sin k\Delta x} \approx e^{ick\Delta t} \quad \text{and} \quad G_2 = -e^{-ir\sin k\Delta x} \approx -1\,. \qquad (22)$$

G_1 and G_2 are *exactly on the unit circle.* With $|G| = 1$ there is no room to move. Numerical diffusion $\alpha(U_{j+1,n} - 2U_{j,n} + U_{j-1,n})$ usually adds extra stability, but not here. So leapfrog for first-order equations can be dangerous.

Wave Equation in Higher Dimensions

The wave equation extends to three-dimensional space (with speed set at $c = 1$):

3D Wave equation $\quad u_{tt} = u_{xx} + u_{yy} + u_{zz}\,. \quad (23)$

Waves go in all directions, and the solution is a superposition of pure harmonics. These plane waves now have three wave numbers k, ℓ, m, and frequency ω:

Plane wave solutions $\quad u(x,y,z,t) = e^{i(kx + \ell y + mz - \omega t)}.$

Substituting into the wave equation gives $\omega^2 = k^2 + \ell^2 + m^2$. So there are two frequencies $\pm\omega$ for the wave-numbers k, ℓ, m. These exponential solutions combine to match the initial wave height $u(x,y,z,0)$ and its velocity $u_t(x,y,z,0)$.

Suppose the initial velocity is a ***three-dimensional delta function*** $\boldsymbol{\delta(x,y,z)}$:

$$\delta(x,y,z) = \delta(x)\delta(y)\delta(z) \quad \text{gives} \quad \iiint f(x,y,z)\,\delta(x,y,z)\,dV = f(0,0,0)\,. \qquad (24)$$

The resulting $u(x,y,z,t)$ will be the Green's function for the wave equation. It is the response to the delta function, which gives equal weight to all harmonics. Rather than computing that superposition we find it from the wave equation itself. Spherical symmetry greatly simplifies $u_{xx} + u_{yy} + u_{zz}$, when u depends only on r and t:

Symmetry produces $u(r,t)$

$$\frac{\partial^2 u}{\partial t^2} = \frac{\partial^2 u}{\partial r^2} + \frac{2}{r}\frac{\partial u}{\partial r}\,. \qquad (25)$$

Multiplying by r, this is a one-dimensional equation $\boldsymbol{(ru)_{tt} = (ru)_{rr}}$! Its solutions ru will be functions of $r - t$ and $r + t$. Starting from a delta function is like sound going out from a bell, or light from a point source. *The solution is nonzero only on the sphere* $r = t$. So every point hears the bell only once, as the sound wave passes by. An impulse in 3D produces a sharp response (this is Huygen's principle).

In 2D, the solution does *not* return to zero for $t > r$. We couldn't hear or see clearly in Flatland. You might imagine a point source in two dimensions as a *line source* in the z-direction in three dimensions. The solution is independent of z, so it satisfies $u_{tt} = u_{xx} + u_{yy}$. But in three dimensions, spheres starting from sources along the line continue to hit the listener. They come from further and further away, so the solution decays—but it is not zero. The wave front passes, but waves keep coming.

Leapfrog Method in Higher Dimensions

In one dimension, two characteristics go out from each point $(x, 0)$. In 2D and 3D, a *characteristic cone* like $x^2 + y^2 = c^2t^2$ goes out from $(x, y, 0)$ and $(x, y, z, 0)$. The condition $r \le 1$ changes in dimension d. And the cost grows with $1/(\Delta x)^{d+1}$.

The leapfrog method replaces u_{xx} and u_{yy} by centered differences at time $n\Delta t$:

Leapfrog for $u_{tt} = u_{xx} + u_{yy}$

$$\frac{U_{n+1} - 2U_n + U_{n-1}}{(\Delta t)^2} = \frac{\Delta_x^2 U_n}{(\Delta x)^2} + \frac{\Delta_y^2 U_n}{(\Delta y)^2}.$$

U_0 and U_1 come from the given initial conditions $u(x, y, 0)$ and $u_t(x, y, 0)$. We look for a solution $U_n = G^n e^{ikx} e^{i\ell y}$ with **separation of variables**. Substituting into the leapfrog equation and canceling $G^{n-1} e^{ikx} e^{i\ell y}$ produces the 2D equation for two G's:

Growth factor

$$\frac{G^2 - 2G + 1}{(\Delta t)^2} = G\,\frac{(2\cos k\,\Delta x - 2)}{(\Delta x)^2} + G\,\frac{(2\cos \ell\,\Delta y - 2)}{(\Delta y)^2}. \tag{26}$$

Again this has the form $G^2 - 2aG + 1 = 0$. You can see a in brackets:

$$G^2 - 2\left[1 - \left(\frac{\Delta t}{\Delta x}\right)^2 (1 - \cos k\,\Delta x) - \left(\frac{\Delta t}{\Delta y}\right)^2 (1 - \cos \ell\,\Delta y)\right] G + 1 = 0. \tag{27}$$

Both roots must have $|G| = 1$ for stability. This still requires $-1 \le a \le 1$. When the cosines are -1 (the dangerous value) we find the stability condition for leapfrog:

Stability $\quad -1 \le 1 - 2\left(\frac{\Delta t}{\Delta x}\right)^2 - 2\left(\frac{\Delta t}{\Delta y}\right)^2$ needs $\left(\frac{\Delta t}{\Delta x}\right)^2 + \left(\frac{\Delta t}{\Delta y}\right)^2 \le 1.$ (28)

On a square grid, this is $\Delta t \le \Delta x/\sqrt{2}$. In three dimensions it would be $\Delta t \le \Delta x/\sqrt{3}$. Those also come from the CFL condition, that the characteristic cone must lie inside the pyramid that gives the leapfrog domain of dependence. Figure 6.11 shows the cone and pyramid just touching, when $\Delta t = \Delta x/\sqrt{2}$.

Cone has circular base for $u_{tt} = u_{xx} + u_{yy}$
Pyramid has diamond base for leapfrog
Cone and pyramid go up to $(0, 0, \Delta t)$

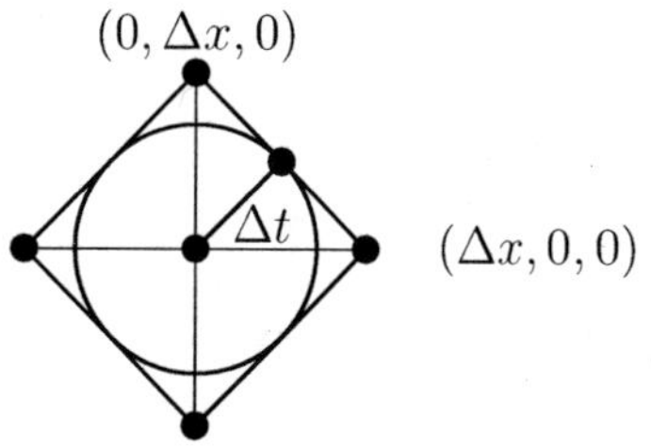

Figure 6.11: The pyramid contains and touches the cone when $(\Delta t)^2 = (\Delta x)^2/2$.

An Equivalent First-order System

I can display a system of two equations $v_t = Av_x$ that is equivalent to $u_{tt} = c^2 u_{xx}$:

First-order system $\partial v/\partial t = A\,\partial v/\partial x$

$$\frac{\partial}{\partial t}\begin{bmatrix} u_t \\ cu_x \end{bmatrix} = \begin{bmatrix} 0 & c \\ c & 0 \end{bmatrix}\frac{\partial}{\partial x}\begin{bmatrix} u_t \\ cu_x \end{bmatrix}. \tag{29}$$

The first equation recovers $u_{tt} = c^2 u_{xx}$. The second is the identity $cu_{xt} = cu_{tx}$. Notice that the 2 by 2 matrix is symmetric and its eigenvalues are the wave velocities $\pm c$.

This "symmetric hyperbolic" form $v_t = Av_x$ is useful in theory and practice. The energy $E(t) = \int \frac{1}{2}\|v(x,t)\|^2\,dx$ is automatically constant in time! Here is the proof for any equation $v_t = Av_x$ with a symmetric (real and non-varying) matrix A:

$$\frac{\partial}{\partial t}\left(\frac{1}{2}\|v\|^2\right) = \sum v_i \frac{\partial v_i}{\partial t} = v^{\mathrm{T}} v_t = v^{\mathrm{T}} A v_x = \frac{\partial}{\partial x}\left(\frac{1}{2} v^{\mathrm{T}} A v\right). \tag{30}$$

When you integrate over all x, the left side is $\partial E/\partial t$. The right side is $\frac{1}{2}v^{\mathrm{T}}Av$ at the limits $x = \pm\infty$. Those limits give zero (no signal has reached that far). So the derivative of the energy $E(t)$ is zero, and $E(t)$ stays constant.

The Euler equations of compressible flow are also a first-order system, but not linear. In physics and engineering, a linear equation deals with a small disturbance. Something from outside acts to change the equilibrium, but not by much:

in acoustics it is a slowly moving body

in aerodynamics it is a slender wing

in elasticity it is a small load

in electromagnetism it is a weak source.

Below some level, the cause-effect relation is very close to linear. In acoustics, the sound speed is steady when pressure is nearly constant. In elasticity, Hooke's law holds until the geometry changes or the material begins to break down. In electromagnetism, nonlinearity comes with relativistic effects (and curved lenses too).

The case to understand has A = constant matrix, with n real eigenvalues λ and eigenvectors w. When $Aw = \lambda w$, look for a solution $v(x,t) = U(x,t)w$. The vector equation $v_t = Av_x$ will split into n scalar one-way wave equations $U_t = \lambda U_x$:

$v_t = Av_x$ has $v = Uw$

$$\frac{\partial U}{\partial t} w = A\frac{\partial U}{\partial x} w = \lambda\frac{\partial U}{\partial x} w \quad \text{so} \quad \frac{\partial U}{\partial t} = \lambda\frac{\partial U}{\partial x}. \tag{31}$$

The complete solution vector v is $v(x,t) = U_1(x + \lambda_1 t)w_1 + \cdots + U_n(x + \lambda_n t)w_n$. ***The equation $v_t = Av_x$ has n signal speeds λ_i and it sends out n waves.***

Example 2 The wave equation has $A = \left[\begin{smallmatrix} 0 & c \\ c & 0 \end{smallmatrix}\right]$ with eigenvalues $\lambda = c$ and $\lambda = -c$. Then the two scalar equations $U_t = \lambda U_x$ produce left and right waves:

$$\begin{aligned} \boldsymbol{\lambda_1 = +c} \qquad & \frac{\partial U_1}{\partial t} = \frac{\partial}{\partial t}(u_t + c\,u_x) = +c\frac{\partial}{\partial x}(u_t + c\,u_x) \\ \boldsymbol{\lambda_2 = -c} \qquad & \frac{\partial U_2}{\partial t} = \frac{\partial}{\partial t}(u_t - c\,u_x) = -c\frac{\partial}{\partial x}(u_t - c\,u_x)\,. \end{aligned} \tag{32}$$

Each equation agrees with $u_{tt} = c^2 u_{xx}$. The one-way left and right waves are $U_1(x+ct)w_1$ and $U_2(x-ct)w_2$. The vector solution $v(x,t)$ is recovered from $U_1 w_1 + U_2 w_2$:

$$v = \begin{bmatrix} u_t \\ c\,u_x \end{bmatrix} = (u_t + c\,u_x)\begin{bmatrix} \frac{1}{2} \\ -\frac{1}{2} \end{bmatrix} + (u_t - c\,u_x)\begin{bmatrix} \frac{1}{2} \\ \frac{1}{2} \end{bmatrix}. \tag{33}$$

Stable difference methods for $v_t = Av_x$ come from stable methods for $u_t = \pm c\,u_x$. Replace c by A in Lax-Friedrichs and Lax-Wendroff, or go to staggered leapfrog.

Leapfrog on a Staggered Grid

The discrete case should copy the continuous case. The two-step leapfrog difference equation should reduce to a pair of one-step equations. But if we don't keep the individual equations centered, they will lose second-order accuracy. **The way to center both first-order equations is to use a staggered grid** (Figure 6.12).

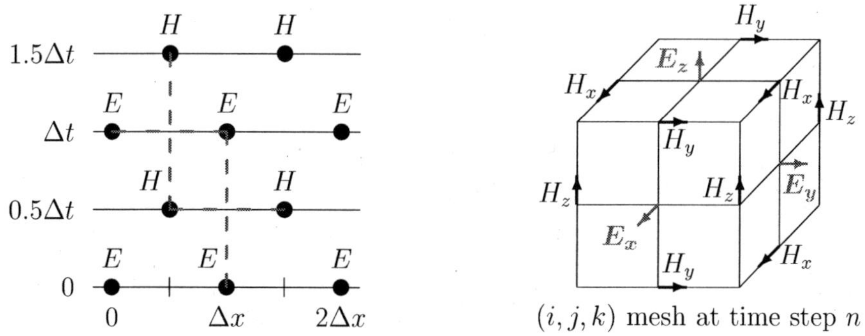

Figure 6.12: $\dfrac{\Delta E}{\Delta t} = c\dfrac{\Delta H}{\Delta x}$ and $\dfrac{\Delta H}{\Delta t} = c\dfrac{\Delta E}{\Delta x}$ are staggered but still centered.

The staggered grid for the wave equation matches *Yee's method for Maxwell's equations.* Yee's idea transformed the whole subject of computational electromagnetics (it is now called the FDTD method: finite differences in the time domain [152]). Previously the moment method, which is Galerkin's method, had been dominant—but staggered grids are so natural for $\boldsymbol{E}$ and $\boldsymbol{H}$. Let me choose units that give the simplest pair of equations:

Waves in 1D $u_t = E,\ cu_x = H$	$\partial E/\partial t = c\,\partial H/\partial x$ $\partial H/\partial t = c\,\partial E/\partial x$	becomes	$\Delta_t E/\Delta t = c\,\Delta_x H/\Delta x$ $\Delta_t H/\Delta t = c\,\Delta_x E/\Delta x$	(34)

I will put E on the standard grid and H on the staggered (half-integer) grid. *Notice how all the differences are centered in Figure 6.12a. This gives second-order accuracy.*

The identities $E_{tx} = E_{xt}$ and $H_{tx} = H_{xt}$ lead to wave equations with $c^2 = \epsilon\,\mu$:

$$\begin{array}{lcl} E_t &=& cH_x \\ H_t &=& cE_x \end{array} \quad \text{becomes} \quad \begin{array}{lclclcl} E_{tt} &=& cH_{xt} &=& cH_{tx} &=& c^2 E_{xx} \\ H_{tt} &=& cE_{xt} &=& cE_{tx} &=& c^2 H_{xx} \end{array} \tag{35}$$

In the discrete case, **eliminating $\boldsymbol{H}$ gives the two-step leapfrog equation for $\boldsymbol{E}$.** Differences copy derivatives. This comes from the finite difference analogue $\Delta_x(\Delta_t U) = \Delta_t(\Delta_x U)$ of the cross-derivative identity $u_{tx} = u_{xt}$:

$$\frac{\partial}{\partial x}\left(\frac{\partial u}{\partial t}\right) = \frac{\partial}{\partial t}\left(\frac{\partial u}{\partial x}\right) \quad \textbf{\textit{corresponds to}} \quad \frac{\Delta_x(\Delta_t U)}{(\Delta x)(\Delta t)} = \frac{\Delta_t(\Delta_x U)}{(\Delta t)(\Delta x)}. \tag{36}$$

With equal denominators, we only need to check the numerators. The same 1's and -1's appear both ways in $\Delta_x \Delta_t$ and $\Delta_t \Delta_x$. Only the order is different:

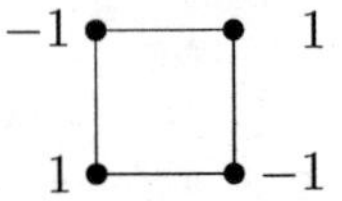

$$\begin{array}{lclcl} \Delta_x(\Delta_t U) &=& (U_{n+1,j+1} - U_{n,j+1}) &-& (U_{n+1,j} - U_{n,j}) \\ \Delta_t(\Delta_x U) &=& (U_{n+1,j+1} - U_{n+1,j}) &-& (U_{n,j+1} - U_{n,j}) \end{array}$$

You could compare (35) with the Cauchy-Riemann equations $u_x = s_y$ and $u_y = -s_x$ for the potential $u(x, y)$ and stream function $s(x, y)$. It would be natural to discretize Cauchy-Riemann on a staggered grid, for Laplace's equation.

May I emphasize that these grids are useful for many other equations too. We will see the "half-point" grid values in Section 6.6 for the flux $F(u)$ in the conservation law $u_t + F(u)_x = 0$, which is a nonlinear extension of the one-way wave equation. Half-point values are centrally important throughout the ***finite volume method***.

Maxwell's Equations

For electrodynamics, the number $c = \sqrt{\epsilon\,\mu}$ in the wave equation is the speed of light. It is the same large number that appears in Einstein's $e = mc^2$. The CFL stability condition $r \le 1/\sqrt{\text{dimension}}$ for the leapfrog method might require very small time steps (on the scale of ordinary life). Often the leapfrog method is entirely appropriate, and we write Maxwell's equations in 3D without source terms:

Maxwell's equations in free space

$$\frac{\partial E}{\partial t} = \frac{1}{\epsilon}\,\text{curl}\,H \quad \text{and} \quad \frac{\partial H}{\partial t} = -\frac{1}{\mu}\,\text{curl}\,E\,. \tag{37}$$

Those six equations begin with the electric field component E_x in the x-direction:

First equation

$$\frac{\partial}{\partial t}\,E_x = \frac{1}{\epsilon}\left[\frac{\partial}{\partial y}\,H_z - \frac{\partial}{\partial z}\,H_y\right]. \tag{38}$$

Yee's difference equation computes E_x at level $n+1$ from E_x at time $n\Delta t$ and the space differences of H_z and H_y ***at level*** $\boldsymbol{n + \frac{1}{2}}$. Figure 6.12 shows the components of the magnetic field $\boldsymbol{H}$ on a staggered grid. We have six difference equations for E_x, E_y, E_z at $n+1$ and then H_x, H_y, H_z at time $(n+1.5)\Delta t$: top of Figure 6.12.

The stability condition $c\,\Delta t \le \Delta x/\sqrt{3}$ is acceptable on a cubic grid. That fixed grid is a big drawback. But the FDTD method has been used with 10^9 meshpoints, which we cannot afford on an unstructured mesh for finite elements.

Finite differences have numerical dispersion—the discrete wave speeds depend on the wave number $\boldsymbol{k} = (k_x, k_y, k_z)$. The true speed c is reduced by a phase factor, like F in equation (11). When dispersion creates significant errors, we can upgrade to fourth-order accuracy—but wider differences make boundaries more difficult. **Material interfaces produce greater errors than numerical dispersion.** I am thinking of **10 meshpoints/wavelength** to resolve the shortest wave.

This is the give and take of numerical analysis: higher accuracy brings greater complexity. We can take larger steps Δt, but every step is slower (and harder to code).

Perfectly Matched Layer

An important application is the reflection of a radar signal by an airplane. The region of interest is ***exterior to the plane***. In principle that region extends infinitely far in all directions. In practice we compute inside a large box, and it is crucial to prevent waves from reflecting back into the box from its sides.

A beautiful way to control reflection was discovered by Berenger [14]. An *absorbing boundary layer* is added to the sides of the box. In that layer the solution decays exponentially, and after less than a wavelength there is very little to reflect. The key is to make this a **perfectly matched layer (PML)** where it meets the computational box. Then the exact solution has no reflection at the box boundary, and the discrete form will have small reflection.

The PML construction can be described as a transformed *material* or a transformed *equation*. Either way, the real coefficients in the wave equation become complex! Suppose the x direction is normal to the boundary:

Complex PML transformation $$\frac{\partial}{\partial x} \quad \text{becomes} \quad \left(1 + i\,\frac{\sigma(x)}{\omega}\right)^{-1} \frac{\partial}{\partial x} \qquad (39)$$

In the differential equation, $\sigma(x)$ could be a step function. That is too sudden for the discrete equation, and in practice σ grows like x^2 or x^3 within the layer.

The important point is the effect on plane waves that hit the layer:

The plane wave $Ae^{i(kx+\ell y+mz-\omega t)}$ **is multiplied by** $e^{-k\int^x \sigma(s)\,ds/\omega}$ (40)

A one-dimensional wave equation has $k/\omega =$ constant. The attenuation rate in the PML layer is *independent of frequency*. A physicist will say that in 3D, the rate depends on the angle (involving ℓy and mz as well as kx) at which the wave hits the boundary: true. A glancing wave has small k/ω. But if the waves radiate from a source well inside the box, their incidence angles will have $\cos\theta > 1/\sqrt{3}$. The reflection is under control.

In the frequency domain, we compute with one ω at a time. But the popularity of the PML method is for finite differences in the time domain (FDTD). The solution involves many waves and we don't see ω explicitly (just t). If all frequencies are near ω_0, the stretching factor can be $1 + (i\sigma/\omega_0)$. Johnson's *PML Notes* on the website describe how the material becomes an anisotropic absorber within the layer.

Those notes are an excellent supplement to the standard PML reference [152]. May I summarize the reflection problem and its successful solution:

1. Free or fixed boundary conditions (Neumann or Dirichlet) give unacceptable reflections at an ordinary boundary. Those reflections decay slowly for wave equations: $1/r^{(d-1)/2}$ in d dimensions.

2. A perfectly matched layer gives exponential decay in the solution to the differential equation. If the width of the layer is $5\Delta x$, the material change (= coordinate change) gives small reflection in the discrete solution.

The Structure of Wave Equations

Scalar wave equations begin with $\partial u/\partial t = c\,\partial u/\partial x$ (one-way). The *antisymmetric* operator $c\,\partial/\partial x$ acts on u. The Schrödinger equation $\partial\psi/\partial t = i(\Delta\psi - V(x)\psi)$ also has antisymmetry (because of the factor i). In his notes on the cse website, Johnson emphasizes that energy conservation and orthogonality of the normal modes follow immediately for $\partial u/\partial t = Lu$, whenever $\boldsymbol{(Lu, w) = -\,(u, Lw)}$:

Conservation of energy	$\frac{\partial}{\partial t}(u,u) = (Lu,u) + (u,Lu) = 0$	(41)
Orthogonality of modes	$u(x,t) = M(x,y,z)e^{-i\omega t}$ means $-\,i\omega M = LM$	(42)

Here L is linear, time-invariant, and antisymmetric. Then iL is Hermitian. Its eigenvalues $\omega_1, \omega_2, \ldots$ are real and its eigenfunctions $M_1, M_2, \ldots$ provide a complete orthogonal basis. Those are deep properties, to be confirmed in each case when the boundary conditions and the inner product are specified.

Example 3 Maxwell's equations (37) have six components of u, and a block L:

$$\textbf{Maxwell as}\quad \frac{\partial \boldsymbol{u}}{\partial \boldsymbol{t}} = \boldsymbol{Lu} \qquad \frac{\partial}{\partial t}\begin{bmatrix} E \\ H \end{bmatrix} = \begin{bmatrix} 0 & (1/\epsilon(x))\,\mathrm{curl} \\ -(1/\mu(x))\,\mathrm{curl} & 0 \end{bmatrix}\begin{bmatrix} E \\ H \end{bmatrix}. \tag{43}$$

The symmetry of curl gives the antisymmetry of L, with the correct inner product:

$$\boldsymbol{(E,E') + (H,H')} \quad ([E\ \ H],[E'\ \ H']) = \frac{1}{2}\iiint (\overline{E}\cdot\epsilon E' + \overline{H}\cdot\mu H')\,dx\,dy\,dz. \tag{44}$$

Integration by parts shows that the block operator L is antisymmetric. (Properly we should say *anti-Hermitian* in this complex case.) The normal mode equation $-i\omega M = LM$

becomes more familiar with curl curl, after $M = [E(x,y,z) \quad H(x,y,z)]$ is separated:

$$\begin{aligned} -i\omega E &= (1/\epsilon)\operatorname{curl} H \\ -i\omega H &= -(1/\mu)\operatorname{curl} E \end{aligned} \quad \text{leads to} \quad \begin{aligned} (1/\epsilon)\operatorname{curl}[(1/\mu)\operatorname{curl} E] &= \omega^2 E \\ (1/\mu)\operatorname{curl}[(1/\epsilon)\operatorname{curl} H] &= \omega^2 H \end{aligned} \qquad (45)$$

Source terms Many important sources have the harmonic form $s = S(x,y,z)e^{-i\omega t}$. Then the solution has the form $u = U(x,y,z)e^{-i\omega t}$. Substitute into $\partial u/\partial t = Lu + s$:

Harmonic source $-i\omega U e^{-i\omega t} = LUe^{-i\omega t} + Se^{-i\omega t}$ becomes $(L+i\omega)U = -S$. (46)

$L + i\omega$ is still anti-Hermitian. $U(x,y,z)$ comes from combining normal modes, or finite differences or finite elements. The name of Helmholtz is applied to our final and most fundamental example: the **scalar wave equation**.

Example 4 The wave equation $u_{tt} = \Delta u = \operatorname{div}(\operatorname{grad} u)$ has an antisymmetric block form:

$$\frac{\partial}{\partial t}\begin{bmatrix} \partial u/\partial t \\ \operatorname{grad} u \end{bmatrix} = \begin{bmatrix} 0 & \operatorname{div} \\ \operatorname{grad} & 0 \end{bmatrix}\begin{bmatrix} \partial u/\partial t \\ \operatorname{grad} u \end{bmatrix}. \qquad (47)$$

1. The energy is the integral of $\frac{1}{2}(u_t^2 + |\operatorname{grad} u|^2) = \frac{1}{2}(u_t^2 + u_x^2 + u_y^2 + u_z^2)$: *constant.*

2. The mode equation (42) is the **Laplace eigenvalue problem** $\Delta M = -\omega^2 M$.

3. The source problem (46) reduces to the **Helmholtz equation** $-\Delta U - \omega^2 U = S$.

Problem Set 6.4

1 A two-way wall of water (box function $u(x,0) = 1$ for $-1 \le x \le 1$) starts from rest with $u_t(x,0) = 0$. Find the solution $u(x,t)$ from (8).

2 Separation of variables gives $u(x,t) = (\sin nx)(\sin nt)$ and three similar 2π-periodic solutions to $u_{tt} = u_{xx}$. What are those three? When does the complex function $e^{ikx}e^{int}$ solve the wave equation?

3 An odd 2π-periodic sawtooth function $ST(x)$ is the integral of an even square wave $SW(x)$. Solve $u_{tt} = u_{xx}$ starting from SW and also ST with $u_t(x,0) = 0$, by a double Fourier series in x and t:

$$SW(x) = \frac{\cos x}{1} - \frac{\cos 3x}{3} + \frac{\cos 5x}{5} \cdots \qquad ST(x) = \frac{\sin x}{1} - \frac{\sin 3x}{9} + \frac{\sin 5x}{25} \cdots$$

4 Draw the graphs of $SW(x)$ and $ST(x)$ for $|x| \le \pi$. If they are extended to be 2π-periodic for all x, what is the d'Alembert solution $u_{SW} = \frac{1}{2}SW(x+t) + \frac{1}{2}SW(x-t)$? Draw its graph at $t = 1$ and $t = \pi$, and similarly for ST.

5 Solve the wave equation $u_{tt} = u_{xx}$ by the leapfrog method (14) starting from rest with $u(x,0) = SW(x)$. Periodic boundary conditions replace u_{xx} by the second difference circulant $-CU/(\Delta x)^2$. Compare with the exact solution in Problem 4 at $t = \pi$, for CFL numbers $\Delta t/\Delta x = 0.8, 0.9, 1.0, 1.1$.

6 Solve the 3D wave equation (25) with rotational symmetry by $ru = F(r+t) + G(r-t)$ if the initial condition is $u(r,0) = 1$ for $0 \le r \le 1$. At what time does the signal reach $(x,y,z) = (1,1,1)$?

7 Plane wave solutions to the 3D wave equation $u_{tt} = \Delta u$ have the form $u = e^{i(k \cdot x - \omega t)}$. How is ω related to $k = (k_1, k_2, k_3)$? Find a corresponding solution to the semidiscrete equation $U_{tt} = (\Delta_x^2 + \Delta_y^2 + \Delta_z^2)U/h^2$.

8 The physical wave equation (1) is $(\rho u_t)_t = (k u_x)_x$ with mass density ρ and stiffness k. If ρ and k are constants, what is the wave speed c in $u_{tt} = c^2 u_{xx}$? What is ω, in the fundamental mode $u = \sin(\pi x/L)\cos\omega t$ of a vibrating string?

9 Suppose the end $x = L$ is moved as in skipping rope by $u(L,t) = \sin\omega t$. With $u_{tt} = c^2 u_{xx}$ and the left end fixed at $u(0,t) = 0$, write $u = U(x,t) + x(\sin\omega t)/L$. Find the differential equation and boundary conditions for U.

10 The small vibrations of a beam satisfy the 4th-order equation $u_{tt} = -c^2 u_{xxxx}$. Separate variables by $u = A(x)B(t)$ and find separate equations for A and B. Then find *four* solutions $A(x)$ that go with $B(t) = a\cos\omega t + b\sin\omega t$.

11 If that beam is clamped ($u = 0$ and $u' = 0$) at both ends $x = 0$ and $x = L$, show that the allowable frequencies ω in Problem 10 must have $(\cos\omega L)(\cosh\omega L) = 1$.

12 For the time-centered leapfrog equation $\Delta_t^2 U/(\Delta t)^2 = -KU/(\Delta x)^2$, find the quadratic equation $G^2 - 2aG + 1 = 0$ for the growth factor in $U = G^n v$ when $Kv = \lambda v$. What stability condition on the real λ and $r = \Delta t/\Delta x$ assures that $|a| \le 1$? Then $|G| = 1$.

13 Write the equation $u_{tt} = u_{xx} + u_{yy}$ as a first-order system $v_t = Av_x + Bv_y$ with the vector unknown $v = (u_t, u_x, u_y)$. The matrices A and B should be symmetric. Then the energy $\frac{1}{2}\int(u_t^2 + u_x^2 + u_y^2)\,dx$ is $E(t) =$ *constant.*

14 How does $v^{\mathrm{T}} A v_x = (\frac{1}{2} v^{\mathrm{T}} A v)_x$ use the symmetry of A? This was the key to conserving energy in equation (30). You could write out $v^{\mathrm{T}} A v = \sum\sum a_{ij} v_i(x) v_j(x)$ and take the derivative of each term by the product rule.

15 Combine Maxwell's equations $\partial E/\partial t = (\operatorname{curl} H)/\epsilon$ and $\partial H/\partial t = -(\operatorname{curl} E)/\mu$ into a 3D wave equation, to find the speed of light c from ϵ and μ.

16 Code a time step of Yee's method on a staggered $x - t$ mesh, for the wave equation $u_{tt} = c^2 u_{xx}$.

17 Write the inhomogeneous wave equation $(bu_t)_t = \operatorname{div}(d \operatorname{grad} u)$ in its block form (47). The correct energy (u, u) is now the integral of $bu_t^2 + d|\operatorname{grad} u|^2$. Show that $(\partial/\partial t)(u, u) = 0$.

18 When Maxwell's equations for $[E, H]$ have a harmonic source $s = [Se^{-i\omega t}, 0]$, reduce the block equation $(L + i\omega)U = -S$ to a "curl curl equation" for the electric field in $E(x, y, z)e^{-i\omega t}$. It is Maxwell's equation in the frequency domain, on the cse website.

6.5 DIFFUSION, CONVECTION, AND FINANCE

The wave equation conserves energy. The heat equation $u_t = u_{xx}$ dissipates energy. The starting conditions for the wave equation can be recovered by going backward in time. The starting conditions for the heat equation can never be recovered. Compare $u_t = cu_x$ with $u_t = u_{xx}$, and look for pure exponential solutions $u(x,t) = G(t)\, e^{ikx}$:

Wave equation: $\boldsymbol{G' = ickG}$ $\quad G(t) = e^{ickt}$ has $|G| = 1$ (conserving energy)

Heat equation: $\boldsymbol{G' = -k^2G}$ $\quad G(t) = e^{-k^2t}$ has $G < 1$ (dissipating energy)

Discontinuities are immediately smoothed out by the heat equation, since G is exponentially small when k is large. This section solves $u_t = u_{xx}$ first analytically and then by finite differences. The key to the analysis is the ***fundamental solution*** starting from a point source (delta function). We will show in equation (8) that this special solution is a bell-shaped curve that gets wider and shorter by $\sqrt{t}$:

$$\boldsymbol{u(x,t) = \frac{1}{\sqrt{4\pi t}}\, e^{-x^2/4t}} \text{ comes from the initial condition } u(x,0) = \delta(x)\,. \tag{1}$$

The convection-diffusion equation $u_t = cu_x + du_{xx}$ smooths a wave as it travels. This is an essential model for environmental and chemical engineering, when particles diffuse. The relative strength of convection by cu_x and diffusion by du_{xx} is given below by the Peclet number. To avoid oscillations, keep $c\,\Delta x < 2d$.

The **Black-Scholes equation** for option pricing comes from *Brownian motion* of stock prices. I hope you enjoy those pages at the end of this section.

For difference equations, explicit methods have strict stability conditions like $\Delta t \le \frac{1}{2}(\Delta x)^2$. This very short time step is much more expensive than $c\Delta t \le \Delta x$. **Implicit methods** avoid instability by computing the space difference $\Delta^2 U$ at the new time level $n+1$. This requires solving a linear system at each time step.

We can already see two major differences between the heat equation and the wave equation (and also one conservation law of $\int u\,dx$ that applies to both):

1. ***Infinite signal speed.*** The initial condition at a single point *immediately* affects the solution at all points. The effect far away is not large, because of the very small exponential $e^{-x^2/4t}$ in the fundamental solution. But it is not zero. (A wave produces no effect at all until the signal arrives, with speed c.)

2. ***Dissipation of energy.*** The energy $\frac{1}{2}\int (u(x,t))^2\,dx$ is a *decreasing* function of t. For proof, multiply the heat equation $u_t = u_{xx}$ by u. Integrate uu_{xx} by parts with $u(\infty) = u(-\infty) = 0$ to produce the integral of $-(u_x)^2$:

Energy decay
$$\frac{d}{dt}\int_{-\infty}^{\infty} \frac{1}{2}u^2\,dx = \int_{-\infty}^{\infty} uu_{xx}\,dx = -\int_{-\infty}^{\infty} (u_x)^2\,dx \le 0\,. \tag{2}$$

3. *Conservation of heat* (analogous to conservation of mass):

Heat is conserved $$\frac{d}{dt}\int_{-\infty}^{\infty} u(x,t)\,dx = \int_{-\infty}^{\infty} u_{xx}\,dx = \Big[u_x(x,t)\Big]_{x=-\infty}^{\infty} = 0\,. \tag{3}$$

Analytic Solution of the Heat Equation

Start with **separation of variables** to find solutions to the heat equation:

$\boldsymbol{u(x,t) = G(t)E(x)}$ $$\frac{\partial u}{\partial t} = \frac{\partial^2 u}{\partial x^2} \text{ gives } G'E = GE'' \text{ and } \frac{G'}{G} = \frac{E''}{E}\,. \tag{4}$$

The ratio G'/G depends only on t. The ratio E''/E depends only on x. Since equation (4) says they are equal, they must be constant. This produces a useful family of solutions to $u_t = u_{xx}$:

$$\frac{E''}{E} = \frac{G'}{G} \text{ is solved by } \boldsymbol{E(x) = e^{ikx}} \text{ and } \boldsymbol{G(t) = e^{-k^2 t}}\,.$$

Two x-derivatives produce the same $-k^2$ as a t-derivative. We are led to exponential solutions $e^{ikx}e^{-k^2t}$ and to their linear combinations (integrals over all k):

General solution $$\boldsymbol{u(x,t) = \frac{1}{2\pi}\int_{-\infty}^{\infty} \widehat{u}_0(k)e^{ikx}e^{-k^2t}\,dk.} \tag{5}$$

At $t = 0$, formula (5) recovers the initial condition $u(x,0)$ because it inverts the Fourier transform $\widehat{u}_0(k)$ (Section 4.5). So we have the analytical solution to the heat equation—not necessarily in an easily computable form! This form usually requires two integrals, one to find the transform $\widehat{u}_0(k)$ of the initial function $u(x,0)$, and the other integral to find the inverse transform of $\widehat{u}_0(k)e^{-k^2t}$ in (5).

Example 1 Suppose the initial function is a bell-shaped Gaussian $u(x,0) = e^{-x^2/2\sigma}$. Then the solution remains a Gaussian. The number σ that measures the width of the bell increases to $\sigma + 2t$ at time t, as heat spreads out. This is one of the few integrals involving e^{-x^2} that we could find exactly. But we don't have to do the integral.

That function $e^{-x^2/2\sigma}$ is the impulse response (fundamental solution) at time $t = 0$ to a delta function $\delta(x)$ that occurred earlier at $t = -\frac{1}{2}\sigma$. So the answer we want (at time t) is the result of starting from that $\delta(x)$ and going forward a total time $\frac{1}{2}\sigma + t$:

Widening Gaussian $$u(x,t) = \frac{\sqrt{\pi(2\sigma)}}{\sqrt{\pi(2\sigma + 4t)}}\, e^{-x^2/(2\sigma + 4t)}\,. \tag{6}$$

This has the right start at $t = 0$ and it satisfies the heat equation (just a time shift).

The Fundamental Solution

For a delta function $u(x,0)=\delta(x)$ at $t=0$, the Fourier transform is $\widehat{u}_0(k)=1$. Then the inverse transform in (5) produces $u(x,t)=\frac{1}{2\pi}\int e^{ikx}e^{-k^2t}\,dk$. One computation of this u uses a neat integration by parts for $\partial u/\partial x$. Three -1's will appear, from the integral of ke^{-k^2t} and the derivative of ie^{ikx} and integration by parts itself:

$$\frac{\partial u}{\partial x}=\frac{1}{2\pi}\int_{-\infty}^{\infty}(e^{-k^2t}k)(ie^{ikx})\,dk=-\frac{1}{4\pi t}\int_{-\infty}^{\infty}(e^{-k^2t})(xe^{ikx})\,dk=-\frac{xu}{2t}. \quad (7)$$

This linear equation $\partial u/\partial x=-xu/2t$ is solved by $u=c\,e^{-x^2/4t}$. The constant $c=1/\sqrt{4\pi t}$ is determined by the requirement $\int u(x,t)\,dx=1$. (This conserves the heat $\int u(x,0)\,dx=\int\delta(x)\,dx=1$ that we started with. It is the area under a bell-shaped curve.) The solution (1) for diffusion from a point source is confirmed:

Fundamental solution from $u(x,0)=\delta(x)$

$$u(x,t)=\frac{1}{\sqrt{4\pi t}}\,e^{-x^2/4t} \quad (8)$$

In two dimensions, we can separate x from y and solve $u_t=u_{xx}+u_{yy}$:

Fundamental solution from $u(x,y,0)=\delta(x)\delta(y)$

$$u(x,y,t)=\left(\frac{1}{\sqrt{4\pi t}}\right)^2 e^{-x^2/4t}\,e^{-y^2/4t}. \quad (9)$$

With patience you can verify that $u(x,t)$ and $u(x,y,t)$ do solve the 1D and 2D heat equations (Problem 1). The zero initial conditions away from $x=0$ are correct as $t\to 0$, because $e^{-x^2/4t}$ goes to zero much faster than $1/\sqrt{t}$ blows up. And since the total heat remains at $\int u\,dx=1$ or $\iint u\,dx\,dy=1$, we have a valid solution.

If the source is at another point $x=s$, then the response just shifts by s. The exponent becomes $-(x-s)^2/4t$ instead of $-x^2/4t$. If the initial $u(x,0)$ is a *combination* of delta functions, then by linearity the solution is the same combination of responses. But every $u(x,0)$ is an integral $\int\delta(x-s)\,u(s,0)\,ds$ of point sources! So the solution to $u_t=u_{xx}$ is an integral of the responses to $\delta(x-s)$. Those responses are fundamental solutions (*Green's functions*) starting from all points $x=s$:

Solution from any $u(x,0)$
Convolve with Green's fcn

$$u(x,t)=\frac{1}{\sqrt{4\pi t}}\int_{-\infty}^{\infty}u(s,0)\,e^{-(x-s)^2/4t}\,ds. \quad (10)$$

Now the formula is reduced to one infinite integral—but still not simple. And for a problem with boundary conditions at $x=0$ and $x=1$ (the temperature on a finite interval, much more realistic), we have to think again. There will also be changes for an equation $u_t=(c(x)u_x)_x$ with variable conductivity or diffusivity. This thinking probably leads us to finite differences.

Three important properties of $u(x,t)$ are immediate from formula (10):

1. *If $u(x,0) \geq 0$ for all x then $u(x,t) \geq 0$ for all x and t.* Nothing in the integral (10) will be negative.

2. *The solution is infinitely smooth.* The Fourier transform $\widehat{u}_0(k)$ in (5) is multiplied by e^{-k^2t}. In (10), we can take all the x and t derivatives we want.

3. *The scaling matches x^2 with t.* A diffusion constant D in the equation $u_t = Du_{xx}$ will lead to the same solution with t replaced by Dt, when we write the equation as $\partial u/\partial(Dt) = \partial^2 u/\partial x^2$. The fundamental solution has $e^{-x^2/4Dt}$ and its Fourier transform has e^{-Dk^2t}.

Example 2 Suppose the initial temperature is a *step function*. Then $u(x,0) = 0$ for negative x and $u(x,0) = 1$ for positive x. The discontinuity is smoothed out immediately, as heat flows to the left. The integral in formula (10) is zero up to the jump:

Starting from step function
$$u(x,t) = \frac{1}{\sqrt{4\pi t}} \int_0^\infty e^{-(x-s)^2/4t}\, ds. \tag{11}$$

No luck with this integral! We can find the area under a complete bell-shaped curve (or half the curve) but there is no elementary formula for the area under a piece of the curve. No elementary function has the derivative e^{-x^2}. That is unfortunate, since those integrals are *cumulative Gaussian probabilities* and statisticians need them all the time. So they have been normalized into the **error function** and tabulated to high accuracy:

Error function
$$\operatorname{erf}(x) = \frac{2}{\sqrt{\pi}} \int_0^x e^{-s^2}\, ds. \tag{12}$$

The integral from $-x$ to 0 is also $\operatorname{erf}(x)$. The normalization by $2/\sqrt{\pi}$ gives $\operatorname{erf}(\infty) = 1$.

We can produce this error function from the heat equation integral (11) by setting $S = (s-x)/\sqrt{4t}$. Then $s = 0$ changes to $S = -x/\sqrt{4t}$ as the lower limit on the integral, and $dS = ds/\sqrt{4t}$. The integral from 0 to ∞ is $\frac{1}{2}$, leaving $-x/\sqrt{4t}$ to 0:

$$u(x,t) = \frac{\sqrt{4t}}{\sqrt{4\pi t}} \int_{-x/\sqrt{4t}}^\infty e^{-S^2}\, dS = \frac{1}{2}\left(1 + \operatorname{erf}\left(\frac{x}{\sqrt{4t}}\right)\right). \tag{13}$$

The only temperature we know exactly is $u = \frac{1}{2}$ at $x = 0$, by left-right symmetry.

Outline The rest of this section discusses three equations in engineering and finance:

1. **Heat equation** (explicit methods need $\Delta t \leq C(\Delta x)^2$, implicit is stable)

2. **Convection-diffusion equation** (flow along streamlines, boundary layers for Peclet number >> 1). The *cell Peclet number* $c\,\Delta x/2d$ controls oscillations.

3. **Black-Scholes equation** (pricing of call options based on Brownian motion).

Explicit Finite Differences

The simplest finite differences are *forward* for $\partial u/\partial t$ and *centered* for $\partial^2 u/\partial x^2$:

$$\textbf{Explicit method} \quad \frac{\Delta_t U}{\Delta t} = \frac{\Delta_x^2 U}{(\Delta x)^2} \qquad \frac{U_{j,n+1} - U_{j,n}}{\Delta t} = \frac{U_{j+1,n} - 2U_{j,n} + U_{j-1,n}}{(\Delta x)^2}. \quad (14)$$

Each new value $U_{j,n+1}$ is given explicitly by $U_{j,n} + R(U_{j+1,n} - 2U_{j,n} + U_{j,n-1})$. The crucial ratio for the heat equation $u_t = u_{xx}$ is now $\boldsymbol{R = \Delta t/(\Delta x)^2}$.

We substitute $U_{j,n} = G^n e^{ikj\Delta x}$ to find the growth factor $G = G(k, \Delta t, \Delta x)$:

$$\textbf{One-step growth factor} \quad G = 1 + R(e^{ik\Delta x} - 2 + e^{-ik\Delta x}) = \boldsymbol{1 + 2R(\cos k\Delta x - 1)}. \quad (15)$$

G is real, just as the exact one-step factor $e^{-k^2\Delta t}$ is real. Stability requires $|G| \le 1$. Again the most dangerous case is when the cosine equals -1 at $k\Delta x = \pi$:

$$\textbf{Stability condition} \quad |G| = |1 - 4R| \le 1 \text{ which requires } \boldsymbol{R = \frac{\Delta t}{(\Delta x)^2} \le \frac{1}{2}}. \quad (16)$$

We might accept that small time step in nonlinear problems and use this simple method. The accuracy from forward Δ_t and centered Δ_x^2 is $|U - u| = O(\Delta t + (\Delta x)^2)$.

That explicit method is just "forward Euler" in time, and centered in space. Normally we expect to do better. Backward Euler is much more stable, and the trapezoidal method combines stability and extra accuracy. Those are coming next in equations (18) and (20).

In practice, we can improve all these single step methods to **multistep**. Complicated new codes are not required, when we call an ODE solver for the system of differential equations (continuous in time, discrete in space). There is one equation for every meshpoint $x = jh$:

$$\textbf{Method of Lines} \quad \frac{d\boldsymbol{U}}{dt} = \frac{\Delta_x^2 \boldsymbol{U}}{(\Delta x)^2} \qquad \frac{dU_j}{dt} = \frac{U_{j+1} - 2U_j + U_{j-1}}{(\Delta x)^2}. \quad (17)$$

This is a **stiff system**, because its matrix $-K$ (second difference matrix) has a large condition number. The ratio $\lambda_{\max}(K)/\lambda_{\min}(K)$ grows like $1/(\Delta x)^2$. When we choose a stiff solver like ode15s, this automatically maintains a suitable stepsize Δt: good.

Implicit Finite Differences

A fully implicit method for $u_t = u_{xx}$ computes $\Delta_x^2 U$ at the new time $(n+1)\Delta t$:

$$\textbf{Implicit} \quad \frac{\Delta_t U_n}{\Delta t} = \frac{\Delta_x^2 U_{n+1}}{(\Delta x)^2} \qquad \frac{U_{j,n+1} - U_{j,n}}{\Delta t} = \frac{U_{j+1,n+1} - 2U_{j,n+1} + U_{j-1,n+1}}{(\Delta x)^2}. \quad (18)$$

The accuracy is still first-order in time and second-order in space. But $R = \Delta t/(\Delta x)^2$ can be large. Stability is *unconditional*, with $0 < G \le 1$ for all k.

To find the implicit growth factor, substitute $U_{j,n} = G^n e^{ijk\Delta x}$ into (18). Canceling those terms leaves an extra G on the right side:

$$G = 1 + RG(e^{ik\Delta x} - 2 + e^{-ik\Delta x}) \quad \text{leads to} \quad G = \frac{1}{1 + 2R(1 - \cos k\Delta x)}. \tag{19}$$

The denominator is at least 1, which ensures that $0 < G \leq 1$. The time step is controlled by accuracy, because stability is no longer a problem.

There is a simple way to improve to second-order accuracy. *Center everything at step* $n + \frac{1}{2}$. Average an explicit $\Delta_x^2 U_n$ with an implicit $\Delta_x^2 U_{n+1}$. This produces the famous ***Crank-Nicolson method*** (like the trapezoidal rule):

Crank-Nicolson (Trapezoidal)
$$\frac{U_{j,n+1} - U_{j,n}}{\Delta t} = \frac{1}{2(\Delta x)^2}\left(\Delta_x^2 U_{j,n} + \Delta_x^2 U_{j,n+1}\right). \tag{20}$$

Now the growth factor G is found by substituting $U_{j,n} = G^n e^{ijk\Delta x}$ into (20):

Growth equation
$$\frac{G - 1}{\Delta t} = \frac{G + 1}{2(\Delta x)^2}(2\cos k\Delta x - 2). \tag{21}$$

Separate out the part involving G, write R for $\Delta t/(\Delta x)^2$, and cancel the 2's:

Unconditional stability
$$G = \frac{1 + R(\cos k\Delta x - 1)}{1 - R(\cos k\Delta x - 1)} \quad \text{has} \quad |G| \leq 1. \tag{22}$$

The numerator is smaller than the denominator, since $\cos k\Delta x \leq 1$. We do notice that $\cos k\Delta x = 1$ whenever $k\Delta x$ is a multiple of 2π. Then $G = 1$ at those frequencies, so Crank-Nicolson does not give the strict decay of the fully implicit method.

Weighting the implicit $\Delta_x^2 U_{n+1}$ by $a \geq \frac{1}{2}$, and the explicit $\Delta_x^2 U_n$ by $1 - a \leq \frac{1}{2}$, will give a whole range of unconditionally stable methods (Problem 7). But only the centered $a = \frac{1}{2}$ has second-order accuracy.

Finite Intervals with Boundary Conditions

We introduced the heat equation on the whole line $-\infty < x < \infty$. But a physical problem will be on a finite interval like $0 \leq x \leq 1$. We are back to Fourier series (not Fourier integrals) for $u(x,t)$. And second differences bring back the great matrices K and T and B that account for these fixed or free boundary conditions:

Absorbing boundary at $x = 0$: The temperature is held at $\boldsymbol{u(0,t) = 0}$.

Insulated boundary: No heat flows through the left boundary if $\boldsymbol{u_x(0,t) = 0}$.

If both boundaries are held at zero temperature, the solution will decay toward $u(x,t) = 0$. If the boundaries are insulated as in a freezer, the solution will approach $u(x,t) =$ *constant.* No heat can escape, and it is evenly distributed as $t \to \infty$. This case still has the conservation law $\int_0^1 u(x,t)\,dx = \text{constant}$.

Example 3 (Fourier series solution) We know that e^{ikx} multiplies e^{-k^2t} to give a solution of the heat equation. Then $u = e^{-k^2t}\sin kx$ is also a solution (combining $+k$ with $-k$). With $u(0,t) = u(1,t) = 0$, the only allowed frequencies are $k = n\pi$ (then $\sin n\pi x = 0$ at both ends $x = 0$ and $x = 1$). The complete solution is a combination:

Complete solution $$u(x,t) = \sum_{n=1}^{\infty} b_n\, e^{-n^2\pi^2 t} \sin n\pi x\,. \tag{23}$$

This example has codes and graphs of $u(x,t)$ on the cse website. The Fourier sine coefficients b_n are chosen to match $u(x,0) = \sum b_n \sin n\pi x$ at $t = 0$.

You can expect cosines to appear for insulated boundaries, where the slope (not the temperature) is zero. Fourier series give exact solutions to compare with finite difference solutions. For finite differences, *absorbing boundary conditions produce the matrix* K (not B or C). With $R = \Delta t/(\Delta x)^2$, the choice between explicit and implicit decides whether we have second differences $-KU$ at time level n or level $n+1$:

Explicit method	$U_{n+1} - U_n = -RKU_n$	(24)
Fully implicit	$U_{n+1} - U_n = -RKU_{n+1}$	(25)
Crank-Nicolson implicit	$U_{n+1} - U_n = -RK(U_n + U_{n+1})/2$	(26)

The explicit stability condition is again $R \le \frac{1}{2}$ (Problem 8). Both implicit methods are unconditionally stable (in theory). The reality test is to try them in practice.

An insulated boundary at $x = 0$ changes K to T. Two insulated boundaries produce the free-free matrix B. Periodic conditions will produce a circulant C. The fact that B and C are singular no longer stops the computations. In the implicit method $(I + RB)U_{n+1} = U_n$, the extra identity matrix makes $I + RB$ invertible.

The **two-dimensional heat equation** $u_t = u_{xx} + u_{yy}$ describes the temperature distribution in a plate. For a square plate with absorbing boundary conditions, K will change to $K2\text{D}$. Its bandwidth jumps from 1 (tridiagonal matrix K) to N (when meshpoints are ordered a row at a time). Each time step of the implicit method (25) is a linear system with matrix $I + R(K2\text{D})$. So implicit methods pay a heavy price per step for stability, to avoid the explicit restriction $\Delta t \le \frac{1}{4}(\Delta x)^2$.

Example 4 Start the heat equation from $u(x,y,0) = (\sin kx)(\sin \ell y)$. The exact solution $u(x,y,t)$ has growth factor $e^{-(k^2+\ell^2)t}$. Sampling at equally spaced points gives an eigenvector of the discrete problem $U_{n+1} = U_n - R\,(K2\text{D})\,U_n$:

$$U_n = G^n U_0 \;\text{ with }\; G = 1 - R(2 - 2\cos k\,\Delta x) - R(2 - 2\cos \ell\,\Delta y).$$

At the worst frequencies $k\,\Delta x = \ell\,\Delta y = \pi$, this is $G = 1 - 8R$. Stability needs $1 - 8R \ge -1$. So $R \le \frac{1}{4}$ is stable in two dimensions (and $R \le \frac{1}{6}$ in 3D).

Convection-Diffusion

Put a chemical into flowing water. It diffuses while it is carried along by the flow. A diffusion term u_{xx} or $u_{xx} + u_{yy}$ appears together with a convection term. This is the model for two of the most important differential equations in engineering:

Convection with diffusion Unsteady 1D and steady 2D	$u_t = cu_x + du_{xx}$	$-\epsilon(u_{xx}+u_{yy})+w\cdot\nabla u=f$	(27)

On the whole line $-\infty < x < \infty$, the flow and the diffusion don't interact. If the flow velocity is c and $h_t = d\,h_{xx}$, convection just carries along that diffusing solution h:

Diffusing traveling wave $$u(x,t) = h(x+ct,t). \tag{28}$$

Substituting into equation (27) confirms that this is the solution (correct at $t=0$):

Chain rule $$\frac{\partial u}{\partial t} = c\frac{\partial h}{\partial x} + \frac{\partial h}{\partial t} = c\frac{\partial h}{\partial x} + d\frac{\partial^2 h}{\partial x^2} = c\frac{\partial u}{\partial x} + d\frac{\partial^2 u}{\partial x^2}. \tag{29}$$

Exponentials also show this separation of convection e^{ikct} from diffusion e^{-dk^2t}:

Starting from e^{ikx} $$u(x,t) = e^{-dk^2t}\,e^{ik(x+ct)}. \tag{30}$$

Convection-diffusion is a terrific model problem, and the constants c and d clearly have different units. We take this small step into *dimensional analysis*:

Convection coefficient c: $\dfrac{\textbf{distance}}{\textbf{time}}$ Diffusion coefficient d: $\dfrac{\textbf{(distance)}^2}{\textbf{time}}$

Suppose L is a typical length scale in the problem. ***The Peclet number*** $\mathrm{Pe} = \boldsymbol{cL/d}$ is dimensionless. It measures the relative importance of convection and diffusion. This Peclet (properly Péclet) number corresponds to the *Reynolds number* for the Navier-Stokes equations in Section 6.7, where c depends on u.

The second problem $-\epsilon(u_{xx}+u_{yy}) + w_1u_x + w_2u_y = f(x,y)$ has a large Peclet number if $\epsilon << \|w\|$. Then diffusion is much less important than convection. This is a key model problem for environmental engineering, when pollution follows the wind velocity $w = (w_1, w_2)$ as it slowly diffuses. *As* $\epsilon \to 0$, *second derivatives disappear.* The elliptic equation for $u(x,y,\epsilon)$ becomes hyperbolic for the limiting $U(x,y,0)$.

Limit equation at $\epsilon = 0$	$w \cdot \operatorname{grad} U = w_1U_x + w_2U_y = f(x,y)$	(31)

The streamlines $s(x,y) =$ constant **are the wind curves with tangent** $w(x,y)$. The dot product $w \cdot \operatorname{grad} s$ is zero. Moving along a streamline $x(t), y(t)$, the limit equation (31) becomes an ordinary differential equation for U in the variable t:

Along the streamlines $$\frac{d}{dt}[U(x(t),y(t))] = \frac{\partial U}{\partial x}\frac{dx}{dt} + \frac{\partial U}{\partial y}\frac{dy}{dt} = (\operatorname{grad} U)\cdot w = f(x(t),y(t)).$$

Steep Gradients and Boundary Layers

The reduction to a first-order equation (31) seems to make the $\epsilon = 0$ problem simple. The smoke follows the wind. But there is a serious catch: The second-order equation (27) came with a boundary condition on u **at both ends of the streamline.** But the limit equation (31) determines U at one end from U at the other end.

When an equation goes from second order to first order, **we cannot expect to satisfy both of the original boundary conditions.** The simplest model is one-dimensional, when the limit equation is just $U' = 1$:

Second order	$-\epsilon u'' + u' = 1$ with $u(0) = 0 = u(1)$	**First order**	$U' = 1$ with $U(0) = 0$	(32)

Both equations have exact solutions. Notice that $u(1) = 0$ but $U(1) \neq 0$:

$u(x)$ has $\epsilon > 0$
$U(x)$ has $\epsilon = 0$

$$u(x) = x - \frac{e^{x/\epsilon} - 1}{e^{1/\epsilon} - 1} \quad \text{and} \quad U(x) = x. \tag{33}$$

The solutions stay together in Figure 6.13a as long as they can. Then the first solution drops quickly to reach $u(1) = 0$. That **boundary layer** is needed to match the outflow condition. The width of the boundary layer is $O(\epsilon)$, as Problem 12 confirms.

The jump between $\epsilon = 0$ and $\epsilon > 0$ is called a **singular** perturbation. A change in any coefficient from 1 to $1 + \epsilon$ is a **regular** perturbation (no layer).

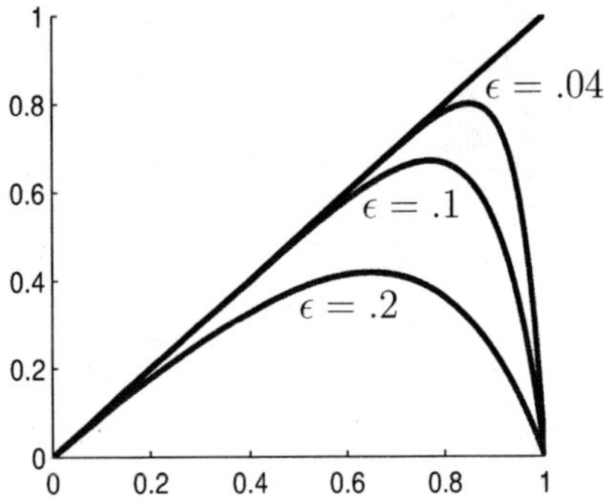

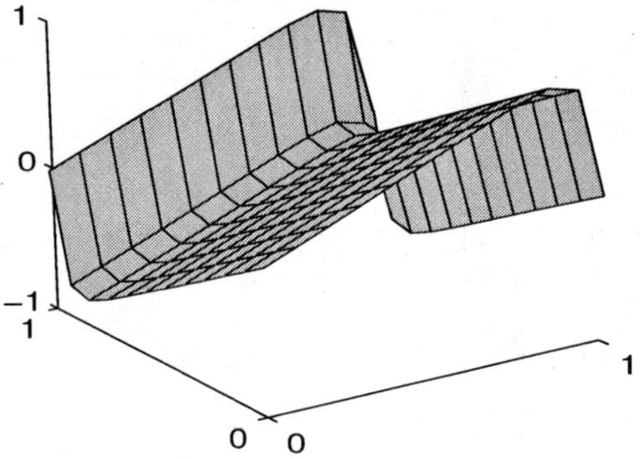

Figure 6.13: Boundary layers in 1D from (33) and in 2D from (35): small ϵ.

Example 5 Diagonal wind and no source in 2D: $-\epsilon(u_{xx} + u_{yy}) + u_x + u_y = 0$. The wind velocity is $w = (1, 1)$. The streamlines $x - y =$ constant go up at a $45°$ angle. The limit equation at $\epsilon = 0$ is $U_x + U_y = 0$. Around a square, the bottom and left sides are inflow boundaries (streamlines enter). The top and right sides have outflow:

$$\textbf{Inflow} \quad w \cdot n < 0 \qquad \textbf{Outflow} \quad w \cdot n > 0 \qquad \textbf{Characteristic} \quad w \cdot n = 0 \tag{34}$$

The unreduced and reduced equations ($U_x + U_y = 0$ for $\epsilon = 0$) have exact solutions:

$$u(x,y) = x - y - \frac{e^{x/\epsilon} - e^{y/\epsilon}}{e^{1/\epsilon} - 1} \qquad U(x,y) = x - y \tag{35}$$

That pair has $u \approx U$ at the inflow boundaries, where $x = 0$ or $y = 0$. The fractional term in $u(x,y)$ is very small. The outflow boundary has $x = 1$ or $y = 1$. Then the fraction increases quickly to give $u \approx 0$ at outflow. This is correct for u in the unreduced equation and it is wrong for U in the limit equation.

The vertical layers in Figure 6.13b show the difference $u - U$. At the upper corner $(x,y) = (1,1)$ the layer disappears and $u = U = 0$. That point is on a streamline from the characteristic inflow point $(x,y) = (0,0)$. Jumps in the inflow conditions will propagate along the streamlines (two rivers in parallel with slow diffusion between them).

Streamline diffusion helps to resolve steep layers parallel to the wind w [47, 98]. It is an extra diffusion $c(w_1\, u_{xx} + w_2\, u_{yy})$, produced by *changing the test functions*. This is the way to move finite element equations from centered toward upwind. The IFISS codes [48] add $cw \cdot \operatorname{grad} \phi$ to the test functions for streamline diffusion.

Finite Differences for Convection-Diffusion

In finite difference equations, the ratios $r = c\Delta t/\Delta x$ and $2R = 2d\Delta t/(\Delta x)^2$ are dimensionless. That is why the stability conditions $r \le 1$ and $2R \le 1$ were natural for the wave and heat equations. The new problem combines $c\, u_x$ with $d\, u_{xx}$ and the ***cell Peclet number P*** uses $\Delta x/2$ as the length scale L in $c\,L/d$:

Cell Peclet Number $$P = \frac{r}{2R} = \frac{c\,\Delta x}{2d} \tag{36}$$

We still don't have agreement on the best finite difference approximation to use! Here are three natural candidates (you may have an opinion after you try them):

1. **Forward in time,** *centered* **convection, centered explicit diffusion**

2. **Forward in time,** *upwind* **convection, centered explicit diffusion**

3. **Explicit convection** (*centered or upwind*), **with implicit diffusion.**

Each method will show the effects of r and R and P (*we replace $r/2$ by RP*):

1. Centered explicit $$\frac{U_{j,n+1} - U_{j,n}}{\Delta t} = c\,\frac{U_{j+1,n} - U_{j-1,n}}{2\Delta x} + d\,\frac{\Delta_x^2\, U_{j,n}}{(\Delta x)^2}\,. \tag{37}$$

Using R and P, every new value $U_{j,n+1}$ is a combination of three values at time n.

Explicit $$U_{j,n+1} = (\mathbf{1} - \mathbf{2R})U_{j,n} + (\boldsymbol{R} + \boldsymbol{RP})U_{j+1,n} + (\boldsymbol{R} - \boldsymbol{RP})U_{j-1,n}\,. \qquad (38)$$

Those three coefficients add to 1, and U = constant certainly solves equation (37). ***If all three coefficients are positive, the method is surely stable.*** More than that, *oscillations will not appear.* Positivity of $1 - 2R$ requires $\boldsymbol{R} \le \frac{1}{2}$, as usual for diffusion. Positivity of the other two coefficients requires $|\boldsymbol{P}| \le \mathbf{1}$. In avoiding numerical oscillations, cell sizes $\Delta x \le 2d/c$ are crucial to the quality of U.

Figure 6.14 from Strikwerda [146] shows the oscillations for $P > 1$. Notice how the initial hat function is smoothed and spread and shrunk by diffusion. The oscillations might pass the usual stability test $|G| \le 1$, but they are unacceptable.

$\boldsymbol{P_{\text{good}}} = \mathbf{0.7143}$
$\boldsymbol{P_{\text{bad}}} = \mathbf{50/3}$
$\boldsymbol{R + 2r} = \mathbf{0.3}$

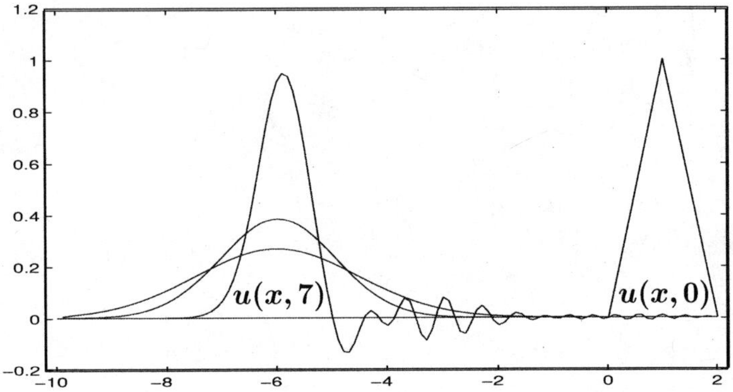

Figure 6.14: Convection-diffusion with and without numerical oscillations from $P > 1$.

2. Upwind convection if $c > 0$ $$\frac{U_{j,n+1} - U_{j,n}}{\Delta t} = c\,\frac{U_{j+1,n} - U_{j,n}}{\Delta x} + d\,\frac{\Delta_x^2 U_{j,n}}{(\Delta x)^2}\,. \qquad (39)$$

The one-sided accuracy has dropped to first order. But oscillations are eliminated whenever $r + 2R \le 1$. That condition ensures three positive coefficients in (39):

$$U_{j,n+1} = (\boldsymbol{r} + \boldsymbol{R})U_{j+1,n} + (\mathbf{1} - \boldsymbol{r} - \mathbf{2R})U_{j,n} + \boldsymbol{R}U_{j-1,n}\,. \qquad (40)$$

Arguments are still going, comparing the centered method and the upwind method. The difference between the two convection terms, **upwind minus centered**, is a diffusion term hidden in (39): this is an interesting identity!

Extra diffusion from upwind $$\frac{U_{j+1} - U_j}{\Delta x} - \frac{U_{j+1} - U_{j-1}}{2\Delta x} = \left(\frac{\Delta x}{2}\right)\frac{U_{j+1} - 2U_j + U_{j-1}}{(\Delta x)^2}\,. \qquad (41)$$

So the upwind method has this extra numerical diffusion or "***artificial viscosity.***" It is a non-physical damping and it reduces the accuracy. The upwind approximation is *distinctly below* the exact solution. Nobody is perfect.

3. Implicit diffusion $$\frac{U_{j,n+1} - U_{j,n}}{\Delta t} = c\,\frac{U_{j+1,n} - U_{j,n}}{\Delta x} + d\,\frac{\Delta_x^2 U_{j,n+1}}{(\Delta x)^2}\,. \qquad (42)$$

Again, the semidiscrete method of lines is an attractive option. The space discretization produces a system of ODE's to be solved without looking.

Stock Prices and Option Prices

The next pages are a guide to a small part of the mathematics of finance. This particular part deals with stock prices and the value of stock options. The whole subject of financial mathematics has grown explosively for two good reasons: the mathematics presents highly interesting problems, often new and difficult, and the applications can be extremely valuable to individuals and firms and countries.

The difficulty in the mathematics comes from the random and unpredictable nature of the market. We have to *model uncertainty*. Equations that describe fluctuating prices (including the price of money) will be **stochastic**. Those models will lead to *decisions*. If we are investors, we decide to buy or sell or hold. Central bankers decide to raise or lower rates. That choice is not simple, and creating a reliable price model on which to base the decision is not simple either.

The two parts are illustrated by the famous equations that model stock prices $S(t)$ (approximately of course) and option prices $V(S,t)$. Notice that S is an output from the stock price model and it is an input to the option price model:

Stochastic equation for stock price S	$dS/S = \sigma\, dW + \mu\, dt$	(43)
Black-Scholes equation for options	$V_t + \frac{1}{2}\sigma^2 S^2 V_{SS} = rV - rSV_S.$	(44)

Stock prices include a random term dW, representing a **Wiener process**. There is no "solution" in the ordinary sense. Every time we run the model, $S(t)$ is different. But this stochastic model for stock prices leads to a deterministic model (depending on the current value of S) for the option price V. We will derive (44) from (43).

The Black-Scholes equation is *parabolic* (with $\partial/\partial t$ and $\partial^2/\partial S^2$) like the heat equation. With constant volatility σ and interest rate r, the right change of variables actually produces $u_t = u_{xx}$. But the real importance of Black-Scholes is its wide application. Any *derivative security* whose value depends only on a primary security and time (S and t) will satisfy a form of this equation. The boundary conditions may be initial, or final, or internal at an unknown "free boundary."

Brownian Motion

The fascination and subtlety of stochastic equations is in the innocent term dW. The random function $W(t)$ has a highly irregular motion. Each $W(t)$ is continuous but it has no derivative dW/dt. The increment dW is **normally distributed with mean zero and variance dt**. Its standard deviation is $\sqrt{dt}$:

Brownian motion	$dW = Z\sqrt{dt}$	At each t, Z comes from $\boldsymbol{N}(0,1)$.	(45)

Every motion $W(t)$ is a **random walk**. The number $Z(t)$ is chosen randomly at each time instant from a standard normal distribution with unit variance:

Probability density $\dfrac{1}{\sqrt{2\pi}}e^{-Z^2/2}$ **Expectations** $\mathrm{E}[Z]=0$ and $\mathrm{E}[Z^2]=1$.

A Monte Carlo simulation constructs a discrete random walk at fixed times t_i:

$$\textbf{Discrete walk} \quad W(t_{i+1}) = W(t_i) + \sqrt{t_{i+1}-t_i}\; Z_{i+1} \quad \text{with} \quad W(0)=0 \qquad (46)$$

That square root instantly shows that this is no ordinary difference equation. **Those have Δt, but this has $\sqrt{\Delta t}$.** Those are not exact, while (46) leads to the exact joint (multivariate) distribution of the values $W(t_1),\ldots,W(t_n)$ of Brownian motion. Of course it says nothing about the wild oscillations in $W(t)$ between those times. If (46) is a random walk, then maybe (45) is a random run.

Lognormal Random Walk

The return on an investment is dS/S. When the rate of return is fixed at $dS/S=\mu\,dt$, the price has $S'=\mu S$ and exponential growth: $S(t)=S_0\,e^{\mu t}$. But stock prices respond to external effects. Those are modeled by the stochastic part $\sigma\,dW$. This produces Brownian motion multiplied by the **volatility** σ:

Lognormal random walk
Normal for log S
$$\frac{dS}{S} = \sigma\,dW + \mu\,dt. \qquad (47)$$

The "drift" is μ and the "diffusion" is σ^2. Notice the **Markov property**. Changes depend only on current prices, not earlier prices. The mean is $\mathrm{E}[dS]=\mu\,S\,dt+0$. The variance is all-important:

$$\textbf{Variance} \quad \mathrm{Var}\,[dS] = \mathrm{E}[(dS-\text{mean})^2] = \mathrm{E}[\sigma^2 S^2 (dW)^2] = \boldsymbol{\sigma^2\,S^2\,dt}. \qquad (48)$$

That expectation $\mathrm{E}[(dW)^2]=dt$ is the most remarkable and confusing equality in financial mathematics. It ruins Taylor series and it introduces **Ito's Lemma**.

The value $V(S,t)$ of a stock option will have a Taylor series expansion:

$$\textbf{Any smooth function } \boldsymbol{V(S,t)} \quad dV = \frac{\partial V}{\partial S}\,dS + \frac{\partial V}{\partial t}\,dt + \frac{1}{2}\frac{\partial^2 V}{\partial S^2}\,(dS)^2 + \cdots \qquad (49)$$

Squaring equation (47), the crucial point is that $(dW)^2$ is of order dt, not $(dt)^2$. The leading term is $(dS)^2=\sigma^2 S^2 dt$ as in (48). Substitute dS and $(dS)^2$ into (49):

$$\textbf{Ito's Lemma} \quad dV = \frac{\partial V}{\partial S}(\sigma\,S\,dW + \mu\,S\,dt) + \frac{\partial V}{\partial t}\,dt + \frac{1}{2}\frac{\partial^2 V}{\partial S^2}\,\sigma^2\,S^2\,dt. \qquad (50)$$

The lemma relates dV to dS, when dW is of order $\sqrt{dt}$. The outcome in (50) is that dV has a random component involving dW and a deterministic component from dt.

Example 6 Choose $V(s) = \log S$, so that $dV/dS = 1/S$ and $d^2V/dS^2 = -1/S^2$:

By Ito's Lemma $$d(\log S) = \sigma\, dW + \left(\mu - \tfrac{1}{2}\sigma^2\right) dt. \tag{51}$$

The sum of normal random variables is also normal. In the limit of a sum, the integral $(\log S - \log S_0)$ is normal with mean $(\mu - \frac{1}{2}\sigma^2)\,t$ and variance $\sigma^2 t$. So the exponent Q in the probability density functions of $\log S$ and S has a familiar form:

Normal for $\log S$	$e^{-Q}/\sigma\sqrt{2\pi t}$	$Q = \left(\log(S/S_0) - \left(\mu - \frac{1}{2}\sigma^2\right) t\right)^2 / 2\sigma^2 t$	(52)
Lognormal for S	$e^{-Q}/\sigma S\sqrt{2\pi t}$		

Stock Options: European Call

The simplest "vanilla option" among financial derivatives is the *European call.* It gives you the option to buy a stock at a fixed date T and a fixed price E (this is the strike price). You will exercise this option if and only if the stock price $S(T)$ at that time is greater than E. The call is "in the money" if $S > E$. So the value $V(S, t)$ of the call option is clearly known at the expiry date $t = T$:

Final value at $t = T$ $$V(S,T) = \max(S - E,\, 0). \tag{53}$$

This is the opposite of a **put**—an option to *sell* the stock is worth $\max(E - S,\, 0)$.

At any time t, the call option value V depends on the current price S and the remaining time $T - t$. It also depends on μ and σ, which describe the expected behavior of S over that time. V is never negative because you can walk away (you bought the option, not the stock). It took genius to derive a differential equation for $V(S, t)$ (even with assumptions that don't always hold). The Nobel Prize in Economics went to Robert Merton and Myron Scholes, after the death of Fischer Black.

The Black-Scholes Equation

The equation will give a value $V(S, t)$ for the call option. We assume continuous trading, no transaction costs, and no arbitrage possibilities. This means that all risk-free investments earn the same return r. The volatility σ is known (and here assumed constant). All these assumptions have been questioned, leading to refinements of the analysis. We follow [170] in deriving the Black-Scholes equation.

Construct a portfolio from the call option **minus** $\Delta = \partial V/\partial S$ **of the stock**:

Portfolio value $$P = V - \frac{\partial V}{\partial S}\, S \qquad dP = dV - \frac{\partial V}{\partial S}\, dS. \tag{54}$$

Ito's Lemma (50) and $dS = S(\mu\, dt + \sigma\, dW)$ give dP with **no stochastic part** $\boldsymbol{dW}$!

$$dP = \frac{\partial V}{\partial S}\,\sigma\, S\, dW + \left(\mu\, S\frac{\partial V}{\partial S} + \frac{\partial V}{\partial t} + \frac{1}{2}\sigma^2 S^2 \frac{\partial^2 V}{\partial S^2}\right) dt - \frac{\partial V}{\partial S}(\mu\, S\, dt + \sigma\, S\, dW). \tag{55}$$

That is a *risk-free* return $dP = \left(\partial V/\partial t + \frac{1}{2}\sigma^2 S^2 \partial^2 V/\partial S^2\right) dt$. This is deterministic. It must equal the return $r\,P\,dt$ from investing the same value P in any other riskless asset. *The absence of arbitrage equalizes all risk-free returns* (this is crucial in Black-Scholes analysis). So dP in (55) equals $r\,P\,dt$ with $P = V - S(\partial V/\partial S)$:

Black-Scholes equation
$$\frac{\partial V}{\partial t} + \frac{1}{2}\sigma^2 S^2 \frac{\partial^2 V}{\partial S^2} = rV - r\,S\,\frac{\partial V}{\partial S}. \tag{56}$$

At first sight, this is not obviously the heat equation $u_t = u_{xx}$. It is linear for V, but the coefficients depend on S. The second derivative V_{SS} has the wrong sign. That would be disaster for an initial-value problem, but we have a *final value.* Equation (56) goes *backward* in time from $V = \max(S-E, 0)$ at the expiry time T.

The variables S and t are replaced by $x = \log S$ and $\tau = \frac{1}{2}\sigma^2(T-t)$ in [170]. Then a scale change $u = e^{ax+b\tau}V$ produces the heat equation. The integral solution (10) yields a direct but complicated formula for $V(S,t)$. That option value is found in Maple as blackscholes(E, $T-t$, S, r, σ).

Note the importance of $\Delta = \partial V/\partial S$. This is the first of the "Greeks" that give derivatives (the sensitivities) of V. Delta correlates the option price V to the underlying stock price S. That number is the key to *hedging*, because the portfolio $P = V - S\Delta$ in (54) is "delta-neutral." A fully hedged investor will sell Δ of unowned stock (*short selling*), to eliminate the random component from dP.

Other sensitivities of the option value are given by other Greeks:

$$\textbf{Gamma}\quad \Gamma = \frac{\partial^2 V}{\partial S^2} \qquad \textbf{Theta}\quad \Theta = -\frac{\partial V}{\partial t} \qquad \textbf{Vega}\quad \frac{\partial V}{\partial \sigma} \qquad \textbf{Rho}\quad \rho = \frac{\partial V}{\partial r} \tag{57}$$

Calculating V and the Greeks is a fundamental problem of computational finance. With special assumptions and boundary conditions, exact formulas are possible. But the reality of market complications makes Black-Scholes a numerical problem. Both finite differences and *Monte Carlo simulation* are popular choices.

Like all sensitivities, the Greeks solve an adjoint problem (a dual problem). Section 8.7 offers a discussion of adjoint methods, and it emphasizes a computational tool that is not yet fully appreciated: *Automatic Differentiation.* The reverse mode of AD computes the key derivatives like $\Delta = \partial V/\partial S$ with great efficiency.

Problem Set 6.5

Problems 1-6 are about exact solutions of the heat equation.

1 Substitute $u(x,t) = e^{-x^2/4t}/\sqrt{4\pi t}$ into $u_t = u_{xx}$ to check that solution. How can you then verify that the $2D$ equation is solved by (9)?

2 Solve $u_t = u_{xx}$ starting from a combination $u(x,0) = \delta(x+1) - 2\delta(x) + \delta(x-1)$ of three delta functions. What is the total heat $\int u(x,t)\,dx$ at time t? Draw a graph of $u(x,1)$ by hand or by MATLAB.

3 Integrating the answer to Problem 2 gives another solution to the heat equation:

$$\text{Show that} \quad w(x,t) = \int_0^x u(X,t)\,dX \quad \text{solves} \quad w_t = w_{xx}\,.$$

Graph the initial function $w(x,0)$ and sketch the solution $w(x,1)$.

4 Integrating once more solves the heat equation $h_t = h_{xx}$ starting from $h(x,0) = \int w(X,0)\,dX =$ *hat function*. Draw the graph of $h(x,0)$. Figure 6.14 shows the graph of $h(x,t)$, shifted along by convection to $h(x+ct,t)$.

5 Another exact integral involving $e^{-x^2/4t}$ is

$$\int_0^\infty x\,e^{-x^2/4t}\,dx = \left[-2t\,e^{-x^2/4t}\right]_0^\infty = 2t\,.$$

From (10), show that the temperature is $u = \sqrt{t}$ at the center point $x = 0$ starting from a ramp $u(x,0) = \max(0,x)$.

6 A ramp is the integral of a step function. So the solution of $u_t = u_{xx}$ starting from a ramp (Problem 5) is the integral of the solution starting from a step function (Example 2 in the text). Then $\sqrt{t}$ must be the total amount of heat that has crossed from $x > 0$ to $x < 0$ in Example 2 by time t. Explain each of those three sentences.

7 For $u_t = u_{xx}$ combine implicit and explicit methods with weights a and $1-a$:

$$\frac{U_{j,n+1} - U_{j,n}}{\Delta t} = \frac{a\,\Delta_x^2 U_{j,n+1} + (1-a)\,\Delta_x^2 U_{j,n}}{(\Delta x)^2}\,.$$

Find the growth factor G by substituting $U_{j,n} = G^n e^{ijk\,\Delta x}$. *If* $a \geq \frac{1}{2}$ *show that* $|G| \leq 1$. If $a < \frac{1}{2}$ find the stability bound on $R = \Delta t/(\Delta x)^2$, probably at $k\,\Delta x = \pi$.

8 On a finite interval, the explicit method (24) is $U_{n+1} = (I - RK)U_n$. What are the eigenvalues G of $I - RK$? Show that $|G| \leq 1$ if $R = \Delta t/(\Delta x)^2 \leq 1/2$. Then show more: $U_{j,n+1}$ is a positive combination of $U_{j,n}$ and $U_{j-1,n}$ and $U_{j+1,n}$.

9 What rescaling of x and t and u will change $u_t = cu_x + du_{xx}$ into the dimensionless equation $U_T = U_X + U_{XX}/\text{Pe}$? The Peclet number is $\text{Pe} = cL/d$.

10 The n eigenvalues of the second difference matrix K are $\lambda_k = 2 - 2\cos\frac{k\pi}{n+1}$. The eigenvectors y_k in Section 1.5 are discrete samples of $\sin k\pi x$. Write the general solutions to the fully explicit and fully implicit equations (14) and (18) after N steps, as combinations of those discrete sines y_k times powers of λ_k.

11 In convection-diffusion, compare the condition $R \le \frac{1}{2}, P \le 1$ (for positive coefficients in the centered method) with $r + 2R \le 1$ (for the upwind method). For which c and d is the upwind condition less restrictive, in avoiding oscillations?

12 The width of the boundary layer in $u(x) = x - (e^{x/\epsilon} - 1)/(e^{1/\epsilon} - 1)$ is $O(\epsilon)$. Evaluate $u(1-\epsilon)$ to see that the solution has started its drop to $u(1) = 0$.

13 In Brownian motion, computing the covariance of $W(s)$ and $W(t)$ for $s < t$ uses the fact that the step $W(t) - W(s)$ is independent of $W(s)$ (and mean zero):

$$\mathrm{E}\,[W(s)W(t)] = \mathrm{E}\,[W(s)^2] + \mathrm{E}\,[W(s)(W(t) - W(s))] = s + 0 = s.$$

Then the covariance matrix for $W = (W(t_1), \ldots, W(t_n)$ is $\Sigma_{ij} = \min(t_i, t_j)$. Write down Σ for $t_i = 1, 2, 3$ and also $t_i = 1, 5, 14$ and factor into $\Sigma = A^{\mathrm{T}}A$. I believe that A^{-1} is bidiagonal and Σ^{-1} is tridiagonal.

14 Verify that $A^{\mathrm{T}}A = \Sigma$ if $\Sigma_{ij} = \min(t_i, t_j)$ for increasing times $t = t_1, \ldots, t_n$:

$$A = \mathsf{chol}(\Sigma) = \begin{bmatrix} \sqrt{t_1} & \sqrt{t_1} & \cdot & \sqrt{t_1} \\ 0 & \sqrt{t_2 - t_1} & \cdot & \sqrt{t_2 - t_1} \\ 0 & 0 & \cdot & \cdot \\ 0 & 0 & 0 & \sqrt{t_n - t_{n-1}} \end{bmatrix}$$

For $t = 1, 2, \ldots, n$
$A =$ sum matrix
$A^{-1} =$ first difference
$\Sigma^{-1} =$ second difference

15 The Brownian random walk (46) is the matrix-vector multiplication $W = A^{\mathrm{T}}Z$. The components $Z_1, \ldots, Z_n$ are independent Gaussians from $\boldsymbol{N}(0,1)$. This multiplication $A^{\mathrm{T}}Z$ looks like $O(n^2)$ but the walk only needs $O(n)$ operations. Show how this is possible by computing the bidiagonal inverse matrix A^{-1}.

16 In a Brownian Bridge, when the future $W_{n+1} = 1$ is fixed, the covariance matrix of $W_1, \ldots, W_n$ changes to $\Sigma = K_n^{-1}/n$. What are the eigenvalues λ_k and eigenvectors y_k of Σ^{-1}? Giles observed that the FFT will quickly execute the sums W of $Z_k\sqrt{\lambda_k}\, y_k$ in Principal Component Analysis [62].

17 The **reaction-diffusion equation** $u_t = \epsilon u_{xx} + u - u^3$ has steady states $u = 1, u = 0, u = -1$. But $u = 0$ is unstable, since a perturbation $u = \epsilon v$ has $v_t = v$ and $v \approx e^t$. Show how $u = 1 + \epsilon V$ leads to $V_t = -2V$ ($u = 1$ is stable). Solve by finite differences from $u(x,0) = x + \sin \pi x$ with $u(0,t) = 0$ and $u(1,t) = 1$, to see $u(x,t)$ flatten out toward 1 and -1. (Convection-diffusion-***reaction*** is on the cse website, for $b_t = d\Delta b - \nabla \cdot (b\nabla c)$, $c_t = D\Delta c - bc$.

6.6 NONLINEAR FLOW AND CONSERVATION LAWS

Nature is nonlinear. The coefficients in the equation *depend on the solution* u. In place of $u_t = c\,u_x$ we will study $u_t + uu_x = 0$ and more generally $u_t + f(u)_x = 0$. These are "conservation laws" and the conserved quantity is the integral of u.

The first part of this book emphasized the **balance equation**: forces balance and currents balance. For steady flow this was Kirchhoff's Current Law: flow in equals flow out. Now the flow is *unsteady*, changing with t. Within any control volume the mass or the energy is changing. So a new $\partial/\partial t$ term will enter the conservation law.

There is flux through the boundaries. **The rate of change of mass inside a region equals the incoming flux.** For any interval $[a, b]$, that is the flux entering at $x = a$ minus the flux $f(u(b,t))$ leaving at $x = b$. The "mass inside" is $\int_a^b u(x,t)\,dx$:

Conservation law Integral form

$$\frac{d}{dt}\int_a^b u(x,t)\,dx = \boldsymbol{f(u(a,t)) - f(u(b,t))}\,. \tag{1}$$

The integral form is fundamental. We can get a differential form by allowing b to approach a. Suppose $b - a = \Delta x$. If $u(x,t)$ is a smooth function, its integral over a distance Δx will have leading term $\Delta x\, u(a,t)$. So if we divide equation (1) by Δx, the limit as Δx approaches zero is $\partial u/\partial t = -\partial f(u)/\partial x$ at the typical point a:

Conservation law Differential form

$$\frac{\partial u}{\partial t} + \frac{\partial}{\partial x} f(u) = \frac{\partial u}{\partial t} + f'(u)\frac{\partial u}{\partial x} = 0\,. \tag{2}$$

In applications, u can be a density of cars along a highway. The integral of u gives the number of cars between a and b. This number changes with time, as cars flow in at point a and out at point b. The traffic flux f is **density u times velocity v.**

Example 1 **Convection equation** Fluid temperature $T(x,t)$, thermal energy $\int T dx$

If the fluid velocity is c, the energy flux is $f(T) = cT$. The heat capacity per unit length has been normalized to 1. The energy balance has two forms (linear equations):

Integral form $\displaystyle \frac{d}{dt}\int_a^b T\,dx = -[cT]_a^b$ **Differential form** $\displaystyle \frac{\partial T}{\partial t} + \frac{\partial}{\partial x}(cT) = 0$ (3)

Example 2 **Diffusion equation** Now the heat flux is due to a temperature difference. The flux is $-k\,dT/dx$, from higher to lower temperature ($k =$ thermal conductivity):

Integral form $\displaystyle \frac{d}{dt}\int_a^b T\,dx = \left[k\frac{\partial T}{\partial x}\right]_a^b$ **Differential form** $\displaystyle \frac{\partial T}{\partial t} = \frac{\partial}{\partial x}\left(k\frac{\partial T}{\partial x}\right)$ (4)

In these examples, the velocity c and conductivity k can depend on the temperature T. Then the equations (**these are conservation laws**) become nonlinear.

Note also: The integral form could be converted by calculus to an integral only.

$$\frac{d}{dt}\int_a^b T\,dx = -[cT]_a^b \text{ is the same as } \int_a^b \left[\frac{\partial T}{\partial t} + \frac{\partial}{\partial x}(cT)\right] dx = 0 \text{ for all } [a,b]. \quad (5)$$

The last expression in brackets must be zero, which is the differential form.

That approach doesn't involve the step with Δx. In two dimensions the step to (5) would use the Divergence Theorem: flux out equals integral of divergence inside. The convection equation would become $\partial T/\partial t + \operatorname{div}(cT) = 0$.

For diffusion in 2D, $\partial T/\partial x$ becomes grad T. Flux through the boundary comes from the divergence inside. Then $\partial/\partial x\,(k\,\partial T/\partial x)$ in Example 2 becomes div $(k$ grad $T)$. This equals $\partial T/\partial t$, with boundary conditions on T:

1. *Dirichlet condition* to specify the boundary temperature T

2. *Neumann condition* for an insulated boundary (adiabatic condition):

   No heat flux $\quad -k\dfrac{\partial T}{\partial x} = 0 \quad$ or $\quad -k \text{ grad } T = 0$

3. *Black-body radiation condition* $\quad -k\dfrac{\partial T}{\partial x} = CT^4.$

Example 4 will include melting. Example 6 has combustion. Example 5 will be a **system of conservation laws** for mass, momentum, and energy in gas dynamics. The outstanding example is *Burgers' equation* $u_t = -uu_x$, which we discuss and solve.

First comes the overall picture of numerical methods for conservation laws.

Three Challenging Goals

Optimally, an algorithm for conservation laws $u_t = -f(u)_x$ would achieve three goals:

1. High accuracy (at least second order)
2. Geometric flexibility (irregular and unstructured meshes)
3. Numerical stability (even when convection dominates diffusion)

The methods in this section can meet two of those tests, but perhaps not all three. It is valuable to see in advance where each one falls short:

I. Finite volume methods don't have high accuracy.

II. Finite difference methods have difficulty with general meshes.

III. Finite element methods are marginally stable (Gibbs-type oscillations).

Those are challenges, not criticisms. Each method is contributing to nonlinear analysis, and has some way of compensating for its one-part weakness. All three methods continue to develop, and at the same time new ideas are proposed and tested.

We mention two proposals that in principle can pass all our tests (but the fourth requirement of *computational efficiency* is a constant challenge to everybody):

IV. Spectral methods (often in the form of "mortared" finite elements)

V. Discontinuous Galerkin (different polynomials within each element)

That list is almost a rough guide to conferences on computational engineering. Look for accuracies $p > 10$ in spectral methods and $p > 4$ in DG methods. For stability, finite volume methods can add diffusion. Finite differences can use upwinding.

This section will explain how $p = 2$ has been attained *without oscillation at shocks*. Nonlinear smoothers are added to Lax-Wendroff (I think only nonlinear terms can truly defeat Gibbs). Do not underestimate that achievement. Second order accuracy is the big step forward, and oscillation was once thought to be unavoidable.

Burgers' Equation and Characteristics

The outstanding example, together with traffic flow, is **Burgers' equation with flux** $\boldsymbol{f(u) = \frac{1}{2}u^2}$. The "inviscid" equation has no viscosity νu_{xx} to prevent shocks:

Inviscid Burgers' equation
$$\frac{\partial u}{\partial t} + \frac{\partial}{\partial x}\left(\frac{u^2}{2}\right) = \frac{\partial u}{\partial t} + u\frac{\partial u}{\partial x} = 0\,. \tag{6}$$

We will approach this conservation law in three ways:

1. By following characteristics until they separate or collide (trouble arrives)
2. By an exact formula (17), which is possible in one space dimension
3. By finite difference and finite volume methods, which are the practical choice.

A fourth (good) way adds νu_{xx}. The limiting u as $\nu \to 0$ is the **viscosity solution**.

Start with the linear equation $u_t = c\,u_x$ and $u(x,t) = u(x+ct, 0)$. The initial value at x_0 is carried along the characteristic line $x + ct = x_0$. Those lines are parallel when the velocity c is a constant. No chance that characteristic lines will meet.

The conservation law $\boldsymbol{u_t + u\,u_x = 0}$ will be solved by $u(x,t) = u(x - ut, 0)$. Every initial value $u_0 = u(x_0, 0)$ is carried along a characteristic line $\boldsymbol{x - u_0 t = x_0}$. Those lines are *not parallel* because their slopes depend on the initial value u_0. For the conservation law $u_t + f(u)_x = 0$, the characteristic lines are $x - f'(u_0)t = x_0$.

Example 3 The formula $\boldsymbol{u(x,t) = u(x - ut, 0)}$ involves u on both sides. It gives the solution "implicitly." If $u(x,0) = 1 - x$ at the start, the formula must be solved for u:

Solution $\boldsymbol{u} = 1 - (\boldsymbol{x - ut})$ gives $(1-t)u = 1 - x$ and $\boldsymbol{u = \dfrac{1-x}{1-t}}$. (7)

This u solves Burgers' equation, since $u_t = (1-x)/(1-t)^2$ is equal to $-uu_x$.

When characteristic lines have different slopes, they can meet (*carrying different* u_0). In this extreme example, all lines $x-(1-x_0)t = x_0$ meet at the same point $x = 1,\ t = 1$. The solution $u = (1-x)/(1-t)$ becomes $0/0$ at that point. Beyond their meeting point, the characteristics cannot decide $u(x,t)$.

A more fundamental example is the **Riemann problem**, which starts from two constant values $u = A$ and $u = B$. Everything depends on whether $A > B$ or $A < B$. On the left side of Figure 6.15, with $A > B$, *the characteristics meet.* On the right side, with $A < B$, *the characteristics separate.* In both cases, we don't have a single characteristic through each point that is safely carrying one correct initial value. This Riemann problem has *two* characteristics through some points, or *none*:

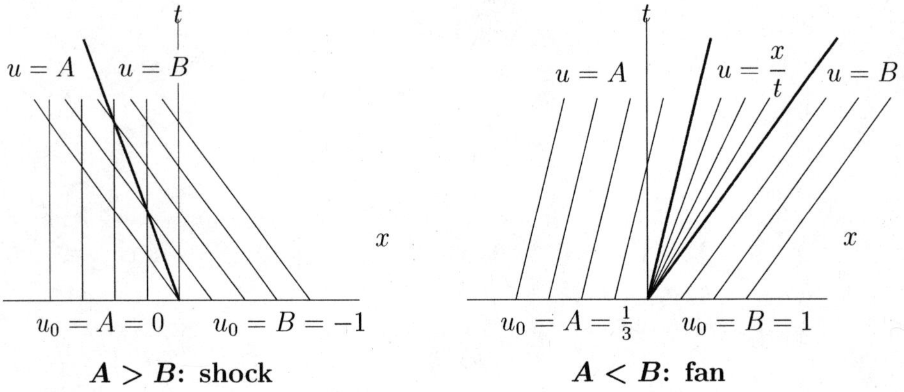

Figure 6.15: A shock when characteristics meet, a fan when they separate.

Shock	Characteristics *collide*	(light goes red: speed drops from 60 to 0)
Fan	Characteristics *separate*	(light goes green: speed up from 0 to 60)

The Riemann problem is how to connect 60 with 0, when the characteristics don't give the answer. A shock will be sharp braking. Drivers only see the car ahead in this model. A fan will be gradual acceleration, as the cars speed up and spread out.

Shocks

After trouble arrives, the *integral form* will guide the choice of the correct solution u. Suppose u has different values u_L and u_R at points $a = x_L$ and $b = x_R$ on the left and right sides, close to the shock. Equation (1) decides where the jump must occur:

Integral form
$$\frac{d}{dt}\int_{x_L}^{x_R} u(x,t)\,dx + f(u_R) - f(u_L) = 0\,. \tag{8}$$

Suppose the position of the shock is $x = X(t)$. Integrate from x_L to X to x_R. The values of $u(x,t)$ inside the integral are close to the constants u_L and u_R:

Left side x_L, u_L
Right side x_R, u_R
$$\frac{d}{dt}\big[(X - x_L)\,u_L + (x_R - X)\,u_R\big] + f(u_R) - f(u_L) \approx 0\,. \tag{9}$$

This connects the speed $s = dX/dt$ of the shock curve to the jumps in u and $f(u)$. Equation (9) says that $s\,u_L - s\,u_R + f(u_R) - f(u_L) = 0$:

Jump condition $\quad$ **Shock speed** $$\boldsymbol{s = \frac{f(u_R) - f(u_L)}{u_R - u_L} = \frac{[\,f\,]}{[\,u\,]}}. \qquad (10)$$

For the Riemann problem, the left and right values u_L and u_R will be constants A and B. The shock speed s is the ratio between the jump $[\,f\,] = f(B) - f(A)$ and the jump $[\,u\,] = B - A$. Since this ratio gives a constant slope, the shock line is straight.

For other problems, the characteristics will carry varying values of u into the shock. So the shock speed s is not constant in (10) and the shock line is curved.

The shock gives the solution when characteristics collide ($A > B$). With $f(u) = \frac{1}{2}u^2$ in Burgers' equation, the shock speed stays halfway between u_L and u_R:

Burgers' equation $\quad$ Shock speed $$s = \frac{1}{2}\frac{u_R^2 - u_L^2}{u_R - u_L} = \frac{1}{2}(u_R + u_L). \qquad (11)$$

The Riemann problem has $u_L = A$ and $u_R = B$. Then s is their average. Figure 6.15 shows how the integral form is solved by the correct placement of the shock.

Fans and Traffic Flow

You might expect the picture to flip over when $A < B$. *Wrong.* The equation is satisfied by a shock, but it is also satisfied by a **fan** (an expansion wave).

The choice between shock and fan is made by the "**entropy condition**." *Characteristics must go into a shock.* They don't come out of it. The wave speed $f'(u)$ must be faster than the shock speed s on the left, and slower than s on the right:

Entropy condition for shocks $$f'(u_L) > s > f'(u_R) \qquad (12)$$

Otherwise a fan in $u_t = -u\,u_x$ $$u = \frac{x}{t} \quad \text{for} \quad At < x < Bt. \qquad (13)$$

Since Burgers' equation has $f'(u) = u$, it only has shocks when u_L is larger than u_R. Otherwise the smaller value $u_L = A$ has to be connected to $u_R = B$ by a fan.

In traffic flow, the velocity $v(u)$ *decreases* as the density u increases. A reasonable model is linear between $v_{\max}$ at zero density and $v = 0$ at maximum density $u_{\max}$. The traffic flux $f(u)$ is a parabola opening down (opposite to $u^2/2$ for Burgers):

Velocity $v(u)$
Flux $f(u) = u\,v(u)$
$$v(u) = v_{\max}\left(1 - \frac{u}{u_{\max}}\right) \quad \text{and} \quad f(u) = v_{\max}\left(u - \frac{u^2}{u_{\max}}\right).$$

Maximum flux for a single lane has been measured at $f = 1600$ vehicles per hour, when the density is $u = 80$ vehicles per mile (50 per kilometer). This highest flow rate has velocity $v = f/u = 20$ miles per hour! Small comfort for a fast driver, but a steady speed is better than braking and accelerating from shocks and fans. This traffic crawl happens when a short green light doesn't let the shock through.

Problems 2 and 3 compute the density $u(x,t)$ when a light goes red (a shock travels backward) and when a light goes green (a fan moves forward). Please look at Figure 6.19. The vehicle trajectories are entirely different from the characteristics.

Solution From a Point Source

Let me comment on three nonlinear equations. They are terrific models, quite special because each one has an exact solution formula—even with the nonlinearity uu_x:

Conservation law	$u_t + u\,u_x = \mathbf{0}$
Burgers with viscosity	$u_t + u\,u_x = \boldsymbol{\nu\, u_{xx}}$
Korteweg - deVries	$u_t + u\,u_x = \boldsymbol{-u_{xxx}}$

The conservation law can develop shocks. This won't happen in the second equation because the u_{xx} viscosity term stops it. That term stays small when the solution is smooth, but u_{xx} prevents breaking when the wave gets steep. So does u_{xxx} in KdV.

To start the conservation law, I will pick a point source $\delta(x)$. We can guess a solution, and check the jump condition and the entropy condition at the shocks. Then we find an exact formula when $\nu\, u_{xx}$ is included, by a neat change of variables that produces $h_t = \nu\, h_{xx}$. When $\nu \to 0$, the limit correctly solves $u_t + u\,u_x = 0$.

Solution with $u(x,0) = \delta(x)$ When $u(x,0)$ jumps upward, we expect a fan. When it drops, we expect a shock. The delta function is an extreme case (very big jumps, very close together). A shock curve $x = X(t)$ sits right at the front of a fan.

Expected solution
Fan ends in shock

$$u(x,t) = \frac{x}{t} \quad \text{for } 0 \le x \le X(t); \quad \text{otherwise } u = 0. \qquad (14)$$

The total mass at the start is $\int \delta(x)\,dx = 1$. The integral of $u(x,t)$ over all x never changes, by the conservation law. Already that locates the shock position $X(t)$:

$$\text{Mass at time } t = \int_0^X \frac{x}{t}\,dx = \frac{X^2}{2t} = 1. \qquad \textbf{The shock is at } \boldsymbol{X(t) = \sqrt{2t}}\,. \qquad (15)$$

Does the drop at X, from $u = X/t = \sqrt{2t}/t$ to $u = 0$, satisfy the jump condition?

$$\text{Shock speed } s = \frac{dX}{dt} = \frac{\sqrt{2}}{2\sqrt{t}} \qquad \text{equals} \qquad \frac{\text{Jump } [\,u^2/2\,]}{\text{Jump } [\,u\,]} = \frac{X^2/2t^2}{X/t} = \frac{X}{2t} = \frac{\sqrt{2t}}{2t}\,.$$

The entropy condition $u_L > s > u_R = 0$ is also satisfied. The solution (14) looks good. It *is* good, but because of the delta function we check the answer another way.

A Solution Formula for Burgers' Equation

We begin with $u_t + u\,u_x = \nu\,u_{xx}$, and solve that equation exactly. If $u(x)$ is $\partial U/\partial x$, then integrating our equation gives $\boldsymbol{U_t + \frac{1}{2}U_x^2 = \nu\,U_{xx}}$. The great change of variables $U = -2\nu \log h$ produces the *linear* heat equation $\boldsymbol{h_t = \nu\,h_{xx}}$ (Problem 7).

The initial value is now $h(x,0) = e^{-U_0(x)/2\nu}$. Section 6.5 solved the heat equation $u_t = u_{xx}$ starting from any function $h(x,0)$. We just change t to νt:

$$\boldsymbol{U}_{\textsf{exact}} = -2\nu \log h(x,t) = -2\nu \log\left[\frac{1}{\sqrt{4\pi\nu t}}\int_{-\infty}^{\infty} e^{-U_0(y)/2\nu}e^{-(x-y)^2/4\nu t}\,dy\right]. \quad (16)$$

It doesn't look easy to let $\nu \to 0$, but it can be done. The exponentials combine into $e^{-B(x,y)/2\nu}$. This is largest when B is smallest. An asymptotic method called "steepest descent" shows that as $\nu \to 0$, the bracketed quantity in (16) approaches $c\,e^{-B_{\textsf{min}}/2\nu}$. Taking its logarithm and multiplying by -2ν, we approach $U = B_{\textsf{min}}$:

Solution at $\nu = 0$ $\boldsymbol{u(x,t) = \partial U/\partial x}$	$U(x,t) = B_{\textsf{min}} = \min\limits_{y}\left[U_0(y) + \dfrac{1}{2t}(x-y)^2\right].$	(17)

This is the solution formula for $U_t + \frac{1}{2}U_x^2 = 0$. Its derivative $u = \partial U/\partial x$ solves the conservation law $u_t + u\,u_x = 0$. By including the viscosity $\nu\,u_{xx}$ with $\nu \to 0$, we are finding the $u(x,t)$ that satisfies the jump condition and the entropy condition.

Point source again Starting from $u(x,0) = \delta(x)$, the integral $U_0(x)$ jumps from 0 to 1. The minimum of B in brackets occurs at $y = x$ or at $y = 0$. Check each case:

$$U(x,t) = B_{\textsf{min}} = \min_{y}\left[\begin{matrix} 0 & (y \le 0) \\ 1 & (y > 0)\end{matrix} + \frac{(x-y)^2}{2t}\right] = \begin{cases} \boldsymbol{0} & \text{for } x \le 0 \\ \boldsymbol{x^2/2t} & \text{for } 0 \le x \le \sqrt{2t} \\ \boldsymbol{1} & \text{for } x \ge \sqrt{2t} \end{cases}$$

The derivative $\partial U/\partial x$ is $\boldsymbol{u = 0}$ then $\boldsymbol{x/t}$ then $\boldsymbol{0}$. This agrees with equation (14). A fan x/t rises from 0. The fan ends in a shock that drops back to 0 at $x = \sqrt{2t}$.

Three Examples of Nonlinear Conservation Laws

Example 4 The melting of ice (**Stefan problem**) becomes a conservation law for energy.

Change in thermal energy E equals heat flux. Giles showed how to express this Stefan problem as a conservation law. The position x_f of the "free boundary" in Figure 6.16 is an important part of the problem. That is the melting point of the ice.

Integral form	$\dfrac{d}{dt}\displaystyle\int_a^x E\,dx = -\left[c\,\dfrac{\partial T}{\partial x}\right]_a^x$	**Differential form**	$\dfrac{\partial E}{\partial t} = \dfrac{\partial}{\partial x}\left(c(E)\,\dfrac{\partial T(E)}{\partial x}\right)$	(18)

Take $T = 0$ as the melting temperature. Express $T(E)$ using the specific heats $h_{\textsf{ice}}$ and $h_{\textsf{water}}$ per unit volume. The conductance $c(E)$ involves $c_{\textsf{ice}}$ and $c_{\textsf{water}}$. Allow an interval of "numerical slush" at the free boundary, normally containing just one meshpoint.

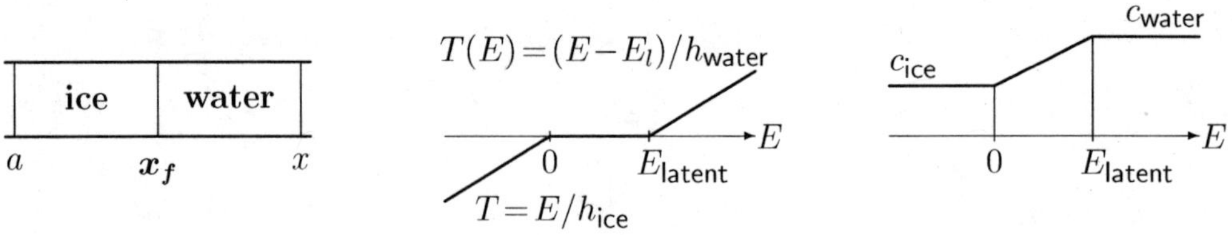

Figure 6.16: The Stefan problem has an unknown boundary x_f at the melting point.

Example 5 The Euler equations for gas dynamics in 3D (compressible, no viscosity)

The five unknowns are the density ρ, the velocity $v = (v_1, v_2, v_3)$, and the pressure p. All five depend on x, y, z and t. Five independent quantities are conserved [113]:

Conservation of mass $$\frac{\partial \rho}{\partial t} + \sum \frac{\partial}{\partial x_j}(\rho v_j) = 0 \tag{19}$$

Conservation of momentum $$\frac{\partial}{\partial t}(\rho v_i) + \sum \frac{\partial}{\partial x_j}(\rho v_i v_j + \delta_{ij} p) = 0 \tag{20}$$

Conservation of energy $$\frac{\partial}{\partial t}(\rho E) + \sum \frac{\partial}{\partial x_j}(\rho E v_j + p v_j) = 0 \tag{21}$$

The total energy E is the sum of kinetic energy $\frac{1}{2}(v_1^2 + v_2^2 + v_3^2)$ and internal energy e. For an ideal gas, a constant $\gamma > 1$ connects e to the temperature and entropy:

Internal energy $e = \dfrac{T}{\gamma - 1}$ **Temperature** $T = \dfrac{p}{\rho}$ **Entropy** $e^S = p e^{-\gamma}$

For small disturbances, we could linearize the gas dynamics equations near a fixed solution and reach the wave equation. The main point here is that those nonlinear Euler equations give a system of conservation laws (and the wave equation does too):

Wave equation $u_{tt} = u_{xx}$
Two conservation laws $$\frac{\partial}{\partial t}\begin{bmatrix} u_x \\ u_t \end{bmatrix} = \frac{\partial}{\partial x}\begin{bmatrix} u_t \\ u_x \end{bmatrix} \tag{22}$$

Example 6 **Combustion and reaction and detonation** (in car engines or explosions)

A chemical reaction (burning) produces a truly difficult nonlinear equation. If Z is the mass fraction of unburnt gas, a sixth conservation law accounts for combustion:

Continuum chemistry $$\frac{\partial}{\partial t}(\rho Z) + \sum \frac{\partial}{\partial x_j}(\rho Z v_j) = -\rho k e^{-E/RT} Z \tag{23}$$

The burnt fraction $1 - Z$ contributes to the internal energy e in the fifth conservation law by $e = Z e_u + (1 - Z) e_b$. We now have source terms on the right side of (23).

That reaction variable Z tells us the state of combustion (there is plenty of energy e_b in the burnt gas). In an automobile engine, shock waves give "knocking" and damage the engine. Combustion is a huge challenge to designers and to computational science.

Example 7 Two-phase flow (oil and water) in a porous medium.

The equation for the water fraction $u(x,t)$ can be written as a conservation law:

Buckley-Leverett $$\frac{\partial u}{\partial t}+\frac{\partial}{\partial x}\left[\frac{u^2}{u^2+a(1-u)^2}\right]=0.$$

These conservation laws *do not include dissipation.* We try to avoid resolving small scale processes like viscosity and diffusion and heat conduction. Their effects will be felt in the "entropy condition" that chooses the physically correct solution (a shock or a fan in 1D).

Difference Methods and Flux Functions

Now we turn to **numerical methods for conservation laws**. The key to a reliable difference method is to maintain the conservation! *Replace $\partial f/\partial x$ by differences Δf of the flux.* Don't take the derivative $\partial f/\partial x = u\,u_x$ and work with u times Δu:

$$\text{Start from}\quad \frac{\partial u}{\partial t}+\frac{\partial}{\partial x}f(u)=0 \quad\text{and not from}\quad \frac{\partial u}{\partial t}+f'(u)\frac{\partial u}{\partial x}=0\,.$$

You will see the idea immediately for the first-order upwind approximation:

Upwind (for $f'>0$) $$\frac{U_{j,n+1}-U_{j,n}}{\Delta t}+\frac{f(U_{j+1,n})-f(U_{j,n})}{\Delta x}=0\,. \qquad (24)$$

By staying with the flux f, this approximation preserves the conservation form. Since the equation is discrete, the integral $\int u(x,t)dx$ is replaced by a ***sum of U_{jn}***. The integral over $a\le x\le b$ in equation (1) becomes a sum of the equations (24) over any integers $A\le j\le B$. The time derivative of u becomes a forward difference:

Discrete conservation $$\frac{1}{\Delta t}\left(\sum_{j=A}^{B}U_{j,n+1}-\sum_{j=A}^{B}U_{j,n}\right)+\frac{1}{\Delta x}(F_{B+1,n}-F_{A,n})=0 \qquad (25)$$

The change in mass $\sum U_{jn}$ still comes from the flux. Notice how the flux $f(U_{jn})$ at intermediate points between A and B was added and subtracted (so it disappeared). The discrete sum form in (25) is parallel to the continuous integral form in (1).

The key decision in nonlinear finite differences is the flux function. Certainly we will want methods other than upwind. They will be nonlinear forms of Lax-Friedrichs and Lax-Wendroff and more. A valuable step for all approximate methods is to see that ***conservation comes automatically from a numerical flux function F***:

Conservation form $$\boldsymbol{U_{j,n+1}-U_{j,n}+\frac{\Delta t}{\Delta x}\left[F_{j+1,n}-F_{j,n}\right]=0}\,. \qquad (26)$$

In the upwind method, the numerical flux is just $F_{j,n}=f(U_{j,n})$. In Lax-Friedrichs and Lax-Wendroff, the flux will involve both $U_{j,n}$ and $U_{j-1,n}$. Other methods have flux functions that depend on several neighboring U's. We need a consistency condition to guarantee that the numerical flux F is in line with the true flux f:

Consistency The flux $F(U_{j+p}, \ldots, U_{j-q})$ satisfies $F(u, \ldots, u) = f(u)$. (27)

Under this condition, a convergent method will solve the right conservation law. The construction of numerical methods rest on a good choice of the flux function F.

Example 8 Watch how nonlinear Lax-Friedrichs fits into this conservation form:

LF $$U_{j,n+1} - \frac{1}{2}\left(U_{j+1,n} + U_{j-1,n}\right) + \frac{\Delta t}{2\Delta x}\left[f(U_{j+1,n}) - f(U_{j-1,n})\right] = 0. \quad (28)$$

To match equation (26), insert $U_{j,n} - U_{j,n}$ into the parentheses and insert $f(U_{j,n}) - f(U_{j,n})$ into the brackets. This produces $\boldsymbol{\Delta_t U}/\Delta t + \boldsymbol{\Delta_x F}/\Delta x = 0$ with a new flux F:

Lax-Friedrichs flux $$F^{\mathrm{LF}} = \frac{1}{2}\left[f(U_j) + f(U_{j+1})\right] - \frac{\Delta x}{2\Delta t}\left(U_{j+1} - U_j\right). \quad (29)$$

Finite Volume Methods

Finite volume methods do *not* think of $U_{j,n}$ as an approximation to $u(j\Delta x, n\Delta t)$. These methods connect directly to the **integral form** of the conservation law. So it is natural for $U_{j,n}$ to approximate the **cell average** $\boldsymbol{\overline{u}_{j,n}}$ from $(j-\frac{1}{2})\Delta x$ to $(j+\frac{1}{2})\Delta x$:

Cell average $U_{j,n}$ approximates $$\boldsymbol{\overline{u}_{j,n}} = \frac{1}{\Delta x}\int_{(j-\frac{1}{2})\Delta x}^{(j+\frac{1}{2})\Delta x} u(x, n\Delta t)\, dx\,. \quad (30)$$

Integrating $u_t + f(u)_x = 0$ over a cell, the exact average satisfies the integral form (1):

Change in cell average $$\frac{d}{dt}\int_{(j-\frac{1}{2})\Delta x}^{(j+\frac{1}{2})\Delta x} u(x,t)\, dx + \left[f(u_{j+\frac{1}{2},n}) - f(u_{j-\frac{1}{2},n})\right] = 0\,. \quad (31)$$

The fluxes are at the midpoints where cells meet. And if we integrate also over a time step, then $u_t + f(u)_x = 0$ is perfectly averaged over a space-time cell:

Cell integrals in x and t have $\Delta_t \overline{u} + \Delta_x \overline{f} = 0$

$$\int_{(j-\frac{1}{2})\Delta x}^{(j+\frac{1}{2})\Delta x} u(x, t_{n+1})\, dx - \int_{(j-\frac{1}{2})\Delta x}^{(j+\frac{1}{2})\Delta x} u(x, t_n)\, dx + \int_{n\Delta t}^{(n+1)\Delta t} f(u_{j+\frac{1}{2}}, t)\, dt - \int_{n\Delta t}^{(n+1)\Delta t} f(u_{j-\frac{1}{2}}, t)\, dt = 0\,. \quad (32)$$

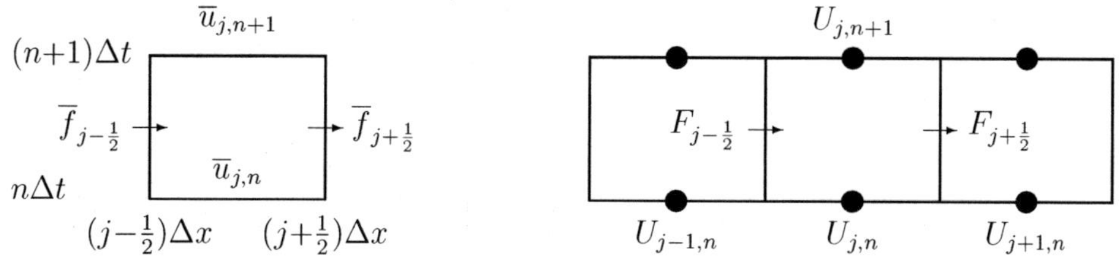

Figure 6.17: Flux balance is exact for $\overline{u}, \overline{f}$ and approximate for U, F in (33).

The total mass in a cell changes between t_n and t_{n+1} by the total flux into that cell. Thus finite volume methods come with a staggered grid in space-time (Figure 6.17). On this staggered grid we must write the numerical flux as $F_{j+\frac{1}{2}}$ rather than F_j:

Finite volume $$\frac{1}{\Delta t}\left(U_{j,n+1} - U_{j,n}\right) + \frac{1}{\Delta x}\left(F_{j+\frac{1}{2},n} - F_{j-\frac{1}{2},n}\right) = 0\,. \qquad (33)$$

Morton and Sonar give a detailed analysis of finite volume methods, with *optimal recovery* to increase accuracy (since all test functions V are piecewise constant) [117].

Upwind and Godunov Fluxes

The simple upwind method is more complex than it looks, because it changes direction with the wind. Information is coming along characteristics. For $u_t = c\,u_x$, the wind direction depends on the (fixed) sign of c. For $u_t + f(u)_x = 0$, the direction depends on the (possibly variable) sign of $f'(u)$. Those signs determine the upwind flux F^{UP}:

The upwind numerical flux $\boldsymbol{F^{\text{UP}}_{j+\frac{1}{2}}}$ ***is either*** $\boldsymbol{f(U_{j,n})}$ ***or*** $\boldsymbol{f(U_{j+1,n})}$**.**

Lax-Friedrichs avoided that sign dependence by using the average in (29), but its accuracy is low. LF is more dissipative than the upwind method. (Lax-Friedrichs uses U_{j+1} and U_{j-1} where upwind stays in one cell.) We need a systematic approach in which the accuracy can be upgraded to reach *high resolution.*

The first step was taken by Godunov (he applied it to gas dynamics):

1. At time $n\Delta t$, construct $\overline{u}(x) = U_{j,n} =$ *constant* in each cell j
2. Solve $u_t + f(u)_x = 0$ starting from this piecewise constant $\overline{u}(x)$ at $n\Delta t$
3. Take the cell averages of that solution at time $(n+1)\Delta t$ as $U_{j,n+1}$.

Since $U_{j,n}$ and $U_{j,n+1}$ match the x-integrals in the exact conservation form (32), that equation tells us Godunov's numerical flux function:

Godunov flux $$F^{\text{GOD}}_{j+\frac{1}{2},n} = \frac{1}{\Delta t}\int_{n\Delta t}^{(n+1)\Delta t} f(\overline{u}(x_{j+\frac{1}{2}}, t))\,dt\,. \qquad (34)$$

Godunov's integral is easy because the solution $\overline{u}$ is *constant* up that line $x = x_{j+\frac{1}{2}}$. It is coming along characteristics from the constant initial value $U_{j,n}$. We only have to ensure that no characteristics coming from neighboring constants $U_{j-1,n}$ or $U_{j+1,n}$ reach that line before the time step ends. The Courant-Friedrichs-Lewy stability condition for Godunov will be $r = |f'(u)|\Delta t/\Delta x \le \frac{1}{2}$, because a characteristic from outside need only cross *half a cell* to reach $x_{j+\frac{1}{2}}$.

For $u_t = c\,u_x$, upwind and Godunov are identical. The important point is that Godunov's method deals naturally with **systems of conservation laws**. Those give n scalar Riemann problems and n characteristics. The bad point is that the piecewise constant construction only allows first-order accuracy. This will be fixed by a combination of Godunov and Lax-Wendroff. Above all, the essential idea is to control oscillations by a "***flux limiter***."

These first-order methods, upwind and Lax-Friedrichs and Godunov, correspond to difference equations $U_{j,n+1} = \sum a_k U_{j+k,n}$ in which *all coefficients have* $a_k \ge 0$. These are ***monotone schemes***, stable but only first-order accurate (Problem 4, Section 6.3). A nonlinear scheme is monotone provided its flux function F decreases when any $U_{j+k,n}$ increases. We move on to Lax-Wendroff, which is not monotone.

Lax-Wendroff with Flux Limiter

For linear $u_t + au_x = 0$ with $r = a\,\Delta t/\Delta x$, the Lax-Wendroff method adds $\frac{1}{2}r^2\Delta_x^2 U_{j,n}$ to the Lax-Friedrichs formula for $U_{j,n+1}$. Equivalently, it adds $\frac{1}{2}(r^2 - r)\Delta_x^2 U_{j,n}$ to the upwind formula. This cancels the first-order error and upgrades the accuracy to second-order. But oscillations come in. We write the Lax-Wendroff flux in this linear case $f(u) = au$, to show the new term that is added to the upwind flux $F^{\mathsf{UP}} = aU$.

Lax-Wendroff flux
$a > 0$, wind from left

$$F^{\mathsf{LW}}_{j+\frac{1}{2}} = aU_j + \frac{a}{2}\left(1 - \frac{a\Delta t}{\Delta x}\right)(U_{j+1} - U_j). \qquad (35)$$

Everybody looks closely at that last term. It has taken a lot of care to modify this formula so that oscillations are controlled. A good measure of the oscillation of both u and U is the **total variation**, which adds all movements up and down:

Total variation

$$\mathbf{TV}(u) = \int_{-\infty}^{\infty} \left|\frac{du}{dx}\right| dx \qquad \mathbf{TV}(U) = \sum_{-\infty}^{\infty} |U_{j+1} - U_j|. \qquad (36)$$

A TVD method (*total variation diminishing*) achieves $\mathrm{TV}(U_{n+1}) \le \mathrm{TV}(U_n)$. This will preserve the property of the true solution, that $\mathrm{TV}(u(t))$ never increases. Shocks can only reduce $\mathrm{TV}(u)$, from the entropy condition in a nonlinear conservation law. But a linear TVD method cannot exceed first-order accuracy. The Lax-Wendroff oscillations increase $\mathrm{TV}(U)$. We need a nonlinear method even for a linear problem!

The key idea is to limit the higher accuracy term in Lax-Wendroff by a "flux limiter" $\phi_{j+\frac{1}{2}}$ that switches away from 1 at a shock. Choosing ϕ is all-important:

Flux-limited Lax-Wendroff
$$F^{\text{limit}}_{j+\frac{1}{2}} = aU_j + \frac{a}{2}\left(1 - \frac{a\Delta t}{\Delta x}\right)\phi_{j+\frac{1}{2}}(U_{j+1} - U_j)\,. \qquad (37)$$

Thus $\phi = 1$ is Lax-Wendroff and $\phi = 0$ is upwind. For best accuracy we come as near to $\phi = 1$ as the TVD condition will allow. How to know when ϕ stops oscillations?

A shock is diagnosed by the slope ratio r_j that compares successive differences:

Slope ratio
$$r_j = \frac{U_j - U_{j-1}}{U_{j+1} - U_j} = \begin{cases} \text{near 0 at a shock} \\ \text{near 1 for smooth } U \end{cases} \qquad (38)$$

The flux factor $\phi_{j+\frac{1}{2}}$ will involve this ratio r_j. A monotone flux function F in (37) and a TVD difference method require two conditions derived in [109, 110]:

TVD conditions
$$0 \le \phi(r) \le 2r \qquad \text{and} \qquad 0 \le \phi(r) \le 2\,. \qquad (39)$$

Summary We have reached high resolution without unacceptable oscillations. Linear Lax-Wendroff violates (39) for small r, but Figure 6.18 shows three choices of the flux limiter $\phi(r)$ that will keep the flux function monotone. A key step forward.

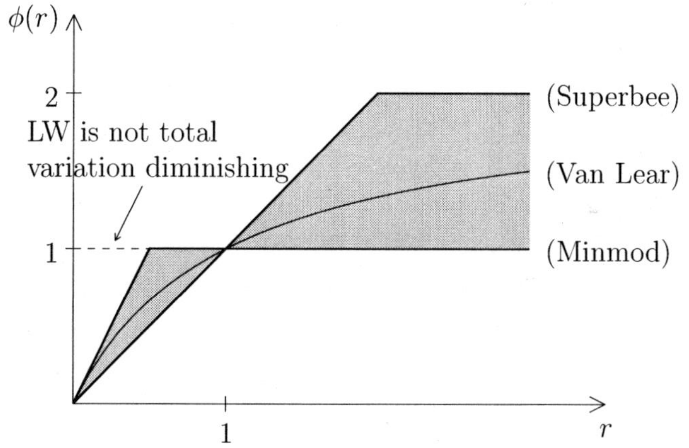

Figure 6.18: Three flux limiters $\phi(r)$ that satisfy the conditions (39) for TVD.

The KdV Equation

Let me end with the Korteweg-deVries equation, not because it is typical but because it is so remarkable. Its unique features are not obvious from the equation itself:

KdV equation
$$u_t + 6u\,u_x + u_{xxx} = 0\,. \qquad (40)$$

Looking for a one-way "**solitary wave**" with speed c, we meet $\operatorname{sech} x = 2/(e^x + e^{-x})$:

Soliton solutions $$u_c(x,t) = F(x - ct) = \frac{c}{2}\operatorname{sech}^2\left(\frac{\sqrt{c}}{2}(x - ct)\right). \tag{41}$$

Since $u_t + 6u\,u_x + u_{xxx} = 0$ is nonlinear, we can't just add solitons. The wave moving with speed $C > c$ catches up with u_c. We can follow their changing shapes numerically. The amazing and unexpected result is that when the faster soliton u_C comes out in front, ***the two solitons go back to their original shapes***.

If the boundary conditions are periodic, the faster wave will come around again to the left boundary. It catches the slower u_c again, interacts, and emerges looking unchanged (with a time delay from the interaction). After many cycles, the solution at a special time $t = T$ is almost exactly the double soliton $u_c + u_C$ at the start.

This is the opposite of "chaos" and "strange attractors." Those are mathematical black holes out of which history cannot be recovered. KdV could go backwards from $t = T$ to $t = 0$, which is impossible for the heat equation.

To explain these computations, the search began with the fact that $\int u\,dx$ and $\int u^2\,dx$ stay constant for KdV solutions. An infinite number of additional conserved quantities were found—very unusual. The real breakthrough was to introduce Schrödinger's eigenvalue problem with $u(x,t)$ as the potential:

Schrödinger equation $$w_{xx} + u(x,t)\,w = \lambda(t)\,w\,. \tag{42}$$

When u solves the KdV equation, *those eigenvalues $\lambda(t)$ stay constant.* This opened the door to exact solutions. Now other "integrable" nonlinear equations have been discovered, and the Sine-Gordon equation $u_{tt} = u_{xx} - \sin u$ is understood. An insight was contributed by Peter Lax, who saw a larger pattern in the constant eigenvalues. This happens whenever the equation comes from a ***Lax pair*** L and B:

Lax equation If $\dfrac{dL}{dt} = BL - LB$ then $L(t) = e^{Bt}L(0)e^{-Bt}$ has constant λ's.

If $L(0)w = \lambda\,w$ then $L(t)(e^{Bt}w) = e^{Bt}L(0)\,w = \lambda(e^{Bt}w)$. Thus $L(t)$ keeps the same eigenvalues λ as $L(0)$. A particular choice of L and B produces the KdV equation.

I hope that some readers will try the famous numerical experiments on solitons. The u_{xxx} term in KdV prevents shocks by dispersion (energy is still conserved). In Burgers and Navier-Stokes, u_{xx} prevents shocks by diffusion (energy goes into heat).

Problem Set 6.6

1 Write down the integral form for conservation of cars when the flux f is the density u times the velocity $v = 80(1-u)$. Then write down the differential equation for u and the jump condition (10) at a shock.

2 A red light at $x = 0$ has density $u_0 = 1$ to the left and $u_0 = 0$ to the right. If the light goes *green* at $t = 0$, a fan of cars goes forward. Explain the solution drawn in the first two figures with no shock.

These figures come from Peraire's Lecture 11: Conservation Laws on ocw.mit.edu [Course 16.920, slides 43–44]. This website is an excellent source to extend Chapter 6 (especially to *integral equations* and *boundary element methods*).

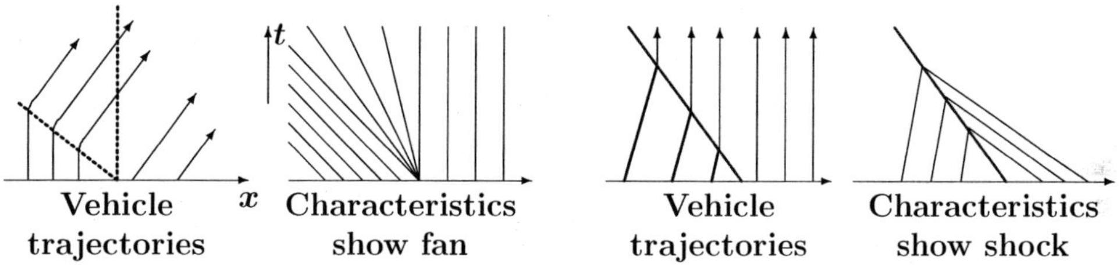

Figure 6.19: Car paths and characteristics after lights go green and red.

3 What is the entropy condition (12) for the shock speed in the traffic equation? When a light turns *red* at $x = 0, t = 0$, the traffic density is zero for $x > 0, t > 0$. *A shock goes backward.* Verify the jump condition and entropy condition for the solution in the last figures.

4 In Example 3, $u = u_0(x - ut)$ gives $u = u(x,t)$ implicitly when $u_t + uu_x = 0$. Start from $u_0(x) = Cx$ and solve for $u(x,t)$. Show that u is constant along the lines $x - u_0 t = x_0$ and draw four of those lines. Which numbers C give shocks?

5 Draw the solution $u(x,1)$ in (14) starting from a point source $\delta(x)$. Sketch how $u(x,1)$ might look for small ν in the viscous Burgers' equation $u_t + uu_x = \nu u_{xx}$.

6 Solve Burgers' equation by formula (17) starting from $u(x,0) = -\delta(x)$.

7 Show that $U = -2\nu \log h$ turns $U_t + \frac{1}{2}U_x^2 = \nu U_{xx}$ into the equation $h_t = \nu h_{xx}$.

8 Solve $u_t + uu_x = 0$ by (17) if u_0 jumps from A to B in the Riemann problem:

$$u(x,t) = \frac{\partial}{\partial x} \min_y \left[\begin{matrix} -Ay\ (y<0) \\ By\ (y>0) \end{matrix} + \frac{1}{2t}(x-y)^2 \right].$$

For $A > B$ this should produce the shock along the line $x = \frac{1}{2}(A+B)t$. For $A < B$ compare with the fan $u = x/t$.

9 Show how the Euler equations (19–21) for an ideal gas are equivalent to

$$\frac{Dp}{Dt} + \gamma p \operatorname{div} v = 0 \qquad \rho \frac{Dv}{Dt} + \operatorname{grad} p = 0 \qquad \frac{DS}{Dt} = 0.$$

Here D/Dt is the convective derivative $\partial/\partial t + \sum v_j \, \partial/\partial x_j$ which will appear in the Transport Rule along particle trajectories in Section 6.7.

10 The linear wave equation $u_{tt} = u_{xx}$ is the system of two conservation laws (22). Write the nonlinear wave equation $u_{tt} = (C(u_x))_x$ in a similar form.

11 Show that the Godunov flux F^{GOD} in (34) is the larger or smaller of $f(U_{j,n})$ and $f(U_{j+1,n})$, depending whether $U_{j,n}$ is larger or smaller than $U_{j+1,n}$.

12 Find equations for the lines bounding the fan in Figure 6.15.

13 *Challenge*: Solve Burgers' equation by (17) starting from $u(x,0) = \delta(x) - \delta(x-1)$.

14 If $u_t + f(u)_x = 0$, find the linear equation for a perturbation $v(x,t)$ by substituting $u + \epsilon v$ into the same conservation law.

6.7 FLUID FLOW AND NAVIER-STOKES

The velocity of a viscous incompressible fluid is governed by the Navier-Stokes equations. The dimensionless form brings out the importance of the Reynolds number Re. The velocity is a divergence-free vector $\boldsymbol{u}$ and the pressure is a scalar p:

Navier-Stokes $$\frac{\partial \boldsymbol{u}}{\partial t} + (\boldsymbol{u}\cdot\nabla)\boldsymbol{u} = -\nabla p + \frac{1}{\mathrm{Re}}\Delta \boldsymbol{u} + \boldsymbol{f} \qquad (1)$$

Continuity equation $$\operatorname{div}\boldsymbol{u} = \nabla\cdot\boldsymbol{u} = 0 \qquad (2)$$

Equation (1) is Newton's Law for the momentum with mass density normalized to 1. The external force $\boldsymbol{f}$ is often absent. Four terms deserve immediate comments:

1. The Laplacian $\Delta\boldsymbol{u}$ applies to each component of $\boldsymbol{u}$. Viscosity produces dissipation.

2. The constraint $\operatorname{div}\boldsymbol{u} = 0$ (no time derivative in this equation) comes from incompressibility and conservation of mass : constant density.

3. The pressure $p(x, y, t)$ is the Lagrange multiplier for that constraint $\nabla\cdot\boldsymbol{u} = 0$. The pressure gradient $-\nabla p$ drives the flow in equation (1).

4. The nonlinear term $(\boldsymbol{u}\cdot\nabla)\boldsymbol{u}$ comes from the movement of the fluid. Newton's Law is applied to moving particles, and as they move we have to follow them. The transport rule (28) will be the key. In 2D the velocity $\boldsymbol{u}$ has components $u(x, y, t)$ and $v(x, y, t)$, and $(\boldsymbol{u}\cdot\nabla)\boldsymbol{u}$ also has two components:

Components of $(\boldsymbol{u}\cdot\nabla)\boldsymbol{u}$ $$\left(u\frac{\partial}{\partial x} + v\frac{\partial}{\partial y}\right)\begin{bmatrix} u \\ v \end{bmatrix} = \begin{bmatrix} uu_x + vu_y \\ uv_x + vv_y \end{bmatrix} \qquad (3)$$

The first term is neater if uu_x is written as $\frac{1}{2}(u^2)_x$. That looks hard to do for vu_y. The product rule for $(uv)_y$ will give an extra term uv_y. But zero divergence saves us with $u_x = -v_y$. Subtracting the unwanted uv_y is the same as adding another uu_x:

Simplify $$uu_x + vu_y = uu_x + (uv)_y + uu_x = (u^2)_x + (uv)_y. \qquad (4)$$

The same device works for $uv_x + vv_y$. (*It also extends to* 3D.) I will write both components of the 2D momentum equation (1) in a form ready for finite differences:

$$\begin{array}{ll} \textbf{x direction} & u_t + p_x = (u_{xx} + u_{yy})/\mathrm{Re} - (u^2)_x - (uv)_y + f_1 \\ \textbf{y direction} & v_t + p_y = (v_{xx} + v_{yy})/\mathrm{Re} - (uv)_x - (v^2)_y + f_2 \end{array} \qquad (5)$$

The derivation of these Navier-Stokes equations is based on conservation of mass and momentum. This will be quite standard (the choice between Euler and Lagrange is important in equation (26) for mass conservation). To progress directly toward a numerical solution we must know some of the possible boundary conditions.

Boundary Conditions in 2D Flow

Suppose that the physical boundaries are in the coordinate directions, horizontal and vertical. The velocity vector $\boldsymbol{u}$ is still (u, v). At a vertical boundary, u is the normal component of velocity and v is the tangential component. We may have an *inflow condition* at the left end and an *outflow condition* (no stress) at the right end:

Inflow across a vertical boundary $\quad u = u_0$ and $v = v_0$ are prescribed $\quad (6)$

Outflow across a vertical boundary $\quad \dfrac{1}{\mathrm{Re}}\dfrac{\partial u}{\partial x} - p = 0$ and $\dfrac{\partial v}{\partial x} = 0 \quad (7)$

In a channel flow, no fluid crosses the upper and lower horizontal boundaries. The *no-slip condition* further requires that the fluid is at rest:

No-slip along a horizontal boundary $\quad u = 0$ (from viscosity) and $v = 0$ (no crossing) $\quad (8)$

Along a sloping boundary, the velocity vector is separated into normal and tangential components. The inflow and no-slip conditions still prescribe both components, and $\partial/\partial x$ in (7) changes to $\partial/\partial n$ for outflow (like a free end). Our examples will show other possibilities, staying with horizontal and vertical boundaries.

If we prescribe the outward flow $\boldsymbol{u} \cdot \boldsymbol{n}$ on the whole boundary, then $\operatorname{div} \boldsymbol{u} = 0$ would require $\int \boldsymbol{u} \cdot \boldsymbol{n}\, ds = 0$. Please note the difference between $\boldsymbol{u} \cdot \boldsymbol{n}$ and $\partial u/\partial n = \nabla u \cdot \boldsymbol{n}$, a normal component and a normal derivative.

The Reynolds Number

To reach the **Reynolds number** Re, the Navier-Stokes equations have been made dimensionless. Physical conservation laws have dimensions. The key to the physics is the relative importance of **inertial forces** and **viscous forces**.

Reynolds number $\quad \mathrm{Re} = \dfrac{\text{inertial forces}}{\text{viscous forces}} \approx \dfrac{(\text{a velocity } U)\ (\text{a length } L)}{(\text{kinematic viscosity } \nu)} \quad (9)$

Example 1 Flow in a long channel Here L would be the width of the channel, and U could be the inflow velocity. The number ν is a ratio μ/ρ of the material constant μ (the dynamic viscosity) to the density ρ.

Experience is needed to identify an appropriate length scale L and velocity U, characteristic of the flow. Here is a light-hearted scale of Re for some familiar motions:

Reynolds number Re	10^{-3}	$\longrightarrow$ *bacteria*	10^{0}	$\longrightarrow$ *blood*	10^{3}	$\longrightarrow$ *baseball*	10^{6}	$\longrightarrow$ *ship*	10^{9}

It is natural to compare Re with the **Péclet number** Pe = convection/diffusion in Section 6.5. When a flow is driven by gravity, the **Froude number** $\mathrm{Fr} = U/\sqrt{Lg}$

is also important (inertial force/gravitational force). The practical importance of Re appears when flight is simulated in a wind tunnel. We might try to keep Re nearly correct (not easy for a model aircraft with reduced length L) by cooling the gas.

More nearly achievable in a laboratory might be oil spill from a tanker imitated by diffusion in glycerine [66]. The point is that flows sharing the same Reynolds number (but looking vastly different) are similar after adjustment of the dimensions.

Example 2 Steady 3D flow $\boldsymbol{u} = (u, 0, 0)$ between planes $y = \pm h$ (**Poiseuille flow**). This is a rare example with simple solutions. Apply Navier-Stokes with $\partial \boldsymbol{u}/\partial t = 0$:

$$\operatorname{div} \boldsymbol{u} = \frac{\partial u}{\partial x} = 0 \text{ so } u \text{ depends only on } y. \text{ Nothing depends on } z.$$

From (5) $$\frac{\partial p}{\partial x} = u_{yy}/\,\text{Re} \quad \text{and} \quad \frac{\partial p}{\partial y} = 0 \quad \text{and} \quad \frac{\partial p}{\partial z} = 0 \quad \text{so } p \text{ depends only on } x.$$

Both sides of $\partial p/\partial x = u_{yy}/\text{Re}$ must be *constant*. Then $u(\pm h) = 0$ for no slip:

Linear pressure $p(x) = cx + p_0$ **Quadratic velocity profile** $u(y) = \dfrac{c\,\text{Re}}{2}(y^2 - h^2)$.

An Example for 2D Fluid Flow

Our primary example will be a **lid-driven cavity**. A square is filled with a fluid. The no-slip conditions $u = v = 0$ hold on three sides. The top side (the lid) moves with fixed horizontal velocity $u = 1$ and vertical velocity $v = 0$. You could imagine a square cut out from one bank of a river. The river velocity $u = 1$ becomes a boundary condition at the top of the square cavity in Figure 6.20.

The fluid will rotate inside that square. In theory, there will be an infinite sequence of eddies and countereddies (rotating in opposite directions). Their size depends on the Reynolds number $UL/\nu = (1)(1)/\nu$. The explicit-implicit calculations by Seibold on the cse website solve this time-dependent problem.

In 2D we will describe the option of replacing the primitive variables u, v by a *stream function* that handles the continuity equation $u_x + v_y = 0$ and a *vorticity* $u_y - v_x$ to eliminate p. Boundary conditions are the key question in such a choice.

Overall, computational fluid dynamics is an enormous subject. At Los Alamos (one of the birthplaces of computational science and engineering) John von Neumann introduced numerical viscosity to control instability. So many ideas have followed. CFD remains a problem of such variety and complexity that any single algorithm and coded example could be quite misleading (but we hope partly useful too).

A Basic Algorithm

A simple and effective Navier-Stokes solver **separates three pieces** of the problem. Convection $(\boldsymbol{u} \cdot \nabla)\boldsymbol{u}$ is explicit, diffusion $\Delta \boldsymbol{u}$ is implicit, and continuity $\operatorname{div} \boldsymbol{u} = 0$

leads to Poisson's equation for the pressure. This splitting method first creates a velocity vector $\boldsymbol{U}^*$ from $\boldsymbol{U}^n$ at the start of the step. Then $\boldsymbol{U}^{n+1}$ comes from $\boldsymbol{U}^*$:

1 **Explicit convection / Implicit diffusion** $$\frac{\boldsymbol{U}^* - \boldsymbol{U}^n}{\Delta t} + (\boldsymbol{U}^n \cdot \nabla)\boldsymbol{U}^n = -\nabla p^n + \frac{\Delta \boldsymbol{U}^*}{\text{Re}} + \boldsymbol{f}^n \quad (10)$$

2 $\boldsymbol{U}^{n+1}$ is the divergence-free part of $\boldsymbol{U}^*$. The pressure p^{n+1} accounts for $\operatorname{div} \boldsymbol{U}^*$:

Poisson for p $$\boldsymbol{U}^* = \boldsymbol{U}^{n+1} + \operatorname{grad}(p^{n+1} - p^n) \text{ yields } \Delta p^{n+1} = \operatorname{div} \boldsymbol{U}^* + \Delta p^n \quad (11)$$

Poisson is the equation we know best (also the most expensive). It separates $\boldsymbol{U}^*$ into a divergence-free part $\boldsymbol{U}^{n+1}$ and a curl-free field $\operatorname{grad}(p^{n+1} - p^n)$. Those subspaces are orthogonal complements, with correct boundary conditions. The computation of p on a finite difference grid is usually called *Chorin's projection method.*

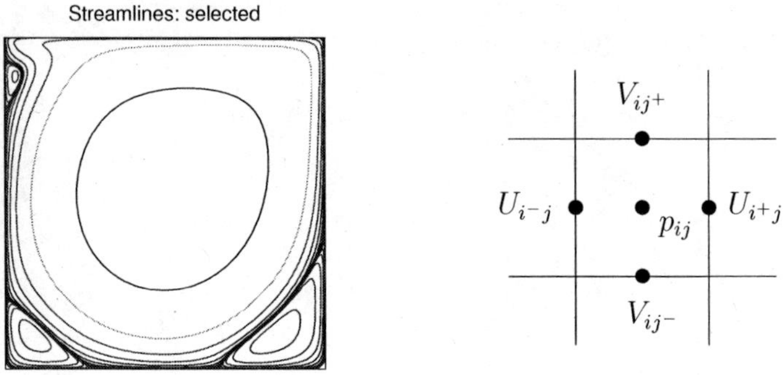

Figure 6.20: Lid-driven cavity flow $\boldsymbol{u} = (u, v)$ in 2D. A triple p, U, V grid in a cell.

Very Staggered Grids

Those steps need to be executed on an actual grid. Normally U, V, and p are defined at different points, as in Figure 6.20. The pressure p_{ij} is located at the **center** of the i, j cell. The horizontal velocity U is level with that point, but on the **edges** of the cell (p and U are staggered on row i). The vertical velocity V is **above** and **below** the center (again on the cell edges so V and p are staggered up each column). The three grids for p, U, V bring many conveniences and some unavoidable problems.

A first question is notation for the grid values of U and V. I shall venture a small proposal. The discrete values on the edges would naturally be $U_{i+\frac{1}{2},j}$ and $V_{i,j+\frac{1}{2}}$, to the right of i, j and above. The inconvenient "$+\frac{1}{2}$" is just removed in [66] to leave $U_{i,j}$ and $V_{i,j}$. But this can be confusing, since i, j refers to three different points.

I suggest simply deleting the "$\frac{1}{2}$" while leaving the + sign as in U_{i+j} and V_{ij+}. Similarly U_{i-j} and V_{ij-} can be values on the left edge and lower edge: see Figure 6.20.

This triple grid avoids a checkerboard oscillation from centered differences p_x and p_y:

Checkerboard pressure $\quad \boldsymbol{p}^*$ on white squares and $\boldsymbol{p}^{**}$ on black squares. $\quad (12)$

It is not good to find a staggered solution on an unstaggered grid. This won't happen on the triple grid. Here are space differences that appear naturally:

Continuity equation $u_x + v_y = 0$ $$\frac{U_{i^+j} - U_{i^-j}}{\Delta x} + \frac{V_{ij^+} - V_{ij^-}}{\Delta y} = 0 \tag{13}$$

Diffusion through right side $$\frac{U_{i+1^+j} - 2U_{i^+j} + U_{i^-j}}{(\Delta x)^2} \tag{14}$$

Pressure gradient $$\frac{p_{i+1,j} - p_{ij}}{\Delta x} \text{ at the vertical edge } i^+j \tag{15}$$

Three other parts of the discretization (and especially $(\boldsymbol{u} \cdot \nabla)\boldsymbol{u}$) need extra attention.

Averaged, Weighted, and Boundary Terms

Equation (5) requires UV but now U and V are on different grids. The three grids have different boundaries. We also hesitate to use centered differences alone on $(u^2)_x$. *Upwind differencing is often needed at high velocities* (and large Re).

A successful compromise identifies a "donor cell" upwind of the needed value. That upwind difference is weighted in (16) by a parameter α. At the i^+j meshpoint, on the right edge of the i, j cell, the term $(u^2)_x$ combines centered and upwind differences. We work with the **averaged velocities** $\overline{U}_{ij} = (U_{i^+j} + U_{i^-j})/2$:

$$(u^2)_x \approx \frac{\overline{U}_{i+1,j}^2 - \overline{U}_{ij}^2}{\Delta x} + \frac{\alpha}{2\Delta x}\left(|\overline{U}_{i+1,j}|(U_{i^+j} - U_{i+1^+j}) - |\overline{U}_{ij}|(U_{i^-j} - U_{i^+j})\right) \tag{16}$$

The code on the cse website uses similar differences of averages for the other nonlinear terms: $(uv)_y$ at that right edge midpoint i^+j, and $(uv)_x + (v^2)_y$ at the upper edge midpoint ij^+. The differences are fully centered for $\alpha = 0$ and fully upwind (from the donor cell) for $\alpha = 1$. For smooth flows, $\alpha = 0$ should be safe.

The boundary values of U and V also involve averaging. *Reason*: V is not defined on vertical boundaries and U is not defined on horizontal boundaries. The no-slip condition $u = v = 0$ uses boundary values of U and V where available, and takes averages where necessary:

No-slip condition $\quad U=0$ and $\overline{V}=0$ (vertical sides) $\quad \overline{U}=0$ and $V=0$ (horizontal sides)

The inflow condition (6) is similar, but with nonzero values. At the outflow boundary, set the velocity U or V equal to the neighboring velocity inside the domain.

Steady Flows from Navier-Stokes

Suppose $\partial \boldsymbol{u}/\partial t = 0$ in the Navier-Stokes equation (1). The velocity and pressure are independent of time. This leaves a nonlinear boundary value problem to be solved:

Steady flow $\left(\dfrac{\partial u}{\partial t} = 0\right)$ $\quad (\boldsymbol{u} \cdot \boldsymbol{\nabla})\boldsymbol{u} - \dfrac{\Delta \boldsymbol{u}}{\text{Re}} + \nabla p = \boldsymbol{f} \quad \nabla \cdot \boldsymbol{u} = 0 \quad (17)$

The boundary conditions are $\boldsymbol{u} = \boldsymbol{u}_0$ at a fixed boundary (Dirichlet part) and $\partial \boldsymbol{u}/\partial n = (\text{Re})p\boldsymbol{n}$ at a free boundary (Neumann part with normal vector $\boldsymbol{n}$). If $\boldsymbol{u} = \boldsymbol{u}_0$ is given on the whole boundary, p is only known up to a constant (hydrostatic pressure).

When the nonlinear convection term $(\boldsymbol{u} \cdot \boldsymbol{\nabla})\boldsymbol{u}$ is large, the solution has layers of rapid change. Finding the right mesh can be difficult. And $\text{Re} \to \infty$ in (17) leaves the **incompressible Euler equations** for non-viscous flow. We mention one steady flow example out of many.

Example 3 **Blasius flow** past a flat plate $0 \le x \le L$, $y = 0$ has an analytic solution

The left boundary at $x = -1$ has horizontal inflow $u = U, v = 0$. The top and bottom $y = \pm 1$ also have $u = U, v = 0$. The outflow boundary $x = L$ has $\partial u/\partial x = (\text{Re})p$ and $\partial v/\partial x = 0$ as usual. Along the internal flat plate, the no-slip condition is $u = v = 0$.

The velocity u has to rise from $u = 0$ to $u = U$, between the plate and the boundaries $y = \pm 1$. This happens quickly near the plate, in a "shear layer" of thickness $1/\sqrt{\text{Re}}$. The IFISS Toolbox [47, 48] provides software for the challenging problem of finite difference / finite element approximation to steady flows using mixed finite elements.

Weak Form and Mixed Finite Elements

In the weak form of Laplace's equation, we multiplied $\Delta u = 0$ by any test function. Then $v\,\Delta u$ was integrated by parts (Gauss-Green identity) to get $\iint u_x v_x + u_y v_y = 0$. Now equation (17) has a second unknown $p(x, y)$. The pressure will have its own test functions $q(x, y)$, which multiply the continuity equation $\operatorname{div} \boldsymbol{u} = 0$:

Weak form of continuity equation $\quad \displaystyle\iint q \operatorname{div} \boldsymbol{u}\, dx\, dy = 0$ for all admissible $q(x, y)$. $\quad (18)$

The momentum equation in (17) is multiplied by *vector* test functions $\boldsymbol{v}(x, y)$:

Weak form of the momentum equation

$$\iint \left[\nabla \boldsymbol{u} \cdot \nabla \boldsymbol{v} / \text{Re} + (\boldsymbol{u} \cdot \nabla \boldsymbol{u}) \cdot \boldsymbol{v} - p(\nabla \cdot \boldsymbol{v}) - \boldsymbol{f} \cdot \boldsymbol{v}\right] dx\, dy = 0 \quad (19)$$

The viscous term $\Delta \boldsymbol{u} \cdot \boldsymbol{v}$ and the pressure term $\nabla p \cdot \boldsymbol{v}$ were integrated by parts. The novelty is in the nonlinear convection term, and the fact that finite elements will require trial and test functions $\phi_i(x, y)$ for velocity and also $Q_i(x, y)$ for pressure:

Finite element approximations $\quad \boldsymbol{U} = \boldsymbol{U}_1 \phi_1 + \cdots + \boldsymbol{U}_N \phi_N + \boldsymbol{U}_b$

Trial functions = test functions $\quad P = P_1 Q_1 + \cdots + P_M Q_M \quad (20)$

The discrete problem replaces $\boldsymbol{u}$ and p in (18) and (19) by $\boldsymbol{U}$ and P. The M test functions Q_i in (18) give M discrete equations. Replace $\boldsymbol{v}$ in both components of (19) by each ϕ_i to get $2N$ equations. The $M+2N$ unknowns are the coefficients P_i and $\boldsymbol{U}_i$. For finite elements (piecewise polynomials) those unknowns will be pressures and velocities at meshpoints.

These are **mixed finite elements**. They represent the primal unknown $\boldsymbol{u}$ and also the Lagrange multiplier p (probably by polynomials of different degrees). An important **inf-sup condition** imposes a requirement on the trial functions ϕ_i and Q_i. For a start, we cannot allow $M > 2N$. The details of the inf-sup condition are developed in Section 8.5 on Stokes flow, which is the linear case of very low velocity when the nonlinear convective term is removed.

With that nonlinear term included here, the $M+2N$ equations for Q_i and $\boldsymbol{U}_i$ are solved by iteration. Section 2.5 offered fixed-point iterations, and Newton iterations using the Jacobian matrix J of the nonlinear terms. Each iteration will be a linear system for the vectors of velocity updates $\Delta \boldsymbol{U}_k$ and pressure updates ΔP_k:

Fixed-point iteration
$$\begin{bmatrix} L+N_k & A \\ A^{\mathrm{T}} & 0 \end{bmatrix} \begin{bmatrix} \Delta \boldsymbol{U}_k \\ \Delta P_k \end{bmatrix} = \begin{bmatrix} \boldsymbol{F}_k \\ 0 \end{bmatrix} \tag{21}$$

Newton iteration
$$\begin{bmatrix} L+N_k+J_k & A \\ A^{\mathrm{T}} & 0 \end{bmatrix} \begin{bmatrix} \Delta \boldsymbol{U}_k \\ \Delta P_k \end{bmatrix} = \begin{bmatrix} \boldsymbol{F}_k \\ 0 \end{bmatrix} \tag{22}$$

The block matrices A and A^{T} represent gradient and divergence (with minus sign). L is the Laplacian matrix like $K2\mathrm{D}$ (two copies in this vector case, divided by the Reynolds number Re). Compared to the splitting and projection in (10) and (11), these methods are "all at once." But large systems need preconditioning (Chapter 7).

The fixed-point "Picard iteration" evaluates N_k using the current velocity U_k as the convection coefficient. This is a discrete *Oseen equation.* Newton's iteration will converge quadratically but it is much less robust (keep control of the step lengths). The terms from nonlinearity in the velocity equation are N and J:

Convection matrix $\quad N_{ij} = \iint (\boldsymbol{U} \cdot \nabla \boldsymbol{\phi}_j)\boldsymbol{\phi}_i \, dx\, dy$

Jacobian matrix $\quad J_{ij} = \iint (\boldsymbol{\phi}_j \cdot \nabla \boldsymbol{U})\boldsymbol{\phi}_i \, dx\, dy$

$$\text{with} \quad \boldsymbol{\phi}_i = \begin{bmatrix} \phi_i \\ \phi_i \end{bmatrix} \tag{23}$$

Those entries N_{ij} and J_{ij} are 2 by 2 blocks. The continuous weak form (18)-(19) and the discrete form using (20) and the iterations (21)-(22) are carefully analyzed in [47]: solvability by the *discrete inf-sup condition*, uniqueness, and error estimates.

The key point for that book and this one is that (21) and (22) involve **saddle point matrices**. The $A^{\mathrm{T}}CA$ structure has come back again for mixed elements. But now the 1, 1 block containing C^{-1} is not diagonal and not simple: it is the Laplacian L in (21). *Multiplication by C is the solution of a discrete Poisson equation.*

Poisson Equations

For unsteady flow, each time step of finite differences or finite elements produces Poisson equations. This is the highest cost. The equations for U and V come from the implicit treatment of the viscosity in (10), to allow a larger Δt. For high Reynolds number those Laplacian terms might change to explicit, with $\boldsymbol{U}^n$ instead of $\boldsymbol{U}^*$. For low Reynolds number, a trapezoidal Crank-Nicolson average $(\boldsymbol{U}^n + \boldsymbol{U}^*)/2$ should give better accuracy. This second-order accuracy is lost by the explicit nonlinear terms, unless a fully second-order approximation is constructed.

The Poisson equations allow all the fast algorithms presented in this book:

1. Fast Poisson Solvers on rectangles with $K2D$ or $B2D$ (Section 3.5)
2. Elimination with node renumbering (Section 7.1)
3. Multigrid with smoothing (Section 7.3)
4. Conjugate gradient methods with preconditioning (Section 7.4)

Boundary conditions can replace the Dirichlet matrix $K2D$ by a Neumann matrix. See the code for one way to deal with the fact that $B2D$ in Section 3.5 is singular. Only pressure differences are required in the momentum equation (10).

Stability places a Courant-Friedrichs-Lewy bound on the allowed step Δt:

Stability $\quad |U|_{\max} \Delta t < \Delta x \quad \text{and} \quad |V|_{\max} \Delta t < \Delta y \quad (24)$

If viscosity is treated explicitly, include $2\Delta t\big(1/(\Delta x)^2 + 1/(\Delta y)^2\big) < \text{Re}$ as a stricter limitation on Δt. Please try the cse code for different viscosities and lid velocities. A good finite element code for this problem and others is in the IFISS Toolbox.

We mention two more important examples before returning to first principles.

Example 4 **Flow around an obstacle** is a classical problem, and highly practical. For flow past a long cylinder, a 2D cross-section is in Figure 6.21a. Between inflow at the left boundary and outflow at the right boundary, the streamlines go around the obstacle. Compared to circulation in the cavity problem, the new feature here is the appearance of a **vortex street** as the Reynolds number increases.

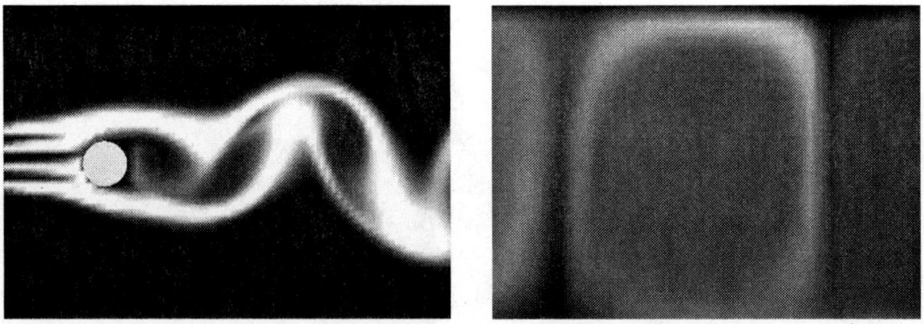

Figure 6.21: (a) The obstacle creates vortices downwind. (b) Heating from below. These figures came from Jos Stam after his inspiring talk at SIAM's CSE meeting.

Example 5 **Rayleigh-Benard cells heated from below**. Fluid rises and circles back

Figure 6.21b shows the effect of heat transfer. The temperature $T(x, y, t)$ enters with a convection-diffusion equation that comes from conservation of energy:

$$\textbf{Heat flow} \qquad \frac{\partial T}{\partial t} + \boldsymbol{u} \cdot \operatorname{grad} T = d\,\Delta T + \text{ heat source.} \tag{25}$$

For fluids, an important effect of temperature is to produce *variations in density.* This produces a buoyancy force in the Navier-Stokes equation. Other dimensionless quantities become crucial when temperature enters the problem. Allow me to mention two of the 37 numbers on Wikipedia. The Prandtl number is Pr ≈ 0.7 for gas, 7 for water, and 1000 for oil:

$$\textbf{Prandtl} \quad \text{Pr} = \frac{\text{viscous diffusion}}{\text{thermal diffusion}} \qquad \qquad \textbf{Rayleigh} \quad \text{Ra} = \frac{\text{heat convection}}{\text{heat conduction}}$$

Euler versus Lagrange

The Navier-Stokes equations determine the velocity at each point in space. That is the **Eulerian** description of the flow. The **Lagrangian** description gives the velocity of each particle, as it moves to different points. The fluid is flowing past Euler, who sits at a point and watches Lagrange go by.

This choice between Euler and Lagrange determines the equations and the choice of numerical method. The difference is clearest in the continuity equation that gives **conservation of mass**, when the density is $\rho(x, y, t)$:

$$\textbf{Euler} \quad \frac{\partial \rho}{\partial t} + \operatorname{div}(\rho \boldsymbol{u}) = 0 \qquad \qquad \textbf{Lagrange} \quad \frac{D\rho}{Dt} + \rho \operatorname{div} \boldsymbol{u} = 0 \tag{26}$$

Steady compressible flow has $\partial\rho/\partial t = 0$. Looking at one point, Euler sees no change in the density. But the **convective derivative $D\rho/Dt$** (the material derivative) will not be zero to Lagrange, if he is carried to points of different density. To make the two forms agree in (26), compare $\operatorname{div}(\rho\boldsymbol{u})$ with $\rho \operatorname{div} \boldsymbol{u} = \rho(\partial u/\partial x + \partial v/\partial y)$:

$$\operatorname{div}(\rho \boldsymbol{u}) = \frac{\partial}{\partial x}(\rho u) + \frac{\partial}{\partial y}(\rho v) = \rho \operatorname{div} \boldsymbol{u} + \boldsymbol{u} \cdot \operatorname{grad} \rho \tag{27}$$

That "convection term" $\boldsymbol{u} \cdot \operatorname{grad} \rho$ is included in the convective derivative $D\rho/Dt$. It accounts for movement of the fluid. The transport rule includes this extra term $\boldsymbol{u} \cdot \operatorname{grad} F$ in the derivative of any function F, not only the density ρ:

$$\textbf{Transport rule} \qquad \frac{DF}{Dt} = \frac{\partial F}{\partial t} + \boldsymbol{u} \cdot \operatorname{grad} F. \tag{28}$$

Euler uses $\partial F/\partial t$, fixed in space. Lagrange uses DF/Dt, moving with the fluid. Newton's Law applies to the momentum $\rho\boldsymbol{u}$ of a particle (*not* $\rho\boldsymbol{u}$ *at a point*). Then Euler-Navier-Stokes has to include that nonlinear term $(\boldsymbol{u} \cdot \operatorname{grad})\rho\boldsymbol{u}$.

Test the transport rule Suppose $F = tx$ in one space dimension, so $\partial F/\partial t = x$. After a small time dt, the particle at x moves to $x + u\,dt$. Lagrange sees the change DF from tx to $(t + dt)(x + u\,dt)$: As always, calculus ignores (dt^2):

$$DF = x\,dt + t\,u\,dt \quad \text{is the transport rule} \quad \frac{DF}{Dt} = \frac{\partial F}{\partial t} + u\frac{\partial F}{\partial x}. \tag{29}$$

Integral form: Transport theorem A more fundamental approach to the continuity equation starts with one of its integral forms, again with no source term:

Mass conservation
$$\frac{\partial}{\partial t}\int_{V_E} \rho\,dV = -\int_{S_E} \rho \boldsymbol{u}\cdot\boldsymbol{n}\,dS \quad \text{or} \quad \frac{D}{Dt}\int_{V_L} \rho\,dV = 0. \tag{30}$$

The first volume V_E is fixed in space; Euler looks at flow into V_E minus flow out. The volume V_L moves with the fluid; Lagrange sees no change of mass inside V_L. The two are connected by integrating the transport rule (26), changing variables from Euler to Lagrange: $D|J|/Dt = |J|\operatorname{div}\boldsymbol{u}$ gives the change in the Jacobian determinant. The momentum equation involves DF/Dt when F is $\boldsymbol{u}$ itself.

Particle methods Instead of finite differences for Navier-Stokes, Lagrange can follow a finite number of particles. These methods will be left for the cse website. We point here to their main difficulty: **The particles bunch up or spread out.** Euler's fixed space mesh is gone, and Lagrange's particle mesh gets badly distorted.

ALE methods Fluid-structure interactions (like blood flow in the heart) can use "*Arbitrary Lagrangian-Eulerian*" methods. The interface between fluid and structure is moving with forces across it and a fixed mesh on Euler's side (where large deformations can be handled). The Lagrange grid follows the motion (but large distortions will ruin that grid, which must be dynamic).

Acceleration and the Balance of Momentum

The Navier-Stokes equations express Newton's Law $F = ma$. In fluids as elsewhere, force equals mass times acceleration. The important point is that the acceleration is not $\partial\boldsymbol{u}/\partial t$. Newton's Law applies to a *fluid particle.* The vector $D\boldsymbol{u}/Dt$ comes from the transport rule for each component of $\boldsymbol{u} = (u, v)$:

Acceleration in the y-direction
$$\frac{Dv}{Dt} = \frac{\partial v}{\partial t} + \boldsymbol{u}\cdot\operatorname{grad} v. \tag{31}$$

Multiplication by the density ρ gives one side of Newton's Law, and the force density comes from the internal stress $\boldsymbol{T}$. Here two main categories of fluids part company:

A ***perfect fluid*** allows no tangential stress: $\boldsymbol{T} = -p\boldsymbol{I}$

A ***viscous fluid*** has friction: $\boldsymbol{T} = -p\boldsymbol{I} + \boldsymbol{\sigma} = -p\boldsymbol{I} + \lambda(\operatorname{div}\boldsymbol{u}) + 2\mu\boldsymbol{D}$

Without viscosity, all the stress comes from pressure. The force on every surface is perpendicular to that surface; a perfect fluid cares nothing for shear.

A viscous fluid has a stress matrix σ with nonzero entries off the diagonal (from shears in D). The difference between solids and fluids is that the fluid is moving! The displacement changes to the displacement *rate*—in other words the velocity $\boldsymbol{u}$. The strain in Section 3.7 changes to the strain rate $D_{ij} = (\partial u_i/\partial x_j + \partial u_j/\partial x_i)/2$:

$$\boxed{\text{velocity } \boldsymbol{u}} \longrightarrow \boxed{\text{strain rate } \boldsymbol{D}} \longrightarrow \boxed{\text{stress } \boldsymbol{T}} \longrightarrow \boxed{\rho \frac{D\boldsymbol{u}}{Dt} = \rho \boldsymbol{f} + \operatorname{div} \boldsymbol{T}.} \tag{32}$$

That is the equation of motion for a Newtonian fluid. The divergence of the stress gives the internal force, as it did for solids. We compute $\operatorname{div} \boldsymbol{T}$ by columns:

Perfect fluids $\qquad \boldsymbol{T} = -p\boldsymbol{I}$ and $\operatorname{div} \boldsymbol{T} = -\operatorname{grad} p$

Viscous incompressible fluids $\qquad \operatorname{div} \boldsymbol{T} = -\operatorname{grad} p + \mu\, \Delta \boldsymbol{u}.$

That last calculation is developed in Problem 3. The pressure $p(\rho, T)$ in compressible flow is a function of density and temperature; there is an equation of state. For incompressible flow p is the Lagrange multiplier for the continuity equation $\operatorname{div} \boldsymbol{u} = 0$. We have reached the two key equations for fluids:

A perfect fluid obeys Euler's equation
$$\rho \frac{D\boldsymbol{u}}{Dt} = \rho \boldsymbol{f} - \operatorname{grad} p \tag{33}$$

A viscous incompressible fluid obeys Navier-Stokes ($\nu = \mu/\rho$)
$$\rho \frac{D\boldsymbol{u}}{Dt} = \rho \boldsymbol{f} - \operatorname{grad} p + \mu \Delta \boldsymbol{u} \tag{34}$$

Incompressibility and continuity are expressed by $D\rho/Dt = 0$ and $\operatorname{div} \boldsymbol{u} = 0$.

Euler and Bernoulli Equations

When every term is a gradient, Euler's equation (33) can be integrated once. The trick is to rewrite the advection by using a vector identity for $\boldsymbol{u} = (u_1, u_2, u_3)$:

$$(\boldsymbol{u} \cdot \operatorname{grad})\, \boldsymbol{u} = \frac{1}{2} \operatorname{grad}(u_1^2 + u_2^2 + u_3^2) - \boldsymbol{u} \times \operatorname{curl} \boldsymbol{u}. \tag{35}$$

Suppose the flow is stationary and irrotational ($\partial \boldsymbol{u}/\partial t = 0$ and $\operatorname{curl} \boldsymbol{u} = 0$), and $\boldsymbol{f}$ is a conservative force like gravity: $\boldsymbol{f} = -\operatorname{grad} G$. Divide Euler's equation by ρ:

Reduced Euler
$$\frac{1}{2} \operatorname{grad}(u_1^2 + u_2^2 + u_3^2) = -\frac{1}{\rho} \operatorname{grad} p - \operatorname{grad} G. \tag{36}$$

If $\rho = \text{constant}$, this says that the gradient of $\frac{1}{2}(u_1^2 + u_2^2 + u_3^2) + p/\rho + G$ is zero. Therefore that function must be constant—which yields the most directly useful equation in nonlinear fluid mechanics:

Bernoulli's equation
$$\frac{1}{2}(u_1^2 + u_2^2 + u_3^2) + \frac{p}{\rho} + G = \text{constant}. \tag{37}$$

Higher velocity $\boldsymbol{u}$ means lower pressure p. This partly accounts for the possibility of throwing a curve ball. When the ball has overspin, the air below it moves faster and lowers the pressure—causing the ball to sink. Bernoulli does not account for a knuckleball, which spins so slowly that it can drift the other way. In fact we would need a different Bernoulli equation—a different first integral of the equation of motion—to permit rotation.

Example 6 A tank has fluid of height h above a hole. How fast does the fluid come out?

Force potential $G = gz$ $$\frac{1}{2}(u_1^2 + u_2^2 + u_3^2) + \frac{p}{\rho} + gz = \text{constant}.$$

At the top of the tank every term is zero. At the hole, the pressure is also zero—because that hole at $z = -h$ is open. Multiplying by 2 and taking square roots, the speed is $|\boldsymbol{u}| = \sqrt{2gh}$—which is curiously the same as if particles were in free fall down to the hole.

To go further than Bernoulli, we need to distinguish 2D flow from 3D. Take the curl of both sides of Euler's equation (33). On the right side the curl of a gradient is zero, and we assume $\boldsymbol{f} = 0$. On the left side the result is extremely satisfactory. The vorticity $\boldsymbol{\omega} = \operatorname{curl} \boldsymbol{u}$ satisfies a straightforward nonlinear equation:

Vorticity equation in 3D $$\frac{D\boldsymbol{\omega}}{Dt} = (\boldsymbol{\omega} \cdot \text{grad})\boldsymbol{u}. \tag{38}$$

In two-dimensional flow with $\boldsymbol{u} = (u, v, 0)$, the vorticity is $\boldsymbol{\omega} = (0, 0, \omega_3)$. Now nothing depends on z. Therefore $D\boldsymbol{\omega}/Dt = 0$ and there is a new conservation law: **The vorticity $\boldsymbol{\omega}$ is conserved along every streamline**, with stream function s:

$$(\boldsymbol{u}, \boldsymbol{v}) = \left(\frac{\partial s}{\partial y}, -\frac{\partial s}{\partial x}\right) \qquad \omega_3 = -\frac{\partial}{\partial x}\left(\frac{\partial s}{\partial x}\right) - \frac{\partial}{\partial y}\left(\frac{\partial s}{\partial y}\right) = -\Delta s. \tag{39}$$

This is the ***vorticity-stream function*** formulation: $D\omega_3/Dt = 0$ is nonlinear for the vorticity, and $\omega_3 = -\Delta s$ is linear for the stream function.

In three dimensions, vortices are stretched and the flow is much more complex. However it is still true that vortex lines and vortex sheets move with the fluid. Equation (38) is the basis for a powerful numerical method—the ***vortex method***. This follows discrete vortices through violent motion: turbulent combustion, boundary layers, instability at high Reynolds numbers, and general breakdown. The vortex method competes with the primitive variables u, v, p for supremacy.

The Onset of Turbulence

When the viscosity terms are too weak to prevent oscillations, **turbulence begins.** At some geometry-dependent point (possibly $\text{Re} \approx 20{,}000$), averaged equations are needed. Point values become too hard to compute and interpret. Small scale motion has an important effect at large scales, and the physics is still hotly debated.

Here are three key choices of numerical methods at the onset of turbulence:

DNS Direct Numerical Solution (of Navier-Stokes)
LES Large Eddy Simulation (of interactions between scales of motion)
RANS Reynolds Averaged Navier-Stokes

The linear convection-diffusion equation $u_t = cu_x + du_{xx}$ shows a similar difficulty. As c/d increases, convection dominates diffusion. The nonlinearity of Navier-Stokes, coming from the fact that c depends on $\boldsymbol{u}$, adds far more difficulty. Section 6.6 on Nonlinear Conservation Laws dealt with $c(u)\, du/dx$ in a stable way.

Example 7 The "ballerina effect" as an ice-skater raises her arms

The velocity $\boldsymbol{v} = (x, -y, 0)$ has no curl and no divergence (potential ϕ and stream function):

Potential flow $\quad \phi = -\frac{1}{2}(x^2 - y^2)$ and $\boldsymbol{v} = \operatorname{grad}\phi$ and $s = xy$.

Rotation comes from a **shear flow**: $\boldsymbol{w} = (0, 0, y)$ has $\operatorname{div}\boldsymbol{w} = 0$ but $\operatorname{curl}\boldsymbol{w} = (1, 0, 0)$. This has a stream function $s = -\frac{1}{2}y^2$ but no potential. The fluid moves in the z-direction (Figure 6.22) but some particles go faster than others. There is rotation around the x-axis (no particle actually goes *around* the axis!) since that is the direction of $\operatorname{curl}\boldsymbol{w}$.

Now we combine the two flows. The velocities $\boldsymbol{v}$ and $\boldsymbol{w}$ cannot be added, since the equations of motion are not linear. The mixture of potential flow $\boldsymbol{v}$ and shear flow $\boldsymbol{w}$ gives an *unsteady* velocity vector $\boldsymbol{u}$, with increasing spin rate e^t:

Solution $\quad \boldsymbol{u} = (x, -y, e^t y)$ with $\operatorname{div}\boldsymbol{u} = 0$ and $\boldsymbol{w} = \operatorname{curl}\boldsymbol{u} = (e^t, 0, 0)$.

The flow is three-dimensional, with particles going up or down while their projection moves along the hyperbolas. The vorticity $\boldsymbol{\omega} = \operatorname{curl}\boldsymbol{u} = (e^t, 0, 0)$ satisfies equation (38). Circles stretch into ellipses that spin around the x-axis because of $\boldsymbol{\omega}$.

The ballerina becomes tall and thin, as her arms go up. She spins faster and faster like an ice-skater. I am a little sorry she is spinning around the x-axis.

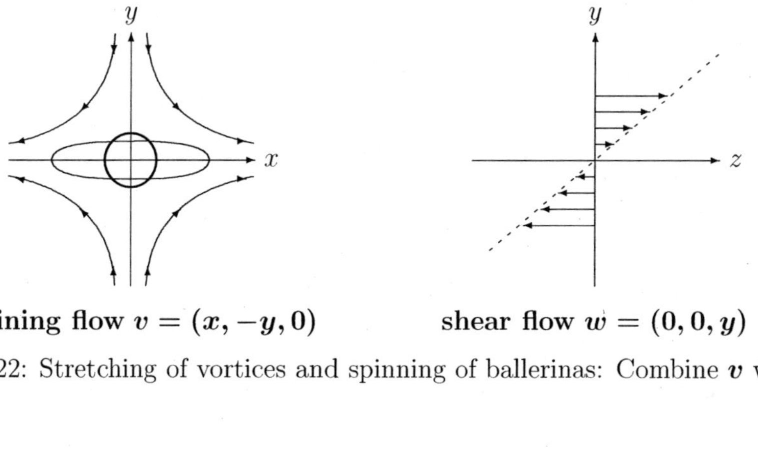

straining flow $\boldsymbol{v} = (x, -y, 0)$ **shear flow $\boldsymbol{w} = (0, 0, y)$**

Figure 6.22: Stretching of vortices and spinning of ballerinas: Combine $\boldsymbol{v}$ with $\boldsymbol{w}$.

Problem Set 6.7

1 Apply the Divergence Theorem to mass conservation (30) in V_E. Then derive Euler's continuity equation $\partial\rho/\partial t + \operatorname{div}(\rho\boldsymbol{u}) = 0$ from $\operatorname{div}^{\mathrm{T}} = -\operatorname{grad}$.

2 Find the material derivatives $D\rho/Dt$ and $D\boldsymbol{u}/Dt$ for these two flows:

$$\rho = x^2 + y^2, \quad \boldsymbol{u} = (y,\ x,\ 0) \quad \text{and} \quad \rho = ze^t, \quad \boldsymbol{u} = (x,\ 0,\ -z).$$

Which satisfies the continuity equation (26) and which is incompressible?

3 A viscous incompressible fluid has $\operatorname{div}\boldsymbol{u} = 0$ and $\sigma_{ij} = \mu(\partial u_i/\partial x_j + \partial u_j/\partial x_i)$. Show that the force $\operatorname{div}\sigma$ from that stress is $\mu\Delta\boldsymbol{u}$. This is the viscosity term in the Navier-Stokes equation.

4 Suppose gravitational acceleration g is added to the Navier-Stokes equation, with the dimension cm/sec^2. Show that the *Froude number* $\mathrm{Fr} = V^2/Lg$ is dimensionless. Two gravity flows are similar if they share both Re and Fr.

5 The *compressible* gas dynamics equation comes from the relation of p to ρ:

$$\rho(\boldsymbol{u}\cdot\operatorname{grad})\boldsymbol{u} = -\operatorname{grad} p = -c^2 \operatorname{grad}\rho \qquad \left(c^2 = \frac{dp}{d\rho} = \text{sound speed}\right).$$

Derive the conservation law in Example 5 of Section 6.6.

6 An ideal fluid is flowing at pressure p and velocity v along a pipe of area A. If the area shrinks to $\frac{1}{2}A$, what is the new velocity (by conservation of fluid)? What is the new pressure (by Bernoulli)?

7 Why does Bernoulli's equation not hold for the Poiseuille flow in Example 2?

8 A viscous fluid in a horizontal pipe has velocity $u = c(y^2 + z^2 - R^2)/4\mu$ and pressure $p = cx + p_0$. There is no slip at the pipe boundary $y^2 + z^2 = R^2$.

(a) Verify that the Navier-Stokes equations are satisfied for $\boldsymbol{u} = (u, 0, 0)$.

(b) By integrating u over the circular cross-section find $-\pi c R^4/8\mu$ as the net flow rate. This is the classical experiment to determine the viscosity μ.

9 (a) Verify the key vector identity (35).

(b) Take the curl of both sides to reach $-(\operatorname{curl}\boldsymbol{u}\cdot\operatorname{grad})\boldsymbol{u}$ when $\operatorname{div}\boldsymbol{u} = 0$.

10 Fluid in a rotating barrel has force potential $G = -gz - \frac{1}{2}\omega^2(x^2 + y^2)$, from gravity and centrifugal force. Its velocity is zero with respect to the barrel. Show from Bernoulli that the surface has the parabolic shape $z = -\omega^2(x^2 + y^2)/2g$.

11 Viscosity leads to an extra boundary condition, for example in 2D flow:

With viscosity	The no-slip condition is $u = 0$ and $v = 0$. *Two* conditions.
Without viscosity	Flow along but not through: $\boldsymbol{u}\cdot\boldsymbol{n} = 0$. *One* condition.

Justify by counting derivatives in the Navier-Stokes and Euler equations.

6.8 LEVEL SETS AND FAST MARCHING

The level sets of $f(x, y)$ are the sets on which the function is constant. For example $f(x, y) = x^2 + y^2$ is constant on circles around the origin. Geometrically, a level plane $z =$ constant will cut through the surface $z = f(x, y)$ on a level set. One attractive feature of working with level sets is that their topology can change (pieces of the level set can separate or come together) just by changing the constant.

Starting from one level set, the **signed distance function** $d(x, y)$ is especially important. It gives the *distance* to the level set, and also the sign: typically $d > 0$ outside and $d < 0$ inside. For the unit circle, $d = r - 1 = \sqrt{x^2 + y^2} - 1$ will be the signed distance function. In the mesh generation algorithm of Section 2.____, it was convenient to describe the region by its distance function $d(x, y)$.

A fundamental fact of calculus: The gradient of $f(x, y)$ is perpendicular to its level sets. Reason: In the tangent direction t to the level set, $f(x, y)$ is not changing and $(\operatorname{grad} f) \cdot t$ is zero. So $\operatorname{grad} f$ is in the normal direction. For the function $x^2 + y^2$, the gradient $(2x, 2y)$ points outward from the circular level sets. The gradient of $d(x, y) = \sqrt{x^2 + y^2} - 1$ points the same way, and it has a special property: **The gradient of a distance function is a unit vector**. It is the *unit* normal $n(x, y)$ to the level sets. For the circles,

$$\operatorname{grad}(\sqrt{x^2 + y^2} - 1) = (\frac{x}{r}, \frac{y}{r}) \qquad \text{and} \qquad |\operatorname{grad}|^2 = \frac{x^2}{r^2} + \frac{y^2}{r^2} = 1\,. \tag{1}$$

You could think of the level set $d(x, y) = 0$ as a wall of fire. This firefront will move normal to itself. If it has constant velocity 1 then at time T the fire will reach all points on the level set $d(x, y) = T$.

That "wall of fire" example brings out an important point when the zero level set has a corner (it might be shaped like a **V**). The points at distance d outside that set (the firefront at time d) will lie on lines parallel to the sides of the **V**, and also on a circular arc of radius d around the corner. For $d < 0$ the **V** moves *inward*. It remains a **V** (with no smoothing of the corner).

The central problem of the level set method is to **propagate a curve** like the firefront. A velocity field $v = (v_1, v_2)$ gives the direction and speed of each point for the movement. At time $t = 0$, the curve is the level set where $d(x, y) = 0$. At later times the curve is the zero level set of a function $\phi(x, y, t)$. The fundamental **level set equation** in its first form is

$$\frac{d\phi}{dt} + v \cdot \operatorname{grad} \phi = 0, \quad \text{with } \phi = d(x, y) \text{ at } t = 0\,. \tag{2}$$

In our wall of fire example, v would be the unit vector in the normal direction to the firefront: $v = n = \operatorname{grad} \phi / |\operatorname{grad} \phi|$. In all cases it is only the normal component $F = v \cdot n$ that moves the curve! Tangential movement (like rotating a circle around its center) gives no change in the curve as a whole. By rewriting $v \cdot \operatorname{grad} \phi$, the level set equation takes a second form that is more useful in computation:

$$v \cdot \operatorname{grad}\phi = v \cdot \frac{\operatorname{grad}\phi}{|\operatorname{grad}\phi|}|\operatorname{grad}\phi| = F|\operatorname{grad}\phi| \quad \text{leads to} \quad \frac{d\phi}{dt} + F|\operatorname{grad}\phi| = 0\,. \quad (3)$$

We only need to know the velocity field v (and only its normal component F) near the *current location* of the level curve–not everywhere else. We are propagating a curve. The velocity field may be fixed (easiest case) or it may depend on the local shape of the curve (nonlinear case). An important example is **motion by mean curvature**: $F = -\kappa$. The neat property $|\operatorname{grad}\phi| = 1$ of distance functions simplifies the formulas for the normal n and curvature κ:

When ϕ is a distance function

$$n = \frac{\operatorname{grad}\phi}{|\operatorname{grad}\phi|} \quad \text{becomes} \quad n = \operatorname{grad}\phi$$
$$\kappa = \operatorname{div} n \quad \text{becomes} \quad \kappa = \operatorname{div}(\operatorname{grad}\phi) = \text{Laplacian of } \phi \quad (4)$$

But here is an unfortunate point for $t > 0$. Constant speed ($F = 1$) in the normal direction does maintain the property $|\operatorname{grad}\phi| = 1$ of a distance function. Motion by mean curvature, and other motions, will destroy this property. To recover the simple formulas (4) for distance functions, the level set method often **reinitializes** the problem—restarting from the current time t_0 and computing the distance function $d(x, y)$ to the current level set $\phi(x, y, t_0) = 0$. This reinitialization was the **Fast Marching Method**, which finds distances from nearby meshpoints to the current level set.

We describe this quick method to compute distances to meshpoints, and then discuss the numerical solution of the level set equation (3) on the mesh.

Fast Marching Method

The problem is to march outward, computing distances from meshpoints to the interface (the current level set where $\phi = 0$). Imagine that we know these distances for the grid points adjacent to the interface. (We describe fast marching but not the full algorithm of reinitialization.) The key step is to compute the distance to the *next nearest meshpoint*. Then the front moves further outward with velocity $F = 1$. When the front crosses a new meshpoint, it will become the next nearest and its distance will be settled next.

So we accept one meshpoint at a time. Distances to further meshpoints are tentative (not accepted). They have to be recomputed using the newly accepted meshpoint and its distance. The Fast Marching Method must quickly take these steps recursively:

1. Find the tentative meshpoint p with smallest distance (to be accepted).

2. Update the tentative distances to all meshpoints adjacent to p.

To speed up step **1**, we maintain a binary tree of unaccepted meshpoints and their tentative distances. The smallest distance is at the top of the tree, which identifies p. When that value is removed from the tree, others move up to form the new tree.

Recursively, each vacancy is filled by the smaller of the two distance values below it. Then step **2** updates those values at points adjacent to p. These updated values may have to move (a little) up or down to reset the tree. In general, the updated values should be smaller (they mostly move up, since they have the latest meshpoint p as a new candidate in finding the shortest route to the original interface).

The Fast Marching Method finds distances to N meshpoints in time $O(N \log N)$. The method applies when the front moves *in one direction only*. The underlying equation is $F|\nabla T| = 1$ (Eikonal equation with $F > 0$). The front never crosses a point twice (and the crossing time is T). If the front is allowed to move in both directions, and F can change sign, we need the initial value formulation (3).

Lagrangian versus Eulerian

A fundamental choice in analyzing and computing fluid flow is between Lagrange and Euler. For the minimizing function in optimization, they arrived at the same "Euler-Lagrange equation". In studying fluids, they chose *very different* approaches:

> **Lagrange follows the path of each particle of fluid.** He moves.
>
> **Euler sees which particles pass through each point.** He sits.

Lagrange is more direct. He "*tracks*" the front. At time zero, points on the front have positions $x(0)$. They move according to vector differential equations $dx/dt = V(x)$. If we mark and follow a finite set of points, equally spaced at the start, serious difficulties can appear. Their spacing can get very tight or very wide (forcing us to remove or add marker points). The initial curve can split apart or cross itself (changes of topology). The level set method escapes from these difficulties by going Eulerian.

For Euler, the x-y coordinate system is fixed. He "*captures*" the front implicitly, as a level set of $\phi(x, y, t)$. When the computational grid is also fixed, we are constantly interpolating to locate level sets and compute distance functions. Squeezing or stretching or tangling of the front appear as changes in ϕ, not as disasters for the mesh.

The velocity v *on the interface* determines its movement. When the level set method needs v at a meshpoint off the interface, a good candidate is the value of v at the nearest point on the interface.

Upwind Differencing

The level set finite difference method is properly developed in the books by its originators: Sethian [133] and Osher and Fedkiw [122]. Here we concentrate on an essential point: *upwind differencing. Recall* from Section 1.2 the three simplest approximations **F**, **B**, **C** to the first derivative $d\phi/dx$: *Forward, Backward, Centered:*

$$\mathbf{F} \quad \frac{\phi(x+h)-\phi(x)}{h} \qquad \mathbf{B} \quad \frac{\phi(x)-\phi(x-h)}{h} \qquad \mathbf{C} \quad \frac{\phi(x+h)-\phi(x-h)}{2h}$$

Which do we use in the simple convection equation $d\phi/dt + a\,d\phi/dx = 0$? Its true solution is $\phi(x-at,0)$. *The choice of finite differences depends on the sign of* a. The flow moves left to right for $a < 0$. Then the *backward* difference is natural—the "upwind" value $\phi(x-h,t)$ on the left should contribute to $\phi(x,t+\Delta t)$. The downwind value $\phi(x+h,t)$ on the right moves further downwind during the time step, and has no influence at x.

When the movement of the solution (and the wind) is right to left (with $a > 0$), then the *forward* difference will use the appropriate upwind value $\phi(x+h,t)$ along with $\phi(x,t)$, in computing the new $\phi(x,t+\Delta t)$.

Notice the time-step limitation $|a|\Delta t \leq h$. In time Δt, the "wind" will bring the true value of ϕ from $x + a\Delta t$ to the point x. If $a > 0$ and finite differences reach upwind to $x+h$, that must be far enough to include information at $x + a\Delta t$. So the *Courant-Friedrichs-Lewy condition* is $a\Delta t \leq h$. The numerical waves must propagate at least as fast as the physical waves (and in the right direction!). Downwind differencing is looking for that information on the wrong side of the point x, and is doomed to failure. Centered differencing in space is unstable for ordinary forward Euler.

By careful choice of the right finite differences, Osher has constructed higher-order essentially non-oscillatory (ENO) schemes. A central idea in nonlinear problems, where the differential equation has multiple solutions (see Section 6.6), is to choose the "*viscosity solution.*" This physically correct solution appears in the limit as an extra ϵu_{xx} diffusion term goes to zero. With good differencing the viscosity solution is the one that appears as $\Delta x \to 0$.

At this point, the level set method does not appear in large production codes. In research papers it has successfully solved a great variety of difficult nonlinear problems.

CHAPTER 7

SOLVING LARGE SYSTEMS

7.1 ELIMINATION WITH REORDERING

Finite elements and finite differences produce large linear systems $KU = F$. *The matrix K is extremely sparse.* It has only a small number of nonzero entries in a typical row. In "physical space" those nonzeros are tightly clustered—they come from neighboring nodes and meshpoints. But we cannot number N^2 nodes in a plane in any way that keeps all neighbors close together! So in 2-dimensional problems, and even more in 3-dimensional problems, we meet three questions right away:

1. How best to number the nodes

2. How to use the sparseness of K (when nonzeros might be widely separated)

3. Whether to choose **direct elimination** or an **iterative method**.

That last point separates this section on elimination (where **node order** is important) from later sections on iterative methods (where **preconditioning** is crucial).

To fix ideas, we will create the n equations $KU = F$ from Laplace's difference equation in an interval, a square, and a cube. With N unknowns in each direction, K has order $n = N$ or N^2 or N^3. There are 3 or 5 or 7 nonzeros in a typical row of the matrix. Second differences in 1D, 2D, and 3D are shown in Figure 7.1.

Along an inside row of the matrix, the entries add to zero. In two dimensions this is $4-1-1-1-1=0$. This "zero sum" remains true for finite elements (the element shapes decide the exact numbers). It reflects the fact that $u = 1$ solves Laplace's equation and $U = \mathsf{ones}(n,1)$ has differences equal to zero.

The constant vector solves $KU = 0$ *except near the boundaries.* When a neighbor is a boundary point, its known value moves onto the right side of $KU = F$. Then that row of K is *not zero sum.* The "boundary rows" of $K2\text{D}$ don't have four -1's. Otherwise the matrix would be singular like $B2\text{D}$, if $K2\text{D} * \mathsf{ones}(\text{n},1) = \mathsf{zeros}(\text{n},1)$.

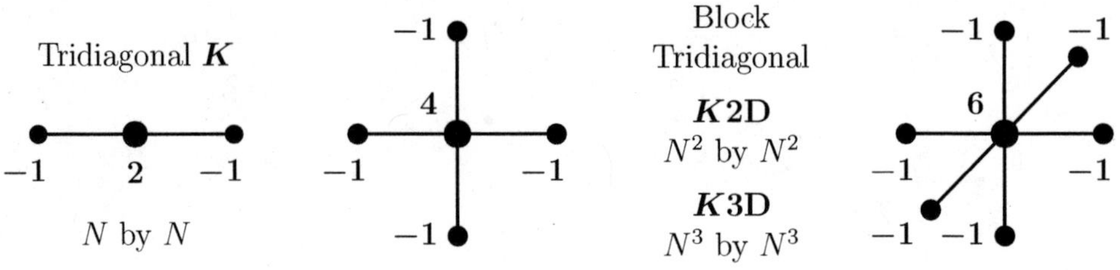

Figure 7.1: $3, 5, 7$-point difference molecules for $-u_{xx}, -u_{xx} - u_{yy}, -u_{xx} - u_{yy} - u_{zz}$.

Using block matrix notation, we can create the matrix $\boldsymbol{K}\mathbf{2D}$ from the familiar N by N second difference matrix K. We number the nodes of the square a row at a time (this "natural numbering" is not necessarily best). Then the -1's for the neighbors above and below are N positions away from the main diagonal of $\boldsymbol{K}\mathbf{2D}$.

The 2D matrix is *block tridiagonal with tridiagonal blocks*:

$$K = \begin{bmatrix} 2 & -1 & & \\ -1 & 2 & -1 & \\ & \cdot & \cdot & \cdot \\ & & -1 & 2 \end{bmatrix} \qquad \boldsymbol{K}\mathbf{2D} = \begin{bmatrix} K+2I & -I & & \\ -I & K+2I & -I & \\ \longleftrightarrow & & \cdot & \cdot \\ \textit{width } w{=}N & & -I & K+2I \end{bmatrix} \tag{1}$$

Size $\boldsymbol{N}$ **Time $\boldsymbol{N}$**

Elimination in this order: Size $\boldsymbol{n = N^2}$
Space $\boldsymbol{nw = N^3}$ Time $\boldsymbol{nw^2 = N^4}$

The matrix $K2D$ has 4's down the main diagonal. Its bandwidth $w = N$ is the distance from the diagonal to the nonzeros in $-I$. Many of the spaces in between are filled during elimination. Then the storage space required for the factors in $K2D = LU$ is of order $nw = N^3$. The time is proportional to $nw^2 = N^4$, when n rows each contain w nonzeros, and w nonzeros below the pivot require elimination.

Again, the operation count grows as nw^2. Each elimination step uses a row of length w. There can be nw nonzeros to eliminate below the diagonal. If some entries stay zero inside the band, elimination could be faster than nw^2—*this is our goal.*

Those counts are not impossibly large in many practical 2D problems (and we show how they can be reduced). The horrifying $\boldsymbol{N^7}$ count will come for elimination on $K3D$. Suppose the 3D cubic grid is numbered a plane at a time. In each plane we see a 2D square, and $K3D$ has blocks of order N^2 from those squares. With each square numbered as above, the blocks come from $\boldsymbol{K}\mathbf{2D}$ and $\boldsymbol{I} = \boldsymbol{I}\mathbf{2D}$:

$$\boldsymbol{K}\mathbf{3D} = \begin{bmatrix} \boldsymbol{K}\mathbf{2D}+2\boldsymbol{I} & -\boldsymbol{I} & & \\ -\boldsymbol{I} & \boldsymbol{K}\mathbf{2D}+2\boldsymbol{I} & -\boldsymbol{I} & \\ \longleftrightarrow & & \cdot & \cdot \\ \textit{width } w = N^2 & & -\boldsymbol{I} & \boldsymbol{K}\mathbf{2D}+2\boldsymbol{I} \end{bmatrix}$$

3D Size $n = N^3$
Bandwidth $w = N^2$
Elimination space N^5
Elimination time $\boldsymbol{N^7}$

The main diagonal of K3D contains 6's, and "inside rows" have six -1's. Next to a face or edge or corner of the cube, we lose one or two or three of those -1's. From any node to the node above it, we count N^2 nodes. The $-I$ blocks are far from the main diagonal and the bandwidth is $w = N^2$. Then $nw^2 = N^7$.

New Nonzeros and New Edges

Let me focus attention immediately on the key problem, when elimination is applied to sparse matrices. *The zeros "inside the band" may fill with nonzeros.* Those nonzeros enter the triangular factors of $K = LL^{\mathrm{T}}$ (Figure 7.2a). We see them by spy(L) and we count the nonzeros by nnz(L). When the pivot row is multiplied by ℓ_{ij} and subtracted from a lower row, *every nonzero in the pivot row will infect that lower row.*

Sometimes a matrix has a full row, from an equation like $\sum U_j = 1$ (see Figure 7.3). That full row better come last! Otherwise all rows below it will fill.

A good way to visualize the nonzero structure (sparsity structure) of K is by a graph. The rows of K are nodes in the graph. A nonzero entry K_{ij} produces an edge between nodes i and j. **The graph of $\boldsymbol{K}$2D is exactly the mesh in $\boldsymbol{x}$-$\boldsymbol{y}$ space.** Filling in a nonzero adds a new edge. Watch how fill-in happens in elimination:

FILL-IN *New nonzero in the matrix* / *New edge in the graph*

Suppose a_{ij} is eliminated. A multiple of row j is subtracted from the later row i. If a_{jk} is nonzero in row j, then $\boldsymbol{a_{ik}^{\text{new}}}$ becomes filled in row i:

Matrix nonzeros $\begin{matrix} a_{jj} & a_{jk} \\ a_{ij} & 0 \end{matrix} \longrightarrow \begin{matrix} a_{jj} & a_{jk} \\ 0 & a_{ik}^{\text{new}} \end{matrix}$ **Graph edges**

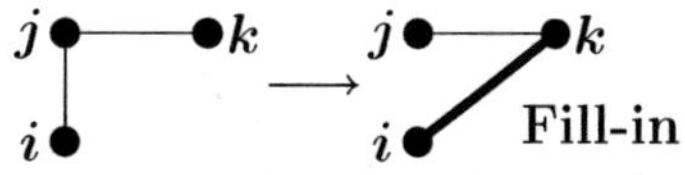

Kronecker Product

One good way to create K2D from K and I (N by N) is the kron(A, B) command. This replaces each number a_{ij} by the block $a_{ij}B$. To take second differences in all columns at the same time, and all rows, kron gives I blocks and K blocks:

$$\boldsymbol{K}\mathbf{2D} = \text{kron}(K, I) + \text{kron}(I, K) = \begin{bmatrix} 2I & -I & \cdot \\ -I & 2I & \cdot \\ \cdot & \cdot & \cdot \end{bmatrix} + \begin{bmatrix} K & & \\ & K & \\ & & \cdot \end{bmatrix} \qquad (2)$$

This sum agrees with $\boldsymbol{K}$**2D** displayed in equation (1). Then a 3D box needs K2D and I2D $=$ kron(I, I) in each plane. This easily adjusts to allow rectangles, with I's and K's of different sizes. For a cube, take second differences inside all planes with kron(K2D$, I$). Then add differences in the z-direction with kron(I2D$, K$):

$$\boldsymbol{K}\mathbf{3D} = \text{kron}(K\text{2D}, I) + \text{kron}(I\text{2D}, K) \quad \text{has size} \quad (N^2)(N) = N^3. \qquad (3)$$

Here K and $K2D$ and $K3D$ of size N and N^2 and N^3 are serving as *models of the type of matrices that we meet.* But we have to say that there are special ways to work with these particular matrices. The x, y, z directions are separable. Section 3.5 on Fast Poisson Solvers uses FFT-type methods in each direction.

MATLAB must know that the matrices are sparse. If we create $I =$ speye(N) and K comes from spdiags as in Section 1.1, the kron command will preserve the sparse treatment. Allow me to display spy($\boldsymbol{L}$) for the triangular factor $\boldsymbol{L}$, before and after reordering $\boldsymbol{K2D}$ by minimum degree. *The latter has much less fill-in.* Your eye may not see this so clearly, but the count of nonzeros (365 to 519) is convincing. ***Even better, look at the minimum degree movie on* math.mit.edu/18086**.

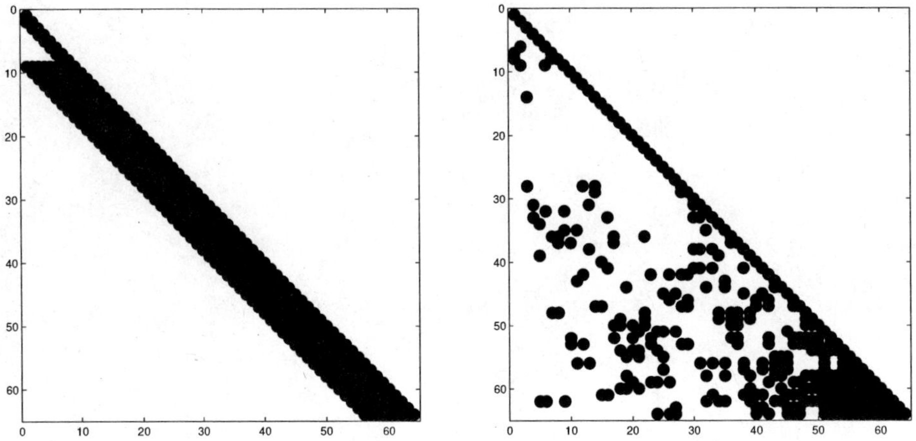

Figure 7.2: (a) The band is filled by elimination. (b) L from good reordering.

Minimum Degree Algorithm

We now describe a useful way to reorder meshpoints and equations in $KU = F$. The ordering achieves *approximate minimum degree* at each step—**the number of nonzeros below the pivot is almost minimized**. This is essentially the algorithm used in MATLAB's command $U = K\backslash F$, when K has been defined as a sparse matrix. Among these functions from the sparfun directory, notice how sparse(find(K)) $= K$:

find	(positions + values of nonzeros)	sparse	(K from positions + values)
spy	(visualize sparsity pattern)	nnz	(number of nonzero entries)

colamd and symamd (approximate minimum degree permutation of K)

You can test and use the minimum degree algorithms without a careful analysis. The approximations are faster than the exact minimum degree permutations colmmd and symmmd. The speed (in two dimensions) and the roundoff errors are quite acceptable.

In the Laplace examples, the minimum degree ordering of nodes is very irregular compared to "a row at a time." The final bandwidth is probably not decreased. But many nonzero entries are postponed as long as possible. That is the key.

For an **arrow matrix** that minimum degree ordering produces large bandwidth, but ***no fill-in***. The triangular L and U keep all the same zeros. *Put the full row last.*

$$\begin{array}{l} \textbf{best} \\ \textbf{when} \\ \textbf{last} \\ \longrightarrow \end{array}
\begin{bmatrix} * & & & \textbf{Faster} & & & * \\ & * & & & & & * \\ & & * & & & & * \\ & & & * & & & * \\ & & & & * & & * \\ & & & & & * & * \\ * & * & * & * & * & * & * \end{bmatrix}
\begin{array}{c} \textbf{Bandwidth} \\ \longleftarrow \text{6 and 3} \longrightarrow \\ \text{diagonals} \\ \\ \textbf{Fill-in} \\ \longleftarrow \text{0 and 6} \longrightarrow \\ \text{entries} \end{array}
\begin{bmatrix} * & & & * & & \textbf{Slower} & \\ & * & & * & & & \\ & & * & * & & & \\ * & * & * & * & * & * & * \\ & & & * & * & \mathbf{F} & \mathbf{F} \\ & & & * & \mathbf{F} & * & \mathbf{F} \\ & & & * & \mathbf{F} & \mathbf{F} & * \end{bmatrix}$$

Figure 7.3: Minimum degree (arrow matrix) defeats minimum bandwidth.

The second ordering in Figure 7.3 reduces the bandwidth from 6 to 3. But when row 4 is used as the pivot row, the entries indicated by **F** are *filled in*. That lower quarter becomes full, with $O(n^2)$ nonzeros in L and U. You see that the whole nonzero "profile" of the matrix decides the fill-in, not just the bandwidth.

Here is another example, from the **red-black ordering** of a square grid. Color the gridpoints like a checkerboard. Then all four neighbors of a red point are black, and vice versa. If we number the red points before the black points, the *permuted* $K2D$ (it is not formed explicitly) has blocks of $4I$ on its diagonal:

Red-black permutation
$$\boldsymbol{P}\,(\boldsymbol{K}\mathbf{2D})\,\boldsymbol{P}^{\mathrm{T}} = \begin{bmatrix} 4\,I_{\text{red}} & -1\text{'s} \\ -1\text{'s} & 4\,I_{\text{black}} \end{bmatrix}. \qquad (4)$$

This pushes the -1's and the fill-in into the lower rows. Notice how P permutes the rows (the equations) and $P^{\mathrm{T}} = P^{-1}$ permutes the columns (the unknowns).

Now the real thing. **Minimum degree algorithms** choose the $(k+1)$st pivot column, after k columns have been eliminated below the diagonal. The algorithms look at the nonzeros in the lower right matrix of size $n-k$.

Symmetric case: Choose the remaining meshpoint with the **fewest neighbors**.
Unsymmetric case: Choose the remaining column with the **fewest nonzeros**.

The component of U corresponding to that column is renumbered $k+1$. So is the meshpoint in the finite difference grid. Of course elimination in that column will normally produce new nonzeros in the remaining columns. Some fill-in is unavoidable. The algorithm keeps track of the new positions of nonzeros, and the actual entries. It is the ***positions*** that decide the ***ordering*** of unknowns (a permutation vector gives the new order). Then the *entries* in K decide the *numbers* in L and U.

Elimination on the Graph of Nodes

The **degree of a node** is the number of connections to other nodes. This is the number of off-diagonal nonzeros in that column of K. In Figure 7.4 the corner nodes $1, 3, 4, 6$ all begin with degree 2. The midpoint nodes 2 and 5 have degree 3. *The degrees change as elimination proceeds*! **Nodes connected to the pivot become connected to each other—and that entry of the matrix fills in.**

You will see how a renumbering of meshpoints preserves the symmetry of K. The rows and columns are reordered in the same way. Then $P K_{\text{old}} P^{\mathrm{T}} = K_{\text{new}} = K_{\text{new}}^{\mathrm{T}}$.

Example 1 Figure 7.4 shows a small example of the minimal degree ordering, for Laplace's 5-point scheme. **Edges in the graph give nonzeros in the matrix**. New edges from elimination give the fill-in **F** in the matrix.

Pivot on row 1 (degree = 2)　　　　Then pivot on row 3

$$\begin{array}{c|cccccc|}
\boxed{1} & \mathbf{P} & \boxed{*} & & \boxed{*} & & \\
2 & \mathbf{0} & * & * & \mathrm{F} & * & \\
3 & & * & * & & & * \\
4 & \mathbf{0} & \mathrm{F} & & * & * & \\
5 & & * & & * & * & * \\
6 & & & * & & * & *
\end{array}
\qquad
\begin{array}{l}
\textbf{Pivots P} \\
\textbf{Fill-in F} \\
\textbf{Pivot row } \square
\end{array}
\qquad
\begin{array}{c|ccccc|}
2 & * & \mathbf{0} & \mathbf{F} & * & \mathrm{F} \\
\boxed{3} & \boxed{*} & \mathbf{P} & & & \boxed{*} \\
 & \mathbf{F} & & * & * & \\
 & * & & * & * & * \\
 & \mathrm{F} & \mathbf{0} & & * & *
\end{array}$$

Figure 7.4: Minimum degree nodes 1 and 3 give pivots **P**. New diagonal edges 2–4 and 2–6 in the graph match the entries **F** that are filled in by elimination.

The first step chooses row 1 as pivot row, because node 1 has minimum degree 2. (Any degree 2 node could come first.) The pivot is **P**, the other nonzeros in that row are boxed. *The two fill-in entries marked by* **F** *change to nonzeros.* This fill-in of the $(2, 4)$ and $(4, 2)$ entries corresponds to the dashed line connecting nodes 2 and 4 in the graph.

Elimination continues on the 5 by 5 matrix (and the graph with 5 nodes). Node 2 still has degree 3, so it is not eliminated next. If we break the tie by choosing node 3, elimination using the new pivot **P** will fill in the $(2, 6)$ and $(6, 2)$ positions. *Node 2 becomes linked to node 6 because they were both linked to the eliminated node 3.*

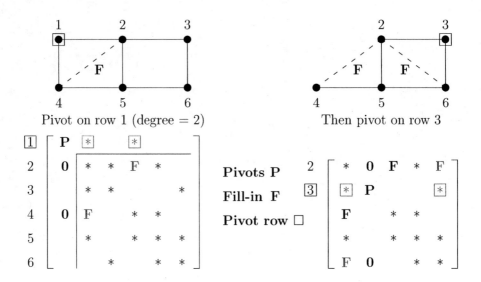

Problem 6 asks you to take the next step—choose a minimum degree node and reduce the 4 by 4 system to 3 by 3. Figure 7.5 shows the start of a minimum degree ordering for a larger grid. Notice how fill-in (16 edges, 32 **F**'s) increases the degrees.

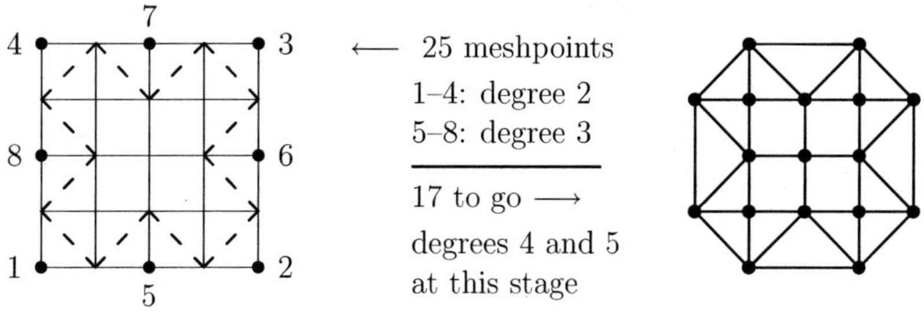

Figure 7.5: Nodes connected to an eliminated node become connected to each other.

Storing the Nonzero Structure = Sparsity Pattern

A large system $KU = F$ needs a fast and economical storage of the node connections (the positions of nonzeros in the matrix). The list of $i, j, s =$ *row*, *column*, *entry* will change as elimination proceeds. Normally we don't see that internal list.

Here we create the list for $N = 4$ by $[i, j, s] = \mathsf{find}(K)$. This has $\mathsf{nnz}(K) = 10$:

$$\boldsymbol{i} = \ \mathbf{1\ 2\ 1\ 2\ 3\ 2\ 3\ 4\ 3\ 4} \qquad \boldsymbol{j} = \ \mathbf{1\ 1\ 2\ 2\ 2\ 3\ 3\ 3\ 4\ 4}$$

$$\uparrow \quad \uparrow \quad \uparrow \quad \uparrow \quad \uparrow$$

$$\boldsymbol{s} = \ \mathbf{2\ \ {-1}\ \ {-1}\ \ 2\ \ {-1}\ \ {-1}\ \ 2\ \ {-1}\ \ {-1}\ \ 2}$$

The fifth nonzero is in row $i = 3$ and column $j = 2$. That entry is $s = K_{32} = -1$.

In that list j of column indices, all we need are the pointers to indicate when a new column appears. In reality j is replaced by this shorter list pointers, easier to update and including a last pointer to position $11 = \mathsf{nnz} + 1$ to signal *stop*:

$$\textbf{pointers} = \ \mathbf{1\ \ 3\ \ 6\ \ 9\ \ 11} \qquad \text{can be updated by } \mathsf{perm(pointers)}$$

Notes on MATLAB's backslash The sparse backslash command $U = K\backslash F$ uses an approximate minimum degree algorithm. First it checks the nonzero pattern to see if row and column permutations P_1 and P_2 can produce a *block triangular form*. The reordered system is $(\boldsymbol{P_1 K P_2^{\mathrm{T}}})(\boldsymbol{P_2 U}) = \boldsymbol{P_1 F}$:

$$\textbf{Block triangular matrix} \qquad \boldsymbol{P_1 K P_2^{\mathrm{T}}} = \begin{bmatrix} B_{11} & B_{12} & \cdot & \cdot \\ 0 & B_{22} & \cdot & \cdot \\ 0 & 0 & \cdot & \cdot \\ 0 & 0 & 0 & B_{mm} \end{bmatrix} \qquad \boldsymbol{P_1 F} = \begin{bmatrix} f_1 \\ f_2 \\ \cdot \\ f_m \end{bmatrix}$$

Block back-substitution starts with the (possibly) smaller problem $B_{mm}U_m = f_m$. That is reordered according to minimum degree. Working upwards, we hope for small blocks B_{ii} on the diagonal. Surprisingly often, they do appear.

To preserve symmetry we need $P_1 = P_2$. In the positive definite case, the Cholesky command chol is preferred to lu, since useless row exchanges can be safely omitted. If diag(K) is positive, there is a chance (not a certainty!) of positive definiteness. Backslash will try chol, and turn to lu if a pivot fails to be positive.

It is understood that MATLAB is not tuned for high performance. Use it for tests and experiments and adjustments. Faster codes often use a version of C.

Graph Separators

Here is another approach to ordering, different from minimum degree. The whole graph or mesh is separated into disjoint pieces by a cut. This separator goes through a small number of nodes or meshpoints. *It is a good idea to number the nodes in the separator last.* Elimination is relatively fast for the disjoint pieces P and Q. It only slows down at the end, for the (smaller) separator S.

The points in P have no direct connections to points in Q. (Both are connected to the separator S.) Numbered in that order P, Q, S, the "block arrow" stiffness matrix has two blocks of zeros. Its $K = LU$ factorization preserves those zero blocks:

$$\boldsymbol{K} = \begin{bmatrix} K_{\mathrm{P}} & \mathbf{0} & K_{\mathrm{PS}} \\ \mathbf{0} & K_{\mathrm{Q}} & K_{\mathrm{QS}} \\ K_{\mathrm{SP}} & K_{\mathrm{SQ}} & K_{\mathrm{S}} \end{bmatrix} \qquad \boldsymbol{L} = \begin{bmatrix} L_{\mathrm{P}} & & \\ \mathbf{0} & L_{\mathrm{Q}} & \\ X & Y & Z \end{bmatrix} \qquad \boldsymbol{U} = \begin{bmatrix} U_{\mathrm{P}} & \mathbf{0} & A \\ & U_{\mathrm{Q}} & B \\ & & C \end{bmatrix} \tag{5}$$

The submatrices K_P and K_Q factor separately. Then come the connections through the separator. The major cost is often that fairly dense system from S. On a rectangular grid, the best cut is down the middle in the shorter direction. Our model problem on a square is actually the hardest, because no cuts are very short.

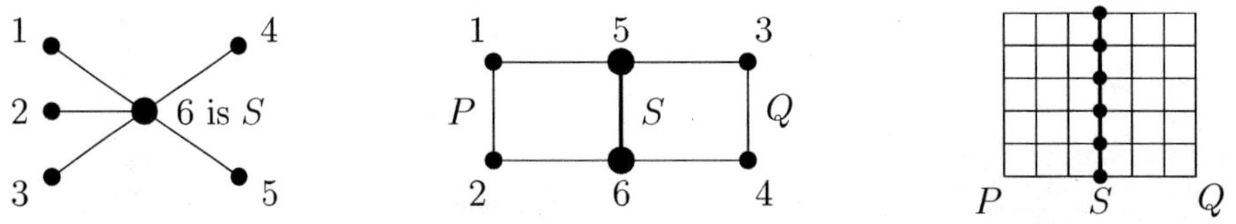

Arrow matrix (Figure 7.3) **Separator comes last** (Figure 7.4) **Blocks P, Q Separator S**

Figure 7.6: A graph separator numbered last produces a block arrow matrix K.

A region shaped like a U (or a radiator in 3D) might look difficult. But actually it allows very short separators. A tree needs *no fill-in at all.*

A separator illustrates the key idea of **domain decomposition**: *Cut the problem into smaller pieces.* This is natural for structural analysis of an airplane: Solve separately for the wings and the fuselage. The smaller system for the separator (where the pieces meet) is like the third row of equation (5). This matches the unknown and its normal derivative (stress or flux) along the separator. We apologize that a full discussion of domain decomposition [155] is impossible here.

Remark MATLAB could use a good subroutine $[P, Q, S] =$ separator(K). Right now this can be put together from a minimum cut and a maximum matching (both discussed in Section 8.6). The cut is an edge separator that produces P^* and Q^* with few edges crossing between. The node separator S could be the P^* endpoints of those crossing edges, or the Q^* endpoints. A smaller S comes partly from P^* and partly from Q^*. A maximum matching of those endpoints finds S so that no edges go from $P = P^*\backslash S$ to $Q = Q^*\backslash S$, as required.

Davis uses symrcm for the cut and dmperm for the matching (google *Csparse*).

Nested Dissection

You could say that the numbering of P then Q then S is **block minimum degree**. But one cut with one separator will not come close to an optimal numbering. It is natural to extend the idea to a nested sequence of cuts. P and Q have their own separators at the next level. This **nested dissection** continues until it is not productive to cut further. It is a strategy of "divide and conquer."

Figure 7.7 illustrates three levels of nested dissection on a 7 by 7 grid. The first separator is down the middle. Then two cuts go across and four cuts go down. Numbering the separators last within each stage, the matrix K of size 49 has arrows inside arrows inside arrows. The spy command will display the pattern of nonzeros.

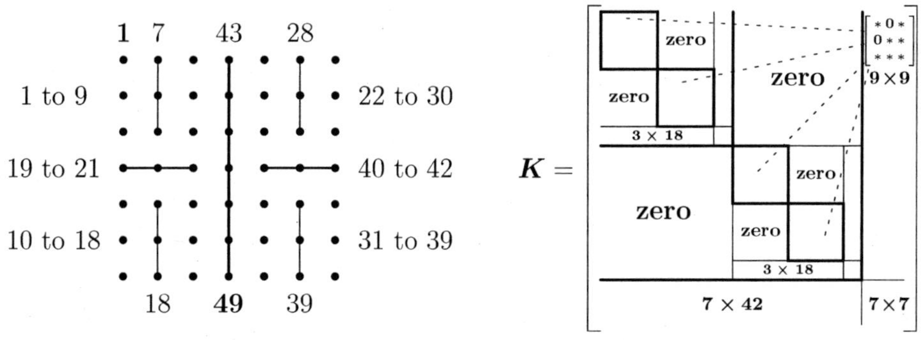

Figure 7.7: Three levels of separators, using nested dissection.

The codes for nested dissection, here and on the cse website, use the function recur in a beautiful way. The new ordering for a rectangle comes recursively from new orderings of the subrectangles P and Q and the separator S.

The 4-line test case for $N = 7$ calls nestdiss which calls recur to find perm(map).

```
N = 7; K = delsq(numgrid('S', N+2));   % 5-point matrix K2D on N by N grid
perm = nestdiss(N, N);                  % order nodes by nested dissection
NZ = nnz(chol(K(perm,perm)))            % count nonzeros in triangular factor
fill = NZ-nnz(tril(K))                  % count fill in triangular factor

function perm = nestdiss(m, n)          % perm(k) = old number of new node k
map = recur(m, n);                      % map(i, j) = new number of old node i, j
perm(map(:)) = 1:m*n;                   % perm is the inverse of map

function map = recur(m, n)              % start with mn nodes numbered by rows
map = zeros(m, n);                      % initialize node map
if m == 0 | n == 0, return; end         % stop when mesh is fully dissected
if m >= n, r = round((m + 1)/2);        % split longer side of the rectangle
  P = recur(r-1, n);                    % recursively dissect the first r-1
  Q = recur(m-r, n);                    % recursively dissect the last m-r
  map(1:r-1, :) = P;                    % nodes of P keep current numbers
  map(r+1:m, :) = (r-1)*n+Q;            % nodes of Q are numbered next
  map(r, :) = (m-1)*n+(1:n);            % nodes of S are numbered last
else
  map = recur(n, m)'; end               % if m < n work with the transpose
```

Summary Separators and nested dissection show how numbering strategies use the **graph of nodes**. Edges between nodes correspond to nonzeros in the matrix K. The fill-in created by elimination (entries **F** in L and U) corresponds to adjacent edges in the graph. In practice, there has to be a balance between simplicity and optimality in the numbering—in scientific computing simplicity is a very good thing!

Here are the complexity estimates for the Laplacian with N^2 or N^3 nodes:

Nested Separators	$n = N^2$ in 2D	$n = N^3$ in 3D
Space (nonzeros from fill-in)	$\boldsymbol{N^2 \log N}$	$\boldsymbol{N^4}$
Time (flops for elimination)	$\boldsymbol{N^3}$	$\boldsymbol{N^6}$

In the last century, nested dissection lost out (too slow) on almost all applications. Now larger problems are appearing and the asymptotics eventually give nested dissection an edge. All planar graphs have separators of size $\sqrt{n}$ into nearly equal pieces (P and Q have sizes at most $2n/3$). Of course a new idea for ordering could still win. We don't recommend the older algorithm of reverse Cuthill-McKee, standing alone.

A reasonable compromise is the backslash command $U = K\backslash F$ that uses a nearly minimum degree ordering in Sparse MATLAB.

The text [59] by George and Liu is the classic reference on ordering of the nodes. The new book [35] and SuiteSparse software by Davis describe how his algorithms are implemented in backslash and UMFPACK for sparse systems. I hope you like and improve the movie on math.mit.edu/18086, removing nodes and creating edges.

Problem Set 7.1

1 Create $K2D$ for a 4 by 4 square grid with $N^2 = 3^2$ interior mesh points (so $n = 9$). Print out its factors $K = LU$ (or its Cholesky factor $C = \text{chol}(K)$ for the symmetrized form $K = C^{\mathrm{T}}C$). How many zeros in these triangular factors? Also print out $\text{inv}(K)$ to see that it is full.

2 In Figure 7.2a, what parts of the LU factors of $K2D$ are filled in?

3 What does Figure 7.2a become for $K3D$? Estimate the number cN^p of nonzeros in L (the most important number is p).

4 Use the tic; ...; toc clocking command (or cpu) to compare the solution time for $K2Du$ = random f in full and sparse MATLAB (where $K2D$ is defined as a sparse matrix). Above what value of N does the sparse $K\backslash f$ win?

5 Compare ordinary vs. sparse solution times for $(K3D)u$ = random f. At which N does the sparse $K\backslash f$ begin to win?

6 Draw the next step after Figure 7.4 when the matrix has become 4 by 4 and the graph has nodes 2–4–5–6. Which nodes have minimum degree? How much new fill-in at this next step?

7 Redraw the right side of Figure 7.4 if row number 2 is chosen as the second pivot row. Node 2 does not have minimum degree. Indicate new edges in the 5-node graph and new nonzeros **F** in the matrix.

8 Any tree has successive levels of branching from a root node. Draw a 12-node tree with a node ordering that produces fill-in (nodes become connected as in Figure 7.4). Then order the 12 nodes to avoid all fill-in.

9 Create a 10-node graph with 20 random edges (find a way to do this). The symmetric adjacency matrix W has 20 random 1's above the diagonal. Count nonzeros in L from factoring $K = 20I - W$. Repeat to find an average $\text{nnz}(L)$.

10 If A is an upper triangular matrix, what does that mean for the edge directions in the corresponding directed graph? If A is block upper triangular, what does that mean for edges inside blocks and edges between blocks?

11 Suppose the unknowns U_{ij} on a square grid are stored in an N by N matrix, and not listed in a vector U of length N^2. Show that the vector result of $(K2\mathrm{D})U$ is now produced by the matrix $KU + UK$.

12 Minimum degree order starts with degree 2 for a square mesh (Figure 7.5). How large do the degrees become as elimination continues (*experimental question*)? For N^2 meshpoints, give instructions for ties in the minimum degree.

13 Experiment with fill-in for a red-black permutation in equation (4). Is the red-black ordering superior (for large N) to the original row-by-row ordering?

14 The commands $K2\mathrm{D} = \mathsf{delsq}(\mathsf{numgrid}(\text{'}S\text{'}, 300))$; $[L, U] = \mathsf{lu}(K2\mathrm{D})$; factor $K2\mathrm{D}$. Count the nonzeros by $\mathsf{nnz}(L)$, not optimal. Use $\mathsf{perm} = \mathsf{symamd}(K2\mathrm{D})$ for an approximate minimum degree ordering. After $[LL, UU] = \mathsf{lu}(K2\mathrm{D}(\mathsf{perm}, \mathsf{perm}))$; count the nonzeros in LL.

15 It is efficient to make space before creating a long vector. Compare times:

1 $n = 1\mathrm{e}5\,;\; x(1) = 1\,;$	*Double the space first*
2 for $k = 2{:}n$	3 if $(k > \mathsf{length}(x))$
5 $\quad x(k) = k\,;$	4 $x(2*\mathsf{length}(x)) = 0\,;$
6 end	*Time is now* $O(n)$ not $O(n^2)$

16 Draw a 5 by 5 square of nodes and enter the 25 numbers from $\mathsf{map} = \mathsf{recur}(5, 5)$. In a second square enter the 25 numbers from $\mathsf{perm} = \mathsf{nestdiff}(5, 5)$.

Why do we work with $K(\mathsf{perm}, \mathsf{perm})$ and not with $K(\mathsf{map}, \mathsf{map})$? Is $F(\mathsf{perm})$ the new right side?

17 Write a nested dissection code for an N by N by N mesh, with the 7-point matrix $K3\mathrm{D}$. Test $N = 5, 7, 9$ to estimate the exponent α in $\mathsf{nnz}(L) \sim N^{\alpha}$ from $[L, U] = \mathsf{lu}(K3\mathrm{D}(\mathsf{perm}, \mathsf{perm}))$.

18 **Challenge** For the 11 by 11 $K2\mathrm{D}$ matrix, find an ordering of the 121 nodes of the mesh that makes $\mathsf{nnz}(\mathsf{chol}(K2\mathrm{D}(\mathsf{perm}, \mathsf{perm})))$ as small as you can. The cse website will publish and update the lowest nnz and the best vector perm that comes to gs@math.mit.edu.

19 **Second competition** Look for an optimal fill-reducing order for the 9 by 9 by 9 $K3\mathrm{D}$ matrix of size 729 (7-point Laplace, ordered non-optimally a plane at a time). A 3D nested dissection code will find a very good perm and nnz—but probably not the absolute best.

20 For the model of a square grid with separator down the middle, create the reordered matrix K in equation (5). Use $\mathsf{spy}(K)$ to print its pattern of nonzeros.

7.2 ITERATIVE METHODS

New solution methods are needed when a problem $Ax = b$ is too large and expensive for ordinary elimination. We are thinking of *sparse matrices* A, so that multiplications Ax are relatively cheap. If A has at most p nonzeros in every row, then ***Ax needs at most pn multiplications***. Typical applications are to large finite difference or finite element equations, where we often write $A = K$.

We are turning from elimination to look at **iterative methods**. There are really two big decisions, the preconditioner P and the choice of the method itself:

1. A good preconditioner P is close to A but much simpler to work with.

2. Options include ***pure iterations*** (6.2), ***multigrid*** (6.3), and ***Krylov methods*** (6.4), including the conjugate gradient method.

Pure iterations compute each new x_{k+1} from $x_k - P^{-1}(Ax_k - b)$. This is called "*stationary*" because every step is the same. Convergence to $x_\infty = A^{-1}b$, studied below, will be fast when all eigenvalues of $M = I - P^{-1}A$ are small. It is easy to suggest a preconditioner, but not so easy to suggest an excellent P (*Incomplete LU is a success*). The older iterations of Jacobi and Gauss-Seidel are less favored (but they are still important, you will see good points and bad points).

Multigrid begins with Jacobi or Gauss-Seidel iterations, for the one job that they do well. They remove high frequency components (rapidly oscillating parts) to leave a smooth error. Then the central idea is to *move to a coarser grid*—where the rest of the error can be destroyed. Multigrid is often dramatically successful.

Krylov spaces contain all combinations of $b, Ab, A^2b, \ldots$ and Krylov methods look for the best combination. Combined with preconditioning, the result is terrific. When the growing subspaces reach the whole space $\mathbf{R}^n$, those methods give the exact solution $A^{-1}b$. But in reality we stop much earlier, long before n steps are complete. The *conjugate gradient method* (*for positive definite A, and with a good preconditioner*) has become truly important.

The goal of numerical linear algebra is clear: **Find a fast stable algorithm that uses the special properties of the matrix.** We meet matrices that are symmetric or triangular or orthogonal or tridiagonal or Hessenberg or Givens or Householder. Those are at the core of matrix computations. The algorithm doesn't need details of the entries (which come from the specific application). By concentrating on the matrix structure, numerical linear algebra offers major help.

Overall, elimination with good numbering is the first choice! But storage and CPU time can become excessive, especially in three dimensions. At that point we turn from elimination to iterative methods, which require more expertise than $K\backslash F$. The next pages aim to help the reader at this frontier of scientific computing.

Stationary Iterations

We begin with old-style pure stationary iteration. The letter K will be reserved for "Krylov" so we leave behind the notation $KU = F$. The linear system becomes $Ax = b$. The large sparse matrix A is not necessarily symmetric or positive definite:

Linear system $Ax = b$ **Residual** $r_k = b - Ax_k$ **Preconditioner** $P \approx A$

The preconditioner P attempts to be close to A and still allow fast iterations. The Jacobi choice P = diagonal of A is one extreme (fast but not very close). The other extreme is $P = A$ (too close). Splitting the matrix A gives a new form of $Ax = b$:

Splitting $$\boldsymbol{Px = (P - A)x + b}\,. \tag{1}$$

This form suggests an iteration, in which every vector x_k leads to the next x_{k+1}:

Iteration $$\boldsymbol{Px_{k+1} = (P - A)x_k + b}\,. \tag{2}$$

Starting from any x_0, the first step finds x_1 from $Px_1 = (P - A)x_0 + b$. The iteration continues to x_2 with the same matrix P, so it often helps to know its triangular factors in $P = LU$. Sometimes P itself is triangular, or L and U are approximations to the triangular factors of A. Two conditions on P make the iteration successful:

1. The new x_{k+1} must be quickly computable. Equation (2) must be fast to solve.
2. The errors $e_k = x - x_k$ should approach zero as rapidly as possible.

Subtract equation (2) from (1) to find the **error equation**. It connects e_k to e_{k+1}:

Error $Pe_{k+1} = (P - A)e_k$ which means $$\boldsymbol{e_{k+1} = (I - P^{-1}A)e_k = Me_k}\,. \tag{3}$$

The right side b disappears in this error equation. Each step multiplies the error vector e_k by M. The speed of convergence of x_k to x (and of e_k to zero) depends entirely on M. *The test for convergence is given by the eigenvalues of* M:

Convergence test Every eigenvalue of $M = I - P^{-1}A$ must have $|\lambda(M)| < 1$.

The largest eigenvalue (in absolute value) is the **spectral radius** $\boldsymbol{\rho(M)} = \max|\lambda(M)|$. Convergence requires $\rho(M) < 1$. The **convergence rate** is set by the largest eigenvalue. For a large problem, we are happy with $\rho(M) = .9$ and even $\rho(M) = .99$.

When the initial error e_0 happens to be an eigenvector of M, the next error is $e_1 = Me_0 = \lambda e_0$. At every step the error is multiplied by λ. *So we must have* $|\lambda| < 1$. Normally e_0 is a combination of all the eigenvectors. When the iteration multiplies by M, each eigenvector is multiplied by its own eigenvalue. After k steps those multipliers are λ^k, and the largest is $(\rho(M))^k$.

If we don't use a preconditioner then $M = I - A$. All the eigenvalues of A must be inside a unit circle centered at 1, for convergence. Our second difference matrices $A = K$ would fail this test ($I - K$ is too large). The first job of a preconditioner is to get the matrix decently scaled. Jacobi will now give $\rho(I - \frac{1}{2}K) < 1$, and a really good P will do more.

Jacobi Iterations

For preconditioner we first propose a simple choice:

Jacobi iteration	$\boldsymbol{P} = $ **diagonal part** $\boldsymbol{D}$ **of** $\boldsymbol{A}$

Typical examples have spectral radius $\rho(M) = 1 - cN^{-2}$, where N counts meshpoints in the longest direction. This comes closer and closer to 1 (too close) as the mesh is refined and N increases. But Jacobi is important, it does part of the job.

For our tridiagonal matrices K, Jacobi's preconditioner is just $P = 2I$ (the diagonal of K). **The Jacobi iteration matrix becomes** $\boldsymbol{M = I - D^{-1}A = I - \frac{1}{2}K}$:

Iteration matrix for a Jacobi step

$$M = I - \frac{1}{2}K = \frac{1}{2}\begin{bmatrix} 0 & 1 & & \\ 1 & 0 & 1 & \\ & 1 & 0 & 1 \\ & & 1 & 0 \end{bmatrix}. \qquad (4)$$

Here is x^{new} from x^{old}, in detail. You see how Jacobi shifts the off-diagonal entries of A to the right-hand side, and divides by the diagonal part $D = 2I$:

$$\begin{aligned} 2x_1 - x_2 &= b_1 \\ -x_1 + 2x_2 - x_3 &= b_2 \\ -x_2 + 2x_3 - x_4 &= b_3 \\ -x_3 + 2x_4 &= b_4 \end{aligned} \quad \text{becomes} \quad \begin{bmatrix} x_1 \\ x_2 \\ x_3 \\ x_4 \end{bmatrix}^{\text{new}} = \frac{1}{2}\begin{bmatrix} & x_2 \\ x_1 + & x_3 \\ x_2 + & x_4 \\ x_3 & \end{bmatrix}^{\text{old}} + \frac{1}{2}\begin{bmatrix} b_1 \\ b_2 \\ b_3 \\ b_4 \end{bmatrix}. \qquad (5)$$

The equation is solved when $x^{\text{new}} = x^{\text{old}}$, but this only happens in the limit. The real question is the number of iterations to get close to convergence, and that depends on the eigenvalues of M. How close is λ_{max} to 1?

Those eigenvalues are simple cosines. In Section 1.5 we actually computed all the eigenvalues $\lambda(K) = 2 - 2\cos(\frac{j\pi}{N+1})$. Since $M = I - \frac{1}{2}K$, we now divide those eigenvalues by 2 and subtract from 1. The eigenvalues $\cos j\theta$ of M are less than 1!

Jacobi eigenvalues $$\lambda_j(M) = 1 - \frac{2 - 2\cos j\theta}{2} = \boldsymbol{\cos j\theta} \quad \text{with } \theta = \frac{\pi}{N+1}. \qquad (6)$$

Convergence is safe (but slow) because $|\cos\theta| < 1$. Small angles have $\cos\theta \approx 1 - \frac{1}{2}\theta^2$. The choice $j = 1$ gives us the first (and largest) eigenvalue of M:

Spectral radius $$\lambda_{\text{max}}(M) = \cos\theta \approx 1 - \frac{1}{2}\left(\frac{\pi}{N+1}\right)^2. \qquad (7)$$

Convergence is slow for the lowest frequency. The matrix M in (4) has the four eigenvalues $\cos\frac{\pi}{5}, \cos\frac{2\pi}{5}, \cos\frac{3\pi}{5}$, and $\cos\frac{4\pi}{5}$ (which is $-\cos\frac{\pi}{5}$) in Figure 7.8.

There is an important point about those Jacobi eigenvalues $\lambda_j(M) = \cos j\theta$. The magnitude $|\lambda_j|$ at $j = N$ is the same as the magnitude at $j = 1$. This is not good for multigrid, where high frequencies need to be strongly damped. So **weighted Jacobi** has a valuable place, with a weighting factor ω in $M = I - \omega D^{-1}A$:

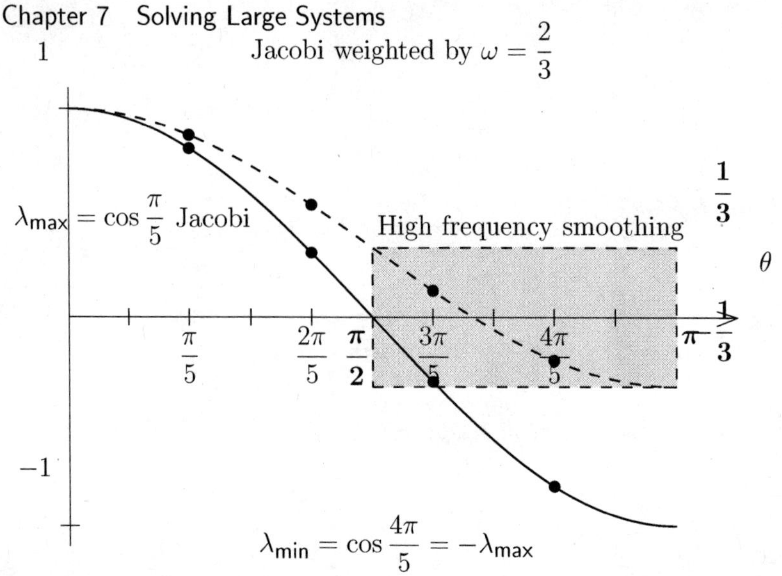

Figure 7.8: The eigenvalues of Jacobi's $M = I - \frac{1}{2}K$ are $\cos j\theta$, starting near $\lambda = 1$ and ending near $\lambda = -1$. Weighted Jacobi has $\lambda = 1 - \omega + \omega \cos j\theta$, ending near $\lambda = 1 - 2\omega$. Both graphs show $j = 1, 2, 3, 4$ and $\theta = \frac{\pi}{N+1} = \frac{\pi}{5}$ (with $\omega = \frac{2}{3}$).

Jacobi's iteration matrix $M = I - D^{-1}A$ changes to $M = I - \omega D^{-1}A$.

The preconditioner is now $P = D/\omega$. Here are the eigenvalues $\lambda(M)$ when $A = K$:

Weighted Jacobi

$$D = 2I \quad \text{and} \quad M = I - \frac{\omega}{2}A \quad \text{and} \quad \omega < 1$$
$$\lambda_j(M) = 1 - \frac{\omega}{2}(2 - 2\cos j\theta) = \mathbf{1 - \omega + \omega \cos j\theta}. \tag{8}$$

The dashed-line graph in Figure 7.8 shows these values $\lambda_j(M)$ for $\omega = \frac{2}{3}$. This ω is optimal in damping the high frequencies ($j\theta$ between $\pi/2$ and π) by at least $\frac{1}{3}$:

$$\text{At } j\theta = \frac{\pi}{2} \qquad \lambda(M) = 1 - \omega + \omega \cos\frac{\pi}{2} = 1 - \frac{2}{3} = \mathbf{\frac{1}{3}}$$

$$\text{At } j\theta = \pi \qquad \lambda(M) = 1 - \omega + \omega \cos\pi = 1 - \frac{4}{3} = \mathbf{-\frac{1}{3}}$$

If we move away from $\omega = \frac{2}{3}$, one of those eigenvalues will increase in magnitude. A weighted Jacobi iteration will be a good smoother within multigrid.

In two dimensions the picture is essentially the same. **The N^2 eigenvalues of K2D are the sums $\lambda_j + \lambda_k$ of the N eigenvalues of K.** All eigenvectors are samples of $\sin j\pi x \sin k\pi y$. (In general, the eigenvalues of $\mathsf{kron}(A, B)$ are $\lambda_j(A)\lambda_k(B)$. For $\mathsf{kron}(K, I) + \mathsf{kron}(I, K)$, sharing eigenvectors means we can add eigenvalues.)

Jacobi has $P = 4I$, from the diagonal of $\boldsymbol{K}$**2D**. So $\boldsymbol{M}\mathbf{2D} = \boldsymbol{I}\mathbf{2D} - \frac{1}{4}\boldsymbol{K}\mathbf{2D}$:

$$\lambda_{jk}(\boldsymbol{M}\mathbf{2D}) = 1 - \frac{1}{4}\left[\lambda_j(K) + \lambda_k(K)\right] = \frac{1}{2}\cos j\theta + \frac{1}{2}\cos k\theta\,. \tag{9}$$

With $j = k = 1$, the spectral radius $\lambda_{\max}(M) = \cos\theta$ is the same $1 - cN^{-2}$ as in 1D.

Numerical Experiments

The multigrid method grew out of the slow convergence of Jacobi iterations. You have to see how typical error vectors e_k begin to decrease and then stall. For weighted Jacobi, the high frequencies disappear long before the low frequencies. Figure 7.9 shows a drop between e_0 and e_{50}, and then very slow decay. We have chosen the second difference matrix and started the iterations with a random right-hand side.

This unacceptably slow convergence is hidden if we only look at the residual $r_k = b - Ax_k$. Instead of measuring the error $x - x_k$ in the solution, r_k measures the error in the equation. That residual error *does* fall quickly. The key that led to multigrid is the rapid drop in r with such a slow drop in e.

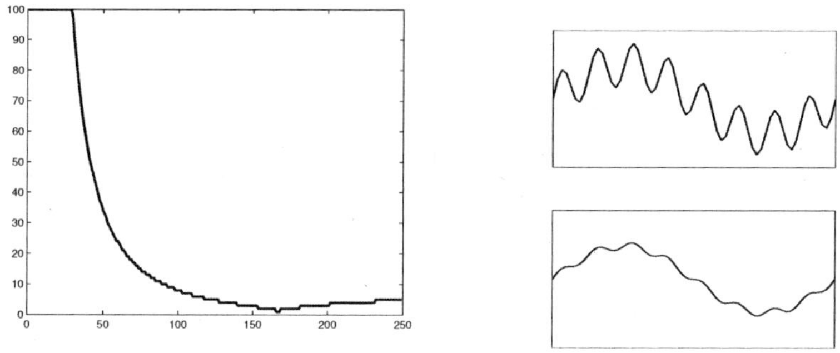

Figure 7.9: (left) Low frequencies take many more iterations to damp out by 1/100. (right) Fast oscillations almost disappear to leave the low frequency [26, p. 23–24].

Gauss-Seidel and the Red-Black Ordering

The Gauss-Seidel idea is to use the components of x^{new} as soon as they are computed. This cuts the storage requirement in half, since x^{old} is overwritten by x^{new}. The preconditioner $P = D + L$ becomes *triangular* instead of diagonal (still easy to use):

Gauss-Seidel iteration $\quad$ $\boldsymbol{P} = $ **lower triangular part of** $\boldsymbol{A}$

Gauss-Seidel gives faster error reduction than ordinary Jacobi, because the Jacobi eigenvalues $\cos j\theta$ become $(\cos j\theta)^2$. The spectral radius is squared, so one Gauss-Seidel step is worth two Jacobi steps. The (large) number of iterations is cut in half, when the -1's below the diagonal stay with the 2's on the *left side* of Px^{new}:

Gauss-Seidel
$\boldsymbol{Px}^{\textbf{new}} =$
$(\boldsymbol{P}-\boldsymbol{A})\boldsymbol{x}^{\textbf{old}} + \boldsymbol{b}$

$$-1\begin{bmatrix} 0 \\ x_1 \\ x_2 \\ x_3 \end{bmatrix}^{\text{new}} + 2\begin{bmatrix} x_1 \\ x_2 \\ x_3 \\ x_4 \end{bmatrix}^{\text{new}} = \begin{bmatrix} x_2 \\ x_3 \\ x_4 \\ 0 \end{bmatrix}^{\text{old}} + \begin{bmatrix} b_1 \\ b_2 \\ b_3 \\ b_4 \end{bmatrix}. \qquad (10)$$

A new x_1 comes from the first equation, because P is triangular. Using x_1^{new} in the second equation gives x_2^{new}, which enters the third equation. Problem 5 shows that

$x^{\text{new}} = (\cos j\theta)^2 x^{\text{old}}$, with the correct eigenvector x^{old}. All the Jacobi eigenvalues $\cos j\theta$ are squared for Gauss-Seidel, so they become smaller.

Symmetric Gauss-Seidel comes from a double sweep, reversing the order of components to make the combined process symmetric. By itself, $I - P^{-1}A$ is not symmetric for triangular P.

A **red-black ordering** produces a neat compromise between Jacobi and Gauss-Seidel. Imagine that a two-dimensional grid is a *checkerboard*. Number the red nodes before the black nodes. The numbering will not change Jacobi's method (which keeps all of x^{old} to create x^{new}). But Gauss-Seidel will be improved. In one dimension, Gauss-Seidel updates all the even (red) components x_{2j} using known black values. Then it updates the odd (black) components x_{2j+1} using the new red values:

$$x_{2j} \longleftarrow \frac{1}{2}\left(x_{2j-1} + x_{2j+1} + b_{2j}\right) \quad \text{and then} \quad x_{2j+1} \longleftarrow \frac{1}{2}\left(x_{2j} + x_{2j+2} + b_{2j+1}\right). \quad (11)$$

In two dimensions, $x_{i,j}$ is red when $i + j$ is even, and black when $i + j$ is odd. Laplace's five-point difference matrix uses four black values to update each center value (red). Then red values update black, giving one example of *block Gauss-Seidel.*

For **line Gauss-Seidel**, each row of grid values forms a block. The preconditioner P is *block triangular.* That is the right way to see P in 2D:

$$P_{\text{red-black}} = \begin{bmatrix} 4I & 0 \\ -1\text{'s} & 4I \end{bmatrix} \quad \text{and} \quad P_{\text{line G-S}} = \begin{bmatrix} K+2I & 0 & 0 \\ -I & K+2I & 0 \\ 0 & -I & K+2I \end{bmatrix}$$

A great feature is the option to compute all red values *in parallel.* They need only black values and can be updated in any order—there are no connections among red values (or within black values in the second half-step). For line Jacobi, the rows in 2D can be updated in parallel (and the plane blocks in 3D). Block matrix computations are efficient.

Overrelaxation (SOR) is a combination of Jacobi and Gauss-Seidel, using a factor ω that almost reaches 2. The preconditioner is $P = D + \omega L$. (By *overcorrecting* from x_k to x_{k+1}, hand calculators noticed that they could finish in a few weeks.) My earlier book and many other references show how ω is chosen to minimize the spectral radius $\rho(M)$, improving $\rho = 1 - cN^{-2}$ to $\rho(M) = 1 - cN^{-1}$. Then convergence is much faster (N steps instead of N^2, to reduce the error by a constant factor like e).

Incomplete LU

A different approach has given much more flexibility in constructing a good P. The idea is to compute an ***incomplete LU factorization*** of the true matrix A:

Incomplete LU $\quad$ $\boldsymbol{P = (approximation\ to\ L)(approximation\ to\ U)}$ (12)

The exact $A = LU$ has fill-in. So does Cholesky's $A = R^{\mathrm{T}}R$. Zero entries in A become nonzero in L and U and R. But $P = L_{\mathsf{approx}}U_{\mathsf{approx}}$ can keep only the fill-in entries $\mathbf{F}$ above a fixed tolerance. The MATLAB commands for incomplete LU are

$$[\,L, U, \mathsf{Perm}\,] = \mathsf{luinc}(A, \mathsf{tol}) \qquad \text{or} \qquad R = \mathsf{cholinc}(A, \mathsf{tol})\,.$$

If you set $\mathsf{tol} = 0$, those letters inc have no effect. This becomes ordinary sparse LU (and Cholesky for positive definite A). A large value of tol will remove all fill-in.

Difference matrices like $K2\mathrm{D}$ can maintain zero row sums by adding entries below tol to the main diagonal (instead of destroying those entries completely). This **modified *ILU*** is a success (mluinc and mcholinc). The variety of options, and especially the fact that the computer can decide automatically how much fill-in to keep, has made incomplete LU a very popular starting point.

In the end, Jacobi and Gauss-Seidel by themselves are too simple. Often the smooth (low frequency) errors decrease too slowly. *Multigrid will fix this.* And pure iteration is choosing one particular vector in a "Krylov subspace." With relatively little work we can make a much better choice of x_k. Multigrid methods and Krylov projections are the state of the art in today's iterative methods.

Problem Set 7.2

Problems 1-5 test iterative methods for the matrix $K_2 = [2\ -1; -1\ 2]$ and K_n.

1 Jacobi's method has the diagonal part of K_2 on the left side:

$$\begin{bmatrix} 2 & 0 \\ 0 & 2 \end{bmatrix} x^{k+1} = \begin{bmatrix} 0 & 1 \\ 1 & 0 \end{bmatrix} x^k + b \text{ has iteration matrix } M = \begin{bmatrix} 2 & 0 \\ 0 & 2 \end{bmatrix}^{-1} \begin{bmatrix} 0 & 1 \\ 1 & 0 \end{bmatrix}$$

Find the eigenvalues of M and the spectral radius $\rho = \cos \frac{\pi}{N+1}$.

2 The Gauss-Seidel method has the lower triangular part on the left:

$$\begin{bmatrix} 2 & 0 \\ -1 & 2 \end{bmatrix} x^{k+1} = \begin{bmatrix} 0 & 1 \\ 0 & 0 \end{bmatrix} x^k + b \text{ has iteration matrix } M = \begin{bmatrix} 2 & 0 \\ -1 & 2 \end{bmatrix}^{-1} \begin{bmatrix} 0 & 1 \\ 0 & 0 \end{bmatrix}.$$

Find the eigenvalues of M. A Gauss-Seidel step for this matrix should match two Jacobi steps: $\rho_{\mathsf{GS}} = (\rho_{\mathsf{Jacobi}})^2$.

3 Successive overrelaxation (**SOR**) has a factor ω to adjust for extra speed:

$$\begin{bmatrix} 2 & 0 \\ -\omega & 2 \end{bmatrix} x^{k+1} = \begin{bmatrix} 2(1-\omega) & \omega \\ 0 & 2(1-\omega) \end{bmatrix} x_k + \omega b \text{ has } M = \begin{bmatrix} 2 & 0 \\ -\omega & 2 \end{bmatrix}^{-1} \begin{bmatrix} 2(1-\omega) & \omega \\ 0 & 2(1-\omega) \end{bmatrix}.$$

The product rule gives $\det M = (\omega - 1)^2$. The optimal ω gives both eigenvalues $= \omega - 1$ and trace $= 2(\omega - 1)$. Set this equal to $\text{trace}(M) = 2 - 2\omega + \frac{1}{4}\omega^2$ to find $\omega = 4(2 - \sqrt{3})$. Compare $\rho_{\mathsf{SOR}} = \omega - 1$ with $\rho_{\mathsf{GS}} = \frac{1}{4}$.

4 For $\theta = \pi/(N+1)$ the largest eigenvalues are $\rho_{\text{Jacobi}} = \cos\theta$, $\rho_{\text{GS}} = \cos^2\theta$, $\rho_{\text{SOR}} = (1-\sin\theta)/(1+\sin\theta)$. Compute those numbers for $N = 21$. If $\log(\rho_{\text{SOR}}) = 30\log(\rho_{\text{Jacobi}})$, why is one SOR step worth 30 Jacobi steps?

5 If $x^{\text{old}} = (\cos\frac{k\pi}{N+1}\sin\frac{k\pi}{N+1}, \cos^2\frac{k\pi}{N+1}\sin\frac{2k\pi}{N+1}, \ldots, \cos^N\frac{k\pi}{N+1}\sin\frac{Nk\pi}{N+1})$ show that the Gauss-Seidel iteration (10) is satisfied with $x^{\text{new}} = \left[\cos^2\frac{k\pi}{N+1}\right] x^{\text{old}}$. This shows that M for Gauss-Seidel has $\lambda = \cos^2\frac{k\pi}{N+1}$ (squares of Jacobi eigenvalues).

6 Eigenvalues are quickly estimated by Gershgorin's circle theorem: *Every eigenvalue of A is in a circle around some diagonal entry a_{ii} with radius $r_i = |a_{i1}| + \cdots + |a_{in}|$ excluding $|a_{ii}|$.* This says that all eigenvalues of the $-1, 2, -1$ matrices are in what circle (and what interval)?

7 $K2\text{D}$ has second differences in x and y. With two points in each direction show that the 4 by 4 matrix M has $\lambda_{\text{max}} > 1$ (complete failure):

$$\begin{bmatrix} K & 0 \\ 0 & K \end{bmatrix} x^{k+1} = \begin{bmatrix} -2I & I \\ I & -2I \end{bmatrix} x^k + b \text{ has } M = \begin{bmatrix} K & 0 \\ 0 & K \end{bmatrix}^{-1} \begin{bmatrix} -2I & I \\ I & -2I \end{bmatrix}. \text{ Find } \lambda_{\text{max}}.$$

The **alternating direction iteration** (ADI) rescues this splitting idea by a second step that exchanges the x and y directions. More on the web!

8 The ADI method is fast because the implicit part multiplying x^{k+1} is tridiagonal. Only east-west or south-north neighbors are on the left side of the iteration. A possibly new idea is to put east-west-south all on the left side (still fast) and alternate with other directions. Experiment with this idea. There could also be speed-up parameters as in ADI.

9 Test $R = \texttt{cholinc}(K2\text{D}, \texttt{tol})$ with different values of tol. Does $P = R^{\text{T}}R$ give the correct nonzeros -1 and 4 in $K2\text{D}$? How does the largest eigenvalue of $I - P^{-1}(K2\text{D})$ depend on tol? Incomplete LU iteration (***ILU***) often removes all fill-in from R with great success—at what value of tol?

10 Find the spectral radius ρ for the red-black ordering of Gauss-Seidel iteration in (11), in 1D and then in 2D ($N = 5$ points in each direction).

7.3 MULTIGRID METHODS

The Jacobi and Gauss-Seidel iterations produce smooth errors. The error vector e has its high frequencies nearly removed in a few iterations. But low frequencies are reduced very slowly. Convergence requires $O(N^2)$ iterations—which can be unacceptable. The extremely effective **multigrid idea** is to change to a coarser grid, on which "smooth becomes rough" and low frequencies act like higher frequencies.

On that coarser grid a big piece of the error is removable. *We iterate only a few times before changing from fine to coarse and coarse to fine.* The remarkable result is that multigrid can solve many sparse and realistic systems to high accuracy in a **fixed number of iterations**, not growing with n.

Multigrid is especially successful for symmetric systems. The key new ingredients are the (rectangular!) matrices R and I that change grids:

1. A ***restriction matrix*** $\boldsymbol{R}$ transfers vectors from the fine grid to the coarse grid

2. An ***interpolation matrix*** $\boldsymbol{I} = \boldsymbol{I}_{2h}^{h}$ returns to the fine grid

3. The original matrix A_h on the fine grid is approximated by $\boldsymbol{A_{2h}} = \boldsymbol{RA_hI}$ on the coarse grid. This A_{2h} is smaller and easier and faster than A_h. I will start with interpolation (a 7 by 3 matrix I that takes 3 v's to 7 u's):

Interpolation $Iv = u$
u on the fine (h) grid
v on the coarse ($2h$) grid

$$\frac{1}{2}\begin{bmatrix} 1 & & \\ 2 & & \\ 1 & 1 & \\ & 2 & \\ & 1 & 1 \\ & & 2 \\ & & 1 \end{bmatrix}\begin{bmatrix} v_1 \\ v_2 \\ v_3 \end{bmatrix} = \begin{bmatrix} v_1/2 \\ v_1 \\ v_1/2+v_2/2 \\ v_2 \\ v_2/2+v_3/2 \\ v_3 \\ v_3/2 \end{bmatrix} = \begin{bmatrix} u_1 \\ u_2 \\ u_3 \\ u_4 \\ u_5 \\ u_6 \\ u_7 \end{bmatrix} \tag{1}$$

This example has $h = \frac{1}{8}$ on the interval $0 \le x \le 1$ with zero boundary conditions. The seven interior values are the u's. The grid with $2h = \frac{1}{4}$ has three interior v's.

Notice that u_2, u_4, u_6 from rows 2, 4, 6 are the same as v_1, v_2, v_3! Those coarse grid values v_j are just moved to the fine grid at the points $x = \frac{1}{4}, \frac{2}{4}, \frac{3}{4}$. The in-between values u_1, u_3, u_5, u_7 on the fine grid are coming from *linear interpolation* between $0, v_1, v_2, v_3, 0$ on the coarse grid:

Linear interpolation in rows 1, 3, 5, 7

$$u_{2j+1} = \frac{1}{2}(v_j + v_{j+1})\,. \tag{2}$$

The odd-numbered rows of the interpolation matrix have entries $\frac{1}{2}$ and $\frac{1}{2}$. We almost always use grid spacings $h, 2h, 4h, \ldots$ with the convenient ratio 2. Other matrices I are possible, but linear interpolation is easy and effective. Figure 7.10a shows the new values u_{2j+1} (open circles) between the transferred values $u_{2j} = v_j$ (solid circles).

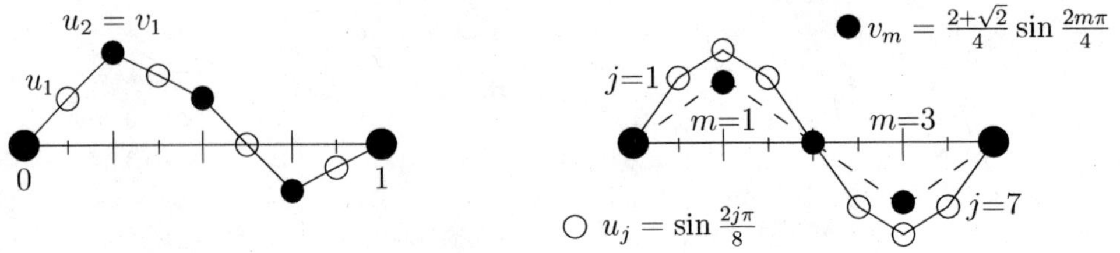

(a) Linear interpolation by $u = I_{2h}^{h} v$ (b) Restriction by $v = Ru = \frac{1}{2} I^{\mathrm{T}} u$

Figure 7.10: **Interpolation** to the h grid (7 u's). **Restriction** to the $2h$ grid (3 v's).

When the v's represent smooth errors on the coarse grid (because Jacobi or Gauss-Seidel has been applied on that grid), interpolation gives a good approximation to the errors on the fine grid. A practical code can use 8 or 10 grids.

The second matrix we need is a **restriction matrix R_h^{2h}**. It transfers u on a fine grid to v on a coarse grid. One possibility is the one-zero "injection matrix" that simply copies v from the values of u at the same points on the fine grid. This ignores the odd-numbered fine grid values u_{2j+1}. Another possibility (which we adopt) is the **full weighting operator R** that comes from transposing I_{2h}^{h}.

Fine grid h to coarse grid 2h by a restriction matrix $R = \frac{1}{2} I^{\mathrm{T}}$

Full weighting $Ru = v$
Fine grid u to coarse grid v

$$\frac{1}{4}\begin{bmatrix} 1 & 2 & 1 & & & & \\ & & 1 & 2 & 1 & & \\ & & & & 1 & 2 & 1 \end{bmatrix} \begin{bmatrix} u_1 \\ u_2 \\ u_3 \\ u_4 \\ u_5 \\ u_6 \\ u_7 \end{bmatrix} = \begin{bmatrix} v_1 \\ v_2 \\ v_3 \end{bmatrix}. \qquad (3)$$

The effect of this restriction matrix is shown in Figure 7.10b. We intentionally chose the special case in which $u_j = \sin(2j\pi/8)$ on the fine grid (*open circles*). Then v on the coarse grid (*dark circles*) is also a pure sine vector. *But the frequency is doubled.* The full cycle takes 4 steps, not 8 steps. So a smooth oscillation on the fine grid becomes "half as smooth" on the coarse grid, which is the effect we wanted.

Interpolation and Restriction in Two Dimensions

Coarse grid to fine grid in two dimensions from bilinear interpolation: Start with values $v_{i,j}$ on a square or rectangular coarse grid. Interpolate to fill in $u_{i,j}$ by a sweep (interpolation) in one direction followed by a sweep in the other direction. We could allow two spacings h_x and h_y, but one meshwidth h is easier to visualize. A horizontal sweep along row i of the coarse grid (which is row $2i$ of the fine grid) will fill in values of u at odd-numbered columns $2j+1$ of the fine grid:

$$\textbf{Horizontal sweep} \qquad u_{2i,2j} = v_{i,j} \quad \text{and} \quad u_{2i,2j+1} = \frac{1}{2}(v_{i,j} + v_{i,j+1}) \quad \text{as in 1D.} \tag{4}$$

Now sweep vertically, up each column of the fine grid. Interpolation will keep those values (4) on even-numbered rows $2i$. On the odd-numbered rows $2i+1$ of the fine grid; we average those values in (4) to find $\boldsymbol{u} = \boldsymbol{I2D}\,\boldsymbol{v}$:

$$\begin{aligned} &\textbf{Vertical sweep} & u_{2i+1,2j} &= (v_{i,j} + v_{i+1,j})/2 \\ &\textbf{Averages of (4)} & u_{2i+1,2j+1} &= (v_{i,j} + v_{i+1,j} + v_{i,j+1} + v_{i+1,j+1})/4\,. \end{aligned} \tag{5}$$

The entries in the tall thin coarse-to-fine interpolation matrix $I2\mathrm{D}$ are 1, $\frac{1}{2}$, and $\frac{1}{4}$.

The full weighting fine-to-coarse restriction operator $R2\mathrm{D}$ is the *transpose* $I2\mathrm{D}^{\mathrm{T}}$, multiplied by $\frac{1}{4}$. That factor is needed (like $\frac{1}{2}$ in one dimension) so that a constant vector of 1's will be restricted to a constant vector of 1's. (The entries along each row of the wide matrix R add to 1.) This restriction matrix has entries $\frac{1}{4}$, $\frac{1}{8}$, and $\frac{1}{16}$ and *each coarse-grid value v is a weighted average of nine fine-grid values u*:

Restriction matrix $\boldsymbol{R} = \frac{1}{4}\boldsymbol{I}^{\mathrm{T}}$

Row $\boldsymbol{i,j}$ of $\boldsymbol{R}$ produces $\boldsymbol{v_{i,j}}$

$\boldsymbol{v_{i,j}}$ uses $\boldsymbol{u_{2i,2j}}$ and 8 neighbors

The nine weights add to 1

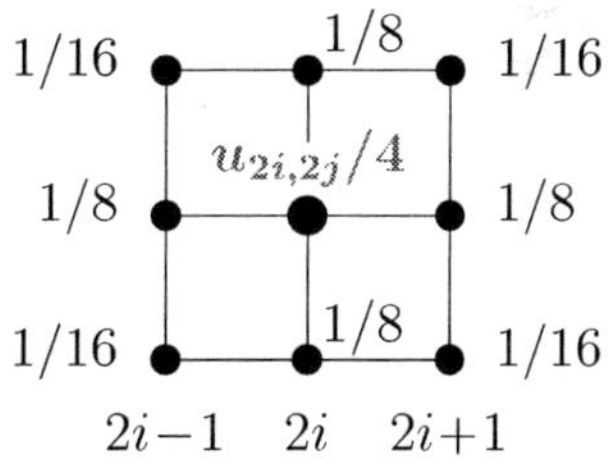

You can see how a sweep along each row with weights $\frac{1}{4}, \frac{1}{2}, \frac{1}{4}$, followed by a sweep down each column, gives the nine coefficients in that "restriction molecule." Its matrix is a *tensor product* or *Kronecker product* $R2\mathrm{D} = \mathsf{kron}(R, R)$. A 3 by 7 matrix R in one dimension becomes a 9 by 49 restriction matrix $R2\mathrm{D}$ in two dimensions.

Now we can transfer vectors between grids. We are ready for the ***geometric multigrid*** method, when the geometry is based on spacings h and $2h$ and $4h$. The idea extends to triangular elements (each triangle splits naturally into four similar triangles). The geometry can be more complicated than our model on a square.

When the geometry becomes too difficult, or A doesn't come with a grid, we turn (in the final paragraph) to ***algebraic multigrid***. This will imitate the multi-scale idea, but it works directly with $Au = b$ and not with any underlying geometric grid.

A Two-Grid V-Cycle (a v-cycle)

Our first multigrid method only involves two grids. The iterations on each grid can use Jacobi's $I - D^{-1}A$ (possibly weighted by $\omega = 2/3$ as in the previous section) or Gauss-Seidel. For the larger problem on the fine grid, iteration converges slowly to the low frequency smooth part of the solution u. *The multigrid method transfers the current residual* $r_h = b - Au_h$ *to the coarse grid.* We iterate a few times on that $2h$ grid, to approximate the coarse-grid error by E_{2h}. Then interpolate back to E_h on the fine grid, make the correction to $u_h + E_h$, and begin again.

This fine-coarse-fine loop is a **two-grid V-cycle**. We call it a **v-cycle** (small v). Here are the steps (remember, the error solves $A_h(u - u_h) = b_h - A_h u_h = r_h$):

1. **Iterate** on $A_h u = b_h$ to reach u_h (say 3 Jacobi or Gauss-Seidel steps).
2. **Restrict** the residual $r_h = b_h - A_h u_h$ to the coarse grid by $r_{2h} = R_h^{2h} r_h$.
3. **Solve** $A_{2h} E_{2h} = r_{2h}$ (or come close to E_{2h} by 3 iterations from $E = 0$).
4. **Interpolate** E_{2h} back to $E_h = I_{2h}^h E_{2h}$. Add E_h to u_h.
5. **Iterate** 3 more times on $A_h u = b_h$ starting from the improved $u_h + E_h$.

Steps **2-3-4** give the restriction-coarse solution-interpolation sequence that is the heart of multigrid. Recall the three matrices we are working with:

$$\begin{aligned} \boldsymbol{A} &= \boldsymbol{A_h} &&= \textit{original matrix} \\ \boldsymbol{R} &= \boldsymbol{R_h^{2h}} &&= \textit{restriction matrix} \\ \boldsymbol{I} &= \boldsymbol{I_{2h}^h} &&= \textit{interpolation matrix}. \end{aligned}$$

Step **3** involves a fourth matrix A_{2h}, to be defined now. A_{2h} is square and it is smaller than the original A_h. In words, we want to "project" the larger matrix A_h onto the coarse grid. There is a natural choice! The variationally correct A_{2h} comes directly and beautifully from R and A and I:

$$\textbf{\textit{The coarse grid matrix is}}\ \boldsymbol{A_{2h} = R_h^{2h} A_h I_{2h}^h = RAI}. \tag{6}$$

When the fine grid has $N = 7$ interior meshpoints, the matrix A_h is 7 by 7. Then the coarse grid matrix RAI is (3 by 7)(7 by 7)(7 by 3) = **3 by 3**.

Example In one dimension, $A = A_h$ might be the second difference matrix K/h^2. Our first example came from $h = \frac{1}{8}$. Now choose $h = \frac{1}{6}$, so that multigrid goes from five meshpoints inside $0 < x < 1$ to two meshpoints (I is 5 by 2 and R is 2 by 5): The neat multiplication (we will use it again later) is $RA_h = RK_5/h^2$:

$$RA = \frac{1}{4}\begin{bmatrix} 1 & 2 & 1 & & \\ & & 1 & 2 & 1 \end{bmatrix} \frac{1}{h^2} \begin{bmatrix} 2 & -1 & & & \\ -1 & 2 & -1 & & \\ & -1 & 2 & -1 & \\ & & -1 & 2 & -1 \\ & & & -1 & 2 \end{bmatrix} = \frac{1}{(2h)^2}\begin{bmatrix} 0 & \mathbf{2} & 0 & \mathbf{-1} & 0 \\ 0 & \mathbf{-1} & 0 & \mathbf{2} & 0 \end{bmatrix}. \tag{7}$$

A natural choice for A_{2h} on the coarse grid is $K_2/(2h)^2$ and multigrid makes this choice:

Coarse grid matrix RAI $$A_{2h} = RAI = \frac{1}{(2h)^2}\begin{bmatrix} 2 & -1 \\ -1 & 2 \end{bmatrix}. \tag{8}$$

The reader will appreciate that the $I^{\mathrm{T}}AI$ rule preserves symmetry and positive definiteness, when A has those properties. The rule arises naturally in Galerkin methods [128], including the finite element method. Notice how the restriction operator R with the factor $\frac{1}{4}$ automatically adjusts $1/h^2$ to $1/(2h)^2$.

Steps **1** and **5** are necessary, but they are really outside the essential multigrid idea. The **smoother** is step **1**, the **post-smoother** is step **5**. Those are normal iterations for which weighted Jacobi or Gauss-Seidel is satisfactory.

We follow the beautiful exposition in [26] to show that multigrid gives full accuracy in $O(n)$ steps. The early vision of Achi Brandt is now a reality.

The Errors e_h and E_h

Suppose we solve the coarse grid equation exactly at step **3**. Is the multigrid error correction E_h then equal to the true fine-grid error $e_h = u - u_h$? No, that is too much to expect! We have only solved the smaller problem on the coarse grid, not the full problem. But the connection between E_h and e_h is simple and crucial for understanding multigrid. We now track down the steps from E to e.

Four matrices multiply e. At step **2**, the residual $r = b - Au_h = A(u - u_h) = Ae$ multiplies by A. The restriction is multiplication by R. The solution step **3** multiplies by $A_{2h}^{-1} = (RAI)^{-1}$. The interpolation step **4** multiplies by I to find the correction E. *Altogether, E is $\boldsymbol{IA_{2h}^{-1}RA_h e}$:*

$$E = I(RAI)^{-1}RAe \quad \text{and we call this} \quad \boldsymbol{E = Se}. \tag{9}$$

When I is 5 by 2 and R is 2 by 5, that matrix S on the right side is 5 by 5. It can't be the identity matrix, since RAI and its inverse are only 2 by 2 (rank two). But $S = I(RAI)^{-1}RA$ has the remarkable property $S^2 = S$. This says that *S is the identity matrix on its 2-dimensional column space.* (Of course S is the zero matrix on its 3-dimensional nullspace.) $S^2 = S$ is easy to check:

$$S^2 = (I(RAI)^{-1}RA)(I(RAI)^{-1}RA) = S \quad \text{because} \quad (RAI)^{-1}RAI = I. \tag{10}$$

So the multigrid correction $E = Se$ is not the whole error e, *it is a projection of e.* The new error is $e - E = e - Se = (I - S)e$. ***This matrix $I - S$ is the two-grid operator.*** $I - S$ plays the same fundamental role in describing the multigrid steps **2–4** that the usual $M = I - P^{-1}A$ plays for each iteration in steps **1** and **5**:

v-cycle matrix $= I - S$ **iteration matrix $= I - P^{-1}A$.**

Example (continued). The 5 by 5 matrix $A_h = K_5/h^2$ and the rectangular I and R led in (8) to $A_{2h} = K_2/(2h)^2$. To find $S = IA_{2h}^{-1}RA_h$, we multiply (7) by A_{2h}^{-1} and I:

$$A_{2h}^{-1}RA_h = \begin{bmatrix} 0 & \mathbf{1} & 0 & \mathbf{0} & 0 \\ 0 & \mathbf{0} & 0 & \mathbf{1} & 0 \end{bmatrix}$$

Now multiply by I to find S

$$S = \begin{bmatrix} 0 & 1/2 & 0 & 0 & 0 \\ 0 & 1 & 0 & 0 & 0 \\ 0 & 1/2 & 0 & 1/2 & 0 \\ 0 & 0 & 0 & 1 & 0 \\ 0 & 0 & 0 & 1/2 & 0 \end{bmatrix}. \qquad (11)$$

The eigenvalues of this S are $1, 1, 0, 0, 0$. If you square S, you recover $S^2 = S$. With its three columns of zeros, the nullspace of S contains all fine-grid vectors of the form $(e_1, 0, e_3, 0, e_5)$. Those are vectors that don't appear on the coarse grid. If the error e had this form, then $E = Se$ would be zero (no improvement from multigrid). *But we don't expect a large component of those high frequency vectors in e, because of the smoothing.*

The column space of S contains column 2 $= (\frac{1}{2}, 1, \frac{1}{2}, 0, 0)$ and column 4 $= (0, 0, \frac{1}{2}, 1, \frac{1}{2})$. These are "mixed-frequency vectors." We do expect them to appear in e, because the smoothing step didn't remove them. But these are vectors for which $E = Se = e$ and they are the errors that multigrid catches! After step **4** they are gone.

High and Low Frequencies in $O(n)$ Operations

Because $S^2 = S$, the only eigenvectors are $\lambda = 0$ and $\lambda = 1$. (If $Su = \lambda u$ we always have $S^2u = \lambda^2 u$. Then $S^2 = S$ gives $\lambda^2 = \lambda$.) Our example has $\lambda = 1, 1, 0, 0, 0$. The eigenvalues of $I - S$ are $0, 0, 1, 1, 1$. **The eigenvectors e reveal what multigrid is doing**:

$E = Se = 0$ In this case multigrid gives no improvement. The correction E added to u_h in step **4** is zero. In the example, this happens for errors $e = (e_1, 0, e_3, 0, e_5)$ that are zero on the coarse grid. Step **3** doesn't see those errors.

$E = Se = e$ In this case multigrid is perfect. The correction E_h added to u_h in step **4** is the whole error e_h. In the example, two eigenvectors of S for $\lambda = 1$ are $e = (1, 2, 2, 2, 1)$ and $e = (1, 2, 0, -2, -1)$. Those have large low-frequency components. They go up and down only once and twice. They are in the column space of I.

These errors e are not perfect sines, but an important part of the low-frequency error is caught and removed. The number of independent vectors with $Se = e$ is the number of coarse gridpoints (here 2). That measures the A_{2h} problem that step **3** deals with. It is the rank of S and R and I. The other $5 - 2$ gridpoints account for the nullspace of S, where $E = Se = 0$ means no improvement from multigrid.

Note The "high-frequency" vectors $(u_1, 0, u_3, 0, u_5)$ with $Su = 0$ are *not exactly* combinations of the last three discrete sines y_3, y_4, y_5. The frequencies are mixed by S, as equations (18–19) will clearly show. The exact statements are *column space of S = column space of I* and *nullspace of S = nullspace of RA*. The mixing of frequencies does not affect our main point: **Iteration handles the high frequencies and multigrid handles the low frequencies.**

You can see that a perfect smoother followed by perfect multigrid (exact solution at step **3**) would leave no error. In reality, this will not happen. Fortunately, a careful (not so simple) analysis will show that a multigrid cycle with good smoothing can reduce the error by a constant factor ρ that is **independent of h**:

$$\|\textbf{error after step 5}\| \leq \rho\,\|\textbf{error before step 1}\| \quad \text{with} \quad \rho < 1\,. \tag{12}$$

A typical value is $\rho = \frac{1}{10}$. Compare with $\rho = .99$ for Jacobi alone. This is the Holy Grail of numerical analysis, to achieve a convergence factor ρ (a spectral radius of the overall iteration matrix) that *does not move up to* 1 *as* $h \to 0$. We can achieve a given relative accuracy in a fixed number of cycles. Since each step of each cycle requires only $O(n)$ operations on sparse problems of size n, **multigrid is an $O(n)$ algorithm**. This does not change in higher dimensions.

There is a further point about the number of steps and the accuracy. The user may want the solution error e to be as small as the discretization error (when the original differential equation was replaced by $Au = b$). In our examples with second differences, this demands that we continue until $e = O(h^2) = O(N^{-2})$. In that case we need more than a fixed number of v-cycles. To reach $\rho^k = O(N^{-2})$ requires $k = O(\log N)$ cycles. Multigrid has an answer for this too.

Instead of repeating v-cycles, or nesting them into V-cycles or W-cycles, it is better to use **full multigrid**: FMG cycles are described below. Then the operation count comes back to $O(n)$ even for this higher required accuracy $e = O(h^2)$.

V-Cycles and W-Cycles and Full Multigrid

Clearly multigrid need not stop at two grids. If it did stop, it would miss the remarkable power of the idea. The lowest frequency is still low on the $2h$ grid, and that part of the error won't decay quickly until we move to $4h$ or $8h$ (or a very coarse $512h$).

The two-grid v-cycle extends in a natural way to more grids. It can go down to coarser grids $(2h, 4h, 8h)$ and back up to $(4h, 2h, h)$. This nested sequence of v-cycles is a **V-cycle** (capital V). *Don't forget that coarse grid sweeps are much faster than fine grid sweeps.* Analysis shows that time is well spent on the coarse grids. So the **W-cycle** that stays coarse longer (Figure 7.11b) is generally superior to a V-cycle.

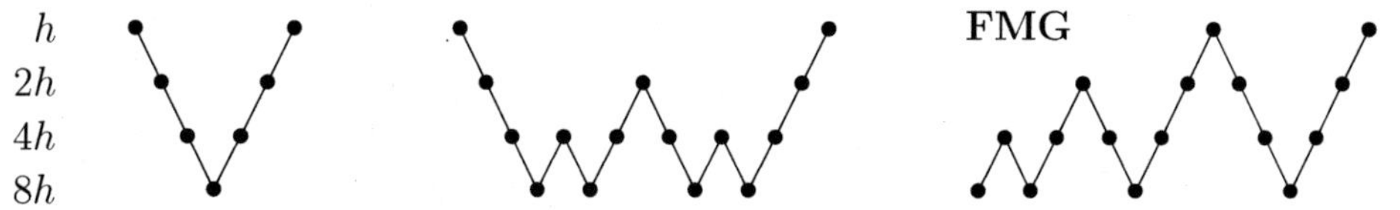

Figure 7.11: V-cycles and W-cycles and FMG use several grids several times.

The **full multigrid cycle** in Figure 7.11c is asymptotically better than V or W. *Full multigrid starts on the coarsest grid.* The solution on the $8h$ grid is interpolated to provide a good initial vector u_{4h} on the $4h$ grid. A v-cycle between $4h$ and $8h$ improves it. Then interpolation predicts the solution on the $2h$ grid, and a deeper V-cycle makes it better (using $2h, 4h, 8h$). Interpolation of that improved solution onto the finest grid gives an excellent start to the last and deepest V-cycle.

The operation counts for a deep V-cycle and for full multigrid are certainly greater than for a two-grid v-cycle, but *only by a constant factor.* That is because the count is divided by a power of 2 every time we move to a coarser grid. For a differential equation in d space dimensions, we divide by 2^d. The cost of a V-cycle (as deep as we want) is less than a fixed multiple of the v-cycle cost:

$$\textbf{V-cycle cost} < \left(1+\frac{1}{2^d}+\left(\frac{1}{2^d}\right)^2+\cdots\right)\textbf{v-cycle cost} = \frac{2^d}{2^d-1}\,\textbf{v-cycle cost}\,. \quad (13)$$

Full multigrid is no more than a series of inverted V-cycles, beginning on a very coarse mesh. By the same reasoning that led to (13),

$$\textbf{Full multigrid cost} < \frac{2^d}{2^d-1}\,\textbf{V-cycle cost} < \left(\frac{2^d}{2^d-1}\right)^2\textbf{v-cycle cost}\,. \quad (14)$$

And the method works in practice. But good programming is required.

Multigrid Matrices

For a 3-grid V-cycle, what matrix S_3 corresponds to the 2-grid v-cycle projection $S = I(RAI)^{-1}RA$? No smoothing is involved here. S and S_3 only project to coarser problems. By itself, S_3 will not be a good solver without smoothers.

To construct A_{4h}, replace the matrix $A_{2h} = RAI$ on the middle grid by using a coarse restriction $R_c = R_{2h}^{4h}$ that transfers down to the $4h$ grid, and an interpolation $I_c = I_{4h}^{2h}$ that comes back to $2h$:

Very coarse matrix $$\boldsymbol{A_{4h} = R_c A_{2h} I_c}\,. \quad (15)$$

If $h = \frac{1}{16}$, that product is $(3 \times 7)(7 \times 7)(7 \times 3)$. The 3 by 3 problem uses A_{4h} on the $4h = \frac{1}{4}$ grid (with three interior unknowns). Then $S_3 = (S_3)^2$ is the matrix that goes down two grids, solves the very coarse problem by A_{4h}^{-1}, and comes back up:

$\boldsymbol{E_{4h} = S_3 e_h =}$ **error removed** $$S_3 = I_{2h}^h I_{4h}^{2h} A_{4h}^{-1} R_{2h}^{4h} R_h^{2h} A\,. \quad (16)$$

The error that remains after an unsmoothed V-cycle will be $(I - S_3)e$. On the $h = \frac{1}{16}$ grid, there are 15 frequencies in the error e. Only the lowest 3 are (approximately) removed by $S_3 e$. We have only solved a 3 by 3 problem with A_{4h}. It is the *smoothers*, on the fine h grid and the middle $2h$ grid, that reduce the high and middle frequency errors in the solution.

Numerical Experiments

The real test of multigrid effectiveness is numerical! Its k-step approximation e_k should approach zero and the graphs will show how quickly this happens. An initial guess u_0 includes an error e_0. Whatever iteration we use, we are trying to drive u_k to u, and e_k to zero. The multigrid method jumps between two or more grids, so as to converge more quickly, and our graphs show the error on the fine grid.

We can work with the equation $Ae = 0$, whose solution is $e = 0$. The initial error has low and high frequencies (drawn as continuous functions rather than discrete values). After three fine-grid sweeps of weighted Jacobi ($\omega = \frac{2}{3}$), Figure 7.9 showed that the high frequency component has greatly decayed. The error $e_3 = (I - P^{-1}A)^3 e_0$ is much smoother than e_0. For our second difference matrix A_h (better known as K), the Jacobi preconditioner from Section 7.2 simply has $P^{-1} = \frac{1}{2}\omega I$.

Now multigrid begins. The current fine-grid residual is $r_h = -A_h e_3$. After restriction to the coarse grid it becomes r_{2h}. Three weighted Jacobi iterations on the coarse grid error equation $A_{2h}E_{2h} = r_{2h}$ start with the guess $E_{2h} = 0$. That produces the crucial error reduction shown in this figure contributed by Bill Briggs.

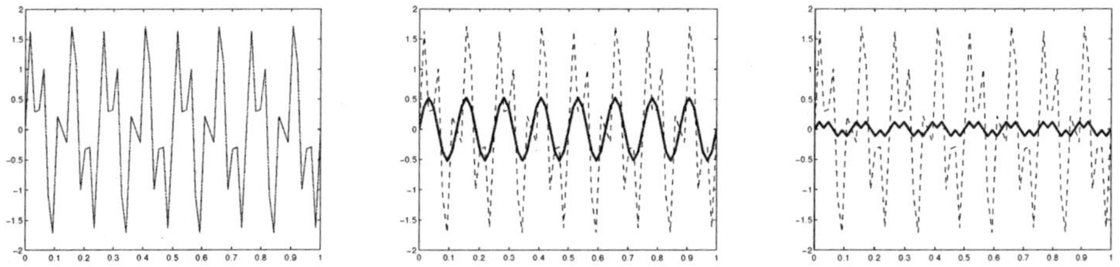

Figure 7.12: (**v-cycle**) Low frequency survives 3 fine grid iterations (center). It is reduced by 3 coarse grid iterations and mapped back to the fine grid by Bill Briggs.

Eigenvector Analysis

The reader will recognize that one matrix (like $I - S$ for a v-cycle) can describe each multigrid step. The eigenvalues of a full multigrid matrix would be nice to know, but they are usually impractical to find. Numerical experiments build confidence. Computation also provides a *diagnostic* tool, to locate where convergence is stalled and a change is needed (often in the boundary conditions). If we want a *predictive* tool, the best is **modal analysis**.

The key idea is to watch the Fourier modes. In our example those are discrete sines, because of the boundary conditions $u(0) = u(1) = 0$. We will push this model problem all the way, to see what the multigrid matrix $I - S$ does to those sine vectors. The final result in (18–19) shows why multigrid works and it also shows how *pairs of frequencies are mixed.* The eigenvectors are mixtures of two frequencies.

The frequencies that mix together are k and $N+1-k$. (We will look only at $k \le N+1-k$.) The discrete sines with those frequencies are y_k and Y_k:

$$y_k = \left(\sin\frac{k\pi}{N+1}, \sin\frac{2k\pi}{N+1}, \ldots\right) \text{ and } Y_k = \left(\sin\frac{(N+1-k)\pi}{N+1}, \sin\frac{2(N+1-k)\pi}{N+1}, \ldots\right).$$

Where y_k goes up and down k times, Y_k does that $N+1-k$ times.

There is something neat you have to see. **Y_k and y_k are the same except for alternating signs!** Cancel $N+1$ with $N+1$ in those components of Y_k:

$$Y_k = \left(\sin\left[\pi - \frac{k\pi}{N+1}\right], \sin\left[2\pi - \frac{2k\pi}{N+1}\right], \ldots\right) = \left(+\sin\frac{k\pi}{N+1}, -\sin\frac{2k\pi}{N+1}, \ldots\right) \quad (17)$$

For our model problem with second differences, we can report the result of multiplying by $S = I(RAI)^{-1}RA$. In fact the true multigrid matrix is $I - S$, to give the error $e - E = (I - S)\,e$ that remains after steps **2**, **3**, **4**. Seeing $I - S$ is even better:

$I - S$ for one v-cycle	$(I - S)\,y_k = \frac{1}{2}\left(1 - \cos\frac{k\pi}{N+1}\right)(y_k + Y_k)$	(18)
Smooth errors reduced		
Frequencies mixed	$(I - S)Y_k = \frac{1}{2}\left(1 + \cos\frac{k\pi}{N+1}\right)(y_k + Y_k)$	(19)

Such beautiful formulas can't be expected in more complicated problems, and we seize this chance to make four key points:

1. **Low frequencies like $k = 1, 2, 3$ are greatly reduced by multigrid.** The cosine in equation (18) will be near 1. The factor $(1 - \cos\frac{k\pi}{N+1})$ is very small, of order $(k/N)^2$. This shows how multigrid is powerful in nearly killing the low frequencies. These are exactly the frequencies on which Jacobi and Gauss-Seidel will stall in the smoothing iterations.

2. **The pair of sines y_k and Y_k is mixed together by multigrid.** We will see that the restriction R and interpolation I are responsible. Those are not like the square matrix A, which keeps frequencies separate (because the sines are its eigenvectors). Aliasing appears for rectangular matrices!

3. **The combinations $e = y_k + Y_k$ are eigenvectors of $I - S$ with $\lambda = 1$.** Just add equations (18) and (19), to get $(I - S)e = e$. Since Y_k has the same components as y_k with alternating signs, $y_k + Y_k$ has the correct form $(e_1, 0, e_3, 0, \ldots)$. Those are the vectors that we discovered earlier in the nullspace $(\lambda = 0)$ of S. They are not touched by $I - S$ since $Se = 0$.

4. **The other eigenvectors of $I - S$ are just Sy_k.** We know that $(I - S)Sy_k = 0$ because $S = S^2$. In our example with $N = 5$, the vectors Sy_1 and Sy_2 are multiples of $(1, 2, 2, 2, 1)$ and $(1, 2, 0, -2, 1)$ that we found explicitly. Those are mostly low frequency, and multigrid removes them from the error.

According to (18), these vectors Sy_k are combinations of y_k and Y_k. To find a good combination e^*, multiply (18) and (19) by $(1 + \cos\frac{k\pi}{N+1})$ and $(1 - \cos\frac{k\pi}{N+1})$. The right-hand sides are now the same and we subtract to find $\boldsymbol{Se^* = e^*}$:

$$(I-S)e^* = (I-S)\left[\left(1+\cos\frac{k\pi}{N+1}\right)y_k - \left(1-\cos\frac{k\pi}{N+1}\right)Y_k\right] = 0. \tag{20}$$

Those mixtures e^* in square brackets are completely killed ($\lambda = 0$) by multigrid. A smooth error vector e_h (after Jacobi iterations have reduced its high frequency components) has only small components along the eigenvectors $y_k + Y_k$. Multigrid doesn't touch those pieces ($\lambda = 1$). The larger components along the e^* will die.

The Restriction R Produces Aliasing

To complete this analysis we have to see where and how a pair of frequencies is mixed. The aliasing comes from the restriction matrix $R = R_h$, when both vectors y_k^h and Y_k^h lead to multiples of the same output vector y_k^{2h}:

$$Ry_k^h = \left(\frac{1}{2} - \frac{1}{2}\cos\frac{k\pi}{N+1}\right)y_k^{2h} \quad \text{and} \quad RY_k^h = \left(-\frac{1}{2} - \frac{1}{2}\cos\frac{k\pi}{N+1}\right)y_k^{2h}. \tag{21}$$

You see the aliasing by R. We cannot hope to decide the input y_k or Y_k if we only know these outputs. This is normal for a short wide matrix. (The matrix R is 3 by 7 and 2 by 5 in our examples.) The coarse mesh output has only about half as many components as the fine mesh input.

The transpose of R does the opposite. Where R mixes two inputs y_k^h and Y_k^h into one output, the interpolation matrix I sends one input frequency on the coarse grid into a pair of frequencies on the fine grid:

$$2\, I_{2h}^h y_k^{2h} = \left(1+\cos\frac{k\pi}{N+1}\right)y_k^h - \left(1-\cos\frac{k\pi}{N+1}\right)Y_k^h. \tag{22}$$

Interpolation of a smooth vector (low k) on a coarse grid will excite an oscillatory mode Y_k^h (high k) on the fine grid. But those oscillations have small amplitude, because the cosine of $k\pi/(N+1)$ is near 1.

The key formulas (18) and (19) that describe multigrid come from assembling (21) for R, (22) for I, and the known eigenvalues for A_h and A_{2h}. I think the calculation of S in (11) shows this best. Its zero columns put $y_k + Y_k$ in its nullspace. The nonzero columns in S come from the interpolation matrix I. So Se captures a part of the whole error e. *Multigrid solves a projection of the original problem.*

Example completed It would be useless to repeat steps **2**, **3**, **4** with no smoothing in between. Nothing would change! The untouched vectors $e = y_k + Y_k$ with $(I-S)e = e$ will still be untouched. It is the smoothing matrix $M = I - P^{-1}A$ that must reduce these high frequency errors.

If we apply Jacobi with weight $w = \frac{2}{3}$ at steps 1 and 5, then $M = I - \frac{1}{3}A$. The overall matrix for all steps 1 to 5 will be $M(I-S)M$. The eigenvalues of that matrix will decide the success (or not) of multigrid. To my amazement, the 5 by 5 matrix $M(I-S)M$ has a *triple eigenvalue of* $\frac{1}{9}$!

The three eigenvalues $\lambda = 1$ of $I - S$ are reduced to $\lambda = \frac{1}{9}$ for $M(I-S)M$.

The largest eigenvalue of M is .91—so you see the value of multigrid. I hope you will try eig$(M * M * (I-S) * M * M)$ with double smoothing (see Problems 3–7).

Fourier Modal Analysis

Pure modal analysis neglects the boundaries completely. It assumes an infinite grid! The vectors y_k in the example were sines because of the boundary conditions. When boundaries are gone, the y_k are replaced by infinitely long vectors y_ω coming from complex exponentials. Now there is a continuum of frequencies ω:

$$\textbf{Fourier modes} \quad y_\omega = (\ldots, e^{-2i\omega}, e^{-i\omega}, 1, e^{i\omega}, e^{2i\omega}, \ldots) \text{ with } -\pi \le \omega \le \pi. \quad (23)$$

We need infinite matrices K_∞ to multiply these infinite vectors. Second differences $-1, 2, -1$ appear on *all rows forever.* The key is that each y_ω is an eigenvector of K_∞. The eigenvalue is $\lambda = 2 - 2\cos\omega$:

$$\boldsymbol{K_\infty y_\omega = (2 - 2\cos\omega)\, y_\omega} \quad \text{because} \quad -e^{i\omega(n+1)} - e^{i\omega(n-1)} = -2\cos\omega\, e^{i\omega n}. \quad (24)$$

This tells us the action of $A_h = K_\infty/h^2$. It also tells us about A_{2h}, when the coarse mesh changes h^2 to $(2h)^2$ and ω to 2ω.

The restriction matrix R still introduces aliasing. The frequencies that mix are now ω and $\omega + \pi$. Notice how increasing ω by π produces a factor $e^{i\pi n} = (-1)^n$ with alternating signs. This is exactly what we saw for y_k and Y_k in (17).

This pure Fourier analysis will go all the way to formulas for the infinite $(I-S)y_\omega$ and $(I-S)y_{\omega+\pi}$, just like equations (18) and (19). In that finite case, those equations explained why multigrid succeeds. They do the same in the infinite case.

Let me emphasize why this pure modal analysis (with no boundaries and constant coefficients) was mentioned. It allows Fourier to work freely. The differential equation $\text{div}(c(x,y)\,\text{grad}\, u) = f(x,y)$ on a general region would lead to giant complications in the eigenvectors for multigrid—impossible to find them. But if we fix $c =$ constant and ignore boundaries, those "interior eigenvectors" return to simple combinations of y_ω and $y_{\omega+\pi}$. That leaves difficulties associated with the boundary conditions, which Fourier doesn't easily resolve.

Algebraic Multigrid

We close this section with a few words about **algebraic multigrid**, when the problem comes as a system of equations $Au = b$. *There is no grid in the background.* We need to find replacements for the key ideas on which geometric multigrid was based: *smooth vectors, connected nodes, coarse meshes.* Replacing the first two is fairly easy. Rescaling A_h to A_{2h} on a (nonexistent) coarse mesh is less clear.

1. **Smooth vectors.** These are vectors for which the norms of u and Au are comparable. High frequencies in u would be greatly amplified by A (just as the second derivative amplifies $\sin kt$ by k^2).

2. **Connected nodes.** On a grid, neighboring nodes are reflected by a nonzero entry in A. When there is no grid, we look directly at the matrix. Its significant nonzero entries (say $|A_{ij}| > A_{ii}/10$) tell us when i is "connected" to j.

3. **Coarse subset of nodes.** Each significant entry A_{ij} indicates that the value of u_j *strongly influences* the value of u_i. Probably the errors e_j and e_i are comparable, when the error is smooth. We don't need both i and j in the "coarse set C" of nodes. On a grid they would be neighbors, not both in C.

   But if i is *not* in C, then every j that strongly influences i should either be in C or be strongly influenced by another J that *is* in C. This heuristic rule is discussed more fully in [74, 75], with an algorithm for constructing C. (In general, too many coarse unknowns are better than too few.)

The excellent book [26] also constructs the coarse-to-fine interpolation matrix I. This starts with the errors E_j for j in C, and leaves them unchanged. If i is not in C, the interpolated value E_i at step **2** of multigrid will be a *weighted combination* of the E_j that do have j in C. In our model problem, that weighted combination E_i was the average of its two neighbors. The model problem had a grid!

The interpolating combination will give greatest weight to the e_j for which j in C strongly influences i. But there may be smaller entries A_{ij} that cannot be completely ignored. The final decision on the weights for each interpolated value is more subtle than a simple average. Algebraic multigrid is more expensive than geometric multigrid, but it applies to a much wider range of sparse matrices A (and the software can control AMG without us). We still expect a "smoothing + multigrid" combination that is close to $O(n)$ steps for an accurate solution of $Au = b$.

Let me mention an important contrast between solid mechanics and fluid mechanics. For solids, the original finite element grid is already relatively coarse. We are typically looking for "engineering accuracy" and we don't have fine scale motions to resolve. Multigrid is not such a common choice for structural problems (elimination is simpler). Fluids do have fine scales so that multigrid becomes a natural idea, not only numerically but physically. Of course fluids don't generally present symmetric matrices, because of the convective terms, and finite element methods may require "upwind adjustments." The analysis of multigrid convergence becomes harder for fluids, just when a multiscale approach becomes attractive.

Problem Set 7.3

1 What is the 3 by 7 matrix $R_{\text{injection}}$ that copies v_1, v_2, v_3 from u_2, u_4, u_6 and ignores u_1, u_3, u_5, u_7?

2 Write down a 9 by 4 bilinear interpolation matrix I that uses the four grid values at the corners of a square (side $2h$) to produce nine values at the (h) gridpoints. What constant should multiply the transpose of I to give a one-element restriction matrix R?

3 In Problem 1, the four small squares (side h) subdivide into 16 smaller squares (side $h/2$). How many rows and columns in the interpolation matrix $I_{h/2}$?

4 If A is the 5-point discrete Laplace matrix (with $-1, -1, 4, -1, -1$ on a typical row) what is a typical row of $A_{2h} = RAI$ using bilinear interpolation as in Problems 1–2?

5 Suppose A comes from the 9-point stencil (8/3 surrounded by eight entries of $-1/3$). What is now the stencil for $A_{2h} = RAI$?

6 Verify $Ry_k^h = \frac{1}{2}(1+\cos\frac{k\pi}{N+1})y_k^{2h}$ in equation (23) for the linear restriction matrix R applied to discrete sines y_k^h with $k \leq \frac{1}{2}(N+1)$.

7 Show that $RY_k^h = \frac{1}{2}(-1-\cos\frac{k\pi}{N+1})y_k^{2h}$ in equation (23) for the "complementary" discrete sines $Y_k^h = y_{N+1-k}$. Now $N+1-k > \frac{1}{2}(N+1)$.

8 Verify equation (24) for linear interpolation applied to the discrete sines y_k^h with $k \leq \frac{1}{2}(N+1)$.

9 With $h = \frac{1}{8}$, use the 7 by 3 and 3 by 7 matrices I and R in equations (1–2) to find the 3 by 3 matrix $A_{2h} = RAI$ with $A = K_7/h^2$.

10 Continue Problem 3 to find the 7 by 7 matrix $S = I(RAI)^{-1}RA$. Verify that $S^2 = S$, and that S has the same nullspace as RA and the same column space as I. What are the seven eigenvalues of S?

11 Continue Problem 4 to find (by MATLAB) the multigrid matrix $I - S$ and the presmoothed/postsmoothed matrix MSM, where M is the Jacobi smoother $I - \omega D^{-1}A = I - \frac{1}{3}K_7$ with $\omega = \frac{2}{3}$. Find the eigenvalues of MSM!

12 Continue Problem 5 to find the eigenvalues of M^2SM^2 with two Jacobi smoothers ($\omega = \frac{2}{3}$) before and after the grid changes.

13 With unweighted Jacobi ($\omega = 1$ and $M = I - \frac{1}{2}K_7$) find MSM and its eigenvalues. Is the weighting useful?

14 Starting from $h = \frac{1}{16}$ and the second difference matrix $A = K_{15}/h^2$, compute the projected 7 by 7 matrix $A_{2h} = RAI$ and the doubly projected 3 by 3 matrix $A_{4h} = R_cA_{2h}I_c$. Use linear interpolation matrices I and I_c, and restriction matrices $R = \frac{1}{2}I^{\mathrm{T}}$ and $R_c = \frac{1}{2}I_c^{\mathrm{T}}$.

15 Use A_{4h} from Problem 6 to compute the projection matrix S_3 in (16). Verify that this 15 by 15 matrix has rank 3, and that $(S_3)^2 = S_3$.

16 The weighted Jacobi smoothers are $M_h = I_{15} - \frac{1}{3}K_{15}$ and $M_{2h} = I_7 - \frac{1}{3}K_7$. With MATLAB, compute the smoothed error reduction matrix V_3 and its eigenvalues:

$$V_3 = M_h I M_{2h} (I_7 - S_{2h}) M_{2h} R A M_h \,.$$

$S_{2h} = I_c A_{4h}^{-1} R_c A_{2h}$ is the projection matrix for the v-cycle within the V-cycle.

17 Compute the $(15 \times 7)(7 \times 3)$ linear interpolation matrix $I_{2h}^{h} I_{4h}^{2h}$. What is the restriction matrix?

7.4 KRYLOV SUBSPACES AND CONJUGATE GRADIENTS

Our original equation is $Ax = b$. *The preconditioned equation is* $P^{-1}Ax = P^{-1}b$. When we write P^{-1}, we never intend that an inverse will be explicitly computed. P may come from Incomplete LU, or a few steps of a multigrid iteration, or "domain decomposition." Entirely new preconditioners are waiting to be invented.

The residual is $\boldsymbol{r_k = b - Ax_k}$. This is the error in $Ax = b$, not the error in x. An ordinary preconditioned iteration corrects x_k by the vector $P^{-1}r_k$:

$$Px_{k+1} = (P - A)x_k + b \quad \text{or} \quad Px_{k+1} = Px_k + r_k \quad \text{or} \quad \boldsymbol{x_{k+1} = x_k + P^{-1}r_k} \tag{1}$$

In describing Krylov subspaces, I should work with $P^{-1}A$. **For simplicity I will only write** A! I am assuming that P has been chosen and used, and the preconditioned equation $P^{-1}Ax = P^{-1}b$ is given the notation $Ax = b$. The preconditioner is now $P = I$. Our new A is probably better than the original matrix with that name.

With $x_1 = b$, look first at two steps of the pure iteration $x_{j+1} = (I - A)x_j + b$:

$$x_2 = (I - A)b + b = \boldsymbol{2b - Ab} \qquad x_3 = (I - A)x_1 + b = \boldsymbol{3b - 3Ab + A^2b}. \tag{2}$$

My point is simple but important: $\boldsymbol{x_j}$ ***is a combination of*** $\boldsymbol{b, Ab, \ldots, A^{j-1}b}$. We can compute those vectors quickly, multiplying at each step by a sparse A. Every iteration involves only one matrix-vector multiplication. Krylov gave a name to ***all*** combinations of those vectors $b, \ldots, A^{j-1}b$, and he suggested that there might be better combinations (closer to $x = A^{-1}b$) than the particular choices x_j in (2).

Krylov Subspaces

The linear combinations of $b, Ab, \ldots, A^{j-1}b$ form the jth Krylov subspace. This space depends on A and b. Following convention, I will write $\boldsymbol{\mathcal{K}_j}$ for that subspace and $\mathbf{K}_j$ for the matrix with those basis vectors in its columns:

		(3)
Krylov matrix	$\mathbf{K}_j = [\, b \;\; Ab \;\; A^2b \;\; \ldots \;\; A^{j-1}b \,]$.	
Krylov subspace	$\mathcal{K}_j =$ ***all combinations of*** $\boldsymbol{b, Ab, \ldots, A^{j-1}b}$.	

Thus $\mathcal{K}_j$ is the column space of $\mathbf{K}_j$. We want to choose the ***best combination*** as our improved x_j. Various definitions of "best" will give various x_j. Here are four different approaches to choosing a good x_j in $\mathcal{K}_j$—this is the important decision:

1. The residual $r_j = b - Ax_j$ is orthogonal to $\mathcal{K}_j$ (**Conjugate Gradients**).
2. The residual r_j has minimum norm for x_j in $\mathcal{K}_j$ (**GMRES** and **MINRES**).
3. r_j is orthogonal to a different space $\mathcal{K}_j(A^{\mathrm{T}})$ (**BiConjugate Gradients**).
4. The error e_j has minimum norm in $\mathcal{K}_j$ (**SYMMLQ**).

In every case we hope to compute the new x_j quickly from the earlier x's. If that step only involves x_{j-1} and x_{j-2} (**short recurrence**) it is especially fast. Short recurrences happen for conjugate gradients and symmetric positive definite A.

The BiCG method extends short recurrences to unsymmetric A (using two Krylov spaces). A stabilized version called **BiCGStab** chooses x_j in $A^{\mathrm{T}}\mathcal{K}_j(A^{\mathrm{T}})$.

As always, computing x_j can be very unstable until we choose a decent basis.

Vandermonde Example

To follow each step of orthogonalizing the basis, and solving $Ax = b$ by conjugate gradients, we need a good example. It has to stay simple! I am happy with this one:

$$A = \begin{bmatrix} 1 & & & \\ & 2 & & \\ & & 3 & \\ & & & 4 \end{bmatrix} \quad b = \begin{bmatrix} 1 \\ 1 \\ 1 \\ 1 \end{bmatrix} \quad Ab = \begin{bmatrix} 1 \\ 2 \\ 3 \\ 4 \end{bmatrix} \quad A^{-1}b = \begin{bmatrix} 1/1 \\ 1/2 \\ 1/3 \\ 1/4 \end{bmatrix}. \tag{4}$$

That constant vector b spans the Krylov subspace $\mathcal{K}_1$. Then Ab, A^2b, and A^3b are the other basis vectors in $\mathcal{K}_4$. They are the columns of $\mathbf{K}_4$, which we will name V:

Vandermonde matrix

$$\mathbf{K}_4 = V = \begin{bmatrix} 1 & 1 & 1 & 1 \\ 1 & 2 & 4 & 8 \\ 1 & 3 & 9 & 27 \\ 1 & 4 & 16 & 64 \end{bmatrix}. \tag{5}$$

Those columns are constant, linear, quadratic, and cubic. The column vectors are independent but not at all orthogonal. The best measure of non-orthogonality starts by computing *inner products of the columns* in the matrix $V^{\mathrm{T}}V$. When columns are orthonormal, their inner products are 0 or 1. (The matrix is called Q, and the inner products give $Q^{\mathrm{T}}Q = I$.) Here $V^{\mathrm{T}}V$ is very far from the identity matrix:

$$V^{\mathrm{T}}V = \begin{bmatrix} 4 & 10 & 30 & 100 \\ 10 & 30 & 100 & 354 \\ 30 & 100 & 354 & 1300 \\ 100 & 354 & 1300 & 4890 \end{bmatrix} \qquad \begin{aligned} 10 &= 1 + 2 + 3 + 4 \\ 30 &= 1^2 + 2^2 + 3^2 + 4^2 \\ 100 &= 1^3 + 2^3 + 3^3 + 4^3 \\ 1300 &= 1^5 + 2^5 + 3^5 + 4^5 \end{aligned}$$

The eigenvalues of this inner product matrix (***Gram matrix***) tell us something important. The extreme eigenvalues are $\lambda_{\mathsf{max}} \approx 5264$ and $\lambda_{\mathsf{min}} \approx .004$. Those are the squares of σ_4 and σ_1, the largest and smallest **singular values of V**. The key measure is their ratio σ_4/σ_1, the **condition number of V**:

$$\operatorname{cond}(V^{\mathrm{T}}V) \approx \frac{5264}{.004} \approx 10^6 \qquad \operatorname{cond}(V) = \sqrt{\frac{\lambda_{\mathsf{max}}}{\lambda_{\mathsf{min}}}} \approx 1000.$$

For such a small example, 1000 is a poor condition number. For an orthonormal basis with $Q^{\mathrm{T}}Q = I$, all eigenvalues = singular values = condition number = 1.

We could improve the condition by rescaling the columns of V to unit vectors. Then V^TV has ones on the diagonal, and the condition number drops to 263. But when the matrix size is realistically large, that rescaling will not save us. In fact we could extend this Vandermonde model from constant, linear, quadratic, and cubic vectors to the functions $1, x, x^2, x^3$. (A multiplies by x.) Please look at what happens:

Continuous Vandermonde matrix $$V_c = [\,1 \quad x \quad x^2 \quad x^3\,]\,. \tag{6}$$

Again, those four functions are far from orthogonal. The inner products in $V_c^TV_c$ change from sums to *integrals*. Working on the interval from 0 to 1, the integrals are $\int_0^1 x^ix^j\,dx = 1/(i+j-1)$. They appear in the ***Hilbert matrix***:

Continuous inner products $$V_c^TV_c = \begin{bmatrix} 1 & \frac{1}{2} & \frac{1}{3} & \frac{1}{4} \\ \frac{1}{2} & \frac{1}{3} & \frac{1}{4} & \frac{1}{5} \\ \frac{1}{3} & \frac{1}{4} & \frac{1}{5} & \frac{1}{6} \\ \frac{1}{4} & \frac{1}{5} & \frac{1}{6} & \frac{1}{7} \end{bmatrix} = \mathsf{hilb}(4)\,. \tag{7}$$

The extreme eigenvalues of this Hilbert matrix are $\lambda_{\max} \approx 1.5$ and $\lambda_{\min} \approx 10^{-4}$. As always, those are the squares of the singular values $\sigma_{\max}$ and $\sigma_{\min}$ of V_c. *The condition number of the power basis* $1, x, x^2, x^3$ *is the ratio* $\sigma_{\max}/\sigma_{\min} \approx 125$. If you want a more impressive number (a numerical disaster), go up to x^9. The condition number of the 10 by 10 Hilbert matrix is $\lambda_{\max}/\lambda_{\min} \approx 10^{13}$. Therefore $1, x, \ldots, x^9$ is a very poor basis for polynomials of degree 9.

To reduce that unacceptably large number, Legendre orthogonalized the basis. He chose the interval from -1 to 1, so that even powers would be automatically orthogonal to odd powers. The first ***Legendre polynomials*** are $1, x, x^2 - \frac{1}{3}, x^3 - \frac{3}{5}x$. Our point is that the Vandermonde matrix example (as we orthogonalize it below) will be completely parallel to the famous functions of Legendre.

In particular, the **three-term recurrence** in the Arnoldi-Lanczos orthogonalization is exactly like Legendre's classical three-term recurrence for his polynomials. These "short recurrences" appear for the same reason—the symmetry of A.

Orthogonalizing the Krylov Basis

The best basis $q_1, \ldots, q_j$ for the Krylov subspace $\mathcal{K}_j$ is orthonormal. Each new q_j comes from orthogonalizing $t = Aq_{j-1}$ to the basis vectors $q_1, \ldots, q_{j-1}$ that are already chosen. The iteration to compute these orthonormal q's is **Arnoldi's method**.

This method is close to the Gram-Schmidt idea (called *modified* Gram-Schmidt when we subtract the projections of the current t onto the q's one at a time, for numerical stability). We display one Arnoldi cycle to find $q_j = q_2$, for the Vandermonde example that has $b = [1 \quad 1 \quad 1 \quad 1]'$ and $A = \mathsf{diag}([1 \quad 2 \quad 3 \quad 4])$:

Arnoldi's orthogonalization of $b, Ab, \ldots, A^{n-1}b$:

0	$q_1 = b/\lVert b \rVert$;	% Normalize b to $\lVert q_1 \rVert = 1$	$q_1 = [1 \;\; 1 \;\; 1 \;\; 1]'/2$
	for $j = 1, \ldots, n-1$	% Start computation of q_{j+1}	
1	$t = Aq_j$;	% one matrix multiplication	$Aq_1 = [1 \;\; 2 \;\; 3 \;\; 4]'/2$
	for $i = 1, \ldots, j$	% t is in the space $\mathcal{K}_{j+1}$	
2	$h_{ij} = q_i^{\mathrm{T}} t$;	% $h_{ij} q_i$ = projection of t on q_i	$h_{11} = 5/2$
3	$t = t - h_{ij} q_i$;	% Subtract that projection	$t = Aq_1 - (5/2)q_1$
	end	% t is orthogonal to $q_1, \ldots, q_j$	$t = [-3 \;\; -1 \;\; 1 \;\; 3]'/4$
4	$h_{j+1,j} = \lVert t \rVert$;	% Compute the length of t	$h_{21} = \sqrt{5}/2$
5	$q_{j+1} = t/h_{j+1,j}$;	% Normalize t to $\lVert q_{j+1} \rVert = 1$	$q_2 = [-3 \;\; -1 \;\; 1 \;\; 3]'/\sqrt{20}$
	end	% $q_1, \ldots, q_n$ are orthonormal	basis for Krylov space

You might like to see the four orthonormal vectors in the Vandermonde example. Those columns q_1, q_2, q_3, q_4 of Q are still constant, linear, quadratic, and cubic. I can also display the matrix H of numbers h_{ij} that produced the q's from the Krylov vectors b, Ab, A^2b, A^3b. (Since Arnoldi stops at $j = n-1$, the last column of H is not actually computed. It comes from a final command $H(:,n) = Q' * A * Q(:,n)$.)

H turns out to be *symmetric and tridiagonal*, when $A^{\mathrm{T}} = A$ (as here).

Arnoldi's method for the Vandermonde example V gives Q and H:

Basis in Q
Multipliers h_{ij}

$$Q = \begin{bmatrix} 1 & -3 & 1 & -1 \\ 1 & -1 & -1 & 3 \\ 1 & 1 & -1 & -3 \\ 1 & 3 & 1 & 1 \\ \hline 2 & \sqrt{20} & 2 & \sqrt{20} \end{bmatrix} \qquad H = \begin{bmatrix} 5/2 & \sqrt{5}/2 & & \\ \sqrt{5}/2 & 5/2 & \sqrt{.80} & \\ & \sqrt{.80} & 5/2 & \sqrt{.45} \\ & & \sqrt{.45} & 5/2 \end{bmatrix}$$

Please notice that H is not upper triangular as in Gram-Schmidt. The usual QR factorization of the original Krylov matrix $\mathbf{K}$ (which is V in our example) has this same Q, but Arnoldi's QH is different from $\mathbf{K} = QR$. The vector t that Arnoldi orthogonalizes against all the previous $q_1, \ldots, q_j$ is $t = Aq_j$. This is not column $j+1$ of $\mathbf{K}$, as in Gram-Schmidt. Arnoldi is factoring AQ!

Arnoldi factorization $AQ = QH$ for the final subspace $\mathcal{K}_n$:

$$AQ = \begin{bmatrix} & & \\ Aq_1 & \cdots & Aq_n \\ & & \end{bmatrix} = \begin{bmatrix} & & \\ q_1 & \cdots & q_n \\ & & \end{bmatrix} \begin{bmatrix} h_{11} & h_{12} & \cdot & h_{1n} \\ h_{21} & h_{22} & \cdot & h_{2n} \\ \mathbf{0} & h_{32} & \cdot & \cdot \\ \mathbf{0} & \mathbf{0} & \cdot & h_{nn} \end{bmatrix}. \qquad (8)$$

This matrix H is upper triangular plus one lower diagonal, which makes it "*upper Hessenberg.*" The h_{ij} in step **2** go down column j as far as the diagonal. Then $h_{j+1,j}$ in step **4** is below the diagonal. We check that the first column of $AQ = QH$ (multiplying by columns) is Arnoldi's first cycle that produces q_2:

Column 1 $\quad Aq_1 = h_{11}q_1 + h_{21}q_2 \quad$ which is $\quad q_2 = (Aq_1 - h_{11}q_1)/h_{21}\,. \qquad (9)$

That subtraction is step **3** in Arnoldi's algorithm. Division by $h_{21} = \|t\|$ is step **5**.

Unless more of the h_{ij} are zero, the cost is increasing at every iteration. The vector operations in step **3** for $j = 1, \ldots, n-1$ give nearly $n^2/2$ updates and n^3 flops. A *short recurrence* means that H is tridiagonal, and the count of floating point operations drops to $O(n^2)$. This big improvement happens when $A = A^{\mathrm{T}}$.

Arnoldi Becomes Lanczos

When A is symmetric, the matrix H is symmetric and therefore tridiagonal. This fact is the foundation of conjugate gradients. For a matrix proof, multiply $AQ = QH$ by Q^{T}. The left side $Q^{\mathrm{T}}AQ$ is symmetric when A is symmetric. The right side $Q^{\mathrm{T}}QH = H$ has one lower diagonal. By symmetry H has one upper diagonal.

This tridiagonal H tells us that computing q_{j+1} only involves q_j and q_{j-1}:

Arnoldi when $A = A^{\mathrm{T}}$
$$Aq_j = h_{j+1,j}\, q_{j+1} + h_{j,j}\, q_j + h_{j-1,j}\, q_{j-1}\,. \tag{10}$$

This is the ***Lanczos iteration***. Each new $q_{j+1} = (Aq_j - h_{j,j}q_j - h_{j-1,j}q_{j-1})/h_{j+1,j}$ involves one multiplication Aq_j, two dot products for h's, and two vector updates.

Allow me an important comment on the **symmetric eigenvalue problem** $Ax = \lambda x$. The matrix $H = Q^{\mathrm{T}}AQ = Q^{-1}AQ$ has the same eigenvalues as A:

Same λ
$$Hy = Q^{-1}AQy = \lambda y \quad \text{gives} \quad A(Qy) = \lambda(Qy)\,. \tag{11}$$

The **Lanczos method** will find, approximately and iteratively and quickly, the leading eigenvalues of a large symmetric matrix A. We just stop the Arnoldi iteration (10) at a small tridiagonal H_k with $k < n$. The full n-step process to reach H_n is too expensive, and often we don't need all n eigenvalues. **Compute the k eigenvalues of H_k instead of the n eigenvalues of H.** These computed λ's (called *Ritz values*) are often excellent approximations to the first k eigenvalues of A [124]. And we have a fast start on the eigenvalue problem for H_{k+1}, if we decide to take a further step.

For the eigenvalues of H_k, we use the "QR method" described in [63, 142, 159, 164].

The Conjugate Gradient Method

We return to iterative methods for $Ax = b$. The Arnoldi algorithm produced orthonormal basis vectors $q_1, q_2, \ldots$ for the growing Krylov subspaces $\mathcal{K}_1, \mathcal{K}_2, \ldots$. Now we select vectors x_k in $\mathcal{K}_k$ that approach the exact solution to $Ax = b$.

We concentrate on the *conjugate gradient method when A is symmetric positive definite.* Symmetry gives a short recurrence. Definiteness prevents division by zero.

The rule for x_k in conjugate gradients is that the residual $r_k = b - Ax_k$ should be orthogonal to all vectors in $\mathcal{K}_k$. Since r_k is in $\mathcal{K}_{k+1}$ (because of Ax_k), it must be a multiple of Arnoldi's next vector q_{k+1}! Since the q's are orthogonal, so are the r's:

Orthogonal residuals $\quad r_i^{\mathrm{T}} r_k = 0 \qquad \text{for } i < k\,. \qquad (12)$

The difference between r_k and q_{k+1} is that the q's are normalized, as in $q_1 = b/\|b\|$.

Similarly r_{k-1} is a multiple of q_k. Then $\Delta r = r_k - r_{k-1}$ is orthogonal to earlier subspaces $\mathcal{K}_i$ with $i < k$. Certainly $\Delta x = x_i - x_{i-1}$ lies in that $\mathcal{K}_i$. Thus $\Delta x^{\mathrm{T}} \Delta r = 0$:

$$(x_i - x_{i-1})^{\mathrm{T}}(r_k - r_{k-1}) = 0 \qquad \text{for } i < k\,. \tag{13}$$

These differences Δx and Δr are directly connected, because the b's cancel in Δr:

$$r_k - r_{k-1} = (b - Ax_k) - (b - Ax_{k-1}) = -A(x_k - x_{k-1})\,. \tag{14}$$

Substituting (14) into (13), ***the updates Δx are "A-orthogonal" or conjugate***:

Conjugate directions $\quad (x_i - x_{i-1})^{\mathrm{T}} A (x_k - x_{k-1}) = 0 \qquad \text{for } i < k\,. \qquad (15)$

Now we have all the requirements. Each conjugate gradient step ends with a "search direction" d_{k-1} for the next $\Delta x = x_k - x_{k-1}$. Steps **1** and **2** compute the correct multiple $\Delta x = \alpha_k d_{k-1}$ to move to x_k. Using (14), step **3** finds the new r_k. Steps **4** and **5** orthogonalize r_k against that search direction d_{k-1}, to find the next d_k.

Here is one cycle of the algorithm, moving in the direction d_{k-1} to find x_k, r_k, d_k. Steps **1** and **3** involve the same matrix-vector multiplication Ad (once per cycle).

Conjugate Gradient Method for Symmetric Positive Definite A

$\boldsymbol{A} = \text{diag}([1\ \ 2\ \ 3\ \ 4])$ **and** $\boldsymbol{b} = [1\ \ 1\ \ 1\ \ 1]'$ **with** $\boldsymbol{d}_0 = \boldsymbol{r}_0 = \boldsymbol{b}$, $\boldsymbol{x}_0 = 0$

1	$\boldsymbol{\alpha_k} = r_{k-1}^{\mathrm{T}} r_{k-1}/d_{k-1}^{\mathrm{T}} A d_{k-1}$	% Step length to next x_k	$\boldsymbol{\alpha}_1 = 4/10 = 2/5$
2	$\boldsymbol{x_k} = x_{k-1} + \alpha_k d_{k-1}$	% Approximate solution	$\boldsymbol{x}_1 = [2\ \ 2\ \ 2\ \ 2]'/5$
3	$\boldsymbol{r_k} = r_{k-1} - \alpha_k A d_{k-1}$	% New residual from (14)	$\boldsymbol{r}_1 = [3\ \ 1\ \ -1\ \ -3]'/5$
4	$\boldsymbol{\beta_k} = r_k^{\mathrm{T}} r_k / r_{k-1}^{\mathrm{T}} r_{k-1}$	% Improvement this step	$\boldsymbol{\beta}_1 = 1/5$
5	$\boldsymbol{d_k} = r_k + \beta_k d_{k-1}$	% Next search direction	$\boldsymbol{d}_1 = [4\ \ 2\ \ 0\ \ -2]'/5$

When there is a preconditioner P (to use even fewer CG steps for an accurate x), step **3** uses $P^{-1}A$ and all inner products in α_k and β_k include an extra factor P^{-1}.

The constants β_k in the search direction and α_k in the update come from (12) and (13) specifically for $i = k-1$. For symmetric A, orthogonality will be automatic for $i < k-1$, as in Arnoldi. This "short recurrence" makes the conjugate gradient method fast. The formulas for α_k and β_k are explained briefly below—and fully by Trefethen-Bau [159] and Shewchuk [136] and many other good references.

Different Viewpoints on Conjugate Gradients

I want to describe the (same!) conjugate gradient method in two different ways:

1. CG solves a tridiagonal system $Hy = f$ recursively in each subspace $\mathcal{K}_j$.
2. CG minimizes the energy $\frac{1}{2}x^{\mathrm{T}}Ax - x^{\mathrm{T}}b$ recursively. This is important.

How does $Ax = b$ change to the tridiagonal $Hy = f$? Those are connected by Arnoldi's orthonormal columns $q_1, \ldots, q_n$ in Q, with $Q^{\mathrm{T}} = Q^{-1}$ and $Q^{\mathrm{T}}AQ = H$:

$$Ax = b \;\text{ is }\; (Q^{\mathrm{T}}AQ)(Q^{\mathrm{T}}x) = Q^{\mathrm{T}}b \;\text{ which is }\; Hy = f = (\|b\|, 0, \ldots, 0)\,. \tag{16}$$

Since q_1 is $b/\|b\|$, the first component of $f = Q^{\mathrm{T}}b$ is $q_1^{\mathrm{T}}b = \|b\|$. The other components of f are $q_i^{\mathrm{T}}b = 0$ because q_i is orthogonal to q_1. The conjugate gradient method is implicitly computing the symmetric tridiagonal H. When the method finds x_k, it also finds $y_k = Q_k^{\mathrm{T}}x_k$ (but it doesn't say so). Here is the third step:

Tridiagonal system $Hy = f$
Implicitly solved by CG

$$H_3y_3 = \begin{bmatrix} h_{11} & h_{12} & \\ h_{21} & h_{22} & h_{23} \\ & h_{32} & h_{33} \end{bmatrix} \begin{bmatrix} \\ y_3 \\ \\ \end{bmatrix} = \begin{bmatrix} \|b\| \\ 0 \\ 0 \end{bmatrix}. \tag{17}$$

This is the equation $Ax = b$ projected by Q_3 onto the third Krylov subspace $\mathcal{K}_3$. When the CG algorithm reaches $k = n$, it finds the exact x. In that sense we have a direct method like elimination, but it takes longer. The crucial point is that *after $k < n$ steps, this algorithm produces something useful.* In fact x_k is often terrific.

These h's never appear in conjugate gradients. We don't want to do Arnoldi too. It is the LDL^{T} factors of H that CG is somehow computing—two new numbers α and β at each step. Those give a fast update from y_{k-1} to y_k. The iterates $x_k = Q_ky_k$ from conjugate gradients approach the exact solution $x_n = Q_ny_n$ which is $x = A^{-1}b$.

Energy By seeing conjugate gradients as an energy minimizing algorithm, we can extend CG to nonlinear problems and use it in optimization. For linear equations $Ax = b$, the energy is $E(x) = \frac{1}{2}x^{\mathrm{T}}Ax - x^{\mathrm{T}}b$. Minimizing $E(x)$ is the same as solving $Ax = b$, when A is positive definite—this was the main point of Section 1.6. **The CG iteration minimizes energy $E(x)$ in the growing Krylov subspaces.**

The first subspace $\mathcal{K}_1$ is the line in the direction $d_0 = r_0 = b$. Minimization of the energy $E(x)$ on this line of vectors $x = \alpha b$ produces the number α_1:

$$E(\alpha b) = \frac{1}{2}\alpha^2 b^{\mathrm{T}}Ab - \alpha b^{\mathrm{T}}b \quad \text{is minimized at} \quad \alpha_1 = \frac{b^{\mathrm{T}}b}{b^{\mathrm{T}}Ab}\,. \tag{18}$$

This α_1 is the constant chosen in step **1** of the first conjugate gradient cycle.

The gradient of $E(x) = \frac{1}{2}x^{\mathrm{T}}Ax - x^{\mathrm{T}}b$ is exactly $Ax - b$. *The steepest descent direction at x_1 is along the negative gradient, which is r_1.* This sounds like the perfect direction d_1 for the next move. But steepest descent is often locally good and globally poor. Little progress along the r's. So step **5** adds the right multiple $\beta_1 d_0$, in order that the new direction $d_1 = r_1 + \beta_1 d_0$ will be A-orthogonal to the first direction d_0.

We move in this conjugate direction d_1 to $x_2 = x_1 + \alpha_2 d_1$. This explains the name *conjugate gradients*. The pure gradients of steepest descent would take small steps across a valley instead of a good step to the bottom (the minimizing x in Figure 7.13). Every cycle of CG chooses α_k to minimize $E(x)$ in the new search direction $x = x_{k-1} + \alpha d_{k-1}$. The last cycle (if we go that far) gives the overall minimizer $x_n = x = A^{-1}b$.

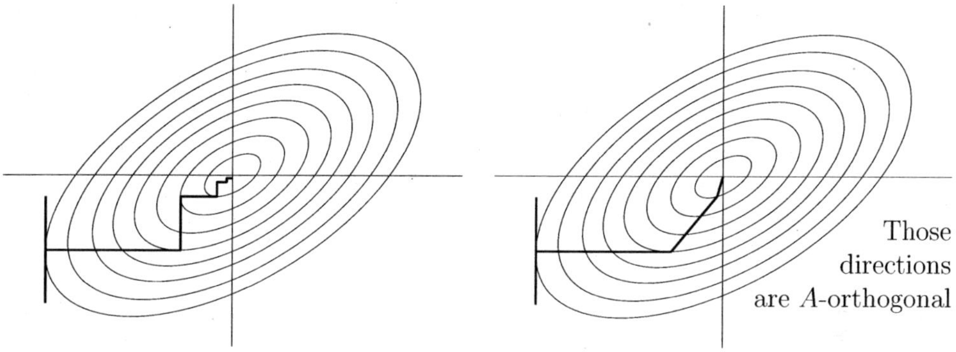

Figure 7.13: Steepest descent (many small steps) vs. conjugate gradients.

The main point is always this. **When you have orthogonality, projections and minimizations can be computed one direction at a time.**

Example of two conjugate gradient steps

$$\text{Suppose} \quad Ax = b \quad \text{is} \quad \begin{bmatrix} 2 & 1 & 1 \\ 1 & 2 & 1 \\ 1 & 1 & 2 \end{bmatrix} \begin{bmatrix} 3 \\ -1 \\ -1 \end{bmatrix} = \begin{bmatrix} 4 \\ 0 \\ 0 \end{bmatrix}.$$

From $x_0 = (0,0,0)$ and $r_0 = d_0 = b$ the first cycle gives $\alpha_1 = \frac{1}{2}$ and $x_1 = \frac{1}{2}b = (2,0,0)$. The new residual is $r_1 = b - Ax_1 = (0,-2,-2)$. Then the CG algorithm yields

$$\beta_1 = \frac{8}{16} \qquad d_1 = \begin{bmatrix} 2 \\ -2 \\ -2 \end{bmatrix} \qquad \alpha_2 = \frac{8}{16} \qquad x_2 = \begin{bmatrix} 3 \\ -1 \\ -1 \end{bmatrix} = A^{-1}b!$$

The correct solution is reached in two steps, where normally CG will take $n = 3$ steps. The reason is that this particular A has only two distinct eigenvalues 4 and 1. In that case $A^{-1}b$ is a combination of b and Ab, and this best combination x_2 is found at cycle 2. The residual r_2 is zero and the cycles stop early—very unusual.

Energy minimization leads in [159] to an estimate of the convergence rate for the error $e = x - x_k$ in conjugate gradients, using the A-norm $\|e\|_A = \sqrt{e^{\mathrm{T}}Ae}$:

$$\textbf{Error estimate} \qquad \|x - x_k\|_A \le 2\left(\frac{\sqrt{\lambda_{\max}} - \sqrt{\lambda_{\min}}}{\sqrt{\lambda_{\max}} + \sqrt{\lambda_{\min}}}\right)^k \|x - x_0\|_A . \tag{19}$$

This is the best-known error estimate, although it doesn't account for good clustering of the eigenvalues of A. It involves only the condition number $\lambda_{\max}/\lambda_{\min}$. The optimal error estimate needs all the eigenvalues of A [159], but it is not so easy to compute. In practice we can bound $\lambda_{\max}$ and $\lambda_{\min}$.

Least Squares and the Normal Equations

To minimize $\|b - Au\|^2$ when A has more rows than columns, the method of choice is LSQR. This is a special implementation of conjugate gradients for the fundamental problem $A^{\mathrm{T}}A\widehat{u} = A^{\mathrm{T}}b$. The iterations begin with $u_1 = b/\|b\|$ and $v_1 = A^{\mathrm{T}}b/\|A^{\mathrm{T}}b\|$. At every step the Lanczos orthogonalization process adds to the lower bidiagonal matrix B_k (and $\overline{B}_k$ has an extra row $[\,0\ \ldots\ 0\ c\,]$):

Bidiagonal B $\quad AV_k = U_{k+1}\overline{B}_k$ and $A^{\mathrm{T}}U_k = V_k B_k^{\mathrm{T}} \quad U_k^{\mathrm{T}}U_k = V_k^{\mathrm{T}}V_k = I_k \quad$ (20)

The key point is that this orthogonalization is stable and fast: B_k and then $\widehat{u}_k = V_k\widehat{y}_k$ are computed with only $2k$ matrix-vector products (k with A and k with A^{T}). Storage is only a few u's and v's at a time. The least squares problem reduces to minimizing the length of $\overline{B}_k y - (\|b\|, 0, \ldots, 0)$.

Minimum Residual Methods

If A is not symmetric positive definite, CG is not guaranteed to solve $Ax = b$. Right away, the denominators $d^{\mathrm{T}}Ad$ in the α's could be zero. We briefly describe the ***minimum norm residual*** approach [162], leading to MINRES and GMRES.

These methods choose x_j in the Krylov subspace $\boldsymbol{\mathcal{K}}_j$ so that $\|b - Ax_j\|$ is minimal. Then $x_j = Q_j y$ is a combination of the orthonormal $q_1, \ldots, q_j$ in the columns of Q_j:

Norm of residual $\quad \|r_j\| = \|b - A\,x_j\| = \|b - A\,Q_j\,y\| = \|b - Q_{j+1}\,H_{j+1,j}\,y\| \quad$ (21)

Here AQ_j uses the first j columns of Arnoldi's formula $AQ = QH$ in (8). The right side only needs $j+1$ columns of Q, because the jth column of H is zero below entry $j+1$.

The norm in (21) is not changed when we multiply by Q_{j+1}^{T}, since $Q_{j+1}^{\mathrm{T}}\,Q_{j+1} = I$. The vector $Q_{j+1}^{\mathrm{T}}b$ is $(\|r_0\|, 0, \ldots, 0)$ as in (16). Our problem has become simpler:

Choose y to minimize $\quad \|r_j\| = \|Q_{j+1}^{\mathrm{T}}b - H_{j+1,j}\,y\|\,. \quad$ (22)

This is an ordinary least squares problem with $j+1$ equations and j unknown y's. The rectangular matrix $H_{j+1,j}$ is upper Hessenberg. We face a completely typical problem of numerical linear algebra: **Use the zeros in H and $Q_{j+1}^{\mathrm{T}}b$ to find a fast algorithm that computes y.** The two favorite algorithms are closely related:

MINRES $\quad A$ is symmetric (likely indefinite, or we use CG) and H is tridiagonal.

GMRES $\quad A$ is *not* symmetric and the upper triangular part of H can be full.

Both cases aim to clear out that nonzero diagonal below the main diagonal of H. The natural way to do that, one entry at a time, is by "*Givens rotations.*" These plane rotations are so useful and simple (their essential part is only 2 by 2) that we complete this section by explaining them.

Givens Rotations

The direct approach to the least squares solution of $Hy = f$ constructs the normal equations $H^{\mathrm{T}}H\widehat{y} = H^{\mathrm{T}}f$. That was the central idea in Chapter 2, but you see what we lose. If H is Hessenberg, with many good zeros, $H^{\mathrm{T}}H$ is full. Those zeros in H should simplify and shorten the computations, so we don't want the normal equations.

The other approach to least squares is by orthogonalization. **We factor H into orthogonal times upper triangular.** Since the letter Q is already used, the orthogonal matrix will be called G (after Givens). The upper triangular matrix is $G^{-1}H$. The 3 by 2 case shows how a rotation in the 1–2 plane can clear out h_{21}:

Plane rotation (Givens rotation)

$$G_{21}^{-1}H = \begin{bmatrix} \cos\theta & \sin\theta & 0 \\ -\sin\theta & \cos\theta & 0 \\ 0 & 0 & 1 \end{bmatrix} \begin{bmatrix} h_{11} & h_{12} \\ h_{21} & h_{22} \\ 0 & h_{32} \end{bmatrix} = \begin{bmatrix} * & * \\ \mathbf{0} & * \\ 0 & \boldsymbol{*} \end{bmatrix}. \qquad (23)$$

That bold zero entry requires $h_{11}\sin\theta = h_{21}\cos\theta$, which determines the rotation angle θ. A second rotation G_{32}^{-1}, in the 2-3 plane, will zero out the 3, 2 entry. Then $G_{32}^{-1}G_{21}^{-1}H$ is a square upper triangular matrix U above a row of zeros!

The Givens orthogonal matrix is $G_{21}G_{32}$ but there is no reason to do this multiplication. We use each G_{ij} as it is constructed, to simplify the least squares problem. Rotations (and all orthogonal matrices) leave the lengths of vectors unchanged:

Triangular least squares

$$\min_y \left\| G_{32}^{-1}G_{21}^{-1}Hy - G_{32}^{-1}G_{21}^{-1}f \right\| = \min_y \left\| \begin{bmatrix} U \\ 0 \end{bmatrix} y - \begin{bmatrix} F \\ e \end{bmatrix} \right\|. \qquad (24)$$

This length is what MINRES and GMRES minimize. The row of zeros below U means that we can't reduce the error e. But we get all other entries exactly right by solving the j by j system $Uy = F$ (here $j = 2$). This gives the best least squares solution y. Going back to the original problem of minimizing the residual $\|r\| = \|b - Ax_j\|$, the best x_j in the jth Krylov space is $Q_j y$. This was also the idea of LSQR.

For non-symmetric A (GMRES rather than MINRES) the recurrence is not short. The upper triangle in H can be full, and *Arnoldi's step j becomes expensive.* Possibly it is inaccurate as j increases. So we may change "full GMRES" to GMRES(m), which restarts the algorithm every m steps. It is not so easy to choose a good m. But GMRES is an important algorithm for unsymmetric A.

Problem Set 7.4

1 Suppose the $-1, 2, -1$ matrix K is preconditioned by $P = T$ ($K_{11} = 2$ changes to $T_{11} = 1$). Show that $\boldsymbol{T^{-1}K = I + \ell e_1^{\mathrm{T}}}$ with $e_1^{\mathrm{T}} = [\,1\; 0\; \ldots\; 0\,]$. Start from $K = T + e_1 e_1^{\mathrm{T}}$. Then $T^{-1}K = I + (T^{-1}e_1)e_1^{\mathrm{T}}$. Verify that $T^{-1}e_1 = \ell$:

$$\boldsymbol{T\ell = e_1} = \begin{bmatrix} 1 & -1 & & \\ -1 & 2 & -1 & \\ & \cdot & \cdot & \cdot \\ & & -1 & 2 \end{bmatrix} \begin{bmatrix} N \\ N-1 \\ \cdot \\ 1 \end{bmatrix} = \begin{bmatrix} 1 \\ 0 \\ \cdot \\ 0 \end{bmatrix}.$$

Multiply $T^{-1}K = I + \ell e_1^{\mathrm{T}}$ times $I - (\ell e_1^{\mathrm{T}})/(N+1)$ to show that this is $K^{-1}T$.

2 Test the $\mathsf{pcg}(K, T)$ MATLAB command on the $-1, 2, -1$ difference matrices.

3 Arnoldi expresses each Aq_j as $h_{j+1,j}q_{j+1} + h_{j,j}q_j + \cdots + h_{1,j}q_1$. Multiply by q_i^{T} to find $h_{i,j} = q_i^{\mathrm{T}}Aq_j$. *If A is symmetric* this is $(Aq_i)^{\mathrm{T}}q_j$. Explain why $(Aq_i)^{\mathrm{T}}q_j = 0$ for $i < j-1$ by expanding Aq_i into $h_{i+1,i}q_{i+1} + \cdots + h_{1,i}q_1$. We have a *short recurrence if* $A = A^{\mathrm{T}}$ (only $h_{j+1,j}$ and $h_{j,j}$ and $h_{j-1,j}$ are nonzero).

4 (This is Problem 3 at the matrix level) The Arnoldi equation $AQ = QH$ gives $H = Q^{-1}AQ = Q^{\mathrm{T}}AQ$. Therefore the entries of H are $h_{ij} = q_i^{\mathrm{T}}Aq_j$.

(a) Which Krylov space contains Aq_j? What orthogonality gives $h_{ij} = 0$ when $i > j+1$? Then H is upper Hessenberg.

(b) If $A^{\mathrm{T}} = A$ then $h_{ij} = (Aq_i)^{\mathrm{T}}q_j$. Which Krylov space contains Aq_i? What orthogonality gives $h_{ij} = 0$ when $j > i+1$? Now H is tridiagonal.

5 If $\mathbf{K} = [\,b\;\; Ab\;\; \ldots\;\; A^{n-1}b\,]$ is a Krylov matrix with $A = A^{\mathrm{T}}$, why is the inner product matrix $\mathbf{K}^{\mathrm{T}}\mathbf{K}$ a **Hankel matrix**? Hankel is constant down each *antidiagonal*, the opposite of Toeplitz. Show that $(\mathbf{K}^{\mathrm{T}}\mathbf{K})_{ij}$ depends on $i + j$.

6 These are famous names associated with linear algebra (and a lot of other mathematics too). All dead. Write one sentence on what they are known for.

Arnoldi	Gram	Jacobi	Schur
Cholesky	Hadamard	Jordan	Schwarz
Fourier	Hankel	Kronecker	Seidel
Frobenius	Hessenberg	Krylov	Toeplitz
Gauss	Hestenes-Stiefel	Lanczos	Vandermonde
Gershgorin	Hilbert	Markov	Wilkinson
Givens	Householder	Schmidt	Woodbury

7 Apply the conjugate gradient method to $Ku = \mathsf{ones}(100, 1)$ using the one-dimensional second difference matrix K of order 100. Plot the errors in the approximate solution at steps $1, \ldots, 100$. Conjugate gradients should give an exact answer (known in Section 1.2) after 100 steps—does it?

8 Apply conjugate gradients to the 5-point Laplace equation $(\mathrm{K2D})u = \mathsf{ones}(100, 1)$ on a 10 by 10 mesh of unknown values. (With boundary the mesh is 12 by 12.) Plot the conjugate gradient errors after $20, 40, 60, 80$ steps compared to a more exact result u^*: the answer after 100 steps or the solution to Poisson's equation $-u_{xx} - u_{yy} = 1$ on a square in Section 3.4.

CHAPTER 8

OPTIMIZATION AND MINIMUM PRINCIPLES

8.1 TWO FUNDAMENTAL EXAMPLES

Within the universe of applied mathematics, optimization is often a world of its own. There are occasional expeditions to other worlds (like differential equations), but mostly the life of optimizers is self-contained: ***Find the minimum of*** $\boldsymbol{F(x_1, .., x_n)}$. That is not an easy problem when F is highly nonlinear. Our F is often quadratic, but with many variables x_j and many constraints on those variables. *Those constraints may require* $Ax = b$ *or* $x_j \geq 0$ *or both or worse.* Whole books and courses and software packages are dedicated to this problem of ***constrained minimization***.

I hope you will forgive the poetry of worlds and universes. I am trying to emphasize the importance of optimization—a key component of engineering mathematics and scientific computing. This chapter will have its own flavor, but it is strongly connected to the rest of this book. To make those connections, I want to begin with two specific examples. **If you read even just this section**, you will see the connections.

Least Squares

Ordinary least squares begins with a matrix A whose n columns are independent. The rank is n, so $A^{\mathrm{T}}A$ is symmetric positive definite. The input vector b has m components, the output $\widehat{u}$ has n components, and $\boldsymbol{m > n}$:

Least squares problem	Minimize $\|\|Au - b\|\|^2$	(1)
Normal equations for best $\widehat{u}$	$A^{\mathrm{T}}A\widehat{u} = A^{\mathrm{T}}b$	

Those equations $A^{\mathrm{T}}A\widehat{u} = A^{\mathrm{T}}b$ say that the error residual $e = b - A\widehat{u}$ solves $\boldsymbol{A^{\mathrm{T}}e = 0}$. Then e is perpendicular to columns $1, 2, \ldots, n$ of A. Write those zero inner products as $(\textbf{column})^{\mathrm{T}}(\boldsymbol{e}) = \mathbf{0}$ to find $A^{\mathrm{T}}A\widehat{u} = A^{\mathrm{T}}b$:

Normal equations
$$\begin{bmatrix} (\text{column } 1)^{\mathrm{T}} \\ \vdots \\ (\text{column } n)^{\mathrm{T}} \end{bmatrix} \begin{bmatrix} \\ e \\ \\ \end{bmatrix} = \begin{bmatrix} 0 \\ \vdots \\ 0 \end{bmatrix} \quad \text{is} \quad \begin{aligned} A^{\mathrm{T}}e &= 0 \\ A^{\mathrm{T}}(b - A\widehat{u}) &= 0 \\ A^{\mathrm{T}}A\widehat{u} &= A^{\mathrm{T}}b\,. \end{aligned} \qquad (2)$$

Graphically, Figure 8.1 shows $A\widehat{u}$ as the *projection of* b. It is the combination of columns of A (the point in the column space) that is nearest to b. We studied least squares in Section 2.3, and now we notice that **a second problem is solved at the same time**.

This second problem (*dual problem*) does not project b down onto the column space. Instead it projects b across onto the perpendicular space. In the 3D picture, that space is a line (its dimension is $3 - 2 = 1$). In m dimensions that perpendicular subspace has dimension $m - n$. *It contains the vectors that are perpendicular to all columns of* A. The line in Figure 8.1a is the **nullspace of** $\boldsymbol{A}^{\mathrm{T}}$.

One of the vectors in that perpendicular space is $e =$ projection of b. Together, e and $\widehat{u}$ solve the two linear equations that express exactly what the figure shows:

Saddle Point
Kuhn-Tucker (KKT)
Primal-Dual
$$\begin{matrix} e & + & A\widehat{u} & = & b & m \text{ equations} \\ A^{\mathrm{T}}e & & & = & 0 & n \text{ equations} \end{matrix} \qquad (3)$$

We took this chance to write down three names for these very simple but so fundamental equations. I can quickly say a few words about each name.

Saddle Point The block matrix S in those equations is not positive definite!

Saddle point matrix
KKT matrix
$$\boldsymbol{S} = \begin{bmatrix} \boldsymbol{I} & \boldsymbol{A} \\ \boldsymbol{A}^{\mathrm{T}} & \mathbf{0} \end{bmatrix} \qquad (4)$$

The first m pivots are all 1's, from the matrix I. When elimination puts zeros in place of A^{T}, *the negative definite Schur complement* $-A^{\mathrm{T}}A$ *enters the zero block.*

Multiply row 1 by $\boldsymbol{A}^{\mathrm{T}}$
Subtract from row 2
$$\begin{bmatrix} I & 0 \\ -A^{\mathrm{T}} & I \end{bmatrix} \begin{bmatrix} I & A \\ A^{\mathrm{T}} & 0 \end{bmatrix} = \begin{bmatrix} I & A \\ 0 & -\boldsymbol{A}^{\mathrm{T}}\boldsymbol{A} \end{bmatrix}. \qquad (5)$$

The final n pivots will all be negative. S is **indefinite**, with pivots of both signs. We don't have a pure minimum or maximum, positive or negative definite. S leads to a *saddle point* $(\widehat{u}, e)$. When we get up more courage, we will try to draw this.

Kuhn-Tucker These are the names most often associated with equations like (3) that solve optimization problems. Because of an earlier Master's Thesis by Karush, you often see " **KKT equations**." In continuous problems, for functions instead of vectors, the right name would be "Euler-Lagrange equations." When the constraints include inequalities like $w \geq 0$ or $Bu = d$, Lagrange multipliers are still the key. For those more delicate problems, Kuhn and Tucker earned their fame.

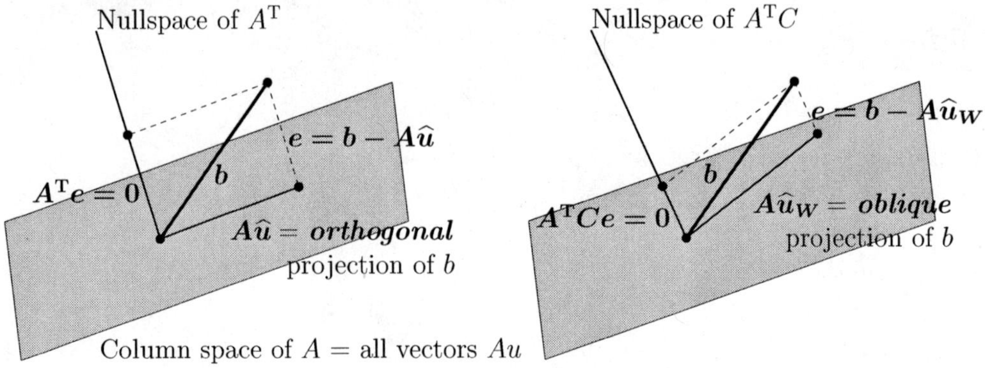

Figure 8.1: Ordinary and weighted least squares: min $\|b - Au\|^2$ and $\|Wb - WAu\|^2$.

Primal-Dual The primal problem is to minimize $\frac{1}{2}\|Au - b\|^2$. This produces $\hat{u}$. **The dual problem minimizes $\frac{1}{2}\|e - b\|^2$, under the constraint that $A^Te = 0$.**

The "Lagrange multiplier" u enters the dual problem to enforce that constraint $A^Te = 0$. The left figure shows $A\hat{u}$ and e (primal and dual). Those solutions are found at the same time and they add to b.

A Small Example

When A has one column ($n = 1$), we can see every step in the primal and dual:

$$A = \begin{bmatrix} 2 \\ 1 \end{bmatrix} \qquad b = \begin{bmatrix} 3 \\ 4 \end{bmatrix} \qquad A^TA = \begin{bmatrix} 5 \end{bmatrix} \qquad A^Tb = \begin{bmatrix} 10 \end{bmatrix}$$

Primal The normal equation $A^TA\hat{u} = A^Tb$ is $5\hat{u} = 10$. Then $\hat{u} = 2$. This gives $A\hat{u}$:

Projection $A\hat{u} = \begin{bmatrix} 2 \\ 1 \end{bmatrix} \begin{bmatrix} 2 \end{bmatrix} = \begin{bmatrix} \mathbf{4} \\ \mathbf{2} \end{bmatrix}$ **Error** $e = b - A\hat{u} = \begin{bmatrix} 3 \\ 4 \end{bmatrix} - \begin{bmatrix} 4 \\ 2 \end{bmatrix} = \begin{bmatrix} \mathbf{-1} \\ \mathbf{2} \end{bmatrix}$

That subtraction splits $b = (3, 4)$ into perpendicular pieces $A\hat{u} = (4, 2)$ and $e = (-1, 2)$.

90° angle $\|b\|^2 = \|A\hat{u}\|^2 + \|e\|^2$ is $25 = 20 + 5$.

Dual The dual problem goes directly to e. Now $\hat{u}$ comes second (as the Lagrange multiplier!). The constraint $A^Te = 2e_1 + e_2 = 0$ puts e on the left line in Figure 8.1. *The dual minimizes $\frac{1}{2}\|e - b\|^2$ with $A^Te = 0$. Its solution gives e and also $\hat{u}$:*

Step 1 Construct Lagrange's function $L = \frac{1}{2}\|e - b\|^2 + u(A^Te)$:

Lagrangian $$L(e_1, e_2, u) = \frac{1}{2}(e_1 - 3)^2 + \frac{1}{2}(e_2 - 4)^2 + u(2e_1 + e_2)\,. \qquad (6)$$

Step 2 Set the derivatives of L to zero, to find both e and $\hat{u}$:

$$\begin{array}{l} \partial L/\partial e_1 = 0 \\ \partial L/\partial e_2 = 0 \\ \partial L/\partial u = 0 \end{array} \qquad \begin{array}{rl} e_1 - 3 + 2\widehat{u} &= 0 \\ e_2 - 4 + \widehat{u} &= 0 \\ 2e_1 + e_2 &= 0 \end{array} \qquad \begin{bmatrix} 1 & & 2 \\ & 1 & 1 \\ 2 & 1 & 0 \end{bmatrix} \begin{bmatrix} e_1 \\ e_2 \\ \widehat{u} \end{bmatrix} = \begin{bmatrix} 3 \\ 4 \\ 0 \end{bmatrix}.$$

You see the saddle point matrix S. Elimination subtracts 2(equation 1)+(equation 2) from the last equation. This leaves $-5\widehat{u} = -10$. That says $A^{\mathrm{T}}A\widehat{u} = A^{\mathrm{T}}b$. Figure 8.1a shows both problems, primal and dual, in three dimensions.

If the matrix A is m by n, then $\widehat{u}$ has n components and e has m components. The primal minimizes $\|b - Au\|^2$, exactly as in this whole book. This "stiffness method" or "displacement method" produces $K = A^{\mathrm{T}}A$ in the normal equations. The dual problem (constrained by $A^{\mathrm{T}}e = 0$, using multipliers u) produces $S = \left[\begin{smallmatrix} \mathbf{I} & \mathbf{A} \\ \mathbf{A}^{\mathrm{T}} & \mathbf{0} \end{smallmatrix}\right]$ in the "saddle point method." Optimization usually leads to these KKT matrices.

Weighted Least Squares

This is a small but very important extension of the least squares problem. It involves the same rectangular A, and a square weighting matrix W. Instead of $\widehat{u}$ we write $\widehat{u}_W$ (this best answer changes with W). You will see that the symmetric positive definite combination $C = W^{\mathrm{T}}W$ is what matters in the end. **The KKT matrix includes** C^{-1}.

Weighted least squares
Normal equations for $\widehat{u}_W$

$$\begin{array}{c} \text{Minimize } \|WAu - Wb\|^2 \\ (WA)^{\mathrm{T}}(WA)\,\widehat{u}_W = (WA)^{\mathrm{T}}(Wb) \end{array} \qquad (7)$$

No new mathematics, just replace A and b by WA and Wb. The equation has become

$$A^{\mathrm{T}}W^{\mathrm{T}}WA\,\widehat{u}_W = A^{\mathrm{T}}W^{\mathrm{T}}Wb \quad \text{or} \quad A^{\mathrm{T}}CA\,\widehat{u}_W = A^{\mathrm{T}}Cb \quad \text{or} \quad A^{\mathrm{T}}C(b - A\,\widehat{u}_W) = 0. \quad (8)$$

The middle equation has that all-important matrix $A^{\mathrm{T}}CA$. In the last equation, $\boldsymbol{A^{\mathrm{T}}e = 0}$ **has changed to** $\boldsymbol{A^{\mathrm{T}}Ce = 0}$. When I made that change in Figure 8.1, I lost the 90° angles. The line is no longer perpendicular to the plane, and the projection is not orthogonal. We are still splitting b into two pieces, $A\widehat{u}_W$ in the column space and e *in the nullspace of* $A^{\mathrm{T}}C$. The equations now include $C = W^{\mathrm{T}}W$:

e is "C-orthogonal"
to the columns of A

$$\begin{array}{rcl} e + A\widehat{u}_W &=& b \\ A^{\mathrm{T}}Ce &=& 0 \end{array} \qquad (9)$$

With a simple change, these equations become symmetric! **Introduce** $\boldsymbol{w = Ce}$ **and** $\boldsymbol{e = C^{-1}w}$ **and shorten** $\boldsymbol{\widehat{u}_W}$ **to** $\boldsymbol{u}$. The right variables are u and w:

Primal-Dual
Saddle Point
Kuhn-Tucker

$$\begin{array}{rcl} C^{-1}w + Au &=& b \\ A^{\mathrm{T}}w &=& 0 \end{array} \qquad (10)$$

This weighted saddle point matrix replaces I by C^{-1} (still positive definite):

Saddle point matrix KKT

$$\boldsymbol{S} = \begin{bmatrix} \boldsymbol{C^{-1}} & \boldsymbol{A} \\ \boldsymbol{A^{\mathrm{T}}} & \boldsymbol{0} \end{bmatrix} \begin{array}{l} m \text{ rows} \\ n \text{ rows} \end{array} \qquad (11)$$

Elimination produces m positive pivots from C^{-1}, and n negative pivots from $-A^{\mathrm{T}}CA$:

$$\begin{bmatrix} C^{-1} & A \\ A^{\mathrm{T}} & 0 \end{bmatrix} \begin{bmatrix} w \\ u \end{bmatrix} = \begin{bmatrix} b \\ 0 \end{bmatrix} \longleftrightarrow \begin{bmatrix} C^{-1} & A \\ \mathbf{0} & -\boldsymbol{A^{\mathrm{T}}CA} \end{bmatrix} \begin{bmatrix} w \\ u \end{bmatrix} = \begin{bmatrix} b \\ -\boldsymbol{A^{\mathrm{T}}Cb} \end{bmatrix}.$$

The Schur complement $-A^{\mathrm{T}}CA$ appears in the 2, 2 block *(negative definite)*. So S is indefinite. We are back to $A^{\mathrm{T}}CAu = A^{\mathrm{T}}Cb$ and all its applications. The constraint was $A^{\mathrm{T}}e = 0$, and now it is $A^{\mathrm{T}}w = 0$ (with $w = Ce$). Soon it will be $A^{\mathrm{T}}w = f$.

How do you minimize a function of e or w when these constraints are enforced? Lagrange showed the way, with his multipliers.

Duality

Figure 8.1 leads to the best example of duality that we can find. There are two different optimization problems (solved by the two projections). Both problems start with the same A and b (and $C = I$ to give the best problem):

1. **Project down to $A\hat{u}$** Minimize $\|b - Au\|^2$
2. **Project across to e** Minimize $\|b - w\|^2$ with $A^{\mathrm{T}}w = 0$.

I am interested in $\|b - Au\|^2$ and $\|b - w\|^2$ for any u and w (always with $A^{\mathrm{T}}w = 0$). Figure 8.2 shows typical choices of Au and w. Those are still perpendicular, because $(Au)^{\mathrm{T}}w = u^{\mathrm{T}}(A^{\mathrm{T}}w) = 0$. But the other right angles are gone, because these Au and w are any vectors in the two spaces, not the projections.

Here is a remarkable fact from geometry (which I never noticed or appreciated). Suppose you have a rectangle, and two perpendicular sides are Au and w. ***Draw lines from b to the four corners of the rectangle.*** Then the sum of two squares $\|b - Au\|^2$ and $\|b - w\|^2$ equals the sum of the other two squares:

Weak duality $\|b - Au\|^2 + \|b - w\|^2 = \|b\|^2 + \|b - Au - w\|^2$. (12)

I asked my class for a proof of this "four-square equation." Most of the students stopped listening to the lecture. By the end we had three proofs of (12), and I will save them for the problem set. (If you find another one, please email.)

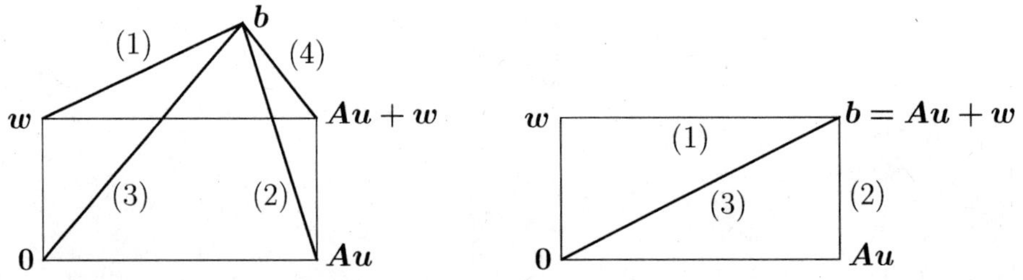

Figure 8.2: Four squares $(1)^2+(2)^2 = (3)^2+(4)^2$ give weak duality. Then $(1)^2+(2)^2 = (3)^2$ is duality. In that case $(4)^2 = \|b - Au - w\|^2 = 0$ splits b into its projections.

This magic identity (12) shows what happens for the minimizing $u = \widehat{u}$ and $w = e$. Those have $b = A\widehat{u} + e$. The fourth square $||b - Au - w||^2$ disappears in Figure 8.2:

Duality (best u and w) $\quad ||b - A\widehat{u}||^2 + ||b - e||^2 = ||b||^2 . \quad (13)$

Weak duality is $(1)^2 + (2)^2 \geq (3)^2$, with a "duality gap" $(4)^2 = ||b - Au - w||^2$. Perfect duality is an equality, when the gap closes to zero. The point b becomes a corner of our rectangle! Then the Pythagoras Law is $a^2 + b^2 = c^2$ with 90° angles and only three squares. The two problems connect at that optimum:

Optimality $\quad$ ***$b - A\widehat{u}$ in Problem 1 equals e in Problem 2.***

In weighted least squares, this optimality $C(b - A\widehat{u}) = \widehat{w}$ will involve C. That middle step in our $A - C - A^{\mathrm{T}}$ framework is the bridge between the two dual problems. It identifies the winners $\widehat{u}$ and $\widehat{w}$ (with $C = I$ in the unweighted example).

Many people see duality as **min = max**. This goes perfectly with a saddle point, and we can have it here. Move the terms in (13) to $||b - e||^2 - ||b||^2 = -||b - A\widehat{u}||^2$. The left side is the minimum of all $||b - w||^2 - ||b||^2$ with $A^{\mathrm{T}}w = 0$. The left side is the maximum (from $-$ sign) of all $-||b - w||^2$. The left side goes down to its minimum, the right side comes up to its maximum. They meet at $u = \widehat{u}$, $w = e$: **duality**.

No gap $\quad \min = ||b - e||^2 - ||b||^2$ *is equal to* $\max = -||b - A\widehat{u}||^2 . \quad (14)$

Minimizing with Constraints

The second example is a line of *two springs and one mass*. The function to minimize is the energy in the springs. The constraint is the balance $A^{\mathrm{T}}w = f$ between internal forces (in the springs) and the external force (on the mass). I believe you can see in Figure 8.3 the fundamental problem of constrained optimization. The forces are drawn as if both springs are stretched with forces $f > 0$, pulling on the mass. Actually spring 2 will be compressed (w_2 is negative).

As I write those words—*spring, mass, energy, force balance*—I am desperately hoping that you won't just say "this is not my area." Changing the example to another area of science or engineering or economics would be easy, the problem stays the same in all languages.

All of calculus trains us to minimize functions: **Set the derivative to zero**. But the basic calculus course doesn't deal properly with constraints. We are minimizing an energy function $E(w_1, w_2)$, but we are constrained to stay on the line $w_1 - w_2 = f$. *What derivatives do we set to zero?*

A direct approach is to replace w_2 by $w_1 - f$, leaving a minimum over w_1. That seems natural, but I want to advocate a different approach (which leads to the same result). Instead of looking for w's that satisfy the constraint, the idea of Lagrange is to *build the constraints into the function.* Rather than removing w_2, we will add a new unknown u. It might seem surprising, but this second approach is better.

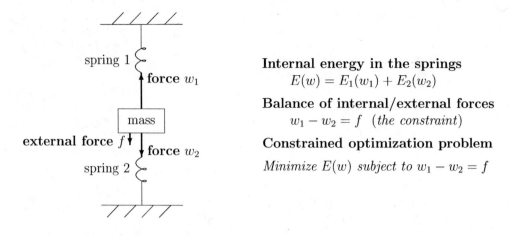

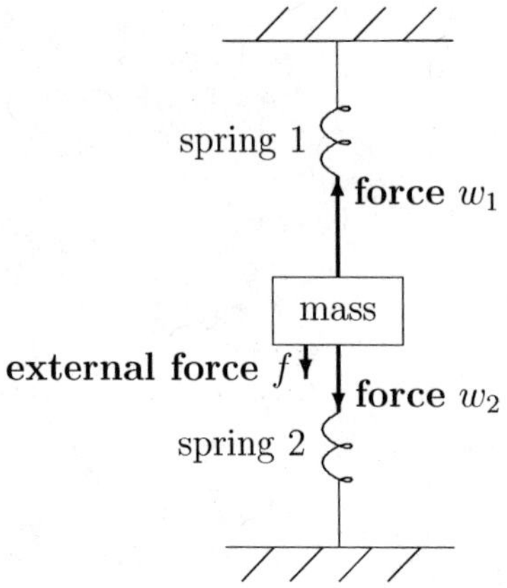

Internal energy in the springs
$E(w) = E_1(w_1) + E_2(w_2)$

Balance of internal/external forces
$w_1 - w_2 = f$ *(the constraint)*

Constrained optimization problem
Minimize $E(w)$ *subject to* $w_1 - w_2 = f$

Figure 8.3: Minimum spring energy $E(w)$ subject to balance of forces on the mass.

With n constraints on m unknowns, Lagrange's method has $m+n$ unknowns. The idea is to add a **Lagrange multiplier** for each constraint. (Books on optimization call this multiplier λ or π, we will call it u.) Our Lagrange function L builds in the constraint $w_1 - w_2 - f = 0$, multiplied (mechanics uses a minus sign) by $-u$:

Lagrange function $\quad L(w_1, w_2, u) = E_1(w_1) + E_2(w_2) - u(w_1 - w_2 - f)\,.$

Calculus can operate on L, by setting derivatives (*three partial derivatives*) to zero:

Kuhn-Tucker optimality equations

$$\frac{\partial L}{\partial w_1} = \frac{\partial E_1}{\partial w_1} - u = 0 \tag{15a}$$

$$\frac{\partial L}{\partial w_2} = \frac{\partial E_2}{\partial w_2} + u = 0 \tag{15b}$$

Lagrange multiplier u

$$\frac{\partial L}{\partial u} = -(w_1 - w_2 - f) = 0 \tag{15c}$$

Notice how the third equation $\partial L/\partial u = 0$ automatically brings back the constraint—because it was just multiplied by $-u$. If we add the first two equations to eliminate u, and substitute $w_1 - f$ for w_2, we are back to the direct approach with one unknown.

But we don't want to eliminate u! That Lagrange multiplier is an important number with a meaning of its own. In this problem, u is the displacement of the mass. In economics, u is the selling price to maximize profit. In all problems, u measures the **sensitivity of the answer** (the minimum energy E_{min}) to a change in the constraint. We will see this sensitivity dE_{min}/df in the linear case.

Linear Case

The force in a linear spring is proportional to the elongation e, by Hooke's Law $w = ce$. Each small stretching step requires work = (force)(movement) = $(ce)(\Delta e)$. Then the integral $\frac{1}{2}ce^2$ that adds up those small steps gives the energy stored in the spring. We can express this energy in terms of e or w:

Energy in a spring
$$E(w) = \frac{1}{2} c\, e^2 = \frac{1}{2} \frac{w^2}{c}\,. \tag{16}$$

Our problem is to minimize a quadratic energy $E(w)$ subject to a linear balance equation $w_1 - w_2 = f$. This is the model problem of optimization.

$$\textbf{Minimize} \quad E(w) = \frac{1}{2}\frac{w_1^2}{c_1} + \frac{1}{2}\frac{w_2^2}{c_2} \quad \textbf{subject to} \quad w_1 - w_2 = f\,. \tag{17}$$

We want to solve this model problem by geometry and then by algebra.

Geometry In the plane of w_1 and w_2, draw the line $w_1 - w_2 = f$. Then draw the ellipse $E(w) = E_{\text{min}}$ that *just touches this line.* The line is tangent to the ellipse. A smaller ellipse from smaller forces w_1 and w_2 will not reach the line—those forces will not balance f. A larger ellipse will not give minimum energy. This ellipse touches the line at the point (w_1, w_2) that minimizes $E(w)$.

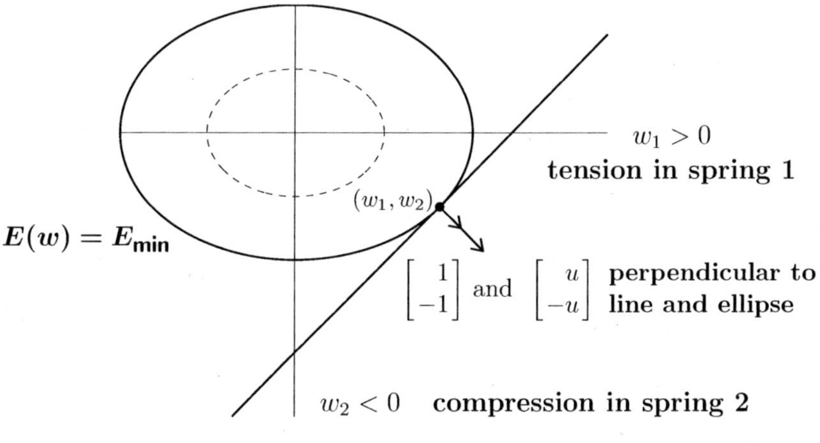

Figure 8.4: The ellipse $E(w) = E_{\text{min}}$ touches $w_1 - w_2 = f$ at the solution (w_1, w_2).

At the touching point in Figure 8.4, the perpendiculars $(1, -1)$ and $(u, -u)$ to the line and the ellipse are parallel. The perpendicular to the line is the vector $(1, -1)$ from the partial derivatives of $w_1 - w_2 - f$. The perpendicular to the ellipse is $(\partial E/\partial w_1, \partial E/\partial w_2)$, from the gradient of $E(w)$. By the optimality equations (15a) and (15b), this is exactly $(u, -u)$. Those parallel gradients at the solution are the algebraic statement that **the line is tangent to the ellipse**.

Algebra To find (w_1, w_2), start with the derivatives of $w_1^2/2\,c_1$ and $w_2^2/2\,c_2$:

Energy gradient $$\frac{\partial E}{\partial w_1} = \frac{w_1}{c_1} \quad \text{and} \quad \frac{\partial E}{\partial w_2} = \frac{w_2}{c_2}. \tag{18}$$

Equations (15a) and (15b) in Lagrange's method become $w_1/c_1 = u$ and $w_2/c_2 = -u$. Now the constraint $w_1 - w_2 = f$ yields $(c_1 + c_2)u = f$ (*both w's are eliminated*):

$$\text{Substitute } w_1 = c_1 u \text{ and } w_2 = -c_2 u. \quad \text{Then } (c_1 + c_2)u = f. \tag{19}$$

I don't know if you recognize $c_1 + c_2$ as our stiffness matrix $A^{\mathrm{T}}CA$! This problem is so small that you could easily miss $K = A^{\mathrm{T}}CA$. The matrix A^{T} in the constraint equation $A^{\mathrm{T}}w = w_1 - w_2 = f$ is only 1 by 2, so *the stiffness matrix K is 1 by 1*:

$$A^{\mathrm{T}} = \begin{bmatrix} 1 & -1 \end{bmatrix} \text{ and } K = A^{\mathrm{T}}CA = \begin{bmatrix} 1 & -1 \end{bmatrix} \begin{bmatrix} c_1 & \\ & c_2 \end{bmatrix} \begin{bmatrix} 1 \\ -1 \end{bmatrix} = \begin{bmatrix} c_1 + c_2 \end{bmatrix}. \tag{20}$$

The algebra of Lagrange's method has recovered $Ku = f$. Its solution is the movement $u = f/(c_1+c_2)$ of the mass. Equation (19) eliminated w_1 and w_2 using (15a) and (15b). Now back substitution finds those energy-minimizing forces:

Spring forces $$w_1 = c_1 u = \frac{c_1 f}{c_1 + c_2} \quad \text{and} \quad w_2 = -c_2 u = \frac{-c_2 f}{c_1 + c_2}. \tag{21}$$

Those forces (w_1, w_2) are on the ellipse of minimum energy $E_{\min}$, tangent to the line:

$$E(w) = \frac{1}{2}\frac{w_1^2}{c_1} + \frac{1}{2}\frac{w_2^2}{c_2} = \frac{1}{2}\frac{c_1 f^2}{(c_1 + c_2)^2} + \frac{1}{2}\frac{c_2 f^2}{(c_1 + c_2)^2} = \boldsymbol{\frac{1}{2}\frac{f^2}{c_1 + c_2}} = \boldsymbol{E_{\min}}. \tag{22}$$

This $E_{\min}$ must be the same minimum $\frac{1}{2}f^{\mathrm{T}}K^{-1}f$ as in Section 2.1, long ago. It is.

We can directly verify the mysterious fact that u measures the sensitivity of $E_{\min}$ to a small change in f. Compute the derivative $dE_{\min}/df$:

Lagrange multiplier = Sensitivity $$\frac{d}{df}\left(\frac{1}{2}\frac{f^2}{c_1 + c_2}\right) = \frac{f}{c_1 + c_2} = u. \tag{23}$$

This sensitivity is linked to the observation in Figure 8.4 that one gradient is u times the other gradient. From (15a) and (15b), that stays true for nonlinear springs. This is the basis for **adjoint methods** to compute $d\,(\text{output})/d\,(\text{input})$.

A Specific Example

I want to insert $c_1 = c_2 = 1$ in this model problem, to see the saddle point of L more clearly. The Lagrange function with built-in constraint depends on w_1 and w_2 and u:

Lagrangian $$\boldsymbol{L = \frac{1}{2}w_1^2 + \frac{1}{2}w_2^2 - uw_1 + uw_2 + uf}. \tag{24}$$

The equations $\partial L/\partial w_1 = 0$ and $\partial L/\partial w_2 = 0$ and $\partial L/\partial u = 0$ produce a beautiful symmetric KKT matrix S:

$$\begin{aligned} \partial L/\partial w_1 &= \quad w_1 - u \quad = 0 \\ \partial L/\partial w_2 &= \quad w_2 + u \quad = 0 \\ \partial L/\partial u \ &= -w_1 + w_2 = f \end{aligned} \quad \text{or} \quad \begin{bmatrix} 1 & 0 & -1 \\ 0 & 1 & 1 \\ -1 & 1 & 0 \end{bmatrix} \begin{bmatrix} w_1 \\ w_2 \\ u \end{bmatrix} = \begin{bmatrix} 0 \\ 0 \\ f \end{bmatrix}. \qquad (25)$$

Is this matrix S positive definite? *No.* It is invertible, and its pivots are $1, 1, -2$. That -2 destroys positive definiteness—it means a saddle point:

Elimination $$\begin{bmatrix} 1 & 0 & -1 \\ 0 & 1 & 1 \\ -1 & 1 & 0 \end{bmatrix} \longrightarrow \begin{bmatrix} \mathbf{1} & 0 & -1 \\ & \mathbf{1} & 1 \\ & & \mathbf{-2} \end{bmatrix} \quad \text{with } L = \begin{bmatrix} 1 & & \\ 0 & 1 & \\ -1 & 1 & 1 \end{bmatrix}.$$

On a symmetric matrix, elimination equals "completing the square." The pivots $1, 1, -2$ are outside the squares. The entries of L are inside the squares:

$$\frac{1}{2}w_1^2 + \frac{1}{2}w_2^2 - uw_1 + uw_2 = \frac{1}{2}\left[1(w_1 - u)^2 + 1(w_2 + u)^2 - 2(u)^2\right]. \qquad (26)$$

The first squares $(w_1 - u)^2$ and $(w_2 + u)^2$ go upwards, but $-2u^2$ goes down. **This KKT matrix gives a saddle point SP = (w_1, w_2, u) in Figure 8.5.**

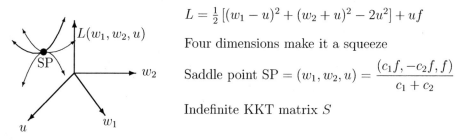

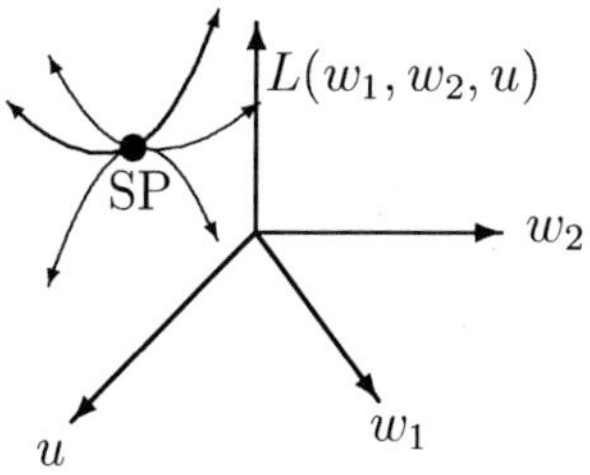

$L = \frac{1}{2}\left[(w_1 - u)^2 + (w_2 + u)^2 - 2u^2\right] + uf$

Four dimensions make it a squeeze

Saddle point SP $= (w_1, w_2, u) = \dfrac{(c_1 f, -c_2 f, f)}{c_1 + c_2}$

Indefinite KKT matrix S

Figure 8.5: $(w_1 - u)^2$ and $(w_2 + u)^2$ go up, $-2u^2$ goes down from the saddle point SP.

The Fundamental Problem

May I describe the full linear case with $w = (w_1, \ldots, w_m)$ and $A^{\mathrm{T}}w = (f_1, \ldots, f_n)$? The problem is to minimize the total energy $E(w) = \frac{1}{2}w^{\mathrm{T}}C^{-1}w$ in the m springs. The n constraints $A^{\mathrm{T}}w = f$ are built in by Lagrange multipliers $u_1, \ldots, u_n$. Multiplying the force balance on the kth mass by $-u_k$ and adding, all n constraints are built into the dot product $u^{\mathrm{T}}(A^{\mathrm{T}}w - f)$. For mechanics, we use a minus sign in L:

Lagrange function $$L(w, u) = \frac{1}{2}w^{\mathrm{T}}C^{-1}w - u^{\mathrm{T}}(A^{\mathrm{T}}w - f). \qquad (27)$$

To find the minimizing w, set the $m + n$ first partial derivatives of L to zero:

KKT equations

$$\partial L/\partial w = C^{-1}w - Au = 0 \qquad (28a)$$

$$\partial L/\partial u = -A^{\mathrm{T}}w + f = 0 \qquad (28b)$$

This is the main point, that Lagrange multipliers lead exactly to the linear equations $w = CAu$ and $A^{\mathrm{T}}w = f$ that we studied in the first chapters of the book. By using $-u$ in the Lagrange function L and introducing $e = Au$, we have the plus signs that appeared for springs and masses:

$$e = Au \qquad w = Ce \qquad f = A^{\mathrm{T}}w \qquad \Longrightarrow \qquad A^{\mathrm{T}}CAu = f\,.$$

Sign Convention Least squares problems have $e = b - Au$ (minus sign from voltage drops). **Then we change to $+u$ in L.** The energy $E = \frac{1}{2}w^{\mathrm{T}}C^{-1}w - b^{\mathrm{T}}w$ now involves b. When Lagrange sets derivatives of L to zero, he finds the KKT matrix S:

$$\begin{aligned} \partial L/\partial w &= C^{-1}w + Au - b = 0 \\ \partial L/\partial u &= A^{\mathrm{T}}w \qquad\quad\; - f = 0 \end{aligned} \qquad \text{or} \qquad \begin{bmatrix} \boldsymbol{C^{-1}} & \boldsymbol{A} \\ \boldsymbol{A^{\mathrm{T}}} & \boldsymbol{0} \end{bmatrix} \begin{bmatrix} \boldsymbol{w} \\ \boldsymbol{u} \end{bmatrix} = \begin{bmatrix} \boldsymbol{b} \\ \boldsymbol{f} \end{bmatrix}. \qquad (29)$$

This system is my top candidate for the fundamental problem of scientific computing.

You could eliminate $w = C(b - Au)$ *but I don't know if you should.* If you do it, $K = A^{\mathrm{T}}CA$ will appear. Usually this is a good plan, going directly to u:

Remove w $\quad A^{\mathrm{T}}w = A^{\mathrm{T}}C(b - Au) = f$ which is $A^{\mathrm{T}}CAu = A^{\mathrm{T}}Cb - f\,.$ (30)

Invertibility of Saddle Point Matrices

For springs, $Ku = f$ comes from the three equations $e = Au, w = Ce$, and $f = A^{\mathrm{T}}w$. This is the straightforward way, eliminating e and w. There is extra insight if we only eliminate $e = C^{-1}w$ and keep both w and u. For networks e is $b - Au$:

Two fundamental equations $\qquad \boldsymbol{C^{-1}w = b - Au}$ and $\boldsymbol{A^{\mathrm{T}}w = f}$

Those equations come from our **saddle-point matrix S** (not positive definite):

Saddle-point system $\qquad \begin{bmatrix} & \boldsymbol{S} & \end{bmatrix} \begin{bmatrix} w \\ u \end{bmatrix} = \begin{bmatrix} C^{-1} & A \\ A^{\mathrm{T}} & 0 \end{bmatrix} \begin{bmatrix} w \\ u \end{bmatrix} = \begin{bmatrix} b \\ f \end{bmatrix}. \qquad$ (31)

This block matrix has size $\boldsymbol{m + n}$ (w has m components and u has n).

Example $\quad S = \begin{bmatrix} C^{-1} & A \\ A^{\mathrm{T}} & 0 \end{bmatrix} = \begin{bmatrix} 1 & 0 & 1 \\ 0 & 1 & -1 \\ 1 & -1 & 0 \end{bmatrix}$ $\quad$ has pivots $1, 1, -2$
 eigenvalues $2, 1, -1$

That example shows the normal situation for this book. C is *positive definite.* A has *full column rank* (independent columns, the rank A is n). **Then $A^{\mathrm{T}}CA$ is invertible and S is invertible.** We factor S into three invertible matrices:

$$S = \begin{bmatrix} C^{-1} & A \\ A^{\mathrm{T}} & 0 \end{bmatrix} = \begin{bmatrix} I & 0 \\ A^{\mathrm{T}}C & I \end{bmatrix} \begin{bmatrix} C^{-1} & 0 \\ 0 & -A^{\mathrm{T}}CA \end{bmatrix} \begin{bmatrix} I & CA \\ 0 & I \end{bmatrix}. \qquad (32)$$

The $2, 2$ block $-A^{\mathrm{T}}CA$ is called the **Schur complement**: the result of elimination.

When C is *indefinite*, S can easily become singular. Change $C_{11} = 1$ to $C_{11} = -1$ in the example, and $(1, 1, 1)$ goes into the nullspace of S. This happens even though A has full rank in the last column, and the first block column also has full rank.

To prove invertibility from the two block columns, the 1, 1 block should be at least semidefinite. Applications can also produce a matrix $-H$ in the 2, 2 block:

Extended saddle-point matrix $$S = \begin{bmatrix} \boldsymbol{G} & \boldsymbol{A} \\ \boldsymbol{A}^{\mathrm{T}} & -\boldsymbol{H} \end{bmatrix} \qquad \begin{array}{l} (\boldsymbol{G} \textbf{ and } \boldsymbol{H} \textbf{ positive semidefinite}) \\ (\text{important case: } H = 0) \end{array} \tag{33}$$

Invertibility is a question in matrix algebra. This answer in Problem 11 is often useful:

$$\boldsymbol{S \textit{ is invertible when its block columns have full ranks } m \textit{ and } n.} \tag{34}$$

Here are examples of an indefinite G (not allowed), and a semidefinite G (but not full rank), and a full rank semidefinite case (to illustrate how (34) succeeds).

$$\left[\begin{array}{cc|c} \mathbf{-1} & 0 & 1 \\ 0 & \mathbf{1} & -1 \\ \hline 1 & -1 & 0 \end{array}\right] \qquad \left[\begin{array}{cc|c} \mathbf{1} & 0 & 1 \\ 0 & \mathbf{0} & 0 \\ \hline 1 & 0 & 0 \end{array}\right] \qquad \left[\begin{array}{cc|c} \mathbf{1} & 0 & 1 \\ 0 & \mathbf{0} & -1 \\ \hline 1 & -1 & 0 \end{array}\right]$$

rank 2 rank 1	rank 1 rank 1	rank 2 rank 1
Singular S	Singular S	Invertible S

To have rank 3 (invertibility) the block columns need ranks 2 and 1. The point of the first matrix (with indefinite G) is that S could still be singular. The point of the last matrix (with semidefinite G) is that ranks 2 and 1 now produce rank 3.

The survey [13] describes applications and algorithms for KKT matrices. They go far beyond networks and structures:

Constrained least squares (in this Section 8.1)

Image reconstruction and restoration (inverse problems in Section 4.7-8.2)

Fluid dynamics and mixed finite elements (in Section 8.5)

Economics and finance (linear programming in Section 8.6)

Interpolation of scattered data

Mesh generation for computer graphics

Optimal control and parameter identification

Problem Set 8.1

1 I just learned a proof of $a^2+b^2=c^2$ for right triangles. Rescale the triangle by a and separately by b. The rescaled triangles fit with common side ab into a larger right triangle (figure below). Its area is $\frac{1}{2}(ac)(bc)$ and also ____ .

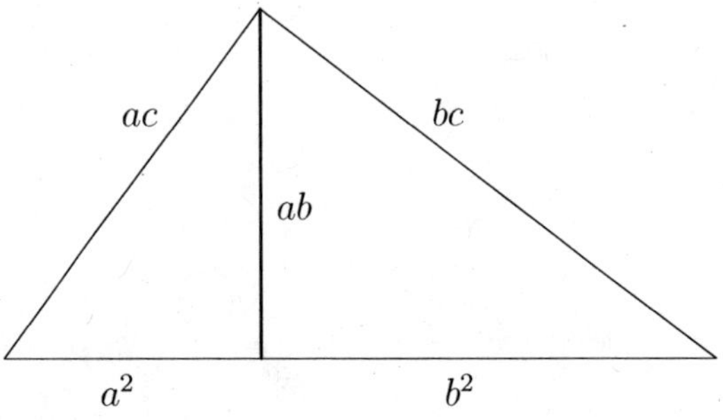

2 **The four squared lengths satisfy $13 + 17 = 25 + 5$.** For any rectangle and any point b outside, find a proof using Pythagoras for four right triangles. Each triangle has one side on the dashed line in the figure.

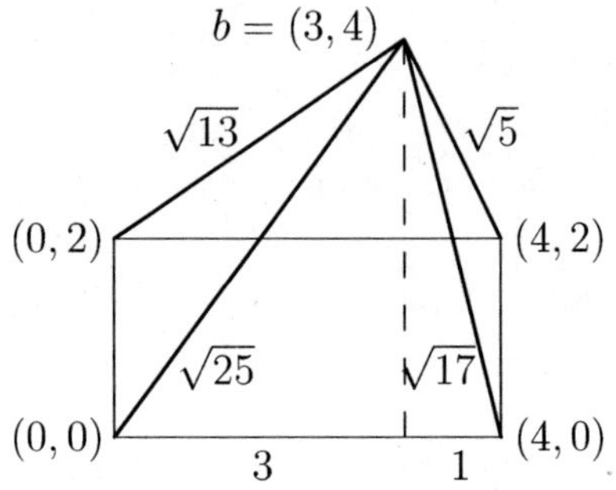

3 In the second figure, write down the four squared lengths using x, y, b_1, b_2. Check the 4-square identity. *Prove it also when b is raised from the page to (b_1, b_2, b_3).*

4 Draw a different rectangle with b *inside*. Check the four-square identity!

5 My proof is in any dimension, since b need not be in the plane of Au and w. Expand $\|b-Au\|^2$ into $b^{\mathrm{T}}b-2b^{\mathrm{T}}Au+(Au)^{\mathrm{T}}Au$. Expand the other three squares in equation (12) and use $A^{\mathrm{T}}w=0$.

6 Kai Borre's trig proof starts from the Law of Cosines (with the angles A and B). In vector notation this produces $\|b\|^2 = \|w\|^2 + \|b-w\|^2 - 2\|w\|\,\|b-w\|\cos A$. The triangle on the right side produces a term $-2\|w\|\,\|b-Au-w\|\cos B$. Those cosine terms are equal by the Law of Sines in the top triangle. Notice $-\cos A = \sin(A-90°)$ and $-\cos B = \sin(B-90°)$. The Law of Sines says that $(\sin\theta)/(\text{length of opposite side})$ is the same for all angles in a triangle.

7 **(Fixed-Free)** Suppose the lower spring in Figure 8.3 holds a mass m_2. This adds a new force balance constraint $w_2 - f_2 = 0$. Build the old and new constraints into $L(w_1, w_2, u_1, u_2)$. Write down *four equations* like (15a)–(15c): partial derivatives of L are zero.

8 Find A in that fixed-free case (Problem 7 with $C = \mathsf{diag}(c_1, c_2)$:

$$\begin{bmatrix} C^{-1} & A \\ A^{\mathrm{T}} & 0 \end{bmatrix} \begin{bmatrix} w \\ u \end{bmatrix} = \begin{bmatrix} 0 \\ f \end{bmatrix} \quad \text{with } w = \begin{bmatrix} w_1 \\ w_2 \end{bmatrix}, u = \begin{bmatrix} u_1 \\ u_2 \end{bmatrix}, f = \begin{bmatrix} f_1 \\ f_2 \end{bmatrix}.$$

Elimination subtracts A^{T} times the first block row from the second. What matrix $-A^{\mathrm{T}}CA$ enters the zero block? Solve for $u = (u_1, u_2)$.

9 Continuing Problem 7 with $C = I$, write down $w = Au$ and compute the energy $E_{\mathbf{min}} = \frac{1}{2}w_1^2 + \frac{1}{2}w_2^2$. Verify that its derivatives with respect to f_1 and f_2 are the Lagrange multipliers u_1 and u_2 (sensitivity analysis).

10 Eigenvalues of $S = [\, I \;\; A; A^{\mathrm{T}} \;\; 0\,]$ connect to singular values of $A = U\Sigma V^{\mathrm{T}}$:

$$\begin{bmatrix} U^{-1} & \\ & V^{-1} \end{bmatrix} \begin{bmatrix} I & U\Sigma V^{\mathrm{T}} \\ V\Sigma^{\mathrm{T}}U^{\mathrm{T}} & 0 \end{bmatrix} \begin{bmatrix} U & \\ & V \end{bmatrix} = \begin{bmatrix} I & \Sigma \\ \Sigma^{\mathrm{T}} & 0 \end{bmatrix} \quad \begin{matrix}\text{has the same} \\ \text{eigenvalues as } S.\end{matrix}$$

That last matrix has n 2 by 2 blocks B_j, after reordering rows and columns:

$$\lambda(S) \text{ from } \Sigma \qquad B_j = \begin{bmatrix} 1 & \sigma_j \\ \sigma_j & 0 \end{bmatrix} \quad \text{has eigenvalues} \quad \lambda^2 - \lambda - \sigma_j^2 = 0\,.$$

Solve for λ and show that S has no eigenvalues in $[0, 1)$. For small σ_j the λ are near $1 + \sigma^2$ and $-\sigma^2$, so S is ill-conditioned. Compute $\mathsf{eig}(S)$ when $A = K_3$.

11 Statement (34) says that if S is singular, at least one block column fails to have full rank. When at least one of w and u is nonzero, we need to show:

$$\begin{bmatrix} G & A \\ A^{\mathrm{T}} & -H \end{bmatrix} \begin{bmatrix} w \\ u \end{bmatrix} = \begin{bmatrix} 0 \\ 0 \end{bmatrix} \text{ forces } \begin{bmatrix} G \\ A^{\mathrm{T}} \end{bmatrix} [w] = \begin{bmatrix} 0 \\ 0 \end{bmatrix} \text{ and } \begin{bmatrix} A \\ -H \end{bmatrix} [u] = \begin{bmatrix} 0 \\ 0 \end{bmatrix}.$$

Proof $Gw + Au = 0$ and $A^{\mathrm{T}}w = Hu$ give $0 = w^{\mathrm{T}}Gw + w^{\mathrm{T}}Au$. This is $w^{\mathrm{T}}Gw + u^{\mathrm{T}}Hu = 0$. *Key step using semidefiniteness*: Explain by factoring $G = M^{\mathrm{T}}M$ and $H = R^{\mathrm{T}}R$ why Gw and Hu must be zero. Then also $A^{\mathrm{T}}w = 0$.

12 Minimize $E = \frac{1}{2}(w_1^2 + \frac{1}{3}w_2^2)$ subject to $w_1 + w_2 = 8$ by solving $\partial L/\partial w = 0$ and $\partial L/\partial u = 0$ for the Lagrangian $L = E + u(w_1 + w_2 - 8)$.

13 Find the minimum by Lagrange multipliers u_1 and u_2 of

(a) $E = \frac{1}{2}(w_1^2 + w_2^2 + w_3^2)$ with $w_1 - w_2 = 1$, $w_2 - w_3 = 2$

(b) $E = w_1^2 + w_1w_2 + w_2^2 + w_2w_3 + w_3^2 - w_3$ with $w_1 + w_2 = 2$

(c) $E = w_1^2 + 2w_1w_2 - 2w_2$ with $w_1 + w_2 = 0$ (watch for maximum).

14 How far is it from $(0,0,0)$ to the plane $w_1 + 2w_2 + 2w_3 = 18$? Write this constraint as $A^{\mathrm{T}}w = 18$ and solve also for the multiplier u:

$$\begin{bmatrix} I & A \\ A^{\mathrm{T}} & 0 \end{bmatrix} \begin{bmatrix} w \\ u \end{bmatrix} = \begin{bmatrix} 0 \\ 18 \end{bmatrix}.$$

15 "The minimum distance from $(0,0,0)$ to points on a line equals the maximum distance to planes through that line." Why is the distance to any point $\geq$ the distance to any plane? This is minimum of primal $\geq$ maximum of dual (weak duality).

16 Minimize $w^{\mathrm{T}}Kw$ subject to the nonlinear constraint $w_1^2 + w_2^2 + w_3^2 = 1$ (K is K_3).
With Lagrange multiplier u, the equation $\partial L/\partial w = 0$ should produce $Kw = uw$. So u is an eigenvalue (which one?) and w is its unit eigenvector. An equivalent statement for any symmetric K is to minimize the **Rayleigh quotient** $w^{\mathrm{T}}Kw/w^{\mathrm{T}}w$.

17 (Important) The minimum value of the **potential energy** $P = \frac{1}{2}u^{\mathrm{T}}A^{\mathrm{T}}CAu - u^{\mathrm{T}}f$ equals the maximum value of the negative **complementary energy** $-Q = -\frac{1}{2}w^{\mathrm{T}}C^{-1}w$ subject to $A^{\mathrm{T}}w = f$.
Introduce Lagrange multipliers u for that constraint. With $L = Q + u^{\mathrm{T}}(A^{\mathrm{T}}w - f)$ show that $\partial L/\partial w = 0$ and $\partial L/\partial u = 0$ give the basic KKT equations, and eliminating w leaves $A^{\mathrm{T}}CAu = f$. The **displacement method** in finite elements minimizes P, the **force method** minimizes Q.

8.2 REGULARIZED LEAST SQUARES

Before this section begins, here is an advance look at what it will bring. You will see the new "two-square problem" right away. It connects to the old problems, but it has its own place and its own applications:

Ordinary least squares	Minimize $\|Au - b\|^2$ by solving	$A^{\mathrm{T}}A\widehat{u} = A^{\mathrm{T}}b$
Weighted least squares	Minimize $(b - Au)^{\mathrm{T}}C(b - Au)$ by	$A^{\mathrm{T}}CA\widehat{u} = A^{\mathrm{T}}Cb$

New problem
Two squares

$$\text{Minimize } \|Au - b\|^2 + \alpha\|Bu - d\|^2 \text{ by solving } (\boldsymbol{A}^{\mathrm{T}}\boldsymbol{A} + \boldsymbol{\alpha}\boldsymbol{B}^{\mathrm{T}}\boldsymbol{B})\widehat{u} = \boldsymbol{A}^{\mathrm{T}}\boldsymbol{b} + \boldsymbol{\alpha}\boldsymbol{B}^{\mathrm{T}}\boldsymbol{d}. \tag{1}$$

This equation (1) is not truly new. It is a special case of weighted least squares, if you adjust the notation to fit A and B into one problem. Then C is $[\,I \;\; 0 \;\; ; \;\; 0 \;\; \alpha I\,]$:

Combined matrix $\begin{bmatrix} \boldsymbol{A} \\ \boldsymbol{B} \end{bmatrix}$

$$\begin{bmatrix} A^{\mathrm{T}} & B^{\mathrm{T}} \end{bmatrix} \begin{bmatrix} I & 0 \\ 0 & \alpha I \end{bmatrix} \begin{bmatrix} A \\ B \end{bmatrix} \widehat{u} = \begin{bmatrix} A^{\mathrm{T}} & B^{\mathrm{T}} \end{bmatrix} \begin{bmatrix} I & 0 \\ 0 & \alpha I \end{bmatrix} \begin{bmatrix} b \\ d \end{bmatrix}. \tag{2}$$

This is equation (1). The solution $\widehat{u}$ depends on the weight α, which appears in that block matrix C. Choosing the parameter α wisely is often the hardest part.

Here are two important applications that lead to this sum of two squares:

Regularized least squares The original problem $A^{\mathrm{T}}A\widehat{u} = A^{\mathrm{T}}b$ can be very "ill-posed." This is typical of **inverse problems**, when we are trying to determine a cause from the effect it produces. The usual solution with $\alpha = 0$ is unreliable when A is highly ill-conditioned. For $A^{\mathrm{T}}A$, the ratio of largest to smallest eigenvalue might be 10^6 or 10^{10} or worse. Extreme examples have $m < n$ and singular $A^{\mathrm{T}}A$.

Adding $\alpha B^{\mathrm{T}}B$ regularizes the matrix $A^{\mathrm{T}}A$. It is like smoothing—we try to reduce the noise but save the signal. The weight α allows us to look for the right balance.

Constrained least squares To achieve $Bu = d$, increase the weight α. In the limit as $\alpha \to \infty$, we expect $\|B\widehat{u}_\alpha - d\|^2 \to 0$. The limiting $\widehat{u}_\infty$ solves a key problem:

Equality constraint $$\textbf{\textit{Minimize}} \;\; \|\boldsymbol{Au} - \boldsymbol{b}\|^2 \;\; \textbf{\textit{subject to}} \;\; \boldsymbol{Bu} = \boldsymbol{d}. \tag{3}$$

Inverse problems have a tremendous range of applications. In most cases the words "least squares" never appear! To impose constraints we use large α. We will apply three leading methods to the simple constraint $Bu = u_1 - u_2 = 8$.

First we mention a key regularizing example (small α). Then come constraints.

Estimating Derivatives

I think this is truly the fundamental ill-posed problem of applied mathematics:

$$\textbf{\textit{Estimate the velocity}}\ \frac{dx}{dt}\ \textbf{\textit{from position}}\ x\ (\textit{not exact})\ \textbf{\textit{at times}}\ t_1, t_2, \ldots$$

Sometimes the problem comes in exactly that form. A GPS receiver gives positions $x(t)$ with great accuracy. It also estimates the velocity dx/dt, but how? The first idea is a finite difference like $x(t_2) - x(t_1)$ divided by $t_2 - t_1$. For high accuracy you need t_2 very near t_1. But when you divide by $t_2 - t_1$, any small position errors (*noise in the data*) are greatly amplified.

This is typical of ill-posed problems. **Small input errors, large output errors.** I will write the same problem as an *integral equation of the first kind*:

Integral equation for v
$$\int_0^t v(s)\,ds = \int_0^t \frac{dx}{ds}\,ds = x(t) - x(0)\,. \tag{4}$$

The function $x(t)$ is given, the function $v(t)$ is the unknown. Many scientific problems look like this, often including a known kernel function $K(t,s)$ inside the integral. The equation is "Volterra" when the endpoints include the variable t, and "Fredholm" when they don't. Second kind equations add an extra term $cv(t)$, much easier.

Derivative estimation goes quickly into high dimensions. Many genes (some important, others not) may act to produce an expression $x(g_1, g_2, \ldots, g_N)$. The sizes of the derivatives $\partial x/\partial g_i$ tell which genes are important. It is an enormous problem to estimate all those derivatives from a limited number of sample values (measurements of x, often very noisy). Usually we discretize and then regularize by a small α. We return to these ill-posed problems after studying the other extreme, when α is large.

Large Penalty

We will minimize $u_1^2 + u_2^2$ with $u_1 - u_2 = 8$. This equality constraint $Bu = d$ fits Problem (3). B has n columns but only p rows (and rank p).

Key example
$$A = \begin{bmatrix} 1 & 0 \\ 0 & 1 \end{bmatrix} \qquad b = \begin{bmatrix} 0 \\ 0 \end{bmatrix} \qquad B = \begin{bmatrix} 1 & -1 \end{bmatrix} \qquad d = \begin{bmatrix} 8 \end{bmatrix}. \tag{5}$$

You could solve that problem without a Ph.D. Just substitute $u_2 = u_1 - 8$ into u_2^2. Minimizing $u_1^2 + (u_1 - 8)^2$ gives $u_1 = 4$. This approach is "the nullspace method" and we will extend it to other problems A, b, B, d. First come two other methods:

1. Large penalty	Minimize $u_1^2 + u_2^2 + \alpha(u_1 - u_2 - 8)^2$ and let $\alpha \to \infty$
2. Lagrange multiplier	Find a saddle point of $L = \frac{1}{2}(u_1^2 + u_2^2) + w(u_1 - u_2 - 8)$
3. Nullspace method	Solve $Bu = d$ and look for the shortest solution.

We start with the large penalty method, which is equation (1). Its big advantage is that we don't need a new computer code, beyond weighted least squares. This practical advantage should not be underestimated, and the key example with $u_1 = u_2 = 4$ will show that *the error in u decreases like* $1/\alpha$.

$$A^{\mathrm{T}}A = I \qquad B^{\mathrm{T}}B = \begin{bmatrix} 1 & -1 \\ -1 & 1 \end{bmatrix} \qquad \begin{bmatrix} 1+\alpha & -\alpha \\ -\alpha & 1+\alpha \end{bmatrix} \begin{bmatrix} u_1 \\ u_2 \end{bmatrix} = \begin{bmatrix} 8\alpha \\ -8\alpha \end{bmatrix} = \alpha\, B^{\mathrm{T}}d. \quad (6)$$

Adding the equations gives $u_1 + u_2 = 0$. Then the first equation is $(1 + 2\alpha)u_1 = 8\alpha$:

$$u_1 = \frac{8\alpha}{1+2\alpha} = \frac{4}{1+(1/2\alpha)} = 4 - \frac{4}{2\alpha} + \cdots \text{ approaches the correct } \quad u_1 = 4. \quad (7)$$

The error is of order $1/\alpha$. So we need large α for good accuracy in u_1 and u_2. In this situation we are intentionally making the problem ill-conditioned. The matrix in (6) has eigenvalues 1 and $1 + 2\alpha$. Roundoff error could be serious at $\alpha = 10^{10}$.

Let me describe without proof the limit $\widehat{u}_\infty$ of the penalty method as $\alpha \to \infty$:

$$\widehat{u}_\infty \textbf{ minimizes } \|Au - b\|^2 \textbf{ among all minimizers of } \|Bu - d\|^2.$$

Large α concentrates first on $\|Bu - d\|^2$. There will be many minimizers when $B^{\mathrm{T}}B$ is singular. Then the limiting $\widehat{u}_\infty$ is the one among them that minimizes the other term $\|Au - b\|^2$. We only require that $\begin{bmatrix} A \\ B \end{bmatrix}$ has full column rank n, so the matrix $A^{\mathrm{T}}A + \alpha\, B^{\mathrm{T}}B$ is invertible.

Here is an interesting point. Suppose I divide equation (1) by α. Then as $\alpha \to \infty$, the equation becomes $B^{\mathrm{T}}B\,\widehat{u}_\infty = B^{\mathrm{T}}d$. All traces of A and b have disappeared from the limiting equation! But the penalty method is smarter than this, when $B^{\mathrm{T}}B$ is singular. Even as A and b fade out, minimizing with the $\|Au - b\|^2$ term included decides which limit $\widehat{u}_\infty$ the large penalty method will approach.

Lagrange Multipliers

The usual way to deal with a constraint $Bu = d$ is by a Lagrange multiplier. Elsewhere in this book, the constraint is $A^{\mathrm{T}}w = f$ and the multiplier is u. Now the constraint applies to u, so the multiplier will be called w. If we have p constraints $Bu = d$, we need p multipliers $w = (w_1, \ldots, w_p)$. The constraints go into L, multiplied by the w's:

$$\textbf{\textit{Lagrangian}}\ L(u, w) = \frac{1}{2}\|Au - b\|^2 + w^{\mathrm{T}}(Bu - d). \quad \textbf{\textit{Set}}\ \frac{\partial L}{\partial u} = \frac{\partial L}{\partial w} = 0.$$

The derivatives of L are zero at the saddle point u, w:

New saddle matrix S^* $$\begin{bmatrix} A^{\mathrm{T}}A & B^{\mathrm{T}} \\ B & 0 \end{bmatrix} \begin{bmatrix} u \\ w \end{bmatrix} = \begin{bmatrix} A^{\mathrm{T}}b \\ d \end{bmatrix} \quad \begin{matrix} (n \text{ rows}) \\ (p \text{ rows}) \end{matrix} \qquad (8)$$

Notice the differences from the saddle-point matrix S in Section 8.1. The new upper left block $A^{\mathrm{T}}A$ might be only positive *semidefinite* (possibly singular). The letters are all different, as expected. S^* will not be invertible unless the p rows of B are independent. Furthermore $\left[\begin{smallmatrix}\mathbf{A}\\ \mathbf{B}\end{smallmatrix}\right]$ must have full column rank n to make $A^{\mathrm{T}}A+B^{\mathrm{T}}B$ invertible—this matrix appears when B^{T} times row 2 is added to row 1.

Our example can be solved in this Lagrange form, without any α:

$$\begin{array}{ll} \boldsymbol{A}=\boldsymbol{I} & \boldsymbol{b}=\mathbf{0} \\ \boldsymbol{B}=\begin{bmatrix}1 & -1\end{bmatrix} & \boldsymbol{d}=\mathbf{8} \end{array} \qquad \begin{bmatrix}1 & 0 & 1\\ 0 & 1 & -1\\ 1 & -1 & 0\end{bmatrix}\begin{bmatrix}4\\ -4\\ -4\end{bmatrix}=\begin{bmatrix}0\\ 0\\ 8\end{bmatrix}. \tag{9}$$

The optimal u_1, u_2 is 4, −4 as earlier. The multiplier is $w=-4$.

The multiplier w always measures the sensitivity of the output P_{min} to the input d. P_{min} is the minimum value of $(u_1^2+u_2^2)/2$. When you solve the problem for any d, you find $u_1=d/2$ and $u_2=w=-d/2$. Then $-w$ is the derivative of P:

$$\textbf{Sensitivity} \qquad P_{\mathrm{min}}=\frac{1}{2}(u_1^2+u_2^2)=\frac{d^2}{4} \quad \text{has derivative} \quad \frac{d}{2}=\frac{8}{2}=-w\,. \tag{10}$$

So Lagrange gives something extra for solving a larger system.

Nullspace Method

The third approach to constrained minimization begins by solving $Bu=d$ directly. For $u_1-u_2=8$, we did that at the start of the section. The result $u_2=8-u_1$ was substituted into $u_1^2+u_2^2$, which we minimized to get $u_1=4$.

When the matrix B is p by n, I could propose the same plan: Solve $Bu=d$ for p of the variables in terms of the other $n-p$. Substitute for those p variables in $\|Au-b\|^2$ and minimize. But this is not really a safe way.

The reason it's not safe is that a p by p block of B might be nearly singular. Then those p variables are the wrong ones to solve for. We would have to exchange columns and test condition numbers to find a good p by p submatrix. Much better to orthogonalize the p rows of B once and for all.

The plan of the nullspace method is simple: ***Solve $\boldsymbol{Bu}=\boldsymbol{d}$ for $\boldsymbol{u}=\boldsymbol{u_n}+\boldsymbol{u_r}$***. The *nullspace* vectors u_n solve $Bu_n=0$. If the $n-p$ columns of Q_n are a basis for the nullspace, then every u_n is a combination Q_nz. One vector u_r in the row space solves $Bu_r=d$. Substitute $\boldsymbol{u}=\boldsymbol{Q_n z}+\boldsymbol{u_r}$ into $\|Au-b\|^2$ and find the minimum:

Nullspace method Minimize $\|A(u_n+u_r)-b\|^2=\|AQ_nz-(b-Au_r)\|^2$

The vector z has only $n-p$ unknowns. Where Lagrange multipliers made the problem larger, this nullspace method makes it smaller. There are no constraints on z and we solve $n-p$ normal equations for the best $\widehat{z}$ in $AQ_nz=b-Au_r$:

$$\textbf{Reduced normal equations} \qquad Q_n^{\mathrm{T}}A^{\mathrm{T}}AQ_n\widehat{z}=Q_n^{\mathrm{T}}A^{\mathrm{T}}(b-Au_r)\,. \tag{11}$$

Then $u=u_r+Q_n\widehat{z}$ minimizes $\|Au-b\|^2$ in the original problem subject to $Bu=d$.

We will solve the example $b_1 - b_2 = 8$ this way. First we keep A, b, B, and d, to construct a MATLAB code for the whole method. It might seem rather strange that only now, near the end of the book, we finally solve $Bu = d$! Linear equations are the centerpiece of this subject, and basic courses use elimination. The "reduced row echelon form" rref(B) gives an answer like $u_2 = u_1 - 8$ in textbooks. But *orthogonalization using* qr(B') gives a better answer in practice.

The usual Gram-Schmidt process converts the p columns of B^{T} into p orthonormal columns. The matrix is being factored into $B^{\mathrm{T}} = QR = (\boldsymbol{n} \text{ by } \boldsymbol{p})(\boldsymbol{p} \text{ by } \boldsymbol{p})$:

Gram-Schmidt $\quad QR = (p \text{ orthonormal columns})(\text{square triangular } R)\,. \qquad (12)$

MATLAB's qr command does more. It adds $n-p$ new orthonormal columns into Q, multiplying $n-p$ new zero rows in R. This is the $(\boldsymbol{n} \text{ by } \boldsymbol{n})(\boldsymbol{n} \text{ by } \boldsymbol{p})$ "unreduced" form. The letter r will stand for *reduced* and also for *row space*; the p columns of Q_r are a basis for the row space of B. The letter n indicates *new* and also *nullspace.*

Matlab: qr(B') is unreduced

$$B^{\mathrm{T}} = \begin{bmatrix} Q_r & Q_n \end{bmatrix} \begin{bmatrix} R \\ 0 \end{bmatrix} \begin{matrix} p & \text{rows} \\ n-p & \text{rows} \end{matrix} \qquad (13)$$

The $n-p$ orthonormal columns of Q_n solve $Bu = 0$ to give the nullspace:

Nullspace of B

$$BQ_n = \begin{bmatrix} R^{\mathrm{T}} & 0 \end{bmatrix} \begin{bmatrix} Q_r^{\mathrm{T}} \\ Q_n^{\mathrm{T}} \end{bmatrix} Q_n = \begin{bmatrix} R^{\mathrm{T}} & 0 \end{bmatrix} \begin{bmatrix} 0 \\ I \end{bmatrix} = 0\,. \qquad (14)$$

The p columns of Q_r are orthogonal to each other ($Q_r^{\mathrm{T}} Q_r = I_p$), and orthogonal to the columns of Q_n. Our particular solution u_r comes from the row space of B:

Particular solution $\quad u_r = Q_r (R^{-1})^{\mathrm{T}} d \quad$ and $\quad Bu_r = (Q_r R)^{\mathrm{T}} Q_r (R^{-1})^{\mathrm{T}} d = d\,. \qquad (15)$

This is the particular solution given by the pseudoinverse, $u_r = B^+ d = \text{pinv}(B) * d$. It is orthogonal to all u_n. Householder's qr algorithm (better than Gram-Schmidt) has produced a square orthogonal matrix $\begin{bmatrix} Q_r & Q_n \end{bmatrix}$. Those two parts Q_r and Q_n lead to very stable forms of u_r and u_n. For an incidence matrix, Q_n will find loops.

We collect the 5 steps of the nullspace method into a MATLAB code:

```
[Q, R] = qr(B');                                % square Q, triangular R has n − p zero rows
Qr = Q(1 : p, :);  Qn = Q(p+1 : n, :);  E = A * Qn;   % split Q into [Qr  Qn]
y = R(1 : p, 1 : p)'\d;  ur = Qr * y;           % particular solution ur to Bu = d
z = (E' * E)\(E' * (b − A * ur));               % best un in the nullspace is Qn * z
uopt = ur + Qn * z;                             % uopt minimizes ||Au − b||^2 with Bu = d
```

Example $(u_1 - u_2 = 8) \quad B^{\mathrm{T}} = \begin{bmatrix} 1 \\ -1 \end{bmatrix}$ factors into $QR = \begin{bmatrix} 1/\sqrt{2} & 1/\sqrt{2} \\ -1/\sqrt{2} & 1/\sqrt{2} \end{bmatrix} \begin{bmatrix} \sqrt{2} \\ 0 \end{bmatrix}$.

The particular solution from $(1, -1)$ in Q_r is $u_r = \begin{bmatrix} 1/\sqrt{2} \\ -1/\sqrt{2} \end{bmatrix} \begin{bmatrix} \sqrt{2} \end{bmatrix}^{-1} \begin{bmatrix} 8 \end{bmatrix} = \begin{bmatrix} 4 \\ -4 \end{bmatrix}$.

The nullspace of $B = \begin{bmatrix} 1 & -1 \end{bmatrix}$ contains all multiples $u_n = Q_n z = \begin{bmatrix} 1/\sqrt{2} \\ 1/\sqrt{2} \end{bmatrix} z$.

In this example the squared distance happens to be a minimum at the particular u_r. **We don't want any of u_n, and the minimizing u has $z = 0$.** This case is very important and we focus on it now. It leads to the *pseudoinverse*.

Notation In most of this book, the constraint has been $A^{\mathrm{T}}w = f$. When B is A^{T}, the first line of the code will take qr(A). We are moving from the *large α problem* with $Bu \approx d$ to the *small α problem* with $Au \approx b$.

The Pseudoinverse

Suppose A is an m by n matrix, and the vector b has m components. The equation $Au = b$ may be solvable or not. The idea of least squares is to find the best solution $\widehat{u}$ from the normal equations $A^{\mathrm{T}}A\widehat{u} = A^{\mathrm{T}}b$. But this only produces $\widehat{u}$ when $A^{\mathrm{T}}A$ is invertible. **The idea of the pseudoinverse is to find the best solution u^+, even when the columns of A are dependent and $A^{\mathrm{T}}A$ is singular**:

Two properties $u^+ = A^+b$ is the **shortest vector** that solves $A^{\mathrm{T}}Au^+ = A^{\mathrm{T}}b$.

The other solutions, which are longer than u^+, have components in the nullspace of A. We will show that u^+ *is the particular solution with no nullspace component.*

There is an n by m matrix A^+ that produces u^+ linearly from b by $\boldsymbol{u^+ = A^+b}$. This matrix A^+ is the ***pseudoinverse*** of A. In case A is square and invertible, $u = A^{-1}b$ is the best solution and A^+ is the same as A^{-1}. When a rectangular A has independent columns, $\widehat{u} = (A^{\mathrm{T}}A)^{-1}A^{\mathrm{T}}b$ is the only solution and then A^+ is $(A^{\mathrm{T}}A)^{-1}A^{\mathrm{T}}$. In case A has *dependent columns* and therefore a nonzero nullspace, those inverses break down. Then the best (shortest) $u^+ = A^+b$ is something new.

You can see u^+ and A^+ in Figure 8.6, which shows how A^+ "inverts" A, from column space back to row space. The Four Fundamental Subspaces are drawn as rectangles. (In reality they are points or lines or planes.) From left to right, A takes all vectors $u = u_{\mathsf{row}} + u_{\mathsf{null}}$ to the column space. Since u_{row} is orthogonal to u_{null}, that nullspace part increases the length of u! The best solution is $u^+ = u_{\mathsf{row}}$.

This vector won't solve $Au^+ = b$ when that is impossible. It does solve $Au^+ = p$, the projection of b onto the column space. So the error $\|e\| = \|b - p\| = \|b - Au^+\|$ is a minimum. Altogether, u^+ is in the row space (*to be shortest*) and $Au^+ = p$ (*to be closest to* b). Then u^+ minimizes e and solves $A^{\mathrm{T}}Au^+ = A^{\mathrm{T}}b$.

How is u^+ computed? The direct way is by the Singular Value Decomposition:

SVD
$$A = U\Sigma V^{\mathrm{T}} = \begin{bmatrix} U_{\mathsf{col}} & U_{\mathsf{null}} \end{bmatrix} \begin{bmatrix} \Sigma_{\mathsf{pos}} & 0 \\ 0 & 0 \end{bmatrix} \begin{bmatrix} V_{\mathsf{row}} & V_{\mathsf{null}} \end{bmatrix}^{\mathrm{T}}. \tag{16}$$

The square matrices U and V have orthonormal columns: $U^{\mathrm{T}}U = I$ and $V^{\mathrm{T}}V = I$. The first r columns U_{col} and V_{row} are bases for the column space and row space of A.

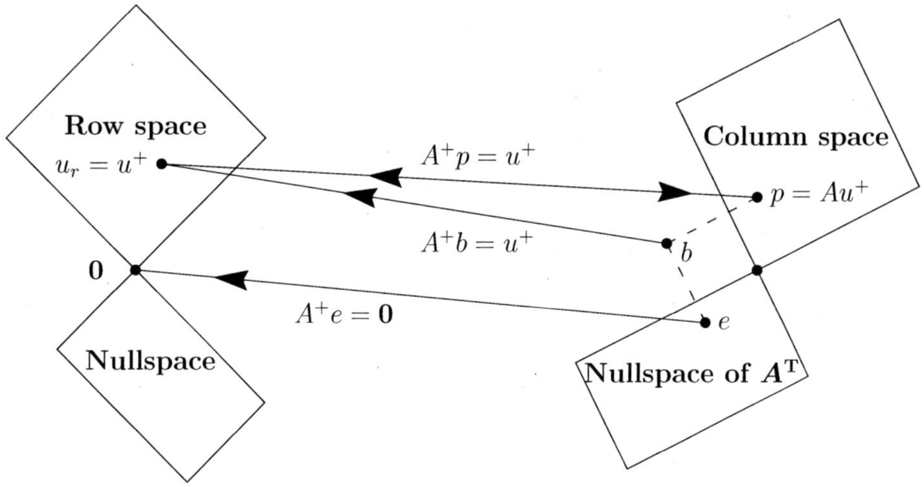

Figure 8.6: The pseudoinverse A^+ inverts A where it can, on the column space.

Those spaces have dimension r = rank of A. The other columns U_{null} and V_{null} are in the nullspaces of A^{T} and A. The pseudoinverse ignores those columns (because it has to). Inversion by A^+ is only possible from column space back to row space:

Pseudoinverse of A $\quad A^+ = (V_{\text{row}})(\Sigma_{\text{pos}})^{-1}(U_{\text{col}})^{\mathrm{T}}.$ (17)

That diagonal matrix Σ_{pos} contains the (positive!) singular values of A. When we multiply $u^+ = A^+b$, this combines the columns in V_{row}. So u^+ is in the row space.

Example $A = \begin{bmatrix} 3 & 4 \\ 3 & 4 \end{bmatrix}$ is singular. Its pseudoinverse is $A^+ = \dfrac{1}{50}\begin{bmatrix} 3 & 3 \\ 4 & 4 \end{bmatrix}$. Show why.

The row space of A with $V_{\text{row}} = (3,4)/5$ is the column space of A^+. The column space of A with $U_{\text{col}} = (3,3)/3\sqrt{2}$ is the row space of A^+. Within those spaces $A^+Av = v$ and $AA^+u = u$. **We find A^+ from the SVD of A**, noticing $AA^{\mathrm{T}} = \begin{bmatrix} 25 & 25 \\ 25 & 25 \end{bmatrix}$ with eigenvalue $\lambda = \sigma^2 = 50$:

$$\boldsymbol{A = U\Sigma V^{\mathrm{T}}} \qquad \begin{bmatrix} 3 & 4 \\ 3 & 4 \end{bmatrix} = \frac{\begin{bmatrix} 1 & 1 \\ 1 & -1 \end{bmatrix}}{\sqrt{2}} \begin{bmatrix} \sqrt{50} & 0 \\ 0 & 0 \end{bmatrix} \frac{\begin{bmatrix} 3 & 4 \\ 4 & -3 \end{bmatrix}^{\mathrm{T}}}{\sqrt{25}} \quad \text{has } \Sigma_{\text{pos}} = \left[\sqrt{50}\right]$$

$$\boldsymbol{A^+ = V_{\text{row}}\Sigma_{\text{pos}}^{-1}U_{\text{col}}^{\mathrm{T}}} \qquad \frac{1}{\sqrt{25}}\begin{bmatrix} 3 \\ 4 \end{bmatrix}\left[\frac{1}{\sqrt{50}}\right]\begin{bmatrix} 1 \\ 1 \end{bmatrix}^{\mathrm{T}}\frac{1}{\sqrt{2}} = \frac{1}{50}\begin{bmatrix} 3 & 3 \\ 4 & 4 \end{bmatrix} = A^+$$

Here A and A^+ have the same rank $r = 1$. **We could have written $A^+ = V\Sigma^+U^{\mathrm{T}}$.** The m by n matrix Σ has Σ_{pos} on its diagonal, and the n by m matrix Σ^+ has $(\Sigma_{\text{pos}})^{-1}$. Both $\Sigma\Sigma^+$ and $\Sigma^+\Sigma$ have r diagonal ones (and then zeros to kill U_{null} and V_{null}).

Regularization Produces u^+

The SVD is great, but it can be expensive to compute. Most likely our working code is written to solve the normal equations. Since $A^{\mathrm{T}}A$ may be singular (that is our problem here), we add on a small multiple αI:

Tychonov Regularization Minimize $\|Au - b\|^2 + \alpha\|u\|^2$ by $(A^{\mathrm{T}}A + \alpha I)\,\widehat{u}_\alpha = A^{\mathrm{T}}b$. (18)

This is our two-square problem with the simple choice $B = I$ and $d = 0$. The regularizing term is just $\alpha\|u\|^2$. By minimizing, we are looking for a short solution $\widehat{u}_\alpha$. And by making α small, we give first importance to minimizing $\|Au - b\|^2$. You will not be surprised by the limit of $\widehat{u}_\alpha$ as the penalty parameter $\alpha \to 0$:

$$(A^{\mathrm{T}}A + \alpha I)^{-1}A^{\mathrm{T}} \textit{ approaches } A^+ \textit{ and } \widehat{u}_\alpha \textit{ approaches } u^+. \tag{19}$$

The easiest proof uses the SVD. But the regularization to $(A^{\mathrm{T}}A + \alpha I)^{-1}$ avoids computing that SVD. Of course we don't get u^+ exactly, with small $\alpha > 0$. And we must decide on the number α. In practice there is uncertainty (noise) in the vector b. The regularized $\widehat{u}_\alpha$ may be just as reliable as u^+, and easier to compute. The noise level in b often indicates a suitable α (see below).

Working with $(A^{\mathrm{T}}A + \alpha I)^{-1}A^{\mathrm{T}}$ produces small new singular values to replace diagonal zeros in the SVD formula (16). Notice how $\sigma/(\sigma^2+\alpha)$ approaches $1/\sigma$ when this is positive, and stays zero when σ is zero. That is the crucial point.

Key Remark We are now choosing a small α. The earlier example with $u_1 - u_2 = 8$ had large α. It is exactly the same problem! *We just exchanged A, b with B, d.* The large α example had $A = I$ and $b = 0$. The small α problem has $B = I$ and $d = 0$:

Large	Minimizing	$\|u\|^2 + \alpha\|Bu - d\|^2$	as $\alpha \to \infty$	gave	$\widehat{u}_\infty = B^+d$
Small	Minimizing	$\|Au - b\|^2 + \alpha\|u\|^2$	as $\alpha \to 0$	gives	$\widehat{u}_0 = A^+b$

In both cases, $\|u\|^2$ regularizes the problem when $B^{\mathrm{T}}B$ (large α) or $A^{\mathrm{T}}A$ (small α) is singular (or close). Our example with $u_1 - u_2 = 8$ had $B = [\,1 \ \ -1\,]$. The best vector $u = (4, -4)$ was in the row space of B. Now the matrix is A and the factor α is small, but no real change. Multiplying A^+ times 8 gives the same $u^+ = (4, -4)$:

$$A = [\,1 \ \ -1\,] \quad \textbf{has pseudoinverse} \quad A^+ = \begin{bmatrix} 1/2 \\ -1/2 \end{bmatrix} \tag{20}$$

The row space of A is the column space of A^+. Every vector v in that space has $A^+Av = v$. The pseudoinverse A^+ inverts A where it can:

$$A^+Av = \begin{bmatrix} 1/2 \\ -1/2 \end{bmatrix} [\,1 \ \ -1\,] \begin{bmatrix} c \\ -c \end{bmatrix} = \begin{bmatrix} c \\ -c \end{bmatrix} \quad \text{and} \quad AA^+ = [\,1 \ \ -1\,] \begin{bmatrix} 1/2 \\ -1/2 \end{bmatrix} = 1. \tag{21}$$

Tychonov Regularization

In reality, we are not given the correct vector b. There is noise in the measurement. When A is ill-conditioned and $\alpha = 0$, that error e will be greatly amplified in the output $\widehat{u}_0^e$ from least squares. The role of αI is to stabilize the least squares solution $\widehat{u}_\alpha^e$, which uses the noisy data $b - e$. We compensate for e by a good choice of α.

If α is too small, the error will still grow with A^{-1}. If α is too large, the excessive smoothing will lose key features of the true $\widehat{u}_0^0$ (coming from $\alpha = 0$ with the true b). *These paragraphs give a guide to α, based on the expected size of e.*

When we separate $\widehat{u}_0^0 - \widehat{u}_\alpha^e$ into $\widehat{u}_0^0 - \widehat{u}_\alpha^0 + \widehat{u}_\alpha^0 - \widehat{u}_\alpha^e$, we get bounds for the two pieces:

Error bounds $$\|\widehat{u}_0^0 - \widehat{u}_\alpha^0\| \le C\alpha\|b\| \qquad \|\widehat{u}_\alpha^0 - \widehat{u}_\alpha^e\| \le \frac{\|e\|}{2\sqrt{\alpha}} \tag{22}$$

We want the sum of those two parts to be small. Reducing Tychonov's penalty factor α brings us closer to exact least squares, in the first error. But the second error $\|e\|/2\sqrt{\alpha}$ will grow as $\alpha \to 0$. Based on this limited information, we could simply choose α to equalize the two parts of the overall error, and add them:

Possible choice of α $$\alpha = \left(\frac{\|e\|}{2C\|b\|}\right)^{2/3} \quad \text{gives error} = \|\widehat{u}_0^0 - \widehat{u}_\alpha^e\| \le (2C\|b\|\,\|e\|^2)^{1/3}. \tag{23}$$

This rule suggests that we know more than we really do. Problem 11 will take a critical look at the error bound. I think the key guidance is the exponent in $\|e\|^{2/3}$, and this 2/3 rule for α is often confirmed in model problems. As far as we can see, it usually works in practice. We now look at the theory behind (22).

The two bounds in (22) can be quickly proved when A is a scalar s (1 by 1). The exact and the penalized normal equations have $A^{\mathrm{T}}A = s^2$:

Without noise $$s^2\,\widehat{u}_0^0 = sb \quad \text{and} \quad (s^2 + \alpha)\,\widehat{u}_\alpha^0 = sb. \tag{24}$$

The difference in the two solutions is the first piece of the error:

$$\widehat{u}_0^0 - \widehat{u}_\alpha^0 = \left(\frac{b}{s} - \frac{s\,b}{s^2 + \alpha}\right)b = \frac{\alpha}{s(s^2 + \alpha)}\,b \le C\,\alpha\,b. \tag{25}$$

This error is $O(\alpha)$ as required in (22). The constant C depends dangerously on $1/s^3$.

Now compare $\widehat{u}_\alpha^0$ with $\widehat{u}_\alpha^e$, by subtracting normal equations with αI included:

$$(s^2+\alpha)\widehat{u}_\alpha^0 = sb \quad \text{and} \quad (s^2+\alpha)\widehat{u}_\alpha^e = s(b-e) \quad \text{give} \quad \boldsymbol{(s^2+\alpha)(\widehat{u}_\alpha^0 - \widehat{u}_\alpha^e) = se}. \tag{26}$$

The second inequality in (22) says that the ratio $s/(s^2 + \alpha)$ is bounded by $1/2\sqrt{\alpha}$. Maximizing that ratio over s, the choice $s = \sqrt{\alpha}$ does give the bound $\sqrt{\alpha}/(\alpha + \alpha)$. Finding that maximum ratio is even quicker without calculus:

$$(s - \sqrt{\alpha})^2 \ge 0 \quad \text{gives} \quad s^2 + \alpha \ge 2s\sqrt{\alpha} \quad \text{and then} \quad \frac{s}{s^2 + \alpha} \le \frac{1}{2\sqrt{\alpha}}. \tag{27}$$

For the matrix case, the SVD produces orthonormal bases $u_1, u_2, \ldots$ and $v_1, v_2, \ldots$ with $\boldsymbol{Av_j = \sigma_j u_j}$ **and** $\boldsymbol{A^{\mathrm{T}} u_j = \sigma_j v_j}$. The SVD diagonalizes A.

Expand the right sides b and e in the basis of u's. Then find the coefficients of each $\widehat{u}$ in the basis of v's. When the input is $b = B_1 u_1 + B_2 u_2 + \cdots$ and the output is $\widehat{u}_\alpha^0 = U_1 v_1 + U_2 v_2 + \cdots$, we just match the terms:

$$\textbf{Term by term} \quad (A^{\mathrm{T}}A + \alpha I)U_j v_j = A^{\mathrm{T}} B_j u_j \quad \text{gives} \quad (\sigma_j^2 + \alpha)U_j = \sigma_j B_j\,. \tag{28}$$

The output coefficient is $U_j = \sigma_j B_j/(\sigma_j^2 + \alpha)$, exactly like (24) with $s = \sigma_j$. Going coefficient by coefficient ($j = 1, 2, \ldots$), the series expansions copy (25) and (26):

$$\widehat{u}_0^0 - \widehat{u}_\alpha^0 = \sum_{j=1}^{\infty} \frac{\alpha\, B_j}{s_j(s_j^2 + \alpha)}\, v_j \quad \text{and} \quad \widehat{u}_\alpha^0 - \widehat{u}_\alpha^e = \sum_{j=1}^{\infty} \frac{s_j\, E_j}{s_j^2 + \alpha}\, v_j\,. \tag{29}$$

Then the norms come from sums of squares, because the v_j are orthonormal:

$$\|\widehat{u}_0^0 - \widehat{u}_\alpha^0\|^2 = \sum \left(\frac{\alpha B_j}{s_j(s_j^2 + \alpha)}\right)^2 \quad \text{and} \quad \|\widehat{u}_\alpha^0 - \widehat{u}_\alpha^e\|^2 = \sum \left(\frac{s_j E_j}{s_j^2 + \alpha}\right)^2. \tag{30}$$

The u's are orthonormal, so $\sum |B_j|^2 = \|b\|^2$ and $\sum |E_j|^2 = \|e\|^2$. This proves (22):

$$\textbf{The two pieces} \quad \|\widehat{u}_0^0 - \widehat{u}_\alpha^0\| \le \frac{\alpha}{s_{\min}{}^3}\, \|b\| \quad \text{and} \quad \|\widehat{u}_\alpha^0 - \widehat{u}_\alpha^e\| \le \frac{\|e\|}{2\sqrt{\alpha}}\,. \tag{31}$$

Learning Gradients from Samples

Learning theory is an important combination of mathematics and statistics, often in high dimensions. Usually regularization is needed, to produce a smooth function from inaccurate samples. Taking mathematical biology as a rich source of fascinating problems, we identify two questions in gene expression:

1. **Classification** Is tissue benign or not? Is treatment successful or not? Determine which class (out of a finite number, like two) best fits the data.

2. **Estimation of derivatives** The state of the cell is measured by the expression levels x_i of thousands of genes. An unknown function $F(x_1, \ldots, x_N)$ describes toxicity. If we can estimate derivatives $F_i' = \partial F/\partial x_i$, we can decide which genes are important. We also estimate covariance, since genes are far from independent.

For classifying types of leukemia, a well-studied data set contains expression levels of $N = 7129$ genes. We use part of the data as a *training set*, to build a classification model (often based on a Support Vector Machine). The rest of the data becomes a *test set*, to judge whether the model is valid. Turning to functions that show covariance (cooperation or not between genes), we are in N dimensions with very few samples.

Probably the data lies close to a "manifold" of much lower dimension, which we don't know. This hidden truth gives our algorithms a chance to succeed, when a strong dependence on 7129 variables would leave us with a hopeless quest.

You will recognize that I cannot do full justice here, either to development of algorithms or to statistics of hypothesis testing. Derivatives can be estimated using Tychonov regularization (a penalty term of size α, to add stability):

Learning F' from b

$$\text{Minimize} \quad \sum_{i,j=1}^{m} w_{ij}\left(b_i - b_j - F_i'(x_j - x_i)\right)^2 + \alpha \|F'\|^2. \tag{32}$$

The measurements b_i are $F(x_i)$. The unknowns F_i' are the slopes in a linear approximation to F, when the Taylor series stops before the second degree terms. This approximation becomes poor when x_j is far from x_i, so the weight $w_{ij} = e^{-(x_j - x_i)^2/2\sigma^2}$ is chosen small in that case.

The new question is the penalty term $\alpha\|F'\|^2$. The matrix problems in this section used the discrete norm $\|F'\|^2 = (F_1')^2 + \cdots + (F_N')^2$. **But now we are learning a function $F(x_1, \ldots, x_N)$. We want the discrete norm to be bounded by the function norm.** The function spaces that allow this link between discrete and continuous have the long name "*reproducing kernel Hilbert spaces*" or RKHS.

Example 1 For smoothing by cubic splines in one dimension, the norm uses d^2f/dx^2:

Spline smoothing

$$\text{Minimize} \quad \frac{1}{m}\sum (b_i - f(x_i))^2 + \alpha \int (f''(x))^2\, dx. \tag{33}$$

Notice the big difference from interpolation, when the first term is forced to be zero. Smoothing by the α term allows for noise in the measurements b_i. We find a spline that compromises between fitting perfectly and staying smooth. If there is a bad outlier b_i, the function cannot go out to match it without a big penalty.

This penalty norm dominates discrete values $f(x_i)$ as an RKHS requires. Wahba [165] explains how spline smoothing $\int (f''(x))^2\, dx$ is also a Bayes estimator in statistics—the basis functions in the RKHS become Gaussian random variables.

Example 2 Change the penalty term to $\alpha \int (f(x))^2\, dx$. Now $f(x)$ can go quickly out and back to reach an outlier b_i, without a large penalty. The integral can be small even when $f(x)$ is very large at a point. Thus the usual Hilbert space L^2 is not an RKHS. Higher derivatives in the penalty would give higher degree splines as minimizers.

For the application to genes in $N = 7129$ dimensions, splines are not practical. We could use the SVD to control the linear algebra (sometimes at significant cost). Or we could choose *radial basis functions* that are better adapted to fit scattered data in high dimensions. Here is a brief description.

Radial Basis Functions

B-splines give a convenient basis in one dimension. They are formed by connecting a few simple pieces (polynomials that fit together smoothly at nodes). Interpolating n sample values by a cubic spline $S(x)$ gives the function that minimizes the integral of $(S''(x))^2$. But as the dimension d increases, simple constructions can go wrong. Tensor product splines $S = S_1(x_1)S_2(x_2)\cdots S_d(x_d)$ become an expensive basis and we look for functions with a simpler dependence on many variables $x_1, \ldots, x_d$.

A function $F(|x - x^0|)$ is a ***radial basis function*** when its value depends on the distance $r = |x - x^0|$ from a center point $x^0 = (x_1^0, \ldots, x_d^0)$ in d-dimensional space. Normally we choose a single function F and a lot of center points $x^{(1)}, x^{(2)}, \ldots$:

Radial basis $\quad F(x) = c_1 F(|x - x^{(1)}|) + c_2 F(|x - x^{(2)}|) + \cdots$

Those basis functions can overlap. Each function decays quickly. Three particular radial basis functions have been the favorites so far:

1. **Thin-plate splines** $\boldsymbol{F(r) = r^2 \log r}$

2. **Multiquadrics** $\boldsymbol{(c > 0)}$ $\boldsymbol{F(r) = \sqrt{r^2 + c^2}}$

3. **Gaussians** $\boldsymbol{(c > 0)}$ $\boldsymbol{F(r) = e^{-cr^2}}$

We won't even touch the question of selecting the best $F(r)$.

Estimating Derivatives from Discrete Data

Numerical differentiation is so important (it was the first step in the book) that we add another approach. It is based on differences of equally spaced data. Start with a centered difference, ***when the exact values u_i are contaminated by errors e_i***:

$$\frac{(u_{i+1} + e_{i+1}) - (u_{i-1} + e_{i-1})}{2\Delta x} = \frac{du}{dx} + \frac{e_{i+1} - e_{i+1}}{2\Delta x} + \frac{1}{6}(\Delta x)^2 \frac{d^3u}{dx^3} + \cdots \tag{34}$$

As $\Delta x \to 0$, two different things happen. Truncation error decreases with $(\Delta x)^2$. But the e's are amplified by $1/\Delta x$. We can expect independent errors e_i with mean zero and variance σ^2. The variance of that noise term $\Delta_0 e/2\Delta x$ gets large:

$$\textbf{Variance} \quad \mathrm{E}\left[\frac{e_{i+1}^2 - 2e_{i-1}e_{i+1} + e_{i-1}^2}{4(\Delta x)^2}\right] = \frac{\sigma^2 + 0 + \sigma^2}{4(\Delta x)^2} = \frac{\sigma^2}{2(\Delta x)^2}. \tag{35}$$

The key question is: Can we use more data (more of the u's, bringing more of the e's) to improve the approximation of du/dx? On the bad side, wider Δx intervals will increase the truncation error. On the good side, ***an average of e's has a smaller variance than a single e.***

We average the r differences $\Delta_0 u/2\Delta x$ for $\Delta x = h, \ldots, jh, \ldots, rh$:

$$\frac{1}{r}\sum_{j=1}^{r}\frac{(u_{i+j}+e_{i+j})-(u_{i-j}+e_{i-j})}{2jh}=\frac{du}{dx}+\sum\frac{\boldsymbol{e_{i+j}-e_{i-j}}}{\boldsymbol{2rjh}}+\sum\frac{\boldsymbol{(jh)^2}}{\boldsymbol{6r}}\frac{\boldsymbol{d^3u}}{\boldsymbol{dx^3}}+\cdots \quad (36)$$

Since $1^2+\cdots+j^2+\cdots+r^2$ is like $\int x^2\,dx$, that final sum grows like $r^3/3$. Multiplying by $h^2/6r$ gives a truncation error close to $r^2h^2u'''/18$. The factor r^2 is the price for widening the interval, but notice $1/r$ in the noise term.

The payoff is a big reduction of the error variance, with $\Delta x = jh$ in (35):

Variance of average
Independent errors
$$\mathrm{E}\left[\left(\sum\frac{e_{i+j}-e_{i-j}}{2rjh}\right)^2\right]=\sum_{j=1}^{r}\frac{\sigma^2}{2r^2(jh)^2}\approx\frac{\sigma^2}{2r^3h^2}\,. \quad (37)$$

In this case the sum $1/1^2+\cdots+1/j^2+\cdots+1/r^2$ is like $\int dx/x^2 = 1/r$. So we have r^2h^2 in the truncation error and $1/r^3h^2$ in the variance. Both can go to zero!

$$\text{If } r=\left(\frac{1}{h}\right)^{\beta} \text{ with } \frac{2}{3}<\beta<1 \text{ then } \boldsymbol{r^2h^2=h^{2-2\beta}\to 0} \text{ and } \frac{\boldsymbol{1}}{\boldsymbol{r^3h^2}}=\boldsymbol{h^{3\beta-2}\to 0}. \quad (38)$$

Test by experiment We add random errors e_i to the exact values of $u(x)=x^3$ at intervals of $h=\frac{1}{8}$. Then $u'''=6=$ constant in the truncation error. We run the test 100 times for each choice of r, the number of centered differences that are averaged.

The first test takes $r=1$ (a normal centered difference). The theory suggests a value between $r=h^{-2/3}=4$ and $r=h^{-1}=8$. We try $r=6$ and report the results on the website.

Readers might like to experiment with second derivatives, and *weighted averages.* For a partial derivative $\partial u/\partial x$, the differences are $u_{i+j,k}-u_{i-j,k}$. You can greatly improve the accuracy (lower the variance) by averaging also over nearby values of k. So the "curse of dimensionality" that afflicts integrals in many dimensions is overturned for derivatives, using this Anderssen-de Hoog averaging.

The whole idea is that ***averages are smoother***. ***Their variances are lower.***

Problem Set 8.2

Problems 1-3 minimize $\|Au-b\|^2$ with $Bu=d$, in three ways (by hand).

$$A=\begin{bmatrix}1&0\\0&2\end{bmatrix}\qquad b=\begin{bmatrix}0\\0\end{bmatrix}\qquad B=\begin{bmatrix}1&3\end{bmatrix}\quad d=20.$$

1 (**Large penalty**) Minimize $\|Au-b\|^2+\alpha\|Bu-d\|^2$. This will involve $A^{\mathrm{T}}A+\alpha B^{\mathrm{T}}B$ and produce a minimizer u_α. Let $\alpha\to\infty$ to find u_∞.

2 (**Lagrange multiplier w**) Solve three equations $\partial L/\partial u=0$ and $\partial L/\partial w=0$ for u_1, u_2, w, with the Lagrangian $L=\frac{1}{2}\|Au-b\|^2+w(u_1+3u_2-20)$.

3 (**Nullspace method**) Find the complete solution $u = u_r + u_n$ to $B_u = d$, which is $u_1 + 3u_2 = 20$. Here u_r in the row space is a particular multiple of (1, 3) and u_n is any multiple $z\,(3, -1)$. Choose z to minimize $\|Au - b\|^2$, with $u = u_r + z\,(3, -1)$.

Problems 4-6 minimize $\|u\|^2 = u_1^2 + \cdots + u_5^2$ with four constraints $u_{i+1} - u_i = 1$. Thus $A = I,\ b = 0,\ B^{\mathrm{T}}B = K_4,\ d = (1, 1, 1, 1)$.

4 (**Large penalty**) Equation (1) is $(I + \alpha K_4)\,u = \alpha(-1, 0, 0, 1)$. Solve by MATLAB or Octave for increasing α = 1,10,100,1000. How many correct digits of u for those α?

5 (**Lagrange multiplier**) Solve the saddle point problem in equation (8). The 4 by 5 matrix $B = \Delta_+$ has $B_{ii} = -1$ and $B_{i,i+1} = 1$.

6 (**Nullspace method**) Use the code to compute uopt. Explain Q_r and Q_n.

7 Find the pseudoinverse $B^+ = \mathsf{pinv}(B)$ of the forward difference matrix in Problem 5. Compute BB^+ and B^+B.

8 Find the pseudoinverse $C^+ = \mathsf{pinv}(C)$ of the 3 by 3 circulant matrix $C = \mathsf{toeplitz}([2 - 1 - 1])$. Also compute $\mathsf{svd}(C)$ as in (16) and verify formula (17) for C^+.

9 Compute $\Delta^+ = \mathsf{pinv}(\Delta)$ for the 3 by 3 centered difference matrix Δ, with second row $(-1, 0, 1)/2$. What are the two singular values of Δ and why only two?

10 The linear position vector $u = 1:10$ would reasonably have constant velocity vector $v = \mathsf{ones(10)}/\Delta t$. Perturb u by random noise $e = \mathsf{rand(1,10)/100}$. Test formula (36) that averages r differences of $u - e$ to estimate the velocities. Take $h = \Delta t = 0.1$ and 0.01, and experiment with different r.

11 The error bound (23) still includes $1/\sigma_{\mathsf{min}}$ if $C = 1/\sigma^3_{\mathsf{min}}$ in (25). That large $\|A^{-1}\| = 1/\sigma_{\mathsf{min}}$ was our reason for regularizing by α in the first place. Probably the actual noise e is less amplified than the worst-case e. Experiment with $A = K_{10}$, $b = \mathsf{ones}(10, 1)$, $e = E * \mathsf{randn(10,1)}$, and different α (depending on E) to come closest to the exact $\widehat{u}_0^0 = K^{-1}b$.

8.3 CALCULUS OF VARIATIONS

One theme of this book is the relation of equations to minimum principles. ***To minimize P is to solve*** $P' = 0$. For a quadratic $P(u) = \frac{1}{2}u^{\mathrm{T}}Ku - u^{\mathrm{T}}f$, there is no difficulty in reaching $P' = Ku - f = 0$. In a continuous problem, the "derivative" of P is not so easy to find. The unknown $u(x)$ or $u(x, y)$ is now a function.

When $P(u)$ is an integral, its derivative $\delta P/\delta u$ is called the *first variation.* ***The "Euler-Lagrange equation"*** $\boldsymbol{\delta P/\delta u = 0}$ ***has a weak form and strong form.*** For an elastic bar, P is the integral of $\frac{1}{2}c(u'(x))^2 - f(x)u(x)$. Then the equation $\delta P/\delta u = 0$ is linear and the problem will have boundary conditions:

Weak form for every $v(x)$	$\int cu'v'\,dx = \int fv\,dx$	**Strong form at every point**	$-(cu')' = f(x)$.

Our goal in this section is to get beyond this first example of weak and strong.

The idea should be simple and it is: ***Perturb*** $\boldsymbol{u(x)}$ ***by a test function*** $\boldsymbol{v(x)}$. Comparing $P(u)$ with $P(u + v)$, the linear term in the difference yields $\delta P/\delta u$. *This linear term must be zero for every admissible* v *(weak form).* That program carries ordinary calculus into the calculus of variations. We do it in several steps:

1. One-dimensional problems $P(u) = \int F(u, u')\,dx$, not necessarily quadratic
2. Constraints with their Lagrange multipliers
3. Two-dimensional problems $P(u) = \iint F(u, u_x, u_y)\,dx\,dy$
4. Time-dependent equations in which $u' = du/dt$.

At each step the examples will be as familiar (and famous) as possible. In two dimensions that means Laplace's equation, and minimal surfaces in the nonlinear case. In time-dependent problems it means Newton's Law, and relativity in the nonlinear case. In one dimension we rediscover the straight line and the circle.

This section is also the opening to ***control theory***—a modern part of the calculus of variations. Its constraints are differential equations, and Pontryagin's maximum principle yields solutions. That is a whole world of good mathematics.

To go from strong form to weak form, ***multiply by*** v ***and integrate.*** For matrices the strong form is $\boldsymbol{A^{\mathrm{T}}CAu = f}$. The weak form is $\boldsymbol{v^{\mathrm{T}}A^{\mathrm{T}}CAu = v^{\mathrm{T}}f}$ for all v.

Notation We will soon write a quadratic $P(u)$ as $\frac{1}{2}\,a(u, u) - \ell(u)$. The weak form will be $\boldsymbol{a(u, v) = \ell(v)}$. For functions with $Au = u'$, this is $\boldsymbol{\int cu'v'\,dx = \int fv\,dx}$.

One-dimensional Problems

The basic problem is to minimize $P(u)$ with a boundary condition at each end:

One-dimensional $$P(u) = \int_0^1 F(u, u')\, dx \text{ with } u(0) = a \text{ and } u(1) = b.$$

The best u defeats every other candidate $u+v$ that satisfies these boundary conditions. Then $(u+v)(0) = a$ and $(u+v)(1) = b$ require that $v(0) = v(1) = 0$. For small v and v', the correction terms come from $\partial F/\partial u$ and $\partial F/\partial u'$. They don't involve v^2:

Inside the integral $$F(u+v, u'+v') = F(u, u') + v\frac{\partial F}{\partial u} + v'\frac{\partial F}{\partial u'} + \cdots$$

After integrating $$P(u+v) = P(u) + \int_0^1 \left(v\frac{\partial F}{\partial u} + v'\frac{\partial F}{\partial u'}\right) dx + \cdots$$

That integrated term is the "first variation" of P. We have already reached $\delta P/\delta u$:

First variation $$\frac{\delta P}{\delta u} = \int_0^1 \left(v\frac{\partial F}{\partial u} + v'\frac{\partial F}{\partial u'}\right) dx = 0 \;\; \textbf{\textit{for every v}}. \tag{1}$$

This is the equation for u. The derivative of P in each direction v must be zero. Otherwise we can make $\delta P/\delta u$ negative, which would mean $P(u+v) < P(u)$: no good.

The weak form comes from integrating $v'(\partial F/\partial u')$ by parts to get $-v(\partial F/\partial u')'$:

Weak form $$\int_0^1 v(x)\left(\frac{\partial F}{\partial u} - \frac{d}{dx}\left(\frac{\partial F}{\partial u'}\right)\right) dx + \left[v\frac{\partial F}{\partial u'}\right]_0^1 = 0. \tag{2}$$

The boundary term vanishes because $v(0) = v(1) = 0$. To guarantee zero for *every* $v(x)$ in the integral, the function multiplying v must be zero (**strong form**):

Euler-Lagrange equation for u $$\frac{\partial F}{\partial u} - \frac{d}{dx}\left(\frac{\partial F}{\partial u'}\right) = 0. \tag{3}$$

Example 1 Find the shortest path $u(x)$ between $(0, a)$ and $(1, b)$: $u(0) = a$ and $u(1) = b$. By Pythagoras, $\sqrt{(dx)^2 + (du)^2}$ is a short step on the path. So $P(u') = \int \sqrt{1 + (u')^2}\, dx$ is the length of the path between the points. This square root $F(u')$ depends only on u' and $\partial F/\partial u = 0$. The derivative $\partial F/\partial u'$ brings the square root into the denominator:

First variation gives weak form $$\frac{\delta P}{\delta u} = \int_0^1 v'\frac{u'}{\sqrt{1+(u')^2}}\, dx = -\int_0^1 v(x)\frac{d}{dx}\left(\frac{u'}{\sqrt{1+(u')^2}}\right) dx = 0. \tag{4}$$

The strong form forces $\partial F/\partial u'$ to be constant. The function multiplying v is zero:

Euler-Lagrange $$-\frac{d}{dx}\left(\frac{\partial F}{\partial u'}\right) = 0 \text{ or } \frac{\partial F}{\partial u'} = \frac{u'}{\sqrt{1+(u')^2}} = c. \tag{5}$$

That integration is always possible when F depends only on u' and not on u. The strong form is simplified to $\partial F/\partial u' = c$. Squaring both sides, *$u$ is linear*:

$$(u')^2 = c^2(1+(u')^2) \quad \text{and} \quad u' = \frac{c}{\sqrt{1-c^2}} \quad \text{and} \quad u = \frac{c}{\sqrt{1-c^2}}x + d\,. \tag{6}$$

The constants c and d are chosen to match $u(0)=a$ and $u(1)=b$. *The shortest curve connecting two points is a straight line.* No surprise! The length $P(u)$ is a minimum, not a maximum or a saddle point, because the second derivative F'' is positive.

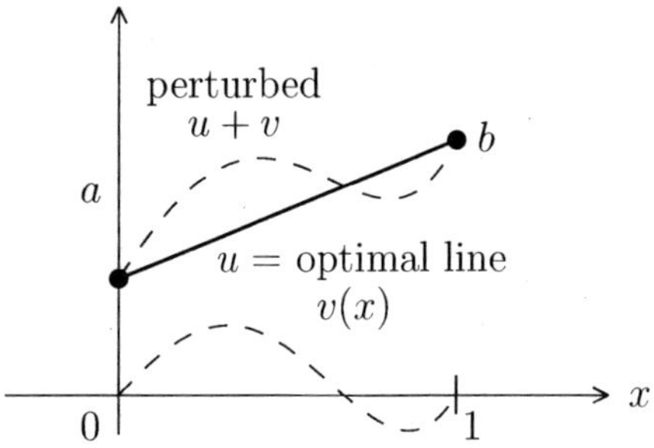

any $v(x)$ adds length

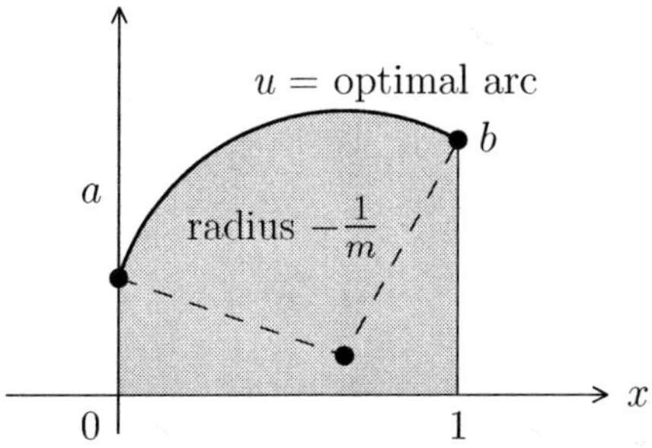

area below arc is A

Figure 8.7: Shortest paths from a to b: straight line and circular arc (constrained).

Constrained Problems

Suppose we cannot go in a straight line because of a constraint. When the constraint is $\int u(x)\,dx = A$, we look for ***the shortest curve that has area A below it***:

$$\text{Minimize} \quad P(u) = \int_0^1 \sqrt{1+(u')^2}\,dx \quad \text{with} \quad u(0)=a,\ u(1)=b,\ \int_0^1 u(x)\,dx = A\,.$$

The area constraint is built into P by a *Lagrange multiplier.* That multiplier m is a number and not a function, because there is one overall constraint rather than a constraint at every point. The Lagrangian L adds in $m(\int u\,dx - A)$:

Lagrangian $\quad L(u,m) = P + (\text{multiplier})(\text{constraint}) = \int (F+mu)\,dx - mA\,.$

Example 2 The equation $\delta L/\delta u = 0$ is exactly like $\delta P/\delta u = 0$ in (3), plus m:

$$\frac{\partial(F+mu)}{\partial u} - \frac{d}{dx}\left[\frac{\partial(F+mu)}{\partial u'}\right] = m - \frac{d}{dx}\frac{u'}{\sqrt{1+(u')^2}} = 0\,. \tag{7}$$

Again this equation is favorable enough to be integrated:

$$mx - \frac{u'}{\sqrt{1+(u')^2}} = c \quad \text{which gives} \quad u' = \frac{mx-c}{\sqrt{1-(mx-c)^2}}\,.$$

After one more integration we reach the equation of a circle in the x-u plane:

$$u(x) = \frac{-1}{m}\sqrt{1-(mx-c)^2} + d \quad \text{and} \quad (mx-c)^2 + (mu-d)^2 = 1. \tag{8}$$

The shortest path is a circular arc. It goes high enough to enclose area A. The three numbers m, c, d are determined by the conditions $u(0) = a, u(1) = b$, and $\int u\,dx = A$. The arc is drawn in Figure 8.7 (and m is negative).

We now summarize the one-dimensional case, allowing F to depend also on u''. That introduces v'' into the weak form. Two integrations by parts will recover v and reach the Euler-Lagrange equation. When F involves a varying coefficient $c(x)$, the form of the equation does not change, because it is u and not x that is perturbed.

The first variation of $\boldsymbol{P(u) = \int_0^1 F(u, u', u'', x)\,dx}$ is zero at a minimum:

Weak form $$\frac{\delta P}{\delta u} = \int_0^1 \left(v\frac{\partial F}{\partial u} + v'\frac{\partial F}{\partial u'} + v''\frac{\partial F}{\partial u''} \right) dx = 0 \text{ for all } v.$$

The Euler-Lagrange equation from integration by parts determines $\boldsymbol{u(x)}$:

Strong form $$\frac{\partial F}{\partial u} - \frac{d}{dx}\left(\frac{\partial F}{\partial u'}\right) + \frac{d^2}{dx^2}\left(\frac{\partial F}{\partial u''}\right) = 0.$$

Constraints on $\boldsymbol{u}$ bring Lagrange multipliers and saddle points as $\boldsymbol{L}$ replaces P.

Applications are everywhere, and we mention one (of many) in sports. What angle is optimal in shooting a basketball? The force of the shot depends on the launch angle—a line drive or a sky hook needs the most push. The force is minimized at 45° if the ball leaves your hand ten feet up; for shorter people the angle is about 50°. What is interesting is that the same angle solves a second optimization problem: to have the largest margin of error and still go through the hoop.

The best strategy has $P' = 0$ in basketball (one shot) and $\delta P/\delta u = 0$ in track—where the strategy to minimize the time $P(u)$ has been analyzed for every distance.

Two-dimensional Problems

In two dimensions the principle is the same. The starting point is a quadratic $P(u)$, without constraints, representing the potential energy over a plane region S:

Minimize $$P(u) = \iint_S \left[\frac{c}{2}\left(\frac{\partial u}{\partial x}\right)^2 + \frac{c}{2}\left(\frac{\partial u}{\partial y}\right)^2 - f(x,y)\,u(x,y) \right] dx\,dy.$$

If this energy has its minimum at $u(x,y)$, then $P(u+v) \geq P(u)$ for every $v(x,y)$. We mentally substitute $u+v$ in place of u, and look for the term that is *linear in* v. That term is the first variation $\delta P/\delta u$, which must be zero for every $v(x,y)$:

Weak form **Linear in v**
$$\frac{\delta P}{\delta u} = \iint \left[c\,\frac{\partial u}{\partial x}\frac{\partial v}{\partial x} + c\,\frac{\partial u}{\partial y}\frac{\partial v}{\partial y} - fv \right] dx\,dy = 0\,. \tag{9}$$

This is the **equation of virtual work**. It holds for all admissible functions $v(x,y)$, and it is the weak form of Euler-Lagrange. The strong form requires as always an integration by parts (Green's formula), in which the boundary conditions take care of the boundary terms. Inside S, that integration moves derivatives away from $v(x,y)$:

Integrate by parts
$$\iint_S \left[-\frac{\partial}{\partial x}\left(c\,\frac{\partial u}{\partial x}\right) - \frac{\partial}{\partial y}\left(c\,\frac{\partial u}{\partial y}\right) - f \right] v(x,y)\,dx\,dy = 0\,. \tag{10}$$

Now the strong form appears. This integral is zero for every $v(x,y)$. By the calculus of variations, the term in brackets is forced to be zero at all points in S:

Strong form
$$-\frac{\partial}{\partial x}\left(c\,\frac{\partial u}{\partial x}\right) - \frac{\partial}{\partial y}\left(c\,\frac{\partial u}{\partial y}\right) = f(x,y) \quad \text{throughout } S\,. \tag{11}$$

This is the Euler-Lagrange equation $A^{\mathrm{T}}CAu = -\nabla\cdot c\nabla u = f$, with $Au = \operatorname{grad} u$.

Boundary conditions can specify u (Dirichlet) or $w\cdot n$ (Neumann). Compare (9) with (10) to see the boundary term $\int (w\cdot n)\,v\,ds$ with $w = c\nabla u$:

Green's formula
$$\iint_S c\nabla u\cdot\nabla v\,dx\,dy = -\iint_S (\nabla\cdot(c\nabla u))v\,dx\,dy + \int_C (c\nabla u\cdot n)v\,ds\,. \tag{12}$$

Both sides equal $\iint fv\,dx\,dy$ for every $v(x,y)$. That is the weak form. The first term on the right yields the strong form $-\operatorname{div}(c\operatorname{grad} u) = f(x,y)$ in the region S. All boundary conditions on u and on $w = c\operatorname{grad} u$ are included in the strong form.

There are two ways to make that boundary integral of $(c\nabla u\cdot n)v$ safely zero. If $u = u_0$ is given, then $u+v = u_0$ and $v = 0$ on the boundary (Dirichlet). That kills the integral. *When u is not given, v is free in the weak form* (Neumann). Then the natural boundary condition $c\nabla u\cdot n = w\cdot n = 0$ appears in the strong form.

A natural condition on w goes with A^{T}. An essential condition on u goes with A.

The notation $P(u) = \frac{1}{2}a(u,u) - \ell(u)$ To deal with a wide range of problems, a good notation is needed. $P(u) = \frac{1}{2}\int c(u')^2\,dx - \int f(x)u(x)\,dx$ has a *quadratic term* $\frac{1}{2}\,a(u,u)$ from the internal energy, and a *linear term* $-\ell(u)$ from the work done by f. Here is the quadratic-linear pair that led to (9) and (10):

$$\boldsymbol{a(u,u)} = \iint \left[\left(\frac{\partial u}{\partial x}\right)^2 + \left(\frac{\partial u}{\partial y}\right)^2\right] dx\,dy \qquad \boldsymbol{\ell(u)} = \iint f(x,y)u(x,y)\,dx\,dy\,. \tag{13}$$

This notation is appearing in engineering and applied mathematics journals. The weak form becomes $\boldsymbol{a(u,v) = \ell(v)}$ for all admissible v. The finite element method (and any Galerkin method) becomes $\boldsymbol{a(U,V) = \ell(V)}$ for all test functions V.

Elliptic, Parabolic, and Hyperbolic

With no extra effort we can go backwards to $P(u)$ from any linear equation:

Second-order equation $$a\frac{\partial^2 u}{\partial x^2}+2b\frac{\partial^2 u}{\partial x\partial y}+c\frac{\partial^2 u}{\partial y^2}=0\,. \tag{14}$$

When a, b, and c are constant, the corresponding quadratic "energy" is $P(u)$:

$$P(u)=\frac{1}{2}\iint\left[a\left(\frac{\partial u}{\partial x}\right)^2+2b\left(\frac{\partial u}{\partial x}\right)\left(\frac{\partial u}{\partial y}\right)+c\left(\frac{\partial u}{\partial y}\right)^2\right]dx\,dy\,.$$

If we minimize P we expect to reach (14) as its Euler equation. But there is more to it than that. To *minimize* P it should be *positive definite*. Inside the integral is an ordinary 2 by 2 quadratic $au_x^2+2bu_xu_y+cu_y^2$. The test for positive-definiteness is still $ac>b^2$, as it was in Chapter 1. (We can make $a>0$ in advance.) That test decides whether equation (14) can be solved with boundary values on $u(x,y)$.

In this positive definite case the equation is called "**elliptic**." Minimization is justified. There are three fundamental classes of partial differential equations:

The partial differential equation $au_{xx}+2bu_{xy}+cu_{yy}=0$ is **elliptic** or **parabolic** or **hyperbolic**, according to the matrix $\begin{bmatrix}a & b\\ b & c\end{bmatrix}$:

E	$ac>b^2$	elliptic boundary-value problem	**(steady state equation)**
P	$ac=b^2$	parabolic initial-value problem	**(heat/diffusion equation)**
H	$ac<b^2$	hyperbolic initial-value problem	**(wave/convection equation)**

Laplace's equation $u_{xx}+u_{yy}=0$ is elliptic; $a=c=1$ produces the identity matrix. The heat equation $u_{xx}-u_t=0$ is parabolic; $b=c=0$ makes the matrix singular. That parabolic borderline needs a lower-order term u_t. The wave equation $u_{xx}-u_{tt}=0$ is hyperbolic with $a=1$ and $c=-1$. It asks for initial values, not boundary values.

Incompressibility of a Fluid

Many fluids are ***incompressible***. The velocity has $\operatorname{div}\boldsymbol{v}=0$. We met this constraint in Navier-Stokes. Now we build $\operatorname{div}\boldsymbol{v}=0$ into the minimum principle.

The Lagrange multiplier will be the pressure $p(x,y)$. This is one more example to show that multipliers have great significance. If the nonlinear $\boldsymbol{v}\cdot\operatorname{grad}\boldsymbol{v}$ can be neglected (slow flow), we get the linear **Stokes problem**. This is a perfect example of a 2D fluid problem with a constraint at every point:

Stokes $$\text{Minimize}\iint\left(\frac{1}{2}|\operatorname{grad}v_1|^2+\frac{1}{2}|\operatorname{grad}v_2|^2-\boldsymbol{f}\cdot\boldsymbol{v}\right)dx\,dy \text{ with } \operatorname{div}\boldsymbol{v}=0. \tag{15}$$

The constraint holds at all points, so its Lagrange multiplier $p(x, y)$ is a function and not a number. Build $p \operatorname{div} \boldsymbol{v}$ into the Lagrangian L, which has a saddle point:

$$L(v_1, v_2, p) = \iint \left(\frac{1}{2} |\operatorname{grad} v_1|^2 + \frac{1}{2} |\operatorname{grad} v_2|^2 - \boldsymbol{f} \cdot \boldsymbol{v} - p \operatorname{div} \boldsymbol{v} \right) dx\, dy\,.$$

$\delta L / \delta p = 0$ brings back the constraint $\operatorname{div} \boldsymbol{v} = 0$. The derivatives $\delta L / \delta v_1 = 0$ and $\delta L / \delta v_2 = 0$ produce the Stokes equations (strong form) that we solve by finite elements in Section 8.5. Green's formula changes $\iint -p \operatorname{div} \boldsymbol{v}$ into $\iint \boldsymbol{v} \cdot \operatorname{grad} p$.

The Minimal Surface Problem

Now we are ready for ***nonlinear*** partial differential equations. A quadratic $P(u)$ is only an approximation to the true energy $E(u)$. Suppose a thin membrane covers S, like a soap bubble. Stretching this membrane requires energy proportional to the surface area of the bubble. The problem is to ***minimize the surface area*** $\boldsymbol{E(u)}$:

Minimal surface Minimize $E(u) = \displaystyle\iint_S \left[1 + \left(\frac{\partial u}{\partial x} \right)^2 + \left(\frac{\partial u}{\partial y} \right)^2 \right]^{1/2} dx\, dy\,.$ (16)

Suppose the bubble is created on a piece of wire that goes around S at height $u_0(x, y)$. This bent wire imposes a boundary condition $u = u_0(x, y)$ at the edge of S. The ***minimal surface problem*** is to find the smallest area $E(u)$ inside the wire.

The test for a minimum is still $E(u) \le E(u + v)$. To compute the term $\delta E / \delta u$ that is linear in v, look at the part F from u alone, and the correction G involving v:

$$F = 1 + \left(\frac{\partial u}{\partial x} \right)^2 + \left(\frac{\partial u}{\partial y} \right)^2 \qquad G = 2 \frac{\partial u}{\partial x} \frac{\partial v}{\partial x} + 2 \frac{\partial u}{\partial y} \frac{\partial v}{\partial y} + O(v^2)\,.$$

For small v, the square root is $\sqrt{F + G} = \sqrt{F} + G / 2\sqrt{F} + \cdots$. Integrate both sides:

$$E(u + v) = E(u) + \iint_S \frac{1}{\sqrt{F}} \left(\frac{\partial u}{\partial x} \frac{\partial v}{\partial x} + \frac{\partial u}{\partial y} \frac{\partial v}{\partial y} \right) dx\, dy + \cdots\,. \tag{17}$$

$\delta E / \delta u$ is exposed as this integral. It is zero for all v. That is the weak form of the minimal surface equation. Because of the square root of A, this is nonlinear in u. (It is always linear in v; that is the whole point of the first variation!) Integrating by parts to move derivatives from v produces the Euler equation in its strong form:

Minimal surface equation

$$-\frac{\partial}{\partial x} \left(\frac{1}{\sqrt{F}} \frac{\partial u}{\partial x} \right) - \frac{\partial}{\partial y} \left(\frac{1}{\sqrt{F}} \frac{\partial u}{\partial y} \right) = 0\,. \tag{18}$$

This is not easy to solve, because of the square root in the denominator. For nearly flat bubbles, linearization approximates $\sqrt{F}$ by 1. *The result is Laplace's equation.* Perhaps it is only natural that the most important nonlinear equation in geometry should reduce to the most important linear equation. But still it is beautiful.

Nonlinear Equations

Shortest distance and minimal surface area are typical nonlinear problems. They start with an integral $E = \iint F\,dx\,dy$. The energy density F depends on x and y and u and one or more derivatives like $\partial u/\partial x$ and $\partial u/\partial y$:

Inside the integral $E(u)$ $$F = F(x, y, u, D_1 u, D_2 u, \ldots).$$

For an elastic bar there was only $D_1 u = \partial u/\partial x$. For a soap bubble there is also $D_2 u = \partial u/\partial y$. Higher derivatives are allowed, and we can think of u itself as $D_0 u$.

The comparison of $E(u)$ with the nearby $E(u+v)$ starts from ordinary calculus: $F(u+v) = F(u) + F'(u)v + O(v^2)$. When F depends on several derivatives of u, this expansion has more terms from $F(u+v) = F(x, y, D_0 u + D_0 v, D_1 u + D_1 v, \ldots)$:

Inside $E(u+v)$ $$F(u+v) = F(u) + \sum \frac{\partial F}{\partial D_i u} D_i v + \cdots. \tag{19}$$

We take the derivatives of F with respect to u and u_x and any other $D_i u$.

$E(u+v) - E(u)$ integrates those linear terms: *integral* $= 0$ *for all* v. The strong form lifts each derivative D_i from v and puts it (as D_i^{T}) onto the part involving u:

Weak to strong (each term) $$\iint \left(\frac{\partial F}{\partial D_i u}\right)(D_i v)\,dx\,dy \longrightarrow \iint \left[D_i^{\mathrm{T}}\left(\frac{\partial F}{\partial D_i u}\right)\right] v\,dx\,dy$$

The transpose is $D^{\mathrm{T}} = -D$ for derivatives of odd order (with an odd number of integrations by parts and minus signs). Derivatives of even order have $D^{\mathrm{T}} = +D$.

Buried inside the calculus of variations is the real source of $A^{\mathrm{T}}CA$! The list of derivatives $e = D_i u$ is $e = Au$. Their "transposes" D_i^{T} give A^{T}. *C can be nonlinear.* ***C times e changes to $C(e)$***. The $A^{\mathrm{T}}CA$ framework becomes $\boldsymbol{A^{\mathrm{T}}C(Au) = f}$.

When F is a pure quadratic $\frac{1}{2}c(Du)^2$, then $D^{\mathrm{T}}\partial F/\partial Du$ is simply $D^{\mathrm{T}}(c\,Du)$—which is exactly the linear $A^{\mathrm{T}}CAu$ that we know so well.

Each problem in the calculus of variations has three forms, with boundary conditions:

Minimum principle **Essential BC on u**	Minimize $E(u) = \iint_S F(x, y, u, D_1 u, D_2 u, \ldots)\,dx\,dy$
Weak form with v **Essential BC on u, v**	$\dfrac{\delta E}{\delta u} = \iint_S \left(\sum \dfrac{\partial F}{\partial D_i u}\right)(D_i v)\,dx\,dy = 0$ for all v
Euler-Lagrange strong form **Boundary-conditions on u, w**	$\sum D_i^{\mathrm{T}}\left(\dfrac{\partial F}{\partial D_i u}\right) = \sum D_i^{\mathrm{T}} w_i = 0.$

Example 3 $F = u^2 + u_x^2 + u_y^2 + u_{xx}^2 + u_{xy}^2 + u_{yy}^2 = (D_0 u)^2 + \cdots + (D_5 u)^2$

The derivatives of F (a pure quadratic) are $2u, 2u_x, 2u_y, \ldots, 2u_{yy}$. They are derivatives with respect to u and u_x and the other $D_i u$, *not* derivatives with respect to x:

Weak form $$2\iint [uv + u_x v_x + u_y v_y + u_{xx} v_{xx} + u_{xy} v_{xy} + u_{yy} v_{yy}]\, dx\, dy = 0\,.$$

We integrate every term by parts to see the strong form (the terms multiplying v):

Strong form $$2\,[u - u_{xx} - u_{yy} + u_{xxxx} + u_{xyxy} + u_{yyyy}] = 0\,. \qquad (20)$$

This is linear because F is quadratic. The minus signs come with odd derivatives in F.

Example 4 $F = (1 + u_x^2)^{1/2}$ and $F = (1 + u_x^2 + u_y^2)^{1/2}$

The derivatives with respect to u_x and u_y bring the square root into the denominator. The shortest path equation and the minimal surface equation are the strong forms:

$$-\frac{d}{dx}\frac{u_x}{(1+u_x^2)^{1/2}} = 0 \quad \text{and} \quad -\frac{\partial}{\partial x}\left(\frac{u_x}{F}\right) - \frac{\partial}{\partial y}\left(\frac{u_y}{F}\right) = 0\,.$$

Every term fits into the pattern of $A^{\mathrm{T}}CA$, and **the framework becomes nonlinear**:

3 steps $\quad e = Au \quad\quad w = C(e) = \dfrac{\partial F}{\partial e} \quad\quad A^{\mathrm{T}}w = A^{\mathrm{T}}C(Au) = f \qquad (21)$

Nonlinear $C(Au)$ from Nonquadratic Energies

That last line was worth a chapter of words. A linear spring has $w = ce$, proportional to e. ***In a nonlinear spring the constitutive law is*** $w = C(e)$. The relation of force to stretching, or current to voltage, or flow to pressure, is no longer a straight line. We need parentheses in $C(e)$! The energy density is still $F(e) = \int C(e)\, de$:

The energy $E(u) = \int [F(Au) - fu]\, dx$ **is minimized when** $A^{\mathrm{T}}C(Au) = f$.

The first variation of E leads to $\int [C(Au)(Av) - fv]\, dx = 0$ for every v (weak form). $A^{\mathrm{T}}C(Au) = f$ is the Euler equation (strong form of the equilibrium equation).

For the nonlinear equivalent of positive definiteness, *the function $C(e)$ should be increasing.* The line $w = ce$ had a constant slope $c > 0$. Now that slope $C' = dC/de$ is changing—but it is still positive. That makes the energy $E(u)$ a **convex function**. The Euler equation $A^{\mathrm{T}}C(Au) = f$ is elliptic—we have a minimum.

Example 5 The *power law* $w = C(e) = e^{p-1}$ has $p > 1$. The energy density is its integral $F = e^p/p$. The stretching is $e = Au = du/dx$. The equilibrium equation is $A^{\mathrm{T}}C(Au) = (-d/dx)(du/dx)^{p-1} = f$. This is linear for $p = 2$. Otherwise nonlinear.

Complementary Energy

The complementary energy is a function of w instead of e. It starts with the *inverse constitutive law* $e = C^{-1}(w)$. In our example $e = w^{1/(p-1)}$. The strain e comes from the stress w; the arrow in the framework is reversed. Graphically, we are looking at Figure 8.8a from the side. ***The area under that curve is the complementary energy density*** $F^*(w) = \int C^{-1}(w)\, dw$. The twin equations come from F and F^*:

Constitutive Laws $\quad w = C(e) = \dfrac{\partial F}{\partial e} \quad$ and $\quad e = C^{-1}(w) = \dfrac{\partial F^*}{\partial w}. \qquad (22)$

The symmetry is perfect and the dual minimum principle applies to $Q(w) = \int F^*(w)\, dx$:

Dual **The complementary energy $Q(w)$ is a minimum subject to $A^{\mathrm{T}}w = f$.**

A Lagrange multiplier $u(x)$ takes Q to $L(w,u) = \int [F^*(w) - uA^{\mathrm{T}}w + uf]\, dx$, with the constraint $A^{\mathrm{T}}w = f$ built in. Its derivatives recover the two equations of equilibrium:

Saddle point	$\partial L/\partial w = 0$	is	$C^{-1}(w) - Au = 0$
of $L(u,w)$	$\partial L/\partial u = 0$	is	$A^{\mathrm{T}}w \qquad = f.$

The first equation gives $w = C(Au)$ and then the second is $A^{\mathrm{T}}C(Au) = f$.

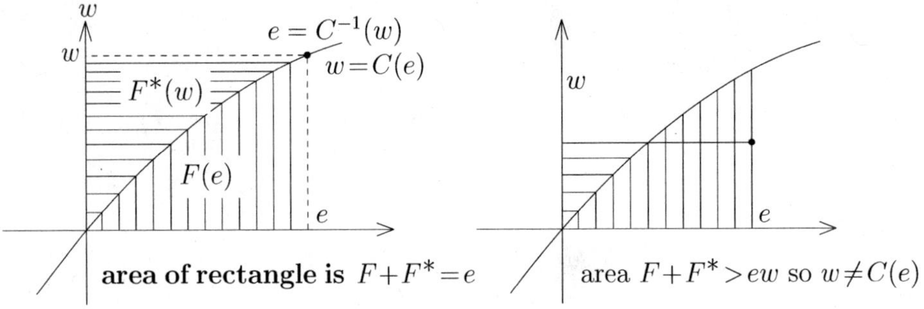

Figure 8.8: The graphs of $w = C(e)$ and $e = C^{-1}(w)$ cover areas $F + F^* = ew$.

Since these nonlinear things are in front of us, why not take the last step? It is never seen in advanced calculus, but there is nothing so incredibly difficult. The link between $F = \int C(e)\, de$ and $F^* = \int C^{-1}(w)\, dw$ is the ***Legendre-Fenchel transform***:

$$F^*(w) = \max_e\, [ew - F(e)] \quad \text{and} \quad F(e) = \max_w\, [ew - F^*(w)]. \qquad (23)$$

For the first maximum, differentiate with respect to e. That brings back $w = \partial F/\partial e$, which is the correct $C(e)$. The maximum itself is $F^* = e\,\partial F/\partial e - F$. Figure 8.8 shows graphically that the areas satisfy $F^* = ew - F$ on the curve and $F^* < ew - F$ off the curve. So the maximum of $ew - F$ is F^* on the curve as desired.

The second maximum in (23) leads to $e = \partial F^*/\partial w$. That is the constitutive law in the other direction $e = C^{-1}(w)$. The whole nonlinear theory is there, provided the material laws are conservative—the energy in the system should be constant. This conservation law seems to be destroyed by dissipation, or more spectacularly by fission, but in some ultimate picture of the universe it must remain true.

The Legendre transform reappears at full strength in constrained optimization. There F and F^* are general convex functions (with nonnegative second derivatives). ***We recognize that*** $\boldsymbol{F^{**} = F}$. Here we compute $F^*(w)$ for the power law:

Example 6 Find $F^*(w)$ for the power law $F(e) = e^p/p$ ($e > 0$ and $w > 0$ and $p > 1$)
Differentiating $ew - F(e)$ gives $w = e^{p-1}$. Then $F^*(w) = w^q/q$ is also a power law:

Dual law $$F^* = ew - \frac{1}{p}e^p = w^{1/(p-1)}w - \frac{1}{p}w^{p/(p-1)} = \frac{p-1}{p}w^{p/(p-1)} = \frac{1}{q}w^q. \qquad (24)$$

The dual exponent is $q = p/(p-1)$. Then w^q/q matches the area under $C^{-1}(w) = w^{1/(p-1)}$, because integration increases that exponent to $1+1/(p-1) = q$. The symmetric relation between the powers is $p^{-1} + q^{-1} = 1$. The power $p = 2 = q$ is self-dual.

Dynamics and Least Action

Fortunately or unfortunately, the world is not in equilibrium. The energy stored in springs and beams and nuclei and people is waiting to be released. When the external forces change, the equilibrium is destroyed. Potential energy is converted to kinetic energy, the system becomes dynamic, and it may or may not find a new steady state.

Feynman's wonderful lectures made "least action" the starting point for physics. When the system conserves energy, the transients will not grow or decay. The energy changes from potential to kinetic to potential to kinetic, but the total energy remains constant. It is like the earth around the sun or a child on a frictionless swing. The force $\delta P/\delta u$ is no longer zero, and the system oscillates. We have dynamics.

To describe the motion we need an equation or a variational principle. Numerically we mostly work with equations (Newton's laws and conservation laws). This section derives those laws from the ***principle of least action***, with Lagrangian $KE - PE$:

The actual path $u(t)$ minimizes the action integral $A(u)$ between $u(t_0)$ and $u(t_1)$:

$$A(u) = \int_{t_0}^{t_1} (\textbf{kinetic energy} - \textbf{potential energy})\, dt = \int_{t_0}^{t_1} L(u, u')\, dt$$

It is better to claim only that $\delta A/\delta u = 0$—the path is always a stationary point but not in every circumstance a minimum. We have a difference of energies, and positive definiteness can be lost (a saddle point). Laplace's equation will be overtaken by the wave equation. First come three examples to show how the ***global law*** of least action (the variational principle $\delta A/\delta u = 0$) produces Newton's ***local law*** $F = ma$.

Example 7 A ball of mass m is attracted by the Earth's gravity

The only degree of freedom is the ball's height $u(t)$. The energies are KE and PE:

$$KE = \textbf{kinetic energy} = \frac{1}{2}m\left(\frac{du}{dt}\right)^2 \quad \text{and} \quad PE = \textbf{potential energy} = mgu\,.$$

The action is $A = \int(\frac{1}{2}m(u')^2 - mgu)\,dt$. Then $\delta A/\delta u$ follows from the rules of this section—with the time variable t replacing the space variable x. The true path u is compared to its neighbors $u + v$. The linear part of $A(u+v) - A(u)$ gives $\delta A/\delta u = 0$:

$$\textbf{Weak form of Newton's Law} \qquad \frac{\delta A}{\delta u} = \int_{t_0}^{t_1} (mu'v' - mgv)\,dt = 0 \quad \text{for every } v.$$

The momentum mu' is the derivative of $\frac{1}{2}m(u')^2$ with respect to the velocity u'.

$$\textbf{Strong form of Newton's Law} \qquad -\frac{d}{dt}\left(m\frac{du}{dt}\right) - mg = 0 \quad \text{which is} \quad ma = f\,. \tag{25}$$

The action integral is minimized by following Newton's Law $A^{\mathrm{T}}CAu = f$.

Our three-step framework has $A = d/dt$ and $A^{\mathrm{T}} = -d/dt$. The usual $w = ce$ changes to $p = mv$. The balance is between **inertial forces** instead of mechanical forces. Figure 8.9 identifies the dual variables u and p as position and momentum.

Example 8 A simple pendulum with mass m and length ℓ moves with least action

The state variable u is the angle θ from the vertical. The height $\ell - \ell\cos\theta$ still enters the potential energy, and the velocity of the mass is $v = \ell\,d\theta/dt$:

$$\textbf{kinetic energy} = \frac{1}{2}m\ell^2\left(\frac{d\theta}{dt}\right)^2 \quad \text{and} \quad \textbf{potential energy} = mg(\ell - \ell\cos\theta)$$

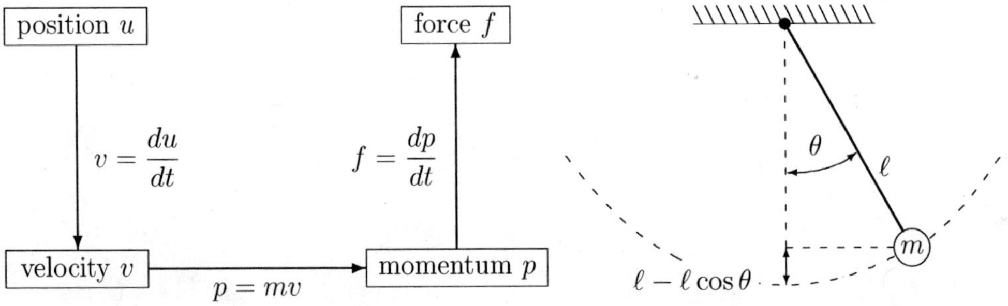

Figure 8.9: Newton's Law is $(mu')' = f$. A pendulum also fits the framework.

In this problem the equation will no longer be linear, because PE involves $\cos\theta$. The Euler equation follows the rule for an integral $\int L(\theta,\theta')\,dt$, with $L = KE - PE$:

Euler equation $$\frac{\partial L}{\partial \theta} - \frac{d}{dt}\left(\frac{\partial L}{\partial \theta'}\right) = 0 \quad \text{or} \quad -mg\ell\sin\theta - \frac{d}{dt}\left(m\ell^2\frac{d\theta}{dt}\right) = 0\,.$$

This is the equation of a simple pendulum. The mass cancels out; clocks keep time!

Pendulum equation $$\frac{d^2\theta}{dt^2} + \frac{g}{\ell}\sin\theta = 0\,. \tag{26}$$

When the angle is small and $\sin\theta$ is approximated by θ, the equation becomes linear. The period changes a little. A linear clock keeps time, but not the right time.

Example 9 A vertical line of springs and masses has $Mu'' + Ku = 0$

The potential energy in the springs is $PE = \frac{1}{2}u^{\mathrm{T}}A^{\mathrm{T}}CAu$. The energy KE has $\frac{1}{2}m_i(u_i')^2$ from each mass. $L = KE - PE$ goes into the action integral, and there is an Euler equation $\delta A/\delta u_i = 0$ for each mass. This is the basic equation of mechanical engineering:

Undamped oscillation $$Mu'' + A^{\mathrm{T}}CAu = 0\,.$$

M is the diagonal mass matrix and $K = A^{\mathrm{T}}CA$ is the positive definite stiffness matrix. The system oscillates around equilibrium and the energy $H = KE + PE$ is constant.

Example 10 Waves in an elastic bar from a *continuum of masses and springs*

The action integral in this continuous case has an integral instead of a sum:

Action $$A(u) = \int_{t_0}^{t_1}\int_{x=0}^{1}\left[\frac{1}{2}m\left(\frac{du}{dt}\right)^2 - \frac{1}{2}c\left(\frac{du}{dx}\right)^2\right]dx\,dt\,.$$

The Euler-Lagrange rules for $\delta A/\delta u = 0$ cover this case of a double integral:

Wave equation $$\frac{\delta A}{\delta u} = -\frac{\partial}{\partial t}\left(m\frac{\partial u}{\partial t}\right) - \frac{\partial}{\partial x}\left(-c\frac{\partial u}{\partial x}\right) = 0\,. \tag{27}$$

That is the **wave equation** $mu_{tt} = cu_{xx}$. With constant density m and elastic constant c, the wave speed is $\sqrt{c/m}$—faster when the bar is stiffer and lighter.

Staying with the calculus of variations, there are two important comments:

1. When u is independent of time (no motion), the kinetic energy is $KE = 0$. The dynamic problem goes back to the static $A^{\mathrm{T}}CAu = f$ that minimizes PE.

2. The dual variable w, from all the evidence, should be found in its usual place in Figure 8.9. It is the ***momentum*** $p = mv = m\,du/dt$.

Lagrangian and Hamiltonian

Hamilton realized that by introducing $w = \partial L/\partial u'$, the Euler-Lagrange equation would have a beautifully symmetric form. The change from u' to $w = \partial L/\partial u'$ carries the Lagrangian $L(u, u') = KE - PE$ into the Hamiltonian $H(u, w)$:

Legendre transform L to H $$H(u,w) = \max_{u'} \left[w^{\mathrm{T}} u' - L(u,u') \right]. \tag{28}$$

The maximum occurs where the derivative of L is $w = \partial L/\partial u'$. The example of masses and springs shows how $w = \partial L/\partial u' = Mu'$ is the momentum:

Lagrangian $$L(u,u') = \tfrac{1}{2}(u')^{\mathrm{T}} M (u') - \tfrac{1}{2} u^{\mathrm{T}} K u = \boldsymbol{KE - PE} \tag{29}$$

Hamiltonian $$H(u,w) = \tfrac{1}{2} w^{\mathrm{T}} M^{-1} w + \tfrac{1}{2} u^{\mathrm{T}} K u = \boldsymbol{KE + PE} \tag{30}$$

Let me show the steps of that transform from Lagrangian L to Hamiltonian H:

Maximum of $\boldsymbol{H(u,w) = w^{\mathrm{T}} u' - L}$ at $\boldsymbol{u' = M^{-1} w}$

$$H = w^{\mathrm{T}} M^{-1} w - \left(\tfrac{1}{2} (M^{-1} w)^{\mathrm{T}} M (M^{-1} w) - \tfrac{1}{2} u^{\mathrm{T}} K u \right) = \tfrac{1}{2} w^{\mathrm{T}} M^{-1} w + \tfrac{1}{2} u^{\mathrm{T}} K u.$$

Using this **momentum** w in place of the velocity u' produces Hamilton's equations:

Hamilton's equations $$\frac{dw}{dt} = -\frac{\partial H}{\partial u} \quad \text{and} \quad \frac{du}{dt} = \frac{\partial H}{\partial w}. \tag{31}$$

The key step was to use Lagrange's equation in $\partial H/\partial u$ when $H = w^{\mathrm{T}} u' - L$:

$$\frac{d}{dt}\left(\frac{\partial L}{\partial u'}\right) = \frac{\partial L}{\partial u} \quad \text{gives} \quad \frac{\partial H}{\partial u} = w^{\mathrm{T}} \frac{\partial u'}{\partial u} - \frac{\partial L}{\partial u} - \left(\frac{\partial L}{\partial u'}\right)^{\mathrm{T}} \frac{\partial u'}{\partial u} = -\frac{\partial L}{\partial u} = -\frac{dw}{dt}.$$

Classical mechanics uses the letters p and q, instead of w and u. The chain rule shows that the Hamiltonian (total complementary energy) is a constant:

H = constant $$\frac{dH}{dt} = \frac{\partial H}{\partial u}\frac{du}{dt} + \frac{\partial H}{\partial w}\frac{dw}{dt} = -w'u' + u'w' = 0. \tag{32}$$

Deeper analysis reveals the property that we mentioned in Section 2.2. The Hamiltonian flows are **symplectic** (preserving areas in phase space, not just the total energy H.) For good long-time integrations, the difference approximations must also be symplectic. Those difference equations are constructed in [76].

Falling Ball and Oscillating Spring

Hamilton found the energy $KE + PE$, using the momentum $w = p$ (*not the velocity*):

Hamilton's equations $$\frac{\partial H}{\partial p} = \frac{p}{m} = \frac{du}{dt} \quad \text{and} \quad \frac{\partial H}{\partial u} = mg = -\frac{dp}{dt}\,. \tag{33}$$

This is the essence of classical mechanics. It is tied to Hamilton and not to Newton. For that reason it survived the revolution brought by Einstein. We will see that H has a relativistic form and even a quantum mechanical form. Comparing a falling ball with an oscillating spring, the key difference in H is between u and u^2:

$$\textbf{(ball)} \quad H = \frac{1}{2m}p^2 + mgu \qquad \textbf{(spring)} \quad H = \frac{1}{2m}p^2 + \frac{1}{2}cu^2$$

Hamilton's equations $\partial H/\partial p = u'$ and $\partial H/\partial u = -p'$ yield Newton's Law:

$$\textbf{(ball)} \qquad \frac{p}{m} = u' \quad \text{and} \quad mg = -p', \quad \text{or} \quad mu'' = -mg \tag{34}$$

$$\textbf{(spring)} \qquad \frac{p}{m} = u' \quad \text{and} \quad cu = -p', \quad \text{or} \quad mu'' + cu = 0\,. \tag{35}$$

The mass on a spring passes through equilibrium at top speed (all energy in KE). The force reverses to stop the motion (all energy goes into PE). In the $u - p$ plane (*the phase plane*) the motion stays on the energy surface $H =$ constant, which is the ellipse in Figure 8.10. Each oscillation of the spring is a trip around the ellipse.

With more springs there are $2n$ axes $u_1, \ldots, u_n, p_1, \ldots, p_n$ and the ellipse becomes an ellipsoid. Hamilton's equations are $\partial H/\partial p_i = du_i/dt$ and $\partial H/\partial u_i = -dp_i/dt$. They lead again to $Mu'' + Ku = 0$, and to the wave equation in the continuous case.

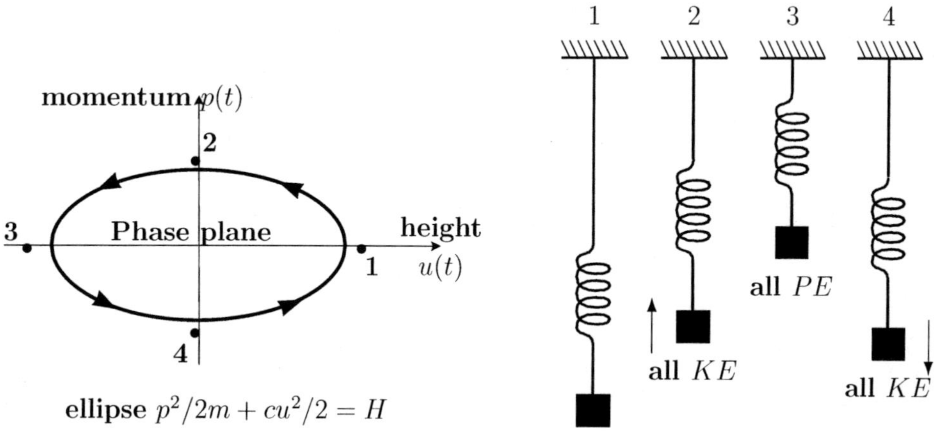

Figure 8.10: **1** tension **2** motion **3** compression **4** motion: Constant $H = KE + PE$.

Relativity and Quantum Mechanics

The next paragraphs are an attempt, by a total amateur, to correct the action integral by the rules of relativity. Feynman's lectures propose the term $-mc^2\sqrt{1-(v/c)^2}$ as the Lagrangian $KE - PE$. At $v = 0$ we see Einstein's formula $\boldsymbol{e = mc^2}$ for the potential energy in a mass m at rest.

As the velocity increases from zero there is also a part corresponding to KE. For small x the square root of $1-x$ is approximately $1-\frac{1}{2}x$, which linearizes the problem and brings back Newton's $\frac{1}{2}mv^2$—just as linearizing the minimal surface equation brought back Laplace. Relativity mixes together KE and PE in the square root:

Linearization $$L(v) = -mc^2\sqrt{1-(v/c)^2} \approx -mc^2\left(1 - \frac{1}{2}\frac{v^2}{c^2}\right) = KE - PE$$

Trusting in duality, we look for the conjugate function L^* as the Hamiltonian. It will be a function of p, not v. The first step is to find that momentum p. Before relativity, L was $\frac{1}{2}mv^2$ and its derivative was $p = mv$. Always p is $\partial L/\partial u' = \partial L/\partial v$:

Momentum (relativistic) $$p = \frac{\partial L}{\partial v} = \frac{mv}{\sqrt{1-(v/c)^2}}. \tag{36}$$

This becomes infinite as v approaches the speed of light. H is the transform L^*:

Hamiltonian $$H = L^* = \max_v\,[\,pv - L(v)\,] = mc^2\sqrt{1+(p/mc)^2}. \tag{37}$$

This maximum occurs at (36)—which we solved for v and substituted into $pv - L(v)$.

The Hamiltonian $H = L^*$ is Einstein's energy $e = mc^2$ when the system is at rest. As p increases from zero, the next term from the square root is Newton's $p^2/2m$:

Newton approximation $$L^* \approx mc^2\left(1 + \frac{1}{2}\frac{p^2}{m^2c^2}\right) = \text{rest energy } + \frac{p^2}{2m}.$$

Newton found the low-order term in the energy that Einstein computed exactly! Perhaps the universe is like a minimal surface in space-time. To Laplace and Newton it looked flat (linearized), but to Einstein it became curved.

It is risky to add anything about quantum mechanics, where u is a probability. This is a mixture of differential equations (Schrödinger) and matrices (Heisenberg). The event at which $\delta A/\delta u = 0$ almost always occurs. Feynman gave each possible trajectory of the system a phase factor $e^{iA/h}$ multiplying its probability amplitude. The small number h (Planck's constant) means that a slight change in the action A completely alters the phase. There are strong canceling effects from nearby paths unless *the phase is stationary*. In other words $\delta A/\delta u = 0$ at the most probable path.

This prediction of "stationary phase" applies equally to light rays and particles. Optics follows the same principles as mechanics, and light travels by the fastest route: ***least action becomes least time***. If Planck's constant could go to zero, the deterministic principles of least action and least time would appear. Then the path of least action would be not only probable but certain.

Problem Set 8.3

1 What are the weak and strong forms of the linear beam equation—the first variation $\delta P/\delta u$ and the Euler-Lagrange equation for $P = \int [\frac{1}{2}c(u'')^2 - fu]\,dx$?

2 Minimizing $P = \int (u')^2 dx$ with $u(0) = a$ and $u(1) = b$ also leads to the straight line through these points. Write down the weak form and the strong form.

3 Find the Euler-Lagrange equations (strong form) for

(a) $P = \int [(u')^2 + e^u]\,dx$ (b) $P = \int uu'\,dx$ (c) $P = \int x^2(u')^2 dx$

4 If $F(u, u')$ is independent of x, as in almost all our examples, show from the Euler equation (3) and the chain rule that $H = u'(\partial F/\partial u') - F$ is constant.

5 If the speed is x, the travel time of a light ray is T:

$$T = \int_0^1 \frac{1}{x}\sqrt{1 + (u')^2}\,dx \quad \text{with} \quad u(0) = 0 \quad \text{and} \quad u(1) = 1\,.$$

(a) From $\delta T/\delta u = 0$ what quantity is constant? This is **Snell's law**.

(b) Can you integrate once more to find the optimal path $u(x)$?

6 With the constraints $u(0) = u(1) = 0$ and $\int u\,dx = A$, show that the minimum value of $P = \int (u')^2 dx$ is $P_{\text{min}} = 12A^2$. Introduce a multiplier m as in (7), solve the Euler equation for u, and verify that $A = -m/24$. Then the derivative dP_{min}/dA equals the multiplier $-m$ as the sensitivity theory predicts.

7 For the shortest path constrained by $\int u\,dx = A$, what is unusual about the solution in Figure 8.7 as A becomes large?

8 Suppose the constraint is $\int u\,dx \geq A$, with inequality allowed. Why does the solution remain a straight line as A becomes small? Where does the multiplier m remain? This is typical of inequality constraints: either the Euler equation is satisfied or the multiplier is zero.

9 Suppose the constrained problem is reversed, and we *maximize* the area $P = \int u\,dx$ subject to fixed length $I = \int \sqrt{1 + (u')^2}\,dx$, with $u(0) = a$ and $u(1) = b$.

(a) Introduce a multiplier M. Solve the Euler equation for u.

(b) How is the multiplier M related to m in the text?

(c) When do the constraints eliminate all functions u?

10 Find by calculus the shortest broken-line path between $(0, 1)$ and $(1, 1)$ that goes first to the horizontal axis $y = 0$ and bounces back. Show that the best path treats this axis like a mirror: angle of incidence = angle of reflection.

11 The principle of *maximum entropy* selects the probability distribution $u(x)$ that maximizes $H = -\int u \log u \, dx$. With Lagrange multipliers for $\int u\, dx = 1$ and $\int xu\, dx = 1/a$, find by differentiation an equation for u. Show that the most likely distribution on the interval $0 \le x < \infty$ is $u = ae^{-ax}$.

12 If the second moment $\int x^2 u\, dx$ is also known, show that Gauss wins again. The maximizing u is the exponential of a quadratic. If only $\int u\, dx = 1$ is known, the most likely distribution is $u =$ constant. The *least* information comes when only one outcome is possible, say $u(6) = 1$, since $u \log u$ is then 1 times 0.

13 A helix climbs around a cylinder with $x = \cos\theta, y = \sin\theta, z = u(\theta)$:

$$\text{The length is} \quad P = \int \sqrt{dx^2 + dy^2 + dz^2} = \int \sqrt{1 + (u')^2}\, d\theta\,.$$

Show that $u' = c$ satisfies Euler's equation. The shortest helix is regular.

14 Multiply the nonlinear equation $-u'' + \sin u = 0$ by v and integrate the first term by parts to find the weak form. What integral P is minimized by u?

15 Find the Euler equations (strong form) for

$$\text{(a)}\ \ P(u) = \frac{1}{2} \iint \left[\left(\frac{\partial^2 u}{\partial x^2}\right)^2 + 2\left(\frac{\partial^2 u}{\partial x \partial y}\right)^2 + \left(\frac{\partial^2 u}{\partial y^2}\right)^2 \right] dx\, dy$$

$$\text{(b)}\ \ P(u) = \frac{1}{2} \iint (y u_x^2 + u_y^2)\, dx\, dy \qquad \text{(c)}\ \ E(u) = \int u\sqrt{1 + (u')^2}\, dx$$

$$\text{(d)}\ \ P(u) = \frac{1}{2} \iint (u_x^2 + u_y^2)\, dx\, dy \quad \text{with} \quad \iint u^2\, dx\, dy = 1.$$

16 Show that the Euler-Lagrange equations for these integrals are the same:

$$\iint \frac{\partial^2 u}{\partial x^2}\frac{\partial^2 u}{\partial y^2}\, dx\, dy \quad \text{and} \quad \iint \left(\frac{\partial^2 u}{\partial x \partial y}\right)^2 dx\, dy$$

Presumably the two integrals are equal if the boundary conditions are zero.

17 Sketch the graph of $p^2/2m + mgu =$ constant in the $u - p$ plane. Is it an ellipse, parabola, or hyperbola? Mark the point where the ball reaches maximum height and begins to fall.

18 Suppose a second spring and mass hang from the first. If the masses are m_1, m_2 and the spring constants are c_1, c_2, the energy is the Hamiltonian H:

$$H = KE + PE = \frac{1}{2m_1} p_1^2 + \frac{1}{2m_2} p_2^2 + \frac{1}{2} c_1 u_1^2 + \frac{1}{2} c_2 (u_2 - u_1)^2\,.$$

Find the four Hamilton's equations $\partial H/\partial p_i = du_i/dt$ and $\partial H/\partial u_i = -dp_i/dt$. Derive the matrix equation $Mu'' + Ku = 0$.

19 Verify that the complementary energy $\frac{1}{2}w^{\mathrm{T}}C^{-1}w$ is the Legendre transform of the energy $\frac{1}{2}e^{\mathrm{T}}Ce$. This means that $\frac{1}{2}w^{\mathrm{T}}C^{-1}w = \max[e^{\mathrm{T}}w - \frac{1}{2}e^{\mathrm{T}}Ce]$.

20 If the pendulum in Figure 8.9 is elastic, a spring energy $\frac{1}{2}c(r-\ell)^2$ is added to $PE = mg(\ell - \ell\cos\theta)$. A kinetic energy $\frac{1}{2}m(r')^2$ is added to $KE = \frac{1}{2}m(\ell\theta')^2$.

(a) Follow Example 8 to obtain two coupled equations for θ'' and r''.

(b) From $H = KE{+}PE$ find Hamilton's four first-order equations for $\theta, r, p_\theta = m\ell\theta'$ and $p_r = mr'$. This and a double pendulum are on the cse website.

21 Important: Our notation for a quadratic potential is $P(u) = \frac{1}{2}a(u,u) - \ell(u)$. What is $P(u+v)$ when you ignore v^2 terms? Subtract to find $\delta P/\delta u = 0$. Show that this weak form is $\boldsymbol{a(u,v) = \ell(v)}$.

22 Find the relativistic Hamiltonian H in (37) by using (36).

Problems 23-28 introduce finite differences and discrete Lagrangians. The key idea is to replace u_x and u_t by $\Delta u/\Delta x$ and $\Delta u/\Delta t$ in the integrals P and E and A. **Discretize the integral and then minimize**. This conserves the energy structure more safely than discretizing the Euler-Lagrange equation.

23 Replace u_x by $(u_{i+1}-u_i)/\Delta x$ to convert $P(u) = \int_0^1 (\frac{1}{2}u_x^2 - 4u)\,dx$ to a sum, with boundary conditions $u_0 = u(0) = 0$ and $u_{n+1} = u(1) = 0$. What are the equations to minimize the discrete sum $P(u_1,\ldots,u_n)$? What equation and what $u(x)$ minimize the integral $P(u)$?

24 Why is the minimum of $P(u) = \int \sqrt{1+u_x^2}\,dx$ still a straight line when u_x changes to $\Delta u/\Delta x$? Find an equation (with Lagrange multiplier m) for the best piecewise line from $u_0 = a$ to $u_{n+1} = b$ when Example 2 adds the area constraint $\int u\,dx = A$. The circular arc becomes piecewise linear.

25 Discretize $\iint (u_x^2 + u_y^2)\,dx\,dy$ by $\Delta u/\Delta x$ and $\Delta u/\Delta y$. When the sum is minimized, what difference equation do you get for $-u_{xx} - u_{yy}$?

26 Discretize $P(u) = \int (u_{xx})^2\,dx$ with $(\Delta^2 u/(\Delta x)^2)^2$ and show how minimization produces a fourth difference $\Delta^4 u$ (with what coefficients?).

27 A ball has $KE = \frac{1}{2}m(u')^2$ and $PE = mg\,u$. Replace u' by $\Delta u/\Delta t$ and minimize $P(u_1,\ldots,u_n)$, the discrete action sum of $\frac{1}{2}m(\Delta u/\Delta t)^2 + mg\,u$.

28 Marsden shows how a satellite could follow a minimum energy path between planets and go far with almost no fuel. Summarize his ideas for discretization.

8.4 ERRORS IN PROJECTIONS AND EIGENVALUES

This section is about the difference between an overall minimizer u^* and a subspace minimizer U^*. Normally u^* is exact and U^* is a numerical solution:

Full problem $P(u^*) = \text{minimum of } P(u)$ for ***all admissible u***

Reduced problem $P(U^*) = \text{minimum of } P(U)$ for U in ***a trial space T***

When we know what controls the error $U^* - u^*$ (it is often the degree of polynomial trial functions), we know how to improve the algorithm. Higher degree allows a closer approximation to u^*. We want to show that U^* comes as close as possible.

$P(u)$ has a linear part $-\ell(u)$ and a symmetric positive definite quadratic part (that property guarantees a minimum). We write P in two ways:

Matrix case $P(u) = \frac{1}{2}u^{\mathrm{T}}Ku - u^{\mathrm{T}}f$ **Continuous case** $P(u) = \frac{1}{2}\,a(u,u) - \ell(u)$

We need to understand $U^* - u^*$, because this situation is so important in scientific computing. The goal is u^* but what we compute is U^*. Four key algorithms in this book (maybe more) fit into this framework of *minimization over a trial subspace*:

Finite element method The trial functions are $U(x,y) = \sum_1^N U_j\phi_j(x,y)$

Multigrid method Trial vectors are interpolated from the coarse grid

Conjugate gradient method Trial vectors are combinations of $f, Kf, K^2f, \ldots$

Sampling and compression Trial functions have low frequencies (band-limited)

Always the trial space has lower dimension than the full space. So we solve a smaller problem. The key insight is to recognize that the computed solution U^* is a ***projection of the true solution u* onto the trial space T***. Measuring distance from the exact u^*, the projection U^* is closer than any other trial function U.

Before proving that fact, I state it in $u^{\mathrm{T}}Ku$ notation and $a(u,u)$ notation.

U^* is closest possible $\|U^* - u^*\|_K^2 \le \|U - u^*\|_K^2$ for every U. (1)

This error bound uses the "K-norm" $\|e\|_K^2 = e^{\mathrm{T}}Ke$. That is the natural "energy norm" for the problem, since the quadratic part of $P(u)$ is the energy $\frac{1}{2}u^{\mathrm{T}}Ku$.

U^* = projection of u^* $a(U^*-u^*, U^*-u^*) \le a(U-u^*, U-u^*)$ for all U. (2)

How do we use this? By choosing any convenient trial function U, the right side gives an upper bound on the left side. That left side measures the error by its energy.

Subspace Minimization and Projection

The U^* in T that minimizes P is also the U^* in T that is closest to the overall minimizer u^*. The subspace T contains all combinations $U = \sum U_i\phi_i$ of the trial functions ϕ_i; and U^* is the best combination. "*Best*" means that U^* minimizes $P(U)$ and it also means that U^* minimizes the distance $a(u^*-U^*, u^*-U^*)$ from u^*.

Those "two properties at once" come directly from this fundamental identity:

Identity for $P(u)$ $\quad \frac{1}{2}\, a(u,u) - \ell(u) = \frac{1}{2}\, a(u-u^*, u-u^*) - \frac{1}{2}\, a(u^*, u^*).$ (3)

When we minimize the left side, restricting u to the subspace T, the winner is U^*. At the same time we are minimizing the right side, restricted to any $u = U$ in T. So the same U^* will minimize that $a(U-u^*, U-u^*)$, and equation (2) is proved. The final term $-\frac{1}{2}a(u^*, u^*)$ in (3) is a constant, so it has no effect.

The proof of (3) expands $\frac{1}{2}a(u-u^*, u-u^*)$ into four terms. The term $\frac{1}{2}a(u,u)$ is in $P(u)$. The next term $-\frac{1}{2}a(u^*, u)$ is $-\frac{1}{2}\ell(u)$ by the weak form. So is $-\frac{1}{2}a(u, u^*)$ by symmetry. And the last term $\frac{1}{2}a(u^*, u^*)$ is subtracted off at the end of (3).

In case that proof looks like magic, let me rewrite (3) for $u^* = K^{-1}f$:

Matrix identity $\quad \frac{1}{2}u^{\mathrm{T}}Ku - u^{\mathrm{T}}f = \frac{1}{2}(u-K^{-1}f)^{\mathrm{T}}K(u-K^{-1}f) - \frac{1}{2}f^{\mathrm{T}}K^{-1}f.$ (4)

On the right side, $(K^{-1}f)^{\mathrm{T}}K(K^{-1}f)$ is the same as $f^{\mathrm{T}}K^{-1}f$. Simplify to get the left side $P(u)$. Equation (4) confirms immediately that the overall minimizer of $P(u)$ is $u^* = K^{-1}f$. The very last term is a constant. Actually that constant is P_{min}, because the previous term is zero when $u = K^{-1}f$. That previous term can never go below zero, since K is positive definite.

Again, minimizing the left side of (4) over the subspace finds U^*. On the right side, this U^* is minimizing the distance to $u^* = K^{-1}f$. That is statement (1), where distance $U^* - u^*$ is measured *in the K-norm.*

The error bounds follow immediately in the next paragraph. First I can express these fundamental facts about U^* in the language of **projections**. In twelve words, ***U^* is the projection of u^* onto T in the energy norm***:

Perpendicular error $\quad a(U^*-u^*, U) = 0 \quad \text{for all} \quad U \text{ in } T$ (5)

I started with the subspace weak form $a(U^*, U) = \ell(U)$. I subtracted the overall weak form $a(u^*, u) = \ell(u)$, which holds for every u and in particular for every U. That subtraction is equation (5), the same perpendicularity as in least squares. *The error vector is always perpendicular to the subspace T.*

Finite Element Errors

The basic 1D example $-u'' = f$ has $a(u,u) = \int (u')^2\, dx$ and $\ell(u) = \int f(x)u(x)\, dx$. If we approximate by linear finite elements, how close is U^* to the exact solution u^*?

With finite differences we used Taylor series. The local error that comes from second differences is $O(h^2)$. If all goes well, the meshpoint errors $u_i - U_i$ are $O(h^2)$ and the slope errors are $O(h)$. To prove this, especially in 2D problems with curved boundaries, would not be fun.

With finite elements, the error is much easier to estimate. The finite element solution $U^*(x)$ is as close as possible (in energy norm) to the true $u^*(x)$. It is closer than the convenient function $U_I(x)$, which gives *linear interpolation* to u^* at the meshpoints. That is equation (2), restated for the particular choice $U = U_I$:

U^* is closer than U_I $$\int \left((U^* - u^*)'\right)^2 dx \leq \int \left((U_I - u^*)'\right)^2 dx. \tag{6}$$

The left side we don't know. But the right side we can estimate.

On an interval from 0 to h, how far is the slope of U_I from the slope of u^*? Those functions are equal at the endpoints 0 and h. The example $u^* = x(h-x)$ is good, because it is zero at both endpoints. The linear interpolating function is $U_I(x) = 0$. Its slope is zero, and the slope of $u^* = x(h-x)$ is $h - 2x$:

Energy in one interval $$\int_0^h (h-2x)^2\, dx = \left[-\frac{1}{6}(h-2x)^3\right]_0^h = \frac{1}{3}h^3. \tag{7}$$

There are $1/h$ intervals, so the right side of (6) is $O(h^2)$. Then the left side is $O(h^2)$. This is the finite element error bound, for linear elements. A little patience will give the bound $ch^2\|u''\|^2$ for interpolating any function, not just $x(h-x)$. This extends to $-(c(x)u')' = f$, and to 2D problems, and to any space dimension:

For linear elements $$a(U^* - u^*, U^* - u^*) \leq a(u_I^* - u^*, u_I^* - u^*) \leq Ch^2. \tag{8}$$

This reveals the true behavior (and success) of the finite element method. Linear interpolation of u^* has slope error $O(h)$. C depends on second derivatives of u^*.

Think for a moment about the 2D problem, with linear elements on triangles. Now we are comparing a curved surface with a flat plane, when they agree at the corners of the triangle. The conclusion is the same, that the error $u_I^* - u^*$ (and therefore $U^* - u^*$) is of order h in the first derivatives. Both derivatives $\partial u/\partial x$ and $\partial u/\partial y$ enter into the 2D energy norm $a(u,u) = \iint c|\operatorname{grad} u|^2\, dx\, dy$.

A separate argument will prove what the numerical output shows, that the pointwise error $U^* - u^*$ is of order h^2 for smooth solutions. That is immediately true for $U_I - u^*$. But the error bound is in the *energy norm*!

Higher Order Trial Functions

Linear approximation has low accuracy $O(h)$ in the slope. Better approximations come from improving to quadratic or cubic elements ($p = 2$ or $p = 3$). It is easy to guess the accuracy, from the *lowest degree* $p+1$ *of the polynomials that are* ***not reproducible*** *from the trial functions*:

$$\textit{The interpolation error } u_I^* - u^* \textit{ is } O(h^{p+1}). \textit{ The slope error is } O(h^p). \tag{9}$$

The error in second derivatives will be $O(h^{p-1})$. That enters the bending energy $a(u,u)$ for beams, plates, and shells. The improvement with increasing degree p comes from matching more terms in the Taylor series for $u^*(x)$ or $u^*(x,y)$. The first unmatched term gives the error. In finite element theory [144], this analysis combines the Bramble-Hilbert lemma for approximation error with the Strang-Fix conditions for reproducing polynomials from combinations of trial functions.

These error bounds explain why there is an ***h-method*** and a ***p-method*** in finite elements. The h-method improves accuracy by refining the mesh (reducing h). The p-method improves accuracy by adding higher degree trial functions (increasing p). Both methods are successful, up to the point where the mesh is too big in the h-method or the trial functions are too complicated in the p-method.

Mesh construction is a whole subject of its own. Section 2.7 gave a quick algorithm to create meshes of triangles and pyramids. Large finite element codes often want rectangles (quads) or 3D boxes (hexes). ***Adaptive mesh refinement*** [8] has had major theoretical attention, using local error estimates to refine the mesh in the right places. Further analysis shows how to choose those right places, when a specific target is desired (like accuracy in the computed drag of an airfoil).

We quickly mention that this theory applies also to **wavelet approximation**. The scaling functions $\phi(x-k)$ in Section 4.7 are not piecewise polynomials, but those strange functions still combine to reproduce polynomials exactly. In that different world, the accuracy p is the number of "vanishing moments" for the wavelets.

Finite differences have no identities like (3) and (4) to give error bounds. They need *stability* to control the error growth. Here, stability comes in an automatic way from the positive definiteness of $a(u,u)$. The eigenvalues in (14) will show why.

The Rayleigh Quotient for Eigenvalues

How do you estimate the eigenvalues and eigenfunctions in differential equations?

Example in 1D
$$-\frac{d^2u}{dx^2} = \lambda\, u(x) \quad \text{with} \quad u(0) = u(1) = 0\,. \tag{10}$$

This example allows exact solutions. The eigenfunctions are $u^*(x) = \sin k\pi x$ and the eigenvalues are $\lambda = k^2\pi^2$. We want a "variational" form of the eigenvalue problem, so we can reduce it to a trial space T and compute approximate eigenfunctions U^*.

The linear term $\ell(u) = \int f(x)u(x)\,dx$ is gone (no source term). The unknown u appears on both sides of the eigenvalue equation $Ku = \lambda u$. Multiplying equation (10) by $u(x)$ and integrating by parts, we discover that λ *is a ratio of two integrals*:

$$\boldsymbol{\lambda = \frac{a(u,u)}{(u,u)}} \qquad \lambda \int_0^1 u^2(x)\,dx = \int_0^1 -u''(x)\,u(x)\,dx = \int_0^1 (u'(x))^2\,dx\,. \tag{11}$$

This ratio is called the **Rayleigh quotient**. It is the key to the eigenvalue problem. In the matrix case we would go from $Ku = \lambda u$ to $u^{\mathrm{T}}Ku = \lambda u^{\mathrm{T}}u$. The "integral" of u times u is $u^{\mathrm{T}}u$. Again $\lambda = u^{\mathrm{T}}Ku/u^{\mathrm{T}}u$ is the Rayleigh quotient.

The insight comes when we **minimize the Rayleigh quotient over all functions**. The minimum ratio is the *lowest eigenvalue* λ_1. The function $u^*(x)$ that produces this minimum ratio is the *lowest eigenfunction* u_1:

Minimizing the Rayleigh quotient $\boldsymbol{\dfrac{a(u,u)}{(u,u)}}$ ***solves the eigenvalue problem***

$$\lambda_1 = \min \frac{a(u,u)}{(u,u)} = \min \frac{\int (u'(x))^2\,dx}{\int (u(x))^2\,dx} \quad \text{with} \quad u(0) = u(1) = 0. \tag{12}$$

Equation (11) produced λ as this ratio, when $u(x)$ is the exact eigenfunction. Equation (12) says that λ_1 is the *minimum ratio*. If you substitute any other $u(x)$ into the Rayleigh quotient, you get a ratio larger than $\lambda_1 = \pi^2$.

Let me check this for a hat function that goes up and down linearly from $u(0) = 0$ to $u(\frac{1}{2}) = 1$ to $u(1) = 0$. The slope is $+2$ followed by -2, so $(u'(x))^2 = 4$:

Hat function $u(x)$

$$\frac{a(u,u)}{(u,u)} = \frac{\int 4\,dx}{\int (\text{hat})^2\,dx} = \frac{4}{1/3} = 12\,. \tag{13}$$

As expected, the ratio 12 is larger than $\lambda_1 = \pi^2$. The minimum ratio equals λ_1.

Our mission is to find *a discretization of the continuous eigenvalue problem.* This small example suggests a good way. Instead of minimizing the Rayleigh quotient over all functions $u(x)$, ***we minimize only over the trial functions $U(x)$***. That gives a discrete eigenvalue problem $KU^* = \Lambda MU^*$. Its lowest eigenvalue Λ_1 is larger than the true λ_1 (but close).

Substitute $U(x) = \sum U_j\phi_j(x)$ in the Rayleigh quotient. Minimizing over all vectors $U = (U_1, \ldots, U_N)$ leads to $KU^* = \Lambda MU^*$. The lowest eigenvalue is Λ_1:

Discrete eigenvalue problem

$$\min \frac{a(U,U)}{(U,U)} = \min \frac{U^{\mathrm{T}}KU}{U^{\mathrm{T}}MU} = \Lambda_1 \geq \lambda_1\,. \tag{14}$$

The approximate eigenfunction is $\sum U_j^*\phi_j(x)$, coming from the discrete eigenvector. For finite elements and second order equations, the eigenvalue error $\Lambda_1 - \lambda_1$ will have the same order $(h^p)^2$ that we found above for the error in energy.

The discrete eigenvalue problem has the "generalized" form $KU = \Lambda MU$ with two positive definite matrices K and M. The best finite element example has linear trial functions with mesh spacing $h = 1/3$. There are two hat functions ϕ_1 and ϕ_2, and the lowest eigenvalue is $\Lambda_1 = 54/5$. Smaller than 12 but larger than π^2:

$$\boldsymbol{KU^* = \Lambda MU^*} \qquad \begin{bmatrix} 6 & -3 \\ -3 & 6 \end{bmatrix} \begin{bmatrix} 1 \\ 1 \end{bmatrix} = \frac{\Lambda}{18} \begin{bmatrix} 4 & 1 \\ 1 & 4 \end{bmatrix} \begin{bmatrix} 1 \\ 1 \end{bmatrix} \quad \text{has} \quad \Lambda = \frac{54}{5}. \tag{15}$$

Problem Set 8.4

1 The solution to $-u'' = 2$ is $u^*(x) = x - x^2$, with $u(0) = 0$ and $u(1) = 0$. Compute $P(u) = \frac{1}{2}\int (u')^2\,dx - \int 2u(x)\,dx$ for this u^*. Compute $P(u)$ also for the hat function $u_H = \min(x, 1-x)$. The theory says $P(u^*) < P(u_H)$.

2 If we tried the constant function $u(x) = 1$, we would find $P(u) = -2$. Why is this lower value unacceptable?

3 For this special problem with $a(u,v) = \int u'v'\,dx$, the linear finite element solution U^* is exactly the interpolant U_I. This was a miracle for finite differences in Section 1.2, now it is automatic for finite elements. Just test equation (5):

Prove $a(U_I - u^*, U) = \int (U_I - u^*)'U'\,dx = 0$ if U is linear and $U_I = u^*$ at the ends.

4 What is $a(u,u)$ for Laplace's equation? What is $P(u)$ for Poisson's equation $u_{xx} + u_{yy} = 4$? Find the solution u^* on the unit square $[0,1]^2$ if $u = 0$ on the sides, and compute $P(u^*)$. Compare with $P(u)$ for $u = (\sin \pi x)(\sin \pi y)$.

5 That function $u = (\sin \pi x)(\sin \pi y)$ solves $-u_{xx} - u_{yy} = \lambda u$. What is its Rayleigh quotient $a(u,u)/\int u^2\,dx\,dy$? Compare with the Rayleigh quotient for the trial function $u = x^2 - x + y^2 - y$.

6 The first variation of $u^{\mathrm{T}}Ku$, when compared with $(u+v)^{\mathrm{T}}K(u+v)$, is $2u^{\mathrm{T}}Kv$. What is the first variation $\delta R/\delta u$ by the quotient rule, for the Rayleigh quotient $R = u^{\mathrm{T}}Ku/u^{\mathrm{T}}Mu$? If $\delta R/\delta u = 0$ for every v, show that $Ku = \lambda Mu$.

7 The least squares equation $A^{\mathrm{T}}A\widehat{u} = A^{\mathrm{T}}b$ was reached through projections: $A\widehat{u}$ is as close as possible to b. The error $b - A\widehat{u}$ is perpendicular to all AU:

$(AU)^{\mathrm{T}}(b - A\widehat{u}) = 0$ for every U (*weak form*) gives $A^{\mathrm{T}}b - A^{\mathrm{T}}A\widehat{u} = 0$ (*strong form*).

Problem Weighted least squares is $(AU)^{\mathrm{T}}C(b - A\widehat{u}) = 0$ for every U. What is the strong form (the equation for $\widehat{u}$)? What is the weighted inner product $a(U,V)$? Then $a(U,U)$ is $U^{\mathrm{T}}KU$ for the usual $K = A^{\mathrm{T}}CA$.

8 The second eigenvector in (15) is $U_2^* = (1, -1)$. Show that $\Lambda_2 > \lambda_2 = 2^2\pi^2$.

8.5 THE SADDLE POINT STOKES PROBLEM

So far the matrix C in A^TCA has been diagonal—no trouble to invert. This section jumps to a fluid flow problem that is still linear (simpler than Navier-Stokes). But now C^{-1} represents the positive definite Laplacian $(-\Delta)$ in the differential equation.

In the matrix problem, C^{-1} will be a discrete Laplacian like $K2D$. **Its inverse C is dense.** In fact $C^{-1}\boldsymbol{v} = \boldsymbol{f}$ involves a serious boundary value problem. In this case we might not reduce the block matrix computation all the way to A^TCA:

Saddle point matrix S
Continuous or discrete

$$\begin{bmatrix} C^{-1} & A \\ A^T & 0 \end{bmatrix} \begin{bmatrix} \boldsymbol{v} \\ p \end{bmatrix} = \begin{bmatrix} -\Delta & \text{grad} \\ -\text{div} & 0 \end{bmatrix} \begin{bmatrix} \boldsymbol{v} \\ p \end{bmatrix} = \begin{bmatrix} \boldsymbol{f} \\ 0 \end{bmatrix}. \quad (1)$$

That block matrix is symmetric but ***indefinite*** (as usual). Its discrete form S will have positive and also negative eigenvalues and pivots (positive pivots from C^{-1}, negative pivots from $-A^TCA$). Finite elements for the velocity $\boldsymbol{v}$ and pressure p have to be carefully matched to ensure that the discrete problem has a good solution. The approximating polynomials are often *one degree higher* for $\boldsymbol{v}$ than for p.

This section discusses the preconditioning of indefinite systems (not only Stokes). The real problem here is indefiniteness, and the **inf-sup condition** to test stability. Two changes will be proposed for S. A new block $-D$ (instead of the zero block) improves stability. And a sign change to $-A^T$ and $+D$ in the second row has opened up entirely new ideas for iterations.

The Stokes Problem

The unknowns in the two-dimensional Stokes problem are the velocity components in $\boldsymbol{v} = (v_1(x,y), v_2(x,y))$ and the pressure $p(x,y)$. The flow is *incompressible* so the velocity vector is constrained by $\text{div}\,\boldsymbol{v} = 0$. Therefore A^T is (minus) the divergence and A must be the gradient. Notice the different letters in our framework (u is changed to p, w is changed to $\boldsymbol{v}$, and b is changed to $\boldsymbol{f}$):

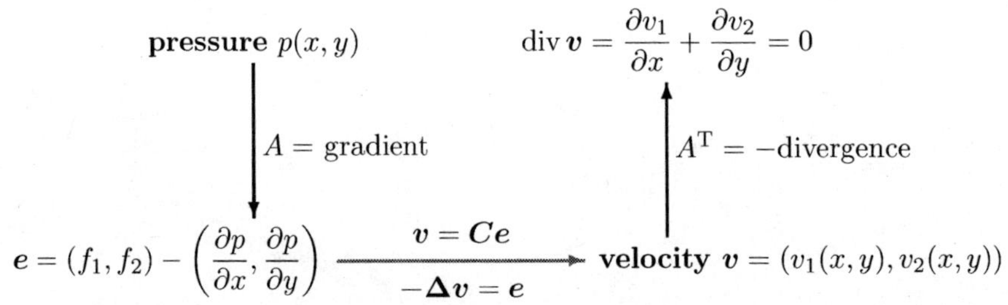

Figure 8.11: The A^TCA framework for the Stokes problem has a difficult C.

The real novelty is in $\boldsymbol{e} = C^{-1}\boldsymbol{v} = (-\Delta v_1, -\Delta v_2)$. The Stokes problem asks us to find a velocity vector (v_1, v_2) and a pressure p that solve $-\Delta \boldsymbol{v} + \operatorname{grad} p = \boldsymbol{f}$ and $\operatorname{div} \boldsymbol{v} = 0$. The viscosity term $-\Delta \boldsymbol{v}$ overwhelms the convection term $\boldsymbol{v} \cdot \operatorname{grad} \boldsymbol{v}$.

Stokes problem

$$\begin{bmatrix} -\Delta & \text{grad} \\ \text{div} & 0 \end{bmatrix} \begin{bmatrix} \boldsymbol{v} \\ p \end{bmatrix} = \begin{bmatrix} \boldsymbol{f} \\ 0 \end{bmatrix} \qquad \begin{aligned} -\left(\frac{\partial^2 v_1}{\partial x^2} + \frac{\partial^2 v_1}{\partial y^2}\right) + \frac{\partial p}{\partial x} &= f_1(x,y) \\ -\left(\frac{\partial^2 v_2}{\partial x^2} + \frac{\partial^2 v_2}{\partial y^2}\right) + \frac{\partial p}{\partial y} &= f_2(x,y) \\ \frac{\partial v_1}{\partial x} + \frac{\partial v_2}{\partial y} \qquad\qquad &= 0 \end{aligned} \tag{2}$$

This describes **slow viscous flow**. It is not for aeronautics! The full Navier-Stokes equations have extra nonlinear terms $\boldsymbol{v} \cdot \operatorname{grad} \boldsymbol{v}$ from the motion of the underlying fluid. The Stokes problem enters in biological applications, not for large-scale blood flow in the heart but for small-scale movements in capillaries (or even in cells). We keep this linear problem simple by omitting discussion of the boundary conditions.

In the language of optimization, the pressure $p(x, y)$ is the Lagrange multiplier that imposes the incompressibility constraint $\operatorname{div} \boldsymbol{v} = 0$ when the energy is minimized:

$$\text{Minimize} \iint \left(|\operatorname{grad} v_1|^2 + |\operatorname{grad} v_2|^2 - 2\boldsymbol{f} \cdot \boldsymbol{v}\right) dx\, dy \;\text{ subject to }\; \operatorname{div} \boldsymbol{v} = 0\,.$$

The Lagrangian $L(\boldsymbol{v}, p)$ includes $\iint p \operatorname{div} \boldsymbol{v}\, dx\, dy$. Then the Euler-Lagrange equations $\delta L/\delta \boldsymbol{v} = 0$ and $\delta L/\delta p = 0$ in Section 8.3 are exactly the Stokes equations (2).

The key point is that we do not eliminate $\boldsymbol{v}$ to reach $K = A^{\mathrm{T}}CA$, because C is *the inverse of the Laplacian.* C is diagonal only in frequency space, not in physical space. The Stokes problem stays in its block form (2) with two unknowns $\boldsymbol{v}$ and p. **Constraints bring saddle points**—the safety of positive definiteness is lost. We cannot use finite elements for $\boldsymbol{v}$ and p without checking their stability.

The Inf-Sup Condition

Restricting K to a subspace never destroys positive definiteness ($u^{\mathrm{T}}Ku$ stays positive). λ_{min} and λ_{max} for the projected submatrix will lie between $\lambda_{\text{min}}(K)$ and $\lambda_{\text{max}}(K)$. An indefinite operator has a *negative* λ_{min}, so this interval includes zero: not safe! We must take particular care that the block matrix S is safely invertible.

These **mixed problems**, or **saddle point problems**, are partly positive and partly negative. The new requirement for a bounded S^{-1} is an ***inf-sup condition***. The inf-sup condition (also named for Babuska and Brezzi) ensures "compatibility" of velocities and pressures. **For every p there must be a v so that**

Inf-sup condition $\qquad \boldsymbol{v}^{\mathrm{T}}Ap \geq \beta\sqrt{\boldsymbol{v}^{\mathrm{T}}C^{-1}\boldsymbol{v}}\,\sqrt{p^{\mathrm{T}}p}\;$ for a fixed $\beta > 0$. $\qquad$ (3)

Condition (3) will immediately fail, if there is a nonzero pressure p with $Ap = 0$. The last n columns of S would be dependent, and S has no chance to be invertible. In particular, the rectangular block A cannot be short and wide.

More exactly, the lower bound (3) on $\boldsymbol{v}^{\mathrm{T}}Ap$ requires that a nonzero pressure p may not be orthogonal to every $A^{\mathrm{T}}\boldsymbol{v}$. The space of all $A^{\mathrm{T}}\boldsymbol{v}$'s must have *at least* the dimension of the space of p's. Thinking of A^{T} as divergence, this indicates why the velocity finite elements are often one polynomial degree above the pressure finite elements. But dimensions of spaces are not sufficient to confirm that (3) is actually true. Each choice of finite elements for $\boldsymbol{v}$ and p requires its own inf-sup analysis.

The inf-sup condition leads to $\|(A^{\mathrm{T}}CA)^{-1}\| \leq 1/\beta^2$ which is stability. Begin by introducing $\boldsymbol{w} = C^{-1/2}\boldsymbol{v}$. The continuous and discrete Laplacians, both called C^{-1}, have positive definite square roots $C^{-1/2}$ (never to be computed). Then the inf-sup condition $\boldsymbol{v}^{\mathrm{T}}Ap \geq \beta\sqrt{\boldsymbol{v}^{\mathrm{T}}C^{-1}\boldsymbol{v}}\sqrt{p^{\mathrm{T}}p}$ has an equivalent form:

$$\textbf{For every } p \textbf{ there must be a } \boldsymbol{w} \textbf{ so that } \quad \frac{\boldsymbol{w}^{\mathrm{T}}C^{1/2}Ap}{\|\boldsymbol{w}\|} \geq \beta\,\|p\|\,. \tag{4}$$

This is where we take the maximum over all $\boldsymbol{w}$ (the ***sup***). On the left, the maximum of $\boldsymbol{w}^{\mathrm{T}}\boldsymbol{z}/\|\boldsymbol{w}\|$ is exactly $\|\boldsymbol{z}\|$. This is attained when $\boldsymbol{w} = \boldsymbol{z}$ (then the cosine is one). Since (4) has $\boldsymbol{z} = C^{1/2}Ap$, this best choice of $\boldsymbol{w}$ simplifies the condition:

$$\textbf{For every } p, \ \|\boldsymbol{z}\| = \|C^{1/2}Ap\| \geq \beta\,\|p\|\,. \tag{5}$$

Square both sides, and minimize their ratio over all p (the ***inf***). The inequality

$$\|C^{1/2}Ap\|^2 \geq \beta^2\|p\|^2 \quad \text{or} \quad p^{\mathrm{T}}A^{\mathrm{T}}CAp \geq \beta^2 p^{\mathrm{T}}p \tag{6}$$

says that the smallest eigenvalue of $A^{\mathrm{T}}CA$ is at least β^2. Singularity is avoided. The matrix $(A^{\mathrm{T}}CA)^{-1}$ is symmetric so its norm is $\leq 1/\beta^2$. Stability is proved.

Correction to $p^{\mathrm{T}}p$: Finite elements are functions $p_h(x,y)$, not just vectors p. So inner products and norms of p_h come from integrals and not sums. The L^2 norm of a pressure trial function $p_h = \sum p_j\psi_j(x,y)$ is connected to the discrete vector p of coefficients p_j through a positive definite "**pressure mass matrix**" Q:

$$\iint (p_h)^2\,dx\,dy = \sum\sum p_i p_j \iint \psi_i\psi_j\,dx\,dy = p^{\mathrm{T}}Qp\,. \tag{7}$$

The correct inf-sup condition changes $p^{\mathrm{T}}p$ in (6) to $p^{\mathrm{T}}Qp$:

$$\textbf{Correction to } (6) \qquad p^{\mathrm{T}}A^{\mathrm{T}}CAp \geq \beta^2\,p^{\mathrm{T}}Qp \tag{8}$$

This makes Q (or even its diagonal part) a simple and useful candidate as preconditioner. Not the best, but it is directly available and it scales the problem correctly.

A key goal of the inf-sup condition is to work with C^{-1} in (3) and not $A^{\mathrm{T}}CA$. *The inf-sup test must be applied to subspaces V_h and P_h of finite element trial functions.* For every pressure p_h in P_h, there must be a velocity $\boldsymbol{v}_h$ in V_h with $\boldsymbol{v}_h^{\mathrm{T}}Ap_h$ bounded below. If and when this test is passed, with a bound β_h that stays away from zero, the **mixed finite element method** using V_h and P_h will be stable.

Testing and Stabilizing Finite Elements

The inf-sup condition can be delicate. The books by Brezzi-Fortin and Elman-Silvester-Wathen are excellent references. From the latter book we report on typical results.

$\boldsymbol{P}_0, \boldsymbol{P}_1, \boldsymbol{P}_2$ contain constant, linear $(a + bx + cy)$, and quadratic polynomials on triangles. The spaces $\boldsymbol{Q}_0, \boldsymbol{Q}_1, \boldsymbol{Q}_2$ are constant, bilinear $(a + bx + cy + dxy)$, and biquadratic on quads, including squares. When the trial functions are $\phi_j(x, y)$ for both v_1 and v_2, and $\psi_k(x, y)$ for pressure, the blocks in C^{-1} and A are integrals:

$$C_{ij}^{-1} = \iint \left(\frac{\partial \phi_i}{\partial x}\frac{\partial \phi_j}{\partial x} + \frac{\partial \phi_i}{\partial y}\frac{\partial \phi_j}{\partial y} \right) dx\, dy \qquad A_{kl} = -\iint \psi_k \begin{bmatrix} \partial \phi_l / \partial x \\ \partial \phi_l / \partial y \end{bmatrix} dx\, dy \qquad (9)$$

The codes on manchester.ac.uk/ifiss construct C^{-1} and A, with inf-sup tests.

1. Velocities in $\boldsymbol{P}_1$ (or $\boldsymbol{Q}_1$), pressures in $\boldsymbol{P}_1$ (or $\boldsymbol{Q}_1$): **failure if both degrees = 1**

2. Velocities in $\boldsymbol{P}_2$ (or $\boldsymbol{Q}_2$), pressures in $\boldsymbol{P}_1$ (or $\boldsymbol{Q}_1$): **success in Figure 8.12**

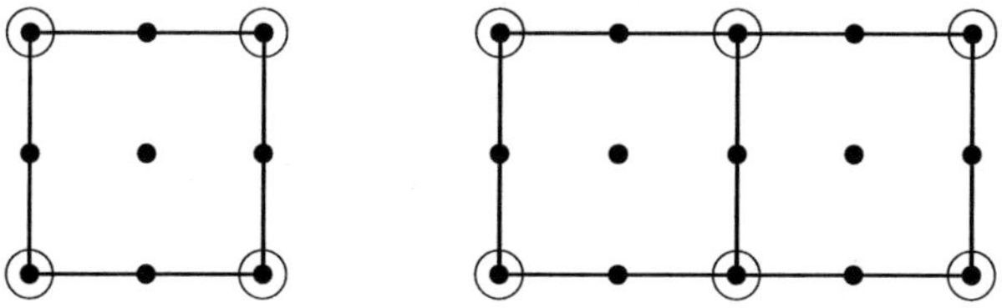

Stability for $\boldsymbol{Q}_2 - \boldsymbol{Q}_1$

Figure 8.12: $\boldsymbol{Q}_2$ velocities • and $\boldsymbol{Q}_1$ pressures ○: one square fails but success on two.

One square has four pressures and only two velocity components at the center for enclosed flow. A is 2 by 4. There must be non-constant solutions to $Ap = 0$: failure.

For two squares, A is 6 by 6 (six pressures and (v_1, v_2) at three internal nodes). Only a constant pressure solves $Ap = 0$, and this *hydrostatic solution* is removed by the boundary conditions (like grounding a node): *success with many squares.*

3. Velocities in $\boldsymbol{P}_1$ (or $\boldsymbol{Q}_1$), pressures in $\boldsymbol{P}_0$ (or $\boldsymbol{Q}_0$): **failure in Figure 8.13**

The list of element pairs also includes linear pressures $\boldsymbol{P}_{-1}$ that are *not continuous* between triangles (this is permitted since delta functions don't appear):

4. Velocities in $\boldsymbol{P}_2$, pressures in $\boldsymbol{P}_{-1}$: **failure**

5. Velocities in $\boldsymbol{Q}_2$, pressures in $\boldsymbol{P}_0$ or $\boldsymbol{P}_{-1}$: **success.**

The failures of $\boldsymbol{Q}_1 - \boldsymbol{Q}_0$ and $\boldsymbol{Q}_1 - \boldsymbol{P}_0$ are especially important. $\boldsymbol{Q}_1$ is the simplest *conforming* element on squares (no delta functions in grad $\boldsymbol{v}$ because $a+bx+cy+dxy$ is made continuous across edges). The next page will rescue $\boldsymbol{Q}_1$ for velocities.

Instability for $Q_1 - Q_0$
$v = a + bx + cy + dxy$ in Q_1
$p =$ *constant* in Q_0 allows $Ap = 0$

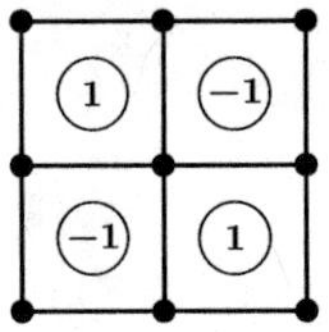

Figure 8.13: Bilinear v's • and constant p's ○ (*unstable checkerboard mode*).

Four squares are not stable because the pressure vector $p = (1, -1, 1, -1)$ satisfies $Ap = 0$. More squares don't help—the checkerboard with "white squares = 1" and "black squares = −1" continues to be a spurious mode satisfying $Ap = 0$. The columns of A, even after $p =$ constant is removed, are still not independent.

$Q_1 - Q_0$ and $Q_1 - P_0$ elements are potentially so useful that they are often stabilized by relaxing the incompressibility equation $A^T\boldsymbol{v} = 0$. We insert a new anti-checkerboard matrix $-D$, chosen to eliminate $(1, -1, 1, -1)$ from the nullspace:

Stabilized matrix $$S = \begin{bmatrix} C^{-1} & A \\ A^T & -\boldsymbol{D} \end{bmatrix} \text{ with } D = \alpha \begin{bmatrix} 1 & -1 & 1 & -1 \\ -1 & 1 & -1 & 1 \\ 1 & -1 & 1 & -1 \\ -1 & 1 & -1 & 1 \end{bmatrix}. \quad (10)$$

Our zero block is replaced by the **negative semidefinite** matrix $-\boldsymbol{D}$. Elimination leaves $-A^TCA - D$ in that block, which is more strongly negative. Now S is uniformly invertible (*also for* $Q_1 - Q_1$) since D times the checkerboard p is not zero.

In this special case we know the guilty p. In other cases D is constructed with only the vector $p =$ constant in its nullspace (which isn't harmful). Then α is chosen small enough so that its positive eigenvalues roughly match those of A^TCA. And the zero eigenvalue of A^TCA (produced by the checkerboard pressure) becomes positive.

Solving the Discrete Saddle Point Problem

Don't forget that this is the fundamental problem of scientific computing:

Saddle matrix S
Positive definite K
$$\begin{bmatrix} C^{-1} & A \\ A^T & 0 \end{bmatrix} \begin{bmatrix} w \\ u \end{bmatrix} = \begin{bmatrix} b \\ f \end{bmatrix} \quad \text{or} \quad A^TCAu = f - A^TCb. \quad (11)$$

In this section, w has become $\boldsymbol{v}$ and u is p. The zero block might become $-D$. When C was a diagonal matrix (or small-block diagonal, in a multidimensional problem), the reduction to A^TCA was very reasonable. Now the Stokes problem illustrates that C^{-1} can be sparse (from finite differences or finite elements) while C is full. In that case we may prefer to compute with the sparse indefinite S.

This page describes established methods for S. The next pages are more exciting.

1. A direct method (not iterative) is appropriate up to $n = 10^4$ or 10^5. Elimination will be used in most problems! The indefinite matrix S may need row exchanges, and a good code will decide that without our intervention.

The pivoting can be organized using 2 by 2 blocks, or we may reorder the unknowns as in Section 7.1 to keep the L and U factors as sparse as possible. If we eliminate in the original order, subtracting $A^{\mathrm{T}}C$ times one block row from the other, then $-K = -A^{\mathrm{T}}CA$ will appear as the **Schur complement** in the lower right block.

2. The conjugate gradient method will be safe for the positive definite $A^{\mathrm{T}}CA$ problem. In each (preconditioned) CG step, the multiplications Ap and $A^{\mathrm{T}}\boldsymbol{v}$ are fast. Multiplying by C amounts to "Poisson solves" $C^{-1}\boldsymbol{v} = Ap$ with the Laplace matrix. An inner iteration like multigrid makes that faster.

A number of iterative methods compute both $\boldsymbol{v}$ and p, based on the block form:

3. **Uzawa's method** alternates $C^{-1}\boldsymbol{v}^{k+1} = \boldsymbol{f} - Ap^k$ and $p^{k+1} = p^k + \alpha A^{\mathrm{T}}\boldsymbol{v}^{k+1}$.

4. **Penalty methods** are described in Section 8.2, adding a stabilizer like $-D$.

5. **Augmented Lagrangian methods** are presented by Glowinsk: and Fortin.

These and more are discussed by Quarteroni-Valli [128] for the Stokes problem. They all involve the Poisson solver associated with C. We turn instead to a closer look at *preconditioners for the general saddle point matrix* S, whether it arises in fluid flow or optimization or network analysis or elsewhere.

Preconditioning Saddle Point Problems

The basic methods for large sparse indefinite problems are **MINRES** and **GMRES** (symmetric and nonsymmetric). Our focus is on constructing a good preconditioner. Look at the block matrix S and its factors:

$$\boldsymbol{S = LDL^{\mathrm{T}}} \qquad \begin{bmatrix} C^{-1} & A \\ A^{\mathrm{T}} & 0 \end{bmatrix} = \begin{bmatrix} I & 0 \\ A^{\mathrm{T}}C & I \end{bmatrix} \begin{bmatrix} C^{-1} & 0 \\ 0 & -A^{\mathrm{T}}CA \end{bmatrix} \begin{bmatrix} I & CA \\ 0 & I \end{bmatrix}. \tag{12}$$

S^{-1} clearly involves C and $(A^{\mathrm{T}}CA)^{-1}$ from the inverse of that middle matrix. Our preconditioners P will keep this m, n block structure. To come close to S^{-1}, P can approximate the blocks of S and invert, or directly approximate C and $(A^{\mathrm{T}}CA)^{-1}$.

When we only know the matrix entries in C^{-1} and A, the code will have to construct P "blindly" from that information. The dividing line is to be *given a matrix or given a problem.* When we know the underlying problem (like Stokes), we can devise a preconditioner by hand. There is a similar separation between algebraic and geometric multigrid (the computer chooses the reduced problem or we do).

Three approximations to S are suggested by Elman-Silvester-Wathen [47]:

$$\textbf{Preconditioners} \qquad P_1 = \begin{bmatrix} \widehat{C}^{-1} & A \\ A^{\mathrm{T}} & 0 \end{bmatrix} \qquad P_2 = \begin{bmatrix} \widehat{C}^{-1} & 0 \\ 0 & \widehat{K} \end{bmatrix} \qquad P_3 = \begin{bmatrix} \widehat{C}^{-1} & A \\ 0 & \widehat{K} \end{bmatrix}$$

P_1 is a "constraint preconditioner"—it keep A unchanged. $\widehat{C}$ approximates the Poisson solver C, and $\widehat{K}$ approximates $K = A^{\mathrm{T}}CA$. Here are two fast algorithms:

1. Replace the Poisson solver C by a single multigrid cycle $\widehat{C}$.

2. Replace K^{-1} by four conjugate gradient steps preconditioned by Q or $\mathsf{diag}(Q)$.

Q is the pressure mass matrix in (7). Fixed multiples of $p^{\mathrm{T}}Qp$ are below and above $p^{\mathrm{T}}Kp$. Usually $\mathsf{diag}(Q)$ also has this "equispectral property" and it rescales S.

A key point about P_2 and P_3: If $\widehat{C} = C$ and $\widehat{K} = K$, then $P_2^{-1}S$ has only *three* different eigenvalues. $P_3^{-1}S$ only has $\lambda = \pm 1$. In that case MINRES and GMRES converge in three or two steps. So those changes from P_1 add very few iterations.

Change Signs to Allow Conjugate Gradients

A neat way to deal with S has recently emerged. Multiply its second row by -1:

Blocks A and $-A^{\mathrm{T}}$
Unsymmetric U
$$U = \begin{bmatrix} C^{-1} & A \\ -A^{\mathrm{T}} & D \end{bmatrix} \qquad (13)$$

It's safe to change signs in the equations (D is a positive semidefinite stabilizer if needed). This unsymmetric U can have complex eigenvalues, but all with $\mathbf{Re}\,\boldsymbol{\lambda} \geq \mathbf{0}$:

$$[\,\overline{w}^{\mathrm{T}}\ \overline{u}^{\mathrm{T}}\,]\,U\begin{bmatrix} w \\ u \end{bmatrix} = \lambda[\,\overline{w}^{\mathrm{T}}\ \overline{u}^{\mathrm{T}}\,]\begin{bmatrix} w \\ u \end{bmatrix} \quad \text{gives} \quad \operatorname{Re}\lambda = \frac{\overline{w}^{\mathrm{T}}C^{-1}w + \overline{u}^{\mathrm{T}}Du}{\overline{w}^{\mathrm{T}}w + \overline{u}^{\mathrm{T}}u} \geq 0. \qquad (14)$$

The off-diagonal part $\overline{w}^{\mathrm{T}}Au - \overline{u}^{\mathrm{T}}A^{\mathrm{T}}w$ is pure imaginary from the sign change.

Something better is true if A is small, provided that C^{-1} is separated from D. This scalar example shows that U then has *real and positive eigenvalues*:

$$U = \begin{bmatrix} 3 & a \\ -a & 1 \end{bmatrix} \quad \lambda^2 - 4\lambda + (3 + a^2) = 0 \quad \lambda = 2 \pm \sqrt{1 - a^2} > 0 \text{ if } a^2 \leq 1 \qquad (15)$$

This is "unsymmetric positive definiteness"—a phrase I never use. It opens the way back to positive definiteness, but with *two matrices* in $U = PR$. The eigenvalues in $PRx = \lambda x$ are real and positive, because λ is the ratio of $\overline{x}^{\mathrm{T}}RPRx$ to $\overline{x}^{\mathrm{T}}Rx$. **Conjugate gradients will apply to $\boldsymbol{PR}$, with $\boldsymbol{P}$ as preconditioner for $\boldsymbol{U}$.**

All this fails if the gap between 3 and 1 is closed, and we lose real eigenvalues:

$$U = \begin{bmatrix} 3 & a \\ -a & 3 \end{bmatrix} \quad \text{has complex eigenvalues } \lambda = 3 \pm ai \text{ with } \operatorname{Re}\lambda > 0. \qquad (16)$$

At this moment we don't know whether CG can be saved. Here we continue with real λ and $C^{-1} > D$ (meaning that the difference is positive definite). Liesen and Parlett discovered symmetric factors in $U = PR$ that are beautifully computable:

$$\text{If } P^{-1} = \begin{bmatrix} C^{-1} - bI & A \\ A^{\mathrm{T}} & bI - D \end{bmatrix} \text{ then } R = P^{-1}U \text{ is also symmetric} \tag{17}$$

$$P^{-1} \text{ is positive definite when } C^{-1} > bI > D \text{ and } bI - D > A^{\mathrm{T}}(C^{-1} - bI)^{-1}A \tag{18}$$

A preconditioned CG method is tested and fully explained in [111]. We hope this can be a breakthrough, to allow the power of conjugate gradients in saddle point problems.

Nonsymmetric Problems and Model Reduction

We turn briefly toward problems more general than Stokes. New ideas for S and U are developed in [13], with many applications. The equations might come from Navier-Stokes and its linearizations. Then C will be unsymmetric, from first derivatives. *Convection joins diffusion* in so many problems from engineering.

The strength of inertia versus viscosity is measured by the **Reynolds number Re** = (density)(velocity)(distance)/(viscosity). This section on Stokes flow is the limiting case Re = 0 for high viscosity and low velocity. The high speed Euler equation $d\boldsymbol{v}/dt = -\operatorname{grad} p + \boldsymbol{f}$ is at the other extreme with Re $= \infty$ and no viscosity.

Beyond computational fluid dynamics are other differential equations with their own constraints. They bring all the algebraic problems of constrained optimization. The *Schur complement* $-BCA$ is always the key, now possibly unsymmetric:

$$\text{Elimination reduces } \begin{bmatrix} C^{-1} & A \\ B & 0 \end{bmatrix} \text{ to } \begin{bmatrix} C^{-1} & A \\ 0 & -BCA \end{bmatrix}. \tag{19}$$

Normally $K = BCA$ will be dense. If it is also large, we look at iterative methods like *algebraic multigrid.* Our discussion is moving from "given a problem" toward "given a matrix." There may be no differential equation in the background.

For $K = BCA$, a "black box" approach to preconditioning reduces C to $\widehat{C}$:

Model reduction $\quad A\widetilde{C} \approx CA \quad$ and then $\quad \widehat{K} = BA\widehat{C} \approx BCA$.

Notice that C is m by m (large) while $\widehat{C}$ is n by n. The reduction rule $CA = A\widehat{C}$ will not be exactly solvable (more equations than unknowns). Weighted least squares will give $\widehat{C}^{-1}$ from $A\widehat{C}^{-1} \approx C^{-1}A$. The meaning of $\approx$ is to be decided by the user!

I expect new ideas will keep coming, for this fundamental saddle point problem.

Problem Set 8.5

Problems 1-4 are about standard finite elements in 2D and 3D.

1 For a standard 3D tetrahedron with corners $(0,0,0), (1,0,0), (0,1,0), (0,0,1)$, the $\boldsymbol{P}_1$ elements are $\phi = a + bX + cY + dZ$. Find the four ϕ's that are zero at three corners and 1 at the fourth corner.

2 The $\boldsymbol{P}_2$ element in 3D also uses the six edge midpoints. Draw the 10 nodes for $\boldsymbol{P}_2$ on a "tet". What combination ϕ of $1, X, Y, Z, X^2, Y^2, Z^2, XY, XZ, YZ$ is zero at all 4 corners and 5 of the edge midpoints, with $\phi(.5, 0, 0) = 1$?

3 The standard $\boldsymbol{Q}_2$ element in the unit square has nine trial functions ϕ_i for the nine nodes with X and Y equal to $0, \frac{1}{2}$, or 1. Draw those 9 nodes in a square. The trial functions ϕ_i have 9 terms $1, X, Y, X^2, XY, Y^2, X^2Y, XY^2, X^2Y^2$. Find $\phi_5(X, Y)$ for the bottom midpoint $(\frac{1}{2}, 0)$ and $\phi_9(X, Y)$ for the center $(\frac{1}{2}, \frac{1}{2})$.

4 How many nodes for a $\boldsymbol{Q}_2$ brick element in 3D? What *bubble function* ϕ is zero at all nodes on the faces and one at the center node $(X, Y, Z) = (\frac{1}{2}, \frac{1}{2}, \frac{1}{2})$?

5 The only 3 eigenvalues of $P^{-1}S$ are $1, (1 \pm \sqrt{5})/2$ for the right preconditioner:

$$Sx = \lambda Px \quad \text{is} \quad \begin{bmatrix} C^{-1} & A \\ A^{\mathrm{T}} & 0 \end{bmatrix} \begin{bmatrix} u \\ p \end{bmatrix} = \lambda \begin{bmatrix} C^{-1} & 0 \\ 0 & A^{\mathrm{T}}CA \end{bmatrix} \begin{bmatrix} u \\ p \end{bmatrix}.$$

(a) Check $\lambda = 1$ with $m - n$ eigenvectors when $A^{\mathrm{T}}u = 0$ and $p = 0$.

(b) Show that $(\lambda^2 - \lambda - 1)\, A^{\mathrm{T}}CAp = 0$ for the other $2n$ eigenvectors. This P is impractical; we are trying to avoid $K = A^{\mathrm{T}}CA$. But it shows that $\widehat{C}^{-1}$ and $\widehat{K}$ can give an excellent preconditioner $P = \mathsf{diag}(\widehat{C}^{-1}, \widehat{K})$.

6 The preconditioner P_3 keeps the block A exactly (but not A^{T}):

$$Sx = \lambda P_3 x \quad \text{is} \quad \begin{bmatrix} C^{-1} & A \\ A^{\mathrm{T}} & 0 \end{bmatrix} \begin{bmatrix} u \\ p \end{bmatrix} = \lambda \begin{bmatrix} C^{-1} & A \\ 0 & A^{\mathrm{T}}CA \end{bmatrix} \begin{bmatrix} u \\ p \end{bmatrix}.$$

The first block equation is $(1-\lambda)(C^{-1}u + Ap) = 0$. Then $\lambda = 1$ or $C^{-1}u = -Ap$. Show that the second block equation then gives $\lambda = -1$. *Convergence takes two iterations.* Again this ideal P_3 is not practical.

7 Use square_stokes in IFISS to find the discrete divergence matrix A^{T} for $\boldsymbol{Q}_1$–$\boldsymbol{Q}_1$ velocities and pressures on a grid of 16 squares with zero outer boundary conditions. This problem is described in [47, p.283] with $B = A^{\mathrm{T}}$. From svd(B) show that the nullspace of A is 8-dimensional.

Problems 8-10 are about the unsymmetric $\boldsymbol{U}$ from a sign change in $\boldsymbol{S}$.

8 The example in (15) has $C^{-1} = 3$ and $D = 1$. When $b = 2$ is their average, show that P^{-1} in (17) is positive definite for $a^2 < 1$.

9 In the same example verify that $P^{-1}U$ is symmetric for all b. Multiply any U in (13) and P^{-1} in (17) to confirm that $P^{-1}U$ is symmetric.

10 If a square matrix $U = V\Lambda V^{-1}$ has positive real eigenvalues in Λ, write U as the product of $V\Lambda V^{\mathrm{T}}$ and another positive definite matrix R.

8.6 LINEAR PROGRAMMING AND DUALITY

Linear programming has equality constraints $Ax = b$ *and also inequalities* $x \geq 0$. The cost $c_1x_1 + \cdots + c_nx_n$ that we minimize is linear. So the inputs to the problem are A, b, c and the output is (usually) the vector x^* of minimum cost. The vector y^* of Lagrange multipliers solves a highly important *dual* linear program, using A^{T}.

If both problems have optimal vectors, which is normal, then $c^{\mathrm{T}}x^* = b^{\mathrm{T}}y^*$. The "duality gap" is closed. *The minimum of* $c^{\mathrm{T}}x$ *equals the maximum of* $b^{\mathrm{T}}y$.

You can see why inequality constraints like $x \geq 0$ are needed. The matrix A is rectangular (with $m < n$). Then $Ax_n = 0$ has many solutions, and some of them probably have negative cost. If we could add large multiples of this x_n to any particular solution of $Ax = b$, we could drive the cost to $-\infty$.

In reality, even Enron could not continue to buy negative amounts of energy and pay negative prices. When the components x_j represent purchases, we expect to see n constraints $x_j \geq 0$. They combine into the vector inequality $x \geq 0$.

Here are the statements of the twin linear programs. The m equations $Ax = b$ have m Lagrange multipliers in y. Notice how n inequalities $x \geq 0$ in the primal produce n inequalities $A^{\mathrm{T}}y \leq c$ in the dual.

Primal	Minimize $c^{\mathrm{T}}x$ with constraints $Ax = b$ and $x \geq 0$	(1)
Dual	Maximize $b^{\mathrm{T}}y$ with constraints $A^{\mathrm{T}}y \leq c$.	(2)

One new word. Vectors are called ***feasible*** when they satisfy the constraints. In each problem, the set of all vectors satisfying the constraints is the ***feasible set***. In general, one or both of the feasible sets could be empty. The primal constraints $x_1 + x_2 = -1$ and $x_1 \geq 0$ and $x_2 \geq 0$ cannot be satisfied by any x_1 and x_2. We don't expect to see this (an empty feasible set) in good applications.

Let me come immediately to the essence of the theory, before the algorithms. Weak duality is easy, and you will see how it uses the inequality $A^{\mathrm{T}}y \leq c$.

Weak duality $\quad b^{\mathrm{T}}y \leq c^{\mathrm{T}}x \quad$ for any feasible x and y $\quad$ (3)

The proof only needs one line, using $Ax = b$ and $x \geq 0$ and $A^{\mathrm{T}}y \leq c$:

Proof
$$b^{\mathrm{T}}y = (Ax)^{\mathrm{T}}y = \boldsymbol{x}^{\mathrm{T}}(\boldsymbol{A}^{\mathrm{T}}\boldsymbol{y}) \leq \boldsymbol{x}^{\mathrm{T}}\boldsymbol{c} = c^{\mathrm{T}}x\,. \tag{4}$$

The step to watch is the inequality. It used both constraints $x \geq 0$ and $A^{\mathrm{T}}y \leq c$. If we only know that $7 \leq 8$, we cannot be sure that $7x \leq 8x$ until we know $x \geq 0$. The inequality $0 \leq x^{\mathrm{T}}(c - A^{\mathrm{T}}y)$ multiplies each $x_j \geq 0$ by a number $s_j \geq 0$. This important number s_j is the "***slack***" in the jth inequality $A^{\mathrm{T}}y \leq c$:

$$\boldsymbol{s} = \boldsymbol{c} - \boldsymbol{A}^{\mathrm{T}}\boldsymbol{y} \text{ is the vector of } \textbf{slack variables}. \text{ Always } \boldsymbol{s} \geq \boldsymbol{0}\,. \tag{5}$$

Weak duality $b^{\mathrm{T}}y \le c^{\mathrm{T}}x$ is simple but valuable. It tells us what must happen for full duality, when the inequality becomes *equality*. Weak duality has $x^{\mathrm{T}}(c - A^{\mathrm{T}}y) \ge 0$. This is $x^{\mathrm{T}}s \ge 0$, for the slack $s = c - A^{\mathrm{T}}y$. ***Full duality has*** $\boldsymbol{x^{\mathrm{T}}s = 0}$.

The components x_j and s_j are never negative, but x and s have a zero dot product $x^{\mathrm{T}}s = 0$ when duality is reached. *For each j, either x_j or s_j must be zero.* This ***complementary slackness*** is the key to duality, at the optimal x^* and y^* and s^*:

Optimality $(\boldsymbol{x^*})^{\mathrm{T}}\boldsymbol{s^*} = \mathbf{0}$ $\qquad x_j^* = 0 \text{ or } s_j^* = 0 \text{ for each } j. \qquad (6)$

The hard part is to show that this actually happens (if both feasible sets are nonempty). When it does happen, we know that the vectors x^* and y^* and s^* must be optimal. ***The minimum of*** $\mathbf{c}^{\mathrm{T}}\boldsymbol{x}$ ***matches the maximum of*** $\mathbf{b}^{\mathrm{T}}\boldsymbol{y}$.

Duality $\qquad$ Optimal vectors x^* and y^* give $\mathbf{c}^{\mathrm{T}}\boldsymbol{x}^* = \mathbf{b}^{\mathrm{T}}\boldsymbol{y}^*$. $\qquad (7)$

The practical problem is how to compute x^* and y^*. Two algorithms are right now in an intense competition: **simplex methods** against **interior point methods.** The simplex method proves duality by actually constructing x^* and y^* (often quite quickly). This fundamental method is explained first, and executed by a short code.

Interior point methods work **inside** the feasible set. They put a logarithmic barrier at the boundary ($\log x$ makes $x \le 0$ impossible). They solve an optimality equation $x^{\mathrm{T}}s = \theta$, often by Newton's method. The solution $x^*(\theta)$ moves along the central path (a terrific name) to reach the optimal x^* when $\theta = 0$.

After those general linear programs, this text focuses on two special problems. One asks for **maximum flow** through a graph. You can guess the equality constraint: *Kirchhoff's Current Law.* Then A is the incidence matrix. Its properties lead to the **max flow-min cut theorem**, and its applications include image segmentation.

The other example brings an explosion of new ideas in sparse compression and sparse sensing. Sparsity comes with ℓ^1 (not ℓ^2). The key is to combine both norms:

Sparse solution from the ℓ^1 penalty $\qquad$ Minimize $\frac{1}{2}\|Ax - b\|_2^2 + \alpha\|x\|_1 \qquad (8)$

The term $\|x\|_1 = \sum |x_i|$ is piecewise linear. Its presence drives x to be sparse. But the slope of $|x_i|$ jumps from -1 to 1, and the derivative fails at $x_i = 0$. LASSO will be our introduction to nonlinear optimization (and our farewell too, if this book is to remain finite). The focus stays on **convex optimization**: the best problems.

Here is a skeleton outline of linear and network and nonlinear optimization:

1. The **simplex method**, moving along the edges of the feasible set.
2. The **interior point barrier method**, moving along the inside central path.
3. The sparsifying influence of the ℓ^1 norm, in **LASSO** and **basis pursuit**.
4. The special problem of **maximum flow-minimum cut**, with applications.

Corners of the Feasible Set

The solutions to m equations $Ax = b$ lie on a "plane" in n dimensions. (Figure 8.14 has $m = 1$ and $n = 3$.) When $b = 0$ the plane goes through $x = 0$. It is the nullspace of A and the equation is $Ax_{\text{null}} = 0$. Normally we have $b \neq 0$ and the solutions are $x = x_{\text{null}} + x_{\text{part}}$. Then the plane is shifted away from the origin by a particular solution x_{part} that solves $Ax = b$.

Linear programming requires $x \geq 0$. This restricts x to the "northeast corner" of $\mathbf{R}^n$. Coordinate planes like $x_1 = 0$ and $x_2 = 0$ will cut through the solution plane to $Ax = b$. Those cuts are faces of the feasible set where $Ax = b$ and $x \geq 0$. In Figure 8.14, the three coordinate planes $x_1 = 0, x_2 = 0, x_3 = 0$ cut out a triangle.

The triangle has three corners. **We claim that one of those corners is an x^*:**

Corner $\quad$ ***$Ax = b$ and $x \geq 0$ and $n - m$ components of x are zero.***

One way to find x^* would be to compute all the corners. Then x^* is the one that minimizes the cost $c^{\mathrm{T}}x$. This is a bad way, because for large m and n there are far too many corners. Which m components of x should be nonzero, solving $Ax = b$?

The winner is a corner because the cost $c^{\mathrm{T}}x$ is linear. If this cost increases in one direction, it will decrease in the opposite direction. A straight line graph on an interval is lowest at an endpoint. (If the cost is constant, all points in the interval are winners.) On a triangle, the cost is a minimum on the boundary. On a boundary edge, the minimum is at a corner. **The simplex method finds that corner x^*.**

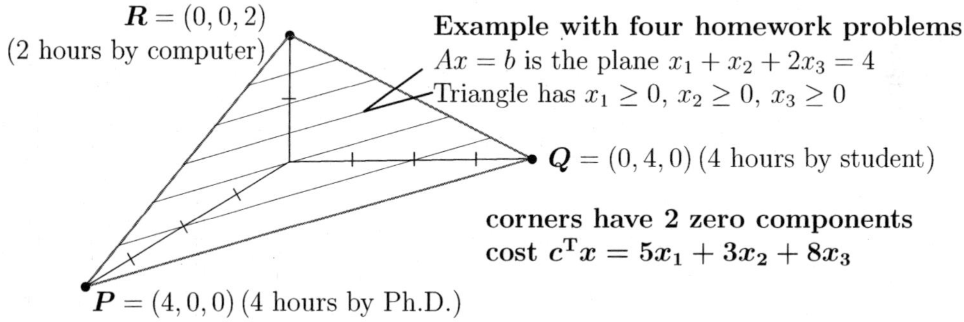

Figure 8.14: A feasible set with corners costing 20, 12, 16. Corner Q is optimal.

The idea is simple. ***Move from corner to corner, decreasing the cost $c^{\mathrm{T}}x$ at every step.*** When you reach a point where all edges going out increase the cost, *stop*. That corner is the optimal x^*. Because the number of corners can grow exponentially with n and m, this simplex method in the worst case could be slow. In practice the best corner is found quickly. Often $2m$ steps bring us to x^*.

The Simplex Method

Each step travels along an edge from one corner x_{old} to the next corner x_{new}. One zero component of x_{old} becomes positive in x_{new} (the **entering** variable x_{in}). One positive component of x_{old} becomes zero in x_{new} (the **leaving** variable x_{out}). The other positive components stay positive as $Ax_{\text{old}} = b$ turns into $Ax_{\text{new}} = b$.

This simplex step solves three m by m systems using the same square matrix B. The "basis matrix" B is a submatrix of A, with m columns that correspond to nonzeros in x_{old}. At x_{new}, only one column changes from B_{old} to B_{new}. So we can update B or B^{-1} instead of solving from scratch the new equations that use B_{new}.

May I quickly describe those three systems. The next page shows an example:

1. $\boldsymbol{Bx_{\text{pos}} = b}$ gives the m positive entries at the corner: $x(\text{basis}) = \text{B}\backslash\text{b}$

2. $\boldsymbol{B^{\mathrm{T}}y = c_B}$ decides the entering variable x_{in} (best edge from x_{old})

3. $\boldsymbol{Bv = A_{\text{in}}}$ decides the leaving variable x_{out} (it is zero at the corner x_{new}).

A little more explanation here. The matrix A and cost vector c split into two parts. Those match the positive and zero components of x at the current corner x_{old}:

$$\boldsymbol{Bx_{\text{pos}} = b} \qquad Ax_{\text{old}} = \begin{bmatrix} B & Z \end{bmatrix} \begin{bmatrix} x_{\text{pos}} \\ \mathbf{0} \end{bmatrix} = b \quad \text{and} \quad c = \begin{bmatrix} c_B \\ c_Z \end{bmatrix} \begin{matrix} \text{size } m \\ \text{size } n-m \end{matrix} \tag{9}$$

The vectors x from $Bx_{\text{pos}} = b$ and y from $B^{\mathrm{T}}y = c_B$ achieve $c^{\mathrm{T}}x = c_B^{\mathrm{T}}B^{-1}b = y^{\mathrm{T}}b$. These x and y might look optimal, but the constraint $A^{\mathrm{T}}y \leq c$ is probably not satisfied. Everything depends on the slack variables $s = c - A^{\mathrm{T}}y$ being positive:

$$\textbf{Slack is} \begin{bmatrix} \mathbf{0} \\ \boldsymbol{r} \end{bmatrix} \qquad s = c - A^{\mathrm{T}}y = \begin{bmatrix} c_B \\ c_Z \end{bmatrix} - \begin{bmatrix} B^{\mathrm{T}} \\ Z^{\mathrm{T}} \end{bmatrix} y = \begin{bmatrix} 0 \\ c_Z - Z^{\mathrm{T}}y \end{bmatrix} = \begin{bmatrix} \mathbf{0} \\ \boldsymbol{r} \end{bmatrix} \tag{10}$$

This ***reduced cost vector*** $\boldsymbol{r}$ is the key. If $r \geq 0$, all edges from x_{old} increase the cost. In that case $s \geq 0$. Then x_{old} is the optimal x^*, and y is the optimal y^*.

Until this optimal corner is reached, at least one component of r is negative. The *most negative* component r_{in} (steepest edge) determines the entering variable x_{in}. Solving $Bv =$ (new column A_{in}) gives the change v in x_{pos} from one unit of x_{in}.

The first component of $x_{\text{pos}} - \alpha v$ to hit zero identifies the leaving variable x_{out}. The edge has ended. A_{in} replaces the column A_{out} in the square basis matrix B_{new}.

That was fast. Every book on linear programming explains the simplex method in more detail (this includes my books on linear algebra, and many others). Equation (12) returns to the reduced costs: $\boldsymbol{r_i} =$ **change in $\mathbf{c}^{\mathrm{T}}\boldsymbol{x}$ when $\boldsymbol{x_i}$ moves from 0 to 1.**

Example of Linear Programming

This example will fit Figure 8.14. The unknowns x_1, x_2, x_3 represent hours of work. Those hours are not negative: $x \geq 0$. The costs per hour are \$5 for a Ph.D., \$3 for a student, and \$8 for a computer. (*I apologize for such low pay.*) The Ph.D. and the student get through one homework problem per hour. *The computer solves two problems in one hour.* In principle they can share out the homework, which has four problems to be solved: $x_1 + x_2 + 2x_3 =$ (Ph.D. plus student plus computer) $= 4$.

Goal: Finish four problems at minimum cost $\boldsymbol{c^{\mathrm{T}}x = 5x_1 + 3x_2 + 8x_3}$.

If all three are working, the job takes one hour: $x_1 = x_2 = x_3 = 1$. The cost is $5 + 3 + 8 = 16$. But certainly the Ph.D. should be put out of work by the student (who is just as fast and costs less—this problem is getting realistic). When the student works two hours and the machine works one, the cost is $6 + 8$ and all four problems get solved. We are on the edge QR because the Ph.D. is unemployed: $x_1 = 0$. But the best point on that edge is the corner $Q = x^* = (0, 4, 0)$. **The student solves all four problems in four hours for \$12**—which is the minimum cost $c^{\mathrm{T}}x^*$.

With only one equation in $Ax = x_1 + x_2 + 2x_3 = 4$, the corner $(0, 4, 0)$ has only one nonzero component. When $Ax = b$ has m equations, corners have m nonzeros. The number of possible corners is the number of ways to choose m components out of n. This number "n choose m" is heavily involved in gambling and probability. With $n = 30$ unknowns and $m = 8$ equations (still small numbers), the feasible set can have $30!/8!\,22!$ corners. That number is $(30)(29)\cdots(23)/8! = 5852925$.

Checking three corners for the minimum cost was fine. Checking five million corners is not the way to go. The simplex method is much faster, as detailed below.

The Dual Problem In optimization with constraints, a minimum problem brings a maximum problem. Here is the dual to our example, where $A = \begin{bmatrix} 1 & 1 & 2 \end{bmatrix}$ is transposed. The vectors $b = [4]$ and $c = (5, 3, 8)$ switch between constraint and cost.

A cheater offers to solve homework problems by looking up the answers. The charge is y dollars per problem, or $4y$ altogether. (Note how $b = 4$ has gone into the cost.) The cheater can't charge more per problem than the Ph.D. or the student or machine: $\boldsymbol{y \leq 5}$ **and** $\boldsymbol{y \leq 3}$ **and** $\boldsymbol{2y \leq 8}$. This is $A^{\mathrm{T}}y \leq c$. The cheater maximizes the income $4y$.

Dual Problem Maximize $y^{\mathrm{T}}b = 4y$ subject to $A^{\mathrm{T}}y \leq c$.

The maximum occurs when $y = 3$. The income is $4y = 12$. The maximum in the dual problem (\$12) equals the minimum in the original problem (\$12). This is duality. Please note that I personally often look up the answers. It's not cheating.

Simplex Example

Start with the computer doing all the work: $x_3 > 0$. Then basis $= [\,3\,]$ has one index from that one nonzero. Column 3 of $A = [1\ \ 1\ \ 2]$ goes into $B = [\,2\,]$. Row 3 of the cost $c = [5\ \ 3\ \ 8]'$ goes into $c_B = [\,8\,]$. A simplex step is quick since $m = 1$:

1. $Bx_{\text{pos}} = b = [\,4\,]$ gives $x_{\text{pos}} = x_3 = 2$. The computer corner is $x_{\text{old}} = (\mathbf{0}, \mathbf{0}, \mathbf{2})$.

2. $B^{\mathrm{T}}y = c_B$ gives $y = 4$. The reduced costs r appear in $c - A^{\mathrm{T}}y = (\mathbf{1}, \mathbf{-1}, \mathbf{0})$. That -1 in r identifies the entering variable $x_{\text{in}} = x_2$ (student goes to work).

3. $Bv = A_{\text{in}}$ is $2v = 1$. The edge from computer to student has $x_1 = 0$, $x_2 = \alpha$, and $x_3 = 2 - \alpha v$. That edge ends when $\alpha = 2/v = 4$. Then $x_{\text{out}} = x_3$ leaves the basis. This student corner has $\alpha = 4$ units of x_{in}, so $x_{\text{new}} = (\mathbf{0}, \mathbf{4}, \mathbf{0})$.

At the next step, the student corner x_{new} becomes x_{old}. Then basis $= [\,2\,]$ and $B = [\,1\,]$ and $x_{\text{pos}} = 4$ is already found (the code only needs step 1 at the starting corner). Step 2 has $c_B = 3$ and $y = 3$ and $c - A^{\mathrm{T}}y = (\mathbf{2}, \mathbf{0}, \mathbf{2})$. *No reduced cost is negative.* So $x^* = (0, 4, 0)$ and $y^* = 3$ are optimal. The student gets the whole job.

Summary The simplex method stops if $c - A^{\mathrm{T}}y \geq 0$. Otherwise r_{min} locates the most negative reduced cost and its index in. Then x_{pos} drops by αv along the edge to x_{new}. The edge ends with $x_{\text{out}} = 0$ when $\alpha = \min(x_i/v_i)$ for $x_i > 0$ and $v_i > 0$.

Different start The first step may not go immediately to the best x^*. The method chooses x_{in} before it knows how much of that variable to include for $Ax = b$. Starting from $x = (4, 0, 0)$ we could have gone first to $x_{\text{machine}} = (0, 0, 2)$. From there we would have found the optimal $x^* = (0, 4, 0)$.

The more of the entering variable we include, the lower the cost. This has to stop when a positive component of x (which is adjusting to keep $Ax = b$) hits zero. *The* ***leaving variable*** x_{out} *is the first positive* x_i *to reach zero*, which signals the new corner. More of x_{in} would make x_{out} negative (not allowed). Start again from x_{new}.

When all reduced costs in r are positive, the current corner is the optimal x^*. The zeros in x^* cannot become positive without increasing $c^{\mathrm{T}}x$. No new variable should enter: stay with $x_Z = 0$. Here is the algebra that explains reduced costs r:

$Ax = b$ along edge
$$Ax = \begin{bmatrix} B & Z \end{bmatrix} \begin{bmatrix} x_B \\ x_Z \end{bmatrix} = b. \quad \text{This gives } x_B = B^{-1}b - B^{-1}Zx_Z\,. \qquad (11)$$

The old corner has $x_Z = 0$ and $x_B = B^{-1}b$. At every x the cost is $c^{\mathrm{T}}x$:

Cost of x along edge
$$c^{\mathrm{T}}x = \begin{bmatrix} c_B^{\mathrm{T}} & c_Z^{\mathrm{T}} \end{bmatrix} \begin{bmatrix} x_B \\ x_Z \end{bmatrix} = c_B^{\mathrm{T}}B^{-1}b + (\boldsymbol{c}_Z^{\mathrm{T}} - \boldsymbol{c}_B^{\mathrm{T}}\boldsymbol{B}^{-1}\boldsymbol{Z})\,\boldsymbol{x}_Z\,. \qquad (12)$$

The last term $\boldsymbol{r}^{\mathrm{T}}\boldsymbol{x}_Z$ is the direct cost $c_Z^{\mathrm{T}}x_Z$ reduced by the savings from a smaller x_B. The constraint (11) updates x_B to maintain $Ax = b$. If $r \geq 0$ we don't want x_Z.

Codes for the Simplex Method

The simplex codes are a gift from Bob Fourer. On the cse website, the code finds a first corner $x \geq 0$ unless the feasible set is empty. In this book, the user inputs m indices in basis to indicate nonzero components of x. The code checks $x \geq 0$.

This code starts from the corner that uses the indices in basis. Each step finds a new index in and an old index out. Notice the neat final command basis(out) = in.

```
function [x, y, cost] = simplex(A, b, c, basis)

x = zeros(size(c)) ; v = zeros(size(c)) ;          % column vectors b, c, x, v, y
B = A(:, basis); x(basis) = B\b; z = .000001       % basis = [m indices <= n]
if any (x < -z)                                     % need x >= 0 and Ax = b to start
  error ('Bad starting basis, x has component < 0'); end
cost = c(basis)' * x(basis) ;                       % cost c^T x at starting corner
for step = 1:100                                    % take <= 100 simplex steps
    y = B'\c(basis) ;                               % this y may not be feasible (>= 0)
    [rmin, in] = min(c - A' * y) ;                  % minimum r and its index in
    if rmin > -z                                    % optimality has been reached, r >= 0
      break; end                                    % current x, y are optimal x*, y*
    v(basis) = B\A(: , in) ;                        % decrease in x from 1 unit of x_in
[alpha, out] = min(x(basis)./max(v(basis), z)) ;    % alpha locates end x_new of the edge
    if v(basis(out)) < z                            % out = index of first x to reach 0
      error ('cost is unbounded on the set of feasible x'); end
    x(in) = alpha ;                                 % new positive component of x
    cost = cost + x(in) * rmin ;                    % lower cost at end of step
    x(basis) = x(basis) - x(in) * v(basis) ;        % update old x to new corner
    basis(out) = in ;                               % replace index out by index in
end
```

Interior Point Methods

The simplex method moves along the edges of the feasible set, eventually reaching the optimal corner x^*. ***Interior point methods move inside the feasible set*** (where $x > 0$). These methods hope to go more directly to x^*. They work well.

One way to stay inside is to put a barrier at the boundary. Add extra cost as a *logarithm that blows up* when any variable x_j touches zero. The best vector has $x > 0$. The number θ is a small parameter that we move toward zero.

Barrier problem Minimize $c^{\mathrm{T}}x - \theta\,(\log x_1 + \cdots + \log x_n)$ with $Ax = b$ (13)

This cost is nonlinear (but linear programming is already nonlinear from inequalities). The constraints $x_j \geq 0$ are not needed because $\log x_j$ becomes infinite at $x_j = 0$.

The barrier gives an *approximate problem* for each θ. It has m constraints $Ax = b$ with Lagrange multipliers $y_1, \ldots, y_m$. The inequalities $x_i \geq 0$ are hidden inside log x_i.

Lagrangian $$L(x, y, \theta) = c^{\mathrm{T}}x - \theta\,(\textstyle\sum \log x_i) - y^{\mathrm{T}}(Ax - b) \qquad (14)$$

$\partial L/\partial y = 0$ brings back $Ax = b$. The derivatives $\partial L/\partial x_j$ are interesting!

Optimality in barrier pbm $$\frac{\partial L}{\partial x_j} = c_j - \frac{\theta}{x_j} - (A^{\mathrm{T}}y)_j = 0 \quad \text{which is} \quad \boldsymbol{x_j s_j = \theta}. \qquad (15)$$

The true problem has $x_j s_j = 0$, the barrier problem has $x_j s_j = \theta$. The solutions $x^*(\theta)$ lie on the ***central path*** to $x^*(0)$. Those n optimality equations $x_j s_j = \theta$ are nonlinear, and we solve this system iteratively by Newton's method.

The current x, y, s will satisfy $Ax = b, x \geq 0$ and $A^{\mathrm{T}}y + s = c$, *but not* $x_j s_j = \theta$. Newton's method takes a step $\Delta x, \Delta y, \Delta s$. By ignoring the second-order term $\Delta x \Delta s$ in $(x + \Delta x)(s + \Delta s) = \theta$, the corrections in x, y, s come from linear equations:

Newton step $$\begin{aligned} A\,\Delta x &= 0 \\ A^{\mathrm{T}}\Delta y + \Delta s &= 0 \\ s_j \Delta x_j + x_j \Delta s_j &= \theta - x_j s_j \end{aligned} \qquad (16)$$

This iteration has quadratic convergence for each θ, and then θ approaches zero. For any m and n, the duality gap $x^{\mathrm{T}}s$ is generally below 10^{-8} after 20 to 60 Newton steps. This algorithm is used almost "as is" in commercial interior-point software, for a large class of nonlinear optimization problems. We will show how an ℓ^1 problem can be made smooth (as Newton wants).

Barrier Method Example

I will try the same 1 by 3 example, apologizing to the Ph.D. who costs way too much:

$$\text{Minimize } c^{\mathrm{T}}x = 5x_1 + 3x_2 + 8x_3 \text{ with } x_i \geq 0 \text{ and } Ax = x_1 + x_2 + 2x_3 = 4.$$

The constraint has one multiplier y. The barrier Lagrangian is L:

$$L = (5x_1 + 3x_2 + 8x_3) - \theta\,(\log x_1 + \log x_2 + \log x_3) - y\,(x_1 + x_2 + 2x_3 - 4). \qquad (17)$$

Seven optimality equations give $x_1, x_2, x_3, s_1, s_2, s_3$, and y (all depending on θ):

$\boldsymbol{s = c - A^{\mathrm{T}}y}$	$s_1 = 5 - y,\ s_2 = 3 - y,\ s_3 = 8 - 2y$	(18)
$\boldsymbol{\partial L/\partial x = 0}$	$x_1 s_1 = x_2 s_2 = x_3 s_3 = \theta$	(19)
$\boldsymbol{\partial L/\partial y = 0}$	$x_1 + x_2 + 2x_3 = 4$	(20)

Start from the interior point $x_1 = x_2 = x_3 = 1$ and $y = 2$, where $s = (3, 1, 4)$. The updates Δx and Δy come from $s_j x_j + s_j \Delta x_j + x_j \Delta s_j = \theta$ and $A\Delta x = 0$:

$$\begin{array}{ll} \boldsymbol{3\Delta x_1 + 1\Delta s_1} & 3\Delta x_1 - 1\Delta y = \theta - 3 \\ \boldsymbol{1\Delta x_2 + 1\Delta s_2} & 1\Delta x_2 - 1\Delta y = \theta - 1 \\ \boldsymbol{4\Delta x_3 + 1\Delta s_3} & 4\Delta x_3 - 2\Delta y = \theta - 4 \\ \boldsymbol{A\,\Delta x = 0} & \Delta x_1 + \Delta x_2 + 2\Delta x_3 = 0 \end{array} \qquad (21)$$

Solving for the updates $\Delta x_1, \Delta x_2, \Delta x_3, \Delta y$ gives x_{new} and y_{new} (not corners!):

$$\begin{bmatrix} x_{\text{new}} \\ y_{\text{new}} \end{bmatrix} = \begin{bmatrix} x_{\text{old}} \\ y_{\text{old}} \end{bmatrix} + \begin{bmatrix} 3 & 0 & 0 & -1 \\ 0 & 1 & 0 & -1 \\ 0 & 0 & 4 & -2 \\ 1 & 1 & 2 & 0 \end{bmatrix}^{-1} \begin{bmatrix} \theta - 3 \\ \theta - 1 \\ \theta - 4 \\ 0 \end{bmatrix} = \begin{bmatrix} 1 \\ 1 \\ 1 \\ 2 \end{bmatrix} + \frac{\theta}{14} \begin{bmatrix} 1 \\ 3 \\ -2 \\ -11 \end{bmatrix} + \frac{1}{7} \begin{bmatrix} -3 \\ 5 \\ -1 \\ 12 \end{bmatrix}.$$

With $\theta = \frac{4}{3}$ this is $\frac{1}{3}(2,6,2,8)$. We are nearer the solution $x^* = (0,4,0)$, $y^* = 3$.

The reader might notice the **saddle-point matrix S** in that equation above. It is ill-conditioned near the $\theta = 0$ solution, where $\mathsf{diag}(S) = c - A^{\mathrm{T}}y^*$ has zeros. Those matrices S just appear everywhere in optimization with constraints.

Optimization in the ℓ^1 Norm

Minimizing $Au - b$ in the ℓ^2 norm leads to $A^{\mathrm{T}}A\widehat{u} = A^{\mathrm{T}}b$ and least squares. Minimizing $Au - b$ in the ℓ^1 norm leads to linear programming and sparse solutions. Section 2.3 noted the benefits of this sparse alternative (and then stayed in ℓ^2 to save linearity). Here $m < n$, and this is **basis pursuit** (sparse fit to the data b).

The ℓ^1 norm adds absolute values, so $\|(1,-5)\|_1 = 6$. Those absolute values are the differences between two linear ramps, $x^+ = (1,0)$ and $x^- = (0,5)$:

$$\text{Write } \boldsymbol{x_k} = \boldsymbol{x_k^+} - \boldsymbol{x_k^-} \text{ with } \boldsymbol{x_k^+} = \max(x_k, 0) \geq 0 \text{ and } \boldsymbol{x_k^-} = \max(-x_k, 0) \geq 0.$$

Then $|\boldsymbol{x_k}| = \boldsymbol{x_k^+} + \boldsymbol{x_k^-}$. So the linear program has $2n$ variables x^+ and x^-:

Basis pursuit $\quad$ Minimize $\sum_{1}^{m}(x_k^+ + x_k^-)$ subject to $Ax^+ - Ax^- = b$ $\quad$ (22)

We require $x_k^+ \geq 0$ and $x_k^- \geq 0$. The minimum never has both $x_k^+ > 0$ and $x_k^- > 0$.

The solution is sparse because it lies at a corner of the feasible set. A has full row rank, and x has $n-m$ zeros. The system $Ax = b$ has many solutions (it is underdetermined, with too few observations in b). The geometry of a polyhedron—*the feasible set*—makes the solution sparse. But we want x to be sparser.

The dual to basis pursuit is neat, involving the $\boldsymbol{\ell^\infty}$ **norm**. The cost vector c is all ones. The constraint matrix $[A \quad -A]$ is transposed according to the dual in (2):

Dual to basis pursuit $\quad$ Maximize $b^{\mathrm{T}}y$ with $\begin{bmatrix} A^{\mathrm{T}} \\ -A^{\mathrm{T}} \end{bmatrix} y \leq \begin{bmatrix} 1 \\ 1 \end{bmatrix}$ $\quad$ (23)

Every component of $A^{\mathrm{T}}y$ is between 1 and -1: *maximum component* $= \|A^{\mathrm{T}}y\|_\infty \leq 1$.

Dual norms $\quad \|y\|_{\text{dual}} = \max\limits_{x \neq 0} y^{\mathrm{T}}x/\|x\|_{\text{primal}} \qquad \|x\|_{\text{primal}} = \max\limits_{y \neq 0} y^{\mathrm{T}}x/\|y\|_{\text{dual}}$

When the primal norm is $\|x\|_1$, the dual norm is $\|y\|_\infty$. Example: If $y = (1,3,5)$ choose $x = (0,0,1)$ to find $y^{\mathrm{T}}x/\|x\|_1 = 5$ which is $\|y\|_\infty$. If $x = (1,3,6)$ choose $y = (1,1,1)$ to find $y^{\mathrm{T}}x/\|y\|_\infty = 10$ which is $\|x\|_1$. The ℓ_2 norm is dual to itself.

LASSO and More Sparsity

Sparse compression wants fewer than m nonzeros in x. So it has to give up on exact solution to the m equations $Ax = b$. We can tighten an ℓ^1 constraint or increase an ℓ^1 penalty, to get more zeros. Increase L or reduce D (the names often get mixed):

Basis Pursuit Denoising	Minimize $\frac{1}{2}\|Ax - b\|_2^2 + L\|x\|_1$	(24)
LASSO: Least Absolute...	Minimize $\|Ax - b\|_2$ subject to $\|x\|_1 \leq D$	(25)

The solution to (24) is also the solution to (25) for some L depending on D. LASSO is slightly more useful because the constraint has a dual variable (Lagrange multiplier) that can tell us how much to change D. The BPDN solution becomes $x = 0$ (totally sparse!) when the penalty coefficient reaches the value $L^* = \|A^{\mathrm{T}}b\|_\infty$.

Section 4.7 on signal processing worked out an instructive example with increasing L. The solution starts from the noiseless basis pursuit (22), with m nonzeros. As L increases, **one of those components moves to zero** (linearly in L). Then another component moves to zero (and stays there). By setting L in (24) or D in (25), we control the sparsity of x—and more zeros mean less accuracy in $Ax \approx b$. For a noisy signal, we are not concerned about perfect reconstruction of b.

May I say: These problems are highly important and the experts are creating fast codes to solve them. The real test is for very large matrices A (a convolution or a randomized sensing matrix, times a wavelet basis matrix). Always there is a competition: Project onto the exact constraints at each step, or move through the interior (but don't slow down for exact Newton steps, that can't win). The cse website will maintain references to both sides, this is remarkable work.

Convex (Nonlinear) Optimization

Least squares and linear programming are convex problems. So are basis pursuit and LASSO. Practically this whole book has dealt with convex functions. Only the Traveling Salesman will leave this best possible world, and that is what makes his task NP-hard. This is our chance to focus on convexity.

A smooth function $f(x)$ is convex if $d^2f/dx^2 \geq 0$ everywhere. With n variables, $f(x_1, \ldots, x_n)$ is convex if its second-derivative matrix H is **positive semidefinite** everywhere: $H_{ij} = \partial^2 f/\partial x_i \partial x_j$. Graphically, the curve or the surface $y = f(x)$ rises above its tangent lines and tangent planes.

The importance of convexity was well stated by Rockafellar (see [20]): **The great watershed in optimization isn't between linearity and nonlinearity, it is between convexity and nonconvexity.** Here are two equivalent statements of a convex optimization problem, when $f_0(x), \ldots, f_m(x)$ are all convex:

Minimize $f_0(x)$ with $f_i(x) \leq b_i$	Minimize $f_0(x)$ in a convex set K	(26)

The absolute value function $f(x) = |x|$ and a vector norm $\|x\|$ are also (and importantly) convex, even though they have no derivative at $x = 0$. They pass the test by **staying below the lines connecting points on their graph**:

Convex function $f(tx + (1-t)X) \le t\,f(x) + (1-t)f(X)$ for $0 \le t \le 1$. (27)

The right side gives a straight line as t goes from 0 to 1. The left side gives a curve (the graph of f). They start equal at $t = 0$ and finish equal at $t = 1$. Straight lines and planes are (barely) convex. Parabolas are (easily) convex if they bend upwards, $\sin x$ is convex between π and 2π but it is **concave** between 0 and π. It is the *bending* upwards (second derivative) and not the *moving* upwards (first derivative) that makes $f(x)$ a convex function.

It is essential to see that the feasible set K (all x that satisfy the m constraints $f_i(x) \le b_i$) is a **convex set** in n-dimensional space:

Convex set The line segment between any points x and X in K stays in K.

Convex functions give convex sets. If $f_1(x) \le b_1$ and $f_1(X) \le b_1$, the right side of (27) stays below b_1—so the left side does too. The same is true for each constraint $f_i(x) \le b_i$. The segment between x and X stays feasible, and K is convex.

Convex sets K give convex functions. The **indicator function** $f_K(x)$ is 0 in K and $+\infty$ outside of K. The condition "x in K" is the same as "$f_K(x) \le 0$". You see why f_K is a convex function: If x and X are in the convex set K, so is the line between them. Then the test (27) is passed.

Example 1 The intersection of convex sets $K_1, \ldots, K_m$ is a convex set K. Especially the intersection of any half-planes $a_i^{\mathrm{T}} x \le b_i$ is a convex set. This is the feasible set when linear programming (**LP**) requires $Ax \le b$. Each new constraint just reduces K.

Example 2 The ball $\|x\| \le 1$ is a convex set in any norm. For the ℓ^2 norm this is truly a ball. For $\|x\|_1 \le 1$ we have a diamond, and $\|x\|_\infty \le 1$ is a box to hold it. The convexity test is the triangle inequality, satisfied by all norms.

Example 3 The set K of all positive semidefinite matrices is a convex set. If $y^{\mathrm{T}}Ay \ge 0$ and $y^{\mathrm{T}}By \ge 0$ then $y^{\mathrm{T}}(tA + (1-t)B)y \ge 0$. A semidefinite program (**SDP**) minimizes over this set of positive semidefinite matrices in matrix space.

A convex primal minimization leads to a concave dual maximization. The primal-dual pair can be solved by interior point methods—central to the computations. The solution is a saddle point and the optimality equations are KKT conditions—central to the framework of $A^{\mathrm{T}}CA$. And most important, **energy is convex**—central to the applications.

Maximum Flow-Minimum Cut

There is a special class of linear programs that have beautiful solutions. By good fortune, those problems have A = *incidence matrix of a graph*. The unknowns in the minimization are potentials u at the nodes. The unknowns w in the dual maximization will be flows on the m edges. The dual problem finds the **maximum flow**.

The flows must satisfy Kirchhoff's Current Law $A^{\mathrm{T}}w = 0$ at every node. Two nodes in the graph are chosen as *the source s and the sink t*. The goal is to maximize the total flow from s to t. (This flow returns directly to the source as w_{ts} along the dotted line.) Each edge flow w_{ij} is bounded by the **capacity** $\boldsymbol{c_{ij}}$ of that edge:

Maximum flow Maximize w_{ts} from t to s subject to $A^{\mathrm{T}}w = 0$ and $w \le c$. (28)

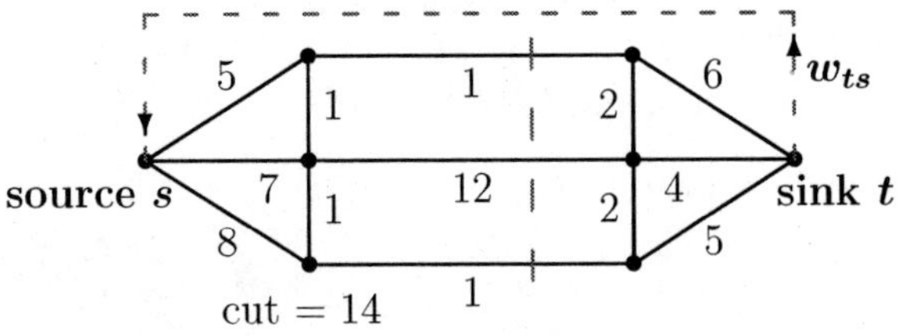

Figure 8.15: Maximize the total flow from s to t with these edge capacities c_{ij}.

The best part of this problem is to solve it without linear algebra. The flow across the middle of the graph is at most $1 + 12 + 1 = 14$. You see a **cut** down the middle, and its total capacity is 14. ***All flow must cross this cut.*** *Please look for a cut with capacity less than* 14. Your cut will give a tighter bound on the total flow.

Eventually you will spot the cut of capacity $1 + 2 + 4 + 2 + 1 = 10$. This is the **minimum cut**, and the total flow across the network flow cannot exceed 10. *Does the minimum cut capacity equal the maximum flow?* The answer must be *yes*, or duality wouldn't hold and we would never have mentioned this problem:

Weak duality All flows $\le$ All cuts **Duality** Max flow = Min cut

The minimum cut is the "bottleneck" in the flow graph. You could easily think of applications to an assembly line. The maximum flow fills that bottleneck to capacity.

Away from the bottleneck, the flow pattern for the 10 units is not unique. There are many optimal solutions w^*. This degeneracy is not at all unusual in large linear programs (the simplex method can change w's with no improvement). There could also be more than one minimum cut. The point is that we find the minimum quickly.

Maximum Flow and Bipartite Matching (Marriage)

The classical Ford-Fulkerson proof of duality (*max flow = min cut*) was algorithmic. At every step they looked for an "augmenting path" that would allow additional flow. This is not quite as fast as a greedy algorithm, which never reverses a decision.

We might have to reduce the flow on some edges (send flow backward) to increase the total flow. The cse website links to a family of fast solvers.

Finding the maximum flow also identifies a minimum cut. That cut separates nodes that could still receive more flow from nodes that can't. So this particular cut is full to capacity, proving that max flow equals min cut.

This augmenting path algorithm is *strongly polynomial.* It solves the problem in $O(mn)$ iterations, independent of the capacities c_{ij}. Its running time has been steadily lowered, and an alternative "Preflow-Push algorithm" is described in [104].

This special network program includes an even more special problem, when the graph is **bipartite** (two parts). All edges go from one set S of nodes to another set T. In the **marriage problem**, an edge goes from a node i in S to j in T when that pair is compatible. All capacities are 1 or 0 (no edge). (At most one marriage, very old-fashioned.) *The maximum flow from S to T is the maximum number of marriages.*

A *perfect matching* connects every node in S along an edge to a node in T. The middle figure shows a maximum flow of 3 (4 marriages are impossible here: no perfect matching). To match the flow problem, Figure 8.16 adds a source s and sink t.

The adjacency matrix has 1's for all eight edges (compatible pairs). Those 1's can be covered by only 3 lines. Equivalently nodes $2, 3, 4$ in S have no edges to $1, 3$ in T (zeros in the matrix). This violates Hall's necessary and sufficient condition for a perfect matching: Every k nodes in S must connect to at least k nodes in T.

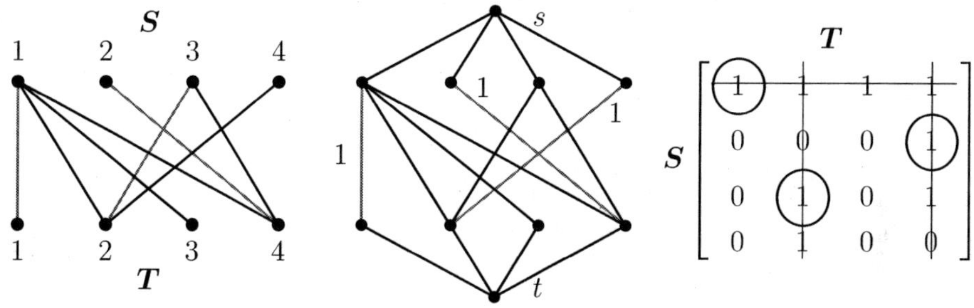

Figure 8.16: This bipartite graph has no perfect matching: $max\ flow = min\ cut = 3$.

Network Problems and Traveling Salesmen

The incidence matrix A has two remarkable properties not yet mentioned in this book:

1. Every square submatrix M of A has $\det(M) = 1, -1$ or 0: **totally unimodular**.

The determinant of M is zero if every row captures both 1 and -1 from A. If a row captures only one of those, removing that row and column leaves a smaller determinant. Eventually we reach a trivial determinant that yields 1 or -1 or 0.

That property tells us that **integer capacities lead to integer maximal flows.** We can require w_{ij} = integer and still have max flow = min cut.

2. The corners of the set where $\sum |u_i - u_j| = 1$ have all $u_i = 1$ or 0 (no fraction).

This property of Au, with components $u_i - u_j$ from the incidence matrix A, tells us that an optimal corner u^* gives a cut (nodes with $u_i^* = 1$ are on one side). So the integer program for cuts has the same minimum as the linear program for potentials.

Another network problem with a beautiful theory has *edge costs* as the c_{ij}:

Transportation problem	Minimize $\sum\sum c_{ij}\, w_{ij}$ with shipments $w_{ij} \geq 0$ and $Aw = b$.	(29)

Those constraints $Aw = b$ are $w_{1j}+\cdots+w_{mj} = b_j$ into market j and $w_{i1}+\cdots+w_{in} = B_i$ from supplier i. The cost from supplier to market is c_{ij}. The transportation problem has mn unknown flows w_{ij} and $m+n$ equality constraints.

Federal Express solves the dual problem, to know how much it can charge. It collects u_j for each unit delivered to market j, and U_i for each unit picked up from supplier i. FedEx cannot charge more than the post office: $u_j + U_i \leq c_{ij}$. With those mn constraints they maximize *income* $= \sum u_j b_j + \sum U_i B_i$.

The optimality condition is complementary slackness on each edge: $u_j + U_i = c_{ij}$ or else $w_{ij} = 0$ (no shipment i to j). FedEx is cheaper only on unused edges.

This problem also has a fast solution. A is now an incidence matrix with only $+1$'s. Integers still win. But not all network problems have fast solutions!

Traveling Salesman Problem	Find the cheapest route in a graph that visits each node exactly once.

If the route could be a tree, the problem is easy. A greedy algorithm finds the shortest spanning tree. But the traveling salesman is not allowed to retrace steps. The route must enter and leave each node once. All known algorithms take exponential time (dynamic programming is $n^2 2^n$) which means hours on a supercomputer.

The traveling salesman problem is NP-hard. Almost nobody believes that an NP-hard problem can be solved in polynomial time $m^\alpha n^\beta$. Linear programs do have polynomial algorithms (**they are in the class P**). Maximum flows have specially fast times. The outstanding unsolved problem brings a million dollar Clay Prize: **Prove that P $\neq$ NP**: there is no polynomial algorithm for the traveling salesman.

Continuous Flows

Kirchhoff's Law $A^{\mathrm{T}} w = f$ for a continuous flow is $\operatorname{div} w = \partial w_1/\partial x + \partial w_2/\partial y = f(x,y)$. *The divergence of w is flow out minus flow in.* Transposing, the gradient is like an incidence matrix. Here is **max flow = min cut in a square**, instead of on graphs:

Flow	Find the flow vector $w(x,y)$ with $\|w\| \leq 1$ and $\operatorname{div} w = C$ that **maximizes** C
Cut	Find the set S in the square that **minimizes** $R =$ (perimeter of S)/(area of S).

To prove $\boldsymbol{C} \leq \boldsymbol{R}$ for all sets S, use the Divergence Theorem and $|w \cdot n| \leq \|w\| \leq 1$:

Weak duality	$\iint (\operatorname{div} w)\, dx\, dy = \int w \cdot n\, ds$	$C(\text{area of } S) \leq (\text{perimeter of } S)$

Minimizing perimeter/area is a classical problem (the Greeks knew that circles win). But hare S lies in the square, partly along its sides. Remove quarter-circles of radius r from the corners. Then calculus finds the best ratio $R = 2 + \sqrt{\pi}$ at $r = 1/R$. That R is the "***Cheeger constant***" of the unit square.

It looks easy, but what is the Cheeger constant (minimum ratio of area to volume) inside a cube?

Application to Image Segmentation

Suppose you have a noisy image of the heart. Which pixels are part of the heart? Where is the boundary? This is image segmentation and restoration and enhancement. We want and expect a piecewise smooth boundary between pieces of the image, while staying close to the observations U.

Assigning pixel values u_p can be expressed as a discrete **energy minimization**:

Regularized energy sum

$$E(u) = E_{\text{data}} + E_{\text{smooth}} = \sum (u_p - U_p)^2 + \sum\sum V(u_p, u_q). \qquad (30)$$

That last smoothing term will penalize edges that are long or erratic or unnecessary. It is a pixel analog of the Mumford-Shah penalty in continuous segmentation:

Regularized energy integral

$$E(u) = \iint \left[(u - U)^2 + A\,|\nabla u|^2\right] dx\, dy + \textbf{edge length} \qquad (31)$$

The difficulty is that those penalty terms are ***not convex***. The energy $E(u)$ has many local minima, and pixel space has high dimension. Minimizing E is NP-hard. These problems have many other names: early vision, Bayesian labeling of Markov random fields, Ising models with 2 labels, Potts models with k labels, and more.

In short, **we need good algorithms for impossibly hard problems**. To come within a guaranteed bound is not impossible. We mention the problem here because graph cuts (*not* the normalized cuts of $*2.9$) have been very effective. "Simulated annealing" was too slow. The goal is to allow many pixel values to improve at once, and the correspondence between cuts and pixel labels [21] opened the door to fast max flow-min cut algorithms. I recommend the Graph Cuts Home Page www.cs.cornell.edu/%7Erdz/graphcuts.html.

Problem Set 8.6

1 Start the example from the Ph.D. corner $x = (4, 0, 0)$ with costs changed to $c = (5, 3, 7)$. Show that the lowest reduced cost r chooses the computer for x_{in}. The student corner $x^* = (0, 4, 0)$ is reached on the second simplex step.

2 Test the simplex code on Problem 1. The input has basis $= [\,1\,]$.

3 Choose a different cost vector c so the Ph.D. gets the job. Find y^* in the dual problem (maximum income to the cheater) for the new c.

4 A six-problem homework on which the Ph.D. is fastest gives a second constraint $2x_1 + x_2 + x_3 = 6$. Then $x = (2, 2, 0)$ shows two hours of work by Ph.D. and student on each homework. Does this x minimize the cost $c^{\mathrm{T}}x$ with $c = (5, 3, 8)$?

5 Draw the region in the xy plane where $x + 2y = 6$ and $x \geq 0$ and $y \geq 0$. Which point in this "feasible set" minimizes the cost $c = x + 3y$? Which corner gives maximum cost instead of minimum?

6 Draw the region in the xy plane where $x + 2y \leq 6$, $2x + y \leq 6$, $x \geq 0$, $y \geq 0$. It has four corners. Which corner minimizes the cost $c = 2x - y$?

7 These two problems are also dual. Prove weak duality, that always $\boldsymbol{y}^{\mathrm{T}}\boldsymbol{b} \leq \boldsymbol{c}^{\mathrm{T}}\boldsymbol{x}$:

Minimize $c^{\mathrm{T}}x$ with $Ax \geq b$ and $x \geq 0$ / Maximize $y^{\mathrm{T}}b$ with $A^{\mathrm{T}}y \leq c$ and $y \geq 0$.

8 Which edges in Figure 8.15 have the bottleneck property? If you increase their capacity by 1, the maximum flow increases from 10 to 11.

9 A graph with source s, sink t, and four other nodes has capacity 1 between all 15 pairs of nodes. What is a maximal flow and a minimal cut?

10 Draw a graph with nodes $0, 1, 2, 3, 4$ and capacity $|i - j|$ between nodes i and j. Find the minimal cut and maximal flow from node 0 to node 4.

11 Suppose there are *node capacities* as well as edge capacities: The flow entering (and therefore leaving) node j cannot exceed C_j. Reduce this to the standard problem by replacing each node j by two nodes j' and j'', connected by an edge of capacity C_j. How should the rest of the network be changed?

12 Suppose A is the 4 by 4 matrix with $a_{ij} = 1$ on the diagonals just above and just below the main diagonal. Is a perfect matching (4 marriages) possible, and is it unique? Draw the corresponding graph with eight vertices.

13 If A is the 5 by 5 matrix with $a_{ij} = 1$ on the diagonals above and below the main diagonal, show that a complete matching is impossible by finding

(i) a set of girls who do not like enough boys

(ii) a set of boys who do not like enough girls

(iii) an r by s zero submatrix with $r + s > n$

(iv) four lines which cover all the 1's in A.

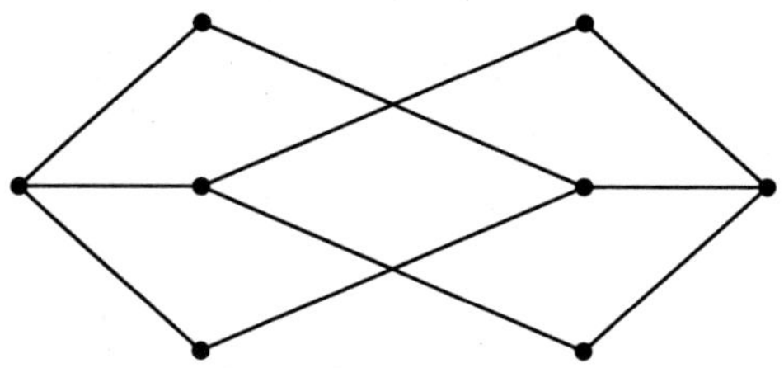

14 The maximum number of paths from s to t with no *edge* in common equals the minimum number of *edges* whose removal disconnects s from t. Verify this equality on the graph above and connect it to the max flow-min cut theorem.

15 If a 7 by 7 matrix has 15 1's, prove that it allows more than two marriages. How many lines to cover the 1's?

16 The feasible set $Ax = b, x \geq 0$ is empty if $A = [-3]$ and $b = [2]$. Show that the dual maximum problem is unbounded (both problems go wrong).

17 Draw a 7-node graph with six edges going around the outer six nodes (a hexagon) and six edges going out from a center node s. If all twelve capacities are 1, what is the maximal flow from s at the center to the sink t (one of the outside nodes)?

8.7 ADJOINT METHODS IN DESIGN

Suppose $u = (u_1, \ldots, u_N)$ is the solution to N equations—linear or nonlinear, continuous or discrete, possibly with initial values or boundary values. Those equations may include M ***control variables*** $p = (p_1, \ldots, p_M)$. These are the design parameters (or decision parameters). Often we want to optimize some scalar function $g(u, p)$. ***The adjoint method is a fast way to find*** $dg/dp = (dg/dp_1, \ldots, dg/dp_M)$.

Those M derivatives measure the ***sensitivity*** of g with respect to changes in p. That is an important quantity! At a given choice of p, dg/dp gives a search direction in p-space to improve g (it is the *gradient direction*). The difficulty is that dg/dp involves the large matrix $\partial u/\partial p$, because of the chain rule:

Gradient of $g(u,p)$
$$\frac{dg}{dp} = \frac{\partial g}{\partial u}\frac{\partial u}{\partial p} + \frac{\partial g}{\partial p} \qquad \begin{matrix} \partial g/\partial u \text{ is } \mathbf{1 \times N} \\ \partial u/\partial p \text{ is } \mathbf{N \times M} \end{matrix} \tag{1}$$

The adjoint method provides a way to avoid computing all the NM derivatives $\partial u_i/\partial p_j$. This is extremely valuable in shape or topology optimization, and other places too, when p includes thousands of parameters (large M). We want to compute dg/dp by solving **one adjoint equation** instead of M direct equations.

Linear Systems

The starting example is a system of N linear equations $Au = b$, when the input b depends on the parameters $p = (p_1, \ldots, p_M)$. The scalar function is $g(u, p) = c^{\mathrm{T}}u$ for a fixed vector c. (The example $c = (1, \ldots, 1)$ would pick out the sum of the u's as the quantity to optimize.) In this case $\partial g/\partial p = 0$ and $\partial g/\partial u = c^{\mathrm{T}}$. It is the row vector $c^{\mathrm{T}}(\partial u/\partial p)$ that we need to know, to move to a better choice of p.

Each $\partial u/\partial p_j$ could come from the derivative of $Au(p) = b(p)$:

Derivatives of u
$$A\frac{\partial u}{\partial p_j} = \frac{\partial b}{\partial p_j}. \tag{2}$$

This is a linear system of size N for every one of the M vectors $\partial u/\partial p_j$. If we can avoid solving all those systems, we will. Remember that the derivatives we actually want in (1) are the components of $c^{\mathrm{T}}(\partial u/\partial p)$, since $g = c^{\mathrm{T}}u$:

Derivatives of g
$$\frac{\partial g}{\partial u}\frac{\partial u}{\partial p} = \underset{1\times N}{c^{\mathrm{T}}}\ \underset{N\times M}{\frac{\partial u}{\partial p}} = \underset{1\times N}{c^{\mathrm{T}}}\ \underset{N\times N}{A^{-1}}\ \underset{N\times M}{\frac{\partial b}{\partial p}}. \tag{3}$$

The whole point of the adjoint method is to compute $\mathbf{c^{\mathrm{T}}A^{-1}}$ first. The calculation to avoid is the last one, $N \times N$ times $N \times M$. All we need for dg/dp is the vector $\lambda^{\mathrm{T}} = c^{\mathrm{T}}A^{-1}$, which involves a single system with coefficient matrix A^{T}:

Adjoint system $\quad A^{\mathrm{T}}\lambda = c \quad$ gives $\quad \lambda^{\mathrm{T}}A = c^{\mathrm{T}} \quad$ and $\quad \lambda^{\mathrm{T}} = c^{\mathrm{T}}A^{-1}$. $\qquad (4)$

For products XYZ of three matrices, **the order $(XY)Z$ could be faster or slower than $X(YZ)$**. Here it is faster. Problem 1 makes the comparison based on shapes. It is the appearance of A^{T} (the ***adjoint***) that gives the method its name.

An **automatic differentiator** (like ADIFOR or AdiMat) is often the best way to compute derivatives of the entries of $b(p)$ and also $A(p)$, which has M derivatives of N^2 entries. Those functions might be specified analytically, or by a FORTRAN code. It is quite amazing to see AD automatically generating codes for the derivatives. When A depends on p, its derivatives go into the last matrix in (3):

$$Z = \frac{\partial b}{\partial p} - \frac{\partial A}{\partial p} u \quad \text{and altogether} \quad \frac{dg}{dp} = c^{\mathrm{T}} A^{-1} Z = \lambda^{\mathrm{T}} Z\,. \tag{5}$$

We thank Mike Giles for a valuable discussion of adjoint methods in design, where changing p gives a new geometry. For an aircraft we may want the change in lift. The methods apply either to the discrete equations or to the PDE's (as in the pioneering papers of Jameson). Steven Johnson gave a beautiful lecture on adjoint methods, with notes on math.mit.edu/~stevenj/18.336/adjoint.pdf. We now follow their applications, to nonlinear problems and eigenvalue problems and initial-value problems.

For many unknowns u and few parameters p, we also explain **direct methods**.

Nonlinear Problems

Suppose the N equations $f(u,p) = 0$ are no longer linear as in $f = Au - b$. The equations determine $u_1, \ldots, u_N$ for the current control variables $p_1, \ldots, p_M$. The scalar function $g(u,p)$ may also be nonlinear. Again we want the gradient dg/dp, in order to know the sensitivity and move to a better p. The derivatives of g in equation (1) involve $\partial u/\partial p$. That N by M matrix now comes from differentiating $f(u,p) = 0$:

Derivatives of f
$$\frac{\partial f}{\partial u}\frac{\partial u}{\partial p} + \frac{\partial f}{\partial p} = 0\,. \tag{6}$$

Substituting into equation (1) gives a formula for the row vector dg/dp:

Sensitivity of g
$$\underset{1\times M}{\frac{dg}{dp}} = \underset{1\times M}{\frac{\partial g}{\partial p}} - \underset{1\times N}{\frac{\partial g}{\partial u}} \underset{N\times N}{\left(\frac{\partial f}{\partial u}\right)^{-1}} \underset{N\times M}{\left(\frac{\partial f}{\partial p}\right)}. \tag{7}$$

Again we have a choice in multiplying three matrices. The better way is to begin with the first two. Their product is the $1 \times N$ row vector λ^{T}. This solves the ***linear adjoint problem*** (linear because we take derivatives at a given p):

Adjoint problem
$$\left(\frac{\partial f}{\partial u}\right)^{\mathrm{T}} \lambda = \left(\frac{\partial g}{\partial u}\right)^{\mathrm{T}} \quad \text{gives} \quad \lambda^{\mathrm{T}} = \frac{\partial g}{\partial u}\left(\frac{\partial f}{\partial u}\right)^{-1}. \tag{8}$$

With $f = Au - b$ and $g = c^{\mathrm{T}}u$, this is $A^{\mathrm{T}}\lambda = c$ as before. Substituting the solution λ^{T} into (6) produces $\lambda^{\mathrm{T}}(\partial f/\partial p)$. We have avoided multiplying two large matrices.

Physical Interpretation of Duality

The adjoint of a matrix (its transpose) is defined by $(\boldsymbol{Au}, \boldsymbol{\lambda}) = (\boldsymbol{u}, \boldsymbol{A}^{\mathrm{T}}\boldsymbol{\lambda})$. The adjoint of $A = d/dx$ is $A^{\mathrm{T}} = -d/dx$, using integration by parts—which is the key to adjoint methods. Section 3.1 showed how boundary conditions appear naturally for the adjoint. Here we are evaluating a scalar g, which can be done in two equivalent ways as $g = c^{\mathrm{T}}u$ or $g = \lambda^{\mathrm{T}}b$ (*direct way* or *adjoint way*):

$$\text{Find } g = c^{\mathrm{T}}u \text{ given } Au = b \qquad \text{Find } g = \lambda^{\mathrm{T}}b \text{ given } A^{\mathrm{T}}\lambda = c \tag{9}$$

The equivalence comes from $\lambda^{\mathrm{T}}b = \lambda^{\mathrm{T}}(Au) = (A^{\mathrm{T}}\lambda)^{\mathrm{T}}u = c^{\mathrm{T}}u$. The choice becomes important when we have M vectors b and u, and L vectors λ and c. We can do M primal calculations or L dual calculations. For large matrices A the cost is in solving linear systems, so the adjoint approach clearly wins for $L << M$ (many design variables). The direct way wins for few variables p, and many g's.

For a physical interpretation of λ, suppose b is a delta vector at position i. Its components are $b_j = \delta_{ij}$. Then $Au = b$ finds the ith column $u = u^i$ of the (discrete) Green's function A^{-1}. The component $\lambda_i = \lambda^{\mathrm{T}}b = c^{\mathrm{T}}u^i$ gives the sensitivity of g to changes at position i, via that column of the Green's function.

Lagrange Variable Viewpoint

The same dual alternatives appear when we see the M variables as Lagrange multipliers. The M constraints in the primal problem are $Au = b$. In the nonlinear case they are $f(u,p) = 0$. The Lagrangian function $L(u,p,\lambda)$ builds in those constraints:

$$\textbf{Lagrange multiplier method} \qquad L = g - \lambda^{\mathrm{T}}f \qquad \frac{dL}{du} = \frac{dg}{du} - \lambda^{\mathrm{T}}\frac{\partial f}{\partial u} \tag{10}$$

The adjoint equation $dL/du = 0$ determines λ, as it did in (8). Then the other part of dL is the sensitivity with respect to p, and we recover equation (7):

$$dL = \frac{dL}{du}\,du + \frac{dL}{dp}\,dp = \left(\frac{dg}{dp} - \lambda^{\mathrm{T}}\frac{\partial f}{\partial p}\right) dp. \tag{11}$$

When the design variables are p, we are minimizing the objective $g(u,p)$. The flow unknowns u are given implicitly by the equations $f(u,p) = 0$. These nonlinear equations, and the linear adjoint equations for λ, are both large systems. We must select an iterative algorithm to compute the minimizing design p^*.

One approach is steepest descent. Another is quasi-Newton (approximating the second derivative matrix $\partial^2 g/\partial p_i \partial p_j$ by low rank BFGS updates at each iteration). Steepest descent is clearly faster per step, because the forward equations $f = 0$ and $dg/du = \lambda^{\mathrm{T}}\partial f/\partial u$ can be solved inexactly (partial convergence of the inner loop).

The serious cost in optimal design problems (inverse problems plus optimization) is in the forward problem that is solved at each iteration. Using AD (Automatic Differentiation) in reverse mode is often essential. Forward AD takes the code to compute f, and uses the rules of differentiation (all linear!) on each command. **In reverse mode, AD computes the adjoint**. Astonishingly, the AD code for derivatives only requires a small multiple of the computing time for the original code for the function [67].

Example 1 Suppose $Au = u' - \epsilon u''$ with fixed end conditions $u(0) = u(1) = 0$

Here A is a convection-diffusion operator in the continuous problem (not a matrix). Integration by parts finds the adjoint operator A^* (or A^{T}) with its boundary conditions. The adjoint variable $\lambda(x)$ is now a function, not a vector:

$$(Au, \lambda) = \int_0^1 \lambda(u' - \epsilon u'')dx = \int_0^1 u(-\lambda' - \epsilon \lambda'')dx + \left[\lambda u - \epsilon \lambda u' + \epsilon u \lambda'\right]_0^1. \quad (12)$$

With zero boundary conditions on λ as well as u, the integrated term vanishes. The adjoint operator $A^*\lambda = -\lambda' - \epsilon \lambda''$ is in the second integral. Notice that the x-direction is reversed in $-\lambda'$. This will reverse causality in the time-dependent problem below, when t replaces x. So the adjoint equation goes *backward in time*.

Initial-value Problems

Suppose $f(u, p) = 0$ is a differential equation like $u_t = B(p)u$, instead of an algebraic equation. We want to adjust $B(p)$ or the initial value $u(0, p)$ to reach a desired result at time T. **The adjoint problem for $\lambda(t)$ will also be a differential equation.** The neat thing is that while $u(t)$ is determined by its initial value, $\lambda(t)$ is determined by its *final value* $\lambda(T)$. We integrate *backwards in time* to compute the adjoint $\lambda(t)$.

The not so neat thing is that the whole history of $u(t)$ seems to be needed to find $\lambda(t)$. For differential equations, the adjoint method can be storage-intensive. *Checkpointing* reduces this storage, at the cost of computing forward in time *twice*:

In the forward computation, save only the checkpoints $u(N\Delta t)$, $u(2N\Delta t), \ldots, u(T)$. The second forward computation goes from the stored $u(T - N\Delta t)$ to $u(T)$. Those last forward values of u give the *first* values of λ, going backward from T. Recomputations of the gaps between u's give backward intervals in $\lambda(t)$, ending at $t = 0$.

When $u(t)$ solves an initial-value problem $u' = f(u, t, p)$, the adjoint solves a final-value problem. That problem depends on $\partial f/\partial u$ and $\partial f/\partial p$. The function we want to optimize might be $g(u, T, p)$ at a specific time T, or it might be an integral of g. To optimize, we need its derivatives with respect to the design variables p:

Find the gradient dG/dp $$G(p) = \int_0^T g(u, t, p)\, dt \quad (13)$$

We have two equations to write down and solve, exactly in parallel with equations (7) and (8). The **sensitivity equation** gives the derivatives in dG/dp from $\partial f/\partial p$ and $\partial g/\partial p$ and the adjoint function $\lambda(t)$. The **adjoint equation** gives $\lambda(t)$ from $\partial f/\partial u$ and $\partial g/\partial u$. Equation (8) was a matrix equation for λ, coming originally from $f(u,p) = 0$. Now we have a *linear differential equation for* λ, coming from $u' = f(u,t,p)$.

Adjoint equation $$\left(\frac{d\lambda}{dt}\right) = -\left(\frac{\partial f}{\partial u}\right)^T \lambda - \left(\frac{\partial g}{\partial u}\right)^T \quad \text{with} \quad \lambda(T) = 0 \tag{14}$$

This imitates (8) with an extra term $d\lambda/dt$, and the minus sign as in Example 1. This minus sign from the antisymmetry of d/dt makes the adjoint equation (14) a **final-value problem**.

The CVODES codes (S for sensitivity) use the checkpointing method to provide $\partial f/\partial u$ and $\partial g/\partial u$, as (14) is integrated backwards. The saved values give a "hot restart" for integrating $u' = f(u,t,p)$ forward between checkpoints.

As in (7), $\lambda(t)$ enters the M sensitivities dG/dp that we want:

Gradient equation $$\frac{dG}{dp} = \lambda^T(0)\,\frac{du}{dp}(0) + \int_0^T \left(\frac{\partial g}{\partial p} + \lambda^T \frac{\partial f}{\partial p}\right) dt \tag{15}$$

Overall, sensitivities come from Lagrange multipliers—not trivial to compute, but highly valuable. Equations (14-15) are implemented in the SUNDIALS package (www.llnl.gov/CASC/sundials) and elsewhere. There is also a pair of equations to give the gradient of $g(u,t,p)$ at the single time point T:

Adjoint equation $$\frac{d\mu}{dt} = -\left(\frac{\partial f}{\partial u}\right)^T \mu \quad \text{backward from} \quad \mu(T) = \left(\frac{\partial g}{\partial u}\right)^T \tag{16}$$

Gradient equation $$\frac{dg}{dp}(T) = \frac{\partial g}{\partial p}(T) + \mu^T(0)\,\frac{du}{dp}(0) + \int_0^T \mu^T \frac{\partial f}{\partial p}\, dt\,. \tag{17}$$

Forward Sensitivity Analysis

The adjoint method finds sensitivities dg/dp of one function g (or a few) with respect to M design variables p. Other problems have only one variable p (or a few) and many functions. In fact we may want ***the sensitivity*** $\boldsymbol{s(t) = du/dp}$ ***of the whole solution*** $\boldsymbol{u(t)}$ ***with respect to*** $\boldsymbol{p}$.

This is a forward problem. Differentiate $u' = f(u,t,p)$ with respect to p:

Sensitivity equation $$\frac{ds}{dt} = \frac{\partial f}{\partial u}\,s + \frac{\partial f}{\partial p} \quad \text{with} \quad s(0) = \frac{\partial u}{\partial p}(0)\,. \tag{18}$$

This is linear and not so difficult. The Jacobian $\partial f/\partial u$ is computed anyway, in an implicit method for the original equation $u' = f(u,t,p)$. The two equations are solved together, at far less than double the cost.

Now increase the number of design variables $p_1, \ldots, p_M$. We have M linear equations (18) for the sensitivities $s_i = \partial u/\partial p_i$, plus the original nonlinear equation $u' = f(u,t,p)$. All share the same Jacobian $\partial f/\partial u$. The solution by backward differences (BDF1 to 5) is highly efficient [ ] until M is large. Then we change to the adjoint method, to compute dg/dp for one functional $g(u)$.

Eigenvalue Problems

Now the unknown u is a unit eigenvector x together with its eigenvalue α. The equations $f(u,p) = 0$ combine $Ax - \alpha x = 0$ and $x^{\mathrm{T}}x - 1 = 0$ (both nonlinear in x and α). *The matrix A depends on control parameters p.* Then x and α depend on p. If A is n by n, we have $N = n+1$ unknowns x and α, and N equations $f(u,p) = 0$:

$$u = \begin{bmatrix} x \\ \alpha \end{bmatrix} \qquad f = \begin{bmatrix} Ax - \alpha x \\ x^{\mathrm{T}}x - 1 \end{bmatrix} \qquad \frac{\partial f}{\partial u} = \begin{bmatrix} A - \alpha I & -x \\ 2x^{\mathrm{T}} & 0 \end{bmatrix} \qquad \lambda = \begin{bmatrix} y \\ c \end{bmatrix}.$$

The adjoint equation $(\partial f/\partial u)^{\mathrm{T}}\lambda = (\partial g/\partial u)^{\mathrm{T}}$ has this block structure:

Adjoint equation $$\begin{bmatrix} A^{\mathrm{T}} - \alpha I & 2x \\ -x^{\mathrm{T}} & 0 \end{bmatrix} \begin{bmatrix} y \\ c \end{bmatrix} = \begin{bmatrix} (\partial g/\partial x)^{\mathrm{T}} \\ \partial g/\partial \alpha \end{bmatrix}. \qquad (19)$$

If we transpose $(A - \alpha I)x = 0$, the first row of (8) determines c:

$$0^{\mathrm{T}}y = x^{\mathrm{T}}(A^{\mathrm{T}} - \alpha I)y = x^{\mathrm{T}}(g_x^{\mathrm{T}} - 2cx) = x^{\mathrm{T}}g_x^{\mathrm{T}} - 2c \quad \text{gives} \quad c = \frac{1}{2}x^{\mathrm{T}}g_x^{\mathrm{T}}. \qquad (20)$$

Now the first row of (9) is $\boldsymbol{(A^{\mathrm{T}} - \alpha I)y = (1 - xx^{\mathrm{T}})g_x^{\mathrm{T}}}$. But the eigenvalue α of A is also an eigenvalue of A^{T}. The matrix $A^{\mathrm{T}} - \alpha I$ is singular with an eigenvector z in its nullspace. (We assume α is a simple real eigenvalue of A and A^{T}. If A is symmetric then z is the same as x.) The second equation $-x^{\mathrm{T}}y = \partial g/\partial\alpha$ in (9) determines the nullspace component βz to include in y. Then λ is all set.

Example 2 The second derivative $-d^2u/dx^2$ with periodic boundary conditions is approximated by $Cu/(\Delta x)^2$, where C is the $-1, 2, -1$ circulant matrix of Section 1.1. *Schrödinger's eigenvalue problem $-u''(x) + V(x)u = Eu$ includes a potential $V(x)$.* Its M meshpoint values in $p = \operatorname{diag}(V(\Delta x), \ldots, V(M\Delta x))$ will be our control vector p.

We adjust p to make the eigenvector in $Cu/(\Delta x)^2 + pu = \alpha u$ close to a desired u_0:

Eigenvector distance $\qquad g(u,p) = \|u - u_0\|^2$ has $\dfrac{\partial g}{\partial u} = 2(u - u_0)^{\mathrm{T}}$.

The cse page links to Johnson's code that computes the vector dg/dp without the explicit matrix $\partial u/\partial p$. The adjoint equation is solved for λ by conjugate gradients.

Problem Set 8.7

1 Suppose X is q by r, Y is r by s, and Z is s by t. Show that multiplying $(XY)Z$ needs $qrs + qst$ multiply-add operations. The same answer from $X(YZ)$ needs $rst + qrt$. Dividing by $qrst$, $(XY)Z$ is faster when $\boldsymbol{t^{-1} + r^{-1} < q^{-1} + s^{-1}}$.

The adjoint method for (3) is a success because $r = s$ with $q = 1$ and $t = M$.

2 (*Forward AD*) An output T comes from an input S by a sequence of intermediate steps $C = f(A, B)$ in the code. At each step the chain rule gives $\partial C/\partial S = (\partial f/\partial A)(\partial A/\partial S) + (\partial f/\partial B)(\partial B/\partial S)$. Then the overall derivative dT/dS comes from that sequence of chain rules.

The code $C = S$^2; $T = S - C$; computes $T = S - S^2$. From the derivatives of the steps, write a code for dT/dS.

3 If the vectors u, v, w have N components, the multiplication $u^{\mathrm{T}}(vw^{\mathrm{T}})$ produces a *matrix* vw^{T} *first*. The multiplication $(u^{\mathrm{T}}v)w^{\mathrm{T}}$ produces a *number* $u^{\mathrm{T}}v$ *first*. Show that the first way costs $2N^2$ multiplications and the second way only costs $2N$ multiplications.

Notes on Automatic Differentiation

The Jacobian matrix J gives the derivatives of outputs $y_1, \ldots, y_p$ with respect to inputs $x_1, \ldots, x_n$. Break this computation into many steps, with simple functions $z_1, \ldots, z_N$. The first n z's are the x's, the last p z's are the y's. Example with $n = 3$: $z_1 = x_1$, $z_2 = x_2$, $z_3 = x_3$, $z_4 = z_1 z_2$, $z_5 = z_4/z_3$. *Each z depends only on earlier z's, so the derivative matrix D_i for each step is* **lower triangular**:

$$z_4' = z_2 z_1' + z_1 z_2' \quad \text{means} \quad D_4 = [\ z_2 \quad z_1 \quad 0 \ldots 0\ ] \quad \text{in row 4.}$$

D_4 is the identity matrix in all other rows. A giant chain rule produces the N by N Jacobian matrix $D = D_N \ldots D_2 D_1$ of z's with respect to earlier z's. This matrix D is still lower triangular. Its lower left corner is J, the derivative of the last z's (those are the y's) with respect to the first z's (the x's). Q and P select this corner:

$$J = QDP^{\mathrm{T}} \quad \text{with} \quad Q = [\ 0 \quad 0 \quad I_p\ ] \quad \text{and} \quad P = [\ I_n \quad 0 \quad 0\ ].$$

Forward AD multiplies $D = D_N(D_{N-1}(\ldots(D_2 D_1)))$ starting with $D_2 D_1$: the normal order. *Reverse AD* finds $D^{\mathrm{T}} = D_1^{\mathrm{T}} \ldots D_N^{\mathrm{T}}$ by multiplying in the opposite order $D_1^{\mathrm{T}}(D_2^{\mathrm{T}}(\ldots(D_{N-1}^{\mathrm{T}} D_N^{\mathrm{T}})))$. The real calculation has shortcuts but this ideal calculation shows the underlying structure.

The fundamental identity in this subject is $y^{\mathrm{T}}(Jx') = (J^{\mathrm{T}}y)^{\mathrm{T}}x'$. We choose the multiplication order (forward or reverse, direct or adjoint) that has fewest steps.

LINEAR ALGEBRA IN A NUTSHELL

One question always comes on the first day of class. *"Do I have to know linear algebra?"* My reply gets shorter every year: *"You soon will."* This section brings together many important points in the theory. It serves as a quick primer, not an official part of the applied mathematics course (like Chapter 1 and 2).

This summary begins with two lists that use most of the key words of linear algebra. The first list applies to invertible matrices. That property is described in 14 different ways. The second list shows the contrast, when A is singular (not invertible). There are more ways to test invertibility of an n by n matrix than I expected.

Nonsingular	Singular
A is invertible	A is not invertible
The columns are independent	The columns are dependent
The rows are independent	The rows are dependent
The determinant is not zero	The determinant is zero
$Ax = 0$ has one solution $x = 0$	$Ax = 0$ has infinitely many solutions
$Ax = b$ has one solution $x = A^{-1}b$	$Ax = b$ has no solution or infinitely many
A has n (nonzero) pivots	A has $r < n$ pivots
A has full rank	A has rank $r < n$
The reduced row echelon form is $R = I$	R has at least one zero row
The column space is all of $\mathbf{R}^n$	The column space has dimension $r < n$
The row space is all of $\mathbf{R}^n$	The row space has dimension $r < n$
All eigenvalues are nonzero	Zero is an eigenvalue of A
$A^{\mathrm{T}}A$ is symmetric positive definite	$A^{\mathrm{T}}A$ is only semidefinite
A has n (positive) singular values	A has $r < n$ singular values

Now we take a deeper look at linear equations, without proving every statement we make. The goal is to discover what $Ax = b$ really means. One reference is my textbook *Introduction to Linear Algebra*, published by Wellesley-Cambridge Press. That book has a much more careful development with many examples (you could look at the course page, with videos of the lectures, on ocw.mit.edu or web.mit.edu/18.06).

The key is to think of every multiplication Ax, a matrix A times a vector x, as a *combination of the columns of A*:

Matrix Multiplication by Columns

$$\begin{bmatrix} 1 & 2 \\ 3 & 6 \end{bmatrix} \begin{bmatrix} C \\ D \end{bmatrix} = C \begin{bmatrix} 1 \\ 3 \end{bmatrix} + D \begin{bmatrix} 2 \\ 6 \end{bmatrix} = \textbf{combination of columns}\,.$$

Multiplying by rows, the first component $C + 2D$ comes from 1 and 2 in the first row of A. But I strongly recommend to think of Ax **a column at a time**. Notice how

$x = (1,0)$ and $x = (0,1)$ will pick out single columns of A:

$$\begin{bmatrix} 1 & 2 \\ 3 & 6 \end{bmatrix} \begin{bmatrix} 1 \\ 0 \end{bmatrix} = \text{first column} \qquad \begin{bmatrix} 1 & 2 \\ 3 & 6 \end{bmatrix} \begin{bmatrix} 0 \\ 1 \end{bmatrix} = \text{last column}\,.$$

Suppose A is an m by n matrix. Then $Ax = 0$ has at least one solution, the all-zeros vector $x = 0$. There are certainly other solutions in case $n > m$ (more unknowns than equations). Even if $m = n$, there might be nonzero solutions to $Ax = 0$; then A is square but not invertible. It is the number r of *independent* rows and columns that counts. That number r is the **rank** of A ($r \le m$ and $r \le n$).

> The **nullspace** of A is the set of all solutions x to $Ax = 0$. This nullspace $\boldsymbol{N}(A)$ contains only $x = 0$ when the columns of A are **independent**. In that case the matrix A has full column rank $r = n$: independent columns.

For our 2 by 2 example, the combination with $C = 2$ and $D = -1$ produces the zero vector. Thus $x = (2, -1)$ is in the nullspace, with $Ax = 0$. The columns $(1,3)$ and $(2,6)$ are "linearly dependent." One column is a multiple of the other column. *The rank is* $r = 1$. The matrix A has a whole line of vectors $cx = c(2,-1)$ in its nullspace:

Nullspace is a line

$$\begin{bmatrix} 1 & 2 \\ 3 & 6 \end{bmatrix} \begin{bmatrix} 2 \\ -1 \end{bmatrix} = \begin{bmatrix} 0 \\ 0 \end{bmatrix} \quad \text{and also} \quad \begin{bmatrix} 1 & 2 \\ 3 & 6 \end{bmatrix} \begin{bmatrix} \boldsymbol{2c} \\ \boldsymbol{-c} \end{bmatrix} = \begin{bmatrix} 0 \\ 0 \end{bmatrix}.$$

If $Ax = 0$ and $Ay = 0$, then every combination $cx + dy$ is in the nullspace. Always $Ax = 0$ asks for a combination of the columns of A that produces the zero vector:

x in nullspace $\quad x_1\,(\text{column } 1) + \cdots + x_n\,(\text{column } n) = \text{zero vector}$

When those columns are independent, the only way to produce $Ax = 0$ is with $x_1 = 0$, $x_2 = 0, \ldots, x_n = 0$. Then $x = (0, \ldots, 0)$ is the only vector in the nullspace of A. Often this will be our requirement (independent columns) for a good matrix A. In that case, $A^{\mathrm{T}}A$ also has independent columns. The square n by n matrix $A^{\mathrm{T}}A$ is then invertible and symmetric and positive definite. If A is good then $A^{\mathrm{T}}A$ is even better.

I will extend this review (*still optional*) to the geometry of $Ax = b$.

Column Space and Solutions to Linear Equations

$Ax = b$ **asks for a linear combination of the columns that equals** b. In our 2 by 2 example, the columns go in the same direction! Then b does too:

Column space

$$Ax = \begin{bmatrix} 1 & 2 \\ 3 & 6 \end{bmatrix} \begin{bmatrix} C \\ D \end{bmatrix} \text{ is always on the line through } \begin{bmatrix} 1 \\ 3 \end{bmatrix}.$$

We can only solve $Ax = b$ when the vector b is on that line. For $b = (1,4)$ there is no solution, it is off the line. For $b = (5,15)$ there are many solutions (5 times column 1 gives b, and this b is on the line). The big step is to look at a space of vectors:

Definition: The *column space* contains all combinations of the columns.

In other words, $C(A)$ contains all possible products A times x. Therefore $Ax = b$ is **solvable** exactly when the vector b is in the column space $C(A)$.

For an m by n matrix, the columns have m components. The column space of A is in m-dimensional space. The word **"space"** indicates that the key operation of linear algebra is allowed: *Any combination of vectors in the space stays in the space.* The zero combination is allowed, so the vector $x = 0$ is in every space.

How do we write down all solutions, when b belongs to the column space of A? Any one solution to $Ax = b$ is a **particular solution** $\boldsymbol{x_p}$. Any vector $\boldsymbol{x_n}$ in the nullspace solves $Ax = 0$. Adding $Ax_p = b$ to $Ax_n = 0$ gives $A(x_p + x_n) = b$. **The complete solution to** $Ax = b$ **has this form** $x = x_p + x_n$:

Complete solution $\quad x = x_{\text{particular}} + x_{\text{nullspace}} = (\text{one } x_p) + (\text{all } x_n)$.

In the example, $b = (5, 15)$ is 5 times the first column, so one particular solution is $x_p = (5, 0)$. To find all other solutions, add to x_p any vector x_n in the nullspace—which is the line through $(2, -1)$. Here is $x_p + (\text{all } x_n)$:

$$\begin{bmatrix} 1 & 2 \\ 3 & 6 \end{bmatrix} \begin{bmatrix} C \\ D \end{bmatrix} = \begin{bmatrix} 5 \\ 15 \end{bmatrix} \quad \text{gives} \quad x_{\text{complete}} = \begin{bmatrix} C \\ D \end{bmatrix} = \begin{bmatrix} 5 \\ 0 \end{bmatrix} + \begin{bmatrix} 2c \\ -c \end{bmatrix}.$$

This line of solutions is drawn in Figure A1. *It is not a subspace.* It does not contain $(0, 0)$, because it is shifted over by the particular solution $(5, 0)$. We only have a "space" of solutions when b is zero (then the solutions fill the nullspace).

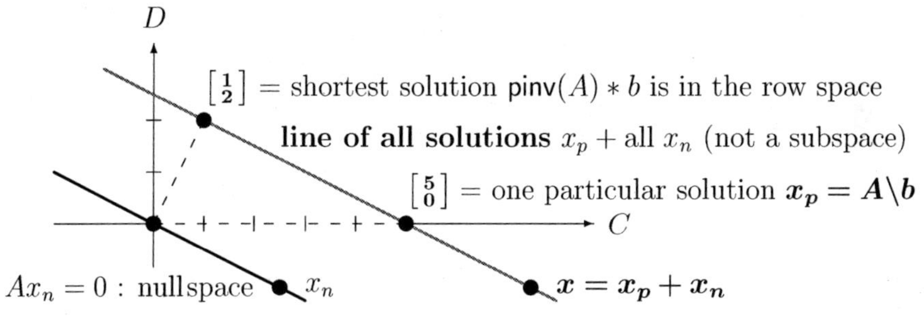

Figure A1: Parallel lines of solutions to $Ax_n = 0$ and $\begin{bmatrix} 1 & 2 \\ 3 & 6 \end{bmatrix}(\boldsymbol{x_p} + \boldsymbol{x_n}) = \begin{bmatrix} 5 \\ 15 \end{bmatrix}$

May I collect three important comments on linear equations $Ax = b$.

1. Suppose A is a square *invertible* matrix (the most common case in practice). Then the nullspace only contains $x_n = 0$. The particular solution $x_p = A^{-1}b$ is the only solution. The complete solution $x_p + x_n$ is $A^{-1}b + 0$. Thus $x = A^{-1}b$.

2. $Ax = b$ has infinitely many solutions in Figure A1. The shortest x always lies in the "row space" of A. That particular solution $(1, 2)$ is found by the *pseudo-inverse* pinv (A). The backslash $A \backslash b$ finds an x with at most m nonzeros.

3. Suppose A is tall and thin $(m > n)$. The n columns are likely to be independent. But if b is not in the column space, $Ax = b$ has no solution. The least squares method minimizes $\|b - Ax\|^2$ by solving $A^{\mathrm{T}} A \widehat{x} = A^{\mathrm{T}} b$.

The Four Fundamental Subspaces

The nullspace $\boldsymbol{N}(A)$ contains all solutions to $Ax = 0$. The column space $\boldsymbol{C}(A)$ contains all combinations of the columns. When A is m by n, $\boldsymbol{N}(A)$ is a subspace of $\mathbf{R}^n$ and $\boldsymbol{C}(A)$ is a subspace of $\mathbf{R}^m$.

The other two fundamental spaces come from the transpose matrix A^{T}. They are $\boldsymbol{N}(A^{\mathrm{T}})$ and $\boldsymbol{C}(A^{\mathrm{T}})$. We call $\boldsymbol{C}(A^{\mathrm{T}})$ the "row space of A" because the rows of A are the columns of A^{T}. What are those spaces for our 2 by 2 example?

$$A = \begin{bmatrix} 1 & 2 \\ 3 & 6 \end{bmatrix} \quad \text{transposes to} \quad A^{\mathrm{T}} = \begin{bmatrix} 1 & 3 \\ 2 & 6 \end{bmatrix}.$$

Both columns of A^{T} are in the direction of $(1, 2)$. The line of all vectors $(c, 2c)$ is $\boldsymbol{C}(A^{\mathrm{T}}) =$ row space of A. The nullspace of A^{T} is in the direction of $(3, -1)$:

Nullspace of $\boldsymbol{A}^{\mathrm{T}}$ $$A^{\mathrm{T}} y = \begin{bmatrix} 1 & 3 \\ 2 & 6 \end{bmatrix} \begin{bmatrix} E \\ F \end{bmatrix} = \begin{bmatrix} 0 \\ 0 \end{bmatrix} \quad \text{gives} \quad \begin{bmatrix} E \\ F \end{bmatrix} = \begin{bmatrix} 3c \\ -c \end{bmatrix}.$$

The four subspaces $\boldsymbol{N}(A)$, $\boldsymbol{C}(A)$, $\boldsymbol{N}(A^{\mathrm{T}})$, $\boldsymbol{C}(A^{\mathrm{T}})$ combine beautifully into the big picture of linear algebra. Figure A2 shows how the nullspace $\boldsymbol{N}(A)$ is perpendicular to the row space $\boldsymbol{C}(A^{\mathrm{T}})$. Every input vector x splits into a row space part x_r and a nullspace part x_n. Multiplying by A always(!) produces a vector in the column space. Multiplication goes from left to right in the picture, from x to $Ax = b$.

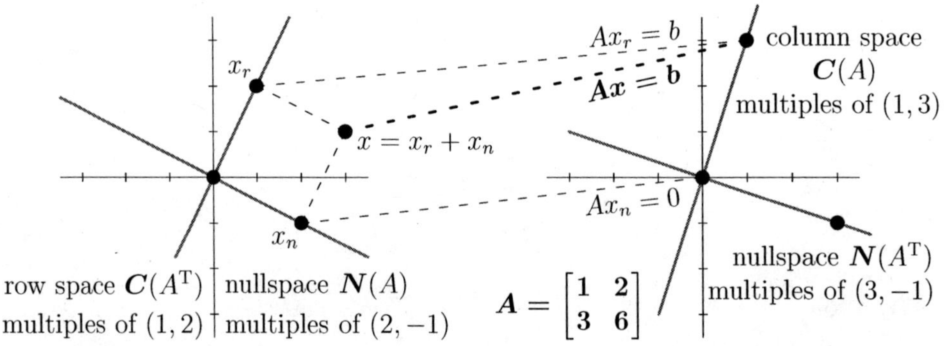

Figure A2: The four fundamental subspaces (lines) for the singular matrix A.

On the right side are the column space $\boldsymbol{C}(A)$ and the fourth space $\boldsymbol{N}(A^{\mathrm{T}})$. **Again they are perpendicular**. The columns are multiples of $(1,3)$ and the y's are multiples of $(3,-1)$. If A were an m by n matrix, its columns would be in m-dimensional space $\mathbf{R}^m$ and so would the solutions to $A^{\mathrm{T}}y=0$. Our singular 2 by 2 example has $m=n=2$, and all four fundamental subspaces in Figure A2 are lines in $\mathbf{R}^2$.

This figure needs more words. Each subspace contains infinitely many vectors, or only the zero vector $x=0$. If u is in a space, so are $10u$ and $-100u$ (and most importantly $0u$). We measure the ***dimension*** of a space not by the number of vectors, which is infinite, but by *the number of independent vectors.* In this example each dimension is 1. A line has one independent vector but not two

Dimension and Basis

A full set of independent vectors is a "**basis**" for a space. This idea is important. The basis has as many independent vectors as possible, and their combinations fill the space. **A basis has not too many vectors, and not too few**:

1. The basis vectors are **linearly independent**.

2. Every vector in the space is a **unique combination** of those basis vectors.

Here are particular bases for $\mathbf{R}^n$ among all the choices we could make:

Standard basis	=	columns of the **identity** matrix
General basis	=	columns of any **invertible** matrix
Orthonormal basis	=	columns of any **orthogonal** matrix

The "dimension" of the space is the number of vectors in a basis.

Difference Matrices

Difference matrices with boundary conditions give exceptionally good examples of the four subspaces (and there is a physical meaning behind them). We choose forward and backward differences that produce 2 by 3 and 3 by 2 matrices:

Forward Δ_+
Backward $-\Delta_-$

$$A=\begin{bmatrix}-1 & 1 & 0\\ 0 & -1 & 1\end{bmatrix} \quad \text{and} \quad A^{\mathrm{T}}=\begin{bmatrix}-1 & 0\\ 1 & -1\\ 0 & 1\end{bmatrix}.$$

A is imposing no boundary conditions (no rows are chopped off). Then A^{T} must impose two boundary conditions and it does: $+1$ disappeared in the first row and -1 in the third row. $A^{\mathrm{T}}w=f$ builds in the boundary conditions $w_0=0$ and $w_3=0$.

The nullspace of A contains $x=(1,1,1)$. Every constant vector $x=(c,c,c)$ solves $Ax=0$, and *the nullspace* $\boldsymbol{N}(A)$ *is a line* in three-dimensional space. The row space of A is the plane through the rows $(-1,1,0)$ and $(0,-1,1)$. Both vectors are perpendicular to $(1,1,1)$ so **the whole row space is perpendicular to the nullspace**. Those two spaces are on the left side (the 3D side) of Figure A3.

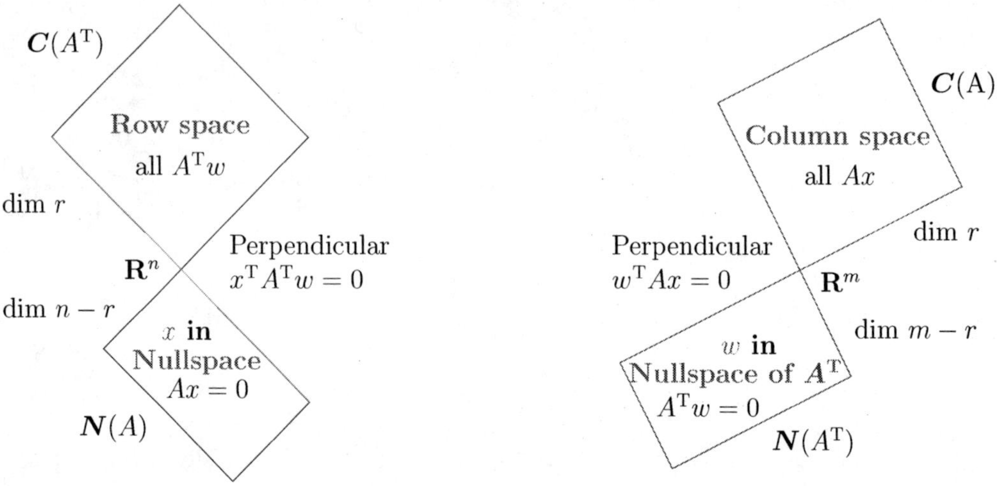

Figure A3: Dimensions and orthogonality for any m by n matrix A of rank r.

Figure A3 shows the Fundamental Theorem of Linear Algebra:

1. The row space in $\mathbf{R}^n$ and column space in $\mathbf{R}^m$ have the same dimension r.
2. The nullspaces $N(A)$ and $N(A^T)$ have dimensions $n-r$ and $m-r$.
3. $N(A)$ is perpendicular to the row space $C(A^T)$.
4. $N(A^T)$ is perpendicular to the column space $C(A)$.

The dimension r of the column space is the "rank" of the matrix. It equals the number of (nonzero) pivots in elimination. The matrix has full column rank when $r = n$ and the columns are linearly independent; the nullspace only contains $x = 0$. Otherwise some nonzero combination x of the columns produces $Ax = 0$.

The dimension of the nullspace is $n - r$. There are n unknowns in $Ax = 0$, and there are really r equations. Elimination leaves $n - r$ columns without pivots. The corresponding unknowns are free (give them any values). This produces $n - r$ independent solutions to $Ax = 0$, a basis for the nullspace.

A good basis makes scientific computing possible:

1 Sines and cosines **2** Finite elements **3** Splines **4** Wavelets

A basis of eigenvectors is often the best.

COMPUTATIONAL SCIENCE AND ENGINEERING

These pages include a few words (plus more on the cse website) about the larger picture of computational science and engineering. The letters CSE often indicate *large scale computations*—the kind that national laboratories do. Certainly, massively parallel computation on supercomputers is more than we can describe in a first course. You can reach that level (I hope you will), but it is not the place to start.

My goal is to present the fundamentals of scientific computing, with short codes to implement the key concepts. You will see a framework for applied mathematics. One theme is the appearance of symmetric positive definite matrices $A^{\mathrm{T}}CA$—stiffness matrices, conductance matrices, multigrid matrices. The geometry is in A, the physical properties are in C. The matrices come from spring-mass systems, and networks, and least squares, and especially from differential equations like $\operatorname{div}(c \operatorname{grad} u) = f$.

Let me *briefly* describe some of the applications that build on those foundations.

Computational Engineering

The **finite element method** is a perfect illustration of what the technical community (led by computational mechanics) has achieved. The ideas and the software represent a highly impressive collective effort of thousands of engineers. This is remarkable.

For the mechanics of structures, finite elements are reliable and efficient. We meet this method early (one-dimensional introduction in Section 3.1, two-dimensional code in Section 3.6). To start, the differential equations are written in **weak form**, integrated against test functions. Then stresses and displacements are approximated by piecewise polynomials, simple to work with and fast to compute.

When computational engineering meets fluid-structure interactions or high-speed impact, finite element codes get stretched (and stressed). A demand for good accuracy is not met by the lowest order elements. If you see how the finite element idea works, you can adjust. For special geometries, we develop fast solvers.

Computational Electromagnetics

The SPICE codes will solve network problems with thousands of circuit elements. Those nonlinear equations $g(u) = 0$ become more difficult with transistors. The codes use variations of **Newton's method** $\boldsymbol{J\Delta u} = \boldsymbol{-g}$, where J is the Jacobian of g and Δu is the step from u^k to u^{k+1}. Section 2.6 develops Newton's method.

For Maxwell's equations, finite differences on a staggered grid (Yee's method) will capture the fundamental laws of physics. The Helmholtz equation separates variables

($e^{i\omega t}$ for time) but the price is an indefinite equation with negative eigenvalues for high frequencies ω. Exterior problems lead to integral equations (and boundary elements).

Computational Physics and Chemistry

Molecular physics and chemistry require large computations over many time steps. Approximations are higher order, simple elements are ruled out, and special functions come in. With finite differences, the resolution needed for high accuracy leads to very large matrices, and solution methods like **multigrid** (Section 7.3). Conservation of energy requires a time evolution staying close to the edge of instability.

Numerically, we can't just damp out the danger by diffusion and dissipation. Solving Newton's Law $mu'' = f(u)$ in Section 2.2 already needs stability and accuracy over many periods. That applies to atomic oscillations and also to orbits in space.

In **computational fluid dynamics**, Sections 6.6-6.7 study convection with diffusion. We apply divergence-free projection to solve the Navier-Stokes equations.

Multiscale problems reach the frontier where the model itself is a major issue. Small scales in high speed flow have strong effects at large scales—how to capture both? Those problems need physics and chemistry, in addition to the computational science that this book presents. *The discretization has to preserve the science.*

Computational Biology

Part of biology can be expressed by differential equations. Another (large) part can't—at least not yet. This part often involves networks of nodes and edges, and combinatorial problems, and probability, and very large amounts of data. Our first line of attack is **least squares** (an ℓ^1 penalty helps to achieve sparsity).

> Microarrays are columns of matrices, from observations of gene expression. Those matrices have a Singular Value Decomposition $A = U\Sigma V^{\mathrm{T}}$. The columns of U and V indicate the orthogonal "eigengenes" in Section 1.8. The singular values in Σ indicate their importance. It is normally *combinations of genes* that produce disease, and the expression data is our key to that information.

Networks and graphs are amazingly useful models in applied mathematics. Section 2.4 studies flows in networks, where the fundamental balance equation is Kirchhoff's Current Law: *Flow in equals flow out.* Conservation laws are the key to modeling.

Data mining is a mixture of probability, statistics, signal processing and optimization. This book can explain each of those parts — Gaussian and Poisson distributions, means and covariances, filters and wavelets, Lagrange multipliers and duality. In a few pages, there is no way to integrate all those tools into a full discussion of machine learning. And that seems premature. The special section $*2.9$ highlights the critical question of **clustering and graph cuts**.

Mathematical biology is a very big subject, because its other parts use physics and chemistry—transport and diffusion and kinetics. Those apply within the cell, and on a larger scale to the whole organism. Stiff differential equations (needing implicit difference methods) come from many sources. This book describes how to solve them: **Choice of basis functions, discretization, stability analysis, sparse matrix methods.**

Computational Simulation and Design

Numerical experiments are often quicker and easier than physical experiments. You can run a series of tests with varying parameters, to approach an optimal design. But are those numerical simulations reliable? They are never exact. The problem of **quantifying uncertainty** is central to computational science. It has two parts:

Validation	"Solving the right equations"
Verification	"Solving the equations right"

The right equations will be simplified, to make them manageable. Modeling is such a crucial part of applied mathematics. "Everything should be made as simple as possible, but not simpler" (Einstein).

A good solution includes an estimate of the numerical error. Classically, that is an $O((\Delta x)^2)$ or $O((\Delta t)^4)$ error from discretization. Derivatives becomes differences, functions become polynomials, integrals become finite sums. The harder part to measure is the error from the wrong material properties. Then the key is a **sensitivity analysis**, to see how the output depends on the input. Section 8.7 describes how the "adjoint problem" measures sensitivity to the control variables.

Optimization of the output can be difficult, because it asks you to adjust the design. Often it is the magic of Lagrange multipliers that yields an estimate of $d(output)/d(input)$. The **inverse problem** finds the input from observing the output. That problem is notoriously ill-posed. **Example: Find velocities $v(t)$ from positions $x(t)$.** Differentiation is the ill-posed inverse problem for $v(t)$, integration is the well-posed forward problem for $x(t)$. Section 8.2 shows how to regularize a nearly singular problem by adding a penalty term.

Optimization of the design shape, or the coefficients in a differential equation, remains a large challenge to modern computational science.

Computational Finance

The fundamental law of finance is best expressed in *Guys and Dolls* (the musical). Nathan Detroit needed \$1000 to find a room for his floating crap game. "*Being I assume the risk, it is only fair I should assume some dough.*"

If one equation is outstanding in the development of mathematical finance, it must be the **Black-Scholes equation**. Depending on the rules of the market (European or American) this equation gives the value of an option to buy or sell an asset. The underlying mathematics is quite subtle: Ito's lemma and Brownian motion. Computationally, we have options of a different kind in Section 6.5:

With **constant volatility**, Black-Scholes reduces to the heat equation $u_t = u_{xx}$.
With **variable volatility**, the natural approach is by finite differences.

Monte Carlo methods are competitive by simulating a random walk. To an outsider, the depth and subtlety of mathematical finance are just astonishing.

Computational Optimization

The problem of optimization is to compute (and understand) a minimum or a maximum subject to constraints. Linear programming is the classic example—and new primal-dual algorithms are overtaking the simplex method. The dual problem finds the all-important **Lagrange multipliers** (the "Greeks" of mathematical finance). Those give the sensitivity of the solution to changes in the data.

Section 8.1 explains duality for least squares. The primal projects onto one subspace, the dual projects onto the orthogonal subspace. The minimax theorem reduces to $a^2 + b^2 = c^2$ for right triangles. Section 8.6 moves to *inequality constraints* $x \geq 0$.

In mechanics the dual problems optimize potential and complementary energy. Physics has Lagrangians and Hamiltonians. This is the **calculus of variations**, when the unknown to be optimized is a function of x or t instead of a vector.

Basics of Scientific Computing

1. **Matrix equations** and the central problems of linear algebra

   lu(A) $Ax = b$ by elimination and $A = LU$ (triangular factors)
   eig(A) $Ax = \lambda x$ leading to diagonalization $A = S\Lambda S^{-1}$ (eigenvalues in Λ)
   qr(A) $Au \approx b$ by solving $A^{\mathrm{T}}A\widehat{u} = A^{\mathrm{T}}b$ with orthogonalization $A = QR$
   svd(A) Best bases from the Singular Value Decomposition $A = U\Sigma V^{\mathrm{T}}$

2. **Differential equations** in space and time: boundary and initial values

   Explicit solution by Fourier and Laplace transforms
   Finite difference solutions with tests for accuracy and stability
   Finite element solutions using polynomials on unstructured meshes
   Spectral methods of exponential accuracy by Fast Fourier Transform

3. **Large sparse systems** of linear and nonlinear equations

   Direct solution by reordering the unknowns before elimination
   Multigrid solution by fast approximation at multiple scales
   Iterative solution by conjugate gradients and MINRES
   Newton's method: linearization with approximate Jacobians

BIBLIOGRAPHY

[1] Y. Achdou and O. Pironneau, *Computational Methods for Option Pricing.* SIAM, 2005.

[2] E. Anderson et al. *LAPACK User's Guide.* SIAM, 3rd edition, 1999.

[3] A. C. Antoulas. *Approximation of Large-Scale Dynamical Systems.* SIAM, 2006.

[4] U. Ascher, R. Mattheij, and R. Russell. *Numerical Solution of Boundary Value Problems for Ordinary Differential Equations.* Prentice-Hall, 1988.

[5] O. Axelsson. *Iterative Solution Methods.* Cambridge, 1994.

[6] O. Axelsson and V. A. Barker. *Finite Element Solution of Boundary Value Problems.* SIAM, 2001.

[7] G. Baker and P. Graves-Morris. *Padé Approximants.* Cambridge, 1996.

[8] W. Bangerth and R. Rannacher. *Adaptive Finite Element Methods for Differential Equations.* Birkhäuser, 2003.

[9] R. E. Bank et al. Transient simulation of silicon devices and circuits. *IEEE Transactions on Electron Devices*, 32:1992–2007, 1985.

[10] K. J. Bathe. *Finite Element Procedures.* Prentice-Hall, 1996.

[11] T. Belytschko and T. J. R. Hughes. *Computational Methods for Transient Analysis.* North-Holland, 1983.

[12] C. M. Bender and S. A. Orszag. *Advanced Mathematical Methods for Scientists and Engineers.* McGraw-Hill, 1978.

[13] M. Benzi, G. H. Golub, and M. Liesen. Numerical Solution of Saddle Point Problems. *Acta Numerica*, 2005.

[14] J. P. Berenger. A perfectly matched layer for the absorption of electromagnetic waves. *J. Computational Physics* 114:185–200, 1994.

[15] D. P. Bertsekas. *Dynamic Programming and Optimal Control.* Athena Press, 2000.

[16] D. A. Bini, G. Latouche, and B. Meini. *Numerical Methods for Structured Markov Chains.* Oxford, 2005.

[17] C. Bischof. *Pattern Recognition and Machine Learning.* Springer, 2006.

[18] A. Björck. *Numerical Methods for Least Squares Problems.* SIAM, 1996.

[19] M. Bonnet. *Boundary Integral Equation Methods for Solids and Fluids.* Wiley, 1999.

[20] S. Boyd and L. Vandenberghe. *Convex Optimization.* Cambridge, 2004.

[21] Y. Boykov, O. Veksler, and R. Zabih. Fast approximate energy minimization via graph cuts. *IEEE Transactions PAMI*, 23:1222–1239, 2001.

[22] R. N. Bracewell. *The Fourier Transform and Its Applications.* McGraw-Hill, 1986.

[23] D. Braess. *Finite Elements: Theory, Fast Solvers and Applications in Solid Mechanics.* Cambridge, 2007.

[24] S. C. Brenner and L. R. Scott. *The Mathematical Theory of Finite Element Methods.* Springer, 1994.

[25] F. Brezzi and M. Fortin. *Mixed and Hybrid Finite Element Methods.* Springer, 1991.

[26] W. L. Briggs, V. E. Henson, and S. F. McCormick. *A Multigrid Tutorial.* SIAM, 2000.

[27] J. Butcher. *The Numerical Analysis of Ordinary Differential Equations.* Wiley, 1987.

[28] B. L. Buzbee, G. H. Golub, and C. W. Nielson. On direct methods for solving Poisson's equation. *SIAM J. Numer. Anal.*, 7:627–656, 1970.

[29] R. Caflisch. Monte Carlo and Quasi-Monte Carlo Methods. *Acta Numerica*, 1998.

[30] C. Canuto, M. Y. Hussaini, A. Quarteroni, and T. A. Zang. *Spectral Methods in Fluid Dynamics.* Springer, 1987.

[31] T. F. Chan and J. H. Shen. *Image Processing and Analysis.* SIAM, 2005.

[32] W. Chew, J. Jin, and E. Michielssen. *Fast and Efficient Algorithms in Computational Electromagnetics.* Artech House, 2001.

[33] F. Chung. *Spectral Graph Theory.* American Mathematical Society, 1997.

[34] P. G. Ciarlet. *The Finite Element Method for Elliptic Problems.* North-Holland, 1978.

[35] T. A. Davis. *Direct Methods for Sparse Linear Systems.* SIAM, 2006.

[36] T. A. Davis and K. Sigmon. *MATLAB Primer.* CRC Press, 2004.

[37] C. deBoor. *A Practical Guide to Splines.* Springer, 2001.

[38] R. Devaney. *An Introduction to Chaotic Dynamical Systems.* Westview, 2003.

[39] I. J. Dhillon, Y. Gi, Y. Guan, and B. Kulis. Weighted graph cuts without eigenvectors: A multilevel approach. *IEEE Trans. PAMI*, 29:1944–1957 2007.

[40] C. Ding and H. Zha. *Spectral Clustering, Ordering, and Ranking.* Springer, 2008.

[41] J. J. Dongarra, I. S. Duff, D. C. Sorensen, and H. Van der Vorst. *Numerical Linear Algebra for High-Performance Computers.* SIAM, 1998.

[42] D. Donoho. Compressed sensing. *IEEE Trans. Inf. Theory* 52:1289–1306, 2006.

[43] I. Duff, A. Erisman, and J. Reid. *Direct Methods for Sparse Matrices.* Oxford, 1986.

[44] D. Duffy. *Advanced Engineering Mathematics with MATLAB.* CRC Press, 2003.

[45] H. Edelsbrunner. *Geometry and Topology for Mesh Generation.* Cambridge, 2006.

[46] L. Eldén. *Matrix Methods in Data Mining and Pattern Recognition.* SIAM, 2007.

[47] H. Elman, D. Silvester, and A. Wathen. *Finite Elements and Fast Iterative Solvers.* Oxford, 2005.

[48] H. C. Elman, A. Ramage, and D. J. Silvester. IFISS: A MATLAB Toolbox for modelling incompressible flows. *ACM Trans. on Mathematical Software*, 2008.

[49] K. Eriksson, D. Estep, P. Hansbo, and C. Johnson. *Computational Differential Equations.* Cambridge, 1996.

[50] L. C. Evans. *Partial Differential Equations.* American Math. Society, 1998.

[51] W. Feller. *Introduction to Probability Theory*, 3rd ed. Wiley, 1968.

[52] L. R. Ford and D.R. Fulkerson. *Flows in Networks.* Princeton, 1962.

[53] B. Fornberg. *A Practical Guide to Pseudospectral Methods.* Cambridge, 1996.

[54] G. Gan, C. Ma, and J. Wu. *Data Clustering: Theory, Algorithms, and Applications.* SIAM, 2007.

[55] W. Gander and J. Hrebicek. *Solving Problems in Scientific Computing Using Maple and* MATLAB. Springer, 2002.

[56] L. Gaul, M. Kogl, and M. Wagner. *Boundary Element Methods for Scientists and Engineers.* Springer, 2003.

[57] W. Gautschi. *Orthogonal Polynomials: Computation and Approximation.* Oxford, 2004.

[58] C. W. Gear. *Numerical Initial Value Problems in Ordinary Differential Equations.* Prentice-Hall, 1971.

[59] A. George and J. W. Liu. *Computer Solution of Large Sparse Positive Definite Systems.* Prentice-Hall, 1981.

[60] A. Gil, J. Segura, and N. Temme. *Numerical Methods for Special Functions.* SIAM, 2007.

[61] M. B. Giles and E. Süli. Adjoint methods for PDEs. *Acta Numerica*, 2002.

[62] P. Glasserman. *Monte Carlo Methods in Financial Engineering.* Springer, 2004.

[63] G. H. Golub and C. F. Van Loan. *Matrix Computations.* Johns Hopkins, 1996.

[64] A. Greenbaum. *Iterative Methods for Solving Linear Systems.* SIAM, 1997.

[65] P. Gresho and R. Sani. *Incompressible Flow and the Finite Element Method: Volume 1: Advection-Diffusion.* Wiley, 1998.

[66] M. Griebel, T. Dornseifer, and T. Neunhoeffer. *Numerical Simulation in Fluid Dynamics.* SIAM, 1998.

[67] A. Griewank. *Evaluating Derivatives: Principles and Techniques of Algorithmic Differentiation.* SIAM, 2000.

[68] D. F. Griffiths and G. A. Watson, editors. *Numerical Analysis.* Longman, 1986.

[69] D. J. Griffiths. *Introduction to Quantum Mechanics.* Prentice-Hall, 2005.

[70] G. Grimmett and D. Stirzaker. *Probability and Random Processes.* Oxford, 2001.

[71] C. M. Grinstead and J. L. Snell. *Introduction to Probability.* American Math. Society.

[72] K. Gröchenig. *Foundations of Time-Frequency Analysis.* Birkhäuser, 2001.

[73] B. Gustafsson, H.-O. Kreiss, and J. Oliger. *Time-Dependent Problems and Difference Methods.* Wiley, 1995.

[74] W. Hackbusch. *Multigrid Methods and Applications.* Springer, 1985.

[75] W. Hackbusch and U. Trottenberg. *Multigrid Methods.* Springer, 1982.

[76] E. Hairer, C. Lubich, and G. Wanner. *Geometric Numerical Integration.* Springer, 2006.

[77] E. Hairer, S. P. Nørsett, and G. Wanner. *Solving Ordinary Differential Equations I: Nonstiff Problems.* Springer, 1987.

[78] E. Hairer and G. Wanner. *Solving Ordinary Differential Equations II: Stiff and Differential-Algebraic Problems.* Springer, 1991.

[79] P. C. Hansen, J. G. Nagy, and D. P. O'Leary. *Deblurring Images: Matrices, Spectra, and Filtering.* SIAM, 2007.

[80] T. Hastie, R. Tibshirani, and J. Friedman. *The Elements of Statistical Learning: Data Mining, Inference, and Prediction.* Springer, 2001.

[81] M. Heath. *Scientific Computing: An Introductory Survey.* McGraw-Hill, 2002.

[82] C. Heij, A. C. M. Ran, and F. van Schagen. *Introduction to Mathematical Systems Theory: Linear Systems, Identification and Control.* Birkhäuser, 2006.

[83] P. Henrici. *Discrete Variable Methods in Ordinary Differential Equations.* Wiley, 1962.

[84] P. Henrici. *Applied and Computational Complex Analysis, III.* Wiley, 1986.

[85] J. Hesthaven and T. Warburton. *Nodal Discontinuous Galerkin Methods.* Springer, 2008.

[86] D. J. Higham. *An Introduction to Financial Option Valuation.* Cambridge, 2004.

[87] D. J. Higham and N. J. Higham. *MATLAB Guide.* SIAM, 2005.

[88] D. J. Higham, G. Kalna, and M. Kibble. Spectral clustering and its use in bioinformatics. *J. Computational and Appl. Mathematics*, 204:25–37, 2007.

[89] N. J. Higham. *Accuracy and Stability of Numerical Algorithms.* SIAM, 1996.

[90] N. J. Higham. *Functions of Matrices: Theory and Computations.* To appear.

[91] L. Hogben. *Encyclopedia of Linear Algebra.* Chapman and Hall/CRC, 2007.

[92] R. Horn and C. Johnson. *Matrix Analysis.* Cambridge, 1985.

[93] T. J. R. Hughes. *The Finite Element Method.* Prentice-Hall, 1987.

[94] W. Hundsdorfer and J. Verwer. *Numerical Solution of Time-Dependent Advection-Diffusion-Reaction Equations.* Springer, 2007.

[95] A. Iserles. *A First Course in the Numerical Analysis of Differential Equations.* Cambridge, 1996.

[96] J. D. Jackson. *Classical Electrodynamics.* Wiley, 1999.

[97] A. K. Jain and R. C. Dubes. *Algorithms for Clustering Data.* Prentice-Hall, 1988.

[98] C. Johnson. *Numerical Solutions of Partial Differential Equations by the Finite Element Method.* Cambridge, 1987.

[99] I. T. Jolliffe. *Principal Component Analysis.* Springer, 2002.

[100] T. Kailath, A. Sayed, and B. Hassibi. *Linear Estimation.* Prentice-Hall, 2000.

[101] J. Kaipio and E. Somersalo. *Statistical and Computational Inverse Problems.* Springer, 2006.

[102] H. B. Keller. *Numerical Solution of Two Point Boundary Value Problems.* SIAM, 1976.

[103] C. T. Kelley. *Iterative Methods for Optimization.* SIAM, 1999.

[104] J. Kleinberg and E. Tardos. *Algorithm Design.* Addison-Wesley, 2006.

[105] D. Kröner. *Numerical Schemes for Conservation Laws.* Wiley-Teubner, 1997.

[106] P. Kunkel and V. Mehrmann. *Differential-Algebraic Equations.* European Mathematical Society, 2006.

[107] J. D. Lambert. *Numerical Methods for Ordinary Differential Systems.* Wiley, 1991.

[108] P. D. Lax. *Hyperbolic Systems of Conservation Laws and the Mathematical Theory of Shock Waves.* SIAM, 1973.

[109] R. J. LeVeque. *Numerical Methods for Conservation Laws.* Birkhäuser, 1992.

[110] R. J. LeVeque. *Finite Difference Methods for Ordinary and Partial Differential Equations.* SIAM, 2007.

[111] J. Liesen and B. N. Parlett. On nonsymmetric saddle point matrices that allow conjugate gradient iterations. *Numerische Mathematik*, 2008.

[112] J. R. Magnus and H. Neudecker. *Matrix Differential Calculus.* Wiley, 1999.

[113] A. Majda. *Compressible Fluid Flow and Systems of Conservation Laws in Several Space Variables.* Springer, 1984.

[114] S. Mallat. *A Wavelet Tour of Signal Processing.* Academic Press, 1999.

[115] G. Meurant. *The Lanczos and Conjugate Gradient Algorithms.* SIAM, 2006.

[116] C. Moler. *Numerical Computing with MATLAB.* SIAM, 2004.

[117] K. W. Morton and T. Sonar. Finite volume methods for hyperbolic conservation laws. *Acta Numerica*, 2007.

[118] N. S. Nise. *Control Systems Engineering.* John Wiley, 2000.

[119] J. Nocedal and S. Wright. *Numerical Optimization.* Springer, 2006.

[120] B. Oksendal. *Stochastic Differential Equations.* Springer, 1992.

[121] A. V. Oppenheim and R. W. Schafer. *Discrete-Time Signal Processing.* Prentice-Hall, 1989.

[122] S. Osher and R. Fedkiw. *Level Set Methods and Dynamic Implicit Surfaces.* Springer, 2003.

[123] N. Paragios, Y. Chen, and O. Faugeras, eds. *Handbook of Mathematical Models in Computer Vision.* Springer, 2006.

[124] B. N. Parlett. *The Symmetric Eigenvalue Problem.* SIAM, 1998.

[125] L. R. Petzold. A description of DASSL—a differential algebraic system solver. *IMACS Trans. Sci. Comp.*, 1:1–65, North Holland, 1982.

[126] W. H. Press, S. A. Teukolsky, W. T. Vetterling, and B. P. Flannery. *Numerical Recipes in C.* Cambridge, 1992. *Numerical Recipes.* Cambridge, 2007.

[127] H. A. Priestley. *Introduction to Complex Analysis.* Oxford, 2003.

[128] A. Quarteroni and A. Valli. *Numerical Approximation of Partial Differential Equations.* Springer, 1997.

[129] R. D. Richtmyer and K. W. Morton. *Difference Methods for Initial-Value Problems.* Wiley, 1967.

[130] Y. Saad. *Iterative Methods for Sparse Linear Systems.* SIAM, 2003.

[131] T. Schlick. *Molecular Modeling and Simulation.* Springer, 2002.

[132] C. Schwab. *p- and hp- Finite Element Methods.* Oxford, 1998.

[133] J. Sethian. *Level Set Methods and Fast Marching Methods.* Cambridge, 1999.

[134] L. F. Shampine and C. W. Gear. A user's view of solving stiff ordinary differential equations. *SIAM Review*, 21:1–17, 1979.

[135] P. Shankar and M. Deshpande. Fluid Mechanics in the Driven Cavity. *Annual Reviews of Fluid Mechanics*, 32:93-136, 2000.

[136] J. R. Shewchuk. The conjugate gradient method without the agonizing pain. www.cs.berkeley.edu/~jrs, 1994.

[137] J. Shi and J. Malik. Normalized cuts and image segmentation. *IEEE Trans. PAMI*, 22:888–905, 2000.

[138] J. Smoller. *Shock Waves and Reaction-Diffusion Equations.* Springer, 1983.

[139] G. A. Sod. *Numerical Methods in Fluid Dynamics.* Cambridge, 1985.

[140] J. Stoer and R. Bulirsch. *Introduction to Numerical Analysis.* Springer, 2002.

[141] G. Strang. *Introduction to Applied Mathematics.* Wellesley-Cambridge, 1986.

[142] G. Strang. *Introduction to Linear Algebra.* Wellesley-Cambridge, 2003.

[143] G. Strang and K. Borre. *Linear Algebra, Geodesy, and GPS.* Wellesley-Cambridge, 1997.
[144] G. Strang and G. J. Fix. *An Analysis of the Finite Element Method.* Prentice-Hall, 1973; Wellesley-Cambridge, 2000. Second edition, 2008.
[145] G. Strang and T. Nguyen. *Wavelets and Filter Banks.* Wellesley-Cambridge, 1996.
[146] J. C. Strikwerda. *Finite Difference Schemes and Partial Differential Equations.* SIAM, 2004.
[147] S. Strogatz. *Nonlinear Dynamics and Chaos.* Perseus, 2001.
[148] A. M. Stuart. Numerical Analysis of Dynamical Systems. *Acta Numerica,* 1994.
[149] E. Süli and D. Mayers. *An Introduction to Numerical Analysis.* Cambridge, 2003.
[150] J. Sundnes et al. *Computing the Electrical Activity in the Heart.* Springer, 2006.
[151] E. Tadmor. Filters, mollifiers, and the computation of the Gibbs phenomenon. *Acta Numerica,* 2007.
[152] A. Taflove and S. C. Hagness. *Computational Electrodynamics: The FDTD Method.* Artech, 2000.
[153] P. N. Tan, M. Steinbach, and V. Kumar. *Introduction to Data Mining.* Addison-Wesley, 2005.
[154] F. Tisseur and K. Meerbergen. The quadratic eigenvalue problem. *SIAM Review,* 41:235–286, 2001.
[155] A. Toselli and O. Widlund. *Domain Decomposition Methods.* Springer, 2005.
[156] L. N. Trefethen. *Finite Difference and Spectral Methods for Ordinary and Partial Differential Equations.* Unpublished lecture notes, 1996.
[157] L. N. Trefethen. *Spectral Methods in MATLAB.* SIAM, 2000.
[158] L. N. Trefethen. Is Gauss quadrature better than Clenshaw-Curtis? *SIAM Review,* to appear.
[159] L. N. Trefethen and D. Bau. *Numerical Linear Algebra.* SIAM, 1997.
[160] J. A. Tropp. Just relax: Convex programming methods for identifying sparse signals. *IEEE Trans. Information Theory,* 51:1030–1051, 2006.
[161] U. Trottenberg, C. Oosterlee, and A. Schüller. *Multigrid.* Academic Press, 2001.
[162] H. Van der Vorst. *Iterative Krylov Methods for Large Linear Systems.* Cambridge, 2003.
[163] E. van Groesen and J. Molenaar. *Continuum Modeling in the Physical Sciences.* SIAM, 2007.
[164] C. F. Van Loan. *Computational Frameworks for the Fast Fourier Transform.* SIAM, 1992.
[165] G. Wahba. *Spline Models for Observational Data.* SIAM, 1990.
[166] D. Watkins. *Fundamentals of Matrix Computations.* Wiley, 2002.
[167] D. J. Watts. *Six Degrees: The Science of a Connected Age.* Norton, 2002.
[168] J. A. C. Weideman and L. N. Trefethen. Parabolic and hyperbolic contours for computing the Bromwich integral. *Math. Comp.,* 76:1341–1356, 2007.
[169] G. B. Whitham. *Linear and Nonlinear Waves.* Wiley, 1974.
[170] P. Wilmott, S. Harrison, and J. Dewynne. *The Mathematics of Financial Derivatives.* Cambridge, 1995.
[171] Y. Zhu and A. Cangellaris. *Multigrid Finite Element Methods for Electromagnetic Modeling.* IEEE Press/Wiley, 2006.

INDEX